GO!

Learn | Practice | Succeed

Microsoft® Office 365®

2019 Edition

Shelley Gaskin | Alicia Vargas | Debra Geoghan | Nancy Graviett

Series Editor: Shelley Gaskin

Pearson

VP Courseware Portfolio Management: Andrew Gilfillan
Executive Portfolio Manager: Jenifer Niles
Team Lead, Content Production: Laura Burgess
Content Producer: Shannon LeMay-Finn
Development Editor: Ginny Munroe
Portfolio Management Assistant: Bridget Daly
Director of Product Marketing: Brad Parkins
Director of Field Marketing: Jonathan Cottrell
Product Marketing Manager: Heather Taylor
Field Marketing Manager: Bob Nisbet
Product Marketing Assistant: Liz Bennett
Field Marketing Assistant: Derrica Moser
Senior Operations Specialist: Diane Peirano

Senior Art Director: Mary Seiner
Interior and Cover Design: Pearson CSC
Cover Photo: Jag_cz/Shutterstock, everything possible/Shutterstock
Senior Product Model Manager: Eric Hakanson
Manager, Digital Studio: Heather Darby
Digital Content Producer, MyLab IT: Becca Golden
Course Producer, MyLab IT: Amanda Losonsky
Digital Studio Producer: Tanika Henderson
Full-Service Project Management: Pearson CSC, Katie Ostler
Composition: Pearson CSC
Printer/Binder: LSC Communications, Inc.
Cover Printer: Phoenix Color/Hagerstown

Credits and acknowledgments borrowed from other sources and reproduced, with permission, in this textbook appear on appropriate page within text.

Google and the Google logo are registered trademarks of Google LLC, used with permission. Found on pages: 124, 147, 213 A&B, 259 A&B, 286, 364, 410, 411, 433, 434, 474, 495, 555, 569, 621, 645, 700, 719, 771, 792, 840, 857, 902, 923.

Microsoft and/or its respective suppliers make no representations about the suitability of the information contained in the documents and related graphics published as part of the services for any purpose. all such documents and related graphics are provided "as is" without warranty of any kind. microsoft and/or its respective suppliers hereby disclaim all warranties and conditions with regard to this information, including all warranties and conditions of merchantability, whether express, implied or statutory, fitness for a particular purpose, title and non-infringement. in no event shall Microsoft and/or its respective suppliers be liable for any special, indirect or consequential damages or any damages whatsoever resulting from loss of use, data or profits, whether in an action of contract, negligence or other tortious action, arising out of or in connection with the use or performance of information available from the services.

The documents and related graphics contained herein could include technical inaccuracies or typographical errors. changes are periodically added to the information herein. microsoft and/or its respective suppliers may make improvements and/or changes in the product(s) and/or the program(s) described herein at any time. partial screen shots may be viewed in full within the software version specified.

Microsoft® and Windows® are registered trademarks of the Microsoft Corporation in the U.S.A. and other countries. Screenshots and icons reprinted with permission from the Microsoft Corporation. This book is not sponsored or endorsed by or affiliated with the Microsoft Corporation.

Many of the designations by manufacturers and seller to distinguish their products are claimed as trademarks. Where those designations appear in this book, and the publisher was aware of a trademark claim, the designations have been printed in initial caps or all caps.

Library of Congress Cataloging-in-Publication Data

On file with the Library of Congress.

ISBN-10: 0-13-541781-3
ISBN-13: 978-0-13-541781-2

3 2019

Brief Contents

Prepare Students to Succeed! xviii

Microsoft Office and Windows 10

Chapter 1   Microsoft Office Features and Windows 10
            File Management 1

Word

Chapter 1   Creating Documents with Microsoft Word 103
Chapter 2   Creating Cover Letters and Using Tables
            to Create Resumes 169
Chapter 3   Creating Research Papers, Newsletters,
            and Merged Mailing Labels 235

Excel

Chapter 1   Creating a Worksheet and Charting Data 315
Chapter 2   Using Functions, Creating Tables, and
            Managing Large Workbooks 385
Chapter 3   Analyzing Data with Pie Charts, Line
            Charts, and What-If Analysis Tools 459

Access

Chapter 1   Getting Started with Microsoft Access 2019 519
Chapter 2   Sort and Query a Database 595
Chapter 3   Forms, Filters, and Reports 671

PowerPoint

Chapter 1 Getting Started with Microsoft PowerPoint **745**

Chapter 2 Formatting PowerPoint Presentations **813**

Chapter 3 Enhancing a Presentation with
Animation, Video, Tables, and Charts **877**

Office Integrated Projects

Chapter 1 Integrating Word, Excel, Access, and PowerPoint .. **945**

Appendixes: Microsoft Office Specialist Mappings **A-1**

Glossary **G-1**

Index **I-1**

Table of Contents

Microsoft Office and Windows 10 1

Chapter 1 Microsoft Office Features and Windows 10 File Management   1

PROJECT IA   Chef Notes   2

Objective 1   Explore Microsoft Office   3
Activity 1.01   Exploring Microsoft Office   4

Objective 2   Create a Folder for File Storage   6
Activity 1.02   Creating a Folder for File Storage   7
More Knowledge   Creating a Microsoft Account   7

Objective 3   Download and Extract Zipped Files, Enter and Edit Text in an Office Application, and Use Editor to Check Documents   10
Activity 1.03   Downloading and Extracting Zipped Files from MyLab IT and Entering and Editing Text in an Office Program   11
Activity 1.04   Checking Spelling   14

Objective 4   Perform Office Commands and Apply Office Formatting   15
Activity 1.05   Performing Commands from a Dialog Box   15
Activity 1.06   Using Undo and Applying Text Effects   18
Activity 1.07   Performing Commands from and Customizing the Quick Access Toolbar   19
Activity 1.08   Performing Commands from the Ribbon   21
Activity 1.09   Minimizing the Ribbon   25
More Knowledge   Displaying KeyTips   25
Activity 1.10   Changing Page Orientation and Zoom Level   25
More Knowledge   Zooming to Page Width   26
Activity 1.11   Formatting Text by Using Fonts, Alignment, Font Colors, and Font Styles   27
Activity 1.12   Using Format Painter   30
Activity 1.13   Using Keyboard Shortcuts and Using the Clipboard to Copy, Cut, and Paste   32
Activity 1.14   Adding Alternative Text for Accessibility   36

Objective 5   Finalize an Office Document   37
Activity 1.15   Inserting a Footer, Inserting Document Info, and Adding Document Properties   37
Activity 1.16   Inspecting a Document   38
Activity 1.17   Inserting a Bookmark and a 3D Model   39
Activity 1.18   Printing a File and Closing a Desktop App   40

More Knowledge   Creating an Electronic Image of Your Document   41

Objective 6   Use the Office Help Features   41
Activity 1.19   Using Microsoft Office Tell Me, Tell Me More, the Help Tab, and Adding Alt Text to an Excel Chart   41
More Knowledge   Don't Type, Talk! With the New Dictate Feature   44

PROJECT 1B   Hotel Files   45

Objective 7   Explore Windows 10   46
Activity 1.20   Recognizing User Accounts in Windows 10   47
Activity 1.21   Turning On Your Computer, Signing In, and Exploring the Windows 10 Environment   49
Activity 1.22   Pinning a Program to the Taskbar   53

Objective 8   Prepare to Work with Folders and Files   54
Activity 1.23   Creating a New Folder to Store a File   54
More Knowledge   Use OneDrive as Cloud Storage   59
Activity 1.24   Creating and Saving a File   59
More Knowledge   Jump to a Lettered Section of the Apps List Quickly   60
More Knowledge   The Hamburger Icon   65
Activity 1.25   Downloading and Extracting Zipped Files   65
Activity 1.26   Locating and Inserting a Saved File Into a PowerPoint Presentation   66
Activity 1.27   Using Snap and Task View   66

Objective 9   Use File Explorer to Extract Zipped Files and to Display Locations, Folders, and Files   70
Activity 1.28   Navigating with File Explorer   71
Activity 1.29   Using File Explorer to Extract Zipped Files   73
Activity 1.30   Using File Explorer to Display Locations, Folders, and Files   74

Objective 10   Start Programs and Open Data Files   78
Activity 1.31   Starting Programs   78
Activity 1.32   Opening Data Files   80
More Knowledge   Do Not Clutter Your Desktop by Creating Desktop Shortcuts or Storing Files   83
Activity 1.33   Searching, Pinning, Sorting, and Filtering in File Explorer   84

Objective 11   Create, Rename, and Copy Files and Folders   85
Activity 1.34   Copying Files from a Removable Storage Device to the Documents Folder on the Hard Disk Drive   85

Activity 1.35 Creating Folders, Renaming Folders, and Renaming Files 87

Activity 1.36 Copying Files 89

Activity 1.37 Moving Files 90

More Knowledge Using Shift + Click to Select Files 91

Activity 1.38 Copying and Moving Files by Snapping Two Windows 92

More Knowledge Deleting Files and Using the Recycle Bin 94

GO! To Work 95

End of Chapter 96

Summary; GO! Learn It Online 96

Glossary 97

INTRODUCTION TO

Microsoft Word 2019   101

Chapter 1 Creating Documents with Microsoft Word 103

PROJECT 1A Flyer 104

Objective 1 Create a New Document and Insert Text 105

Activity 1.01 Creating a New Word Document 105

More Knowledge Word's Default Settings Are Easier to Read Online 107

Activity 1.02 Inserting Text from Another Document 107

Objective 2 Insert and Format Graphics 108

Activity 1.03 Formatting Text by Using Text Effects 108

More Knowledge Clear Existing Formatting 109

Activity 1.04 Inserting Pictures 109

Activity 1.05 Wrapping Text Around a Picture Using Layout Options 110

Activity 1.06 Resizing Pictures and Using Live Layout 111

Activity 1.07 Positioning a Picture 112

Activity 1.08 Applying Picture Effects 114

More Knowledge Applying Picture Styles 114

Activity 1.09 Applying Artistic Effects 114

Activity 1.10 Adding a Page Border 115

Objective 3 Insert and Modify Text Boxes and Shapes 116

Activity 1.11 Inserting, Sizing, and Positioning a Shape 116

Activity 1.12 Typing Text in a Shape and Formatting a Shape 117

Activity 1.13 Inserting a Text Box 118

Activity 1.14 Sizing and Positioning a Text Box and Formatting a Text Box Using Shape Styles 119

Objective 4 Preview and Print a Document 120

Activity 1.15 Adding a File Name to the Footer by Inserting a Field 120

Activity 1.16 Adding Document Properties and Previewing and Printing a Document 122

GO! With Google Docs 124

Objective Create a Flyer Using Google Docs 124

PROJECT 1B Information Handout 126

Objective 5 Change Document and Paragraph Layout 127

Activity 1.17 Setting Margins 127

Activity 1.18 Aligning Paragraphs 128

Activity 1.19 Setting Line Spacing 130

Activity 1.20 Indenting Text 131

Activity 1.21 Setting Space Before and After Paragraphs 133

Objective 6 Create and Modify Lists 134

Activity 1.22 Creating a Bulleted List 134

Activity 1.23 Creating a Numbered List 135

More Knowledge To End a List 137

Activity 1.24 Customizing Bullets 137

Objective 7 Set and Modify Tab Stops 139

Activity 1.25 Setting Tab Stops 139

Activity 1.26 Modifying Tab Stops 141

Objective 8 Insert and Format a SmartArt Graphic and an Icon 143

Activity 1.27 Inserting a SmartArt Graphic 143

Activity 1.28 Sizing and Formatting a SmartArt Graphic 144

Activity 1.29 Inserting an Icon 145

GO! With Google Docs 147

Objective Create an Information Handout 147

GO! To Work 149

End of Chapter 150

Summary; GO! Learn It Online; GO! Collaborative Team Project 150

Project Guide for Word Chapter 1 151

Glossary 152

Chapter Review 153

Content-Based Assessments: Mastery, Critical Thinking, and Problem Solving 159

Content-Based Assessment Rubric 167

GO! Think 168

Chapter 2 Creating Cover Letters and Using Tables to Create Resumes 169

PROJECT 2A Resume 170

Objective 1 Create a Table for a Resume 171

Activity 2.01 Inserting a Table by Defining Table Dimensions 171

Activity 2.02 Typing Text in a Table 172

Activity 2.03 Inserting Text From a File and Using Resume Assistant 173

Activity 2.04 Creating Bulleted Lists in a Table 176

Objective 2	**Format a Table**	**177**
Activity 2.05	Changing the Width of Table Columns and Using AutoFit	177
More Knowledge	Changing Column Widths	178
Activity 2.06	Using One-Click Row/Column Insertion to Modify Table Dimensions	178
Activity 2.07	Adjusting Cell Margins and Merging Table Cells	179
Activity 2.08	Setting Tabs in a Table	181
Activity 2.09	Using Spacing After in a Table	181
Activity 2.10	Modifying Table Borders, Using Spacing Before, and Viewing Gridlines in a Table	183
More Knowledge	Converting a Table to Text	186
Objective 3	**Present a Word Document Online**	**186**
Activity 2.11	Presenting a Word Document Online	186
GO! With Google Docs		**188**
Objective	**Edit a Resume in Google Docs**	**188**
PROJECT 2B	**Cover Letter and Envelope**	**190**
Objective 4	**Create a Letterhead for a Cover Letter**	**191**
Activity 2.12	Inserting a Manual Line Break	191
Activity 2.13	Applying a Bottom Border to a Paragraph	193
Objective 5	**Create a Cover Letter and Correct and Reorganize Text**	**194**
Activity 2.14	Adding AutoCorrect Entries	194
Activity 2.15	Inserting the Current Date and Creating a Cover Letter	195
Activity 2.16	Finding and Replacing Text	197
Activity 2.17	Selecting Text and Moving Text by Using Drag and Drop	199
Activity 2.18	Inserting a Table into a Document and Applying a Table Style	200
Objective 6	**Use the Word Editor to Check Your Document**	**201**
Activity 2.19	Using the Word Editor to Check for Spelling, Grammar, and Writing Issues	202
Activity 2.20	Using the Thesaurus	205
Objective 7	**Print an Envelope, Change a Style Set, Create a Word Template, and Use Learning Tools**	**206**
Activity 2.21	Addressing and Printing an Envelope	206
Activity 2.22	Changing a Style Set	207
Activity 2.23	Creating a Word Template	208
Activity 2.24	Using Learning Tools and Read Aloud	210
GO! With Google Docs		**212**
Objective	**Create a Table in Google Docs**	**212**
GO! To Work		**214**
End of Chapter		**215**

Summary; GO! Learn It Online; GO! Collaborative Team Project		215
Project Guide for Word Chapter 2		216
Glossary		217
Chapter Review		218
Mastering Word		224
Rubric		232
GO! Think		233

Chapter 3 Creating Research Papers, Newsletters, and Merged Mailing Labels 235

PROJECT 3A	**Research Paper**	**236**
Objective 1	**Create a Research Paper**	**237**
Activity 3.01	Formatting the Spacing and First-Page Information for a Research Paper	237
Activity 3.02	Formatting the Page Numbering and Paragraph Indents for a Research Paper	238
More Knowledge	Suppressing the Page Number on the First Page of a Document	240
Objective 2	**Insert Footnotes in a Research Paper**	**240**
Activity 3.03	Inserting Footnotes	240
More Knowledge	Using Symbols Rather Than Numbers for Notes	241
Activity 3.04	Modifying a Footnote Style	241
Objective 3	**Create Citations and a Bibliography in a Research Paper**	**244**
Activity 3.05	Adding Citations for a Book	244
Activity 3.06	Editing Citations	245
More Knowledge	Word Formats the MLA Style for Two or More Authors Automatically	247
Activity 3.07	Adding Citations for a Website	247
More Knowledge	Including URLs of Web Sources	248
Activity 3.08	Inserting Page Breaks	248
Activity 3.09	Creating a Reference Page	249
Activity 3.10	Managing and Modifying Sources for a Document	249
Activity 3.11	Using the Navigation Pane to Go to a Specific Page	250
Activity 3.12	Managing Document Properties	251
Activity 3.13	Using Smart Lookup, Researcher, Text Highlighting, Cover Pages, and Side to Side Page Movement	252
Objective 4	**Use Read Mode, PDF Reflow, and Save Documents in Alternative File Formats**	**255**
Activity 3.14	Using Read Mode, PDF Reflow, and Saving Documents in Alternative File Formats	256

Table of Contents **vii**

GO! With Google Docs		259
Objective	Use the Research Bar in Google Docs	259
PROJECT 3B	**Newsletter with Optional Mailing Labels**	261
Objective 5	**Format a Multiple-Column Newsletter**	262
Activity 3.15	Changing One Column of Text to Two Columns	262
Activity 3.16	Formatting Multiple Columns	264
More Knowledge	Justifying Column Text	265
Activity 3.17	Inserting a Column Break	265
Activity 3.18	Inserting a Picture	266
Activity 3.19	Cropping a Picture and Resizing a Picture by Scaling	268
Activity 3.20	Setting Transparent Color and Recoloring a Picture	271
Activity 3.21	Adjusting the Brightness and Contrast of a Picture	272
Activity 3.22	Applying a Border to a Picture and Flipping a Picture	273
Activity 3.23	Inserting and Formatting a Screen Clipping	274
More Knowledge	Inserting a Link in a Document	274
Objective 6	**Use Special Character and Paragraph Formatting**	275
Activity 3.24	Applying the Small Caps Font Effect	275
Activity 3.25	Inserting Symbols and Special Characters	276
Activity 3.26	Adding Borders and Shading to a Paragraph	277
Objective 7	**Create Mailing Labels Using Mail Merge**	280
Activity 3.27	Starting the Mail Merge Wizard	280
Activity 3.28	Completing the Mail Merge	282
Activity 3.29	Previewing and Printing Mail Merge Results	283
GO! With Google Docs		285
Objective	Format a Newsletter in Google Docs	285
GO! To Work		287
End of Chapter		288
Summary; GO! Learn It Online; GO! Collaborative Team Project		288
Project Guide for Word Chapter 3		289
Glossary		290
Chapter Review		291
Mastering Word		299
Rubric		310
GO! Think		311

INTRODUCTION TO

Microsoft Excel 2019 313

Chapter 1	**Creating a Worksheet and Charting Data**	315
PROJECT 1A	**Sales Report with Embedded Column Chart and Sparklines**	316
Objective 1	**Create, Save, and Navigate an Excel Workbook**	317
Activity 1.01	Starting Excel, Navigating Excel, and Naming and Saving a Workbook	317
Objective 2	**Enter Data in a Worksheet**	320
Activity 1.02	Entering Text, Using AutoComplete, and Using the Name Box to Select a Cell	320
Activity 1.03	Using Auto Fill and Keyboard Shortcuts	321
Activity 1.04	Aligning Text and Adjusting the Size of Columns	323
Activity 1.05	Entering Numbers	325
Objective 3	**Construct and Copy Formulas and Use the SUM Function**	326
Activity 1.06	Constructing a Formula and Using the SUM Function	326
Activity 1.07	Copying a Formula by Using the Fill Handle	328
Objective 4	**Format Cells with Merge & Center, Cell Styles, and Themes**	329
Activity 1.08	Using Merge & Center and Applying Cell Styles	329
Activity 1.09	Formatting Financial Numbers	330
Activity 1.10	Changing the Workbook Theme	332
More Knowledge	Formatting a Cell's Font, Style, Size, or Color with Individual Commands	332
Objective 5	**Chart Data to Create a Column Chart and Insert Sparklines**	332
Activity 1.11	Charting Data and Using Recommended Charts to Select and Insert a Column Chart	332
Activity 1.12	Using the Chart Tools to Apply Chart Styles	335
Activity 1.13	Creating and Formatting Sparklines	338
Objective 6	**Print a Worksheet, Display Formulas, and Close Excel**	339
Activity 1.14	Creating a Footer and Centering a Worksheet	339
Activity 1.15	Adding Document Properties and Printing a Workbook	341
Activity 1.16	Printing a Section of the Worksheet	342
Activity 1.17	Changing Page Orientation and Displaying, Printing, and Hiding Formulas	342

GO! With Google Sheets   345

    Objective   Create a Sales Report with
                 an Embedded Column Chart
                 Using Google Sheets   345

PROJECT 1B Inventory Valuation   347

    Objective 7 Check Spelling in a Worksheet   348
    Activity 1.18   Checking Spelling in a Worksheet   348

    Objective 8 Enter Data by Range   350
    Activity 1.19   Entering Data by Range   350

    Objective 9 Construct Formulas for
                 Mathematical Operations   351
    Activity 1.20   Using Arithmetic Operators   351
    Activity 1.21   Using the Quick Analysis Tool   352
    Activity 1.22   Copying Formulas Containing
                 Absolute Cell References   354
  More Knowledge   Calculate a Percentage if You Know
                 the Total and the Amount   356

    Objective 10 Edit Values in a Worksheet   356
    Activity 1.23   Editing Values in a Worksheet   356
    Activity 1.24   Formatting Cells with the
                 Percent Style   357

    Objective 11 Format a Worksheet   358
    Activity 1.25   Inserting and Deleting Rows
                 and Columns   358
    Activity 1.26   Adjusting Column Widths and
                 Wrapping Text   359
    Activity 1.27   Changing Theme Colors   360

GO! With Google Sheets   363

    Objective   Creating an Inventory
                 Valuation Report   363

GO! To Work   365
End of Chapter   366
Summary; GO! Learn It Online; GO! Collaborative
Team Project   366
Glossary   368
Chapter Review   370
Project Guide for Excel Chapter 1   367
Mastering Excel   376
Rubric   383
GO! Think   384

**Chapter 2 Using Functions,
Creating Tables, and
Managing Large
Workbooks**   **385**

PROJECT 2A Inventory Status Report   386

    Objective 1 Use Flash Fill and the SUM,
                AVERAGE, MEDIAN, MIN, and
                MAX Functions   387
    Activity 2.01   Using Flash Fill   387

    Activity 2.02   Moving a Column   388
    Activity 2.03   Using the SUM and AVERAGE
                 Functions   389
    Activity 2.04   Using the MEDIAN Function   391
    Activity 2.05   Using the MIN and MAX Functions   392

    Objective 2 Move Data, Resolve Error
                Messages, and Rotate Text   392
    Activity 2.06   Moving Data and Resolving
                 a ##### Error Message   393
    Activity 2.07   Merging Cells and Rotating Text   394

    Objective 3 Use COUNTIF and IF
                Functions and Apply
                Conditional Formatting   395
    Activity 2.08   Using the COUNTIF Function   395
    Activity 2.09   Using the IF Function   396
    Activity 2.10   Applying Conditional Formatting
                 by Using Highlight Cells Rules and
                 Data Bars   397
    Activity 2.11   Using Find and Replace   399

    Objective 4 Use Date & Time Functions
                and Freeze Panes   400
    Activity 2.12   Using the NOW Function to Display
                 a System Date   400
  More Knowledge   NOW Function Recalculates Each
                 Time a Workbook Opens   400
    Activity 2.13   Freezing and Unfreezing Panes   400
  More Knowledge   Freeze Columns or Freeze Both
                 Rows and Columns   401

    Objective 5 Create, Sort, and Filter an
                Excel Table   402
    Activity 2.14   Creating an Excel Table and
                 Applying a Table Style   402
    Activity 2.15   Sorting an Excel Table   403
    Activity 2.16   Filtering an Excel Table and
                 Displaying a Total Row   404
  More Knowledge   Band Rows and Columns in a Table   405
    Activity 2.17   Clearing Filters   405
  More Knowledge   Converting a Table to a Range   405

    Objective 6 View, Format, and Print a
                Large Worksheet   406
    Activity 2.18   Modifying and Shrinking the
                 Worksheet View   406
    Activity 2.19   Splitting a Worksheet Window
                 into Panes   406
    Activity 2.20   Printing Titles and Scaling to Fit   407
  More Knowledge   Scaling for Data That Is Slightly
                 Larger Than the Printed Page   409

GO! With Google Sheets   410

    Objective   Summarize an
                 Inventory List   410

PROJECT 2B Weekly Sales Summary   412

    Objective 7 Navigate a Workbook and
                Rename Worksheets   413

Activity 2.21 Navigating Among Worksheets, Renaming Worksheets, and Changing the Tab Color of Worksheets 413
More Knowledge Copying a Worksheet 414

Objective 8 Enter Dates, Clear Contents, and Clear Formats 414
Activity 2.22 Entering and Formatting Dates 414
Activity 2.23 Clearing Cell Contents and Formats 416
More Knowledge Clearing an Entire Worksheet 417

Objective 9 Copy and Paste by Using the Paste Options Gallery 417
Activity 2.24 Copying and Pasting by Using the Paste Options Gallery 417

Objective 10 Edit and Format Multiple Worksheets at the Same Time 418
Activity 2.25 Grouping Worksheets for Editing 418
More Knowledge Hide Worksheets 420
Activity 2.26 Formatting and Constructing Formulas on Grouped Worksheets 420
Activity 2.27 Determining Multiple Totals at the Same Time 423
Activity 2.28 Formatting Grouped Worksheets 423
Activity 2.29 Ungrouping Worksheets 423

Objective 11 Create a Summary Sheet with Column Sparklines 424
Activity 2.30 Inserting a Worksheet 424
Activity 2.31 Constructing Formulas That Refer to Cells in Another Worksheet 425
Activity 2.32 Changing Values in a Detail Worksheet to Update a Summary Worksheet 425
Activity 2.33 Inserting Column Sparklines 427
Activity 2.34 Determining Bonus Based on Sales Using the IFS Function 427

Objective 12 Format and Print Multiple Worksheets in a Workbook 429
Activity 2.35 Moving a Worksheet, Repeating Footers, and Formatting Multiple Worksheets in a Workbook 429
Activity 2.36 Printing All or Individual Worksheets in a Workbook 431

GO! With Google Sheets 433
Objective Calculate Weekly Sales 433

GO! To Work 435
End of Chapter 436
Summary; GO! Learn It Online; GO! Collaborative Team Project 436
Project Guide for Excel Chapter 2 437
Glossary 438
Chapter Review 439
Mastering Excel 446
Rubric 456
GO! Think 457

Chapter 3 Analyzing Data with Pie Charts, Line Charts, and What-If Analysis Tools 459

PROJECT 3A Enterprise Fund Pie Chart 460
Objective 1 Chart Data with a Pie Chart 461
Activity 3.01 Calculating Values for a Pie Chart 461
Activity 3.02 Creating a Pie Chart and Moving a Chart to a Chart Sheet 462

Objective 2 Format a Pie Chart 464
Activity 3.03 Formatting a Chart Title by Applying a WordArt Style and Changing Font Size 464
Activity 3.04 Formatting Chart Elements by Removing a Legend and Adding and Formatting Data Labels 464
Activity 3.05 Formatting a Data Series with 3-D Effects 466
Activity 3.06 Formatting a Data Series with a Shadow Effect 468
Activity 3.07 Rotating a Pie Chart by Changing the Angle of the First Slice 468
Activity 3.08 Exploding and Coloring a Pie Slice 469
Activity 3.09 Formatting the Chart Area 469

Objective 3 Edit a Workbook and Update a Chart 470
Activity 3.10 Editing a Workbook and Updating a Chart 470

Objective 4 Use Goal Seek to Perform What-If Analysis 471
Activity 3.11 Using Goal Seek to Perform What-If Analysis 471
Activity 3.12 Preparing and Printing a Workbook with a Chart Sheet 473

GO! With Google Sheets 474
Objective Analyze Expenditures with a Pie Chart 474

PROJECT 3B Tourism Spending Projection and Analysis 475

Objective 5 Design a Worksheet for What-If Analysis 476
Activity 3.13 Using Parentheses in a Formula to Calculate a Percentage Rate of Increase 476
More Knowledge Use of Parentheses in a Formula 477
Activity 3.14 Using Format Painter 478
More Knowledge Percentage Calculations 478
Activity 3.15 Calculating a Value After an Increase 478
More Knowledge Percent Increase or Decrease 479

Objective 6 Answer What-If Questions by Changing Values in a Worksheet 480

Activity 3.16 Answering What-If Questions and Using Paste Special 480

Objective 7 Chart Data with a Line Chart 482

Activity 3.17 Inserting Multiple Rows and Creating a Line Chart 483
Activity 3.18 Formatting Axes in a Line Chart 485
Activity 3.19 Formatting the Chart Area in a Line Chart 488
Activity 3.20 Formatting the Plot Area Gridlines and Axis Fonts in a Line Chart 490

Objective 8 Create a Map Chart and a Funnel Chart 491

Activity 3.21 Creating and Sizing a Map Chart 491
Activity 3.22 Creating and Sizing a Funnel Chart 493

GO! With Google Sheets 495

Objective Analyze Trends with a Line Chart 495

GO! To Work 496
End of Chapter 497

Summary; GO! Learn It Online; GO! Collaborative Team Project 497
Project Guide for Excel Chapter 3 498
Glossary 499
Chapter Review 500
Mastering Excel 507
Rubric 515
GO! Think 516

INTRODUCTION TO

Microsoft Access 2019   517

Chapter 1   Getting Started with Microsoft Access 2019 519

PROJECT 1A Student Advising Database with Two Tables 520

Objective 1 Identify Good Database Design 521
Activity 1.01 Using Good Design Techniques to Plan a Database 521

Objective 2 Create a Table and Define Fields in a Blank Desktop Database 522
Activity 1.02 Starting with a Blank Database 523
Activity 1.03 Assigning the Data Type and Name to Fields 525
More Knowledge Create Fields by Entering Data 527
Activity 1.04 Renaming Fields, Changing Data Types, and Setting Field Size in a Table 527
Activity 1.05 Adding a Record to a Table 528

More Knowledge Renaming or Deleting a Table 530
Activity 1.06 Adding Additional Records to a Table 530
Activity 1.07 Importing Data from an Excel Workbook into an Existing Access Table 530

Objective 3 Change the Structure of Tables and Add a Second Table 533
Activity 1.08 Deleting a Table Field in Design View 533
Activity 1.09 Adding Field Descriptions and Changing Field Size 535
More Knowledge Add a Table Description 536
Activity 1.10 Viewing the Primary Key in Design View 536
Activity 1.11 Adding a Second Table to a Database by Importing an Excel Spreadsheet 537
Activity 1.12 Adjusting Column Widths and Viewing a Table in Print Preview 540
Activity 1.13 Viewing a Table in Print Preview 542

Objective 4 Create a Query, Form, and Report 545
Activity 1.14 Creating a Query by Using the Simple Query Wizard 545
Activity 1.15 Creating a Form 548
Activity 1.16 Creating and Modifying a Report 550

Objective 5 Close a Database and Close Access 553
Activity 1.17 Closing a Database and Closing Access 553

GO! With Google 554

Objective Export an Access Table to an Excel Spreadsheet, Open as a Google Sheet, Edit a Record, and Save to Your Computer 554

PROJECT 1B Student Workshops Database 557

Objective 6 Use a Template to Create a Database 558
Activity 1.18 Using a Template to Create a Database 558
Activity 1.19 Building a Table by Entering Records in a Multiple-Items Form and a Single-Record Form 559
Activity 1.20 Appending Records by Importing from an Excel Spreadsheet 561

Objective 7 Organize Objects in the Navigation Pane 562
Activity 1.21 Grouping Database Objects in the Navigation Pane 562

Objective 8 Create a New Table in a Database Created with a Template 564
Activity 1.22 Using the Table Tool to Create a New Table 564

More Knowledge Create a Table from a Template with
Application Parts   565
Activity 1.23 Entering Records Into a New Table   565

Objective 9 View a Report   567
Activity 1.24 Viewing a Report   567

GO! With Google   568

Objective **Export an Access Table to
a Word Document, Save to
Google Drive, Add a Record,
and Save to Your Computer**   568

GO! To Work   570
End of Chapter   571
Summary; GO! Learn It Online; GO! Collaborative
Team Project   571
Project Guide for Access Chapter 1   572
Glossary   573
Chapter Review   575
Mastering Access   582
Rubric   592
GO! Think   593

Chapter 2 Sort and Query
a Database   595

PROJECT 2A Instructors and Courses   595

**Objective 1 Open and Save an Existing
Database**   597
Activity 2.01 Opening an Existing Database and
Resolving Security Alerts   597

Objective 2 Create Table Relationships   598
Activity 2.02 Selecting the Tables and Common
Field to Establish the Table
Relationship   598
Activity 2.03 Setting Relationship Options   601
More Knowledge Edit or Delete a Relationship   602
Activity 2.04 Saving a Relationship Report   603
Activity 2.05 Displaying Subdatasheet Records   603
More Knowledge Other Types of Relationships:
One-to-One and Many-to-Many   604
Activity 2.06 Testing Cascade Options   604

Objective 3 Sort Records in a Table   606
Activity 2.07 Sorting Records in a Table in
Ascending or Descending Order   606
Activity 2.08 Sorting Records in a Table on
Multiple Fields   607

Objective 4 Create a Query in Design View   608
Activity 2.09 Creating a New Select Query in
Design View   609
Activity 2.10 Running, Saving, and Closing a Query   610

**Objective 5 Create a New Query From an
Existing Query**   611
Activity 2.11 Copying an Existing Query   612
More Knowledge Rename a Query   612

Activity 2.12 Modifying the Design of a Query   612
Objective 6 Sort Query Results   614
Activity 2.13 Sorting Query Results   614
More Knowledge Sorting in Design View
or Datasheet View   615

Objective 7 Specify Criteria in a Query   615
Activity 2.14 Specifying Text Criteria in a Query   615
Activity 2.15 Specifying Criteria and Hiding the
Field in the Query Results   617
Activity 2.16 Using *Is Null* Criteria to Find Empty
Fields   618

GO! With Google   620

Objective **Export a Relationship Report
to a PDF File, Save the PDF
File to Google Drive, and then
Share the File**   620

PROJECT 2B Athletic Scholarships Database   622

**Objective 8 Specify Numeric Criteria in a
Query**   623
Activity 2.17 Opening an Existing Database and
Importing a Spreadsheet as a New
Table   623
Activity 2.18 Creating a One-to-Many Table
Relationship   624
Activity 2.19 Specifying Numeric Criteria in a Query   626
Activity 2.20 Using Comparison Operators in
Criteria   626
Activity 2.21 Using the Between . . . And
Comparison Operator   627

**Objective 9 Use Compound Criteria
in a Query**   628
Activity 2.22 Using AND Criteria in a Query   628
Activity 2.23 Using OR Criteria in a Query   629

**Objective 10 Create a Query Based on More
Than One Table**   630
Activity 2.24 Creating a Query Based on More
Than One Table   630

Objective 11 Use Wildcards in a Query   632
Activity 2.25 Using a Wildcard in a Query   632
More Knowledge Using the ? Wildcard Character
to Search for a Single Unknown
Character   633

**Objective 12 Create Calculated Fields
in a Query**   634
Activity 2.26 Creating a Calculated Field in a Query   634
Activity 2.27 Creating a Second Calculated Field
in a Query   635
Activity 2.28 Formatting Calculated Fields   636

**Objective 13 Calculate Statistics and Group
Data in a Query**   637
Activity 2.29 Using the Min, Max, Avg, and Sum
Functions in a Query   637
Activity 2.30 Grouping Records in a Query   638

Objective 14 Create a Crosstab Query 639

Activity 2.31 Creating a Crosstab Query Using
the Query Wizard 639

More Knowledge Creating a Crosstab Query Using
Data From Two Related Tables 641

Objective 15 Create a Parameter Query 641

Activity 2.32 Creating a Parameter Query With
One Criteria 641

More Knowledge Parameter Query Prompts 643

GO! With Google 644

Objective Export an Access Query to an
Excel Spreadsheet, Save it in
Google Drive, and Create a
Chart 644

GO! To Work 646

End of Chapter 647

Summary; GO! Learn It Online; GO! Collaborative
Team Project 647

Project Guide for Access Chapter 2 648

Glossary 649

Chapter Review 650

Mastering Access 659

Rubric 669

GO! Think 670

**Chapter 3 Forms, Filters, and
Reports 671**

PROJECT 3A Students and Majors Database 672

**Objective 1 Create and Use a Form to Add
and Delete Records** 673

Activity 3.01 Opening and Saving an Existing
Database and Viewing a Table
Relationship 673

Activity 3.02 Creating a Form and Viewing Records 674

Activity 3.03 Creating a Second Form 676

Activity 3.04 Adding Records to a Table by Using
a Form 677

Activity 3.05 Deleting Records from a Table by
Using a Form 679

Objective 2 Filter Records 680

Activity 3.06 Filtering Data by Selection of One
Field 680

Activity 3.07 Using Filter By Form 682

Activity 3.08 Using Advanced Filter/Sort 684

More Knowledge Using the Filter Button 685

**Objective 3 Create a Form by Using the
Form Wizard** 686

Activity 3.09 Creating a Form by Using the Form
Wizard 686

**Objective 4 Modify a Form in Layout View
and in Design View** 687

Activity 3.10 Grouping Controls in Layout View 688

Activity 3.11 Applying a Theme and Formatting a
Form in Layout View 689

Activity 3.12 Adding, Resizing, and Moving
Controls in Layout View 690

Activity 3.13 Formatting Controls in Layout View 692

Activity 3.14 Modifying a Form in Design View 694

Activity 3.15 Printing a Single Form 697

GO! With Google 699

Objective Export an Access Form to
an Excel Spreadsheet, Save
to Google Drive as a Google
Sheet, Edit a Record, and Save
to Your Computer 699

PROJECT 3B Job Openings Database 701

**Objective 5 Create a Report by Using the
Report Tool and Modify the
Report in Layout View** 702

Activity 3.16 Opening and Saving an Existing
Database, Renaming Objects, and
Viewing a Table Relationship 702

Activity 3.17 Creating a Report by Using the
Report Tool and Applying a Theme
to the Report 703

Activity 3.18 Modifying a Report in Layout View 704

**Objective 6 Create a Report by Using the
Report Wizard** 706

Activity 3.19 Creating a Report by Using the
Report Wizard 707

Objective 7 Modify the Design of a Report 709

Activity 3.20 Formatting and Deleting Controls in
Layout View 709

Activity 3.21 Modifying Controls in Layout View 710

Activity 3.22 Aligning Controls in Design View 713

**Objective 8 Keep Grouped Data Together
in a Printed Report** 714

Activity 3.23 Keeping Grouped Data Together in a
Printed Report 715

GO! With Google 718

Objective Export an Access Report to
a Word File, Upload the Word
File to Google Drive, and Edit
the Report in Google Docs 718

GO! To Work 720

End of Chapter 721

Summary; GO! Learn It Online; GO! Collaborative
Team Project 721

Project Guide for Access Chapter 3 722

Glossary 723

Chapter Review 724

Mastering Access 732

Rubric 740

GO! Think 741

INTRODUCTION TO
Microsoft PowerPoint 2019 743

Chapter 1 Getting Started with Microsoft PowerPoint 745

PROJECT 1A Company Overview Presentation 746

Objective 1 Create a New Presentation 747
Activity 1.01 Identifying Parts of the PowerPoint Window 747
Activity 1.02 Entering Presentation Text 749
Activity 1.03 Applying a Presentation Theme 750

Objective 2 Edit a Presentation in Normal View 751
Activity 1.04 Inserting a New Slide 751
Activity 1.05 Increasing and Decreasing List Levels 754
Activity 1.06 Adding Speaker Notes to a Presentation 755
Activity 1.07 Displaying and Editing Slides in the Slide Pane 755

Objective 3 Add Pictures to a Presentation 757
Activity 1.08 Inserting a Picture from a File 757
Activity 1.09 Applying a Style to a Picture 759
Activity 1.10 Applying and Removing Picture Artistic Effects 760

Objective 4 Print and View a Presentation 761
Activity 1.11 Viewing a Slide Show 761
Activity 1.12 Using Presenter View 762
Activity 1.13 Inserting Headers and Footers on Slide Handouts 764
Activity 1.14 Inserting Slide Numbers on Slides 765
Activity 1.15 Printing Presentation Handouts 767
Activity 1.16 Printing Speaker Notes 769

GO! With Google Slides 770
Objective Create a Company Overview Presentation in Google Slides 770

PROJECT 1B Itinerary Presentation 772

Objective 5 Edit an Existing Presentation 773
Activity 1.17 Changing Slide Size 773
Activity 1.18 Inserting Slides from an Existing Presentation 774
More Knowledge Inserting All Slides 775
Activity 1.19 Displaying and Editing the Presentation Outline 776
Activity 1.20 Deleting and Moving a Slide 777
Activity 1.21 Finding and Replacing Text 778

Objective 6 Format a Presentation 778
Activity 1.22 Applying a Theme Variant 778
Activity 1.23 Changing Fonts and Font Sizes 779
Activity 1.24 Changing Font Styles and Font Colors 780
Activity 1.25 Aligning Text 781
Activity 1.26 Changing Line Spacing 782

Activity 1.27 Changing the Slide Layout 783

Objective 7 Use Slide Sorter View 783
Activity 1.28 Deleting Slides in Slide Sorter View 784
Activity 1.29 Moving a Single Slide in Slide Sorter View 784
Activity 1.30 Selecting Contiguous and Noncontiguous Slides and Moving Multiple Slides 785

Objective 8 Apply Slide Transitions 787
Activity 1.31 Applying Slide Transitions to a Presentation 787
Activity 1.32 Setting Slide Transition Timing Options 788
Activity 1.33 Displaying a Presentation in Reading View 789

GO! With Google Slides 791
Objective Create an Itinerary Presentation in Google Slides 791

GO! To Work 793
End of Chapter 794
Summary; GO! Learn It Online; GO! Collaborative Team Project 794
Project Guide for PowerPoint Chapter 1 795
Glossary 796
Chapter Review 797
Mastering PowerPoint 803
Rubric 810
GO! Think 811

Chapter 2 Formatting PowerPoint Presentations 813

PROJECT 2A Employee Training Presentation 814

Objective 1 Format Numbered and Bulleted Lists 815
Activity 2.01 Selecting Placeholder Text 815
Activity 2.02 Changing a Bulleted List to a Numbered List 816
Activity 2.03 Changing the Shape and Color of a Bulleted List Symbol 817
More Knowledge Using Other Symbols as Bullet Characters 818
Activity 2.04 Removing a Bullet Symbol from a Bullet Point 818

Objective 2 Insert Online Pictures 819
Activity 2.05 Inserting Online Pictures in a Content Placeholder 819
Activity 2.06 Inserting Pictures in Any Location on a Slide 821
Activity 2.07 Sizing a Picture 821
Activity 2.08 Using Smart Guides and the Ruler to Position a Picture 822
More Knowledge Moving an Object by Using the Arrow Keys 823

Activity 2.09   Cropping a Picture   823
Activity 2.10   Using the Crop to Shape Command
                to Change the Shape of a Picture   825
Objective 3   Insert Text Boxes and Shapes   826
Activity 2.11   Inserting a Text Box   826
Activity 2.12   Inserting and Sizing a Shape   827
Activity 2.13   Adding Text to Shapes   830
Objective 4   Format Objects   830
Activity 2.14   Applying Shape Fills and Outlines   830
Activity 2.15   Using the Eyedropper to Change
                Color   831
Activity 2.16   Applying Shape Styles   833
Activity 2.17   Applying Shape and Picture Effects   833
Activity 2.18   Duplicating Objects   834
Activity 2.19   Aligning and Distributing Objects
                Relative to the Slide   835
Activity 2.20   Aligning and Distributing Objects
                Relative to Each Other   837
Activity 2.21   Grouping Objects   837
GO! With Google Slides   839
**Objective   Create an Informational
                Presentation in Google Slides   839**
PROJECT 2B   Event Announcement   842
**Objective 5   Remove Picture Backgrounds
                and Insert WordArt   843**
Activity 2.22   Removing the Background from
                a Picture and Applying Soft Edge
                Options   843
Activity 2.23   Applying WordArt Styles to Existing
                Text   844
Activity 2.24   Changing the Text Fill and Text
                Outline Colors of a WordArt Object   844
Activity 2.25   Inserting and Aligning a WordArt
                Object   845
Activity 2.26   Adding Text Effects to a WordArt   846
**Objective 6   Create and Format
                a SmartArt Graphic   847**
Activity 2.27   Creating a SmartArt Graphic from
                Bulleted Points   847
Activity 2.28   Adding Shapes in a
                SmartArt Graphic   850
Activity 2.29   Inserting a SmartArt Graphic Using
                a Content Layout   850
Activity 2.30   Inserting Pictures and Text in a
                SmartArt Graphic   851
Activity 2.31   Changing the Size and Shape of
                SmartArt Elements   851
Activity 2.32   Changing the SmartArt Layout   852
Activity 2.33   Changing the Color and Style of a
                SmartArt Graphic   852
Activity 2.34   Converting a SmartArt to Text   853
Objective 7 Insert a 3D Object   854
Activity 2.35   Inserting 3D Objects   854
GO! With Google Slides   856

**Objective   Create an Advertisement
              Presentation in Google Slides   856**
GO! To Work   858
End of Chapter   859
Summary; GO! Learn It Online   859
Review and Assessment Guide for
PowerPoint Chapter 2   860
Glossary   861
Chapter Review   862
Mastering PowerPoint   867
Rubric   874
GO! Think   875

**Chapter 3   Enhancing a
              Presentation with
              Animation, Video,
              Tables, and Charts   877**

PROJECT 3A   Parks and Trails Presentation   878
**Objective 1   Customize Slide Backgrounds
                and Themes   879**
Activity 3.01   Changing Theme Colors   879
Activity 3.02   Changing Theme Fonts   880
Activity 3.03   Applying a Background Style   881
Activity 3.04   Hiding Background Graphics   882
More Knowledge Hiding Background Objects from All
                Slides in a Presentation   883
Activity 3.05   Applying a Background Fill Color to
                a Slide   883
More Knowledge Applying a Fill Color to All the Slides
                in a Presentation   884
Activity 3.06   Applying a Background Texture   884
Activity 3.07   Applying a Picture to the Slide
                Background and Adjusting
                Transparency   885
Activity 3.08   Resetting a Slide Background   887
Objective 2   Animate a Slide Show   888
Activity 3.09   Applying Animation Entrance Effects
                and Effect Options   888
Activity 3.10   Reordering Animation   891
Activity 3.11   Setting Animation Start Options   891
Activity 3.12   Setting Animation Duration and
                Delay Timing Options   892
Activity 3.13   Using Animation Painter and
                Removing Animation   893
Objective 3   Insert a Video   895
Activity 3.14   Inserting a Video and Using Media
                Controls   895
Activity 3.15   Sizing and Aligning a Video   896
Activity 3.16   Changing the Style
                and Shape of a Video   897
Activity 3.17   Trimming and Compressing a Video
                and Setting Playback Options   898

GO! With Google Slides 901
    Objective Create an Informational Presentation Using Google Slides 901
PROJECT 3B Summary and Analysis Presentation 903

Objective 4 Create and Modify Tables 904
Activity 3.18 Creating a Table 904
Activity 3.19 Inserting Rows and Columns in a Table 905
More Knowledge Deleting Rows and Columns 906
Activity 3.20 Sizing a Table 906
Activity 3.21 Distributing Rows and Aligning Table Text 907
More Knowledge Distributing Columns 908
Activity 3.22 Applying and Modifying a Table Style 908
Activity 3.23 Applying Table Effects and Font Formatting 909

Objective 5 Create and Modify Charts 910
Activity 3.24 Inserting a Column Chart 910
Activity 3.25 Entering Chart Data 911
More Knowledge Editing the Chart Data After Closing the Worksheet 913
Activity 3.26 Applying a Chart Style and Modifying Chart Elements 913
Activity 3.27 Creating a Line Chart and Deleting Chart Data 915
Activity 3.28 Formatting a Line Chart 917
Activity 3.29 Animating a Chart 918
Activity 3.30 Animating a Chart with the Morph Transition 919

GO! With Google Slides 922
    Objective Create a Summary and Analysis Presentation in Google Slides 922

GO! To Work 924
End of Chapter 925
Summary; GO! Learn It Online; GO! Collaborative Team Project 925
Project Guide for PowerPoint Chapter 3 926
Glossary 927
Chapter Review 928
Mastering PowerPoint 934
Rubric 942
GO! Think 943

Office Integrated Projects

Chapter 1 Integrating Word, Excel, Access, and PowerPoint 945

PROJECT 1A State Sales 946
Objective 1 Export Access Data to Excel 947
Activity 1.01 Exporting Access Data to Excel 947
Activity 1.02 Creating and Sorting an Excel Table 949
Activity 1.03 Inserting a Total Row in an Excel Table 950

Objective 2 Create an Excel Worksheet from a Word Table 951
Activity 1.04 Formatting a Word Table 947
Activity 1.05 Copying and Pasting a Word Table into an Excel Workbook 949
Activity 1.06 Using the SUM Function and Fill Handle in Excel 949

Objective 3 Copy and Paste an Excel Chart into Other Programs 951
Activity 1.07 Creating and Formatting a Bar Chart in Excel 955
Activity 1.08 Creating and Formatting a Pie Chart in Excel 957
Activity 1.09 Copying and Pasting an Excel Chart into Word 960
Activity 1.10 Pasting an Excel Chart in PowerPoint 961

Objective 4 Copy and Paste an Object from PowerPoint into Excel 962
Activity 1.11 Inserting a SmartArt Graphic 962
Activity 1.12 Copying and Pasting a SmartArt Graphic 963

PROJECT 1B Taos Welcome 966
Objective 5 Using Paste Special to Link Files 967
Activity 1.13 Inserting a SmartArt Graphic 966

Objective 6 Using Paste Special to Link Files 967
Activity 1.14 Updating the Linked Data 968

Objective 7 Create a Table in Word from Access Data 969
Activity 1.15 Exporting an Access Table to an RTF File 969
Activity 1.16 Inserting Access Data into a Word Document 970

Objective 8 Use Access Data to Complete a Mail Merge in Word 971
Activity 1.17 Adding Records to an Access Table 971
Activity 1.18 Starting Mail Merge in Word 972
Activity 1.19 Inserting Merge Fields 973

Appendix A-1
Glossary G-1
Index I-1

About the Authors

Shelley Gaskin, Series Editor, is a professor in the Business and Computer Technology Division at Pasadena City College in Pasadena, California. She holds a bachelor's degree in Business Administration from Robert Morris College (Pennsylvania), a master's degree in Business from Northern Illinois University, and a doctorate in Adult and Community Education from Ball State University (Indiana). Before joining Pasadena City College, she spent 12 years in the computer industry, where she was a systems analyst, sales representative, and director of Customer Education with Unisys Corporation. She also worked for Ernst & Young on the development of large systems applications for their clients. She has written and developed training materials for custom systems applications in both the public and private sector, and has also written and edited numerous computer application textbooks.

This book is dedicated to my husband Fred, and to my students, who inspire me every day.

Alicia Vargas is a faculty member in Business Information Technology at Pasadena City College. She holds a master's and a bachelor's degree in business education from California State University, Los Angeles, and has authored several textbooks and training manuals on Microsoft Word, Microsoft Excel, and Microsoft PowerPoint.

This book is dedicated with all my love to my husband Vic, who makes everything possible; and to my children Victor, Phil, and Emmy, who are an unending source of inspiration and who make everything worthwhile.

Debra Geoghan is a Professor of Computer Science in the STEM department at Bucks County Community College, teaching computer classes ranging from basic computer literacy to cybercrime, computer forensics, and networking. She has certifications from Microsoft, CompTIA, and Apple. Deb has taught at the college level since 1996 and also spent 11 years in the high school classroom. She holds a B.S. in Secondary Science Education from Temple University and an M.A. in Computer Science Education from Arcadia University.

Throughout her teaching career Deb has worked with educators to integrate technology across the curriculum. At BCCC she serves on many technology committees, presents technology workshops for BCCC faculty, and heads the Computer Science Area. Deb is an avid user of technology, which has earned her the nickname "gadget lady."

This book is dedicated to my colleagues and students at Bucks County Community College: for your suggestions and encouragement throughout this process. You inspire me every day. And most importantly—my family. My husband and sons for your patience, help, and love— I couldn't have done this without your love and support.

Nancy Graviett is a professor and department chair in Business Technology at St. Charles Community College in Cottleville, Missouri. She holds a bachelor's degree in marketing and a master's degree in business education from the University of Missouri and has completed a certificate in online education. Nancy has authored textbooks on WordPerfect, Google, Microsoft Outlook, and Microsoft Access.

This book is dedicated to my husband, Dave, and my children, Matthew and Andrea. I cannot thank my family enough for the love and support they share everyday.

GO! with Microsoft Office 365, 2019 Edition

Introducing seamless digital instruction, practice, and assessment

Using GO! with MyLab IT has never been better! With the integrated etext and pre-built learning modules, instructors can assign learning easily and students can get started quickly.

▶ **Proven content and pedagogical approach of *guided instruction, guided practice*, and *mastery*** is effective for all types of learners and all types of course delivery—face-to-face in the classroom, online, and hybrid.

▶ **Students learn Microsoft Office skills by creating practical projects** they will see in their academic and professional lives.

▶ **With GO! MyLab IT students can learn, practice, and assess live or in authentic simulations of Microsoft Office.**

- **Microsoft Office autograded Grader** projects for the instructional, mastery, and assessment projects allow students to work live in Excel, Word, Access, or PPT so that during each step of the learning process, they can receive immediate, autograded feedback!

- **Microsoft Office authentic simulations** allow students to practice what they are learning in a safe environment with learning aids for instant help—*Read*, *Watch*, or *Practice*. Authentic simulations can also be used for assessment without learning aids.

What's New?

- The **book (print or etext) is the student's guide** to completing all autograded Grader projects for instruction, practice, and assessment.

- The **GO! *Learn How* videos**, integrated in the etext, give students an instructor-led, step-by-step guide through the A & B projects.

- **Improved business case connection** throughout the instruction so students always understand the *what* and *why*.

- **Mac tips** ⌨ are woven into the instruction for each project so Mac students can proceed successfully.
  - All text and Grader projects created and tested by the authors on both a Mac and a PC.
  - Content not limited by Mac compatibility! Everything students need to know for MOS exams, Excel, and Access that are not possible on the Mac are still covered!

- **MyLab IT Prebuilt Learning modules** make course setup a snap. The modules are based on research and customer use, and can be easily customized to meet your course requirements.

- **Critical Thinking assessments and badges** expand coverage of Employability Skills.

- **New combined Office Features and Windows chapter** with Grader projects and autograded Windows projects for a fast and concise overview of these important features. Shorter and easier to assign.

- **Regular content updates to stay current with Office 365** updates and new features:
  - New *Semester Updates* for the etext and Grader projects through MyLab IT
  - New *Lessons on the GO!* to help you teach new features

What's New for Grader Projects

- **Autograded *Integrated Projects*** covering Word, Excel, Access, and PPT.
- Projects **A & B Grader reports now include *Learning Aids*** for immediate remediation.
- Autograded Critical Thinking Quizzes and Badges
  - Critical Thinking Modules include a Capstone and Quiz that enable students to earn a Critical Thinking Badge
  - Critical Thinking quizzes for the A & B instructional projects
- A **final output image** is provided so students can visualize what their solution should look like.
- **Mac Compatibility:** All Grader projects are built for PC and Mac users, excluding Access. Only projects that have features not supported on the Mac are not 100% compatible.

What's New for Simulations

- Simulations are updated by the authors for improved reinforcement of the software navigation in each instructional project—as always, they are matched one-to-one with the text Activities.
- *Student Action Visualization* provides an immediate playback for review by students and instructors when there's a question about why an action is marked as incorrect.

The Program

The GO! series has been used for over 17 years to teach students Microsoft Office successfully because of the *Quality of Instruction, Ease of Implementation*, and *Excellence in Assessment*. Using the hallmark Microsoft Procedural Syntax and Teachable Moment approach, students understand how to navigate the Microsoft Office ribbon so they don't get lost, and they get additional instruction and tips *when* they need them. Learning by doing is a great approach for skill-based learning, and creating a real-world document, spreadsheet, presentation, or database puts the skills in context for effective learning!

To improve student results, we recommend pairing the text content with **MyLab IT,** which is the teaching and learning platform that empowers you to reach every student. By combining trusted author content with digital tools and a flexible platform, MyLab personalizes the learning experience and will help your students learn and retain key course concepts while developing skills that future employers are seeking in their candidates.

Solving Teaching and Learning Challenges

The GO! series continues to evolve based on author interaction and experience with real students. GO! is written to ensure students know where they are going, how to get there, and why. Today's software is cloud based and changes frequently, so students need to know how the software functions so they can adapt quickly.

Each chapter is written with two instructional projects organized around **student learning outcomes** and **numbered objectives,** so that students understand what they will learn and be able to do when they finish the chapter. The **project approach** clusters the learning objectives around the projects rather than around the software features. This tested pedagogical approach teaches students to solve real problems as they practice and learn the software features. By using the textbook (print or digital), students can complete the A & B instructional projects as autograded Grader projects in MyLab IT. The *Learn How* videos, integrated in the etext or learning modules, give students an instructor-led, step-by-step guide through the project. This unique approach enhances learning and engages students because they receive immediate feedback. Additionally, students can practice the skills they are learning in the MyLab IT simulations, where they also get immediate feedback and help when needed! Both *Graders* and *Simulations* are available in assessment form so that students can demonstrate mastery.

The **Clear Instruction** in the project steps is written following *Microsoft Procedural Syntax* to guide students where to go and *then* what to do, so they never get lost! With the **Teachable Moment** approach, students learn important concepts when they need to as they work through the instructional projects. No long paragraphs of text. And with the integrated etext in MyLab IT, students can access their book anywhere, anytime.

The page design drives effective learning; textbook pages are clean and uncluttered, with screenshots that validate the student's actions and engage visual learners. Important information is boxed within the text so that students won't miss or skip the *Mac Tips, Another Way, By Touch, Note, Alert,* or *More Knowledge* details. **Color-Coded Steps** guide students through the projects with colors coded by project and the **End-of-Project Icon** helps students know when they have completed the project, which is especially useful in self-paced or online environments.

Students can engage in a wide variety of end-of-chapter projects where they apply what they learned in outcomes-based, problem-solving, and critical thinking projects—many of which require students to create a complete project from scratch.

Within the GO! etext and MyLab IT, students also have access to the *GO! Learn How* training videos, the *GO! to Work* videos (which demonstrate how Microsoft Office is used in a variety of jobs), the GO! for Job Success videos (which teach essential employability skills), and the *Where We're Going* videos, which provide a clear and concise overview of the instructional projects to ensure student success!

This complete, highly effective offering ensures students can learn the skills they need to succeed!

Developing Employability Skills

For students to succeed in a rapidly changing job market, they should be aware of their career options and how to go about developing a variety of skills. With MyLab IT and GO! we focus on developing these skills in the following ways:

High-Demand Office Skills are taught to help students gain these skills and prepare for the Microsoft Office Specialist (MOS) certification exams. The MOS objectives are covered throughout the content and highlighted with the MOS icons.

Essential Employability Skills are taught throughout the chapters using GO! for Job Success Videos and discussions, along with the new Critical Thinking badge students can earn by successfully completing the Critical Thinking Modules.

Employability Skills Matrix (ESM)								
	Grader Projects	Project K	Project M	Project O Group Project	Critical Thinking Projects and Badge	GO! To Work and Job Success Videos	MOS Practice Exams	MOS Badges
Critical Thinking	X	X	X		X		X	X
Communication	X			X		X		
Collaboration				X		X		
Knowledge Application and Analysis	X	X	X		X		X	X
Social Responsibility						X		

Creating a Worksheet and Charting Data — 1

◁ Real-World Projects and GO! To Work Videos

The projects in GO! help you learn skills you'll need in the workforce and everyday life. And the GO! to Work videos give you insight into how people in a variety of jobs put Microsoft Office into action every day.

◁ Projects in GO! are real-world projects you create from start to finish, so that you are using the software features and skills as you will on the job and in everyday life.

GO! to Work videos feature people from a variety of real jobs
◁ explaining how they use Microsoft Office every day to help you see the relevance of learning these programs.

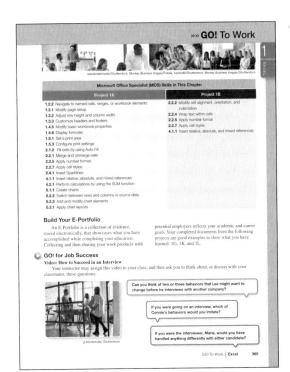

GO! for Job Success Videos and Discussions

Important professional skills you need to succeed in a work environment, such as Accepting Criticism, Customer Service, and Interview Skills, are covered in a video with discussion questions or an overall discussion topic. These are must-have skills.

Skills Badging

Within MyLab IT 2019, you can earn digital badges that demonstrate mastery of specific skills related to Office 2019 or Critical Thinking. These badges can be easily shared across social networks, such as LinkedIn, leading to real opportunities to connect with potential employers.

Applied Learning Opportunities

Throughout the chapters there are two projects for instruction, two for review, and a variety of outcomes-based projects to demonstrate mastery, critical thinking, and problem solving. In addition, within MyLab IT, GO! Learn How videos walk students through the A & B instructional project objectives. Grader projects and simulations provide hands-on instruction, training, and assessment.

▼ Live-in-the-Application Grader Projects

The MyLab IT Grader projects are autograded so students receive immediate feedback on their work. By completing these projects, students gain real-world context as they work live in the application, to learn and demonstrate an understanding of how to perform specific skills to complete a project.

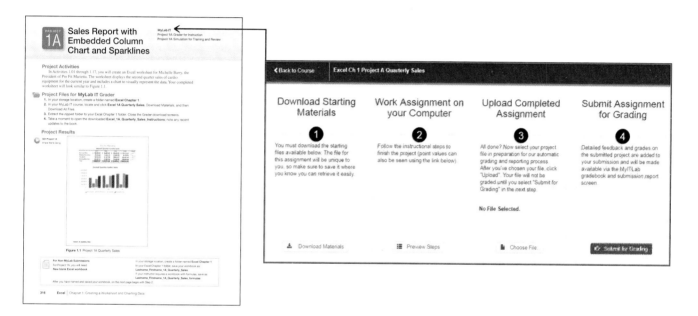

▼ Microsoft Office Simulations

The realistic and hi-fidelity simulations help students feel like they are working in the real Microsoft applications and enable them to explore, use 96% of Microsoft methods, and do so without penalty.

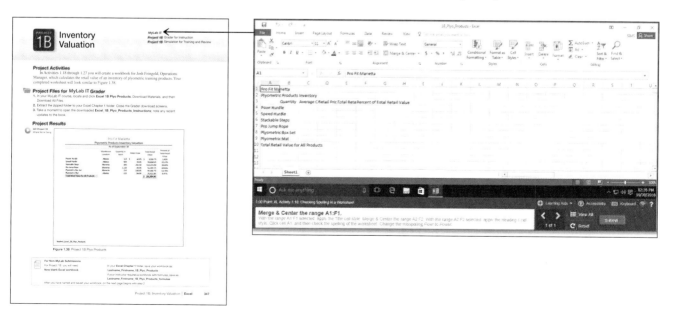

Instructor Teaching Resources

This program comes with the following teaching resources.

Resources available to instructors at www.pearsonhighered.com/go	Features of the Resources
Annotated Instructor Edition Tabs	Available for each chapter and include: • Suggested course implementation strategies and resources for the instructional portion of the chapter • Suggested strategies and resources for the Review, Practice, and Assessment portion of the chapter • Teaching tips
Annotated Solution Files	Annotated solution files in PDF feature callouts to enable easy grading.
Answer Keys for Chapter, MOS, and Critical Thinking Quizzes	Answer keys for each matching and multiple choice question in the chapter.
Application Capstones	Capstone projects for Word, Excel, Access, and PowerPoint that cover the objectives from all three chapters of each application. These are available as autograded Grader projects in MyLab IT, where students can also earn a proficiency badge if they score 90% or higher.
Collaborative Team Project	An optional exercise to assign to students to learn to work in groups.
Content Updates	A living document that features any changes in content based on Microsoft Office 365 changes as well as any errata.
Critical Thinking Quiz and Answers	Additional quiz and answers.
End-of-Chapter Online Projects H-J and M-O	Additional projects that can be assigned at instructor discretion.
Image Library	Every image in the book.
Instructor Manual	Available for each chapter and includes: • Suggested course implementation strategies and resources for the instructional portion of the chapter • Suggested strategies and resources for the Review, Practice, and Assessment portion of the chapter • Objectives • Teaching notes • Discussion questions
List of Objectives and Outcomes	Available for each chapter to help you determine what to assign • Includes every project and identifies which outcomes, objectives, and skills are included from the chapter
Lessons on the GO!	Projects created to teach new features added to Office 365. Available online only.
MOS Mapping and Additional Content	Based on the Office 2019 MOS Objectives • Includes a full guide of where each objective is covered in the textbook. • For any content not covered in the textbook, additional material is available in the Online Appendix document.
PowerPoint Presentations	PowerPoints for each chapter cover key topics, feature key images from the text, and include detailed speaker notes in addition to the slide content. PowerPoints meet accessibility standards for students with disabilities. Features include, but are not limited to: • Keyboard and screen reader access • Alternative text for images • High color contrast between background and foreground colors Audio PPTs contain spoken audio within traditional PowerPoint presentations.
Prepared Exams by Project, Chapter, and Application	An optional exercise that can be used to assess students' ability to perform the skills from each project, chapter, or across all chapters in an application • Each Prepared Exam folder includes the needed data files, instruction file, solution, annotated solution, and scorecard.

Resources available to instructors at www.pearsonhighered.com/go	Features of the Resources
Scorecards and Rubrics	Scorecards allow for easy scoring when hand-grading projects with definitive solutions. Rubrics are for projects without a definitive solution. These are available in Microsoft Word format, enabling instructors to customize the assignments for their classes.
Scripted Lectures	A lecture guide that provides the actions and language to help instructors demonstrate skills from the chapter.
Skills and Procedures Summary Charts	Concise list of key skills, including software icon and keyboard shortcut.
Solution Files, Solution File PDFs, and Solution Files with Formulas (Excel only)	Available for all exercises with definitive solutions.
Student Assignment Trackers	Document with a grid of suggested student deliverables per chapter that can be provided to students with columns for Due Date, Possible Points, and Actual Points.
Student Data Files	Files that students need to complete projects that are not delivered as Grader projects in MyLab IT.
Syllabus Template	Syllabus templates set up for 8-week, 12-week, and 16-week courses.
TestGen and Test Bank	TestGen enables instructors to: • Customize, save, and generate classroom tests • Edit, add, or delete questions from the Test Item Files • Analyze test results • Organize a database of tests and student results. The Test Gen contains approximately 75–100 total questions per chapter, made up of multiple-choice, fill-in-the blank, true/false, and matching. Questions include these annotations: • Correct answer • Difficulty level • Learning objective Alternative versions of the Test Bank are available for the following LMS: Blackboard CE/Vista, Blackboard, Desire2Learn, Moodle, Sakai, and Canvas.
Transition Guide	A detailed spreadsheet that provides a clear mapping of content from GO! Microsoft Office 2016 to GO! Microsoft Office 365, 2019 Edition.

Reviewers of the GO! Series

Carmen Montanez	Allan Hancock College
Jody Derry	Allan Hancock College
Roberta McDonald	Anoka-Ramsey Community College
Paula Ruby	Arkansas State University
Buffie Schmidt	Augusta University
Julie Lewis	Baker College
Melanie Israel	Beal College
Suzanne Marks	Bellevue College
Ellen Glazer	Broward College
Charline Nixon	Calhoun Community College
Joseph Cash	California State University, Stanislaus
Shaun Sides	Catawba Valley Community College
Linda Friedel	Central Arizona College
Vicky Semple	Central Piedmont Community College
Amanda Davis	Chattanooga State Community College
Randall George	Clarion University of Pennsylvania
Beth Zboran	Clarion University of Pennsylvania
Lee Southard	College of Coastal Georgia
Susan Mazzola	College of the Sequoias
Vicki Brooks	Columbia College
Leasa Richards-Mealy	Columbia College
Heidi Eaton	Elgin Community College
Ed Pearson	Friends University
Nancy Woolridge	Fullerton College
Wayne Way	Galveston College
Leslie Martin	Gaston College
Don VanOeveren	Grand Rapids Community College

Therese ONeil	Indiana University of Pennsylvania
Bradley Howard	Itawamba Community College
Edna Tull	Itawamba Community College
Pamela Larkin	Jefferson Community and Technical College
Sonya Shockley	Madisonville Community College
Jeanne Canale	Middlesex Community College
John Meir	Midlands Technical College
Robert Huyck	Mohawk Valley Community College
Mike Maesar	Montana Tech
Julio Cuz	Moreno Valley College
Lynn Wermers	North Shore Community College
Angela Mott	Northeast Mississippi Community College
Connie Johnson	Owensboro Community & Technical College
Kungwen Chu	Purdue University Northwest
Kuan Chen	Purdue University Northwest
Janette Nichols	Randolph Community College
Steven Zhang	Roane State Community College
Elizabeth Drake	Santa Fe College
Sandy Keeter	Seminole State
Pat Dennis	South Plains College
Tamara Dawson	Southern Nazarene University
Richard Celli	SUNY Delhi
Lois Blais	Walters State Community College
Frederick MacCormack	Wilmington University
Jessica Brown	Wilmington University
Doreen Palucci	Wilmington University
Rebecca Anderson	Zane State College

Microsoft Office Features and Windows 10 File Management

PROJECT 1A

Outcomes
Use the features common across all Microsoft Office applications to create and save a Microsoft Word document.

Objectives
1. Explore Microsoft Office
2. Create a Folder for File Storage
3. Download and Extract Zipped Files, Enter and Edit Text in an Office Application, and use Editor to Check Documents
4. Perform Office Commands and Apply Office Formatting
5. Finalize an Office Document
6. Use the Office Help Features

PROJECT 1B

Outcomes
Use Windows 10 features and the File Explorer program to manage files and folders.

Objectives
7. Explore Windows 10
8. Prepare to Work with Folders and Files
9. Use File Explorer to Extract Zipped Files and to Display Locations, Folders, and Files
10. Start Programs and Open Data Files
11. Create, Rename, and Copy Files and Folders

Petar Djordjevic/Shutterstock

In This Chapter

In this chapter, you will practice using the features of Microsoft Office that work similarly across Word, Excel, Access, and PowerPoint. These features include performing commands, adding document properties, applying formatting to text, and searching for Office commands quickly. You will also practice using the file management features of Windows 10 so that you can create folders, save files, and find your documents easily.

The projects in this chapter relate to the **Bell Orchid Hotels**, headquartered in Boston, and which own and operate restaurants, resorts, and business-oriented hotels. Resort property locations are in popular destinations, including Honolulu, Orlando, San Diego, and Santa Barbara. The resorts offer deluxe accommodations and a wide array of dining options. Other Bell Orchid hotels are located in major business centers and offer the latest technology in their meeting facilities. Bell Orchid offers extensive educational opportunities for employees. The company plans to open new properties and update existing properties over the next decade.

Chef Notes

Project Activities

In Activities 1.01 through 1.19, you will create a handout for the Executive Chef at Skyline Metro Grill to give to her staff at a meeting where they will develop new menu ideas for wedding rehearsal dinners. The restaurant is located within Bell Orchid's San Diego resort hotel. Your completed notes will look similar to Figure 1.1.

Project Files for **MyLab IT** Grader

1. For Project 1A, you will start with a blank Word document, and then you will learn how to create a folder for your MyLab IT files as you work through the Project instruction. At the appropriate point in the Project, you will be instructed to download your files from your MyLab IT course.

Project Results

GO! Project 1A

Where We're Going

Figure 1.1 (Wavebreakmedia/Shutterstock)

For Non-MyLab Submissions   **Start with a blank Word document**

For Project 1A, you will begin with a blank Word document and then learn how to create a folder and save a Word document as you work through the Project instruction.

Tap an item to click it.

Press and hold for a few seconds to right-click; release when the information or commands display.

Touch the screen with two or more fingers and then pinch together to zoom out or stretch your fingers apart to zoom in.

Slide your finger on the screen to scroll—slide left to scroll right and slide right to scroll left.

Slide to rearrange—similar to dragging with a mouse.

Swipe to select—slide an item a short distance with a quick movement—to select an item and bring up commands, if any.

Objective 1   Explore Microsoft Office

ALERT   Because Office 365 is a cloud-based subscription service that receives continuous updates, you may encounter some variations in what appears on your screen and what is shown in this instruction. Microsoft Office 365 is fully installed on your PC or Mac; no internet access is necessary to create or edit documents. When you *are* connected to the internet, you will receive monthly upgrades and new features, so you always have the latest versions of Office apps as soon as they are available. Your subscription gives you continuous free access to the latest innovations and refinements.

ALERT   Is Your Screen More Colorful and a Different Size Than the Figures in This Textbook?

Your installation of Microsoft Office may use the default Colorful theme, where the ribbon in each application is a vibrant color and the title bar displays with white text. In this textbook, figures shown use the White theme, but you can be assured that all the commands are the same. You can keep your Colorful theme, or if you prefer, you can change your theme to White to match the figures here. To do so, open any application and display a new document. On the ribbon, click the File tab, and then on the left, click Options. With General selected on the left, under Personalize your copy of Microsoft Office, click the Office Theme arrow, and then click White. Change the Office Background to No Background. (In macOS, display the menu bar, click the application name—Word, Excel, and so on—click Preferences, and then click General. Under Personalize, click the Office Theme arrow to select either Colorful or Classic.)

Additionally, the figures in this book were captured using a screen resolution of 1280 x 768. If that is not your screen resolution, your screen will closely resemble, but not match, the figures shown. To view or change your screen's resolution, on the desktop, right-click in a blank area, click Display settings, click the Resolution arrow, and then select the resolution you want.

GO! Learn How
Video OF1-1

The term ***desktop application*** or ***desktop app*** refers to a computer program that is installed on your PC and that requires a computer operating system such as Microsoft Windows to run. The programs in Office 365 and in Microsoft Office 2019 are considered to be desktop apps. A desktop app typically has hundreds of features and takes time to learn.

Activity 1.01 | Exploring Microsoft Office

1 On the computer you are using, start Microsoft Word, and then compare your screen with Figure 1.2.

Depending on which operating system you are using and how your computer is set up, you might start Word from the taskbar or from the Start menu. On an Apple Mac computer, you might start the program from the Dock.

On the left, the Home tab is active in this view, referred to as *Backstage view*, which is a centralized space for all your file management tasks such as opening, saving, printing, publishing, or sharing a file—all the things you can do *with* a file. In macOS the File tab is on the menu bar.

Documents that you have recently opened, if any, display under the Recent tab. You can also click the Pinned tab to see documents you have pinned there, or you can click the Shared with Me tab to see documents that have been shared with you by others.

On the left, you can click New to find a *template*—a preformatted document that you can use as a starting point and then change to suit your needs. Or you can click Open to navigate to your files and folders. You can also look at Account information, give feedback to Microsoft, or look at the Word Options dialog box.

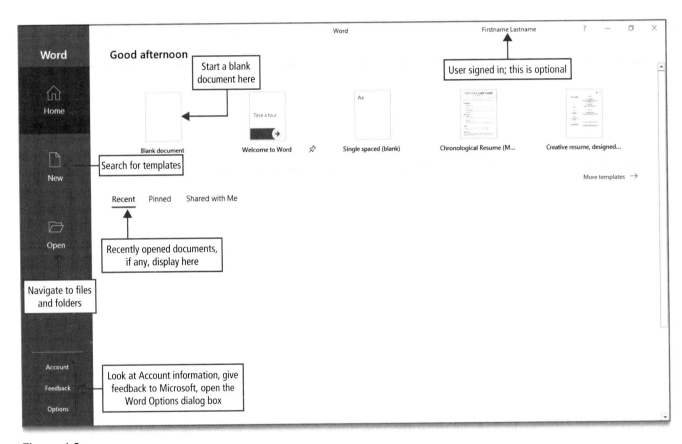

Figure 1.2

2 Click **Blank document**. Compare your screen with Figure 1.3, and then take a moment to study the description of the screen elements in the table in Figure 1.4.

Figure 1.3

Screen Element	Description
AutoSave (off unless your document is saved to OneDrive using an Office 365 subscription)	Saves your document every few seconds so you don't have to. On a Windows system, AutoSave is available in Word, Excel, and PowerPoint for Office 365 subscribers. AutoSave is enabled only when a file is stored on OneDrive, OneDrive for Business, or SharePoint Online. Changes to your document are saved to the cloud as you are working, and if other people are working on the same file, AutoSave lets them see your changes in a matter of seconds.
Comments	Displays a short menu from which you can add a comment to your document or view other comments already in the document.
File tab	Displays Microsoft Office Backstage view, which is a centralized space for all your file management tasks such as opening, saving, printing, publishing, or sharing a file—all the things you can do *with* a file. (In macOS the File tab is on the menu bar.)
Group names	Indicate the name of the groups of related commands on the displayed ribbon tab.
Quick Access Toolbar	Displays buttons to perform frequently used commands and resources with a single click. The default commands include Save, Undo, and Redo. You can add and delete buttons to customize the Quick Access Toolbar for your convenience.
Ribbon	Displays a group of task-oriented tabs that contain the commands, styles, and resources you need to work in Microsoft Office desktop apps. The look of your ribbon depends on your screen resolution. A high resolution will display more individual items and button names on the ribbon.
Ribbon Display Options	Displays three ways you can display the ribbon: Auto-hide Ribbon, Show Tabs, or Show Tabs and Commands; typically, you will want to use Show Tabs and Commands, especially while you are learning Office.
Ribbon tabs	Display the names of the task-oriented tabs relevant to the open document.
Share	Opens the Share dialog box from which you can save your file to the cloud—your OneDrive—and then share it with others so you can collaborate. Here you can also email the Office file or a PDF of the file directly from Outlook if you are using Outlook to view and send email. A *dialog box* enables you to make decisions about an individual object or topic.
Signed-in user	Identifies the user who is signed in to Office.
Status bar	Displays file information on the left; on the right displays buttons for Read Mode, Print Layout, and Web Layout views; on the far right edge, displays Zoom controls.
Tell me what you want to do	Provides a search feature for Microsoft Office commands that you activate by typing what you are looking for in the *Tell me what you want to do* area. As you type, every keystroke refines the results so that you can click the command as soon as it displays.
Title bar	Displays the name of the file and the name of the program; the window control buttons are grouped on the right side of the title bar.
Window control buttons	Displays buttons for commands to Minimize, Restore Down, or Close the window.

Figure 1.4

Objective 2 **Create a Folder for File Storage**

GO! Learn How
Video OF1-2

A *location* is any disk drive, folder, or other place in which you can store files and folders. A *file* is information stored on a computer under a single name. A *folder* is a container in which you store files. Where you store your files depends on how and where you use your data. For example, for your college classes, you might decide to store your work on a removable USB flash drive so that you can carry your files to different locations and access your files on different computers.

If you do most of your work on a single computer, for example your home desktop system or your laptop computer that you take with you to school or work, then you can store your files in one of the folders on your hard drive provided by your Windows operating system—Documents, Music, Pictures, or Videos.

The best place to store files if you want them to be available anytime, anywhere, from almost any device is on your *OneDrive*, which is Microsoft's free *cloud storage* for anyone with a free Microsoft account. Cloud storage refers to online storage of data so that you can access your data from different places and devices. *Cloud computing* refers to applications and services that are accessed over the internet, rather than to applications that are installed on your local computer.

Besides being able to access your documents from any device or location, OneDrive also offers *AutoSave*, which saves your document every few seconds, so you don't have to. On a Windows system, AutoSave is available in Word, Excel, and PowerPoint for Office 365 subscribers. Changes to your document are saved to the cloud as you are working, and if other people are working on the same file—referred to as *real-time co-authoring*—AutoSave lets them see your changes in a matter of seconds.

If you have an *Office 365* subscription—one of the versions of Microsoft Office to which you subscribe for an annual fee or download for free with your college *.edu* address—your storage capacity on OneDrive is a terabyte or more, which is more than most individuals would ever require. Many colleges provide students with free Office 365 subscriptions. The advantage of subscribing to Office 365 is that you receive monthly updates with new features.

Because many people now have multiple computing devices—desktop, laptop, tablet, smartphone—it is common to store data *in the cloud* so that it is always available. *Synchronization*, also called *syncing*—pronounced SINK-ing—is the process of updating computer files that are in two or more locations according to specific rules. So, if you create and save a Word document on your OneDrive using your laptop, you can open and edit that document on your tablet in OneDrive. When you close the document again, the file is properly updated to reflect your changes. Your OneDrive account will guide you in setting options for syncing files to your specifications. You can open and edit Office files by using Office apps available on a variety of device platforms, including iOS, Android, in a web browser, and in Windows.

MORE KNOWLEDGE **Creating a Microsoft Account**

Use a free Microsoft account to sign in to Microsoft Office so that you can work on different PCs and use your free OneDrive cloud storage. If you already sign in to a Windows PC or tablet, or you sign in to Xbox Live, Outlook.com, or OneDrive, use that account to sign in to Office. To create a new Microsoft account, in your browser, search for *sign up for a Microsoft account*. You can use any email address as the user name for your new Microsoft account—including addresses from Outlook.com or Gmail.

Activity 1.02 | Creating a Folder for File Storage

Your computer's operating system, either Windows or macOS, helps you to create and maintain a logical folder structure, so always take the time to name your files and folders consistently.

NOTE **This Activity is for Windows PC users. Mac users refer to the document** *Creating a Folder for File Storage on a Mac.*

Mac users can refer to the document Creating a Folder for File Storage on a Mac available within MyLab IT or, for non-MyLab users, your instructor can provide this document to you from the Instructor Resource Center.

In this Activity, you will create a folder in the storage location you have chosen to use for your files, and then you will save your file. This example will use the Documents folder on the PC at which you are working. If you prefer to store on your OneDrive or on a USB flash drive, you can use similar steps.

1 Decide where you are going to store your files for this Project.

As the first step in saving a file, determine where you want to save the file, and if necessary, insert a storage device.

2 At the top of your screen, in the title bar, notice that *Document1 – Word* displays.

The Blank option on the opening screen of an Office program displays a new unsaved file with a default name—*Document1, Presentation1*, and so on. As you create your file, your work is temporarily stored in the computer's memory until you initiate a Save command, at which time you must choose a file name and a location in which to save your file.

3 In the upper left corner of your screen, click the **File tab** to display **Backstage** view, and then on the left, if necessary, click **Info**. Compare your screen with Figure 1.5.

Recall that Backstage view is a centralized space that groups commands related to *file* management; that is why the tab is labeled *File*. File management commands include opening, saving, printing, or sharing a file. The ***Backstage tabs***—*Info, New, Open, Save, Save As, Print, Share, Export*, and *Close*—display along the left side. The tabs group file-related tasks together.

Here, the ***Info tab*** displays information—*info*—about the current file, and file management commands display under Info. For example, if you click the Protect Document button, a list of options that you can set for this file that relate to who can open or edit the document displays.

On the right, you can also examine the ***document properties***. Document properties, also known as ***metadata***, are details about a file that describe or identify it, such as the title, author name, subject, and keywords that identify the document's topic or contents.

Figure 1.5

4 On the left, click **Save As**, and notice that, if you are signed into Office with a Microsoft account, one option for storing your files is your **OneDrive**. Compare your screen with Figure 1.6.

When you are saving something for the first time, for example a new Word document, the Save and Save As commands are identical. That is, the Save As commands will display if you click Save or if you click Save As.

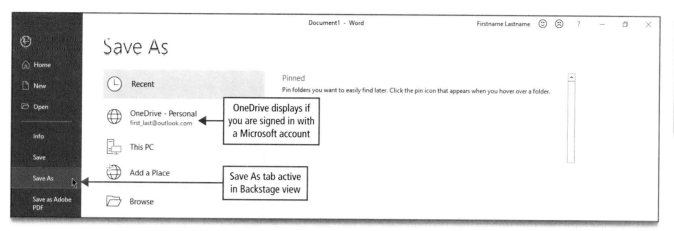

Figure 1.6

5 To store your Word file in the **Documents** folder on your PC, click **Browse** to display the **Save As** dialog box. On the left, in the **navigation pane**, scroll down; if necessary click > to expand This PC, and then click **Documents**. Compare your screen with Figure 1.7.

In the Save As dialog box, you must indicate the name you want for the file and the location where you want to save the file. When working with your own data, it is good practice to pause at this point and determine the logical name and location for your file.

In the Save As dialog box, a *toolbar* displays, which is a row, column, or block of buttons or icons, that displays across the top of a window and that contains commands for tasks you perform with a single click.

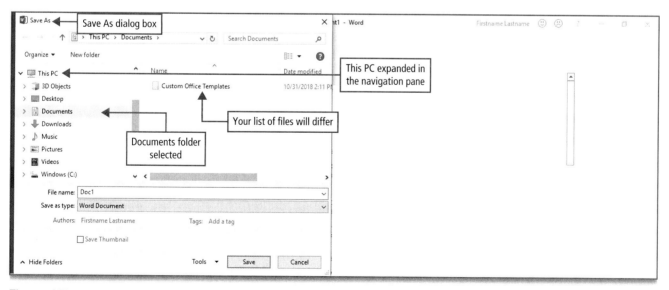

Figure 1.7

6 On the toolbar, click **New folder**.

In the file list, Windows creates a new folder, and the text *New folder* is selected.

7 Type **Office Features Chapter 1** and press [Enter]. In the **file list**, double-click the name of your new folder to open it and display its name in the **address bar**. Compare your screen with Figure 1.8.

In Windows-based programs, the [Enter] key confirms an action.

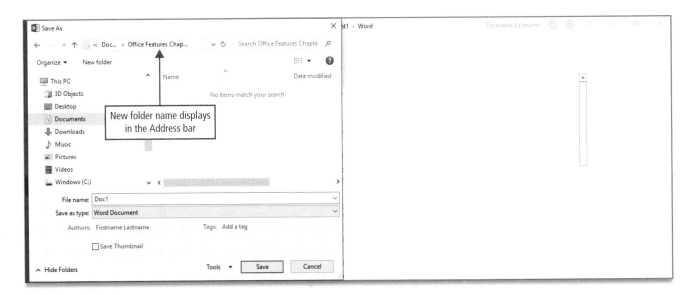

Figure 1.8

8 In the lower right corner of the **Save As** dialog box, click **Cancel**. In the upper left corner of Backstage view, click the **Back** arrow [←].

9 In the upper right corner of the Word window, click **Close** [X]. If prompted to save your changes, click Don't Save. Close any other open windows or programs.

Objective 3	**Download and Extract Zipped Files, Enter and Edit Text in an Office Application, and Use Editor to Check Documents**

GO! Learn How
Video OF1-3

Download refers to the action of transferring or copying a file from another location—such as a cloud storage location, your college's Learning Management System, or from an internet site like MyLab IT—to your computer. Files that you download are frequently *compressed files*, which are files that have been reduced in size, take up less storage space, and can be transferred to other computers faster than uncompressed files.

A compressed folder might contain a group of files that were combined into one compressed folder, which makes it easier to share a group of files. To *extract* means to decompress, or pull out, files from a compressed form. The terms *zip* and *unzip* refer to the process of compressing (zipping) and extracting (unzipping). Windows 10 includes *Compressed Folder Tools*, available on the ribbon, to assist you in extracting compressed files. Similar tools are available in macOS. You do not need to install a separate program to zip or unzip files; modern operating systems like Windows and macOS provide sophisticated tools for these tasks.

All programs in Microsoft Office require some typed text. Your keyboard is still the primary method of entering information into your computer. Techniques to enter text and to *edit*—make changes to—text are similar across all Microsoft Office programs.

For Non-MyLab Submissions

Start Word and click Blank document. Click the File tab, on the left click Save As, click Browse, and then navigate to your **Office Features Chapter 1 folder.** At the bottom of the **Save As** dialog box, in the **File name** box, using your own name, name the file **Lastname_Firstname_Office_Features_1A_Chef_Notes** and then click Save. Then, move to Step 3 in Activity 1.03.

---

1 Sign in to your MyLab IT course. Locate and click the Grader project **Office Features 1A Chef Notes**, click **Download Materials**, and then click **Download All Files**. Using the Chrome browser (if you are using a different browser see notes below), extract the zipped folder to your **Office Features Chapter 1 folder** as follows (or use your favorite method to download and extract files):

- In the lower left, next to the downloaded zipped folder, click the small **arrow**, and then click **Show in folder**. The zipped folder displays in *File Explorer*—the Windows program that displays the contents of locations, folders, and files on your computer—in the Downloads folder. (Unless you have changed default settings, downloaded files go to the Downloads folder on your computer.)
- With the zipped folder selected, on the ribbon, under **Compressed Folder Tools**, click the **Extract tab**, and then at the right end of the ribbon, click **Extract all** (you may have to wait a few seconds for the command to become active).
- In the displayed **Extract Compressed (Zipped) Folders** dialog box, click **Browse**. In the **Select a destination** dialog box, use the navigation pane on the left to navigate to your **Office Features Chapter 1 folder**, and double-click its name to open the folder and display its name in the **Address bar**.
- In the lower right, click **Select Folder**, and then in the lower right, click **Extract**; when complete, a new File Explorer window displays showing the extracted files in your chapter folder. Take a moment to open **Office_Features_1A_Chef_Notes_Instructions**; note any recent updates to the book.
- **Close** ☒ both File Explorer windows, close any open documents, and then close the Grader download screens. You can also close MyLab IT and, if open, your Learning Management system.

NOTE   Using the Edge Browser or Firefox Browser to Extract Files

Microsoft Edge: At the bottom, click Open, click Extract all, click Browse, navigate to and open your Chapter folder, click Select Folder, click Extract.

Firefox: In the displayed dialog box, click OK, click Extract all, click Browse, navigate to and open your Chapter folder, click Select Folder, and then click Extract.

MAC TIP   Using the Chrome browser, in MyLab IT, after you click Download Materials, in the lower left, to the right of the zipped folder, click the arrow. Click Open. Click the blue folder containing the unzipped files. Use Finder commands to move or copy the files to your Office Features Chapter 1 folder.

2 On the Windows taskbar, click **File Explorer** ▣. Navigate to your **Office Features Chapter 1 folder**, and then double-click the Word file you downloaded from MyLab IT that displays your name—**Student_Office_Features_1A_Chef_Notes**. In this empty Word document, if necessary, at the top, click **Enable Editing**.

MAC TIP   When the Word application is not open, on the Dock, use the macOS Finder commands to locate your Word document. When the Word application is open, use the File tab on the menu bar.

3 On the ribbon, on the **Home tab**, in the **Paragraph group**, if necessary, click **Show/Hide** ¶ so that it is active—shaded. On the **View tab**, if necessary, in the **Show group**, select the **Ruler** check box so that rulers display below the ribbon and on the left side of your window, and then redisplay the **Home tab**.

The *insertion point*—a blinking vertical line that indicates where text or graphics will be inserted—displays. In Office programs, the mouse *pointer*—any symbol that displays on your screen in response to moving your mouse device—displays in different shapes depending on the task you are performing and the area of the screen to which you are pointing.

When you press Enter, Spacebar, or Tab on your keyboard, characters display to represent these keystrokes. These screen characters do not print and are referred to as *formatting marks* or *nonprinting characters*.

When working in Word, display the rulers so that you can see how margin settings affect your document and how text and objects align. Additionally, if you set a tab stop or an indent, its location is visible on the ruler.

MAC TIP To display group names on the ribbon, display the menu bar, click Word, click Preferences, click View, under Ribbon, select the Show group titles check box.

NOTE   **Activating Show/Hide in Word Documents**

When Show/Hide is active—the button is shaded—formatting marks display. Because formatting marks guide your eye in a document—like a map and road signs guide you along a highway—these marks will display throughout this instruction. Expert Word users keep these marks displayed while creating documents.

4 Type **Skyline Grille Info** and notice how the insertion point moves to the right as you type. Point slightly to the right of the letter *e* in *Grille* and click to place the insertion point there. Compare your screen with Figure 1.9.

A *paragraph symbol* (¶) indicates the end of a paragraph and displays each time you press Enter. This is a type of formatting mark and does not print.

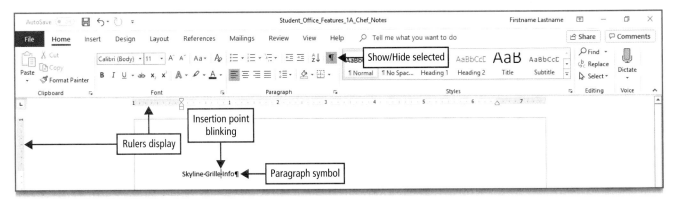

Figure 1.9

5 On your keyboard, locate and then press the Backspace key one time to delete the letter *e*.

Pressing Backspace removes a character to the left of the insertion point.

MAC TIP Press delete.

6 Press → one time to place the insertion point to the left of the *I* in *Info*. Type **Chef** and then press Spacebar one time.

By *default*, when you type text in an Office program, existing text moves to the right to make space for new typing. Default refers to the current selection or setting that is automatically used by a program unless you specify otherwise.

7 Press Del four times to delete *Info* and then type **Notes**

Pressing Del removes a character to the right of the insertion point.

MAC TIP Press fn + delete to delete characters to the right of the insertion point.

8 With your insertion point blinking after the word *Notes*, on your keyboard, hold down the Ctrl key. While holding down Ctrl, press ← three times to move the insertion point to the beginning of the word *Grill*.

> This is a **keyboard shortcut**—a key or combination of keys that performs a task that would otherwise require a mouse. This keyboard shortcut moves the insertion point to the beginning of the previous word.
>
> A keyboard shortcut is indicated as Ctrl + ← (or some other combination of keys) to indicate that you hold down the first key while pressing the second key. A keyboard shortcut can also include three keys, in which case you hold down the first two and then press the third. For example, Ctrl + Shift + ← selects one word to the left.

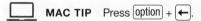 **MAC TIP** Press option + ←.

9 With the insertion point blinking at the beginning of the word *Grill*, type **Metro** and press Spacebar one time.

10 Click to place the insertion point after the letter *s* in *Notes* and then press Enter one time. With the insertion point blinking, type the following and include the spelling error: **Exective Chef, Madison Dunham** (If Word autocorrects *Exective* to *Executive*, delete *u* in the word.)

11 With your mouse, point slightly to the left of the *M* in *Madison*, hold down the left mouse button, and then **drag**—hold down the left mouse button while moving your mouse—to the right to select the text *Madison Dunham* but not the paragraph mark following it, and then release the mouse button. Compare your screen with Figure 1.10.

> The **mini toolbar** displays commands that are commonly used with the selected object, which places common commands close to your pointer. When you move the pointer away from the mini toolbar, it fades from view.
>
> **Selecting** refers to highlighting—by dragging or clicking with your mouse—areas of text or data or graphics so that the selection can be edited, formatted, copied, or moved. The action of dragging includes releasing the left mouse button at the end of the area you want to select.
>
> The Office programs recognize a selected area as one unit to which you can make changes. Selecting text may require some practice. If you are not satisfied with your result, click anywhere outside of the selection, and then begin again.

MAC TIP The mini toolbar may not display; use ribbon commands.

BY TOUCH Tap once on *Madison* to display the gripper—a small circle that acts as a handle—directly below the word. This establishes the start gripper. If necessary, with your finger, drag the gripper to the beginning of the word. Then drag the gripper to the end of *Dunham* to select the text and display the end gripper.

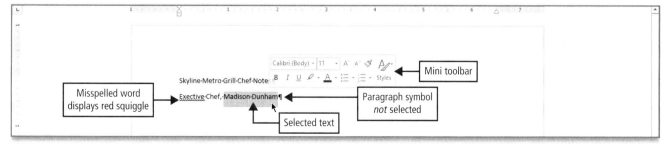

Figure 1.10

12 With the text *Madison Dunham* selected, type **Sarah Jackson**

In any Windows-based program, such as the Microsoft Office programs, selected text is deleted and then replaced when you begin to type new text. You will save time by developing good techniques for selecting and then editing or replacing selected text, which is easier than pressing `Backspace` or `Del` numerous times to delete text.

Activity 1.04 | Checking Spelling

Microsoft Office has a dictionary of words against which all entered text is checked. In Word and PowerPoint, words that are not in the dictionary display a red squiggle, indicating a possible misspelled word, a proper name, or an unusual word—none of which are in the Office dictionary. In Excel and Access, you can initiate a check of the spelling, but red squiggles do not display.

1 Notice that the misspelled word *Exective* displays with a red squiggle.

2 Point to *Exective* and then **right-click**—click your right mouse button one time.

A **shortcut menu** displays, which displays commands and options relevant to the selected text or object. These are **context-sensitive commands** because they relate to the item you right-clicked. These are also referred to as **context menus**. Here, the shortcut menu displays commands related to the misspelled word.

BY TOUCH   Tap and hold a moment—when a square displays around the misspelled word, release your finger to display the shortcut menu.

3 Press `Esc` two times to cancel the shortcut menus, and then in the lower left corner of your screen, on the status bar, click the **Proofing** icon, which displays an *X* because some errors are detected. In the **Editor** pane that displays on the right, if necessary, click the Results button, and then under **Suggestions**, to the right of *Executive*, click, and then compare your screen with Figure 1.11.

The Editor pane displays on the right. **Editor**, according to Microsoft, is your digital writing assistant in Word and also in Outlook. Editor displays misspellings, grammatical mistakes, and writing style issues as you type by marking red squiggles for spelling, blue double underlines for grammar, and dotted underlines for writing style issues.

Here you have many more options for checking spelling than you have on the shortcut menu. The suggested correct word, *Executive*, displays under Suggestions. The displayed menu provides additional options for the suggestion. For example, you can have the word read aloud, hear it spelled out, change all occurrences in the document, or add to AutoCorrect options.

In the Editor pane, you can ignore the word one time or in all occurrences, change the word to the suggested word, select a different suggestion, or add a word to the dictionary against which Word checks.

MAC TIP   In the Spelling and Grammar dialog box, click Executive, and then click Change. The Editor pane is not available on a Mac.

Figure 1.11

 ANOTHER WAY Press [F7] to display the Editor pane; or, on the Review tab, in the Proofing group, you can check your document for Spelling.

4 In the **Editor** pane, under **Suggestions**, click *Executive* to correct the spelling. In the message box that displays, click **OK**.

5 If necessary **Close** the **Editor** pane by clicking ☒ in the upper right corner.

Objective 4 **Perform Office Commands and Apply Office Formatting**

GO! Learn How
Video OF1-4

Formatting refers to applying Office commands to make your document easy to read and to add visual touches and design elements to make your document inviting to the reader. This process establishes the overall appearance of text, graphics, and pages in your document.

Activity 1.05 │ **Performing Commands from a Dialog Box**

MOS
1.2.4

In a dialog box, you make decisions about an individual object or topic. In some dialog boxes, you can make multiple decisions in one place.

1 On the ribbon, click the **Design tab**, and then in the **Page Background group**, click **Page Color**.

2 At the bottom of the menu, notice the command **Fill Effects** followed by an **ellipsis** (. . .). Compare your screen with Figure 1.12.

An *ellipsis* is a set of three dots indicating incompleteness. An ellipsis following a command name indicates that a dialog box will display when you click the command.

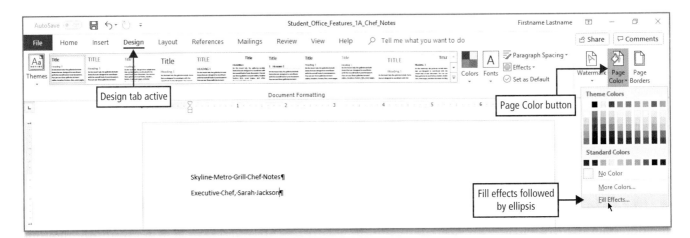

Figure 1.12

3 Click **Fill Effects** to display the **Fill Effects** dialog box. Compare your screen with Figure 1.13.

Fill is the inside color of a page or object. Here, the dialog box displays a set of tabs across the top from which you can display different sets of options. Some dialog boxes display the option group names on the left. The Gradient tab is active. In a *gradient fill*, one color fades into another.

📱 **MAC TIP**   Click More Colors to display the Colors dialog box.

Figure 1.13

4 ▶ Under **Colors**, click the **One color** option button.

The dialog box displays settings related to the *One color* option. An *option button* is a round button that enables you to make one choice among two or more options.

🖥️ **MAC TIP** On the first tab, drag your cursor on the color wheel until you see a color in the small box similar to the background color shown in Figure 1.1.

5 ▶ Click the **Color 1 arrow**—the arrow under the text *Color 1*—and then in the eighth column, point to the second color to display a ScreenTip with the name of the color.

When you click an arrow in a dialog box, additional options display. A *ScreenTip* displays useful information about mouse actions, such as pointing to screen elements or dragging.

6 ▶ Click the color, and then notice that the fill color displays in the **Color 1** box. In the **Dark Light** bar, click the **Light arrow** as many times as necessary until the scroll box is all the way to the right—or drag the scroll box all the way to the right. Under **Shading styles**, click the **From corner** option button. Under **Variants**, click the **upper right variant**. Compare your screen with Figure 1.14.

This dialog box is a good example of the many different elements you may encounter in a dialog box. Here you have option buttons, an arrow that displays a menu, a slider bar, and graphic options that you can select.

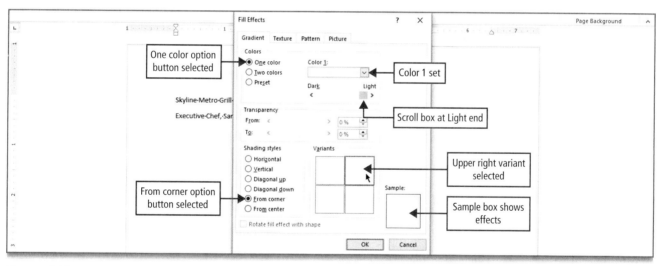

Figure 1.14

👆 **BY TOUCH** In a dialog box, you can tap option buttons and other commands just as you would click them with a mouse. When you tap an arrow to display a color palette, a larger palette displays than if you used your mouse. This makes it easier to select colors with your finger in a dialog box.

7 ▶ At the bottom of the dialog box, click **OK**, and notice the subtle page color.

In Word, the gold shading page color will not print—even on a color printer—unless you set specific options to do so. However, a subtle background page color is effective if people will be reading the document on a screen. Microsoft's research indicates that two-thirds of people who open Word documents on a screen never print or edit them; they only read them.

Activity 1.06 | Using Undo and Applying Text Effects

1 Point to the *S* in *Skyline*, and then drag down and to the right to select both paragraphs of text and include the paragraph marks. On the mini toolbar, click **Styles**, and then *point to* but do not click **Title**. Compare your screen with Figure 1.15.

A *style* is a group of formatting commands, such as font, font size, font color, paragraph alignment, and line spacing that can be applied to a paragraph with one command.

Live Preview is a technology that shows the result of applying an editing or formatting change as you point to possible results—before you actually apply it.

MAC TIP The mini toolbar and Live Preview are not available; use ribbon commands.

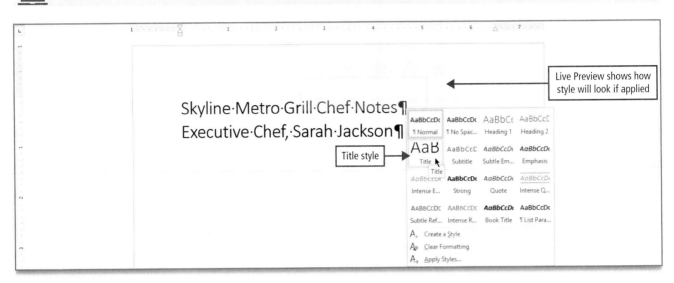

Figure 1.15

2 In the **Styles** gallery, click **Title**.

A *gallery* is an Office feature that displays a list of potential results.

MAC TIP On the Home tab, in the Styles gallery, click Title.

3 On the ribbon, on the **Home tab**, in the **Paragraph group**, click **Center** to center the two paragraphs.

Alignment refers to the placement of paragraph text relative to the left and right margins. *Center alignment* refers to text that is centered horizontally between the left and right margins. You can also align text at the left margin, which is the default alignment for text in Word, or at the right.

ANOTHER WAY Press Ctrl + E to use the Center command.

MAC TIP Press command ⌘ + E to use the Center command.

4 With the two paragraphs still selected, on the **Home tab**, in the **Font Group**, click **Text Effects and Typography** to display a gallery.

5 In the second row, click the first effect. Click anywhere to *deselect*—cancel the selection—the text and notice the text effect.

6 Because this effect might be difficult to read, in the upper left corner of your screen, on the Quick Access Toolbar, click **Undo**.

The *Undo* command reverses your last action.

ANOTHER WAY Press Ctrl + Z as the keyboard shortcut for the Undo command.

MAC TIP Press command ⌘ + Z as the keyboard shortcut for the Undo command.

7 Select the two paragraphs of text again, display the **Text Effects and Typography** gallery again, and then in the first row, click the fifth effect. Click anywhere to deselect the text and notice the text effect. Compare your screen with Figure 1.16.

As you progress in your study of Microsoft Office, you will practice using many dialog boxes and commands to apply interesting effects such as this to your Word documents, Excel worksheets, Access database objects, and PowerPoint slides.

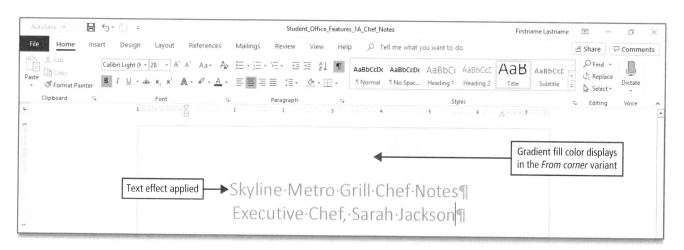

Figure 1.16

Activity 1.07 | Performing Commands from and Customizing the Quick Access Toolbar

The ribbon that displays across the top of the program window groups commands in the way that you would most logically use them. The ribbon in each Office program is slightly different, but all contain the same three elements: *tabs*, *groups*, and *commands*.

Tabs display across the top of the ribbon, and each tab relates to a type of activity; for example, laying out a page. Groups are sets of related commands for specific tasks. Commands—instructions to computer programs—are arranged in groups and might display as a button, a menu, or a box in which you type information.

You can also minimize the ribbon so only the tab names display, which is useful when working on a smaller screen such as a tablet computer where you want to maximize your screen viewing area.

1 In the upper left corner of your screen, above the ribbon, locate the **Quick Access Toolbar**.

Recall that the Quick Access Toolbar contains commands that you use frequently. By default, only the commands Save, Undo, and Redo display, but you can add and delete commands to suit your needs. Possibly the computer at which you are working already has additional commands added to the Quick Access Toolbar.

2 At the end of the **Quick Access Toolbar**, click the **Customize Quick Access Toolbar** button [⏷], and then compare your screen with Figure 1.17.

A list of commands that Office users commonly add to their Quick Access Toolbar displays, including New, Open, Email, Quick Print, and Print Preview and Print. Commands already on the Quick Access Toolbar display a check mark. Commands that you add to the Quick Access Toolbar are always just one click away.

Here you can also display the More Commands dialog box, from which you can select any command from any tab to add to the Quick Access Toolbar.

👉 **BY TOUCH** Tap once on Quick Access Toolbar commands.

Figure 1.17

3 On the list, click **Print Preview and Print**, and then notice that the icon is added to the **Quick Access Toolbar**. Compare your screen with Figure 1.18.

The icon that represents the Print Preview command displays on the Quick Access Toolbar. Because this is a command that you will use frequently while building Office documents, you might decide to have this command remain on your Quick Access Toolbar.

🔄 **ANOTHER WAY** Right-click any command on the ribbon, and then on the shortcut menu, click Add to Quick Access Toolbar.

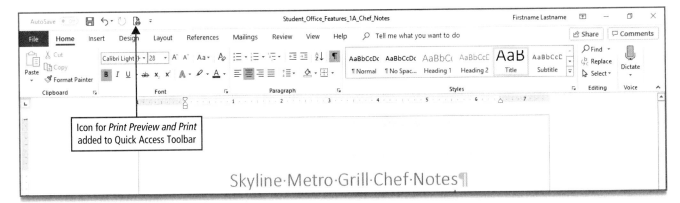

Figure 1.18

Activity 1.08 | Performing Commands from the Ribbon

1 In the second line of text, click to place the insertion point to the right of the letter *n* in *Jackson*. Press [Enter] three times. Compare your screen with Figure 1.19.

Word creates three new blank paragraphs, and no Text Effect is applied.

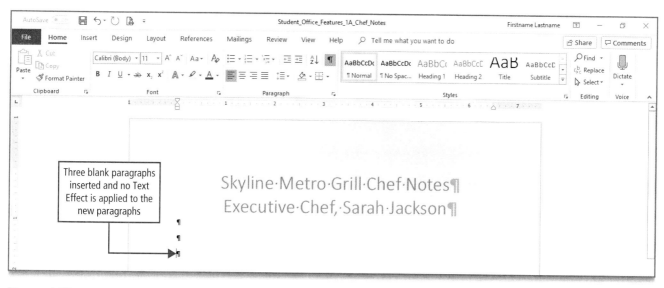

Figure 1.19

2 Click to position the insertion point to the left of the **second blank paragraph** that you just inserted. On the ribbon, click the **Insert tab**. In the **Illustrations group**, *point* to **Pictures** to display its ScreenTip.

Many buttons on the ribbon have this type of *enhanced ScreenTip*, which displays useful descriptive information about the command.

3 Click **Pictures**. In the **Insert Picture** dialog box, navigate to your **Office Features Chapter 1 folder**, double-click the **of01A_Chefs** picture, and then compare your screen with Figure 1.20.

The picture displays in your Word document.

MAC TIP Click Picture from File, then navigate to your Office Features Chapter 1 folder.

For Non-MyLab Submissions
The of01A_Chefs picture is included with this chapter's Student Data Files, which you can obtain from your instructor or by downloading the files from www.pearsonhighered.com/go

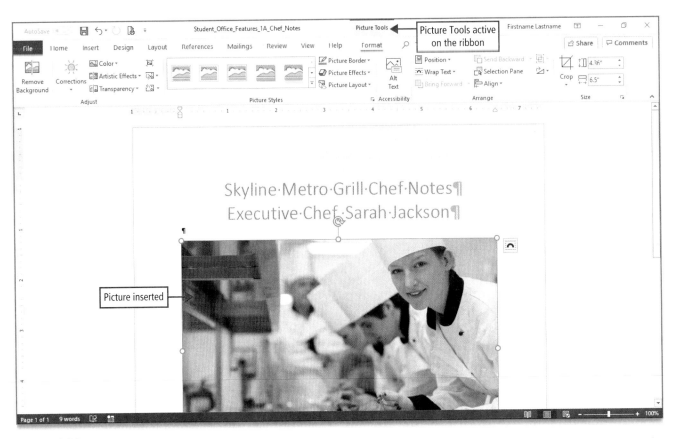

Figure 1.20

4 In the upper right corner of the picture, point to the **Layout Options** button ⌞☑⌝ to display its ScreenTip, and then compare your screen with Figure 1.21.

Layout Options enable you to choose how the *object*—in this instance an inserted picture—interacts with the surrounding text. An object is a picture or other graphic such as a chart or table that you can select and then move and resize.

When a picture is selected, the Picture Tools become available on the ribbon. Additionally, *sizing handles*—small circles or squares that indicate an object is selected—surround the selected picture.

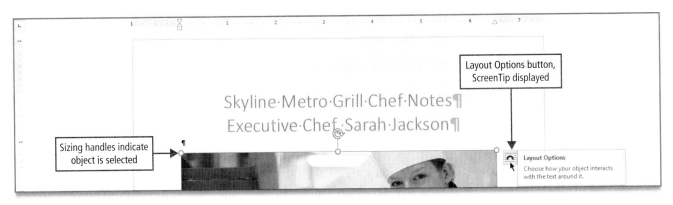

Figure 1.21

5 With the image selected, click **Layout Options** ⌞☑⌝, and then under **With Text Wrapping**, in the second row, click the first layout—**Top and Bottom**. In the upper right corner of the Layout Options dialog box, click **Close** ⌞✕⌝.

6 On the ribbon, with the **Picture Tools Format tab** active, at the right, in the **Size group**, click in the **Shape Height** box ⟦ 0.29" ⟧ to select the existing text. Type **2** and press Enter.

7 On the **Picture Tools Format tab**, in the **Arrange group**, click **Align**, and then at the bottom of the list, locate **Use Alignment Guides**. If you do not see a checkmark to the left of **Use Alignment Guides**, click the command to enable the guides.

8 If necessary, click the image again to select it. Point to the image to display the ⟦⟧ pointer, hold down the left mouse button and move your mouse slightly to display a green line at the left margin, and then drag the image to the right and down slightly until a green line displays in the center of the image as shown in Figure 1.22, and then release the left mouse button.

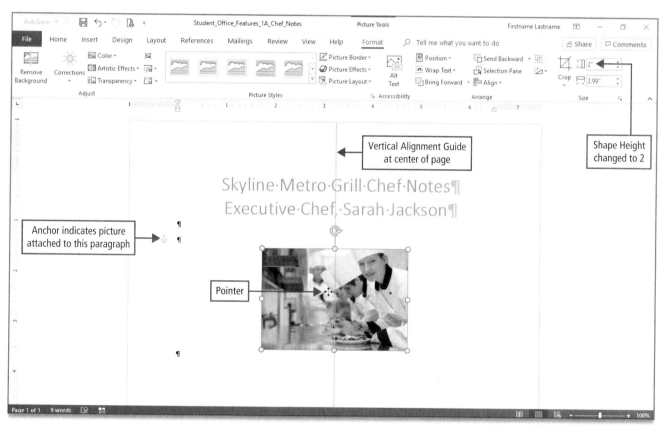

Figure 1.22

9 Be sure that there are two blank paragraphs above the image and that the anchor symbol is attached to the second blank paragraph mark—if necessary, drag the picture up slightly or down slightly. If you are not satisfied with your result, on the Quick Access Toolbar, click Undo ⟲ and begin again.

Alignment guides are green lines that display to help you align objects with margins or at the center of a page.

Inserted pictures anchor—attach to—the paragraph at the insertion point location—as indicated by an anchor symbol.

10 On the ribbon, on the **Picture Tools Format tab**, in the **Picture Styles group**, point to the first style to display the ScreenTip *Simple Frame, White*, and notice that the image displays with a white frame.

MAC TIP   Preview may not be available.

NOTE   The Size of Groups on the Ribbon Varies with Screen Resolution

Your monitor's screen resolution might be set higher than the resolution used to capture the figures in this book. At a higher resolution, the ribbon expands some groups to show more commands that are available with a single click, such as those in the Picture Styles group. Or, the group expands to add descriptive text to some buttons, such as those in the Arrange group. Regardless of your screen resolution, all Office commands are available to you. In higher resolutions, you will have a more robust view of the ribbon commands.

11 Watch the image as you point to the second picture style, and then to the third, and then to the fourth.

Recall that Live Preview shows the result of applying an editing or formatting change as you point to possible results—*before* you actually apply it.

12 In the **Picture Styles group**, click the fourth style—**Drop Shadow Rectangle**. Reposition the picture up or down so that it is anchored to the second blank paragraph above the image, and then click anywhere outside of the image to deselect it. Notice that the Picture Tools no longer display on the ribbon. Compare your screen with Figure 1.23.

Contextual tabs on the ribbon display only when you need them.

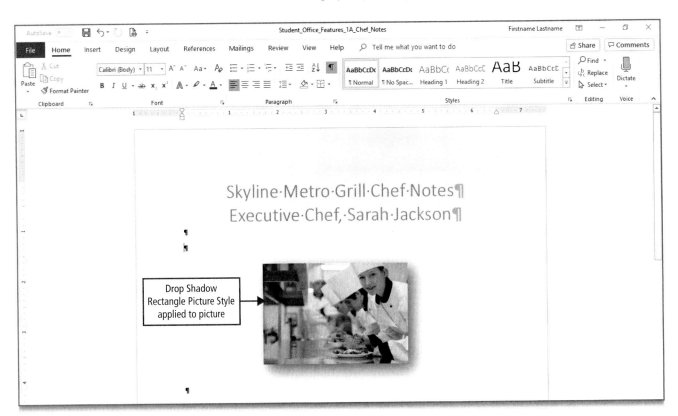

Figure 1.23

13 On the **Quick Access Toolbar**, click **Save** 🖫 to save the changes you have made.

Activity 1.09 | Minimizing the Ribbon

1 Point to any tab on the ribbon and right-click to display a shortcut menu.

> Here you can choose to display the Quick Access Toolbar below the ribbon or collapse the ribbon to maximize screen space. You can also customize the ribbon by adding, removing, renaming, or reordering tabs, groups, and commands, although this is not recommended until you become an expert Word user.

2 Click **Collapse the Ribbon** and notice that only the ribbon tabs display. Click the **Home tab** to display the commands. Click in the last blank paragraph—or anywhere in the document—and notice that the ribbon goes back to the collapsed display.

MAC TIP To minimize the ribbon, click the up arrow on the top right of the screen.

3 Right-click any ribbon tab, and then click **Collapse the Ribbon** again to remove the check mark from this command.

> Most expert Office users prefer the full ribbon display.

4 Point to any tab on the ribbon, and then on your mouse device, roll the mouse wheel. Notice that different tabs become active as you roll the mouse wheel.

> You can make a tab active by using this technique, instead of clicking the tab.

MORE KNOWLEDGE **Displaying KeyTips**

Instead of a mouse, some individuals prefer to navigate the ribbon by using keys on the keyboard. You can do this by activating the *KeyTip* feature where small labels display on the ribbon tabs and also on the individual ribbon commands. Press Alt to display the KeyTips on the ribbon tabs, and then press N to display KeyTips on the ribbon commands. Press Esc to turn the feature off. NOTE: This feature is not yet available on a Mac.

Activity 1.10 | Changing Page Orientation and Zoom Level

1.2.1

1 On the ribbon, click the **Layout tab**. In the **Page Setup group**, click **Orientation**, and notice that two orientations display—*Portrait* and *Landscape*. Click **Landscape**.

> In ***portrait orientation***, the paper is taller than it is wide. In ***landscape orientation***, the paper is wider than it is tall.

2 In the lower right corner of the screen, locate the **Zoom slider**.

> Recall that to zoom means to increase or decrease the viewing area. You can zoom in to look closely at a section of a document, and then zoom out to see an entire page on the screen. You can also zoom to view multiple pages on the screen.

3 Drag the **Zoom slider** ▬▬▬|▬▬▬ to the left until you have zoomed to approximately *60%*. Compare your screen with Figure 1.24.

Figure 1.24

🖐 **BY TOUCH** Drag the Zoom slider with your finger.

4 Use the technique you just practiced to change the **Orientation** back to **Portrait**.

The default orientation in Word is Portrait, which is commonly used for business documents such as letters, reports, and memos.

5 In the lower right corner, click the **Zoom In** button **+** as many times as necessary to return to the **100%** zoom setting.

Use the zoom feature to adjust the view of your document for editing and for your viewing comfort.

🔄 **ANOTHER WAY** You can also control Zoom from the ribbon. On the View tab, in the Zoom group, you can control the Zoom level and also zoom to view multiple pages.

6 On the **Quick Access Toolbar**, click **Save** 🖫.

MORE KNOWLEDGE **Zooming to Page Width**

Some Office users prefer *Page Width*, which zooms the document so that the width of the page matches the width of the window. Find this command on the View tab, in the Zoom group.

Activity 1.11 | Formatting Text by Using Fonts, Alignment, Font Colors, and Font Styles

MOS
2.2.5

1 If necessary, on the right edge of your screen, drag the vertical scroll box to the top of the scroll bar. To the left of *Executive Chef, Sarah Jackson*, point in the margin area to display the ⬩ pointer and click one time to select the entire paragraph. Compare your screen with Figure 1.25.

Use this technique to select complete paragraphs from the margin area—drag downward to select multiple-line paragraphs—which is faster and more efficient than dragging through text.

Figure 1.25

2 On the **Home tab**, in the **Font Group**, click **Clear All Formatting** ⬩. Compare your screen with Figure 1.26.

This command removes all formatting from the selection, leaving only the normal, unformatted text.

Figure 1.26

3 With the text still selected, on the **Home tab**, in the **Paragraph group**, click **Center** ☰.

4 With the text still selected, on the **Home tab**, in the **Font group**, click the **Font button arrow** Calibri (Body) ▾. On the alphabetical list of font names, scroll down and then locate and *point to* **Cambria**.

A *font* is a set of characters with the same design and shape. The default font in a Word document is Calibri, which is a *sans serif font*—a font design with no lines or extensions on the ends of characters.

The Cambria font is a *serif font*—a font design that includes small line extensions on the ends of the letters to guide the eye in reading from left to right.

The list of fonts displays as a gallery showing potential results. For example, in the Font gallery, you can point to see the actual design and format of each font as it would look if applied to text.

5 Point to several other fonts and observe the effect on the selected text. Then, scroll back to the top of the **Font** gallery. Under **Theme Fonts**, click **Calibri Light**.

A *theme* is a predesigned combination of colors, fonts, line, and fill effects that look good together and is applied to an entire document by a single selection. A theme combines two sets of fonts— one for text and one for headings. In the default Office theme, Calibri Light is the suggested font for headings.

6 With the paragraph *Executive Chef, Sarah Jackson* still selected, on the **Home tab**, in the **Font group**, click the **Font Size button arrow** [11 ▾], point to **20**, and then notice how Live Preview displays the text in the font size to which you are pointing. Compare your screen with Figure 1.27.

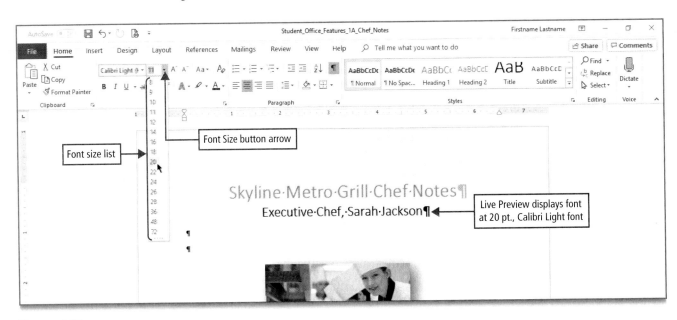

Figure 1.27

7 On the list of font sizes, click **20**.

Fonts are measured in *points*, with one point equal to 1/72 of an inch. A higher point size indicates a larger font size. Headings and titles are often formatted by using a larger font size. The word *point* is abbreviated as *pt*.

8 With *Executive Chef, Sarah Jackson* still selected, on the **Home tab**, in the **Font group**, click the **Font Color button arrow** [A ▾]. Under **Theme Colors**, in the sixth column, click the fifth (next to last) color, and then click in the last blank paragraph to deselect the text.

9 With your insertion point in the blank paragraph below the picture, type **Rehearsal Dinner Menu Ideas** and then press [Enter] two times.

10 Type **Appetizers** and press ⌈Enter⌉ two times. Type **Salads** and press ⌈Enter⌉ two times. Type **Main Dishes** and press ⌈Enter⌉ two times.

11 Type **Desserts** and press ⌈Enter⌉ four times. Compare your screen with Figure 1.28.

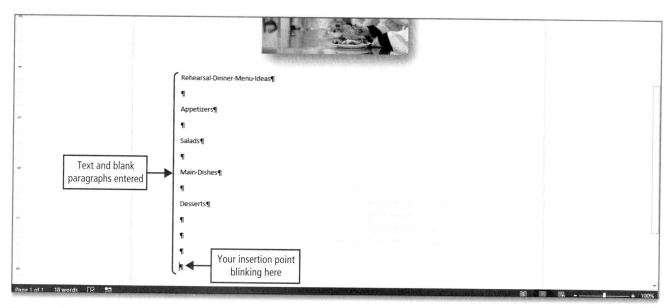

Rehearsal·Dinner·Menu·Ideas¶

¶

Appetizers¶

¶

Salads¶

¶

Main·Dishes¶

¶

Desserts¶

¶

¶

¶

Text and blank
paragraphs entered

Your insertion point
blinking here

Page 1 of 1   18 words

Figure 1.28

12 Click anywhere in the word *Dinner* and then ***triple-click***—click the left mouse button three times—to select the entire paragraph. If the entire paragraph is not selected, click in the paragraph and begin again.

13 With the paragraph selected, on the mini toolbar, click the **Font Color** button 🅰·, and notice that the text color of the selected paragraph changes.

> The font color button retains its most recently used color—the color you used to format *Executive Chef, Sarah Jackson* above. As you progress in your study of Microsoft Office, you will use other commands that behave in this manner; that is, they retain their most recently used format. This is commonly referred to as ***MRU***—most recently used.

> Recall that the mini toolbar places commands that are commonly used for the selected text or object close by so that you reduce the distance you must move your mouse to access a command. If you are using a touch screen device, most commands that you need are close and easy to touch.

MAC TIP   Use commands on the ribbon, on the Home tab.

14 With the paragraph *Rehearsal Dinner Menu Ideas* still selected and the mini toolbar displayed, on the mini toolbar, click **Bold** ⎍B⎍ and **Italic** ⎍I⎍.

> ***Font styles*** include bold, italic, and underline. Font styles emphasize text and are a visual cue to draw the reader's eye to important text.

15 On the mini toolbar, click **Italic** I again to turn off the Italic formatting. Click anywhere to deselect, and then compare your screen with Figure 1.29.

A *toggle button* is a button that can be turned on by clicking it once, and then turned off by clicking it again.

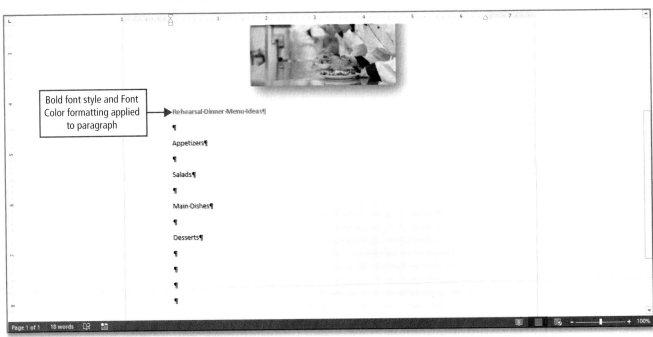

Bold font style and Font Color formatting applied to paragraph

Figure 1.29

Activity 1.12 | Using Format Painter

Use the ***Format Painter*** to copy the formatting of specific text or copy the formatting of a paragraph and then apply it in other locations in your document.

1 To the left of *Rehearsal Dinner Menu Ideas*, point in the left margin to display the pointer, and then click one time to select the entire paragraph. Compare your screen with Figure 1.30.

Use this technique to select complete paragraphs from the margin area. This is particularly useful if there are many lines of text in the paragraph. You can hold down the left mouse button and drag downward instead of trying to drag through the text.

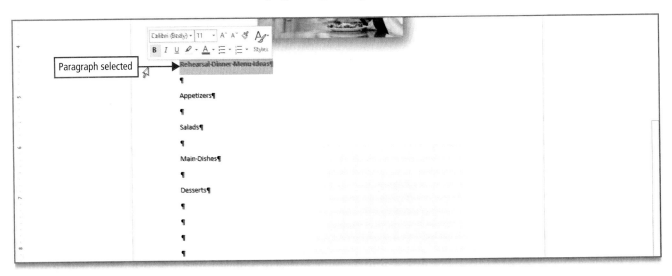

Paragraph selected

Figure 1.30

2 With *Rehearsal Dinner Menu Ideas* still selected, on the mini toolbar, click **Format Painter** 🖌️. Then, move your mouse to the right of the word *Appetizers*, and notice the 📌I mouse pointer. Compare your screen with Figure 1.31.

> The pointer takes the shape of a paintbrush and contains the formatting information from the paragraph where the insertion point is positioned or from what is selected. Information about the Format Painter and how to turn it off displays in the status bar.

🖥️ **MAC TIP** On the Home tab, in the Clipboard group, click Format Painter.

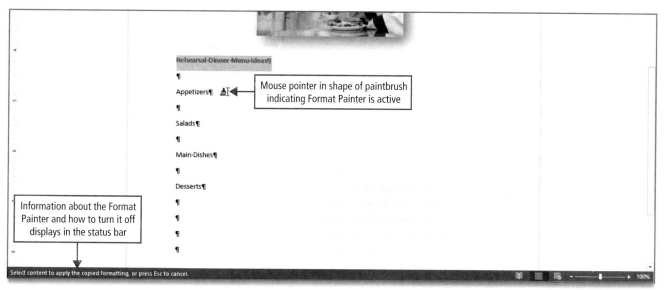

Rehearsal·Dinner·Menu·Ideas¶

Appetizers¶ 📌I ◀— Mouse pointer in shape of paintbrush indicating Format Painter is active

Salads¶

Main·Dishes¶

Desserts¶

Information about the Format Painter and how to turn it off displays in the status bar

Select content to apply the copied formatting, or press Esc to cancel.

Figure 1.31

---

3 With the 📌I pointer, drag to select the paragraph *Appetizers* and notice that the font color and Bold formatting is applied. Then, click anywhere in the word *Appetizers*, right-click to display the mini toolbar, and on the mini toolbar, *double-click* **Format Painter** 🖌️.

4 Select the paragraph *Salads* to copy the font color and Bold formatting, and notice that the pointer retains the 📌I shape. You might have to move the mouse slightly to see the paintbrush shape.

> When you *double-click* the Format Painter button, the Format Painter feature remains active until you either click the Format Painter button again, or press Esc to cancel it—as indicated on the status bar.

5 With Format Painter still active, drag to select the paragraph *Main Dishes*, and then on the ribbon, on the **Home tab**, in the **Clipboard group**, notice that **Format Painter** is selected, indicating that it is active. Compare your screen with Figure 1.32.

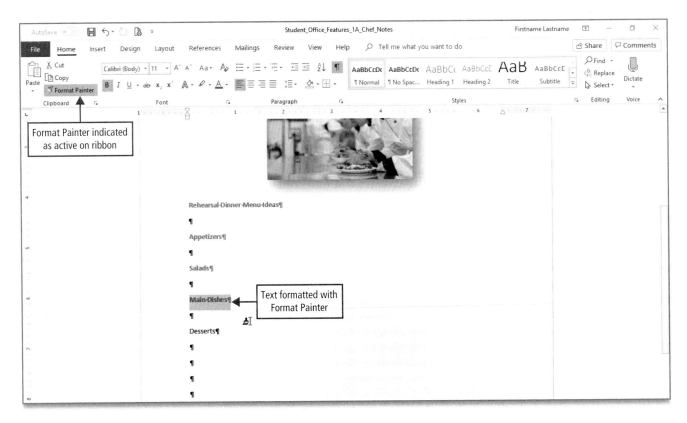

Figure 1.32

6 Select the paragraph *Desserts* to copy the format, and then on the ribbon, click **Format Painter** to turn the command off.

🔄 **ANOTHER WAY**   Press Esc to turn off Format Painter.

---

7 On the **Quick Access Toolbar**, click **Save** 🔲 to save the changes you have made to your document.

Activity 1.13 | Using Keyboard Shortcuts and Using the Clipboard to Copy, Cut, and Paste

The **Clipboard** is a temporary storage area that holds text or graphics that you select and then cut or copy. When you *copy* text or graphics, a copy is placed on the Clipboard and the original text or graphic remains in place. When you *cut* text or graphics, a copy is placed on the Clipboard, and the original text or graphic is removed—cut—from the document.

After copying or cutting, the contents of the Clipboard are available for you to *paste*—insert—in a new location in the current document, or into another Office file.

1 ▷ On your keyboard, hold down Ctrl and press Home to move to the beginning of your document, and then take a moment to study the table in Figure 1.33, which describes similar keyboard shortcuts with which you can navigate quickly in a document.

🖥 **MAC TIP** Press command ⌘ + fn + to move to the top of a document.

To Move	On a Windows PC press:	On a Mac press:
To the beginning of a document	Ctrl + Home	command ⌘ + fn + ←
To the end of a document	Ctrl + End	command ⌘ + fn + →
To the beginning of a line	Home	command ⌘ + ←
To the end of a line	End	command ⌘ + →
To the beginning of the previous word	Ctrl + ←	option + ←
To the beginning of the next word	Ctrl + →	option + →
To the beginning of the current word (if insertion point is in the middle of a word)	Ctrl + ←	option + ←
To the beginning of the previous paragraph	Ctrl + ↑	command ⌘ + ↑
To the beginning of the next paragraph	Ctrl + ↓	command ⌘ + ↓
To the beginning of the current paragraph (if insertion point is in the middle of a paragraph)	Ctrl + ↑	command ⌘ + ↑
Up one screen	PgUp	fn + ↑
Down one screen	PgDn	fn + ↓

Figure 1.33

2 ▷ To the left of *Skyline Metro Grill Chef Notes*, point in the left margin area to display the 𝒜 pointer, and then click one time to select the entire paragraph. On the **Home tab**, in the **Clipboard group**, click **Copy** 🗐.

Because anything that you select and then copy—or cut—is placed on the Clipboard, the Copy command and the Cut command display in the Clipboard group of commands on the ribbon. There is no visible indication that your copied selection has been placed on the Clipboard.

🔄 **ANOTHER WAY** Right-click the selection, and then click Copy on the shortcut menu; or, use the keyboard shortcut Ctrl + C.

🖥 **MAC TIP** Press command ⌘ + C as a keyboard shortcut for the Copy command.

3 On the **Home tab**, in the **Clipboard group**, to the right of the group name *Clipboard*, click the **Dialog Box Launcher** button ⌐, and then compare your screen with Figure 1.34

The Clipboard pane displays with your copied text. In any ribbon group, the *Dialog Box Launcher* displays either a dialog box or a pane related to the group of commands. It is not necessary to display the Clipboard in this manner, although sometimes it is useful to do so.

Figure 1.34

4 In the upper right corner of the **Clipboard** pane, click **Close** ☒.

5 Press Ctrl + End to move to the end of your document. On the **Home tab**, in the **Clipboard group**, point to **Paste**, and then click the *upper* portion of this split button.

The Paste command pastes the most recently copied item on the Clipboard at the insertion point location. If you click the lower portion of the Paste button, a gallery of Paste Options displays. A *split button* is divided into two parts; clicking the main part of the button performs a command, and clicking the arrow displays a list or gallery with choices.

ANOTHER WAY   Right-click, on the shortcut menu under Paste Options, click the desired option button; or, press Control + V.

6 Below the pasted text, click **Paste Options** 📋 as shown in Figure 1.35.

Here you can view and apply various formatting options for pasting your copied or cut text. Typically, you will click Paste on the ribbon and paste the item in its original format. If you want some other format for the pasted item, you can choose another format from the *Paste Options gallery*, which provides a Live Preview of the various options for changing the format of the pasted item with a single click. The Paste Options gallery is available in three places: on the ribbon by clicking the lower portion of the Paste button—the Paste button arrow; from the Paste Options button that displays below the pasted item following the paste operation; or on the shortcut menu if you right-click the pasted item.

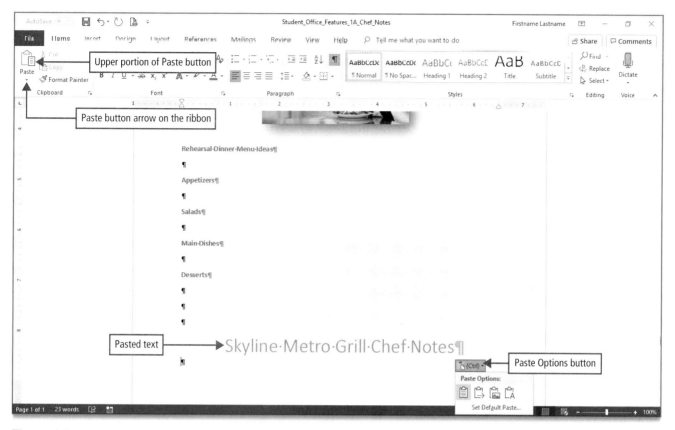

Figure 1.35

> **7** In the **Paste Options** gallery, *point* to each option to see the Live Preview of the format that would be applied if you clicked the button.
>
> The contents of the Paste Options gallery are contextual; that is, they change based on what you copied and where you are pasting.
>
> **8** Press Esc to close the gallery; the button will remain displayed until you take some other screen action.
>
> **9** On your keyboard, press Ctrl + Home to move to the top of the document, and then click the **chefs image** one time to select it. While pointing to the selected image, right-click, and then on the shortcut menu, click **Cut**.
>
> Recall that the Cut command cuts—removes—the selection from the document and places it on the Clipboard.

🔄 **ANOTHER WAY** On the Home tab, in the Clipboard group, click the Cut button; or use the keyboard shortcut Ctrl + X.

💻 **MAC TIP** Press command ⌘ + X as a keyboard shortcut for the Cut command..

> **10** Press Ctrl + End to move to the end of the document.

11 With the insertion point blinking in the blank paragraph at the end of the document, right-click, and notice that the **Paste Options** gallery displays on the shortcut menu. Compare your screen with Figure 1.36.

Figure 1.36

12 On the shortcut menu, under **Paste Options**, click the first button—**Keep Source Formatting**.

MAC TIP On the shortcut menu, click Paste, click the Paste Options button, and then click Keep Source Formatting.

13 Point to the picture to display the ⬚ pointer, and then drag to the right until the center green **Alignment Guide** displays and the blank paragraph is above the picture. Release the left mouse button.

MAC TIP In the Arrange group, on the Picture Format tab, click Align, click Align Center.

14 Above the picture, select the text *Chef Notes*, type **Festive Salad** and then compare your screen with Figure 1.37.

Figure 1.37

15 Click **Save** 🖫.

Activity 1.14 | Adding Alternative Text for Accessibility

MOS
5.4.3

1 Point to the **chefs picture** and right-click. On the shortcut menu, click **Edit Alt Text** to display the **Alt Text** pane.

Alternative text helps people using a *screen reader*, which is software that enables visually impaired users to read text on a computer screen to understand the content of pictures. *Alt text* is the term commonly used for this feature.

2 ▶ In the **Alt Text** pane, notice that Word generates a suggested description of the picture. Click in the box, select the existing text, and then type **Young chefs making salads in a restaurant kitchen** and then compare your screen with Figure 1.38.

Anyone viewing the document with a screen reader will see the alternative text displayed instead of the picture.

Figure 1.38

3 ▶ **Close** ☒ the **Alt Text** pane. Press Ctrl + Home to move to the top of your document. On the Quick Access Toolbar, click **Save** 🔲 to the changes you have made to your document.

Objective 5 | **Finalize an Office Document**

GO! Learn How

Video OF1-5

There are steps you will want to take to finalize your documents. This typically includes inserting a footer for identifying information and adding Document Properties to facilitate searching. Recall that Document Properties—also known as metadata—are details about a file that describe or identify it, such as the title, author name, subject, and keywords that identify the document's topic or contents. You might also want to take some security measures or mark information to find later.

Activity 1.15 | Inserting a Footer, Inserting Document Info, and Adding Document Properties

MOS

1.3.2

1 ▶ On the **Insert tab**, in the **Header & Footer group**, click **Footer**. At the bottom of the list, click **Edit Footer**, and then with the **Header & Footer Tools Design tab** active, in the **Insert group**, click **Document Info**. Click **File Name** to add the file name to the footer.

A *footer* is a reserved area for text and graphics that displays at the bottom of each page in a document. It is common in organizations to add the file name to the footer of documents so that documents are easily identified.

 MAC TIP In the Insert group, click Field. In the dialog box, under Categories, click Document Information. Then under Field names, click FileName. Click OK.

2 ▶ On the right end of the ribbon, click **Close Header and Footer**.

3 ▶ On the **Quick Access Toolbar**, point to the **Print Preview and Print** button 🖨 you placed there, right-click, and then click **Remove from Quick Access Toolbar**.

> If you are working on your own computer and you want to do so, you can leave the icon on the toolbar; in a college lab, you should return the software to its original settings.

4 ▶ Click the **File tab** to display **Backstage** view. With the **Info tab** active, in the lower right corner, click **Show All Properties**. Click in the **Tags** box, and then type **rehearsal dinners, menus**

> *Tags*—also referred to as *keywords*—are custom file properties in the form of words that you associate with a document to give an indication of the document's content. Use tags to assist in searching for and organizing files.

⌨ **MAC TIP**   On the menu bar, click File, click Properties, click the Summary tab, and then type the tags in the Keywords box. Click OK.

5 ▶ Click in the **Subject** box, and then type your course name and number—for example, *CIS 10, #5543*. Under **Related People**, be sure your name displays as the author. (To edit the Author, right-click the name, click Edit Property, type the new name, click in a white area to close the list, and then click OK.)

6 ▶ On the left, click **Save** to save your document and return to the Word window.

Activity 1.16 │ Inspecting a Document

Word, Excel, and PowerPoint all have the same commands to inspect a file before sharing it.

⌨ **MAC TIP**   On the menu bar, click Tools. Here you can click Protect Document and Check Accessibility.

1.4.1,1.4.2, 1.4.3

1 ▶ With your document displayed, click the **File tab**, on the left, if necessary, click **Info**, and then on the right, click **Check for Issues**.

2 ▶ On the list, click **Inspect Document**.

> The *Inspect Document* command searches your document for hidden data or personal information that you might not want to share publicly. This information could reveal company details that should not be shared.

3 ▶ In the lower right corner of the **Document Inspector** dialog box, click **Inspect**.

> The Document Inspector runs and lists information that was found and that you could choose to remove.

4 ▶ In the lower right corner of the dialog box, click **Close**, and then click **Check for Issues** again. On the list, click **Check Accessibility**.

> The *Check Accessibility* command checks the document for content that people with disabilities might find difficult to read. The Accessibility Checker pane displays on the right and lists objects that might require attention.

5 ▶ Close ☒ the **Accessibility Checker** pane, and then click the **File tab**.

6 ▶ Click **Check for Issues**, and then click **Check Compatibility**.

> The *Check Compatibility* command checks for features in your document that may not be supported by earlier versions of the Office program. This is only a concern if you are sharing documents with individuals with older software.

7 ▶ Click **OK**. Leave your Word document displayed for the next Activity.

Activity 1.17 | Inserting a Bookmark and a 3D Model

1.1.2, 5.2.6

A *bookmark* identifies a word, section, or place in your document so that you can find it quickly without scrolling. This is especially useful in a long document.

3D models are a new kind of shape that you can insert from an online library of ready-to-use three-dimensional graphics. A 3D model is most powerful in a PowerPoint presentation where you can add transitions and animations during your presentation, but you can also insert a 3D model into a Word document for an impactful image that you can position in various ways.

1 In the paragraph *Rehearsal Dinner Menu Items*, select the word *Menu*.

2 On the **Insert tab**, in the **Links group**, click **Bookmark**.

3 In the **Bookmark** name box, type **menu** and then click **Add**.

4 Press Ctrl + Home to move to the top of your document.

5 On the **Home tab**, at the right end of the ribbon, in the **Editing group**, click the **Find button arrow**, and then click **Go To**.

ANOTHER WAY Press Ctrl + G, which is the keyboard shortcut for the Go To command.

MAC TIP On the menu bar, click Edit, point to Find, click Go To. In the dialog box, click Bookmark.

6 Under **Go to what**, click **Bookmark**, and then with *menu* indicated as the bookmark name, click **Go To**. **Close** the **Find and Replace** dialog box, and notice that your bookmarked text is selected for you.

7 Click to position your insertion point at the end of the word *Desserts*. On the **Insert tab**, in the **Illustrations group**, click the upper portion of the **3D Models** button to open the **Online 3D Models** dialog box.

NOTE 3D Models Not Available?

If the 3D Models command is not available on your system, in the **Illustrations group**, click **Pictures**, and then from the files downloaded with this project, click of01A_Cupcake. Change the Height to .75" and then move to Step 12.

8 In the search box, type **cupcake** and then press Enter.

9 Click the image of the **cupcake in a pink and white striped wrapper**—or select any other cupcake image. At the bottom, click **Insert**.

10 Point to the **3D control** in the center of the image, hold down the left mouse button, and then rotate the image so the top of the cupcake is pointing toward the upper right corner of the page—your rotation need not be exact. Alternatively, in the 3D Model Views group, click the More button ▾, and then locate and click Above Front Left.

11 With the cupcake image selected, on the **3D Model Tools Format tab**, in the **Size group**, click in the **Height** box, type **.75"** and press Enter.

12 In the **Arrange group**, click **Wrap Text**, and then click **In Front of Text**. Then, in the **Arrange group**, click **Align**, and click **Align Right** to position the cupcake at the right margin.

13 Press Ctrl + Home to move to the top of your document. On the **Quick Access Toolbar**, click **Save** ▪.

Activity 1.18 | Printing a File and Closing a Desktop App

1 Click the **File tab** to return to **Backstage** view, on the left click **Print**, and then compare your screen with Figure 1.39.

Here you can select any printer connected to your system and adjust the settings related to how you want to print. On the right, the ***Print Preview*** displays, which is a view of a document as it will appear on paper when you print it. Your page color effect will not display in Print Preview nor will the shading print. This effect appears only to anyone viewing the document on a screen.

At the bottom of the Print Preview area, in the center, the number of pages and page navigation arrows with which you can move among the pages in Print Preview display. On the right, the Zoom slider enables you to shrink or enlarge the Print Preview. ***Zoom*** is the action of increasing or decreasing the viewing area of the screen.

ANOTHER WAY From the document screen, press Ctrl + P or Ctrl + F2 to display Print in Backstage view.

MAC TIP Press command ⌘ + P.

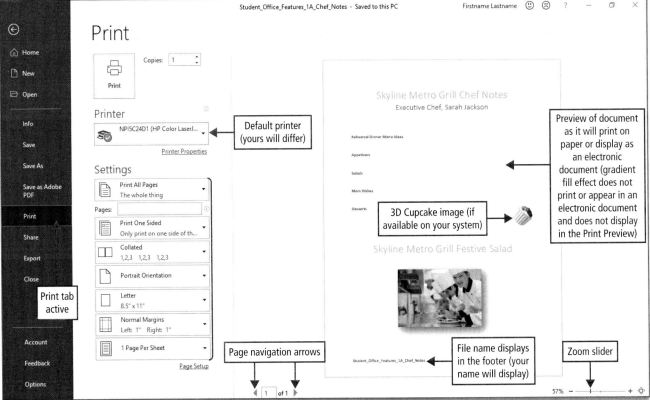

Figure 1.39

2 On the left, click **Save**. In the upper right corner of your screen, click **Close** X to close Word. If a message displays regarding copied items, click No.

MAC TIP On the menu bar, click File, click Close.

3 In **MyLab IT**, locate and click the Grader Project **Office Features 1A Chef Notes**. In **step 3**, under **Upload Completed Assignment**, click **Choose File**. In the **Open** dialog box, navigate to your **Office Features Chapter 1 folder**, and then click your **Student_Office_Features_1A_ Chef_Notes** file one time to select it. In the lower right corner of the **Open** dialog box, click **Open**.

The name of your selected file displays above the Upload button.

4 To submit your file to MyLab IT for grading, click **Upload**, wait a moment for a green **Success!** message, and then in **step 4**, click the blue **Submit for Grading** button. Click **Close Assignment** to return to your list of **Course Materials**.

MORE KNOWLEDGE **Creating an Electronic Image of Your Document**

You can create an electronic image of your document that looks like a printed document. To do so, in Backstage view, on the left click Export. On the right, click Create PDF/XPS, and then click the Create PDF/XPS button to display the Publish as PDF or XPS dialog box.

PDF stands for **Portable Document Format**, which is a technology that creates an image that preserves the look of your file. This is a popular format for sending documents electronically, because the document will display on most computers. **XPS** stands for **XML Paper Specification**—a Microsoft file format that also creates an image of your document and that opens in the XPS viewer.

ALERT **The Remaining Activities in This Chapter Are Optional**

The following Activities describing the Office Help features are recommend but are optional to complete.

Objective 6 Use the Office Help Features

GO! Learn How
Video OF1-6

Within each Office program, you will see the *Tell Me* feature at the right end of the ribbon— to the right of the Help tab. This is a search feature for Microsoft Office commands that you activate by typing in the *Tell me what you want to do* box. Another way to use this feature is to point to a command on the ribbon, and then at the bottom of the displayed ScreenTip, click *Tell me more*.

Activity 1.19 | **Using Microsoft Office Tell Me, Tell Me More, the Help Tab, and Adding Alt Text to an Excel Chart**

5.3.3

1 Start Excel and open a **Blank workbook**. With cell **A1** active, type **456789** and press Enter. Click cell **A1** again to make it the active cell.

2 At the top of the screen, click in the *Tell me what you want to do* box, and then type **format as currency** In the displayed list, to the right of **Accounting Number Format**, click the ▶ arrow. Compare your screen with Figure 1.40.

> As you type, every keystroke refines the results so that you can click the command as soon as it displays. This feature helps you apply the command immediately; it does not explain how to locate the command.

MAC TIP   Click the Help tab on the menu bar.

Figure 1.40

3 Click **$ English (United States)**.

4 On the **Home tab**, in the **Font group**, *point* to the **Font Color** button to display its ScreenTip, and then click **Tell me more**.

> *Tell me more* is a prompt within a ScreenTip that opens the Office online Help system with explanations about how to perform the command referenced in the ScreenTip.

5 In the **Help** pane that displays on the right, if necessary, click **Change the color of text**. Compare your screen with Figure 1.41.

> As you scroll down, you will notice that the Help pane displays extensive information about the topic of changing the color of text, including how to apply a custom color.

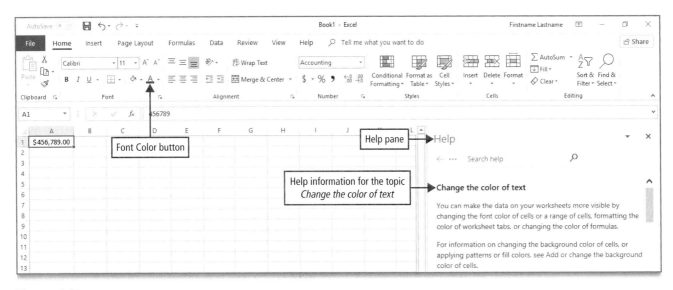

Figure 1.41

6 Close ☒ the **Help** pane.

7 On the ribbon, click the **Help tab**. In the **Help** group, click **Help**. In the **Help** pane, type **3D models** and then click the **Search** button. Click **Get creative with 3D models**, and then compare your screen with Figure 1.42.

Some Help topics include videos like this one to demonstrate and explain the topic.

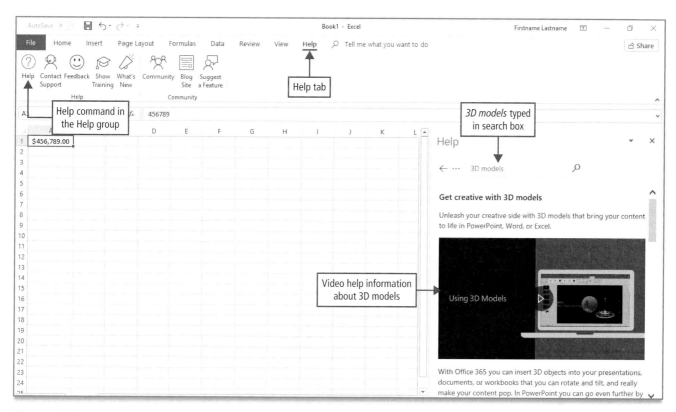

Figure 1.42

8 In the **Help** group and the **Community** group, look at the buttons.

Here you can Contact Support, send Feedback, Show Training developed by Microsoft, and see new features. In the Community group, you can visit the Excel Community, read the Excel Blog, and suggest new features.

9 Click **Show Training**, and then compare your screen with Figure 1.43.

Here you can view training videos developed by Microsoft.

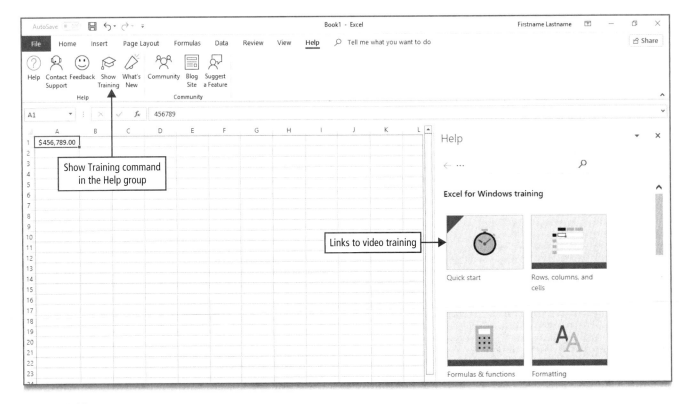

Figure 1.43

10 Click cell **A1**, and then click the **Insert tab**. In the **Charts group**, click **Recommended Charts**, and then in the **Insert Chart** dialog box, with the first chart selected, click **OK**.

11 Click the **Chart Tools Format tab**, and then in the **Accessibility group**, click **Alt Text**.

Here you can add text to describe the chart, similar to the Alt Text you added for the chef's image.

12 **Close** ☒ the **Help** pane, **Close** ☒ the **Alt Text** pane, and then in the upper right corner of the Excel window, click **Close** ☒. Click **Don't Save**.

MORE KNOWLEDGE **Don't Type, Talk! With the New Dictate Feature**

Office 365 subscribers will see the *Dictate* feature in Word, PowerPoint, Outlook, and OneNote for Windows 10. When you enable Dictate, you start talking and as you talk, text appears in your document or slide. Dictate is one of Microsoft's Office Intelligent Services, which adds new cloud-enhanced features to Office. Dictate is especially useful in Outlook when you must write lengthy emails. The Dictate command is on the Home tab in Word and PowerPoint and on the Message tab in Outlook.

You have completed Project 1A **END**

Hotel Files

Project Activities

In Activities 1.20 through 1.38, you will assist Barbara Hewitt and Steven Ramos, who work for the Information Technology Department at the Boston headquarters office of the Bell Orchid Hotels. Barbara and Steven must organize some of the files and folders that comprise the corporation's computer data. As you progress through the project, you will insert screenshots of windows that you create into a PowerPoint presentation with five slides that will look similar to Figure 1.44.

Project Files for MyLab IT Grader

For Project 1B, you will start with the Windows 10 desktop displayed, and then learn how to create a folder for your MyLab IT files as you work through the project instruction. At the appropriate point in the project, you will be instructed to download your files from your MyLab IT course.

Project Results

GO! Project 1B
Where We're Going

Figure 1.44

For Non-MyLab Submissions Start with the Windows 10 Desktop Displayed

For Project 1B, you will start with the Windows 10 desktop displayed and learn how to create a folder and save a new PowerPoint presentation as you work through the project instruction. Additionally, you will need the Student Data Files **win01_1B_Bell_Orchid** from your instructor or from www.pearsonhighered.com/go.

Objective 7   Explore Windows 10

ALERT   Because Windows 10 periodically checks for and then automatically downloads updates, you are assured that your device is up to date with the latest features and security improvements. Therefore, you may encounter some variations in what appears on your screen and what is shown in this instruction. Microsoft Office 365 is fully installed on your PC or Mac; no internet access is necessary to create or edit documents. When you *are* connected to the internet, you will receive monthly upgrades and new features, so you always have the latest versions of Office apps as soon as they are available. Your subscription gives you continuous free access to the latest innovations and refinements.

GO! Learn How
Video OF1-7

A *program* is a set of instructions that a computer uses to accomplish a task. A computer program that helps you perform a task for a specific purpose is referred to as an *application*. As an example, there are applications to create a document using word processing software, to play a game, to view the latest weather report, to edit photos or videos, or to manage financial information.

An *operating system* is a specific type of computer program that manages the other programs on a computing device such as a desktop computer, a laptop computer, a smartphone, a tablet computer, or a game console. You need an operating system to:

- Use application programs.
- Coordinate the use of your computer hardware such as a keyboard, mouse, touchpad, touchscreen, game controller, or printer.
- Organize data that you store on your computer and access data that you store on your own computer and in other locations.

Windows 10 is an operating system developed by Microsoft Corporation that works with mobile computing devices and also with traditional desktop and laptop PCs.

The three major tasks of an operating system are to:

- Manage your computer's hardware—the printers, scanners, disk drives, monitors, and other hardware attached to it.
- Manage the application software installed on your computer—programs like those in Microsoft Office and other programs you might install to edit photos and videos, play games, and so on.
- Manage the *data* generated from your application software. Data refers to the documents, worksheets, pictures, songs, and so on that you create and store during the day-to-day use of your computer.

The Windows 10 operating system continues to perform these three tasks, and additionally is optimized for touchscreens; for example, tablets of all sizes and convertible laptop computers. Windows 10 works equally well with any input device, including a mouse, keyboard, touchscreen, and *pen*—a pen-shaped stylus that you tap on a computer screen.

In most instances, when you purchase a computer, the operating system software is already installed. The operating system consists of many smaller programs, stored as system files, which transfer data to and from the disk and transfer data in and out of your computer's memory. Other functions performed by the operating system include hardware-specific tasks such as checking to see if a key has been pressed on the keyboard and, if it has, displaying the appropriate letter or character on the screen.

Windows 10, in the same manner as other operating systems and earlier versions of the Windows operating system, uses a *graphical user interface*—abbreviated as *GUI* and pronounced *GOO-ee*. A graphical user interface uses graphics such as an image of a file folder or wastebasket that you click to activate the item represented. A GUI commonly incorporates the following:

- A *pointer*—any symbol that displays on your screen in response to moving your mouse and with which you can select objects and commands.
- An *insertion point*—a blinking vertical line that indicates where text will be inserted when you type or where an action will take place.
- A *pointing device*, such as a mouse or touchpad, to control the pointer.
- *Icons*—small images that represent commands, files, applications, or other windows.
- A *desktop*—a simulation of a real desk that represents your work area; here you can arrange icons such as shortcuts to programs, files, folders, and various types of documents in the same manner you would arrange physical objects on top of a desk.

In Windows 10, you also have a Start menu with tiles that display when you click the Start button in the lower left corner of your screen. The array of tiles serves as a connected dashboard to all of your important programs, sites, and services. On the Start menu, your view is tailored to your information and activities.

The physical parts of your computer such as the central processing unit (CPU), memory, and any attached devices such as a printer, are collectively known as *resources*. The operating system keeps track of the status of each resource and decides when a resource needs attention and for how long.

Application programs enable you to do work on, and be entertained by, your computer—programs such as Word and Excel found in the Microsoft Office suite of products, Adobe Photoshop, and computer games. No application program, whether a larger desktop app or smaller *Microsoft Store app*—a smaller app that you download from the Store—can run on its own; it must run under the direction of an operating system.

For the everyday use of your computer, the most important and most often used function of the operating system is managing your files and folders—referred to as *data management*. In the same manner that you strive to keep your paper documents and file folders organized so that you can find information when you need it, your goal when organizing your computer files and folders is to group your files so that you can find information easily. Managing your data files so that you can find your information when you need it is one of the most important computing skills you can learn.

Activity 1.20 │ Recognizing User Accounts in Windows 10

On a single computer, Windows 10 can have multiple user accounts. This is useful because you can share a computer with other people in your family or organization and each person can have his or her own information and settings—none of which others can see. Each user on a single computer is referred to as a ***user account***. Figure 1.45 shows the Settings screen where you can add additional users to your computer.

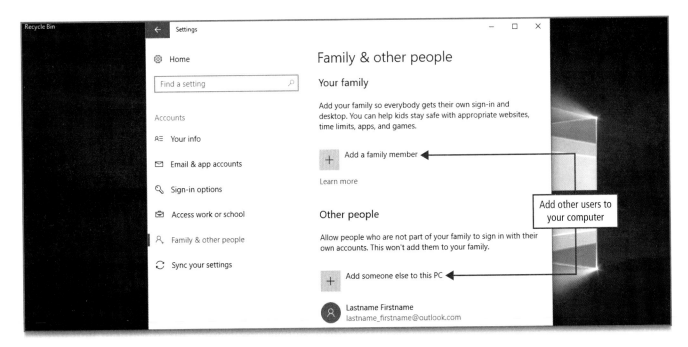

Figure 1.45

ALERT   Variations in Screen Organization, Colors, and Functionality Are Common in Windows 10

Individuals and organizations can determine how Windows 10 displays; therefore, the colors and the organization of various elements on the screen can vary. Your college or organization may customize Windows 10 to display a college picture or company logo or restrict access to certain features. The basic functions and structure of Windows 10 are not changed by such variations. You can be confident that the skills you will practice in this instruction apply to Windows 10 regardless of available functionality or differences between the figures shown and your screen.

NOTE   Comparing Your Screen with the Figures in This Textbook

Your screen will more closely match the figures shown in this textbook if you set your screen resolution to 1280 x 768. At other resolutions, your screen will closely resemble, but not match, the figures shown. To view your screen's resolution, on the desktop, right-click in a blank area, click *Display settings*, and then click the Resolution arrow. To adjust the resolution, select the desired setting, and then click OK.

With Windows 10, you can create a ***Microsoft account***, and then use that account to sign in to *any* Windows 10 computer on which you have, or create, a user account. By signing in with a Microsoft account you can:

- Download apps from the Microsoft Store
- Get your online content—email, social network updates, updated news—automatically displayed in an app when you sign in

Optionally, you can create a local account for use only on a specific PC. On your own Windows 10 computer, you must establish and then sign in with either a local account or a Microsoft account. Regardless of which one you select, you must provide an email address to associate with the user account name. If you create and then sign in with a local account, you can still connect to the internet, but you will not have the advantage of having your personal arrangement of apps displayed on your Start menu every time you sign in to that PC. You can use any email address to create a local account—similar to other online services where an email address is your user ID. You can also use any email address to create a Microsoft account.

To enjoy and get the full benefit of Windows 10, Microsoft Office, Skype, and free OneDrive cloud storage, if you have not already done so, create a Microsoft account. To do so, in your preferred web search engine, search for *create a Microsoft account*.

You can create an account using any email address. By signing in with a Microsoft account, your computer becomes your connected device where *you*—not your files—are the center of activity. At your college or place of employment, sign-in requirements will vary, because those computers are controlled by the organization's IT (Information Technology) professionals who are responsible for maintaining a secure computing environment for the entire organization.

Activity 1.21 | Turning On Your Computer, Signing In, and Exploring the Windows 10 Environment

Before you begin any computer activity, you must, if necessary, turn on your computer. This process is commonly referred to as ***booting the computer***. Because Windows 10 does not require you to completely shut down your computer except to install or repair a hardware device, in most instances moving the mouse or pressing a key will wake your computer in a few seconds. So, most of the time you will skip the lengthier boot process.

In this Activity, you will turn on your computer and sign in to Windows 10. Within an organization, the sign-in process may differ from that of your own computer.

ALERT **The look and features of Windows 10 will differ between your own PC and a PC you might use at your college or workplace.**

The Activities in this project assume that you are working on your own PC and signed in with a Microsoft account, or that you are working on a PC at your college or workplace where you are permitted to sign into Windows 10 with your own Microsoft account.

If you do not have a Microsoft account, or are working at a computer where you are unable to sign in with your Microsoft account, you can still complete the Activities, but some steps will differ.

On your own computer, you created your user account when you installed Windows 10 or when you set up your new computer that came with Windows 10. In a classroom or lab, check with your instructor to see how you will sign in to Windows 10.

NOTE **Create your Microsoft account if you have not already done so.**

To benefit from this instruction and understand your own computer, be sure that you know your Microsoft account login and password and use that to set up your user account. If you need to create a Microsoft account, in your preferred web search engine, search for *create a Microsoft account* and click the appropriate link.

1 If necessary, turn on your computer, and then examine Figure 1.46.

The Windows 10 *lock screen* fills your computer screen with a background—this might be a default picture from Microsoft such as one of the ones shown in the Lock screen settings in Figure 1.46 or a picture that you selected if you have personalized your system already. You can also choose to have a slide show of your own photos display on the lock screen.

Figure 1.46

2 Determine whether you are working with a mouse and keyboard system or with a touchscreen system. If you are working with a touchscreen, determine whether you will use a stylus pen or the touch of your fingers.

NOTE   This Book Assumes You Are Using a Mouse and Keyboard, but You Can Also Use Touch

This instruction uses terminology that assumes you are using a mouse and keyboard, but you need only touch gestures (described at the beginning of Project 1A in this chapter) to move through the instruction easily using touch. If a touch gesture needs more clarification, a *By Touch* box will assist you in using the correct gesture. Because more precision is needed for desktop operations, touching with a stylus pen may be preferable to touch using your fingers. When working with Microsoft Store apps, finger gestures are usually precise enough.

---

3 Press Enter to display the Windows 10 sign-in screen. If you are already signed in, go to Step 5.

BY TOUCH   On the lock screen, swipe upward to display the sign-in screen. Tap your user image if necessary to display the Password box.

---

4 If you are the displayed user, type your password (if you have established one) and press Enter. If you are not the displayed user, click your user image if it displays or click the Switch user arrow → and then click your user image. Type your password.

The Windows 10 desktop displays with a default desktop background, a background you have selected, or perhaps a background set by your college or workplace.

5 In the lower left corner of your screen, move the mouse pointer over—***point to***—**Start** ⊞ and then ***click***—press the left button on your mouse pointing device—to display the **Start menu**. Compare your screen with Figure 1.47, and then take a moment to study the table in Figure 1.48. If your list of programs does not display, in the upper left, click the ≡ .

The ***mouse pointer*** is any symbol that displays on your screen in response to moving your mouse.

The Windows 10 ***Start menu*** displays a list of installed programs on the left and a customizable group of square and rectangular boxes—referred to as ***tiles***—on the right. You can customize the arrangement of tiles from which you can access apps, websites, programs, folders, and tools for using your computer by simply clicking or tapping them.

Think of the right side of the Start menu as your connected ***dashboard***—a one-screen view of links to information and programs that matter to *you*—through which you can connect with the people, activities, places, and apps that you care about.

Some tiles are referred to as ***live tiles***, because they are constantly updated with fresh information relevant to you—the number of new email messages you have or new sports scores that you are interested in. Live tiles are at the center of your Windows 10 experience.

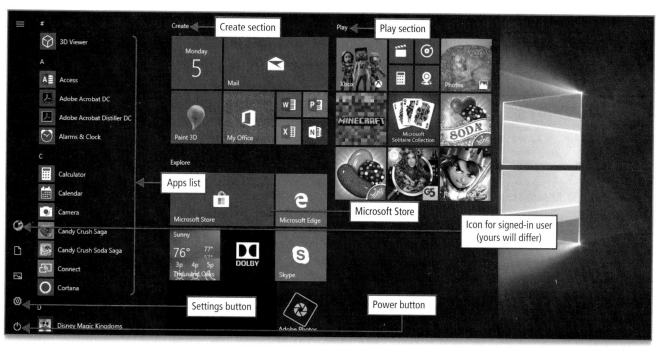

Figure 1.47

Parts of the Windows 10 Start Menu

Create	Apps pinned to the Start menu that relate to your own information; for example, your Mail, your Calendar, and apps with which you create things; for example, your Office apps.
Apps list	Displays a list of the apps available on your system (yours will differ).
Play and Explore	Apps pinned to the Start menu that relate to games or news apps that you have installed; you can change this heading or delete it.
Power button	Enables you to set your computer to Sleep, Shut down, or Restart.
Settings	Displays the Settings menu to change any Windows 10 setting.
Signed-in User	Displays the icon for the signed-in user.

Figure 1.48

6 Click **Start** ⊞ again to close the Start menu. Compare your screen with Figure 1.49, and then take a moment to study the parts of the Windows desktop as shown in the table in Figure 1.50.

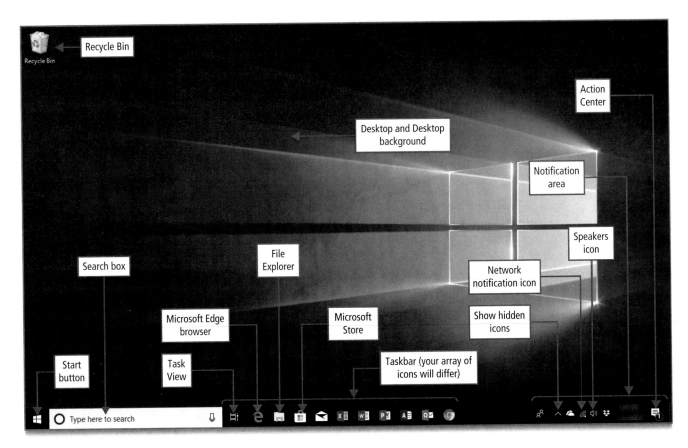

Figure 1.49

Parts of the Windows 10 Desktop	
Action Center	Displays the Action Center in a vertical pane on the right of your screen where you can see notifications—such as new mail or new alerts from social networks—at the top and access commonly used settings at the bottom.
Desktop	Serves as a surface for your work, like the top of an actual desk. Here you can arrange icons— small pictures that represent a file, folder, program, or other object.
Desktop background	Displays the colors and graphics of your desktop; you can change the desktop background to look the way you want it, such as using a picture or a solid color. Also referred to as *wallpaper*.
File Explorer	Launches the File Explorer program, which displays the contents of folders and files on your computer and on connected locations and also enables you to perform tasks related to your files and folders such as copying, moving, and renaming. If your File Explorer icon does not display, search for it, right-click its name in the search results, and then click Pin to taskbar.
Microsoft Edge browser	Launches Microsoft Edge, the web browser program developed by Microsoft that is included with Windows 10.
Microsoft Store	Opens the Microsoft Store where you can select and download Microsoft Store apps.
Network notification icon	Displays the status of your network.
Notification area	Displays notification icons and the system clock and calendar; sometimes referred to as the *system tray*.
Recycle Bin	Contains files and folders that you delete. When you delete a file or folder, it is not actually deleted; it stays in the Recycle Bin if you want it back, until you take an action to empty the Recycle Bin.
Search box	If *Cortana*—Microsoft's intelligent personal assistant—is enabled, a small circle will display on the left edge of the Search box. If Cortana is not enabled, a search icon displays at the left edge.

Parts of the Windows 10 Desktop

Show hidden icons	Displays additional icons related to your notifications.
Speakers icon	Displays the status of your computer's speakers (if any).
Start button	Displays the Start menu.
Task View	Displays your desktop background with a small image of all open programs and apps. Click once to open, click again to close. May also display the Timeline.
Taskbar	Contains buttons to launch programs and buttons for all open programs; by default, it is located at the bottom of the desktop, but you can move it. You can customize the number and arrangement of buttons.

Figure 1.50

Activity 1.22 | Pinning a Program to the Taskbar

Snipping Tool is a program within Windows 10 that captures an image of all or part of your computer's screen. A *snip*, as the captured image is called, can be annotated, saved, copied, or shared via email. Any capture of your screen is referred to as a *screenshot*, and there are many other ways to capture your screen in addition to the Snipping Tool.

> **NOTE** **Snip & Sketch Offers Improved Snipping Capabilities**
>
> Although Snipping Tool will be available for several more years, a newer tool for snipping, called Snip & Sketch, will roll out to Windows 10 users. Find it by typing Snip & Sketch in the search box.

1 In the lower left corner of your screen, click in the **Search box**.

Search relies on *Bing*, Microsoft's search engine, which enables you to conduct a search on your PC, your apps, and the web.

2 With your insertion point in the search box, type **snipping** Compare your screen with Figure 1.51.

BY TOUCH On a touchscreen, tap in the Search box to display the onscreen keyboard, and then begin to type *snipping*.

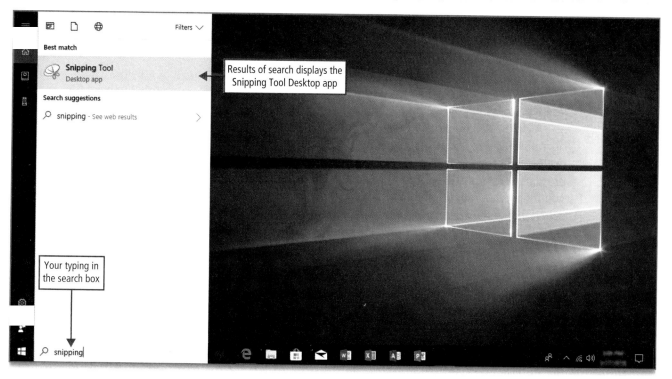

Figure 1.51

3 With the **Snipping Tool Desktop app** shaded and displayed at the top of the search results, press Enter one time.

The Snipping Tool program's *dialog box*—a small window that displays options for completing a task—displays on the desktop, and on the taskbar, the Snipping Tool program button displays underlined and framed in a lighter shade to indicate that the program is open.

BY TOUCH   In the search results, tap the Snipping Tool app.

4 On the taskbar, point to the **Snipping Tool** button and then *right-click*—click the right mouse button one time. On the displayed **Jump List**, click **Pin to taskbar**.

A *Jump List* displays destinations and tasks from a program's taskbar icon when you right-click the icon.

BY TOUCH   On the taskbar, use the *Swipe to select* technique—swipe upward with a short quick movement—to display the Jump List. On the list, tap *Pin to taskbar*.

5 Point to the upper right corner of the **Snipping Tool** dialog box, and then click **Close** ☒.

Because Snipping Tool is a useful tool, while completing the Projects in this textbook, it is recommended that you leave Snipping Tool pinned to your taskbar.

Objective 8   Prepare to Work with Folders and Files

GO! Learn How
Video OF1-8

A *file* is a collection of information stored on a computer under a single name. Examples of a file include a Word document, an Excel workbook, a picture, a song, or a program. A *folder* is a container in which you store files. Windows 10 organizes and keeps track of your electronic files by letting you create and label electronic folders into which you can place your files.

Activity 1.23 │ Creating a New Folder to Store a File

In this Activity, you will create a new folder and save it in a location of your choice. You might decide to use a *removable storage device*, such as a USB flash drive, which is commonly used to transfer information from one computer to another. Such devices are also useful when you want to work with your files on different computers. For example, you probably have files that you work with at your college, at home, and possibly at your workplace.

A *drive* is an area of storage that is formatted with a file system compatible with your operating system and is identified by a drive letter. For example, your computer's *hard disk drive*—the primary storage device located inside your computer where some of your files and programs are typically stored—is usually designated as drive *C*. Removable storage devices that you insert into your computer will be designated with a drive letter—the letter designation varies depending on how many input ports you have on your computer.

You can also use *cloud storage*—storage space on an internet service that can also display as a drive on your computer. When you create a Microsoft account, free cloud storage called *OneDrive* is provided to you. If you are signed in with your Microsoft account, you can access OneDrive from File Explorer.

Increasingly, the use of removable storage devices for file storage is becoming less common, because having your files stored in the cloud where you can retrieve them from any device is more convenient and efficient.

ALERT   The steps in this project use the example of creating your Windows 10 Chapter 1 folder on a USB flash drive. If you want to store your folder in a different location, such as the Documents folder on your computer's hard drive or a folder on your OneDrive, you can still complete the steps, but your screens will not match exactly those shown.

1 Be sure your Windows desktop is still displayed. If you want to do so, insert your USB flash drive. If necessary, close any messages.

Plugging in a device results in a chime sound—if sound is enabled. You might see a message in the taskbar or on the screen that the device software is being installed.

2 On your taskbar, check to see if the **File Explorer** icon ▣ displays. If it does, move to Step 3. If not, in the search box, type **file explorer** under **Best match**, point to **File Explorer Desktop app**, right-click, and then click **Pin to taskbar**.

In an enterprise environment such as a college or business, File Explorer may not be pinned to the taskbar by default, so you might have to pin it there each time you use the computer. Windows 10 Home, the version of Windows that comes on most consumer PCs, typically has File Explorer pinned to the taskbar by default.

3 On the taskbar, click **File Explorer** ▣. If necessary, in the upper right corner of the **File Explorer** window, click Expand the Ribbon ▣.

File Explorer is the program that displays the contents of locations, folders, and files on your computer and also in your OneDrive and other cloud storage locations.

The *ribbon* is a user interface in Windows 10 that groups commands for performing related tasks on tabs across the upper portion of a window. Commands for common tasks include copying and moving, creating new folders, emailing and zipping items, and changing the view.

Use the *navigation pane*—the area on the left side of File Explorer window—to get to locations—your OneDrive, folders on your PC, devices and drives connected to your PC, and other PCs on your network.

4 On the ribbon at the top of the window, click the **View tab**, and then in the **Layout group**, click **Tiles**. Compare your screen with Figure 1.52, and then take a moment to study the parts of the File Explorer window as shown in the table in Figure 1.53.

The *File Explorer window* displays with the Quick access area selected by default. A File Explorer window displays the contents of the current location and contains helpful parts so you can *navigate*—explore within the file organizing structure of Windows. A *location* is any disk drive, folder, network, or cloud storage area in which you can store files and folders.

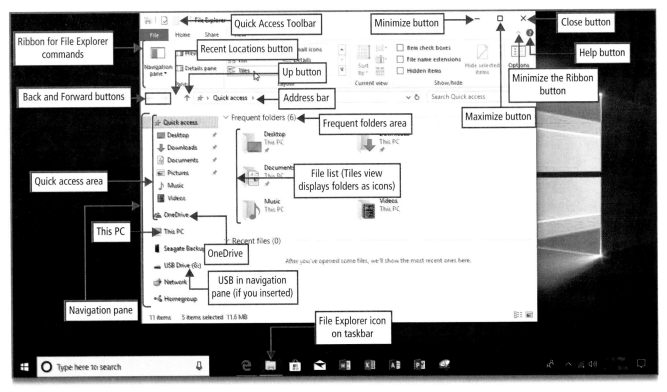

Figure 1.52

Parts of the File Explorer Window	
Address bar	Displays your current location in the folder structure as a series of links separated by arrows.
Back and Forward buttons	Provides the ability to navigate to other folders you have already opened without closing the current folder window. These buttons work with the address bar; that is, after you use the address bar to change folders, you can use the Back button to return to the previous folder.
Close button	Closes the window.
File list	Displays the contents of the current folder or location; if you type text into the Search box, only the folders and files that match your search will display here—including files in subfolders.
Frequent folders area	When Quick access is selected in the navigation pane, displays the folders you use frequently.
Help button	Opens a Bing search for Windows 10 help.
Maximize button	Increases the size of a window to fill the entire screen.
Minimize button	Removes the window from the screen without closing it; minimized windows can be reopened by clicking the associated button in the taskbar.

Parts of the File Explorer Window

Minimize the Ribbon button	Collapses the ribbon so that only the tab names display.
Navigation pane	Displays—for the purpose of navigating to locations—the Quick access area, your OneDrive if you have one and are signed in, locations on the PC at which you are working, any connected storage devices, and network locations to which you might be connected.
OneDrive	Provides navigation to your free file storage and file sharing service provided by Microsoft that you get when you sign up for a Microsoft account; this is your personal cloud storage for files.
Quick access area	Displays commonly accessed locations—such as Documents and Desktop—that you want to access quickly.
Quick Access Toolbar	Displays commonly used commands; you can customize this toolbar by adding and deleting commands and by showing it below the ribbon instead of above the ribbon.
Recent Locations button	Displays the path to locations you have visited recently so that you can go back to a previously working directory quickly.
Ribbon for File Explorer commands	Groups common tasks such as copying and moving, creating new folders, emailing and zipping items, and changing views.
Search box	Locates files stored within the current folder when you type a search term.
This PC	Provides navigation to your internal storage and attached storage devices including optical media such as a DVD drive.
Up button	Opens the location where the folder you are viewing is saved—also referred to as the *parent folder*.

Figure 1.53

5 In the **navigation pane**, click **This PC**. On the right, under **Devices and drives**, locate **Windows (C:)**—or **OS (C:)**—point to the device name to display the ☐ pointer, and then right-click to display a shortcut menu. Compare your screen with Figure 1.54.

A *shortcut menu* is a context-sensitive menu that displays commands and options relevant to the active object. The Windows logo on the C: drive indicates this is where the Windows 10 operating system is stored.

BY TOUCH Press and hold briefly to display a shaded square and then release.

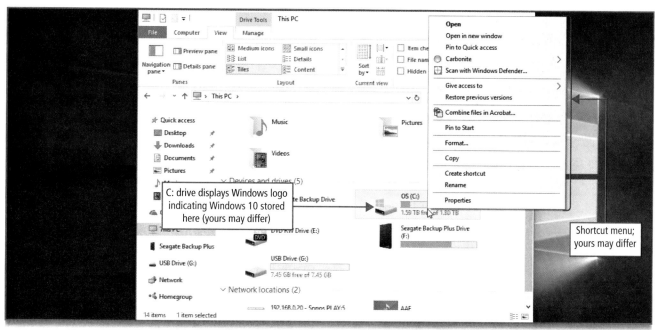

Figure 1.54

6 On the shortcut menu, click **Open** to display the *file list* for this drive.

A file list displays the contents of the current location. This area is also referred to as the *content pane*. If you enter a search term in the search box, your results will also display here. Here, in the C: drive, Windows 10 stores various files related to your operating system.

ANOTHER WAY Point to the device name and double-click to display the file list for the device.

7 On the ribbon, notice that the **Drive Tools** tab displays above the **Manage tab**.

This is a *contextual tab*, which is a tab added to the ribbon automatically when a specific object is selected and that contains commands relevant to the selected object.

8 To the left of the **address bar**, click **Up** ↑ to move up one level in the drive hierarchy and close the file list.

The *address bar* displays your current location in the folder structure as a series of links separated by arrows. Use the address bar to enter or select a location. You can click a part of the path to go to that level. Or, click at the end of the path to select the path for copying.

9 Under **Devices and drives**, click your **USB flash drive** to select it—or click the folder or location where you want to store your file for this project—and notice that the drive or folder is highlighted in blue, indicating it is selected. At the top of the window, on the ribbon, click the **Computer tab**, and then in the **Location group**, click **Open**. Compare your screen with Figure 1.55.

The file list for the selected location displays. There may be no files or only a few files in the location you have selected. You can open a location by double-clicking its name, using the shortcut menu, or by using this ribbon command.

Figure 1.55

10 On the ribbon, on the **Home tab**, in the **New group**, click **New folder**.

11 With the text *New folder* highlighted, type **Windows 10 Chapter 1** and then press Enter to confirm the folder name and select—highlight—the new folder. With the folder selected, press Enter again to open the File Explorer window for your **Windows 10 Chapter 1** folder. Compare your screen with Figure 1.56.

Windows creates a new folder in the location you selected. The address bar indicates the *path* from This PC to your folder. A path is a sequence of folders that leads to a specific file or folder.

To *select* means to specify, by highlighting, a block of data or text on the screen with the intent of performing some action on the selection.

BY TOUCH You may have to tap the keyboard icon in the lower right corner of the taskbar to display the onscreen keyboard.

Figure 1.56

MORE KNOWLEDGE **Use OneDrive as Cloud Storage**

OneDrive is Microsoft's *cloud storage* product. Cloud storage means that your data is stored on a remote server that is maintained by a company so that you can access your files from anywhere and from any device. The idea of having all your data on a single device—your desktop or laptop PC—has become old fashioned. Because cloud storage from large companies like Microsoft are secure, many computer users now store their information on cloud services like OneDrive. Anyone with a Microsoft account has a large amount of free storage on OneDrive, and if you have an Office 365 account—free to most college students—you have 1 terabyte or more of OneDrive storage that you can use across all Microsoft products. That amount of storage is probably all you will ever need—even if you store lots of photos on your OneDrive. OneDrive is integrated into the Windows 10 operating system.

Activity 1.24 | **Creating and Saving a File**

1 In the upper right corner of your **Windows 10 Chapter 1** folder window, click **Close** ⊠.

2 In the lower left corner, click **Start** ⊞.

3 Point to the right side of the **apps list** to display a **scroll bar**, and then drag the **scroll box** down to view apps listed under **T**. Compare your screen with Figure 1.57.

To *drag* is to move something from one location on the screen to another while holding down the left mouse button; the action of dragging includes releasing the mouse button at the desired time or location.

A vertical *scroll bar* displays on the right side of the menu area. A scroll bar displays when the contents of a window or pane are not completely visible. A scroll bar can be vertical as shown or horizontal and displayed at the bottom of a window.

Within the scroll bar, you can move the *scroll box* to bring the contents of the window into view. The position of the scroll box within the scroll bar indicates your relative position within the window's contents. You can click the *scroll arrow* at either end of the scroll bar to move within the window in small increments.

Figure 1.57

MORE KNOWLEDGE   **Jump to a Lettered Section of the Apps List Quickly**

To move quickly to an alphabetic section of the apps list, click an alphabetic letter on the list to display an onscreen alphabet, and then click the letter of the alphabet to which you want to jump.

---

4 Click **Tips**. If necessary, in the upper right, click **Maximize** ☐ so that the **Tips** window fills your entire screen. Then, move your mouse pointer to the right edge of the screen to display the **scroll bar**. Compare your screen with Figure 1.58.

In any window, the *Maximize* button will maximize the size of the window to fill the entire screen.

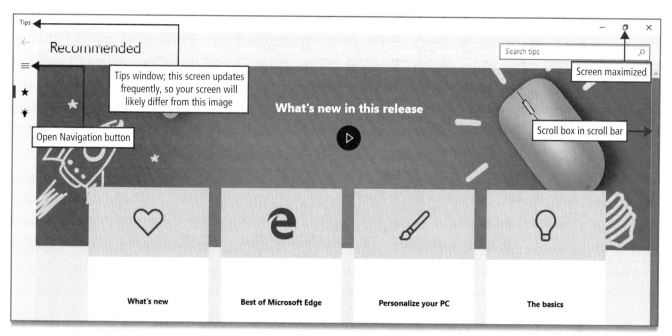

Figure 1.58

5 In the upper left corner, click **Open Navigation** ≡.

This icon is commonly referred to as a *menu icon* or a *hamburger menu* or simply a *hamburger*. The name derives from the three lines that bring to mind a hamburger on a bun. This type of button is commonly used in mobile applications because it is compact to use on smaller screens.

When you click the hamburger icon, a menu expands to identify the icons on the left—Recommended and Collections.

6 Click **Collections**, and then click **Windows**. Click **Get organized**. Move your mouse within the center right side of the screen to display a slideshow arrow ▷, and then click the arrow until you get to the tip **Snap apps side by side**; if this tip is not available, pause at another interesting tip. Compare your screen with Figure 1.59.

To find interesting new things about Windows, Office, Microsoft Mixed Reality, and other topics, take time to explore the Tips app.

Figure 1.59

7 On the taskbar, click **Snipping Tool** 🖼 to display the small **Snipping Tool** dialog box over the screen.

8 On the **menu bar** of the **Snipping Tool** dialog box, to the right of *Mode*, click the **arrow**. Compare your screen with Figure 1.60.

This *menu*—a list of commands within a category—displays four types of snips. A group of menus at the top of a program window is referred to as the *menu bar*.

Use a *free-form snip* to draw an irregular line such as a circle around an area of the screen. Use a *rectangular snip* to draw a precise box by dragging the mouse pointer around an area of the screen to form a rectangle. Use a *window snip* to capture the entire displayed window. Use a *full-screen snip* to capture the entire screen.

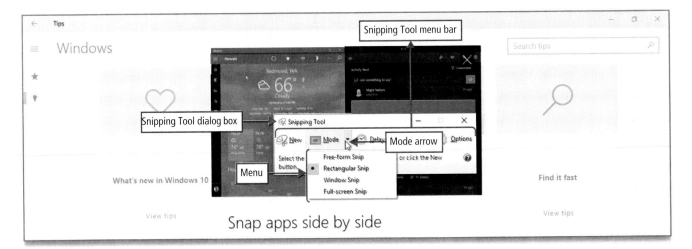

Figure 1.60

9 On the menu, click **Rectangular Snip**, and move your mouse slightly. Notice that the screen dims and your pointer takes the shape of a plus sign ⊞.

10 Move the ⊞ pointer to the upper left corner of the slide portion of the screen, hold down the left mouse button, and then drag down and to the right until you have captured the slide portion of the screen, as shown in Figure 1.61 and then release the mouse button. If you are not satisfied with your result, close the Snipping Tool window and begin again.

The Snipping Tool mark-up window displays the portion of the screen that you snipped. Here you can annotate—mark or make notes on—save, copy, or share the snip.

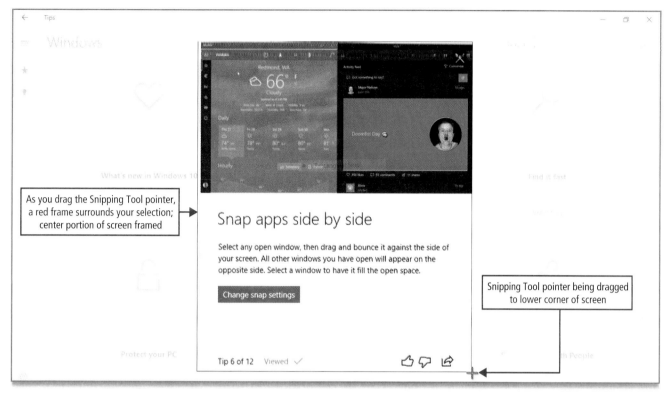

Figure 1.61

11 On the toolbar of the displayed **Snipping Tool** mark-up window, click the **Pen button arrow** ✏, and then click **Red Pen**. Notice that your mouse pointer displays as a red dot.

12 On the snip—remember that you are now looking at a picture of the portion of the screen you captured—use the red mouse pointer to draw a circle around the text *Snap apps side by side*—or whatever the name of the tip you selected is. The circle need not be precise. If you are not satisfied with your circle, on the toolbar, click the Eraser button 🧽, point anywhere on the red circle, click to erase, and then begin again. Compare your screen with Figure 1.62.

Figure 1.62

13 On the **Snipping Tool** mark-up window's toolbar, click **Save Snip** 🖫 to display the **Save As** dialog box.

14 In the **Save As** dialog box, in the **navigation pane**, drag the scroll box down as necessary to find and then click the location where you created your **Windows 10 Chapter 1** folder.

15 In the **file list**, scroll as necessary, locate and *double-click*—press the left mouse button two times in rapid succession while holding the mouse still—your **Windows 10 Chapter 1** folder. Compare your screen with Figure 1.63.

 ANOTHER WAY   Right-click the folder name and click Open.

Figure 1.63

NOTE   **Successful Double-Clicking Requires a Steady Hand**

Double-clicking needs a steady hand. The speed of the two clicks is not as important as holding the mouse still between the two clicks. If you are not satisfied with your result, try again.

---

16 At the bottom of the **Save As** dialog box, locate **Save as type**, click anywhere in the box to display a list, and then on the displayed list click **JPEG file**.

JPEG, which is commonly pronounced *JAY-peg* and stands for Joint Photographic Experts Group, is a common file type used by digital cameras and computers to store digital pictures. JPEG is popular because it can store a high-quality picture in a relatively small file.

17 At the bottom of the **Save As** dialog box, click in the **File name** box to select the text *Capture*, and then using your own name, type **Lastname_Firstname_1B_Tip_Snip**

Within any Windows-based program, text highlighted in blue—selected—in this manner will be replaced by your typing.

NOTE   **File Naming in This Textbook**

Windows 10 recognizes file names with spaces. You can use spaces in file names, however, some programs, especially when transferring files over the internet, may insert the extra characters %20 in place of a space. In this instruction you will be instructed to save files using an underscore instead of a space. The underscore key is the shift of the ⎡-⎤ key—on most keyboards located two or three keys to the left of ⎡Backspace⎤.

---

18 In the lower right corner of the window, click **Save**.

19 Close ⊠ the **Snipping Tool** mark-up window, and then Close ⊠ the **Tips** window.

20 Close any open windows and display your Windows desktop.

You have successfully created a folder and saved a file within that folder.

MORE KNOWLEDGE | **The Hamburger**

For a brief history of the hamburger icon, visit http://blog.placeit.net/history-of-the-hamburger-icon

---

For Non-MyLab Submissions

Start PowerPoint and click Blank Presentation. Click the File tab, on the left click Save As, click Browse, and then navigate to your Windows 10 Chapter 1 folder. At the bottom of the Save As dialog box, in the File name box, using your own name, name the file **Lastname_Firstname_Windows_10_1B_Hotel_Files** and then click Save. Move to Activity 1.26.

Activity 1.25 | Downloading and Extracting Zipped Files

1 If the Microsoft PowerPoint application is not pinned to your taskbar, use the same technique you used to search for and pin the Snipping Tool application to search for and pin the PowerPoint application to your taskbar.

2 Sign in to your MyLab IT course. In your course, locate and click **Windows 10 1B Hotel Files**, click Download Materials, and then click Download All Files. Using the Chrome browser (if you are using a different browser see notes below), use the steps below to extract the zipped folder to your **Windows 10 Chapter 1** (or use your favorite method to download and extract files):

- In the lower left, next to the downloaded zipped folder, click the small **arrow**, and then click **Show in folder**. The zipped folder displays in *File Explorer*—the Windows program that displays the contents of locations, folders, and files on your computer—in the Downloads folder. (Unless you have changed default settings, downloaded files go to the Downloads folder on your computer.)
- With the zipped folder selected, on the ribbon, under **Compressed Folder Tools**, click the **Extract tab**, and then at the right end of the ribbon, click **Extract all**.
- In the displayed **Extract Compressed (Zipped) Folders** dialog box, click **Browse**. In the **Select a destination** dialog box, use the navigation pane on the left to navigate to your **Windows 10 Chapter 1 folder**, and double-click its name to open the folder and display its name in the **Address bar**.
- In the lower right, click **Select Folder**, and then in the lower right, click **Extract**; when complete, a new File Explorer window displays showing the extracted files in your chapter folder. For this Project, you will see a PowerPoint file with your name and another zipped folder named **win01_1B_Bell_Orchid**, which you will extract later, a result file to check against, and an Instruction file. Take a moment to open **Windows_10_1B_Hotel_Files_Instructions**; note any recent updates to the book.
- **Close** ⊠ both File Explorer windows, close the Grader download screens, and close any open documents For this Project, you should close MyLab and any other open windows in your browser.

3 From the taskbar, click **File Explorer**, navigate to and reopen your **Windows 10 Chapter 1 folder**, and then double-click the PowerPoint file you downloaded from MyLab IT that displays your name—**Student_Windows_10_1B_Hotel_Files**. In your blank PowerPoint presentation, if necessary, at the top click **Enable Editing**.

Activity 1.26 | Locating and Inserting a Saved File Into a PowerPoint Presentation

1 Be sure your PowerPoint presentation with your name is displayed. Then, on the **Home tab,** in the **Slides group**, click **Layout**. In the displayed gallery, click **Title Only**. If necessary, on the right, close the Design Ideas pane. Click anywhere in the text *Click to add title*, and then type **Tip Snip**

2 Click anywhere in the empty space below the title you just typed. Click the **Insert tab**, and then in the **Images group**, click **Pictures**. In the **navigation pane**, click the location of your **Windows 10 Chapter 1** folder, open the folder, and then in the **Insert Picture** dialog box, click one time to select your **Lastname_Firstname_1B_Tip_Snip** file. In the lower right corner of the dialog box, click **Insert**. If necessary, close the Design Ideas pane on the right. If necessary, drag the image to the right so that your slide title *Tip Snip* displays.

3 On the Quick Access Toolbar, click **Save** 🖫, and then in the upper right corner of the PowerPoint window, click **Minimize** ⎯ so that PowerPoint remains open but not displayed on your screen; you will need your PowerPoint presentation as you progress through this project.

4 **Close** ☒ the File Explorer window and close any other open windows.

Activity 1.27 | Using Snap and Task View

Use **Snap** to arrange two or more open windows on your screen so that you can work with multiple screens at the same time.

Snap with the mouse by dragging the **title bar**—the bar across the top of the window that displays the program, file, or app name—of one app to the left until it snaps into place, and then dragging the title bar of another app to the right until it snaps into place.

Snap with the keyboard by selecting the window you want to snap, and then pressing ⊞ + ◄. Then select another window and press ⊞ + ►. This is an example of a **keyboard shortcut**—a combination of two or more keyboard keys used to perform a task that would otherwise require a mouse.

1 ▷ From your desktop, click **Start** ⊞. In the list of apps, click the letter **A** to display the alphabet, and then click **W**. Under **W**, click **Weather**. If necessary, personalize your weather content by typing your zip code into the Search box, selecting your location, and clicking Start.

2 ▷ By using the same technique to display the alphabet, click **C**, and then click **Calculator**. On the taskbar, notice that icons display to show that the Weather app and the Calculator app are open. Notice also that on the desktop, the most recently opened app displays on top and is also framed on the taskbar. Compare your screen with Figure 1.64.

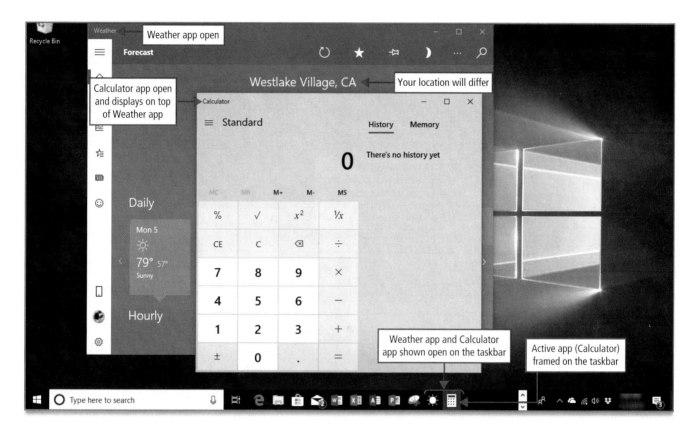

Figure 1.64

3 Point to the word *Calculator* at the top of this open app, hold down your left mouse button, drag your mouse pointer to the left edge of your screen until an outline displays to show where the window will snap, and then release the mouse button. Compare your screen with Figure 1.65.

On the right, all open windows display—your PowerPoint presentation and the Weather app. This feature is ***Snap Assist***—after you have snapped a window, all other open windows display as ***thumbnails*** in the remaining space. A thumbnail is a reduced image of a graphic.

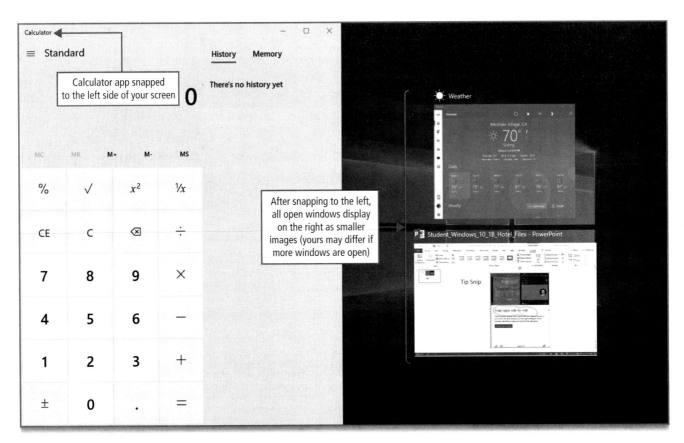

Figure 1.65

4 Click the **Weather** app to have it fill the right half of your screen.

5 In the lower left of your keyboard, press and hold down ⊞ and then in upper right of your keyboard, locate and press and release (PrintScrn). Notice that your screen dims momentarily.

This is another method to create a screenshot. This screenshot file is automatically stored in the Screenshots folder in the Pictures folder of your hard drive; it is also stored on the Clipboard if you want to copy it immediately.

A screenshot captured in this manner is saved as a *.png* file, which is commonly pronounced PING, and stands for Portable Network Graphic. This is an image file type that can be transferred over the internet.

6 On the taskbar, click **Task View** 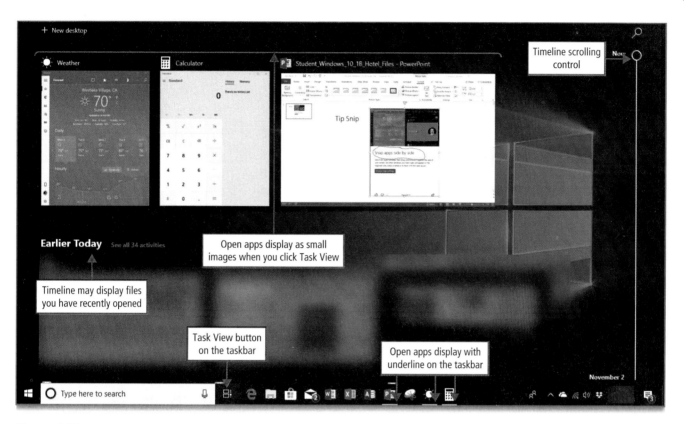, point to one of the open apps, and then compare your screen with Figure 1.66.

Use the *Task View* button on the taskbar to see and switch between open apps—including desktop apps. You may see the Windows 10 feature *Timeline*, with which, when you click the Task View button, you can see your activities and files you have recently worked on across your devices. For example, you can find a document, image, or video you worked on yesterday or a week ago.

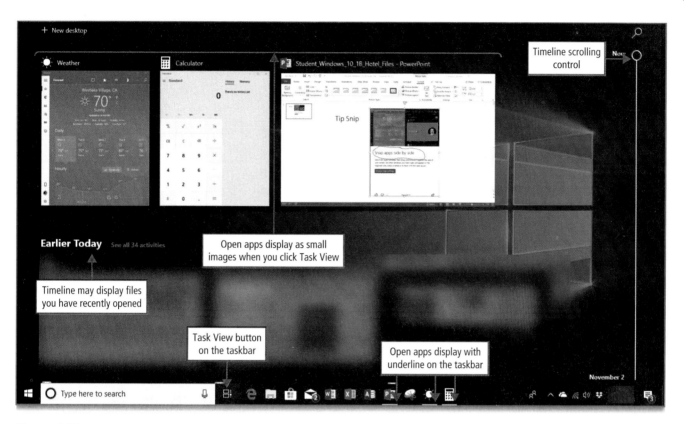

Figure 1.66

7 From **Task View**, click your **PowerPoint** window. On the **Home tab**, in the **Slides group**, click the upper portion of the **New Slide** button to insert a new slide in the same layout as your previous slide.

An arrow attached to a button will display a menu when clicked. Such a button is referred to as a *split button*—clicking the main part of the button performs a command and clicking the arrow opens a menu with choices.

8 As the title type **Side by Side** and then click in the blank space below the title. On the ribbon, on the **Home tab**, in the **Clipboard group**, click the upper portion of the **Paste** button to paste your screenshot into the slide.

Recall that by creating a screenshot using the [⊞] + [PrintScrn] command, a copy was placed on the Clipboard. A permanent copy is also stored in the Screenshots folder of your Pictures folder. This is a convenient way to create a quick screenshot.

9 With the image selected, on the ribbon, under **Picture Tools**, click **Format**. In the **Size group**, click in the **Shape Height** box [□ 0.05″ ⸋], type 5 and press Enter. Drag the image down and into the center of the space so that your slide title is visible. Compare your screen with Figure 1.67.

Figure 1.67

10 On the Quick Access Toolbar, click **Save** [💾], and then in the upper right corner of the PowerPoint window, click **Minimize** [−] so that PowerPoint remains open but not displayed on your screen.

11 **Close** [✕] the **Calculator** app and the **Weather** app to display your desktop.

Objective 9 **Use File Explorer to Extract Zipped Files and to Display Locations, Folders, and Files**

GO! Learn How
Video OF1-9

A file is the fundamental unit of storage that enables Windows 10 to distinguish one set of information from another. A folder is the basic organizing tool for files. In a folder, you can store files that are related to one another. You can also place a folder inside of another folder, which is then referred to as a **subfolder**.

Windows 10 arranges folders in a structure that resembles a **hierarchy**—an arrangement where items are ranked and where each level is lower in rank than the item above it. The hierarchy of folders is referred to as the **folder structure**. A sequence of folders in the folder structure that leads to a specific file or folder is a **path**.

Activity 1.28 | Navigating with File Explorer

Recall that File Explorer is the program that displays the contents of locations, folders, and files on your computer and also in your OneDrive and other cloud storage locations. File Explorer also enables you to perform tasks related to your files and folders such as copying, moving, and renaming. When you open a folder or location, a window displays to show its contents. The design of the window helps you navigate—explore within the file structure so you can find your files and folders—and so that you can save and find your files and folders efficiently.

In this Activity, you will open a folder and examine the parts of its window.

1 With your desktop displayed, on the taskbar, *point to* but do not click **File Explorer**, and notice the ScreenTip *File Explorer*.

A *ScreenTip* displays useful information when you perform various mouse actions, such as pointing to screen elements.

2 Click **File Explorer** to display the **File Explorer** window.

File Explorer is at work anytime you are viewing the contents of a location or the contents of a folder stored in a specific location. By default, the File Explorer button on the taskbar opens with the *Quick access* location—a list of files you have been working on and folders you use often—selected in the navigation pane and in the address bar.

The default list will likely display the Desktop, Downloads, Documents, and Pictures folders, and then folders you worked on recently or work on frequently will be added automatically, although you can change this behavior.

The benefit of the Quick access list is that you can customize a list of folders that you go to often. To add a folder to the list quickly, you can right-click a folder in the file list and click Pin to Quick Access.

For example, if you are working on a project, you can pin it—or simply drag it—to the Quick access list. When you are done with the project and not using the folder so often, you can remove it from the list. Removing it from the list does not delete the folder, it simply removes it from the Quick access list.

3 On the left, in the **navigation pane**, scroll down if necessary, and then click **This PC** to display folders, devices, and drives in the **file list** on the right. Compare your screen with Figure 1.68.

Figure 1.68

4 If necessary, in the upper right corner, click Expand the Ribbon ⌄. In the **file list**, under **Folders**—click **Documents** one time to select it, and then on the ribbon, on the **Computer tab**, in the **Location group**, click **Open**.

5 On the ribbon, click the **View tab**. In the **Show/Hide group**, be sure that **Item check boxes** is selected—select it if necessary, and then in the **Layout group**, if necessary, click **Details**.

The window for the Documents folder displays. You may or may not have files and folders already stored here. Because this window typically displays the file list for a folder, it is also referred to as the *folder window*. Item check boxes make it easier to select items in a file list and also to see which items are selected in a file list.

🔁 **ANOTHER WAY** Point to Documents, right-click to display a shortcut menu, and then click Open; or, point to Documents and double-click.

6 Compare your screen with Figure 1.69, and then take a moment to study the parts of the window as described in the table in Figure 1.70.

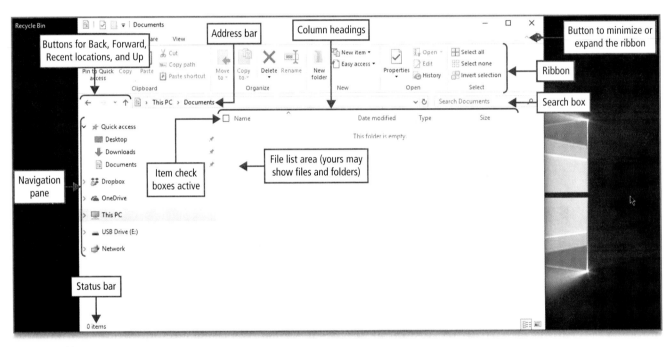

Figure 1.69

Parts of the File Explorer Window	
Window Part	**Function**
Address bar	Displays your current location in the file structure as a series of links separated by arrows. Tap or click a part of the path to go to that level or tap or click at the end to select the path for copying.
Back, Forward, Recent locations, and Up buttons	Enable you to navigate to other folders you have already opened without closing the current window. These buttons work with the address bar; that is, after you use the address bar to change folders, you can use the Back button to return to the previous folder. Use the Up button to open the location where the folder you are viewing is saved—also referred to as the *parent folder*.
Column headings	Identify the columns in Details view. By clicking the column heading name, you can change how the files in the file list are organized; by clicking the arrow on the right, you can select various sort arrangements in the file list. By right-clicking a column heading, you can select other columns to add to the file list.
File list	Displays the contents of the current folder or location. If you type text into the Search box, a search is conducted on the folder or location only, and only the folders and files that match your search will display here—including files in subfolders.
Minimize the Ribbon or Expand the Ribbon button	Changes the display of the ribbon. When minimized, the ribbon shows only the tab names and not the full ribbon.
Navigation pane	Displays locations to which you can navigate; for example, your OneDrive, folders on This PC, devices and drives connected to your PC, folders listed under Quick access, and possibly other PCs on your network. Use Quick access to open your most commonly used folders and searches. If you have a folder that you use frequently, you can drag it to the Quick access area so that it is always available.
Ribbon	Groups common tasks such as copying and moving, creating new folders, emailing and zipping items, and changing views of the items in the file list.
Search box	Enables you to type a word or phrase and then searches for a file or subfolder stored in the current folder that contains matching text. The search begins as soon as you begin typing; for example, if you type *G*, all the file and folder names that start with the letter *G* display in the file list.
Status bar	Displays the total number of items in a location, or the number of selected items and their total size.

Figure 1.70

7 Move your ⟨pointer⟩ pointer anywhere into the **navigation pane**, and notice that a downward pointing arrow ˅ displays to the left of *Quick access* to indicate that this item is expanded, and a right-pointing arrow > displays to the left of items that are collapsed.

You can click these arrows to collapse and expand areas in the navigation pane.

Activity 1.29 | Using File Explorer to Extract Zipped Files

 For Non-MyLab Users
From your instructor or from www.pearsonhighered.com/go download the zipped folder **win01_1B_Bell_Orchid** to your **Windows 10 Chapter 1** folder.

1 In the **navigation pane**, if necessary expand **This PC**, scroll down if necessary, and then click your **USB flash drive** (or the location where you have stored your chapter folder) one time to display its contents in the **file list**. Double-click to open your **Windows 10 Chapter 1 folder** and locate the zipped folder **win01_1B_Bell_Orchid**.

2 Use the steps below to extract this zipped folder to your **Windows 10 Chapter 1 folder** as follows (or use your favorite method to unzip):

- On the **Home tab**, click **New folder**, and then name the folder **win01_1B_Bell_Orchid**
- Click the zipped folder **win01_1B_Bell_Orchid** one time to select it.

- With the zipped folder selected, on the ribbon, under **Compressed Folder Tools**, click the **Extract tab**, and then at the right end of the ribbon, click **Extract all**.
- In the displayed **Extract Compressed (Zipped) Folders** dialog box, click **Browse**. In the **Select a destination** dialog box, use the navigation pane on the left to navigate to your **Windows 10 Chapter 1 folder**, and then double-click the name of the new folder you just created to open the folder and display its name in the **Address bar**.
- In the lower right, click **Select Folder**, and then in the lower right, click **Extract**. When complete, click the Up button ⬆ one time. You will see the extracted folder and the zipped folder.
- To delete the unneeded zipped version, click it one time to select it, and then on the **Home tab**, in the **Organize group**, click **Delete**. If necessary, click Yes. Now that the files are extracted, you do not need the zipped copy.

3 Close ⊠ all File Explorer windows to display your desktop.

Activity 1.30 | **Using File Explorer to Display Locations, Folders, and Files**

1 From the taskbar, open **File Explorer** 🗀. In the **navigation pane**, if necessary expand **This PC**, scroll down if necessary, and then click your **USB flash drive** (or the location where you have stored your chapter folder) one time to display its contents in the **file list**. In the **file list**, double-click your **Windows 10 Chapter 1 folder** to display its contents. Compare your screen with Figure 1.71.

In the navigation pane, *This PC* displays all of the drive letter locations attached to your computer, including the internal hard drives, CD or DVD drives, and any connected devices such as a USB flash drive.

Your PowerPoint file, your *Tip_Snip* file, and your extracted folder *win01_1B_Bell_Orchid* folder display if this is your storage location.

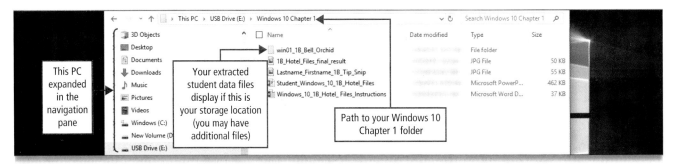

Figure 1.71

2 In the **file list**, double-click the **win01_1B_Bell_Orchid** folder to display the subfolders and files.

Recall that the corporate office of the Bell Orchid Hotels is in Boston. The corporate office maintains subfolders labeled for each of its large hotels in Honolulu, Orlando, San Diego, and Santa Barbara.

ANOTHER WAY Right-click the folder, and then click Open; or, select the folder and then on the ribbon, on the Home tab, in the Open group, click Open.

3 In the **file list**, double-click **Orlando** to display the subfolders, and then look at the **address bar** to view the path. Compare your screen with Figure 1.72.

Within each city's subfolder, there is a structure of subfolders for the Accounting, Engineering, Food and Beverage, Human Resources, Operations, and Sales and Marketing departments.

Because folders can be placed inside of other folders, such an arrangement is common when organizing files on a computer.

In the address bar, the path from the flash drive to the win01_1B_Bell_Orchid folder to the Orlando folder displays as a series of links.

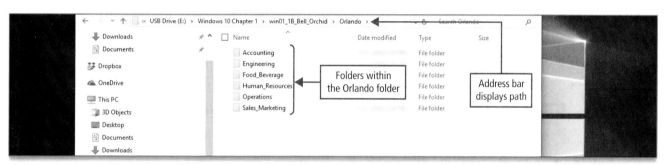

Figure 1.72

4 In the **address bar**, to the right of **win01_1B_Bell_Orchid**, click the ⟩ arrow to display a list of the subfolders in the **win01_1B_Bell_Orchid** folder. On the list that displays, notice that **Orlando** displays in bold, indicating it is open in the file list. Then, on the list, click **Honolulu**.

The subfolders within the Honolulu folder display.

5 In the **address bar**, to the right of **win01_1B_Bell_Orchid**, click the ⟩ arrow again to display the subfolders in that folder. Then, on the **address bar**—not on the list—point to **Honolulu** and notice that the list of subfolders in the **Honolulu** folder displays.

After you display one set of subfolders in the address bar, all of the links are active and you need only point to them to display the list of subfolders.

Clicking an arrow to the right of a folder name in the address bar displays a list of the subfolders in that folder. You can click a subfolder name to display its contents. In this manner, the address bar is not only a path, but it is also an active control with which you can step from the current folder directly to any other folder above it in the folder structure just by clicking a folder name.

6 On the list of subfolders for **Honolulu**, click **Sales_Marketing** to display its contents in the **file list**. On the **View tab**, in the **Layout group**, if necessary, click **Details**. Compare your screen with Figure 1.73.

🔄 **ANOTHER WAY**   In the file list, double-click the Sales_Marketing folder.

The files in the Sales_Marketing folder for Honolulu display in the Details layout. To the left of each file name, an icon indicates the program that created each file. Here, there is one PowerPoint file, one Excel file, one Word file, and four JPEG images.

Figure 1.73

7 In the upper left portion of the window, click **Back** ⬅ one time.

The Back button retraces each of your clicks in the same manner as clicking the Back button when you are browsing the internet.

8 In the **file list**, point to the **Human_Resources** folder, and then double-click to open the folder.

9 In the **file list**, click one time to select the PowerPoint file **HO_HR_New_Employee_ Presentation**, and then on the ribbon, click the **View tab**. In the **Panes group**, click **Details pane**, and then compare your screen with Figure 1.74.

The ***Details pane*** displays the most common ***file properties*** associated with the selected file. File properties refer to information about a file, such as the author, the date the file was last changed, and any descriptive ***tags***—properties that you create to help you find and organize your files.

Additionally, a thumbnail image of the first slide in the presentation displays, and the status bar displays the number of items in the folder.

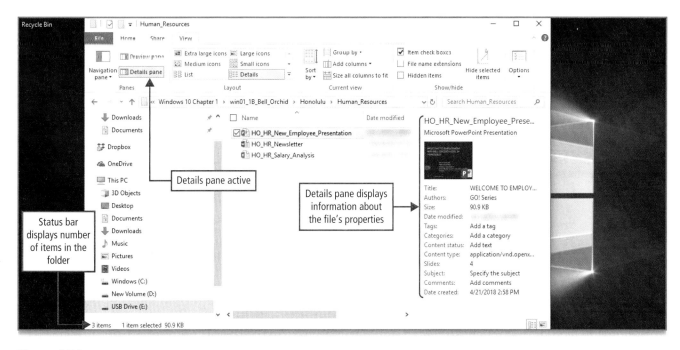

Figure 1.74

> **10** On the right, in the **Details pane**, click **Add a tag**, type **New Employee meeting** and then at the bottom of the pane click **Save**.
>
> Because you can search for tags, adding tags to files makes them easier to find.

ANOTHER WAY With the file selected, on the Home tab, in the Open group, click Properties to display the Properties dialog box for the file, and then click the Details tab.

> **11** On the ribbon, on the **View tab**, in the **Panes group**, click **Preview pane** to replace the **Details pane** with the **Preview pane**. Compare your screen with Figure 1.75.
>
> In the Preview pane that displays on the right, you can use the scroll bar to scroll through the slides in the presentation; or, you can click the up or down scroll arrow to view the slides as a miniature presentation.

Figure 1.75

12 ▶ On the ribbon, click **Preview pane** to close the right pane.

Use the Details pane to see a file's properties and the Preview pane when you want to look at a file quickly without actually opening it.

13 ▶ **Close** ☒ the **Human_Resources** window.

Objective 10   Start Programs and Open Data Files

GO! Learn How
Video OF1-10

When you are using the software programs installed on your computer, you create and save data files—the documents, workbooks, databases, songs, pictures, and so on that you need for your job or personal use. Therefore, most of your work with Windows 10 desktop applications is concerned with locating and starting your programs and locating and opening your files.

Activity 1.31   Starting Programs

You can start programs from the Start menu or from the taskbar by pinning a program to the taskbar. You can open your data files from within the program in which they were created, or you can open a data file from a window in File Explorer, which will simultaneously start the program and open your file.

1 ▶ Be sure your desktop displays and that your PowerPoint presentation is still open but minimized on the taskbar. You can point to the PowerPoint icon to have a small image of the active slide display. Click **Start** ▦ to place the insertion point in the search box, type **wordpad** and then click the **WordPad Desktop app**.

2 ▶ With the insertion point blinking in the document window, type your first and last name.

3 ▶ From the taskbar, open your PowerPoint presentation. On the **Home tab**, click the upper portion of the **New Slide** button to insert a blank slide in the Title Only layout. Click anywhere in the text *Click to add title*, and then type **Wordpad**

4 ▶ Click anywhere in the lower portion of the slide. On the **Insert tab**, in the **Images group**, click **Screenshot**, and then under **Available Windows**, click the image of the WordPad program with your name typed to insert the image in the PowerPoint slide. Click in a blank area of the slide to deselect the image; if necessary, close the Design Ideas pane on the right. As necessary, drag the image down so that the title displays, and if necessary, use the Shape Height box to decrease the size of the screenshot slightly. Compare your screen with Figure 1.76.

Figure 1.76

5 On the Quick Access toolbar, click **Save** 🖫 and then in the upper right corner of the PowerPoint window, click **Minimize** ─ so that PowerPoint remains open but not displayed on your screen.

6 Close ✕ **WordPad**, and then click **Don't Save**.

Activity 1.32 | Opening Data Files

1 Open **Microsoft Word** from your taskbar, or click **Start** ⊞, type **Microsoft word** and then open the **Word** desktop app. Compare your screen with Figure 1.77.

The Word program window has features that are common to other programs you have opened; for example, commands are arranged on tabs. When you create and save data in Word, you create a Word document file.

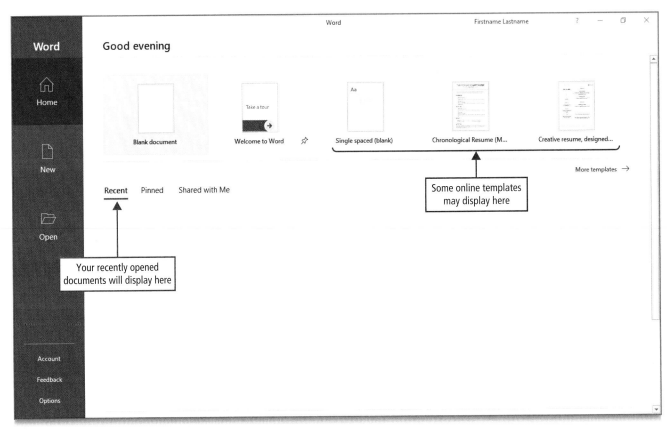

Figure 1.77

2 On the left, click **Open**. Notice the list of places from which you can open a document, including your OneDrive if you are logged in. Click **Browse** to display the **Open** dialog box. Compare your screen with Figure 1.78, and then take a moment to study the table in Figure 1.79.

Recall that a dialog box is a window containing options for completing a task; the layout of the Open dialog box is similar to that of a File Explorer window. When you are working in a desktop application, use the Open dialog box to locate and open existing files that were created in the desktop application.

When you click Browse, typically the Documents folder on This PC displays. You can use the skills you have practiced to navigate to other locations on your computer, such as your removable USB flash drive.

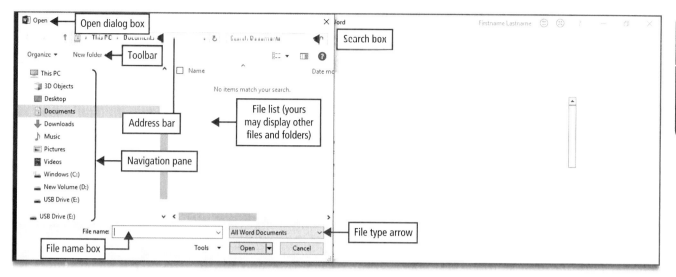

Figure 1.78

Dialog Box Element	Function
Address bar	Displays the path in the folder structure.
File list	Displays the list of files and folders that are available in the folder indicated in the address bar.
File name box	Enables you to type the name of a specific file to locate it—if you know it.
File type arrow	Enables you to restrict the type of files displayed in the file list; for example, the default *All Word Documents* restricts (filters) the type of files displayed to only Word documents. You can click the arrow and adjust the restrictions (filters) to a narrower or wider group of files.
Navigation pane	Navigate to files and folders and get access to Quick access, OneDrive, and This PC.
Search box	Search for files in the current folder. Filters the file list based on text that you type; the search is based on text in the file name (and for files on the hard drive or OneDrive, in the file itself), and on other properties that you can specify. The search takes place in the current folder, as displayed in the address bar, and in any subfolders within that folder.
Toolbar	Displays relevant tasks; for example, creating a new folder.

Figure 1.79

3 In the **navigation pane**, scroll down as necessary, and then under **This PC**, click your **USB flash drive** or whatever location where you have stored your files for this project. In the **file list**, double-click your **win01_1B_Bell_Orchid** folder to open it and display its contents.

4 In the upper right portion of the **Open** dialog box, click the **More options arrow** ⌄, and then set the view to **Large icons**. Compare your screen with Figure 1.80.

The Live Preview feature indicates that each folder contains additional subfolders.

Figure 1.80

5 In the **file list**, double-click the **Corporate** folder, and then double-click the **Accounting** folder.

The view returns to the Details view.

6 In the **file list**, notice that only one document—a Word document—displays. In the lower right corner, locate the **File type** button, and notice that *All Word Documents* displays as the file type. Click the **File type arrow**, and then on the displayed list, click **All Files**. Compare your screen with Figure 1.81.

When you change the file type to *All Files*, you can see that the Word file is not the only file in this folder. By default, the Open dialog box displays only the files created in the active program; however, you can display variations of file types in this manner.

Microsoft Office file types are identified by small icons, which is a convenient way to differentiate one type of file from another. Although you can view all the files in the folder, you can open only the files that were created in the active program, which in this instance is Microsoft Word.

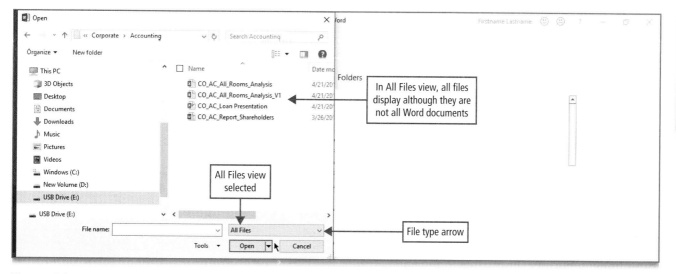

Figure 1.81

7 ▶ Change the file type back to **All Word Documents**. Then, in the **file list**, double-click the **CO_AC_Report_Shareholders** Word file to open the document. Take a moment to scroll through the document. If necessary, Maximize ☐ the window.

8 ▶ **Close** ☒ the Word window.

9 ▶ Click **Start** ⊞, and then search for **.txt** At the top, click **Filters**, click **Documents**, and then on the list, click **Structure.txt in Future_Hotels**.

> The file opens using the Windows 10 *Notepad* desktop app—a basic text-editing program included with Windows 10 that you can use to create simple documents.
>
> In the search box, you can search for files on your computer, and you can search for a file by its *file name extension*—a set of characters at the end of a file name that helps Windows understand what kind of information is in a file and what program should open it. A *.txt file* is a simple file consisting of lines of text with no formatting that almost any computer can open and display.

10 ▶ **Close** ☒ the Notepad program.

MORE KNOWLEDGE **Do Not Clutter Your Desktop by Creating Desktop Shortcuts or Storing Files**

On your desktop, you can add or remove *desktop shortcuts*, which are desktop icons that can link to items accessible on your computer such as a program, file, folder, disk drive, printer, or another computer. In previous versions of Windows, many computer users commonly did this.

Now the Start menu is your personal dashboard for all your programs and online activities, and increasingly you will access programs and your own files in the cloud. So do not clutter your desktop with shortcuts—doing so is more confusing than useful. Placing desktop shortcuts for frequently used programs or folders directly on your desktop may seem convenient, but as you add more icons, your desktop becomes cluttered and the shortcuts are not easy to find. A better organizing method is to use the taskbar for shortcuts to programs. For folders and files, the best organizing structure is to create a logical structure of folders within your Documents folder or your cloud-based OneDrive.

You can also drag frequently-used folders to the Quick access area in the navigation pane so that they are available any time you open File Explorer. As you progress in your use of Windows 10, you will discover techniques for using the taskbar and the Quick access area of the navigation pane to streamline your work instead of cluttering your desktop.

Activity 1.33 | Searching, Pinning, Sorting, and Filtering in File Explorer

1 From the taskbar, open **File Explorer**. On the right, at the bottom, you may notice that under **Recent files**, you can see files that you have recently opened.

2 In the **navigation pane**, click your **USB flash drive**—or click the location where you have stored your files for this project. Double-click your **Windows 10 Chapter 1 folder** to open it. In the upper right, click in the **Search** box, and then type **pool** Compare your screen with Figure 1.82.

Files that contain the word *pool* in the title display. If you are searching a folder on your hard drive or OneDrive, files that contain the word *pool* within the document will also display. Additionally, Search Tools display on the ribbon.

Figure 1.82

3 In the search box, clear the search by clicking ☒, and then in the search box type **Paris.jpg** Notice that you can also search by using a file extension as part of the search term.

4 **Clear** ☒ the search. Double-click your **win01_1B_Bell_Orchid** folder to open it.

5 On the **Home tab**, in the **Clipboard group**, click **Pin to Quick access**. If necessary, scroll up in the navigation pane. Compare your screen with Figure 1.83.

You can pin frequently used folders to the Quick access area, and then unpin them when you no longer need frequent access. Folders that you access frequently will also display in the Quick access area without the pin image. Delete them by right-clicking the name and clicking Unpin from Quick access.

Figure 1.83

ANOTHER WAY In the file list, right-click a folder name, and then click Pin to Quick access; or, drag the folder to the Quick access area in the navigation pain and release the mouse button when the ScreenTip displays Pin to Quick access.

6 In the **file list**—double-click the **Corporate** folder and then double-click the **Engineering** folder.

7 On the **View tab, in the Current view group**, click **Sort by**, and then click **Type**. Compare your screen with Figure 1.84.

> Use this technique to sort files in the file list by type. Here, the JPG files display first, and then the Microsoft Excel files, and so on—in alphabetic order by file type.

Figure 1.84

8 Point to the column heading **Type**, and then click **∧**.

9 Point to the column heading **Type** again, and on the right, click ☑. On the displayed list, click **Microsoft PowerPoint Presentation**, and notice that the file list is filtered to show only PowerPoint files.

> A *filtered list* is a display of files that is limited based on specified criteria.

10 To the right of the **Type** column heading, click the check mark and then click **Microsoft PowerPoint Presentation** again to clear the Microsoft PowerPoint filter and redisplay all of the files.

11 **Close** ☒ the File Explorer window.

ALERT   Allow Time to Complete the Remainder of This Project in One Session

If you are working on a computer that is not your own, for example in a college lab, plan your time to complete the remainder of this project in one working session. Allow 45 to 60 minutes.

Because you will need to store and then delete files on the hard disk drive of the computer at which you are working, it is recommended that you complete this project in one working session—*unless you are working on your own computer or you know that the files will be retained.* In your college lab, files you store on the computer's hard drive will not be retained after you sign off.

Objective 11   Create, Rename, and Copy Files and Folders

GO! Learn How
Video OF1-11

File management includes organizing, copying, renaming, moving, and deleting the files and folders you have stored in various locations—both locally and in the cloud.

Activity 1.34 | Copying Files from a Removable Storage Device to the Documents Folder on the Hard Disk Drive

Barbara and Steven have the assignment to transfer and then organize some of the corporation's files to a computer that will be connected to the corporate network. Data on such a computer can be accessed by employees at any of the hotel locations through the use of sharing technologies. For example, *SharePoint* is a Microsoft technology that enables employees in an organization to access information across organizational and geographic boundaries.

1 Close any open windows, but leave your open PowerPoint presentation minimized on the taskbar.

2 From the taskbar, open **File Explorer**. In the **navigation pane**, if necessary expand **This PC**, and then click your USB flash drive or the location where you have stored your chapter folder to display its contents in the file list.

> Recall that in the navigation pane, under This PC, you have access to all the storage areas inside your computer, such as your hard disk drives, and to any devices with removable storage, such as CDs, DVDs, or USB flash drives.

3 Open your **Windows 10 Chapter 1** folder, and then in the **file list**, click **win01_1B_Bell_ Orchid** one time to select the folder. Compare your screen with Figure 1.85.

Figure 1.85

4 With the **win01_1B_Bell_Orchid** folder selected, on the ribbon, on the **Home tab**, in the **Clipboard group**, click **Copy**.

> The Copy command places a copy of your selected file or folder on the *Clipboard* where it will be stored until you use the Paste command to place the copy somewhere else. The Clipboard is a temporary storage area for information that you have copied or moved from one place and plan to use somewhere else.

> In Windows 10, the Clipboard can hold only one piece of information at a time. Whenever something is copied to the Clipboard, it replaces whatever was there before. In Windows 10, you cannot view the contents of the Clipboard nor place multiple items there in the manner that you can in Microsoft Word.

ANOTHER WAY With the item selected in the file list, press Ctrl + C to copy the item to the clipboard.

5 To the left of the address bar, click **Up** ↑ two times. In the **file list**, double-click your **Documents** folder to open it, and then on the **Home tab**, in the **Clipboard group**, click **Paste**.

> A *progress bar* displays in a dialog box and also displays on the taskbar button with green shading. A progress bar indicates visually the progress of a task such as a copy process, a download, or a file transfer.

> The Documents folder is one of several folders within your *personal folder* stored on the hard disk drive. For each user account—even if there is only one user on the computer—Windows 10 creates a personal folder labeled with the account holder's name.

ANOTHER WAY With the destination location selected, press Ctrl + V to paste the item from the clipboard to the selected location. Or, on the Home tab, in the Organize group, click Copy to, find and then click the location to which you want to copy. If the desired location is not on the list, use the Choose location command at the bottom.

6 Close ☒ the **Documents** window.

Activity 1.35 | Creating Folders, Renaming Folders, and Renaming Files

Barbara and Steven can see that various managers have been placing files related to new European hotels in the *Future_Hotels* folder. They can also see that the files have not been organized into a logical structure. For example, files that are related to each other are not in separate folders; instead they are mixed in with other files that are not related to the topic.

In this Activity, you will create, name, and rename folders to begin a logical structure of folders in which to organize the files related to the European hotels project.

1 From the taskbar, open **File Explorer** 📁, and then use any of the techniques you have practiced to display the contents of the **Documents** folder in the **file list**.

NOTE **Using the Documents Folder and OneDrive Instead of Your USB Drive**

In this modern computing era, you should limit your use of USB drives to those times when you want to quickly take some files to another computer without going online. Instead of using a USB drive, use your computer's hard drive, or better yet, your free OneDrive cloud storage that comes with your Microsoft account.

There are two good reasons to stop using USB flash drives. First, searching is limited on a USB drive—search does not look at the content inside a file. When you search files on your hard drive or OneDrive, the search extends to words and phrases actually *inside* the files. Second, if you delete a file or folder from a USB drive, it is gone and cannot be retrieved. Files you delete from your hard drive or OneDrive go to the Recycle Bin where you can retrieve them later.

---

2 In the **file list**, double-click the **win01_1B_Bell_Orchid** folder, double-click the **Corporate** folder, double-click the **Information_Technology** folder, and then double-click the **Future_Hotels** folder to display its contents in the file list; sometimes this navigation is written as *Documents > win01_1B_Bell_Orchid > Corporate > Information_Technology > Future_Hotels*.

Some computer users prefer to navigate a folder structure by double-clicking in this manner. Others prefer using the address bar as described in the following Another Way box. Use whatever method you prefer—double-clicking in the file list, clicking in the address bar, or expanding files in the Navigation pane.

🔄 **ANOTHER WAY** In the navigation pane, click Documents, and expand each folder in the navigation pane. Or, In the address bar, to the right of Documents, click >, and then on the list, click win01_1B_Bell_Orchid. To the right of win01_1B_Bell_Orchid, click the > and then click Corporate. To the right of Corporate, click > and then click Information_Technology. To the right of Information_Technology, click >, and then click Future_Hotels.

3 In the **file list**, be sure the items are in alphabetical order by **Name**. If the items are not in alphabetical order, recall that by clicking the small arrow in the column heading name, you can change how the files in the file list are ordered.

4 On the ribbon, click the **View tab**, and then in the **Layout group**, be sure **Details** is selected.

The *Details view* displays a list of files or folders and their most common properties.

🔄 **ANOTHER WAY** Right-click in a blank area of the file list, point to View, and then click Details.

5 On the ribbon, click the **Home tab**, and then in the **New group**, click **New folder**. With the text *New folder* selected, type **Paris** and press ⏎. Click **New folder** again, type **Venice** and then press ⏎. Create a third **New folder** named **London**

In a Windows 10 file list, folders are listed first, in alphabetic order, followed by individual files in alphabetic order.

6 Click the **Venice** folder one time to select it, and then on the ribbon, on the **Home tab**, in the **Organize group**, click **Rename**. Notice that the text *Venice* is selected. Type **Rome** and press Enter.

ANOTHER WAY   Point to a folder or file name, right-click, and then on the shortcut menu, click Rename.

7 In the **file list**, click one time to select the Word file **Architects**. With the file name selected, click the file name again to select all the text. Click the file name again to place the insertion point within the file name, edit the file name to **Architects_Local** and press Enter. Compare your screen with Figure 1.86.

You can use any of the techniques you just practiced to change the name of a file or folder.

Figure 1.86

8 On the taskbar, click the **PowerPoint** icon to redisplay your **Windows_10_1B_Hotel_Files** presentation, and then on the **Home tab**, click the upper portion of the **New Slide** button to insert a new slide with the Title Only layout.

9 Click anywhere in the text *Click to add title*, type **Europe Folders** and then click anywhere in the empty space below the title.

10 On the **Insert tab**, in the **Images group**, click **Screenshot**, and then under **Available Windows**, click the image of your file list. On the **Picture Tools Format tab**, in the **Size group**, click in the **Shape Height** box, type **5** and then press Enter. As necessary, drag the image down so that the title you typed is visible; your presentation contains four slides.

11 Above the **File tab**, on the Quick Access toolbar, click **Save** 🖫, and then in the upper right corner, click **Minimize** ⊟ so that PowerPoint remains open but not displayed on your screen.

12 **Close** ⊠ the **Future_Hotels** window.

Activity 1.36 | Copying Files

Copying, moving, renaming, and deleting files and folders comprise the most heavily used features within File Explorer. Probably half or more of the steps you complete in File Explorer relate to these tasks, so mastering these techniques will increase your efficiency.

When you *copy* a file or a folder, you make a duplicate of the original item and then store the duplicate in another location. In this Activity, you will assist Barbara and Steven in making copies of the Staffing_Plan file, and then placing the copies in each of the three folders you created— London, Paris, and Rome.

1 From the taskbar, open **File Explorer** ▣, and then by double-clicking in the file list or following the links in the address bar, navigate to **This PC > Documents > win01_1B_Bell_ Orchid > Corporate > Information_Technology > Future_Hotels**.

2 In the upper right corner, **Maximize** □ the window. On the **View tab**, if necessary set the **Layout** to **Details**, and then in the **Current view group**, click **Size all columns to fit** ▦.

3 In the **file list**, click the file **Staffing_Plan** one time to select it, and then on the **Home tab**, in the **Clipboard group**, click **Copy**.

4 At the top of the **file list**, double-click the **London folder** to open it, and then in the **Clipboard group**, click **Paste**. Notice that the copy of the **Staffing_Plan** file displays. Compare your screen with Figure 1.87.

Figure 1.87

🔄 **ANOTHER WAY** Right-click the file you want to copy, and on the menu click Copy. Then right-click the folder into which you want to place the copy, and on the menu click Paste. Or, select the file you want to copy, press [Ctrl] + [C] to activate the Copy command, open the folder into which you want to paste the file, and then press [Ctrl] + [V] to activate the Paste command.

5 With the **London** window open, by using any of the techniques you have practiced, rename this copy of the **Staffing_Plan** file to London_Staffing_Plan

6 To the left of the **address bar**, click **Up** ↑ to move up one level in the folder structure and to redisplay the **file list** for the **Future_Hotels** folder.

🔄 **ANOTHER WAY** In the address bar, click Future_Hotels to redisplay this window and move up one level in the folder structure.

7 Click the **Staffing_Plan** file one time to select it, hold down Ctrl, and then drag the file upward over the **Paris** folder until the ScreenTip + *Copy to Paris* displays, and then release the mouse button and release Ctrl.

> When dragging a file into a folder, holding down Ctrl engages the Copy command and places a *copy* of the file at the location where you release the mouse button. This is another way to copy a file or copy a folder.

8 Open the **Paris** folder, and then rename the **Staffing_Plan** file **Paris_Staffing_Plan** Then, move up one level in the folder structure to redisplay the **Future_Hotels** window.

9 Double-click the **Rome** folder to open it. With your mouse pointer anywhere in the **file list**, right-click, and then from the shortcut menu click **Paste**.

> A copy of the Staffing_Plan file is copied to the folder. Because a copy of the Staffing_Plan file is still on the Clipboard, you can continue to paste the item until you copy another item on the Clipboard to replace it.

10 Rename the file **Rome_Staffing_Plan**

11 On the **address bar**, click **Future_Hotels** to move up one level and open the **Future_Hotels** window—or click Up ↑ to move up one level. Leave this folder open for the next Activity.

Activity 1.37 | Moving Files

When you *move* a file or folder, you remove it from the original location and store it in a new location. In this Activity, you will move items from the Future_Hotels folder into their appropriate folders.

1 With the **Future_Hotels** folder open, in the **file list**, click the Excel file **Financials_London** one time to select it. On the **Home tab**, in the **Clipboard group**, click **Cut**.

> The file's Excel icon dims. This action places the item on the Clipboard.

> **ANOTHER WAY**   Right-click the file or folder, and then on the shortcut menu, click Cut; or, select the file or folder, and then press Ctrl + X.

2 Double-click the **London** folder to open it, and then on the **Home tab**, in the **Clipboard group**, click **Paste**.

> **ANOTHER WAY**   Right-click the folder, and then on the shortcut menu, click Paste; or, select the folder, and then press Ctrl + V.

3 Click **Up** ↑ to move up one level and redisplay the **Future_Hotels** folder window. In the **file list**, point to **Financials_Paris**, hold down the left mouse button, and then drag the file upward over the **Paris** folder until the ScreenTip *Move to Paris* displays, and then release the mouse button.

4 Open the **Paris** folder, and notice that the file was moved to this folder. Click **Up** ↑—or on the address bar, click Future_Hotels to return to that folder.

5 In the **file list**, click **Loans_London** one time to select it. hold down (Ctrl), and then click the
photo image **London** and the Word document **Marketing_London** to select the three files.
Release the (Ctrl) key. Compare your screen with Figure 1.88.

Use this technique to select a group of noncontiguous items in a list.

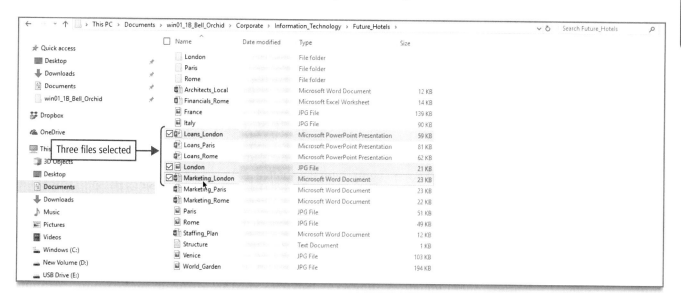

Figure 1.88

6 Point to any of the selected files, hold down the left mouse button, and then drag upward
over the **London** folder until the ScreenTip →*Move to London* displays and *3* displays over
the files being moved, and then release the mouse button.

You can see that by keeping related files together—for example, all the files that relate to the
London hotel—in folders that have an appropriately descriptive name, it will be easier to locate
information later.

7 By dragging, move the **Architects_Local** file into the **London** folder.

8 In an empty area of the file list, right-click, and then click **Undo Move**. Leave the
Future_Hotels window open for the next Activity.

Any action that you make in a file list can be undone in this manner.

ANOTHER WAY   Press (Ctrl) + (Z) to undo an action in the file list.

MORE KNOWLEDGE   **Using Shift + Click to Select Files**

If a group of files to be selected are contiguous (next to each other in the file list), click the first file to be selected, hold down
(Shift) and then click the left mouse button on the last file to select all of the files between the top and bottom file selections.

Activity 1.38 | Copying and Moving Files by Snapping Two Windows

Sometimes you will want to open, in a second window, another instance of a program that you are using; that is, two copies of the program will be running simultaneously. This capability is especially useful in the File Explorer program, because you are frequently moving or copying files from one location to another.

In this Activity, you will open two instances of File Explorer, and then use snap, which you have already practiced in this chapter, to display both instances on your screen.

To copy or move files or folders into a different level of a folder structure, or to a different drive location, the most efficient method is to display two windows side by side and then use drag and drop or copy (or cut) and paste commands.

In this Activity, you will assist Barbara and Steven in making copies of the Staffing_Plan files for the corporate office.

1 In the upper right corner, click **Restore Down** ⬜ to restore the **Future_Hotels** window to its previous size and not maximized on the screen.

> Use the *Restore Down* command ⬜ to resize a window to its previous size.

2 Hold down ⊞ and press ← to snap the window so that it occupies the left half of the screen.

3 On the taskbar, *point* to **File Explorer** ⬛ and then right-click. On the jump list, click **File Explorer** to open another instance of the program. With the new window active, hold down ⊞ and press → to snap the window so that it occupies the right half of the screen.

4 In the window on the right, click in a blank area to make the window active. Then navigate to **Documents > win01_1B_Bell_Orchid > Corporate > Human_Resources**. Compare your screen with Figure 1.89.

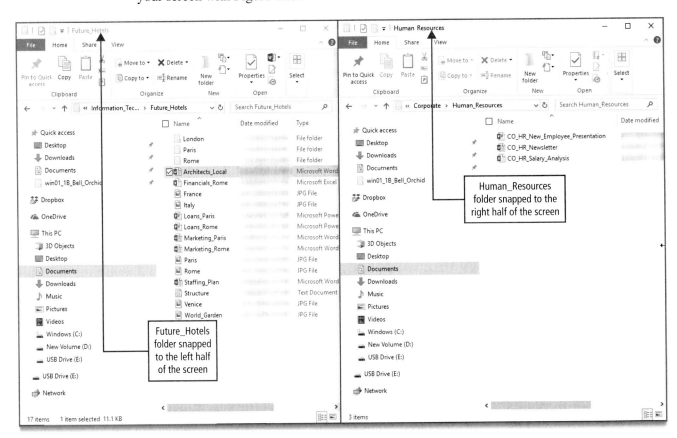

Figure 1.89

5 In the left window, double-click to open the **Rome** folder, and then click one time to select the file **Rome_Staffing_Plan**.

6 Hold down Ctrl, and then drag the file into the right window, into an empty area of the **Human_Resources file list**, until the ScreenTip + *Copy to Human_Resources* displays and then release the mouse button and Ctrl.

7 In the left window, on the **address bar**, click **Future_Hotels** to redisplay that folder. Open the **Paris** folder, point to **Paris_Staffing_Plan** and right-click, and then click **Copy**.

> You can access the Copy command in various ways; for example, from the shortcut menu, on the ribbon, or by using the keyboard shortcut Ctrl + C.

8 In the right window, point anywhere in the **file list**, right-click, and then click **Paste**.

9 On the taskbar, click the PowerPoint icon to redisplay your **Windows_10_1B_Hotel_Files** presentation, and then on the **Home tab**, click the upper portion of the **New Slide** button to insert a new slide with the **Title Only** layout; this will be your fifth slide.

10 Click anywhere in the text *Click to add title*, type **Staffing Plan Files** and then click anywhere in the empty space below the title.

11 On the **Insert tab**, in the **Images group**, click **Screenshot**, and then click **Screen Clipping**. When the dimmed screen displays, move the ✛ pointer to the upper left corner of the screen, hold down the left mouse button, and drag to the lower right corner but do not include the taskbar. Then release the mouse button.

> Because you have two windows displayed side by side, each window displays under Available Windows. Recall that to capture an entire screen that contains more than one window, use the Screen Clipping tool with which you can capture a snapshot of your screen.

12 If necessary, close the Design Ideas pane on the right. On the **Picture Tools Format tab**, in the **Size group**, click in the **Shape Height** box, type **5** and press Enter. As necessary, drag the image down so that the title you typed is visible.

13 Click outside of the image to deselect it, and then press Ctrl + Home to display the first slide in your presentation; your presentation contains five slides.

14 In the upper right, **Close** ✕ the **PowerPoint** window, and when prompted, click **Save**. **Close** ✕ all open windows.

For Non-MyLab Submissions Determine What Your Instructor Requires for Submission
As directed by your instructor, submit your completed PowerPoint file.

---

15 In **MyLab IT**, locate and click the Grader Project **Windows 10 1B Hotel Files**. In **step 3**, under **Upload Completed Assignment**, click **Choose File**. In the **Open** dialog box, navigate to your **Windows 10 Chapter 1 folder**, and then click your **Student_Windows_10_1B_Hotel_Files** file one time to select it. In the lower right corner of the **Open** dialog box, click **Open**.

> The name of your selected file displays above the Upload button.

16 To submit your file to MyLab IT for grading, click **Upload**, wait a moment for a green **Success!** message, and then in **step 4**, click the blue **Submit for Grading** button. Click **Close Assignment** to return to your list of **Course Materials**.

Deleting Files and Using the Recycle Bin

It is good practice to delete files and folders that you no longer need from your hard disk drive and removable storage devices. Doing so makes it easier to keep your data organized and also frees up storage space.

When you delete a file or folder from any area of your computer's hard disk drive or from OneDrive, the file or folder is not immediately deleted. Instead, the deleted item is stored in the *Recycle Bin* and remains there until the Recycle Bin is emptied. Thus, you can recover an item deleted from your computer's hard disk drive or OneDrive so long as the Recycle Bin has not been emptied. Items deleted from removable storage devices like a USB flash drive and from some network drives are immediately deleted and cannot be recovered from the Recycle Bin.

To permanently delete a file without first moving it to the Recycle Bin, click the item, hold down [Shift], and then press [Delete]. A message will display indicating *Are you sure you want to permanently delete this file?* Use caution when using [Shift] + [Delete] to permanently delete a file because this action is not reversible.

You can restore items by dragging them from the file list of the Recycle Bin window to the file list of the folder window in which you want to restore. Or, you can restore them to the location they were deleted from by right-clicking the items in the file list of the Recycle Bin window and selecting Restore.

You have completed Project 1B   **END**

1

OFFICE AND WINDOWS

Microsoft Office Specialist (MOS) Skills in this Chapter

Project 1A

Microsoft Word

1.1.2 Search for text

1.2.1 Set up document pages

1.2.4 Configure page background elements

1.2.4 Modify basic document properties

1.3.2 Modify basic document properties

1.4.1 Locate and remove hidden properties and personal information

1.4.2 Locate and correct accessibility issues

1.4.3 Locate and correct compatibility issues

2.2.5 Clear formatting

5.2.6 Format 3D models

5.4.3 Add alternative text to objects for accessibility

Microsoft Excel

5.3.3 Add alternative text to charts for accessibility

Build Your E-Portfolio

An E-Portfolio is a collection of evidence, stored electronically, that showcases what you have accomplished while completing your education. Collecting and then sharing your work products with potential employers reflects your academic and career goals. Your completed documents from the following projects are good examples to show what you have learned: 1A and 1B.

▶ GO! for Job Success

Discussion: Managing Your Computer Files

Your instructor may assign this discussion to your class, and then ask you to think about, or discuss with your classmates, these questions:

g-stockstudio/Shutterstock

> **Why do you think it is important to follow specific guidelines when naming and organizing your files?**

> **Why is it impractical to store files and shortcuts to programs on your desktop?**

> **How are you making the transition from storing all your files on physical media, such as flash drives or the hard drive of your computer, to storing your files in the cloud where you can access them from any computer with an internet connection?**

End of Chapter

Summary

Many Office features and commands, such as accessing the Open and Save As dialog boxes, performing commands from the ribbon and from dialog boxes, and using the Clipboard are the same in all Office desktop apps.

A desktop app is installed on your computer and requires a computer operating system such as Microsoft Windows or Apple's macOS to run. The programs in Microsoft Office 365 and Office 2019 are considered to be desktop apps.

The Windows 10 Start menu is your connected dashboard—this is your one-screen view of information that updates continuously with new information and personal communications that are important to you.

File Explorer is at work anytime you are viewing the contents of a location, a folder, or a file. Use File Explorer to navigate your Windows 10 folder structure that stores and organizes the files you create.

GO! Learn It Online

Review the concepts, key terms, and MOS skills in this chapter by completing these online challenges, which you can find at **MyLab IT**.

Chapter Quiz: Answer matching and multiple-choice questions to test what you have learned in this chapter.

Lessons on the GO!: Learn how to use all the new apps and features as they are introduced by Microsoft.

Quiz: Answer questions to review the MOS skills that you practiced in this chapter.

Monkey Business Images/Fotolia

Glossary

.png file An image file type that can be transferred over the internet, an acronym for Portable Network Graphic.

.txt file A simple file consisting of lines of text with no formatting that almost any computer can open and display.

3D models A new kind of shape that you can insert from an online library of ready-to-use three-dimensional graphics.

Address bar In a File Explorer window, the area that displays your current location in the folder structure as a series of links separated by arrows.

Alignment The placement of text or objects relative to the margins.

Alignment guides Green lines that display when you move an object to assist in alignment.

Alt text Text added to a picture or object that helps people using a screen reader understand what the object is; also called *alternative text*.

Alternative text Text added to a picture or object that helps people using a screen reader understand what the object is; also called *alt text*.

Application A computer program that helps you perform a task for a specific purpose.

AutoSave An Office 365 feature that saves your document every few seconds—if saved on OneDrive, OneDrive for Business, or SharePoint Online—and enables you to share the document with others for real-time co-authoring.

Backstage tabs The area along the left side of Backstage view with tabs to display screens with related groups of commands.

Backstage view A centralized space for file management tasks; for example, opening, saving, printing, publishing, or sharing a file.

Bing Microsoft's search engine.

Bookmark A command that marks a word, section, or place in a document so that you can jump to it quickly without scrolling.

Booting the computer The process of turning on the computer.

Center alignment The alignment of text or objects centered horizontally between the left and right margin.

Check Accessibility A command that checks a document for content that people with disabilities might find difficult to read.

Check Compatibility A command that searches your document for features that may not be supported by older versions of Office.

Click The action of pressing the left button of the mouse pointing device.

Clipboard A temporary storage area that holds text or graphics that you select and then cut or copy.

Cloud computing Applications and services that are accessed over the internet.

Cloud storage Online storage of data so that you can access your data from different places and devices.

Commands An instruction to a computer program that causes an action to be carried out.

Compressed Folder Tools A command available in File Explorer with which you can extract compressed files.

Compressed files Files that have been reduced in size, take up less storage space, and can be transferred to other computers faster than uncompressed files.

Content pane In a File Explorer window, another name for the file list.

Context menus Menus that display commands and options relevant to the selected text or object; also called *shortcut menus*.

Context-sensitive commands Commands that display on a shortcut menu that relate to the object or text that is selected.

Contextual tab A tab added to the ribbon automatically when a specific object is selected and that contains commands relevant to the selected object.

Copy A command that duplicates a selection and places it on the Clipboard.

Cortana Microsoft's intelligent personal assistant in Windows 10 and also available on other devices; named for the intelligent female character in the video game Halo.

Cut A command that removes a selection and places it on the Clipboard.

Dashboard The right side of the Start menu that is a one-screen view of links to information and programs that matter to you.

Data The documents, worksheets, pictures, songs, and so on that you create and store during the day-to-day use of your computer.

Data management The process of managing files and folders.

Default The term that refers to the current selection or setting that is automatically used by a computer program unless you specify otherwise.

Deselect The action of canceling the selection of an object or block of text by clicking outside of the selection.

Desktop A simulation of a real desk that represents your work area; here you can arrange icons such as shortcuts to files, folders, and various types of documents in the same manner you would arrange physical objects on top of a desk.

Desktop app A computer program that is installed on your PC and requires a computer operating system such as Microsoft Windows to run; also known as a *desktop application*.

Desktop application A computer program that is installed on your PC and requires a computer operating system such as Microsoft Windows to run; also known as a *desktop app*.

Desktop shortcuts Desktop icons that can link to items accessible on your computer such as a program, file, folder, disk drive, printer, or another computer.

Details pane When activated in a folder window, displays—on the right—the most common file properties associated with the selected file.

Details view A command that displays a list of files or folders and their most common properties.

Dialog box A small window that displays options for completing a task.

Dictate A feature in Word, PowerPoint, Outlook, and OneNote for Windows 10; when you enable Dictate, you start talking and as you talk, text appears in your document or slide.

Dialog Box Launcher A small icon that displays to the right of some group names on the ribbon and that opens a related dialog box or pane providing additional options and commands related to that group.

Document properties Details about a file that describe or identify it, including the title, author name, subject, and keywords that identify the document's topic or contents; also known as *metadata*.

Double-click The action of pressing the left mouse button two times in rapid succession while holding the mouse still.

Glossary

Download The action of transferring or copying a file from another location—such as a cloud storage location, your college's Learning Management System, or from an internet site—to your computer.

Drag The action of holding down the left mouse button while moving your mouse.

Drive An area of storage that is formatted with a file system compatible with your operating system and is identified by a drive letter.

Edit The process of making changes to text or graphics in an Office file.

Editor A digital writing assistant in Word and Outlook that displays misspellings, grammatical mistakes, and writing style issues.

Ellipsis A set of three dots indicating incompleteness; an ellipsis following a command name indicates that a dialog box will display if you click the command.

Enhanced ScreenTip A ScreenTip that displays useful descriptive information about the command.

Extract To decompress, or pull out, files from a compressed form.

File Information stored on a computer under a single name.

File Explorer The Windows program that displays the contents of locations, folders, and files on your computer.

File Explorer window A window that displays the contents of the current location and contains helpful parts so that you can navigate—explore within the file organizing structure of Windows.

File list In a File Explorer window, the area that displays the contents of the current location.

File name extension A set of characters at the end of a file name that helps Windows understand what kind of information is in a file and what program should open it.

File properties Information about a file, such as the author, the date the file was last changed, and any descriptive tags.

Fill The inside color of an object.

Filtered list A display of files that is limited based on specified criteria.

Folder A container in which you can store files.

Folder structure The hierarchy of folders.

Folder window A window that typically displays the File List for a folder.

Font A set of characters with the same design and shape.

Font styles Formatting emphasis such as bold, italic, and underline.

Footer A reserved area for text or graphics that displays at the bottom of each page in a document.

Format Painter The command to copy the formatting of specific text or to copy the formatting of a paragraph and then apply it in other locations in your document; when active, the pointer takes the shape of a paintbrush.

Formatting The process of applying Office commands to make your documents easy to read and to add visual touches and design elements to make your document inviting to the reader; establishes the overall appearance of text, graphics, and pages in an Office file—for example, in a Word document.

Formatting marks Characters that display on the screen, but do not print, indicating where the Enter key, the Spacebar, and the Tab key were pressed; also called *nonprinting characters*.

Free-form snip From the Snipping Tool, a command that draws an irregular line such as a circle around an area of the screen.

Full-screen snip From the Snipping Tool, a command that captures the entire screen.

Gallery An Office feature that displays a list of potential results.

Gradient fill A fill effect in which one color fades into another.

Graphical user interface Graphics such as an image of a file folder or wastebasket that you click to activate the item represented.

Groups On the Office ribbon, the sets of related commands that you might need for a specific type of task.

GUI An abbreviation of the term graphical user interface.

Hamburger Another name for a hamburger menu.

Hamburger menu Another name for a menu icon, deriving from the three lines that bring to mind a hamburger on a bun.

Hard disk drive The primary storage device located inside your computer where some of your files and programs are typically stored, usually designated as drive C.

Hierarchy An arrangement where items are ranked and where each level is lower in rank than the item above it

Icons Small images that represent commands, files, applications, or other windows.

Info tab The tab in Backstage view that displays information about the current file.

Insertion point A blinking vertical line that indicates where text or graphics will be inserted.

Inspect Document A command that searches your document for hidden data of personal information that you might not want to share publicly.

JPEG An acronym that stands for *Joint Photographic Experts Group* and that is a common file type used by digital cameras and computers to store digital pictures.

Jump List A display of destinations and tasks from a program's taskbar icon when you right-click the icon.

Keyboard shortcut A combination of two or more keyboard keys, used to perform a task that would otherwise require a mouse.

KeyTip The letter that displays on a command in the ribbon and that indicates the key you can press to activate the command when keyboard control of the ribbon is activated.

Keywords Custom file properties in the form of words that you associate with a document to give an indication of the document's content.

Landscape orientation A page orientation in which the paper is wider than it is tall.

Layout Options A button that displays when an object is selected and that has commands to choose how the object interacts with surrounding text.

Live Preview A technology that shows the result of applying an editing or formatting change as you point to possible results—*before* you actually apply it.

Live tiles Tiles that are constantly updated with fresh information.

Location Any disk drive, folder, or other place in which you can store files and folders.

Lock screen A background that fills the computer screen when the computer boots up or wakes up from sleep mode.

Maximize A window control button that will enlarge the size of the window to fill the entire screen.

Menu A list of commands within a category.

Menu bar A group of menus at the top of a program window.

Menu icon A button consisting of three lines that, when clicked, expands a menu; often used in mobile applications because it is compact to use on smaller screens—also referred to as a *hamburger menu*.

Glossary

Metadata Details about a file that describe or identify it, including the title, author name, subject, and keywords that identify the document's topic or contents; also known as *document properties*.

Microsoft account A user account with which you can sign in to any Windows 10 computer on which you have, or create, an account.

Microsoft Store app A smaller app that you download from the Microsoft Store.

Mini toolbar A small toolbar containing frequently used formatting commands that displays as a result of selecting text or objects.

Minimize A window control button that will keep a program open but will remove it from screen view.

Move In File Explorer, the action of removing a file or folder from its original location and storing it in a new location.

Mouse pointer Any symbol that displays on the screen in response to moving the mouse.

MRU Acronym for *most recently used*, which refers to the state of some commands that retain the characteristic most recently applied; for example, the Font Color button retains the most recently used color until a new color is chosen.

Navigate A process for exploring within the file organizing structure of Windows.

Navigation pane The area on the left side of the File Explorer window to access your OneDrive, folders on your PC, devices and drives connected to your PC, and other PCs on your network.

Nonprinting characters Characters that display on the screen, but do not print, indicating where the Enter key, the Spacebar, and the Tab key were pressed; also called *formatting marks*.

Notepad A basic text-editing program included with Windows 10 that you can use to create simple documents.

Object A text box, picture, table, or shape that you can select and then move and resize.

Office 365 A version of Microsoft Office to which you subscribe for an annual fee.

OneDrive Microsoft's free cloud storage for anyone with a free Microsoft account.

Operating system A specific type of computer program that manages the other programs on a computing device such as a desktop computer, a laptop computer, a smartphone, a tablet computer, or a game console.

Option button In a dialog box, a round button that enables you to make one choice among two or more options.

Page Width A command that zooms the document so that the width of the page matches the width of the window.

Paragraph symbol The symbol ¶ that represents the end of a paragraph.

Parent folder The location in which the folder you are viewing is saved.

Paste The action of placing text or objects that have been copied or cut from one location to another location.

Paste Options gallery A gallery of buttons that provides a Live Preview of all the Paste options available in the current context.

Path A sequence of folders that leads to a specific file or folder.

PDF The acronym for Portable Document Format, which is a file format that creates an image that preserves the look of your file, but that cannot be easily changed; a popular format for sending documents electronically, because the document will display on most computers.

Pen A pen-shaped stylus that you tap on a computer screen.

Personal folder The folder created on the hard drive for each Windows 10 user account on a computer; for each user account—even if there is only one user on the computer—Windows 10 creates a personal folder labeled with the account holder's name.

Point to The action of moving the mouse pointer over a specific area.

Pointer Any symbol that displays on your screen in response to moving your mouse.

Pointing device A mouse or touchpad used to control the pointer.

Points A measurement of the size of a font; there are 72 points in an inch.

Portable Document Format A file format that creates an image that preserves the look of your file, but that cannot be easily changed; a popular format for sending documents electronically, because the document will display on most computers.

Portrait orientation A page orientation in which the paper is taller than it is wide.

Print Preview A view of a document as it will appear when you print it.

Program A set of instructions that a computer uses to accomplish a task.

Progress bar A bar that displays in a dialog box—and also on the taskbar button—that indicates visually the progress of a task such as a copy process, a download, or a file transfer.

pt The abbreviation for *point* when referring to a font size.

Quick access In the navigation pane in a File Explorer window, a list of files you have been working on and folders you use often.

Real-time co-authoring A process where two or more people work on the same file at the same time and see changes made by others in seconds.

Rectangular snip From the Snipping Tool, a command that draws a precise box by dragging the mouse pointer around an area of the screen to form a rectangle.

Recycle Bin The area where deleted items are stored until you empty the bin; enables you to recover deleted items until the bin is emptied.

Removable storage device A device such as a USB flash drive used to transfer information from one computer to another.

Resources The collection of the physical parts of your computer such as the central processing unit (CPU), memory, and any attached devices such as a printer.

Restore Down A command that resizes a window to its previous size.

Ribbon In Office applications, displays a group of task-oriented tabs that contain the commands, styles, and resources you need to work in an Office desktop app. In a File Explorer window, the area at the top that groups common tasks on tabs. such as copying and moving, creating new folders, emailing and zipping items, and changing the view on related tabs.

Right-click The action of clicking the right mouse button one time.

Sans serif font A font design with no lines or extensions on the ends of characters.

Screen reader Software that enables visually impaired users to read text on a computer screen to understand the content of pictures.

Screenshot Any captured image of your screen.

ScreenTip A small box that displays useful information when you perform various mouse actions such as pointing to screen elements or dragging.

Glossary

Scroll arrow An arrow found at either end of a scroll bar that can be clicked to move within the window in small increments.

Scroll bar A vertical bar that displays when the contents of a window or pane are not completely visible; a scroll bar can be vertical, displayed at the side of the window, or horizontal, displayed at the bottom of a window.

Scroll box Within a scroll bar, a box that you can move to bring the contents of the window into view.

Select To specify, by highlighting, a block of data or text on the screen with the intent of performing some action on the selection.

Selecting Highlighting, by dragging with your mouse, areas of text or data or graphics, so that the selection can be edited, formatted, copied, or moved.

Serif font A font design that includes small line extensions on the ends of the letters to guide the eye in reading from left to right.

SharePoint A Microsoft technology that enables employees in an organization to access information across organizational and geographic boundaries.

Shortcut menu A menu that displays commands and options relevant to the selected text or object; also called a *context menu*.

Sizing handles Small circles or squares that indicate a picture or object is selected.

Snap An action to arrange two or more open windows on your screen so that you can work with multiple screens at the same time.

Snap Assist A feature that displays all other open windows after one window is snapped.

Snip An image captured by the Snipping tool that can be annotated, saved, copied, or shared via email.

Snipping tool A Windows 10 program that captures an image of all or part of your computer's screen.

Split button A button divided into two parts and in which clicking the main part of the button performs a command and clicking the arrow opens a menu with choices.

Start menu A Windows 10 menu that displays as a result of clicking the Start button and that displays a list of installed programs on the left and a customizable group of tiles on the right that can act as a user dashboard.

Style A group of formatting commands, such as font, font size, font color, paragraph alignment, and line spacing that can be applied to a paragraph with one command.

Subfolder The term for a folder placed within another folder.

Synchronization The process of updating computer files that are in two or more locations according to specific rules— also called *syncing*.

Syncing The process of updating computer files that are in two or more locations according to specific rules— also called *synchronization*.

System tray Another term for the notification area on the taskbar that displays notification icons and the system clock and calendar.

Tabs (ribbon) On the Office ribbon, the name of each activity area.

Tags Custom file properties in the form of words that you associate with a document to give an indication of the document's content; used to help find and organize files. Also called keywords.

Task View A taskbar button that displays your desktop background with small images of all open programs and apps and from which you can see and switch between open apps, including desktop apps.

Taskbar The bar at the bottom of your Windows screen that contains buttons to launch programs and buttons for all open apps.

Tell Me A search feature for Microsoft Office commands that you activate by typing what you are looking for in the Tell Me box.

Tell me more A prompt within a ScreenTip that opens the Office online Help system with explanations about how to perform the command referenced in the ScreenTip.

Template A preformatted document that you can use as a starting point and then change to suit your needs.

Theme A predesigned combination of colors, fonts, and effects that look good together and that is applied to an entire document by a single selection.

Timeline A Windows 10 feature that when you click the Task view button, you can see activities you have worked on across your devices; for example, you can find a document, image, or video you worked on yesterday or a week ago.

Thumbnail A reduced image of a graphic.

Tiles A group of square and rectangular boxes that display on the start menu.

Title bar The bar across the top of the window that displays the program, file, or app name.

Toggle button A button that can be turned on by clicking it once and then turned off by clicking it again.

Toolbar A row, column, or block of buttons or icons that displays across the top of a window and that contains commands for tasks you perform with a single click.

Triple-click The action of clicking the left mouse button three times in rapid succession.

Undo On the Quick Access Toolbar, the command that reverses your last action.

Unzip The process of extracting files that have been compressed.

User account A user on a single computer.

Wallpaper Another term for the Desktop background.

Window snip From the Snipping Tool, a command that captures the entire displayed window.

Windows 10 An operating system developed by Microsoft Corporation that works with mobile computing devices and also with traditional desktop and laptop PCs.

XML Paper Specification A Microsoft file format that creates an image of your document and that opens in the XPS viewer.

XPS The acronym for *XML Paper Specification*—a Microsoft file format that creates an image of your document and that opens in the XPS viewer.

Zip The process of compressing files.

Zoom The action of increasing or decreasing the size of the viewing area on the screen.

Introducing Microsoft Word 2019

WORD 2019

TippaPatt/Shutterstock

Word 2019: Introduction Introduction to Word

Content! Defined by Merriam-Webster's online dictionary as "the topic or matter treated in a written work" and also as "the principal substance (as written matter, illustrations, or music) offered by a World Wide Web site," content is what you consume when you read on paper or online, when you watch video, or when you listen to any kind of music—live or recorded.

Content is what you *create* when your own words or performances are recorded in some form. For creating content in the form of words, Microsoft Word is a great choice. Rather than just a tool for word processing, Word is now a tool for you to communicate and collaborate with others. When you want to communicate with pictures or images, Microsoft Word has many features to help you do so. You can use Word to complete complex tasks, such as creating sophisticated tables, embedding graphics, writing blogs, and creating publications. Word is a program that you can learn gradually, and then add more advanced skills one at a time.

Best of all, Microsoft Word is integrated into the cloud. If you save your documents to your cloud-based storage that comes with any free Microsoft account, you can retrieve them from any device and continue to work with and share your documents.

Creating Documents with Microsoft Word

WORD 2019

PROJECT 1A

Outcomes
Create a flyer with a picture.

Objectives
1. Create a New Document and Insert Text
2. Insert and Format Graphics
3. Insert and Modify Text Boxes and Shapes
4. Preview and Print a Document

PROJECT 1B

Outcomes
Format text, paragraphs, and documents.

Objectives
5. Change Document and Paragraph Layout
6. Create and Modify Lists
7. Set and Modify Tab Stops
8. Insert and Format a SmartArt Graphic and an Icon

Roman Belogorodov/Shutterstock

In This Chapter

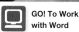

GO! To Work
with Word

In this chapter, you will begin your study of Microsoft Word, one of the most popular computer software applications and one that almost everyone has a reason to use. You can use Microsoft Word to perform basic word processing tasks, such as writing a memo, a report, or a letter. In this chapter, you will insert and format objects such as pictures, text boxes, SmartArt, and shapes, to improve the appearance of your documents and to better communicate your message. You will also practice formatting fonts, paragraphs, and the layout of your pages.

The projects in this chapter relate to **Sturgeon Point Productions**, an independent film company based in Miami with offices in Detroit and Milwaukee. The film professionals produce effective broadcast and branded content for many industries and provide a wide array of film and video production services. Sturgeon Point Productions has won awards for broadcast advertising, business media, music videos, and social media. The mission of the company is to help clients tell their stories—whether the story is about a social issue, a new product, a geographical location, a company, or a person.

Flyer

Project Activities

In Activities 1.01 through 1.16, you will create a flyer for Sharon Matsuo, Creative Director for Sturgeon Point Productions, announcing two internships for a short documentary. Your completed document will look similar to Figure 1.1.

 ## Project Files for **MyLab IT Grader**

1. In your storage location, create a folder named **Word Chapter 1**.
2. In your **MyLab IT** course, locate and click **Word 1A Flyer**, Download Materials, and then Download All Files.
3. Extract the zipped folder to your Word Chapter 1 folder. Close the Grader download screens.
4. Take a moment to open the downloaded **Word_1A_Flyer_Instructions**; note any recent updates to the book.

Project Results

GO Project 1A
Where We're Going

Figure 1.1 Project 1A Internship Flyer

NOTE   If You Are Using a Touch Screen

Tap an item to click it.

Press and hold for a few seconds to right-click; release when the information or commands display.

Touch the screen with two or more fingers and then pinch together to zoom out or stretch your fingers apart to zoom in.

Slide your finger on the screen to scroll—slide left to scroll right and slide right to scroll left.

Slide to rearrange—similar to dragging with a mouse.

Swipe to select—slide an item a short distance with a quick movement—to select an item and bring up commands, if any.

Objective 1   Create a New Document and Insert Text

ALERT   Because Office 365 is a cloud-based subscription service that receives continuous updates, you may encounter some variations in what appears on your screen and what is shown in this instruction. Microsoft Office 365 is fully installed on your PC or Mac; no internet access is necessary to create or edit documents. When you *are* connected to the internet, you will receive monthly upgrades and new features, so you always have the latest versions of Office apps as soon as they are available. Your subscription gives you continuous free access to the latest innovations and refinements.

GO! Learn How

Video W1-1

When you create a new document, you can type all the document text, or you can type some of the text and then insert additional text from another source. Sharon Matsuo, Creative Director for Sturgeon Point Productions, created some of the document text in a Word document that you can insert in the flyer you are creating.

Activity 1.01 | Creating a New Word Document

1.1.4

1 Navigate to your **Word Chapter 1 folder**, and then double-click the Word file you downloaded from **MyLab IT** that displays your name—**Student_Word_1A_Flyer**. In your blank document, if necessary, at the top click **Enable Editing**.

MAC TIP   If you are not submitting your file in MyLab IT, from the student data files that accompany this project, open the file Mac_w01A_Flyer. This is a blank document with default settings necessary to complete this project.

2 On the **Home tab**, in the **Paragraph group**, if necessary click Show/Hide ¶ so that it is active and the formatting marks display. If the rulers do not display, click the View tab, and then in the Show group, select the Ruler check box.

MAC TIP   To display group names on the ribbon, display the menu, click Word, click Preferences, click View, select the Show group titles check box.

3 Type **Internships Available** and then press Enter two times. Then, type the following text: **This summer, Sturgeon Point Productions will be filming a short documentary in Costa Rica about its native birds and has positions available for two interns.**

As you type, the insertion point moves to the right, and when it approaches the right margin, Word determines whether the next word in the line will fit within the established right margin. If the word does not fit, Word moves the entire word down to the next line. This is **word wrap** and means that you press Enter *only* when you reach the end of a paragraph—it is not necessary to press Enter at the end of each line of text.

NOTE   Spacing Between Sentences

Although you might have learned to add two spaces following end-of-sentence punctuation, the common practice now is to space only one time at the end of a sentence. Be sure to press Spacebar only one time following end-of-sentence punctuation.

4 Press Spacebar and then take a moment to study the table in Figure 1.2 to become familiar with the default document settings in Microsoft Word. Compare your screen with Figure 1.3.

When you press Enter, Spacebar, or Tab on your keyboard and Show/Hide is active, characters display in your document to represent these keystrokes. These characters do not print and are referred to as *formatting marks* or *nonprinting characters*. These marks will display throughout this instruction.

Default Document Settings in a New Word Document	
Setting	**Default format**
Font and font size	The default font is Calibri, and the default font size is 11 points.
Margins	The default left, right, top, and bottom page margins are 1 inch.
Line spacing	The default line spacing is 1.08, which provides slightly more space between lines than single spacing does.
Paragraph spacing	The default spacing after a paragraph is 8 points, which is slightly less than the height of one blank line of text.
View	The default view is Print Layout view, which displays the page borders and displays the document as it will appear when printed.

Figure 1.2

Figure 1.3

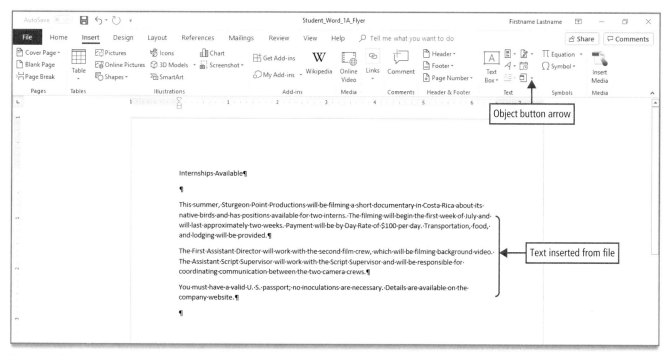

Activity 1.02 | Inserting Text from Another Document

You can create text in one Word document and insert it in another. Sharon Matsuo, Creative Director for Sturgeon Point Productions, created some of the document text for your flyer. You will insert the text from her document into the flyer you are creating.

1 ▶ On the ribbon, click the **Insert tab**. In the **Text group**, click the **Object button arrow**, and then click **Text from File**.

2 ▶ In the **Insert File** dialog box, navigate to the files you downloaded for this project, locate and select **w01A_Text**, and then click **Insert**. Compare your screen with Figure 1.4.

A *copy* of the text from the w01A_Text file displays at the insertion point location; the text is not removed from the original file.

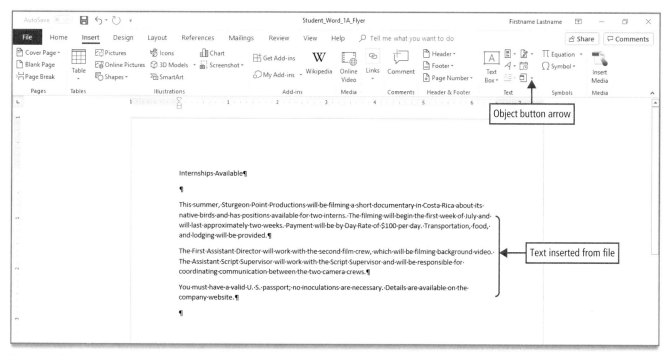

Figure 1.4

🔄 **ANOTHER WAY**   Open the file, copy the required text, close the file, and then paste the text into the current document.

3 ▶ On the **Quick Access Toolbar**, click **Save** 🖫.

GO! Learn How
Video W1-2

To add visual interest to a document, insert *graphics*. Graphics include pictures, online pictures, charts, and *drawing objects*—shapes, diagrams, lines, and so on. For additional visual interest, you can apply an attractive graphic format to text; add, resize, move, and format pictures; and add a page border.

Activity 1.03 │ Formatting Text by Using Text Effects

Text effects are decorative formats, such as shadowed or mirrored text, text glow, 3-D effects, and colors that make text stand out. The flyer you are creating will be printed and posted online, and the use of text effects will draw attention to some of the important information.

1 Including the paragraph mark, select the first paragraph of text—*Internships Available*. On the **Home tab**, in the **Font group**, click **Text Effects and Typography** [A ▾].

2 In the **Text Effects and Typography** gallery, in the third row, click the first effect to apply it to the selection.

3 With the text still selected, in the **Font group**, click in the **Font Size** box [11 ▾] to select the existing font size. Type **52** and then press Enter.

> When you want to change the font size of selected text to a size that does not display in the Font Size list, type the number in the Font Size box and press Enter to confirm the new font size.

4 With the text still selected, in the **Paragraph group**, click **Center** [≡] to center the text. Compare your screen with Figure 1.5.

Figure 1.5

5 With the text still selected, in the **Font group**, click the **Font Color button arrow** [A ▾] to display the Font Color palette. Under **Theme Colors**, in the sixth column, click the first color.

6 With the text still selected, in the **Font group**, click **Text Effects and Typography** [A ▾]. Point to **Shadow**, and then under **Outer**, in the second row, click the third style.

7 Click anywhere in the document to deselect the text, click **Save** [💾], and then compare your screen with Figure 1.6.

Figure 1.6

Activity 1.04 | Inserting Pictures

MOS
5.1.2

Pictures that reflect document content can focus the reader's attention on the message. Sharon Matsuo asked that you insert a picture in the flyer that depicts the types of images that a photographer might capture during the internship.

1 In the paragraph that begins *This summer*, click to position the insertion point at the beginning of the paragraph.

2 On the **Insert tab**, in the **Illustrations group**, click **Pictures**. In the **Insert Picture** dialog box, navigate to the files you downloaded for this project, locate and click **w01A_Bird**, and then click **Insert**.

Word inserts the picture as an *inline object*; that is, the picture is positioned directly in the text at the insertion point, just like a character in a sentence. The Layout Options button displays to the right of the picture. You can change the *Layout Options* to control the manner in which text wraps around a picture or other object. Sizing handles surround the picture indicating it is selected.

MAC TIP To insert the picture, on the Insert tab, click Pictures, and then click Picture from File.

3 Notice the sizing handles around the selected picture, as shown in Figure 1.7.

The corner sizing handles resize the graphic proportionally. The center sizing handles resize a graphic vertically or horizontally only; however, sizing with these will distort the graphic. A *rotation handle*, with which you can rotate the graphic to any angle, displays above the top center sizing handle.

Figure 1.7

Activity 1.05 | Wrapping Text Around a Picture Using Layout Options

MOS
5.4.2

Recall that Layout Options enable you to control ***text wrapping***—the manner in which text displays around an object.

1 Be sure the picture is selected—you know it is selected if the sizing handles display.

2 To the right of the picture, click **Layout Options** 🔲 to display a gallery of text wrapping arrangements. Point to each icon layout option to view its ScreenTip.

Each icon visually depicts how text will wrap around an object.

ANOTHER WAY On the Format tab, in the Arrange group, click Wrap Text.

MAC TIP On the Picture Format tab, click Wrap Text, and then choose the layout option that you want to apply.

3 From the gallery, under **With Text Wrapping**, click the first layout—**Square**. Compare your screen with Figure 1.8.

Select Square text wrapping when you want to wrap the text to the left or right of an image. To the left of the picture, an ***object anchor*** displays, indicating that the selected object is anchored to the text at this location in the document.

Figure 1.8

4 ▸ **Close** ✕ the **Layout Options**, and then **Save** 🔲 your document.

Activity 1.06 | Resizing Pictures and Using Live Layout

When you move or size a picture, *Live Layout* reflows text as you move or size an object so that you can view the placement of surrounding text.

1 ▸ If necessary, scroll your document so the entire picture displays. At the lower right corner of the picture, point to the sizing handle until the 🔲 pointer displays. Drag slightly upward and to the left. As you drag, a green alignment guide may display. Compare your screen with Figure 1.9.

Alignment guides may display when you are moving or sizing a picture to help you with object placement, and Live Layout shows you how the document text will flow and display on the page.

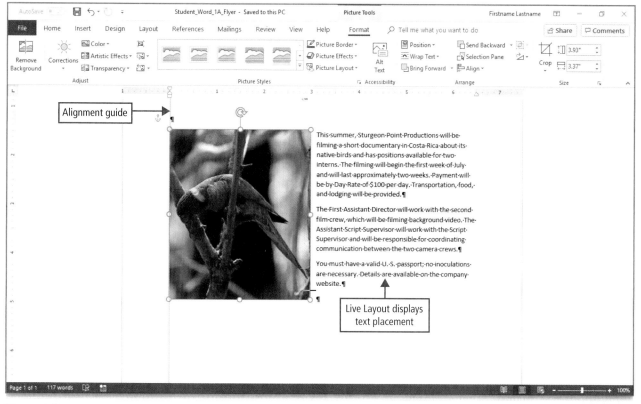

Figure 1.9

2 Continue to drag up and to the left until the bottom of the graphic is aligned at approximately **4 inches on the vertical ruler**. Notice that the graphic is proportionally resized.

3 On the **Quick Access Toolbar**, click **Undo** to restore the picture to its original size.

ANOTHER WAY On the Format tab, in the Adjust group, click Reset Picture.

4 On the ribbon, under **Picture Tools**, on the **Format tab**, in the **Size group**, click in the **Shape Height box** to select the number. Type **3.8** and then press Enter. If necessary, scroll down to view the entire picture on your screen, and then compare your screen with Figure 1.10.

When you use the Shape Height and Shape Width boxes to change the size of a graphic, the graphic will resize proportionally; that is, the width adjusts as you change the height and vice versa.

Figure 1.10

ANOTHER WAY A *spin box* is a small box with an upward- and downward-pointing arrow that lets you move rapidly through a set of values by clicking. You can change the height or width of a picture or object by clicking the Shape Height or Shape Width spin box arrows.

5 Save your document.

Activity 1.07 | Positioning a Picture

5.4.1

There are two ways to move a picture in a document. You can point to the picture and then drag it to a new position. You can also change the picture settings in a dialog box, which gives you more precise control over the picture location.

1 Be sure the picture is selected. On the ribbon, click the **Format tab**. In the **Arrange group**, click **Position**, and then click **More Layout Options**.

2 In the **Layout** dialog box, be sure the **Position tab** is selected. Under **Horizontal**, click the **Alignment** option button. To the right of **Alignment**, click the **arrow**, and then click **Right**. To the right of **relative to**, click the **arrow**, and then click **Margin**.

3 Under **Vertical**, click the **Alignment** option button. Change the **Alignment** options to **Top relative to Line**. Compare your screen with Figure 1.11.

> With these alignment settings, the picture will move to the right margin of the page and the top edge will align with the top of the first line of the paragraph to which it is anchored.

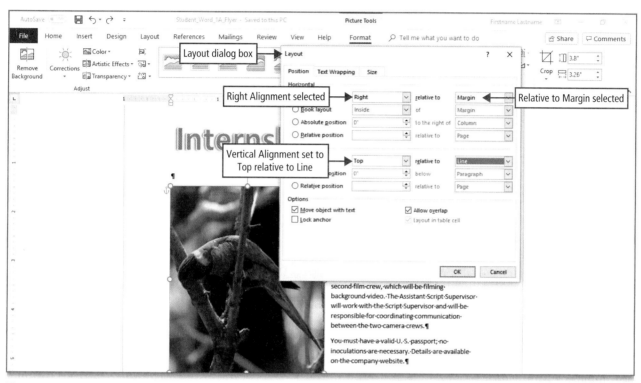

Figure 1.11

4 At the bottom of the **Layout** dialog box, click **OK**, and then on the **Quick Access Toolbar**, click **Save**. Notice that the picture moves to the right margin, and the text wraps on the left side of the picture. Compare your screen with Figure 1.12.

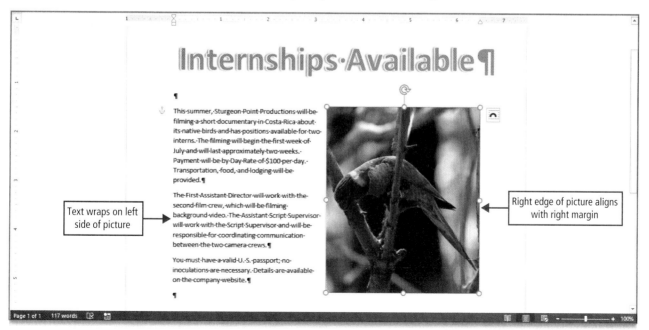

Figure 1.12

Activity 1.08 | Applying Picture Effects

5.2.2

Picture styles include shapes, shadows, frames, borders, and other special effects with which you can stylize an image. *Picture Effects* enhance a picture with effects such as a shadow, glow, reflection, or 3-D rotation.

1 Be sure the picture is selected. On the **Format tab**, in the **Picture Styles group**, click **Picture Effects**.

2 Point to **Soft Edges**. Use the ScreenTips to locate and then click **5 Point**.

The Soft Edges feature fades the edges of the picture. The number of points you choose determines how far the fade goes inward from the edges of the picture.

3 Compare your screen with Figure 1.13, and then **Save** 💾 your document.

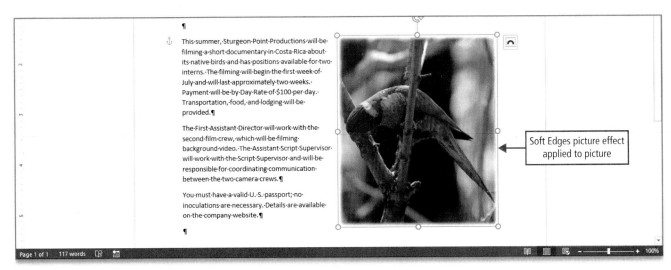

Figure 1.13

MORE KNOWLEDGE | **Applying Picture Styles**

To apply a picture style, select the picture. On the Format tab, in the Picture Styles group, click More, and then click the Picture Style that you want to apply.

Activity 1.09 | Applying Artistic Effects

5.2.1

Artistic effects are formats that make pictures look more like sketches or paintings.

1 Be sure the picture is selected. On the **Format tab**, in the **Adjust group**, click **Artistic Effects**.

2 In the first row of the gallery, point to, but do not click, the third effect.

Live Preview displays the picture with the third effect added.

3 In the second row of the gallery, click the third effect—**Paint Brush**. Paint Brush may be in another location in the gallery. If necessary, use the ScreenTips to locate the Paint Brush effect.

4 **Save** 💾 your document, and then notice that the picture looks more like a painting than a photograph. Compare your screen with Figure 1.14.

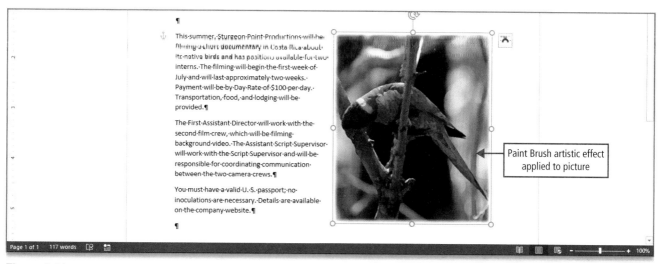

Figure 1.14

Activity 1.10 | Adding a Page Border

Page borders frame a page and help to focus the information on the page.

1 Click anywhere outside the picture to deselect it. On the **Design tab**, in the **Page Background group**, click **Page Borders**.

2 In the **Borders and Shading** dialog box, on the **Page Border tab**, under **Setting**, click **Box**. Under **Style**, scroll the list and click the seventh style—double lines.

3 Click the **Color arrow**, and then in the sixth column, click the first color.

4 Under **Apply to**, be sure *Whole document* is selected, and then compare your screen with Figure 1.15.

Figure 1.15

5 At the bottom of the **Borders and Shading** dialog box, click **OK**. Press Ctrl + Home to move to the top of the document.

⌨ **MAC TIP** To move to the top of a document, press command ⌘ + fn + ←.

6 **Save** 🖫 your document, and then compare your screen with Figure 1.16.

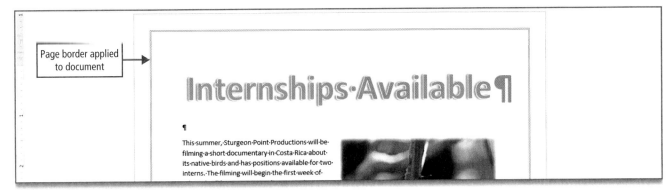

Figure 1.16

Objective 3 | Insert and Modify Text Boxes and Shapes

GO! Learn How
Video W1-3

Word has predefined *shapes* and *text boxes* that you can add to your documents. A shape is an object such as a line, arrow, box, callout, or banner. A text box is a movable, resizable container for text or graphics. Use these objects to add visual interest to your document.

Activity 1.11 | Inserting, Sizing, and Positioning a Shape

MOS
5.1.1

Important information in a document needs to be easily recognized and noticed. Ms. Matsuo asked that you insert a shape with text in it to draw attention to the important information in the flyer.

1 Click in the blank paragraph below the title. Press Enter four times to create additional space for a text box, and then notice that the picture anchored to the paragraph moves with the text.

2 Press Ctrl + End to move to the bottom of the document, and then notice that your insertion point is positioned in the empty paragraph at the end of the document. Press Delete to remove the blank paragraph.

3 Click the **Insert tab**, and then in the **Illustrations group**, click **Shapes** to display the Shapes gallery. Compare your screen with Figure 1.17.

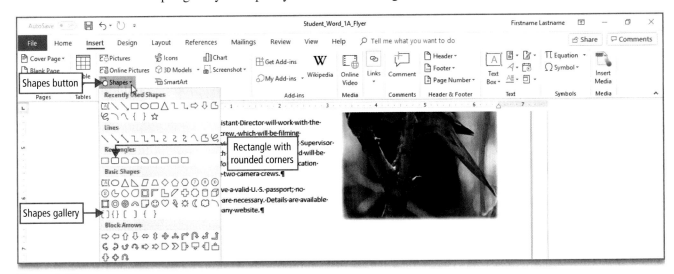

Figure 1.17

4 Under **Rectangles**, click the second shape—the rectangle that includes rounded corners, and then move your pointer. Notice that the ⊞ pointer displays.

5 Position the ⊞ pointer near the left margin at approximately **8 inches on the vertical** ruler. Click one time to insert a 1-inch by 1-inch rounded rectangle. The exact location is not important.

> A blue rectangle with rounded edges displays.

MAC TIP You may need to drag your mouse to insert the rectangle. The exact size and location are not important as you will adjust both in a later step.

6 To the right of the rectangle object, click **Layout Options** 🖾, and then at the bottom of the gallery, click **See more** to display the Layout dialog box.

MAC TIP On the Shape Format tab, click Arrange, click Position, and then click More Layout Options.

7 In the **Layout** dialog box, under **Horizontal**, click **Alignment**. To the right of **Alignment**, click the **arrow**, and then click **Centered**. To the right of **relative to**, click the **arrow**, and then click **Page**. Under **Vertical**, select the existing number in the **Absolute position** box. Type **1** and then to the right of **below**, be sure that **Paragraph** displays. Click **OK**.

> This action centers the rectangle on the page and positions the rectangle one inch below the last paragraph.

8 On the **Format tab**, in the **Shape Height box** 🔟 0.29" ⏼ select the existing number. Type **1.5** and then click in the **Shape Width box** 🔟 1.07" ⏼. Select the existing number, type **4.5** and then press Enter.

9 Compare your screen with Figure 1.18, and then **Save** 🖫 your document.

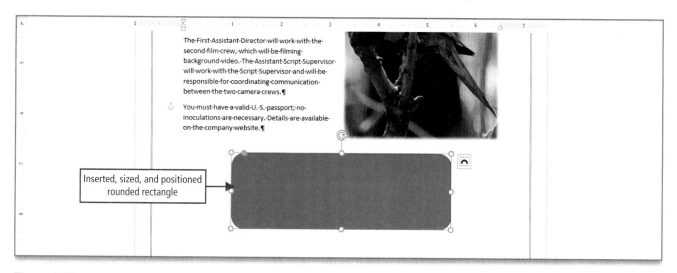

> Inserted, sized, and positioned rounded rectangle

Figure 1.18

Activity 1.12 | Typing Text in a Shape and Formatting a Shape

MOS
5.2.4 and 5.3.2

1 If necessary, select the rectangle shape. Type **To set up an interview, apply online at:** and then press Enter. Type **www.SturgeonPointProductions.com**

2 Press Ctrl + A to select all of the text in the shape. Right-click over the selected text to display the mini toolbar, and then click **Bold** B. With the text still selected, click **Increase Font Size** A˄ three times to increase the font size to **16 pt**.

> Use the keyboard shortcut Ctrl + A to select all of the text in a text box.

3 ▸ With the text still selected, on the **Home tab**, click the **Font Color button arrow**. Under
Theme Colors, in the second column, click the first color.

4 ▸ Click outside the shape to deselect the text. Click the border of the shape to select the shape
but not the text. On the **Format tab**, in the **Shape Styles group**, click **Shape Fill**. In the
sixth column, click the fourth color.

5 ▸ With the shape still selected, in the **Shape Styles group**, click **Shape Outline**. In the sixth
column, click the first color. Compare your screen with Figure 1.19, and then **Save** 🖫 your
document.

Figure 1.19

Activity 1.13 | Inserting a Text Box

A text box is useful to differentiate portions of text from other text on the page. Because it is a
floating object—a graphic that can be moved independently of the surrounding text characters—
you can place a text box anywhere on the page.

1 ▸ Press Ctrl + Home to move to the top of the document.

2 ▸ On the **Insert tab**, in the **Text group**, click **Text Box**. At the bottom of the gallery, click
Draw Text Box.

3 ▸ Position the ⊞ pointer over the first blank paragraph—aligned with the left margin and at
approximately 1 inch on the vertical ruler. Drag down and to the right to create a text box
approximately **1.5 inches** high and **4 inches** wide—the exact size and location need not be
precise.

4 With the insertion point blinking in the text box, type the following, pressing Enter after each of the first *two* lines to create a new paragraph:

Interviews will be held.
Friday and Saturday, January 14 and 15
In the Career Services Conference Room

5 Compare your screen with Figure 1.20, and then **Save** 🖫 your document

Internships·Available¶

Text box with text → Interviews·will·be·held:¶
Friday·and·Saturday,·January·14·and·15¶
In·the·Career·Services·Conference·Room¶

Figure 1.20

Activity 1.14 | **Sizing and Positioning a Text Box and Formatting a Text Box Using Shape Styles**

1 Point to the text box border to display the ⬚ pointer. In the space below the *Internships Available* title, by dragging, move the text box until a horizontal green alignment guide displays above the first blank paragraph mark and a vertical green alignment guide displays in the center of the page, as shown in Figure 1.21. If the alignment guides do not display, drag the text box to position it approximately as shown in the figure.

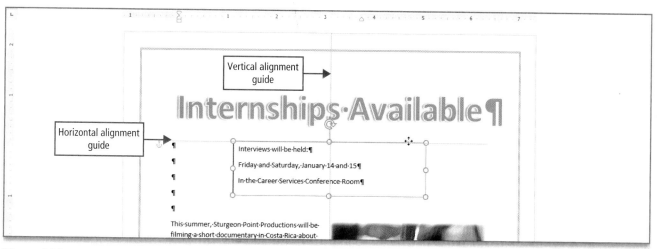

Vertical alignment guide

Internships·Available¶

Horizontal alignment guide →
¶
¶ Interviews·will·be·held:¶
¶ Friday·and·Saturday,·January·14·and·15¶
¶ In·the·Career·Services·Conference·Room¶
¶
¶

This·summer,·Sturgeon·Point·Productions·will·be·
filming·a·short·documentary·in·Costa·Rica·about·

Figure 1.21

2 To place the text box precisely, on the **Format tab**, in the **Arrange group**, click **Position**, and then click **More Layout Options**.

3 In the **Layout** dialog box, under **Horizontal**, click **Alignment**. To the right of **Alignment**, click the **arrow**, and then click **Centered**. To the right of **relative to**, click the **arrow**, and then click **Page**.

4 Under **Vertical**, click in the **Absolute position** box, select the existing number, and then type **1.25** To the right of **below**, click the **arrow**, and then click **Margin**.

5 In the **Layout** dialog box, click the **Size tab**. Under **Height**, select the number in the **Absolute** box. Type **1.25** and then under **Width**, select the number in the **Absolute** box. Type **4** and then click **OK**.

The text box is sized correctly, centered horizontally, and the top edge is positioned 1.25 inches below the top margin of the document.

6 On the **Format tab**, in the **Shape Styles group**, click **More** ⌄, and then in the first row, click the third style.

MAC TIP The More button is located below the Shape Styles.

7 On the **Format tab**, in the **Shape Styles group**, click **Shape Effects**. Point to **Shadow**, and then under **Outer**, in the first row, click the first effect.

8 Click in the text box, and then select all the text in the text box. On the **Home tab**, change the **Font Size** to **16** and apply **Bold** B. In the **Paragraph group**, click **Center** ☰.

ANOTHER WAY The keyboard shortcut to center text in a document is Ctrl + E.

9 Click anywhere in the document to deselect the text box. Compare your screen with Figure 1.22, and then **Save** 💾 your document.

Figure 1.22

Objective 4 **Preview and Print a Document**

GO! Learn How
Video W1-4

While you are creating your document, it is useful to preview your document periodically to be sure that you are getting the result you want. Then, before printing or distributing electronically, make a final preview to be sure the document layout is what you intended.

Activity 1.15 | **Adding a File Name to the Footer by Inserting a Field**

MOS
1.3.4

Information in headers and footers helps to identify a document when it is printed or displayed electronically. Recall that a header is information that prints at the top of every page and a footer is information that prints at the bottom of every page. In this text book, you will insert the file name in the footer of every Word document.

1 Click the **Insert tab**, and then in the **Header & Footer group**, click **Footer**.

2 At the bottom of the gallery, click **Edit Footer**.

The footer area displays with the insertion point blinking at the left edge, and on the ribbon, the Header & Footer Tools display.

🔄 **ANOTHER WAY**   At the bottom edge of the page, right-click; from the shortcut menu, click Edit Footer.

---

3 On the ribbon, under the **Header & Footer Tools**, on the **Design tab**, in the **Insert group**, click **Document Info**, and then click **File Name**. Compare your screen with Figure 1.23.

💻 **MAC TIP**   To insert the filename in the footer, on the Insert tab, click Footer, and then click Edit Footer. On the Header & Footer tab, click Field, and then under Categories, click Document Information. Under Field Names, click FileName, and then click OK.

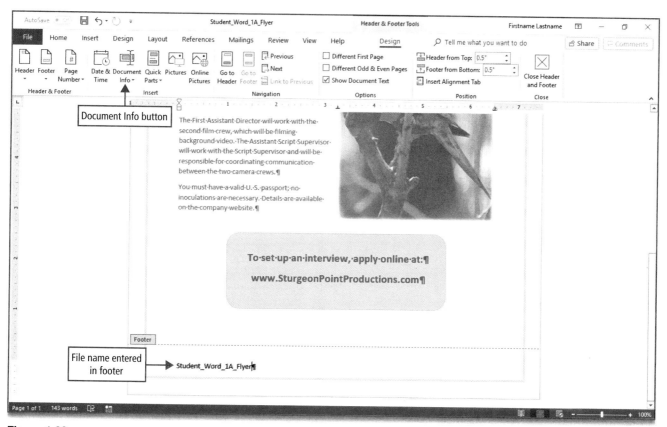

Figure 1.23

4 On the **Design tab**, click **Close Header and Footer**, and then **Save** 🖫 your document.

When the body of the document is active, the footer text is dimmed—it displays in gray. Conversely, when the footer area is active, the footer text is not dimmed; instead, the document text is dimmed.

🔄 **ANOTHER WAY**   Double-click in the document outside of the footer area to close the footer and return to the document.

Activity 1.16 | Adding Document Properties and Previewing and Printing a Document

1.3.2 and 1.3.3

1 ▶ Press `Ctrl` + `Home` to move the insertion point to the top of the document. In the upper left corner of your screen, click the **File tab** to display **Backstage** view. Click **Info**, and then at the bottom of the **Properties** list, click **Show All Properties**.

2 ▶ As the **Tags** type **internship, documentary** In the **Subject** box, type your course name and section number. Be sure that your name displays in the **Author** box and edit if necessary.

MAC TIP To enter document properties, click File. At the bottom of the menu, click Properties, and then click the Summary tab. Click in the Keywords box to type the tags internship, documentary. Click in the Subject box, type your course name and section number, edit the Author if necessary, and then click OK. To print, click File, and then click Print.

---

3 ▶ On the left, click **Print** to display the **Print Preview**. Compare your screen with Figure 1.24.

Here you can select any printer connected to your system and adjust the settings related to how you want to print. On the right, Print Preview displays your document exactly as it will print; the formatting marks do not display. At the bottom of the Print Preview area, the number of pages and arrows with which you can move among the pages in Print Preview display. On the right, Zoom settings enable you to shrink or enlarge the Print Preview.

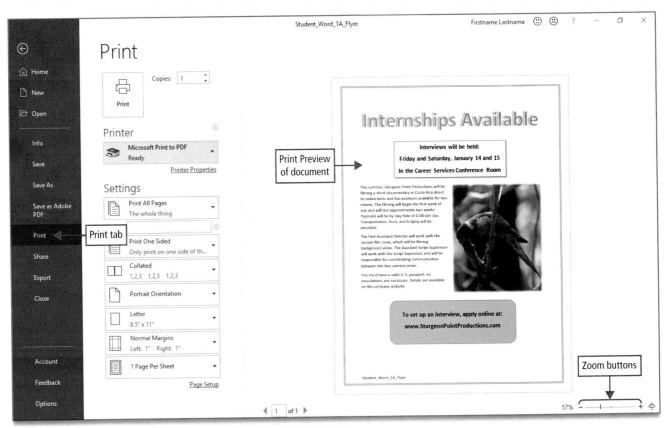

Figure 1.24

4 ▶ In the lower right corner of the window, click **Zoom In** ➕ several times to view the document at a larger size, and notice that a larger preview is easier to read. Click **Zoom to Page** ▣ to view the entire page.

5 If you want to print your document on paper using the default printer on your system, in the upper left portion of the screen, click **Print**. If you do not print, click Save.

> The document will print on your default printer; if you do not have a color printer, colors will print in shades of gray. Backstage view closes and your file redisplays in the Word window.

6 **Save** 🖫 your document. In the upper right corner of the Word window, click **Close** ⊠.

For Non-MyLab Submissions Determine What Your Instructor Requires
As directed by your instructor, submit your completed Word file.

---

7 In **MyLab IT**, locate and click the Grader Project **Word 1A Flyer**. In **step 3**, under **Upload Completed Assignment**, click **Choose File**. In the **Open** dialog box, navigate to your **Word Chapter 1 folder**, and then click your **Student_Word_1A_Flyer** file one time to select it. In the lower right corner of the **Open** dialog box, click **Open**.

> The name of your selected file displays above the Upload button.

8 To submit your file to **MyLab IT** for grading, click **Upload**, wait a moment for a green **Success!** message, and then in **step 4**, click the blue **Submit for Grading** button. Click **Close Assignment** to return to your list of **Course Materials**.

You have completed Project 1A **END**

»»GO! With Google Docs

ALERT   Working with Web-Based Applications and Services

Computer programs and services on the web receive continuous updates and improvements, so the steps to complete this web-based Activity may differ from the ones shown. You can often look at the screens and the information presented to determine how to complete the Activity.

If you do not already have a Google account, you will need to create one before you begin this Activity. Go to **http://google.com** and in the upper right corner, click Sign In. On the Sign In screen, click Create Account. On the Create your Google Account page, complete the form, read and agree to the Terms of Service and Privacy Policy, and then click Next step. On the Welcome screen, click Get Started.

Activity | Creating a Flyer

In this Activity, you will use Google Docs to create a flyer.

1 From the desktop, open your browser, navigate to http://google.com, and then sign in to your Google account. In the upper right corner of your screen, click **Google apps** ⊞, and then click **Drive**.

2 To create a folder in which to store your web projects, click **New**, and then click **Folder**. In the **New folder** box, type **GO! Web Projects** and then click **Create** to create a folder on your Google drive. Double-click your **GO! Web Projects** folder to open it.

3 In the left pane, click **New**, and then click **Google Docs** to open a new tab in your browser and to start an Untitled document. At the top of the window, click **Untitled document** and then, using your own name as the file name, type **Lastname_Firstname WD_1A_Web** and then press Enter to change the file name.

4 To the right of the file name, point to the small file folder to display the ScreenTip **Move to**. Click the file folder and notice that your file is saved in the GO! Web Projects folder. Compare your screen with Figure A.

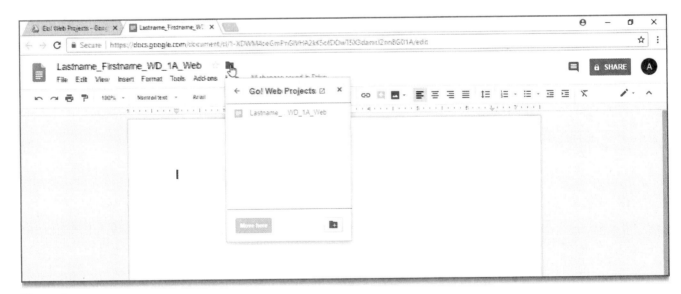

Figure A

5 Click in your document to close the Move to folder dialog box and to position the insertion point at the top of the document. Type **Internships Available** and then press Enter two times. Type **Interviews will be held Friday and Saturday, January 14 and 15 in the Career Services Conference Room.**

6 Press Ctrl + A to select all of the text. Click the **Font size arrow** 10, and then click **24**. With the text still selected, click **Center** ≣.

7 Press Ctrl + End to move to the end of the document, and then press Enter. Click **Insert**, and then click **Image**. Click **Upload from computer**, and then navigate to your student data files. Click **w01A_Bird**, and then click **Open** to insert the picture.

8 Click the picture to select it, and then point to the square sizing handle at the upper left corner of the picture. Drag down and to the right until the sizing handle aligns with approximately **3 inches on the ruler**.

9 If necessary scroll up to view the image and the text above it. Click to the right of the picture and then press Enter twice. Type **Join our production crew in Costa Rica as we film a short documentary about its native birds. We are hiring two interns!**

10 Select the title *Internships Available* and then click **Text color** A. In the first column, click the last color, and then apply **Bold** B. Your document will look similar to Figure B.

11 Your document will be saved automatically. Sign out of your Google account. Submit as instructed by your instructor.

Internships Available

Interviews will be held Friday and Saturday, January 14 and 15 in the Career Services Conference Room.

Join our production crew in Costa Rica as we film a short documentary about its native birds. We are hiring two interns!

Figure B

Project Activities

In Activities 1.17 through 1.29, you will format an information handout from Sturgeon Point Productions that describes internships available to students. Your completed document will look similar to Figure 1.25.

 Project Files for MyLab IT Grader

1. In your **MyLab IT** course, locate and click **Word 1B Programs**, Download Materials, and then Download All Files.
2. Extract the zipped folder to your Word Chapter 1 folder. Close the Grader download screens.
3. Take a moment to open the downloaded **Word_1B_Programs_Instructions**; note any recent updates to the book.

Project Results

GO! Project 1B
Where We're Going

Figure 1.25 Project 1B Information Handout

For Non-MyLab Submissions

For Project 1B, you will need:

w01B_Programs

In your Word Chapter 1 folder, save your document as:

Lastname_Firstname_1B_Programs

After you have named and saved your document, on the next page continue with Step 2.

Objective 5   Change Document and Paragraph Layout

GO! Learn How
Video W1-5

Document layout includes *margins*—the space between the text and the top, bottom, left, and right edges of the paper. Paragraph layout includes line spacing, indents, and tabs. In Word, the information about paragraph formats is stored in the paragraph mark at the end of a paragraph. When you press Enter, the new paragraph mark contains the formatting of the previous paragraph, unless you take steps to change it.

Activity 1.17 │ Setting Margins

1.2.1

1 Navigate to your **Word Chapter 1 folder**, and then double-click the Word file you downloaded from **MyLab IT** that displays your name —**Student_Word_1B_Programs**. If necessary, at the top click **Enable Editing**. On the **Home tab**, in the **Paragraph group**, be sure **Show/Hide** ¶ is active so that you can view the formatting marks.

2 Click the **Layout tab**. In the **Page Setup group**, click **Margins**, and then take a moment to study the settings in the Margins gallery.

> If you have recently used custom margins settings, they will display at the top of this gallery. Other commonly used settings also display.

3 At the bottom of the **Margins** gallery, click the command followed by an ellipsis—**Custom Margins . . .** —to display the **Page Setup** dialog box.

4 In the **Page Setup** dialog box, under **Margins**, press Tab as necessary to select the value in the **Left** box, and then, with *1.25″* selected, type **1**

> This action will change the left margin to 1 inch on all pages of the document. You do not need to type the inch (″) mark.

5 Press Tab to select the margin in the **Right** box, and then type **1** At the bottom of the dialog box, notice that the new margins will apply to the **Whole document**. Compare your screen with Figure 1.26.

Figure 1.26

6 ▶ Click **OK** to apply the new margins and close the dialog box. If the ruler below the ribbon is not displayed, on the View tab, in the Show group, select the Ruler check box.

7 ▶ Scroll to position the bottom of **Page 1** and the top of **Page 2** on your screen. Notice that the page edges display, and the page number and total number of pages display on the left side of the status bar.

8 ▶ Near the bottom edge of **Page 1**, point anywhere in the bottom margin area, right-click, and then click **Edit Footer** to display the footer area. On the ribbon, under the **Header & Footer Tools**, on the **Design tab**, in the **Insert group**, click **Document Info**, and then click **File Name**.

🖥 **MAC TIP** In the bottom margin area, hold down [control] and then click to display the shortcut menu. Click Edit Footer. On the Header & Footer tab, click Field, and then under Categories, click Document Information. Under Field Names, click FileName, and then click OK.

---

9 ▶ Double-click anywhere in the document to close the footer area, and then **Save** 🖫 your document.

Activity 1.18 | Aligning Paragraphs

Alignment refers to the placement of paragraph text relative to the left and right margins. Most paragraph text uses *left alignment*—aligned at the left margin, leaving the right margin uneven. Three other types of paragraph alignment are: *center alignment*—centered between the left and right margins; *right alignment*—aligned at the right margin with an uneven left margin; and *justified alignment*—text aligned evenly at both the left and right margins. The table in Figure 1.27 shows examples of these alignment types.

Types of Paragraph Alignment		
Alignment	**Button**	**Description and Example**
Align Left	☰	Align Left is the default paragraph alignment in Word. Text in the paragraph aligns at the left margin, and the right margin is uneven.
Center	☰	Center alignment aligns text in the paragraph so that it is centered between the left and right margins.
Align Right	☰	Align Right aligns text at the right margin. Using Align Right, the left margin, which is normally even, is uneven.
Justify	☰	The Justify alignment option adds additional space between words so that both the left and right margins are even. Justify is often used when formatting newspaper-style columns.

Figure 1.27

1 Scroll to position the middle of **Page 2** on your screen, look at the left and right margins, and notice that the text is justified—both the right and left margins of multiple-line paragraphs are aligned evenly at the margins. On the **Home tab**, in the **Paragraph group**, notice that **Justify** ☰ is active.

> To achieve a justified right margin, Word adjusts the size of spaces between words, which can result in unattractive spacing in a document that spans the width of a page. Many individuals find such spacing difficult to read.

2 Press Ctrl + A to select all the text in the document, and then on the **Home tab**, in the **Paragraph group**, click **Align Left** ☰.

ANOTHER WAY On the Home tab, in the Editing group, click Select, and then click Select All.

MAC TIP Use command ⌘ + A to select all the text in a document.

3 Press Ctrl + Home to move to the beginning of the document. In the left margin area, point to the left of the first paragraph—*Sturgeon Point Productions*—until the ⌐ pointer displays, and then click one time to select the paragraph.

> Use this technique to select entire lines of text.

4 On the mini toolbar, in the **Font Size** box, select the existing number, type **40** and then press Enter.

> Use this technique to change the font size to a size that is not available on the Font Size list.

MAC TIP On the Home tab, in the Font Size, select the existing number and type 40.

5 Select the second paragraph—*Internship Guide*—and then using the mini toolbar or the ribbon, change the **Font Size** to **26 pt**. Point to the left of the first paragraph—*Sturgeon Point Productions*—to display the ⌐ pointer again, and then drag down to select the first two paragraphs, which form the title and subtitle of the document.

6 On the **Home tab**, in the **Paragraph group**, click **Center** ☰ to center the title and subtitle between the left and right margins, and then compare your screen with Figure 1.28.

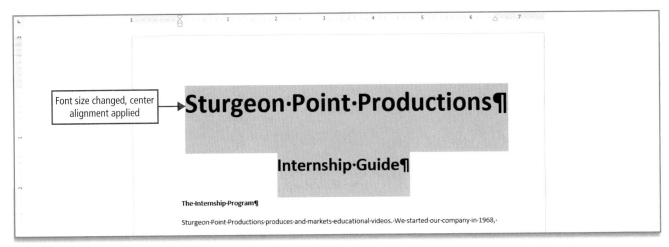

Figure 1.28

7 Near the top of **Page 1**, locate the first bold subheading—*The Internship Program*. Point to the left of the paragraph to display the ⌖ pointer, and then click one time to select the text.

8 With *The Internship Program* selected, use your mouse wheel or the vertical scroll bar to bring the bottom portion of **Page 1** into view. Locate the subheading *Requirements*. Move the pointer to the left of the paragraph to display the ⌖ pointer, hold down Ctrl, and then click one time. Release Ctrl, and then scroll to the middle of **Page 2**. Use the same technique to select the third subheading—*Introduction to Upcoming Internships*.

Three subheadings are selected; in Windows-based programs, you can hold down Ctrl to select multiple items.

MAC TIP Hold down command ⌘ when selecting multiple items.

9 Click **Center** ≡ to center all three subheadings, and then click **Save** 🖫.

Activity 1.19 │ Setting Line Spacing

2.2.3

Line spacing is the distance between lines of text in a paragraph. Three of the most commonly used line spacing options are shown in the table in Figure 1.29.

Line Spacing Options	
Spacing	**Description, Example, and Information**
Single spacing	**This text in this example uses single spacing**. Single spacing was once the most commonly used spacing in business documents. Now, because so many documents are read on a computer screen rather than on paper, single spacing is becoming less popular.
Multiple 1.08 spacing	**This text in this example uses multiple 1.08 spacing**. The default line spacing in Microsoft Word is 1.08, which is slightly more than single spacing to make the text easier to read on a computer screen. Many individuals now prefer this spacing, even on paper, because the lines of text appear less crowded.
Double spacing	**This text in this example uses double spacing**. College research papers and draft documents that need space for notes are commonly double-spaced; there is space for a full line of text between each document line.

Figure 1.29

1 Move to the beginning of the document, and then press [Ctrl] + [A] to select all of the text in the document.

2 With all of the text in the document selected, on the **Home tab**, in the **Paragraph group**, click **Line and Paragraph Spacing** ![icon], and notice that the text in the document is double spaced—**2.0** is checked. Compare your screen with Figure 1.30.

🔊 **BY TOUCH** Tap the ribbon commands.

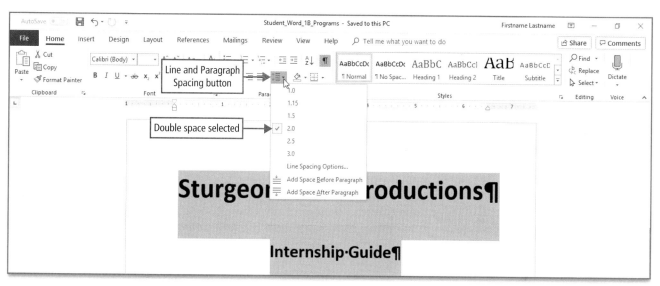

Figure 1.30

3 On the **Line Spacing** menu, click **1.5**, and then click anywhere in the document to deselect the text. Compare your screen with Figure 1.31, and then **Save** ![icon] your document.

Figure 1.31

Activity 1.20 │ Indenting Text

MOS
2.2.3

Indenting the first line of each paragraph is a common technique to distinguish paragraphs.

1 Below the title and subtitle of the document, click anywhere in the paragraph that begins *Sturgeon Point Productions produces*.

2 On the **Home tab**, in the **Paragraph group**, click the **Dialog Box Launcher** ![icon].

⬜ **MAC TIP** Click the Line and Paragraph Spacing button, and then click Line Spacing Options.

3 In the **Paragraph** dialog box, on the **Indents and Spacing tab**, under **Indentation**, click the **Special arrow**, and then click **First line** to indent the first line by 0.5", which is the default indent setting. Compare your screen with Figure 1.32.

Figure 1.32

4 Click **OK**, and then click anywhere in the next paragraph, which begins *As an intern*. On the ruler under the ribbon, drag the **First Line Indent** marker ▽ to **0.5 inches on the horizontal ruler**, and then compare your screen with Figure 1.33.

Figure 1.33

5 By using either of the techniques you just practiced, apply a first line indent of **0.5"** to the paragraph that begins *Here is a partial*

6 Save 🖫 your document.

Activity 1.21 | Setting Space Before and After Paragraphs

MOS
2.2.3

Adding space after each paragraph is another technique to differentiate paragraphs.

1 Press Ctrl + A to select all the text in the document. Click the **Layout tab**, and then in the **Paragraph group**, under **Spacing**, click the **After spin box up arrow** one time to change the value to **6 pt**.

To change the value in the box, you can also select the existing number, type a new number, and then press Enter. This document will use 6 pt spacing after paragraphs to add space.

🔁 **ANOTHER WAY** On either the Home tab or the Layout tab, display the Paragraph dialog box from the Paragraph group, and then under Spacing, click the spin box arrows as necessary.

2 Press Ctrl + Home, and then compare your screen with Figure 1.34.

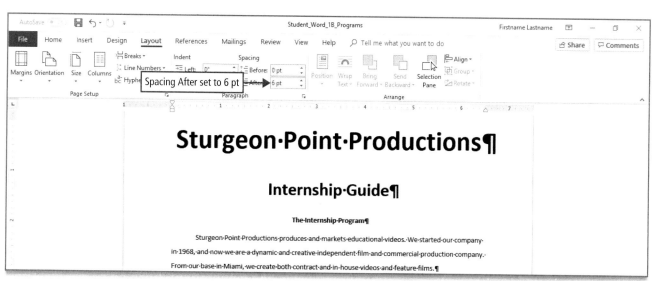

Figure 1.34

3 Near the top of **Page 1**, select the subheading *The Internship Program*, including the paragraph mark following it. Scroll down using the vertical scroll bar, hold down Ctrl, and then select the *Requirements* and *Introduction to Upcoming Internships* subheadings.

🖥 **MAC TIP** Use command ⌘ to select multiple items.

ALERT **Did your screen zoom when you were selecting?**

Holding down Ctrl and using the mouse wheel at the same time will zoom your screen.

4 With all three subheadings selected, in the **Paragraph group**, under **Spacing**, click the **Before up spin box arrow** two times to set the **Spacing Before** to **12 pt**. Compare your screen with Figure 1.35, and then **Save** 🖫 your document.

This action increases the amount of space above each of the subheadings, which will make them easy to distinguish in the document. The formatting is applied only to the selected paragraphs.

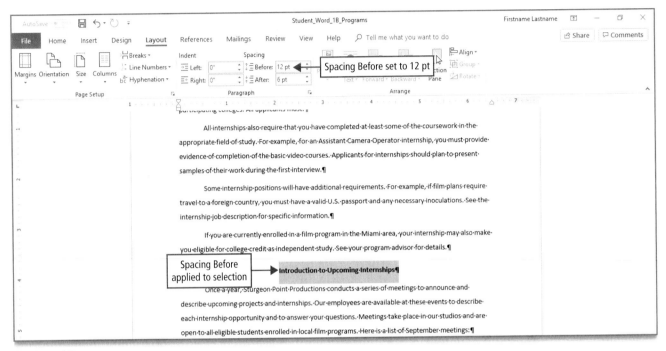

Figure 1.35

Objective 6   Create and Modify Lists

GO! Learn How
Video W1-6

To display a list of information, you can choose a ***bulleted list***, which uses ***bullets***—text symbols such as small circles or check marks—to introduce each item in a list. You can also choose a ***numbered list***, which uses consecutive numbers or letters to introduce each item in a list.

Use a bulleted list if the items in the list can be introduced in any order; use a numbered list for items that have definite steps, a sequence of actions, or are in chronological order.

Activity 1.22 | **Creating a Bulleted List**

3.3.1

1 In the upper portion of **Page 1**, locate the paragraph *Short feature films*, and then point to this paragraph from the left margin area to display the 🔏 pointer. Drag down to select this paragraph and the next five paragraphs—ending with the paragraph *Recordings of live concerts*.

2 On the **Home tab**, in the **Paragraph group**, click **Bullets** ≔▾ to change the selected text to a bulleted list.

The spacing between each of the bulleted points is removed and each bulleted item is automatically indented.

3 On the ruler, point to **First Line Indent** ▽ and read the ScreenTip, and then point to **Hanging Indent** △. Compare your screen with Figure 1.36.

> By default, Word formats bulleted items with a first line indent of 0.25" and adds a Hanging Indent at 0.5". The hanging indent maintains the alignment of text when a bulleted item is more than one line.

> You can modify the list indentation by using Decrease Indent ⬅ or Increase Indent ➡. Decrease Indent moves your paragraph closer to the margin. Increase Indent moves your paragraph farther away from the margin.

Figure 1.36

4 Scroll down slightly, and then by using the ⟋ pointer from the left margin area, select the five internship positions, beginning with *Production Assistant* and ending with *Assistant Set Designer*. In the **Paragraph group**, click **Bullets** ☰▾.

5 Scroll down to view **Page 2**. Apply bullets to all of the paragraphs that indicate the September meetings and meeting dates, beginning with *Technical* and ending with *Music*.

6 **Save** 🖫 your document.

Activity 1.23 | Creating a Numbered List

MOS
3.3.1

1 Under the subheading *Requirements*, in the paragraph that begins *The exact requirements*, click to position the insertion point at the *end* of the paragraph, following the colon. Press Enter to create a blank paragraph. Notice that the paragraph is indented because the First Line Indent from the previous paragraph carried over to the new paragraph.

2 To change the indent formatting for this paragraph, on the ruler, drag the **First Line Indent** marker ▽ to the left so that it is positioned directly above the lower button.

3 Being sure to include the period, type **1.** and press Spacebar. Compare your screen with Figure 1.37.

> Word determines that this paragraph is the first item in a numbered list and formats the new paragraph accordingly, indenting the list in the same manner as the bulleted list. The space after the number changes to a tab, and the AutoCorrect Options button displays to the left of the list item. The tab is indicated by a right arrow formatting mark.

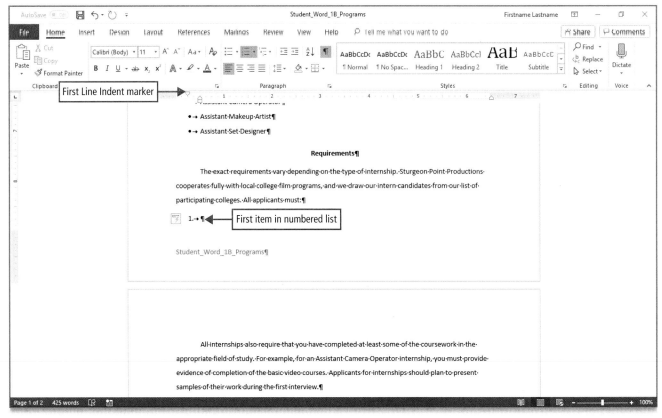

Figure 1.37

4 Click **AutoCorrect Options** [icon], and then compare your screen with Figure 1.38.

From the displayed list, you can remove the automatic formatting here, or stop using the automatic numbered lists option in this document. You also have the option to open the AutoCorrect dialog box to *Control AutoFormat Options*.

Figure 1.38

5 Click **AutoCorrect Options** 📋 again to close the menu without selecting any of the commands. Type **Be enrolled in an accredited film program** and press Enter. Notice that the second number and a tab are added to the next line.

6 Type **Be available during the entire production schedule** and press Enter. Type **Submit two faculty recommendation letters** and then compare your screen with Figure 1.39. **Save** 💾 your document.

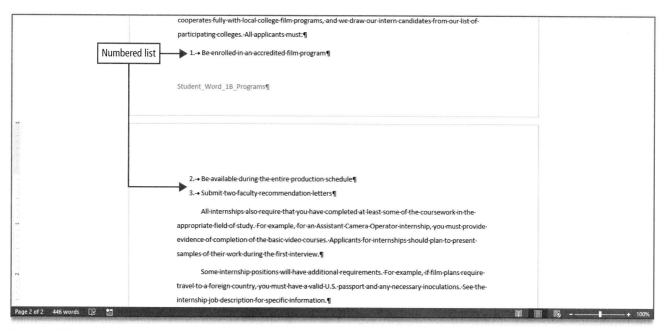

Figure 1.39

Activity 1.24 | Customizing Bullets

3.3.2

You can use any symbol from any font for your bullet characters.

1 Press Ctrl + End to move to the end of the document, and then scroll up as necessary to display the bulleted list containing the list of meetings.

2 Point to the left of the first list item to display the ⬚ pointer, and then drag down to select all six meetings in the list—the bullet symbols are not selected.

3 On the mini toolbar, click the **Bullets button arrow** ⬚ to display the Bullet Library, and then compare your screen with Figure 1.40.

⬚ **MAC TIP** On the Home tab, click the Bullets button arrow.

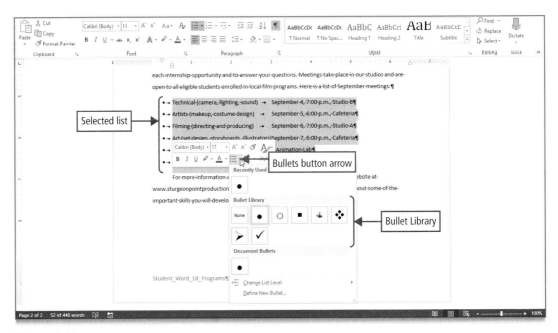

Figure 1.40

4 ▶ Under **Bullet Library**, click the **check mark** symbol.

MAC TIP   If the check mark bullet is not available, click Define New Bullet. Click Bullet, click the Font arrow, click Wingdings, and then locate and click the check mark symbol. Click OK two times.

5 ▶ With the bulleted list still selected, on the **Home tab**, in the **Clipboard group**, double-click **Format Painter** 🖌 to activate it for multiple use.

6 ▶ Use the vertical scroll bar or your mouse wheel to scroll to view **Page 1**. Move the pointer to the left of the first item in the first bulleted list to display the 🔏 pointer, and then drag down to select all six items in the list and to apply the format of the third bulleted list—the check mark bullets—to this list. Repeat this procedure to change the bullets in the second list to check marks. Press Esc to turn off **Format Painter**, and then **Save** 💾 your document. Compare your screen with Figure 1.41.

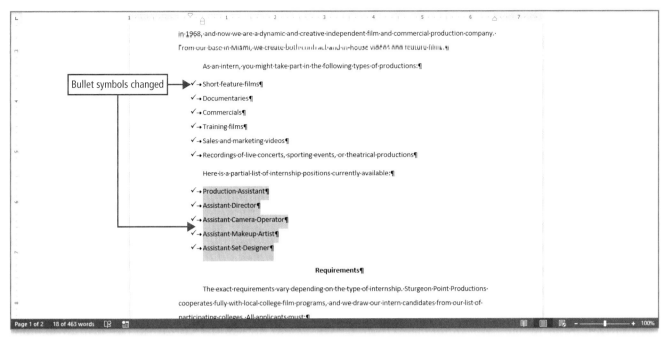

Figure 1.41

Objective 7 | Set and Modify Tab Stops

GO! Learn How

Video W1-7

Tab stops mark specific locations on a line of text. Use tab stops to indent and align text and use the ⟨Tab⟩ key to move to tab stops.

Activity 1.25 | Setting Tab Stops

1 Scroll to view **Page 2**, and then by using the ⟨pointer⟩ pointer at the left of the first item, select all the items in the bulleted list. Notice that there is a tab mark between the name of the meeting and the date.

The arrow that indicates a tab is a nonprinting formatting mark.

2 To the left of the horizontal ruler, point to **Tab Alignment** ⟨L⟩ to display the *Left Tab* ScreenTip, and then compare your screen with Figure 1.42.

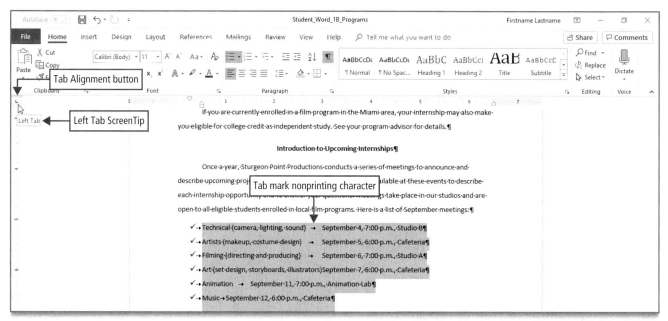

Figure 1.42

> **3** Click **Tab Alignment** ⌊ several times to view the tab alignment options shown in the table in Figure 1.43.

Tab Alignment Options		
Type	**Tab Alignment Button Displays This Marker**	**Description**
Left	⌊	Text is left aligned at the tab stop and extends to the right.
Center	⊥	Text is centered around the tab stop.
Right	⌋	Text is right aligned at the tab stop and extends to the left.
Decimal	⊥	The decimal point aligns at the tab stop.
Bar	|	A vertical bar displays at the tab stop.
First Line Indent	▽	Text in the first line of a paragraph indents.
Hanging Indent	△	Text in all lines indents except for the first line in the paragraph.

Figure 1.43

> **4** Display **Left Tab** ⌊. Along the lower edge of the horizontal ruler, point to and then click at **3.5 inches on the horizontal ruler**. Notice that all of the dates left align at the new tab stop location, and the right edge of the column is uneven.

> **5** Compare your screen with Figure 1.44, and then **Save** 🖫 your document.

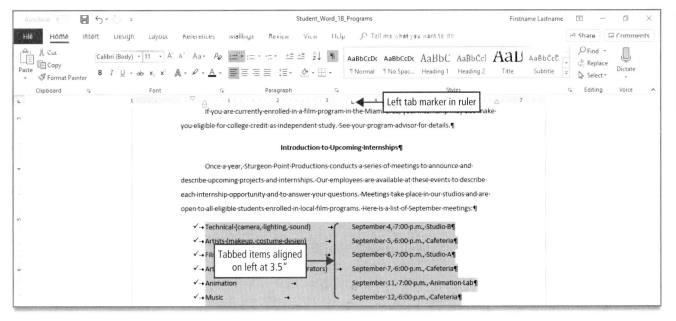

Figure 1.44

Activity 1.26 | Modifying Tab Stops

Tab stops are a form of paragraph formatting. Therefore, the information about tab stops is stored in the paragraph mark in the paragraphs to which they were applied.

1 With the bulleted list still selected, on the ruler, point to the new tab marker at *3.5 inches on the horizontal ruler*, and then when the *Left Tab* ScreenTip displays, drag the tab marker to **4 inches on the horizontal ruler**.

In all of the selected lines, the text at the tab stop left aligns at 4 inches.

2 On the ruler, point to the tab marker that you moved to display the *Left Tab* ScreenTip, and then double-click to display the **Tabs** dialog box.

ANOTHER WAY On the Home tab, in the Paragraph group, click the Dialog Box Launcher. At the bottom of the Paragraph dialog box, click the Tabs button.

3 In the **Tabs** dialog box, under **Tab stop position**, if necessary select *4"*, and then type **6**

MAC TIP At the bottom of the Tabs dialog box, click Clear All. In the Tab stops box type 6. Under Alignment, click Right. Under Leader, click the option that is a series of dots, and then skip to step 6.

4 Under **Alignment**, click the **Right** option button. Under **Leader**, click the **2** option button. Near the bottom of the **Tabs** dialog box, click **Set**.

Because the Right tab will be used to align the items in the list, the tab stop at 4" is no longer necessary.

5 In the **Tabs** dialog box, in the **Tab stop position** box, click **4"** to select this tab stop, and then in the lower portion of the **Tabs** dialog box, click the **Clear** button to delete this tab stop, which is no longer necessary. Compare your screen with Figure 1.45.

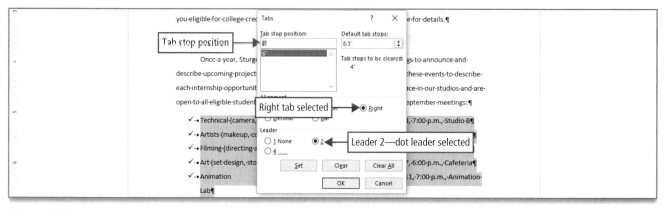

Figure 1.45

> **6** Click **OK**. On the ruler, notice that the left tab marker at *4″* no longer displays, a right tab marker displays at *6″*, and a series of dots—a ***dot leader***—displays between the columns of the list. Notice also that the right edge of the column is even. Compare your screen with Figure 1.46.
>
> > A ***leader character*** creates a solid, dotted, or dashed line that fills the space to the left of a tab character and draws the reader's eyes across the page from one item to the next. When the character used for the leader is a dot, it is commonly referred to as a dot leader.

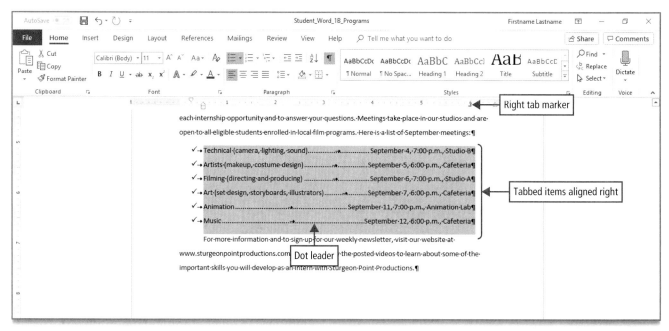

Figure 1.46

> **7** In the bulleted list that uses dot leaders, locate the *Art* meeting, and then click to position the insertion point at the end of that line, after the word *Cafeteria*. Press Enter to create a new blank bullet item.
>
> **8** Type **Video Editing** and press Tab. Notice that a dot leader fills the space to the tab marker location.
>
> **9** Type **September 10, 7:00 p.m., Cafeteria** and notice that the text moves to the left to maintain the right alignment of the tab stop.
>
> **10** **Save** 🖫 your document.

Objective 8 Insert and Format a SmartArt Graphic and an Icon

GO! Learn How
Video W1-8

SmartArt graphics are designer-quality visual representations of information, and Word provides many different layouts from which you can choose. *Icons* are pictures composed of straight and curved lines. SmartArt graphics and icons can communicate your messages or ideas more effectively than plain text, and these objects add visual interest to a document or web page.

Activity 1.27 │ Inserting a SmartArt Graphic

MOS
5.1.4 and 5.3.3

1 Press Ctrl + Home to move to the top of the document, and then click to the right of the subtitle *Internship Guide*.

2 Click the **Insert tab**, and then in the **Illustrations group**, point to **SmartArt** to display its ScreenTip. Read the ScreenTip, and then click **SmartArt**.

3 In the center portion of the **Choose a SmartArt Graphic** dialog box, examine the numerous types of SmartArt graphics available.

4 On the left, click **Process**, and then by using the ScreenTips, locate and click **Basic Chevron Process**. Compare your screen with Figure 1.47.

At the right of the dialog box, a preview and description of the SmartArt displays.

Figure 1.47

5 Click **OK** to insert the SmartArt graphic.

To the left of the inserted SmartArt graphic, the text pane may display. The *text pane* is used to type text and edit text in your SmartArt graphic. If you choose not to use the text pane to enter text, you can close it.

6 On the ribbon, under **SmartArt Tools**, on the **Design tab**, in the **Create Graphic group**, notice the Text Pane button. If the text pane button is selected, click **Text Pane** to close the pane.

7 In the SmartArt graphic, in the first blue arrow, click **[Text]**, and notice that *[Text]* is replaced by a blinking insertion point.

The word *[Text]* is called *placeholder text*, which is nonprinting text that indicates where you can type.

8 Type **Apply Online**

9 Click the placeholder text in the middle arrow. Type **Interview** and then click the placeholder text in the third arrow. Type **Train on the Job** and then compare your screen with Figure 1.48.

Figure 1.48

10 **Save** 🖫 your document.

Activity 1.28 | Sizing and Formatting a SmartArt Graphic

5.2.5

1 Click the **SmartArt solid border** to select it. Be sure that none of the arrows have sizing handles around their border, which would indicate the arrow was selected, not the entire graphic.

2 Click the **SmartArt Tools Format tab**, and then in the **Size group**, if necessary, click Size to display the Shape Height and Shape Width boxes.

3 Set the **Height** to **1.75"** and the **Width** to **6.5"**, and then compare your screen with Figure 1.49.

Figure 1.49

4 With the SmartArt graphic still selected, click the **SmartArt Tools Design tab**, and then in the **SmartArt Styles group**, click **Change Colors**. Under **Colorful**, click the fourth style—**Colorful Range - Accent Colors 4 to 5**.

5 On the **SmartArt Tools Design tab**, in the **SmartArt Styles group**, click **More** ⊡. Under **3-D**, click the second style—**Inset**. Compare your screen with Figure 1.50.

Sturgeon·Point·Productions¶

Internship·Guide

SmartArt color changed and SmartArt 3-D style applied

Apply Online

Interview

Train on the Job

Figure 1.50

6 **Save** 🖫 your document.

Activity 1.29 | Inserting an Icon

Many of the marketing materials at Sturgeon Point Productions use a clapperboard icon to represent the filmmaking and video production aspect of the business. In this Activity, you will insert a clapperboard icon at the end of the document.

1 Press Ctrl + End to move to the end of the document. Press Enter to insert a blank line and notice that a first line indent is applied. On the ruler, drag the **First Line Indent** marker back to the left margin.

2 On the **Insert tab**, in the **Illustrations group**, click **Icons**. On the left side of the **Insert Icons** dialog box, click **Arts**. Under **Arts**, click the **clapperboard icon** as shown in Figure 1.51 so that a check mark displays.

⬜ **MAC TIP** In the Icons pane, click the Jump to arrow, and then click Arts. Click the Clapperboard icon.

Figure 1.51

> **3** Click **Insert** to insert the icon. On the **Home tab**, in the **Paragraph group**, click **Center**.

> **4** **Save** 🖫 your document. In the upper right corner of the Word window, click **Close** ☒.

For Non-MyLab Submissions Determine What Your Instructor Requires
As directed by your instructor, submit your completed Word file.

> **5** In **MyLab IT**, locate and click the Grader Project **Word 1B Programs**. In step 3, under **Upload Completed Assignment**, click **Choose File**. In the **Open** dialog box, navigate to your **Word Chapter 1 folder**, and then click your **Student_Word_1B_Programs** file one time to select it. In the lower right corner of the **Open** dialog box, click **Open**.

The name of your selected file displays above the Upload button.

> **6** To submit your file to **MyLab IT** for grading, click **Upload**, wait a moment for a green **Success!** message, and then in **step 4**, click the blue **Submit for Grading** button. Click **Close Assignment** to return to your list of **Course Materials**.

You have completed Project 1B **END**

Objective   Create an Information Handout

ALERT   Working with Web-Based Applications and Services

Computer programs and services on the web receive continuous updates and improvements, so the steps to complete this web-based Activity may differ from the ones shown. You can often look at the screens and the information presented to determine how to complete the Activity.

If you do not already have a Google account, you will need to create one before you begin this Activity. Go to http://google .com and in the upper right corner, click **Sign In**. On the Sign In screen, click **Create Account**. On the Create your Google Account page, complete the form, read and agree to the Terms of Service and Privacy Policy, and then click **Next step**. On the Welcome screen, click **Get Started**.

Activity │ Creating a Handout with Bulleted and Numbered Lists

In this Activity, you will use Google Docs to create an information handout.

1 From the desktop, open your browser, navigate to http://google.com. In the upper right corner of your screen, click **Google apps** ⊞, and then click **Drive** ☁. Sign in to your Google account, and then double-click your **GO! Web Projects** folder to open it. If you have not created this folder, refer to the instructions in the first Google Docs project in this chapter.

2 Click **New**, and then click **Google Docs**. Click **File**, and then click **Open**. Click **Upload**, and then click **Select a file from your computer**. From your student data files, click **w01_1B_Web** and then click **Open**.

3 In the upper left corner of the Google Docs window, select **w01_1B_Web**. Type **Lastname_Firstname_WD_1B_Web** and then press Enter to rename the file.

4 Press Ctrl + A to select all of the text. Click **Line spacing** ☷▾, and then click **1.5**. Click **Left align** ▤.

5 Select the six lines of text beginning with *Short feature films* and ending with *Recording of live concerts*, and then click **Bulleted list** ☰ to apply bullets to the selected text. Select the list of internship positions beginning with *Production Assistant* and ending with *Assistant Set Designer*, and then click **Bulleted list**. Compare your screen with Figure A.

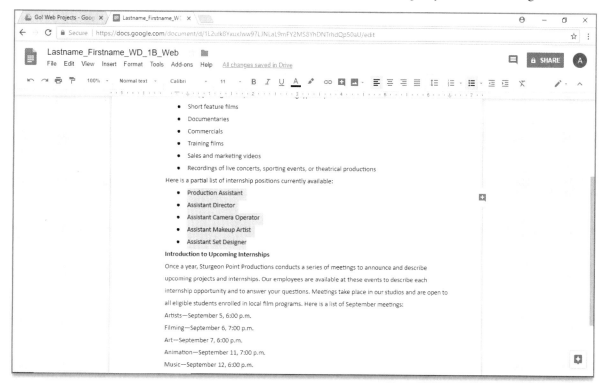

Figure A

»»» GO! With Google continues on next page

6 Select the last five lines of the document beginning with *Artists* and ending with *Music*. To create a numbered list from the selection, click **Numbered list**.

7 Select the first three lines of text in the document, and then click **Center**. Click in the *Introduction to Upcoming Internships* heading, and then click **Center**.

8 Click at the beginning of the paragraph that begins *Sturgeon Point Production produces and markets*, and then press Tab. Look at the ruler and notice that the first line indent is applied.

9 With the insertion point in the same paragraph, double-click **Paint format**. Then, click in the paragraphs that begin *As an intern*, *Here is a partial list*, and *Once a year* to apply the first line indent to each of the paragraphs. Click **Paint format** to turn it off. Compare your document with Figure B.

10 Your document will be saved automatically. Sign out of your Google account, and then submit as instructed by your instructor.

Sturgeon Point Productions

Internship Guide

The Internship Program

Sturgeon Point Productions produces and markets educational videos. We started our company in 1968, and now we are a dynamic and creative independent film and commercial production company. From our base in Miami, we create both contract and in-house videos and feature films.

As an intern, you might take part in the following types of productions:

- Short feature films
- Documentaries
- Commercials
- Training films
- Sales and marketing videos
- Recordings of live concerts, sporting events, or theatrical productions

Here is a partial list of internship positions currently available:

- Production Assistant
- Assistant Director
- Assistant Camera Operator
- Assistant Makeup Artist
- Assistant Set Designer

Introduction to Upcoming Internships

Once a year, Sturgeon Point Productions conducts a series of meetings to announce and describe upcoming projects and internships. Our employees are available at these events to describe each internship opportunity and to answer your questions. Meetings take place in our studios and are open to all eligible students enrolled in local film programs. Here is a list of September meetings:

1. Artists—September 5, 6:00 p.m.
2. Filming—September 6, 7:00 p.m.
3. Art—September 7, 6:00 p.m.
4. Animation—September 11, 7:00 p.m.
5. Music—September 12, 6:00 p.m.

Figure B

wavebreakmedia/Shutterstock, Monkey Business Images/Fotolia, Ivanko80/Shutterstock, Monkey Business Images/Shutterstock

Microsoft Office Specialist (MOS) Skills in this Chapter	
Project A	**Project B**
1.1.4 Show or hide formatting symbols and hidden text	**1.2.1** Set up document pages
1.2.3 Insert and modify headers and footers	**2.2.3** Set line and paragraph spacing and indentation
1.3.2 Modify basic document properties	**3.3.1** Format paragraphs as numbered and bulleted lists
1.3.3 Modify print settings	**3.3.2** Change bullet characters and number formats
5.1.1 Insert shapes	**5.1.4** Insert SmartArt graphics
5.1.2 Insert pictures	**5.2.5** Format SmartArt graphics
5.1.6 Insert text boxes	**5.3.3** Add and modify SmartArt graphic content
5.2.1 Apply artistic effects	
5.2.2 Apply picture effects and picture styles	
5.2.4 Format graphic elements	
5.3.2 Add and modify text in shapes	
5.4.1 Position objects	
5.4.2 Wrap text around objects	

Build Your E-Portfolio

An E-Portfolio is a collection of evidence, stored electronically, that showcases what you have accomplished while completing your education. Collecting and then sharing your work products with potential employers reflects your academic and career goals. Your completed documents from the following projects are good examples to show what you have learned: 1G, 1K, and 1L

Go! For Job Success

Video: How to Succeed in an Interview

Your instructor may assign this video to your class, and then ask you to think about, or discuss with your classmates, these questions:

g-stockstudio/Shutterstock

> Can you think of two or three behaviors that Lee might want to change before he interviews with another company?

> If you were going on an interview, which of Connie's behaviors would you imitate?

> If you were the interviewer, Maria, would you have handled anything differently with either candidate?

End of Chapter

Summary

In this chapter, you started Word and practiced navigating the Word window, and you entered, edited, and formatted text. You also inserted text from another Word file.

Graphics include pictures, shapes, and text boxes. In this chapter, you formatted objects by applying styles, effects, and text-wrapping options, and you sized and positioned objects on the page.

SmartArt graphics visually represent your ideas, and there are many SmartArt graphics from which to choose. You added an icon to your document to provide visual interest.

Word documents can be formatted to display your information attractively. You can add a page border, add bulleted and numbered lists, change margins and tabs, and modify paragraph and line spacing.

GO! Learn It Online

Review the concepts, key terms, and MOS skills in this chapter by completing these online challenges, which you can find at **MyLab IT**.

Chapter Quiz: Answer matching and multiple-choice questions to test what you learned in this chapter.

Lessons on the GO!: Learn how to use all the new apps and features as they are introduced by Microsoft.

MOS Prep Quiz: Answer questions to review the MOS skills that you practiced in this chapter.

GO! Collaborative Team Project (Available in Instructor Resource Center)

If your instructor assigns this project to your class, you can expect to work with one or more of your classmates—either in person or by using Internet tools—to create work products similar to those that you created in this chapter. A **team** is a group of workers who work together to solve a problem, make a decision, or create a work product. **Collaboration** is when you work together with others as a team in an intellectual endeavor to complete a shared task or achieve a shared goal.

Monkey Business Images/Fotolia

Project Guide for Word Chapter 1

Your instructor will assign Projects from this list to ensure your learning and assess your knowledge.

Project	Apply Skills from These Chapter Objectives	Project Type	Project Location
1A MyLab IT	Objectives 1–4 from Project 1A	**1A Instructional Project (Grader Project)** **Instruction** Guided instruction to learn the skills in Project A.	In **MyLab IT** and in text
1B MyLab IT	Objectives 5–8 from Project 1B	**1B Instructional Project (Grader Project)** **Instruction** Guided instruction to learn the skills in Project B.	In **MyLab IT** and in text
1C	Objectives 1–4 from Project 1A	**1C Skills Review (Scorecard Grading)** **Review** A guided review of the skills from Project 1A.	In text
1D	Objectives 5–8 from Project 1B	**1D Skills Review (Scorecard Grading)** **Review** A guided review of the skills from Project 1B.	In text
1E MyLab IT	Objectives 1–4 from Project 1A	**1E Mastery (Grader Project)** **Mastery and Transfer of Learning** A demonstration of your mastery of the skills in Project 2A with extensive decision-making.	In **MyLab IT** and in text
1F MyLab IT	Objectives 5–8 from Project 1B	**1F Mastery (Grader Project)** **Mastery and Transfer of Learning** A demonstration of your mastery of the skills in Project 1B with extensive decision-making.	In **MyLab IT** and in text
1G MyLab IT	Objectives 1–8 from Projects 1A and 1B	**1G Mastery (Grader Project)** **Mastery and Transfer of Learning** A demonstration of your mastery of the skills in Projects 1A and 1B with extensive decision-making.	In **MyLab IT** and in text
1H	Combination of Objectives from Projects 1A and 1B	**1H GO! Fix It (Scorecard Grading)** **Critical Thinking** A demonstration of your mastery of the skills in Projects 1A and 1B by creating a correct result from a document that contains errors you must find.	IRC
1I	Combination of Objectives from Projects 1A and 1B	**1I GO! Make It (Scorecard Grading)** **Critical Thinking** A demonstration of your mastery of the skills in Projects 1A and 1B by creating a result from a supplied picture.	IRC
1J	Combination of Objectives from Projects 1A and 1B	**1J GO! Solve It (Rubric Grading)** **Critical Thinking** A demonstration of your mastery of the skills in Projects 1A and 1B, your decision-making skills, and your critical thinking skills. A task-specific rubric helps you self-assess your result.	IRC
1K	Combination of Objectives from Projects 1A and 1B	**1K GO! Solve It (Rubric Grading)** **Critical Thinking** A demonstration of your mastery of the skills in Projects 1A and 1B, your decision-making skills, and your critical thinking skills. A task-specific rubric helps you self-assess your result.	In text
1L	Combination of Objectives from Projects 1A and 1B	**1L GO! Think (Rubric Grading)** **Critical Thinking** A demonstration of your understanding of the chapter concepts applied in a manner that you would outside of college. An analytic rubric helps you and your instructor grade the quality of your work by comparing it to the work an expert in the discipline would create.	In text
1M	Combination of Objectives from Projects 1A and 1B	**1M GO! Think (Rubric Grading)** **Critical Thinking** A demonstration of your understanding of the chapter concepts applied in a manner that you would outside of college. An analytic rubric helps you and your instructor grade the quality of your work by comparing it to the work an expert in the discipline would create.	IRC
1N	Combination of Objectives from Projects 1A and 1B	**1N You and GO! (Rubric Grading)** **Critical Thinking** A demonstration of your understanding of the chapter concepts applied in a manner that you would in a personal situation. An analytic rubric helps you and your instructor grade the quality of your work.	IRC
1O	Combination of Objectives from Projects 1A and 1B	**1O Cumulative Group Project for Word Chapter 1** A demonstration of your understanding of concepts and your ability to work collaboratively in a group role-playing assessment, requiring both collaboration and self-management.	IRC

Glossary

Glossary of Chapter Key Terms

Alignment The placement of paragraph text relative to the left and right margins.

Alignment guide A green vertical or horizontal line that displays when you are moving or sizing an object to assist you with object placement.

Artistic effects Formats applied to images that make pictures resemble sketches or paintings.

Bulleted list A list of items with each item introduced by a symbol such as a small circle or check mark, and which is useful when the items in the list can be displayed in any order.

Bullets Text symbols such as small circles or check marks that precede each item in a bulleted list.

Center alignment The alignment of text or objects that is centered horizontally between the left and right margin.

Collaboration The action of working together with others as a team in an intellectual endeavor to complete a shared task or achieve a shared goal.

Dot leader A series of dots preceding a tab that guides the eye across the line.

Drawing objects Graphic objects, such as shapes, diagrams, lines, or circles.

Floating object A graphic that can be moved independently of the surrounding text characters.

Formatting marks Characters that display on the screen, but do not print, indicating where the Enter key, the Spacebar, and the Tab key were pressed; also called nonprinting characters.

Graphics Pictures, charts, or drawing objects.

Icons Pictures composed of straight and curved lines.

Inline object An object or graphic inserted in a document that acts like a character in a sentence.

Justified alignment An arrangement of text in which the text aligns evenly on both the left and right margins.

Layout Options Picture formatting options that control the manner in which text wraps around a picture or other object.

Leader character Characters that form a solid, dotted, or dashed line that fills the space preceding a tab stop.

Left alignment An arrangement of text in which the text aligns at the left margin, leaving the right margin uneven.

Line spacing The distance between lines of text in a paragraph.

Live Layout A feature that reflows text as you move or size an object so that you can view the placement of surrounding text.

Margins The space between the text and the top, bottom, left, and right edges of the paper.

Nonprinting characters Characters that display on the screen, but do not print; also called formatting marks.

Numbered list A list that uses consecutive numbers or letters to introduce each item in a list.

Object anchor The symbol that indicates to which paragraph an object is attached.

Picture effects Effects that enhance a picture, such as a shadow, glow, reflection, or 3-D rotation.

Picture styles Frames, shapes, shadows, borders, and other special effects that can be added to an image to create an overall visual style for the image.

Placeholder text Nonprinting text that holds a place in a document where you can type.

Right alignment An arrangement of text in which the text aligns at the right margin, leaving the left margin uneven.

Rotation handle A symbol with which you can rotate a graphic to any angle; displays above the top center sizing handle.

Shapes Lines, arrows, stars, banners, ovals, rectangles, and other basic shapes with which you can illustrate an idea, a process, or a workflow.

SmartArt A designer-quality visual representation of your information that you can create by choosing from among many different layouts to effectively communicate your message or ideas.

Spin box A small box with an upward- and downward-pointing arrow that lets you move rapidly through a set of values by clicking.

Tab stop A specific location on a line of text, marked on the Word ruler, to which you can move the insertion point by pressing the Tab key, and which is used to align and indent text.

Team A group of workers tasked with working together to solve a problem, make a decision, or create a work product.

Text box A movable resizable container for text or graphics.

Text effects Decorative formats, such as shadowed or mirrored text, text glow, 3-D effects, and colors that make text stand out.

Text pane A pane that displays to the left of a SmartArt graphic and is used to type text and edit text in a SmartArt graphic.

Text wrapping The manner in which text displays around an object.

Toggle button A button that can be turned on by clicking it once, and then turned off by clicking it again.

Word wrap The feature that moves text from the right edge of a paragraph to the beginning of the next line as necessary to fit within the margins.

Chapter Review

Skills Review | **Project 1C Photography**

Apply 1A skills from these Objectives:

1. Create a New Document and Insert Text
2. Insert and Format Graphics
3. Insert and Modify Text Boxes and Shapes
4. Preview and Print a Document

In the following Skills Review, you will create a flyer advertising a photography internship with Sturgeon Point Productions. Your completed document will look similar to Figure 1.52.

Project Files

For Project 1C, you will need the following files:

New blank Word document
w01C_Building
w01C_Job_Description
You will save your document as:
Lastname_Firstname_1C_Photography

Project Results

Internship Available for

Still Photographer

This position requires skill in the use of:

Professional full-frame DSLR cameras

Tilt-shift lenses for tall buildings

This fall, Sturgeon Point Productions will film a documentary on the historic architecture in and around Milwaukee, Wisconsin.

The filming will take place during the last two weeks of September. If the weather is not conducive to outdoor shooting, it is possible that filming will continue into the first week of October.

The still photographer will accompany the director during the first two weeks of September to scout locations and take photographs for the purpose of planning the filming schedule. The photographer will also accompany the film crew throughout filming.

Photographs taken during pre-production and filming will be used for advertising and marketing and published in an upcoming book on the history of the city of Milwaukee.

Submit Your Application by June 30!

Student_Word_1C_Photography

Figure 1.52

Chapter Review

1 ▶ Start Word and then click **Blank document**. On the **Home tab**, in the **Paragraph group**, if necessary, click Show/Hide to display the formatting marks. If the rulers do not display, click the View tab, and then in the Show group, select the Ruler check box. (Mac users, from your student data files, open Mac_w01C_Photography and use this file instead of a new blank document.) **Save** the file in your **Word Chapter 1** folder as **Lastname_Firstname_1C_Photography**

a. Type **Internship Available for Still Photographer** and then press [Enter] two times. Type the following text: **This fall, Sturgeon Point Productions will film a documentary on the historic architecture in and around Milwaukee, Wisconsin.** Press [Enter].

b. On the ribbon, click the **Insert tab**. In the **Text group**, click the **Object button arrow**, and then click **Text from File**. In the **Insert File** dialog box, from your student data files, locate and select **w01C_Job_Description**, and then click **Insert**. Delete the blank paragraph at the end of the document.

c. Including the paragraph mark, select the first paragraph of text—*Internship Available for Still Photographer*. On the **Home tab**, in the **Font group**, click **Text Effects and Typography**. In the **Text Effects and Typography** gallery, in the first row, click the fourth effect.

d. With the text still selected, in the **Font group**, click in the **Font Size** box to select the existing font size. Type **44** and then press [Enter]. In the **Font group**, click the **Font Color button arrow**. Under **Theme Colors**, in the fourth column, click the first color.

e. With the text still selected, in the **Font group**, click **Text Effects and Typography**. Point to **Shadow**, and then under **Outer**, in the second row, click the third style. In the **Paragraph group**, click **Center**.

2 ▶ In the paragraph that begins *The filming*, click to position the insertion point at the beginning of the paragraph. On the **Insert tab**, in the **Illustrations group**, click **Pictures**. (Mac users, after clicking Pictures, click Picture form File.) In the **Insert Picture** dialog box, navigate to your student data files, locate and click **w01C_Building**, and then click **Insert**.

a. To the right of the selected picture, click the **Layout Options** button, and then under **With Text Wrapping**, click the first option—**Square**. **Close** the Layout Options. (Mac users, on the Picture Format tab, click Wrap Text.)

b. On the **Format tab**, in the **Size group**, click in the **Shape Height** box to select the value, type **2.7** and then press [Enter].

c. With the picture selected, on the **Format tab**, in the **Arrange group**, click **Position**, and then click **More Layout Options**. In the **Layout** dialog box, on the **Position tab**, in the middle of the dialog box under **Vertical**, click the **Alignment** option button. To the right of **Alignment**, click the arrow, and then click **Top**. To the right of **relative to**, click the arrow, and then click **Line**. Click **OK**.

d. On the **Format tab**, in the **Picture Styles group**, click **Picture Effects**. Point to **Soft Edges**, and then click **5 Point**. On the **Format tab**, in the **Adjust group**, click **Artistic Effects**. Use the ScreenTips to locate and click **Crisscross Etching**.

e. Click anywhere outside the picture to deselect it. On the **Design tab**, in the **Page Background group**, click **Page Borders**. In the **Borders and Shading** dialog box, on the **Page Border tab**, under **Setting**, click **Box**. Under **Style**, scroll the list and then click the third style from the bottom—a black line that fades to gray.

f. Click the **Color arrow**, and then in the next to last column, click the first color. Under **Apply to**, be sure **Whole document** is selected, and then click **OK**. Click **Save**.

3 ▶ Click the **Insert tab**, and then in the **Illustrations group**, click **Shapes** to display the gallery. Under **Basic Shapes**, use the ScreenTips to locate and then click **Frame**.

a. Position the ⊞ pointer anywhere in the blank area at the bottom of the document. Click one time to insert a 1" by 1" frame. The exact location need not be precise. To the right of the shape, click the **Layout Options** button, and at the bottom, click **See more**. (Mac users, drag a 1 × 1 shape, click to insert the shape. To display the Layout dialog box, on the Shape Format tab, click Arrange, click Position, click More Layout Options.)

b. In the **Layout** dialog box, under **Horizontal**, click the **Alignment** option button. To the right of **Alignment**, click the arrow, and then click **Centered**. To the right of **relative to**, click the arrow, and then click **Page**. Under **Vertical**, click the **Absolute position** option button. In the **Absolute position** box, select the existing number, and then type **1** To the right of **below**, click the arrow, and then click **Paragraph**. Click **OK**.

(continues on next page)

Chapter Review

c. On the **Format tab**, click in the **Shape Height** box. Type **1.5** and then select the number in the **Shape Width** box. Type **5.5** and then press Enter.

d. If necessary, select the frame shape. On the **Format tab**, in the **Shape Styles group**, click **More**. In the **Shape Styles** gallery, in the first row, click the sixth style. With the shape selected, type **Submit Your Application by June 30!** Select the text you just typed, and then change the **Font Size** to **22**.

4 Click outside of the frame to deselect it, and then to move to the top of the document. Click in the blank paragraph below the title. Press Enter four times to make space for a text box.

a. On the **Insert tab**, in the **Text group**, click **Text Box**. At the bottom of the gallery, click **Draw Text Box**. Position the ⊞ pointer over the first blank paragraph at the left margin. Drag down and to the right to create a text box approximately 1.5 inches high and 4 inches wide—the exact size and location need not be precise.

b. With the insertion point blinking in the text box, type the following, pressing Enter after the first two lines to create a new paragraph:

This position requires skill in the use of:
Professional full-frame DSLR cameras
Tilt-shift lenses for tall buildings

c. To precisely place the text box, on the **Format tab**, in the **Arrange group**, click **Position**, and then click **More Layout Options**. In the **Layout** dialog box, under **Horizontal**, click the **Alignment** button. To the right of **Alignment**, click the arrow, and then click **Centered**. To the right of **relative to**, click the arrow, and then click **Page**.

d. Under **Vertical**, click the **Absolute position** button. In the **Absolute position** box, select the existing number. Type **2** To the right of **below**, click the arrow, and then click **Margin**.

e. In the **Layout** dialog box, click the **Size tab**. Under **Height**, select the number in the **Absolute** box. Type **1** and then under **Width**, select the number in the **Absolute** box. Type **3.75** and then click **OK**.

f. In the text box, select all of the text. On the **Home tab**, change the **Font Size** to **12**, apply **Bold**, and then **Center** the text.

g. On the **Format tab**, in the **Shape Styles group**, click **Shape Effects**. Point to **Shadow**, and then under **Outer**, in the first row, click the first style.

h. In the **Shape Styles group**, click **Shape Outline**. In the fifth column, click the first color to change the color of the text box border. Click **Shape Fill**, and then in the fifth column, click the second color. Click **Save**.

5 Click the **Insert tab**, and then in the **Header & Footer group**, click **Footer**. At the bottom of the menu, click **Edit Footer**. On the **Header & Footer Tools Design tab**, in the **Insert group**, click **Document Info**, and then click **File Name**. Double-click in the document outside of the footer area to close the footer and return to the document. (Mac users, on the Header & Footer tab, click Field, click Document Information, click FileName.)

a. In the upper left corner of your screen, click the **File tab** to display **Backstage** view. Click **Info**, and then at the bottom of the **Properties list**, click **Show All Properties**. On the list of Properties, click to the right of **Tags**, and then type **internship, documentary** Click to the right of **Subject**, and then type your course name and section #. Under **Related People**, be sure that your name displays as the author. If necessary, right-click the author name, click Edit Property, type your name, and click OK. ((Mac users, click File, click Properties, click Summary. In the Keywords box type the tags. Type the Subject and Author. Click OK.)

b. **Save** and **Close** your document. Print or submit your workbook electronically as directed by your instructor.

Chapter Review

Apply 1B skills from
these Objectives:

5. Change
   Document and
   Paragraph Layout
6. Create and
   Modify Lists
7. Set and Modify
   Tab Stops
8. Insert and Format
   a SmartArt
   Graphic and an
   Icon

Skills Review   Project 1D Internship

In the following Skills Review, you will edit an information handout regarding production and development internships with Sturgeon Point Productions. Your completed document will look similar to Figure 1.53.

Project Files

For Project 1D, you will need the following file:

w01D_Internship

You will save your document as:

Lastname_Firstname_1D_Internship

Project Results

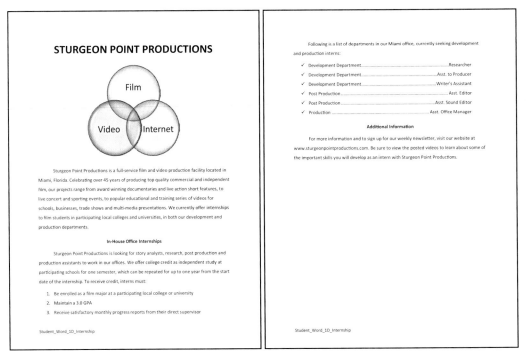

Figure 1.53

(continues on next page)

Chapter Review

1 From your student data files, open **w01D_Internship**. On the **Home tab**, in the **Paragraph group**, be sure **Show/Hide** is active. **Save** the document to your **Word Chapter 1** folder, as **Lastname_Firstname_1D_Internship**

a. Click the **Layout tab**. In the **Page Setup group**, click **Margins**, and then click **Custom Margins**. In the **Page Setup** dialog box, press Tab as necessary to select the value in the **Left** box. Type **1** and then press Tab to select the value in the **Right** box. Type **1** and then click **OK**.

b. Scroll down to view the bottom of **Page 1**, point anywhere in the bottom margin area, right-click, and then click **Edit Footer** to display the footer area. On the **Header & Footer Tools Design tab**, in the **Insert group**, click **Document Info**, and then click **File Name**. Double-click anywhere in the document to close the footer area. (Mac users, double-click in the footer area. On the Header & Footer tab, click Field.)

c. Press Ctrl + A to select all the text in the document. (Mac users, press command ⌘ + A.) On the **Home tab**, in the **Paragraph group**, click **Align Left**.

d. Press Ctrl + Home. (Mac users, press command ⌘ + fn + ←.) Select the document title, and then on the **Home tab**, in the **Paragraph group**, click **Center**.

e. Locate the first bold subheading—*In-House Office Internships*. Point to the left of the paragraph to display the ⟋ pointer, and then click one time to select the text. With *In-House Office Internships* selected, locate the subheading *Additional Information*. Move the pointer to the left of the paragraph to display the ⟋ pointer, hold down Ctrl, and then click one time to select both paragraphs. (Mac users, press command ⌘.) In the **Paragraph group**, click **Center**.

f. Select all of the text in the document. On the **Home tab**, in the **Paragraph group**, click **Line and Paragraph Spacing**, and then click **1.5**.

2 Below the title of the document, click anywhere in the paragraph that begins *Sturgeon Point Productions is a full-service*. On the **Home tab**, in the **Paragraph group**, click the **Dialog Box Launcher**. (Mac users, on the Home tab, click Line and Paragraph Spacing, click Line Spacing Options.)

a. In the **Paragraph** dialog box, on the **Indents and Spacing tab**, under **Indentation**, click the **Special arrow**, and then click **First line** to indent the first line by 0.5". Click **OK**, and then click anywhere in the paragraph that begins *Sturgeon Point Productions is looking for*. On the ruler under the ribbon, drag the **First Line Indent** marker to **0.5 inches on the horizontal ruler**.

b. Select all the text in the document. Click the **Layout tab**, and then in the **Paragraph group**, under **Spacing**, click the **After spin box up arrow** one time to change the value to **6 pt**.

c. Select the subheading *In-House Office Internships*, including the paragraph mark following it. Scroll down, hold down Ctrl, and then select the subheading *Additional Information*. With both subheadings selected, in the **Paragraph group**, under **Spacing**, click the **Before up spin box arrow** two times to set the **Spacing Before** to **12 pt**. **Save** your document.

3 Locate the first paragraph that begins *Development Department*, and then point to this paragraph from the left margin area to display the ⟋ pointer. Drag down to select this paragraph and the next five paragraphs so that six paragraphs are selected. On the **Home tab**, in the **Paragraph group**, click **Bullets** to change the selected text to a bulleted list.

a. Under the subheading *In-House Office Internships*, in the paragraph that begins *Sturgeon Point Productions is looking*, click to position the insertion point at the *end* of the paragraph, following the colon. Press Enter to create a blank paragraph. On the ruler, drag the **First Line Indent** marker to the left so that it is positioned directly above the lower button. Being sure to include the period, type **1.** and then press Spacebar to create the first item in a numbered list.

b. Type **Be enrolled as a film major at a participating local college or university** and then press Enter. Type **Maintain a 3.0 GPA** and then press Enter. Type **Receive satisfactory monthly progress reports from their direct supervisor**

c. Scroll down to view the bulleted list of departments, and then select all six bulleted items in the list. On the mini toolbar, click the **Bullets button arrow**, and then under **Bullet Library**, click the **check mark** symbol. If the check mark is not available, choose another bullet symbol.

4 With the list selected, move the pointer to the horizontal ruler, and then point to and click at **3.5 inches on the horizontal ruler** to align the job titles at the tab mark.

a. With the bulleted list still selected, on the ruler, point to the new tab marker at **3.5 inches on the horizontal ruler**, and then when the *Left Tab* ScreenTip displays, drag the tab marker to **4 inches on the horizontal ruler**.

(continues on next page)

Chapter Review

b. With the list still selected, on the ruler, point to the tab marker that you moved to display the *Left Tab* ScreenTip, and then double-click to display the **Tabs** dialog box.

c. In the **Tabs** dialog box, under **Tab stop position**, if necessary select *4"*, and then type **6** Under **Alignment**, click the **Right** option button. Under **Leader**, click the **2** option button. Near the bottom of the **Tabs** dialog box, click **Set**. Under **Tab stop position**, select *4"*, and then click **Clear** to delete the tab stop. (Mac users, click Clear All. In the Tab stops box, type 6, click Right, and then Under Leader, click the dot leader style.) Click **OK**. **Save** your document.

5 ▶ Press Ctrl + Home to move to the top of the document, and then in the title, click to the right of the *S* in *PRODUCTIONS*.

a. Click the **Insert tab**, and then in the **Illustrations group**, click **SmartArt**. On the left, click **Relationship**, and then scroll the list to the bottom. Locate and then click **Basic Venn**. Click **OK** to insert the SmartArt graphic. If necessary, close the Text Pane.

b. In the SmartArt graphic, click on *[Text]* in the top circle shape. Type **Film** and then in the lower left shape, click on the placeholder *[Text]*. Type **Video** and then in the third circle, type **Internet**

c. Click the SmartArt graphic border to select it. Click the **Format tab**, and then in the **Size group**, if necessary click **Size** to display the **Shape Height** and **Shape Width** boxes. Set the **Height** to **3"**.

d. With the SmartArt graphic still selected, on the ribbon, under **SmartArt Tools**, click the **Design tab**, and then in the **SmartArt Styles group**, click **Change Colors**. (Mac users, use the SmartArt Design tab.) Under **Colorful**, click the third style—**Colorful Range - Accent Colors 3 to 4**. On the **Design tab**, in the **SmartArt Styles group**, click **More**. Under **3-D**, click **Cartoon**.

e. Click the **File tab**, click **Info**, and then, click **Show All Properties**. In the **Tags** box, type **internship** and in the **Subject** box type your course name and section number. If necessary, in the **Author** box, replace the existing text with your first and last name. Click **Save**.

f. Click the **File tab** to display **Backstage** view, and then click **Print** to display **Print Preview**. At the bottom of the preview, click the **Next Page** and **Previous Page** buttons to move between pages. If necessary, return to the document and make any necessary changes.

g. **Save** and **Close** your document. Print or submit your workbook electronically as directed by your instructor.

You have completed Project 1D **END**

Content-Based Assessments (Mastery and Transfer of Learning)

Apply 1A skills from these Objectives:

1. Create a New Document and Insert Text
2. Insert and Format Graphics
3. Insert and Modify Text Boxes and Shapes
4. Preview and Print a Document

In the following Mastery project, you will create a flyer announcing a special event being hosted by Sturgeon Point Productions. Your printed results will look similar to those in Figure 1.54.

Project Files for MyLab IT Grader

1. In your **MyLab IT** course, locate and click **Word 1E Documentary**, Download Materials, and then Download All Files.
2. Extract the zipped folder to your Word Chapter 1 folder. Close the Grader download screens.
3. Take a moment to open the downloaded **Word_1E_Documentary_Instructions**; note any recent updates to the book.

Project Results

Sturgeon Point Productions

Presents Aria Pacheco

Sturgeon Point Productions will be hosting its **5th Annual Script to Screen** series, every Friday night this April in our Studio G screening room. All employees, interns, and film students with current school ID are welcome to share in this totally free, exciting evening, where our award-winning filmmakers from our Documentary and Short Feature Film Departments give a first-hand account of the filmmaking process and the challenges that went into their particular projects, from the script phase through production and finally, in distribution and marketing.

This year, we are proud to kick off the series with Aria Pacheco, who will discuss her multi-award winning documentary, **"Through the Cold."** This film documents the perils and triumphs of a team of scientists living in Antarctica. This compelling story, rich in visual complexity, follows the team as they prepare for the six months of darkness in the winter season. Celebrated film critic, Georges Harold, will be conducting an interview with Ms. Pacheco and select members of her crew following a screening of the film, which will take place on Friday, April 5th at 8 p.m. This event is guaranteed to fill up fast, so we suggest you get in line at least one hour prior to the screening.

"Through the Cold" has been heralded by critics across the country. Don't miss this chance to meet one of our greatest documentary filmmakers.

Date: April 5

Time 8 p.m.

Place: Studio G Screening Room

Student_Word_1E_Documentary

Figure 1.54 (Volodymyr Goinyk/Shutterstock)

For Non-MyLab Submissions

For Project 1E, you will need:
New blank Word Document
w01E_Antarctica
w01E_Filmmaker

In your Word Chapter 1 folder, save your document as:
Lastname_Firstname_1E_Documentary

Start with a new blank document. After you have named and saved your document, on the next page, begin with Step 2. After Step 16, save and submit your file as directed by your instructor.

Content-Based Assessments (Mastery and Transfer of Learning)

1 Navigate to your **Word Chapter 1 folder**, and then double-click the Word file you downloaded from **MyLab IT** that displays your name—**Student_Word_1E_Documentary**. In your document, if necessary, at the top click **Enable Editing**. Display the rulers and verify that **Show/Hide** is active. (Mac users, If you are not submitting your file in **MyLab IT**, from the student data files that accompany this project, open the file **Mac_w01E_Documentary**.)

2 Type **Sturgeon Point Productions Presents Aria Pacheco** and then press [Enter]. From your downloaded files, insert the text file **w01E_Filmmaker**.

3 Select the title and then from the **Text Effects and Typography** gallery, in the first row apply the second effect. Change the **Font Size** to **36**.

4 With the title still selected, display the **Font Color** palette, and then in the fourth column apply the first color. Then, from the **Shadow** gallery, under **Outer**, apply the first **Shadow** style. **Center** the title.

5 Position the insertion point at the beginning of the paragraph that begins with *This year*, and then from your downloaded files, insert the picture **w01E_Antarctica**.

6 Change the **Layout Options** to **Square** and then change the **Height** of the picture to **2.25**

7 Using the **Position** command, display the **Layout** dialog box, and then change the **Horizontal Alignment** to **Right relative to** the **Margin**.

8 Apply a **10 Point Soft Edges** picture effect to the image, and then display the **Artistic Effects** gallery. Apply the **Paint Brush** effect.

9 Deselect the picture. Apply a **Page Border** to the document using the **Shadow** setting, and then select the double lines style.

10 Below the last paragraph, draw a **Text Box** and then change the **Height** to **1.5** and the **Width** to **4.5**

11 To precisely place the text box, display the **Layout** dialog box. Change the **Horizontal Alignment** to **Centered, relative to** the **Page**, and then change the **Vertical Absolute position** to **0.5** below the **Paragraph**.

12 In the text box, type the following text:

> **Date: April 5**
> **Time: 8 p.m.**
> **Place: Studio G Screening Room**

13 In the text box, change the font size of all the text to **18**. Apply **Bold** and **Center**.

14 Apply a **Shape Style** to the text box—under **Theme Styles**, in the last row, select the second style.

15 Insert the **File Name** in the footer, and then display the document properties. As the **Tags**, type **documentary, interview** and as the **Subject**, type your course and section number. Be sure your name is indicated as the **Author**. **Save** your file.

16 Display the **Print Preview** and, if necessary, return to the document and make any necessary changes. **Save** your document and **Close** Word.

17 In **MyLab IT**, locate and click the Grader Project **Word 1E Documentary**. In **step 3**, under **Upload Completed Assignment**, click **Choose File**. In the **Open** dialog box, navigate to your **Word Chapter 1 folder**, and then click your **Student_Word_1E_Documentary** file one time to select it. In the lower right corner of the **Open** dialog box, click **Open**.

The name of your selected file displays above the Upload button.

18 To submit your file to **MyLab IT** for grading, click **Upload**, wait a moment for a green **Success!** message, and then in step 4, click the blue **Submit for Grading** button. Click **Close Assignment** to return to your list of **Course Materials**.

You have completed Project 1E   END

Content-Based Assessments (Mastery and Transfer of Learning)

MyLab IT Grader   **Mastering Word**   **Project 1F Pitch Festival**

Apply 1B skills from these Objectives:

5. Change Document and Paragraph Layout
6. Create and Modify Lists
7. Set and Modify Tab Stops
8. Insert and Format a SmartArt Graphic and an Icon

In the following Mastery project, you will edit a document with information regarding an event that Sturgeon Point Productions is holding for college students. Your printed results will look similar to those in Figure 1.55.

Project Files for MyLab IT Grader

1. In your **MyLab IT** course, locate and click **Word 1F Pitch Festival**, Download Materials, and then Download All Files. Close the Grader download screens.
2. Extract the zipped folder to your Word Chapter 1 folder. Close the Grader download screens.
3. Take a moment to open the downloaded **Word_1F_Pitch_Festival_Instructions**; note any recent updates to the book.

Project Results

Student_Word_1F_Pitch_Festival

Figure 1.55

For Non-MyLab Submissions

For Project 1F, you will need: In your Word Chapter 1 folder, save your document as:

w01F_Pitch_Festival   **Lastname_Firstname_1F_Pitch_Festival**

After you have named and saved your document, on the next page, begin with Step 2.
After Step 13, save and submit your file as directed by your instructor.

Mastering Word: Project 1F Pitch Festival (continued)

1 Navigate to your **Word Chapter 1 folder**, and then double-click the Word file you downloaded from **MyLab IT** that displays your name—**Student_Word_1F_Pitch_Festival**. In your document, if necessary, at the top, click **Enable Editing**. Display the rulers and verify that **Show/Hide** is active.

2 Insert the **File Name** in the footer, and then change the **Line Spacing** for the entire document to **1.5. Center** the document title, and then change the title font size to **24**. Change the **Top** and **Bottom** margins to **0.5**

3 Select the paragraph below the title, and then apply a **First line** indent of **0.5"**. Then, apply the same indent to the paragraphs below the picture that begin *Sturgeon Point Productions* and *The Pitch Festival.*

4 Select the entire document, and then change the **Spacing Before** to **6 pt** and the **Spacing After** to **6 pt.**

5 Select the last three paragraphs containing the dates, and then apply the filled square bullets. With the bulleted list selected, set a **Right** tab with **dot leaders** at **6"**.

6 Locate the paragraph that begins *Sturgeon Point Productions*, and then click at the end of the paragraph, after the colon. Press Enter and remove the first line indent from the new paragraph.

7 In the blank line you inserted, create a numbered list with the following three numbered items:

Human interest or educational
Political or journalistic
Biographical or documentary

8 Position the insertion point at the end of the document after the word *Pitches*. Do *not* insert a blank line. Display the **SmartArt** gallery and the **Process** category. Select and insert the **Equation** SmartArt. Select the outside border of the SmartArt, and then change the **Height** of the SmartArt to **1** and the **Width** to **6.5**

9 With the SmartArt selected, change the layout to **Square**, and change the **Horizontal Alignment** to **Centered relative to** the **Page**. Change the **Vertical Alignment** to **Bottom relative to** the **Margin**.

10 In the first circle, type **Your Ideas** and in the second circle, type **Our Experts** In the third circle, type **Pitch Festival!**

11 Change the SmartArt color to **Colorful Range – Accent Colors 4 to 5**. Apply the **3-D Polished** style.

12 Display the document properties. As the **Tags**, type **pitch festival** and in the **Subject** box, type your course name and section number. In the **Author** box, replace the existing text with your first and last name. **Save** the file.

13 Display the **Print Preview** and if necessary, return to the document and make any necessary changes. **Save** your document and **Close** Word.

14 In **MyLab IT**, locate and click the Grader Project **Word 1F Pitch Festival**. In **step 3**, under **Upload Completed Assignment**, click **Choose File**. In the **Open** dialog box, navigate to your **Word Chapter 1 folder**, and then click your **Student_Word_1F_Pitch_Festival** file one time to select it. In the lower right corner of the **Open** dialog box, click **Open**.

The name of your selected file displays above the Upload button.

15 To submit your file to **MyLab IT** for grading, click **Upload**, wait a moment for a green **Success!** message, and then in step 4, click the blue **Submit for Grading** button. Click **Close Assignment** to return to your list of **Course Materials**.

You have completed Project 1F | END

Content-Based Assessments (Mastery and Transfer of Learning)

Mastering Word | **Project 1G Educational Website**

Apply 1A and 1B skills from these Objectives:

1. Create a New Document and Insert Text
2. Insert and Format Graphics
3. Insert and Modify Text Boxes and Shapes
4. Preview and Print a Document
5. Change Document and Paragraph Layout
6. Create and Modify Lists
7. Set and Modify Tab Stops
8. Insert and Format a SmartArt Graphic and an Icon

In the following Mastery project, you will create a flyer that details a new educational website that Sturgeon Point Productions has developed for instructors. Your printed results will look similar to those in Figure 1.56.

Project Files for MyLab IT Grader

1. In your **MyLab IT** course, locate and click **Word 1G Educational Website**, Download Materials, and then Download All Files. Close the Grader download screens.
2. Extract the zipped folder to your Word Chapter 1 folder. Close the Grader download screens.
3. Take a moment to open the downloaded **Word_1G_Educational_Website_Instructions**; note any recent updates to the book.

Project Results

Figure 1.56

For Non-MyLab Submissions

For Project 1G, you will need:
New blank document
w01G_Education
w01G_Media

In your Word Chapter 1 folder, save your document as:
Lastname_Firstname_1G_Educational_Website

After you have named and saved your document, on the next page, begin with Step 2.
After Step 19, save and submit your file as directed by your instructor.

(continues on next page)

1 Navigate to your **Word Chapter 1 folder**, and then double-click the Word file you downloaded from **MyLab IT** that displays your name— **Student_Word_1G_Educational_Website**. In your document, if necessary, at the top click **Enable Editing**. Display the rulers and verify that **Show/Hide** is active. (Mac users, If you are not submitting your file in MyLab IT, from the student data files that accompany this project, open the file **Mac_w01G_Educational_Website**.)

2 Type **Educational Websites** and then press Enter. Type **Sturgeon Point Productions is offering website tie-ins with every educational video in our catalog, at no additional cost.** Press Spacebar, and then with the insertion point positioned at the end of the sentence that you typed, insert the text from your downloaded file **w01G_Education**.

3 Change the **Line Spacing** for the entire document to **1.5** and the spacing **After** to **6 pt**. To each of the four paragraphs that begin *Sturgeon Point Productions*, *As educators*, *When submitting*, and *Additional information*, apply a **First Line** indent of **0.5"**.

4 Change the **font size** of the title to **50** and the **Line Spacing** to **1.0. Center** the title. With the title selected, display the **Text Effects and Typography** gallery. In the first row, apply the second effect.

5 Click at the beginning of the paragraph below the title, and then from your downloaded files, insert the picture **w01G_Media**. Change the picture **Height** to **2** and the **Layout Options** to **Square**. Format the picture with **Soft Edges** in **10 Point**.

6 Use the **Position** command to display the **Layout** dialog box. Change the picture position so that the **Horizontal Alignment** is **Right relative to** the **Margin**. Change the **Vertical Alignment** to **Top relative to** the **Line**.

7 Select the five paragraphs beginning with *Historic interactive timelines* and ending with *Quizzes and essay exams*, and then apply checkmark bullets. (Mac users, if the check mark bullet style does not display, click Define New Bullet, click Bullet, change the font to Wingdings, click the check mark symbol, and then click OK.)

8 In the paragraph below the bulleted list, click after the colon. Press Enter and remove the first line indent. Type a numbered list with the following three numbered items:

> **The title in which you are interested**
> **The name of the class and subject**
> **Online tools you would like to see created**

9 With the insertion point located at the end of the numbered list, insert a **SmartArt** graphic. In the **Process** category, locate and select the **Basic Chevron Process**. In the first shape, type **View** In the second shape, type **Interact** and in the third shape, type **Assess**

10 Change the SmartArt color to **Colorful Range – Accent Colors 4 to 5**, and then apply the **3-D Flat Scene** style. Change the **Height** of the SmartArt to **1** and the **Width** to **6.5** Change the **Layout Options** to **Square**, the **Horizontal Alignment** to **Centered relative to** the **Page**, and the **Vertical Alignment** to **Bottom relative to** the **Margin**.

11 Select the days and times at the end of the document, and then set a **Right** tab with **dot leaders** at **6"**.

12 In the middle of **Page 2**, insert a **Shape**—the rectangle with rounded corners. The exact location need not be precise. Change the **Shape Height** to **1.5** and the **Shape Width** to **6.5** and then display the **Shape Styles** gallery. In the first row, apply the second style.

13 Use the **Position** command to display the **Layout** dialog box, and then change the position so that both the **Horizontal** and **Vertical Alignment** are **Centered relative to** the **Margin**. In the rectangle, type **Sturgeon Point Productions** and then press Enter. Type **Partnering with Educators to Produce Rich Media Content** and then change the font size to **16**.

14 Move to the top of the document and insert a **Text Box** above the title. The exact location need not be precise. Change the **Height** of the text box to the **0.5** and the **Width** to **3.7** Type **Sturgeon Point Productions** and then change the font size of all the text in the text box to **22. Center** the text.

15 Use the **Position** command to display the **Layout** dialog box, and then position the text box so that the **Horizontal Alignment** is **Centered relative to** the **Page** and the **Vertical Absolute position** is **0.5 below** the **Page**.

16 With the text box selected, display the **Shape Fill** gallery, and then in the next to last column, select the second color. Change the **Shape Outline** to the same color.

17 Deselect the text box. Apply a **Page Border** to the document. Use the **Box** setting, and then choose the first style. Display the **Color** palette, and then in the second to last column, apply the first color.

18 Change the **Top** margin to **1.25** and insert the **File Name** in the footer.

(continues on next page)

Content-Based Assessments (Mastery and Transfer of Learning)

Mastering Word: Project 1G Educational Website (continued)

19 Display the document properties. As the **Tags**, type **website** and as the **Subject**, type your course and section number. Be sure your name displays in the **Author** box. **Save** your document and **Close** Word.

20 In **MyLab IT**, locate and click the Grader Project **Word 1G Educational Website**. In **step 3**, under **Upload Completed Assignment**, click **Choose File**. In the **Open** dialog box, navigate to your **Word Chapter 1 folder**, and then click your **Student_Word_1G_Educational_ Website** file one time to select it. In the lower right corner of the **Open** dialog box, click **Open**.

The name of your selected file displays above the Upload button.

21 To submit your file to **MyLab IT** for grading, click **Upload**, wait a moment for a green **Success**! message, and then in step 4, click the blue **Submit for Grading** button. Click **Close Assignment** to return to your list of **Course Materials**.

You have completed Project 1G END

Content-Based Assessments (Critical Thinking)

Apply a
combination of
the 1A and 1B skills

GO! Fix It	**Project 1H Casting Call**	IRC
GO! Make It	**Project 1I Development Team**	IRC
GO! Solve It	**Project 1J Softball**	IRC
GO! Solve It	**Project 1K Production**	

Project Files

For Project 1K, you will need the following files:

w01K_Production
w01K_Studio

You will save your document as:

Lastname_Firstname_1K_Production

The Marketing Director for Sturgeon Point Productions is developing marketing materials aimed at filmmakers. From the student files that accompany this textbook, locate and open the file w01K_Production. Format the document using techniques you learned in this chapter to create an appropriate flyer aimed at filmmakers. From your student data files, insert the picture w01K_Studio, and then format the picture with an artistic effect. Insert a SmartArt graphic that illustrates two or three important points about the company. Use text effects so that the flyer is easy to read and understand and has an attractive design. Save the file in your Word Chapter 1 folder as **Lastname_Firstname_1K_Production** and submit it as directed.

		Performance Level		
		Exemplary: You consistently applied the relevant skills	**Proficient: You sometimes, but not always, applied the relevant skills.**	**Developing: You rarely or never applied the relevant skills.**
Performance Criteria	**Use text effects**	Text effects applied to text in an attractive and appropriate manner.	Text effects are applied but do not appropriately display text.	Text effects not used.
	Insert and format a picture	The picture is inserted; text wrapping and an artistic effect are applied.	The picture is inserted but not formatted properly.	No picture is inserted in the document.
	Insert and format SmartArt	The SmartArt is inserted and appropriately formatted.	The SmartArt is inserted but no formatting is applied.	A SmartArt is not inserted in the document.

You have completed Project 1K | END

Outcomes-Based Assessments (Critical Thinking)

Rubric

The following outcomes-based assessments are *open-ended assessments*. That is, there is no specific correct result; your result will depend on your approach to the information provided. Make *Professional Quality* your goal. Use the following scoring rubric to guide you in *how* to approach the problem and then to evaluate *how well* your approach solves the problem.

The *criteria*—Software Mastery, Content, Format and Layout, and Process—represent the knowledge and skills you have gained that you can apply to solving the problem. The *levels of performance*—Professional Quality, Approaching Professional Quality, or Needs Quality Improvements—help you and your instructor evaluate your result.

	Your completed project is of Professional Quality if you:	Your completed project is Approaching Professional Quality if you:	Your completed project Needs Quality Improvements if you:
1-Software Mastery	Choose and apply the most appropriate skills, tools, and features and identify efficient methods to solve the problem.	Choose and apply some appropriate skills, tools, and features, but not in the most efficient manner.	Choose inappropriate skills, tools, or features, or are inefficient in solving the problem.
2-Content	Construct a solution that is clear and well organized, contains content that is accurate, appropriate to the audience and purpose, and is complete. Provide a solution that contains no errors of spelling, grammar, or style.	Construct a solution in which some components are unclear, poorly organized, inconsistent, or incomplete. Misjudge the needs of the audience. Have some errors in spelling, grammar, or style, but the errors do not detract from comprehension.	Construct a solution that is unclear, incomplete, or poorly organized, contains some inaccurate or inappropriate content, and contains many errors of spelling, grammar, or style. Do not solve the problem.
3-Format and Layout	Format and arrange all elements to communicate information and ideas, clarify function, illustrate relationships, and indicate relative importance.	Apply appropriate format and layout features to some elements, but not others. Overuse features, causing minor distraction.	Apply format and layout that does not communicate information or ideas clearly. Do not use format and layout features to clarify function, illustrate relationships, or indicate relative importance. Use available features excessively, causing distraction.
4-Process	Use an organized approach that integrates planning, development, self-assessment, revision, and reflection.	Demonstrate an organized approach in some areas, but not others; or, use an insufficient process of organization throughout.	Do not use an organized approach to solve the problem.

Outcomes-Based Assessments (Critical Thinking)

Apply a combination of the 1A and 1B skills.

GO! Think   **Project 1L Classes**

Project Files

For Project 1L, you will need the following file:

New blank Word document

You will save your document as:

Lastname_Firstname_1L_Classes

The Human Resources director at Sturgeon Point Productions needs to create a flyer to inform full-time employees of educational opportunities beginning in September. The courses are taught each year by industry professionals and are designed to improve skills in motion picture and television development and production. Employees who have been with Sturgeon Point Productions for at least two years are eligible to take the courses free of cost. The classes provide employees with opportunities to advance their careers, gain valuable skills, and achieve technical certification. All courses take place in Studio G. Interested employees should contact Elana Springs in Human Resources to sign up. Information meetings are being held at 5:30 according to the following schedule: television development on June 15; motion picture production on June 17; and recording services on June 21.

Create a flyer with basic information about the courses and information meetings. Be sure the flyer is easy to read and understand and has an attractive design. Save the document as **Lastname_Firstname_1L_Classes** and submit it as directed.

You have completed Project 1L   END

GO! Think	**Project 1M Store**	IRC
You and GO!	**Project 1N Family Flyer**	IRC
GO! Cumulative Team Project	**Project 1O Bell Orchid Hotels**	IRC

Creating Cover Letters and Using Tables to Create Resumes

2

WORD 2019

Dragan Grkic/Shutterstock

In This Chapter

GO! To Work with Word

Tables are useful for organizing and presenting data. Because a table is so easy to use, many individuals prefer to arrange tabular information in a Word table rather than setting a series of tabs. For example, you can use a table when you want to present rows and columns of information or to create a format for a document such as a resume.

When using Word to write business or personal letters, use a commonly approved letter format, and always use a clear writing style. You will make a good impression with prospective employers if you use a standard business letter style when you are writing a cover letter for a resume.

The projects in this chapter relate to the **College Career Center at Florida Port Community College** in St. Petersburg, Florida, a coastal port city near the Florida High Tech Corridor. With 60 percent of Florida's high tech companies and a third of the state's manufacturing companies located in the St. Petersburg and Tampa Bay areas, the college partners with businesses to play a vital role in providing a skilled workforce. The College Career Center assists students in exploring careers, finding internships, and applying for jobs. The Center offers workshops for resume and cover letter writing and for practice interviews.

PROJECT 2A Resume

Project Activities

In Activities 2.01 through 2.11, you will create a table to use as the format for a resume. The director of the Career Center, Mary Walker-Huelsman, will use this model when assisting students with building their resumes. Your completed document will look similar to Figure 2.1.

Project Files for **MyLab IT** Grader

1. In your storage location, create a folder named **Word Chapter 2**.
2. In your **MyLab IT** course, locate and click **Word 2A Resume**, click Download Materials, and then click Download All Files.
3. Extract the zipped folder to your Word Chapter 2 folder. Close the Grader download screens.
4. Take a moment to open the downloaded **Word_2A_Resume_Instructions**; note any recent updates to the book.

Project Results

GO! Project 2A
Where We're Going

Figure 2.1 Project 2A Resume

For Non-MyLab Submissions

For Project 2A, you will need:
New blank Word document
w02A_Experience

In your storage location, create a folder named **Word Chapter 2**
In your Word Chapter 2 folder, save your document as:
Lastname_Firstname_2A_Resume

After you have named and saved your document, on the next page, begin with Step 2.

ALERT   Because Office 365 is a cloud-based subscription service that receives continuous updates, you may encounter some variations in what appears on your screen and what is shown in this instruction. Microsoft Office 365 is fully installed on your PC or Mac; no internet access is necessary to create or edit documents. When you are connected to the internet, you will receive monthly upgrades and new features, so you always have the latest versions of Office apps as soon as they are available. Your subscription gives you continuous free access to the latest innovations and refinements.

GO! Learn How
Video W2-1

A *table* is an arrangement of information organized into rows and columns. The intersection of a row and a column in a table creates a box called a *cell* into which you can type. Tables are useful to present information in a logical and orderly format. Using a Word table to create a resume will assure that your information is presented in an easy-to-read format.

Activity 2.01 | Inserting a Table by Defining Table Dimensions

MOS
1.1.4, 1.2.3, 3.1.3

1 Navigate to your **Word Chapter 2** folder, and then double-click the Word file you downloaded from **MyLab IT** that displays your name—**Student_Word_2A_Resume**. In your blank Word document, if necessary, at the top click **Enable Editing**.

MAC TIP   If you are not submitting your file in MyLab IT, from the student data files that accompany this project, open the file Mac_w02A_Resume. This is a blank document with default settings necessary to complete this project.

To display group names, display the menu bar, click Word, click Preferences, click View, select Show group titles.

2 On the **Home tab**, in the **Paragraph group**, if necessary click **Show/Hide** ¶ to display the formatting marks. If the rulers do not display, click the View tab, and then in the Show group, select the Ruler check box.

3 On the **Insert tab**, in the **Header & Footer group**, click **Footer**, and then at the bottom of the list, click **Edit Footer**. On the ribbon, in the **Insert group**, click **Document Info**, click **File Name**, and then at the right end of the ribbon, click **Close Header and Footer**.

MAC TIP   On the Header & Footer tab, in the Insert group, click Field. Under Categories, click Document Information. Under Field names, click FileName. Click OK.

4 On the **Insert tab**, in the **Tables group**, click **Table**. In the **Insert Table** grid, in the fourth row, point to the second square, and notice that the cells are bordered in orange and *2x4 Table* displays at the top of the grid. Compare your screen with Figure 2.2.

MAC TIP   Cells are shaded in blue.

Figure 2.2

5 Click one time to create the table. Notice that formatting marks in each cell indicate the end of the contents of each cell; the mark to the right of each *row* indicates the row end. Compare your screen with Figure 2.3.

A table with four rows and two columns displays at the insertion point location, and the insertion point displays in the upper left cell. The table fills the width of the page from the left margin to the right margin. On the ribbon, Table Tools and two additional tabs—*Design* and *Layout*—display. Borders display around each cell in the table.

Figure 2.3

Activity 2.02 | Typing Text in a Table

In a Word table, each cell behaves similarly to a document. For example, as you type in a cell, when you reach the right border of the cell, wordwrap moves the text to the next line. When you press Enter, the insertion point moves down to a new paragraph in the same cell. You can also insert text from another document into a table cell.

There are numerous acceptable formats for resumes, many of which can be found in Business Communications textbooks. The layout in this project is suitable for a recent college graduate and places topics in the left column and details in the right column.

1 With the insertion point blinking in the first cell in the first row, type **OBJECTIVE** and then press Tab.

Pressing Tab moves the insertion point to the next cell in the row, or, if the insertion point is already in the last cell in the row, pressing Tab moves the insertion point to the first cell in the following row.

2 Type **Technology writing and editing position in the robotics industry, using research and advanced editing skills to communicate with customers.** Notice that the text wraps in the cell and the height of the row adjusts to fit the text.

3 Press Tab to move to the first cell in the second row. Type **SUMMARY OF QUALIFICATIONS** and then press Tab. Type the following, pressing Enter at the end of each line *except* the last line:

Two years' experience in robotics lab for Aerospace Instruction Team

Excellent interpersonal and communication skills

Proficiency using Microsoft Office and page layout and design software

Fluency in spoken and written Spanish

The default font and font size in a table are the same as for a document—Calibri 11 pt. The default line spacing in a table is single spacing with no space before or after paragraphs, which differs from the defaults for a document.

4 **Save** 🖫 your document, and then compare your screen with Figure 2.4.

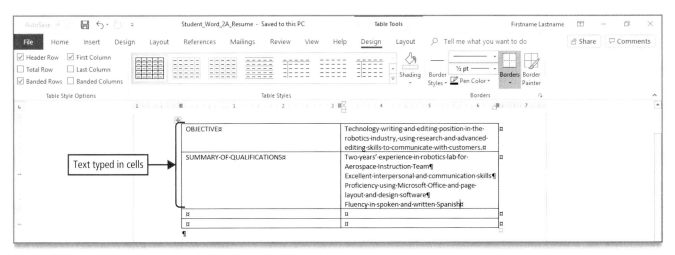

Figure 2.4

Activity 2.03 | Inserting Text From a File and Using Resume Assistant

Use the *Text from File* command to insert text from another file into your document. If you have text already created, this is much easier than retyping.

Resume Assistant enables you to view suggestions from *LinkedIn* to help you update your resume. LinkedIn is professional networking website that focuses on business and employment-oriented services and on which you can build and share your professional identity and connect with others in your field of interest. If you have not yet set up a LinkedIn profile, it's a good idea to do so to begin building your professional online presence. And it's a good place to find a new job!

1 Press Tab to move to the first cell in the third row. Type **EXPERIENCE** and then press Tab.

2 Be sure your insertion point is positioned in the second column to the left of the cell marker. Compare your screen with Figure 2.5.

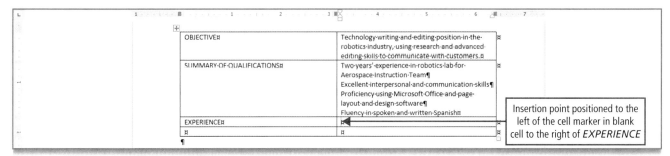

Figure 2.5

> **3** On the **Insert tab**, in the **Text group**, click the **Object button arrow**, and then click **Text from File**. Navigate to the downloaded files that accompany this project, select **w02A_Experience**, and then click **Insert**.
>
> All of the text from the w02A_Experience document is added to the document at the insertion point.

ANOTHER WAY Open the second document and select the text you want. Copy the text, and then paste at the desired location.

> **4** At this point, you might see a message indicating *Working on a resume?* On the **Review tab**, in the **Resume group**, click **Resume Assistant**. If you do not have the Resume Assistant, just examine Steps 5–9 and the Figures that follow and begin with Step 9.
>
> Resume Assistant is part of an Office 365 subscription. If your Resume Assistant button is dimmed, go to File > Options > General tab and then under **LinkedIn Features**, click *Enable (or Show) LinkedIn features in my Office applications*.

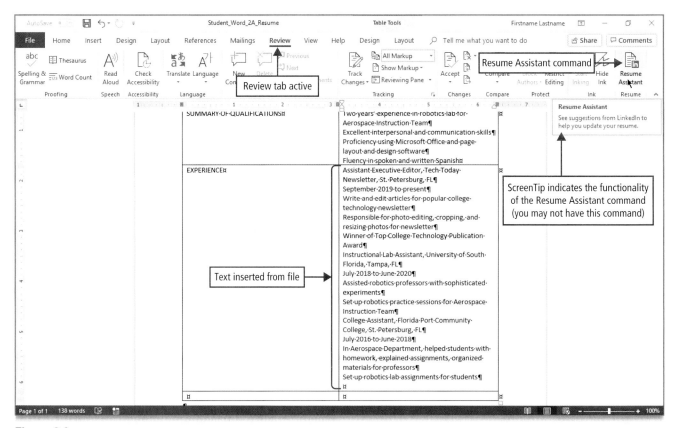

Figure 2.6

5 Click **Resume Assistant**. In the **Resume Assistant** pane on the right, if necessary, click **Get started**. Click **Add role**, and then type **Executive Editor** as shown in Figure 2.7.

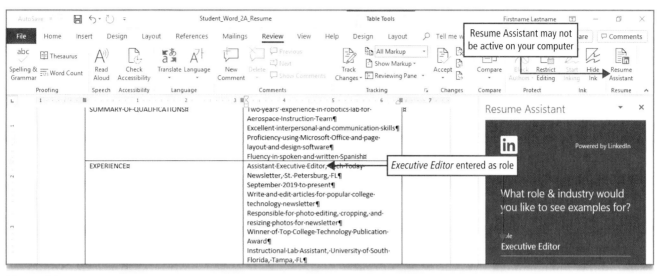

Figure 2.7

6 Click in **Add industry**, type **technology** and then click **Information Technology and Services**. Click **See examples**. Compare your screen with Figure 2.8.

Certainly you cannot copy someone else's resume. But you can see how people who are looking for the same type of job you are have talked about their experience. It can give you ideas about how you could word your own resume to make it more interesting and more descriptive of your experience.

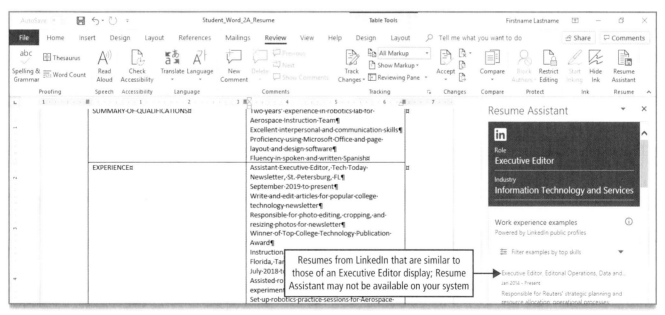

Figure 2.8

7 In the **Resume Assistant** pane, scroll down to view more resumes, interesting articles, and a link to get started on LinkedIn.

8 **Close** ☒ the **Resume Assistant** pane.

9 Locate, or click to position, the insertion point at the bottom of the text you just inserted, and then press ⟨Backspace⟩ one time to remove the blank line at the end of the inserted text. Compare your screen with Figure 2.9.

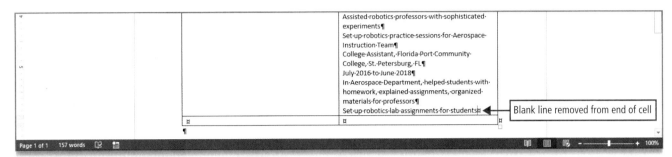

Figure 2.9

10 Press ⟨Tab⟩ to move to the first cell in the fourth row. Type **HONORS AND ACTIVITIES** and then press ⟨Tab⟩.

11 Type the following, pressing ⟨Enter⟩ at the end of each item *except* the last one:

Elected to Pi Tau Sigma, honor society for mechanical engineers
Qualified for Dean's List, six semesters
Student Mentor, helped other students in engineering programs

12 **Save** 🖫 your document, and then compare your screen with Figure 2.10.

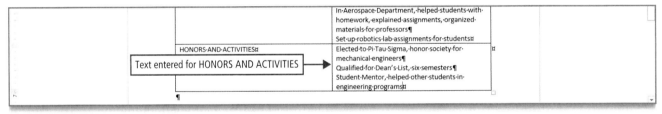

Figure 2.10

Activity 2.04 | Creating Bulleted Lists in a Table

2.2.2, 3.3.1, 3.3.4

1 Press ⟨Ctrl⟩ + ⟨Home⟩ to move to the top of your document, and then in the cell to the right of *SUMMARY OF QUALIFICATIONS*, select all of the text.

MAC TIP Press ⟨command ⌘⟩ + ⟨fn⟩ + ⟨←⟩.

2 On the **Home tab**, in the **Paragraph group**, click **Bullets** 🔽.

The selected text displays as a bulleted list to make each qualification more distinctive.

3 In the **Paragraph group**, click **Decrease Indent** one time to align the bullets at the left edge of the cell.

4 Scroll as necessary so that you can view the entire *EXPERIENCE* and *HONORS AND ACTIVITIES* sections on your screen. With the bulleted text still selected, in the **Clipboard group**, double-click **Format Painter**.

5 In the cell to the right of *EXPERIENCE*, select the third, fourth, and fifth paragraphs—beginning with *Write* and *Responsible* and *Winner*—to create the same style of bulleted list as you did in the previous step.

6 In the same cell, under *Instructional Lab Assistant*, select the two paragraphs that begin *Assisted* and *Set up* to create another bulleted list aligned at the left edge of the cell.

7 In the same cell, select the paragraphs that begin *In Aerospace* and *Set up robotics* to create the same type of bulleted list.

8 In the cell below, select the paragraphs that begin *Elected*, *Qualified*, and *Student* to create a bulleted list.

9 Press [Esc] to turn off the **Format Painter**. Click anywhere in the table to deselect the text; if blue lines display, right-click over them and click Ignore Once. **Save** 🖫 your document, and then compare your screen with Figure 2.11.

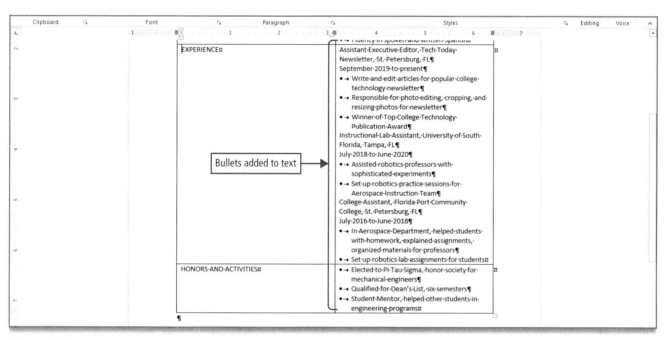

Figure 2.11

Format a Table

GO! Learn How
Video W2-2

Use Word's formatting tools to make your tables attractive and easy to read. Types of formatting you can add to a table include changing the row height and the column width, removing or adding borders, increasing or decreasing the paragraph or line spacing, and enhancing the text.

Activity 2.05 | **Changing the Width of Table Columns and Using AutoFit**

3.2.4

When you create a table, all of the columns are of equal width. In this Activity, you will change the width of the columns.

1 Press [Ctrl] + [Home]. Click anywhere in the first column, and then on the ribbon, under **Table Tools**, click the **Layout tab**. In the **Cell Size group**, notice the **Width** box, which displays the width of the active column.

2 Look at the horizontal ruler and locate the **1.5-inch mark**. Then, in the table, in any row, point to the vertical border between the two columns to display the ⊹ pointer.

3 Hold down the left mouse button and drag the column border to the left until the white arrow on the ruler is at approximately **1.5 inches on the horizontal ruler** and then release the left mouse button.

4 In the **Cell Size group**, click the **Width box down spin arrow** as necessary to set the column width to **1.4"** and notice that the right border of the table moves to the left.

> Adjusting column width by dragging a column border adjusts only the width of the column; adjusting column width with the Width box simultaneously adjusts the right border of the table.

5 In the **Cell Size group**, click **AutoFit**, and then click **AutoFit Window** to stretch the table across the page within the margins so that the right border of the table is at the right margin. **Save** and then compare your screen with Figure 2.12.

ANOTHER WAY You can adjust column widths by dragging the Move Table Column markers on the ruler. To maintain the right border of the table at the right margin, hold down Shift while dragging. To display measurements on the ruler, hold down Alt while dragging the marker.

Figure 2.12

MORE KNOWLEDGE **Changing Column Widths**

You will typically get the best results if you change the column widths starting at the left side of the table, especially in tables with three or more columns. Word can also calculate the best column widths for you. To do this, select the table. Then, on the Layout tab, in the Cell Size group, click the AutoFit button and click AutoFit Contents.

Activity 2.06 | Using One-Click Row/Column Insertion to Modify Table Dimensions

One of the most common actions you will take in a table is adding another row or another column. By using *One-click Row/Column Insertion* you can do so in context by pointing to the left or top edge where you want the row or column to appear and then clicking the ⊕ button to add it.

1 Scroll to view the lower portion of the table. On the left border of the table, *point* to the upper left corner of the cell containing the text *HONORS AND ACTIVITIES* to display the **One-click Row/Column Insertion** button. Compare your screen with Figure 2.13.

MAC TIP In your table, click where you want to add a row or column. To the right of the Table Design tab, click the Layout tab, and then use the commands in the Rows & Columns group.

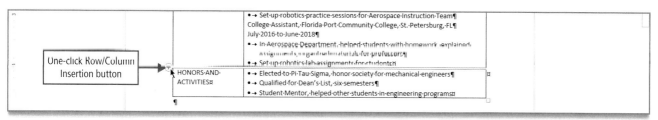

Figure 2.13

2 Click ⊕ one time to insert a new row above the *HONORS AND ACTIVITIES* row.

3 Click in the left cell of the new row, type **EDUCATION** and then press [Tab].

4 Type the following, pressing [Enter] at the end of each item *except* the last one:

> **University of South Florida, Tampa, FL**
> **Bachelor of Science, Mechanical Engineering, June 2020**
> **Florida Port Community College, St. Petersburg, FL**
> **Associate of Arts, Journalism, June 2018**

5 **Save** 🖫 your document, and then compare your screen with Figure 2.14.

Figure 2.14

🔄 **ANOTHER WAY** When the insertion point is in the last cell in the bottom row of a table, you can add a row by pressing the TAB key; the insertion point will display in the first cell of the new row.

Activity 2.07 | Adjusting Cell Margins and Merging Table Cells

3.2.3

Cell margins refer to the space inside a table cell between the text and the cell borders—top, bottom, left, and right. By increasing the cell margins, you can avoid having text so close to the cell borders that it is difficult to read.

The title of a table typically spans all of the columns. In this Activity, you will increase the cell margins and then merge cells so that you can position the personal information across both columns.

1 Click anywhere in the top row of the table, and then on the **Table Tools Layout tab**, in the **Alignment group**, click **Cell Margins**.

The Table Options dialog box displays showing the default cell margins.

2 In the **Table Options** dialog box, use the spin box arrows to change the **Top** cell margin to **0.04** and the **Bottom** cell margin to **0.04**. Compare your screen with Figure 2.15.

Figure 2.15

> **3** Click **OK**, and then compare your screen with Figure 2.16.
>
> The space between the text and the top and bottom of each cell increases, making it easier to read the text with in the table.

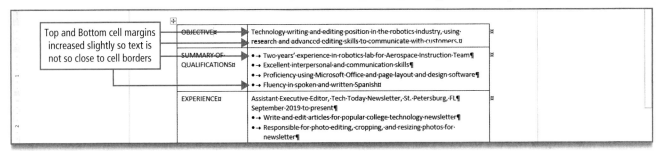

Figure 2.16

> **4** Click anywhere in the top row of the table, and then on the **Table Tools Layout tab**, in the **Rows & Columns group**, click **Insert Above**.
>
> A new row displays above the row that contained the insertion point, and the new row is selected. This is another method to insert rows and columns in a table; use this method to insert a new row at the top of a table.

ANOTHER WAY   Right-click in the top row, point to Insert, and then click Insert Rows Above.

> **5** Be sure the two cells in the top row are selected; if necessary, drag across both cells to select them.
>
> **6** On the **Table Tools Layout tab**, in the **Merge group**, click **Merge Cells**.
>
> The cell border between the two cells no longer displays.

ANOTHER WAY   Right-click the selected row and click Merge Cells on the shortcut menu.

Activity 2.08 | Setting Tabs in a Table

1 With the merged cell still selected, on the **Home tab**, in the **Paragraph group**, click the **Dialog Box Launcher** ⌐ to display the **Paragraph** dialog box.

⊡ **MAC TIP** To display the Paragraph dialog box, on the Home tab, in the Paragraph group, click Line and Paragraph Spacing. Click Line Spacing Options.

2 On the **Indents and Spacing tab**, in the lower left corner, click **Tabs** to display the **Tabs** dialog box.

3 Under **Tab stop position**, type **6.5** and then under **Alignment**, click the **Right** option button. Click **Set**, and then click **OK** to close the dialog box.

⊡ **MAC TIP** Instead of Set, click the add button (+).

4 Type **Josh Hayes** Hold down [Ctrl] and then press [Tab]. Notice that the insertion point moves to the right-aligned tab stop at 6.5".

In a Word table, you must use [Ctrl] + [Tab] to move to a tab stop, because pressing [Tab] is reserved for moving the insertion point from cell to cell.

5 Type **(727) 555-0313** and then press [Enter].

6 Type **1541 Dearborn Lane, St. Petersburg, FL 33713** Hold down [Ctrl] and then press [Tab].

7 Type **jhayes@alcona.net Save** 🖫 your document, and then compare your screen with Figure 2.17.

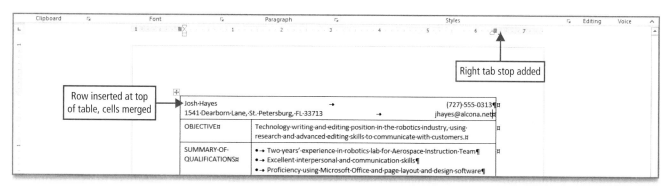

Figure 2.17

Activity 2.09 | Using Spacing After in a Table

1 In the first row of the table, select the name *Josh Hayes*, and then from the mini toolbar, apply **Bold** [B] and change the **Font Size** to **16**.

⊡ **MAC TIP** Use ribbon commands on the Home tab, in the Font group.

2 Under *Josh Hayes*, click anywhere in the second line of text, which contains the address and email address.

3 On the **Layout tab**, in the **Paragraph group**, click the **Spacing After up spin arrow** three times to add **18 pt** spacing between the first row of the table and the second row. Compare your screen with Figure 2.18.

> This action separates the personal information from the body of the resume and adds focus to the name.

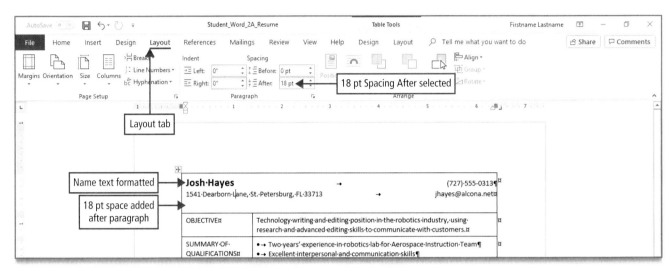

Figure 2.18

4 By using the technique you just practiced, in the second column, click in the last line of *every cell* and add **18 pt Spacing After** including the last row; later you will add a border to the bottom of the table, so spacing will be needed between the last row and the border.

5 In the second row, point to the word *OBJECTIVE*, hold down the left mouse button, and then drag downward in the first column only to select all the headings in uppercase letters. From the mini toolbar, click **Bold** B.

NOTE   **Selecting Only One Column**

When you drag downward to select the first column, a fast mouse might also begin to select the second column when you reach the bottom. If this happens, drag upward slightly to deselect the second column and select only the first column.

6 In the cell to the right of *EXPERIENCE*, without selecting the following comma, select *Assistant Executive Editor* and then on the mini toolbar, click **Bold** B.

7 In the same cell, apply **Bold** B to the other job titles—*Instructional Lab Assistant* and *College Assistant*.

8 In the cell to the right of *EDUCATION*, apply **Bold** B to *University of South Florida, Tampa, FL* and *Florida Port Community College, St. Petersburg, FL*.

9 In the same cell, click anywhere in the line beginning *Bachelor*. On the **Layout tab**, in the **Paragraph group**, click the **Spacing After up spin arrow** two times to add **12 pt** spacing after the paragraph.

10 In the cell to the right of *EXPERIENCE*, under *Assistant Executive Editor*, click anywhere in the third bulleted item, and then add **12 pt Spacing After** the item.

11 In the same cell, repeat this process for the last bulleted item under *Instructional Lab Assistant*.

12 Scroll to view the top of your document, **Save** 🖫 your document, and then compare your screen with Figure 2.19.

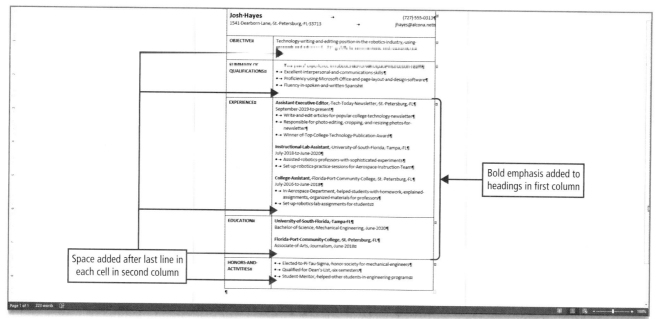

Figure 2.19

Activity 2.10 | Modifying Table Borders, Using Spacing Before, and Viewing Gridlines in a Table

MOS
1.3.2

When you create a table, all of the cells have black 1/2-point, single-line, solid-line borders that print unless you remove them. Most resumes do not display any cell borders. A border at the top and bottom of the resume, however, is attractive and adds a professional look to the document.

1 Scroll as necessary to view the top margin area above the table, and then click anywhere in the top row of the table. In the upper left corner of the table, notice the **table move handle** ⊞, which indicates the table is active.

2 On the **Table Tools Layout tab**, in the **Table group**, click **Select**, and then click **Select Table**. Notice that the row markers at the end of each row are also selected.

Shaded row markers indicate that the entire row is selected.

🔄 **ANOTHER WAY** Click the table move handle ⊞ to select the table.

3 On the ribbon, click the **Table Tools Design tab**. In the **Borders group**, click the **Borders button arrow**, and then click **No Border**.

The black borders no longer display.

4 Click the **Borders button arrow** again, and then at the bottom of the menu, if necessary, click **View Gridlines** to view the gridlines in your table. Compare your screen with Figure 2.20.

When you turn off the display of borders, you can show table gridlines to help you see where each cell is located. Table gridlines do not print, but can be useful in visualizing a table in which borders do not display. This command is a toggle—clicking it once turns on the display of gridlines, clicking it again turns off the display of gridlines.

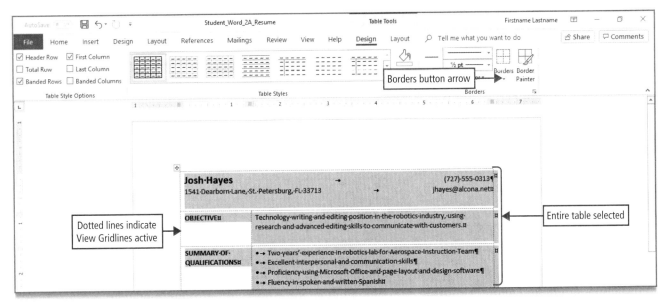

Figure 2.20

5 Click the **Borders button arrow** again, and then at the bottom of the menu, click **View Gridlines** to cancel the display of gridlines.

6 Press Ctrl + P, which is the keyboard shortcut to view the **Print Preview**, and notice that no borders display in the preview. Then, press **Back** ⊕ to return to your document.

MAC TIP   Press command ⌘ + P; then click Cancel.

7 With the table still selected, on the **Table Tools Design tab**, in the **Borders group**, click the **Borders button arrow**, and then at the bottom of the **Borders** gallery, click **Borders and Shading**.

8 In the **Borders and Shading** dialog box, on the **Borders tab**, under **Setting**, click **Custom**. Under **Style**, scroll down about one-third of the way, and then click the style with a **thick upper line and a thin lower line**.

9 In the **Preview** box at the right, point to the *top* border of the small preview and click one time.

ANOTHER WAY   Click the top border button, which is one of the buttons that surround the Preview.

10 Under **Style**, scroll down if necessary, click the opposite style—with the **thin upper line and the thick lower line**, and then in the **Preview** box, click the *bottom* border of the preview. Compare your screen with Figure 2.21.

Figure 2.21

11 Click **OK**, click anywhere to cancel the selection, and then notice that there is only a small amount of space between the upper border and the first line of text.

12 Click anywhere in the text *Josh Hayes*, and then on the **Layout tab**, in the **Paragraph group**, click the **Spacing Before up spin arrow** as necessary to add **6 pt** spacing before the first paragraph.

13 Click the **File tab**, and then on the left click **Print** to display the Print Preview. Compare your screen with Figure 2.22.

MAC TIP Display the menu bar, click File, click Print.

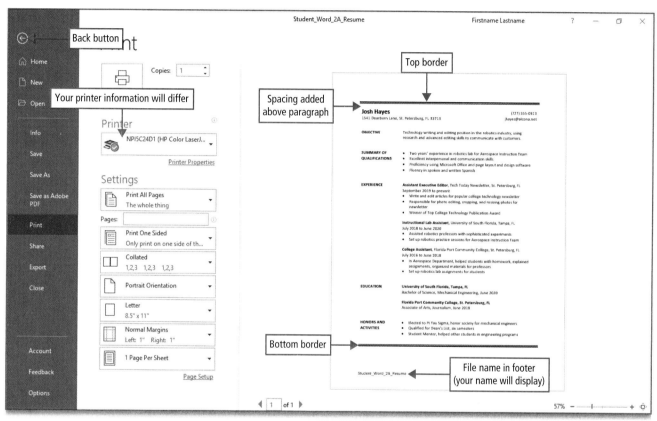

Figure 2.22

14 On the left, click **Info**, and then in the lower right corner, click **Show All Properties**. In the **Tags** box, type **resume, Word table** and in the **Subject** box, type your course name and section number. In the **Author** box, be sure your name is indicated and edit if necessary.

MAC TIP On the menu bar, click File, click Properties, click the Summary tab. For Tags, use Keywords.

15 Press **Back** ⊕ to return to your document, and then on the Quick Access Toolbar, click **Save** 🖫.

MAC TIP Click OK to return to your document.

16 In the upper right corner of the Word window, click **Close** ✕.

> **For Non-MyLab Submissions Determine What Your Instructor Requires for Submission**
> As directed by your instructor, submit your completed Word file.

17 In **MyLab IT**, locate and click the Grader Project **Word 2A Resume**. In **step 3**, under **Upload Completed Assignment**, click **Choose File**. In the **Open** dialog box, navigate to your **Word Chapter 2 folder**, and then click your **Student_Word_2A_Resume** file one time to select it. In the lower right corner of the **Open** dialog box, click **Open**.

> The name of your selected file displays above the Upload button.

18 To submit your file to **MyLab IT** for grading, click **Upload**, wait a moment for a green **Success!** message, and then in **step 4**, click the blue **Submit for Grading** button. Click **Close Assignment** to return to your list of **Course Materials**.

MORE KNOWLEDGE | **Converting a Table to Text**

You can convert a table to regular text and choose which text character to use to separate the columns. To do so, on the Table Tools Layout tab, in the Data group, click Convert to Text.

You have completed Project 2A | **END**

Objective 3 | Present a Word Document Online

ALERT | **This Activity in Objective 3 is Optional**

This Activity is optional. Check with your instructor to see if you should complete this Activity. This Activity is not included in the **MyLab IT** Grader system for this project; however, you may want to practice this on your own.

GO! Learn How

Video W2-3

Office Presentation Service enables you to present your Word document to others who can watch in a web browser. No preliminary setup is necessary; Word creates a link to your document that you can share with others via email or instant message. Anyone to whom you send the link can see your document while you are presenting online.

Individuals watching your presentation can navigate within the document independently of you or others in the presentation, so they can use a mouse, keyboard, or touch input to move around in the document while you are presenting it. If an individual is viewing a different portion of the document than the presenter, an alert displays on his or her screen. To return to the portion of the document that the presenter is showing, a Follow Presenter button displays.

While you are presenting, you can make minor edits to the document. If you want to share a copy of the document to the presentation attendees, you can select *Enable remote viewers to download the document* when you start the presentation. You can also share any meeting notes that you or others created in OneNote.

Activity 2.11 | Presenting a Word Document Online

If you are creating your own resume, it will be valuable to get feedback from your friends, instructors, or Career Center advisors before you submit your resume for a job application. In this Activity, you will present the resume document online for others to look at.

NOTE | **You must sign in with your Microsoft account.**

You must sign in with your Microsoft account, even if you are already signed in, to present your document online.

1 With your resume document displayed, click **Save** 🖫.

2 Click the **File tab**, on the left click **Share**, and then under **Share**, click **Present Online**

3 On the right, click **Present Online**. Wait a moment for the service to connect, and then compare your screen with Figure 2.23.

> There are several methods to send your meeting invitation to others. You can click Copy Link to copy and paste the hyperlink; for example, you could copy the link into a *Skype* window. Skype is a Microsoft product with which you can make voice calls, make video calls, transfer files, or send messages—including instant messages and text messages—over the internet.
>
> You can also select Send in Email, which will open your Outlook email window if you use Outlook as your mail client.

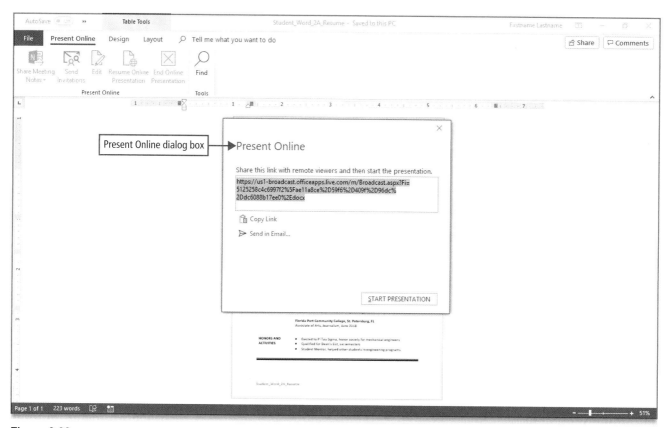

Figure 2.23

4 If you want to do so, identify a classmate or friend who is at a computer and available to view your presentation, select one of the methods to share, click **START PRESENTATION**, and when you are finished, on the ribbon, click **End Online Presentation**. Otherwise, **Close** ☒ the **Present Online** dialog box.

> If you present online, you will need to initiate voice communication using Skype or by simply phoning the other person.

You have completed the optional portion of this project | END

»»» GO! With Google Docs

Objective	Edit a Resume in Google Docs

ALERT   Working with Web-Based Applications and Services

Computer programs and services on the web receive continuous updates and improvements, so the steps to complete this web-based Activity may differ from the ones shown. You can often look at the screens and the information presented to determine how to complete the Activity.

If you do not already have a Google account, you will need to create one before you begin this Activity. Go to http://google.com and, in the upper right corner, click Sign In. On the Sign In screen, click Create Account. On the Create your Google Account page, complete the form, read and agree to the Terms of Service and Privacy Policy, and then click Next step. On the Welcome screen, click Get Started.

Activity | Editing a Resume in Google Docs

In this Activity, you will use Google Docs to open and edit a Word table containing a resume similar to the resume you created in Project 2A.

1 From the desktop, open your browser, navigate to **http://google.com**, and then click the **Google apps** menu ⊞. Click **Drive**, and then if necessary, sign in to your Google account.

2 Open your **GO! Web Projects** folder—or click New to create and then open this folder if necessary.

3 In the upper left corner, click **New**, and then click **File upload**. In the **Open** dialog box, navigate to the files you downloaded with this chapter, and then in the **File List**, double-click to open **w02_2A_Web**.

4 When the upload is complete, in the **Google Drive file list**, double-click the document to open it in Google Docs. If necessary, at the top of the screen, click Open with Google Docs.

5 Click anywhere in the word *OBJECTIVE*. On the menu bar, click **Format**, point to **Table**, and then click **Insert row above**. In the first cell of the new row, type **Daniela Frank** Select the text you just typed, and then on the toolbar, click the **Font size arrow**, and then click **18**.

6 Press [Tab] to move to the second cell of the new row, and then type **1343 Siena Lane, Deerfield, WI 53531** Hold down [Shift] and press [Enter]. Type **(608) 555-0588** Hold down [Shift] and press [Enter]. Type **dfrank@alcona.net** Select all the text in the second cell that you just typed, and then on toolbar, locate and click **Right align**.

7 Drag to select the two cells in the top row, right-click over the selection, and then click **Merge cells**. With the newly merged cell still selected, right-click over the selection again, and then click **Table properties**.

8 Under **Cell background color**, click the arrow, and then in the top row, click the seventh color—**light gray 1**. Click **OK**.

9 Scroll down and click anywhere in the *EXPERIENCE* cell. Right-click, and then click **Insert row below**. In the first cell of the new row, type **EDUCATION**

10 Press [Tab] to move to the second cell in the new row, and then type **Madison Area Technical College, Madison, WI** Hold down [Shift] and press [Enter].

11 On the toolbar, click **Bold** [B] to turn off bold formatting, and then type **Associate of Arts in Information Systems, June 2020** and press [Enter].

12 Press [Ctrl] + [P] to view the Print Preview, and then compare your screen with Figure A.

13 In the upper left corner, click **Cancel** to close the Print Preview. Submit the file as directed by your instructor. In the upper right, click your user name, and then click **Sign out**. **Close** your browser window. Your file is automatically saved in your Google Drive.

Figure A

PROJECT 2B

Cover Letter and Envelope

Project Activities

In Activities 2.12 through 2.20, you will create a letterhead, and then use the letterhead to create a cover letter to accompany a resume. Optionally, in Activities 2.21 through 2.24 you will format and print an envelope, change a style set, create a Word template for a letterhead, and use Word's Learning Tools. Your completed cover letter will look similar to Figure 2.24.

Project Files for MyLab IT Grader

1. In your **MyLab IT** course, locate and click **Word 2B Cover Letter**, Download Materials, and then Download All Files.
2. Extract the zipped folder to your Word Chapter 2 folder. Close the Grader download screens.
3. Take a moment to open the downloaded **Word_2B_Cover_Letter_Instructions**; note any recent updates to the book.

Project Results

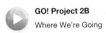
GO! Project 2B
Where We're Going

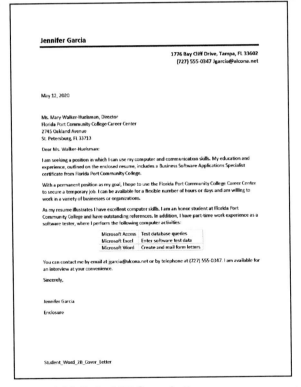

Figure 2.24 Project 2B Cover Letter

For Non-MyLab Submissions
For Project 2B, you will need:
New blank Word document
w02B_Cover_Letter_Text

In your **Word Chapter 2** folder, save your document as:
Lastname_Firstname_2B_Cover_Letter

After you have named and saved your document, on the next page, begin with Step 2.

ALERT   Because Office 365 is a cloud-based subscription service that receives continuous updates, you may encounter some variations in what appears on your screen and what is shown in this instruction. Microsoft Office 365 is fully installed on your PC or Mac; no internet access is necessary to create or edit documents. When you are connected to the internet, you will receive monthly upgrades and new features, so you always have the latest versions of Office apps as soon as they are available. Your subscription gives you continuous free access to the latest innovations and refinements.

GO! Learn How
Video W2-4

A *letterhead* is the personal or company information that displays at the top of a letter, and which commonly includes a name, address, and contact information. The term also refers to a piece of paper imprinted with such information at the top.

Activity 2.12 | Inserting a Manual Line Break

In this Activity, you will create a personal letterhead for the top of your cover letter.

1 Navigate to your **Word Chapter 2 folder**, and then double-click the Word file you downloaded from **MyLab IT** that displays your name—**Student_Word_2B_Cover_Letter**. If necessary, at the top click **Enable Editing**.

2 On the **Design tab**, in the **Document Formatting group**, click **Paragraph Spacing**. Notice that **Default** is shaded in blue indicating this is the active Style Set for paragraphs in this document. (If this is not the active style set, click Default to make it active.)

A *style set* is a collection of character and paragraph formatting that is stored and named.

MAC TIP   If you are not submitting your file in MyLab IT, from the student data files that accompany this project, open the file Mac_w02B_Cover_Letter and begin with that file instead of a blank document. If group names do not display on your ribbon, display the menu bar, click Word, click Preferences, under Authoring and Proofing tools, click View, and then at the bottom of the View dialog box, select the Show group titles check box. Close the dialog box.

3 *Point* to **Default**, and then compare your screen with Figure 2.25.

MAC TIP   No ScreenTip displays.

This is the default paragraph spacing for a new Word document when you open Word and click Blank document, which is 0 points of blank space before a paragraph, 8 points of blank space following a paragraph, and line spacing of 1.08. This is also referred to as the Normal style. Microsoft's research shows that these settings make documents easier to read both on paper and on a screen.

Figure 2.25

4 On the list, under **Built-In**, *point* to **No Paragraph Space**, and then examine the ScreenTip. Compare your screen with Figure 2.26.

The *No Paragraph Space* style inserts *no* extra space before or after a paragraph and uses line spacing of 1. This is the format commonly referred to as *single spacing*.

Some Business Communications texts describe business letters, for example a cover letter, in terms of single spacing. However, it is more modern, and will make your documents easier to read, if you use Word's default paragraph spacing for all of your documents.

Single spacing—where you must press Enter two times to create a new paragraph and where the lines of text within a paragraph are very close together—is an old-fashioned method designed for typewriters in the previous century!

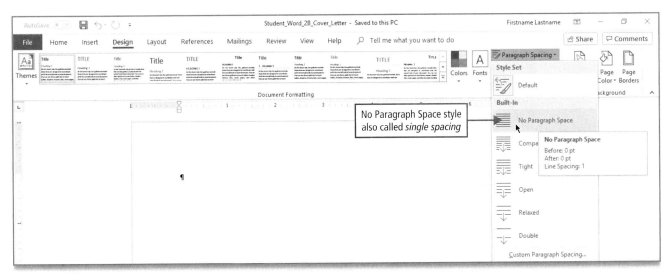

Figure 2.26

5 Be sure that **Default** is the active style set, and then click anywhere outside of the menu to close the menu without making any changes.

6 As the first paragraph, type **Jennifer Garcia** and then press Enter.

7 Type **1776 Bay Cliff Drive, Tampa, FL 33602** hold down Shift and then press Enter. Compare your screen with Figure 2.27.

Holding down Shift while pressing Enter inserts a *manual line break*, which moves the text to the right of the insertion point to a new line while keeping the text in the same paragraph. A *line break indicator*, in the shape of a bent arrow, indicates a manual line break.

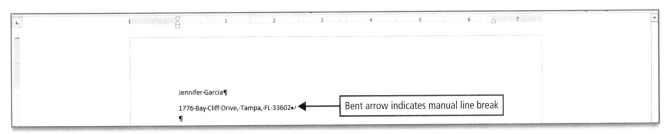

Figure 2.27

8 Type **(727) 555-0347 jgarcia@alcona.net** and then press Enter. If the email address changes to blue text, right-click the address, and then click **Remove Hyperlink**. (Mac users: Point to the beginning of the hyperlink, click AutoCorrect Options button, click Undo Hyperlink.)

9 Select the first paragraph—*Jennifer Garcia*—and then apply **Bold** B and change the **Font Size** to **16**.

10 Select the two address lines that form the second paragraph. Apply **Bold** **B** and change the **Font Size** to **12**.

11 With the two-line paragraph still selected, on the **Home tab**, in the **Paragraph group**, click **Align Right** ▤.

ANOTHER WAY Press Ctrl + R to align text to the right.

Activity 2.13 | Applying a Bottom Border to a Paragraph

1 Click anywhere in the first paragraph—*Jennifer Garcia*. In the **Paragraph group**, click the **Borders button arrow** ▦, and then at the bottom, click **Borders and Shading**.

2 In the **Borders and Shading** dialog box, on the **Borders tab**, under **Style**, be sure the first style—a single solid line—is selected.

3 Click the **Width arrow**, and then click **3 pt**. To the right, under **Preview**, click the bottom border of the diagram. Under **Apply to**, be sure *Paragraph* displays. Compare your screen with Figure 2.28.

Figure 2.28

ANOTHER WAY Under Preview, click the bottom border button ▥. Mac users: press command ⌘ + R.

4 Click **OK** to display a 3 pt line below *Jennifer Garcia*, which extends from the left margin to the right margin.

The border is a paragraph command and uses the same margins as the paragraph to which it is applied.

5 On the **Insert tab**, in the **Header & Footer** group, click **Footer**, at the bottom click **Edit Footer**, and then in the **Insert group**, click **Document Info**. Click **File Name**, and then click **Close Header and Footer**.

MAC TIP On the Header & Footer tab, in the Insert group, click Field, click Document Information, click FileName.

6 **Save** 🖫 your document.

GO! Learn How
Video W2-5

A ***cover letter*** is a document that you send with your resume to provide additional information about your skills and experience. An effective cover letter includes specific information about why you are qualified for the job for which you are applying. Use the cover letter to explain your interest in the position and the organization.

Business letters follow a standard format and contain the following parts: the current date, referred to as the ***dateline***; the name and address of the person receiving the letter, referred to as the ***inside address***; a greeting, referred to as the ***salutation***; the text of the letter, usually referred to as the ***body*** of the letter; a closing line, referred to as the ***complimentary closing***; and the ***writer's identification***, which includes the name of the writer and sometimes the writer's job title and which is also referred to as the ***writer's signature block***.

Some letters also include the initials of the person who prepared the letter, an optional ***subject line*** that describes the purpose of the letter, or a list of ***enclosures***—documents included with the letter.

Activity 2.14 │ Adding AutoCorrect Entries

Word's ***AutoCorrect*** feature corrects commonly misspelled words automatically; for example *teh* instead of *the*. If you have words that you frequently misspell, you can add them to the list for automatic correction.

1 ▶ Click the **File tab** to display **Backstage** view. On the left, click **Options** to display the **Word Options** dialog box.

💻 **MAC TIP**   Display the menu bar, click Tools, click AutoCorrect; move to Step 3.

2 ▶ On the left side of the **Word Options** dialog box, click **Proofing**, and then under **AutoCorrect options**, click the **AutoCorrect Options** button.

3 ▶ In the **AutoCorrect** dialog box, click the **AutoCorrect tab**. Under **Replace**, type **resumee** and under **With**, type **resume**

If another student has already added this AutoCorrect entry, a Replace button will display.

4 ▶ Click **Add**. If the entry already exists, click Replace instead, and then click Yes.

5 ▶ In the **AutoCorrect** dialog box, under **Replace**, with the existing text highlighted in blue, type **computr** and under **With**, type **computer** Compare your screen with Figure 2.29.

Figure 2.29

6 Click **Add** (or Replace) and then click **OK** two times to close the dialog boxes.

Activity 2.15 | Inserting the Current Date and Creating a Cover Letter

Typically you send a cover letter with your resume to provide additional information about your skills and experience. An effective cover letter includes specific information about why you are qualified for the job for which you are applying. Use the cover letter to explain your interest in the position and the organization.

By using the *Date & Time* command, you can select from a variety of formats to insert the current date and time in a document.

For cover letters, there are a variety of accepted letter formats that you will see in reference manuals and Business Communications texts. The one used in this chapter is a block format following the style in Courtland Bovee and John Thill, *Business Communication Today*, Fourteenth Edition, Pearson, 2018, p. 584.

1 Press Ctrl + End to move the insertion point to the blank line below the letterhead, and then press Enter two times.

🖥 **MAC TIP**   Press command ⌘ + fn + →.

2 On the **Insert tab**, in the **Text group**, click **Insert Date & Time**, and then click the third date format. Click **OK** to create the dateline. Compare your screen with Figure 2.30

Most Business Communication texts recommend that the dateline be positioned at least 0.5 inch below the letterhead; or, position the dateline approximately 2 inches from the top edge of the paper.

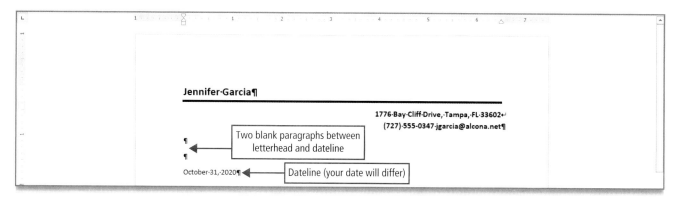

Figure 2.30

3 Press Enter two times. Type **Ms. Mary Walker-Huelsman, Director** and press Enter.

The recommended space between the dateline and inside address varies slightly among experts in Business Communication texts and office reference manuals. However, all indicate that the space can be from 2 to 10 blank paragraphs (sometimes referred to as blank *lines* in a single-spaced document) depending on the length of your letter. You can adjust the number of blank paragraphs to balance the layout of your letter.

4 Type **Florida Port Community College Career Center** and press Enter. Type **2745 Oakland Avenue** and press Enter.

5 Type **St. Petersburg, FL 33713** and press Enter.

6 Select the first three lines of the inside address, and then on the **Layout tab**, in the **Paragraph group**, change **Spacing After** to **0**. Compare you screen with Figure 2.31.

Two parts of a business letter—the inside address and the writer's signature block if it is more than one line—are commonly described in terms of single-spaced paragraphs where there is no blank space following a paragraph. By changing the spacing after paragraphs for all but the last line of the inside address, you will be following the prescribed format of a letter.

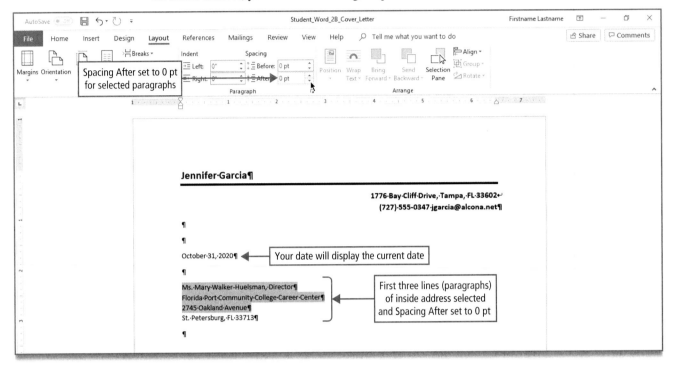

Figure 2.31

7 Click in the blank paragraph below the inside address. Type the salutation **Dear Ms. Walker-Huelsman:** and then press `Enter`.

Because the Word default settings automatically apply 8 pt spacing after a paragraph, pressing `Enter` one time to begin a new paragraph inserts appropriate space between the parts of the letter.

8 Type, exactly as shown, the following opening paragraph that includes an intentional word usage error: **I am seek a position in which I can use my** and press `Spacebar`. Type, exactly as shown, **computr** and then watch *computr* as you press `Spacebar`.

The AutoCorrect feature recognizes the misspelled word, and then changes *computr* to *computer* when you press `Spacebar`, `Enter`, or type a punctuation mark.

9 Type the following, including the misspelled last word: **and communication skills. My education and experience, outlined on the enclosed resumee** and then type **,** (a comma). Notice that when you type the comma, AutoCorrect replaces *resumee* with *resume*.

10 Press `Spacebar`, and then complete the paragraph by typing **includes a Business Software Applications Specialist certificate from FPCC.** Compare your screen with Figure 2.32.

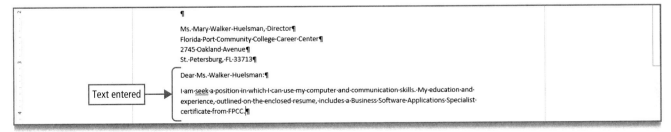

Figure 2.32

11 Press Enter. On the **Insert tab**, in the **Text group**, click the **Object button arrow**, and then click **Text from File**. From the files downloaded with this project, locate and **Insert** the file **w02B_Cover_Letter_Text**.

> Some of the words in the cover letter text display red squiggles and double blue underlines. You may also see brown dotted underlines. These indicate potential spelling, grammar, or writing style errors, and will be addressed before the end of this project.

12 Scroll as necessary to display the lower half of the letter on your screen, and be sure your insertion point is positioned in the blank paragraph at the end of the document.

13 Type **Sincerely,** as the complimentary closing, and then press Enter two times to leave space between the complimentary closing and the writer's identification.

> This allows space for the writer to sign the letter above his or her name.

14 Type **Jennifer Garcia** as the writer's identification, and then press Enter.

15 Type **Enclosure** to indicate that a document is included with the letter. **Save** 🖫 your document, and then compare your screen with Figure 2.33.

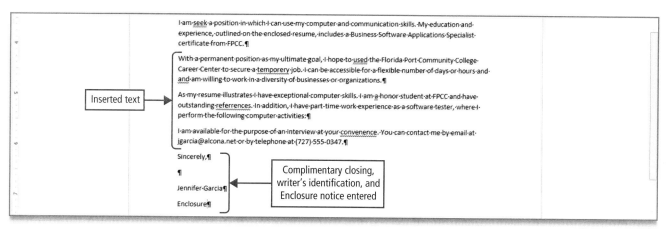

Figure 2.33

Activity 2.16 | Finding and Replacing Text

MOS
1.1.1, 2.1.1

Use the Find command to locate text in a document quickly. Use the Find and Replace command to make the same change, or to make more than one change at a time, in a document.

1 Press Ctrl + Home to position the insertion point at the beginning of the document.

> Because a find operation—or a find and replace operation—begins from the location of the insertion point and proceeds to the end of the document, it is good practice to position the insertion point at the beginning of the document before initiating the command.

2 On the **Home tab**, in the **Editing group**, click **Find**.

> The Navigation pane displays on the left side of the screen with a search box at the top of the pane.

 MAC TIP Display the menu, click Edit, point to Find, click Replace; use this navigation pane for Steps 3–5.

3 In the search box, type **ac** If necessary, scroll down slightly in your document to view the entire body text of the letter, and then compare your screen with Figure 2.34.

> In the document, the search letters *ac* are selected and highlighted in yellow for both words that begin with the letters *ac* and also for the word *contact*, which contains this letter combination. In the Navigation pane, the three instances are shown in context—*ac* displays in bold.

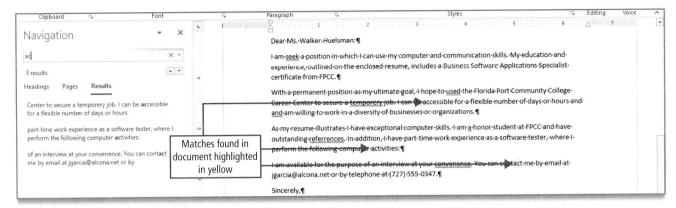

Figure 2.34

4 Click in the search box again, and type as necessary to display the word *accessible* in the search box.

> One match for the search term displays in context in the Navigation pane and is highlighted in the document.

5 In the document, double-click the yellow highlighted word *accessible*, and then type **available** to replace the word.

MAC TIP Complete this step in the Find and Replace navigation pane; move to Step 7 (do not close the pane).

6 Close ☒ the **Navigation** pane.

7 On the **Home tab**, in the **Editing group**, click **Replace**.

MAC TIP Click the Settings icon, click Advanced Find & Replace, click the Replace tab.

8 In the **Find and Replace** dialog box, in the **Find what** box, replace the existing text by typing **FPCC** In the **Replace with** box, type **Florida Port Community College** and then compare your screen with Figure 2.35.

Figure 2.35

9 In the lower left corner of the dialog box, click **More** to expand the dialog box, and then under **Search Options**, select the **Match case** check box.

> The acronym *FPCC* appears in the document two times. In a formal letter, the reader may not know what the acronym means, so you should include the full text instead of an acronym. In this instance, you must select the *Match case* check box so that the replaced text will match the case you typed in the Replace with box, and *not* display in all uppercase letters in the manner of *FPCC*.

MAC TIP Be sure All appears in the Search list box.

10 In the **Find and Replace** dialog box, click **Replace All** to replace both instances of *FPCC*. Click **OK** to close the message box.

11 In the **Find and Replace** dialog box, clear the **Match case** check box, click **Less**, and then **Close** the dialog box.

The Find and Replace dialog box opens with the settings used the last time it was open. Therefore, it is good practice to reset this dialog box to its default settings each time you use it.

MAC TIP   Close the Find & Replace pane.

12 Save 🖫 your document.

Activity 2.17 | Selecting Text and Moving Text by Using Drag and Drop

By using Word's ***drag-and-drop*** feature, you can use the mouse to drag selected text from one location to another. This method is most useful when the text you are moving is on the same screen as the destination location.

1 Take a moment to study the table in Figure 2.36 to become familiar with the techniques you can use to select text in a document quickly.

Selecting Text in a Document	
To select this:	**Do this:**
A portion of text	Click to position the insertion point at the beginning of the text you want to select, hold down Shift, and then click at the end of the text you want to select. Alternatively, hold down the left mouse button and drag from the beginning to the end of the text you want to select.
A word	Double-click the word.
A sentence	Hold down Ctrl and click anywhere in the sentence. (Mac users: Hold down command ⌘)
A paragraph	Triple-click anywhere in the paragraph; or, move the pointer to the left of the line, into the margin area. When the 🔖 pointer displays, double-click.
A line	Move the pointer to the left of the line. When the 🔖 pointer displays, click one time.
One character at a time	Position the insertion point to the left of the first character, hold down Shift, and press ← or → as many times as desired.
A string of words	Position the insertion point to the left of the first word, hold down Shift and Ctrl, and then press ← or → as many times as desired. (Mac users: Hold down command ⌘. This will select the rest of the text in the line before or after the insertion point.)
Consecutive lines	Position the insertion point to the left of the first word, hold down Shift and press ↑ or ↓.
Consecutive paragraphs	Position the insertion point to the left of the first word, hold down Shift and Ctrl and press ↑ or ↓. (Mac users: Hold down command ⌘)
The entire document	Hold down Ctrl and press A. Alternatively, move the pointer to the left of any line in the document. When the 🔖 pointer displays, triple-click. (Mac users: Hold down command ⌘)

Figure 2.36

2 Be sure you can view the entire body of the letter on your screen. In the paragraph that begins *With a permanent position*, in the second line, locate and double-click *days*.

3 Point to the selected word to display the ▷ pointer.

4 Drag to the right until the dotted vertical line that floats next to the pointer is positioned to the right of the word *hours* in the same line, as shown in Figure 2.37.

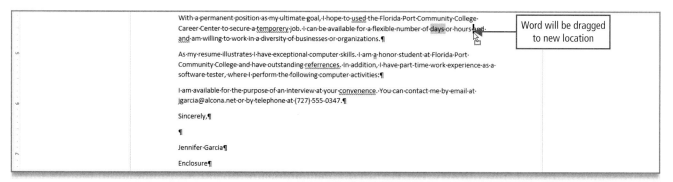

Figure 2.37

5 Release the mouse button to move the text. Select the word *hours* and drag it to the left of the word *or*—the previous location of the word *days*. Click anywhere in the document to deselect the text.

6 Examine the text that you moved, and add or remove spaces as necessary.

7 Hold down Ctrl, and then in the paragraph that begins *I am available*, click anywhere in the first sentence to select the entire sentence.

MAC TIP   Hold down command ⌘.

8 Release Ctrl. Drag the selected sentence to the end of the paragraph by positioning the small vertical line that floats with the pointer to the left of the paragraph mark. **Save** 🖫 your document, and then compare your screen with Figure 2.38.

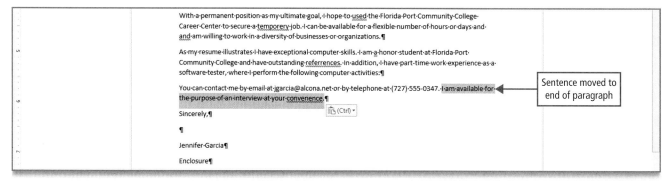

Figure 2.38

Activity 2.18 | Inserting a Table into a Document and Applying a Table Style

1 Locate the paragraph that begins *You can contact me*, and then click to position the insertion point at the beginning of the paragraph. Press Enter one time, and then press ↑ one time to position the insertion point in the new blank paragraph.

2 With the insertion point in the new blank paragraph, on the **Insert tab**, in the **Tables group**, click **Table**. In the **Table** grid, in the third row, click the second square to insert a 2x3 table.

3 In the first cell of the table, type **Microsoft Access** and then press ⌜Tab⌝. Type **Test database queries** and then press ⌜Tab⌝. Complete the table using the following information:

Microsoft Excel	Enter software test data
Microsoft Word	Create and mail form letters

4 On the **Table Tools Layout tab**, in the **Table group**, click **Select**, and then click **Select Table**.

5 On the **Table Tools Layout tab**, in the **Cell Size group**, click **AutoFit**, and then click **AutoFit Contents** to have Word choose the best column widths for the two columns based on the text you entered.

6 With the table still selected, under **Table Tools**, click the **Design tab**. In the **Table Styles group**, click **More** ⌐⌐. Under **Plain Tables**, click the second style—**Table Grid Light**.

Use Table Styles to change the visual style of a table.

7 With the table still selected, on the **Home tab**, in the **Paragraph group**, click **Center** ≡ to center the table between the left and right margins. Click anywhere to deselect the table.

8 Select the blank paragraph under the table, and then on the **Layout tab**, in the **Paragraph group**, change the **Spacing After** to **0 pt**.

9 **Save** ⊞ and then compare your screen with Figure 2.39.

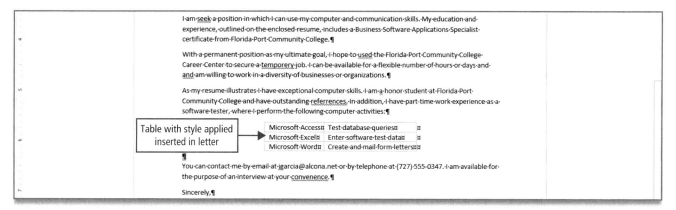

Figure 2.39

Objective 6   Use the Word Editor to Check Your Document

ALERT   **Activating Proofing**

If you do not see any red squiggles or double blue underlines under words, the automatic spelling and/or grammar checking has been turned off on your system. To activate the spelling and grammar checking, display Backstage view, click Options, click Proofing, and then under *When correcting spelling in Microsoft Office programs*, select the first four check boxes. Under *When correcting spelling and grammar in Word*, select the first four check boxes, and then click the Writing Style arrow and click Grammar & Refinements. Under *Exceptions for*, clear both check boxes. To display the flagged items, click the Recheck Document button, and then close the dialog box.

GO! Learn How
Video W2-6

The best way to check your document is to use the Word *Editor*, which, according to Microsoft, is your digital writing assistant in Word. Editor flags misspellings, grammatical mistakes, and writing style issues as you type by marking red squiggles for spelling, blue double underlines for grammar—for example, the misuse of *their*, *there*, and *they're*—and brown dotted underlines for writing issues such as clarity and concise language.

Word will not flag the word *sign* as misspelled even though you intended to type *sing a song* rather than *sign a song*, because both are words contained within Word's dictionary. Your own knowledge and proofreading skills are still required, even when using a sophisticated word processing program like Word.

Activity 2.19 | Using the Word Editor to Check for Spelling, Grammar, and Writing Issues

There are two ways to respond to spelling, grammar, and writing items flagged by Word. You can right-click a flagged word or phrase, and then from the shortcut menu choose a correction or action. Or, you can launch Editor, which provides more options than the shortcut menus.

ALERT   The Word Editor may vary in flagging items; your results may not match the screens and steps exactly but you will be able to make appropriate adjustments to the text.

1 Position the body of the letter on your screen, and then examine the text to locate the various items that Word has flagged as potential errors.

A list of grammar rules applied by a computer program like Word can never be exact, and a computer dictionary cannot contain all known words and proper names. Therefore, you will need to check any words flagged by Word, and you will also need to proofread for content errors.

2 In the lower left corner of your screen, in the status bar, locate and point to the 🔲 icon to display the ScreenTip *Word found proofing errors. Click or tap to correct them.* Compare your screen with Figure 2.40.

If this button displays, you know there are potential errors identified in the document.

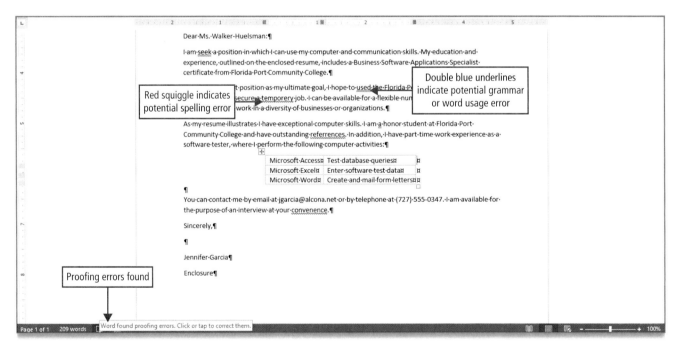

Figure 2.40

3 In the paragraph that begins *With a permanent*, in the second line, locate the word *temporery* with the red squiggle. Point to the word and right-click, and then click **temporary** to correct the spelling error.

⌨ **MAC TIP**   Hold down control and click the misspelled word to display the shortcut menu.

4 In the next line, locate the word *and* that displays with a red squiggle, point to the word and right-click, and then on the shortcut menu, click **Delete Repeated Word** to delete the duplicate word.

5 Press Ctrl + Home to move the insertion point to the beginning of the document. Click the **Review tab**, and then in the **Proofing group**, click **Check Document** (or yours may indicate *Spelling & Grammar*). If the proper name *Huelsman* is flagged, you can Ignore All.

> Word's dictionary contains only very common proper names—unusual names like this may be flagged as a potential spelling error. If this is a name that you frequently type, consider adding it to the dictionary.

 ANOTHER WAY press F7 to start the Editor; Mac users, fn + F7.

ALERT The Order of Flagged Items May Vary

Your Editor pane might consolidate issues. If you see a Results button, click it, and proceed with correcting spelling and grammar and writing issues. The order of flagged items may differ from the Steps below.

6 Compare your screen with Figure 2.41.

> The word *seek* is highlighted as a grammar error, and *seeking* is suggested.

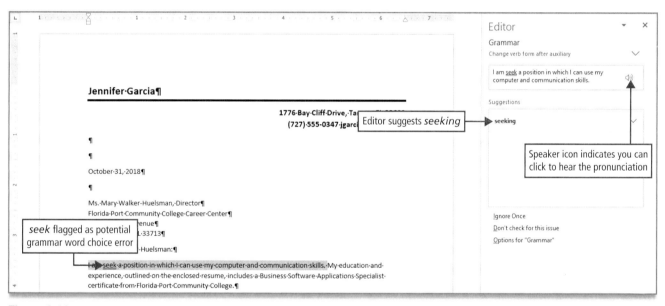

Figure 2.41

7 In the **Editor** pane, under **Suggestions**, click **seeking** to change to the correct usage.

> The next marked word—a possible grammar error—displays.

MAC TIP Click Change.

8 Compare your screen with Figure 2.42 to see the next flagged item.

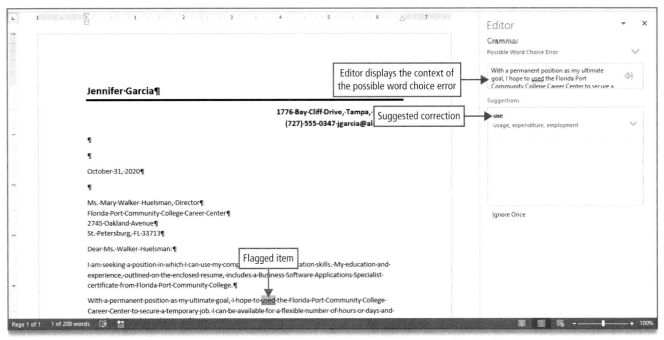

Figure 2.42

> **9** Under **Suggestions**, click **use** to change *used* to *use*. Compare your screen with Figure 2.43.
>
> For the next flagged item, Word indicates a writing issue for clarity and conciseness. Indicating that you have an "ultimate goal" might be an overstatement—Word suggests using only "goal."

NOTE Depending on recent updates to Word, the order of corrections in the next steps may vary. Use the suggestions to make appropriate corrections until you reach Step 12.

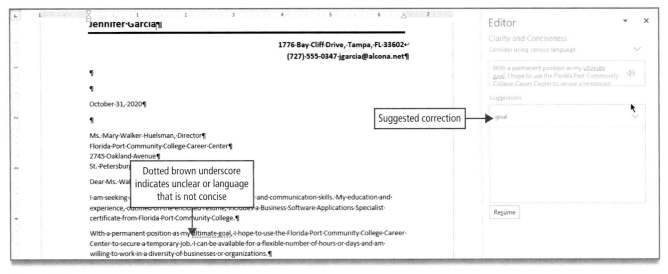

Figure 2.43

> **10** Under **Suggestions**, click **goal** to delete the word *ultimate*; or make this change manually.
>
> **11** Under **Suggestions**, click **references** to correct the spelling error, and then under **Suggestions**, click **an** to correct the grammar error. Click **convenience** to correct the spelling error.

NOTE If Word does not flag this on your system, edit your document to make this change.

12 To use more concise language, click **for** to replace the phrase *for the purpose of*, or if this is not flagged on your system, in the paragraph above *Sincerely*, delete the words *the purpose of*.

13 In the message box indicating the check is complete, click **OK**.

14 Save 🖫 your document. If necessary, Close the Editor pane.

Activity 2.20 | Using the Thesaurus

MOS
1.3.2

A *thesaurus* is a research tool that lists *synonyms*—words that have the same or similar meaning to the word you selected.

1 Scroll so that you can view the body of the letter. In the paragraph that begins *With a permanent*, in the last line, double-click to select the word *diversity*, and then in the **Proofing** group, click **Thesaurus**.

> The Thesaurus pane displays on the right with a list of synonyms; the list will vary in length depending on the selected word.

🔄 **ANOTHER WAY**   Right-click the word, on the shortcut menu, point to Synonyms, and then click Thesaurus.

2 In the **Thesaurus** pane, point to the word *variety*, and then click the arrow that displays. Click **Insert** to change *diversity* to *variety*.

⌨️ **MAC TIP**   Hold down ⌃ctrl, click *variety*, click Insert.

3 In the paragraph that begins *As my resume*, double-click the word *exceptional*, and then on the ribbon, click **Thesaurus** again.

4 In the **Thesaurus** pane, point to *excellent*, click the **arrow**, and then click **Insert**. Compare your screen with Figure 2.44.

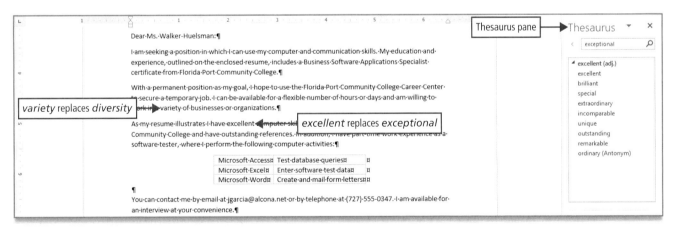

Figure 2.44

5 Close ✕ the **Thesaurus** pane.

6 Click the **File tab** to display **Backstage** view, and then on the **Info tab**, in the lower right portion of the screen, click **Show All Properties**.

⌨️ **MAC TIP**   Display the menu bar, click File, click Properties, click the Summary tab. For Tags, use Keywords.

7 In the **Tags** box, type **cover letter** and in the **Subject** box, type your course name and section number. In the **Author** box, be sure your name is indicated and edit if necessary.

8 On the left, click **Save**. In the upper right corner of the Word window, click **Close** ☒.

MAC TIP Click Save on the Quick Access Toolbar.

For Non-MyLab Submissions Determine What Your Instructor Requires for Submission
As directed by your instructor, submit your completed Word file.

---

9 In **MyLab IT**, locate and click the Grader Project **Word 2B Cover Letter**. In **step 3**, under **Upload Completed Assignment**, click **Choose File**. In the **Open** dialog box, navigate to your **Word Chapter 2 folder**, and then click your **Student_Word_2B_Cover_Letter** file one time to select it. In the lower right corner of the **Open** dialog box, click **Open**.

The name of your selected file displays above the Upload button.

10 To submit your file to **MyLab IT** for grading, click **Upload**, wait a moment for a green **Success!** message, and then in **step 4**, click the blue **Submit for Grading** button. Click **Close Assignment** to return to your list of **Course Materials**.

You have completed Project 2B **END**

Objective 7 **Print an Envelope, Change a Style Set, Create a Word Template, and Use Learning Tools**

ALERT The remaining activities in this Project are optional. Activities 2.21, 2.22, and 2.23, in which you print an envelope, change a style set, create a Word template, and use Learning Tools, are optional. Check with your instructor to see if you should complete these Activities. These Activities are not included in the **MyLab IT** Grader system.

Student Training
Video W2-7

Word's command to Create Envelopes enables you to choose the envelope size, format the addresses, and add electronic postage to an envelope. Changing the Style Set is easily accomplished from the Design tab. You can create your own custom templates in Word, and you might also want to use one of Word's thousands of pre-formatted templates, for which you can search from Word's opening screen. Learning Tools assist with reading.

Activity 2.21 | **Addressing and Printing an Envelope**

Use Word's Envelopes command on the Mailings tab to format and print an envelope.

1 Display your **2B_Cover_Letter**, select the four lines that comprise the inside address.

2 On the **Mailings tab**, in the **Create group**, click **Envelopes** and notice that the selected text is filled in as the **Delivery address**.

3 Click in the **Return address** box.

MAC TIP Deselect *Use my address.*

4 Type **Jennifer Garcia** and press [Enter]. Type **1776 Bay Cliff Drive** and then press [Enter]. Type **Tampa, FL 33602**

5 In the lower portion of the **Envelopes and Labels** dialog box, click **Options**, and then compare your screen with Figure 2.45.

> The default envelope size is a standard business envelope referred to as a Size 10.

 MAC TIP Click Custom.

Figure 2.45

6 Click **OK** to close the **Envelope Options** dialog box. As shown under **Feed**, insert an envelope in your printer and then click **Print**.

> Depending on the type and brand of printer you are using, your feed area may vary.

7 If necessary, **Close** [X] the **Envelopes and Labels** dialog box. Leave your **2B_Cover_Letter** open for the next Activity.

Activity 2.22 | Changing a Style Set

MOS
1.2.2, 2.2.4

The Paragraph Spacing command offers various options for changing the style set so that you can set the line and paragraph spacing of your entire document. A gallery of predefined values displays; or you can create your own custom paragraph spacing.

1 With your **2B_Cover_Letter** displayed, click the **File tab**, on the left click **Save As**, click **Browse**, navigate to your **Word Chapter 2** folder, and then using your own name, save this document as **Lastname_Firstname_2B_Cover_Letter_No_Paragraph_Space**

2 On the **Home tab**, in the **Editing group**, click **Select**, and then click **Select All**.

3 On the **Design tab**, in the **Document Formatting group**, click **Paragraph Spacing**, and then under **Built-In**, click **No Paragraph Space**.

> With no spacing after a paragraph, to use this style set, you will need to insert blank paragraphs to create appropriate space within your letter.

4 Click at the end of the dateline, and then press [Enter] four times to move the first line of the inside address to approximately two inches from the top of the paper.

5 Click after the ZIP code in the inside address and press [Enter] one time. Click at the end of the salutation and press [Enter] one time.

6 Click at the end of the first paragraph of body text and press Enter one time. Click at the end of the second paragraph of body text and press Enter one time.

7 Click after the colon above the table and press Enter one time. Click at the end of the last paragraph of body text and press Enter one time.

8 Click at the end of the closing and press Enter two times to leave three blank paragraphs between the closing and the writer's identification. Click after *Garcia* and press Enter one time to leave a blank paragraph between the writer's identification and the Enclosure notation. Compare your screen with Figure 2.46.

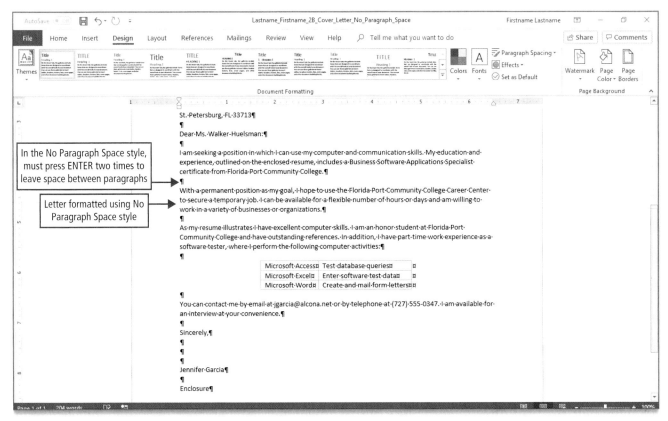

Figure 2.46

9 Save your document and in the upper right corner of the Word window, click **Close** ✕. Submit if directed to do so by your instructor.

Activity 2.23 | Creating a Word Template

A *template* is a file you use as a starting point for a *new* document. A template has a predefined document structure and defined settings, such as font, margins, and available styles. On Word's opening screen, you can select from among many different templates—or you can create your own custom template.

When you open a template as the starting point for a new document, the template file opens a copy of itself, unnamed, and then you use the structure—and possibly some content, such as headings—as the starting point for a new document.

All documents are based on a template. When you create a new blank document, it is based on Word's *Normal template*, which serves as the starting point for all blank Word documents.

1 Start Word and click **Blank document**. Type **Jennifer Garcia** and then press Enter.

2 Type **1776 Bay Cliff Drive, Tampa, FL 33602** hold down Shift and then press Enter.

3 Type **(727) 555-0347 jgarcia@alcona.net** and then press Enter. If the email address changes to blue text, right-click the email address, and then click **Remove Hyperlink**.

4 Select the first paragraph—*Jennifer Garcia*—and then on the mini toolbar, apply **Bold** B and change the **Font Size** to **16**.

5 Select the two address lines that form the second paragraph. On the mini toolbar, apply **Bold** B and change the **Font Size** to **12**.

6 With the two-line paragraph still selected, on the **Home tab**, in the **Paragraph group**, click **Align Right** ☰.

7 Click anywhere in the first paragraph—*Jennifer Garcia*. In the **Paragraph group**, click the **Borders button arrow** ⊞ ▾, and then at the bottom, click **Borders and Shading**.

8 In the **Borders and Shading** dialog box, on the **Borders tab**, under **Style**, be sure the first style—a single solid line—is selected.

9 Click the **Width arrow**, and then click **3 pt**. To the right, under **Preview**, click the bottom border of the diagram. Under **Apply to**, be sure *Paragraph* displays.

10 Click **OK** to display a 3 pt line below *Jennifer Garcia*, which extends from the left margin to the right margin.

11 Click the **File tab**, on the left click **Save As**, and then click **Browse** to display the **Save As** dialog box.

12 In the lower portion of the **Save As** dialog box, click the **Save as type arrow**, and then on the list click **Word Template**. At the top of the **Save As** dialog box, examine the path in the **address bar** as shown in Figure 2.47.

By default, Word stores template files that you create on the hard drive of your computer in your user folder, in a folder named Custom Office Templates. By doing so, the template is always available to you from this folder.

MAC TIP Click the File Format arrow.

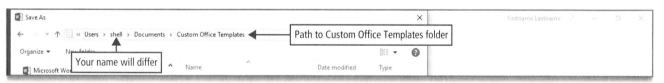

Figure 2.47

13 Click in the **File name** box, and then using your own name, type **Lastname_Firstname_2B_Letterhead_Template** Click **Save**.

MAC TIP Click in the Save As box.

14 In the upper right corner of the Word window, click **Close** ✕.

15 In **File Explorer**, navigate to the **Documents** folder on your hard drive, and then double-click to open the folder **Custom Office Templates**. Double-click your **Lastname_Firstname_2B_Letterhead_Template** document. Compare your screen with Figure 2.48.

Word opens a copy of your 2B_Letterhead_Template in the form of a new Word document. The title bar indicates *Document* followed by a number. You are not opening the original template file, and changes that you make to this new document will not affect the contents of your stored 2B_Letterhead_Template file. You can insert text into the document, and then save it with an appropriate name.

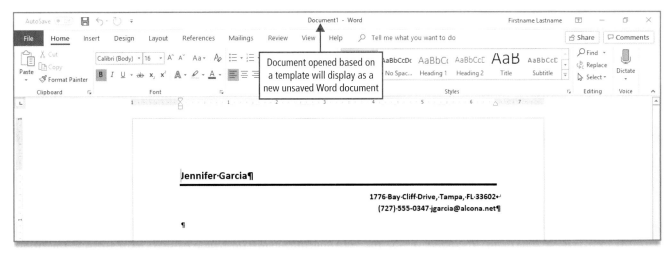

Figure 2.48

16 In the upper right corner of the Word window, click **Close** ✕.

Activity 2.24 | Using Learning Tools and Read Aloud

Learning Tools are features in Word that add visual changes to assist with reading fluency and comprehension. You enable Learning Tools from the View tab, and depending on how you want to focus on your document while viewing it on your screen, you can enable various commands.

The *Page Color* command changes the color to make the text easy to scan and consume; for example, you can set the Page color to *Sepia* (pale yellow with print feel) or to *Inverse* (black background with white text).

The *Column Width* command changes the width of the line length to fit more or less text on each line. Options include Very Narrow, Narrow, Moderate, or Wide. The *Text Spacing* command increases spacing between words, characters, and lines.

The *Syllables* command shows breaks between syllables of words. If you are editing, you can type and make edits to your document and the syllable marks will appear in real time as you type.

The *Read Aloud* command reads text out loud and highlights each word as it is read. This command is available in both Word and Outlook. If you start typing while this feature is enabled, the narration will pause so you can make edits and then resume the narration. The Read Aloud command is also available on the Review tab so you can use it in any of Word's views.

1 Open your completed **2B_Cover_Letter** document, and then click to position your insertion point at the beginning of the paragraph that begins *I am seeking*.

2 Be sure that your computer speaker is on, and if you are in a college lab or public space, use headphones. On the **Review tab**, in the **Speech group**, click **Read Aloud** to hear a narration of the text, and notice that as each word is read aloud, it is highlighted.

3 Click **Read Aloud** again to stop the narration.

4 Click the **View tab**, and then in the **Immersive group**, click **Learning Tools**.

5 Click **Column Width**, and then click **Very Narrow**. Click **Page Color**, and then click **Sepia**. If necessary, click **Text Spacing**. Click **Syllables**, and then compare your screen with Figure 2.49.

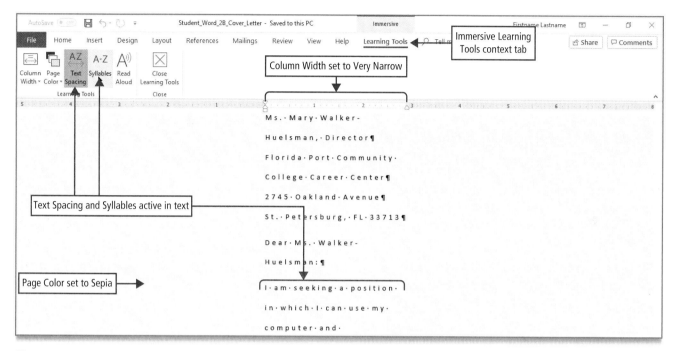

Figure 2.49

6 On the ribbon, click **Close Learning Tools**.

7 In the upper right corner of the Word window, click **Close** ⨯.

You have completed the optional portion of this Project **END**

»» GO! With Google Docs

Objective	Create a Table in Google Docs

ALERT   **Working with Web-Based Applications and Services**

Computer programs and services on the web receive continuous updates and improvements, so the steps to complete this web-based Activity may differ from the ones shown. You can often look at the screens and the information presented to determine how to complete the Activity.

   If you do not already have a Google account, you will need to create one before you begin this Activity. Go to http://google.com and, in the upper right corner, click Sign In. On the Sign In screen, click Create Account. On the Create your Google Account page, complete the form, read and agree to the Terms of Service and Privacy Policy, and then click Next step. On the Welcome screen, click Get Started.

Activity | Creating a Table in Google Docs

In this Activity, you will use Google Docs to create a table within a document similar to Project 2B.

1 From the desktop, open your browser, navigate to **http://google.com**, and then click the **Google Apps** menu ▦. Click **Drive**, and then if necessary, sign in to your Google account.

2 Open your **GO! Web Projects** folder—or click New to create and then open this folder if necessary.

3 In the upper left, click **New**, and then click **File upload**. In the **Open** dialog box, navigate to the files you downloaded with this project, and then in the **File List**, double-click to open **w02_2B_Web**.

4 When the upload is complete, in the **Google Drive file list**, double-click the document to open it in Google Docs. If necessary, click Open with Google Docs.

5 Click in the document and then press Ctrl + End to move to the end of the document. Press Enter one time.

6 On the menu bar, click **Insert**, point to **Table**, and then insert a 3x4 table.

7 Type **Position** and press Tab. Type **Type** and press Tab. Type **Location** and press Tab.

8 In the second row type **Paralegal** and press Tab. Type **Part-time** and press Tab. Type **Tampa** and press Tab. Compare your screen with Figure A.

9 Type **Legal Records Clerk** and press Tab. Type **Full-time, 2 months** and press Tab. Type **North Tampa** and press Tab.

10 Right-click in the last row of the table, and then click **Delete row**.

11 Drag to select all the cells in the first row. On the toolbar, click the **Normal text button arrow** , and then click **Heading 2**. With the three column titles still selected, on the toolbar, locate and click **Center**.

12 Press Ctrl + Home to move to the top of the document, and then compare your screen with Figure B.

13 Submit the file as directed by your instructor. In the upper right, click your user name, and then click **Sign out**. **Close** your browser window. Your file is automatically saved in your Google Drive.

Figure A

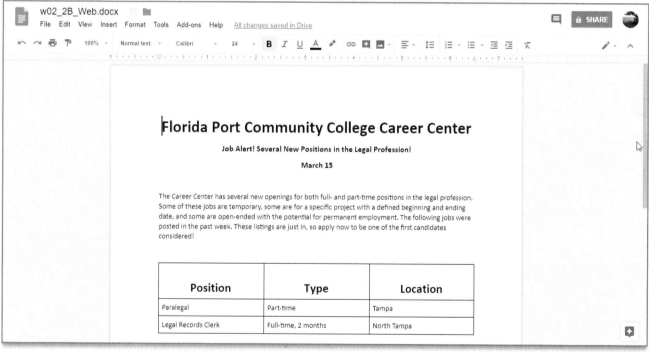

Figure B

»»» GO! To Work

wavebreakmedia/Shutterstock, Monkey Business Images/Fotolia, Ivanko80/Shutterstock, Monkey Business Images/Shutterstock

Microsoft Office Specialist (MOS) Skills in this Chapter

Project 2A	Project 2B
1.1.4 Show and hide formatting symbols and hidden text	**1.1.1** Search for text
1.2.3 Insert and modify headers and footers	**1.2.2** Apply style sets
1.3.2 Modify basic document properties	**1.3.2** Modify basic document properties
2.2.2 Apply formatting by using Format Painter	**2.1.1** Find and replace text
3.1.3 Create tables by specifying rows and columns	**2.2.4** Apply built-in styles to text
3.2.3 Merge and split cells	
3.2.4 Resize tables, rows, and columns	
3.3.1 Format paragraphs as numbered and bulleted lists	
3.3.4 Increase and decrease list levels	

Build Your E-Portfolio

An E-Portfolio is a collection of evidence, stored electronically, that showcases what you have accomplished while completing your education. Collecting and then sharing your work products with potential employers reflects your academic and career goals. Your completed documents from the following projects are good examples to show what you have learned: 2G, 2K, and 2L.

▶ GO! For Job Success

Video: Resume and Cover Letter Tips

Your instructor may assign this video to your class, and then ask you to think about, or discuss with your classmates, these questions:

g-stockstudio/Shutterstock

A cover letter should contain information that is different from but complimentary to the information than the facts on your resume and be tailored to the specific job you are applying for. Name two different things that you could mention in a cover letter.

Why should you avoid fancy layout techniques or elaborate templates for your resume document?

Why is creating and then including a LinkedIn page on your resume a good idea?

End of Chapter

Summary

Word tables enable you to present information in a logical and orderly format. Each cell in a Word table behaves like a document; as you type in a cell, wordwrap moves text to the next line.

A good source of information for resume formats is a Business Communications textbook. A simple two-column table created in Word is suitable to create an appropriate resume for a recent college graduate.

Instead of switching to old-fashioned single-spacing to create a letter, use Word's default settings and then apply Spacing after of 0 pt to all but the last line of the inside address.

Business letters follow a standard format and should always contain a dateline, an inside address, a salutation, body text, a complimentary closing, and the writer's identification.

GO! Learn It Online

Review the concepts, key terms, and MOS skills in this chapter by completing these online challenges, which you can find at **MyLab IT**.

Chapter Quiz: Answer matching and multiple choice questions to test what you learned in this chapter.

Lessons on the GO!: Learn how to use all the new apps and features as they are introduced by Microsoft.

MOS Prep Quiz: Answer questions to review the MOS skills that you practiced in this chapter.

GO! Collaborative Team Project (Available in Instructor Resource Center)

If your instructor assigns this project to your class, you can expect to work with one or more of your classmates—either in person or by using internet tools—to create work products similar to those that you created in this chapter. A team is a group of workers who work together to solve a problem, make a decision, or create a work product. Collaboration is when you work together with others as a team in an intellectual endeavor to complete a shared task or achieve a shared goal.

Monkey Business Images/Fotolia

Project Guide for Word Chapter 2

Your instructor will assign Projects from this list to ensure your learning and assess your knowledge.

	Project Guide for Word Chapter 2		
Project	**Apply Skills from These Chapter Objectives**	**Project Type**	**Project Location**
2A MyLab IT	Objectives 1-3 from Project 2A	**2A Instructional Project (Grader Project)** **Instruction** Guided instruction to learn the skills in Project A.	In **MyLab IT** and in text
2B MyLab IT	Objectives 4-7 from Project 2B	**2B Instructional Project (Grader Project)** **Instruction** Guided instruction to learn the skills in Project B.	In **MyLab IT** and in text
2C	Objectives 1-3 from Project 2A	**2C Skills Review (Scorecard Grading)** **Review** A guided review of the skills from Project 2A.	In text
2D	Objectives 4-7 from Project 2B	**2D Skills Review (Scorecard Grading)** **Review** A guided review of the skills from Project 2B.	In text
2E MyLab IT	Objectives 1-3 from Project 2A	**2E Mastery (Grader Project)** **Mastery and Transfer of Learning** A demonstration of your mastery of the skills in Project 2A with extensive decision-making.	In **MyLab IT** and in text
2F MyLab IT	Objectives 4-7 from Project 2B	**2F Mastery (Grader Project)** **Mastery and Transfer of Learning** A demonstration of your mastery of the skills in Project 2B with extensive decision-making.	In **MyLab IT** and in text
2G MyLab IT	Objectives 1 -7 from Projects 2A and 2B	**2G Mastery (Grader Project)** **Mastery and Transfer of Learning** A demonstration of your mastery of the skills in Projects 2A and 2B with extensive decision-making.	In **MyLab IT** and in text
2H	Combination of Objectives from Projects 2A and 2B	**2H GO! Fix It (Scorecard Grading)** **Critical Thinking** A demonstration of your mastery of the skills in Projects 2A and 2B by creating a correct result from a document that contains errors you must find.	IRC
2I	Combination of Objectives from Projects 2A and 2B	**2I GO! Make It (Scorecard Grading)** **Critical Thinking** A demonstration of your mastery of the skills in Projects 2A and 2B by creating a result from a supplied picture.	IRC
2J	Combination of Objectives from Projects 2A and 2B	**2J GO! Solve It (Rubric Grading)** **Critical Thinking** A demonstration of your mastery of the skills in Projects 2A and 2B, your decision-making skills, and your critical thinking skills. A task-specific rubric helps you self-assess your result.	IRC
2K	Combination of Objectives from Projects 2A and 2B	**2K GO! Solve It (Rubric Grading)** **Critical Thinking** A demonstration of your mastery of the skills in Projects 2A and 2B, your decision-making skills, and your critical thinking skills. A task-specific rubric helps you self-assess your result.	In text
2L	Combination of Objectives from Projects 2A and 2B	**2L GO! Think (Rubric Grading)** **Critical Thinking** A demonstration of your understanding of the Chapter concepts applied in a manner that you would outside of college. An analytic rubric helps you and your instructor grade the quality of your work by comparing it to the work an expert in the discipline would create.	In text
2M	Combination of Objectives from Projects 2A and 2B	**2M GO! Think (Rubric Grading)** **Critical Thinking** A demonstration of your understanding of the Chapter concepts applied in a manner that you would outside of college. An analytic rubric helps you and your instructor grade the quality of your work by comparing it to the work an expert in the discipline would create.	IRC
2N	Combination of Objectives from Projects 2A and 2B	**2N You and GO! (Rubric Grading)** **Critical Thinking** A demonstration of your understanding of the Chapter concepts applied in a manner that you would in a personal situation. An analytic rubric helps you and your instructor grade the quality of your work.	IRC
2O	Combination of Objectives from Projects 2A and 2B	**2O Collaborative Team Project for Word Chapter 2** **Critical Thinking** A demonstration of your understanding of concepts and your ability to work collaboratively in a group role-playing assessment, requiring both collaboration and self-management.	IRC

Glossary

Glossary of Chapter Key Terms

AutoCorrect A feature that corrects common typing and spelling errors as you type, for example changing *teh* to *the*.

Body The text of a letter.

Cell The box at the intersection of a row and column in a Word table.

Cell margins The space inside a table cell between the text and the cell borders—top, bottom, left, and right.

Column Width A Learning Tools command that changes the width of the line length to fit more or less text on each line; options include Very Narrow, Narrow, Moderate, or Wide.

Complimentary closing A parting farewell in a business letter.

Cover letter A document that you send with your resume to provide additional information about your skills and experience.

Date & Time A command with which you can automatically insert the current date and time into a document in a variety of formats.

Dateline The first line in a business letter that contains the current date and which is positioned just below the letterhead if a letterhead is used.

Drag-and-drop A technique by which you can move, by dragging, selected text from one location in a document to another.

Editor A digital writing assistant in Word that flags misspellings, grammatical errors, and writing style issues.

Enclosures Additional documents included with a business letter.

Inside address The name and address of the person receiving the letter; always positioned below the date line.

Inverse A Page Color in Learning Tools that displays the text in white on a black background.

Learning Tools Features in Word that add visual changes to assist with reading fluency and comprehension.

Letterhead The personal or company information that displays at the top of a letter, and which commonly includes a name, address, and contact information.

Line break indicator A formatting mark in the shape of a bent arrow that indicates a manual line break.

LinkedIn A professional networking website that focuses on business and employment-oriented services and on which you can build and share your professional identify and connect with others in your field of interest.

Manual line break A line break that moves the text to the right of the insertion point to a new line while keeping the text in the same paragraph.

No Paragraph Space The built-in paragraph style—available from the Paragraph Spacing command—that inserts *no* extra space before or after a paragraph and uses line spacing of 1.

Normal template The template that serves as a basis for all Word documents.

Office Presentation Service A Word feature to present your Word document to others who can watch in a web browser.

One-click Row/Column Insertion A Word table feature with which you can insert a new row or column by pointing to the desired location and then clicking.

Page Color A Learning Tools command that changes the color of the page to make the text easy to scan and consume.

Read Aloud A Learning Tools command that reads text out loud and highlights each word as it is read; this command is available in both Word and Outlook.

Resume Assistant A feature in Word with which you can see suggestions from LinkedIn to help you update your resume.

Salutation The greeting line of a business letter.

Sepia A Page Color command in Learning Tools that shades the screen in pale yellow with a print feel.

Single spacing The common name for line spacing in which there is *no* extra space before or after a paragraph; uses line spacing of 1.

Skype A Microsoft product with which you can make voice calls, make video calls, transfer files, or send messages—including instant messages and text messages—over the Internet.

Style set A collection of character and paragraph formatting that is stored and named.

Subject line The optional line following the inside address in a business letter that states the purpose of the letter.

Syllables A Learning Tools command that shows breaks between syllables of words.

Synonyms Words with the same or similar meaning.

Table (Word) An arrangement of information organized into rows and columns.

Template An existing document that you use as a starting point for a new document; it opens a copy of itself, unnamed, and then you use the structure—and possibly some content, such as headings—as the starting point for a new document.

Text from File A command to insert text from another file into your document.

Text Spacing A Learning Tools command that increases the spacing between words, characters, and lines.

Thesaurus A research tool that provides a list of synonyms.

Writer's identification The name and title of the author of a letter placed near the bottom of the letter under the complimentary closing—also referred to as the *writer's signature block*.

Writer's signature block The name and title of the author of a letter placed near the bottom of the letter, under the complimentary closing—also referred to as the *writer's identification*.

Chapter Review

Apply 2A skills from these Objectives:

1. Create a Table for a Resume
2. Format a Table
3. Present a Word Document Online

In the following Skills Review, you will use a table to create a resume for Ashley Kent. Your completed resume will look similar to the one shown in Figure 2.50.

Project Files

For Project 2C, you will need the following files:

New blank Word document

w02C_Skills

w02C_Experience

You will save your document as:

Lastname_Firstname_2C_Student_Resume

Project Results

Ashley Kent

2212 Bramble Road
St. Petersburg, FL 33713
(727) 555-0237
ashleykent@alcona.net

OBJECTIVE A computer programmer position in a small startup company that requires excellent computer programming skills, systems analysis experience, and knowledge of database design.

SKILLS **Computer Programming**
- Advanced C/C++
- Java
- Ruby on Rails
- SQL

Leadership
- Secretary, Florida Port Community College Computer Club
- Vice President, Associated Students, Bay Hills High School

Additional Skills
- Microsoft Office
- Adobe Creative Suite
- Adobe Acrobat Pro

EXPERIENCE **Database Designer** (part-time), Admissions and Records Florida Port Community College, St. Petersburg, FL September 2019 to present

Software Tester (part-time), Macro Games Inc., Tampa, FL September 2016 to September 2019

EDUCATION **Florida Port Community College**, Computer Science major September 2020 to present

Graduate of Bay Hills High School June 2019

Student_Word_2C_Student_Resume

Figure 2.50

(continues on next page)

Chapter Review

1 Start Word and display a blank document. Be sure that formatting marks and rulers display. **Save** the document in your **Word Chapter 2** folder, using your own name, as **Lastname_Firstname_2C_Student_Resume**

a. Add the file name to the footer, and then close the footer area. (Mac users: from your student data files, open Mac_w02C_Student_Resume and use this file instead of a new blank document. On the Header & Footer tab, in the Insert group, click Field. Under Categories, click Document Information. Under Field names, click FileName. Click OK.)

b. Click the **Insert tab**, and then in the **Tables group**, click **Table**. In the **Table** grid, in the fourth row, click the second square to insert a **2x4** table.

c. In the first cell of the table, type **Ashley Kent** and then press Enter. Type the following text, pressing Enter after each line *except* the last line:

2212 Bramble Road
St. Petersburg, FL 33713
(727) 555-0237
ashleykent@alcona.net

d. Press ↓ to move to the first cell in the second row. Type **SKILLS** and then press ↓ to move to the first cell in the third row.

e. Type **EXPERIENCE** and then press ↓. Type **EDUCATION**

f. In the first cell, if the email address displays in blue, right-click the email address, and then on the shortcut menu, click **Remove Hyperlink**. **Save** your document.

2 Click in the cell to the right of *SKILLS*, and then type the following, pressing Enter after each line including the last line:

Computer Programming
Advanced C/C++
Java
Ruby on Rails
SQL

a. With the insertion point in the new line at the end of the cell, click the **Insert tab**. In the **Text group**, click the **Object button arrow**, and then click **Text from File**.

b. Navigate to the files downloaded with this project, select **w02C_Skills**, and then click **Insert**. Press Backspace one time to remove the blank line.

c. Click in the cell to the right of *EXPERIENCE*, and then insert the file **w02C_Experience**. Press Backspace one time to remove the blank line.

d. Click in the cell to the right of *EDUCATION*, and then type the following four items, pressing Enter after all items *except* the last four items:

Florida Port Community College, Computer Science major
September 2020 to present
Graduate of Bay Hills High School
June 2019

3 Point to the upper left corner of the *SKILLS* cell, and then click the **Row Insertion** button. (Mac users: Point to the upper left corner of the cell, right-click, point to Insert, click Rows Above.)

In the first cell of the new row, type **OBJECTIVE** and then press Tab.

a. Type **A computer programmer position in a small startup company that requires excellent computer programming skills, systems analysis experience, and knowledge of database design.**

b. In any row, point to the vertical border between the two columns to display the ┼ pointer. Drag the column border to the left to approximately **1.5 inches on the horizontal ruler**.

c. Under **Table Tools**, on the **Layout tab**, in the **Cell Size group**, click **AutoFit**, and then click **AutoFit Window** to be sure that your table stretches across the page within the margins.

d. In the **Alignment group**, click **Cell Margins**, and then increase the **Top** and **Bottom** cell margins to **0.04**. Click **OK**.

e. In the first row of the table, drag across both cells to select them. On the **Table Tools Layout tab**, in the **Merge group**, click **Merge Cells**. Right-click over the selected cell, and then on the mini toolbar, click **Center**.

f. In the top row, select the first paragraph of text— *Ashley Kent*. On the mini toolbar, increase the **Font Size** to **20** and apply **Bold**.

g. In the second row, point to the word *OBJECTIVE*, hold down the left mouse button, and then drag down to select the row headings in uppercase letters. On the mini toolbar, click **Bold**. **Save** your document.

(continues on next page)

Chapter Review

4 ▶ Click in the cell to the right of *OBJECTIVE*. On the **Layout tab**, in the **Paragraph group**, click the **Spacing After up spin arrow** three times to change the spacing to **18 pt**.

a. In the cell to the right of *SKILLS*, apply **Bold** to the words *Computer Programming*, *Leadership*, and *Additional Skills*. Then, under each bold heading in the cell, select the lines of text, and create a bulleted list.

b. In the first two bulleted lists, click in the last bullet item, and then on the **Layout tab**, in the **Paragraph group**, set the **Spacing After** to **12 pt**.

c. In the last bulleted list, click in the last bullet item, and then set the **Spacing After** to **18 pt**.

d. In the cell to the right of *EXPERIENCE*, apply **Bold** to *Database Designer* and *Software Tester*. Click in the line *September 2019 to present* and apply **Spacing After** of **12 pt**. Click in the line *September 2016 to September 2019* and apply **Spacing After** of **18 pt**.

e. In the cell to the right of *EDUCATION*, apply **Bold** to *Florida Port Community College* and *Graduate of Bay Hills High School*.

f. In the same cell, click in the line *September 2020 to present* and apply **Spacing After** of **12 pt**.

g. In the first row, click in the last line—*ashleykent@alcona.net*—and then change the **Spacing After** to **18 pt**. Click in the first line—*Ashley Kent*—and set the **Spacing Before** to **30 pt** and the **Spacing After** to **6 pt**.

5 ▶ On the **Table Tools Layout tab**, in the **Table group**, click **Select**, and then click **Select Table**. On the **Table Tools Design tab**, in the **Borders group**, click the **Borders button arrow**, and then click **No Border**.

a. In the **Borders group**, click the **Borders button arrow** again, and then at the bottom of the gallery, click **Borders and Shading**. In the **Borders and Shading** dialog box, under **Setting**, click **Custom**. Under **Style**, scroll down slightly, and then click the style with two equal lines.

b. Click the **Width arrow**, and then click **1 1/2 pt**. Under **Preview**, click the top border of the preview box, and then click **OK**.

c. Click the **File tab** to display **Backstage** view, on the left click **Info**, and then in the lower right portion of the screen, click **Show All Properties**. In the **Tags** box, type **resume, table** and in the **Subject** box, type your course name and section number. In the **Author** box, be sure your name is indicated and edit if necessary. (Mac users: On the menu bar, click File, click Properties, click Summary tab. For Tags, use Keywords.)

d. On the left, click **Print** to display **Print Preview**.

e. On the left, click **Save**, and then if you want to do so, present your document online to a fellow classmate. If directed by your instructor to do so, submit your paper printout, your electronic image of your document that looks like a printed document, or your original Word file. Close Word.

You have completed Project 2C　**END**

Chapter Review

Skills Review | **Project 2D Cover Letter**

Apply 2B skills from these Objectives:

4. Create a Letterhead for a Cover Letter
5. Create a Cover Letter and Correct and Reorganize Text
6. Use the Word Editor to Check Your Document
7. Print an Envelope, Change a Style Set, Create a Word Template, and Use Learning Tools

In the following Skills Review, you will create a cover letter with a letterhead to accompany a resume. Your completed document will look similar to Figure 2.51.

Project Files

For Project 2D, you will need the following files:

New blank Word document

w02D_Cover_Letter_Text

You will save your document as:

Lastname_Firstname_2D_Cover_Letter

Project Results

Sarah Villmosky

7279 Rambling Brook Way, St. Petersburg, FL 33713
(727) 555-0117 svillmosky@alcona.net

May 12, 2020

Ms. Mary Walker-Huelsman, Director
Florida Port Community College Career Center
2745 Oakland Avenue
St. Petersburg, FL 33713

Dear Ms. Walker-Huelsman:

I am seeking the assistance of the Career Center in my job search.

Having recently graduated from Florida Port Community College with an Associate of Arts in Media Studies, I am interested in working for a newspaper, a magazine, or a publishing company.

I have previous work experience in the publishing industry as a writer and section editor for the local activities section of the St. Petersburg News and Times. I have the following skills that I developed while working at the St. Petersburg News and Times. I believe these skills would be a good fit with a local or national newspaper or publication:

Editorial Experience:	Writing, editing, interviewing
Computer proficiency:	Adobe InDesign, Quark Express, Microsoft Publisher
Education focus:	Media Studies and Journalism

I am willing to consider temporary positions that might lead to a permanent position. Please contact me at sarahvillmosky@alcona.net or by phone at (727) 555-0117. I am available immediately for an interview or for further training at the Career Center that you think would be beneficial in my job search.

Sincerely,

Sarah Villmosky

Enclosure

Student_Word_2D_Cover_Letter

Figure 2.51

(continues on next page)

Chapter Review

1 ▶ Start Word and display a blank document; be sure that formatting marks and rulers display. (Mac users: from your student data files, open Mac_w02D_Cover_Letter and use this file instead of a new blank document.)

a. Type **Sarah Villmosky** and then press Enter. Type **7279 Rambling Brook Way, St. Petersburg, FL 33713** hold down Shift, and then press Enter to insert a manual line break.

b. Type **(727) 555-0117 svillmosky@alcona.net** and then press Enter. If the email address changes to blue text, right-click the address, and then click **Remove Hyperlink**.

c. Select the first paragraph—*Sarah Villmosky*—and then on the mini toolbar, apply **Bold**, and change the **Font Size** to **16**.

d. Select the two lines that form the second paragraph, and then on the mini toolbar, apply **Bold** and change the **Font Size** to **12**.

e. Click anywhere in the first paragraph—*Sarah Villmosky*. On the **Home tab**, in the **Paragraph group**, click the **Borders button arrow**, and then click **Borders and Shading**. Under **Style**, click the first style—a single solid line. Click the **Width arrow**, and then click **3 pt**. In the **Preview** area, click the bottom border, and then click **OK**.

f. Click the **File tab**, click **Save As**, click **Browse**, and then navigate to your **Word Chapter 2 folder**. Using your own name, save the document as **Lastname_Firstname_2D_Cover_Letter**

g. On the **Insert tab**, in the **Header & Footer group**, click **Footer**, click **Edit Footer**, and then in the **Insert group**, click **Document Info**. Click **File Name**, and then click **Close Header and Footer**. Click **Save**.

2 ▶ Click the **File tab**. On the left, click **Options**. On the left side of the **Word Options** dialog box, click **Proofing**, and then under **AutoCorrect options**, click the **AutoCorrect Options** button. (Mac users: On the menu bar, click Tools, click AutoCorrect.)

a. In the **AutoCorrect** dialog box, click the **AutoCorrect tab**. Under **Replace**, type the misspelled word **assistence** and under **With**, type **assistance** Click **Add**. If the entry already exists, click Replace instead, and then click Yes. Click **OK** two times to close the dialog boxes.

b. Press Ctrl + End, and then press Enter two times. On the **Insert tab**, in the **Text group**, click **Date & Time**, and then click the third date format. Click **OK**.

c. Press Enter two times. Type **Ms. Mary Walker-Huelsman, Director** and press Enter. Type **Florida Port Community College Career Center** and press Enter. Type **2745 Oakland Avenue** and press Enter. Type **St. Petersburg, FL 33713** and press Enter.

d. Select the first three lines of the inside address, and then on the **Layout tab**, in the **Paragraph group**, change the **Spacing After** to **0 pt**.

e. Click in the blank paragraph below the inside address. Type **Dear Ms. Walker-Huelsman:** and then press Enter one time. Type, exactly as shown with the intentional misspelling, and then watch *assistence* as you press Spacebar: **I am seeking the assistence**

f. Type **of the Career Center in my job search.** Press Enter one time.

g. On the **Insert tab**, in the **Text Group**, click the **Object button arrow**, and then click **Text from File**. From the files downloaded with this project, locate and insert the file **w02D_Cover_Letter_Text**.

h. Scroll to view the lower portion of the page, and be sure your insertion point is in the empty paragraph mark at the end. Type **Sincerely,** and then press Enter two times. Type **Sarah Villmosky** and press Enter one time. Type **Enclosure** and then **Save** your document.

i. Press Ctrl + Home. On the **Home tab**, in the **Editing group**, click **Find**. In the **Navigation** pane, click in the search box, and then type **Journalism** In the letter, double-click the yellow highlighted word *Journalism* and type **Media Studies** (Mac users, in the next step, do not close the pane; click the Settings icon, click Advanced Find & Replace, click the Replace tab.)

j. **Close** the **Navigation** pane, and then on the **Home tab**, in the **Editing group**, click **Replace**. In the **Find and Replace** dialog box, in the **Find what** box, replace the existing text by typing **SPNT** In the **Replace with** box, type **St. Petersburg News and Times** Click **More** to expand the dialog box, select the **Match case** check box, click **Replace All**, and then click **OK**. Clear the **Match case** check box, click **Less**, and then **Close** the **Find and Replace** dialog box.

k. In the paragraph that begins *I am available*, hold down Ctrl, and then click anywhere in the first sentence. Release Ctrl, and then drag the selected sentence to the end of the paragraph by positioning the small vertical line that floats with the insertion point to the left of the paragraph mark.

(continues on next page)

Chapter Review

3 Click at the beginning of the paragraph that begins *I am willing*, and then press Enter one time to insert a new blank paragraph. Press ↑ one time to position your insertion point in the new blank paragraph. On the **Insert tab**, in the **Tables group**, click **Table**. In the **Table grid**, in the third row, click the second square to insert a 2x3 table. Type the following information in the table:

Editorial experience:	Writing, editing, interviewing
Computer proficiency:	Adobe InDesign, QuarkXPress, Microsoft Publisher
Education focus:	Media Studies and Journalism

a. Click anywhere inside the table. On the **Table Tools Layout tab**, in the **Table group**, click **Select**, and then click **Select Table**. In the **Cell Size group**, click **AutoFit**, and then click **AutoFit Contents**.

b. With the table selected, on the **Design tab**, in the **Table Styles group**, click **More** ⊡. Under **Plain Tables**, click the second style—**Table Grid Light**.

c. With the table still selected, on the **Home tab**, in the **Paragraphs group**, click **Center**. Select the blank paragraph below the table, and then on the **Layout tab**, set the **Spacing After** to **0** pt. **Save** your document.

4 Press Ctrl + Home. On the **Review tab**, in the **Proofing group**, click **Check Document** (or *Spelling & Grammar*) to open the **Editor** pane. For the spelling of *Villmosky*, in the **Editor** pane, click **Ignore All**. If necessary, for the spelling of *Huelsman*, click **Ignore All**.

a. For the grammar error *a*, click **an**. (Mac users: Click Change.) For the spelling error *intrested*, click **interested**. Click **Delete Repeated Word** to delete the duplicated word *for*. Change *activitys* to **activities**. Change *benificial* to **beneficial**. Click **OK** when the check is complete.

b. In the paragraph that begins *I am willing*, in the third line, double-click the word *preparation*. In the **Proofing group**, click **Thesaurus**.

c. In the **Thesaurus** pane, point to *training*, click the **arrow**, and then click **Insert**. **Close** the **Thesaurus** pane. (Mac users: Hold down Ctrl, click *training*, click Insert.)

d. Click **File tab**, on the left, click **Info**, and then in the lower right portion of the screen, click **Show All Properties**. In the **Tags** box, type **cover letter** and in the **Subject** box, type your course name and section number. (Mac users: Display the menu bar, click File, click Properties, click the Summary tab.)

e. In the **Author** box, be sure your name is indicated and edit if necessary. On the left, click **Save**. If directed by your instructor to do so, submit your paper printout, your electronic image of your document that looks like a printed document, or your original Word file. **Close** Word.

You have completed Project 2D **END**

MyLab IT Grader
Mastering Word Project 2E Table of Job Listings

Apply 2A skills from these Objectives:

1. Create a Table
2. Format a Table
3. Present a Word Document Online

In the following Mastering Word project, you will use a Word table to create an announcement for new job postings at the Career Center. Your completed document will look similar to Figure 2.52.

Project Files for MyLab IT Grader

1. In your **MyLab IT** course, locate and click **Word 2E Job Listings**, Download Materials, and then Download All Files.
2. Extract the zipped folder to your Word Chapter 2 folder. Close the Grader download screens.
3. Take a moment to open the downloaded **Word_2E_Job_Listings_Instructions**; note any recent updates to the book.

Project Results

Florida Port Community College Career Center

Job Alert! New Positions for Computer Science Majors!

April 11

Florida Port Community College Career Center has new jobs available for both part-time and full-time positions in Computer Science. Some of these jobs are temporary, some are for a specific project with a defined beginning and ending date, and some are open-ended with the potential for permanent employment. The following jobs were posted in the past week. These listings are just in, so apply now to be one of the first candidates considered!

For further information about any of these new jobs, or a complete listing of jobs that are available through the Career Center, please call Mary Walker-Huelsman at (727) 555-0030 or visit our website at www.fpcc.pro/careers.

New Computer Science Listings for the Week of April 11

POSITION	TYPE	LOCATION
Computer Engineer	Full-time, two months	Clearwater
Project Assistant	Full-time, three months	Coral Springs
Software Developer	Full-time, open-ended	Tampa
UI Designer	Part-time, two months	St. Petersburg

To help prepare yourself before applying for these jobs, we recommend that you review the following articles on our website at www.fpcc.pro/careers.

Topic	Article Title
Research	Working in Computer Science Fields
Interviewing	Interviewing in Startup Companies

Student_Word_2E_Job_Listings

Figure 2.52

For Non-MyLab Submissions

For Project 2E, you will need:
A new blank Word document
w02E_New_Jobs

In your Word Chapter 2 folder, save your document as:
Lastname_Firstname_2E_Job_Listings

After you have named and saved your document, on the next page, begin with Step 2. (Mac users: See MAC TIP in Activity 2.01 to change settings.)
After Step 11, save and submit your file as directed by your instructor.

(continues on next page)

Content-Based Assessments (Mastery and Transfer of Learning)

1 Navigate to your **Word Chapter 2 folder**, and then double-click the Word file you downloaded from **MyLab IT** that displays your name—**Student_Word_2E_Job_Listings**. If necessary, at the top, click **Enable Editing**. (Mac users: if you are not submitting your file in MyLab IT, from the student data files that accompany this project, open Mac_w02E_New_Jobs and use this file instead of a new blank document.)

2 Type **Florida Port Community College Career Center** and press Enter. Type **Job Alert! New Positions for Computer Science Majors!** and press Enter. Type **April 11** and press Enter. Insert the text from the file you downloaded with this project named **w02E_New_Jobs** by using the **Text from File** command.

3 At the top of the document, select and **Center** the three title lines. Select the title *Florida Port Community College Career Center*, change the **Font Size** to **20 pt** and apply **Bold**. Apply **Bold** to the second and third title lines. Locate the paragraph that begins *For further*, and then below that paragraph, position the insertion point in the second blank paragraph. **Insert** a three-column, four-row (**3x4**) table. Enter the following text into the table:

POSITION	TYPE	LOCATION
Computer Engineer	Full-time, two months	Clearwater
Software Developer	Full-time, open-ended	Tampa
UI Designer	Part-time, two months	St. Petersburg

4 In the table, point to the upper left corner of the cell *Software Developer* to display the **Row Insertion** button, and then click to insert a new row. In the new row, type the following information so that the job titles remain in alphabetic order: (Mac users: In your table, click where you want to add a row or column. To the right of the Table Design tab, click the Layout tab, and then use the commands in the Rows & Columns group.)

Project Assistant	Full-time, three months	Coral Springs

5 Select the entire table. From the **Table Tools Layout tab**, apply **AutoFit Contents**. With the table still selected, on the **Home tab**, **Center** the table between the left and right margins, and then add **6 pt Spacing Before** and **6 pt Spacing After**.

6 With the table still selected, remove all table borders, and then add a **Custom 1 pt** solid line top border and bottom border. Select all three cells in the first row, apply **Bold**, and then **Center** the text. Click anywhere in

the first row, and then on the **Table Tools Layout tab**, in the **Rows & Columns group**, insert a row above. Merge the three cells in the new top row, and then type **New Computer Science Listings for the Week of April 11** Notice that the new row keeps the formatting of the row from which it was created.

7 Move to the end of the document, and then **Insert** a two-column, three-row (2x3) table. Enter the following text into the table:

Topic	Article Title
Research	Working in Computer Science Fields
Interviewing	Interviewing in Startup Companies

8 Select the entire table. On the **Layout tab**, in the **Cell Size group**, use the **AutoFit** button to **AutoFit Contents**. On the **Home tab**, **Center** the table. On the **Layout tab**, add **6 pt Spacing Before** and **6 pt Spacing After**.

9 With the table still selected, remove all table borders, and then add a **Custom 1 pt** solid line top border and bottom border. Select the cells in the first row, apply **Bold** and **Center**.

10 Insert the **File Name** in the footer. Display **Backstage** view, click **Info**, and then in the lower right portion of the screen, click **Show All Properties**. In the **Tags** box type **new listings, computer science** and in the **Subject** box type your course name and section number. In the **Author** box, be sure your name is indicated and edit if necessary. (Mac users: To insert the file name, on the Header & Footer tab, in the Insert group, click Field. Under Categories, click Document Information. Under Field names, click FileName. To show properties, on the menu bar click File, click Properties, click the Summary tab. For Tags, use Keywords.)

11 On the left, click **Save**. In the upper right corner of the Word window, click **Close** ⊠.

12 In **MyLab IT**, locate and click the Grader Project **Word 2E Job Listings**. In **step 3**, under **Upload Completed Assignment**, click **Choose File**. In the **Open** dialog box, navigate to your **Word Chapter 2 folder**, and then click your **Student_Word_2E_Job_Listings** file one time to select it. In the lower right corner of the **Open** dialog box, click **Open**.

The name of your selected file displays above the Upload button.

13 To submit your file to **MyLab IT** for grading, click **Upload**, wait a moment for a green **Success!** message, and then in **step 4**, click the blue **Submit for Grading** button. Click **Close Assignment** to return to your list of **Course Materials**.

You have completed Project 2E | **END**

Content-Based Assessments (Mastery and Transfer of Learning)

Apply 2B skills from these Objectives:

4. Create a Letterhead for a Cover Letter
5. Create a Cover Letter and Correct and Reorganize Text
6. Use the Word Editor to Check Your Document
7. Print an Envelope, Change a Style Set, Create a Word Template, and Use Learning Tools

In the following Mastering Word project, you will create a memo that includes job tips for students and graduates using the services of the Florida Port Community College Career Center. Your completed document will look similar to Figure 2.53.

Project Files for MyLab IT Grader

1. In your **MyLab IT** course, locate and click **Word 2F Career Tips**, Download Materials, and then Download All Files.
2. Extract the zipped folder to your Word Chapter 2 folder. Close the Grader download screens.
3. Take a moment to open the downloaded **Word_2F_Career_Tips_Instructions**; note any recent updates to the book.

Project Results

Florida Port Community College Career Center

Memo

DATE: January 12, 2021

TO: Florida Port Community College Students and Graduates

FROM: Mary Walker-Huelsman, Director

SUBJECT: Using the Career Center

Tips for Students and Recent Graduates of Florida Port Community College

It is no surprise that after you leave college, you will be entering one of the most competitive job markets on record. That doesn't mean it's impossible to get your dream job. It does, however, mean that it's critical that you know how to put your best self forward to job interviewers and that you highlight all your academic, personal, and professional achievements in a way that will help you stand out from the crowd. An Associate degree from Florida Port Community College is just the first step on your journey to getting the professional career that you want.

Give 100 Percent to Every Job

Treat every job as a career. Be willing to go beyond your assignment and complete tasks not delegated to you. Take the initiative to see ways to contribute to the company. Be willing to stay if there is unfinished work. You never know who you will meet on any job. Making a positive impression every time will give you a network of people who may help you down the road. Networking is an established means that professionals use to further their careers. You can always benefit from networking. You will distinguish yourself from potential competitors if you truly give 100 percent to each job. Always remember these job basics:

Job Item	Tip for Success
Time Management	Show up on time and don't hurry to leave
Attire	Dress appropriately for the job
Work Area	Keep your work area neat and organized

Use the Career Center

Here at the Career Center and on our website, we offer tips on how to write a stellar resume and a cover letter that puts your hard work up front and center. Have you volunteered somewhere? Have you participated at a club at school? Were you a TA or a tutor? Did you make the Dean's list or graduate with honors? These are the kinds of achievements interviewers want to see. Meet with your career guidance counselor and together, come up with a plan to find the jobs that you want and get the important interview.

Student_Word_2F_Career_Tips

Figure 2.53

For Non-MyLab Submissions

For Project 2F, you will need:
w02F_Career_Tips
w02F_Memo_Text

In your Word Chapter 2 folder, save your w02F_Career_Tips document as:
Lastname_Firstname_2F_Career_Tips

After you have named and saved your document, on the next page, begin with Step 2.

After Step 12, save and submit your file as directed by your instructor.

(continues on next page)

Content-Based Assessments (Mastery and Transfer of Learning)

1 Navigate to your **Word Chapter 2 folder**, and then double-click the Word file you downloaded from **MyLab IT** that displays your name—**Student_Word_2F_Career_Tips**. If necessary, at the top, click **Enable Editing**.

2 Insert the **File Name** in the footer. If necessary, display formatting marks. By using the information below, complete the memo headings by positioning your insertion point to the left of the paragraph mark for each heading.

DATE:	January 12, 2021
TO:	Florida Port Community College Students and Graduates
FROM:	Mary Walker-Huelsman, Director
SUBJECT:	Using the CC

3 Position the insertion point in the blank paragraph below the memo heading. **Insert** the file **w02F_Memo_Text**, and then press (Backspace) one time to remove the blank line at the end of the inserted text.

4 Position the insertion point at the top of the document. From the **Review tab**, display the **Editor** pane. By clicking the suggested words in the **Editor**, correct *too* to **to**, *proffessionals* to **professionals**, *benifit* to **benefit**, *Deans* to **Dean's**, *guidence* to **guidance**, and *interveiw* to **interview**.

5 In the paragraph that begins *Treat every job*, in the second line, locate and double-click the word *donate*. (Mac users: Hold down (control), click *donate* in the Thesaurus pane, and then click Insert "donate".) Use the **Thesaurus** to replace the word with *contribute*. In the last line of the same paragraph, right-click the word *fundamentals*, point to **Synonyms**, and then click *basics*. If necessary, close the Thesaurus pane.

6 In the paragraph that begins *An Associate degree*, move the first sentence to the end of the paragraph.

7 Below the paragraph that begins *Treat every job*, click in the blank paragraph, and then **Insert** a **2x4** table.

8 Type the following information in the table:

Job Item	Tip for Success
Time Management	Show up on time and don't hurry to leave
Attire	Dress appropriately for the job
Work Area	Keep your work area neat and organized

9 Select the entire table. **AutoFit Contents**, and then apply the **Grid Table 1 Light – Accent 1** table style. **Center** the table between the left and right margins.

10 Position the insertion point at the top of the document, and then by using the **Match case** option, replace all instances of *CC* with *Career Center*.

11 Display **Backstage** view, click **Info**, and then click **Show All Properties**. As the **Tags**, type **memo, job tips** (Note: Mac users use the Keywords box.) As the **Subject**, type your course name and section number. Be sure your name is indicated as the **Author**, and edit if necessary.

12 On the left, click **Save**. In the upper right corner of the Word window, click **Close** ☒.

13 In **MyLab IT**, locate and click the Grader Project **Word 2F Career Tips**. In **step 3**, under **Upload Completed Assignment**, click **Choose File**. In the **Open** dialog box, navigate to your **Word Chapter 2 folder**, and then click your **Student_Word_2F_Career_Tips** file one time to select it. In the lower right corner of the **Open** dialog box, click **Open**.

The name of your selected file displays above the Upload button.

14 To submit your file to **MyLab IT** for grading, click **Upload**, wait a moment for a green **Success!** message, and then in **step 4**, click the blue **Submit for Grading** button. Click **Close Assignment** to return to your list of **Course Materials**.

You have completed Project 2F ▮ **END**

Apply 2A and 2B skills from these Objectives:

1. Create a Table for a Resume
2. Format a Table
3. Present a Word Document Online
4. Create a Letterhead for a Cover Letter
5. Create a Cover Letter and Correct and Reorganize Text
6. Use the Word Editor to Check Your Document
7. Print an Envelope, Change a Style Set, Create a Word Template, and Use Learning Tools

In the following Mastering Word project, you will create a cover letter and resume. Your completed documents will look similar to Figure 2.54.

Project Files for MyLab IT Grader

1. In your **MyLab IT** course, locate and click **Word 2G Letter and Resume**, Download Materials, and then Download All Files.
2. Extract the zipped folder to your Word Chapter 2 folder. Close the Grader download screens.
3. Take a moment to open the downloaded **Word_2G_Letter_and_Resume_Instructions**; note any recent updates to the book.

Project Results

Figure 2.54

For Non-MyLab Submissions

For Project 2G, you will need:

w02G_Letter_and_Resume
w02G_Letter_Text

In your Word Chapter 2 folder, save your w02G_Letter_and_Resume document as:

Lastname_Firstname_2G_Letter_and_Resume

After you have named and saved your document, on the next page, begin with Step 2.
After Step 15, save and submit your file as directed by your instructor.

(continues on next page)

Content-Based Assessments (Mastery and Transfer of Learning)

1 Navigate to your **Word Chapter 2 folder**, and then double-click the Word file you downloaded from **MyLab IT** that displays your name—**Student_Word_2G_Letter_and_Resume**. If necessary, at the top, click **Enable Editing**.

2 Add the **File Name** to the footer. Be sure that rulers and formatting marks display. On **Page 1**, click in the blank paragraph below the letterhead, and then press Enter two times. Use the **Date & Time** command to insert the current date using the third format. Press Enter two times. Type **Ms. Mary Walker-Huelsman, Director** and press Enter. Type **Florida Port Community College Career Center** and press Enter. Type **2745 Oakland Avenue** and press Enter. Type **St. Petersburg, FL 33713** and press Enter. Select the first three lines of the inside address, and then set **Spacing After** to **0 pt**.

3 Click in the blank paragraph below the inside address. Type **Dear Ms. Walker-Huelsman:** and press Enter. **Insert** the text from the file **w02G_Letter_Text** and press Backspace one time to remove the blank line at the bottom of the inserted text.

4 Press Ctrl + Home to move to the top of the document. From the **Review tab**, display the **Editor** pane. Take appropriate action on each flagged item including removing the comma from the conjunction.

5 Press Ctrl + Home to move to the top of the document again, and then replace all instances of **posting** with **listing**

6 In the paragraph that begins *The job description*, use the Thesaurus pane or the Synonyms command on the shortcut menu to change *specific* to *explicit* and *credentials* to *qualifications*.

7 In the paragraph that begins *I currently live in Tampa* select the first sentence of the paragraph and drag it to the end of the same paragraph.

8 Click at the beginning of the paragraph that begins *I could be available*, press Enter to insert a new blank paragraph, and then press ↑ to position your insertion point in the new blank paragraph. **Insert** a **2x3** table, and then type the text shown in Table 1 at the bottom of the page.

9 Select the entire table. **AutoFit Contents**, and then apply the **Table Grid Light** table style—under **Plain Tables**, in the first row, the first style. **Center** the table between the left and right margins. Select the blank paragraph mark below the table and apply **Spacing After** of **0 pt**.

10 In the resume on **Page 2**, insert a new second row in the table. In the first cell of the new row, type **OBJECTIVE** and press Tab. Type **To obtain a Business Programmer Analyst position that will use my technical and communications skills and computer support experience.** Add **12 pt Spacing After** to the text you just typed and apply **Bold** to the word *OBJECVTIVE*. (Mac users: When inserting a row above in a table, the formatting style of the row below is applied. Deselect bold formatting as necessary.)

11 Select the entire resume table and apply **AutoFit Contents**. Remove the table borders, and then from the **Borders and Shading** dialog box, apply a **Custom** single solid line **1 1/2 pt** top border to the table.

12 In the first row of the resume table, select both cells and then **Merge Cells**. **Center** the five lines and apply **Bold**. In the first row, select *William Franklin* and change the **Font Size** to **20 pt** and add **24 pt Spacing Before**. Click in the email address at the bottom of the first row, and then add **24 pt Spacing After**.

13 In the cell to the right of *RELEVANT EXPERIENCE*, below the line that begins *January 2018*, apply bullets to the six lines that comprise the job duties. Create a similar bulleted list for the duties as a Computer Technician.

14 Display **Backstage** view, click **Info**, and then click **Show All Properties**. As the **Tags**, type **cover letter, resume** (Mac users; use Keywords.) As the **Subject**, type your course name and section number. Be sure your name is indicated as the **Author**, and edit if necessary.

Table 1

Education	Bachelor of Science, Business Management
Experience	Two years Computer Support experience at a major university
Required Certifications	MCSA BI Reporting, MCSA Microsoft Dynamics 365

(continues on next page)

Mastering Word: Project 2G Application Letter and Resume (continued)

15 On the left, click **Save**. In the upper right corner of the Word window, click **Close** ☒.

16 In **MyLab IT**, locate and click the Grader Project **Word 2G Letter and Resume**. In **step 3**, under **Upload Completed Assignment**, click **Choose File**. In the **Open** dialog box, navigate to your **Word Chapter 2 folder**, and then click your **Student_Word_2G_Letter_and_Resume** file one time to select it. In the lower right corner of the **Open** dialog box, click **Open**.

The name of your selected file displays above the Upload button.

17 To submit your file to **MyLab IT** for grading, click **Upload**, wait a moment for a green **Success!** message, and then in **step 4**, click the blue **Submit for Grading** button. Click **Close Assignment** to return to your list of **Course Materials**.

You have completed Project 2G   **END**

Content-Based Assessments (Critical Thinking)

Apply a combination of the 2A and 2B skills.

GO! Fix It	**Project 2H New Jobs**	IRC
GO! Make It	**Project 2I Training**	IRC
GO! Solve It	**Project 2J Job Postings**	IRC
GO! Solve It	**Project 2K Agenda**	

Project Files

For Project 2K, you will need the following file:

Agenda template from Word's Online templates

You will save your document as:

Lastname_Firstname_2K_Agenda

Start Word, on the left click New, and then search for an online template using the search term **formal meeting agenda** Click the agenda and then click Create. Save the agenda in your Word Chapter 2 folder as **Lastname_Firstname_2K_Agenda** Use the following information to prepare an agenda for an FPCC Career Center meeting.

The meeting will be chaired by Mary Walker-Huelsman. It will be the monthly meeting of the Career Center's staff—Kevin Rau, Marilyn Kelly, André Randolph, Susan Nguyen, and Charles James. The meeting will be held on March 15 at 3:00 p.m. The old business agenda items (open issues) include 1) seeking more job listings related to the printing and food service industries; 2) expanding the alumni website, and 3) the addition of a part-time trainer. The new business agenda items will include 1) writing a grant so the center can serve more students and alumni; 2) expanding the training area with 20 additional workstations; 3) purchase of new computers for the training room; and 4) renewal of printing service contract.

Add the file name to the footer, add your name, your course name, the section number, and then add the keywords **agenda, monthly staff meeting** to the Properties area. Submit as directed.

	Performance Level		
	Exemplary: You consistently applied the relevant skills	**Proficient: You sometimes, but not always, applied the relevant skills**	**Developing: You rarely or never applied the relevant skills**
Select an agenda template	Agenda template is appropriate for the information provided for the meeting.	Agenda template is used, but does not fit the information provided.	No template is used for the agenda.
Add appropriate information to the template	All information is inserted in the appropriate places.	All information is included, but not in the appropriate places.	Information is missing.
Format template information	All text in the template is properly aligned and formatted.	All text is included, but alignment or formatting is inconsistent.	No additional formatting has been added.

Performance Criteria

You have completed Project 2K | **END**

Rubric

The following outcomes-based assessments are *open-ended assessments*. That is, there is no specific correct result; your result will depend on your approach to the information provided. Make *Professional Quality* your goal. Use the following scoring rubric to guide you in *how* to approach the problem and then to evaluate *how well* your approach solves the problem.

The *criteria*—Software Mastery, Content, Format and Layout, and Process—represent the knowledge and skills you have gained that you can apply to solving the problem. The *levels of performance*—Professional Quality, Approaching Professional Quality, or Needs Quality Improvements—help you and your instructor evaluate your result.

	Your completed project is of Professional Quality if you:	Your completed project is Approaching Professional Quality if you:	Your completed project Needs Quality Improvements if you:
1-Software Mastery	Choose and apply the most appropriate skills, tools, and features and identify efficient methods to solve the problem.	Choose and apply some appropriate skills, tools, and features, but not in the most efficient manner.	Choose inappropriate skills, tools, or features, or are inefficient in solving the problem.
2-Content	Construct a solution that is clear and well organized, contains content that is accurate, appropriate to the audience and purpose, and is complete. Provide a solution that contains no errors of spelling, grammar, or style.	Construct a solution in which some components are unclear, poorly organized, inconsistent, or incomplete. Misjudge the needs of the audience. Have some errors in spelling, grammar, or style, but the errors do not detract from comprehension.	Construct a solution that is unclear, incomplete, or poorly organized, contains some inaccurate or inappropriate content, and contains many errors of spelling, grammar, or style. Do not solve the problem.
3-Format and Layout	Format and arrange all elements to communicate information and ideas, clarify function, illustrate relationships, and indicate relative importance.	Apply appropriate format and layout features to some elements, but not others. Overuse features, causing minor distraction.	Apply format and layout that does not communicate information or ideas clearly. Do not use format and layout features to clarify function, illustrate relationships, or indicate relative importance. Use available features excessively, causing distraction.
4-Process	Use an organized approach that integrates planning, development, self-assessment, revision, and reflection.	Demonstrate an organized approach in some areas, but not others; or, use an insufficient process of organization throughout.	Do not use an organized approach to solve the problem.

Outcomes-Based Assessments (Critical Thinking)

GO! Think	Project 2L Workshops

Apply a combination of the 2A and 2B skills.

Project Files

For Project 2L, you will need the following files:

New blank Word document

w02L_Workshop_Information

You will save your document as:

Lastname_Firstname_2L_Workshops

The Florida Port Community College Career Center offers a series of workshops for both students and alumni. Any eligible student or graduate can attend the workshops, and there is no fee. Currently, the Career Center offers a three-session workshop covering Excel and Word, a two-session workshop covering Business Communication, and a one-session workshop covering Creating a Resume.

Print the w02L_Workshop_Information file and use the information to complete this project. Create an announcement with a title, an introductory paragraph, and a table listing the workshops and the topics covered in each workshop. Use the file w02L_Workshop_Information for help with the topics covered in each workshop. Format the table cells appropriately. Add an appropriate footer and document properties. Save the document as **Lastname_Firstname_2L_Workshops** and submit it as directed.

You have completed Project 2L   **END**

GO! Think	Project 2M Schedule	IRC
You and GO!	Project 2N Personal Resume	IRC
GO! Cumulative Team Project	Project 2O Bell Orchid Hotels	IRC

Creating Research Papers, Newsletters, and Merged Mailing Labels

WORD 2019

PROJECT 3A

Outcomes
Create a research paper that includes citations and a bibliography.

Objectives
1. Create a Research Paper
2. Insert Footnotes in a Research Paper
3. Create Citations and a Bibliography in a Research Paper
4. Use Read Mode, PDF Reflow, and Save Documents in Alternate Formats

PROJECT 3B

Outcomes
Create a multiple-column newsletter and merged mailing labels.

Objectives
5. Format a Multiple-Column Newsletter
6. Use Special Character and Paragraph Formatting
7. Create Mailing Labels Using Mail Merge

create jobs 51/Shutterstock

In This Chapter

 GO! To Work with Word

Microsoft Word provides many tools for creating complex documents. For example, Word has tools that enable you to create a research paper that includes citations, footnotes, and a bibliography, and to research information from other sources directly from within Word. You can also create multiple-column newsletters, format the nameplate at the top of the newsletter, use special character formatting to create distinctive title text, and add borders and shading to paragraphs to highlight important information.

In this chapter, you will edit and format a research paper, create a two-column newsletter, and optionally create a set of mailing labels to mail the newsletter to multiple recipients.

The projects in this chapter relate to **University Medical Center**, which is a patient-care and research institution serving the metropolitan area of Memphis, Tennessee. Because of its outstanding reputation in the medical community and around the world, University Medical Center can attract top physicians, scientists, and researchers in all fields of medicine and achieve a level of funding that allows it to build and operate state-of-the-art facilities. A program in biomedical research was recently added. Individuals throughout the eastern United States travel to University Medical Center for diagnosis and care.

Research Paper

Project Activities

In Activities 3.01 through 3.14, you will edit and format a research paper that contains an overview of a new area of study. This paper was created by Gerard Foster, a medical intern at University Medical Center, for distribution to his classmates studying various physiologic monitoring devices. Your completed document will look similar to Figure 3.1.

Project Files for **MyLab IT Grader**

1. In your storage location, create a folder named **Word Chapter 3**
2. In your MyLab IT course, locate and click **Word 3A Quantitative Technology**, Download Materials, and then Download All Files.
3. Extract the zipped folder to your Word Chapter 3 folder. Close the Grader download screens.
4. Take a moment to open the downloaded **Word_3A_Quantitative_Technology_Instructions**; note any recent updates to the book.

Project Results

GO! Project 3A
Where We're Going

Figure 3.1 Project 3A Quantitative Technology

 For Non-MyLab Submissions

For Project 3A, you will need:
w03A_Quantitative_Technology

In your storage location, create a folder named **Word Chapter 3**
In your Word Chapter 3 folder, save your document as:
Lastname_Firstname_3A_Quantitative_Technology

After you have named and saved your document, on the next page, begin with Step 2.

Objective 1 Create a Research Paper

ALERT   Because Office 365 is a cloud-based subscription service that receives continuous updates, you may encounter some variations in what appears on your screen and what is shown in this instruction. Microsoft Office 365 is fully installed on your PC or Mac; no internet access is necessary to create or edit documents. When you *are* connected to the internet, you will receive monthly upgrades and new features, so you always have the latest versions of Office apps as soon as they are available. Your subscription gives you continuous free access to the latest innovations and refinements.

GO! Learn How
Video W3-1

When you write a research paper or a report for college or business, follow a format prescribed by one of the standard *style guides*—a manual that contains standards for the design and writing of documents. The two most commonly used styles for research papers are those created by the *Modern Language Association (MLA)* and the *American Psychological Association (APA)*; there are several others.

Activity 3.01 | Formatting the Spacing and First-Page Information for a Research Paper

2.2.3

When formatting the text for your research paper, refer to the standards for the style guide that you have chosen. In this Activity, you will create a research paper using the MLA style. The MLA style uses 1-inch margins, a 0.5" first line indent, and double spacing throughout the body of the document with no extra space above or below paragraphs.

1 ▸ Navigate to your **Word Chapter 3 folder**, and then double-click the Word file you downloaded from MyLab IT that displays your name—**Student_Word_3A_Quantitative_Technology**. If necessary, at the top click **Enable Editing**.

2 ▸ On the **Review tab**, from the **Proofing group**, display the Word **Editor**, and then click **Ignore Once** for each instance of any flagged items—this will remove any red squiggles or other markings from your document. When complete, click **OK**, and if necessary, close the Editor pane.

▭ **MAC TIP** To display group names on the ribbon, display the menu, click Word, click Preferences, click View, select the Show group titles check box.

3 ▸ Press Ctrl + A to select all the text in the document. With the entire document selected, on the **Home tab**, in the **Paragraph group**, click **Line and Paragraph Spacing** ⌄≡⌄, and then change the line spacing to **2.0**. On the **Layout tab**, in the **Paragraph group**, change the **Spacing After** to **0 pt**.

▭ **MAC TIP** Press command ⌘ + A to select the entire document.

↻ **ANOTHER WAY** On the Home tab, in the Editing group, click Select, and then click Select All to select the entire document.

4 ▸ Press Ctrl + Home to deselect and move to the top of the document. Press Enter one time to create a blank line at the top of the document, and then click to position the insertion point in the new blank paragraph. Type **Gerard Foster** and press Enter.

▭ **MAC TIP** Press command ⌘ + fn + ←.

5 Type **Dr. Hillary Kim** and press Enter. Type **Biomedical Research 617** and press Enter. Type **February 15, 2021** and press Enter.

6 Type **Quantified Self Movement Gains Momentum** and then press Ctrl + E, which is the keyboard shortcut to center a paragraph of text. Click **Save** 🖫, and then compare your screen with Figure 3.2.

> To create the document heading for a research paper, on the first line, type the report author. On the second line, type the person for whom the report is prepared—for example, your professor or supervisor. On the third line, type the name of the class or business. On the fourth line, type the date. On the fifth line, type the report title and center it.

🖥 **MAC TIP** Press command ⌘ + E to center a paragraph.

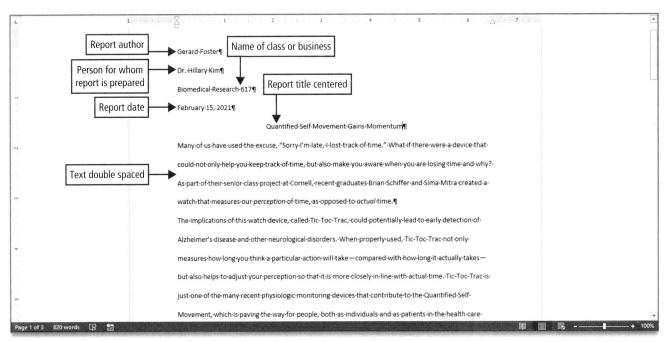

Figure 3.2

Activity 3.02 | Formatting the Page Numbering and Paragraph Indents for a Research Paper

MOS
2.2.3

1 On the **Insert tab**, in the **Header & Footer group**, click **Header**, and then at the bottom of the list, click **Edit Header**.

2 Type **Foster** and then press Spacebar one time.

> Recall that the text you insert into a header or footer displays on every page of a document. Within a header or footer, you can insert many types of information; for example, automatic page numbers, the date, the time, the file name, or pictures.

3 Under **Header and Footer Tools**, on the **Design tab**, in the **Header & Footer group**, click **Page Number**, and then point to **Current Position**. In the gallery, under **Simple**, click **Plain Number**. Compare your screen with Figure 3.3.

Word will automatically number the pages using this number format.

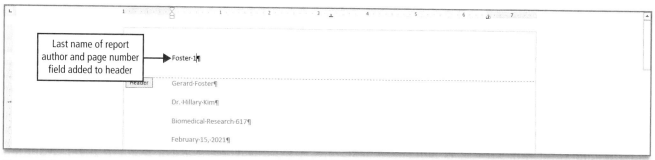

Figure 3.3

4 On the **Home tab**, in the **Paragraph group**, click **Align Right** 🗏. Double-click anywhere in the document to close the Header area.

MAC TIP Click Page Number; in the Alignment box, click Right, click OK.

5 Near the top of **Page 1**, locate the paragraph beginning *Many of us*, and then click to position the insertion point at the beginning of the paragraph. On the right of your screen, by moving the vertical scroll box, scroll down to view the end of the document, hold down Shift, and then click to the right of the last paragraph mark to select all of the text from the insertion point to the end of the document. Release Shift.

6 With the text selected, in the **Paragraph group**, click the **Dialog Box Launcher** button ⤢ to display the **Paragraph** dialog box.

MAC TIP Click Line and Paragraph Spacing. Click Line Spacing Options to open the Paragraph dialog box.

7 On the **Indents and Spacing tab**, under **Indentation**, click the **Special arrow**, and then click **First line**. In the **By** box, be sure **0.5"** displays. Click **OK**. Compare your screen with Figure 3.4.

The MLA style uses 0.5-inch indents at the beginning of the first line of every paragraph. *Indenting*— moving the beginning of the first line of a paragraph to the right or left of the rest of the paragraph— provides visual cues to the reader to help divide the document text and make it easier to read.

Figure 3.4

ANOTHER WAY On the ruler, point to the First Line Indent button ⬚, and then drag the button to 0.5" on the horizontal ruler.

8 Press `Ctrl` + `Home` to deselect and move to the top of the document. On the **Insert tab**, in the **Header & Footer group**, click **Footer**, and then at the bottom of the list click **Edit Footer**.

9 In the **Insert group**, click **Document Info**, and then click **File Name**. On the ribbon, click **Close Header and Footer**.

The file name in the footer is *not* part of the research report format, but it is included in projects in this instruction so that you and your instructor can identify your work.

🖳 **MAC TIP** Click Field. In the Field dialog box, under Categories, click Document Information. Under Field names, click FileName.

10 Save 🖫 your document.

MORE KNOWLEDGE **Suppressing the Page Number on the First Page of a Document**

Some style guidelines require that the page number and other header and footer information on the first page be hidden from view—*suppressed*. To hide the information contained in the header and footer areas on Page 1 of a document, double-click in the header or footer area. Then, under Header and Footer Tools, on the Design tab, in the Options group, select the Different First Page check box.

| Objective 2 | **Insert Footnotes in a Research Paper** |

GO! Learn How
Video W3-2

Within report text, numbers mark the location of ***notes***—information that expands on the topic being discussed but that does not fit well in the document text. The numbers refer to *footnotes*—notes placed at the bottom of the page containing the note, or to ***endnotes***—notes placed at the end of a document or chapter.

Activity 3.03 | **Inserting Footnotes**

4.1.1

You can add footnotes as you type your document or after your document is complete. Word renumbers the footnotes automatically, so footnotes do not need to be entered in order, and if one footnote is removed, the remaining footnotes automatically renumber.

1 Scroll to view the upper portion of **Page 2**, and then locate the paragraph that begins *Accurate records*. In the third line of the paragraph, click to position the insertion point to the right of the period after *infancy*.

2 On the **References tab**, in the **Footnotes group**, click **Insert Footnote**.

Word creates space for a footnote in the footnote area at the bottom of the page and adds a footnote number to the text at the insertion point location. Footnote *1* displays in the footnote area, and the insertion point moves to the right of the number. A short black line is added just above the footnote area. You do not need to type the footnote number.

3 Type **The U.S. Department of Health & Human Services indicates that the widespread use of Health Information Technology will improve the quality of health care.**

This is an explanatory footnote; the footnote provides additional information that does not fit well in the body of the report.

4 Scroll to view the top of **Page 1**, and then locate the paragraph that begins *Many of us*. At the end of the paragraph, click to position the insertion point to the right of the period following *time*.

5 On the **References tab**, in the **Footnotes group**, click **Insert Footnote**. Type **Organizations such as airlines and the military could benefit because many employees are involved in time-sensitive operations.** Notice that the footnote you just added becomes the new footnote *1*. Click **Save** 🖫, and then compare your screen with Figure 3.5.

The first footnote that you typed, which is on Page 2 and begins *The U.S. Department of Health*, is renumbered as footnote *2*.

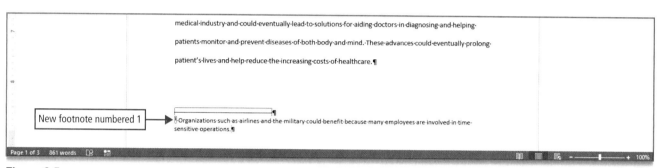

medical·industry·and·could·eventually·lead·to·solutions·for·aiding·doctors·in·diagnosing·and·helping·

patients·monitor·and·prevent·diseases·of·both·body·and·mind.·These·advances·could·eventually·prolong·

patient's·lives·and·help·reduce·the·increasing·costs·of·healthcare.¶

New footnote numbered 1 → ⁸·Organizations·such·as·airlines·and·the·military·could·benefit·because·many·employees·are·involved·in·time-sensitive·operations.¶

Page 1 of 3   861 words

Figure 3.5

MORE KNOWLEDGE | **Using Symbols Rather Than Numbers for Notes**

Instead of using numbers to designate footnotes, you can use standard footnote symbols. The seven traditional symbols, available from the Footnote and Endnote dialog box, in order, are * (asterisk), † (dagger), ‡ (double dagger), § (section mark), ‖ (parallels), ¶ (paragraph mark), and # (number or pound sign). This sequence can be continuous, which is the default setting, or it can begin anew with each page.

Activity 3.04 | Modifying a Footnote Style

4.1.2, 2.3.2 (Expert)

Microsoft Word contains built-in paragraph formats called *styles*—groups of formatting commands, such as font, font size, font color, paragraph alignment, and line spacing—that can be applied to a paragraph with one command.

The default style for footnote text is a single-spaced paragraph that uses a 10-point Calibri font and no paragraph indents. MLA style specifies double-spaced text in all areas of a research paper—including footnotes. According to the MLA style, first lines of footnotes must also be indented 0.5 inch and use the same font size as the report text.

1 Click the **Home tab**, and then in the **Paragraph group**, examine the font size and line spacing settings. Notice that the new footnote displays in 10 pt font size and is single-spaced, even though the font size of the document text is 11 pt and the text is double-spaced, as shown in Figure 3.6.

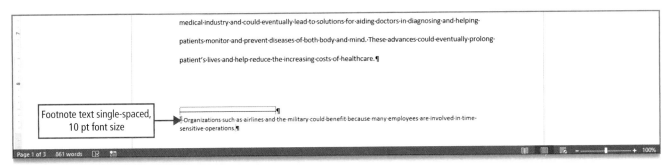

medical·industry·and·could·eventually·lead·to·solutions·for·aiding·doctors·in·diagnosing·and·helping·

patients·monitor·and·prevent·diseases·of·both·body·and·mind.·These·advances·could·eventually·prolong·

patient's·lives·and·help·reduce·the·increasing·costs·of·healthcare.¶

> Footnote text single-spaced, 10 pt font size

⁸·Organizations·such·as·airlines·and·the·military·could·benefit·because·many·employees·are·involved·in·time-sensitive·operations.¶

Page 1 of 3   861 words

Figure 3.6

2 At the bottom of **Page 1**, point anywhere in the footnote text you just typed, right-click, and then on the shortcut menu, click **Style**. Compare your screen with Figure 3.7.

The Style dialog box displays, listing the styles currently in use in the document, in addition to some of the word processing elements that come with special built-in styles. Because you right-clicked in the footnote text, the selected style is the Footnote Text style.

Figure 3.7

3 In the **Style** dialog box, click **Modify**, and then in the **Modify Style** dialog box, locate the small **Formatting** toolbar in the center of the dialog box. Click the **Font Size button arrow**, click **11**, and then compare your screen with Figure 3.8.

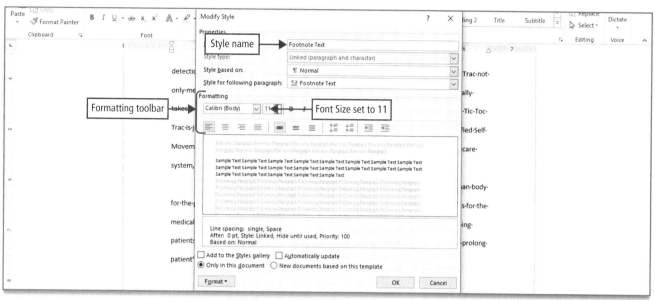

Figure 3.8

4 In the lower left corner of the dialog box, click **Format**, and then click **Paragraph**. In the **Paragraph** dialog box, on the **Indents and Spacing tab**, under **Indentation**, click the **Special arrow**, and then click **First line**.

5 Under **Spacing**, click the **Line spacing arrow**, and then click **Double**. Compare your dialog box with Figure 3.9.

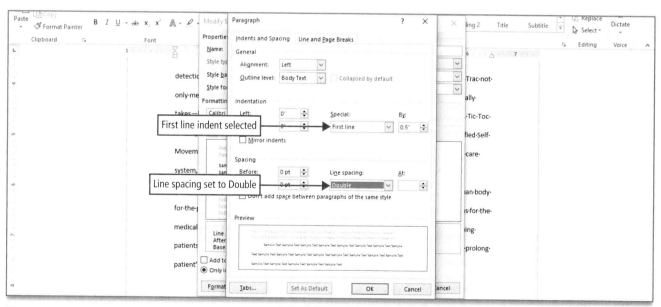

Figure 3.9

6 Click **OK** to close the **Paragraph** dialog box, click **OK** to close the **Modify Style** dialog box, and then click **Apply** to apply the new style and close the dialog box. Compare your screen with Figure 3.10.

Word formats your inserted footnotes with the modified Footnote Text paragraph style; any new footnotes that you insert will also use this format.

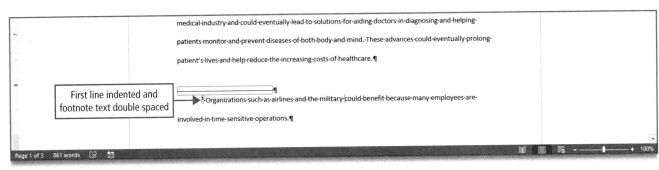

medical·industry·and·could·eventually·lead·to·solutions·for·aiding·doctors·in·diagnosing·and·helping·

patients·monitor·and·prevent·diseases·of·both·body·and·mind.·These·advances·could·eventually·prolong·

patient's·lives·and·help·reduce·the·increasing·costs·of·healthcare.¶

First line indented and footnote text double spaced

·Organizations·such·as·airlines·and·the·military·could·benefit·because·many·employees·are·

involved·in·time-sensitive·operations.¶

Figure 3.10

7 Scroll to view the bottom of **Page 2** to confirm that the new format was also applied to the second footnote, and then **Save** your document.

Objective 3 | Create Citations and a Bibliography in a Research Paper

GO! Learn How
Video W3-3

Reports and research papers typically include information that you find in other sources, and these sources of information must be credited. When you use quotations from or detailed summaries of other people's work, you must specify the source of the information. A ***citation*** is a note inserted into the text of a report or research paper that refers the reader to a source in the ***bibliography***. Create a bibliography at the end of a research paper to list the sources you have referenced. Such a list is typically titled ***Works Cited*** (in MLA style), *Bibliography*, *Sources*, or *References*.

Activity 3.05 | Adding Citations for a Book

MOS
4.1.3, 4.1.4

When writing a long research paper, you will likely reference numerous books, articles, and websites. Some of your research sources may be referenced many times, others only one time. References to sources within the text of your research paper are indicated in an *abbreviated* manner. However, as you enter a citation for the first time, you can also enter the *complete* information about the source. Then, when you have finished your paper, you will be able to automatically generate the list of sources that must be included at the end of your research paper.

1 On the **References tab**, in the **Citations & Bibliography group**, click the **Style button arrow**, and then click **MLA** to insert a reference using MLA bibliography style.

2 Scroll to view the middle of **Page 2**. In the paragraph that begins *Accurate records*, at the end of the paragraph, click to position the insertion point to the right of the quotation mark.

The citation in the document points to the full source information in the bibliography, which typically includes the name of the author, the full title of the work, the year of publication, and other publication information.

3 ▶ Click **Insert Citation**, and then click **Add New Source**. Click the **Type of Source arrow**, and then click **Book**. Add the following information, and then compare your screen with Figure 3.11:

Author:	**Sopol, Eric J.**
Title:	**The Creative Destruction of Medicine**
Year:	**2012**
City:	**New York**
Publisher:	**Basic Books**
Medium:	**Print**

🖥 **MAC TIP** The order of fields is Author, Title, City, Publisher, Year; there is no Medium field.

Figure 3.11

4 ▶ Click **OK** to insert the citation. Point to *(Sopol)* and click one time to select the citation.

> In the MLA style, citations that refer to items on the *Works Cited* page are placed in parentheses and are referred to as **parenthetical references**—references that include the last name of the author or authors and the page number in the referenced source, which you add to the reference. No year is indicated, and there is no comma between the name and the page number. Both MLA and APA styles use parenthetical references for source citations rather than using footnotes.

5 ▶ **Save** 🖫 the document.

NOTE **Citing Corporate Authors and Indicating the Medium**

If the author of a document is only identified as the name of an organization, select the Corporate Author check box and type the name of the organization in the Corporate Author box.

In the 7th edition of the *MLA Handbook for Writers of Research Papers*, the category Medium was added and must be included for any item on the Works Cited page. Entries for this category can include Print, Web, Performance, and Photograph, among many others.

Activity 3.06 | Editing Citations

4.1.3

1 ▶ In the lower right corner of the box that surrounds the selected reference, point to the small arrow to display the ScreenTip *Citation Options*. Click this **Citation Options arrow**, and then on the list of options, click **Edit Citation**.

2 In the **Edit Citation** dialog box, under **Add**, in the **Pages** box, type **5** to indicate that you are citing from page 5 of this source. Compare your screen with Figure 3.12.

Figure 3.12

3 Click **OK** to display the page number of the citation. Click outside of the citation box to deselect it.

4 Type a period to the right of the citation.

5 Delete the period to the left of the quotation mark.

> In the MLA style, if the reference occurs at the end of a sentence, the parenthetical reference always displays to the left of the punctuation mark that ends the sentence.

6 Press [Ctrl] + [End] to move to the end of the document, and then click to position the insertion point after the letter *e* in *disease* and to the left of the period.

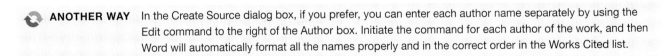

MAC TIP Press [command ⌘] + [fn] + [→].

7 In the **Citations & Bibliography group**, click **Insert Citation**, and then click **Add New Source**. Click the **Type of Source arrow**, if necessary scroll to the top of the list, click **Book**. Being sure to include the period following the name *Salzberg*, add the following information:

Author:	**Glaser, John P., and Claudia Salzberg.**
Title:	**The Strategic Application of Information Technology in Health Care Organizations**
Year:	**2011**
City:	**San Francisco**
Publisher:	**Jossey-Bass**
Medium:	**Print**

8 Click **OK**. Click the inserted citation to select it, click the **Citation Options arrow**, and then click **Edit Citation**.

ANOTHER WAY In the Create Source dialog box, if you prefer, you can enter each author name separately by using the Edit command to the right of the Author box. Initiate the command for each author of the work, and then Word will automatically format all the names properly and in the correct order in the Works Cited list.

9 In the **Edit Citation** dialog box, under **Add**, in the **Pages** box, type **28** to indicate that you are citing from page 28 of this source. Click **OK**.

10 On the **References tab**, in the **Citations & Bibliography group**, click **Manage Sources**, and then compare your screen with Figure 3.13.

> The Source Manager dialog box displays. Other citations on your computer might display in the Master List box. The citations for the current document display in the Current List box. Word

maintains the Master List so that if you use the same sources regularly, you can copy sources from your Master List to the current document. A preview of the bibliography entry also displays at the bottom of the dialog box.

▭ **MAC TIP** Click Citations, at the bottom of the pane, click Settings. Click Citation Source Manager. There is no preview.

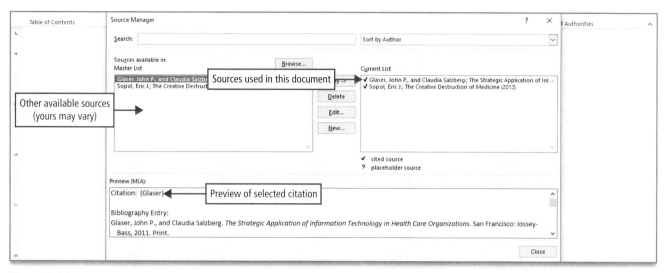

Figure 3.13

11 At the bottom of the **Source Manager** dialog box, click **Close**. Click anywhere in the document to deselect the parenthetical reference, and then **Save** ▤ your document.

MORE KNOWLEDGE **Word Formats the MLA Style for Two or More Authors Automatically**

According to MLA Style, to cite a book by two or more authors, reverse only the name of the first author and place a period after the name of the last author. In this example, you typed the exact MLA style, however, if you type *John P. Glaser; Claudia Salzberg* Word will automatically format the Works Cited page properly, inserting all necessary punctuation and putting the names in the proper order.

Activity 3.07 │ **Adding Citations for a Website**

MOS
4.1.4

1 In the lower portion of **Page 2**, in the paragraph that begins *Doctors have long urged*, in the third line, click to position the insertion point after the *s* in *States* and to the left of the period.

2 In the **Citations & Bibliography group**, click **Insert Citation**, and then click **Add New Source**. Click the **Type of Source arrow**, scroll down as necessary, and then click **Web site**. Type the following information (Mac users: there is no Medium field.):

Author:	**Ogden, Cynthia L.**
Name of Web Page:	**NCHS Data Brief Number 82**
Year:	**2012**
Month:	**January**
Day:	**15**
Year Accessed:	**2021**
Month Accessed:	**January**
Day Accessed:	**17**
Medium	**Web**

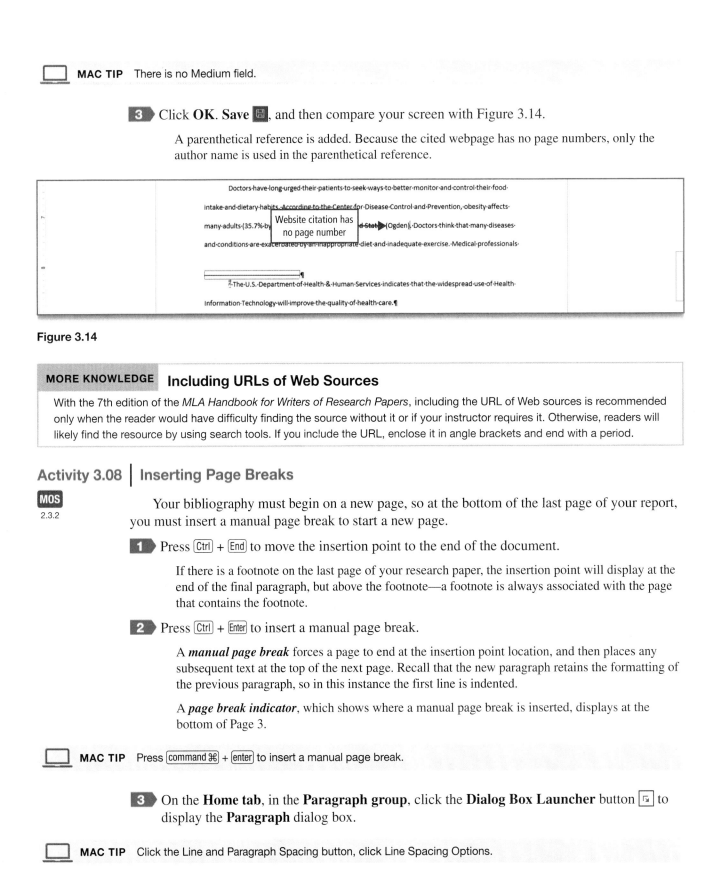

MAC TIP   There is no Medium field.

3 Click **OK**. **Save** 🖫, and then compare your screen with Figure 3.14.

A parenthetical reference is added. Because the cited webpage has no page numbers, only the author name is used in the parenthetical reference.

Doctors·have·long·urged·their·patients·to·seek·ways·to·better·monitor·and·control·their·food·

intake·and·dietary·habits.·According·to·the·Center·for·Disease·Control·and·Prevention,·obesity·affects·

many·adults·(35.7%·by   ～～～～   d·States)·(Ogden).·Doctors·think·that·many·diseases·

      Website citation has
      no page number

and·conditions·are·exacerbated·by·an·inappropriate·diet·and·inadequate·exercise.·Medical·professionals·

¶

ᵃ·The·U.S.·Department·of·Health·&·Human·Services·indicates·that·the·widespread·use·of·Health·

Information·Technology·will·improve·the·quality·of·health·care.¶

Figure 3.14

MORE KNOWLEDGE   **Including URLs of Web Sources**

With the 7th edition of the *MLA Handbook for Writers of Research Papers*, including the URL of Web sources is recommended only when the reader would have difficulty finding the source without it or if your instructor requires it. Otherwise, readers will likely find the resource by using search tools. If you include the URL, enclose it in angle brackets and end with a period.

Activity 3.08 | Inserting Page Breaks

MOS
2.3.2

Your bibliography must begin on a new page, so at the bottom of the last page of your report, you must insert a manual page break to start a new page.

1 Press Ctrl + End to move the insertion point to the end of the document.

If there is a footnote on the last page of your research paper, the insertion point will display at the end of the final paragraph, but above the footnote—a footnote is always associated with the page that contains the footnote.

2 Press Ctrl + Enter to insert a manual page break.

A *manual page break* forces a page to end at the insertion point location, and then places any subsequent text at the top of the next page. Recall that the new paragraph retains the formatting of the previous paragraph, so in this instance the first line is indented.

A *page break indicator*, which shows where a manual page break is inserted, displays at the bottom of Page 3.

MAC TIP   Press command ⌘ + enter to insert a manual page break.

3 On the **Home tab**, in the **Paragraph group**, click the **Dialog Box Launcher** button 🡖 to display the **Paragraph** dialog box.

MAC TIP   Click the Line and Paragraph Spacing button, click Line Spacing Options.

4 On the **Indents and Spacing tab**, under **Indentation**, click the **Special arrow**, and then if necessary, click **(none)**. Click **OK**, and then **Save** 🖫 your document.

ANOTHER WAY   On the ruler, point to the First Line Indent button ▽ , and then drag the button to 0" on the horizontal ruler.

Activity 3.09 | Creating a Reference Page

4.1.4, 4.2.3

At the end of a report or research paper, include a list of each source referenced. *Works Cited* is the reference page heading used in the MLA style guidelines. Other styles may refer to this page as a *Bibliography* (Business Style) or *References* (APA Style). Always display this information on a separate page.

1 With the insertion point blinking in the first paragraph of **Page 4**, on the **References tab**, in the **Citations & Bibliography group**, in the **Style** box, be sure *MLA* displays.

2 In the **Citations & Bibliography group**, click **Bibliography**, and then near the bottom of the list, click **Works Cited**.

3 Select the paragraph *Works Cited*. On the **Home tab**, in the **Font group**, change the **Font** to **Calibri**, and then change the **Font Size** to **11**. Click the **Font Color arrow** [A ⋅], and then in the second column, click the first color. With the text *Works Cited* still selected, in the **Paragraph group**, click **Center** [≡].

4 Click to the left of *Works Cited* and then drag down to select the title *Works Cited* and the three citations. On the **Layout tab**, in the **Paragraph group**, click the **Dialog Box Launcher** button [⌐], and then in the **Paragraph** dialog box, change the **Spacing Before** to **0 pt**, change the **Spacing After** to **0 pt**, and then set the **Line spacing** to **Double**. Click **OK**.

🖥 **MAC TIP** Click the Line and Paragraph Spacing button, click Line Spacing Options.

The bibliography entries that you created display as a field, which is indicated by the gray shading. This field links to the Source Manager for the citations. The references display alphabetically by the author's last name.

The entries display according to MLA guidelines; the text is double-spaced, and each entry uses a *hanging indent*—the first line of each entry extends 0.5 inch to the left of the remaining lines of the entry.

5 At the bottom of **Page 4**, click in the last blank paragraph to deselect the text, and then compare your screen with Figure 3.15. **Save** [💾] your document.

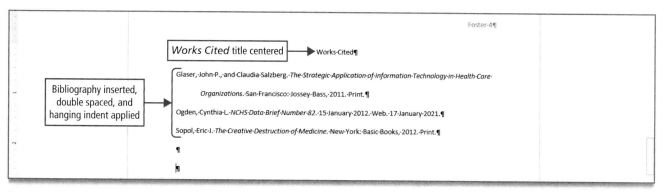

Figure 3.15

Activity 3.10 | Managing and Modifying Sources for a Document

Use the Source Manager to organize the sources cited in your document. For example, in the Source Manager dialog box, you can copy sources from the master list to the current list, delete a source, edit a source, or search for a source. You can also display a preview of how your citations will appear in your document.

1 On the **References tab**, in the **Citations & Bibliography group**, click **Manage Sources**.

MAC TIP On the References tab, click Citations, click the settings button in the bottom right corner of the Citations pane. Click Citation Source Manager. Click the reference for Sopol, click Edit, edit the name *Sopol* to *Topol*. Click OK, click Close. On Page 2, click the Topol reference, click the arrow, click Update Citations and Bibliography. Then move to the Activity 3.11.

2 On the left, in the **Master List**, click the entry for *Sopol, Eric J.* and then between the **Master List** and the **Current List**, click **Edit**.

The name of this source should be *Topol* instead of *Sopol*.

3 In the **Edit Source** dialog box, in the **Author** box, delete *S* and type **T**

4 Click **OK**. When the message box indicates *This source exists in your master list and current document. Do you want to update both lists with these changes?* click **Yes**. Compare your screen with Figure 3.16.

In the lower portion of the Source Manager dialog box, a preview of the corrected entry displays.

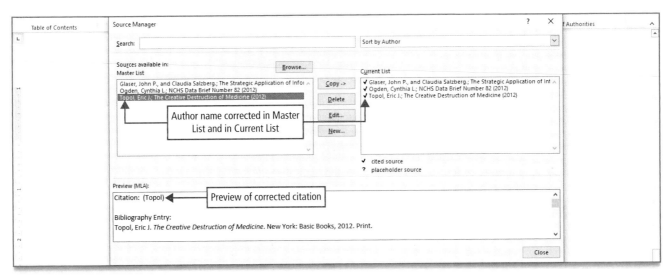

Figure 3.16

5 In the lower right corner, click **Close**. On your **Works Cited page**, notice that the author name is *not* corrected. Scroll to view the lower portion of **Page 2** and notice that the author name *is* corrected and the citation is selected.

6 On the selected citation *(Topol 5)*, click the **Citation Options arrow**, and then click **Update Citations and Bibliography**. Scroll to view your **Works Cited page** and notice that this action updates the Works Cited page with the corrected name but also changes the line spacing of the citations.

Editing a source in Source Manager updates only the sources in the document; to update the Works Cited page, use the Update Citations and Bibliography command on the citation.

7 On the *Works Cited* page, drag to select the three citations, and then from the **Home tab**, redisplay the **Paragraph** dialog box. Reset the **Spacing Before** and **Spacing After** to **0 pt** and the **Line spacing** to **Double**. Click **OK**. Click **Save** 🖫.

Activity 3.11 | Using the Navigation Pane to Go to a Specific Page

MOS
1.1.1, 1.1.3

In a multipage document, use the Navigation pane to move to a specific page or to find specific objects in the document.

1 Press Ctrl + Home to move to the top of the document. Click the **View tab**, and then in the **Show group**, select the **Navigation Pane** check box.

 MAC TIP   At the top of the Navigation pane, click the Find and Replace icon (magnifying glass). Click the Settings button, click Advanced Find & Replace, and then click the Go To tab. Under Go to what, select Footnote.

2 In the **Navigation** pane, on the right end of the **Search document** box, click the **Search for more things arrow**, and then compare your screen with Figure 3.17.

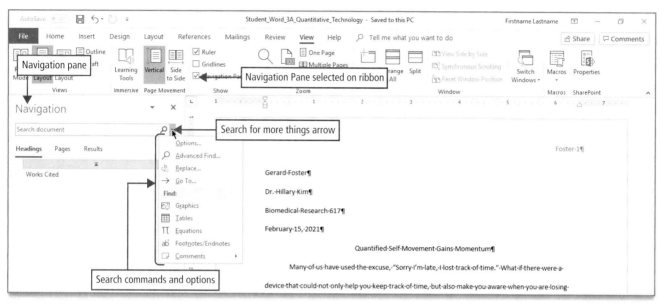

Figure 3.17

3 Under **Find**, click **Footnotes/Endnotes**. Notice that the first numbered footnote is selected.

4 In the **Navigation** pane, to the right of *Result 1 of 2*, click the ▼ arrow to move to the next numbered footnote.

5 Click the **Search for more things arrow** again, and then click **Go To**. In the **Find and Replace** dialog box, under **Go to what**, be sure **Page** is selected, and then in the **Enter page number** box, type **4**

6 Click **Go To**, and then click **Close**. Notice that **Page 4** displays.

The Navigation pane is useful when you need to navigate to find various elements, especially in a very long document.

7 In the **Navigation pane**, click **Pages**, and notice that you can view thumbnail images of your document's pages.

Here you can scroll quickly through the pages of a long document.

8 **Close** ⊠ the **Navigation** pane.

Activity 3.12 | Managing Document Properties

For a research paper, you may want to add additional document properties.

1 Press Ctrl + Home to return to the top of your document. From the **File tab**, display **Backstage** view, click **Info**, and then in the lower right corner of the screen, click **Show All Properties**.

2 As the document **Title**, type **Quantified Self Movement Gains Momentum** and then as the **Tags**, type **quantified self, research paper**

3 Click in the **Comments** box and type **draft copy of report for class** and then in the **Categories** box, type **biomedical research**

4 In the **Subject** box, type your course name and section number. In the **Company** box, select and delete any existing text, and then type **University Medical Center**

5 Click in the **Manager** box and type **Dr. Hillary Kim** If necessary, click outside of the Manager box to close it. Be sure your name displays as the **Author** and edit if necessary.

6 At the top of the **Properties** list, click the text *Properties*, and then click **Advanced Properties**. In the dialog box, if necessary click the **Summary tab**, and then compare your screen with Figure 3.18.

In the Advanced Properties dialog box, you can view and modify additional document properties.

Figure 3.18

7 Click the **Statistics tab**.

The document statistics show the number of revisions made to the document, the last time the document was edited, and the number of paragraphs, lines, words, and characters in the document. Additional information categories are available by clicking the Custom tab.

8 **Close** ⊠ the dialog box. On the left, click **Save** to save and return to your document.

Activity 3.13 | **Using Smart Lookup, Researcher, Text Highlighting, Cover Pages, and Side to Side Page Movement**

Smart Lookup is a Word feature with which you can get information about text you select. Smart Lookup can show definitions, images, and results from various online sources.

Researcher is a Word feature that helps you find topics and reliable sources for your research paper. For sources that you select, citation information is available.

Text Highlight Color is a Word command with which you can apply a highlight color to selected text.

1 Scroll to view **Page 2** of your document, and then in the paragraph that begins *Accurate records*, in the fifth line of the paragraph, locate and select *Dr. Eric Topol.*

2 With *Dr. Eric Topol* selected, on the **References tab**, in the **Research group**, click **Smart Lookup**. Compare your screen with Figure 3.19.

The Smart Lookup pane displays on the right. Here you can see that Dr. Topol is an American cardiologist, geneticist, and digital medicine researcher.

NOTE You may have to enable Office intelligent services to use Smart Lookup and Researcher. To do so, click the File tab, on the left click Options, in the Word Options dialog box, on the left click General, and then under Office intelligent services, select the Enable services check box.

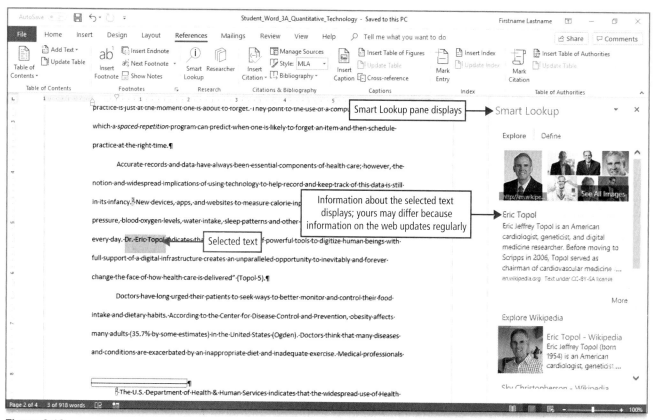

Figure 3.19

3 In the **Smart Lookup pane**, scroll down and then click the **blue text** for any of the additional informational sources about Dr. Topol; for example, his Wikipedia page, information about the Scripps Genomic Health Initiative, Dr. Topol's faculty page at The Scripps Research Institute, or the page related to the book cited in your research paper—*The Creative Destruction of Medicine.*

Smart Lookup enables you to search for information about a topic from within Word without having to open a browser and begin a new search.

4 **Close** ✕ your browser window, and then **Close** ✕ the **Smart Lookup pane**.

5 On the **References tab**, in the **Research group**, click **Researcher** to display the **Researcher pane** on the right.

6 With the insertion point blinking in the search box, type, including the quotation marks, **"quantified self"** and then press Enter. Under **Top sources for "quantified self"** click **Journals**. Compare your screen with Figure 3.20.

Here you can search for scholarly journal articles about a topic from within Word. You can scroll down and find links to many articles related to the topic *quantified self*.

When searching for a phrase or a concept that contains two or more words, use quotation marks so that the search engine conducts the search on the entire phrase. The search engine in Researcher is Microsoft's Bing.

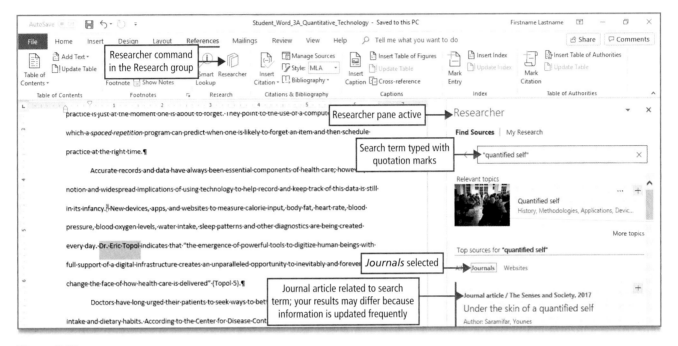

Figure 3.20

7 Close ☒ the **Researcher pane**.

8 On **Page 2**, in the paragraph that begins *Gary Wolf, who along*, in the first line of the paragraph, select the text *Quantified Self*.

9 On the **Home tab**, in the **Font group**, click the **Text Highlight Color arrow** [✎▾], and then click **Bright Green** as shown in Figure 3.21.

This highlighting will serve as a reminder to conduct additional research about the topic *quantified self* by using the Researcher feature in Word.

MAC TIP On the Home tab, in the Font group, click the Highlight arrow.

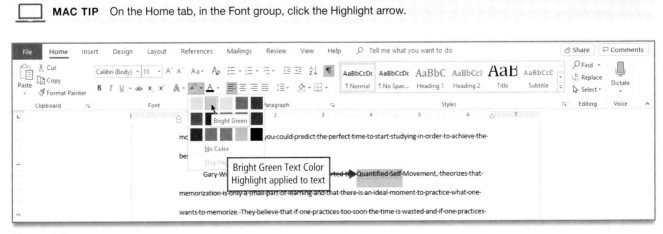

Figure 3.21

10 On the **View tab**, in the **Page Movement group**, click **Side to Side**, and then click the horizontal scroll arrows to slide pages left or right

The *Side to Side* command enables you to see whole pages by sliding each page from right to left or left to right. This is convenient when you have multiple pages and you want to see how the pages look side by side. Depending on your screen size and screen resolution, there may be variations in how the Side to Side view displays on your computer.

11 On the **View tab**, in the **Page Movement group**, click **Vertical** to return to the default setting.

Vertical is the default Page Movement setting, meaning you can use the vertical scroll arrows to move the pages up or down on your screen.

12 On the **Insert tab**, in the **Pages group**, click **Cover Page**, and then in the gallery, click **Banded**—or select any other cover page design. Press Ctrl + Home to see the cover page.

Academic research papers do not typically include a stylized cover page. In business organizations, or for informal college term papers, adding a cover page is appropriate. Here you can choose from many styles that are pre-built, and you can further customize those with different fonts and colors.

13 On the Quick Access toolbar, click **Undo** —you will not include a cover page for this project.

14 Click **Save** .

Objective 4 Use Read Mode, PDF Reflow, and Save Documents in Alternative File Formats

GO! Learn How
Video W3-4

Read Mode optimizes the view of the Word screen for the times when you are *reading* Word documents on the screen and not creating or editing them. Microsoft's research indicates that two-thirds of user sessions in Word contain no editing—meaning that people are simply reading the Word document on the screen. The Column Layout feature of Read Mode reflows the document to fit the size of the device you are reading so that the text is as easy to read on a tablet device as it is to read on a standard desktop computer screen. The Object Zoom feature of Read Mode resizes graphics to fit the screen you are using, but you can click or tap to zoom in on the graphic.

PDF Reflow enables you to import PDF files into Word so that you can transform a PDF into a fully editable Word document. This is useful if you have lost the original Word file or if someone sends you a PDF that you would like to modify. PDF Reflow is not intended to act as a viewer for PDF files—for that you will still want to use a PDF reader such as Adobe Reader. In Windows 10, the Microsoft Edge browser also serves as a PDF reader.

Activity 3.14 | Using Read Mode, PDF Reflow, and Saving Documents in Alternative File Formats

MOS
1.3.1

1 ▶ Press [Ctrl] + [Home] to move to the top of your document. On the **View tab**, in the **Views group**, click **Read Mode**, and notice that Read Mode keeps footnotes displayed on the page associated with the footnote.

> Read Mode displays differently for different screen sizes and screen resolution settings; if you have a different resolution setting, your screens may differ slightly than those shown here.

🔄 **ANOTHER WAY** On the right side of the status bar, click the Read Mode button 📖.

💻 **MAC TIP** Focus mode is similar—the page fills the screen and eliminates distractions. On the View tab, in the Focus group, click Focus, move your mouse to the top of the screen to display the focus view toolbar. Tools may not be available. To exit Focus mode, display the menu, and then click Exit. Move to Step 6.

2 ▶ In the upper left corner, click **Tools**.

> You can use these tools to find something within the document or use Smart Lookup to conduct an internet search.

3 ▶ Click **Find**, and then in the **Search** box, type **Topol** Notice that Word displays the first page where the search term displays and highlights the term in yellow. Compare your screen with Figure 3.22.

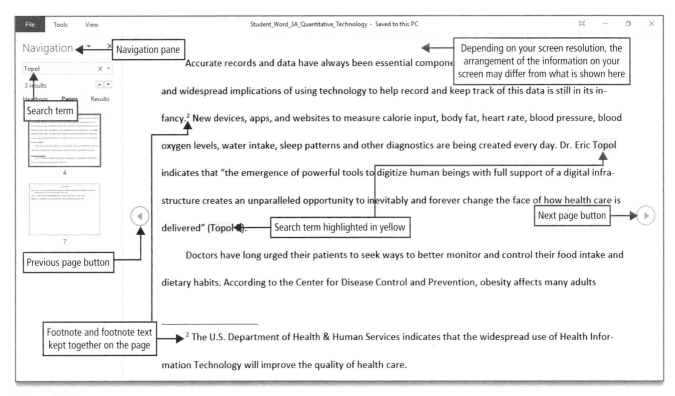

Figure 3.22

4 In the upper left corner, click **View**, and then take a moment to study the table in Figure 3.23.

View Commands in Read Mode	
View Command	**Action**
Edit Document	Return to Print Layout view to continue editing the document.
Navigation Pane	Search for specific text or click a heading or page to move to that location.
Show Comments	See comments, if any, within the document.
Column Width	Change the display of the document to fit more or less text on each line.
Page Color	Change the colors used to show the document to make it easier to read. Some readers prefer a sepia (brownish-gray) shading as the background or a black background with white text.
Layout	Read in different layouts. Select Column Layout, which is the default, or Paper Layout, which mimics the 8.5 x 11 format but without the ribbon.
A–Z Syllables	Show the breaks between the syllables.
A–Z Text Spacing	Increase spacing between words, characters, and lines.
Read Aloud	Read text out loud and highlight each word as it's read.

Figure 3.23

5 On the **View** menu, click **Edit Document** to return to **Print Layout** view. **Close** ☒ the **Navigation** pane.

 ANOTHER WAY On the status bar on the right, click the Print Layout button 🗏.

6 **Save** 🖫 your document. In the upper right corner of the Word window, click **Close** ☒.

 For Non-MyLab Submissions Determine What Your Instructor Requires for Submission
As directed by your instructor, submit your completed Word document.

7 In **MyLab IT**, locate and click the Grader Project **Word 3A Quantitative Technology**. In **step 3**, under **Upload Completed Assignment**, click **Choose File**. In the **Open** dialog box, navigate to your **Word Chapter 3 folder**, and then click your **Student_Word_3A_ Quantitative_Technology** file one time to select it. In the lower right corner of the **Open** dialog box, click **Open**.

The name of your selected file displays above the Upload button.

8 To submit your file to MyLab IT for grading, click **Upload**, wait a moment for a green **Success!** message, and then in **step 4**, click the blue **Submit for Grading** button. Click **Close Assignment** to return to your list of **Course Materials**.

You have completed Project 3A 　END

ALERT **The Remaining Steps in this Activity are Optional**

The remaining steps in the Activity are optional and are not included in the MyLab IT Grader system for this project. Your instructor may want you to complete these steps; or you may want to practice these steps on your own to see how PDF Reflow works and to see how to save Word documents in alternative file formats.

9 ▸ Start Word, and then on the left, click **Open**.

Recall that PDF Reflow enables you to import PDF files into Word so that you can transform a PDF into a fully editable Word document.

You can save a Word document in many different file formats, and there are times when you will want to do this. For example, you can save a Word document as a PDF or as a Plain Text file, which is a simple file consisting of lines of text with no formatting that almost any computer can open and display. Files saved in this file format will have the file name extension of .txt.

10 ▸ Click **Browse**, and then in the **Open** dialog box, navigate to the files you downloaded with this project. Click **w03A_PDF_optional**.

NOTE   Locating Your w03A_PDF_optional File

Your instructor can provide this file to you from the Instructor Resource Center, or you can download the student data files from www.pearsonhighered.com/go.

11 ▸ In the lower right corner, click **Open**. When a message indicates that *Word will now convert the PDF to an editable Word document . . .* , click **OK**.

12 ▸ If necessary, click **Enable Editing**, click **OK** again, and then compare your screen with Figure 3.24.

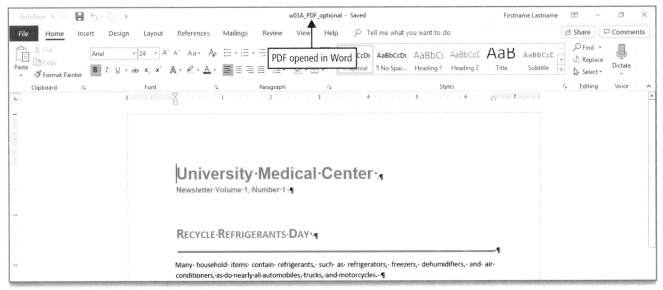

Figure 3.24

13 ▸ Click the **File tab**, and then on the left click **Save As**. Click **Browse**, and then navigate to your **Word Chapter 3** folder. In the **File name** box, using your own name, type **Lastname_Firstname_3A_Alt_File_Format** and then click the **Save as type arrow**.

14 ▸ On the **Save as type** list, notice the many file types you can use to save a Word document. Then, on the list, click **Plain Text**, and click **Save**. In the **File Conversion** dialog box, click **OK**.

15 ▸ **Close** ⊠ Word. Submit your Plain Text file if directed to do so by your instructor.

You have completed the optional portion of Project 3A   **END**

Objective   Use the Research Bar in Google Docs

ALERT   **Working with Web-Based Applications and Services**

Computer programs and services on the web receive continuous updates and improvements, so the steps to complete this web-based Activity may differ from the ones shown. You can often look at the screens and the information presented to determine how to complete the Activity.

If you do not already have a Google account, you will need to create one before you begin this Activity. Go to http://google.com and in the upper right corner, click Sign In. On the Sign In screen, click Create Account. On the Create your Google Account page, complete the form, read and agree to the Terms of Service and Privacy Policy, and then click Next step. On the Welcome screen, click Get Started.

Activity | Using the Research Bar in Google Docs

Google Docs provides a research tool that you can use to find studies and academic papers on many topics. You can narrow your search results by selecting "Scholar" from the drop-down menu in the search bar. After you find the study, you can insert it as a citation or a footnote. You can also choose to use the MLA, APA, or Chicago citation formatting.

1 From the desktop, open your browser, navigate to **http://google.com**, and then click the **Google Apps** menu ▦. Click **Drive**, and then if necessary, sign in to your Google account.

2 Open your **GO! Web Projects** folder—or click New to create and then open this folder if necessary.

3 In the upper left corner, click **New**, and then click **File upload**. In the **Open** dialog box, navigate to the files you downloaded for this chapter, and then in the **File List**, double-click to open **w03_3A_Web**.

4 Point to the uploaded file **w03_3A_Web**, and then right-click. On the shortcut menu, scroll as necessary, and then click **Rename**. Using your own last name and first name, type **Lastname_Firstname_WD_3A_Web** and then click **OK** to rename the file.

5 Point to the file in the file list, right-click, on the shortcut menu point to **Open with**, and then click **Google Docs**.

6 Press Ctrl + End to move to the end of the document, and then press Enter one time. Type **There are many studies related to the quantified self movement conducted by Melanie Swan, who is interested in crowdsourced health research.**

7 On the menu bar, click **Tools**, and then click **Explore** to open the **Explore pane** on the right.

8 At the top of the **Explore pane**, click in the search box, and then—being sure to include the quotation marks and uppercase letters as indicated—type **"quantified self" AND "Melanie Swan"** Press Enter.

9 *Point* to the first item in the list and point to the quotation marks that display to the right; compare your screen with Figure A.

»» **GO!** With Google continues on next page

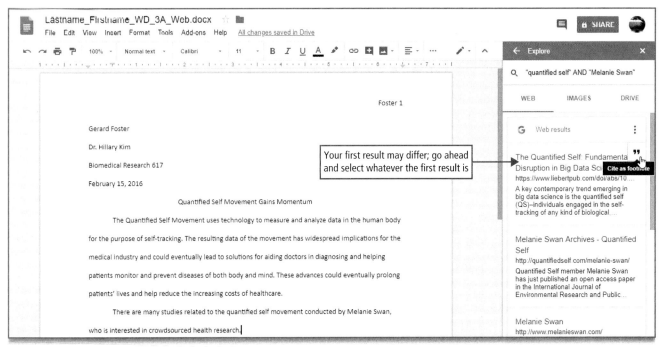

Figure A

10 Click **Cite as footnote**. Notice that a footnote number is inserted at the end of the sentence. Scroll down to view the bottom of the page, and then compare your screen with Figure B.

11 Submit the file as directed by your instructor. In the upper right, click your user name or picture, and then click **Sign out**. **Close** your browser window. Your file is automatically saved in your Google Drive.

Figure B

PROJECT 3B

Newsletter with Optional Mailing Labels

Mylab IT
Project 3B Grader for Instruction
Project 3B Simulation for Training and Review

Project Activities

In Activities 3.15 through 3.29, you will edit a newsletter that University Medical Center is sending to the board of directors; optionally, you can create the necessary mailing labels. Your completed documents will look similar to Figure 3.25.

Project Files for MyLabIT Grader

1. In your MyLab IT course, locate and click **Word 3B Environment Newsletter**, Download Materials, and then Download All Files.
2. Extract the zipped folder to your Word Chapter 3 folder. Close the Grader download screens.
3. Take a moment to open the downloaded **Word_3B_Environment_Newsletter_Instructions**; note any recent updates to the book.

Project Results

GO! Project 3B
Where We're Going

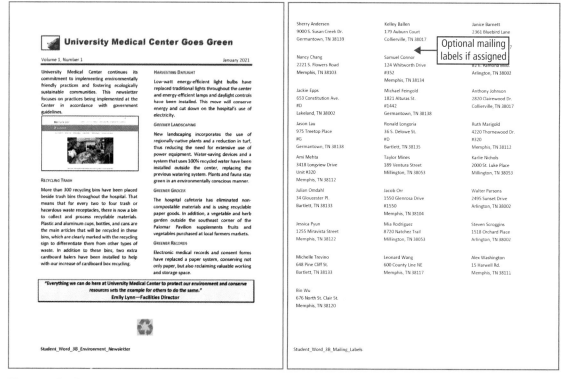

Figure 3.25 Project 3B Environment Newsletter

For Non-MyLab Submissions

For Project 3B, you will need:
w03B_Environment_Newsletter
w03B_Recycle_Symbol
w03B_Recycling
w03B_Addresses (optional if labels assigned)

In your Word Chapter 3 folder, save your document as:
Lastname_Firstname_3B_Environment_Newsletter
Lastname_Firstname_3B_Mailing_Labels (optional if labels assigned)

After you have named and saved your document, on the next page, begin with Step 2.

ALERT   Because Office 365 is a cloud-based subscription service that receives continuous updates, you may encounter some variations in what appears on your screen and what is shown in this instruction. Microsoft Office 365 is fully installed on your PC or Mac; no internet access is necessary to create or edit documents. When you *are* connected to the internet, you will receive monthly upgrades and new features, so you always have the latest versions of Office apps as soon as they are available. Your subscription gives you continuous free access to the latest innovations and refinements.

GO! Learn How
Video W3-5

A *newsletter* is a periodical that communicates news and information to a specific group. Newsletters, as well as all newspapers and most magazines, use multiple columns for articles because text in narrower columns is easier to read than text that stretches across a page.

You can create a newsletter in Word by changing a single column of text into two or more columns. If a column does not end where you want it to, you can end the column at a location of your choice by inserting a *manual column break*—an artificial end to a column to balance columns or to provide space for the insertion of other objects.

Activity 3.15 | Changing One Column of Text to Two Columns

2.3.1, 2.3.2

Newsletters are usually two or three columns wide. When using 8.5 × 11-inch paper in portrait orientation, avoid creating four or more columns because they are so narrow that word spacing looks awkward, often resulting in one long word on a line by itself.

1 Navigate to your **Word Chapter 3 folder**, and then double-click the Word file you downloaded from MyLab IT that displays your name—**Student_Word_3B_Environment_ Newsletter**. If necessary, at the top click **Enable Editing**.

2 On the **Insert tab**, in the **Header & Footer group**, click **Footer**, and then at the bottom click **Edit Footer**. On the **Header & Footer Tools Design tab**, in the **Insert group**, click **Document Info**, and then click **File Name** to insert the file name in the footer. On the ribbon, click **Close Header and Footer**.

3 Select the first two paragraphs—the title and the Volume information and date. On the mini toolbar, click the **Font Color button arrow** [A ▾], and then under **Theme Colors**, in the fifth column, click the last color.

⬛ **MAC TIP**   Use ribbon commands.

4 With the text still selected, on the **Home tab**, in the **Paragraph group**, click the **Borders button arrow** [⊞ ▾], and then at the bottom, click **Borders and Shading**.

5 In the **Borders and Shading** dialog box, on the **Borders tab**, click the **Color arrow**, and then under **Theme Colors**, in the fifth column, click the last color.

6 Click the **Width arrow**, and then click **3 pt**. In the **Preview** box at the right, point to the *bottom* border of the preview and click one time. Compare your screen with Figure 3.26.

Figure 3.26

↻ **ANOTHER WAY**   In the Preview area, click the Bottom Border button ⊞▾.

7 In the **Borders and Shading** dialog box, click **OK**.

The line visually defines the newsletter's ***nameplate***—the banner on the front page of a newsletter that identifies the publication.

8 Below the Volume information, click at the beginning of the paragraph that begins *University Medical Center continues*. By using the vertical scroll box, scroll to view the lower portion of the document, hold down Shift, and then click after the paragraph mark at the end of the paragraph that begins *Electronic medical records* to select all of the text between the insertion point and the sentence ending with the word *space*. Be sure that the paragraph mark is included in the selection. Compare your screen with Figure 3.27.

Use Shift to define a selection that may be difficult to select by dragging.

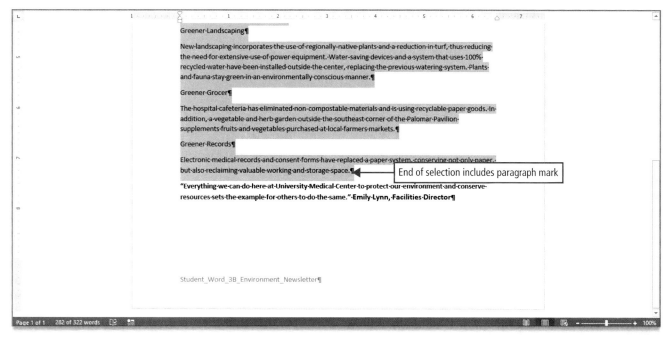

Figure 3.27

9 On the **Layout tab**, in the **Page Setup group**, click **Columns**, and then click **Two**. Compare your screen with Figure 3.28, and then **Save** 🔲 your newsletter.

Word divides the selected text into two columns and inserts a ***section break*** at the end of the selection, dividing the one-column section of the document from the two-column section of the document. A ***section*** is a portion of a document that can be formatted differently from the rest of the document. A section break marks the end of one section and the beginning of another section.

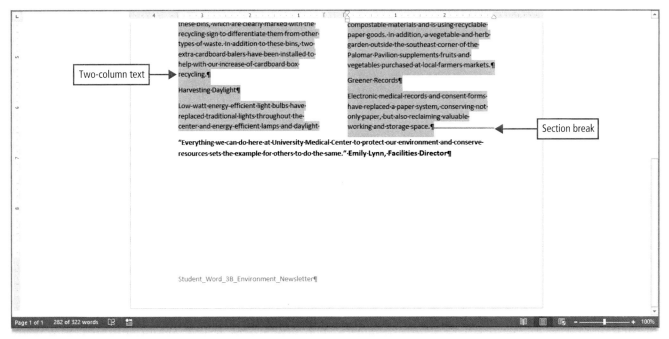

Two-column text

Section break

these bins, which are clearly marked with the recycling sign to differentiate them from other types of waste. In addition to these bins, two extra cardboard balers have been installed to help with our increase of cardboard box recycling.

Harvesting Daylight

Low-watt energy-efficient light bulbs have replaced traditional lights throughout the center and energy-efficient lamps and daylight

compostable materials and is using recyclable paper goods. In addition, a vegetable and herb garden outside the southeast corner of the Palomar Pavilion supplements fruits and vegetables purchased at local farmers markets.

Greener Records

Electronic medical records and consent forms have replaced a paper system, conserving not only paper, but also reclaiming valuable working and storage space.

"Everything we can do here at University Medical Center to protect our environment and conserve resources sets the example for others to do the same." Emily Lynn, Facilities Director

Student_Word_3B_Environment_Newsletter

Page 1 of 1   282 of 322 words   100%

Figure 3.28

Activity 3.16 | Formatting Multiple Columns

MOS
2.3.1

The uneven right margin of a single page-width column is easy to read. When you create narrow columns, justified text is sometimes preferable. Depending on the design and layout of your newsletter, you might decide to reduce extra space between paragraphs and between columns to improve the readability of the document.

1 With the two columns of text still selected, on the **Layout tab**, in the **Paragraph group**, click the **Spacing After down spin arrow** one time to change the spacing after to **6 pt**.

2 On the **Home tab**, in the **Paragraph group**, click **Justify** 🔲.

3 ▶ Click anywhere in the document to deselect the text, compare your screen with Figure 3.29, and then **Save** 🖫.

Figure 3.29

MORE KNOWLEDGE **Justifying Column Text**

Although many magazines and newspapers still justify text in columns, there are a variety of opinions about whether to justify the columns, or to use left alignment and leave the right edge uneven. Justified text tends to look more formal and cleaner, but in a word processing document, it also results in uneven spacing between words. It is the opinion of some authorities that justified text is more difficult to read, especially in a page-width document. Let the overall look of your newsletter be your guide.

Activity 3.17 │ Inserting a Column Break

1 ▶ Near the bottom of the first column, click to position the insertion point at the beginning of the line *Harvesting Daylight*.

2 ▶ On the **Layout tab**, in the **Page Setup group**, click **Breaks**. Under **Page Breaks**, click **Column**, and then if necessary, scroll to view the bottom of the first column.

A column break displays at the bottom of the first column; text to the right of the column break moves to the top of the next column.

3 Compare your screen with Figure 3.30, and then **Save** 🖫.

A *column break indicator*—a dotted line containing the words *Column Break*—displays at the bottom of the column.

Figure 3.30

Activity 3.18 | Inserting a Picture

MOS

5.4.1, 5.4.2

Pictures can make your newsletter visually appealing and more interesting.

1 Press Ctrl + End to move to the end of the document.

2 On the **Insert tab**, in the **Illustrations group**, click **Pictures**. Navigate to your **Word Chapter 3** folder, and then double-click the file **w03B_Recycle_Symbol** to insert the image at the insertion point. If a blue message regarding *Automatic Alt Text* displays, click Got it. Compare your screen with Figure 3.31.

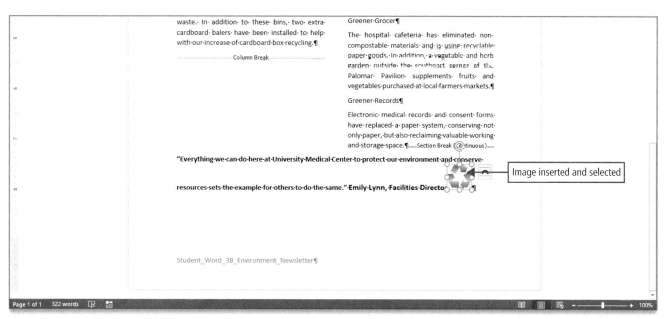

Figure 3.31

> **3** With the image selected, on the **Picture Tools Format tab**, in the **Size group**, click in the **Height** box. If necessary, type **0.5** and then press Enter.

> **4** On the **Picture Tools Format tab**, in the **Arrange group**, click **Wrap Text**, and then click **Square**. In the **Arrange group**, click **Position**, and then at the bottom of the gallery, click **More Layout Options**. Compare your screen with Figure 3.32.

MAC TIP   On the Picture Format tab, in the Arrange group, click the Wrap Text button, and then click Square.

ANOTHER WAY   To the right of the picture, click the Layout Options button, and then click Square.

Figure 3.32

5 In the **Layout** dialog box, on the **Position tab**, under **Horizontal**, click the **Alignment** option button. Click the **Alignment arrow**, and then click **Centered**. Click the **relative to arrow** and then click **Page**.

6 Under **Vertical**, click the **Alignment** option button. Click the **Alignment arrow**, and then click **Bottom**. Click the **relative to arrow**, and then click **Margin**. Compare your screen with Figure 3.33.

Figure 3.33

7 Click **OK**, scroll to the bottom of the page, and then notice that the recycle image is centered in the lower portion of your document. **Save** the document.

ANOTHER WAY   Drag the image to visually position the image.

Activity 3.19 │ Cropping a Picture and Resizing a Picture by Scaling

MOS

5.1.2, 5.4.1

In this Activity, you will insert a picture and edit the picture by cropping and scaling. When you ***crop*** a picture, you remove unwanted or unnecessary areas of the picture. When you ***scale*** a picture, you resize it to a percentage of its size.

1 Press Ctrl + Home to move to the top of the document. On the **Insert tab**, in the **Illustrations group**, click **Pictures**. In the **Insert Picture** dialog box, navigate to the files you downloaded with this project, and then double-click **w03B_Recycling** to insert it.

2 With the picture selected, on the **Picture Tools Format tab**, in the **Size group**, click the upper portion of the **Crop** button to display crop handles around the picture. Compare your screen with Figure 3.34.

Crop handles are used like sizing handles to define unwanted areas of the picture.

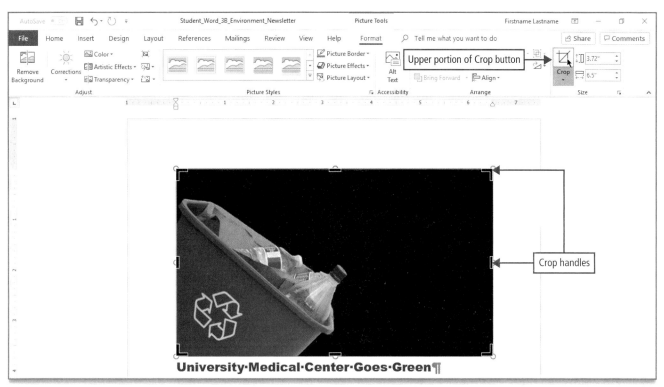

Figure 3.34

3 Point to the center right crop handle to display the ⊢ pointer. Compare your screen with Figure 3.35.

Use the *crop pointer* to crop areas of a picture.

Figure 3.35

4 With the crop pointer displayed, hold down the left mouse button and drag to the left to approximately **5 inches on the horizontal ruler**, and then release the mouse button. Compare your screen with Figure 3.36.

The portion of the image to be removed displays in gray.

Picture cropped to 5 inches on the horizontal ruler

Gray area indicates portion of picture to be removed

Figure 3.36

5 Click anywhere in the document outside of the image to apply the crop.

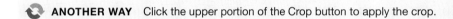

ANOTHER WAY   Click the upper portion of the Crop button to apply the crop.

6 Click to select the picture again. On the **Picture Tools Format tab**, in the **Size group**, click the **Dialog Box Launcher** button ⌐.

7 In the **Layout** dialog box, on the **Size tab**, in the lower portion of the dialog box under **Scale**, be sure that the **Lock aspect ratio** and **Relative to original picture size** check boxes are selected. Under **Scale**, select the percentage number in the **Height box**, type **10** and then press Tab. Compare your screen with Figure 3.37.

When *Lock aspect ratio* is selected, the height and width of the picture are sized proportionately and only one scale value is necessary. The second value—in this instance Width—adjusts proportionately. When *Relative to original picture size* is selected, the scale is applied as a percentage of the original picture size.

MAC TIP   In the Arrange group, click Wrap Text, click More Layout Options, and then click the Size tab.

Height value

Width value

Check boxes selected

Figure 3.37

8 In the **Layout** dialog box, click the **Text Wrapping tab**. Under **Wrapping style**, click **Square**.

9 Click the **Position tab**, and then under **Horizontal**, click the **Alignment** option button. Be sure that the **Alignment** indicates **Left** and **relative to Column**. Under **Vertical**, click the **Alignment** option button, and then change the alignment to **Top relative to Margin**. Click **OK**, and then compare your screen with Figure 3.38.

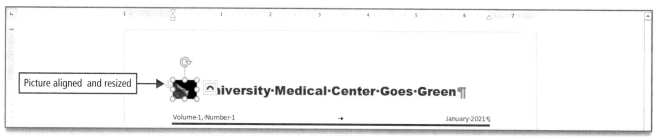

Figure 3.38

Activity 3.20 | Setting Transparent Color and Recoloring a Picture

MOS
5.2.3

You can make one color in a picture transparent using the Set Transparent Color command. When you *recolor* a picture, you change all the colors in the picture to shades of a single color.

1 On the **View tab**, in the **Zoom group**, click **Zoom**, and then click **200%**. Click **OK**. Drag the scroll boxes as necessary so that you can view the recycle bin picture at the top of the document.

2 If necessary, select the recycle bin picture. Click the **Picture Tools Format tab**. In the **Adjust group**, click **Color**, and then below the gallery, click **Set Transparent Color**. Move the pointer into the document to display the pointer.

3 Point anywhere in the black background of the recycle bin picture, and then click to apply the transparent color to the background. Compare your screen with Figure 3.39.

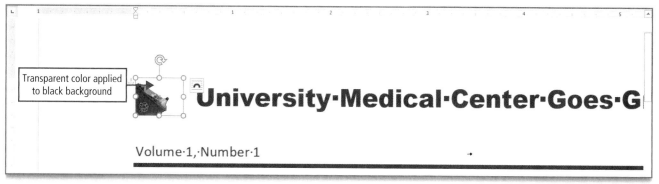

Figure 3.39

4 Press Ctrl + End to move to the end of your document, and then select the picture of the recycle symbol. Click the **Picture Tools Format tab**, and then in the **Adjust group**, click **Color** to display a gallery of recoloring options. Under **Recolor**, point to one of the Recolor options that are blue, for example the one shown in Figure 3.40.

Figure 3.40

5 Click the blue recolor option to apply it, or select any of the blue options, and then **Save** 💾 the document.

Activity 3.21 | Adjusting the Brightness and Contrast of a Picture

MOS
5.2.4

Brightness is the relative lightness of a picture. *Contrast* is the difference between the darkest and lightest area of a picture.

1 If necessary, select the recycle symbol. On the **Format tab**, in the **Adjust group**, click **Corrections**. Under **Brightness/Contrast**, point to several of the options to view the effect that the settings have on the picture.

🖥 **MAC TIP**   Live Preview while pointing to options is not available.

2 Under **Brightness/Contrast**, use the ScreenTips to locate the setting **Brightness: -40% Contrast: +40%** as shown in Figure 3.41.

Figure 3.41

3 Click to apply **Brightness: -40% Contrast: +40%** to the recycle image.

4 On the **View tab**, in the **Zoom group**, click **100%**, if necessary, click **OK**, and then **Save** 🖫 your document.

Activity 3.22 | Applying a Border to a Picture and Flipping a Picture

MOS
5.2.4

The *flip* commands create a reverse image of a picture or object.

1 Press [Ctrl] + [Home] to move to the top of the document, and then select the picture of the recycle bin. Click the **Picture Tools Format tab**, and then in the **Picture Styles group**, click the **Picture Border button**. Under **Theme Colors**, in the fourth column, click the first color.

2 Click **Picture Border** again, and then point to **Weight**. Click **1 1/2 pt** to change the thickness of the border.

3 On the **Format tab**, in the **Arrange group**, click **Rotate Objects** ⬚ˏ, and then click **Flip Horizontal**. Click anywhere in the document to deselect the picture. **Save** 🖫, and then compare your screen with Figure 3.42.

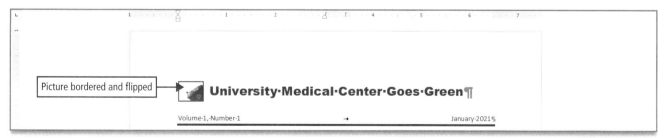

Figure 3.42

Activity 3.23 | Inserting and Formatting a Screen Clipping

A *screenshot* is an image of an active window on your computer that you can paste into a document. Screenshots are especially useful when you want to insert an image of a website into your Word document. You can also insert a screenshot by using **Screen Clipping**, a tool with which you can take a quick snapshot of part of the screen, and then add it to your document.

1 In the paragraph that begins *University Medical Center continues*, click after the period at the end of the paragraph. Start your web browser, and then navigate to the site **www.data.gov/ecosystems/** (If this website is not available, go to another section of the data.gov site or go to www.epa.gov.)

2 From the taskbar, redisplay your **3B_Environment_Newsletter** document.

3 With the insertion point still positioned at the end of the paragraph, on the **Insert tab**, in the **Illustrations group**, click **Screenshot**, and then click **Screen Clipping**.

4 When the dimmed screen displays, move the ⊞ pointer to the upper left corner of the screen just below the address bar, hold down the left mouse button, and drag to the lower right corner but do not include the taskbar. Then release the mouse button to insert the image in your document. Compare your screen with Figure 3.43.

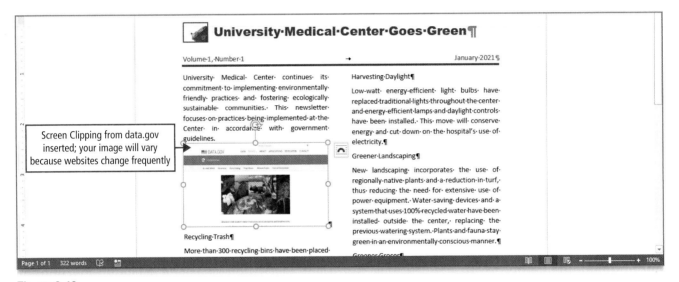

Figure 3.43

5 With the inserted screenshot selected, on the **Format tab**, in the **Picture Styles group**, click **Picture Border**, and then under **Theme Colors**, in the second column, click the first color.

6 Save 🖫 the document.

MORE KNOWLEDGE | **Inserting a Link in a Document**

You can create a link in your document for quick access to webpages and files. To insert a link in a document, first position the insertion point where you want the link to appear. On the Insert tab, in the Links group, click Hyperlink. In the Insert Hyperlink dialog box, in the Text to display box, type the text that will display in the document as a blue hyperlink. At the bottom, in the Address box, type the URL and then click OK.

Objective 6 | Use Special Character and Paragraph Formatting

GO! Learn How
Video W3-6

Special text and paragraph formatting is useful to emphasize text, and it makes your newsletter look more professional. For example, you can place a border around one or more paragraphs or add shading to a paragraph. When adding shading, use light colors; dark shading can make the text difficult to read.

Activity 3.24 | Applying the Small Caps Font Effect

MOS
2.2.1

For headlines and titles, *small caps* is an attractive font effect. The effect changes lowercase letters to uppercase letters, but with the height of lowercase letters.

1 Under the screenshot, select the paragraph *Recycling Trash* including the paragraph mark.

2 Right-click the selected text, and then on the shortcut menu, click **Font** to display the **Font** dialog box. Click the **Font color arrow**, and then in the fifth column, click the last color.

3 Under **Font style**, click **Bold**. Under **Effects**, select the **Small caps** check box. Compare your screen with Figure 3.44.

The Font dialog box provides more options than are available on the ribbon and enables you to make several changes at the same time. In the Preview box, the text displays with the selected formatting options applied.

MAC TIP Display the menu bar, click Format, click Font, under Effects, select the Small caps check box; or, right-click over the selected text and click Font to display the Font dialog box.

Figure 3.44

4 Click **OK**. With the text still selected, point to the text and right-click, and then on the mini toolbar, double-click **Format Painter** ☑ so that you can apply the selected format multiple times. Then, in the second column, with the ▲I pointer, select each of the heading paragraphs—*Harvesting Daylight*, *Greener Landscaping*, *Greener Grocer*, and *Greener Records*—to apply the same formats. Press [Esc] to turn off Format Painter.

MAC TIP On the Home tab, in the Clipboard group, double-click the Format Painter icon.

5 In the first column, below the screenshot, notice that the space between the *Recycling Trash* subheading and the screenshot is fairly small. Click anywhere in the *Recycling Trash* subheading, and then on the **Layout tab**, in the **Paragraph group**, click the **Before up spin arrow** two times to set the **Spacing Before** to **12 pt**.

6 Compare your screen with Figure 3.45, and then **Save** 💾 your document.

Figure 3.45

Activity 3.25 | Inserting Symbols and Special Characters

2.1.2

You can insert symbols and special characters in a Word document, including copyright symbols, trademark symbols, and em dashes. An ***em dash*** is a punctuation symbol used to indicate an explanation or emphasis.

1 Press ⌃Ctrl + End to move to the end of the document, and then after the name *Emily Lynn* delete the comma and the space that separates her name from her job title—*Facilities Director*.

2 With the insertion point positioned before the *F* in *Facilities*, on the **Insert tab**, in the **Symbols group**, click **Symbol**. Below the gallery, click **More Symbols** to display the **Symbol** dialog box.

Here you can choose the symbol that you want to insert in your document.

3 In the **Symbol** dialog box, click the **Special Characters tab**. Scroll the list to view the types of special characters that you can insert; notice that some of the characters can be inserted using a Shortcut key.

4 Click **Em Dash**, and then in the lower right portion of the dialog box, click **Insert**. If necessary, drag the title bar of the Symbol window up or to the side, and then compare your screen with Figure 3.46.

An em dash displays between the name *Lynn* and the word *Facilities*.

Figure 3.46

5 In the **Symbol** dialog box, click **Close**, and then **Save** 🖫 your document.

Activity 3.26 | Adding Borders and Shading to a Paragraph

Paragraph borders provide strong visual cues to the reader. You can use paragraph shading with or without borders; however, combined with a border, light shading can be very effective in drawing the reader's eye to specific text.

1 At the end of the document, being sure to include the paragraph mark at the end, select the two lines of bold text that begin *"Everything we can do.*

The recycle picture may also be selected because it is anchored to the paragraph.

2 On the **Home tab**, in the **Paragraph group**, click the **Borders button arrow** ⊞ ▾, and then click **Borders and Shading**.

3 In the **Borders and Shading** dialog box, be sure the **Borders tab** is selected. Under **Setting**, click **Shadow**. Click the **Color arrow**, and then in the fifth column, click the last color. Click the **Width arrow**, and then click **1 pt**. Compare your screen with Figure 3.47

In the lower right portion of the Borders and Shading dialog box, the *Apply to* box indicates *Paragraph*. The *Apply to* box directs where the border will be applied—in this instance, the border will be applied to the selected paragraph.

Figure 3.47

NOTE   Adding Simple Borders to Text

You can add simple borders from the Borders button gallery, located in the Paragraph group. This button offers less control over the border appearance, however, because the line thickness and color applied will match the most recently used on the computer at which you are working. The Borders and Shading dialog box enables you to make your own custom selections.

---

4 At the top of the **Borders and Shading** dialog box, click the **Shading tab**.

5 Click the **Fill arrow**, and then in the fifth column, click the second color. Notice that the shading change is reflected in the Preview area on the right side of the dialog box.

6 Click **OK**. On the **Home tab**, in the **Paragraph group**, click **Center** ≡.

7 Click anywhere in the document to deselect, and then compare your screen with Figure 3.48.

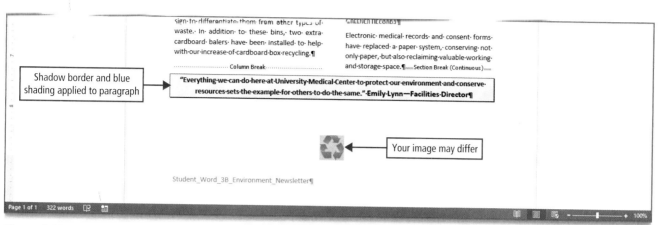

sign to differentiate them from other types of waste. In addition to these bins, two extra cardboard balers have been installed to help with our increase of cardboard box recycling.¶

·········· Column Break ··········

Shadow border and blue shading applied to paragraph

"Everything we can do here at University Medical Center to protect our environment and conserve resources sets the example for others to do the same." Emily Lynn—Facilities Director¶

GREENER RECORDS¶

Electronic medical records and consent forms have replaced a paper system, conserving not only paper, but also reclaiming valuable working and storage space.¶ ···Section Break (Continuous)···

Your image may differ

Student_Word_3B_Environment_Newsletter¶

Figure 3.48

8 In the shaded paragraph, in the second line, click in front of the *E* in the name *Emily*. Hold down Shift and then press Enter.

Holding down Shift while pressing Enter inserts a ***manual line break***, which moves the text to the right of the insertion point to a new line while keeping the text in the same paragraph. A ***line break indicator***, in the shape of a bent arrow, indicates a manual line break.

9 Press Ctrl + Home to move the insertion point to the top of the document. Click the **File tab** to display **Backstage** view, and then on the left click **Info**. On the right, at the bottom of the **Properties** list, click **Show All Properties**.

10 On the list of **Properties**, click to the right of **Tags**, and then type newsletter, January

11 Click to the right of **Subject**, and then type your course name and section number. Under **Related People**, be sure that your name displays as the author. If necessary, right-click the author name, click Edit Property, type your name, and click OK.

12 On the left, click **Save**. In the upper right corner of the Word window, click **Close** ☒.

For Non-MyLab Submissions Determine What Your Instructor Requires for Submission
As directed by your instructor, submit your completed Word document.

---

13 In **MyLab IT**, locate and click the Grader Project **Word 3B Environment Newsletter**. In **step 3**, under **Upload Completed Assignment**, click **Choose File**. In the **Open** dialog box, navigate to your **Word Chapter 3 folder**, and then click your **Student_Word_3B_ Environment_Newsletter** file one time to select it. In the lower right corner of the **Open** dialog box, click **Open**.

The name of your selected file displays above the Upload button.

14 To submit your file to MyLab IT for grading, click **Upload**, wait a moment for a green **Success!** message, and then in **step 4**, click the blue **Submit for Grading** button. Click **Close Assignment** to return to your list of **Course Materials**.

You have completed Project 3B **END**

ALERT   The Remaining Activities in this Chapter are Optional

Activities 3.28, 3.29, and 3.30, in which you create a set of mailing labels for the newsletter, are optional. Check with your instructor to see if you should complete these three Activities. These Activities are *not* included in the MyLab IT Grader system; you will need to obtain the starting file from your instructor or from www.pearsonhighered.com/go.

GO! Learn How
Video W3-7

Word's *mail merge* feature joins a *main document* and a *data source* to create customized letters or labels. The main document contains the text or formatting that remains constant. For labels, the main document contains the formatting for a specific label size. The data source contains information including the names and addresses of the individuals for whom the labels are being created. Names and addresses in a data source might come from an Excel worksheet or an Access database.

The easiest way to perform a mail merge is to use the Mail Merge Wizard, which asks you questions and, based on your answers, walks you step by step through the mail merge process.

Activity 3.27 | Starting the Mail Merge Wizard

MOS
4.3.1
(Expert)

In this Activity, you will open the data source for the mail merge, which is an Excel worksheet containing names and addresses.

1 Start Word and display a new blank document. Display formatting marks and rulers. Using your own name, **Save** the document in your **Word Chapter 3** folder as **Lastname_Firstname_Word_3B_Mailing_Labels**

2 Click the **Mailings tab**. In the **Start Mail Merge group**, click **Start Mail Merge**, and then click **Step-by-Step Mail Merge Wizard** to display the **Mail Merge** pane on the right.

3 In the **Mail Merge** pane, under **Select document type**, click **Labels**. At the bottom of the **Mail Merge** pane, click **Next: Starting document** to display Step 2 of 6.

4 Under **Select starting document**, be sure **Change document layout** is selected, and then under **Change document layout**, click **Label options**.

5 In the **Label Options** dialog box, under **Printer information**, click the **Tray arrow**, and then if necessary, click Default tray (Automatically Select)—the exact wording may vary depending on your printer, but select the *Default* or *Automatic* option so that you can print the labels on regular paper rather than manually inserting labels in the printer.

6 Under **Label information**, click the **Label vendors arrow**, and then click **Avery US Letter**. Under **Product number**, scroll about halfway down the list, and then click **5160 Address Labels**. Compare your screen with Figure 3.49.

The Avery 5160 address label is a commonly used label. The precut sheets contain three columns of 10 labels each—for a total of 30 labels per sheet.

Figure 3.49

7 At the bottom of the **Label Options** dialog box, click **OK**. If a message box displays, click OK to set up the labels. If the gridlines that define each label do not display, on the Table Tools Layout tab, in the Table group, click View Gridlines.

8 At the bottom of the **Mail Merge** pane, click **Next: Select recipients**. In the **Mail Merge** pane, under **Select recipients**, be sure the **Use an existing list** option button is selected. Under **Use an existing list**, click **Browse**.

> The label page is set up with three columns and ten rows. Here, in Step 3 of the Mail Merge Wizard, you must identify the recipients—the data source. For your recipient data source, you can choose to use an existing list—for example, a list of names and addresses that you have in an Access database, an Excel worksheet, or your Outlook contacts list. If you do not have an existing data source, you can create a new list at this point in the wizard.

9 In the **Select Data Source** dialog box, navigate to the files you downloaded with this chapter, click one time to select the Excel file **w03B_Addresses**, and then click **Open** to display the **Select Table** dialog box. Compare your screen with Figure 3.50.

> In the Select Table dialog box, the sheet name of the Excel workbook is selected, and at the bottom the check box for *First row of data contains column headers* is selected.

> Each row of information in the Excel worksheet that contains data for one person is referred to as a *record*. The column headings—for example, *Last Name* and *First Name*—are referred to as *fields*.

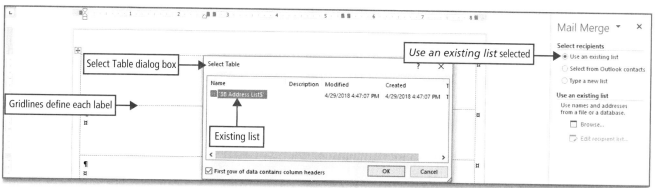

Figure 3.50

10 In the **Select Table** dialog box, click **OK**, and then compare your screen with Figure 3.51.

> The Mail Merge Recipients dialog box displays. Here you can perform various actions on the list; for example, you can sort, filter, find duplicates in, locate a specific recipient, or validate addresses.

> You can also select the path in the Data Source to enable editing to add additional recipients to the list.

Figure 3.51

11 In the lower right corner of the **Mail Merge Recipients** dialog box, click **OK**.

The labels in the Word document display, and *<<Next Record>>* displays in each label cell.

Activity 3.28 | Completing the Mail Merge

MOS
4.3.2
(Expert),
4.3.4
(Expert)

1 At the bottom of the **Mail Merge** pane, click **Next: Arrange your labels**.

2 Under **Arrange your labels**, click **Address block**. In the **Insert Address Block** dialog box, under **Specify address elements**, examine the various formats for names. If necessary, under *Insert recipient's name in this format*, select the *Joshua Randall Jr.* format. Compare your dialog box with Figure 3.52.

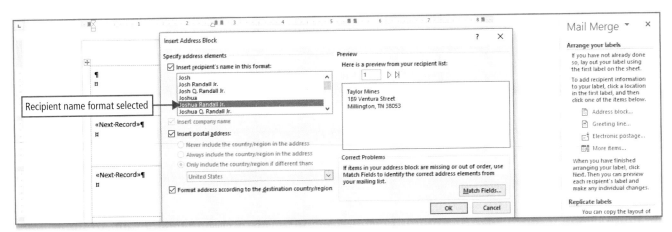

Figure 3.52

3 In the lower right corner of the **Insert Address Block** dialog box, click **Match Fields**.

If your field names are descriptive, the Mail Merge program will identify them correctly, as is the case with most of the information in the *Required for Address Block* section. However, the Address 2 field is unmatched—in the source file, this column is named *Unit*.

4 Click the **Address 2 arrow**, and then from the list of available fields, click **Unit** to match the Mail Merge field with the field in your data source.

5 At the bottom of the **Match Fields** dialog box, click **OK**. At the bottom of the **Insert Address Block** dialog box, click **OK**.

6 In the **Mail Merge** pane, under **Replicate labels**, click **Update all labels** to insert an address block in each label space for each subsequent record.

7 At the bottom of the **Mail Merge** pane, click **Next: Preview your labels**. Notice that for addresses with four lines, the last line of the address is cut off.

8 Press Ctrl + A to select all of the label text, click the **Layout tab**, and then in the **Paragraph group**, click in the **Spacing Before** box. Type **3** and press Enter to adjust the spacing in your label.

9 Click in any label to deselect, and notice that 4-line addresses are no longer cut off. Compare your screen with Figure 3.53.

Labels with 4 lines display correctly

All fields updated with address data

Figure 3.53

10 At the bottom of the **Mail Merge** pane, click **Next: Complete the merge**.

Step 6 of the Mail Merge displays. At this point, you can print or edit your labels, although this is done more easily in the document window.

11 **Save** 🖫 your labels, and then on the right, **Close** ☒ the **Mail Merge** pane.

Activity 3.29 | Previewing and Printing Mail Merge Results

If you discover that you need to make further changes to your labels, you can still make them even though the Mail Merge task pane is closed.

1 Add the file name to the footer, close the footer area, and then move to the top of Page 2. Click anywhere in the empty table row, and then click the **Table Tools Layout tab**. In the **Rows & Columns group**, click **Delete**, and then click **Delete Rows**.

Adding footer text to a label sheet replaces the last row of labels on a page with the footer text and moves the last row of labels to the top of the next page. In this instance, a blank second page is created, which you can delete by deleting the blank row.

2 Notice that the labels do not display in alphabetical order. Click the **Mailings tab**, and then in the **Start Mail Merge group**, click **Edit Recipient List** to display the list of names and addresses.

3 In the **Mail Merge Recipients** dialog box, click the **Last Name** field heading, and notice that the names are sorted alphabetically by the recipient's last name.

Mailing labels are often sorted by either last name or by ZIP Code.

4 Click the **Last Name** field heading again, and then notice that the last names are sorted in descending order. Click the **Last Name** field one more time to return to ascending order, and then click **OK**. Press Ctrl + Home, and then compare your screen with Figure 3.54.

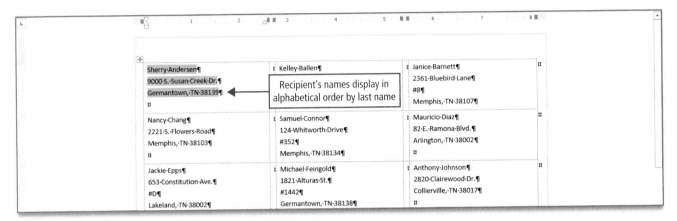

Figure 3.54

5 From the **File tab**, display **Backstage** view, on the left click **Info**, and in the lower right, click **Show All Properties**. On the list of **Properties**, click to the right of **Tags**, and then type **labels**

6 Click to the right of **Subject**, and then type your course name and section number. Be sure that your name displays as the author. If necessary, right-click the author name, click Edit Property, type your name, and click OK.

7 On the left, click **Save**. In the upper right corner of the Word window, click **Close** ✕. If directed by your instructor to do so, submit your Lastname_Firstname_3B_Mailing_Labels file as a paper printout, an electronic image of your document that looks like a printed document, or your completed Word file.

If you print, the labels will print on whatever paper is in the printer; unless you have preformatted labels available, the labels will print on a sheet of paper. Printing the labels on plain paper enables you to proofread the labels before you print them on more expensive label sheets.

You have completed the optional portion of this project **END**

Objective | Format a Newsletter in Google Docs

ALERT Working with Web-Based Applications and Services

Computer programs and services on the web receive continuous updates and improvements, so the steps to complete this web-based Activity may differ from the ones shown. You can often look at the screens and the information presented to determine how to complete the Activity.

If you do not already have a Google account, you will need to create one before you begin this Activity. Go to http://google.com and, in the upper right corner, click Sign In. On the Sign In screen, click Create Account. On the Create your Google Account page, complete the form, read and agree to the Terms of Service and Privacy Policy, and then click Next step. On the Welcome screen, click Get Started.

Activity | Formatting a Two-Column Newsletter in Google Docs

In this Activity, you will use Google Docs to edit a newsletter similar to the one you edited in Project 3B.

1 From the desktop, open your browser, navigate to **http://google.com**, and then click the **Google Apps** menu. Click **Drive**, and then if necessary, sign in to your Google account.

2 Open your **GO! Web Projects** folder—or click New to create and then open this folder if necessary.

3 On the left, click **New**, and then click **File upload**. In the **Open** dialog box, navigate to the files you downloaded for this chapter, and then in the **File List**, double-click to open **w03_3B_Web**.

4 Point to the uploaded file **w03_3B_Web**, and then right-click. On the shortcut menu, scroll as necessary, and then click **Rename**. Using your own last name and first name, type **Lastname_Firstname_WD_3B_Web** and then click **OK** to rename the file.

5 Right-click the file you just renamed, point to **Open with**, and then click **Google Docs**.

6 Drag to select the newsletter title—*University Medical Center Goes Green*. On the toolbar, click the **Font size arrow**, and then click **18**. With the newsletter title still selected, on the toolbar, click the **Text color button**, and then in the second row, click the third from last color—**blue**.

Apply the same **Font Color** to the five subheadings—*Recycling Trash*, *Harvesting Daylight*, *Greener Landscaping*, *Greener Grocer*, and *Greener Records*.

7 Press Ctrl + End to move to the end of the document, and then press Enter. On the menu bar, click **Insert**, point to **Image**, and then click **Upload from computer**. In the **Open** dialog box, navigate to the files downloaded with this chapter, and then double-click **w03B_Recycle_Symbol**.

8 Select the image and then on the toolbar, click **Center**.

9 Click at the beginning of the paragraph heading *Recycling Trash*, and then drag down to select the text for the five articles—ending with the period after the word *space*.

10 With the five headings and their accompanying paragraphs selected, on the toolbar, click **Format**. Point to **Columns**, and then click the second option—text with two columns. Click anywhere to deselect, and then compare your screen with Figure A.

11 Submit the file as directed by your instructor. In the upper right, click your user name, and then click **Sign out**. **Close** your browser window. Your file is automatically saved in your Google Drive.

»»GO! With Google Docs

Figure A

wavebreakmedia/Shutterstock, Monkey Business Images/Fotolia, Ivanko80/Shutterstock, Monkey Business Images/Shutterstock

Microsoft Office Specialist (MOS) Skills in this Chapter

Project A	Project B
1.1.1 Search for text	**2.1.2** Insert symbols and special characters
1.1.3 Move to specific locations and objects in a document	**2.2.1** Apply text effects
	2.3.2 Insert page, section, and column breaks
1.3.1 Save documents in alternative file formats	**4.3.1** (Expert) Manage recipient lists
1.3.2 Modify basic document properties	**4.3.2** (Expert) Insert merged fields
2.2.3 Set line and paragraph spacing and indentation	**4.3.3** (Expert) Preview merge results
2.3.1 Format text in multiple columns	**4.3.4** (Expert) Create merged documents, labels, and envelopes
2.3.2 Insert page, section, and column breaks	
2.3.2 (Expert) Modify existing styles	**5.1.2** Insert pictures
4.1.1 Insert footnotes and endnotes	**5.1.5** Insert screenshots and screen clippings
4.1.2 Modify footnote and endnote properties	**5.2.3** Remove picture backgrounds
4.1.3 Create and modify bibliography citation sources	**5.2.4** Format graphic elements
4.1.4 Insert citations for bibliographies	**5.4.1** Position objects
4.2.3 Insert bibliographies	**5.4.2** Wrap text around objects

Build Your E-Portfolio

An E-Portfolio is a collection of evidence, stored electronically, that showcases what you have accomplished while completing your education. Collecting and then sharing your work products with potential employers reflects your academic and career goals. Your completed documents from the following projects are good examples to show what you have learned: 3G, 3K, and 3L.

Go! For Job Success

Video: Interview Walkthru

Your instructor may assign this video to your class, and then ask you to think about, or discuss with your classmates, these questions:

g-stockstudio/ Shutterstock

> What kind of information should you gather before going to a job interview?

> What items should you take with you to an interview?

> What things will the interviewer be noticing about you to determine if you are prepared for the interview?

End of Chapter

Summary

Word assists you in formatting a research paper for college or business by providing built-in styles and formats for the most commonly used footnote and citation styles for research papers—MLA and APA.

Word helps you create the bibliography for your research paper by recording all of your citations in the Source Manager, and then generating the bibliography—in MLA, called Works Cited—for you.

Newsletters are often used by organizations to communicate information to a specific group. A newsletter can be formatted in two columns with a nameplate at the top that identifies the publication.

The Mail Merge Wizard enables you to easily merge a main document and a data source to create customized letters or labels. The data source can be a Word table, Excel spreadsheet, or Access database.

GO! Learn It Online

Review the concepts, key terms, and MOS skills in this chapter by completing these online challenges, which you can find at **MyLab IT**.

Chapter Quiz: Answer matching and multiple choice questions to test what you learned in this chapter.

Lessons on the GO!: Learn how to use all the new apps and features as they are introduced by Microsoft.

MOS Prep Quiz: Answer questions to review the MOS skills that you practiced in this chapter.

GO! Collaborative Team Project (Available in Instructor Resource Center)

If your instructor assigns this project to your class, you can expect to work with one or more of your classmates—either in person or by using internet tools—to create work products similar to those that you created in this chapter. A team is a group of workers who work together to solve a problem, make a decision, or create a work product. Collaboration is when you work together with others as a team in an intellectual endeavor to complete a shared task or achieve a shared goal.

Monkey Business Images/Fotolia

Project Guide for Word Chapter 3

Your instructor may assign one or more of these projects to help you review the chapter and assess your mastery and understanding of its contents.

	Project Guide for Word Chapter 3		
Project	**Apply Skills from These Chapter Objectives**	**Project Type**	**Project Location**
3A MyLab IT	Objectives 1-4 from Project 3A	**3A Instructional Project (Grader Project)** Instruction Guided instruction to learn the skills in Project A.	In **MyLab IT** and in text
3B MyLab IT	Objectives 5-7 from Project 3B	**3B Instructional Project (Grader Project)** Instruction Guided instruction to learn the skills in Project B.	In **MyLab IT** and in text
3C	Objectives 1-4 from Project 3A	**3C Skills Review** Review A guided review of the skills from Project 3A. In text	In text
3D	Objectives 5-7 from Project 3B	**3D Skills Review Review** Review A guided review of the skills from Project 3B.	In text
3E MyLab IT	Objectives 1-4 from Project 3A	**3E Mastery (Grader Project)** **Mastery and Transfer of Learning** A demonstration of your mastery of the skills in Project 3A with extensive decision-making.	In **MyLab IT** and in text
3F MyLab IT	Objectives 5-7 from Project 3B	**3F Mastery (Grader Project)** **Mastery and Transfer of Learning** A demonstration of your mastery of the skills in Project 3B with extensive decision-making.	In **MyLab IT** and in text
3G MyLab IT	Objectives 1-7 from Projects 3A and 3B	**3G Mastery (Grader Project)** **Mastery and Transfer of Learning** A demonstration of your mastery of the skills in Projects 3A and 3B with extensive decision-making.	In **MyLab IT** and in text
3H	Combination of Objectives from Projects 3A and 3B	**3H GO! Fix It (Scorecard Grading** **Critical Thinking** A demonstration of your mastery of the skills in Projects 3A and 3B by creating a correct result from a document that contains errors you must find.	Online
3I	Combination of Objectives from Projects 3A and 3B	**3I GO! Make It (Scorecard Grading** **Critical Thinking** A demonstration of your mastery of the skills in Projects 3A and 3B by creating a result from a supplied picture.	Online
3J	Combination of Objectives from Projects 3A and 3B	**3J GO! Solve It (Rubric Grading)** **Critical Thinking** A demonstration of your mastery of the skills in Projects 3A and 3B, your decision-making skills, and your critical thinking skills. A task-specific rubric helps you self-assess your result.	Online
3K	Combination of Objectives from Projects 3A and 3B	**3K GO! Solve It (Rubric Grading)** **Critical Thinking** A demonstration of your mastery of the skills in Projects 3A and 3B, your decision-making skills, and your critical thinking skills. A task-specific rubric helps you self-assess your result.	In text
3L	Combination of Objectives from Projects 3A and 3B	**3L GO! Think (Rubric Grading)** **Critical Thinking** A demonstration of your understanding of the Chapter concepts applied in a manner that you would outside of college. An analytic rubric helps you and your instructor grade the quality of your work by comparing it to the work an expert in the discipline would create.	In text
3M	Combination of Objectives from Projects 3A and 3B	**3M GO! Think (Rubric Grading)** **Critical Thinking** A demonstration of your understanding of the Chapter concepts applied in a manner that you would outside of college. An analytic rubric helps you and your instructor grade the quality of your work by comparing it to the work an expert in the discipline would create.	IRC
3N	Combination of Objectives from Projects 3A and 3B	**3N You and GO! (Rubric Grading)** **Critical Thinking** A demonstration of your understanding of the Chapter concepts applied in a manner that you would in a personal situation. An analytic rubric helps you and your instructor grade the quality of your work.	IRC
3O	Combination of Objectives from Projects 3A and 3B	**3O Cumulative Team Project for Word Chapter 3** **Critical Thinking** A demonstration of your understanding of concepts and your ability to work collaboratively in a group role-playing assessment, requiring both collaboration and self-management.	IRC
Capstone Project for Word Chapters 1-3	Combination of Objectives from Projects 1A, 1B, 2A, 2B, 3A, and 3B	**Word Capstone (Grader Project)** **Mastery and Transfer of Learning** A demonstration of your mastery of the skills in Chapters 1-3 with extensive decision making.	In **MyLab IT**

Glossary

Glossary of Chapter Key Terms

American Psychological Association (APA) One of two commonly used style guides for formatting research papers.

Bibliography A list of cited works in a report or research paper; also referred to as Works Cited, Sources, or References, depending upon the report style.

Brightness The relative lightness of a picture.

Citation A note inserted into the text of a research paper that refers the reader to a source in the bibliography.

Column break indicator A dotted line containing the words *Column Break* that displays at the bottom of the column.

Contrast The difference between the darkest and lightest area of a picture.

Crop A command that removes unwanted or unnecessary areas of a picture.

Crop handles Handles used to define unwanted areas of a picture.

Crop pointer The pointer used to crop areas of a picture.

Data source A document that contains a list of variable information, such as names and addresses, that you merge with a main document to create customized form letters or labels.

Em dash A punctuation symbol that indicates an explanation or emphasis.

Endnote In a research paper, a note placed at the end of a document or chapter.

Fields In a mail merge, the column headings in the data source.

Flip A command that creates a reverse image of a picture or object.

Footnote In a research paper, a note placed at the bottom of the page.

Hanging indent An indent style in which the first line of a paragraph extends to the left of the remaining lines and that is commonly used for bibliographic entries.

Indenting Moving the beginning of the first line of a paragraph to the right or left of the rest of the paragraph to provide visual cues to the reader to help divide the document text and make it easier to read.

Line break indicator A non-printing character in the shape of a bent arrow that indicates a manual line break.

Mail merge A feature that joins a main document and a data source to create customized letters or labels.

Main document In a mail merge, the document that contains the text or formatting that remains constant.

Manual column break An artificial end to a column to balance columns or to provide space for the insertion of other objects.

Manual line break A break that moves text to the right of the insertion point to a new line while keeping the text in the same paragraph.

Manual page break The action of forcing a page to end and placing subsequent text at the top of the next page.

Modern Language Association (MLA) One of two commonly used style guides for formatting research papers.

Nameplate The banner on the front page of a newsletter that identifies the publication.

Newsletter A periodical that communicates news and information to a specific group.

Note In a research paper, information that expands on the topic, but that does not fit well in the document text.

Page break indicator A dotted line with the text *Page Break* that indicates where a manual page break was inserted.

Parenthetical references References that include the last name of the author or authors, and the page number in the referenced source.

PDF Reflow The ability to import PDF files into Word so that you can transform a PDF back into a fully editable Word document.

Read Mode A view in Word that optimizes the Word screen for the times when you are reading Word documents on the screen and not creating or editing them.

Recolor A feature that enables you to change all colors in the picture to shades of a single color.

Record Each row of information that contains data for one person.

Researcher A Word feature that helps you find topics and reliable sources for a research paper; for sources that you select, citation information is available.

Scale A command that resizes a picture to a percentage of its size.

Screen Clipping A tool with which you can take a quick snapshot of part of a screen, and then add it to your document.

Screenshot An image of an active window on your computer that you can paste into a document.

Section A portion of a document that can be formatted differently from the rest of the document.

Section break A double dotted line that indicates the end of one section and the beginning of another section.

Side to Side A Page Movement setting that enables you to see whole pages by sliding each page from right to left or left to right.

Small caps A font effect that changes lowercase letters to uppercase letters, but with the height of lowercase letters.

Smart Lookup A Word feature with which you can get more information about text you select; shows definitions, images, and results from various online sources.

Style A group of formatting commands, such as font, font size, font color, paragraph alignment, and line spacing, that you can apply to a paragraph with one command.

Style guide A manual that contains standards for the design and writing of documents.

Suppress A Word feature that hides header and footer information, including the page number, on the first page of a document.

Text Highlight Color A Word command with which you can apply a highlight color to selected text.

Works Cited In the MLA style, a list of cited works placed at the end of a research paper or report.

Chapter Review

Skills Review | **Project 3C Diet and Exercise Report**

Apply **3A** skills from
these Objectives:

1. Create a Research Paper
2. Insert Footnotes in a Research Paper
3. Create Citations and a Bibliography in a Research Paper
4. Use Read Mode, PDF Reflow, and Save Documents in Alternate Formats

In the following Skills Review, you will edit and format a research paper that contains information about the effects of diet and exercise. This paper was created by Rachel Holder, a medical intern at University Medical Center, for distribution to her classmates studying physiology. Your completed document will look similar to the one shown in Figure 3.55.

Project Files

For Project 3C, you will need the following file:

w03C_Diet_Exercise

You will save your document as:

Lastname_Firstname_3C_Diet_Exercise

Project Results

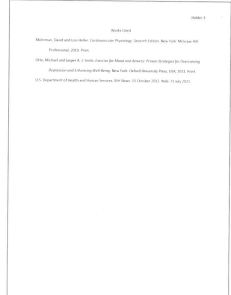

Figure 3.55

(continues on next page)

Chapter Review

1 ▶ Start Word. On Word's opening screen, on the left, click **Open**. Navigate to the files downloaded with this project, and then locate and open the document **w03C_Diet_Exercise**. Display the formatting marks and rulers. **Save** the file in your **Word Chapter 3** folder as Lastname_Firstname_3C_Diet_Exercise

a. Press Ctrl + A to select all the text. On the **Home tab**, in the **Paragraph group**, click **Line and Paragraph Spacing**, and then change the line spacing to **2.0**. On the **Layout tab**, change the **Spacing After** to **0 pt**.

b. Press Ctrl + Home, press Enter to create a blank line at the top of the document, and then click to position the insertion point in the new blank line. Type **Rachel Holder** and press Enter. Type **Dr. Hillary Kim** and press Enter. Type **Physiology 621** and press Enter. Type **August 31, 2021** and press Enter.

c. Type **Effects of Diet and Exercise** and then press Ctrl + E to center the title you just typed.

2 ▶ On the **Insert tab**, in the **Header & Footer group**, click **Header**, and then at the bottom of the list, click **Edit Header**. Type **Holder** and then press Spacebar.

a. Under **Header and Footer Tools**, on the **Design tab**, in the **Header & Footer group**, click **Page Number**, and then point to **Current Position**. Under **Simple**, click **Plain Number**.

b. On the **Home tab**, in the **Paragraph group**, click **Align Right**. Double-click anywhere in the document to close the Header area.

c. Near the top of **Page 1**, locate the paragraph beginning *The scientific evidence*, and then click to position the insertion point at the beginning of that paragraph. Scroll to the end of the document, hold down Shift, and then click to the right of the last paragraph mark to select all of the text from the insertion point to the end of the document.

d. On the **Home tab**, in the **Paragraph group**, click the **Dialog Box Launcher** button ⌐. In the **Paragraph** dialog box, on the **Indents and Spacing tab**, under **Indentation**, click the **Special arrow**, and then click **First line**. Click **OK**.

e. On the **Insert tab**, in the **Header & Footer group**, click **Footer**, and then click **Edit Footer**. In the **Insert group**, click **Document Info**, and then click **File Name**. Click **Close Header and Footer**.

3 ▶ Scroll to view the top of **Page 2**, locate the paragraph that begins *Exercise also has*, and then at the end of that paragraph, click to position the insertion point to the right of the period following *Irwin*. On the **References tab**, in the **Footnotes group**, click **Insert Footnote**.

a. As the footnote text, type **Physical activity may provide a low-risk method of preventing weight gain. Unlike diet-induced weight loss, exercise-induced weight loss increases cardiorespiratory fitness levels.**

b. In the upper portion of **Page 1**, locate the paragraph that begins *Regular cardiovascular exercise*. Click to position the insertion point at the end of the paragraph and insert a footnote.

c. As the footnote text, type **The objective of the study was to examine the effects of exercise on total and intra-abdominal body fat overall and by level of exercise. Save** your document.

4 ▶ At the bottom of **Page 1**, right-click in the footnote you just typed. On the shortcut menu, click **Style**. In the **Style** dialog box, click **Modify**. In the **Modify Style** dialog box, locate the small **Formatting** toolbar in the center of the dialog box, click the **Font Size button arrow**, and then click **11**.

a. In the lower left corner of the dialog box, click **Format**, and then click **Paragraph**. In the **Paragraph** dialog box, under **Indentation**, click the **Special arrow**, and then click **First line**. Under **Spacing**, click the **Line spacing arrow**, and then click **Double**.

b. Click **OK** to close the **Paragraph** dialog box, click **OK** to close the **Modify Style** dialog box, and then click **Apply** to apply the new style. **Save** your document.

5 ▶ Scroll to view the top of **Page 1**, and then in the paragraph that begins *The scientific evidence*, click to position the insertion point to the left of the period at the end of the paragraph.

(continues on next page)

Chapter Review

a. On the **References tab**, in the **Citations & Bibliography group**, click the **Style button arrow**, and then click **MLA** to insert a reference using MLA style. Click **Insert Citation**, and then click **Add New Source**. Click the **Type of Source arrow**, scroll as necessary to locate and click **Book**, and then add the following information: (Mac users: there is no Medium field; the order of the fields differs slightly.)

Author	Otto, Michael and Jasper A. J. Smits.
Title	Exercise for Mood and Anxiety: Proven Strategies for Overcoming Depression and Enhancing Well-Being
Year	2011
City	New York
Publisher	Oxford University Press, USA
Medium	Print

b. Click **OK** to insert the citation. In the paragraph, click to select the citation, click the **Citation Options arrow**, and then click **Edit Citation**. In the **Edit Citation** dialog box, under **Add**, in the **Pages** box, type **3** and then click **OK**.

c. On the upper portion of **Page 2**, in the paragraph that begins *Other positive effects*, in the second line, click to position the insertion point to the left of the period following *substantially*. In the **Citations & Bibliography group**, click **Insert Citation**, and then click **Add New Source**. Click the **Type of Source arrow**, click **Book**, and then add the following information: (Mac users: There is no Medium field; order of the fields differs slightly.)

Author	Lohrman, David and Lois Heller.
Title	Cardiovascular Physiology, Seventh Edition
Year	2010
City	New York
Publisher	McGraw-Hill Professional
Medium	Print

d. Click **OK**. Click to select the citation in the paragraph, click the **Citation Options arrow**, and then click **Edit Citation**. In the **Edit Citation** dialog box, under **Add**, in the **Pages** box, type **195** and then click **OK**.

6 ▶ Press Ctrl + End to move to the end of the last paragraph in the document. Click to the left of the period following *loss*. In the **Citations & Bibliography group**, click **Insert Citation**, and then click **Add New Source**. Click the **Type of Source arrow**, click **Web site**, and then select the **Corporate Author** check box. Add the following information: (Mac users: There is no Medium field; the order of the fields differs slightly.)

Corporate Author	U.S. Department of Health and Human Services
Name of Web Page	NIH News
Year	2012
Month	October
Day	15
Year Accessed	2021
Month Accessed	July
Day Accessed	21
Medium	Web

a. Click **OK**. Press Ctrl + End to move the insertion point to the end of the document. Press Ctrl + Enter to insert a manual page break. On the **Home tab**, in the **Paragraph group**, click the **Dialog Box Launcher** button. In the **Paragraph** dialog box, on the **Indents and Spacing tab**, under **Indentation**, click the **Special arrow**, and then click **(none)**. Click **OK**. (Mac users: To display the Paragraph dialog box, on the Home tab, in the Paragraph group, click the Line and Paragraph Spacing button, click Line Spacing Options.)

b. On the **References tab**, in the **Citations & Bibliography group**, be sure **MLA** displays in the **Style** box. In the **Citations & Bibliography group**, click **Bibliography**, and then at the bottom, click **Works Cited**.

c. Select the paragraph *Works Cited*. On the **Home tab**, in the **Font group**, change the **Font** to **Calibri**, and then change the **Font Size** to **11**. Click the **Font Color arrow**, and then in the second column, click the first color. With the text *Works Cited* still selected, in the **Paragraph group**, click **Center**.

d. Click to the left of *Works Cited* and then drag down to select the title *Works Cited* and the three citations. Display the **Paragraph** dialog box, change the **Spacing Before** to **0 pt**, change the **Spacing After** to **0 pt**, and then set **Line spacing** to **Double**. Click **OK**. **Save** your document.

(continues on next page)

Chapter Review

7 ▶ On the **References tab**, in the **Citations & Bibliography group**, click **Manage Sources**. On the left, on the **Master List**, click the entry for *Lohrman, David*, and then click **Edit**. In the **Edit Source** dialog box, in the **Author** box, change the *L* in *Lohrman* to **M** Click **OK**, click **Yes**, and then click **Close**.

(Mac users: On the References tab, click Citations, click the Settings button in the bottom right corner of the Citations pane. Click Citation Source Manager. Click the reference for Lohrman, click Edit, edit the name *Lohrman* to *Mohrman*. Click OK, and then click Close. On Page 2 of the document, click the *Lohrman* reference, click the arrow, and then click Update Citations and Bibliography. Move to step b.)

a. On **Page 2**, in the paragraph that begins *Other positive effects*, in the third line, on the selected citation, click the **Citation Options arrow**, and then click **Update Citations and Bibliography**.

b. On the *Works Cited* page, drag to select the three citations, and then from the **Home tab**, redisplay the **Paragraph** dialog box. Reset the **Spacing Before** and **Spacing After** to **0 pt** and the **Line spacing** to **Double**. Click **OK**.

c. From the **File tab**, display **Backstage** view, on the left click **Info**, and then in the lower right, click **Show All Properties**. Add the following information:

Title	**Diet and Exercise**
Tags	**weight loss, exercise, diet**
Comments	**Draft copy of report for class**
Categories	**biomedical research**
Company	**University Medical Center**
Manager	**Dr. Hillary Kim**

d. Click outside of the **Manager** box to close it. In the **Subject** box, type your course name and section number. Be sure that your name displays as the Author and edit if necessary. On the left, click **Save** to redisplay your document.

8 ▶ On **Page 1**, in the paragraph that begins *Regular cardiovascular*, in the third line, select the text *Melinda Irwin*. On the **References tab**, in the **Research group**, click **Smart Lookup**. In the **Smart Lookup** pane, scroll down to view the results—you will likely see Dr. Irwin's page in the Public Health department at Yale University. If you want to do so, click this link to see more of Dr. Irwin's research.

a. **Close** the **Smart Lookup** pane. On the **References tab**, in the **Research group**, click **Researcher**. In the **Researcher** pane, in the search box, type—being sure to include the quotation marks and uppercase letters as indicated—**"aerobic exercise" AND "endorphins"** and then press [Enter].

b. Under **Top sources**, click **Websites**, and notice the websites you can visit regarding this topic.

c. On **Page 2** of your research paper, in the paragraph that begins *Other positive effects*, in the third line, select the text *aerobic exercise can also produce endorphins*. With the text selected, on the **Home tab**, in the **Font group**, click the **Text Highlight Color arrow**, and then apply **Yellow** highlighting.

d. **Close** the **Researcher** pane.

e. Press [Ctrl] + [Home] to move to the top of your document. On the **View tab**, in the **Views group**, click **Read Mode**. In the upper left, click **Tools**, click **Find**, and then in the search box, type **Yale** and notice that the text you searched for is highlighted in the document.

f. In the upper left, click **View**, and then click **Edit Document** to return to Print Layout view. **Close** the **Navigation** pane. **Save** your document, and view the Print Preview. If directed by your instructor to do so, submit your paper printout, your electronic image of your document that looks like a printed document, or your Word file. **Close** Word.

You have completed Project 3C **END**

Chapter Review

Skills Review | **Project 3D Career Newsletter**

Apply 3B skills from these Objectives:

5. Format a Multiple-Column Newsletter
6. Use Special Character and Paragraph Formatting
7. Create Mailing Labels Using Mail Merge

In the following Skills Review, you will format a newsletter regarding professional development opportunities offered by University Medical Center, and you will create mailing labels for staff interested in these opportunities. Your completed document will look similar to Figure 3.56.

Project Files

For Project 3D, you will need the following files:

New blank Word document
w03D_Career_Newsletter
w03D_Career_Sign (optional)
w03D_Medical_Symbol
w03D_Addresses

You will save your documents as:

Lastname_Firstname_3D_Career_Newsletter
Lastname_Firstname_3D_Mailing_Labels

Project Results

Figure 3.56

(continues on next page)

Chapter Review

1 Start Word. On Word's opening screen, on the left click **Open**. Navigate to the files you downloaded with this project, and then locate and open **w03D_Career_Newsletter**. Using your own name, **Save** the file in your **Word Chapter 3** folder as **Lastname_Firstname_3D_Career_Newsletter** and then add the file name to the footer.

a. Select the first two lines of the document. On the mini toolbar, change the **Font** to **Arial Black** and the **Font Size** to **18**. Select the first three lines of the document. Click the **Font Color button arrow**, and then under **Theme Colors**, in the fifth column, click the last color.

b. With the text still selected, on the **Home tab**, in the **Paragraph group**, click the **Borders button arrow**, and then at the bottom, click **Borders and Shading**. In the **Borders and Shading** dialog box, on the **Borders tab**, click the **Color arrow**, and then under **Theme Colors**, in the fifth column, click the last color.

c. Click the **Width arrow**, and then click **3 pt**. In the **Preview** box, click the bottom border. Click **OK**.

d. Click at the beginning of the paragraph that begins *Professional Development*. Scroll the document, hold down Shift, and then click after the paragraph mark at the end of the *Internship Essentials* line. On the **Layout tab**, in the **Page Setup group**, click **Columns**, and then click **Two**. With the two columns of text selected, on the **Home tab**, in the **Paragraph group**, click **Justify**.

e. In the first column, click at the beginning of the paragraph that begins *Courses are taught*. On the **Layout tab**, in the **Page Setup group**, click **Breaks**. Under **Page Breaks**, click **Column**.

2 Press Ctrl + Home. On the **Insert tab**, in the **Illustrations group**, click **Pictures**. From the files downloaded with this project, insert the file **w03D_Career_Sign**.

a. With the image selected, on the **Format tab**, in the **Size group**, click the **Dialog Box Launcher** button. In the **Layout** dialog box, on the **Size tab**, under **Scale**, be sure the **Lock aspect ratio** and **Relative to original picture size** check boxes are selected. Select the number in the **Height box**, type **15** and then press Tab.

b. In the **Layout** dialog box, click the **Text Wrapping tab**. Under **Wrapping style**, click **Square**.

c. Click the **Position tab**, and then under **Horizontal**, click the **Alignment** option button. Be sure that the **Alignment** indicates **Left** and **relative to Column**. Under **Vertical**, click the **Alignment** option button, and then change the alignment to **Top relative to Margin**. Click **OK**. Compare the picture size and placement with Figure 3.56 and adjust the size of the image if necessary. **Save** your newsletter.

3 Press Ctrl + End to move to the end of the document. On the **Insert tab**, in the **Illustrations group**, click **Pictures**, and then from your student data files, insert the picture **w03D_Medical_Symbol**.

a. With the image selected, on the **Picture Tools Format tab**, in the **Adjust group**, click **Color**, and then under **Recolor**, in the last row, click one of the paler images such as blue or gray or purple.

b. With the picture selected, on the **Picture Tools Format tab**, in the **Size group**, click in the **Height** box. If necessary, type **1** and then press Enter. To the right of the picture, click the **Layout Options** button, and then click **Square**. At the bottom of the **Layout Options gallery**, click **See more** to display the **Layout** dialog box.

c. On the **Position tab**, under **Horizontal**, click the **Alignment** option button, and then change the **Alignment** to **Centered relative to Page**. Under **Vertical**, click the **Alignment** option button, and then change **Alignment** to **Bottom relative to Margin**. Click **OK**.

d. On the **Picture Tools Format tab**, in the **Picture Styles group**, click the **Picture Border button**. Under **Theme Colors**, in the fifth column, click the second color. Click the **Picture Border button arrow** again, and then point to **Weight**. Click **1 pt**.

4 In the paragraph that begins *University Medical Center is a dynamic*, click after the period at the end of the paragraph, and then press Enter one time. With the insertion point in the new blank paragraph, open your web browser, and then navigate to **www.ahrq.gov/clinic/**

a. From the taskbar, redisplay your **3D_Career_Newletter** document. With the insertion point positioned in the new blank paragraph, on the **Insert tab**, in the **Illustrations group**, click **Screenshot**. Click **Screen Clipping**, position the ✛ pointer in the upper left corner of the website—below the address bar—and then drag down to the lower right corner—do not include the taskbar.

(continues on next page)

Chapter Review

b. Select the subheading *Professional Development at UMC* including the paragraph mark. Right-click the selected text, and then on the shortcut menu, click **Font**. In the **Font** dialog box, click the **Font color arrow**, and then in the fifth column, click the last color. Under **Font style**, click **Bold**, and then under **Effects**, select **Small caps**. Click **OK**.

c. With the text still selected, right-click, and then on the mini toolbar, double-click **Format Painter**. In the second column, with the [🔖I] pointer, select each of the subheadings—*What to Expect from Coursework at UMC* and *Examples of Courses at UMC*. Press [Esc] to turn off Format Painter.

5 ▶ Press [Ctrl] + [End] to move to the end of the document, and then select the two lines of bold text—the graphic will also be selected. On the **Home tab**, in the **Paragraph group**, click the **Borders button arrow**, and then click **Borders and Shading**.

a. In the **Borders and Shading** dialog box, on the **Borders tab**, under **Setting**, click **Shadow**. Click the **Color arrow**, and then in the fifth column, click the last color. Click the **Width arrow**, and then click **1 pt**.

b. In the **Borders and Shading** dialog box, click the **Shading tab**. Click the **Fill arrow**, and then in the fifth column, click the second color. Click **OK**. On the **Home tab**, in the **Paragraph group**, click **Center**. In the shaded paragraph, click in front of the *D* in the word *Director*. Hold down [Shift] and then press [Enter].

c. Press [Ctrl] + [Home], and then click the **File tab**. On the left, click **Info**, and then at the bottom right, click **Show All Properties**. Click to the right of **Tags**, and then type **newsletter, careers** Click to the right of **Subject**, and then type your course name and section number. Under **Related People**, if necessary, type your name in the Author box. Display the **Print Preview** and make any necessary corrections. **Save** the document; close Word and close your browser window. Submit this file as directed by your instructor.

6 ▶ (NOTE: The remainder of this Project, which is the creation of mailing labels, is optional. Complete only if assigned by your instructor.)

Start Word and display a new blank document. **Save** the document in your **Word Chapter 3** folder as **Lastname_Firstname_3D_Mailing_Labels**

a. Click the **Mailings tab**. In the **Start Mail Merge group**, click **Start Mail Merge**, and then click **Step-by-Step Mail Merge Wizard**. In the **Mail Merge** pane, under **Select document type**, click **Labels**. At the bottom of the **Mail Merge** pane, click **Next: Starting document**.

b. Under **Select starting document**, under **Change document layout**, click **Label options**. In the **Label Options** dialog box, under **Printer information**, be sure that the **Default tray** is selected.

c. Under **Label information**, click the **Label vendors arrow**, and then click **Avery US Letter**. Under **Product number**, scroll about halfway down the list, and then click **5160 Address Labels**. At the bottom of the **Label Options** dialog box, click **OK**. At the bottom of the **Mail Merge** pane, click **Next: Select recipients**.

d. In the **Mail Merge** pane, under **Select recipients**, under **Use an existing list**, click **Browse**. In the **Select Data Source** dialog box, navigate to the files downloaded for this project, click the Excel file **w03D_Addresses** one time to select it, and then click **Open** to display the **Select Table** dialog box. Click **OK**.

7 ▶ In the lower left portion of the **Mail Merge Recipients** dialog box, in the **Data Source** box, click the file name *w03D_Addresses*. Then, at the bottom of the **Mail Merge Recipients** dialog box, click **Edit**. In the lower left corner of the displayed **Edit Data Source** dialog box, click **New Entry**. In the blank record—the blue shaded row at the bottom of the list—type the following, pressing [Tab] to move from field to field:

First Name	Mia
Last Name	Orr
Address 1	1378 Lima Ave.
Unit	#82
City	Memphis
State	TN
ZIP Code	38123

a. In the lower right corner of the **Edit Data Source** dialog box, click **OK**, and then in the displayed message, click **Yes**. At the bottom of the **Mail Merge Recipients** dialog box, click **OK**.

b. At the bottom of the **Mail Merge** pane, click **Next: Arrange your labels**. Under **Arrange your labels**, click **Address block**. In the lower right corner of the **Insert Address Block** dialog box, click **Match Fields**.

(continues on next page)

Chapter Review

c. Click the **Address 2 arrow**, and then from the list of available fields, click **Unit**. Click **OK** two times.

d. In the **Mail Merge** pane, under **Replicate labels**, click **Update all labels**. At the bottom of the **Mail Merge** pane, click **Next: Preview your labels**. Press [Ctrl] + [A] to select all of the label text, click the **Layout tab**, and then in the **Paragraph group**, click in the **Spacing Before** box. Type **3** and press [Enter]. At the bottom of the **Mail Merge** pane, click **Next: Complete the merge**.

e. Click the **Mailings tab**, and then in the **Start Mail Merge group**, click **Edit Recipient List** to display the list of names and addresses. In the **Mail Merge Recipients** dialog box, click the **Last Name** field heading to sort the names. Click **OK**. **Close** the **Mail Merge** pane.

f. Scroll the document and then click anywhere in the empty table row at the bottom. Click the **Table Tools Layout tab**. In the **Rows & Columns group**, click **Delete**, and then click **Delete Rows**. Add the file name to the footer, close the footer area, and then in Backstage view, display **Show All Properties**. As the **Tags**, type **labels** and as the **Subject**, type your course name and section number. Be sure your name displays as the **Author**, and then **Save** your file.

g. If directed by your instructor to do so, submit your paper printout, your electronic image of your document, or your original Word files. **Close** Word.

You have completed Project 3D | **END**

Content-Based Assessments (Mastery and Transfer of Learning)

MyLab IT Grader	Mastering Word	Project 3E Skin Protection Report

Apply 3A skills from these Objectives:

1. Create a Research Paper
2. Insert Footnotes in a Research Paper
3. Create Citations and a Bibliography in a Research Paper
4. Use Read Mode, PDF Reflow, and Save Documents in Alternate Formats

In the following Mastering Word project, you will edit and format a research paper that contains information about skin protection and the use of sunblocks and sunscreens. This paper was created by Rachel Holder, a medical intern at University Medical Center, for distribution to her classmates studying dermatology. Your completed document will look similar to the one shown in Figure 3.57.

Project Files for MyLab IT Grader

1. In your **MyLab IT** course, locate and click **Word 3E Skin Protection**, Download Materials, and then Download All Files.
2. Extract the zipped folder to your Word Chapter 3 folder. Close the Grader download screens.
3. Take a moment to open the downloaded **Word_3E_Skin_Protection_Instructions** document; note any recent updates to the book.

Project Results

Figure 3.57

(continues on next page)

For Non-MyLab Submissions

For Project 3E, you will need:
w03E_Skin_Protection

In your Word Chapter 3 folder, save your document as:
Lastname_Firstname_3E_Skin_Protection

After you have named and saved your document, on the next page, begin with Step 2.
After Step 17, save and submit your file as directed by your instructor.

Mastering Word: Project 3E Skin Protection Report (continued)

1 Navigate to your **Word Chapter 3 folder**, and then double-click the Word file you downloaded from MyLab IT that displays your name—**Student_Word_3E_Skin_Protection**. If necessary, at the top, click **Enable Editing**.

2 Select all the text, change the **Line Spacing** to **2.0**, and then change the **Spacing After** to **0 pt**.

3 At the top of the document, insert a new blank paragraph, and then in the new blank paragraph, type **Rachel Holder** and press Enter. Type **Dr. Hillary Kim** and press Enter. Type **Dermatology 544** and press Enter. Type **August 31, 2021** and press Enter.

4 In the new blank paragraph, type **Skin Protection** Center the title *Skin Protection*. Insert a header, type **Holder** and then press Spacebar one time. Display the **Page Number** gallery, and then in the **Current Position**, add the **Plain Number** style (Mac users, in the Header & Footer group, click Page Number, on the menu click Page Number; under Alignment, be sure Right is selected.)

5 Apply **Align Right** formatting to the header. Insert a footer with the file name. To the paragraph that begins *One way to prevent*, apply a **First line** indent of **0.5**.

6 On **Page 2**, at the end of the paragraph that begins *In the medical field*, immediately following the period at the end of the paragraph, insert a footnote with the following text (one footnote is already inserted): **The American Academy of Dermatology recommends using a broad spectrum sunscreen with an SPF of 30 or more.** Be sure to type the period at the end of the footnote.

7 Modify the **Footnote Text** style so that the **Font Size** is **11**, there is a **First line indent** of **0.5"**, and the spacing is **Double**. Then, apply the style.

8 On **Page 1**, at the end of the paragraph that begins *According to an article*, click to the left of the period. Using **MLA** format, insert a citation for a **Journal Article** with the following information: (Note: Mac users, select Article in a journal. Fill in only the fields indicated; there is no Medium field.)

Author	Brash, D. E.
Title	Sunlight and Sunburn in Human Skin Cancer
Journal Name	The Journal of Investigative Dermatology
Year	1996
Pages	136-142
Medium	Print

9 In the report, select the citation you just created, display the **Citation Options**, and then edit the citation to include **Pages 136-142**

10 At the top of **Page 2**, at the end of the paragraph that begins *According to Dr. Lawrence*, click to the left of the period, and then insert a citation for a **Web site** with the following information: (Mac users: there is no Medium field.)

Author	Gibson, Lawrence E.
Name of Web Page	Does Sunscreen Expire?
Year	2011
Month	April
Day	01
Year Accessed	2021
Month Accessed	June
Day Accessed	30
Medium	Web

11 On **Page 3**, at the end of the last paragraph of the report that begins *Because the effect*, click to the left of the period, and then using MLA format, insert a citation for a **Book** with the following information: (Mac users: there is no Medium field.)

Author	Leffell, David.
Title	Total Skin: The Definitive Guide to Whole Skin Care for Life
Year	2000
City	New York
Publisher	Hyperion
Medium	Print

12 In the report, select the citation you just created, display the **Citation Options**, and then edit the citation to include **Page 96**

13 Move to the end of the document, and then insert a manual page break to create a new page. On the new **Page 4**, display the **Paragraph** dialog box, and then change the **Indentation** under **Special** to **(none)**.

14 On the **References tab**, click **Bibliography**, and at the bottom click **Works Cited**. Select the paragraph *Works Cited*, change the **Font** to **Calibri**, change the **Font Size** to **11**. Display the **Font Color** gallery, and then in the second column, click the first color. Then center the *Works Cited* title.

(continues on next page)

Content-Based Assessments (Mastery and Transfer of Learning)

15 Click to the left of *Works Cited* and then drag down to select *Works Cited* and the three citations. Display the **Paragraph** dialog box, change the **Spacing Before** to **0 pt**, change the **Spacing After** to **0 pt**, and set the **Line spacing** to **Double**.

16 Move to the top of your document. From the **References tab**, open **Researcher**, and then—including the quotation marks—search for **"sun protection factor"** and press Enter. Under **Top sources**, click **Journals**, and notice the extensive number of journal articles on this topic. **Close** the **Researcher pane**, and then on **Page 1**, in the paragraph that begins *Most sunburns*, in the fifth line, select the text *sun protection factor*. To the selected text, apply **Yellow Text Highlight Color**.

17 **Save** 🖫 your document. In the upper right corner of the Word window, click **Close** ⊠.

18 In **MyLab IT**, locate and click the Grader Project **Word 3E Skin Protection**. In **step 3**, under **Upload Completed Assignment**, click **Choose File**. In the **Open** dialog box, navigate to your **Word Chapter 3 folder**, and then click your **Student_Word_3E_Skin_Protection** file one time to select it. In the lower right corner of the **Open** dialog box, click **Open**.

The name of your selected file displays above the Upload button.

19 To submit your file to MyLab IT for grading, click **Upload**, wait a moment for a green **Success!** message, and then in **step 4**, click the blue **Submit for Grading** button. Click **Close Assignment** to return to your list of **Course Materials**.

You have completed Project 3E **END**

| MyLab IT Grader | Mastering Word | Project 3F Dogs Newsletter and Mailing Labels |

Apply 3B skills from these Objectives:

5. Format a Multiple-Column Newsletter
6. Use Special Character and Paragraph Formatting
7. Create Mailing Labels Using Mail Merge

In the following Mastering Word project, you will format a newsletter with information about the therapy dogs handled by volunteers at the University Medical Center. As an optional activity, you can create mailing labels so the newsletter can be sent to the volunteer staff. Your completed documents will look similar to Figure 3.58.

Project Files for MyLab IT Grader

1. In your **MyLab IT** course, locate and click **Word 3F Dogs Newsletter**, Download Materials, and then Download All Files.
2. Extract the zipped folder to your Word Chapter 3 folder. Close the Grader download screens.
3. Take a moment to open the downloaded **Word_3F_Dogs_Newsletter_Instructions**; note any recent updates to the book.

Project Results

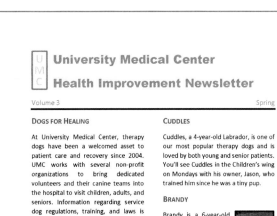

Optional mailing labels (if assigned)

Figure 3.58

For Non-MyLab Submissions

For Project 3E, you will need:
w03F_Dogs_Newsletter
w03F_Dog
w03F_Logo
w03F_Addresses (Optional: For use only if you are completing the Mailing Labels portion of this project)
After you have named and saved your document, on the next page, begin with Step 2.
After Step 10, save and submit your file as directed by your instructor.

In your Word Chapter 3 folder, save your document as:
Lastname_Firstname_3F_Dogs_Newsletter

(continues on next page)

Content-Based Assessments (Mastery and Transfer of Learning)

1 Navigate to your **Word Chapter 3 folder**, and then double-click the Word file you downloaded from MyLab IT that displays your name—**Student_Word_3F_ Dogs_Newsletter**. If necessary, at the top, click **Enable Editing**.

2 Add the **File Name** to the footer of your document. Select the first three paragraphs of the document that form the newsletter's nameplate, and then from the **Font Color** gallery, in the seventh column, click the fifth color. With the text still selected, display the **Borders and Shading** dialog box. Apply a **3 pt** bottom border, and as the border color, click the **Color arrow**, and then in the second column, click the first color.

3 Click at the beginning of the newsletter title *University Medical Center*. From your downloaded files, insert the picture **w03F_Logo**. If necessary, change the image **Height** to **1"** Change the **Brightness/Contrast** to **Brightness: 0% (Normal) Contrast: +40%**. Change the **Text Wrapping** to **Square**. Change the **Horizontal Alignment** of the image to **Left relative** to **Margin** and the **Vertical Alignment** to **Top relative** to **Margin**.

4 Starting with the paragraph that begins *Dogs for Healing*, select all of the text from that point to the end of the document. Change the **Spacing After** to **10 pt** Format the selected text in two columns, and then apply **Justify** alignment. Insert a **Column** break before the subheading *Cuddles*.

5 Click at the beginning of the sentence that begins with *Brandy is a 6-year-old Beagle*. From the files downloaded with this project, insert the picture **w03F_Dog**. Rotate the picture using **Flip Horizontal**. Change the picture **Width** to **1"**

6 Set the wrapping style of the picture to **Square**. Change the **Horizontal Alignment** to **Right relative** to **Margin** and the **Vertical Alignment** to **Top relative** to **Line**. Apply a **Picture Border** using the first color in the second column and change the **Weight** to **2 1/4 pt**. **Save** your file.

7 Open your web browser and if necessary, maximize the window. Navigate to **https://www.cdc.gov/healthypets/pets/dogs.html** If the website is not available, choose another page on the www.cdc.gov website. From the taskbar, redisplay your **3F_Dogs_Newsletter**, click at the end of the paragraph below the *Dogs for Healing* subheading. Insert a **Screen Clipping** of the website—do not include the address bar at the top or the taskbar at the bottom. To the screenclipping, apply a **Picture Border** using the first color in the second column, and set the **Weight** to **3 pt**.

8 Select the subheading *Dogs for Healing* including the paragraph mark. By using the **Font** dialog box, change the **Size** to **16**, apply **Bold**, and apply the **Small caps** effect. Click the **Font color arrow**, and then in the seventh column, click the last color. Apply the same formatting to the subheadings *Benefits to Patients*, *Cuddles*, and *Brandy*.

9 Select the last paragraph in the newsletter including the paragraph mark, and then from the **Borders and Shading** dialog box, apply a **1 pt Shadow** border using the first color in the second column. From the **Shading tab**, apply a **Fill color**—in the seventh column, click the second color.

10 **Save** 🖫 your document. In the upper right corner of the Word window, click **Close** ☒.

11 In **MyLab IT**, locate and click the Grader Project **Word 3F Dogs Newsletter**. In **step 3**, under **Upload Completed Assignment**, click **Choose File**. In the **Open** dialog box, navigate to your **Word Chapter 3 folder**, and then click your **Student_Word_3F_Dogs_Newsletter** file one time to select it. In the lower right corner of the **Open** dialog box, click **Open**.

The name of your selected file displays above the Upload button.

12 To submit your file to MyLab IT for grading, click **Upload**, wait a moment for a green **Success!** message, and then in **step 4**, click the blue **Submit for Grading** button. Click **Close Assignment** to return to your list of **Course Materials**.

You have completed Project 3F **END**

Content-Based Assessments (Mastery and Transfer of Learning)

1 Start Word and display a new blank document. **Save** the document in your **Word Chapter 3** folder as Lastname_Firstname_3F_Mailing_Labels

2 Start the **Step-by-Step Mail Merge Wizard** and as the document type create **Labels**. Move to the next step of the Mail Merge wizard. Click **Label options**, be sure that the **Default tray** is selected and that the label vendor is **Avery US Letter**. As the **Product number**, click **5160 Address Labels**. Move to the next step of the Mail Merge wizard, and then click **Use an existing list**. Click **Browse**, navigate to your downloaded files, click the Excel file **w03F_Addresses**, click **Open**, and then click **OK** two times.

3 Move to the next step of the Mail Merge Wizard, and then click **Address block**. Click **OK**, and then **Update all labels**. Move to the next step of the Mail Merge Wizard to preview the labels. Then **Complete the merge**. Delete the last two rows from the bottom of the table, and then add the file name to the footer.

4 **Save** your file. As directed by your instructor, print or submit electronically.

You have completed the optional portion of this project   **END**

Content-Based Assessments (Mastery and Transfer of Learning)

| MyLab IT Grader | **Mastering Word** | **Project 3G Research Paper, Newsletter, and Mailing Labels** |

Apply 3A and 3B skills from these Objectives:

1. Create a Research Paper
2. Insert Footnotes in a Research Paper
3. Create Citations and a Bibliography in a Research Paper
4. Use Read Mode, PDF Reflow, and Save Documents in Alternate Formats
5. Format a Multiple-Column Newsletter
6. Use Special Character and Paragraph Formatting
7. Create Mailing Labels Using Mail Merge

In the following Mastering Word project, you will edit and format a research paper and a newsletter. Optionally, you will create mailing labels. Your completed documents will look similar to Figure 3.59.

Project Files for MyLab IT Grader

1. In your MyLab IT course, locate and click **Word 3G Newsletter and Research Paper**, Download Materials, and then Download All Files.
2. Extract the zipped folder to your Word Chapter 3 folder. Close the Grader download screens.
3. Take a moment to open the downloaded **Word_3G_Newsletter_and_Research_Paper_Instructions**; note any recent updates to the book.

Project Results

Figure 3.59

For Non-MyLab Submissions

For Project 3G, you will need:
w03G_Newsletter_and_Research_Paper
w03G_Logo
w03G_Addresses (Optional: For use only if you are completing the Mailing Labels portion of this project)
After you have named and saved your document, on the next page, begin with Step 2.
After step 18, save and submit your file as directed by your instructor.

In your Word Chapter 3 folder, save your document as:
Lastname_Firstname_3G_Newsletter_and_Research_Paper

(continues on next page)

Content-Based Assessments (Mastery and Transfer of Learning)

1 Navigate to your **Word Chapter 3 folder**, and then double-click the Word file you downloaded from MyLab IT that displays your name—**Student_Word_3G_ Newsletter_and_Research_Paper**. If necessary, at the top, click **Enable Editing**.

2 Add the **File Name** to the footer. Scroll down to **Page 2**, which is the first page of the research paper. Click anywhere on the page, and then because this is a separate section, add the **File Name** to the footer again so that it appears in both sections of the document. Press Ctrl + Home to move back to the top of the newsletter on **Page 1**. On **Page 1**, click at the beginning of the newsletter title. From your downloaded files, insert the picture **w03G_Logo**. If necessary, change the **Height** to **0.4"** Recolor the logo by applying a blue recolor option in a light shade. To the logo image, apply a **Picture Border** using the second color in the first column.

3 Change the **Text Wrapping** of the logo image to **Square**. Change the **Horizontal Alignment** to **Left relative** to **Margin** and the **Vertical Alignment** to **Top relative** to **Margin**.

4 Starting with the subheading paragraph *New Research on Electronic Health Records*, select all of the text from that point to the end of the page—include the paragraph mark but do not include the Section Break in your selection. Format the selected text in two columns, and then apply **Justify** alignment. Insert a **Column** break before the subheading *Health Information Privacy and Security*.

5 Open your web browser, and then navigate to **www.healthit.gov** Redisplay your document, and then click at the end of the paragraph below the *New Research on Electronic Health Records* subheading. Insert a **Screen Clipping** of the website—do not include the address bar or the taskbar. To the inserted screenshot, apply a **Picture Border** using the first color in the second column, and change the **Weight** to **1 pt**, If necessary, set the **Height** of the screen clipping to **1.5"**.

6 Select the subheading *New Research on Electronic Health Records* including the paragraph mark. From the **Font** dialog box, apply **Bold** and **Small caps**. Click the **Font color arrow**, and then in the fourth column, click the first color. Apply the same formatting to the subheadings *Doctors Define Meaningful Use, Health Information Privacy and Security* and *Research Sources Aid in EHR Implementation*. Select the *Doctors Define Meaningful Use* subheading and then change the **Spacing Before** to **18 pt**.

7 Select the last paragraph in the newsletter—the text in bold italic that begins *Ensuring the privacy* including the paragraph mark but not the Section Break lines. From the **Borders and Shading** dialog box, apply a **1 pt Shadow** border and as the **Color**, in the second column click the first color. On the **Shading tab**, click the **Fill arrow**, and then in the fourth column, click the second color. **Center** the paragraph text. **Save** your document.

8 On **Page 2**, beginning with *Janet Eisler*, select all of the text on the page but not the Page Break line. With the text on **Page 2** selected, change the **Line Spacing** to **2.0**, and then change the **Spacing After** to **0 pt**.

9 To the paragraph that begins *There is often a discrepancy*, apply a **First line** indent of **0.5** inches.

10 In the paragraph that begins *Linder claims that*, in the next to last line of text, after the period at the end of the sentence that ends *if they had it*, insert a footnote with the following text: **The EMR (electronic medical record) is the patient record created in hospitals and ambulatory environments; it serves as a data source for other systems.** Be sure to type the period at the end of the footnote text.

11 Right-click anywhere in the footnote text, and then modify the **Footnote Text** style to set the **Font Size** to **11** and the format of the Footnote Text paragraph to include a **First line** indent of **0.5"** and **Double** spacing. Apply the new style to the footnote text.

12 On the first page of the research paper, at the end of the paragraph that begins *Those clinical practices*, click to the left of the period, and then using **MLA** format, insert a citation for a **Web site** with the following information: (Mac users, there is no Medium field.)

Author	**Gabriel, Barbara A.**
Name of Web Page	**Do EMRS Make You a Better Doctor?**
Year	**2008**
Month	**July**
Day	**15**
Year Accessed	**2021**
Month Accessed	**June**
Day Accessed	**30**
Medium	**Web**

(continues on next page)

Content-Based Assessments (Mastery and Transfer of Learning)

13 On the second page of the research paper, at the end of the paragraph that begins *Further research*, click to the left of the period, and then using **MLA** format, insert a citation for a **Book** with the following information: (Mac users, there is no Medium field.)

Author	DeVore, Amy.
Title	The Electronic Health Record for the Physician's Office, 1e
Year	2010
City	Maryland Heights
Publisher	Saunders
Medium	Print

14 In the report, select the citation you just created, display the **Citation Options**, and then edit the citation to include **Pages 253**

15 From the **References tab**, open **Researcher**, and then—including the quotation marks—search for **"electronic health records"** and press Enter. Under **Top sources**, click **Journals**, and notice the extensive number of journal articles on this topic. **Close** the **Researcher pane**, and then on the first page of the research paper, in the paragraph that begins *There is often a discrepancy*, in the fourth line, select the text *electronic health records*. To the selected text, apply **Yellow Text Highlight Color**.

16 On the last page of the research paper click in the blank paragraph. On the **References tab**, click **Bibliography**, and then at the bottom of the list, click **Works Cited**.

17 Select the paragraph *Works Cited*, and then change the font to **Calibri**, change the font size to **11**, and then change the font color to **Black, Text 1**. Center the text *Works Cited*.

18 Click to the left of the title *Works Cited*, and then drag down to select the title *Works Cited* and the two citations. From the **Paragraph** dialog box, change the **Spacing Before** to **0 pt**, change the **Spacing After** to **0 pt**, and set the **Line spacing** to **Double**. Move to the top of your document and **Save**.

19 In **MyLab IT**, locate and click the Grader Project **Word 3G Newsletter and Research Paper**. In **step 3**, under **Upload Completed Assignment**, click **Choose File**. In the **Open** dialog box, navigate to your **Word Chapter 3 folder**, and then click your **Student_Word_3G_Newsletter_and_Research_Paper** file one time to select it. In the lower right corner of the **Open** dialog box, click **Open**.

The name of your selected file displays above the Upload button.

20 To submit your file to MyLab IT for grading, click **Upload**, wait a moment for a green **Success!** message, and then in **step 4**, click the blue **Submit for Grading** button. Click **Close Assignment** to return to your list of **Course Materials**.

You have completed Project 3G **END**

Content-Based Assessments (Mastery and Transfer of Learning)

1 Start Word and display a new blank document. **Save** the document in your **Word Chapter 3** folder as **Lastname_Firstname_3G_Mailing_Labels**

2 Start the **Step-by-Step Mail Merge Wizard** and as the document type create **Labels**. Move to the next step of the Mail Merge wizard. Click **Label options**, be sure that the **Default tray** is selected and that the label vendor is **Avery US Letter**. As the **Product number**, click **5160 Address Labels**. Move to the next step of the Mail Merge wizard, and then click **Use an existing list**. Click **Browse**, navigate to your downloaded student data files, click the Excel file **w03G_Addresses**, click **Open**, and then click **OK** two times.

3 Move to the next step of the Mail Merge Wizard, and then click **Address block**. Click **OK**, and then **Update all labels**. Move to the next step of the Mail Merge Wizard to preview the labels. Then **Complete the merge**. Delete the last two rows from the bottom of the table, and then add the file name to the footer.

4 **Save** your file. As directed by your instructor, print or submit electronically.

You have completed the optional portion of this project   **END**

Content-Based Assessments (Critical Thinking)

GO! Fix It	**Project 3H Hospital Materials**	**IRC**
GO! Make It	**Project 3I Health Newsletter**	**IRC**
GO! Solve It	**Project 3J Colds and Flu**	**IRC**
GO! Solve It	**Project 3K Cycling Newsletter**	

Apply a combination of the 3A and 3B skills

Project Files

For Project 3K, you will need the following files:

w03K_Cycling_Newsletter

w03K_Bicycle

You will save your document as:

Lastname_Firstname_3K_Cycling_Newsletter

The University Medical Center Emergency Department publishes a monthly newsletter focusing on safety and injury prevention. The topic for the current newsletter is bicycle safety. From your student data files, open **w03K_Cycling_Newsletter**, add the file name to the footer, and then save the file in your Word Chapter 3 folder as **Lastname_Firstname_3K_Cycling_Newsletter**

Using the techniques that you practiced in this chapter, format the document in two-column, newsletter format. Format the newsletter heading so that it is clearly separate from the body of the newsletter and is easily identified as the heading. Insert column breaks as necessary and apply appropriate formatting to subheadings. Insert and format the bicycle picture, and insert a Screen Clipping of a relevant website. Apply a border and shading to the last paragraph so that it is formatted attractively.

Add your name, your course name and section number, and the keywords **safety, newsletter** to the Properties area. Submit as directed.

		Performance Level		
		Exemplary: You consistently applied the relevant skills	**Proficient: You sometimes, but not always, applied the relevant skills**	**Developing: You rarely or never applied the relevant skills**
Performance Criteria	**Format newsletter heading**	The nameplate is formatted attractively and in a manner that clearly indicates that it is the nameplate.	The nameplate includes some formatting but is not clearly separated from the body of the newsletter.	The newsletter does not include a nameplate.
	Insert and format picture	The image is sized and positioned appropriately.	The image is inserted but is formatted or positioned poorly.	No image is included.
	Border and shading added to a paragraph	The last paragraph displays an attractive border with shading that enables the reader to read the text.	A border or shading is displayed but not both; or the shading is too dark to enable the reader to easily read the text.	No border or shading is added to a paragraph.
	Insert a screenshot	A screenshot is inserted in one of the columns; the screenshot is related to the content of the article.	A screenshot is inserted in the document but does not relate to the content of the article.	No screenshot is inserted.

You have completed Project 3K **END**

Outcomes-Based Assessments (Critical Thinking)

Rubric

The following outcomes-based assessments are *open-ended assessments*. That is, there is no specific correct result; your result will depend on your approach to the information provided. Make *Professional Quality* your goal. Use the following scoring rubric to guide you in *how* to approach the problem and then to evaluate *how well* your approach solves the problem.

The *criteria*—Software Mastery, Content, Format and Layout, and Process—represent the knowledge and skills you have gained that you can apply to solving the problem. The *levels of performance*—Professional Quality, Approaching Professional Quality, or Needs Quality Improvements—help you and your instructor evaluate your result

	Your completed project is of Professional Quality if you:	Your completed project is Approaching Professional Quality if you:	Your completed project Needs Quality Improvements if you:
1-Software Mastery	Choose and apply the most appropriate skills, tools, and features and identify efficient methods to solve the problem.	Choose and apply some appropriate skills, tools, and features, but not in the most efficient manner.	Choose inappropriate skills, tools, or features, or are inefficient in solving the problem.
2-Content	Construct a solution that is clear and well organized, contains content that is accurate, appropriate to the audience and purpose, and is complete. Provide a solution that contains no errors of spelling, grammar, or style.	Construct a solution in which some components are unclear, poorly organized, inconsistent, or incomplete. Misjudge the needs of the audience. Have some errors in spelling, grammar, or style, but the errors do not detract from comprehension.	Construct a solution that is unclear, incomplete, or poorly organized, contains some inaccurate or inappropriate content, and contains many errors of spelling, grammar, or style. Do not solve the problem.
3-Format and Layout	Format and arrange all elements to communicate information and ideas, clarify function, illustrate relationships, and indicate relative importance.	Apply appropriate format and layout features to some elements, but not others. Overuse features, causing minor distraction.	Apply format and layout that does not communicate information or ideas clearly. Do not use format and layout features to clarify function, illustrate relationships, or indicate relative importance. Use available features excessively, causing distraction.
4-Process	Use an organized approach that integrates planning, development, self-assessment, revision, and reflection.	Demonstrate an organized approach in some areas, but not others; or, use an insufficient process of organization throughout.	Do not use an organized approach to solve the problem.

310 **Word** | Chapter 3: Creating Research Papers, Newsletters, and Merged Mailing Labels

Content-Based Assessments (Critical Thinking)

GO! Think	Project 3L Influenza Report

Apply a combination of the 3A and 3B skills.

Project Files

For Project 3L, you will need the following file:

New blank Word document

You will save your document as:

Lastname_Firstname_3L_Influenza

As part of the ongoing research conducted by University Medical Center in the area of community health and contagious diseases, Dr. Hillary Kim has asked Sarah Stanger to create a report on influenza—how it spreads and how it can be prevented in the community.

Create a new file and save it as **Lastname_Firstname_3L_Influenza** Create the report in MLA format. The report should include at least two footnotes, at least two citations, and should include a *Works Cited* page.

The report should contain an introduction and information about what influenza is, how it spreads, and how it can be prevented. A good place to start is at http://health.nih.gov/topic/influenza.

Add the file name to the footer. Add appropriate information to the Document Properties and submit it as directed.

You have completed Project 3L | END

GO! Think	Project 3M Volunteer Newsletter	IRC
You and GO!	Project 3N College Newsletter	IRC
GO! Cumulative Team Project	Project 3O Bell Orchid Hotels	IRC

Introducing Microsoft Excel 2019

Kheng Guan Toh/Shutterstock

Excel 2019: Introduction

 Introduction to Excel

Quantitative information! Defined as a type of information that can be counted or that communicates the quantity of something, quantitative information can be either easy or hard to understand—depending on how it is presented. According to Stephen Few, in his book *Show Me the Numbers:* "Quantitative information forms the core of what businesses must know to operate effectively."

Excel 2019 is a tool to communicate quantitative business information effectively. Sometimes you need to communicate quantitative relationships. For example, the number of units sold per geographic region shows a relationship of sales to geography. Sometimes you need to

summarize numbers. A list of every student enrolled at your college along with his or her major is not as informative as a summary of the total number of students in each major. In business, the most common quantitative information is some measure of money—costs, sales, payroll, expenses and so on.

Rather than just a tool for making calculations, Excel is also a tool for you to communicate and collaborate with others. When you want to communicate visually with tables and graphs, Excel 2019 has many features to help you do so. If you engage in Business Intelligence activities, you will find rich tools for forecasting and for delivering insights about your organization's data.

Creating a Worksheet and Charting Data

EXCEL 2019

PROJECT 1A

Outcomes
Create a sales report with an embedded column chart and sparklines.

Objectives
1. Create, Save, and Navigate an Excel Workbook
2. Enter Data in a Worksheet
3. Construct and Copy Formulas and Use the SUM Function
4. Format Cells with Merge & Center, Cell Styles, and Themes
5. Chart Data to Create a Column Chart and Insert Sparklines
6. Print a Worksheet, Display Formulas, and Close Excel

PROJECT 1B

Outcomes
Calculate the value of an inventory.

Objectives
7. Check Spelling in a Worksheet
8. Enter Data by Range
9. Construct Formulas for Mathematical Operations
10. Edit Values in a Worksheet
11. Format a Worksheet

Wavebreakmedia/Shutterstock

In This Chapter

 GO! To Work with Excel

In this chapter, you will use Microsoft Excel to create and analyze data organized into columns and rows. After entering data in a worksheet, you can perform complex calculations, analyze the data to make logical decisions, and create attractive charts that help readers visualize your data in a way they can understand and that is meaningful. In this chapter, you will create and modify Excel workbooks. You will practice the basics of worksheet design, create a footer, enter and edit data in a worksheet, and chart data. You will save, preview, and print workbooks, and you will construct formulas for mathematical operations.

The projects in this chapter relate to **Pro Fit Marietta**, a distributor of fitness equipment and apparel to private gyms, personal trainers, health clubs, corporate wellness centers, hotels, college athletic facilities, physical therapy practices, and multi-unit residential properties. The company's mission is to find, test, and distribute the highest quality fitness products in the world to its customers for the benefit of consumers. The company's blog provides useful tips on how to use the latest workout and fitness equipment. The company is in Marietta, Georgia, which is metropolitan Atlanta's largest suburb.

PROJECT

1A

Sales Report with
Embedded Column
Chart and Sparklines

MyLab IT
Project 1A Grader for Instruction
Project 1A Simulation for Training and Review

Project Activities

In Activities 1.01 through 1.17, you will create an Excel worksheet for Michelle Barry, the President of Pro Fit Marietta. The worksheet displays the second quarter sales of cardio equipment for the current year and includes a chart to visually represent the data. Your completed worksheet will look similar to Figure 1.1.

Project Files for MyLab IT Grader

1. In your storage location, create a folder named **Excel Chapter 1**.
2. In your MyLab IT course, locate and click **Excel 1A Quarterly Sales**, Download Materials, and then Download All Files.
3. Extract the zipped folder to your Excel Chapter 1 folder. Close the Grader download screens.
4. Take a moment to open the downloaded **Excel_1A_Quarterly_Sales_Instructions**; note any recent updates to the book.

Project Results

GO! Project 1A
Where We're Going

Figure 1.1 Project 1A Quarterly Sales

For Non-MyLab Submissions

For Project 1A, you will need:

New blank Excel workbook

In your storage location, create a folder named **Excel Chapter 1**

In your Excel Chapter 1 folder, save your workbook as:

Lastname_Firstname_1A_Quarterly_Sales

If your instructor requires a workbook with formulas, save as:

Lastname_Firstname_1A_Quarterly_Sales_formulas

After you have named and saved your workbook, on the next page begin with Step 2.

Objective 1   Create, Save, and Navigate an Excel Workbook

GO Learn How
Video E1-1

On startup, Excel displays a new blank *workbook*—the Excel document that stores your data—which contains one or more pages called a *worksheet*. A worksheet—or *spreadsheet*—is stored in a workbook and is formatted as a pattern of uniformly spaced horizontal rows and vertical columns. The intersection of a column and a row forms a box referred to as a *cell*.

Activity 1.01 | **Starting Excel, Navigating Excel, and Naming and Saving a Workbook**

   1 ▸ Navigate to your **Excel Chapter 1 folder**, and then double-click the Excel file you downloaded from **MyLab IT** that displays your name—**Student_Excel_1A_Quarterly_ Sales**. In your blank workbook, if necessary, at the top click **Enable Editing**.

   2 ▸ In the lower right corner of the window, on the status bar, if necessary, click the **Normal** button ▦, and then to the right, locate the zoom—magnification—level.

     Your zoom level should be 100%, although some figures in this textbook may be shown at a higher zoom level. The *Normal view* maximizes the number of cells visible on your screen and keeps the column letters and row numbers closer.

3 Compare your screen with Figure 1.2, and then take a moment to study the Excel window parts in the table in Figure 1.3.

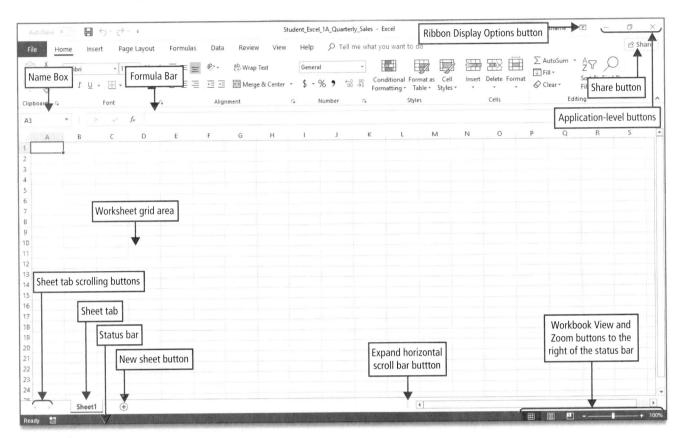

Figure 1.2

Parts of the Excel Window	
Screen Part	**Description**
Application-level buttons	Minimize, close, or restore the previous size of the displayed workbook window.
Expand horizontal scroll bar button	Increases or decreases the width of the horizontal scroll bar by sliding left or right.
Formula Bar	Displays the value or formula contained in the active cell; also permits entry or editing.
Name Box	Displays the name of the selected cell, table, chart, or object.
New sheet button	Inserts an additional worksheet.
Ribbon Display Options button	Displays various ways you can display the ribbon—Show Tabs and Commands is shown here.
Share button	Opens the Share dialog box or the Share pane from which you can save your file to the cloud—for example, your OneDrive—and then share it with others so you can collaborate.
Sheet tab	Identifies the worksheet in the workbook.
Sheet tab scrolling buttons	Display sheet tabs that are not in view when there are numerous sheet tabs.
Status bar	Displays the current cell mode (here in Ready mode) and possibly Macro information as shown here. To the right of the status bar, Workbook View buttons and Zoom buttons display. Here, numerical data and common calculations such as Sum and Average may display.
Worksheet grid area	Displays the columns and rows that intersect to form the worksheet's cells.

Figure 1.3

4 Take a moment to study Figure 1.4 and the table in Figure 1.5 to become familiar with the Excel workbook window.

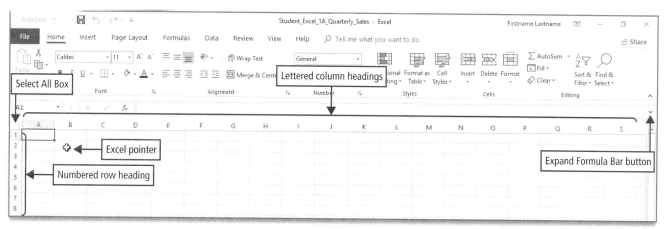

Figure 1.4

Excel Workbook Window Elements	
Workbook Window Element	**Description**
Excel pointer	Displays the location of the pointer.
Expand Formula Bar button	Increases the height of the Formula Bar to display lengthy cell content.
Lettered column headings	Indicate the column letter.
Numbered row headings	Indicate the row number.
Select All box	Selects all the cells in a worksheet.

Figure 1.5

5 In the lower right corner of the screen, in the horizontal scroll bar, click the **right scroll arrow** one time to shift **column A** out of view.

A *column* is a vertical group of cells in a worksheet. Beginning with the first letter of the alphabet, *A*, a unique letter identifies each column—this is called the *column heading*. Clicking one of the horizontal scroll bar arrows shifts the window either left or right one column at a time.

6 Point to the **right scroll arrow**, and then hold down the left mouse button until the columns begin to scroll rapidly to the right; release the mouse button when you begin to see pairs of letters as the column headings.

🖥 **MAC TIP** For rapid scrolling, swipe your finger to the left or right on the mouse or track pad.

👆 **BY TOUCH** Anywhere on the worksheet, slide your finger to the left to scroll to the right.

7 Slowly drag the horizontal scroll box to the left, and notice that just above the scroll box, ScreenTips with the column letters display as you drag. Drag the horizontal scroll box left or right—or click the left or right scroll arrow—as necessary to position **column Z** near the center of your screen.

Column headings after column Z use two letters starting with AA, AB, and so on through ZZ. After that, columns begin with three letters beginning with AAA. This pattern provides 16,384 columns. The last column is XFD.

🖥 **MAC TIP** Drag the scroll box, there are no ScreenTips.

8 In the vertical scroll bar, click the **down scroll arrow** one time to move **row 1** out of view.

A *row* is a horizontal group of cells. Beginning with number 1, a unique number identifies each row—this is the *row heading*, located at the left side of the worksheet. A single worksheet can have 1,048,576 rows of data.

9 Use the skills you just practiced to scroll horizontally to display **column A**, and if necessary, **row 1**.

10 Point to and then click the cell at the intersection of **column A** and **row 1** to make it the *active cell*—the cell is outlined and ready to accept data.

The intersecting column letter and row number form the *cell reference*—also called the *cell address*. When a cell is active, its column letter and row number are highlighted. The cell reference of the selected cell, *A1*, displays in the Name Box.

11 With cell **A1** as the active cell, type the worksheet title **Pro Fit Marietta** and then press ⏎. Compare your screen with Figure 1.6. Click **Save** 🖫.

Text or numbers in a cell are referred to as *data*. You must confirm the data you type in a cell by pressing ⏎ or by some other keyboard movement, such as pressing Tab or an arrow key. Pressing ⏎ moves the active cell to the cell below.

Figure 1.6

Objective 2 | Enter Data in a Worksheet

GO! Learn How
Video E1-2

Cell content, which is anything you type in a cell, can be one of two things: either a *constant value*—referred to simply as a *value*—or a *formula*. A formula is an equation that performs mathematical calculations on values in your worksheet. The most commonly used values are *text values* and *number values*, but a value can also include a date or a time of day. A text value is also referred to as a *label*.

Activity 1.02 | Entering Text, Using AutoComplete, and Using the Name Box to Select a Cell

1.2.2

A text value usually provides information about number values in other worksheet cells. In this worksheet for Pro Fit Marietta, the title *Second Quarter Cardio Sales* gives the reader an indication that data in the worksheet relates to information about sales of cardio equipment during the three-month period April through June.

1 In cell **A1**, notice that the text does not fit; the text extends into cell **B1** to the right.

If text is too long for a cell and cells to the right are empty, the text will display. If the cells to the right contain other data, only the text that will fit in the cell displays.

2 In cell **A2**, type the worksheet subtitle **Second Quarter Cardio Sales** and then press ⏎. Compare your screen with Figure 1.7.

Figure 1.7

> **3** Above **column A**, click in the **Name Box** to select the cell reference *A3*, and then type **a4** Press [Enter] to make cell **A4** the active cell. In cell **A4**, type **Exercise Bikes** to form the first row title, and then press [Enter].

> The text characters that you typed align at the left edge of the cell—referred to as *left alignment*—and cell A5 becomes the active cell. Left alignment is the default for text values. You can type a cell address in the Name Box and press [Enter] to move to a specific cell quickly.

> **4** In cell **A5**, type **E** and notice the text from the previous cell displays.

> If the first characters you type in a cell match an existing entry in the column, Excel fills in the remaining characters for you. This feature, called *AutoComplete*, assists only with alphabetic values.

> **5** Continue typing the remainder of the row title **lliptical Machines** and press [Enter].

> The AutoComplete suggestion is removed when the entry you are typing differs from the previous value.

> **6** In cell **A6**, type **Treadmills** and press [Enter]. In cell **A7**, type **Rowing Machines** and press [Enter]. In cell **A8**, type **Total** and press [Enter]. On the Quick Access Toolbar, click **Save** 🖫.

🔄 **ANOTHER WAY**   Use the keyboard shortcut [Ctrl] + [S] to save changes to your workbook.

⌨ **MAC TIP**   Use the keyboard shortcut [command ⌘] + [S] to save changes to your workbook.

Activity 1.03 | Using Auto Fill and Keyboard Shortcuts

MOS
2.1.2

> **1** Click cell **B3**. Type **A** and notice that when you begin to type in a cell, on the **Formula Bar**, the **Cancel** and **Enter** buttons become active, as shown in Figure 1.8.

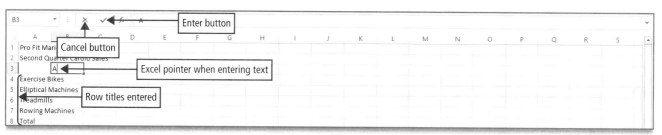

Figure 1.8

2 Continue to type **pril** On the **Formula Bar**, notice that values you type in a cell also display there, and then on the **Formula Bar**, click **Enter** ☑ to confirm the entry and keep cell **B3** active.

3 With cell **B3** active, locate the small square in the lower right corner of the selected cell.

You can drag this *fill handle*—the small square in the lower right corner of a selected cell—to adjacent cells to fill the cells with values based on the first cell.

4 Point to the **fill handle** until the ⊞ pointer displays, hold down the left mouse button, drag to the right to cell **D3**, and as you drag, notice the ScreenTips *May* and *June*. Release the mouse button.

5 Under the text that you just filled, click the **Auto Fill Options** button ⊞ that displays, and then compare your screen with Figure 1.9.

Auto Fill generates and extends a *series* of values into adjacent cells based on the value of other cells. A series is a group of things that come one after another in succession; for example, *April, May, June*.

The Auto Fill Options button displays options to fill the data; options vary depending on the content and program from which you are filling, and the format of the data you are filling.

Fill Series is selected, indicating the action that was taken. Because the options are related to the current task, the button is referred to as being *context sensitive*.

Figure 1.9

6 Click in any cell to cancel the display of the list.

The list no longer displays; the button will display until you perform some other screen action.

7 Press Ctrl + Home, which is the keyboard shortcut to make cell **A1** active.

MAC TIP Press control + fn + ← to make cell A1 active.

8 On the Quick Access Toolbar, click **Save** 💾 to save the changes you have made to your workbook.

9 Take a moment to study the table in Figure 1.10 to become familiar with keyboard shortcuts with which you can navigate the Excel worksheet.

Keyboard Shortcuts to Navigate the Excel Window		
To Move the Location of the Active Cell:	**On a Windows PC Press:**	**On a Mac Press:**
Up, down, right, or left one cell	↑, ↓, →, ←	↑, ↓, →, ←
Down one cell	Enter	enter
Up one cell	Shift + Enter	shift + enter
Up one full screen	PgUp	fn + ↑
Down one full screen	PgDn	fn + ↓
To column A of the current row	Home	fn + ←
To the last cell on a worksheet, to the lowest used row of the rightmost used column	Ctrl + End	control + fn + →
To cell A1	Ctrl + Home	control + fn + ←
Right one cell	Tab	tab
Left one cell	Shift + Tab	shift + tab
To one screen to the right in a worksheet	Alt + PgDn	fn + option + ↓
To one screen to the left in a worksheet	Alt + PgUp	fn + option + ↑

Figure 1.10

Activity 1.04 | Aligning Text and Adjusting the Size of Columns

MOS
1.3.2

1 In the **column heading area**, point to the vertical line between **column A** and **column B** to display the ⊞ pointer, press and hold down the left mouse button, and then compare your screen with Figure 1.11.

A ScreenTip displays information about the width of the column. The default width of a column is 64 *pixels*. A pixel, short for *picture element*, is a point of light measured in dots per square inch. Sixty-four pixels equal 8.43 characters, which is the average number of characters that will fit in a cell using the default font. The default font in Excel is Calibri and the default font size is 11.

MAC TIP The default font size on a Mac is 12.

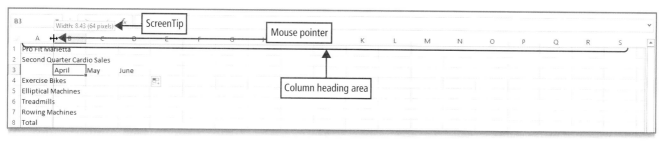

Figure 1.11

2 ▶ Drag to the right, and when the number of pixels indicated in the ScreenTip reaches **120 pixels**, release the mouse button. If you are not satisfied with your result, click Undo 🔄 on the Quick Access Toolbar and begin again.

This width accommodates the longest row title in cells A4 through A8—*Elliptical Machines*. The worksheet subtitle in cell A2 spans more than one column and still does not fit in column A.

⬜ **MAC TIP**   Change the width to 16.50 (104 pixels).

3 ▶ Point to cell **B3** and then drag across to select cells **B3**, **C3**, and **D3**. Compare your screen with Figure 1.12; if you are not satisfied with your result, click anywhere and begin again.

The three cells, B3 through D3, are selected and form a *range*—two or more cells on a worksheet that are adjacent (next to each other) or nonadjacent (not next to each other). This range of cells is referred to as *B3:D3*. When you see a colon (:) between two cell references, the range includes all the cells between the two cell references.

A range of cells you select this way is indicated by a dark border, and Excel treats the range as a single unit so you can make the same changes to more than one cell at a time. The selected cells in the range are highlighted except for the first cell in the range, which displays in the Name Box.

When you select a range of data, the *Quick Analysis tool* displays in the lower right corner of the selected range, with which you can analyze your data by using Excel tools such as charts, color-coding, and formulas.

Figure 1.12

👉 **BY TOUCH**   To select a range, tap and hold the first cell, and then when the circular gripper displays, drag it to the right, or to the right and down, to define the beginning and end of a range.

4 ▶ With the range **B3:D3** selected, point anywhere over the selected range, right-click, and then on the mini toolbar, click **Center** ▤. On the Quick Access Toolbar, click **Save** 💾.

The column titles *April*, *May*, *June* align in the center of each cell.

⬜ **MAC TIP**   Press command ⌘ + E to center align.

Activity 1.05 | Entering Numbers

MOS
2.2.5

To type number values, use either the number keys across the top of your keyboard or the numeric keypad if you have one—laptop computers may not have a numeric keypad.

In this Activity, you will enter the data that Michelle has given you that represents the sales of cardio equipment in the second quarter of the year.

1 Under *April*, click cell **B4**, type **68991.12** and then on the **Formula Bar**, click **Enter** ☑ to maintain cell **B4** as the active cell. Compare your screen with Figure 1.13.

By default, *number* values align at the right edge of the cell. The default *number format*—a specific way in which Excel displays numbers—is the *general format*. In the default general format, whatever you type in the cell will display, with the exception of trailing zeros to the right of a decimal point. For example, in the number 237.50 the *0* following the *5* is a trailing zero and would not display.

Data that displays in a cell is the *displayed value*. Data that displays in the Formula Bar is the *underlying value*. The number of digits or characters that display in a cell—the displayed value—depends on the width of the column. Calculations on numbers will always be based on the underlying value, not the displayed value.

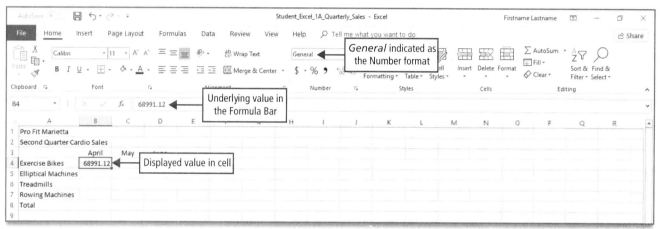

Figure 1.13

2 Press Tab to make cell **C4** active. Type **86894.82** and then press Tab to move to cell **D4**. Type **99650.58** and then press Enter to move to cell **B5** in the next row. Then, by using the same technique, enter the remaining sales numbers as shown:

	April	May	June
Elliptical Machines	28836	22634.23	22828.78
Treadmills	59519.78	82337.98	99823.87
Rowing Machines	81267.17	87867.50	91669.98

3 Compare the numbers you entered with Figure 1.14, and then **Save** 🖫 your workbook.

In the default General format, trailing zeros to the right of a decimal point will not display. For example, when you type *87867.50*, the cell displays 87867.5 instead.

Figure 1.14

GO! Learn How
Video E1-3

A cell contains either a constant value (text or numbers) or a formula. A formula is an equation that performs mathematical calculations on values in other cells, and then places the result in the cell containing the formula. You can create formulas or use a *function*—a prewritten formula that looks at one or more values, performs an operation, and then returns a value.

Activity 1.06 | **Constructing a Formula and Using the SUM Function**

4.2.1

In this Activity, you will practice three different ways to sum a group of numbers in Excel so that Michelle can see totals for each month and for each category of equipment sold.

1 Click cell **B8** to make it the active cell and type **=**

The equal sign (=) displays in the cell with the insertion point blinking, ready to accept more data.

All formulas begin with the = sign, which signals Excel to begin a calculation. The Formula Bar displays the = sign, and the Formula Bar Cancel and Enter buttons display.

2 At the insertion point, type **b4** and then compare your screen with Figure 1.15.

A list of Excel functions that begin with the letter *B* may briefly display—as you progress in your study of Excel, you will use functions of this type. A blue border with small corner boxes surrounds cell B4, which indicates that the cell is part of an active formula. The color used in the box matches the color of the cell reference in the formula.

Figure 1.15

3 At the insertion point, type **+** and then type **b5**

A border of another color surrounds cell B5, and the color matches the color of the cell reference in the active formula. When typing cell references, it is not necessary to use uppercase letters.

4 At the insertion point, type **+b6+b7** and then press Enter.

The result of the formula calculation—*238614.1*—displays in the cell. Recall that in the default General format, trailing zeros do not display. (Mac users: yours may display *238614.07*)

> **5** Click cell **B8** again, look at the **Formula Bar**, and then compare your screen with Figure 1.16.

The formula adds the values in cells B4 through B7, and the result displays in cell B8. In this manner, you can construct a formula by typing. Although cell B8 displays the *result* of the formula, the formula itself displays in the Formula Bar. This is referred to as the ***underlying formula***.

Always view the Formula Bar to be sure of the exact content of a cell—*a displayed number may actually be a formula*.

Figure 1.16

> **6** Click cell **C8** and type = to signal the beginning of a formula. Then, point to cell **C4** and click one time.

The reference to the cell C4 is added to the active formula. A moving border surrounds the referenced cell, and the border color and the color of the cell reference in the formula are color coded to match.

> **7** At the insertion point, type + and then click cell **C5**. Repeat this process to complete the formula to add cells **C6** and **C7**, and then press [Enter].

The result of the formula calculation—*279734.5*—displays in the cell. This method of constructing a formula is the ***point and click method*** (Mac users: yours may display *279734.53*).

> **8** Click cell **D8**. On the **Home tab**, in the **Editing group**, click **AutoSum**, and then compare your screen with Figure 1.17.

SUM is an Excel function—a prewritten formula. A moving border surrounds the range D4:D7 and =*SUM(D4:D7)* displays in cell D8.

The = sign signals the beginning of a formula, *SUM* indicates the type of calculation that will take place (addition), and *(D4:D7)* indicates the range of cells on which the sum calculation will be performed. A ScreenTip provides additional information about the action.

MAC TIP To display group names on the ribbon, display the menu, click Excel, click Preferences, click View, under In Ribbon, select the Group Titles check box.

Figure 1.17

9 Look at the **Formula Bar** and notice that the formula also displays there. Then, look again at the cells surrounded by the moving border.

When you activate the *Sum function*, Excel first looks *above* the active cell for a range of cells to sum. If no range is above the active cell, Excel will look to the *left* for a range of cells to sum. If the proposed range is not what you want to calculate, you can select a different group of cells.

10 Press [Enter] to construct a formula by using the prewritten SUM function.

Your total is *313973.2*. (Mac users: yours may display *313973.21*) Because the Sum function is frequently used, it has its own button in the Editing group on the Home tab of the ribbon. A larger version of the button also displays on the Formulas tab in the Function Library group. This button is also referred to as *AutoSum*.

11 Notice that the totals in the range **B8:D8** display only one decimal place. Click **Save** 🖫.

Number values that are too long to fit in the cell do *not* spill over into the unoccupied cell to the right in the same manner as text values. Rather, Excel rounds the number to fit the space.

Rounding is a procedure that determines which digit at the right of the number will be the last digit displayed and then increases it by one if the next digit to its right is 5, 6, 7, 8, or 9.

 MAC TIP The total may display 2 decimal places.

Activity 1.07 | Copying a Formula by Using the Fill Handle

MOS
4.1.1

You have practiced three ways to create a formula—by typing, by using the point and click technique, and by using a Function button from the ribbon. You can also copy formulas. When you copy a formula from one cell to another, Excel adjusts the cell references to fit the new location of the formula.

1 Click cell **E3**, type **Total** and then press [Enter].

The text in cell E3 is centered because the centered format continues from the adjacent cell.

2 With cell **E4** as the active cell, hold down [Alt], and then press [=]. Compare your screen with Figure 1.18.

[Alt] + [=] is the keyboard shortcut for the Sum function. Recall that Excel first looks above the selected cell for a proposed range of cells to sum, and if no data is detected, Excel looks to the left and proposes a range of cells to sum.

 MAC TIP Press [command ⌘] + [shift] + [T] as the keyboard shortcut to total.

Figure 1.18

3 On the **Formula Bar**, click **Enter** ✓ to display the result and keep cell **E4** active.

The total dollar amount of *Exercise Bikes* sold in the quarter is *255536.5*. In cells E5:E8, you can see that you need a formula similar to the one in E4, but formulas that refer to the cells in row 5, row 6, and so on.

4 With cell **E4** active, point to the fill handle in the lower right corner of the cell until the ➕ pointer displays. Then, drag down through cell **E8**; if you are not satisfied with your result, on the Quick Access Toolbar, click Undo ↺ and begin again. Compare your screen with Figure 1.19.

Figure 1.19

5 Click cell **E5**, look at the **Formula Bar**, and notice the formula =*SUM(B5:D5)*. Click cell **E6**, look at the **Formula Bar**, and then notice the formula =*SUM(B6:D6)*.

In each row, Excel copied the formula but adjusted the cell references *relative to* the row number. This is called a ***relative cell reference***—a cell reference based on the relative position of the cell that contains the formula and the cells referred to in the formula.

The calculation is the same, but it is performed on the cells in that particular row. Use this method to insert numerous formulas into spreadsheets quickly.

6 Click cell **F3**, type **Trend** and then press Enter. **Save** 🖫 your workbook.

Objective 4 | Format Cells with Merge & Center, Cell Styles, and Themes

GO! Learn How
Video E1-4

Format—change the appearance of—cells to make your worksheet attractive and easy to read.

Activity 1.08 | Using Merge & Center and Applying Cell Styles

2.2.1

In this Activity, you will apply formatting to the worksheet so that Michelle and her staff can present a visually attractive worksheet to the company.

1 Select the range **A1:F1**, and then in the **Alignment group**, click **Merge & Center**. Then, select the range **A2:F2** and click **Merge & Center**.

The ***Merge & Center*** command joins selected cells into one larger cell and centers the contents in the merged cell; individual cells in the range B1:F1 and B2:F2 can no longer be selected—they are merged into cells A1 and A2, respectively.

🔄 **ANOTHER WAY** Select the range, right-click over the selection, and then on the mini toolbar, click the Merge & Center button.

2 ▶ Click cell **A1**. In the **Styles group**, click **Cell Styles**, and then compare your screen with Figure 1.20.

> A *cell style* is a defined set of formatting characteristics, such as font, font size, font color, cell borders, and cell shading.

Figure 1.20

3 ▶ In the displayed gallery, under **Titles and Headings**, click **Title** and notice that the row height adjusts to accommodate the larger font size.

4 ▶ Click cell **A2**, display the **Cell Styles** gallery, and then under **Titles and Headings**, click **Heading 1**.

> Use cell styles to maintain a consistent look in a worksheet and across worksheets in a workbook.

5 ▶ Select the horizontal range **B3:F3**, hold down Ctrl, and then select the vertical range **A4:A8** to select the column titles and the row titles.

> Use this technique to select two or more ranges that are nonadjacent—not next to each other.

⌨ **MAC TIP** Hold down command ⌘ and then select the vertical range.

---

6 ▶ Display the **Cell Styles** gallery, click **Heading 4** to apply this cell style to the column titles and row titles, and then **Save** 🖫 your workbook.

Activity 1.09 | Formatting Financial Numbers

MOS
2.2.5, 2.2.7

To present a clear and accurate worksheet, Michelle likes to apply appropriate formatting when reporting financial information such as sales.

In this Activity, you will apply formatting to financial numbers.

1 ▶ Select the range **B4:E4**, hold down Ctrl, and then select the range **B8:E8**.

> This range is referred to as *b4:e4,b8:e8* with a comma separating the references to the two nonadjacent ranges.

ANOTHER WAY   In the Name Box type b4:e4,b8:e8 and then press [Enter].

2 ▶ On the **Home tab**, in the **Number group**, click **Accounting Number Format** $ ▾ . Compare your screen with Figure 1.21.

The *Accounting Number Format* applies a thousand comma separator where appropriate, inserts a fixed U.S. dollar sign aligned at the left edge of the cell, applies two decimal places, and leaves a small amount of space at the right edge of the cell to accommodate parentheses when negative numbers are present. Excel widens the columns to accommodate the formatted numbers.

At the bottom of your screen, in the status bar, Excel displays the results for some common calculations that might be made on the range; for example, the Average of the numbers selected and the Count—the number of items selected.

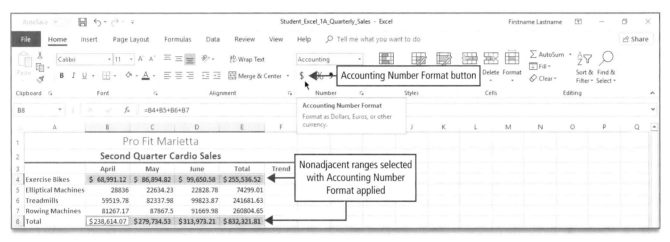

Figure 1.21

ANOTHER WAY   Display the Cell Styles gallery, and under Number Format, click Currency.

3 ▶ Select the range **B5:E7**, and then in the **Number group**, click **Comma Style** ▾ .

The *Comma Style* inserts a thousand comma separator where appropriate and applies two decimal places. Comma Style also leaves space at the right to accommodate a parenthesis when negative numbers are present.

When preparing worksheets with financial information, the first row of dollar amounts and the total row of dollar amounts are formatted in the Accounting Number Format; that is, with thousand comma separators, dollar signs, two decimal places, and space at the right to accommodate a parenthesis for negative numbers, if any. Rows that are *not* the first row or the total row should be formatted with the Comma Style.

4 ▶ Select the range **B8:E8**. In the **Styles group**, display the **Cell Styles** gallery, and then under **Titles and Headings**, click **Total**. Click any blank cell to cancel the selection, and then compare your screen with Figure 1.22.

This is a common way to apply borders to financial information. The single border indicates that calculations were performed on the numbers above, and the double border indicates that the information is complete. Sometimes financial documents do not display values with cents; rather, the values are rounded up. You can do this by selecting the cells, and then clicking the Decrease Decimal button two times.

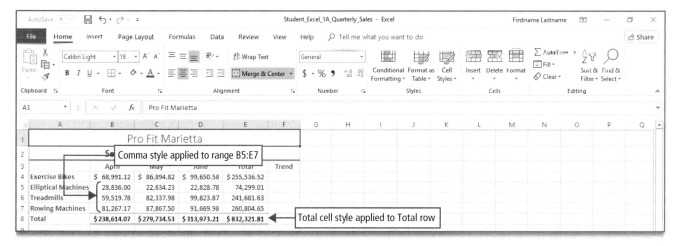

Figure 1.22

Activity 1.10 | Changing the Workbook Theme

A *theme* is a predefined set of colors, fonts, lines, and fill effects that coordinate for an attractive look.

1 ▸ Click the **Page Layout tab**, and then in the **Themes group**, click **Themes**.

2 ▸ Click the **Retrospect** theme, and notice that the cell styles change to match the new theme. Click **Save** 🖫.

MORE KNOWLEDGE **Formatting a Cell's Font, Style, Size, or Color with Individual Commands**

Instead of using Cell Styles, you could use a combination of individual commands to format a cell. For example, on the Home tab, in the Font group, you can change a cell's font by clicking the Font arrow and selecting a different font. You can change the font size by clicking the Font Size arrow and selecting a size. From the same group, you can apply various styles to the cell—such as Bold, Italic, or Underline. To change a cell's font color, in the Font group, click the Font Color arrow and select a different color.

Objective 5 **Chart Data to Create a Column Chart and Insert Sparklines**

GO! Learn How
Video E1-5

A *chart* is a graphic representation of data in a worksheet. Data in a chart is easier to understand than a table of numbers. *Sparklines* are tiny charts embedded in a cell that give a visual trend summary alongside your data. A sparkline makes a pattern more obvious to the eye.

Activity 1.11 | Charting Data and Using Recommended Charts to Select and Insert a Column Chart

MOS
5.1.1, 5.2.2

Recommended Charts is an Excel feature that displays a customized set of charts that, according to Excel's calculations, will best fit your data based on the range of data that you select.

In this Activity, you will create a ***column chart*** showing the monthly sales of cardio equipment by category during the second quarter. A column chart is useful for illustrating comparisons among related numbers. The chart will enable the company president, Michelle Barry, to see a pattern of overall monthly sales.

1 Select the range **A3:D7**.

When charting data, typically you should *not* include totals—include only the data you want to compare.

2 With the data that you want to compare selected, click the **Insert tab**, and then in the **Charts group**, click **Recommended Charts**. Compare your screen with Figure 1.23.

The Insert Chart dialog box displays a list of recommended charts on the left and a preview of the first chart, which is selected, on the right. The second tab of the Insert Chart dialog box includes all chart types—even those that are not recommended by Excel for this type of data.

By using different ***chart types***, you can display data in a way that is meaningful to the reader— common examples are column charts, pie charts, and line charts.

MAC TIP Instead of an Insert Chart dialog box, you may see a drop-down menu of recommended charts; click the second Clustered Column chart.

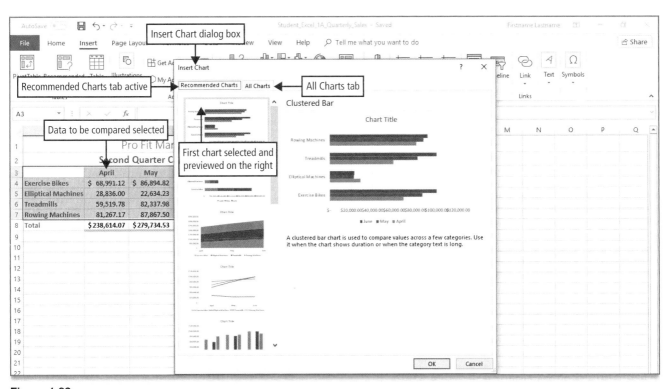

Figure 1.23

3 In the **Insert Chart** dialog box, use the scroll bar to scroll down about one-third of the way, and then click the second Clustered Column chart to view it in the preview area of the **Insert Chart** dialog box. Compare your screen with Figure 1.24.

Here, *each type of cardio equipment* displays its *sales for each month*. A clustered column chart is useful to compare values across a few categories, especially if the order of categories is not important.

MAC TIP Because there is no preview, do not click the chart; if you clicked it and it embedded in your worksheet, on the Quick Access toolbar, click Undo.

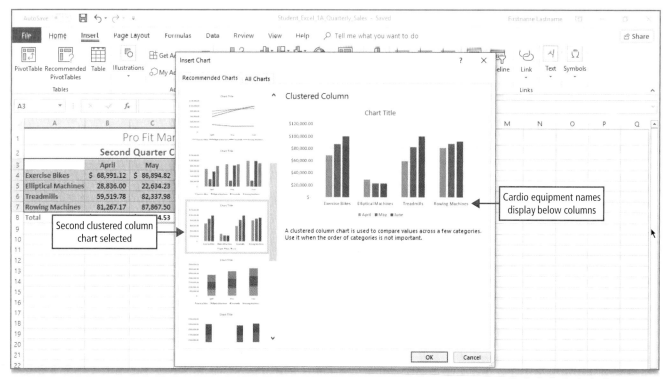

Figure 1.24

> **4** In the **Insert Chart** dialog box, click the chart directly above the selected chart—the first clustered column chart that shows the month names below the columns. Compare your screen with Figure 1.25.
>
> > In this clustered column chart, *each month* displays its *sales for each type of cardio equipment*. When constructing a chart, you can switch the row and column data in this manner to display the data in a way that is most useful to the reader. Here, the president of Pro Fit Marietta wants to compare sales of each type of equipment by month to detect patterns.
> >
> > The comparison of data—either by month or by type of equipment—depends on the type of analysis you want to perform. You can select either chart, or, after your chart is complete, you can use the *Switch/Row Column* command on the ribbon to swap the data over the axis; that is, data being charted on the vertical axis will move to the horizontal axis and vice versa.

Figure 1.25

5 In the lower right corner of the **Insert Chart** dialog box, click **OK** to insert the selected chart into the worksheet. Compare your screen with Figure 1.26,

Your selected column chart displays in the worksheet, and the charted data is bordered by colored lines. Because the chart object is selected—surrounded by a border and displaying sizing handles—contextual tools named *Chart Tools* display and add contextual tabs next to the standard tabs on the ribbon.

MAC TIP   Click the chart to insert it.

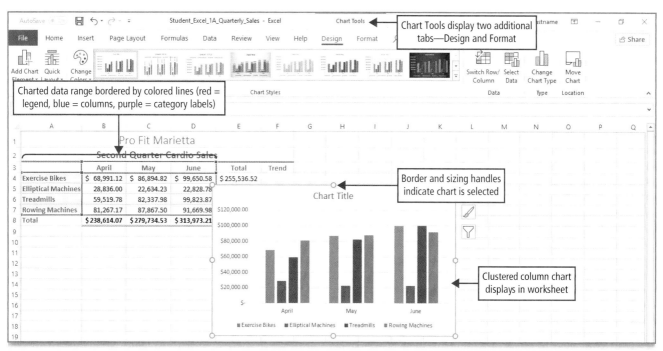

Figure 1.26

Activity 1.12 | Using the Chart Tools to Apply Chart Styles

5.2.3, 5.3.1

1 On the ribbon, locate the contextual tabs under **Chart Tools**—**Design** and **Format**.

When a chart is selected, Chart Tools become available and these two tabs provide commands for enhancing the design and format of the chart.

Based on the data you selected in your worksheet and the chart you selected in the Insert Chart dialog box, Excel constructs a column chart and adds *category labels*—the labels that display along the bottom of the chart to identify the category of data. This area is referred to as the *category axis* or the *x-axis*.

Depending on which arrangement of row and column data you select in the Insert Chart dialog box, Excel arranges either the row titles or the column titles as the category names. Here, based on your selection, the column titles that form the category labels are bordered in purple, indicating the cells that contain the category names.

On the left side of the chart, Excel includes a numerical scale on which the charted data is based; this is the *value axis* or the *y-axis*. Along the lower edge of the chart, a *legend*, which is a chart element that identifies the patterns or colors that are assigned to the categories in the chart, displays. Here, the row titles are bordered in red, indicating the cells containing the legend text.

2 To the right of the chart, notice the three buttons, and then point to each button to display its ScreenTip, as shown in Figure 1.27.

The *Chart Elements button* enables you to add, remove, or change chart elements such as the title, legend, gridlines, and data labels.

The *Chart Styles button* enables you to set a style and color scheme for your chart.

The *Chart Filters button* enables you to change which data displays in the chart—for example, to see only the data for *May* and *June* or only the data for *Treadmills* and *Rowing Machines*.

⬚ **MAC TIP** Chart buttons may not display; use menu commands instead.

Figure 1.27

3 In the worksheet data, locate the group of cells bordered in blue.

Each of the twelve cells bordered in blue is referred to as a *data point*—a value that originates in a worksheet cell. Each data point is represented in the chart by a *data marker*—a column, bar, area, dot, pie slice, or other symbol in a chart that represents a single data point.

Related data points form a *data series*; for example, there is a data series for *April*, for *May*, and for *June*. Each data series has a unique color or pattern represented in the chart legend.

4 On the **Design tab**, in the **Chart Layouts group**, click **Quick Layout**, and then compare your screen with Figure 1.28.

In the Quick Layout gallery, you can change the overall layout of the chart by selecting a predesigned *chart layout*—a combination of chart elements, which can include a title, legend, labels for the columns, and the table of charted cells.

Figure 1.28

5 *Point* to several different layouts to see how Live Preview displays the effect on your chart, and then click the **Quick Layout** button again without changing the layout.

6 In the chart, click anywhere in the text *Chart Title* to select the title box, watch the **Formula Bar** as you begin to type **Second** and notice that AutoComplete fills in the subtitle for you. Press [Enter] at any point to insert the worksheet subtitle as the chart title.

7 Click in a white area just slightly *inside* the chart border to deselect the chart title but keep the chart selected. To the right of the chart, click **Chart Styles** ✐, and then at the top of the **Chart Styles** gallery, be sure that **Style** is selected. Compare your screen with Figure 1.29.

The **Chart Styles gallery** displays an array of pre-defined **chart styles**—the overall visual look of the chart in terms of its colors, backgrounds, and graphic effects such as flat or shaded columns. You can also select Chart Styles from the Chart Styles group on the ribbon, but having the gallery closer to the chart makes it easier to use a touch gesture on a touch device to format a chart.

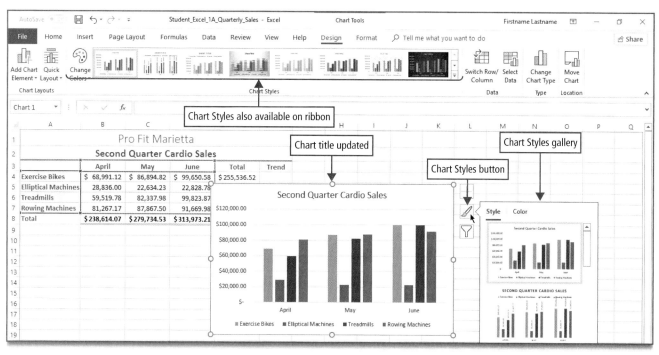

Figure 1.29

8 On the right side of the **Style** gallery, scroll down about halfway, and then by using the ScreenTips as your guide, locate and click **Style 6**.

This style uses a white background, formats the columns with theme colors, and applies a slight shadowed effect to the columns. With this clear visual representation of the data, the president can see the sales of all product categories in each month, and can see that sales of exercise bikes and treadmills have risen markedly during the quarter.

9 At the top of the gallery, click **Color**. Under **Colorful**, point to the third row of colors to display the ScreenTip, and then click to apply this variation of the theme colors.

10 ▶ Point to the top border of the chart to display the ⬚ pointer, and then drag the upper left corner of the chart just inside the upper left corner of cell **A10**, approximately as shown in Figure 1.30.

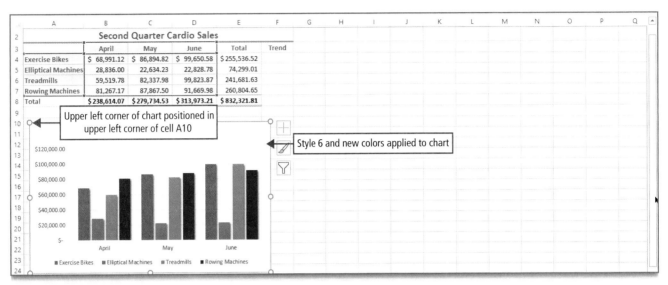

Figure 1.30

11 ▶ Click any cell to deselect the chart, and notice that the chart buttons no longer display to the right of the chart and the Chart Tools no longer display on the ribbon. Click **Save** 🖫.

Contextual tabs display on the ribbon when an object is selected and then are removed from view when the object is deselected.

Activity 1.13 │ Creating and Formatting Sparklines

By creating sparklines, you provide a context for your numbers. Michelle and her colleagues at Pro Fit Marietta will be able to see the relationship between a sparkline and its underlying data quickly.

1 ▶ Select the range **B4:D7**, which represents the monthly sales figures for each product and for each month. Click the **Insert tab**, and then in the **Sparklines group**, click **Line**. In the displayed **Create Sparklines** dialog box, notice that the selected range *B4:D7* displays. Compare your screen with Figure 1.31.

Figure 1.31

2 With the insertion point in the **Location Range** box, type **f4:f7** which is the range of cells where you want the sparklines to display.

 ANOTHER WAY In the worksheet, select the range F4:F7 to insert it into the Location Range box.

3 Click **OK** to insert the sparklines in the range **F4:F7**, and then on the **Design tab**, in the **Show group**, click the **Markers** check box to select it.

Alongside each row of data, the sparkline provides a quick visual trend summary for sales of each cardio item over the three-month period. For example, you can see instantly that of the four items, only Elliptical Machines had declining sales for the period.

4 On the **Design tab**, in the **Style group**, click **More**. In the first row, click the third style. Press Ctrl + Home to deselect the range and make cell **A1** the active range. Click **Save**, and then compare your screen with Figure 1.32.

Use markers, colors, and styles in this manner to further enhance your sparklines.

[computer icon] **MAC TIP** Select the third style in the first row of the drop-down gallery, not from the row of styles that remain on the toolbar.

Figure 1.32

Objective 6 | Print a Worksheet, Display Formulas, and Close Excel

GO! Learn How
Video E1-6

Use the Show Formulas command to display the formula in each cell instead of the resulting value. Use the commands on the Page Layout tab to prepare for printing.

Activity 1.14 | Creating a Footer and Centering a Worksheet

MOS
1.3.1

For each Excel project in this textbook, you will create a footer containing the file name, which includes your name and the project name. You will also center the data horizontally on the page to create an attractive result if your worksheet is shared with others electronically or printed.

1 If necessary, click cell **A1** to deselect the chart. Click the **Page Layout tab**, and then in the **Page Setup group**, click **Margins**. At the bottom of the **Margins** gallery, click **Custom Margins** to display the **Page Setup** dialog box. Compare your screen with Figure 1.33.

Figure 1.33

> **2** On the **Margins tab**, under **Center on page**, select the **Horizontally** check box.

This action will center the data and chart horizontally on the page, as shown in the Preview area.

> **3** Click the **Header/Footer tab**, and then in the center of the dialog box, click **Custom Footer**. In the **Footer** dialog box, with your insertion point blinking in the **Left section**, on the row of buttons, click **Insert File Name** 📄. Compare your screen with Figure 1.34.

&[File] displays in the Left section. Here you can type or insert information from the row of buttons into the left, middle, or right section of the footer. The Custom Header button displays a similar screen to enter information in the header of the worksheet.

Figure 1.34

> **4** Click **OK** two times.

The vertical dotted line between columns indicates that as currently arranged, only the columns to the left of the dotted line will print on the first page. The exact position of the vertical line may depend on your default printer setting.

🔄 **ANOTHER WAY** Deselect the chart. On the Insert tab, in the Text group, click Header & Footer to display Page Layout view. Click in the left section of the displayed footer, and then in the Header & Footer Elements group, click File Name. Click any cell in the workbook to deselect the footer area, and then on the status bar, click the Normal button to return to Normal view.

Activity 1.15 | Adding Document Properties and Printing a Workbook

Michelle likes to add tags and other identifying properties to all company documents so they are easily searchable. In this Activity, you will add searchable document properties to the workbook.

1 In the upper left corner of your screen, click the **File tab** to display **Backstage** view. If necessary, on the left, click the **Info tab**. In the lower right corner, click **Show All Properties**.

☐ **MAC TIP** Click File, at the bottom of the menu, click Properties, click the Summary tab; for Tags use Keywords.

2 As the **Tags**, type **cardio sales** In the **Subject** box, type your course name and section number. Be sure your name displays in the **Author** box and edit if necessary.

3 On the left, click **Print** to view the **Print Preview**. Compare your screen with Figure 1.35.

☐ **MAC TIP** Click OK to close Properties dialog box first. Click File, then click Print.

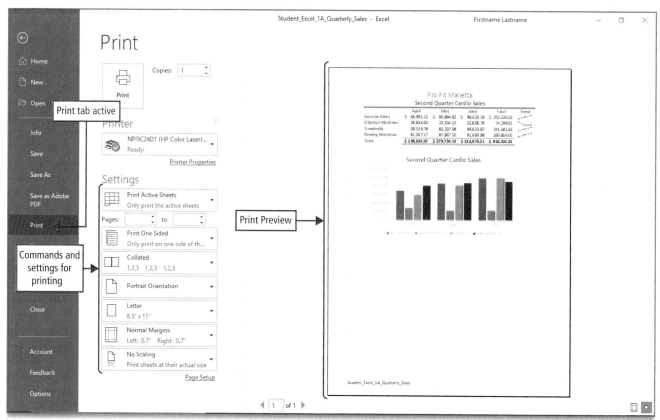

Figure 1.35

4 Note any adjustments that need to be made, and then on the left, click **Save** to save and return to the workbook.

☐ **MAC TIP** Click Close to close the Print dialog box, then Save your workbook.

Activity 1.16 | Printing a Section of the Worksheet

1.5.1, 1.5.3

From Backstage view, you can print only the portion of the worksheet that you select, and there are times you might want to do this. For example, sometimes Michelle wants to see data for only one or two types of equipment when she is evaluating various brands of equipment.

1 Select the range **A2:F5** to select only the subtitle and the data for *Exercise Bikes* and *Elliptical Machines* and the column titles.

2 Click the **File tab**, on the left, click **Print** to display **Print Preview**, and then under **Settings**, click the first arrow, which currently displays *Print Active Sheets*. On the list that displays, click **Print Selection**, and then compare your screen with Figure 1.36.

🖥 **MAC TIP**   On the File menu, point to Print Area, and then click Set Print Area. When finished, go back to Print Area and click Clear Print Area.

Figure 1.36

📄 **For Non-MyLab Submissions: Determine if Your Instructor Requires a Submission for Printing a Section of a Worksheet**
If directed by your instructor, print the selection on paper or create an electronic image. Then press [Ctrl] + [Home] and click Save 🖫.

3 Click the **Print Selection arrow** again, and then click **Print Active Sheets** to return this setting to the default. In the upper left, click **Back** ⊖ to return to your document. Press [Ctrl] + [Home] to make cell **A1** the active cell, and then click **Save** 🖫.

Activity 1.17 | Changing Page Orientation and Displaying, Printing, and Hiding Formulas

1.3.1, 1.3.2,
1.4.6, 1.5.3

When you type a formula in a cell, the cell displays the *results* of the formula calculation. Recall that this value is called the displayed value. You can view and print the underlying formulas in the cells. When you do so, a formula often takes more horizontal space to display than the result of the calculation.

1 If necessary, redisplay your worksheet. Because you will make some temporary changes to your workbook, on the Quick Access Toolbar, click **Save** 🖫 to be sure your work is saved up to this point.

2 On the **Formulas tab**, in the **Formula Auditing group**, click **Show Formulas**.

🔄 **ANOTHER WAY**   Hold down [Ctrl], and then press [~] (usually located below [Esc]).

3 In the **column heading area**, point to the **column A** heading to display the ⬇ pointer, hold down the left mouse button, and then drag to the right to select columns **A:F**. Compare your screen with Figure 1.37.

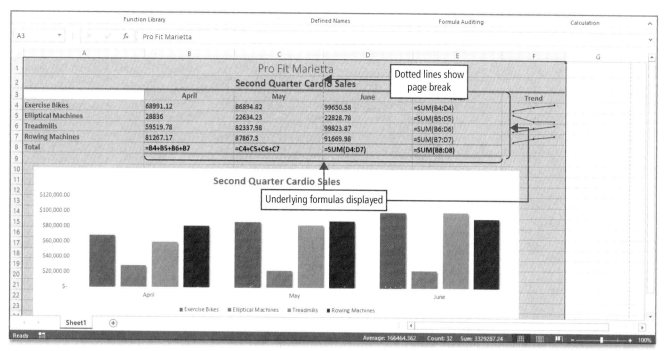

Figure 1.37

NOTE   Turning the Display of Formulas On and Off

The Show Formulas button is a toggle button. Clicking it once turns the display of formulas on—the button will be shaded. Clicking the button again turns the display of formulas off.

4 Point to the column heading boundary between any two of the selected columns to display the ➕ pointer, and then double-click to AutoFit the selected columns.

AutoFit adjusts the width of a column to fit the cell content of the *widest* cell in the column.

🔄 **ANOTHER WAY**   With the columns selected, on the Home tab, in the Cells group, click Format, and then click AutoFit Column Width.

5 On the **Page Layout tab**, in the **Page Setup group**, click **Orientation**, and then click **Landscape**. In the **Scale to Fit** group, click the **Width arrow**, and then click **1 page** to scale the data to fit onto one page.

Scaling shrinks the width or height of the printed worksheet to fit a maximum number of pages and is convenient for printing formulas. Although it is not always the case, formulas frequently take up more space than the actual data.

🔄 **ANOTHER WAY**   In the Scale to Fit group, click the Dialog Box Launcher button to display the Page tab of the Page Setup dialog box. Then, under Scaling, click the Fit to option button.

6 In the **Page Setup group**, click **Margins**, click **Custom Margins**, and then on the **Margins tab**, under **Center on page**, be sure the **Horizontally** check box is selected—select it if necessary.

7 Click **OK** to close the dialog box. Click cell **A1**. Check to be sure your chart is centered below the data and the left and right edges are slightly inside column A and column F—use the pointer to drag a chart edge and then deselect the chart if necessary.

8 Click the **File tab**, and then on the left click **Print** to display the **Print Preview**. Under **Settings**, if necessary, switch back to the option to **Print Active Sheets**.

9 On the left, click **Close**, and when prompted, click **Don't Save** so that you do *not* save the changes you made—displaying formulas, changing column widths and orientation, and scaling—to print your formulas.

10 In the upper right corner of your screen, click **Close** ☒ to close Excel.

For Non-MyLab Submissions: Determine What Your Instructor Requires for Submission

As directed by your instructor, submit your completed Excel workbook.

---

11 In **MyLab IT**, locate and click the Grader Project **Excel 1A Quarterly Sales**. In **step 3**, under **Upload Completed Assignment**, click **Choose File**. In the **Open** dialog box, navigate to your **Excel Chapter 1 folder**, and then click your **Student_Excel_1A_Quarterly_Sales** file one time to select it. In the lower right corner of the **Open** dialog box, click **Open**.

The name of your selected file displays above the Upload button.

12 To submit your file to **MyLab IT** for grading, click **Upload**, wait a moment for a green **Success!** message, and then in **step 4**, click the blue **Submit for Grading** button. Click **Close Assignment** to return to your list of **Course Materials**.

You have completed Project 1A **END**

EXCEL

1

Objective | Create a Sales Report with an Embedded Column Chart Using Google Sheets

ALERT   **Working with Web-Based Applications and Service**

Computer programs and services on the web receive continuous updates and improvements, so the steps to complete this web-based Activity may differ from the ones shown. You can often look at the screens and the information presented to determine how to complete the Activity.

If you do not already have a Google account, you will need to create one before you begin this Activity. Go to **http://google.com** and in the upper right corner, click Sign In. On the Sign In screen, click Create Account. On the Create your Google Account page, complete the form, read and agree to the Terms of Service and Privacy Policy, and then click Next step. On the Welcome screen, click Get Started.

Activity | Creating a Sales Report with an Embedded Column Chart Using Google Sheets

In this Activity, you will use Google Sheets to create a sales report and chart similar to the one you created in Project 1A.

1 From the desktop, open your browser (use a browser other than Edge), navigate to **https://www.google.com**, and then click the **Google apps** menu ⊞. Click **Drive**, and then if necessary, sign in to your Google account.

2 Open your **GO! Web Projects** folder—or click New to create and then open this folder if necessary.

3 In the upper left corner, click **New**, and then click **Google Sheets**. From your Windows taskbar, open **File Explorer**, navigate to the files you downloaded for this chapter, and then in the **File List**, double-click to open **e01A_Web**.

4 In the displayed Excel worksheet, select the range **A1:E8**, right-click over the selection, click **Copy**, and then **Close** Excel. **Close** the **File Explorer** window.

5 In your blank Google Sheet, with cell **A1** active, point to cell **A1**, right-click, and then click **Paste**; by copying and pasting the data, you can create this Project faster without having to do extra typing. In the column heading area, point to the border between **column A** and **column B** to display the ⟷ pointer, and then widen **column A** slightly so that all of the data displays.

6 Select the range **A1:E1**. On the toolbar, click **Merge cells** ⊞. On the toolbar, click the **Horizontal Align button arrow** ▤ and then click **Center** ▤. Repeat for the range **A2:E2**, and then apply **Bold** ⓑ to cells **A1** and **A2**.

7 Select the range with the month names, center them, and apply **Bold** ⓑ. Apply **Bold** ⓑ to the totals in the range **B8:E8**.

8 Select the range **A3:D7**—the data without the totals and without the titles. On the menu bar, click **Insert**, and then click **Chart**. On the right, in the **Chart editor** pane, be sure the **DATA tab** is active.

9 In the Chart editor pane, scroll down as necessary, and then select the **Switch rows/columns** check box.

10 At the top of the **Chart editor** pane, click the **CUSTOMIZE tab**. Click the **Chart & axis titles arrow**, and then click in the **Chart title** box. Type **Second Quarter Cardio Sales**

11 Click the **Legend arrow**, click the **Position arrow**, and then click **None**. Click the **Chart style arrow**, click the **Background color arrow**, and then in the fourth column, click the third color—**light yellow 3**.

12 Point anywhere inside the selected chart, hold down the left mouse button and begin to drag to display the 🖑 pointer, and then drag the chart slightly below the data. Then using the corner sizing handles, resize and reposition the chart so that it is the width of columns **A:E** and displays below the data.

13 At the top of the worksheet window, click the text *Untitled spreadsheet*, and then using your own name, type **Lastname_Firstname_EX_1A_Web** and press ⏎.

»» **GO!** With Google continues on next page

»» GO! With Google Sheets

14 If you are instructed to submit your file to your instructor, you can either share the file through Google Drive, or create a PDF or Excel file. Ask your instructor in what format he or she would like to receive your file.

15 **Close** ✕ the browser tab—a new Google Sheet always opens in a new window in your browser; your work is automatically saved. Notice that your new Google Sheet displays in the file list on your Google Drive. Sign out of your Google account.

Figure A

PROJECT 1B

Inventory Valuation

Project Activities

In Activities 1.18 through 1.27 you will create a workbook for Josh Feingold, Operations Manager, which calculates the retail value of an inventory of plyometric training products. Your completed worksheet will look similar to Figure 1.38.

Project Files for MyLab IT Grader

1. In your MyLab IT course, locate and click **Excel 1B Plyo Products**, Download Materials, and then Download All Files.
2. Extract the zipped folder to your Excel Chapter 1 folder. Close the Grader download screens.
3. Take a moment to open the downloaded **Excel_1B_Plyo_Products_Instructions**; note any recent updates to the book.

Project Results

GO! Project 1B
Where We're Going

Pro Fit Marietta
Plyometric Products Inventory Valuation

	Warehouse Location	Quantity in Stock	Retail Price	Total Retail Value	Percent of Total Retail Value
As of September 30					
Power Hurdle	Atlanta	125	$ 32.95	$ 4,118.75	1.41%
Speed Hurdle	Atlanta	995	59.95	59,650.25	20.37%
Stackable Steps	Marietta	450	251.59	113,215.50	38.65%
Pro Jump Rope	Marietta	1,105	49.95	55,194.75	18.84%
Plyometric Box Set	Marietta	255	158.05	40,302.75	13.76%
Plyometric Mat	Atlanta	215	94.99	20,422.85	6.97%
Total Retail Value for All Products				$ 292,904.85	

Student_Excel_1B_Plyo_Products

Figure 1.38 Project 1B Plyo Products

For Non-MyLab Submissions

For Project 1B, you will need:

New blank Excel workbook

In your **Excel Chapter 1** folder, save your workbook as:

Lastname_Firstname_1B_Plyo_Products

If your instructor requires a workbook with formulas, save as:

Lastname_Firstname_1B_Plyo_Products_formulas

After you have named and saved your workbook, on the next page begins with step 2.

ALERT Because Office 365 is a cloud-based subscription service that receives continuous updates, you may encounter some variations in what appears on your screen and what is shown in this instruction. Microsoft Office 365 is fully installed on your PC or Mac; no internet access is necessary to create or edit documents. When you *are* connected to the internet, you will receive monthly upgrades and new features, so you always have the latest versions of Office apps as soon as they are available. Your subscription gives you continuous free access to the latest innovations and refinements.

GO! Learn How
Video E1-7

In Excel, the spelling checker performs similarly to the way it behaves in other Microsoft Office programs.

Activity 1.18 | Checking Spelling in a Worksheet

MOS
2.2.7

1 Navigate to your **Excel Chapter 1 folder**, and then double-click the Excel file you downloaded from **MyLab IT** that displays your name—**Student_Excel_1B_Plyo_ Products**. In your blank workbook, if necessary, at the top click **Enable Editing**.

2 In cell **A1**, type **Pro Fit Marietta** and press Enter. In cell **A2**, type **Plyometric Products Inventory** and press Enter.

MAC TIP To display group names on the ribbon, display the menu, click Excel, click Preferences, click View, under In Ribbon, select the Group Titles check box.

3 Press Tab to move to cell **B3**, type **Quantity** and press Tab. In cell **C3**, type **Average Cost** and press Tab. In cell **D3**, type **Retail Price** and press Tab.

4 Click cell **C3**, and then look at the **Formula Bar**. Notice that in the cell, the displayed value is cut off; however, in the **Formula Bar**, the entire text value—the underlying value—displays. Compare your screen with Figure 1.39.

Text that is too long to fit in a cell extends into cells on the right only if they are empty. If the cell to the right contains data, the text in the cell to the left is truncated—cut off. The entire value continues to exist, but it is not completely visible.

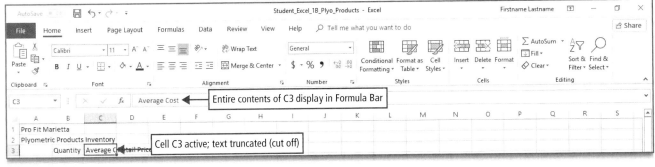

Figure 1.39

5 Click cell **E3**, type **Total Retail Value** and press Tab. In cell **F3**, type **Percent of Total Retail Value** and press Enter.

6 Click cell **A4**. *Without* correcting the spelling error, type **Powr Hurdle** Press ⏎. In the range **A5:A10**, type the remaining row titles shown below. Then compare your screen with Figure 1.40.

> Speed Hurdle
>
> Stackable Steps
>
> Pro Jump Rope
>
> Plyometric Box Set
>
> Plyometric Mat
>
> Total Retail Value for All Products

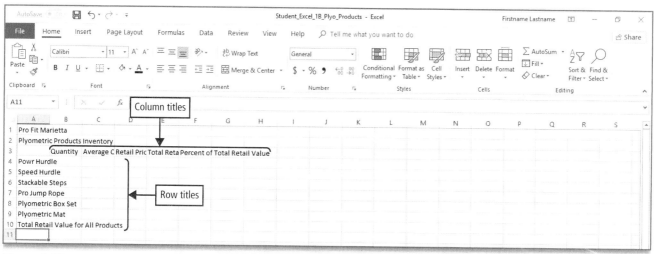

Figure 1.40

7 In the **column heading area**, point to the right boundary of **column A** to display the ⟷ pointer, and then drag to the right to widen **column A** to **215** pixels.

🖥️ **MAC TIP** Change the width to 30 (185 pixels).

8 Select the range **A1:F1**, **Merge & Center** the text, and then from the **Cell Styles** gallery, apply the **Title** style.

9 Select the range **A2:F2**, **Merge & Center** the text, and then from the **Cell Styles** gallery, apply the **Heading 1** style. Press Ctrl + Home to move to cell **A1** at the top of your worksheet.

🖥️ **MAC TIP** Press control + E + ← to move to cell A1.

10 With cell **A1** as the active cell, click the **Review tab**, and then in the **Proofing group**, click **Spelling**. Compare your screen with Figure 1.41.

Figure 1.41

 ANOTHER WAY Press [F7], which is the keyboard shortcut for the Spelling command.

11 In the **Spelling** dialog box, under **Not in Dictionary**, notice the word *Powr*.

The spelling tool does not have this word in its dictionary. Under *Suggestions*, Excel provides a list of suggested spellings.

12 Under **Suggestions**, if necessary click **Power**, and then click **Change**.

Powr, a typing error, is changed to *Power*. A message box displays *Spell check complete. You're good to go!*—unless you have additional unrecognized words. Because the spelling check begins its checking process starting with the currently selected cell, it is good practice to return to cell A1 before starting the Spelling command.

13 Correct any other errors you may have made. When the message displays, *Spell check complete. You're good to go!*, click **OK. Save** 🖫 your workbook.

Objective 8 Enter Data by Range

GO! Learn How
Video E1-8

You can enter data by first selecting a range of cells. This is a time-saving technique, especially if you use a numeric keypad to enter the numbers.

Activity 1.19 │ Entering Data by Range

1 Select the range **B4:D9**, type **125** and then press [Enter].

The value displays in cell B4, and cell B5 becomes the active cell.

2 With cell **B5** active in the range, and pressing [Enter] after each entry, type the following, and then compare your screen with Figure 1.42:

1125

450

1105

255

215

After you enter the last value and press [Enter], the active cell moves to the top of the next column within the selected range. Although it is not required to enter data in this manner, you can see that selecting the range before you enter data saves time because it confines the movement of the active cell to the selected range. When you select a range of data, the Quick Analysis button displays. (Mac users: you may not see the Quick Analysis button.)

Figure 1.42

3 With the selected range still active, from the following table, beginning in cell **C4** and pressing Enter after each entry, enter the data for the **Average Cost** column and then the **Retail Price** column. If you prefer, deselect the range to enter the values—typing in a selected range is optional.

Average Cost	Retail Price
15.50	32.95
29.55	59.95
125.95	251.59
18.75	49.95
85.25	159.05
49.95	94.99

Recall that the default number format for cells is the *General* number format, in which numbers display exactly as you type them and trailing zeros do not display, even if you type them.

4 Click any blank cell, and then compare your screen with Figure 1.43. Correct any errors you may have made while entering data, and then click **Save** 🖫.

Figure 1.43

Objective 9 ┃ Construct Formulas for Mathematical Operations

GO! Learn How
Video E1-9

Operators are symbols with which you can specify the type of calculation you want to perform in a formula.

Activity 1.20 ┃ Using Arithmetic Operators

1 Click cell **E4**, type **=b4*d4** and notice that the two cells are outlined as part of an active formula. Then, press Enter.

The *Total Retail Value* of all *Power Hurdle* items in inventory—*4118.75*—equals the *Quantity* (125) times the *Retail Price* (selling price) of 32.95. In Excel, the asterisk (*) indicates multiplication.

2 Take a moment to study the symbols you will use to perform basic mathematical operations in Excel as shown in the table in Figure 1.44, which are referred to as *arithmetic operators*.

Symbols Used in Excel for Arithmetic Operators	
Operator Symbol	**Operation**
+	Addition
-	Subtraction (also negation)
*	Multiplication
/	Division
%	Percent
^	Exponentiation

Figure 1.44

3 Click cell **E4**.

You can see that in cells E5:E9 you need a formula similar to the one in E4, but one that refers to the cells in row 5, row 6, and so on. Recall that you can copy formulas and the cell references will change *relative to* the row number.

4 With cell **E4** selected, position your pointer over the fill handle in the lower right corner of the cell until the ⊞ pointer displays. Then, drag down through cell **E9** to copy the formula.

5 Select the range **B4:B9**, and then on the **Home tab**, in the **Number group**, click **Comma Style** [,]. In the **Number group**, click **Decrease Decimal** [ ] two times to remove the decimal places from these values.

Comma Style formats a number with two decimal places; because these are whole numbers referring to quantities, no decimal places are necessary.

 ANOTHER WAY   Select the range, display the Cell Styles gallery, and then under Number Format, click Comma [0].

6 Select the range **E4:E9**, and then at the bottom of your screen, in the status bar, notice the displayed values for **Average**, **Count**, and **Sum**—*50158.89167, 6,* and *300953.35*.

When you select a range of numerical data, Excel's *AutoCalculate* feature displays three calculations in the status bar by default—Average, Count, and Sum. Here, Excel indicates that if you averaged the selected values, the result would be *50158.89167*, there are *6* cells in the selection that contain values, and that if you added the values the result would be *300953.35*.

You can display three additional calculations to this area by right-clicking the status bar and selecting them—Numerical Count, Minimum, and Maximum.

Activity 1.21 | Using the Quick Analysis Tool

2.2.5, 2.2.7

Recall that the Quick Analysis button displays when you select a range of data. Quick Analysis is convenient because it keeps common commands close to your mouse pointer and also displays commands in a format that is easy to touch with your finger if you are using a touchscreen device.

1 With the range **E4:E9** selected, in the lower right corner of the selected range, click **Quick Analysis** [ ]. In the displayed gallery, click **Totals**. *Point to*, but do not click, the first **Sum** button, which shows blue cells at the bottom. Compare your screen with Figure 1.45.

Here, the shaded cells on the button indicate what will be summed and where the result will display, and a preview of the result displays in the cell bordered with a gray shadow.

MAC TIP   Quick Analysis is not available, use AutoSum.

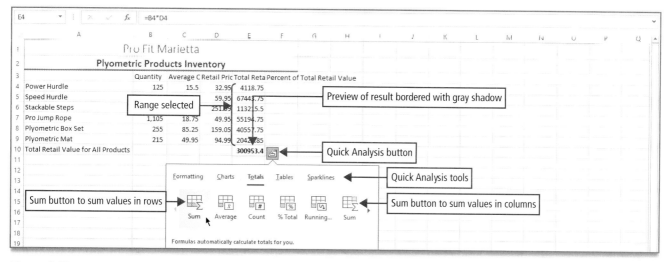

Figure 1.45

> **2** Click the first **Sum** button to display the column total *300953.4* formatted in Bold.
>
> Sums calculated using the Quick Analysis tool are formatted in Bold.

⌨ **MAC TIP** Select the range E4:E9, and then on the Home tab, click AutoSum. In the Font group, click Bold.

> **3** Select the range **C5:E9** and apply the **Comma Style** ⎾,⏌; notice that Excel widens the columns to accommodate the data.
>
> **4** Select the range **C4:E4**, hold down Ctrl, and then click cell **E10**. Release Ctrl, and then apply the **Accounting Number Format** ⎾$ ▾⏌. Notice that Excel widens the columns as necessary.
>
> **5** Click cell **E10**, and then from the **Cell Styles** gallery, apply the **Total** style. Click any blank cell, **Save** 🖫 your workbook, and then compare your screen with Figure 1.46.

Figure 1.46

Activity 1.22 | Copying Formulas Containing Absolute Cell References

4.1.1

In a formula, a relative cell reference refers to a cell by its position *relative to* the cell that contains the formula. An ***absolute cell reference***, on the other hand, refers to a cell by its *fixed* position in the worksheet, for example, the total in cell E10.

A relative cell reference automatically adjusts when a formula is copied. In some calculations, you do *not* want the cell reference to adjust; rather, you want the cell reference to remain the same when the formula is copied.

1 Click cell **F4**, type = and then click cell **E4**. Type **/** and then click cell **E10**.

The formula =*E4/E10* indicates that the value in cell E4 will be *divided* by the value in cell E10 because Mr. Feingold wants to know the percentage by which each product's Total Retail Value makes up the Total Retail Value for All Products.

Arithmetically, the percentage is computed by dividing the *Total Retail Value* for each product by the *Total Retail Value for All Products*. The result will be a percentage expressed as a decimal.

2 Press Enter. Click cell **F4** and notice that the formula displays in the **Formula Bar**. Then, point to cell **F4** and double-click.

The formula, with the two referenced cells displayed in color and bordered with the same color, displays in the cell. This feature, called the ***range finder***, is useful for verifying formulas because it visually indicates which workbook cells are included in a formula calculation.

3 Press Enter to redisplay the result of the calculation in the cell, and notice that .013686, which is approximately 1% of the total retail value of the inventory, is made up of Power Hurdles.

4 Click cell **F4** again, and then drag the fill handle down through cell **F9**. Compare your screen with Figure 1.47.

Each cell displays an error message—*#DIV/0!* and a green triangle in the upper left corner of each cell indicates that Excel detects an error.

Like a grammar checker, Excel uses rules to check for formula errors and flags errors in this manner. Additionally, the Auto Fill Options button displays, from which you can select formatting options for the copied cells.

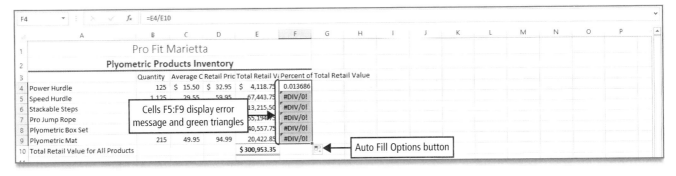

Figure 1.47

5 Click cell **F5**, and then to the left of the cell, point to the **Error Checking** button to display its ScreenTip—*The formula or function used is dividing by zero or empty cells.*

In this manner, Excel suggests the cause of an error.

MAC TIP On the Formulas tab, click Error Checking.

6 Look at the **Formula Bar** and examine the formula.

The formula is =E5/E11. The cell reference to E5 is correct, but the cell reference following the division operator (/) is *E11*, and E11 is an *empty* cell.

7 Click cell **F6**, point to the **Error Checking** button, and in the **Formula Bar**, examine the formula.

Because the cell references are relative, Excel builds the formulas by increasing the row number for each equation. But in this calculation, the divisor must always be the value in cell E10—the *Total Retail Value for All Products*.

8 Point to cell **F4**, and then double-click to place the insertion point within the cell.

9 Within the cell, use the arrow keys as necessary to position the insertion point to the left of *E10*, and then press ⟨F4⟩. Compare your screen with Figure 1.48.

Dollar signs ($) display, which changes the reference to cell E10 to an absolute cell reference. The use of the dollar sign to denote an absolute reference is not related in any way to whether or not the values you are working with are currency values. It is simply the symbol that Excel uses to denote an absolute cell reference.

MAC TIP Press ⟨command ⌘⟩ + ⟨T⟩ to make a cell reference in a formula absolute.

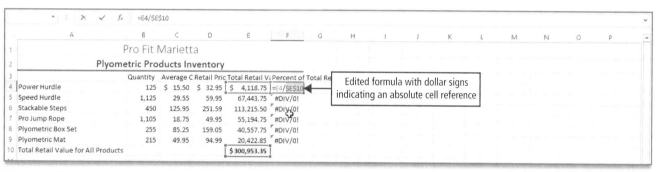

Figure 1.48

ANOTHER WAY Edit the formula so that it indicates =E4/$E$10.

10 On the **Formula Bar**, click **Enter** ✓ so that **F4** remains the active cell. Then, drag the fill handle to copy the new formula down through cell **F9**. Compare your screen with Figure 1.49.

Figure 1.49

11 Click cell **F5**, examine the formula in the **Formula Bar**, and then examine the formulas for cells **F6**, **F7**, **F8**, and **F9**.

For each formula, the cell reference for the *Total Retail Value* of each product changed relative to its row; however, the value used as the divisor—*Total Retail Value for All Products* in cell E10—remained absolute. You can see that by using either relative or absolute cell references, it is easy to duplicate formulas without typing them.

12 Save 🖫 your workbook.

MORE KNOWLEDGE **Calculate a Percentage if You Know the Total and the Amount**

Using the equation *amount/total = percentage*, you can calculate the percentage by which a part makes up a total—with the percentage formatted as a decimal. For example, if on a test you score 42 points correctly out of 50, your percentage of correct answers is 42/50 = 0.84 or 84%.

Objective 10 Edit Values in a Worksheet

GO! Learn How
Video E1-10

Excel performs calculations on numbers; that is why you use Excel. If you make changes to the numbers, Excel automatically *re*-calculates the results. This is one of the most powerful and valuable features of Excel.

Activity 1.23 | Editing Values in a Worksheet

You can edit text and number values directly within a cell or in the Formula Bar.

Josh needs to edit some of the worksheet's information, so in this Activity, you will correct the quantity of Speed Hurdles from 1,125 to 995, change the Retail Price of Plyometric Box Sets from $159.05 to $158.05, edit the subtitle to include the word *Valuation*, and edit the column title in cell B3.

1 In cell **E10**, notice the column total *$300,953.35*. Click cell **B5**, and then change its value by typing **995** Watch cell **E5** and press Enter.

Excel formulas *re-calculate* if you change the value in a cell that is referenced in a formula. It is not necessary to delete the old value in a cell; selecting the cell and typing a new value replaces the old value with your new typing.

The *Total Retail Value* of all *Speed Hurdle* items recalculates to *59,650.25* and the total in cell E10 recalculates to *$293,159.85*. Additionally, all of the percentages in column F recalculate.

2 Point to cell **D8**, and then double-click to place the insertion point within the cell. Use the arrow keys to move the insertion point to the left or right of *9*, and use either Del or Backspace to delete *9* and then type **8** so that the new Retail Price is *158.05*.

3 Watch cell **E8** and **E10** as you press Enter, and then notice the recalculation of the formulas in those two cells.

Excel recalculates the value in cell E8 to *40,302.75* and the value in cell E10 to *$292,904.85*. Additionally, all of the percentages in column F recalculate because the *Total Retail Value for All Products* recalculated.

4 Point to cell **A2** so that the ✛ pointer is positioned slightly to the right of the word *Inventory*, and then double-click to place the insertion point in the cell. Edit the text to add the word **Valuation** pressing Spacebar as necessary, and then press Enter.

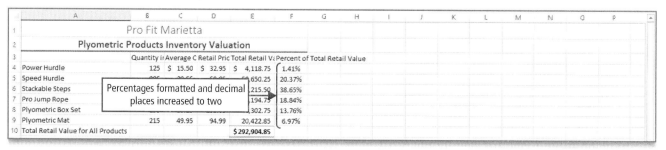

5 ▶ Click cell **B3**, and then in the **Formula Bar**, click to place the insertion point after the letter *y*. Press [Spacebar] one time, type **in Stock** and then on the **Formula Bar**, click **Enter** ✓. Click **Save** 🖫, and then compare your screen with Figure 1.50.

Recall that if text is too long to fit in the cell and the cell to the right contains data, the text is truncated—cut off—but the entire value still exists as the underlying value.

B3	▼ : ✕ ✓ ƒx	Quantity in Stock ◄	*in Stock* added to column title													
	A	B	C	D	E	F	G	H	I	J	K	L	M	N	O	P
1	Pro Fit Marietta															
2	Plyometric Products Inventory Valuation ◄			*Valuation* added to subtitle												
3		Quantity i	Average C	Retail Pric	Total Retail Va	Percent of Total Retail Value										
4	Power Hurdle	125	$ 15.50	$ 32.95	$ 4,118.75	0.014062										
5	Speed Hurdle	995	◄ 29.5	New value in cell B5		0.203651										
6	Stackable Steps	450	125.9			0.386527										
7	Pro Jump Rope	1,105	18.75	49.95	55,1											
8	Plyometric Box Set	255	85.25	158.05 ◄	New value in cell D8											
9	Plyometric Mat	215	49.95	94.99	20,4											
10	Total Retail Value for All Products				$ 292,904.85											

Figure 1.50

Activity 1.24 | Formatting Cells with the Percent Style

[MOS]

2.2.2

A percentage is part of a whole expressed in hundredths. For example, 75 cents is the same as 75 percent of one dollar. The Percent Style button formats the selected cell as a percentage rounded to the nearest hundredth. In this Activity, you will format the percentage values in column F with the Percent Style.

1 ▶ Click cell **F4**, and then in the **Number group**, click **Percent Style** %.

Your result is 1%, which is *0.014062* rounded to the nearest hundredth and expressed as a percentage. Percent Style displays the value of a cell as a percentage.

2 ▶ Select the range **F4:F9**. On the **Home tab**, in the **Number group**, click **Percent Style** %, and then click **Increase Decimal** ⬚ two times. Then in the **Alignment group**, click **Center** ☰.

⌨ **MAC TIP** Use commands on the Home tab.

Percent Style may not offer a percentage precise enough to analyze important financial information—adding additional decimal places to a percentage makes data more precise.

🔁 **ANOTHER WAY** Right-click over the selected range, and then click the commands on the mini toolbar.

3 ▶ Click any cell to cancel the selection, **Save** 🖫 your workbook, and then compare your screen with Figure 1.51.

	A	B	C	D	E	F	G	H	I	J	K	L	M	N	O	P
1	Pro Fit Marietta															
2	Plyometric Products Inventory Valuation															
3		Quantity ir	Average C	Retail Pric	Total Retail Va	Percent of Total Retail Value										
4	Power Hurdle	125	$ 15.50	$ 32.95	$ 4,118.75	1.41%										
5	Speed Hurdle				650.25	20.37%										
6	Stackable Steps	Percentages formatted and decimal			215.50	38.65%										
7	Pro Jump Rope	places increased to two			194.75	18.84%										
8	Plyometric Box Set				302.75	13.76%										
9	Plyometric Mat	215	49.95	94.99	20,422.85	6.97%										
10	Total Retail Value for All Products				$ 292,904.85											

Figure 1.51

Objective 11 | Format a Worksheet

GO! Learn How
Video E1-11

Formatting refers to the process of specifying the appearance of cells and the overall layout of your worksheet. Formatting is accomplished through various commands on the ribbon, for example, applying Cell Styles, and also from commands on shortcut menus, using keyboard shortcuts, and in the Format Cells dialog box.

Activity 1.25 | Inserting and Deleting Rows and Columns

MOS
2.1.3

In the next Activities, you will format the worksheet attractively so that Josh and his staff can view the information easily.

1 In the **row heading area** on the left side of your screen, point to the row heading for **row 3** to display the ➡ pointer, and then right-click to simultaneously select the row and display a shortcut menu.

2 On the shortcut menu, click **Insert** to insert a new **row 3** above the selected row.

> The rows below the new row 3 move down one row, and the Insert Options button displays. By default, the new row uses the formatting of the row *above*.

ANOTHER WAY Select the row, on the Home tab, in the Cells group, click the Insert button arrow, and then click Insert Sheet Rows. Or, select the row and click the Insert button—the default setting of the button inserts a new sheet row above the selected row.

3 Click cell **E11**. On the **Formula Bar**, notice that the range changed to sum the new range **E5:E10**. Compare your screen with Figure 1.52.

> If you move formulas by inserting additional rows or columns in your worksheet, Excel automatically adjusts the formulas. Here, Excel adjusted all of the formulas in the worksheet that were affected by inserting this new row.

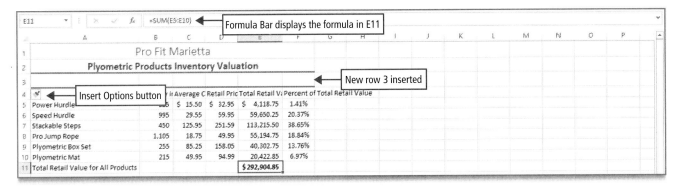

Formula Bar displays the formula in E11

New row 3 inserted

Insert Options button

		Average C	Retail Pric	Total Retail V:	Percent of Total Retail Value
Pro Fit Marietta					
Plyometric Products Inventory Valuation					
Power Hurdle		$ 15.50	$ 32.95	$ 4,118.75	1.41%
Speed Hurdle	995	29.55	59.95	59,650.25	20.37%
Stackable Steps	450	125.95	251.59	113,215.50	38.65%
Pro Jump Rope	1,105	18.75	49.95	55,194.75	18.84%
Plyometric Box Set	255	85.25	158.05	40,302.75	13.76%
Plyometric Mat	215	49.95	94.99	20,422.85	6.97%
Total Retail Value for All Products				$ 292,904.85	

Figure 1.52

4 Click cell **A3**, type **As of September 30** and then on the **Formula Bar**, click **Enter** ✓ to maintain **A3** as the active cell. **Merge & Center** the text across the range **A3:F3**, and then apply the **Heading 2** cell style.

5 In the **column heading area**, point to **column B** to display the ⬇ pointer, right-click, and then click **Insert**.

A column is inserted to the left of column B. By default, the new column uses the formatting of the column to the *left*.

⟳ ANOTHER WAY Select the column, on the Home tab, in the Cells group, click the Insert button arrow, and then click Insert Sheet Columns. Or, select the column and click the Insert button—the default setting of the button inserts a new sheet column to the right of the selected column.

6 Click cell **B4**, type **Warehouse Location** and then press Enter.

7 In cell **B5**, type **Atlanta** and then type **Atlanta** again in cells **B6** and **B10**. Use AutoComplete to speed your typing by pressing Enter as soon as the AutoComplete suggestion displays. In cells **B7**, **B8**, and **B9**, type **Marietta**

8 In the **column heading area**, point to **column D**, right-click, and then click **Delete**.

The remaining columns shift to the left, and Excel adjusts all the formulas in the worksheet accordingly. You can use a similar technique to delete a row in a worksheet.

9 Compare your screen with Figure 1.53, and then **Save** 💾 your workbook.

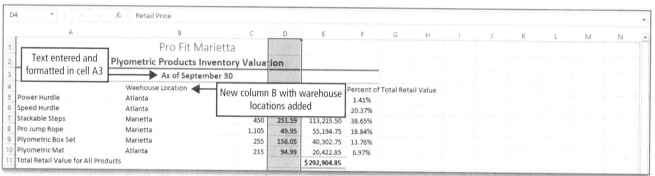

Figure 1.53

Activity 1.26 | Adjusting Column Widths and Wrapping Text

MOS
1.3.2, 2.2.4

Use the Wrap Text command to display the contents of a cell on multiple lines.

1 In the **column heading area**, point to the **column B** heading to display the ⬇ pointer, and then drag to the right to select **columns B:F**.

2 With the columns selected, in the **column heading area**, point to the right boundary of any of the selected columns to display the ➕ pointer, and then drag to set the width to **95 pixels**.

Use this technique to format multiple columns or rows simultaneously.

⌨ MAC TIP Set the width of columns B:F to 12.83. (82 pixels)

3 Select the range **B4:F4** that comprises the column headings, and then on the **Home tab**, in the **Alignment group**, click **Wrap Text** 📖. Notice that the row height adjusts to display the column titles on multiple lines.

4 With the range **B4:F4** still selected, in the **Alignment group**, click **Center** ≡ and **Middle Align** ≡. With the range **B4:F4** still selected, apply the **Heading 4** cell style.

> The *Middle Align* command aligns text so that it is centered between the top and bottom of the cell.

5 Select the range **B5:B10**, and then in the **Alignment group**, click **Center** ≡. Click cell **A11**, and then from the **Cell Styles** gallery, under **Themed Cell Styles**, click **40% - Accent1**. **Save** 💾 your workbook.

Activity 1.27 | Changing Theme Colors

You can change only the theme *colors* of a workbook—without changing the theme fonts or effects.

1 On the **Page Layout tab**, in the **Themes group**, click **Colors**, and then click **Green** to change the Theme Color. Click any blank cell, and then compare your screen with Figure 1.54.

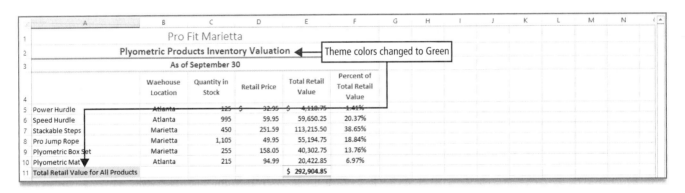

Figure 1.54

2 On the **Page Layout tab**, in the **Page Setup group**, click **Margins**, and then click **Custom Margins**.

3 In the **Page Setup** dialog box, on the **Margins tab**, under **Center on page**, select the **Horizontally** check box.

> This action will center the data and chart horizontally on the page, as shown in the Preview area.

4 Click the **Header/Footer tab**, and then in the center of the dialog box, click **Custom Footer**. In the **Footer** dialog box, with your insertion point blinking in the **Left section**, on the row of buttons, click **Insert File Name** 📄.

> *&[File]* displays in the Left section. Here you can type or insert information from the row of buttons into the left, middle, or right section of the footer. The Custom Header button displays a similar screen to enter information in the header of the worksheet.

5 Click **OK** two times.

6 Click the **File tab** to display Backstage view, on the left click the **Info tab**, and then in the lower right corner, click **Show All Properties**.

7 As the **Tags**, type **plyo products, inventory** and as the **Subject**, type your course name and section number. Be sure your name displays in the **Author box**, or edit it if necessary.

8 On the left, click **Print** to view the **Print Preview**. At the bottom of the **Print Preview**, click **Next Page** ▶, and notice that as currently formatted, the worksheet occupies two pages.

9 Under **Settings**, click **Portrait Orientation**, and then click **Landscape Orientation**. Compare your screen with Figure 1.55.

You can change the orientation on the Page Layout tab, or here, in Print Preview. Because it is in the Print Preview that you will often see adjustments that need to be made, commonly used settings display on the Print tab in Backstage view.

 MAC TIP At the bottom of the Print dialog box, click Show Details. Select and click the Landscape Orientation button.

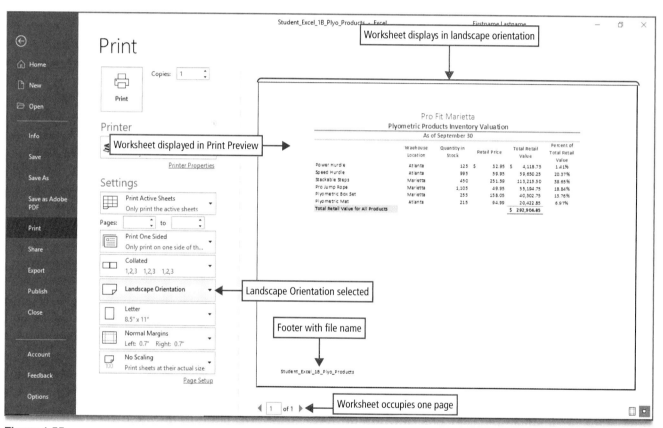

Figure 1.55

10 On the left, click **Save**.

11 In the upper right corner of your screen, click **Close** ✕ to close Excel.

For Non-MyLab Submissions: Determine What Your Instructor Requires for Submission

As directed by your instructor, submit your completed Excel workbook.

---

12 In **MyLab IT**, locate and click the Grader Project **Excel 1B Plyo Products**. In **step 3**, under **Upload Completed Assignment**, click **Choose File**. In the **Open** dialog box, navigate to your **Excel Chapter 1 folder**, and then click your **Student_Excel_1B_Plyo_Products** file one time to select it. In the lower right corner of the **Open** dialog box, click **Open**.

The name of your selected file displays above the Upload button.

13 To submit your file to **MyLab IT** for grading, click **Upload**, wait a moment for a green **Success!** message, and then in **step 4**, click the blue **Submit for Grading** button. Click **Close Assignment** to return to your list of **Course Materials**.

You have completed Project 1B `END`

Objective | Creating an Inventory Valuation Report

ALERT   Working with Web-Based Applications and Service

Computer programs and services on the web receive continuous updates and improvements, so the steps to complete this web-based Activity may differ from the ones shown. You can often look at the screens and the information presented to determine how to complete the Activity.

   If you do not already have a Google account, you will need to create one before you being this Activity. Go to **http://google.com** and in the upper right corner, click Sign In. On the Sign In screen, click Create Account. On the Create your Google Account page, complete the form, read and agree to the Terms of Service and Privacy Policy, and then click Next step. On the Welcome screen, click Get Started.

Activity | Creating an Inventory Valuation Report Using Google Sheets

   In this Activity, you will use Google Sheets to create an inventory valuation report similar to the one you created in Project 1B.

1 From the desktop, open your browser (a browser other than Edge), navigate to **https://www.google.com** and then click the **Google Apps** menu ⊞. Click **Drive**, and then if necessary, sign in to your Google account.

2 Open your **GO! Web Projects** folder—or click New to create and then open this folder if necessary.

3 In the upper left, click **New**, and then click **Google Sheets**. From your Windows taskbar, open **File Explorer**, navigate to the files you downloaded for this chapter, and then in the **File List**, double-click the Word document **e01B_Web**. To complete this project quickly and eliminate extra typing, you will copy the data from a Word document.

4 In the displayed Word document, click anywhere in the text, and then in the upper left corner, click to select the **Table Select** icon ⊞ to select the entire Word table. Right-click anywhere over the selection, and then click **Copy**. **Close** Word. **Close** the **File Explorer** window.

5 In your blank Google Sheet, with cell **A1** active, point to cell **A1**, right-click, and then click **Paste**. In the column heading area, point to the border between **column A** and **column B** to display the ↔ pointer, and then widen **column A** slightly so that all of the data displays.

6 Select the range **A1:E1** and on the toolbar, click **Merge cells**. On the toolbar, click the **Horizontal Align button arrow** ≣ and then click **Center** ≣. Repeat for the range **A2:E2**, and then apply **Bold** B to cells **A1** and **A2**.

7 Select the range **B3:E3**, on the menu bar click **Format**, point to **Text wrapping**, and then click **Wrap**. **Center** these column titles and apply **Bold** B.

8 Select the range **C4:C9**, on the menu bar click **Format**, point to **Number**, click **Number**, and then on the toolbar, click **Decrease decimal places** ≣ two times.

9 Click cell **E4**, type = and then click cell **C4**. Type * and then click cell **D4**. Press Enter. Click cell **E4**, point to the fill handle in the lower right corner of the cell, and then drag down to cell **C9**.

10 Select the range **E4:E9**. On the toolbar, click **Functions** Σ ·, click **SUM**, and then press Enter to total the column and place the result in cell **E10**.

11 Select the range **D4:E4**, hold down Ctrl, and then select cell **D10**. On the menu bar, click **Format**, point to **Number**, and then click **Currency**.

12 Select cell **A10**, hold down Ctrl, and then select cell **E10**. Apply **Bold** B.

13 Click cell **A1**, hold down Ctrl, and then click cell **A2**, cell **A10**, and cell **E10**. With the four cells selected, on the toolbar, click **Fill color** ◆ ·, and then in the fourth column, click the third color—**light yellow 3**.

14 At the top of the worksheet, click the text *Untitled spreadsheet*, and then using your own name, type **Lastname_Firstname_Ex_1B_Web** and press Enter.

»» **GO!** With Google continues on next page

»» GO! With Google Sheets

15 If you are instructed to submit your file to your instructor, you can either share the file through Google Drive, or create a PDF or Excel file. Ask your instructor in what format he or she would like to receive your file.

16 Close ⊞ the browser tab—a new Google Sheet always opens in a new window in your browser; your work is automatically saved. Notice that your new Google Sheet displays in the file list on your Google Drive. Sign out of your Google account.

Figure 1A

wavebreakmedia/Shutterstock, Monkey Business Images/Fotolia, Ivanko80/Shutterstock, Monkey Business Images/Shutterstock

Microsoft Office Specialist (MOS) Skills in This Chapter	
Project 1A	**Project 1B**
1.2.2 Navigate to named cells, ranges, or workbook elements	**2.2.2** Modify cell alignment, orientation, and indentation
1.3.1 Modify page setup	**2.2.4** Wrap text within cells
1.3.2 Adjust row height and column width	**2.2.5** Apply number format
1.3.3 Customize headers and footers	**2.2.7** Apply cell styles
1.4.5 Modify basic workbook properties	**4.1.1** Insert relative, absolute, and mixed references
1.4.6 Display formulas	
1.5.1 Set a print area	
1.5.3 Configure print settings	
2.1.2 Fill cells by using Auto Fill	
2.2.1 Merge and unmerge cells	
2.2.5 Apply number format	
2.2.7 Apply cell styles	
2.4.1 Insert Sparklines	
4.1.1 Insert relative, absolute, and mixed references	
4.2.1 Perform calculations by using the SUM function	
5.1.1 Create charts	
5.2.2 Switch between rows and columns in source data	
5.2.3 Add and modify chart elements	
5.3.1 Apply chart layouts	

Build Your E-Portfolio

An E-Portfolio is a collection of evidence, stored electronically, that showcases what you have accomplished while completing your education. Collecting and then sharing your work products with potential employers reflects your academic and career goals. Your completed documents from the following projects are good examples to show what you have learned: 1G, 1K, and 1L.

GO! for Job Success

Video: How to Succeed in an Interview

Your instructor may assign this video to your class, and then ask you to think about, or discuss with your classmates, these questions:

g-stockstudio/ Shutterstock

> Can you think of two or three behaviors that Lee might want to change before he interviews with another company?

> If you were going on an interview, which of Connie's behaviors would you imitate?

> If you were the interviewer, Maria, would you have handled anything differently with either candidate?

End of Chapter

Summary

In Excel, you work with worksheets that are contained in a workbook. A worksheet is formatted as a pattern of uniformly spaced horizontal rows and vertical columns, the intersection of which forms a cell.

A cell can contain a constant value—referred to as a value—or a formula, which is an equation that performs mathematical calculations on the values in your worksheet. Common values are text and numbers.

Charts provide a graphic representation of data in a worksheet. Use the Recommended Charts feature to display customized charts that, according to Excel's calculations, will best represent your data.

You can insert sparklines in an Excel worksheet, which are tiny charts embedded in a cell that give a visual trend summary alongside your data. A sparkline makes a pattern more obvious to the eye.

GO! Learn It Online

Review the concepts, key terms, and MOS skills in this chapter by completing these online challenges, which you can find at **MyLab IT**.

Chapter Quiz: Answer matching and multiple choice questions to test what you learned in this chapter.

Lessons on the GO!: Learn how to use all the new apps and features as they are introduced by Microsoft.

MOS Prep Quiz: Answer questions to review the MOS skills that you practiced in this chapter.

GO! Collaborative Team Project (Available in Instructor Resource Center)

If your instructor assigns this project to your class, you can expect to work with one or more of your classmates—either in person or by using internet tools—to create work products similar to those that you created in this chapter. A team is a group of workers who work together to solve a problem, make a decision, or create a work product. Collaboration is when you work together with others as a team in an intellectual endeavor to complete a shared task or achieve a shared goal.

Monkey Business Images/ Fotolia

Project Guide for Excel Chapter 1

Your instructor will assign Projects from this list to ensure your learning and assess your knowledge.

Project	Apply Skills from These Chapter Objectives	Project Type		Project Location
1A MyLab IT	Objectives 1-6 from Project 1A	**1A Instructional Project (Grader Project)** Guided instruction to learn the skills in Project 1A.	Instruction	In **MyLab IT** and in text
1B MyLab IT	Objectives 7–11 from Project 1B	**1B Instructional Project (Grader Project)** Guided instruction to learn the skills in Project 1B.	Instruction	In **MyLab IT** and in text
1C	Objectives 1–6 from Project 1A	**1C Skills Review (Scorecard Grading)** A guided review of the skills from Project 1A.	Review	In text
1D	Objectives 7–11 from Project 1B	**1D Skills Review (Scorecard Grading)** A guided review of the skills from Project 1B.	Review	In text
1E MyLab IT	Objectives 1–6 from Project 1A	**1E Mastery (Grader Project)** A demonstration of your mastery of the skills in Project 1A with extensive decision-making.	Mastery and Transfer of Learning	In **MyLab IT** and in text
1F MyLab IT	Objectives 7–11 from Project 1B	**1F Mastery (Grader Project)** A demonstration of your mastery of the skills in Project 1B with extensive decision-making.	Mastery and Transfer of Learning	In **MyLab IT** and in text
1G MyLab IT	Objectives 1–11 from Projects 1A and 1B	**1G Mastery (Grader Project)** A demonstration of your mastery of the skills in Projects 1A and 1B with extensive decision-making.	Mastery and Transfer of Learning	In **MyLab IT** and in text
1H	Combination of Objectives from Projects 1A and 1B	**1H GO! Fix It (Scorecard Grading)** A demonstration of your mastery of the skills in Projects 1A and 1B by creating a correct result from a document that contains errors you must find.	Critical Thinking	IRC
1I	Combination of Objectives from Projects 1A and 1B	**1I GO! Make It (Scorecard Grading)** A demonstration of your mastery of the skills in Projects 1A and 1B by creating a result from a supplied picture.	Critical Thinking	IRC
1J	Combination of Objectives from Projects 1A and 1B	**1J GO! Solve It (Rubric Grading)** A demonstration of your mastery of the skills in Projects 1A and 1B, your decision-making skills, and your critical thinking skills. A task-specific rubric helps you self-assess your result.	Critical Thinking	IRC
1K	Combination of Objectives from Projects 1A and 1B	**1K GO! Solve It (Rubric Grading)** A demonstration of your mastery of the skills in Projects 1A and 1B, your decision-making skills, and your critical thinking skills. A task-specific rubric helps you self-assess your result.	Critical Thinking	In text
1L	Combination of Objectives from Projects 1A and 1B	**1L GO! Think (Rubric Grading)** A demonstration of your understanding of the Chapter concepts applied in a manner that you would outside of college. An analytic rubric helps you and your instructor grade the quality of your work by comparing it to the work an expert in the discipline would create.	Critical Thinking	In text
1M	Combination of Objectives from Projects 1A and 1B	**1M GO! Think (Rubric Grading)** A demonstration of your understanding of the Chapter concepts applied in a manner that you would outside of college. An analytic rubric helps you and your instructor grade the quality of your work by comparing it to the work an expert in the discipline would create.	Critical Thinking	IRC
1N	Combination of Objectives from Projects 1A and 1B	**1N You and GO! (Rubric Grading)** A demonstration of your understanding of the Chapter concepts applied in a manner that you would in a personal situation. An analytic rubric helps you and your instructor grade the quality of your work.	Critical Thinking	IRC
1O	Combination of Objectives from Projects 1A and 1B	**1O Cumulative Group Project for Excel Chapter 1** A demonstration of your understanding of concepts and your ability to work collaboratively in a group role-playing assessment, requiring both collaboration and self-management.		IRC

Glossary

Glossary of Chapter Key Terms

Absolute cell reference A cell reference that refers to cells by their fixed position in a worksheet; an absolute cell reference remains the same when the formula is copied.

Accounting Number Format The Excel number format that applies a thousand comma separator where appropriate, inserts a fixed U.S. dollar sign aligned at the left edge of the cell, applies two decimal places, and leaves a small amount of space at the right edge of the cell to accommodate a parenthesis for negative numbers.

Active cell The cell, surrounded by a black border, ready to receive data or be affected by the next Excel command.

Arithmetic operators The symbols +, -, *, /, %, and ^ used to denote addition, subtraction (or negation), multiplication, division, percentage, and exponentiation in an Excel formula.

Auto Fill An Excel feature that generates and extends values into adjacent cells based on the values of selected cells.

AutoCalculate A feature that displays three calculations in the status bar by default—Average, Count, and Sum—when you select a range of numerical data.

AutoComplete A feature that speeds your typing and lessens the likelihood of errors; if the first few characters you type in a cell match an existing entry in the column, Excel fills in the remaining characters for you.

AutoFit An Excel feature that adjusts the width of a column to fit the cell content of the widest cell in the column.

AutoSum A button that provides quick access to the SUM function.

Category axis The area along the bottom of a chart that identifies the categories of data; also referred to as the x-axis.

Category labels The labels that display along the bottom of a chart to identify the categories of data; Excel uses the row titles as the category names.

Cell The intersection of a column and a row.

Cell address Another name for a cell reference.

Cell content Anything typed into a cell.

Cell reference The identification of a specific cell by its intersecting column letter and row number.

Cell style A defined set of formatting characteristics, such as font, font size, font color, cell borders, and cell shading.

Chart The graphic representation of data in a worksheet; data presented as a chart is usually easier to understand than a table of numbers.

Chart Elements button A button that enables you to add, remove, or change chart elements such as the title, legend, gridlines, and data labels.

Chart Filters button A button that enables you to change which data displays in the chart.

Chart layout The combination of chart elements that can be displayed in a chart such as a title, legend, labels for the columns, and the table of charted cells.

Chart style The overall visual look of a chart in terms of its graphic effects, colors, and backgrounds; for example, you can have flat or beveled columns, colors that are solid or transparent, and backgrounds that are dark or light.

Chart Styles button A button that enables you to set a style and color scheme for your chart.

Chart Styles gallery A group of predesigned chart styles that you can apply to an Excel chart.

Chart types Various chart formats used in a way that is meaningful to the reader; common examples are column charts, pie charts, and line charts.

Column A vertical group of cells in a worksheet.

Column chart A chart in which the data is arranged in columns and that is useful for showing data changes over a period of time or for illustrating comparisons among items.

Column heading The letter that displays at the top of a vertical group of cells in a worksheet; beginning with the first letter of the alphabet, a unique letter or combination of letters identifies each column.

Comma Style The Excel number format that inserts thousand comma separators where appropriate and applies two decimal places; Comma Style also leaves space at the right to accommodate a parenthesis when negative numbers are present.

Constant value Numbers, text, dates, or times of day that you type into a cell.

Context sensitive A command associated with the currently selected or active object; often activated by right-clicking a screen item.

Data Text or numbers in a cell.

Data marker A column, bar, area, dot, pie slice, or other symbol in a chart that represents a single data point; related data points form a data series.

Data point A value that originates in a worksheet cell and that is represented in a chart by a data marker.

Data series Related data points represented by data markers; each data series has a unique color or pattern represented in the chart legend.

Displayed value The data that displays in a cell.

Excel pointer An Excel window element with which you can display the location of the pointer.

Expand Formula Bar button An Excel window element with which you can increase the height of the Formula Bar to display lengthy cell content.

Expand horizontal scroll bar button An Excel window element with which you can increase the width of the horizontal scroll bar.

Fill handle The small square in the lower right corner of a selected cell.

Format Changing the appearance of cells and worksheet elements to make a worksheet attractive and easy to read.

Formula An equation that performs mathematical calculations on values in a worksheet.

Formula Bar An element in the Excel window that displays the value or formula contained in the active cell; here you can also enter or edit values or formulas.

Function A predefined formula—a formula that Excel has already built for you—that performs calculations by using specific values in a particular order.

General format The default format that Excel applies to numbers; this format has no specific characteristics—whatever you type in the cell will display, with the exception that trailing zeros to the right of a decimal point will not display.

Label Another name for a text value, and which usually provides information about number values.

Glossary

Left alignment The cell format in which characters align at the left edge of the cell; this is the default for text entries and is an example of formatting information stored in a cell.

Legend A chart element that identifies the patterns or colors that are assigned to the categories in the chart.

Lettered column headings The area along the top edge of a worksheet that identifies each column with a unique letter or combination of letters.

Merge & Center A command that joins selected cells in an Excel worksheet into one larger cell and centers the contents in the merged cell.

Middle Align An alignment command that centers text between the top and bottom of a cell.

Name Box An element of the Excel window that displays the name of the selected cell, table, chart, or object.

Normal view A screen view that maximizes the number of cells visible on your screen and keeps the column letters and row numbers close to the columns and rows.

Number format A specific way in which Excel displays numbers in a cell.

Number values Constant values consisting of only numbers.

Numbered row headings The area along the left edge of a worksheet that identifies each row with a unique number.

Operators The symbols with which you can specify the type of calculation you want to perform in an Excel formula.

Picture element A point of light measured in dots per square inch on a screen; 64 pixels equals 8.43 characters, which is the average number of characters that will fit in a cell in an Excel worksheet using the default font.

Pixel The abbreviated name for a picture element.

Point and click method The technique of constructing a formula by pointing to and then clicking cells; this method is convenient when the referenced cells are not adjacent to one another.

Quick Analysis Tool A tool that displays in the lower right corner of a selected range, with which you can analyze your data by using Excel tools such as charts, color-coding, and formulas.

Range Two or more selected cells on a worksheet that are adjacent or nonadjacent; because the range is treated as a single unit, you can make the same changes or combination of changes to more than one cell at a time.

Range finder An Excel feature that outlines cells in color to indicate which cells are used in a formula; useful for verifying which cells are referenced in a formula.

Recommended Charts An Excel feature that displays a customized set of charts that, according to Excel's calculations, will best fit your data based on the range of data that you select.

Relative cell reference In a formula, the address of a cell based on the relative positions of the cell that contains the formula and the cell referred to in the formula.

Rounding A procedure in which you determine which digit at the right of the number will be the last digit displayed and then increase it by one if the next digit to its right is 5, 6, 7, 8, or 9.

Row A horizontal group of cells in a worksheet.

Row heading The numbers along the left side of an Excel worksheet that designate the row numbers.

Scaling The process of shrinking the width and/or height of printed output to fit a maximum number of pages.

Select All box A box in the upper left corner of the worksheet grid that, when clicked, selects all the cells in a worksheet.

Series A group of things that come one after another in succession; for example, January, February, March, and so on.

Sheet tab scrolling buttons Buttons to the left of the sheet tabs used to display Excel sheet tabs that are not in view; used when there are more sheet tabs than will display in the space provided.

Sheet tabs The labels along the lower border of the Excel window that identify each worksheet.

Show Formulas A command that displays the formula in each cell instead of the resulting value.

Sparkline A tiny chart in the background of a cell that gives a visual trend summary alongside your data; makes a pattern more obvious.

Spreadsheet Another name for a worksheet.

Status bar The area along the lower edge of the Excel window that displays, on the left side, the current cell mode, page number, and worksheet information; on the right side, when numerical data is selected, common calculations such as Sum and Average display.

SUM function A predefined formula that adds all the numbers in a selected range of cells.

Switch Row/Column A charting command to swap the data over the axis—data being charted on the vertical axis will move to the horizontal axis and vice versa.

Text values Constant values consisting of only text, and which usually provide information about number values; also referred to as labels.

Theme A predefined set of colors, fonts, lines, and fill effects that coordinate with each other.

Underlying formula The formula entered in a cell and visible only on the Formula Bar.

Underlying value The data that displays in the Formula Bar.

Value Another name for a constant value.

Value axis A numerical scale on the left side of a chart that shows the range of numbers for the data points; also referred to as the y-axis.

Workbook An Excel file that contains one or more worksheets.

Worksheet The primary document that you use in Excel to work with and store data, and which is formatted as a pattern of uniformly spaced horizontal and vertical lines.

Worksheet grid area A part of the Excel window that displays the columns and rows that intersect to form the worksheet's cells.

X-axis Another name for the horizontal (category) axis.

Y-axis Another name for the vertical (value) axis.

Chapter Review

In the following Skills Review, you will create a new Excel worksheet with a chart that summarizes the first quarter sales of fitness equipment for step training. Your completed worksheet will look similar to Figure 1.56.

Apply 1A skills from these Objectives:

1. Create, Save, and Navigate an Excel Workbook
2. Enter Data in a Worksheet
3. Construct and Copy Formulas and Use the SUM Function
4. Format Cells with Merge & Center, Cell Styles, and Themes
5. Chart Data to Create a Column Chart and Insert Sparklines
6. Print a Worksheet, Display Formulas, and Close Excel

Project Files

For Project 1C, you will need the following file:

New blank Excel workbook

You will save your workbook as:

Lastname_Firstname_1C_Step_Sales

Project Results

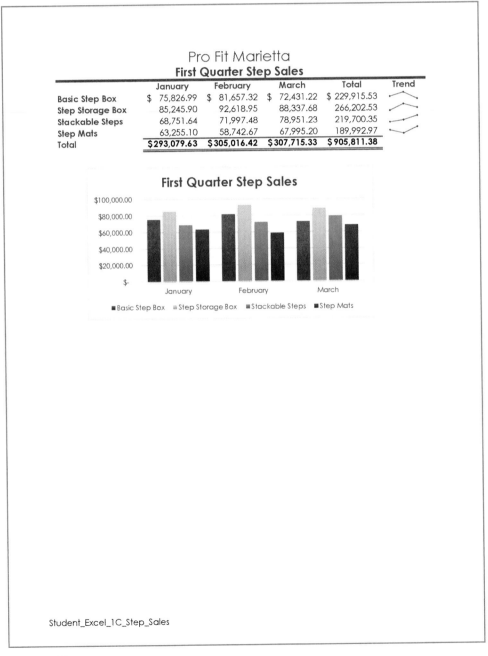

Figure 1.56

Chapter Review

Skills Review: Project 1C Step Sales (continued)

1 Start Excel and open a new blank workbook. Click the **File tab** to display **Backstage** view, click **Save As**, and then navigate to your **Excel Chapter 1** folder. In the **File name** box, using your own name, type **Lastname_Firstname_1C_Step_Sales** and press Enter.

a. With cell **A1** as the active cell, type the worksheet title **Pro Fit Marietta** and then press Enter. In cell **A2**, type the worksheet subtitle **First Quarter Step Sales** and then press Enter.

b. Click in cell **A4**, type **Basic Step Box** and then press Enter. In cell **A5**, type **Step Storage Box** and then press Enter. In cell **A6**, type **Stackable Steps** and then press Enter. In cell **A7**, type **Step Mats** and then press Enter. In cell **A8**, type **Total** and then press Enter.

c. Click cell **B3**. Type **January** and then in the **Formula Bar**, click **Enter** to keep cell **B3** the active cell. With **B3** as the active cell, point to the fill handle in the lower right corner of the selected cell, drag to the right to cell **D3**, and then release the mouse button to enter the text *February* and *March*.

d. Press Ctrl + Home to make cell **A1** the active cell. In the **column heading area**, point to the vertical line between **column A** and **column B** to display the ✛ pointer, hold down the left mouse button, and drag to the right to increase the width of **column A** to **130 pixels**.

e. Point to cell **B3**, and then drag across to select cells **B3** and **C3** and **D3**. With the range **B3:D3** selected, on the **Home tab**, in the **Alignment group**, click **Center**.

f. Click cell **B4**, type **75826.99** and press Tab to make cell **C4** active. Enter the remaining values, as shown in **Table 1** below, pressing Tab to move across the rows and pressing Enter to move down the columns.

2 Click cell **B8** to make it the active cell and type =

a. At the insertion point, type **b4** and then type + Type **b5** and then type **+b6+b7** Press Enter. Your result is *293079.6*.

b. Click in cell **C8**. Type = and then click cell **C4**. Type + and then click cell **C5**. Repeat this process to complete the formula to add cells **C6** and **C7** to the formula, and then press Enter. Your result is *305016.4*.

c. Click cell **D8**. On the **Home tab**, in the **Editing group**, click **AutoSum**, and then press Enter to construct a formula by using the SUM function. Your result is *307715.3*.

d. In cell **E3** type **Total** and press Enter. With cell **E4** as the active cell, on the **Home tab**, in the **Editing group**, click **AutoSum**. On the **Formula Bar**, click **Enter** to display the result and keep cell **E4** active.

e. With cell **E4** active, point to the fill handle in the lower right corner of the cell. Drag down through cell **E8**, and then release the mouse button to copy the formula with relative cell references down to sum each row.

3 Click cell **F3**. Type **Trend** and then press Enter.

a. Select the range **A1:F1**, and then on the **Home tab**, in the **Alignment group**, click **Merge & Center**. Select the range **A2:F2** and **Merge & Center** the selection.

b. Click cell **A1**. In the **Styles group**, click **Cell Styles**. Under **Titles and Headings**, click **Title**. Click cell **A2**, display the **Cell Styles** gallery, and then click **Heading 1**.

c. Select the range **B3:F3**, hold down Ctrl, and then select the range **A4:A8**. From the **Cell Styles** gallery, click **Heading 4** to apply this cell style to the column and row titles.

d. Select the range **B4:E4**, hold down Ctrl, and then select the range **B8:E8**. On the **Home tab**, in the **Number group**, click **Accounting Number Format**. Select the range **B5:E7**, and then in the **Number group**, click **Comma Style**. Select the range **B8:E8**. From the **Styles group**, display the **Cell Styles** gallery, and then under **Titles and Headings**, click **Total**.

Table 1			
	January	February	March
Basic Step Box	75826.99	81657.32	72431.22
Step Storage Box	85245.90	92618.95	88337.68
Stackable Steps	68751.64	71997.48	78951.23
Step Mats	63255.10	58742.67	67995.20

Chapter Review

e. On the ribbon, click the **Page Layout tab**, and then in the **Themes group**, click **Themes** to display the **Themes** gallery. Click the **Ion** theme. (This theme widens the columns slightly.) On the Quick Access Toolbar, click **Save**.

4 Select the range **A3:D7**, which includes the row titles, the column titles and the data without the totals. Click the **Insert tab**, and then in the **Charts group**, click **Recommended Charts**. In the **Insert Chart** dialog box, scroll down and click the **Clustered Column** chart in which *each month* displays its *sales for each type of step training equipment*. Click **OK**.

a. In the chart, click anywhere in the text *Chart Title* to select the text box. Watch the **Formula Bar** as you type **First** and then let AutoComplete complete the title by pressing [Enter].

b. Click in a white area just slightly *inside* the chart border to deselect the chart title but keep the chart selected. To the right of the chart, click the second button—the **Chart Styles** button [✏].

Be sure the **Style tab** is active. Use the scroll bar to scroll down, and then by using the ScreenTips, locate and click **Style 6**.

c. At the top of the gallery, click **Color**. Under **Colorful**, click the second row of colors to apply this variation of the theme colors.

d. Point to the top border of the chart to display the [↖] pointer, and then drag the upper left corner of the chart just to the center of cell **A10** to visually center it below the data.

5 Click an empty cell to deselect the chart, and then select the range **B4:D7**. Click the **Insert tab**, and then in the **Sparklines group**, click **Line**. In the **Create Sparklines** dialog box, in the **Location Range** box, type **f4:f7** and then click **OK** to insert the sparklines.

a. On the **Design tab**, in the **Show group**, select the **Markers** check box to display markers in the sparklines.

b. On the **Design tab**, in the **Style group**, click **More** [▾] and then in the first row, click the second style.

6 Click cell **A1** to deselect the chart. Click the **Page Layout tab**, and then in the **Page Setup group**, click **Margins**. Click **Custom Margins**. In the **Page Setup** dialog box, on the **Margins tab**, under **Center on page**, select the **Horizontally** check box.

a. Click the **Header/Footer tab**, and then click **Custom Footer**. With your insertion point in the **Left section**, click **Insert File Name**. Click **OK** two times.

b. Click the **File tab** to display **Backstage** view; if necessary, on the left, click the **Info tab**. In the lower right corner, click **Show All Properties**. As the **Tags**, type **step sales, 1st quarter** In the **Subject** box, type your course name and section number. Be sure your name displays as the author—edit if necessary.

c. On the left, click **Save**.

d. Print or submit your workbook electronically as directed by your instructor. If required by your instructor, print or create an electronic version of your worksheet with formulas displayed by using the instructions at the end of Project 1A. **Close** Excel without saving so that you do not save the changes you made to print formulas. (Mac users: if necessary to fit on one page, on the Page Layout tab, in the Scale to Fit group, set the Width and Height to 1 page.)

You have completed Project 1C **END**

Chapter Review

Skills Review | **Project 1D Band and Tubing Inventory**

Apply 1B skills from these Objectives:

7. Check Spelling in a Worksheet
8. Enter Data by Range
9. Construct Formulas for Mathematical Operations
10. Edit Values in a Worksheet
11. Format a Worksheet

In the following Skills Review, you will create a worksheet that summarizes the inventory of band and tubing exercise equipment. Your completed worksheet will look similar to Figure 1.57.

Project Files

For Project 1D, you will need the following file:

New blank Excel workbook

You will save your workbook as:

Lastname_Firstname_1D_Band_Inventory

Project Results

Pro Fit Marietta
Band and Tubing Inventory
As of June 30

	Material	Quantity in Stock	Retail Price	Total Retail Value	Percent of Total Retail Value
Super Strength Bands	Latex	225	$ 48.98	$ 11,020.50	25.16%
Medium Tubing	Rubber	198	27.95	5,534.10	12.64%
Resistance Band, Average	Latex	165	42.95	7,086.75	16.18%
Mini Bands, Medium	Latex	245	25.95	6,357.75	14.52%
Mini Bands, Heavy	Rubber	175	32.95	5,766.25	13.17%
Heavy Tubing	Latex	187	42.95	8,031.65	18.34%
Total Retail Value for All Products				$ 43,797.00	

Student_Excel_1D_Band_Inventory

Figure 1.57

Chapter Review

1 Start Excel and display a new blank workbook. **Save** the workbook in your **Excel Chapter 1** folder as **Lastname_Firstname_1D_Band_Inventory** In cell **A1**, type **Pro Fit Marietta** and in cell **A2**, type **Band and Tubing Inventory**

a. Click cell **B3**, type **Quantity in Stock** and press [Tab]. In cell **C3**, type **Average Cost** and press [Tab]. In cell **D3**, type **Retail Price** and press [Tab]. In cell **E3**, type **Total Retail Value** and press [Tab]. In cell **F3**, type **Percent of Total Retail Value** and press [Enter].

b. Click cell **A4**, type **Super Strength Bands** and press [Enter]. In the range **A5:A10**, type the remaining row titles as shown below, including any misspelled words.

   Medium Tubing
   Resistnce Band, Average
   Mini Bands, Medium
   Mini Bands, Heavy
   Heavy Tubing
   Total Retail Value for All Products

c. Press [Ctrl] + [Home] to move to the top of your worksheet. On the **Review tab**, in the **Proofing group**, click **Spelling**. Correct *Resistnce* to **Resistance** and any other spelling errors you may have made, and then when the message displays, *Spell check complete. You're good to go!* click **OK**.

d. In the **column heading area**, point to the right boundary of **column A** to display the [+] pointer, and then drag to the right to widen **column A** to **225** pixels.

e. In the **column heading area**, point to the **column B** heading to display the [↓] pointer, and then drag to the right to select **columns B:F**. With the columns selected, in the **column heading area**, point to the right boundary of any of the selected columns, and then drag to the right to set the width to **100 pixels**.

f. Select the range **A1:F1.** On the **Home tab**, in the **Alignment group**, click **Merge & Center**, and then from the **Cell Styles** gallery, apply the **Title** style. Select the range **A2:F2. Merge & Center** the text across the selection, and then from the **Cell Styles** gallery, apply the **Heading 1** style.

2 On the **Page Layout tab**, in the **Themes group**, change the **Colors** to **Blue Green**. Select the empty range **B4:D9**. With cell **B4** active in the range, type **225** and then press [Enter].

a. With cell **B5** active in the range, and pressing [Enter] after each entry, type the following data in the *Quantity in Stock* column:

   198
   265
   245
   175
   187

b. With the selected range still active, from the following table, beginning in cell **C4** and pressing [Enter] after each entry, enter the following data for the **Average Cost** column and then the **Retail Price** column. If you prefer, type without selecting the range first; recall that this is optional.

Average Cost	Retail Price
22.75	48.98
15.95	27.95
26.90	42.95
12.95	25.95
18.75	32.95
26.90	42.95

3 In cell **E4**, type **=b4*d4** and then press [Enter] to construct a formula that calculates the *Total Retail Value* of the *Super Strength Bands* (Quantity in Stock X Retail Price).

a. Click cell **E4**, position your pointer over the fill handle, and then drag down through cell **E9** to copy the formula with relative cell references.

b. Select the range **B4:B9**, and then on the **Home tab**, in the **Number group**, click **Comma Style**. Then, in the **Number group**, click **Decrease Decimal** two times to remove the decimal places from these non-currency values.

Chapter Review

c. To calculate the *Total Retail Value for All Products*, select the range **E4:E9**, and then in the lower right corner of the selected range, click the **Quick Analysis** button.

d. In the gallery, click **Totals**, and then click the *first* **Sum** button, which visually indicates that the column will be summed with a result at the bottom of the column.

e. Select the range **C5:E9** and apply the **Comma Style**. Select the range **C4:E4**, hold down Ctrl, and then click cell **E10**. With the nonadjacent cells selected, apply the **Accounting Number Format**. Click cell **E10**, and then from the **Cell Styles** gallery, apply the **Total** style.

f. Click cell **F4**, type = and then click cell **E4**. Type / and then click cell **E10**. Press F4 to make the reference to cell *E10* absolute, and then on the **Formula Bar**, click **Enter** so that cell **F4** remains the active cell. (Mac users: press command ⌘ + T.)

g. Drag the fill handle to copy the formula down through cell **F9**. Point to cell **B6**, and then double-click to place the insertion point within the cell. Use the arrow keys to move the insertion point to the left or right of *2*, and use either Del or Backspace to delete *2*, and then type **1** and press Enter so that the new *Quantity in Stock* is *165*. Notice the recalculations in the worksheet.

4 Select the range **F4:F9**, and then in the **Number group**, click **Percent Style**. Click **Increase Decimal** two times, and then **Center** the selection.

a. In the **row heading area** on the left side of your screen, point to **row 3** to display the → pointer, and then right-click to simultaneously select the row and display a shortcut menu. On the shortcut menu, click **Insert** to insert a new **row 3**.

b. Click cell **A3**, type **As of June 30** and then on the **Formula Bar**, click **Enter** to keep cell **A3** as the active cell. **Merge & Center** the text across the range **A3:F3**, and then apply the **Heading 2** cell style.

5 In the **column heading area**, point to **column B**. When the ↓ pointer displays, right-click, and then click **Insert** to insert a new column.

a. Click cell **B4**, type **Material** and then press Enter. In cell **B5**, type **Latex** and then press Enter. In cell **B6**, type **Rubber** and then press Enter.

b. Using AutoComplete to speed your typing by pressing Enter as soon as the AutoComplete suggestion displays, in cells **B7**, **B8**, and **B10**, type **Latex** and in cell **B9**, type **Rubber**

c. In the **column heading area**, point to the right boundary of **column B**, and then drag to the left and set the width to **90 pixels**. In the **column heading area**, point to **column D**, right-click, and then click **Delete**.

d. Select the column titles in the range **B4:F4**, and then on the **Home tab**, in the **Alignment group**, click **Wrap Text**, **Center**, and **Middle Align**. With the range still selected, apply the **Heading 4** cell style.

e. Click cell **A11**, and then from the **Cell Styles** gallery, under **Themed Cell Styles**, click **40% - Accent1**.

6 Click the **Page Layout tab**, and then in the **Page Setup group**, click **Margins**. Click **Custom Margins**. In the **Page Setup** dialog box, on the **Margins tab**, under **Center on page**, select the **Horizontally** check box.

a. Click the **Header/Footer tab**, and then click **Custom Footer**. With your insertion point in the **Left section**, click **Insert File Name**. Click **OK** two times.

b. In the **Page Setup group**, click **Orientation**, and then click **Landscape**.

c. Click the **File tab** to display **Backstage** view; if necessary, on the left click the **Info tab**. In the lower right corner, click **Show All Properties**. As the **Tags**, type **bands, tubing, inventory** In the **Subject** box, type your course name and section number. Be sure your name displays as the author—edit if necessary.

d. On the left, click **Save** to be sure that you have saved your work up to this point.

e. Print or submit your workbook electronically as directed by your instructor. (Mac users: if necessary to fit on one page, on the Page Layout tab, in the Scale to Fit group, set the Width and Height to 1 page.)

f. If required by your instructor, print or create an electronic version of your worksheet with formulas displayed by using the instructions at the end of Project 1A. **Close** Excel without saving so that you do not save the changes you made to print formulas.

You have completed Project 1D　　**END**

Content-Based Assessments (Mastery and Transfer of Learning)

Mastering Excel | **Project 1E Gym Sales**

In the following Mastering Excel project, you will create a worksheet comparing the sales of different types of home gym equipment sold in the second quarter. Your completed worksheet will look similar to Figure 1.58.

Project Files for **MyLab IT** Grader

1. In your **MyLab IT** course, locate and click **Excel 1E Gym Sales**, Download Materials, and then Download All Files.
2. Extract the zipped folder to your Excel Chapter 1 folder. Close the Grader download screens.
3. Take a moment to open the downloaded **Excel_1E_Gym_Sales_Instructions**; note any recent updates to the book.

Project Results

Figure 1.58

For Non-MyLab Submissions

For Project 1E, you will need:
e01E_Gym_Sales

In your Excel Chapter 1 folder, save your workbook as:
Lastname_Firstname_1E_Gym_Sales
If your instructor requires a workbook with formulas, save as:
Lastname_Firstname_1E_Gym_Sales_formulas

After you have named and saved your workbook, on the next page, begin with Step 2.
After Step 16, submit your file as directed by your instructor.

Content-Based Assessments (Mastery and Transfer of Learning)

1 Navigate to your **Excel Chapter 1 folder**, and then double-click the Excel file you downloaded from **MyLab IT** that displays your name—**Student_1E_Gym_Sales**. If necessary, at the top, click **Enable Editing**.

2 Change the workbook theme to **Wisp**. If the Wisp theme is not available on your computer, in the Themes gallery, click Browse for Themes, and then select the theme from your downloaded student files.

3 In cell **B3**, use the fill handle to fill the months *May* and *June* in the range **C3:D3**.

4 **Merge & Center** the title across the range **A1:F1**, and then apply the **Title** cell style. **Merge & Center** the subtitle across the range **A2:F2**, and then apply the **Heading 1** cell style. **Center** the column titles in the range **B3:F3**.

5 Widen **column A** to **180 pixels**, and then widen columns **B:F** to **115 pixels**. (Mac users: set column A to a width of 21.83 or 136 pixels and columns B:F to a width of 13.83 or 88 pixels.) In the range **B7:D7**, enter the monthly sales figures for the Elite Home Gym for April, May, and June as shown in the table below:

	April	May	June
Elite Home Gym	137727.85	121691.64	128964.64

6 In cell **B8**, on the **Home tab**, use the **AutoSum** button to sum the April sales. Copy the resulting formula across to cells **C8:D8** to sum the May monthly sales and the June monthly sales. In cell **E4**, use the **AutoSum** button to sum the *Basic Home Gym* sales. Copy the formula down to cells **E5:E8**.

7 Apply the **Heading 4** cell style to the row titles and the column titles. Apply the **Total** cell style to the totals in the range **B8:E8**.

8 Apply the **Accounting Number Format** to the first row of sales figures and to the total row. Apply the **Comma Style** to the remaining sales figures.

9 To compare the monthly sales of each product visually, select the range that represents the sales figures for the three months, including the month names and the product names—do not include any totals in the range. With this data selected, use the **Recommended Charts** command to insert a **Clustered Column** chart with the month names displayed on the category axis and the product names displayed in the legend.

10 Move the chart so that its upper left corner is positioned in the center of cell **A10**. Then drag the center right sizing handle to the right until the right edge of the chart aligns with the right edge of **column E**; this will display the legend on one row and, after you add the sparklines, center the chart below the data.

11 Apply **Chart Style 6** and change the colors by applying the second row of colors under **Colorful**. Change the **Chart Title** to Second Quarter Home Gym Sales

12 In the range **F4:F7**, insert **Line** sparklines that compare the monthly data. Do not include the totals. Show the sparkline **Markers**. Display the sparkline **Style** gallery, and then in the first row, apply the second style.

13 Center the worksheet **Horizontally** on the page, and then insert a **Footer** with the **File Name** in the **left section**.

14 Change the **Orientation** to **Landscape**. Display the document properties, and then as the **Tags** type **home gym, sales** As the **Subject**, type your course name and section number. Be sure your name displays as the **Author**. Check your worksheet by previewing it in **Print Preview**, and then make any necessary corrections.

15 On the left, click **Save**.

16 In the upper right corner of your screen, click **Close** ☒ to close Excel.

17 In **MyLab IT**, locate and click the Grader Project **Excel 1E Gym Sales**. In **step 3**, under **Upload Completed Assignment**, click **Choose File**. In the **Open** dialog box, navigate to your **Excel Chapter 1 folder**, and then click your **Student_Excel_1E_Gym_Sales** file one time to select it. In the lower right corner of the **Open** dialog box, click **Open**.

The name of your selected file displays above the Upload button.

18 To submit your file to **MyLab IT** for grading, click **Upload**, wait a moment for a green **Success!** message, and then in **step 4**, click the blue **Submit for Grading** button. Click **Close Assignment** to return to your list of **Course Materials**.

You have completed Project 1E **END**

Content-Based Assessments (Mastery and Transfer of Learning)

Apply 1B skills from these Objectives:

7. Check Spelling in a Worksheet
8. Enter Data by Range
9. Construct Formulas for Mathematical Operations
10. Edit Values in a Worksheet
11. Format a Worksheet

In the following Mastering Excel project, you will create a worksheet that summarizes the sales of balance and stabilization equipment that Pro Fit Marietta is marketing. Your completed worksheet will look similar to Figure 1.59.

Project Files for **MyLab IT** Grader

1. In your **MyLab IT** course, locate and click **Excel 1F Balance Sales**, Download Materials, and then Download All Files.
2. Extract the zipped folder to your Excel Chapter 1 folder. Close the Grader download screens.
3. Take a moment to open the downloaded **Excel_1F_Balance_Sales_Instructions**; note any recent updates to the book.

Project Results

Figure 1.59

For Non-MyLab Submissions

For Project 1F, you will need:
e01F_Gym_Sales

After you have named and saved your workbook, on the next page, begin with Step 2.

After Step 18, submit your file as directed by your instructor.

In your Excel Chapter 1 folder, save your workbook as:
Lastname_Firstname_1F_Balance_Sales

If your instructor requires a workbook with formulas, save as:
Lastname_Firstname_1F_Balance_Sales_formulas

Mastering Excel: Project 1F Balance Sales (continued)

1 Navigate to your Excel Chapter 1 folder, and then double-click the Excel file you downloaded from **MyLab IT** that displays your name—**Student_Excel_1F_Balance_Sales**. If necessary, at the top, click **Enable Editing**.

2 **Merge & Center** the title and then the subtitle across **columns A:F** and apply the **Title** and **Heading 1** cell styles respectively.

3 Make cell **A1** the active cell, and then check spelling in your worksheet. Correct *Silde* to **Slide**. Widen **column A** to **180 pixels** and widen **columns B:F** to **95 pixels**. (Mac users: set column A to 141 pixels and widen columns B:F to75 pixels.)

4 In cell **E4**, construct a formula to calculate the *Total Sales* of the *Balance Pillow* by multiplying the *Quantity Sold* times the *Retail Price*. Copy the formula down for the remaining products.

5 Select the range **E4:E10**, and then use the **Quick Analysis** tool to **Sum** the *Total Sales for All Products*, which will be formatted in bold. To the total in cell **E11**, apply the **Total** cell style. (Mac users: instead of the Quick Analysis tool, use the Sum button. Complete the step as specified.)

6 Using absolute cell references as necessary so that you can copy the formula, in cell **F4**, construct a formula to calculate the *Percent of Total Sales* for the first product. Copy the formula down for the remaining products.

7 To the computed percentages, apply **Percent Style** with two decimal places, and then **Center** the percentages.

8 Apply the **Comma Style** with no decimal places to the *Quantity Sold* figures. To cells **D4**, **E4**, and **E11** apply the **Accounting Number Format**.

9 To the range **D5:E10**, apply the **Comma Style**.

10 Change the *Retail Price* of the *Slide Board* to **75.50** and the *Quantity Sold* of the *Balance Pad* to **150**.

11 Delete **column B**.

12 Insert a new **row 3**. In cell **A3**, type **Month Ending March 31** and then **Merge & Center** the text across the range **A3:E3**. Apply the **Heading 2** cell style.

13 To cell **A12**, apply the **20%-Accent1** cell style.

14 Select the four column titles. Apply **Wrap Text**, **Middle Align**, and **Center** formatting, and then apply the **Heading 3** cell style.

15 Center the worksheet **Horizontally** on the page, and then insert a **Footer** with the **File Name** in the **left section**.

16 Display the document properties, and then as the **Tags**, type **balance, stability, sales** In the **Subject** box, add your course name and section number. Be sure your name displays as the Author.

17 On the left, click **Save**.

18 In the upper right corner of your screen, click **Close** ☒ to close Excel.

19 In **MyLab IT**, locate and click the Grader Project **Excel 1F Balance Sales**. In **step 3**, under **Upload Completed Assignment**, click **Choose File**. In the **Open** dialog box, navigate to your **Excel Chapter 1 folder**, and then click your **Student_Excel_1F_Balance_Sales** file one time to select it. In the lower right corner of the **Open** dialog box, click **Open**.

The name of your selected file displays above the Upload button.

20 To submit your file to **MyLab IT** for grading, click **Upload**, wait a moment for a green **Success!** message, and then in **step 4**, click the blue **Submit for Grading** button. Click **Close Assignment** to return to your list of **Course Materials**.

You have completed Project 1F | END

Content-Based Assessments (Mastery and Transfer of Learning)

Apply a combination of 1A and 1B skills:

1. Create, Save, and Navigate an Excel Workbook
2. Enter Data in a Worksheet
3. Construct and Copy Formulas and Use the SUM Function
4. Format Cells with Merge & Center, Cell Styles, and Themes
5. Chart Data to Create a Column Chart and Insert Sparklines
6. Print a Worksheet, Display Formulas, and Close Excel
7. Check Spelling in a Worksheet
8. Enter Data by Range
9. Construct Formulas for Mathematical Operations
10. Edit Values in a Worksheet
11. Format a Worksheet

In the following Mastering Excel project, you will create a new worksheet that compares annual sales by region. Your completed worksheet will look similar to Figure 1.60.

Project Files for **MyLab IT** Grader

1. In your **MyLab IT** course, locate and click **Excel 1G Regional Sales**, Download Materials, and then Download All Files.
2. Extract the zipped folder to your Excel Chapter 1 folder. Close the Grader download screens.
3. Take a moment to open the downloaded **Excel_1G_Regional_Sales_Instructions**; note any recent updates to the book.

Project Results

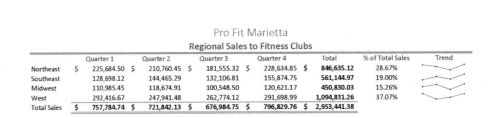

Pro Fit Marietta
Regional Sales to Fitness Clubs

	Quarter 1	Quarter 2	Quarter 3	Quarter 4	Total	% of Total Sales	Trend
Northeast	$ 225,684.50	$ 210,760.45	$ 181,555.32	$ 228,634.85	$ 846,635.12	28.67%	
Southeast	128,698.12	144,465.29	132,106.81	155,874.75	561,144.97	19.00%	
Midwest	110,985.45	118,674.91	100,548.50	120,621.17	450,830.03	15.26%	
West	292,416.67	247,941.48	262,774.12	291,698.99	1,094,831.26	37.07%	
Total Sales	$ 757,784.74	$ 721,842.13	$ 676,984.75	$ 796,829.76	$ 2,953,441.38		

Student_Excel_1G_Regional_Sales

Figure 1.60

For Non-MyLab Submissions

For Project 1G, you will need:
e01G_Regional_Sales

In your Excel Chapter 1 folder, save your workbook as:
Lastname_Firstname_1G_Regional_Sales
If your instructor requires a workbook with formulas, save as:
Lastname_Firstname_1G_Regional_Sales_formulas

After you have named and saved your workbook, on the next page, begin with Step 2.

After Step 18, submit your file as directed by your instructor. (Mac users: if necessary to fit on one page, on the Page Layout tab, in the Scale to Fit group, set the width to 1 page.)

Content-Based Assessments (Mastery and Transfer of Learning)

1 Navigate to your **Excel Chapter 1 folder**, and then double-click the Excel file you downloaded from **MyLab IT** that displays your name—**Student_1G_Regional_Sales**. If necessary, at the top, click **Enable Editing**.

2 Change the **Theme** to **Retrospect**. Set the width of **column A** to **80 pixels** and the width of columns **B:H** to **110 pixels**. (Mac users: Set Column A to 68 pixels and columns B:H to 95 pixels.)

3 **Merge & Center** the title across the range **A1:H1**, and then apply the **Title** cell style. **Merge & Center** the subtitle across the range **A2:H2**, and then apply the **Heading 1** cell style.

4 Select the seven column titles, apply **Center** formatting, and then apply the **Heading 4** cell style.

5 By using the **Quick Analysis** tool, **Sum** the *Quarter 1* sales, and then copy the formula across for the remaining Quarters; the Quick Analysis tool formats totals in bold. (Mac users: use AutoSum and apply bold.)

6 Select the *Northeast* sales for the four quarters, and then display the **Quick Analysis** gallery for **Totals**. Click the second **Sum** option—the sixth item in the gallery—which displays the column selection in yellow. Copy the formula down through cell **F7**; recall that the Quick Analysis tool applies bold formatting to sums. (Mac users: use AutoSum and apply bold.)

7 Apply the **Accounting Number Format** to the first row of sales figures and to the total row, and the **Comma Style** to the remaining sales figures. Format the totals in **row 7** with the **Total** cell style.

8 **Insert** a new **row 6** with the row title **Midwest** and the following sales figures for each quarter: **110985.45** and **118674.91** and **100548.50** and **120621.17** Copy the formula in cell **F5** down to cell **F6** to sum the new row.

9 Using absolute cell references as necessary so that you can copy the formula, in cell **G4** construct a formula to calculate the *Percent of Total Sales* for the first region. Copy the formula down for the remaining regions.

10 To the computed percentages, apply **Percent Style** with two decimal places, and then **Center** the percentages.

11 Insert **Line** sparklines in the range **H4:H7** that compare the quarterly data. Do not include the totals. Show the sparkline **Markers** and apply a style to the sparklines using the second style in the second row. (Mac users: Select the first color in the second row.)

12 **Save** your workbook. To compare the quarterly sales of each region visually, select the range that represents the sales figures for the four quarters, including the quarter names and each region—do not include any totals in the range. With this data selected, by using the **Recommended Charts** command, insert a **Clustered Column** with the regions as the category axis and the Quarters as the legend.

13 Apply **Chart Style 8**. Change the colors by applying the third row of colors under Colorful. Position the upper middle sizing handle of the chart on the line between **column D** and **column E** and just below **row 9**.

14 Change the **Chart Title** to **Regional Sales to Fitness Clubs**

15 Deselect the chart. Change the page **Orientation** to **Landscape**, center the worksheet **Horizontally** on the page, and then insert a footer with the file name in the left section.

16 Show the document properties. As the **Tags**, type **fitness clubs, regional sales** In the **Subject** box, type your course name and section number. Be sure your name displays as the Author.

17 On the left, click **Save**.

18 In the upper right corner of your screen, click **Close** ✕ to close Excel.

19 In **MyLab IT**, locate and click the Grader Project **Excel 1G Regional Sales**. In **step 3**, under **Upload Completed Assignment**, click **Choose File**. In the **Open** dialog box, navigate to your **Excel Chapter 1 folder**, and then click your **Student_Excel_1G_Regional_Sales** file one time to select it. In the lower right corner of the **Open** dialog box, click **Open**.

The name of your selected file displays above the Upload button.

20 To submit your file to **MyLab IT** for grading, click **Upload**, wait a moment for a green **Success!** message, and then in **step 4**, click the blue **Submit for Grading** button. Click **Close Assignment** to return to your list of **Course Materials**.

You have completed Project 1G | **END**

Content-Based Assessments (Critical Thinking)

GO! Fix It	**Project 1H Team Sales**	IRC
GO! Make It	**Project 1I Agility Sales**	IRC
GO! Solve It	**Project 1J Kettlebell Sales**	IRC
GO! Solve It	**Project 1K Commission**	

Project Files

For Project 1K, you will need the following file:

e01K_Commission

You will save your workbook as:

Lastname_Firstname_1K_Commission

Open the file e01K_Commission and save it as **Lastname_Firstname_1K_Commission** Complete the worksheet by using Auto Fill to complete the month headings, and then calculating the Total Commission for each month and for each region. Insert and format appropriate sparklines in the Trend column. Format the worksheet attractively with a title and subtitle, check spelling, adjust column width, and apply appropriate financial formatting. Insert a chart that compares the total sales commission for each region with the months displaying as the categories, and format the chart attractively. Include the file name in the footer, add appropriate properties, and submit as directed.

		Performance Level		
		Exemplary: You consistently applied the relevant skills	**Proficient: You sometimes, but not always, applied the relevant skills**	**Developing: You rarely or never applied the relevant skills**
Performance Criteria	**Create formulas**	All formulas are correct and are efficiently constructed.	Formulas are correct but not always constructed in the most efficient manner.	One or more formulas are missing or incorrect; or only numbers were entered.
	Create a chart	Chart created properly.	Chart was created but incorrect data was selected.	No chart was created.
	Insert and format sparklines	Sparklines inserted and formatted properly.	Sparklines were inserted but incorrect data was selected or sparklines were not formatted.	No sparklines were inserted.
	Format attractively and appropriately	Formatting is attractive and appropriate.	Adequately formatted but difficult to read or unattractive.	Inadequate or no formatting.

You have completed Project 1K   END

Outcomes-Based Assessments (Critical Thinking)

Rubric

The following outcomes-based assessments are *open ended assessments*. That is, there is no specific correct result; your result will depend on your approach to the information provided. Make *Professional Quality* your goal. Use the following scoring rubric to guide you in *how* to approach the problem and then to evaluate *how well* your approach solves the problem.

The *criteria*—Software Mastery, Content, Format and Layout, and Process—represent the knowledge and skills you have gained that you can apply to solving the problem. The *levels of performance*—Professional Quality, Approaching Professional Quality, or Needs Quality Improvements—help you and your instructor evaluate your result.

	Your completed project is of Professional Quality if you:	Your completed project is Approaching Professional Quality if you:	Your completed project Needs Quality Improvements if you:
1-Software Mastery	Choose and apply the most appropriate skills, tools, and features and identify efficient methods to solve the problem.	Choose and apply some appropriate skills, tools, and features, but not in the most efficient manner.	Choose inappropriate skills, tools, or features, or are inefficient in solving the problem.
2-Content	Construct a solution that is clear and well organized, contains content that is accurate, appropriate to the audience and purpose, and is complete. Provide a solution that contains no errors of spelling, grammar, or style.	Construct a solution in which some components are unclear, poorly organized, inconsistent, or incomplete. Misjudge the needs of the audience. Have some errors in spelling, grammar, or style, but the errors do not detract from comprehension.	Construct a solution that is unclear, incomplete, or poorly organized, contains some inaccurate or inappropriate content, and contains many errors of spelling, grammar, or style. Do not solve the problem.
3-Format and Layout	Format and arrange all elements to communicate information and ideas, clarify function, illustrate relationships, and indicate relative importance.	Apply appropriate format and layout features to some elements, but not others. Overuse features, causing minor distraction.	Apply format and layout that does not communicate information or ideas clearly. Do not use format and layout features to clarify function, illustrate relationships, or indicate relative importance. Use available features excessively, causing distraction.
4-Process	Use an organized approach that integrates planning, development, self-assessment, revision, and reflection.	Demonstrate an organized approach in some areas, but not others; or, use an insufficient process of organization throughout.	Do not use an organized approach to solve the problem.

Outcomes-Based Assessments (Critical Thinking)

Apply a combination of the 1A and 1B skills.

| GO! Think | **Project 1L Video Sales** |

Project Files

For Project 1L, you will need the following file:

New blank Excel workbook

You will save your workbook as:

Lastname_Firstname_1L_Video_Sales

Michelle Barry, President of Pro Fit Marietta, needs a worksheet that summarizes the following data regarding the first quarter sales of training videos. Michelle would like the worksheet to include a calculation of the total sales for each type of video and a total of the sales of all of the videos. She would also like to know each type of video's percentage of total sales.

	Number Sold	Price
Pilates	156	29.99
Step	392	14.99
Weight Training	147	54.99
Kickboxing	282	29.99
Yoga	165	34.99

Create a worksheet that provides Michelle with the information needed. Include appropriate worksheet, column, and row titles. Using the formatting skills that you practiced in this chapter, format the worksheet in a manner that is professional and easy to read and understand. Insert a footer with the file name and add appropriate document properties. Save the file as **Lastname_Firstname_1L_Video_Sales** and print or submit as directed by your instructor.

You have completed Project 1L | END

| GO! Think | **Project 1M Planner** | IRC |

| You and GO! | **Project 1N Personal Resume** | IRC |

| GO! Collaborative Group Project | **Project 1O Bell Orchid Hotels** | IRC |

Using Functions, Creating Tables, and Managing Large Workbooks

2
EXCEL 2019

PROJECT 2A

Outcomes
Analyze inventory by applying statistical and logical calculations to data and by sorting and filtering data.

Objectives
1. Use Flash Fill and the SUM, AVERAGE, MEDIAN, MIN, and MAX Functions
2. Move Data, Resolve Error Messages, and Rotate Text
3. Use COUNTIF and IF Functions and Apply Conditional Formatting
4. Use Date & Time Functions and Freeze Panes
5. Create, Sort, and Filter an Excel Table
6. View, Format, and Print a Large Worksheet

PROJECT 2B

Outcomes
Summarize the data on multiple worksheets.

Objectives
7. Navigate a Workbook and Rename Worksheets
8. Enter Dates, Clear Contents, and Clear Formats
9. Copy and Paste by Using the Paste Options Gallery
10. Edit and Format Multiple Worksheets at the Same Time
11. Create a Summary Sheet with Column Sparklines
12. Format and Print Multiple Worksheets in a Workbook

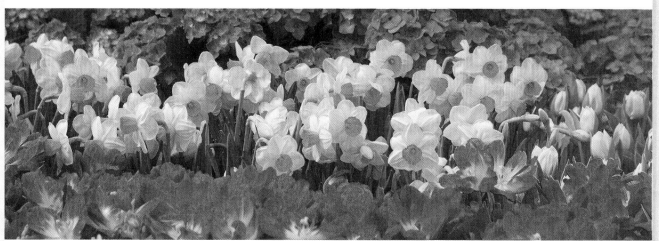

joloei/Shutterstock

In This Chapter

GO! To Work with Excel

In this chapter, you will use the Statistical functions to calculate the average of a group of numbers and perform other summary calculations. You will also use Logical and Date & Time functions. Excel's statistical functions are useful for common calculations that you probably encounter frequently. You will also use Excel's Flash Fill feature to automatically fill in values, use the counting functions, and apply different types of conditional formatting to make data easy to visualize. You will create a table to organize related information and analyze the table's information by sorting and filtering. You will summarize a workbook that contains multiple worksheets.

The projects in this chapter relate to **Rosedale Landscape and Garden**, which grows and sells trees and plants suitable for all areas of North America. Throughout its 75-year history, the company has introduced many new plants for the enjoyment of home gardeners. The company has nurseries and stores in the major metropolitan areas in the United States and Canada. In addition to high-quality plants and trees, Rosedale sells garden tools and outdoor furniture. Rosedale also offers professional landscape design and installation for both commercial and residential clients. The company headquarters is in Pasadena, California.

Project Activities

In Activities 2.01 through 2.20, you will edit a worksheet for Jacob Hill, President of Rosedale Landscape and Garden, detailing the current inventory of trees at the Pasadena nursery. Your completed worksheet will look similar to Figure 2.1.

Project Files for **MyLab IT Grader**

1. In your storage location, create a folder named **Excel Chapter 2**.
2. In your **MyLab IT** course, locate and click **Excel 2A Tree Inventory**, Download Materials, and then Download All Files.
3. Extract the zipped folder to your Excel Chapter 2 folder. Close the Grader download screens.
4. Take a moment to open the downloaded **Excel_2A_Tree_Inventory_Instructions**; note any recent updates to the book.

Project Results

GO! Project 2A

Where We're Going

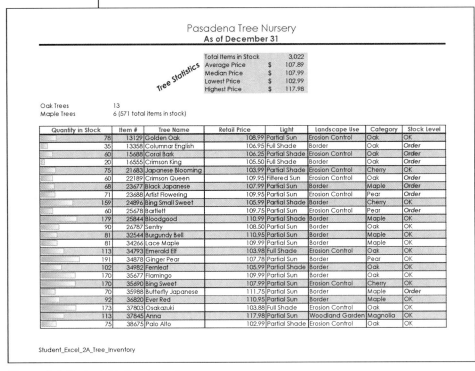

Figure 2.1 Project 2A Tree Inventory

For Non-MyLab Submissions

For Project 2A, you will need:

e02A_Tree_Inventory

In your storage location, create a folder named **Excel Chapter 2**

In your Excel Chapter 2 folder, save your workbook as:

Lastname_Firstname_2A_Tree_Inventory

If your instructor requires a workbook with formulas, save as:

Lastname_Firstname_2A_Tree_Inventory_formulas

After you have named and saved your workbook, on the next page, begin with Step 2.

Use Flash Fill and the SUM, AVERAGE, MEDIAN, MIN, and MAX Functions

ALERT   Because Office 365 is a cloud-based subscription service that receives continuous updates, you may encounter some variations in what appears on your screen and what is shown in this instruction. Microsoft Office 365 is fully installed on your PC or Mac; no internet access is necessary to create or edit documents. When you *are* connected to the internet, you will receive monthly upgrades and new features, so you always have the latest versions of Office apps as soon as they are available. Your subscription gives you continuous free access to the latest innovations and refinements.

GO! Learn How

Video E2-1

Flash Fill recognizes a pattern in your data and then automatically fills in values when you enter examples of the output that you want. Use Flash Fill to split data into two or more cells or to combine data from two cells.

A *function* is the name given to a predefined formula—a formula that Excel has already built for you—that performs calculations by using specific values that you insert in a particular order or structure. *Statistical functions*, which include the AVERAGE, MEDIAN, MIN, and MAX functions, are useful to analyze a group of measurements.

Activity 2.01 | Using Flash Fill

MOS

2.1.3, Expert 2.1.1

1 Navigate to your **Excel Chapter 2 folder**, and then double-click the Excel file you downloaded from **MyLab IT** that displays your name—**Student_Excel_2A_Tree_Inventory**.

2 Scroll down. Notice that the worksheet contains data related to types of trees in inventory, including information about the *Quantity in Stock, Item #/Category, Tree Name, Retail Price, Light,* and *Landscape Use.*

3 In the **column heading area**, point to **column C** to display the ⬇ pointer, and then drag to the right to select **columns C:D**. On the **Home tab**, in the **Cells group**, click the **Insert button arrow**, and then click **Insert Sheet Columns**.

New columns for C and D display and the remaining columns move to the right.

 MAC TIP   To display group names on the ribbon, display the menu, click Excel, click Preferences, click View, select the Show group titles check box.

ANOTHER WAY   Select the columns, right-click anywhere over the selected columns, and then on the shortcut menu, click Insert.

4 Click cell **C11**, type **13129** and then on the **Formula Bar**, click **Enter** ☑ to confirm the entry and keep **C11** as the active cell.

5 On the **Home tab**, in the **Editing group**, click **Fill**, and then click **Flash Fill**. Compare your screen with Figure 2.2.

> Use this technique to split a column of data based on what you type. Flash Fill looks to the left and sees the pattern you have established, and then fills the remaining cells in the column with only the Item #. The Flash Fill Options button displays.

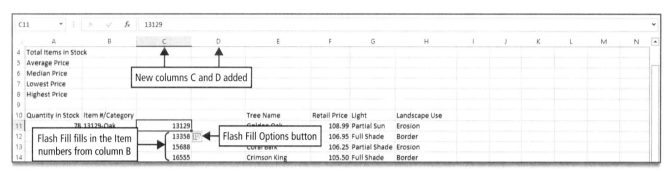

Figure 2.2

6 Near the lower right corner of cell **C11**, click the **Flash Fill Options** button, and notice that here you can *Undo Flash Fill*, *Accept suggestions*, or *Select all 28 changed cells*, for example, to apply specific formatting. Click the button again to close it.

> If Excel is not sure what pattern to use, it suggests a pattern by filling with pale gray characters, and then you can use the Accept suggestions command to accept or start again.

7 Click cell **D11**, type **Oak** and then on the **Formula Bar**, click **Enter** ☑ to confirm the entry and keep **D11** as the active cell. Press Ctrl + E, which is the keyboard shortcut for Flash Fill.

> Flash Fill extracts the text from the *Item#/Category* column and also inserts *Category* as the column name. Now that *Item #* and *Category* are in two separate columns, the data can be sorted and filtered by both Item # and Category.

8 Select **column B**, and then on the **Home tab**, in the **Cells group**, click the **Delete button arrow**. Click **Delete Sheet Columns**. **Save** 🖫 your file.

ANOTHER WAY   Select the column, right-click anywhere over the selected column, and then on the shortcut menu, click Delete.

Activity 2.02 | Moving a Column

1 In cell **B10**, type **Item #** and then press Enter. Select **column C**, and then on the **Home tab**, in the **Clipboard group**, click **Cut** ✂. Click cell **H1**, and then in the **Clipboard group**, click the upper portion of the **Paste** button.

ANOTHER WAY   Press Ctrl + X to cut and Ctrl + V to paste.

2 Select and then delete **column C**. Select **columns A:G**. In the **Cells group**, click **Format**, and then click **AutoFit Column Width**.

ANOTHER WAY   Select the columns, in the column heading area, point to any of the selected column borders to display the ⊞ pointer, and then double-click to AutoFit the columns.

3 **Merge & Center** cell **A1** across the range **A1:H1**, and then apply the **Title** cell style. **Merge & Center** cell **A2** across the range **A2:H2**, and then apply the **Heading 1** cell style. Compare your screen with Figure 2.3. **Save** 🖫 your workbook.

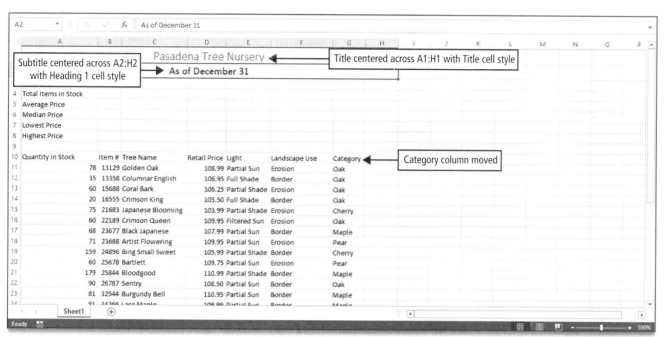

Figure 2.3

Activity 2.03 | Using the SUM and AVERAGE Functions

MOS
4.2.1

In this Activity, you will use the SUM and AVERAGE functions to gather information about the product inventory.

1 Click cell **B4**. Click the **Formulas tab**, and then in the **Function Library group**, click the upper portion of the **AutoSum** button. Compare your screen with Figure 2.4.

The *SUM function* is a predefined formula that adds all the numbers in a selected range of cells. Because it is frequently used, there are several ways to insert the function. For example, you can insert the function from the Home tab's Editing group, or by using the keyboard shortcut [Alt] + [=], or from the Function Library group on the Formulas tab, or from the Math & Trig button in that group.

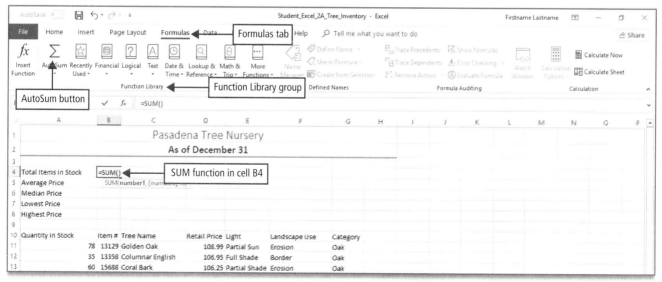

Figure 2.4

2 With the insertion point blinking in the function, type the cell range **a11:a39** to sum all the values in the *Quantity in Stock* column, and then press [Enter]; your result is *3022*.

3 Click cell **B4**, look at the **Formula Bar**, and then compare your screen with Figure 2.5.

SUM is the name of the function. The values in parentheses are the ***arguments***—the values that an Excel function uses to perform calculations or operations. In this instance, the argument consists of the values in the range A11:A39.

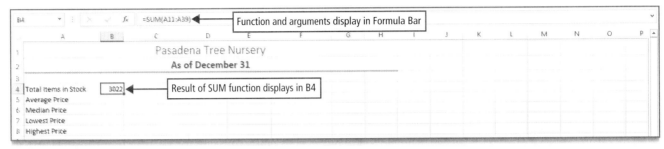

Figure 2.5

4 Click cell **B5**. On the **Formulas tab**, in the **Function Library group**, click **More Functions**, point to **Statistical**, point to **AVERAGE**, and notice the ScreenTip. Compare your screen with Figure 2.6.

The ScreenTip describes how the AVERAGE function will compute the calculation.

Figure 2.6

5 Click **AVERAGE**, and then if necessary, drag the title bar of the Function Arguments dialog box down and to the right so you can view the Formula Bar and cell B5.

The ***AVERAGE function*** adds a group of values, and then divides the result by the number of values in the group. In the cell, the Formula Bar, and the dialog box, Excel proposes to average the value in cell B4. Recall that Excel functions will propose a range if there is data above or to the left of a selected cell.

6 In the **Function Arguments** dialog box, notice that *B4* is highlighted. Press [Del] to delete the existing text, type **d11:d39** and then compare your screen with Figure 2.7.

Because you want to average the retail price values in the range D11:D39—and not cell B4—you must edit the proposed range.

MAC TIP When you click Average, the Formula Builder displays at the right side of the Excel window. In the Formula Builder, under Number1, delete B4, type d11:d39, and then click Done. Leave the Formula Builder open for the next Activity.

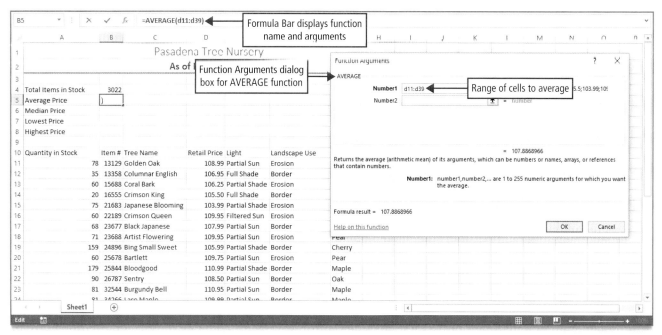

Figure 2.7

7 In the **Function Arguments** dialog box, click **OK**, and then click **Save** 🖫.

The result indicates that the average Retail Price of all products is *107.89*.

Activity 2.04 | Using the MEDIAN Function

The ***MEDIAN function*** is a statistical function that describes a group of data—it is commonly used to describe the price of houses in a particular geographical area. The MEDIAN function finds the middle value that has as many values above it in the group as are below it. It differs from AVERAGE in that the result is not affected as much by a single value that is greatly different from the others.

1 Click cell **B6**. In the **Function Library group**, click **More Functions**, display the list of **Statistical** functions, scroll down as necessary, and then click **MEDIAN**.

2 Delete the text in the **Number1** box. Type **d11:d39** and then compare your screen with Figure 2.8.

When indicating which cells you want to use in the function's calculation—known as *defining the arguments*—you can either select the values with your mouse or type the range of values, whichever you prefer.

Figure 2.8

3 Click **OK** to display *107.99* in cell **B6**. Click **Save** and compare your screen with Figure 2.9.

In the range of prices, 107.99 is the middle value. Half of all trees in inventory are priced *above* 107.99 and half are priced *below* 107.99.

Figure 2.9

Activity 2.05 | Using the MIN and MAX Functions

4.2.1

The statistical ***MIN function*** determines the smallest value in a selected range of values. The statistical ***MAX function*** determines the largest value in a selected range of values.

1 Click cell **B7**. On the **Formulas tab**, in the **Function Library group**, click **More Functions**, display the list of **Statistical** functions, scroll as necessary, and then click **MIN**.

2 Delete the text in the **Number1** box. Type **d11:d39** and then click **OK**.

The lowest Retail Price is *102.99*.

3 Click cell **B8**, and then by using a similar technique, insert the **MAX** function to determine the highest **Retail Price**, and then check to see that your result is *117.98*.

4 Press Ctrl + Home. Point to cell **B4**, right-click, and then on the mini toolbar, click **Comma Style** one time and **Decrease Decimal** two times.

MAC TIP Close the Formula Builder. Press Control + fn + ←. Click cell B4, and then on the Home tab, click Comma Style. Click Decrease Decimal two times.

5 Select the range **B5:B8**, apply the **Accounting Number Format**, click **Save**, and then compare your screen with Figure 2.10.

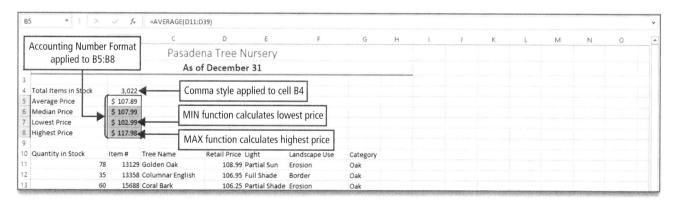

Figure 2.10

Objective 2   Move Data, Resolve Error Messages, and Rotate Text

GO! Learn How
Video E2-2

When you move a formula, the cell references within the formula do not change, no matter what type of cell reference you use.

If you move cells into a column that is not wide enough to display number values, Excel will display a message so that you can adjust as necessary.

You can reposition data within a cell at an angle by rotating the text.

Activity 2.06 | Moving Data and Resolving a # # # # # Error Message

1 Select **column E** and set the width to **50 pixels**. Select the range **A4:B8**. Point to the right edge of the selected range to display the ⊹ pointer, and then compare your screen with Figure 2.11.

Figure 2.11

2 Drag the selected range to the right until the ScreenTip displays *D4:E8*, release the mouse button, and then notice that a series of # symbols displays in **column E**. Point to any of the cells that display # symbols, and then compare your screen with Figure 2.12.

Using this technique, cell contents can be moved from one location to another; this is referred to as *drag and drop*.

If a cell width is too narrow to display the entire number, Excel displays the ##### message, because displaying only a portion of a number would be misleading. The underlying values remain unchanged and are displayed in the Formula Bar for the selected cell. An underlying value also displays in the ScreenTip if you point to a cell containing # symbols.

Figure 2.12

3 Select **columns D:E**, and then in the **column heading area**, point to the right boundary of **column E** to display the ╋ pointer. Double-click to AutoFit the columns to accommodate the widest entry in each column.

4 Select the range **D4:E8**. On the **Home tab**, in the **Styles group**, display the **Cell Styles** gallery. Under **Themed Cell Styles**, click **20%-Accent1**. Click **Save** 🖫.

Activity 2.07 | Merging Cells and Rotating Text

MOS

2.2.1, 2.2.2, 2.2.6

1 In cell **C6**, type **Tree Statistics** and then press [Enter].

2 Select the range **C4:C8**, right-click over the selection, and then on the shortcut menu, click **Format Cells**.

MAC TIP Hold down [Control] and click the selection. On the shortcut menu, click Format Cells.

3 In the **Format Cells** dialog box, click the **Alignment tab**. Under **Text control**, select the **Merge cells** check box. Under **Orientation**, click in the **Degrees** box to select the value, type **30** and then compare your screen with Figure 2.13.

Figure 2.13

🔄 **ANOTHER WAY** In the upper right portion of the dialog box, under Orientation, point to the red diamond, and then drag the diamond upward until the Degrees box indicates 30.

4 In the lower right corner of the **Format Cells** dialog box, click **OK** to apply the merge cell and text rotation settings.

5 On the **Home tab**, in the **Font group**, change the **Font Size** 11 ▾ to **14**, and then apply **Bold** B and **Italic** I. Click the **Font Color arrow** A▾, and then in the fifth column, click the first color.

6 In the **Alignment group**, apply **Align Right** ☰. Move to cell **A1**, and then compare your screen with Figure 2.14.

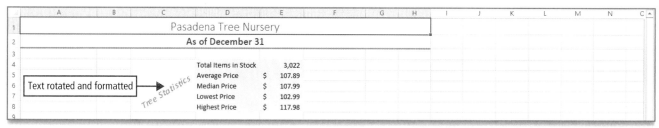

Figure 2.14

7 In the **row heading area**, point to **row 9**, and then right-click to select the row and display the shortcut menu. Click **Insert**, and then press [F4] two times to repeat the last action and insert two additional blank rows.

[F4] is useful to repeat commands in Microsoft Office programs. Most commands can be repeated in this manner.

MAC TIP To insert rows, from the row heading area, drag to select rows 9:11. On the Home tab, click Insert to insert three rows.

8 ▶ From the **row heading area**, select **rows 9:11**. On the **Home tab**, in the **Editing group**, click **Clear** ⊘, and then click **Clear Formats** to remove the blue accent color in columns D and E from the new rows. Click **Save** 🖫.

> When you insert rows or columns, formatting from adjacent rows or columns repeats in the new cells.

9 ▶ Click cell **E4**, look at the **Formula Bar**, and then notice that the arguments of the **SUM** function adjusted and refer to the appropriate cells in rows 14:42.

> The referenced range updates to *A14:A42* after you insert the three new rows. In this manner, Excel adjusts the cell references in a formula relative to their new locations.

Use COUNTIF and IF Functions and Apply Conditional Formatting

GO! Learn How
Video E2-3

Recall that statistical functions analyze a group of measurements. Another group of Excel functions, referred to as *logical functions*, test for specific conditions. Logical functions typically use conditional tests to determine whether specified conditions—called *criteria*—are true or false.

Activity 2.08 | Using the COUNTIF Function

The *COUNT function* counts the number of cells in a range that contain numbers. The *COUNTIF function* is a statistical function that counts the number of cells within a range that meet the given condition—the criteria that you provide. The COUNTIF function has two arguments—the range of cells to check and the criteria.

The trees of Rosedale Landscape and Garden will be featured on an upcoming segment of a TV gardening show. In this Activity, you will use the COUNTIF function to determine the number of *Oak* trees currently available in inventory that can be featured in the TV show.

1 ▶ In cell **A10**, type **Oak Trees** and then press `Tab`.

2 ▶ With cell **B10** as the active cell, on the **Formulas tab**, in the **Function Library group**, click **More Functions**, and then display the list of **Statistical** functions. Click **COUNTIF**.

> Recall that the COUNTIF function counts the number of cells within a range that meet the given condition.

3 ▶ In the **Range** box, type **g14:g42** and then click in the **Criteria** box. Type **Oak** and then compare your screen with Figure 2.15.

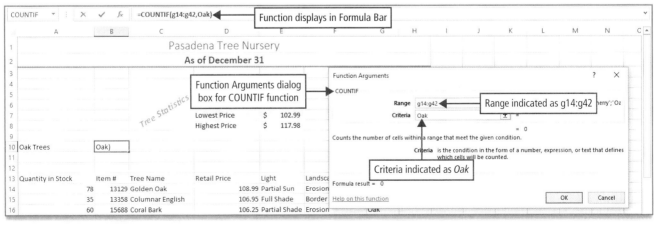

Figure 2.15

4 In the lower right corner of the **Function Arguments** dialog box, click **OK**.

There are *13* different *Oak* trees available to feature on the TV show.

5 On the **Home tab**, in the **Alignment group**, click **Align Left** ≡ to place the result closer to the row title. **Save** 🖫 your workbook.

Activity 2.09 | Using the IF Function

A *logical test* is any value or expression that you can evaluate as being true or false. The *IF function* uses a logical test to check whether a condition is met, and then returns one value if true, and another value if false.

For example, *C14=228* is an expression that can be evaluated as true or false. If the value in cell C14 is equal to 228, the expression is true. If the value in cell C14 is not 228, the expression is false.

In this Activity, you will use the IF function to evaluate the inventory levels and determine if more products should be ordered.

1 Click cell **H13**, type **Stock Level** and then press Enter.

2 In cell **H14**, on the **Formulas tab**, in the **Function Library group**, click **Logical**, and then in the list, click **IF**. Drag the title bar of the **Function Arguments** dialog box up or down to view **row 14** on your screen.

3 With the insertion point in the **Logical_test** box, type **a14<75**

This logical test will look at the value in cell A14, which is *78*, and then determine whether the number is less than 75. The expression *<75* includes the *< comparison operator*, which means *less than*. Comparison operators compare values.

4 Examine the table in Figure 2.16 for a list of comparison operator symbols and their definitions.

Comparison Operators	
Comparison Operators	**Symbol Definition**
=	Equal to
>	Greater than
<	Less than
>=	Greater than or equal to
<=	Less than or equal to
<>	Not equal to

Figure 2.16

5 Press Tab to move the insertion point to the **Value_if_true** box, and then type **Order**

If the result of the logical test is true—the Quantity in Stock is less than 75—cell H14 will display the text *Order*, indicating that additional trees must be ordered.

6 ▸ Press Tab to move to the **Value_if_false** box, type **OK** and then compare your screen with Figure 2.17.

> If the result of the logical test is false—the Quantity in Stock is *not* less than 75—then Excel will display *OK* in the cell, indicating that no order is necessary at this time.

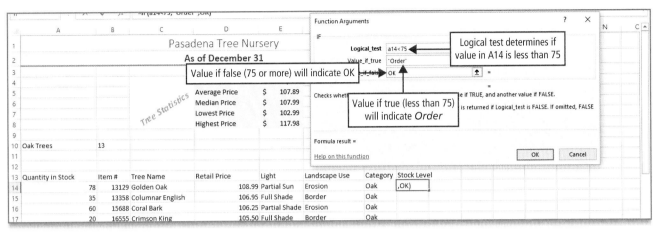

Figure 2.17

7 ▸ Click **OK** or press Enter to display the result *OK* in cell **H14**.

8 ▸ Using the fill handle, copy the function in cell **H14** down through cell **H42**. Then scroll as necessary to view cell **A18**, which contains the value *75*. Look at cell **H18** and notice that the **Stock Level** is indicated as *OK*. **Save** 🖫 your workbook. Compare your screen with Figure 2.18.

> The comparison operator indicated <75 (less than 75) and therefore a value of *exactly* 75 is indicated as OK.

Figure 2.18

Activity 2.10 | Applying Conditional Formatting by Using Highlight Cells Rules and Data Bars

2.4.2

> A ***conditional format*** changes the appearance of a cell based on a condition—a criteria. If the condition is true, the cell is formatted based on that condition; if the condition is false, the cell is *not* formatted. In this Activity, you will use conditional formatting as another way to draw attention to the Stock Level of trees.

1 Be sure the range **H14:H42** is selected. On the **Home tab**, in the **Styles group**, click **Conditional Formatting**. In the list, point to **Highlight Cells Rules**, and then click **Text that Contains**.

2 In the **Text That Contains** dialog box, with the insertion point blinking in the first box, type **Order** and notice that in the selected range, the text *Order* displays with the default format—Light Red Fill with Dark Red Text.

3 In the second box, click the **arrow**, and then in the list, click **Custom Format**.

Here, in the Format Cells dialog box, you can select any combination of formats to apply to the cell if the condition is true. The custom format you specify will be applied to any cell in the selected range if it contains the text *Order*.

MAC TIP To apply conditional formatting, in the New Formatting Rule box, be sure that the dialog box includes the following settings: Classic, Format only cells that contain, Specific Text, and containing. To the right of containing, type Order. Click the Format with arrow, and then click Custom Format.

4 On the **Font tab**, under **Font style**, click **Bold Italic**. Click the **Color arrow**, and then under **Theme Colors**, in the last column, click the first color. Click the **Fill** tab. Under **Background color**, click **No Color**. Click **OK**. Compare your screen with Figure 2.19.

In the range, if the cell meets the condition of containing *Order*, the font color will change to Bold Italic, Green, Accent 6.

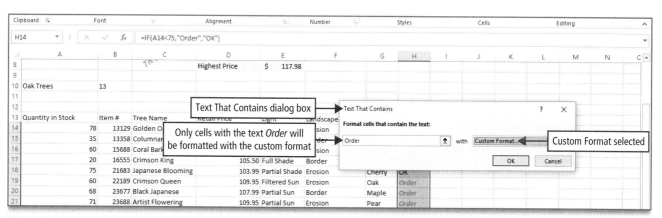

Figure 2.19

5 In the **Text That Contains** dialog box, click **OK**.

MAC TIP In the New Formatting Rule dialog box, click OK.

6 Select the range **A14:A42**. In the **Styles group**, click **Conditional Formatting**. Point to **Data Bars**, and then under **Gradient Fill**, click **Orange Data Bar**. Click anywhere to cancel the selection, click **Save** 🖫, and then compare your screen with Figure 2.20.

A *data bar* provides a visual cue to the reader about the value of a cell relative to other cells. The length of the data bar represents the value in the cell. A longer bar represents a higher value and a shorter bar represents a lower value. Data bars are useful for identifying higher and lower numbers quickly within a large group of data, such as very high or very low levels of inventory.

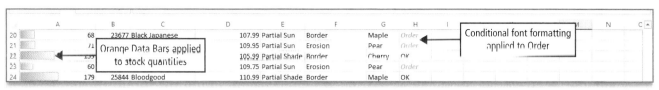

Figure 2.20

Activity 2.11 | Using Find and Replace

MOS
1.2.1

The ***Find and Replace*** feature searches the cells in a worksheet—or in a selected range—for matches, and then replaces each match with a replacement value of your choice.

Comments from customers on the company's blog indicate that using the term *Erosion Control* would be clearer than *Erosion* when describing the best landscape use for specific trees. Therefore, all products of this type will be relabeled accordingly. In this Activity, you will replace all occurrences of *Erosion* with *Erosion Control*.

1 Select the range **F14:F42**. On the **Home tab**, in the **Editing group**, click **Find & Select**, and then click **Replace**.

Restrict the find and replace operation to a specific range in this manner, especially if there is a possibility that the name occurs elsewhere.

MAC TIP Press Control + F to display the Find dialog box, and then click Replace.

2 In the **Find what** box, type **Erosion** and then press Tab. In the **Replace with** box, type **Erosion Control** and then compare your screen with Figure 2.21.

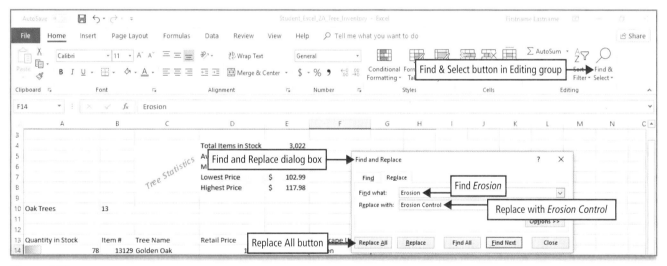

Figure 2.21

3 Click **Replace All**. In the message box, notice that 13 replacements were made, and then click **OK**. In the lower right corner of the **Find and Replace** dialog box, click **Close**, and then click **Save** 🖫.

GO! Learn How
Video E2-4

Excel can obtain the date and time from your computer's calendar and clock and display this information on your worksheet.

By freezing or splitting panes, you can view two areas of a worksheet and lock rows and columns in one area. When you freeze panes, you select the specific rows or columns that you want to remain visible when scrolling in your worksheet.

Activity 2.12 | Using the NOW Function to Display a System Date

MOS
Expert 3.3.1

The *NOW function* retrieves the date and time from your computer's calendar and clock and inserts the information into the selected cell. The result is formatted as a date and time.

1 To the left of the **Formula Bar**, click in the **Name Box**, type **a44** and then press Enter. Notice that cell A44 is the active cell.

2 With cell **A44** as the active cell, on the **Formulas tab**, in the **Function Library group**, click **Date & Time**. In the list of functions, click **NOW**. Compare your screen with Figure 2.22.

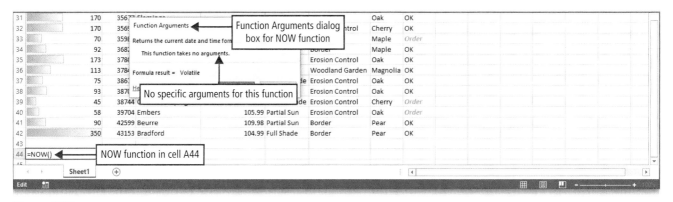

Figure 2.22

3 Read the description in the **Function Arguments** dialog box and notice that this result is *Volatile*.

The Function Arguments dialog box displays a message indicating that this function does not require an argument. It also states that this function is *volatile*, meaning the date and time will not remain as entered, but rather the date and time will automatically update each time you open this workbook.

4 In the **Function Arguments** dialog box, click **OK** to close the dialog box to display the current date and time in cell **A44**. **Save** 🖫 your workbook.

🖵 **MAC TIP** In the Formula Builder, click Done, and then close the Formula Builder.

MORE KNOWLEDGE **NOW Function Recalculates Each Time a Workbook Opens**

The NOW function updates each time the workbook is opened. With the workbook open, you can force the NOW function to update by pressing F9 , for example, to update the time.

Activity 2.13 | Freezing and Unfreezing Panes

MOS
1.4.3

In a large worksheet, if you scroll down more than 25 rows or scroll beyond column O (the exact row number and column letter varies, depending on your screen size and screen resolution), you will no longer see the top rows or first column of your worksheet where identifying information about the data is usually placed. You will find it easier to work with your data if you can always view the identifying row or column titles.

The *Freeze Panes* command enables you to select one or more rows or columns and then freeze (lock) them into place. The locked rows and columns become separate panes. A *pane* is a portion of a worksheet window bounded by and separated from other portions by vertical or horizontal bars.

1 Press Ctrl + Home to make cell **A1** the active cell. Scroll down until **row 21** displays at the top of your Excel window, and notice that all of the identifying information in the column titles is out of view.

MAC TIP Press Control + fn + ← to move to cell A1.

2 Press Ctrl + Home again, and then from the **row heading area**, select **row 14**. Click the **View tab**, and then in the **Window group**, click **Freeze Panes**. In the list, click **Freeze Panes**. Click any cell to deselect the row, and then notice that a line displays along the upper border of **row 14**.

> By selecting row 14, the rows above—rows 1–13—are frozen in place and will not move as you scroll down.

3 Watch the row numbers below **row 13**, and then begin to scroll down to bring **row 21** into view again. Notice that rows 1:13 are frozen in place. Compare your screen with Figure 2.23.

> The remaining rows of data continue to scroll. Use this feature when you have long or wide worksheets.

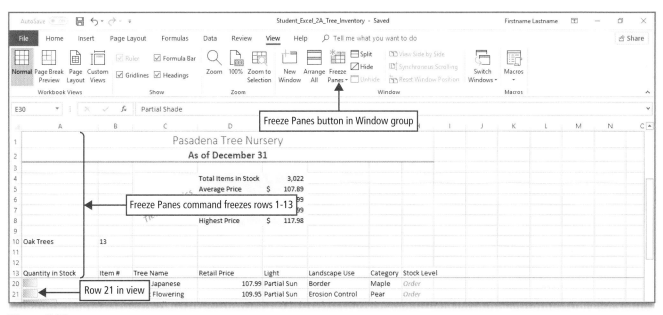

Figure 2.23

4 In the **Window group**, click **Freeze Panes**, and then click **Unfreeze Panes** to unlock all rows and columns. **Save** your workbook.

MORE KNOWLEDGE **Freeze Columns or Freeze Both Rows and Columns**

You can freeze columns that you want to remain in view on the left. Select the column to the right of the column(s) that you want to remain in view while scrolling to the right, and then click the Freeze Panes command. You can also use the command to freeze both rows and columns; click a *cell* to freeze the rows *above* the cell and the columns to the *left* of the cell.

GO! Learn How
Video E2-5

To analyze a group of related data, you can convert a range of cells to an *Excel table*. An Excel table is a series of rows and columns that contains related data that is managed independently from the data in other rows and columns in the worksheet.

Activity 2.14 | Creating an Excel Table and Applying a Table Style

3.1.1 and 3.1.2

1 Be sure that you have applied the Unfreeze Panes command—no rows on your worksheet are locked. Click any cell in the data below **row 13**. Click the **Insert tab**. In the **Tables group**, click **Table**. In the **Create Table** dialog box, if necessary, click to select the My table has headers check box. Verify that in the dialog box, **$A$13:$H$42** displays, and then compare your screen with Figure 2.24.

The column titles in row 13 will form the table headers. By clicking in a range of contiguous data, Excel will suggest the range as the data for the table. You can adjust the range if necessary.

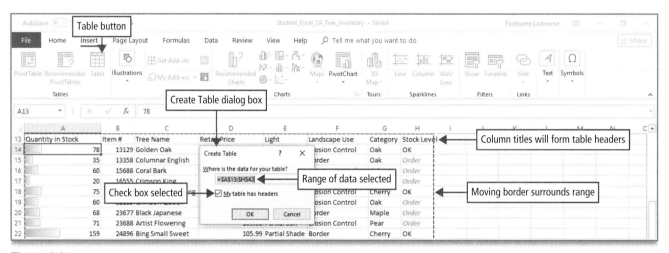

Figure 2.24

🔄 **ANOTHER WAY**   Select the range of cells that make up the table, including the header row, and then click the Table button.

2 Click **OK**. With the range still selected, on the ribbon, notice that the **Table Tools** contextual tab is active.

3 On the **Design tab**, in the **Table Styles group**, click **More** ⊡, and then under **Light**, locate and click **Light Blue, Table Style Light 16**. If this table style is not available, choose a similar style.

4 Make cell **A1** the active cell. Click **Save** 🖫, and then compare your screen with Figure 2.25.

Sorting and filtering arrows display in the table's header row.

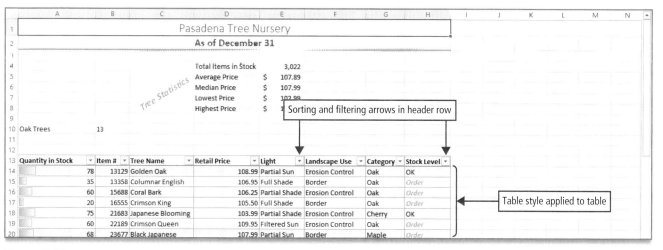

Figure 2.25

Activity 2.15 | Sorting an Excel Table

MOS
3.3.2

You can *sort* tables—arrange all the data in a specific order—in ascending or descending order.

1 In the header row of the table, click the **Retail Price arrow**, and then on the menu, click **Sort Smallest to Largest**. Next to the arrow, notice the small **up arrow** indicating an ascending (smallest to largest) sort.

This action sorts the rows in the table from the lowest retail price to highest retail price.

MAC TIP In the Retail Price dialog box, under Sort, click Ascending, and then click Close.

2 In the table's header row, click the **Category arrow**, and then click **Sort Z to A**.

This action sorts the rows in the table in reverse alphabetic order by Category name, and the small arrow points downward, indicating a descending (Z to A) sort. The Retail Price continues to be sorted from smallest to largest within each category.

MAC TIP In the Category dialog box, under Sort, click Descending.

3 Click the **Category arrow**, and then sort from **A to Z**. Next to the arrow, notice the small **up arrow** indicating an ascending (A to Z) sort.

This action sorts the rows in the table alphabetically by Category, and within a Category, it sorts the rows from smallest to largest by Retail Price.

MAC TIP In the Category dialog box, under Sort, click Ascending, and then click Close.

4 In the table header row, click the **Item # arrow**, and then click **Sort Smallest to Largest**, which will apply an ascending sort to the data using the *Item #* column.

MAC TIP In the Item # dialog box, under Sort, click Ascending, and close the dialog box.

Activity 2.16 | Filtering an Excel Table and Displaying a Total Row

3.2.3 and
3.3.1

You can *filter* tables—display only a portion of the data based on matching a specific value—to show only the data that meets the criteria that you specify.

1 Click the **Category arrow**. Click the **(Select All)** check box to clear all the check boxes. Click to select only the **Maple** check box, and then click **OK**. Compare your screen with Figure 2.26.

Only the rows containing *Maple* in the Category column display—the remaining rows are hidden from view. A small funnel—the filter icon—indicates that a filter is applied to the data in the table. Additionally, the row numbers display in blue to indicate that some rows are hidden from view. A filter hides entire rows in the worksheet.

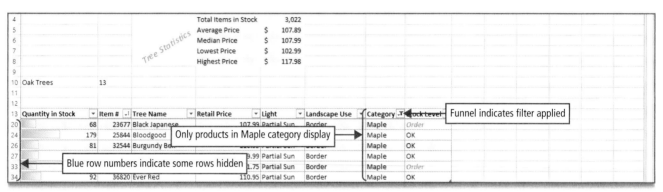

Figure 2.26

2 Point to the right of *Category* and notice that *Equals "Maple"* displays to indicate the filter criteria.

3 Click any cell in the table so that the table is selected. On the **Table Tools Design tab**, in the **Table Style Options group**, select the **Total Row** check box.

Total displays in cell A43. In cell H43, the number *6* indicates that six rows currently display.

4 Click cell **A43**, click the **arrow** that displays to the right of cell **A43**, and then in the list, click **Sum**.

Excel sums only the visible rows in Column A and indicates that 571 products in the Maple category are in stock. In this manner, you can use an Excel table to quickly find information about a group of data.

5 Click cell **A11**, type **Maple Trees** and press Tab. In cell **B11**, type **6 (571 total items in stock)** and then press Enter.

6 In the table header row, click the **Category arrow**, and then click **Clear Filter From "Category"**.

All the rows in the table redisplay.

MAC TIP To clear the filter, click the Category arrow, click Clear Filter, and then click Close.

7 Click the **Landscape Use arrow**, click the **(Select All)** check box to clear all the check boxes, and then click to select the **Erosion Control** check box. Click **OK**.

8 ▶ Click the **Category arrow**, click the **(Select All)** check box to clear all the check boxes, and then click the **Oak** check box. Click **OK**, **Save** 🖫 your workbook, and then compare your screen with Figure 2.27.

By applying multiple filters, you can determine quickly that eight tree names identified with a *Landscape Use* of *Erosion Control* are in the *Oak* tree category with a total of 710 such trees in stock.

	Quantity in Stock	Item #	Tree Name	Retail Price	Light	Landscape Use	Category	Stock Level
10	Oak Trees	13						
11	Maple Trees	6 (571 total items in stock)						
12								
13	Quantity in Stock	Item #	Tree Name	Retail Price	Light	Landscape Use	Category	Stock Level
14	78	13129	Golden Oak	108.99	Partial Sun	Erosion Control	Oak	OK
16	60	15688	Coral Bark	106.25	Partial Shade	Erosion Control	Oak	Order
19	60	22189	Crimson Queen	109.95	Filtered Sun	Erosion Control	Oak	Order
28	113	34793	Emerald Elf	103.98	Full Shade	Erosion Control	Oak	OK
35	173	37803	Osakazuki	103.88	Full Shade	Erosion Control	Oak	OK
37	75	38675	Palo Alto	102.99	Partial Shade	Erosion Control	Oak	OK
38	93	38700	Pacific Fire	103.75	Full Shade	Erosion Control	Oak	OK
40	58	39704	Embers	105.99	Partial Sun	Erosion Control	Oak	Order
43	710							8

8 tree types in Oak category can be used for Erosion Control

Figure 2.27

MORE KNOWLEDGE **Band Rows and Columns in a Table**

You can band rows to format even rows differently from odd rows, making them easier to read. To band rows or columns, on the Design tab, in the Table Style Options group, select the Banded Rows or Banded Columns check box.

Activity 2.17 | Clearing Filters

When you are finished answering questions about the data in a table, you can clear the filters and remove the total row.

1 ▶ Click the **Category arrow**, and then click **Clear Filter From "Category"**. Use the same technique to remove the filter from the **Landscape Use** column.

2 ▶ Click anywhere in the table to activate the table. On the **Table Tools Design tab**, in the **Table Style Options group**, click the **Total Row** check box to clear the check mark and remove the Total row from the table.

3 ▶ Click **Save** 🖫, and then compare your screen with Figure 2.28.

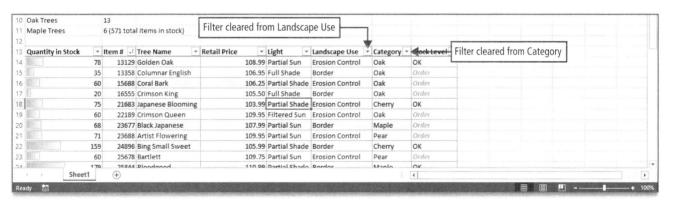

Filter cleared from Landscape Use

Filter cleared from Category

Figure 2.28

MORE KNOWLEDGE **Converting a Table to a Range**

When you are finished answering questions about the data in a table by sorting, filtering, and totalling, you can convert the table into a normal range. Doing so is useful if you want to use the Table feature only to apply an attractive Table Style to a range of cells. For example, you can insert a table, apply a Table Style, and then convert the table to a normal range of data but keep the formatting. To convert a table to a range, on the Design tab, in the Tools group, click Convert to Range. In the message box, click Yes. Or, with any table cell selected, right-click, point to Table, and then click Convert to Range.

GO! Learn How
Video E2-6

You can magnify or shrink the view of a worksheet on your screen to either zoom in to view specific data or zoom out to see the entire worksheet. You can also split a worksheet window into panes to view different parts of a worksheet at the same time.

A worksheet might be too wide, too long—or both—to print on a single page. Use Excel's **Print Titles** and **Scale to Fit** commands to create pages that are attractive and easy to read.

The Print Titles command enables you to specify rows and columns to repeat on each printed page. Scale to Fit commands enable you to stretch or shrink the width, height, or both, of printed output to fit a maximum number of pages.

Activity 2.18 | Modifying and Shrinking the Worksheet View

1 Press Ctrl + Home to display the top of your worksheet. On the **View tab**, in the **Zoom group**, click **Zoom**.

 MAC TIP Press Control + fn + ←. On the View tab, click the Zoom arrow.

2 In the **Zoom** dialog box, click the **75%** option button, and then click **OK.** Notice that by zooming out in this manner, you can see additional rows of your worksheet on the screen.

3 In the lower right corner of your worksheet, in the status bar, click the **Zoom In** button ➕ until the worksheet redisplays at 100%.

Activity 2.19 | Splitting a Worksheet Window into Panes

MOS
1.4.4

The **Split** command splits the window into multiple resizable panes that contain views of your worksheet. This is useful to view multiple distant parts of your worksheet at one time.

1 Click cell **F9**. On the **View tab**, in the **Window group**, click **Split**.

Horizontal and vertical split bars display. You can drag the split bars to view any four portions of the worksheet. On the right, separate vertical scroll bars display for the upper and lower panes and at the bottom, separate horizontal scroll bars display for the left and right panes.

2 Drag the lower vertical scroll box down to the bottom of the scroll bar to view **row 43**. Compare your screen with Figure 2.29.

Here it could be useful to isolate the Tree Statistics at the top and then scroll to the bottom to browse the inventory items.

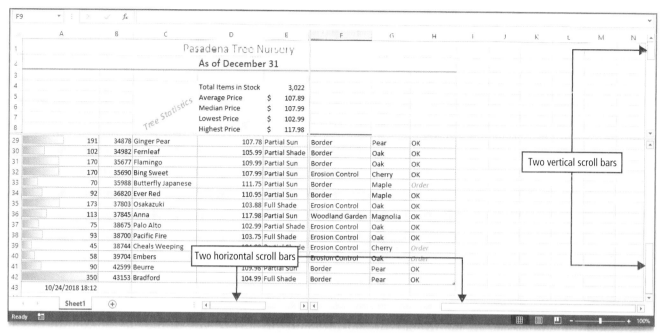

Figure 2.29

> **3** ▶ Click **Split** again to remove the split bars.

> **4** ▶ Press [Ctrl] + [Home] to display the top of your worksheet. On the **Page Layout tab**, in the **Themes group**, click **Themes**, and then click **Slice**.

> **5** ▶ Select the range **A13:H13**. On the **Home tab**, from the **Styles group**, apply the **Heading 4** cell style, and then apply **Center** ☰. Click cell **A1**.

Activity 2.20 | Printing Titles and Scaling to Fit

1.5.3

> **1** ▶ Click the **Page Layout tab**, and then in the **Page Setup group**, click **Margins**. At the bottom of the gallery, click **Custom Margins** to display the **Page Setup** dialog box. Under **Center on page**, select the **Horizontally** check box.

> **2** ▶ Click the **Header/Footer tab**, and then in the center of the dialog box, click **Custom Footer**. In the **Footer** dialog box, with your insertion point blinking in the **Left section**, on the row of buttons, click **Insert File Name** 🖼. Click **OK** two times.

> **3** ▶ In the **Page Setup group**, click **Orientation**, and then click **Landscape**.

> The dotted line indicates that as currently formatted, column H will not fit on the page.

> **4** ▶ On the **File tab**, click **Print** to display the **Print Preview**. At the bottom of the **Print Preview**, click **Next Page** ▶.

> As currently formatted, the worksheet will print on four pages, and the columns will span multiple pages. Additionally, after Page 1, no column titles are visible to identify the data in the columns.

> **5** ▶ Click **Next Page** ▶ two times to display **Page 4** and notice that one column moves to an additional page.

> **6** ▶ In the upper left corner of **Backstage** view, click **Back** ⊚ to return to the worksheet. In the **Page Setup group**, click **Print Titles**. Under **Print titles**, click in the **Rows to repeat at top** box, and then at the right, click **Collapse Dialog** 🔼.

7 From the **row heading area**, select **row 13**, and then in the **Page Setup – rows to repeat at top:** dialog box, click **Expand Dialog** [⬚]. Click **OK** to print the column titles in row 13 at the top of every page.

> You can collapse and then expand dialog boxes on your screen to enable a better view of your data.

8 Display the **Print Preview** again. At the bottom of the **Settings group**, click the **No Scaling arrow**, and then on the displayed list, point to **Fit All Columns on One Page**. Compare your screen with Figure 2.30.

> This action will shrink the width of the printed output to fit all the columns on one page. You can make adjustments like this on the Page Layout tab, or here, in the Print Preview.

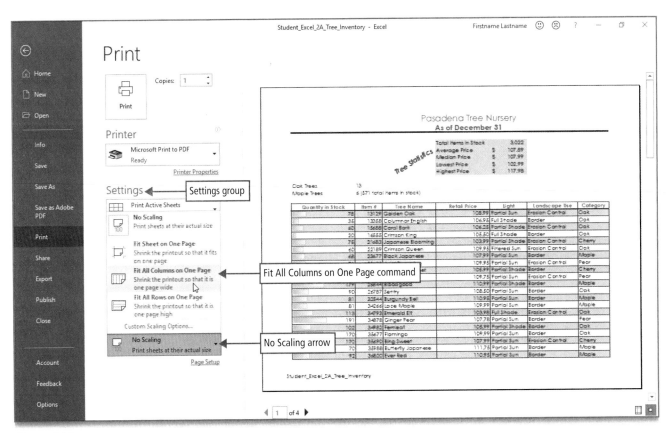

Figure 2.30

🖥️ **MAC TIP** To fit the worksheet width on one page, close the Print dialog box. On the Page Layout tab, click the Width button arrow, and then click 1 page.

9 Click **Fit All Columns on One Page**. Notice in the **Print Preview** that all the columns display on one page.

🔄 **ANOTHER WAY** With the worksheet displayed, on the Page Layout tab, in the Scale to Fit group, click the Width button arrow, and then click 1 page.

10 At the bottom of the **Print Preview**, click **Next Page** [▶] one time. Notice that the output will now print on two pages and that the column titles display at the top of **Page 2**. Compare your screen with Figure 2.31.

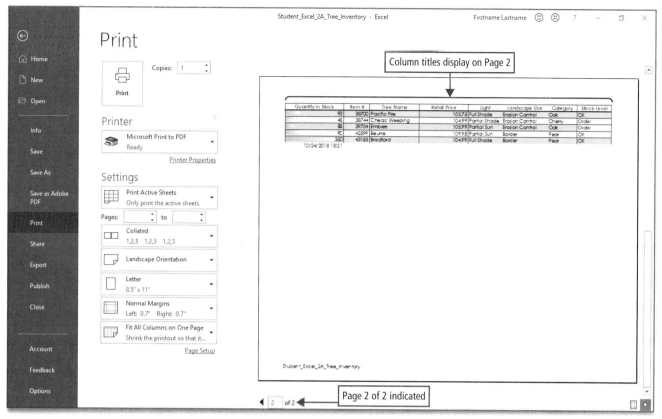

Figure 2.31

11 Display the workbook **Properties**. As the **Tags**, type **tree inventory, Pasadena** and as the **Subject**, type your course name and section number. Be sure your name displays as the Author; edit if necessary. **Save** your worksheet and then **Close** Excel.

MAC TIP To edit the document properties, click File, and then click Properties. Click Summary, and then edit the properties as necessary.

MORE KNOWLEDGE   Scaling for Data That Is Slightly Larger Than the Printed Page

If your data is just a little too large to fit on a printed page, you can scale the worksheet to make it fit. Scaling reduces both the width and height of the printed data to a percentage of its original size or by the number of pages that you specify. On the Page Layout tab, in the Scale to Fit group, click the Scale arrows to select a percentage.

For Non-MyLab Submissions Determine What Your Instructor Requires for Submission
As directed by your instructor, submit your completed Excel workbook.

---

12 In **MyLab IT**, locate and click the Grader Project **Excel 2A Tree Inventory**. In **step 3**, under **Upload Completed Assignment**, click **Choose File**. In the **Open** dialog box, navigate to your **Excel Chapter 2 folder**, and then click your **Student_Excel_2A_Tree_Inventory** file one time to select it. In the lower right corner of the **Open** dialog box, click **Open**.

The name of your selected file displays above the Upload button.

13 To submit your file to **MyLab IT** for grading, click **Upload**, wait a moment for a green **Success!** message, and then in **step 4**, click the blue **Submit for Grading** button. Click **Close Assignment** to return to your list of **Course Materials**.

You have completed Project 2A   END

»»» GO! With Google Sheets

Objective | Summarize an Inventory List

ALERT Working with Web-Based Applications and Services

Computer programs and services on the web receive continuous updates and improvements, so the steps to complete this web-based activity may differ from the ones shown. You can often look at the screens and the information presented to determine how to complete the activity.

If you do not already have a Google account, you will need to create one before you begin this activity. Go to http://google.com and in the upper right corner, click Sign In. On the Sign In screen, click Create Account. On the Create your Google Account page, complete the form, read and agree to the Terms of Service and Privacy Policy, and then click Next step. On the Welcome screen, click Get Started.

Activity | Create SUM, AVERAGE, COUNTIF, and IF functions

1 From the desktop, open your browser, navigate to http://google.com, and then click **Google Apps** ⊞. Click **Drive** ◢, and then if necessary, sign in to your Google account.

2 Open your **GO! Web Projects** folder—or click **New** to create and then open this folder if necessary. In the left pane, click **New** and then click **File upload**. Navigate to your student data files, click **e02_2A_Web**, and then click **Open**.

3 Right-click the file you uploaded, point to **Open with**, and then click **Google Sheets**.

4 Select the range **A1:H1**. Click **Merge cells** ⊞. Click **Format**, point to **Align**, and then click **Center**. With **A1** selected, click **Paint format** 🖌, and then click cell **A2**.

5 Select **A1:A2**, and then click the **Font size arrow** 10. Click **18**.

6 Click cell **B4**. On the ribbon, click **Functions** Σ ·, and then click **SUM**. Within the formula's parentheses, type **a11:a33** and press Enter for a result of *2311*. Click **B4**, and then on the ribbon, click **More formats** 123 ·. Click **Number**, and then click **Decrease decimal places** .0. two times.

7 Click cell **B5**, click **Functions** Σ ·, and then click **AVERAGE**. Within the parentheses, type **d11:d33** and press Enter. Click **B5**, and then on the ribbon, click **Format as currency** $.

8 Click cell **B7**. Type **=countif(g11:g33,"Oak")** and then press Enter to create a function that counts the number of Oak trees in the category column. Compare your screen with Figure A.

	A	B	C	D	E	F	G	H	I	J	K	L	M	N	O	P
1				Austin Tree Nursery												
2				As of March 30												
3																
4	Total Items in Stock	2,311														
5	Average Price	$108.52														
6																
7	Oak Trees:	10														
8																
9																
10	Quantity in Stock	Item #	Tree Name	Retail Price	Light		Landscape Use	Category	Stock Level							
11	78	13129	Golden Oak	108.99	Partial Sun		Erosion	Oak								
12	35	13358	Columnar English	106.95	Full Shade		Border	Oak								
13	60	15688	Coral Bark	106.25	Partial Shade		Erosion	Oak								
14	20	16555	Crimson King	105.5	Full Shade		Border	Oak								
15	75	21683	Japanese Blooming	103.99	Partial Shade		Erosion	Cherry								
16	60	22189	Crimson Queen	109.95	Filtered Sun		Erosion	Oak								
17	68	23677	Black Japanese	107.99	Partial Sun		Border	Maple								

Figure A

9 Click cell **H11**. Type **=if(a11<75,"Order","OK")** and then press **Enter**. Click cell **H11**, and then drag the fill handle down through cell **H33**.

10 With the range **H11:H33** selected, click **Format**, and then click **Conditional formatting**. On the right side of the window, in the **Apply to range** box, make sure that **H11:H33** displays. Under **Format cells if . . .** , click the displayed box, and then click **Text contains**. Click in the **Value or formula** box, and then type **Order** Under

Formatting style, click **Bold**. Click **Done** to apply the default conditional format and bold to all cells containing the word *Order*.

11 Close the Conditional Format rules pane, click cell **A1** and compare your screen with Figure B.

12 Submit your file as directed by your instructor. Sign out of your Google account and close your browser.

Figure B

Project 2B Weekly Sales Summary

MyLab IT
Project 2B Grader for Instruction
Project 2B Simulation for Training and Review

Project Activities

In Activities 2.21 through 2.36, you will edit an existing workbook for the Sales Director, Mariam Daly. The workbook summarizes the online and in-store sales of products during a one-week period in May. The worksheets of your completed workbook will look similar to Figure 2.32.

Project Files for MyLab IT Grader

1. In your MyLab IT course, locate and click **Excel 2B Weekly Sales**, Download Materials, and then Download All Files.

2. Extract the zipped folder to your Excel Chapter 2 folder. Close the Grader download screens.

3. Take a moment to open the downloaded **Excel_2B_Weekly_Sales_Instructions**; note any recent updates to the book.

Project Results

GO! Project 2B

Where We're Going

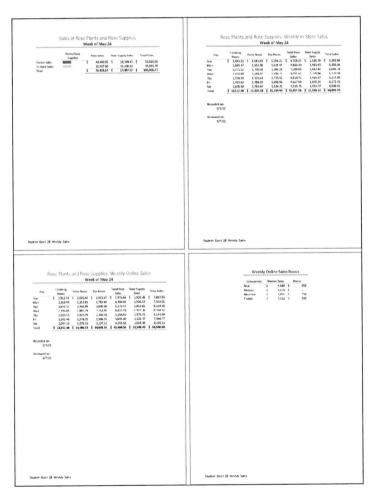

Figure 2.32 Project 2B Weekly Sales

For Non-MyLab Submissions

For Project 2B, you will need:

e02B_Weekly_Sales

In your Excel Chapter 2 folder, save your workbook as:

Lastname_Firstname_2B_Weekly_Sales

If your instructor requires a workbook with formulas, save as:

Lastname_Firstname_2B_Weekly_Sales_formulas

After you have named and saved your workbook, on the next page, begin with Step 2.

Objective 7   Navigate a Workbook and Rename Worksheets

ALERT   Because Office 365 is a cloud-based subscription service that receives continuous updates, you may encounter some variations in what appears on your screen and what is shown in this instruction. Microsoft Office 365 is fully installed on your PC or Mac; no internet access is necessary to create or edit documents. When you *are* connected to the internet, you will receive monthly upgrades and new features, so you always have the latest versions of Office apps as soon as they are available. Your subscription gives you continuous free access to the latest innovations and refinements.

GO! Learn How
Video E2-7

Use multiple worksheets in a workbook to organize data in a logical arrangement. When you have more than one worksheet in a workbook, you can *navigate* (move) among worksheets by clicking the *sheet tabs*. Sheet tabs identify each worksheet in a workbook and display along the lower left edge of the workbook window. When you have more worksheets in the workbook than can display in the sheet tab area, use the sheet tab scrolling buttons to move sheet tabs into and out of view.

Activity 2.21 │ Navigating Among Worksheets, Renaming Worksheets, and Changing the Tab Color of Worksheets

Excel names the first worksheet in a workbook *Sheet1* and each additional worksheet that you add in order—*Sheet2*, *Sheet3*, and so on. Most Excel users rename their worksheets with meaningful names. In this Activity, you will navigate among worksheets, rename worksheets, and change the tab color of sheet tabs.

1 Navigate to your **Excel Chapter 2 folder**, and then double-click the Excel file you downloaded from **MyLab IT** that displays your name—**Student_Excel_2B_Weekly_Sales**.

In this workbook two worksheets display, into which some data has already been entered. For example, on the first worksheet, the days of the week and sales data for the one-week period displays.

2 Along the bottom of the Excel window, point to and then click the **Sheet2 tab**.

The second worksheet in the workbook displays and becomes the active worksheet. *Sheet2* displays in bold.

3 In cell **A1**, notice the text *In-Store*—this worksheet will contain data for in-store sales.

4 Click the **Sheet1 tab**. Then, point to the **Sheet1 tab**, and double-click to select the sheet tab name. Type **Online Sales** and press Enter.

The first worksheet becomes the active worksheet, and the sheet tab displays *Online Sales*.

5 Point to the **Online Sales sheet tab** and right-click. Point to **Tab Color**, and then in the next to last column, point to the first color. Compare your screen with Figure 2.33.

ANOTHER WAY   On the Home tab, in the Cells group, click the Format button, and then on the displayed list, point to Tab Color. Mac users may also use this method.

MAC TIP   To display the shortcut menu, point to the Online Sales sheet tab, hold down Control, and then click.

Figure 2.33

6 In the second to last column, click the first color to change the tab color.

7 Point to the **Sheet2 tab**, right-click, and then from the shortcut menu, click **Rename**. Type **In-Store Sales** and press Enter.

> You can either double-click the sheet name or use the shortcut menu to rename a sheet tab.

8 Point to the **In-Store Sales sheet tab** and right-click. Point to **Tab Color**, and then in the last column, click the first color. **Save** your workbook.

MORE KNOWLEDGE **Copying a Worksheet**

To copy a worksheet to the same workbook, right-click the sheet tab, on the shortcut menu click Move or Copy, click the sheet before which you want to insert the copied sheet, select the Create a copy check box, and then click OK. To copy to a different workbook, in the Move or Copy dialog box, click the To book arrow, and then select the workbook into which you want to insert the copy.

Objective 8 **Enter Dates, Clear Contents, and Clear Formats**

GO! Learn How
Video E2-8

Dates represent a type of value that you can enter in a cell. When you enter a date, Excel assigns a serial value—a number—to the date. This makes it possible to treat dates like other numbers. For example, if two cells contain dates, you can find the number of days between the two dates by subtracting the older date from the more recent date.

Activity 2.22 | Entering and Formatting Dates

In this Activity, you will examine the various ways that Excel can format dates in a cell. Date values entered in any of the following formats will be recognized by Excel as a date:

Value Typed	Example
m/d/yy	7/4/2016
d-mmm	4-Jul
d-mmm-yy	4-Jul-16
mmm-yy	Jul-16

On your keyboard, $\boxed{-}$ (the hyphen key) and $\boxed{/}$ (the forward slash key) function identically in any of these formats and can be used interchangeably. You can abbreviate the month name to three characters or spell it out. You can enter the year as two digits, four digits, or even leave it off. When left off, the current year is assumed but does not display in the cell.

A two-digit year value of 30 through 99 is interpreted by the Windows operating system as the four-digit years of 1930 through 1999. All other two-digit year values are assumed to be in the 21st century. If you always type year values as four digits, even though only two digits may display in the cell, you can be sure that Excel interprets the year value as you intended. Examples are shown in Figure 2.34.

How Excel Interprets Dates	
Date Typed As:	**Completed by Excel As:**
7/4/15	7/4/2015
7/4/98	7/4/1998
7/4	4-Jul (current year assumed)
7-4	4-Jul (current year assumed)
July 4	4-Jul (current year assumed)
Jul 4	4-Jul (current year assumed)
Jul/4	4-Jul (current year assumed)
Jul-4	4-Jul (current year assumed)
July 4, 1998	4-Jul-98
July 2012	Jul-12 (first day of month assumed)
July 1998	Jul-98 (first day of month assumed)

Figure 2.34

1 Click the **Online Sales sheet tab** to make it active. Click cell **A16** and notice that the cell displays *6/3*. In the **Formula Bar**, notice that the full date of June 3, 2022 displays in the format *6/3/2022*.

2 With cell **A16** selected, on the **Home tab**, in the **Number group**, click the **Number Format arrow**. At the bottom, click **More Number Formats** to display the **Number tab** of the **Format Cells** dialog box.

Under Category, *Date* is selected, and under Type, *3/14* is selected. Cell A16 uses this format type; that is, only the month and day display in the cell.

MAC TIP To display group names on the ribbon, display the menu, click Word, click Preferences, click View, select the Show group titles check box.

3 In the displayed dialog box, under **Type**, click several other date types and watch the **Sample** area to see how applying the selected date format will format your cell. When you are finished, click the **3/14/12** type, and then compare your screen with Figure 2.35.

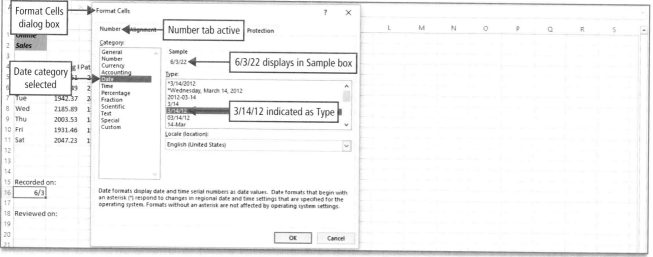

Figure 2.35

4 At the bottom of the dialog box, click **OK**. Click cell **A19**, type **6-7-22** and then press [Enter].

Cell A19 has no special date formatting applied and displays in the default date format *6/7/2022*.

5 Click cell **A19** again. Hold down [Ctrl] and press [;] (semicolon). Press [Enter] to confirm the entry.

Excel enters the current date, obtained from your computer's internal calendar, in the selected cell using the default date format. [Ctrl] + [;] is a quick method to enter the current date.

6 Click cell **A19** again, type **6/7/22** and then press [Enter].

Because the year *22* is less than 30, Excel assumes a 21st century date and changes *22* to *2022* to complete the four-digit year. Typing *98* would result in *1998*. For two-digit years that you type that are between 30 and 99, Excel assumes a 20th century date.

7 Click cell **A16**, and then on the **Home tab**, in the **Clipboard group**, click **Format Painter**. Click cell **A19** and notice that the date format from cell **A16** is copied to cell **A19**. **Save** your workbook.

Activity 2.23 │ Clearing Cell Contents and Formats

2.2.8

A cell has *contents*—a value or a formula—and a cell may also have one or more *formats* applied, for example, bold and italic font styles, fill color, font color, and so on. You can choose to clear—delete—the *contents* of a cell, the *formatting* of a cell, or both.

Clearing the contents of a cell deletes the value or formula typed there, but it does *not* clear formatting applied to a cell. In this Activity, you will clear the contents of a cell and then clear the formatting of a cell that contains a date to see its underlying content.

1 In the **Online Sales** worksheet, click cell **A1**. In the **Editing group**, click **Clear**, and then click **Clear Contents**. Notice that the text is cleared, but the green formatting remains.

2 Click cell **A2**, and then press [Delete].

You can use either of these two methods to delete the *contents* of a cell. Deleting the contents does not, however, delete the formatting of the cell; you can see that the green fill color format applied to the two cells still displays.

3 In cell **A1**, type **Online Sales** and then on the **Formula Bar**, click **Enter** so that cell **A1** remains the active cell.

In addition to the green fill color, the bold italic text formatting remains with the cell.

4 In the **Editing group**, click **Clear**, and then click **Clear Formats**.

Clearing the formats deletes formatting from the cell—the green fill color and the bold and italic font styles—but does not delete the cell's contents.

5 Use the same technique to clear the green fill color from cell **A2**. Click cell **A16**, click **Clear**, and then click **Clear Formats**. In the **Number group**, notice that *General* displays as the number format of the cell.

The box in the Number group indicates the current Number format of the selected cell. Clearing the date formatting from the cell displays the date's serial number. The date, June 3, 2022, is stored as a serial number that indicates the number of days since January 1, 1900. This date is the 44,715th day since the reference date of January 1, 1900.

6 On the **Quick Access Toolbar**, click **Undo** 5· to restore the date format. **Save** 🖫 your workbook, and then compare your screen with Figure 2.36.

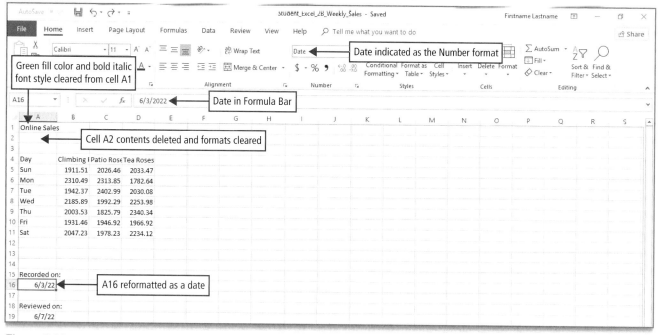

Figure 2.36

MORE KNOWLEDGE **Clearing an Entire Worksheet**

To clear an entire worksheet, in the upper left corner of the worksheet, click the Select All button, and then on the Home tab, in the Editing group, click Clear, and then click Clear All.

Objective 9 Copy and Paste by Using the Paste Options Gallery

GO! Learn How
Video E2-9

Data in cells can be copied to other cells in the same worksheet, to other sheets in the same workbook, or to sheets in another workbook. The action of placing cell contents that have been copied or moved to the Clipboard into another location is called *paste*.

Activity 2.24 | Copying and Pasting by Using the Paste Options Gallery

2.1.2

Recall that the Clipboard is a temporary storage area maintained by your Windows operating system. When you select one or more cells, and then perform the Copy command or the Cut command, the selected data is placed on the Clipboard. From the Clipboard storage area, the data is available for pasting into other cells, other worksheets, other workbooks, and even into other Office programs. When you paste, the *Paste Options gallery* displays, which includes Live Preview to preview the Paste formatting that you want.

1 With the **Online Sales** worksheet active, select the range **A4:A19**.

A range of cells identical to this one is required for the *In-Store Sales* worksheet.

2 Right-click over the selection, and then click **Copy** to place a copy of the cells on the Clipboard. The copied cells may display a moving border.

🔄 **ANOTHER WAY** Use the keyboard shortcut for Copy, which is Ctrl + C; or on the Home tab, click Copy.

⌨️ **MAC TIP** On the Home tab, click Copy.

---

3 At the bottom of the workbook window, click the **In-Store Sales sheet tab** to make it the active worksheet. Point to cell **A4**, right-click, and then on the shortcut menu, under **Paste Options**, *point* to the first button—**Paste**. Compare your screen with Figure 2.37.

> Live Preview displays how the copied cells will be placed in the worksheet if you click the Paste button. In this manner, you can experiment with different paste options, and then be sure you are selecting the paste operation that you want. When pasting a range of cells, you need only point to or select the cell in the upper left corner of the *paste area*—the target destination for data that has been cut or copied using the Clipboard.

 MAC TIP On the Home tab, click Paste.

Figure 2.37

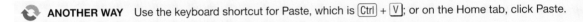 **ANOTHER WAY** Use the keyboard shortcut for Paste, which is [Ctrl] + [V]; or on the Home tab, click Paste.

4 Click the first button, **Paste**. In the status bar, notice the message that displays, indicating that you can paste your selection to another destination.

5 Display the **Online Sales** worksheet. Press [Esc] to cancel the moving border. **Save** 🖫 your workbook.

> The status bar no longer displays the message.

Objective 10 Edit and Format Multiple Worksheets at the Same Time

GO! Learn How
Video E2-10

> You can enter or edit data on several worksheets at the same time by selecting and grouping multiple worksheets. Data that you enter or edit on the active sheet is reflected in all selected sheets. If the sheet tab displays with a solid background color, you know the sheet is not selected.

Activity 2.25 │ Grouping Worksheets for Editing

MOS
2.2.4

> In this Activity, you will group the two worksheets, and then format both worksheets at the same time.

1 With the **Online Sales** sheet active, press [Ctrl] + [Home] to make cell **A1** the active cell. Point to the **Online Sales sheet tab**, right-click, and then click **Select All Sheets**.

 MAC TIP To display the shortcut menu, point to the Online Sales sheet tab, hold down [Control], and then click.

2 At the top of your screen, notice that *Group* displays in the title bar. Compare your screen with Figure 2.38.

> Both worksheets are selected, as indicated by *Group* in the title bar and the sheet tab names underlined. Data that you enter or edit on the active sheet will also be entered or edited in the same manner on all the selected sheets in the same cells.

Figure 2.38

3 Select **columns A:G**, and then set their width to **85 pixels**.

4 Click cell **A2**, type **Week of May 24** and then on the **Formula Bar**, click **Enter** ☑ to keep cell **A2** as the active cell. **Merge & Center** 🔲 the text across the range **A2:G2**, and then apply the **Heading 1** cell style.

5 Click cell **E4**, type **Total Rose Sales** and then press ⌨Tab. In cell **F4**, type **Rose Supply Sales** and then press ⌨Tab. In cell **G4**, type **Total Sales** and then press ⌨Enter.

6 Select the range **A4:G4**, and then apply the **Heading 3** cell style. In the **Alignment group**, click **Center** ☰, **Middle Align** ☰, and **Wrap Text**. **Save** 🖫 your workbook.

7 Display the **In-Store Sales** worksheet to cancel the grouping, and then compare your screen with Figure 2.39.

> When you select a single sheet that was not a sheet that was active when you selected all sheets, the grouping of the sheets is cancelled and *Group* no longer displays in the title bar. Because the sheets were grouped, the same new text and formatting were applied to both sheets. In this manner, you can make the same changes to all the sheets in a workbook at one time.

ANOTHER WAY Right-click any sheet tab, and then click Ungroup Sheets.

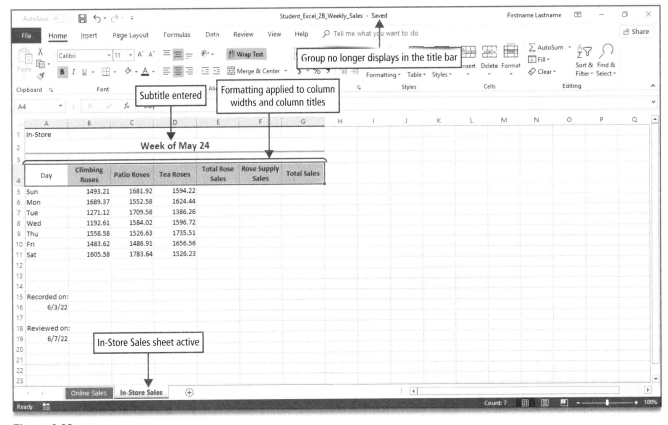

Figure 2.39

> **MORE KNOWLEDGE** **Hide Worksheets**
>
> You can hide any worksheet in a workbook to remove it from view using this technique:
> Select the sheet tabs of the worksheets you want to hide, right-click any of the selected sheet tabs, and then click Hide.

Activity 2.26 | Formatting and Constructing Formulas on Grouped Worksheets

Recall that formulas are equations that perform calculations on values in your worksheet and that a formula starts with an equal sign (=). Operators are the symbols with which you specify the type of calculation that you want to perform on the elements of a formula. In this Activity, you will enter sales figures for Rose Supply items from both Online and In-Store sales, and then calculate the total sales.

1 Display the **Online Sales** worksheet. Verify that the sheets are not grouped—*Group* does *not* display in the title bar.

2 Click cell **A1**, replace *Online Sales* by typing **Rose Plants and Rose Supplies: Weekly Online Sales** and then on the **Formula Bar**, click **Enter** ☑ to keep cell **A1** as the active cell. **Merge & Center** 🖃▾ the text across the range **A1:G1**, and then apply the **Title** cell style.

3 In the column titled *Rose Supply Sales*, click cell **F5**. In the range **F5:F11**, type the following data for Rose Supply Sales, and then compare your screen with Figure 2.40.

	Rose Supply Sales
Sun	1926.49
Mon	1526.03
Tue	1853.82
Wed	1922.36
Thu	1973.73
Fri	2121.47
Sat	2025.55

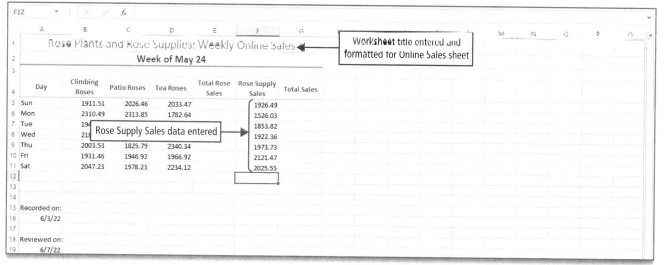

Figure 2.40

4 Display the **In-Store Sales** sheet. In cell **A1**, replace *In-Store* by typing **Rose Plants and Rose Supplies: Weekly In-Store Sales** and then on the **Formula Bar**, click **Enter** ☑ to keep cell **A1** as the active cell. **Merge & Center** the text across the range **A1:G1**, and then apply the **Title** cell style.

5 In the column titled *Rose Supply Sales*, click cell **F5**, in the range **F5:F11**, type the following data for Rose Supply Sales, and then compare your screen with Figure 2.41.

	Rose Supply Sales
Sun	1626.59
Mon	1483.69
Tue	1693.82
Wed	1778.94
Thu	1416.37
Fri	1645.24
Sat	1493.47

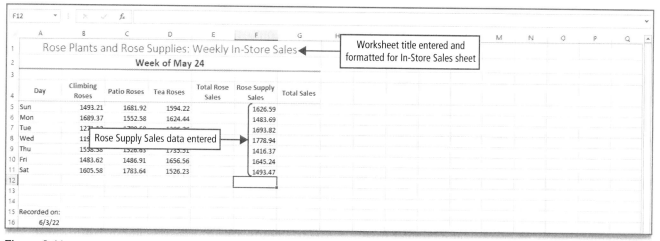

Figure 2.41

6 Save 🔲 your workbook. Right-click the **Online Sales sheet tab**, and then click **Select All Sheets**.

The first worksheet becomes the active sheet, and the worksheets are grouped, *Group* displays in the title bar, and the sheet tabs are underlined, indicating they are selected as part of the group. Recall that when grouped, any action that you perform on the active worksheet is *also* performed on any other selected worksheets.

🖥 **MAC TIP** To display the shortcut menu, point to the Online Sales sheet tab, hold down (Control), and then click.

7 With the sheets *grouped* and the **Online Sales** sheet active, click cell **E5**. On the **Home tab**, in the **Editing group**, click **AutoSum**. Compare your screen with Figure 2.42.

Recall that when you enter the SUM function, Excel looks first above and then left for a proposed range of cells to sum.

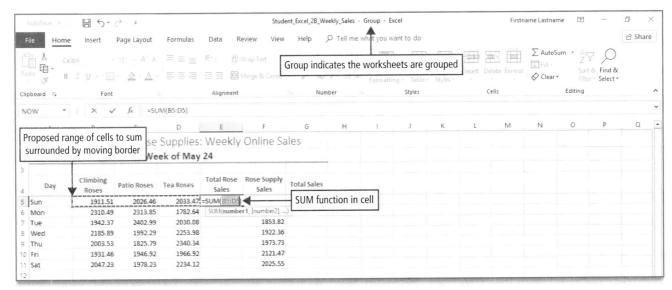

Figure 2.42

8 Press (Enter) to display Total Rose Sales for Sunday, which is *5971.44*.

9 Click cell **E5**, and then drag the fill handle down to copy the formula through cell **E11**.

10 Click cell **G5**, type = click cell **E5**, type + click cell **F5**, and then compare your screen with Figure 2.43.

Using the point-and-click technique to construct this formula is only one of several techniques you can use. Alternatively, you could use any other method to enter the SUM function to add the values in these two cells.

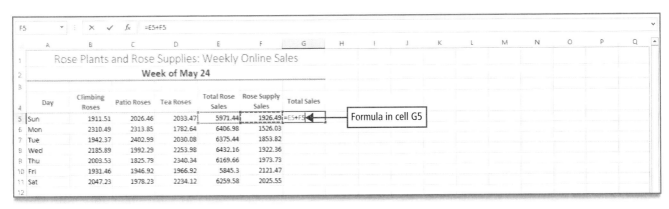

Figure 2.43

11 Press Enter to display the result *7897.93*, and then copy the formula down through cell **G11**. Save 🖫 your workbook.

Activity 2.27 | Determining Multiple Totals at the Same Time

You can select a contiguous range of cells adjacent to rows or columns of numbers and then click the AutoSum button—or use Alt + = —to enter the SUM function for each row or column.

1 With the two worksheets still grouped, in cell **A12**, type **Total** and then select the range **B5:G12**, which is all of the sales data and the empty cells at the bottom of each column of sales data.

2 With the range **B5:G12** selected, hold down Alt and press = to enter the **SUM** function in each empty cell. Click **Save** 🖫.

Selecting a range in this manner and then clicking the AutoSum button, or entering the SUM function with the keyboard shortcut Alt + = , places the SUM function in the empty cells at the bottom of each column.

⌨ **MAC TIP** With the range B5:G12 selected, on the Home tab, click AutoSum.

Activity 2.28 | Formatting Grouped Worksheets

1 With the two worksheets still grouped, select the range **A5:A12**, and then apply the **Heading 4** cell style.

2 To apply financial formatting to the worksheets, select the range **B5:G5**, hold down Ctrl, and then select the range **B12:G12**. With the nonadjacent ranges selected, apply the **Accounting Number Format** $ -.

⌨ **MAC TIP** To select nonadjacent ranges, select the first range, hold down command ⌘, and then select the next range.

3 Select the range **B6:G11** and apply **Comma Style** 9. Select the range **B12:G12** and apply the **Total** cell style. Press Ctrl + Home to move to the top of the worksheet; compare your screen with Figure 2.44.

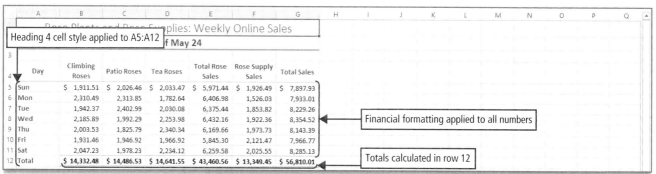

Figure 2.44

Activity 2.29 | Ungrouping Worksheets

1 Right-click the **Online Sales sheet tab**. On the shortcut menu, click **Ungroup Sheets** to cancel the grouping.

⌨ **MAC TIP** To display the shortcut menu, hold down Control and then click Ungroup Sheets.

2 Click the **In-store Sales sheet tab**. Click **Save** 🖫, and then compare your screen with Figure 2.45.

With your worksheets grouped, the calculations and formatting on the first worksheet were also added on the second worksheet.

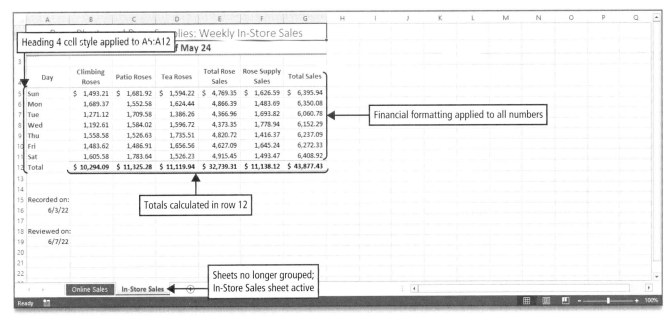

Figure 2.45

Create a Summary Sheet with Column Sparklines

GO! Learn How
Video E2-11

A *summary sheet* is a worksheet where totals from other worksheets are displayed and summarized. Recall that sparklines are tiny charts within a single cell that show a data trend.

Activity 2.30 | Inserting a Worksheet

1 To the right of the **In-Store Sales** sheet tab, click **New sheet** ⊕.

2 Rename the new worksheet tab **Summary** and display the **Tab Color** gallery. In the eighth column, select the first color.

3 Widen **columns A:E** to **110** pixels. In cell **A1**, type **Sales of Rose Plants and Rose Supplies** and then **Merge & Center** the title across the range **A1:E1**. Apply the **Title** cell style.

4 In cell **A2**, type **Week of May 24** and then **Merge & Center** across **A2:E2**; apply the **Heading 1** cell style.

5 Leave **row 3** blank. To form column titles, in cell **B4**, type **Roses/Rose Supplies** and press Tab. In cell **C4**, type **Rose Sales** and press Tab. In cell **D4**, type **Rose Supply Sales** and press Tab. In cell **E4**, type **Total Sales** and press Enter.

6 Select the range **B4:E4**. Apply the **Heading 3** cell style. In the **Alignment group**, click **Center** ≡, **Middle Align** ≡, and **Wrap Text**.

7 To form row titles, in cell **A5**, type **Online Sales** In cell **A6**, type **In-Store Sales**

8 **Save** 🖫, and then compare your screen with Figure 2.46.

Figure 2.46

Activity 2.31 | Constructing Formulas That Refer to Cells in Another Worksheet

In this Activity, you will construct formulas in the Summary worksheet to display the total sales for both online sales and in-store sales that will update the Summary worksheet whenever changes are made to the other worksheet totals.

1 Click cell **C5**. Type **=** and then click the **Online Sales sheet tab**. On the **Online Sales** worksheet, click cell **E12**, and then press Enter to redisplay the **Summary** worksheet and insert the total **Rose Sales** amount of *$43,460.56*.

2 Click cell **C5** to select it again. Look at the **Formula Bar**, and notice that instead of a value, the cell contains a formula that is equal to the value in another cell in another worksheet. Compare your screen with Figure 2.47.

The value in this cell is equal to the value in cell E12 of the *Online Sales* worksheet. The Accounting Number Format applied to the referenced cell is carried over. By using a formula of this type, changes in cell E12 on the *Online Sales* worksheet will be automatically updated in this *Summary* worksheet.

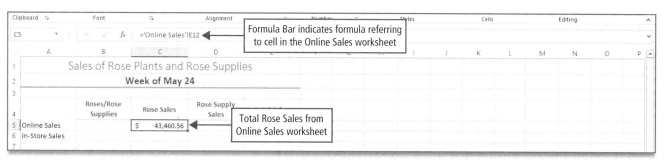

Figure 2.47

3 Click cell **D5**. Type **=** and then click the **Online Sales sheet tab**. Click cell **F12**, and then press Enter to redisplay the **Summary** worksheet and insert the total **Rose Supply Sales** amount of *$13,349.45*.

4 By using the techniques you just practiced, in cells **C6** and **D6** insert the total **Rose Sales** and **Rose Supply Sales** data from the **In-Store Sales** worksheet. Click **Save** 💾, and then compare your screen with Figure 2.48.

Figure 2.48

Activity 2.32 | Changing Values in a Detail Worksheet to Update a Summary Worksheet

The formulas in cells C5:D6 display the totals from the other two worksheets. Changes made to any of the other two worksheets—sometimes referred to as *detail sheets* because the details of the information are contained there—that affect their totals will display on this Summary worksheet. In this manner, the Summary worksheet accurately displays the current totals from the other worksheets.

1 In cell **A7**, type **Total** Select the range **C5:E6**, and then on the **Home tab**, in the **Editing group**, click **AutoSum** to total the two rows.

This technique is similar to selecting the empty cells at the bottom of columns and then inserting the SUM function for each column. Alternatively, you could use any other method to sum the rows. Recall that cell formatting carries over to adjacent cells unless two cells are left blank.

2 Select the range **C5:E7**, and then click **AutoSum** to total the three columns. Compare your screen with Figure 2.49.

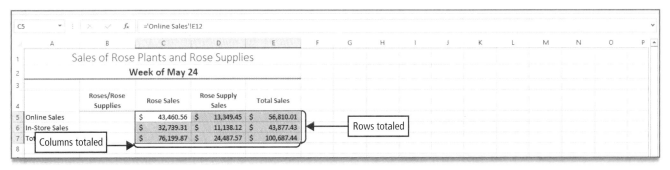

Figure 2.49

3 Notice that in cell **C6**, Rose Sales for In-Store Sales is $32,739.31, and in cell **C7**, the total is $76,199.87. Display the **In-Store Sales** worksheet, click cell **B8**, type **1410.88** and then press Enter. Notice that the formulas in the worksheet recalculate.

4 Display the **Summary** worksheet, and notice that in the **Rose Sales** column, both the total for the *In-Store Sales* and the *Total* were recalculated.

In this manner, a Summary sheet recalculates any changes made in the other worksheets.

5 On the **Summary** worksheet, select the range **C6:E6** and change the format to **Comma Style**. Select the range **C7:E7**, and then apply the **Total** cell style. Select the range **A5:A7** and apply the **Heading 4** cell style. **Save** your workbook. Click cell **A1**, and then compare your screen with Figure 2.50.

Figure 2.50

Activity 2.33 | Inserting Column Sparklines

2.4.1

In this Activity, you will insert column sparklines to visualize the ratio of Rose sales to Rose Supply sales for both Online and In-Store.

1 On the **Summary** worksheet, click cell **B5**. On the **Insert tab**, in the **Sparklines group**, click **Column**. In the **Create Sparklines** dialog box, with the insertion point blinking in the **Data Range** box, type **c5:d5** and then compare your screen with Figure 2.51.

Figure 2.51

2 Click **OK**. Click cell **B6**, and then **Insert** a **Column Sparkline** for the range **c6:d6**

3 With cell **B6** selected, on the **Design tab**, in the **Style group**, click **More**, and then in the third row, click the fourth style. Press Ctrl + Home, click **Save**, and then compare your screen with Figure 2.52.

You can see, at a glance, that for both Online and In-Store sales, Rose sales are greater than Rose Supply sales.

MAC TIP In the Sparkline Style gallery, use the ScreenTips to locate Gold, Sparkline Style Accent 4, (no dark or light).

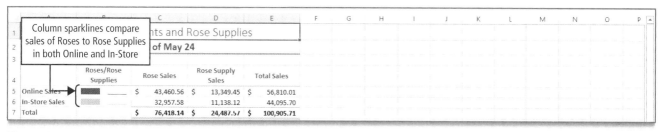

Figure 2.52

Activity 2.34 | Determining Bonus Based on Sales Using the IFS Function

Expert 3.1.1

The *IFS function* checks whether one or more conditions—logical tests—are met, and then returns a value corresponding to the first TRUE condition.

The salespeople who handle commercial online sales are eligible for bonuses each week based on sales. Weekly sales between $3,000 and $3,999 qualify the salesperson for a $250 bonus. Weekly sales between $4,000 and $4,999 qualify the salesperson for a $350 bonus. Weekly sales greater than $4,999 qualify the salesperson for a $500 bonus. In this Activity, you will use the IFS function to determine the bonus for which each salesperson is eligible.

1 To the right of the **Summary** sheet tab, click **New sheet** ⊕. **Rename** the new worksheet tab **Bonus** and display the **Tab Color** gallery. In the sixth column, select the first color.

2 Widen columns **A:C** to **95 pixels**. In cell **A1**, type Weekly Online Sales Bonus and then **Merge & Center** the title across the range **A1:C1**. Apply the **Heading 1** cell style.

3 In cell **A3**, type Salesperson and then press Tab. In cell **B3**, type Weekly Sales and then press Tab. In cell **C3**, type **Bonus** and then press Enter. Select **A3:C3**, and then apply the **Heading 3** cell style. **Center** ≡ the headings.

4 In the range **A4:B7**, type the data for each salesperson:

Salesperson	Weekly Sales
Arce	4588
Matsuo	2575
Morrison	3851
Tindall	5162

5 Click cell **C4**. On the **Formulas tab**, in the **Function Library group**, click **Logical**, and then click **IFS**. If necessary, drag the dialog box to the right so that columns A:C are visible.

MAC TIP Skip steps 6–10 and follow these instructions instead. At the right of the Mac window, in the Formula Builder, click in the Logical_test1 box. Type b4>4999 and then below the Logical_test1 box, click +. In the Value_if_true1 box, type 500. Click + and then use this same technique to add three more conditions and TRUE values as follows: b4>3999, 350; b4>2999, 250; b4>0, 0. When you are finished entering the conditions, click Done and then Close the Formula Builder. Then continue with step 11.

6 In the **Logical_test1 box**, type **b4>4999** and then press ⎡Tab⎤. In the **Value_if_true1 box**, type **500** and then press ⎡Tab⎤. Compare your screen with Figure 2.53.

The first logical test determines whether the Weekly Sales for Arce is greater than $4,999. In this case, the result is FALSE; Weekly Sales of $4,588 are less than $4,999.

When entering the logical tests for the IFS function, begin with the largest value because the IFS function returns a value based on the *first* condition that meets the criteria.

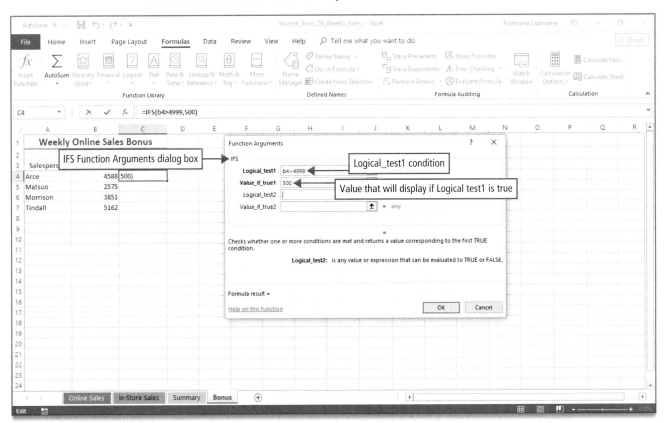

Figure 2.53

7 In the **Logical_test2 box**, type **b4>3999** and then press ⎡Tab⎤. In the **Value_if_true2 box**, type **350** and then press ⎡Tab⎤.

To the right of the Logical_test2 box, *TRUE* displays, indicating that Weekly Sales for Arce are greater than $3,999. Since this is the first *TRUE* condition, the Value_if_true—*350*—will display in cell C4.

> **8** In the **Logical_test3 box**, type **b4>2999** and then press Tab. In the **Value_if_true3 box**, type **250** and then press Tab.

> **9** In the **Logical_test4 box**, type **b4>0** and then press Tab. In the **Value_if_true4 box**, type **0** and then press Tab.

This IFS function contains four logical tests. It is important to include a default value that displays if none of the conditions are met. When no default value is included, an error message displays if no TRUE conditions are found. In this case, the default value is 0.

> **10** Click **OK** and notice that in cell **C4**, the IFS function determined that a bonus of 350 was earned.

> **11** Drag the fill handle down through cell **C7**, and then compare your screen with Figure 2.54.

Based on the conditions specified in the IFS function, three of the four salespersons earned bonuses based on their weekly sales.

In the Formula bar, the IFS statement arguments indicate each of the conditions and the TRUE values.

Figure 2.54

> **12** Select the range **B4:C7**, and then apply **Accounting Number Format** $ ▾. Click **Decrease Decimal** two times. **Save** your workbook.

Objective 12 Format and Print Multiple Worksheets in a Workbook

GO! Learn How
Video E2-12

Each worksheet within a workbook can have different formatting, for example, different headers or footers. If all the worksheets in the workbook will have the same header or footer, you can select all the worksheets and apply formatting common to all of the worksheets; for example, you can set the same footer in all of the worksheets.

Activity 2.35 │ Moving a Worksheet, Repeating Footers, and Formatting Multiple Worksheets in a Workbook

In this Activity, you will move the Summary sheet to become the first worksheet in the workbook. Then you will format and prepare your workbook for printing. The four worksheets can be formatted simultaneously.

> **1** Point to the **Summary sheet tab**, hold down the left mouse button to display a small black triangle—a caret—and then notice that a small paper icon attaches to the mouse pointer.

2 Drag to the left until the caret and mouse pointer are to the left of the **Online Sales sheet tab**, as shown in Figure 2.55, and then release the left mouse button.

Use this technique to rearrange the order of worksheets within a workbook.

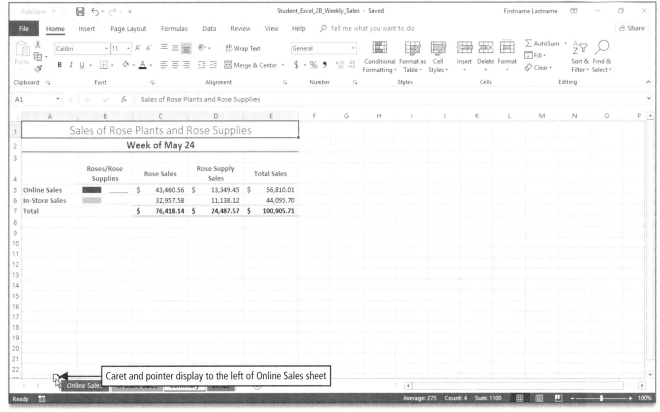

Figure 2.55

3 Be sure the **Summary** worksheet is the active sheet, point to its sheet tab, right-click, and then click **Select All Sheets** to display *Group* in the title bar.

MAC TIP Hold down Control, and then click the Summary sheet tab to display the shortcut menu.

4 Click the **Page Layout tab**. In the **Page Setup group**, click **Margins**, and then at the bottom of the gallery, click **Custom Margins** to display the **Page Setup** dialog box.

5 In the **Page Setup** dialog box, on the **Margins tab**, under **Center on page**, select the **Horizontally** check box.

6 Click the **Header/Footer tab**, and then in the center of the dialog box, click **Custom Footer**. In the **Footer** dialog box, with your insertion point blinking in the **Left section**, on the row of buttons, click **Insert File Name**.

7 Click **OK** two times.

The dotted line indicates the page break as currently formatted.

8 Press Ctrl + Home; verify that *Group* still displays in the title bar.

By selecting all sheets, you can apply the same formatting to all the worksheets at the same time, for example to repeat headers or footers.

9 Click the **File tab**, click **Info**, and then display the **Properties**. As the **Tags**, type **weekly sales** and then in the **Subject** box, type your course name and section number. Be sure your name displays as the **Author**; edit if necessary.

10 On the left, click **Print** to display the **Print Preview**, and then compare your screen with Figure 2.56.

By grouping, you can view all sheets in Print Preview. If you do not see *1 of 4* at the bottom of the Preview, redisplay the workbook, select all the sheets again, and then redisplay Print Preview.

Figure 2.56

11 At the bottom of the **Print Preview**, click **Next Page** ▶ as necessary and take a moment to view each page of your workbook.

MAC TIP If the Print Preview indicates more than 4 pages, in the Print dialog box, click Cancel. With the worksheets grouped, on the Page Layout tab, click the Width arrow, and then click 1 page.

Activity 2.36 | Printing All or Individual Worksheets in a Workbook

MOS
1.5.3

1 In **Backstage** view, click **Save** to save your workbook before printing. In the displayed workbook, right-click the **Summary sheet tab**, and then click **Ungroup Sheets**.

2 On the **File tab**, click **Print** to display the **Print Preview**, and then at the bottom of the window, notice that *1 of 1* is indicated.

Because the worksheets are no longer grouped, only the active sheet is available for printing.

3 On the left, under **Settings**, click **Print Active Sheets**, and then click **Print Entire Workbook**.

At the bottom of the window, *1 of 4* is indicated. You can use this command to print an entire workbook.

MAC TIP In the Print dialog box, click the Pages arrow, and then click All to print all sheets, click Single to specify one page, and click Range to specify multiple pages. After you view the Pages options, click Cancel.

4 Click **Save** and then **Close** Excel.

 For Non-MyLab Submissions Determine What Your Instructor Requires for Submission
As directed by your instructor, submit your completed Excel workbook.

5 In **MyLab IT**, locate and click the Grader Project **Excel 2B Weekly Sales**. In **step 3**, under **Upload Completed Assignment**, click **Choose File**. In the **Open** dialog box, navigate to your **Excel Chapter 2 folder**, and then click your **Student_Excel_2B_Weekly_Sales** file one time to select it. In the lower right corner of the **Open** dialog box, click **Open**.

The name of your selected file displays above the Upload button.

6 To submit your file to **MyLab IT** for grading, click **Upload**, wait a moment for a green **Success!** message, and then in **step 4**, click the blue **Submit for Grading** button. Click **Close Assignment** to return to your list of **Course Materials**.

You have completed Project 2B **END**

Objective Calculate Weekly Sales

ALERT **Working with Web-Based Applications and Services**

Computer programs and services on the web receive continuous updates and improvements, so the steps to complete this web-based activity may differ from the ones shown. You can often look at the screens and the information presented to determine how to complete the activity.

If you do not already have a Google account, you will need to create one before you begin this activity. Go to http://google.com and, in the upper right corner, click Sign In. On the Sign In screen, click Create Account. On the Create your Google Account page, complete the form, read and agree to the Terms of Service and Privacy Policy, and then click Next step. On the Welcome screen, click Get Started.

Activity | Calculating Weekly Sales with Google Sheets

1 From the desktop, open your browser, navigate to http://google.com, and then click **Google Apps** ⊞. Click **Drive** ▲, and then if necessary, sign in to your Google account.

2 Open your **GO! Web Projects** folder—or click **New** to create and then open this folder if necessary. Click **New** and then click **File upload**. Navigate to your student data files, click **e02_2B_Web**, and then click **Open**.

3 Right-click the file you uploaded, point to **Open with**, and then click **Google Sheets**.

4 Click cell **E5**. On the ribbon, click **Functions** Σ ▾, and then click **SUM**. Select **B5:D5** and then press Enter to total the rose sales for Sunday. Click cell **E5**, and then drag the fill handle down through cell **E11**. Select **E6:E11**, and then on the ribbon, click **More Formats** 123 ▾. Click **Number**.

5 Click cell **G5** and then enter a formula to add cells **E5** and **F5**. Fill the formula down through cell **G11**, and then format the range **G6:G11** with **Number** format. Click cell **A1** and then compare your screen with Figure A.

6 Select the range **B5:B11**. Click **Functions** Σ ▾, click **SUM**, and then press Enter to sum the selected range and place the result in cell **B12**. With **B12** selected, fill the formula across to cell **G12**.

7 Click cell **H5**. To calculate the percent that the Sunday sales are of the total sales, type **=g5/g12** and then press F4 to make the cell reference to G12 absolute. Press Enter and then fill the formula down through cell **H11**. With the range **H5:H11** selected, click **Format as percent** % .

8 Select the range **B5:G5**. Hold down Ctrl, and then select **B12:G12**. With both ranges selected, click **Format as Currency** $.

	Rose Plants and Rose Supplies: Austin Sales						
	Week of May 24						
Day	Climbing Roses	Patio Roses	Tea Roses	Total Rose Sales	Rose Supply Sales	Total Sales	Percent of Sales
Sun	$911.51	$26.46	$33.47	$971.44	$1,926.49	$2,897.93	
Mon	310.49	313.85	782.64	1,406.98	1,526.03	2,933.01	
Tue	942.37	402.99	30.08	1,375.44	1,853.82	3,229.26	
Wed	185.89	992.29	253.98	1,432.16	1,922.36	3,354.52	
Thu	3.53	825.79	340.34	1,169.66	1,973.73	3,143.39	
Fri	931.46	946.92	966.92	2,845.30	2,121.47	4,966.77	
Sat	47.23	978.23	234.12	1,259.58	2,025.55	3,285.13	
Total Sales							

Figure A

»» **GO!** With Google continues on next page

»»» GO! With Google Sheets

9 Click cell **A1** and then compare your screen with Figure B.

10 Submit your file as directed by your instructor. Sign out of your Google account and close your browser.

fx | Rose Plants and Rose Supplies: Austin Sales

Day	Climbing Roses	Patio Roses	Tea Roses	Total Rose Sales	Rose Supply Sales	Total Sales	Percent of Sales
Rose Plants and Rose Supplies: Austin Sales							
Week of May 24							
Sun	$911.51	$26.46	$33.47	$971.44	$1,926.49	$2,897.93	12.17%
Mon	310.49	313.85	782.64	1,406.98	1,526.03	2,933.01	12.32%
Tue	942.37	402.99	30.08	1,375.44	1,853.82	3,229.26	13.56%
Wed	185.89	992.29	253.98	1,432.16	1,922.36	3,354.52	14.09%
Thu	3.53	825.79	340.34	1,169.66	1,973.73	3,143.39	13.20%
Fri	931.46	946.92	966.92	2,845.30	2,121.47	4,966.77	20.86%
Sat	47.23	978.23	234.12	1,259.58	2,025.55	3,285.13	13.80%
Total Sales	$3,332.48	$4,486.53	$2,641.55	$10,460.56	$13,349.45	$23,810.01	

Figure B

wavebreakmedia/Shutterstock, Monkey Business Images/Fotolia, Ivanko80/Shutterstock, Monkey Business Images/Shutterstock

Microsoft Office Specialist (MOS) Skills in This Chapter

Project 2A	Project 2B
1.2.1 Search for data within a workbook	**2.4.1** Insert sparklines
1.4.3 Freeze worksheet rows and columns	**4.1.1** Insert relative, absolute, and mixed references
1.4.4 Change window views	
1.5.3 Configure print settings	
2.1.3 Insert and delete multiple columns or rows	
2.2.1 Merge and unmerge cells	
2.2.2 Modify cell alignment, orientation, and indentation	
2.2.4 Wrap text within cells	
2.2.6 Apply cell formats from the Format Cells dialog box	
2.2.8 Clear cell formatting	
2.4.2 Apply built-in conditional formatting	
3.1.1 Create Excel tables from cell ranges	
3.1.2 Apply styles to tables	
3.2.3 Insert and configure total rows	
3.3.1 Filter records	
3.3.2 Sort data by multiple columns	
4.2.1 Perform calculations by using the AVERAGE( ), MAX( ), MIN( ), and SUM( ) functions	
4.2.3 Perform conditional operations by using the IF( ) function	
Expert 2.1.1 Fill cells by using Flash Fill	
Expert 3.1.1 Perform logical operations by using nested functions including the IF( ), IFS( ), SWITCH( ), SUMIF( ), AVERAGEIF( ), COUNTIF( ), SUMIFS( ), AVERAGEIFS( ), COUNTIFS( ), MAXIFS( ), MINIFS( ), AND( ), OR( ), and NOT( ) functions	
Expert 3.3.1 Reference date and time by using the NOW( ) and TODAY ( ) functions	

Build Your E-Portfolio

An E-Portfolio is a collection of evidence, stored electronically, that showcases what you have accomplished while completing your education. Collecting and then sharing your work products with potential employers reflects your academic and career goals. Your completed documents from the following projects are good examples to show what you have learned: 2G, 2K, and 2L.

Go! For Job Success

Video: Workplace Goal Setting

Your instructor may assign this video to your class, and then ask you to think about, or discuss with your classmates, these questions:

g-stockstudio/Shutterstock

Is there anything you would change about Theo's behavior at his performance evaluation? Why or Why not?

SMART goals are goals that are specific, measurable, achievable, realistic, and time frame specific. Is Theo's first goal of beating his sales numbers by 10% next year a SMART goal?

How important do you think it is to set career development goals for yourself? Why?

End of Chapter

Summary

Use Flash Fill to recognize a pattern in data and automatically fill in values when you enter examples of desired output. Flash Fill can split data from two or more cells or combine data from two cells.

Functions are formulas that Excel provides and that perform calculations by using specific values in a particular order or structure. Statistical functions are useful to analyze a group of measurements.

You can navigate among worksheets in a workbook by clicking the sheet tabs, which identify each worksheet in a workbook. Use multiple worksheets in a workbook to organize data in a logical arrangement.

Dates are a value you can enter in a cell to which Excel assigns a serial value—a number—so that you can treat dates like other numbers. For example, you can find the number of days between two dates.

GO! Learn It Online

Review the concepts, key terms, and MOS skills in this chapter by completing these online challenges, which you can find at **MyLab IT**.

Chapter Quiz: Answer matching and multiple choice questions to test what you learned in this chapter.

Lessons on the GO!: Learn how to use all the new apps and features as they are introduced by Microsoft.

MOS Prep Quiz: Answer questions to review the MOS skills that you practiced in this chapter.

GO! Collaborative Team Project (Available in Instructor Resource Center)

If your instructor assigns this project to your class, you can expect to work with one or more of your classmates—either in person or by using internet tools—to create work products similar to those that you created in this chapter. A team is a group of workers who work together to solve a problem, make a decision, or create a work product. Collaboration is when you work together with others as a team in an intellectual endeavor to complete a shared task or achieve a shared goal.

Monkey Business Images/Fotolia

Project Guide for Excel Chapter 2

Your instructor will assign Projects from this list to ensure your learning and assess your knowledge.

		Project Guide for Excel Chapter 2		
Project	**Apply Skills from These Chapter Objectives**	**Project Type**		**Project Location**
2A MyLab IT	Objectives 1–6 from Project 2A	**2A Instructional Project (Grader Project)** Guided instruction to learn the skills in Project 2A.	Instruction	In **MyLab IT** and in text
2B MyLab IT	Objectives 7–12 from Project 2B	**2B Instructional Project (Grader Project)** Guided instruction to learn the skills in Project 2B.	Instruction	In **MyLab IT** and in text
2C	Objectives 1–6 from Project 2A	**2C Skills Review (Scorecard Grading)** A guided review of the skills from Project 2A.	Review	In text
2D	Objectives 7–12 from Project 2B	**2D Skills Review (Scorecard Grading)** A guided review of the skills from Project 2B.	Review	In text
2E MyLab IT	Objectives 1–6 from Project 2A	**2E Mastery (Grader Project)** A demonstration of your mastery of the skills in Project 2A with extensive decision making.	Mastery and Transfer of Learning	In **MyLab IT** and in text
2F MyLab IT	Objectives 7–12 from Project 2B	**2F Mastery (Grader Project)** A demonstration of your mastery of the skills in Project 2B with extensive decision making.	Mastery and Transfer of Learning	In **MyLab IT** and in text
2G MyLab IT	Objectives 1–12 from Projects 2A and 2B	**2G Mastery (Grader Project)** A demonstration of your mastery of the skills in Projects 2A and 2B with extensive decision making.	Mastery and Transfer of Learning	In **MyLab IT** and in text
2H	Combination of Objectives from Projects 2A and 2B	**2H GO! Fix It (Scorecard Grading)** A demonstration of your mastery of the skills in Projects 2A and 2B by creating a correct result from a document that contains errors you must find.	Critical Thinking	IRC
2I	Combination of Objectives from Projects 2A and 2B	**2I GO! Make It (Scorecard Grading)** A demonstration of your mastery of the skills in Projects 2A and 2B by creating a result from a supplied picture.	Critical Thinking	IRC
2J	Combination of Objectives from Projects 2A and 2B	**2J GO! Solve It (Rubric Grading)** A demonstration of your mastery of the skills in Projects 2A and 2B, your decision-making skills, and your critical thinking skills. A task-specific rubric helps you self-assess your result.	Critical Thinking	IRC
2K	Combination of Objectives from Projects 2A and 2B	**2K GO! Solve It (Rubric Grading)** A demonstration of your mastery of the skills in Projects 2A and 2B, your decision-making skills, and your critical thinking skills. A task-specific rubric helps you self-assess your result.	Critical Thinking	In text
2L	Combination of Objectives from Projects 2A and 2B	**2L GO! Think (Rubric Grading)** A demonstration of your understanding of the chapter concepts applied in a manner that you would outside of college. An analytic rubric helps you and your instructor grade the quality of your work by comparing it to the work an expert in the discipline would create.	Critical Thinking	In text
2M	Combination of Objectives from Projects 2A and 2B	**2M GO! Think (Rubric Grading)** A demonstration of your understanding of the chapter concepts applied in a manner that you would outside of college. An analytic rubric helps you and your instructor grade the quality of your work by comparing it to the work an expert in the discipline would create.	Critical Thinking	IRC
2N	Combination of Objectives from Projects 2A and 2B	**2N You and GO! (Rubric Grading)** A demonstration of your understanding of the chapter concepts applied in a manner that you would in a personal situation. An analytic rubric helps you and your instructor grade the quality of your work.	Critical Thinking	IRC
2O	Combination of Objectives from Projects 2A and 2B	**2O Collaborative Team Project for EXCEL Chapter 2** A demonstration of your understanding of concepts and your ability to work collaboratively in a group role-playing assessment, requiring both collaboration and self-management.	Critical Thinking	IRC

Glossary

Chapter Key Terms

Arguments The values that an Excel function uses to perform calculations or operations.

AVERAGE function An Excel function that adds a group of values, and then divides the result by the number of values in the group.

Comparison operators Symbols that evaluate each value to determine if it is the same (=), greater than (>), less than (<), or in between a range of values as specified by the criteria.

Conditional format A format that changes the appearance of a cell—for example, by adding cell shading or font color—based on a condition; if the condition is true, the cell is formatted based on that condition, and if the condition is false, the cell is *not* formatted.

COUNT function A statistical function that counts the number of cells in a range that contains numbers.

COUNTIF function A statistical function that counts the number of cells within a range that meet the given condition and that has two arguments—the range of cells to check and the criteria.

Criteria Conditions that you specify in a logical function.

Data bar A cell format consisting of a shaded bar that provides a visual cue to the reader about the value of a cell relative to other cells; the length of the bar represents the value in the cell—a longer bar represents a higher value and a shorter bar represents a lower value.

Detail sheets The worksheets that contain the details of the information summarized on a summary sheet.

Drag and drop The action of moving a selection by dragging it to a new location.

Excel table A series of rows and columns that contains related data that is managed independently from the data in other rows and columns in the worksheet.

Filter The process of displaying only a portion of the data based on matching a specific value to show only the data that meets the criteria that you specify.

Find and Replace A command that searches the cells in a worksheet—or in a selected range—for matches and then replaces each match with a replacement value of your choice.

Flash Fill Recognizes a pattern in your data, and then automatically fills in values when you enter examples of the output that you want. Use it to split data from two or more cells or to combine data from two cells.

Freeze Panes A command that enables you to select one or more rows or columns and freeze (lock) them into place; the locked rows and columns become separate panes.

Function A predefined formula—a formula that Excel has already built for you—that performs calculations by using specific values in a particular order or structure.

IF function A function that uses a logical test to check whether a condition is met, and then returns one value if true, and another value if false.

IFS function A function that checks whether one or more conditions—logical tests—are met, and then returns a value corresponding to the first TRUE condition.

Logical functions A group of functions that test for specific conditions and that typically use conditional tests to determine whether specified conditions are true or false.

Logical test Any value or expression that can be evaluated as being true or false.

MAX function An Excel function that determines the largest value in a selected range of values.

MEDIAN function An Excel function that finds the middle value that has as many values above it in the group as are below it; it differs from AVERAGE in that the result is not affected as much by a single value that is greatly different from the others.

MIN function An Excel function that determines the smallest value in a selected range of values.

Navigate The process of moving within a worksheet or workbook.

NOW function An Excel function that retrieves the date and time from your computer's calendar and clock and inserts the information into the selected cell.

Pane A portion of a worksheet window bounded by and separated from other portions by vertical and horizontal bars.

Paste The action of placing cell contents that have been copied or moved to the Clipboard into another location.

Paste area The target destination for data that has been cut or copied using the Office Clipboard.

Paste Options gallery A gallery of buttons that provides a Live Preview of all the Paste options available in the current context.

Print Titles An Excel command that enables you to specify rows and columns to repeat on each printed page.

Scale to Fit Excel commands that enable you to stretch or shrink the width, height, or both, of printed output to fit a maximum number of pages.

Sheet tabs The labels along the lower border of the workbook window that identify each worksheet.

Sort The process of arranging data in a specific order based on the value in each field.

Split Splits the window into multiple resizable panes that contain views of your worksheet. This is useful to view multiple distant parts of your worksheet at one time.

Statistical functions Excel functions, including the AVERAGE, MEDIAN, MIN, and MAX functions, which are useful to analyze a group of measurements.

SUM function A predefined formula that adds all the numbers in a selected range of cells.

Summary sheet A worksheet where totals from other worksheets are displayed and summarized.

Volatile A term used to describe an Excel function that is subject to change each time the workbook is reopened; for example, the NOW function updates itself to the current date and time each time the workbook is opened.

Chapter Review

Apply 2A skills from these Objectives:

1. Use Flash Fill and the SUM, AVERAGE, MEDIAN, MIN, and MAX Functions
2. Move Data, Resolve Error Messages, and Rotate Text
3. Use COUNTIF and IF Functions and Apply Conditional Formatting
4. Use Date & Time Functions and Freeze Panes
5. Create, Sort, and Filter an Excel Table
6. View, Format, and Print a Large Worksheet

Skills Review | **Project 2C Roses**

In the following Skills Review, you will edit a worksheet detailing the current inventory of roses at the Pasadena nursery. Your completed workbook will look similar to Figure 2.57.

Project Files

For Project 2C, you will need the following file:

e02C_Roses

You will save your workbook as:

Lastname_Firstname_2C_Roses

Project Results

Quantity in Stock	Item #	Rose Name	Retail Price	Color	USDA Zone	Stock Level
62	12934	River 2	11.99	White	Zone 3	OK
46	12647	New Dawn	12.5	Pink	Zone 1	OK
29	12398	Lace Christmas	12.95	Black	Zone 7	Order
65	12556	Many Shades	12.95	Red	Zone 5	OK
56	12841	Double Fantasy	12.95	Black	Zone 6	OK
49	12489	Woodland Red	12.98	Burgundy	Zone 1	OK
43	12493	Azurri Lace	12.98	Burgundy	Zone 3	OK
45	12223	Gushing Pride	12.99	Red	Zone 5	OK
56	12225	Julia Peony	13.75	Merlot	Zone 5	OK
29	12564	Woodland Pink	13.95	Pink	Zone 1	Order
36	12954	Aphrodite	13.95	Red	Zone 2	Order
46	12664	Winter Bliss	13.97	Pink	Zone 6	OK

Pasadena Nursery: Roses Inventory
As of June 30

Rose Statistics

Total Items in Stock		2,303
Average Price	$	14.23
Median Price	$	12.95
Lowest Price	$	6.99
Highest Price	$	39.95

Yellow Rose Types	3
Red Rose Types	13 595 total items in stock

Quantity in Stock	Item #	Rose Name	Retail Price	Color	USDA Zone	Stock Level
49	12485	Clown Mallow	6.99	White	Zone 8	OK
26	12365	Sensation Meadow	7.59	Apricot	Zone 7	Order
42	12465	Singing Winter	7.95	Burgundy	Zone 6	OK
46	12534	Queen Bishops	7.95	Red	Zone 8	OK
85	12894	Blue Bird	7.95	Burgundy	Zone 4	OK
46	12893	Berry Pie	7.98	Purple	Zone 1	OK
46	12553	Rose Satin	8.75	Purple	Zone 6	OK
23	12968	Racer Lenten	8.95	Orange	Zone 3	Order
28	12113	Sunny Days	8.99	Yellow	Zone 5	Order
39	12312	Tropical Rose	8.99	Red	Zone 8	Order
49	12642	Winter Blossom	8.99	Red	Zone 7	OK
28	12895	Bennett Rock	9.55	Red	Zone 3	Order
46	12455	Heritage Strain	9.78	Pink	Zone 7	OK
65	12347	Perfume Delight	9.95	Burgundy	Zone 2	OK
45	12582	White Chiffon	9.95	Burgundy	Zone 4	OK
37	2616	Honey Bun	9.95	Burgundy	Zone 1	Order
36	12663	Rose Marianne	9.95	Burgundy	Zone 7	Order
49	12221	Coral Bells	9.97	Red	Zone 5	OK
26	12892	Origami	9.97	Burgundy	Zone 3	Order
42	12668	Apricot Bloom	10.95	Apricot	Zone 4	OK
45	12336	China Bloom	11.95	Burgundy	Zone 6	OK
32	12457	Wildberry	11.95	Red	Zone 2	Order
36	12783	Warley Rock	11.95	Pink	Zone 8	Order

Student_Excel_2C_Roses

Figure 2.57

(continues on next page)

Chapter Review

1 From the files downloaded with this chapter, locate and open **e02C_Roses**. **Save** the file in your **Excel Chapter 2** folder as **Lastname_Firstname_2C_Roses**

a. In the **column heading area**, point to **column C** to display the ↓ pointer, and then drag to the right to select **columns C:D**. On the **Home tab**, in the **Cells group**, click the **Insert button arrow**, and then click **Insert Sheet Columns**.

b. Click cell **C14**, type **12113** and then on the **Formula Bar**, click **Enter** to confirm the entry and keep cell **C14** as the active cell. On the **Home tab**, in the **Editing group**, click **Fill**, and then click **Flash Fill**.

c. Click cell **D14**, type **Zone 5** On the **Formula Bar**, click **Enter** to confirm the entry and keep the cell active. Press Ctrl + E, which is the keyboard shortcut for Flash Fill.

d. Select **column B**, and then on the **Home tab**, in the **Cells group**, click the **Delete button arrow**. Click **Delete Sheet Columns**.

2 In cell **B13** type **Item #** and press Enter.

a. Select **column C**, and then on the **Home tab**, in the **Clipboard group**, click **Cut**. Click cell **G1**, and then in the **Clipboard group**, click the upper portion of the **Paste** button.

b. Select and then delete **column C**. In cell **F13**, type **USDA Zone** and in cell **G13**, type **Stock Level**

c. Select columns **A:G**. In the **Cells group**, click **Format**, and then click **AutoFit Column Width**.

d. **Merge & Center** cell **A1** across the range **A1:G1**, and then apply the **Title** cell style. **Merge & Center** cell **A2** across the range **A2:G2**, and then apply the **Heading 1** cell style. Click **Save**.

3 Click cell **B4**. On the **Formulas tab**, in the **Function Library group**, click **AutoSum**, and then within the parentheses, type **a14:a68** which is the range containing the quantities for each item. Press Enter.

a. With cell **B5** active, on the **Formulas tab**, in the **Function Library group**, click **More Functions**. Point to **Statistical**, click **AVERAGE**, and then in the **Number1** box, type **d14:d68** which is the range containing the *Retail Price* for each item. Click **OK**. (Mac users, in the Formula Builder, under Number1, type d14:d68 and then click Done.)

b. Click cell **B6**. In the **Function Library group**, click **More Functions**, point to **Statistical**, and then click **MEDIAN**. In the **Function Arguments** dialog box, type **d14:d68** and then click **OK**. (Mac users, in the Formula Builder, under Number1, type d14:d68, and then click Done.)

c. Click cell **B7**, and then insert the **MIN** function to determine the lowest **Retail Price**. Click cell **B8**, and then insert the **MAX** function to determine the highest **Retail Price**.

4 Select cell **B4**. On the **Home tab**, apply **Comma Style**, and then click **Decrease Decimal** two times. Select the range **B5:B8**, and then apply **Accounting Number Format**.

a. Select the range **A4:B8**. Point to the right edge of the selected range to display the ⟨pointer⟩ pointer. Drag the selected range to the right until the ScreenTip displays *D4:E8*, and then release the mouse button. AutoFit **column D**.

b. With the range **D4:E8** selected, on the **Home tab**, in the **Styles group**, display the **Cell Styles** gallery, and then apply **20% - Accent1**.

c. In cell **C6**, type **Rose Statistics** Select the range **C4:C8**, right-click over the selection, and then click **Format Cells**. (Mac users, hold down Ctrl and click the selection. On the shortcut menu, click Format Cells.) In the **Format Cells** dialog box, click the **Alignment tab**. Under **Text control**, select the **Merge cells** check box.

d. In the upper right portion of the dialog box, under **Orientation**, change the value in the **Degrees** box to **20** and then click **OK**.

e. With the merged cell still selected, change the **Font Size** to **14**, and then apply **Bold** and **Italic**. Apply **Middle Align** and **Center** to the cell.

5 Click cell **B10**. On the **Formulas tab**, in the **Function Library group**, click **More Functions**, and then display the list of **Statistical** functions. Click **COUNTIF**.

a. As the range, type **e14:e68** which is the range with the color of each item. Click in the **Criteria** box, type **Yellow** and then click **OK** to calculate the number of yellow rose types. (Mac users, type the range and criteria in the Formula Builder, and then click Done.)

(continues on next page)

Chapter Review

b. Click cell **G14**. On the **Formulas tab**, in the **Function Library group**, click **Logical**, and then on the list, click **IF**. If necessary, drag the title bar of the **Function Arguments** dialog box up or down so that you can view **row 14** on your screen.

c. With the insertion point in the **Logical_test** box, click cell **A14**, and then type **<40** Press Tab to move the insertion point to the **Value_if_true** box, and then type **Order** Press Tab to move the insertion point to the **Value_if_false** box, type **OK** and then click **OK**. (Mac users, use the Formula Builder to create the arguments for the IF function, and then click Done. Close the Formula Builder.)

d. Using the fill handle, copy the function in cell **G14** down through cell **G68**.

6 With the range **G14:G68** selected, on the **Home tab**, in the **Styles group**, click **Conditional Formatting**. In the list, point to **Highlight Cells Rules**, and then click **Text that Contains**. (Mac users, skip steps a and b. Instead, do the following to apply conditional formatting: in the New Formatting Rule box, be sure that the dialog box includes the following settings: Classic, Format only cells that contain, Specific Text, and Containing. To the right of Containing, type Order. Click the Format with arrow, and then click Custom Format. Under Font Style, click Bold Italic, click the Color arrow, and then click Automatic. Click the Fill tab, and then click No Color. Click OK two times.)

a. In the **Text That Contains** dialog box, with the insertion point blinking in the first box, type **Order** and then in the second box, click the **arrow**. On the list, click **Custom Format**.

b. In the **Format Cells** dialog box, on the **Font tab**, under **Font style**, click **Bold Italic**. Click the **Color arrow**, and then click **Automatic**. Click the **Fill tab**, and then click **No Color**. Click **OK** two times to apply bold and italic to the cells that contain the word *Order*.

c. Select the range **A14:A68**. In the **Styles group**, click **Conditional Formatting**. In the list, point to **Data Bars**, and then under **Gradient Fill**, click **Red Data Bar**. Click anywhere to cancel the selection.

d. Select the range **E14:E68**. On the **Home tab**, in the **Editing group**, click **Find & Select**, and then click **Replace**. (Mac users, press Ctrl + F. In the Find dialog box, click Replace.) In the **Find and Replace** dialog box, in the **Find what** box, type **Deep Burgundy** and then in the **Replace with** box, type **Burgundy** Click **Replace All** and then click **OK**. In the lower right corner of the **Find and Replace** dialog box, click **Close**.

e. Scroll down as necessary, and then click cell **A70**. Type **Edited by Maria Rios** and then press Enter. With cell **A71** as the active cell, on the **Formulas tab**, in the **Function Library group**, click **Date & Time**. In the list of functions, click **NOW**, and then click **OK** to enter the current date and time. (Mac users, in the Formula Builder, click Done and then Close the Formula Builder.)

f. **Save** your workbook.

7 Click any cell in the data below row 13. Click the **Insert tab**, and then in the **Tables group**, click **Table**. In the **Create Table** dialog box, be sure the **My table has headers** check box is selected and that the range **$A$13:$G$68** displays, and then click **OK**. On the **Design tab**, in the **Table Styles group**, click **More**, and then under **Light**, locate and click **Blue, Table Style Light 9**. If the style is not available, choose another style.

a. In the header row of the table, click the **Retail Price arrow**, and then from the menu, click **Sort Smallest to Largest**. (Mac users, click Ascending and then close the Retail Price dialog box.) Click the **Color arrow**. On the menu, click the **(Select All)** check box to clear all the check boxes. Scroll as necessary and then select only the **Red** check box. Click **OK**.

b. Click anywhere in the table. On the **Table Tools Design tab**, in the **Table Style Options group**, select the **Total Row** check box. Click cell **A69**, click the arrow that displays to the right of cell **A69**, and then click **Sum**. In cell **B11**, type the result **13** and then press Tab. In cell **C11**, type **595 total items in stock** and then press Enter.

c. In the header row of the table, click the **Color arrow** and then click **Clear Filter From "Color"** to redisplay all of the data. (Mac users, click Clear Filter and then Close the Color dialog box.) Click anywhere in the table. Click the **Table Tools Design tab**, in the **Table Style Options group**, clear the **Total Row** check box.

8 On the **Page Layout tab**, in the **Themes group**, click **Themes** and then click the **Ion** theme. Change the **Orientation** to **Landscape**.

a. In the **Page Setup group**, click **Margins**, and then click **Custom Margins** to display the **Page Setup** dialog box.

(continues on next page)

Chapter Review

b. On the **Margins tab**, under **Center on page**, select the **Horizontally** check box. On the **Header/Footer tab**, display the **Custom Footer**, and then in the **Left section**, insert the file name. Click **OK** two times.

c. In the **Page Setup** group, click **Print Titles** to redisplay the **Page Setup** dialog box. Under **Print titles**, click in the **Rows to repeat at top** box, and then at the right, click **Collapse Dialog**. From the **row heading area**, select **row 13**, and then click **Expand Dialog**. Click **OK** to print the column titles in row 13 at the top of every page.

d. Click the **File tab** and then click **Print**. At the bottom of the **Settings group**, click **No Scaling**, and then on the displayed list, click **Fit All Columns on**

One Page. (Mac users, to fit the worksheet width on one page, close the Print dialog box. On the Page Layout tab, click the Width button arrow, and then click 1 page.)

e. Display the **Properties**. As the **Tags**, type **inventory, roses** In the **Subject** box, type your course name and section number. Be sure your name displays as the author. (Mac users, click File, and then click Properties. Click Summary, and then type the Keywords, Subject, and Author name).

9 **Save** your workbook. Print or submit your workbook electronically as directed by your instructor.

You have completed Project 2C `END`

Chapter Review

Skills Review **Project 2D Canada**

Apply 2B skills from these Objectives:

7. Navigate a Workbook and Rename Worksheets
8. Enter Dates, Clear Contents, and Clear Formats
9. Copy and Paste by Using the Paste Options Gallery
10. Edit and Format Multiple Worksheets at the Same Time
11. Create a Summary Sheet with Column Sparklines
12. Format and Print Multiple Worksheets in a Workbook

In the following Skills Review, you will edit a workbook that summarizes sales in the Eastern and Western region of Canada. Your completed workbook will look similar to Figure 2.58.

Project Files

For Project 2D, you will need the following file:

e02D_Canada

You will save your workbook as:

Lastname_Firstname_2D_Canada

Project Results

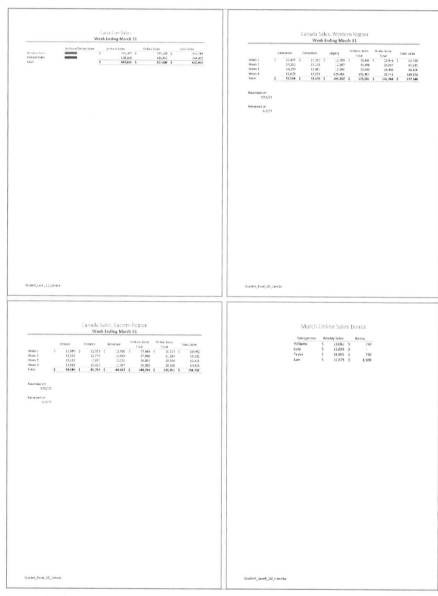

FIGURE 2.58

(continues on next page)

Chapter Review

1 From the files downloaded with this chapter, locate and open **e02D_Canada**. **Save** the file in your **Excel Chapter 2** folder as **Lastname_Firstname_2D_Canada**

a. Point to the **Sheet1 tab**, and then double-click to select the sheet tab name. Type **Western Sales** and then press Enter.

b. Point to the **Sheet2 tab**, right-click, and then from the shortcut menu, click **Rename**. Type **Eastern Sales** and press Enter. (Mac users, to display the shortcut menu, point to the Sheet2 tab, hold down Ctrl, and then click.)

c. Point to the **Western Sales sheet tab** and right-click. On the shortcut menu, point to **Tab Color**, and then in the last column, click the first color. Change the **Tab Color** of the **Eastern Sales sheet tab**—in the fifth column, click the first color.

d. Click the **Western Sales sheet tab**, and then click cell **A13**. On the **Home tab**, in the **Number group**, click the **Number Format arrow**. At the bottom of the list, click **More Number Formats** to display the **Number tab** of the **Format Cells** dialog box. Click the **3/14/12** type, and then click **OK**.

e. Click cell **A16**, type **4/5/22** and then press Enter. Click cell **A13**, and then on the **Home tab**, in the **Clipboard group**, click **Format Painter**. Click cell **A16** to copy the date format from cell **A13** to cell **A16**.

f. Click cell **A1**. In the **Editing group**, click **Clear**, and then click **Clear Formats**.

g. Select the range **A5:A16**. On the **Home tab**, in the **Clipboard group**, click **Copy**. At the bottom of the workbook window, click the **Eastern Sales sheet tab** to make it the active worksheet. Click cell **A5**, and then on the **Home tab**, in the **Clipboard group**, click **Paste**. Display the **Western Sales** sheet. Press Esc to cancel the moving border.

2 With the **Western Sales** sheet active, make cell **A1** the active cell. Point to the sheet tab, right-click, and then on the shortcut menu, click **Select All Sheets**. Verify that *Group* displays in the title bar. (Mac users, hold down Ctrl, and then click the Western Sales sheet tab to display the shortcut menu.)

a. **Merge & Center** the text in cell **A1** across the range **A1:G1**, and then apply the **Title** cell style. Select **columns A:G**, and then set their widths to **100 pixels**.

b. Click cell **A2**, type **Week Ending March 31** and then on the **Formula Bar**, click the **Enter** button to keep cell **A2** as the active cell. **Merge & Center** the text across the range **A2:G2**, and then apply the **Heading 1** cell style.

c. Select the range **B4:G4**, and then apply the **Heading 3** cell style. In the **Alignment group**, click **Center**, **Middle Align**, and **Wrap Text**.

d. With the sheets still grouped and the **Western Sales** sheet active, click cell **E5**. On the **Home tab**, in the **Editing group**, click the **AutoSum** button, and then press Enter. Click cell **E5**, and then drag the fill handle down to copy the formula through cell **E8**.

e. Click cell **G5**, type = click cell **E5**, type + click cell **F5**, and then press Enter. Copy the formula down through cell **G8**. In cell **A9**, type **Total** Select the range **B5:G9**, and then on the **Home tab**, in the **Editing group**, click the **AutoSum** button to enter the SUM function for all the columns. Select the range **A5:A9**, and then apply the **Heading 4** cell style.

f. Select the range **B5:G5**, hold down Ctrl, and then select the range **B9:G9**. (Mac users, hold down command ⌘.) Apply the **Accounting Number Format** and decrease the decimal places to zero. Select the range **B6:G8**, and then apply **Comma Style** with zero decimal places. Select the range **B9:G9**, and then apply the **Total** cell style.

3 Click the **Eastern Sales sheet tab** to cancel the grouping and display the second worksheet.

a. To the right of the **Eastern Sales sheet tab**, click the **New sheet** button. **Rename** the new worksheet tab **Summary** and then change the **Tab Color**—in the eight column, click the first color.

b. Widen **columns A:E** to **150** pixels. In cell **A1**, type **Canadian Sales** and then **Merge & Center** the title across the range **A1:E1**. Apply the **Title** cell style. In cell **A2**, type **Week Ending March 31** and then **Merge & Center** the text across the range **A2:E2**. Apply the **Heading 1** cell style. In cell **A5**, type **Western Sales** and in cell **A6**, type **Eastern Sales**

c. In cell **B4**, type **In-Store/Online Sales** and in cell **C4**, type **In-Store Sales** In cell **D4**, type **Online Sales** and in cell **E4**, type **Total Sales** Select the range **B4:E4**, apply the **Heading 3** cell style, and then **Center** these column titles.

d. Click cell **C5**. Type = and then click the **Western Sales sheet tab**. In the **Western Sales** worksheet, click cell **E9**, and then press Enter. Click cell **D5**. Type = and then click the **Western Sales sheet tab**. Click cell **F9**, and then press Enter.

(continues on next page)

Chapter Review

e. By using the same technique, in cells **C6** and **D6**, insert the total **In-Store Sales** and **Online Sales** data from the **Eastern Sales** worksheet.

f. Select the range **C5:E6**, and then click **AutoSum** to total the two rows. In cell **A7**, type **Total** and then in **C7** sum the range **C5:C6**. Fill the formula across to **D7:E7**.

g. Select the nonadjacent ranges **C5:E5** and **C7:E7**, and then apply **Accounting Number Format** with zero decimal places. Select the range **C6:E6**, and then apply **Comma Style** with zero decimal places. Select the range **C7:E7**, and then apply the **Total** cell style. Select the range **A5:A7** and apply the **Heading 4** cell style.

h. Click cell **B5**. On the **Insert tab**, in the **Sparklines group**, click **Column**. In the **Create Sparklines** dialog box, with the insertion point blinking in the **Data Range** box, select the range **C5:D5** and then click **OK**.

i. Click cell **B6**, and then insert a **Column Sparkline** for the range **C6:D6**. With the **Eastern Sales** sparkline selected, in the **Style group**, in the first row, apply the second style.

4 To the right of the **Summary** sheet tab, click **New sheet**. **Rename** the new worksheet tab **Bonus** and display the **Tab Color** gallery. In the sixth column, select the first color. Widen columns **A:C** to **95 pixels**.

a. In cell **A1**, type **March Online Sales Bonus** and then **Merge & Center** the title across the range **A1:C1**. Apply the **Title** cell style. In cell **A3**, type **Salesperson** In cell **B3**, type **Weekly Sales** In cell

Salesperson	Weekly Sales
Williams	23062
Cote	15895
Taylor	18901
Lam	31675

C3, type **Bonus** and then select **A3:C3**. Apply the **Heading 3** cell style and **Center** the headings.

b. In the range **A4:B7**, type the data for each salesperson:

c. Click cell **C4**. On the **Formulas tab**, in the **Function Library group**, click **Logical**, and then click **IFS**.

d. In the **Logical_test1 box**, type **b4>30000** and then press Tab. In the **Value_if_true1 box**, type 1500 and then press Tab. In the **Logical_test2 box**, type

b4>18000 and then press Tab. In the **Value_if_true2 box**, type 750 and then press Tab. In the **Logical_test3 box**, type **b4>0** and then press Tab. In the **Value_if_true3 box**, type **0** and then click **OK**. (Mac users, in the Formula Builder, click in the Logical_test1 box. Type b4>30000 and then below the Logical_test1 box, click +. In the Value_if_true1 box, type 1500. Click + and then use this same technique to add two more conditions and TRUE values as follows: b4>18000, 750; b4>0,0. Click Done and then close the Formula Builder.)

e. Drag the fill handle down through cell **C7**. Select the range **B4:C7**, and then apply **Accounting Number Format**. Click **Decrease Decimal** two times.

5 Point to the **Summary sheet tab**, hold down the left mouse button to display a small black triangle, drag to the left until the triangle and mouse pointer are to the left of the **Western Sales sheet tab**, and then release the left mouse button to move the sheet to the first position in the workbook.

a. Be sure the **Summary** worksheet is the active sheet and then click cell **A1**. Point to the **Summary sheet tab**, right-click, and then click **Select All Sheets** to display *Group* in the title bar. (Mac users, hold down ctrl, click the Summary sheet tab, and then click Select All Sheets.)

b. On the **Page Layout tab**, in the **Page Setup group**, click **Margins**, and then click **Custom Margins** to display the **Page Setup** dialog box. On the **Margins tab**, center the worksheets **Horizontally**. On the **Header/Footer tab**, insert the file name in the **left section** of the footer.

c. Display the **Print Preview** of the worksheets. Under **Settings**, click **No Scaling**, and then click **Fit All Columns on One Page**. Use the **Next** button to view all four worksheets. (Mac users, on the Page Layout tab, click the Width arrow, and then click 1 page.)

d. Display the **Properties**. As the **Tags**, type **Canada, sales** In the **Subject** box, type your course name and section number. Be sure your name displays as the author. (Mac users, click File, and then click Properties. Click Summary, and then enter the Subject, Keywords, and Author.)

6 **Save** and **Close** your workbook. Print or submit your workbook electronically as directed by your instructor.

You have completed Project 2D `END`

Content-Based Assessments (Mastery and Transfer of Learning)

Apply 2A skills from these Objectives:

1. Use Flash Fill and the SUM, AVERAGE, MEDIAN, MIN, and MAX Functions
2. Move Data, Resolve Error Messages, and Rotate Text
3. Use COUNTIF and IF Functions and Apply Conditional Formatting
4. Use Date & Time Functions and Freeze Panes
5. Create, Sort, and Filter an Excel Table
6. View, Format, and Print a Large Worksheet

In the following project, you will edit a worksheet detailing the current inventory of plants at the Pasadena facility. Your completed worksheet will look similar to Figure 2.59.

Project Files for **MyLab IT** Grader

1. In your **MyLab IT** course, locate and click **Excel 2E Plants**, Download Materials, and then Download All Files.
2. Extract the zipped folder to your Excel Chapter 2 folder. Close the Grader download screens.
3. Take a moment to open the downloaded **Excel_2E_Plants_Instructions**; note any recent updates to the book.

Project Results

Figure 2.59

For Non-MyLab Submissions

For Project 2E, you will need:

e02E_Plants

In your Excel Chapter 2 folder, save your workbook as:

Lastname_Firstname_2E_Plants

If your instructor requires a workbook with formulas, save as:

Lastname_Firstname_2E_Plants_formulas

After you have named and saved your document, on the next page, begin with Step 2.

After Step 16, save and submit your file as directed by your instructor.

(continues on next page)

Mastering Excel: Project 2E Plants (continued)

1 Navigate to your **Excel Chapter 2 folder**, and then double-click the Excel file you downloaded from **MyLab IT** that displays your name—**Student_Excel_2E_Plants**.

2 To the right of **column B**, insert two new columns to create **new blank columns C and D**. By using **Flash Fill** in the two new columns, split the data in **column B** into a column for *Item #* in **column C** and *Category* in **column D**. As necessary, type **Item #** as the column title in **column C** and **Category** as the column title in **column D**. Delete **column B**.

3 By using the **Cut** and **Paste** commands, cut **column C**—*Category*—and paste it to **column H**, and then delete the empty **column C**. Apply **AutoFit** to **columns A:G**.

4 In cell **B4**, insert a function to calculate the **Total Items in Stock** by summing the **Quantity in Stock** data, and then apply **Comma Style** with zero decimal places to the result.

5 In each cell in the range **B5:B8**, insert functions to calculate the Average, Median, Lowest, and Highest retail prices, and then apply the **Accounting Number Format** to each result.

6 Move the range **A4:B8** to the range **D4:E8**, apply the **40% - Accent4** cell style to the range, and then select **columns D:E** and **AutoFit**.

7 In cell **C6**, type **Statistics** and then select the range **C4:C8**. Display the **Format Cells** dialog box, merge the selected cells, and change the text **Orientation** to **25 Degrees**. Format the cell with **Bold** and change the **Font Size** to **14 pt**. Apply **Middle Align** and **Align Right**.

8 In the **Category** column, **Replace All** occurrences of **Vine Roses** with **Patio Roses**

9 In cell **B10**, use the **COUNTIF** function to count the number of **Specialty** plant types in the **Category** column.

10 In cell **H13**, type **Stock Level** In cell **H14**, enter an **IF** function to determine the items that must be ordered. If the **Quantity in Stock** is less than **50** the **Value_if_true** is **Order** Otherwise, the **Value_if_false** is **OK** Fill the formula down through cell **H42**.

11 Apply **Conditional Formatting** to the **Stock Level** column so that cells that contain the text **Order** are formatted with **Bold Italic**. Change the font **Color** to **Automatic**, and the **Fill** color to **No Color**. Apply conditional formatting to the **Quantity in Stock** column by applying a **Gradient Fill Green Data Bar**.

12 Format the range **A13:H42** as a **Table** with headers, and apply the style **Light Blue, Table Style Light 20**. If the table style is not available, choose another style. Sort the table from **A to Z** (Ascending order) by **Item Name**, and then filter on the **Category** column to display the **Specialty** types.

13 Display a **Total Row** in the table, and then in cell **A43**, **Sum** the **Quantity in Stock** for the **Specialty** items. Type the result in cell **B11**. Click in the table, and then remove the total row from the table. Clear the **Category** filter.

14 **Merge & Center** the title and subtitle across **columns A:H** and apply **Title** and **Heading 1** styles respectively. Change the theme to **Mesh**, and then **AutoFit** all the columns.

15 Set the orientation to **Landscape**. In the **Page Setup** dialog box, center the worksheet **Horizontally**, insert a custom footer in the **left section** with the file name, and set **row 13** to repeat at the top of each page. Fit all the columns to one page.

16 Display the workbook **Properties**. As the **Tags**, type **plants inventory, Pasadena** As the **Subject**, type your course name and section number. Be sure your name displays as the **Author**. **Save** your workbook and then **Close** Excel.

(continues on next page)

Content-Based Assessments (Mastery and Transfer of Learning)

17 In **MyLab IT**, locate and click the Grader Project **Excel 2E Plants**. In **step 3**, under **Upload Completed Assignment**, click **Choose File**. In the **Open** dialog box, navigate to your **Excel Chapter 2 folder**, and then click your **Student_Excel_2E_Plants** file one time to select it. In the lower right corner of the **Open** dialog box, click **Open**.

> The name of your selected file displays above the Upload button.

18 To submit your file to **MyLab IT** for grading, click **Upload**, wait a moment for a green **Success!** message, and then in **step 4**, click the blue **Submit for Grading** button. Click **Close Assignment** to return to your list of **Course Materials**.

You have completed Project 2E **END**

Content-Based Assessments (Mastery and Transfer of Learning)

Mastering Excel **Project 2F Bonus**

Apply 2B skills from these Objectives:

7. Navigate a Workbook and Rename Worksheets
8. Enter Dates, Clear Contents, and Clear Formats
9. Copy and Paste by Using the Paste Options Gallery
10. Edit and Format Multiple Worksheets at the Same Time
11. Create a Summary Sheet with Column Sparklines
12. Format and Print Multiple Worksheets in a Workbook

In the following project, you will edit a workbook that summarizes the compensation for the commercial salespersons who qualified for bonuses in Northern and Southern California. Your completed worksheets will look similar to Figure 2.60.

Project Files for **MyLab IT Grader**

1. In your **MyLab IT** course, locate and click **Excel 2F Bonus**, Download Materials, and then Download All Files.
2. Extract the zipped folder to your Excel Chapter 2 folder. Close the Grader download screens.
3. Take a moment to open the downloaded **Excel_2F_Bonus_Instructions**; note any recent updates to the book.

Project Results

Figure 2.60

For Non-MyLab Submissions

For Project 2F, you will need:
e02F_Bonus

After you have named and saved your document, on the next page, begin with Step 2.

After Step 17, save and submit your file as directed by your instructor.

In your Excel Chapter 2 folder, save your workbook as:
Lastname_Firstname_2F_Bonus
If your instructor requires a workbook with formulas, save as:
Lastname_Firstname_2F_Bonus_formulas

(continues on next page)

Content-Based Assessments (Mastery and Transfer of Learning)

Mastering Excel: Project 2F Bonus (continued)

1 Navigate to your **Excel Chapter 2 folder**, and then double-click the Excel file you downloaded from **MyLab IT** that displays your name—**Student_Excel_2F_Bonus**.

2 Rename **Sheet1** as **Northern** and rename **Sheet2** as **Southern**

3 Click the **Northern sheet tab** to make it the active sheet, and then group the worksheets. In cell **A1**, type **Rosedale Landscape and Garden** and then **Merge & Center** the text across the range **A1:F1**. Apply the **Title** cell style. **Merge & Center** the text in cell **A2** across the range **A2:F2**, and then apply the **Heading 3** cell style.

4 The bonus rates for each salesperson are determined by sales amounts using the following scale: Sales **greater than $35,000** earn a bonus rate of **5%**, sales **greater than $25,000** earn a bonus rate of **4%**. All other sales (any amount greater than 0) earn a bonus rate of **2%**. With the sheets still grouped, in cell **C5** use an **IFS** function to determine the bonus rate for the first salesperson whose sales are in cell **B5**. Fill the formula down through cell **C8**.

5 In cell **D5**, calculate **Bonus** for *Reid* by multiplying the **Sales Eligible for Bonus** times the **Bonus Rate**. **Copy** the formula down through cell **D8**.

6 In cell **F5**, calculate **Total Compensation** by summing the **Bonus** and **Base Salary** for *Reid*. Copy the formula down through the cell **F8**.

7 In **row 9**, sum the columns for **Sales Eligible for Bonus**, **Bonus**, **Base Salary**, and **Total Compensation**. Apply the **Accounting Number Format** with two decimal places to the appropriate cells in **row 5** and **row 9** (do not include the percentages).

8 Apply the **Comma Style** with two decimal places to the appropriate cells in **rows 6:8** (do not include the percentages). Apply the **Total** cell style to **B9** and **D9:F9**.

9 **Ungroup** the sheets, and then insert a new worksheet. Change the sheet name to **Summary** and then widen **column A** to **210** pixels and **columns B:E** to **155** pixels.

10 Move the **Summary** sheet so that it is the first sheet in the workbook. In cell **A1** of the **Summary** sheet, type **Rosedale Landscape and Garden** and then **Merge & Center** the title across the range **A1:E1**. Apply the **Title** cell style. In cell **A2**, type **June Commercial Salesperson Bonus Summary: California** and then **Merge & Center** the text across the range **A2:E2**. Apply the **Heading 1** cell style.

11 In the range **A5:A7**, type the following row titles and then apply the **Heading 4** cell style:

Bonus

Base Salary

Total Compensation

12 In the range **B4:E4**, type the following column titles, and then **Center** and apply the **Heading 3** cell style.

Northern/Southern

Northern

Southern

Total

13 In cell **C5**, enter a formula that references cell **D9** in the **Northern** worksheet so that the total bonus amount for the Northern region displays in cell **C5**. Create similar formulas to enter the total **Base Salary** for the **Northern** region in cell **C6**. Using the same technique, enter formulas in the range **D5:D6** so that the **Southern** totals display.

14 Sum the **Bonus** and **Base Salary** rows, and then calculate **Total Compensation** for the **Northern**, **Southern**, and **Total** columns.

15 In cell **B5**, insert a **Column Sparkline** for the range **C5:D5**. In cells **B6** and **B7**, insert **Column** sparklines for the appropriate ranges to compare Northern totals with Southern totals.

16 **Group** the three worksheets, and then center the worksheets **Horizontally** on the page and insert a **Custom Footer** in the **left section** with the file name. Change the **Orientation** to **Landscape** and fit the columns to **1 page**.

17 Display the workbook **Properties**. As the **Tags**, type **June, bonus** As the **Subject**, type your course name and section number. Be sure your name displays as the **Author** and then **Save** the workbook and **Close** Excel.

(continues on next page)

Content-Based Assessments (Mastery and Transfer of Learning)

18 In **MyLab IT**, locate and click the Grader Project **Excel 2F Bonus**. In **step 3**, under **Upload Completed Assignment**, click **Choose File**. In the **Open** dialog box, navigate to your **Excel Chapter 2 folder**, and then click your **Student_Excel_2F_Bonus** file one time to select it. In the lower right corner of the **Open** dialog box, click **Open**.

The name of your selected file displays above the Upload button.

19 To submit your file to **MyLab IT** for grading, click **Upload**, wait a moment for a green **Success!** message, and then in **step 4**, click the blue **Submit for Grading** button. Click **Close Assignment** to return to your list of **Course Materials**.

You have completed Project 2F | END

Content-Based Assessments (Mastery and Transfer of Learning)

Mastering Excel   **Project 2G Inventory**

Apply a combination of 2A and 2B skills:

1. Use Flash Fill and the SUM, AVERAGE, MEDIAN, MIN, and MAX Functions
2. Move Data, Resolve Error Messages, and Rotate Text
3. Use COUNTIF and IF Functions and Apply Conditional Formatting
4. Use Date & Time Functions and Freeze Panes
5. Create, Sort, and Filter an Excel Table
6. View, Format and Print a Large Worksheet
7. Navigate a Workbook and Rename Worksheets
8. Enter Dates, Clear Contents, and Clear Formats
9. Copy and Paste by Using the Paste Options Gallery
10. Edit and Format Multiple Worksheets at the Same Time
11. Create a Summary Sheet with Column Sparklines
12. Format and Print Multiple Worksheets in a Workbook

In the following project, you will edit a worksheet that summarizes the inventory of bulbs and trees at the Pasadena facility. Your completed workbook will look similar to Figure 2.61.

Project Files for **MyLab IT Grader**

1. In your **MyLab IT** course, locate and click **Excel 2G Inventory**, Download Materials, and then Download All Files.
2. Extract the zipped folder to your Excel Chapter 2 folder. Close the Grader download screens.
3. Take a moment to open the downloaded **Excel_2G_Inventory_Instructions** note any recent updates to the book.

Project Results

Figure 2.61

For Non-MyLab Submissions

For Project 2G, you will need: In your Excel Chapter 2 folder, save your workbook as:

e02G_Inventory   **Lastname_Firstname_2G_Inventory**

If your instructor requires a workbook with formulas, save as:

Lastname_Firstname_2G_Inventory _formulas

After you have named and saved your document, on the next page, begin with Step 2.

After Step 24, save and submit your file as directed by your instructor.

(continues on next page)

Content-Based Assessments (Mastery and Transfer of Learning)

1 Navigate to your **Excel Chapter 2 folder**, and then double-click the Excel file you downloaded from **MyLab IT** that displays your name—**Student_Excel_2G_Inventory**.

2 Change the **Theme** to **Slice**. Rename **Sheet1** as **Bulbs** and **Sheet2** as **Trees** and then make the **Bulbs sheet** the active sheet.

3 To the right of **column B**, insert two new columns to create **new blank columns C and D**. By using **Flash Fill** in the two new columns, split the data in **column B** into a column for *Item #* in **column C** and *Category* in **column D**.

4 Type **Item #** as the column title in **column C** and **Category** as the column title in **column D**. Delete **column B**. By using the **Cut** and **Paste** commands, cut **column C**—*Category*—and paste it to **column G**, and then delete the empty **column C**. Apply **AutoFit** to **columns A:F**.

5 Display the **Trees** worksheet, and then repeat steps 3 and 4 on this worksheet.

6 Make the following calculations in each of the two worksheets *without* grouping the sheets:

- In cell **B4**, enter a function to sum the **Quantity in Stock** data, and then apply **Comma Style** with zero decimal places to the result.

- In cells **B5:B8**, enter formulas to calculate the Average, Median, Lowest, and Highest retail prices, and then apply the **Accounting Number Format**.

7 In each of the two worksheets, make the following calculation *without* grouping the sheets:

- In cell **B10**, enter a COUNTIF function to determine how many different types of **Tulips** are in stock on the **Bulbs** sheet and how many different types of **Evergreens** are in stock on the **Trees** worksheet.

8 Without grouping the worksheets, complete the following in each worksheet:

- In cell **G14**, type **Stock Level**

- In cell **G15**, construct an **IF** function to determine the items that must be ordered. If the **Quantity in Stock** is less than **75** the **Value_if_true** is **Order** Otherwise the **Value_if_false** is **OK** Fill the formula down through all the rows.

9 Without grouping the worksheets, apply conditional formatting as follows to both worksheets:

- Apply **Conditional Formatting** to the **Stock Level** column so that cells that contain the text *Order* are formatted with **Bold Italic,** font **Color** set to **Automatic,** and **Fill** color set to **No color**.

- Apply **Gradient Fill Blue Data Bars** to the **Quantity in Stock** column.

10 In the **Bulbs** sheet, format the range **A14:G42** as a table with headers and apply **Light Orange, Table Style Light 20**. If the style isn't available, choose another style. Insert a **Total Row**, filter by **Category** for **Tulips**, and then **Sum** the **Quantity in Stock** column. Record the result in cell **B11**.

11 Select the table, clear the filter, **Sort** the table on the **Item #** column from **Smallest to Largest** (Ascending) and then remove the **Total Row**. On the **Page Layout tab**, set **Print Titles** so that **row 14** repeats at the top of each page.

12 In the **Trees** sheet, format the range **A14:G42** as a table with headers and apply **Light Green, Table Style Light 19**. If the style isn't available, choose another style. Insert a **Total Row**, filter by **Category** for **Evergreens**, and then **Sum** the **Quantity in Stock** column. Record the result in cell **B11**.

13 Select the table, clear the filter, **Sort** the table on the **Item #** column from **Smallest to Largest** (Ascending), and then remove the **Total Row**. On the **Page Layout tab**, set **Print Titles** so that **row 14** repeats at the top of each page, and then **Save** your workbook.

14 **Group** the two worksheets. **Merge & Center** the title in cell **A1** across the range **A1:G1** and apply the **Title** cell style. **Merge & Center** the subtitle in cell **A2** across the range **A2:G2** and apply the **Heading 1** cell style. **AutoFit** Column A.

15 With the worksheets still grouped, **Center** the worksheets **Horizontally**, change the **Orientation** to **Landscape**, and insert a footer in the left section with the file name. Display the **Print Preview**, and then change the **Settings** to **Fit All Columns on One Page**. (Mac users, on the Page Layout tab, change the Width to 1 page.)

(continues on next page)

Mastering Excel: Project 2G Inventory (continued)

16 **Save** your workbook and then ungroup the sheets. Make the **Trees** sheet the active sheet, and then insert a new worksheet. Change the new sheet name to **Summary** and then widen **columns A:D** to **170** pixels. Move the **Summary** sheet so that it is the first sheet in the workbook.

17 In cell **A1**, type **Pasadena Inventory Summary** **Merge & Center** the title across the range **A1:D1**, and then apply the **Title** cell style. In cell **A2**, type **As of December 31** and then **Merge & Center** the text across the range **A2:D2**. Apply the **Heading 1** cell style.

18 On the **Bulbs sheet**, **Copy** the range **A4:A8**. Display the **Summary sheet** and **Paste** the selection to cell **A5**. Apply the **Heading 4** cell style to the selection.

19 In the **Summary sheet**, in cell **B4**, type **Bulbs** In cell **C4**, type **Trees** In cell **D4**, type **Bulbs/Trees** and then **Center** the column titles. Apply the **Heading 3** cell style.

20 In cell **B5**, enter a formula that references cell **B4** in the **Bulbs sheet** so that the **Bulbs Total Items in Stock** displays in **B5**. Create similar formulas to enter the **Average Price**, **Median Price**, **Lowest Price**, and **Highest Price** from the **Bulbs sheet** into the **Summary** sheet in the range **B6:B9**.

21 Enter formulas in the range **C5:C9** that reference the Total Items in stock and the Average Price, Median Price, Lowest Price, and Highest Price cells in the **Trees** worksheet.

22 In cells **D5**, **D6**, **D7**, **D8**, and **D9**, insert **Column** sparklines using the values in the *Bulbs* and *Trees* columns. Format each sparkline using the first five Sparkline styles in the first row.

23 To the range **B5:C5**, apply **Comma Style** with zero decimal places, and to the range **B6:C9**, apply **Accounting Number Format**. Center the **Summary** worksheet **Horizontally** and change the **Orientation** to **Landscape**. Insert a footer in the left section with the **File Name**.

24 Display the workbook **Properties**. As the **Tags**, type **Pasadena inventory** As the **Subject**, type your course name and section number. Be sure your name displays as the **Author**. **Save** your workbook and **Close** Excel.

25 In **MyLab IT**, locate and click the Grader Project **Excel 2G Inventory**. In **step 3**, under **Upload Completed Assignment**, click **Choose File**. In the **Open** dialog box, navigate to your **Excel Chapter 2 folder**, and then click your **Student_Excel_2G_Inventory** file one time to select it. In the lower right corner of the **Open** dialog box, click **Open**.

The name of your selected file displays above the Upload button.

26 To submit your file to **MyLab IT** for grading, click **Upload**, wait a moment for a green **Success!** message, and then in **step 4**, click the blue **Submit for Grading** button. Click **Close Assignment** to return to your list of **Course Materials**.

You have completed Project 2G **END**

Content-Based Assessments (Critical Thinking)

Apply a combination of the 2A and 2B skills.

GO! Fix It	**Project 2H Planters**	IRC
GO! Make It	**Project 2I Salary**	IRC
GO! Solve It	**Project 2J Sod**	IRC
GO! Solve It	**Project 2K Products**	

Project Files

For Project 2K, you will need the following file:

e02K_Products

You will save your workbook as:

Lastname_Firstname_2K_Products

From your student data files, open the file e02K_Products and save it as **Lastname_Firstname_2K_Products** This workbook contains two worksheets: one for U.S. sales data by product and one for Canadian sales data by product. Complete the two worksheets by calculating totals by product and by month. Then calculate the Percent of Total for all products by dividing the Product Total by the Monthly Total, using absolute cell references as necessary. Format the percentages with two decimal places and center in the cells. Format the worksheets attractively and apply financial formatting. Insert a new worksheet that summarizes the monthly totals for the U.S. and Canada. Enter the months as the column titles and the countries as the row titles. Include a Product Total column and a column for sparklines titled **April/May/June** Format the Summary worksheet attractively with a title and subtitle, insert column sparklines that compare the months, and apply financial formatting. Include the file name in the footer, add appropriate document properties, and submit as directed.

		Performance Level		
		Exemplary: You consistently applied the relevant skills	**Proficient: You sometimes, but not always, applied the relevant skills**	**Developing: You rarely or never applied the relevant skills**
Performance Criteria	**Create formulas**	All formulas are correct and are efficiently constructed.	Formulas are correct but not always constructed in the most efficient manner.	One or more formulas are missing or incorrect; or only numbers were entered.
	Create Summary worksheet	Summary worksheet created properly.	Summary worksheet was created but the data, sparklines, or formulas were incorrect.	No Summary worksheet was created.
	Formatting is attractive and appropriate.	Format attractively and appropriately	Adequately formatted but difficult to read or unattractive.	Inadequate or no formatting.

You have completed Project 2K END

Outcomes-Based Assessments (Critical Thinking)

Rubric

The following outcomes-based assessments are open ended assessments. That is, there is no specific correct result; your result will depend on your approach to the information provided. Make Professional Quality your goal. Use the following scoring rubric to guide you in how to approach the problem and then to evaluate how well your approach solves the problem.

The *criteria*—Software Mastery, Content, Format and Layout, and Process—represent the knowledge and skills you have gained that you can apply to solving the problem. The *levels of performance*—Professional Quality, Approaching Professional Quality, or Needs Quality Improvements—help you and your instructor evaluate your result.

	Your completed project is of Professional Quality if you:	Your completed project is Approaching Professional Quality if you:	Your completed project Needs Quality Improvements if you:
1-Software Mastery	Choose and apply the most appropriate skills, tools, and features and identify efficient methods to solve the problem.	Choose and apply some appropriate skills, tools, and features, but not in the most efficient manner.	Choose inappropriate skills, tools, or features, or are inefficient in solving the problem.
2-Content	Construct a solution that is clear and well organized, contains content that is accurate, appropriate to the audience and purpose, and is complete. Provide a solution that contains no errors of spelling, grammar, or style.	Construct a solution in which some components are unclear, poorly organized, inconsistent, or incomplete. Misjudge the needs of the audience. Have some errors in spelling, grammar, or style, but the errors do not detract from comprehension.	Construct a solution that is unclear, incomplete, or poorly organized, contains some inaccurate or inappropriate content, and contains many errors of spelling, grammar, or style. Do not solve the problem.
3-Format and Layout	Format and arrange all elements to communicate information and ideas, clarify function, illustrate relationships, and indicate relative importance.	Apply appropriate format and layout features to some elements, but not others. Overuse features, causing minor distraction.	Apply format and layout that does not communicate information or ideas clearly. Do not use format and layout features to clarify function, illustrate relationships, or indicate relative importance. Use available features excessively, causing distraction.
4-Process	Use an organized approach that integrates planning, development, self-assessment, revision, and reflection.	Demonstrate an organized approach in some areas, but not others; or, use an insufficient process of organization throughout.	Do not use an organized approach to solve the problem.

Outcomes-Based Assessments (Critical Thinking)

Apply a combination of the 2A and 2B skills.

GO! Think   **2L Palms**

Project Files

For Project 2L, you will need the following file:

e02L_Palms

You will save your workbook as:

Lastname_Firstname_2L_Palms

Melanie Castillo, Product Manager for Rosedale Landscape and Garden, has requested a worksheet that summarizes the current palm tree inventory data. Melanie would like the worksheet to include the total Quantity in Stock and Number of Items for each of the four categories of palm trees, and she would like the items to be sorted from lowest to highest retail price. She would also like a separate column for Item # and for Category.

Edit the file e02L_Palms to provide Melanie with the information requested, and use the Table feature to find the data requested. Format the worksheet titles and data and include an appropriately formatted table so that the worksheet is professional and easy to read and understand. Insert a footer with the file name, and add appropriate document properties. Save the file as **Lastname_Firstname_2L_Palms** and print or submit as directed by your instructor.

You have completed Project 2L   END

GO! Think   **Project 2M Contracts**   IRC

You and GO!   **Project 2N Annual Expenses**   IRC

GO! Cumulative Team Project   **Project 2O Bell Orchid Hotels**   IRC

Analyzing Data with Pie Charts, Line Charts, and What-If Analysis Tools

EXCEL 2019

PROJECT 3A

Outcomes
Present fund data in a pie chart.

Objectives

1. Chart Data with a Pie Chart
2. Format a Pie Chart
3. Edit a Workbook and Update a Chart
4. Use Goal Seek to Perform What-If Analysis

PROJECT 3B

Outcomes
Make projections using what-if analysis and present projections in a line chart.

Objectives

5. Design a Worksheet for What-If Analysis
6. Answer What-If Questions by Changing Values in a Worksheet
7. Chart Data with a Line Chart
8. Create a Map Chart and a Funnel Chart

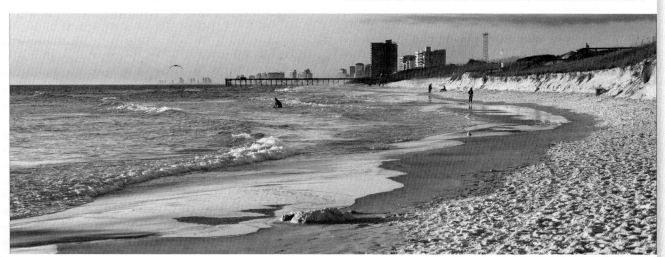

Rob Hainer/Shutterstock

In This Chapter

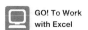

GO! To Work with Excel

In this chapter, you will work with two different types of commonly used charts that make it easy to visualize data. You will create a pie chart in a separate chart sheet to show how the parts of a fund contribute to a total fund. Pie charts are one type of chart you can use to show part-to-whole relationships. You will also practice using parentheses in a formula, calculate the percentage rate of an increase, answer what-if questions, and then chart data in a line chart to show the flow of data over time. In this chapter, you will also create a map chart and a funnel chart.

The projects in this chapter relate to the city of **Pacifica Bay**, a coastal city south of San Francisco. The city's access to major transportation provides both residents and businesses an opportunity to compete in the global marketplace. The city's mission is to create a more beautiful and more economically viable community for its residents. Each year the city welcomes a large number of tourists who enjoy exploring the rocky coastline and seeing the famous landmarks in San Francisco. The city encourages best environmental practices and partners with cities in other countries to promote sound government at the local level.

PROJECT
3A

Enterprise Fund
Pie Chart

MyLab IT
Project 3A Grader for Instruction
Project 3A Simulation for Training and Review

Project Activities

In Activities 3.01 through 3.12, you will edit a worksheet for Michael Larsen, City Manager, that reports the adjusted figures for Enterprise Fund Expenditures for the next fiscal year, and then present the data in a pie chart. Your completed worksheets will look similar to Figure 3.1.

Project Files for MyLab IT Grader

1. In your storage location, create a folder named **Excel Chapter 3**.
2. In your **MyLab IT** course, locate and click **Excel 3A Enterprise Fund**, Download Materials, and then Download All Files.
3. Extract the zipped folder to your Excel Chapter 3 folder. Close the Grader download screens.
4. Take a moment to open the downloaded **Excel_3A_Enterprise_Fund_Instructions**; note any recent updates to the book.

Project Results

GO! Project 3A
Where We're Going

Figure 3.1 Project 3A Enterprise Fund Pie Chart

For Non-MyLab Submissions

For Project 3A, you will need:
e03A_Enterprise_Fund

In your storage location, create a folder named **Excel Chapter 3**
In your Excel Chapter 3 folder, save your workbook as:
Lastname_Firstname_3A_Enterprise_Fund
If your instructor requires a workbook with formulas, save as:
Lastname_Firstname_3A_Enterprise_Fund_formulas

After you have named and saved your workbook, on the next page, begin with Step 2.

ALERT Because Office 365 is a cloud-based subscription service that receives continuous updates, you may encounter some variations in what appears on your screen and what is shown in this instruction. Microsoft Office 365 is fully installed on your PC or Mac; no internet access is necessary to create or edit documents. When you *are* connected to the internet, you will receive monthly upgrades and new features, so you always have the latest versions of Office apps as soon as they are available. Your subscription gives you continuous free access to the latest innovations and refinements.

GO! Learn How
Video E3-1

A *pie chart* shows the relationship of each part to a whole. The size of each pie slice is equal to its value compared to the total value of all the slices. A pie chart displays data that is arranged in a single column or single row and shows the size of items in a single data series proportional to the sum of the items. Whereas a column or bar chart can have two or more data series in the chart, a pie chart can have only one data series.

Consider using a pie chart when you have only one data series to plot; you do not have more than seven categories, and the categories represent parts of a total value.

Activity 3.01 | **Calculating Values for a Pie Chart**

A *fund* is a sum of money set aside for a specific purpose. In a municipal government like the city of Pacifica Bay, the *general fund* is money set aside for the normal operating activities of the city, such as police, fire, and administering the everyday functions of the city.

Municipal governments also commonly establish an *enterprise fund* to report income and expenditures related to municipal services for which a fee is charged in exchange for goods or services. For example, Pacifica Bay receives income from airport landing fees, parking fees, water usage fees, and rental fees along public beaches, but there are costs—expenditures—related to building and maintaining these facilities and services from which income is received.

1 Navigate to your **Excel Chapter 3 folder**, and then double-click the Excel file you downloaded from **MyLab IT** that displays your name—**Student_Excel_3A_Enterprise_Fund**.

> The worksheet indicates the originally proposed and adjusted expenditures from the Enterprise Fund for the next fiscal year.

2 Click cell **D5**, and then type = to begin a formula.

3 Click cell **C5**, which is the first value that is part of the total adjusted Fund Expenditures, to insert it into the formula. Type **/** to indicate division, and then click cell **C11**, which is the total adjusted expenditures.

> Recall that to determine the percentage by which a value makes up a total, you must divide the value by the total. The result will be a percentage expressed as a decimal.

4 Press F4 to make the reference to the value in cell **C11** absolute, which will enable you to copy the formula. Compare your screen with Figure 3.2.

> Recall that an *absolute cell reference* refers to a cell by its fixed position in the worksheet—the cell reference will not change when you copy the formula. The reference to cell C5 is a *relative cell reference*, because when you copy the formula, you want the reference to change *relative* to its row. In the formula, dollar signs display to indicate that a cell reference is absolute.

MAC TIP Press command ⌘ + T to make a cell reference in a formula absolute.

Figure 3.2

5 On the **Formula Bar**, click **Enter** ✓ to confirm the entry and to keep cell **D5** the active cell.

6 Copy the formula down through cell **D10**, and then compare your screen with Figure 3.3.

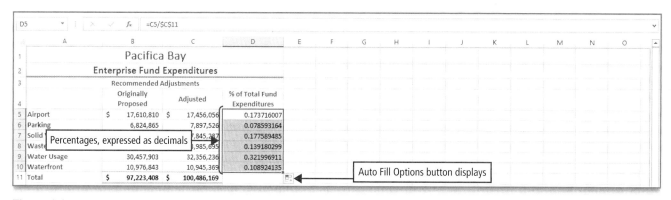

Figure 3.3

7 With the range **D5:D10** still selected, apply **Percent Style** % and then **Center** ≡ the selection. Click cell **A1** to cancel the selection, and then **Save** 💾 your workbook. Compare your screen with Figure 3.4.

	A	B	C	D	E	F	G	H	I	J	K	L	M	N	O
1		Pacifica Bay													
2		Enterprise Fund Expenditures													
3		Recommended Adjustments													
4		Originally Proposed	Adjusted	% of Total Fund Expenditures											
5	Airport	$ 17,610,810	$ 17,456,056	17%											
6	Parking	6,824,865	7,897,526	8%											
7	Solid Waste	18,695,222	17,845,287	18%											
8	Wastewater	12,657,765	13,985,695	14%											
9	Water Usage	30,457,903	32,356,236	32%											
10	Waterfront	10,976,843	10,945,369	11%											
11	Total	$ 97,223,408	$ 100,486,169												
12															

Percent of Total for each item calculated, expressed as percentages

Figure 3.4

Activity 3.02 | Creating a Pie Chart and Moving a Chart to a Chart Sheet

MOS
5.1.1 and 5.1.2

1 Select the range **A5:A10**, hold down Ctrl, and then select the range **C5:C10** to select the nonadjacent ranges with the item names and the adjusted expenditure for each item.

🖥 **MAC TIP** With the first range selected, press command ⌘ while selecting the second range.

To create a pie chart, you must select two ranges. One range contains the labels for each slice of the pie chart, and the other range contains the values that add up to a total. The two ranges must have the same number of cells and the range with the values should *not* include the cell with the total.

The item names (Airport, Parking, and so on) are the category names and will identify the slices of the pie chart. Each adjusted expenditure is a ***data point***—a value that originates in a worksheet cell and that is represented in a chart by a ***data marker***. In a pie chart, each pie slice is a data marker. Together, the data points form the ***data series***—related data points represented by data markers—and determine the size of each pie slice.

2 With the nonadjacent ranges selected, click the **Insert tab**, and then in the **Charts group**, click **Insert Pie or Doughnut Chart** ⊙▾. Under **3-D Pie**, click the chart **3-D Pie** to create the chart on your worksheet and to display the Chart Tools contextual tabs on the ribbon.

MAC TIP To display group names on the ribbon, display the menu, click Excel, click Preferences, click View, select the Group Titles check box.

3 On the **Design tab**, at the right end of the ribbon in the **Location group**, click **Move Chart**. In the **Move Chart** dialog box, click the **New sheet** option button.

4 In the **New sheet** box, replace the highlighted text *Chart1* by typing **Expenditures Chart** and then click **OK** to display the chart on a separate worksheet in your workbook. Compare your screen with Figure 3.5.

The pie chart displays on a separate new sheet in your workbook, and a ***legend*** identifies the pie slices. Recall that a legend is a chart element that identifies the patterns or colors assigned to the categories in the chart.

A ***chart sheet*** is a workbook sheet that contains only a chart; it is useful when you want to view a chart separately from the worksheet data. The sheet tab indicates *Expenditures Chart*.

Figure 3.5

GO! Learn How

Video E3-2
Activity 3.03 | Formatting a Chart Title by Applying a WordArt Style and Changing Font Size

1 Click the text *Chart Title* to surround it with selection handles, and then watch the **Formula Bar** as you type **Enterprise Fund Expenditures** Press Enter to create the new chart title in the box.

MAC TIP Select the title text before typing the new chart title. Do not press Enter after typing the new title.

2 Click the **Format tab**, and then in the **WordArt Styles group**, click **More** . In the first row, click the last style.

MAC TIP Select the title text and then apply the WordArt style. Be sure to display the entire WordArt Styles gallery to locate the last style in the first row.

3 Drag to select the chart title text, and then change the **Font Size** to **32**. Click the edge of the chart to deselect the title, and then compare your screen with Figure 3.6.

4 **Save** your workbook.

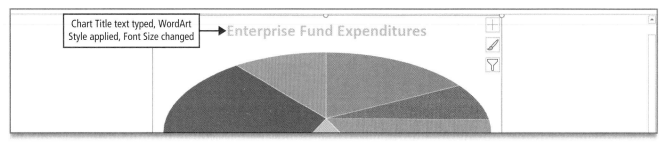

Chart Title text typed, WordArt Style applied, Font Size changed → Enterprise Fund Expenditures

Figure 3.6

Activity 3.04 | Formatting Chart Elements by Removing a Legend and Adding and Formatting Data Labels

MOS
5.2.3

In your worksheet, for each budget item, you calculated the percent of the total in column D. These percentages can also be calculated by the Chart feature and added to the pie slices as labels.

1 If necessary, click the edge of the chart to display the three chart buttons on the right, and then click **Chart Elements** . Compare your screen with Figure 3.7.

Use the Chart Elements button to add, remove, or change chart elements such as the chart title, the legend, and the data labels.

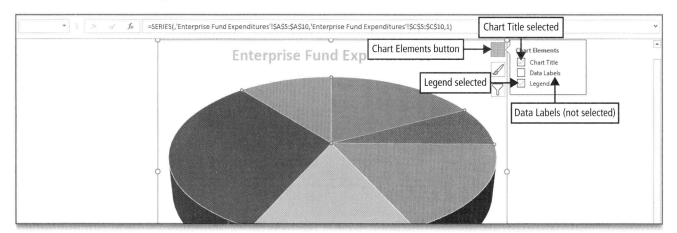

=SERIES(,'Enterprise Fund Expenditures'!$A$5:$A$10,'Enterprise Fund Expenditures'!$C$5:$C$10,1)

Chart Title selected

Enterprise Fund Exp... | Chart Elements button

Chart Elements
- Chart Title
- Data Labels
- Legend

Legend selected

Data Labels (not selected)

Figure 3.7

2 Click the **Legend** check box to deselect it and remove the legend from the bottom of the chart.

🖥 **MAC TIP**   On the Chart Design tab, click Add Chart Element, point to Legend, and then click None.

3 Point to **Data Labels**, and then click the ▶ **arrow** to display a menu. At the bottom of the menu, click **More Options** to display the **Format Data Labels** pane on the right.

The Format Data Labels pane displays and data labels representing the values display on each pie slice.

🖥 **MAC TIP**   On the Chart Design tab, click Add Chart Element, point to Data Labels, and then click More Data Label Options.

4 In the **Format Data Labels** pane, under **Label Options**, click as necessary to select the **Category Name** and **Percentage** check boxes. Click to *clear* any other check boxes in this group. Under **Label Position**, click the **Center** option button. Compare your screen with Figure 3.8.

All of the data labels are selected and display both the category name and the percentage. In the worksheet, you calculated the percent of the total in column D. Here, the percentage will be calculated by the Chart feature and added to the chart as a label.

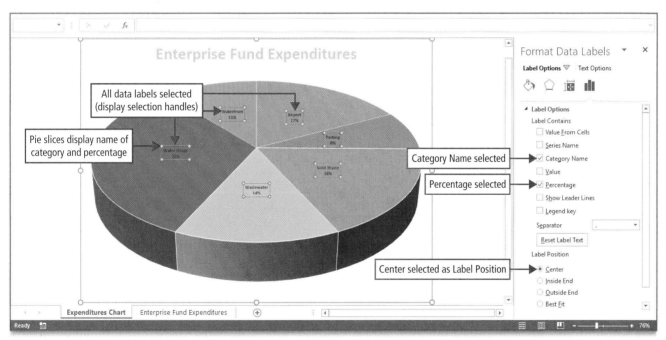

Figure 3.8

5 Point to any of the selected data labels, right-click to display a shortcut menu, and then click **Font** to display the **Font** dialog box.

🖥 **MAC TIP**   Press control and then click a data label to display the Shortcut menu.

6 On the **Font tab**, click the **Font style arrow**, and then click **Bold Italic**. In the **Size** box, drag to select 9 and type **11** Compare your screen with Figure 3.9.

Figure 3.9

7 Click **OK** to close the dialog box and apply the formatting to the data labels. In the upper right corner of the **Format Data Labels** pane, click **Close** ☒. **Save** 🖫 your workbook.

Activity 3.05 | Formatting a Data Series with 3-D Effects

3-D, which is short for *three-dimensional*, refers to an image that appears to have all three spatial dimensions—length, width, and depth.

1 In any pie slice, point anywhere outside of the selected label, and then double-click to display the **Format Data Series** pane on the right.

ANOTHER WAY Right-click outside the label of any pie slice, and then click Format Data Series to display the Format Data Series pane. Or, on the Format tab, in the Current Selection group, click the Chart Elements arrow, click Series 1, and then click Format Selection.

2 In the **Format Data Series** pane, under **Series Options**, click **Effects** 🔾, and then click **3-D Format**. Compare your screen with Figure 3.10.

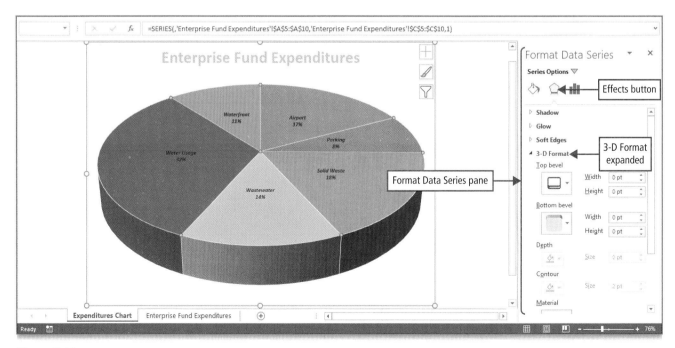

Figure 3.10

3 ▸ Click the **Top bevel arrow**, and then in the gallery, under **Bevel**, click the first bevel, as shown in Figure 3.11.

> *Bevel* is a shape effect that uses shading and shadows to make the edges of a shape appear to be curved or angled.

Figure 3.11

4 ▸ Under **Top bevel**, in the **Width** box, select the existing text and type **512** Change the **Height** to **512** and then press Enter.

5 ▸ Under **Bottom bevel**, use the technique you just practiced to apply the first bevel in the first row with a **Width** of **512** and **Height** of **512** Compare your screen with Figure 3.12.

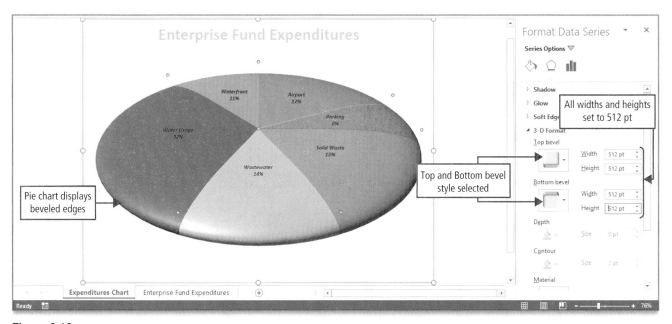

Figure 3.12

6 ▸ In the **Format Data Series** pane, scroll down as necessary, and then click the **Material arrow**. Under **Standard**, click the third material—**Plastic**.

7 ▸ **Save** 🖫 your workbook.

Activity 3.06 | Formatting a Data Series with a Shadow Effect

> **1** In the **Format Data Series pane**, scroll back to the top of the pane, and then click **Shadow** to expand the options for this effect.

> **2** Under **Shadow**, click the **Presets arrow**, use the scroll bar to move to the bottom of the gallery, and then under **Perspective**, in the first row, point to the third effect to display the ScreenTip. Compare your screen with Figure 3.13.

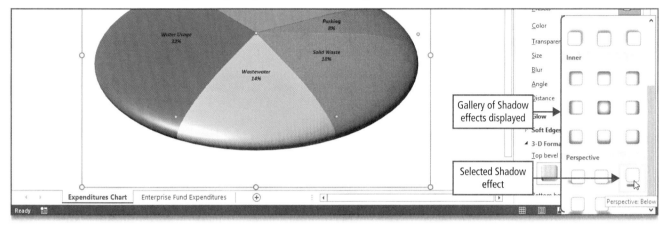

Figure 3.13

> **3** Click **Perspective: Below** to apply the shadow to the chart. **Save** 🖫 your workbook.

Activity 3.07 | Rotating a Pie Chart by Changing the Angle of the First Slice

The order in which the data series in pie charts are plotted in Excel is determined by the order of the data on the worksheet. To gain a different view of the chart, you can rotate the chart within the 360 degrees of the circle of the pie shape to present a different visual perspective of the chart.

> **1** Notice the position of the **Water Usage** and **Waterfront** slices in the chart. Then, with the pie chart still selected—sizing handles surround the pie—in the **Format Data Series** pane, under **Series Options**, click **Series Options** 📊.

> **2** Under **Angle of first slice**, in the box to the right, drag to select **0°**, type **250** and then press Enter to rotate the chart 250 degrees to the right.

🔄 **ANOTHER WAY** Drag the slider to 250°, or click the spin box up arrow as many times as necessary.

> **3** Click **Save** 🖫, and then compare your screen with Figure 3.14.

Rotating the chart can provide a better perspective to the chart. Here, rotating the chart in this manner emphasizes that Water Usage is the largest enterprise fund expenditure.

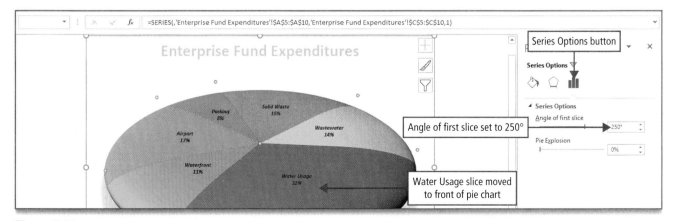

Figure 3.14

Activity 3.08 | Exploding and Coloring a Pie Slice

You can pull out—*explode*—one or more slices of a pie chart to emphasize a specific slice or slices.

1 In the **Format Data Series** pane, under **Series Options**, notice the slider and box for *Pie Explosion*.

When all the pie slices are selected, as they currently are, you can use this command to explode *all* of the pie pieces away from the center by varying degrees to emphasize all the individual slices of the pie chart. An exploded pie chart illustrates the contribution of each value to the total, while at the same time emphasizing individual values.

2 On the pie chart, click the **Waterfront** slice to select only that slice, and then on the right, notice that the **Format Data Point** pane displays.

Excel adjusts the pane, depending on what you have selected, so that the commands you need are available.

3 In the **Format Data Point** pane, in the **Point Explosion** box, select the existing text, type **10%** and then press [Enter].

4 With the **Waterfront** slice still selected, in the **Format Data Point** pane, under **Series Options**, click **Fill & Line** 🎨, and then click **Fill** to expand its options.

5 Click the **Gradient fill** option button, click the **Preset gradients arrow**, and then in the fourth row, click the last gradient. Click **Save** 💾, and then compare your screen with Figure 3.15.

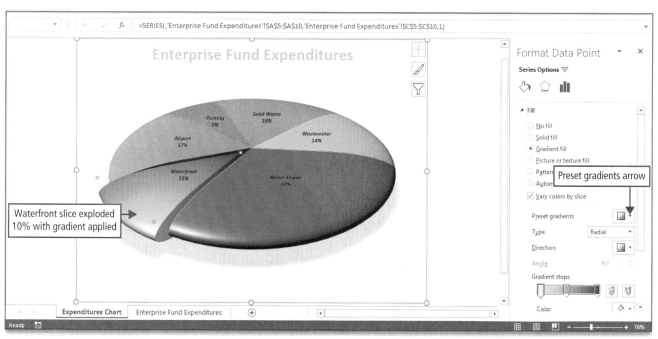

Figure 3.15

Activity 3.09 | Formatting the Chart Area

The entire chart and all of its elements comprise the ***chart area***.

1 Point to the white area just inside the border of the chart to display the ScreenTip *Chart Area*. Click one time, and notice that on the right, the **Format Chart Area** pane displays.

2 Under **Chart Options**, click **Fill & Line** 🎨, and be sure the **Fill** options are still displayed.

3 Click the **Gradient fill** option button, click the **Preset gradients arrow**, and then in the fourth row, click the first gradient.

4 In the **Format Chart Area** pane, click **Fill** to collapse the options, and then click **Border** to expand its options.

5 Under **Border**, click **Solid line**, click the **Color arrow** to display the Outline colors, and then in the fourth column, click the first color. In the **Width** box, drag to select the existing width, type **5** and then press Enter.

6 **Close** ☒ the **Format Chart Area** pane, and then click outside of the Chart Area to deselect the chart. Click **Save** ▣, and then compare your screen with Figure 3.16.

Figure 3.16

Objective 3 | **Edit a Workbook and Update a Chart**

GO! Learn How
Video E3-3

Activity 3.10 | **Editing a Workbook and Updating a Chart**

If you edit the data in your worksheet, the chart data markers—in this instance the pie slices—will adjust automatically to accurately represent the new values.

1 On the pie chart, notice that *Airport* represents 17% of the total projected expenses.

2 In the sheet tab area at the bottom of the workbook, click the **Enterprise Fund Expenditures tab** to redisplay the worksheet.

3 Click cell **C5**, type **18,121,067** and then press Enter. Notice that the Accounting Number Format is retained in the cell.

ANOTHER WAY Double-click the cell to position the insertion point in the cell and edit.

4 Notice that the total in cell **C11** recalculated to *$101,151,180* and the percentages in **column D** also recalculated.

5 ▶ Display the **Expenditures Chart** sheet. Notice that the pie slices adjust to show the recalculation—*Airport* is now *18%* of the adjusted expenditures. Click **Save** 💾, and then compare your screen with Figure 3.17.

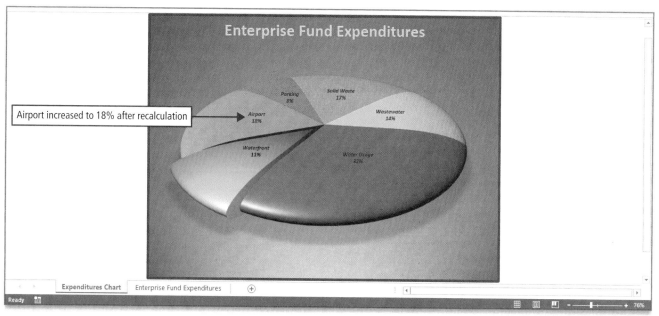

Figure 3.17

Objective 4 | **Use Goal Seek to Perform What-If Analysis**

GO! Learn How

Video E3-4

Activity 3.11 | Using Goal Seek to Perform What-If Analysis

MOS

Expert 3.4.2

The process of changing the values in cells to see how those changes affect the outcome of formulas in your worksheet is referred to as ***what-if analysis***. One what-if analysis tool in Excel is ***Goal Seek***, which finds the input needed in one cell to arrive at the desired result in another cell.

1 ▶ Click the **Enterprise Fund Expenditures sheet tab** to redisplay the worksheet.

2 ▶ Select the range **D5:D10**, and then increase the number of decimal places to two. Compare your screen with Figure 3.18.

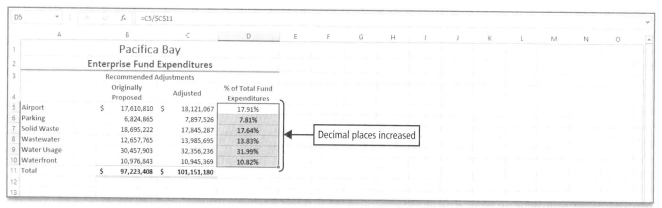

Figure 3.18

3 Click the cell containing the *Adjusted Total*, cell **C11**. On the **Data tab**, in the **Forecast group**, click **What-If Analysis**, and then click **Goal Seek**.

4 In the **Goal Seek** dialog box, notice that the active cell, **C11**, is indicated in the **Set cell** box. Press Tab to move to the **To value** box, and then type **100,000,000**

C11 is the cell in which you want to set a specific value; $100,000,000 is the total expenditures budgeted for the Enterprise Fund. The Set cell box contains the formula that calculates the information you seek.

5 Press Tab to move the insertion point to the **By changing cell** box, and then click cell **C10**. Compare your screen with Figure 3.19.

Cell C10 contains the value that Excel changes to reach the goal. In the Goal Seek dialog box, Excel formats this cell as an absolute cell reference.

Figure 3.19

6 Click **OK**. In the displayed **Goal Seek Status** dialog box, click **OK**.

7 Press Ctrl + Home, click **Save** 💾, and then compare your screen with Figure 3.20.

Excel calculates that the city must budget for *$9,794,189* in Waterfront expenditures in order to maintain a total Enterprise Fund Expenditure budget of $100,000,000.

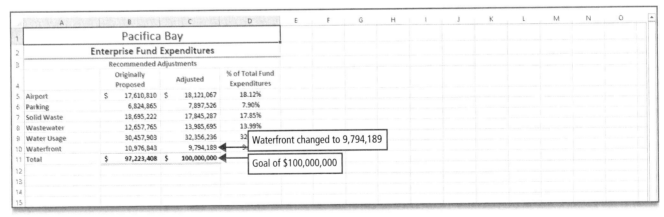

Figure 3.20

Activity 3.12 | Preparing and Printing a Workbook with a Chart Sheet

1 Click the **Page Layout tab**. In the **Page Setup group**, click **Margins**, and then click **Custom Margins**.

2 In the **Page Setup** dialog box, on the **Margins tab**, under **Center on page**, select the **Horizontally** check box.

3 Click the **Header/Footer tab**, and then in the center of the dialog box, click **Custom Footer**. In the **Footer** dialog box, with the insertion point blinking in the **Left section**, on the row of buttons, click **Insert File Name** ⊞. Click **OK** two times.

> The dotted line indicates the page break as currently formatted.

4 Display the **Expenditures Chart**, which must have its footer formatted separately. In the **Page Setup group**, click the **Dialog Box Launcher** ⌐.

> Chart sheets are automatically centered on the page.

🖳 **MAC TIP** On the Page Layout tab, click Page Setup to display the Page Setup dialog box.

5 Click the **Header/Footer tab**, and then in the center of the dialog box, click **Custom Footer**. In the **Footer** dialog box, with the insertion point blinking in the **Left section**, on the row of buttons, click **Insert File Name** ⊞. Click **OK** two times.

6 Right-click the **Expenditures Chart sheet tab**, and then click **Select All Sheets**. Verify that *Group* displays in the title bar.

> Recall that by selecting all sheets, you can view all of the workbook pages in Print Preview.

🖳 **MAC TIP** Press [control] and then click the Expenditures Chart sheet to display the shortcut menu.

7 Click **File**, and then click **Print** to display the **Print Preview**. Examine the first page, and then at the bottom of the **Print Preview**, click **Next Page** ▶ to view the second page of your workbook.

8 Display the workbook properties. As the **Tags**, type enterprise fund, expenditures As the **Subject**, type your course name and section number. Be sure your name displays as the **Author**. **Save** 🖫 the workbook and **Close** Excel.

📄 **For Non-MyLab Submissions Determine What Your Instructor Requires**
As directed by your instructor, submit your completed Excel file.

---

9 In **MyLab IT**, locate and click the Grader Project **Excel 3A Enterprise Fund**. In **step 3**, under **Upload Completed Assignment**, click **Choose File**. In the **Open** dialog box, navigate to your **Excel Chapter 3 folder**, and then click your **Student_Excel_3A_Enterprise_Fund** file one time to select it. In the lower right corner of the **Open** dialog box, click **Open**.

> The name of your selected file displays above the Upload button.

10 To submit your file to **MyLab IT** for grading, click **Upload**, wait a moment for a green **Success!** message, and then in **step 4**, click the blue **Submit for Grading** button. Click **Close Assignment** to return to your list of **Course Materials**.

You have completed Project 3A END

Objective	Analyze Expenditures with a Pie Chart

ALERT   Working with Web-Based Applications and Services

Computer programs and services on the web receive continuous updates and improvements, so the steps to complete this web-based Activity may differ from the ones shown. You can often look at the screens and the information presented to determine how to complete the Activity.

If you do not already have a Google account, you will need to create one before you begin this Activity. Go to **http://google.com** and, in the upper right corner, click Sign In. On the Sign In screen, click Create Account. On the Create your Google Account page, complete the form, read and agree to the Terms of Service and Privacy Policy, and then click Next step. On the Welcome screen, click Get Started.

Activity | Creating a Pie Chart

1 From the desktop, open your browser, navigate to http://google.com, and then click **Google apps** ▦. Click **Drive** 🔺, and then if necessary, sign in to your Google account.

2 Open your **GO! Web Projects** folder—or click **New** to create and then open this folder if necessary. Click **New**, and then click **File upload**. Navigate to your student data files, click **e03_3A_Web**, and then click **Open**.

3 Right-click the file you uploaded, point to **Open with**, and then click **Google Sheets**.

4 Click cell **D5**. Type = and then click cell **C5**. Type / and then click **C11** and press F4 to make the cell reference absolute. Press Enter to create a formula to calculate % of Total Fund Expenditures.

5 Click cell **D5**, and then apply percent formatting ％. Fill the formula down through cell **D10**. Click the **Format tab**, point to **Align**, and then click **Center.**

6 Select the range **A5:A10**, hold down Ctrl, and then select **C5:C10**. Click the **Insert tab**, and then click **Chart**. In the **Chart editor pane**, click the **Chart type arrow**. To the right of the chart gallery, point to the vertical scroll

bar and drag down to display the Pie charts. Click the third chart—**3D pie chart** to insert the chart in the worksheet.

7 Point to the chart and then drag down and to the left to position the pie chart under the worksheet data so that its left edge aligns with the left edge of cell **A13**. Click the **Chart title** to display a box in which you can type the chart title. Type **Enterprise Fund Expenditures** and then press Enter. In the **Chart editor pane**, click the **Title font size arrow**, and then click **30**. Click anywhere in the chart outside of the title so that the title is not selected.

8 In the **Chart editor pane**, on the **Customize tab**, click **Chart style**. Click the **Background color arrow**, and then in the seventh column, click the third color—**light cornflower blue 3**. Click **Legend**, and then click the **Position arrow**. Click **Right**. Click **Pie Chart**, and then click the **Slice label arrow**. Click **Percentage** and then close the **Chart Editor pane**.

9 Click cell **A1** and then scroll down to view the entire chart. Compare your screen with Figure A.

10 Submit your file as directed by your instructor. Sign out of your Google account and close your browser.

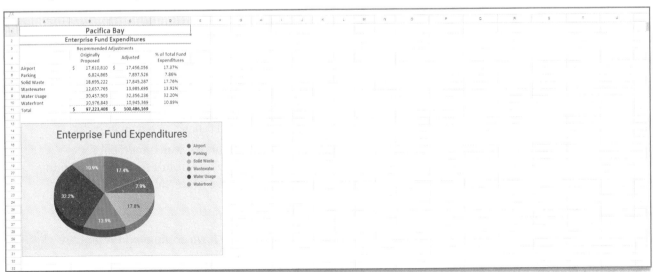

Figure A

Tourism Spending Projection and Analysis

Project Activities

In Activities 3.13 through 3.22, you will assist Michael Larsen, City Manager, in creating a worksheet to estimate future tourism spending based on two possible growth rates. You will also create a line chart to display past visitor spending and a map chart and funnel chart to analyze tourism advertising and event spending. Your resulting worksheet and chart will look similar to Figure 3.21.

Project Files for MyLab IT Grader

1. In your **MyLab IT** course, locate and click **Excel 3B Tourism**, Download Materials, and then Download All Files.

2. Extract the zipped folder to your Excel Chapter 3 folder. Close the Grader download screens.

3. Take a moment to open the downloaded **Excel_3B_Tourism_Instructions**; note any recent updates to the book.

Project Results

GO! Project 3B

Where We're Going

Figure 3.21 Project 3B Tourism Spending Projection and Analysis

ALERT Because Office 365 is a cloud-based subscription service that receives continuous updates, you may encounter some variations in what appears on your screen and what is shown in this instruction. Microsoft Office 365 is fully installed on your PC or Mac; no internet access is necessary to create or edit documents. When you *are* connected to the internet, you will receive monthly upgrades and new features, so you always have the latest versions of Office apps as soon as they are available. Your subscription gives you continuous free access to the latest innovations and refinements.

GO! Learn How

Video E3-5

If you change the value in a cell referenced in a formula, Excel automatically recalculates the result of the formula. This means that you can change cell values to see what would happen if you tried different values. This process of changing the values in cells to see how those changes affect the outcome of formulas in your worksheet is referred to as what-if analysis.

Activity 3.13 | Using Parentheses in a Formula to Calculate a Percentage Rate of Increase

Mr. Larsen has the city's tourism spending figures for the recent 5-year period. In each year, tourism spending has increased. In this Activity, you will construct a formula to calculate the *percentage rate of increase*—the percent by which one number increases over another number—for each year since 2016. From this information, future tourism spending growth can be estimated.

Excel follows a set of mathematical rules called the ***order of operations***, which has four basic parts:

- Expressions within parentheses are processed first.
- Exponentiation, if present, is performed before multiplication and division.
- Multiplication and division are performed before addition and subtraction.
- Consecutive operators with the same level of precedence are calculated from left to right.

1 ▶ Navigate to your **Excel Chapter 3 folder**, and then double-click the Excel file you downloaded from **MyLab IT** that displays your name—**Student_Excel_3B_Tourism**.

2 ▶ In cell **B4**, type **2016** and then press ⟨Tab⟩. In cell **C4**, type **2017** and then press ⟨Tab⟩. Select the range **B4:C4**, and then drag the fill handle to the right through cell **F4** to extend the series to *2020*. Compare your screen with Figure 3.22.

By establishing a pattern of 1-year intervals with the first two cells, you can use the fill handle to continue the series. The AutoFill feature will do this for any pattern that you establish with two or more cells.

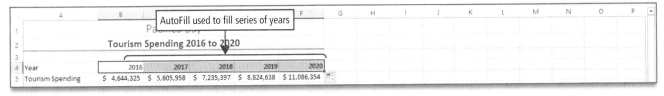

Figure 3.22

3 ▶ Click cell **C6**. Being sure to include the parentheses, type **=(c5-b5)/b5** and then on the **Formula Bar**, click **Enter** ☑ to keep cell **C6** active. Notice that your result displays as *$0.21* because Excel retains the Accounting Number Format of the cells referenced in the formula.

As you type, a list of Excel functions that begin with the letters *C* and *B* may briefly display. This is ***Formula AutoComplete***, an Excel feature which, after typing an = (equal sign) and the beginning letter or letters of a function name, displays a list of function names that match the typed letter(s). In this instance, the letters represent cell references, *not* the beginning of a function name.

4 With cell **C6** selected, apply **Percent Style** %, and then compare your screen with Figure 3.23.

C6			f_x	=(C5-B5)/B5 ◄—— Formula Bar displays formula													
	A	B	C	D	E	F	G	H	I	J	K	L	M	N	O	P	
1			Pacifica Bay														
2			Tourism Spending 2016 to 2020														
3																	
4	Year		2016	2017	2018	2019	2020										
5	Tourism Spending		$ 4,644,325	$ 5,605,958	$ 7,235,397	8,824,638	11,086,354										
6	Percent Increase		21% ◄—— Formula result in cell C6														
7																	

Figure 3.23

5 With cell **C6** selected, drag the fill handle to the right to copy the formula through cell **F6**.

Because this formula uses relative cell references—that is, for each year, the formula is the same but the values used are relative to the formula's location—you can copy the formula in this manner. For example, the result for 2018 uses the 2017 value as the base, the result for 2019 uses the 2018 value as the base, and the result for 2020 uses the 2019 value as the base.

6 Click cell **C6** and look at the **Formula Bar**.

The mathematical formula *rate = amount of increase/base* is used to calculate the percentage rate of tourism spending increase from 2016 to 2017. The formula is applied as follows:

First, determine the *amount of increase* by subtracting the *base*—the starting point represented by the 2016 tourism spending—from the 2017 tourism spending. Therefore, the *amount of increase* = $5,605,958 – $4,644,325 or $961,633. Between 2016 and 2017, tourism spending increased by $961,633. In the formula, this calculation is represented by C5-B5.

Second, calculate the *rate*—what the amount of increase ($961,633) represents as a percentage of the base (2016's tourism spending of $4,644,325). Determine this by dividing the amount of increase ($961,633) by the base ($4,644,325). Therefore, $961,633 divided by $4,644,325 is equal to *0.207055492* or, when formatted as a percent and rounded up, 21%.

7 In the **Formula Bar**, locate the parentheses enclosing *C5-B5*.

Recall that Excel follows a set of mathematical rules called the order of operations, in which expressions within parentheses are processed first, multiplication and division are performed before addition and subtraction, and consecutive operators with the same level of precedence are calculated from left to right.

8 **Save** 💾 your workbook, and then compare your screen with Figure 3.24.

C6			f_x	=(C5-B5)/B5													
	A	B	C	D	E	F	G	H	I	J	K	L	M	N	O	P	
1			Pacifica Bay														
2			Tourism Spending 2016 to 2020														
3																	
4	Year		2016	2017	2018	2019	2020										
5	Tourism Spending		$ 4,644,325	$ 5,605,958	$ 7,235,397	$ 8,824,638	$ 11,086,354										
6	Percent Increase		21%	29%	22%	26% ◄—— Formula filled across row											
7																	

Figure 3.24

MORE KNOWLEDGE **Use of Parentheses in a Formula**

When writing a formula in Excel, use parentheses to specify the order in which the operations should occur. For example, to average three test scores of 100, 50, and 90 that you scored on three different tests, you would add the test scores and then divide by the number of test scores in the list. If you write this formula as = 100 + 50 + 90/3, the result would be 180, because Excel would first divide 90 by 3 and then add 100 + 50 + 30. Excel would do so because the order of operations states that multiplication and division are calculated *before* addition and subtraction.

The correct way to write this formula is = (100 + 50 + 90)/3. Excel will add the three values, and then divide the result by 3, or 240/3 resulting in a correct average of 80. Parentheses play an important role in ensuring that you get the correct result in your formulas.

Activity 3.14 | Using Format Painter

2.2.3

In this Activity, you will use Format Painter to copy formatting.

1 Click cell **A2**, and then on the **Home tab**, in the **Clipboard group**, click **Format Painter** ✑. Click cell **A8** to copy the format.

>The format of cell A2 is *painted*—applied to—cell A8, including the merging and centering of the text across the range A8:F8.

2 Point to cell **F5**, display the shortcut menu, and then click **Copy**. Point to cell **B13**, right-click, and then on the shortcut menu, under **Paste Options**, click **Paste** ⬚. Compare your screen with Figure 3.25, and then **Save** 🖫 your workbook.

🖥 **MAC TIP** Press [control] and then click cell B13. Click Paste.

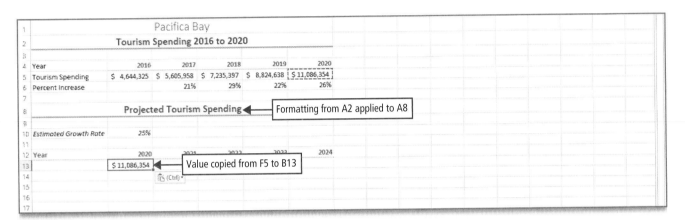

Figure 3.25

MORE KNOWLEDGE **Percentage Calculations**

When you type a percentage into a cell—for example 25%—the percentage format, without decimal points, displays in both the cell and the Formula Bar. Excel will, however, use the decimal value of 0.25 for actual calculations.

Activity 3.15 | Calculating a Value After an Increase

A growth in tourism spending means that the city can plan for additional revenues and also plan more hotel and conference space to accommodate the increasing number of visitors. Therefore, city planners in Pacifica Bay want to estimate how much tourism spending will increase in the future. The calculations you made in the previous Activity show that tourism spending has increased at varying rates during each year from 2016 to 2020, ranging from a low of 21% to a high of 29% per year.

Economic data suggests that future growth will trend close to that of the recent past. To plan for the future, Mr. Larsen wants to prepare a forecast of tourism spending based on the percentage increase halfway between the high of 29% and the low of 21%; that is, for 25%. In this Activity, you will calculate the tourism spending that would result from a 25% increase.

1 Click cell **C13**. Type **=b13*(100%+b10)** and then on the **Formula Bar**, click **Enter** ✓ to display a result of *13857942.5*.

2 Point to cell **B13**, right-click, click **Format Painter** ✑, and then click cell **C13** to copy the format. Compare your screen with Figure 3.26.

>This formula calculates what tourism spending will be in the year 2021 assuming an increase of 25% over 2020's tourism spending. Use the mathematical formula ***value after increase = base × percent for new value*** to calculate a value after an increase as follows:

First, establish the *percent for new value*. The **percent for new value = base percent + percent of increase**. The *base percent* of 100% represents the base tourism spending and the *percent of increase*—in this instance, 25%. Therefore, the tourism spending will equal 100% of the base year plus 25% of the base year. This can be expressed as 125% or 1.25. In this formula, you will use 100% + the rate in cell B10, which is 25%, to equal 125%.

Second, enter a reference to the cell that contains the *base*—the tourism spending in 2020. The base value resides in cell B13—*$11,086,354*.

Third, calculate the *value after increase*. Because in each future year the increase will be based on 25%—an absolute value located in cell B10—this cell reference can be formatted as absolute by typing dollar signs.

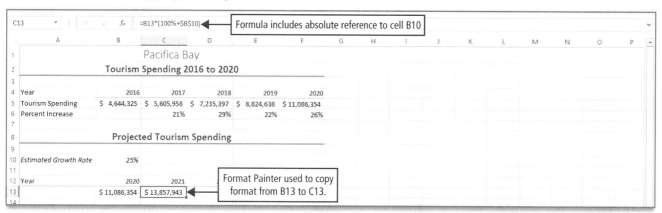

Figure 3.26

3 With cell **C13** as the active cell, drag the fill handle to copy the formula to the range **D13:F13**. Click an empty cell to cancel the selection, click **Save** and then compare your screen with Figure 3.27.

The formula in cell C13 uses a relative cell address—B13—for the *base*; the tourism spending in the previous year is used in each of the formulas in cells D13:F13 as the *base* value. Because the reference to the *percent of increase* in cell B10 is an absolute reference, each *value after increase* is calculated with the value from cell B10.

The tourism spending projected for 2021—*$13,857,943*—is an increase of 25% over the spending in 2020. The projected spending in 2022—*$17,322,428*—is an increase of 25% over the spending in 2021, and so on.

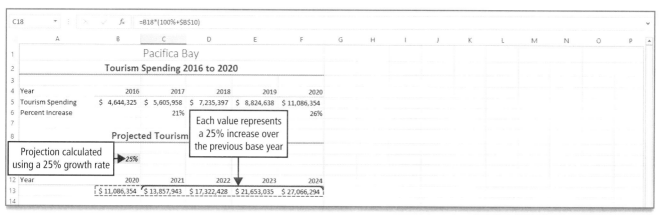

Figure 3.27

MORE KNOWLEDGE **Percent Increase or Decrease**

The basic formula for calculating an increase or decrease can be done in two parts. First determine the percent by which the base value will be increased or decreased, and then add or subtract the results to the base. The formula can be simplified by using (1+amount of increase) or (1–amount of decrease), where 1, rather than 100%, represents the whole. Therefore, the formula used in Step 1 of Activity 3.15 could also be written =b13*(1+b10), or =(b13*b10)+b13.

Objective 6   Answer What-If Questions by Changing Values in a Worksheet

GO! Learn How

Video E3-6

If a formula depends on the value in a cell, you can see what effect it will have if you change the value in that cell. Then, you can copy the value computed by the formula and paste it into another part of the worksheet where you can compare it to other values.

Activity 3.16 | Answering What-If Questions and Using Paste Special

2.1.1

A growth rate of 25% in tourism spending in each year will result in tourism spending of approximately $27 million by 2018. The city planners will likely ask: *What if* tourism spending grows at the lowest rate of 21%?

Because the formulas are constructed to use the growth rate displayed in cell B10, Mr. Larsen can answer that question quickly by entering a different percentage into that cell. To keep the results of the new calculation so it can be compared, you will paste the results of the what-if question into another area of the worksheet.

1   Click cell **A15**. Type **Estimated Growth in Tourism Spending 2020 to 2024** and then press Enter. Use **Format Painter** 🖌 to copy the format from cell **A8** to cell **A15**.

2   Select the range **A10:B10**, right-click to display the mini toolbar, click the **Fill Color button arrow** 🎨▾, and then under **Theme Colors**, in the first column, click the third color.

🖥 **MAC TIP**   On the Home tab, click the Fill Color button arrow

3   Leave **row 16** blank, and then in the range **A17:A19**, type the following row titles:

Year

25% Growth Rate

21% Growth Rate

4   Select the range **B12:F12**, right-click over the selection, and then on the shortcut menu, click **Copy**.

🖥 **MAC TIP**   Press control + C; or, on the Home tab, click Copy.

5   Point to cell **B17**, right-click, and then on the shortcut menu, under **Paste Options**, click **Paste** 📋.

> Recall that when pasting a group of copied cells to a target range, you need only point to or select the first cell of the range.

🖥 **MAC TIP**   On the Home tab, click Paste.

6   Select and **Copy** the range **B13:F13**, and then **Paste** it beginning in cell **B18**.

7   Click cell **C18**. On the **Formula Bar**, notice that the *formula* was pasted into the cell, as shown in Figure 3.28.

> This is *not* the desired result. The actual *calculated values*—not the formulas—are needed in the range.

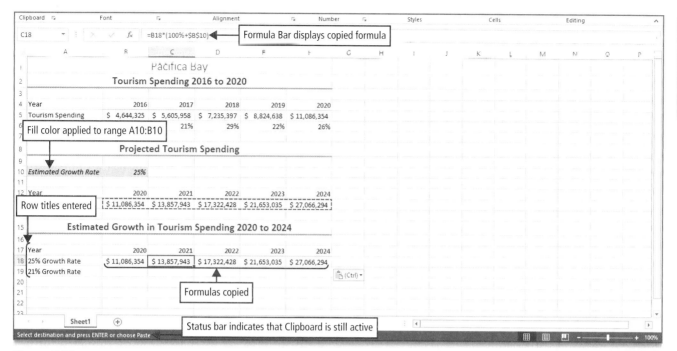

Figure 3.28

8 On the **Quick Access Toolbar**, click **Undo** 🔄. With the range **B13:F13** still copied to the Clipboard—as indicated by the message in the status bar and the moving border—point to cell **B18**, and then right-click to display the shortcut menu.

⌨ **MAC TIP** On the Home tab, click the Paste *arrow*, and then click Values & Number Formatting. Skip to Step 11.

9 Under **Paste Options**, point to **Paste Special** to display another gallery, and then under **Paste Values**, point to **Values & Number Formatting** 📋 to display the ScreenTip as shown in Figure 3.29.

The ScreenTip *Values & Number Formatting (A)* indicates that you can paste the calculated values that result from the calculation of formulas along with the formatting applied to the copied cells. *(A)* is the keyboard shortcut for this command.

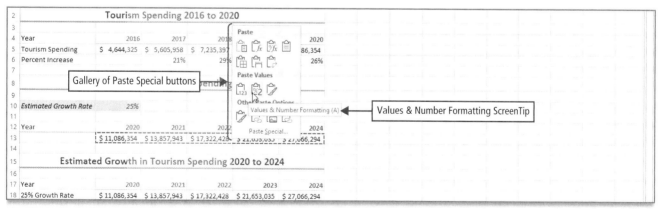

Figure 3.29

10 Click **Values & Number Formatting** 📋.

11 Click cell **C18** and notice on the **Formula Bar** that the cell contains a *value*, not a formula. Press (Esc) to cancel the moving border. Compare your screen with Figure 3.30.

The calculated estimates based on a 25% growth rate are pasted along with their formatting.

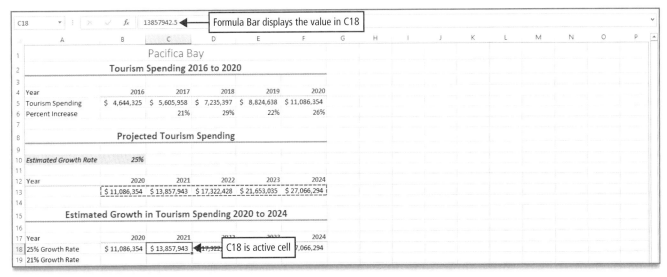

Figure 3.30

12 Click cell **B10**. Type **21** and then watch the values in **C13:F13** *recalculate* as, on the **Formula Bar**, you click **Enter** ✓.

The value *21%* is the lowest percent increase for the past 5-year period.

13 Select and **Copy** the new values in the range **B13:F13**. Point to cell **B19**, right-click, and then on the shortcut menu, point to **Paste Special**. Under **Paste Values**, click **Values & Number Formatting** 📋.

14 Press (Esc) to cancel the moving border, click cell **A1**, click **Save** 💾, and then compare your screen with Figure 3.31.

With this information, Mr. Larsen can answer what-if questions about the projected increase in tourism spending based on the rates of increase over the past five years.

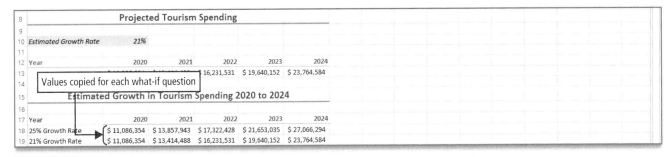

Figure 3.31

Objective 7   **Chart Data with a Line Chart**

GO! Learn How
Video E3-7

A *line chart* displays trends over time. Time is displayed along the bottom axis and the data point values connect with a line. The curve and direction of the line make trends obvious to the reader.

The columns in a column chart and the pie slices in a pie chart emphasize the distinct values of each data point. A line chart, on the other hand, emphasizes the flow from one data point value to the next.

Activity 3.17 | Inserting Multiple Rows and Creating a Line Chart

2.1.3, 6.1.1

So that City Council members can see how tourism spending has increased over a 5-year period, in this Activity, you will chart the actual tourism spending from 2016 to 2020 in a line chart.

1 Click the **Page Layout tab**. In the **Themes group**, click **Colors**, and then change the **Theme Colors** to **Orange**.

2 In the **row header area**, point to **row 8** to display the → pointer, and then drag down to select **rows 8:24**. Right-click over the selection, and then click **Insert** to insert the same number of blank rows as you selected. Compare your screen with Figure 3.32.

Use this technique to insert multiple rows quickly.

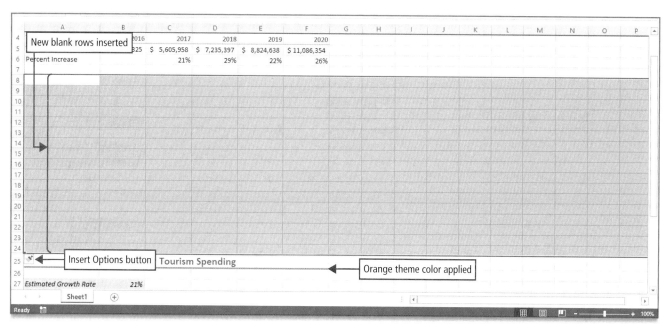

Figure 3.32

3 Near **row 25**, click **Insert Options** , and then click the **Clear Formatting** option button to clear any formatting from these rows.

You will use this blank area to position your line chart.

MAC TIP On the Home tab, click Clear, and then click Clear Formats.

4 Press Ctrl + Home to deselect the rows and move to the top of your worksheet. Select the range **A5:F5**. On the **Insert tab**, in the **Charts group**, click **Insert Line or Area Chart** .

5 In the gallery of line charts, under **2-D Line**, point to the fourth chart type to display the ScreenTip *Line with Markers*. Compare your screen with Figure 3.33.

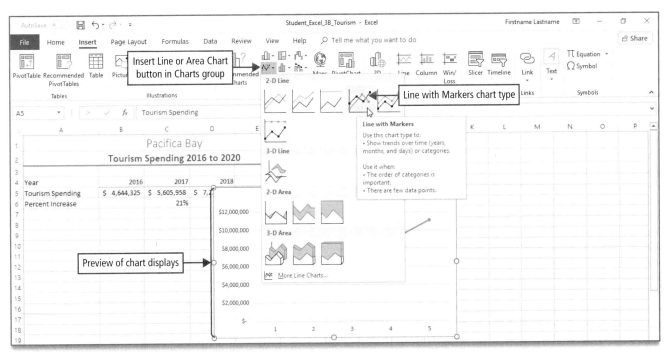

Figure 3.33

6 Click the **Line with Markers** chart type to create the chart in the worksheet.

7 Point to the border of the chart to display the pointer, and then drag the chart so that its upper left corner is positioned in cell **A8**, aligned approximately under the *t* in the word *Percent* above.

Excel uses the label in cell A5—*Tourism Spending*—as the suggested chart title.

8 Point to the **Chart Title** *Tourism Spending* and right-click to display the shortcut menu. On the shortcut menu, click **Edit Text** to place the insertion point at the beginning of the title. Type **Pacifica Bay** and press Enter. Press End to move to the end of *Spending*, press Spacebar, and then type **2016 to 2020**

9 Click the dashed border surrounding the **Chart Title** so that it is a solid line, indicating the entire title is selected. Right-click over the title, and then click **Font**. In the **Font** dialog box, click the **Font style arrow**, and then click **Bold**. Click the **Font color arrow**, and then in the second column, click the first color. Click **OK** and then compare your screen with Figure 3.34.

Figure 3.34

Activity 3.18 | Formatting Axes in a Line Chart

MOS
5.2.1

An *axis* is a line that serves as a frame of reference for measurement; it borders the chart *plot area*. The plot area is the area bounded by the axes, including all the data series. In a line chart, the area along the bottom of a chart that identifies the categories of data is referred to as the *category axis* or the *x-axis*. The area along the left side of a chart that shows the range of numbers for the data points is referred to as the *value axis* or the *y-axis*.

In this Activity, you will change the category axis to include the years 2016 to 2020 and adjust the numeric scale of the value axis.

1 Be sure the chart is still selected. At the bottom of the chart, point to any of the numbers *1* through *5* to display the ScreenTip *Horizontal (Category) Axis*, and then right-click. On the shortcut menu, click **Select Data**.

MAC TIP On the Chart Design tab, click Select Data. Click in the Horizontal (Category) axis labels box, and then select the range B4:F4. Click OK. Skip Steps 2, 3, and 4.

ANOTHER WAY Click the Design tab, and then in the Data group, click Select Data.

2 On the right side of the **Select Data Source** dialog box, under **Horizontal (Category) Axis Labels**, locate **Edit**, as shown in Figure 3.35.

Here you can change the labels on the category axis to the years that are represented in the chart.

Figure 3.35

3 In the right column, click **Edit**. If necessary, drag the title bar of the Axis Labels dialog box to the right of the chart so that it is not blocking your view of the data. Select the years in the range **B4:F4**. Compare your screen with Figure 3.36.

Figure 3.36

4 In the **Axis Labels** dialog box, click **OK**, and notice that in the right column of the **Select Data Source** dialog box, the years display as the category labels. Click **OK** to close the **Select Data Source** dialog box. Compare your screen with Figure 3.37.

Figure 3.37

5 With the **Horizontal (Category) Axis** selected, click the **Chart Elements** button ⊞, point to **Axes**, click the ▶ **arrow**, and then click **More Options** to display the **Format Axis** pane.

MAC TIP Select the Category Axis. On the Chart Design tab, click Add Chart Element, point to Axes, and then click More Axis Options.

6 Under **Axis Options**, click **Fill & Line** ◇, and then if necessary, click Line to expand the options. Click the **No line** option button and then **Close** ✕ the **Format Axis** pane.

7 On the chart, notice that the orange line—the data series—does not display in the lower portion of the chart. On the left side of the chart, point to any of the dollar values to display the ScreenTip *Vertical (Value) Axis*, and then right-click. On the shortcut menu, click **Format Axis** to display the **Format Axis** pane on the right. Compare your screen with Figure 3.38.

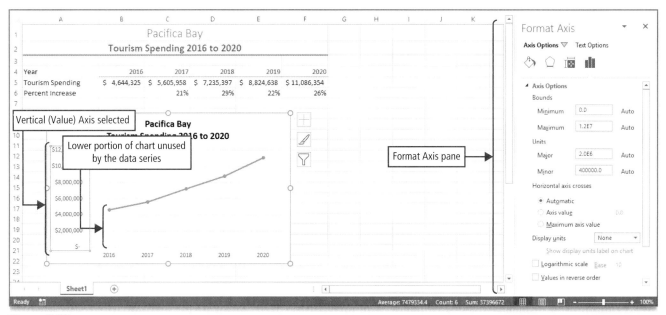

Figure 3.38

ANOTHER WAY On the Format tab, in the Current Selection group, click the Chart Elements arrow, click Vertical (Value) Axis, and then click Format Selection. Or, click the Chart Elements button, point to Axes, click the arrow, click More Options, and then in the Format Axis pane, click the Axis Options arrow. On the displayed list, click Vertical (Value) Axis.

8 In the **Format Axis** pane, under **Bounds**, click in the **Minimum** box, and then select the existing text *0.0*. Type **4000000** and then press Enter.

Because none of the spending figures are under $4,000,000, changing the Minimum number to $4,000,000 will enable the data series to occupy more of the plot area.

9 Under **Units**, in the **Major** box, select the text *1.0E6*, type **2000000** and press Enter. Click **Save** 🖫, and then compare your screen with Figure 3.39.

The *Major unit* value determines the spacing between the gridlines in the plot area. By default, Excel started the values at zero and increased in increments of $2,000,000. By setting the Minimum value on the value axis to $4,000,000, the Major unit is changed to 1.0E6—$1,000,000. Changing the Minimum value to $4,000,000 and setting the Major unit back to $2,000,000 displays a clearer and more pronounced trend in tourism spending.

Numbers that display E + a number are expressed by Excel in the Scientific format, which displays a number in exponential notation.

Figure 3.39

Activity 3.19 | Formatting the Chart Area in a Line Chart

An Excel chart has two background elements—the plot area and the chart area—which by default display a single fill color. To add visual appeal to a chart, you can insert a graphic image as the background.

1 Near the top of the **Format Axis** pane, click the **Axis Options arrow**, and then click **Chart Area** to display the **Format Chart Area** pane. Click **Fill & Line** 🖌.

When formatting chart elements, Excel provides multiple ways to display the panes that you need. You can right-click the area you want to format and choose a command on the shortcut menu. You can use an existing pane to move to a different pane, and you can use the Format tab on the ribbon to navigate among various chart elements in the Current Selection group. Use whatever method is easiest for you.

ANOTHER WAY On the Format tab, in the Current Selection group, click the Chart Elements arrow, click Chart Area, and then click Format Selection. Or, right-click slightly inside the chart to display the shortcut menu, and then click Format Chart Area.

MAC TIP With the Format Axis pane open, point to a blank area in the upper right corner of the chart until the ScreenTip Chart Area displays, and then click to display the Format Chart Area pane.

2 In the **Format Chart Area** pane, click **Fill** to expand the options, and then click the **Picture or texture fill** option button.

A default texture displays in the chart area.

3 In the **Format Chart Area** pane, under **Insert picture from**, click **File**. In the **Insert Picture** dialog box, navigate to the files you downloaded with this project, and then click **e03B_Surfers**. Click **Insert**, and then compare your screen with Figure 3.40.

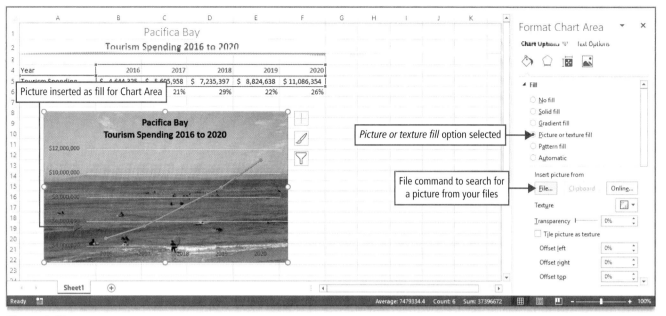

Figure 3.40

---

4 In the **Format Chart Area** pane, click **Fill** to collapse the options, and then if necessary, click Border to expand the options. Click the **Solid line** option button, click the **Color arrow**, and then under **Theme Colors**, in the fifth column, if necessary, click the first color.

5 Set the **Width** to **4 pt** either by selecting the existing text in the Width box and typing or by clicking the up spin box arrow as necessary.

6 Use the scroll bar on the right side of the Format Chart Area pane if necessary to scroll to the bottom of the pane, and then select the **Rounded corners** check box. On the Quick Access Toolbar, click **Save**, and then compare your screen with Figure 3.41.

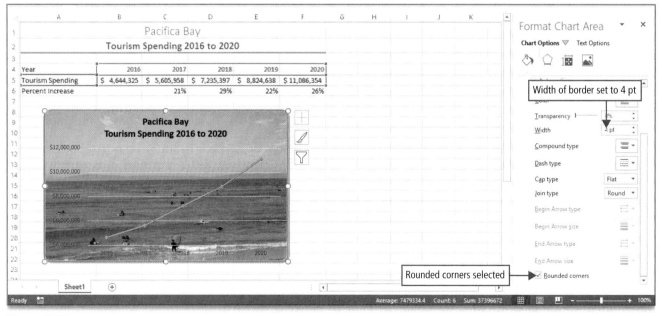

Figure 3.41

Activity 3.20 | Formatting the Plot Area Gridlines and Axis Fonts in a Line Chart

1 To the right of the chart, if necessary, click Chart Elements ⊞ to display the list of elements. Point to **Gridlines**, click the **arrow**, and then click **More Options** to display the **Format Major Gridlines** pane. Compare your screen with Figure 3.42.

Figure 3.42

MAC TIP On the Chart Design tab, click the Add Chart Element button. Point to Gridlines, and then click More Gridline Options.

---

2 Click the **Solid line** option button. Click the **Color arrow**, and be sure that in the fifth column, the first color is selected.

3 Set the **Width** to **1 pt**.

4 In the chart, point to any of the dollar values on the **Vertical (Value) Axis**, right-click, and then click **Font**.

5 In the **Font** dialog box, change the **Font style** to **Bold**, and then change the **Font color**—in the second column, click the first color. Click **OK**.

6 Use the same technique to format the font of the **Horizontal (Category) Axis** with the same color applied in Step 5. Apply **Bold**.

7 **Close** ☒ the **Format Axis** pane. Click cell **A1** to deselect the chart. Click **Save** 🖫, and then compare your screen with Figure 3.43.

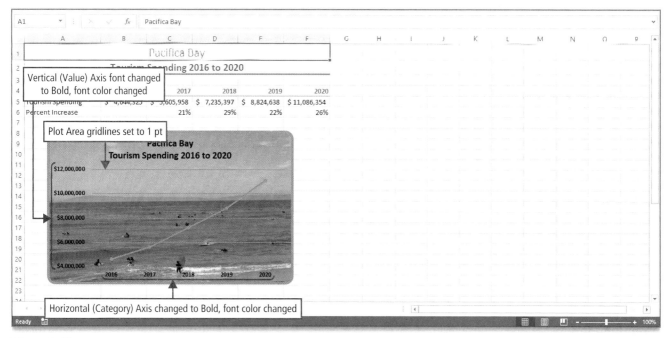

A1 | Pacifica Bay

Vertical (Value) Axis font changed to Bold, font color changed

Plot Area gridlines set to 1 pt

Pacifica Bay
Tourism Spending 2016 to 2020

$12,000,000
$10,000,000
$8,000,000
$6,000,000
$4,000,000

2016   2017   2018   2019   2020

Horizontal (Category) Axis changed to Bold, font color changed

Figure 3.43

Objective 8 Create a Map Chart and a Funnel Chart

GO! Learn How
Video E3-8

A ***map chart*** compares values and shows categories across geographical regions; for example, across countries, states, counties, and regions. The charted regions display in map form, and each region displays shading to indicate the values in the data series.

Funnel charts show values across the stages in a process. Typically, the values decrease gradually, allowing the bars to resemble a funnel.

Activity 3.21 Creating and Sizing a Map Chart

4.1.2

To encourage visitors to come to the city, the Pacifica Bay Tourism Office conducts advertising campaigns in five states—Oregon, Arizona, Washington, New York, and Illinois. In this Activity, you will create a map chart to depict how the advertising budget is allocated across these five states.

1 Double-click the **Sheet1** tab, type **Expenditures** and then press Enter to rename the sheet. To the right of the **Expenditures** sheet, click **New sheet** ⊕, and then rename the sheet **Advertising**

2 In the **Advertising** sheet, in cell **A1**, type **Tourism Advertising** and then press Enter. In cell **A2**, type **By State** and then press Enter. **Merge & Center** the titles across columns **A:B**. To cell **A1**, apply the **Title** cell style and to cell **A2**, apply the **Heading 1**. Set the width of columns **A:B** to **100 pixels**.

3 In the range **A3:B8**, type the following data:

State	Expenditures
Arizona	48500
Illinois	62350
New York	51300
Oregon	75200
Washington	68500

4 Select the range **B4:B8**, and then apply **Accounting Number Format** with zero decimal places. Select the range **A3:B3**, and then apply the **Heading 2** cell style. **Center** ≡ the range.

5 Select the range **A3:B8**. On the **Insert tab**, in the **Charts group**, click **Maps**, and then click **Filled Map**. If a message box displays, click I Accept. Compare your screen with Figure 3.44.

A map of the United States displays to the right of the data. The five states display varying shades of orange. Arizona—the state in which the fewest advertising dollars are spent—is the lightest shade of orange. Oregon—the state in which the most advertising dollars are spent—is the darkest shade of orange. The legend displays the Expenditures scale from highest to lowest.

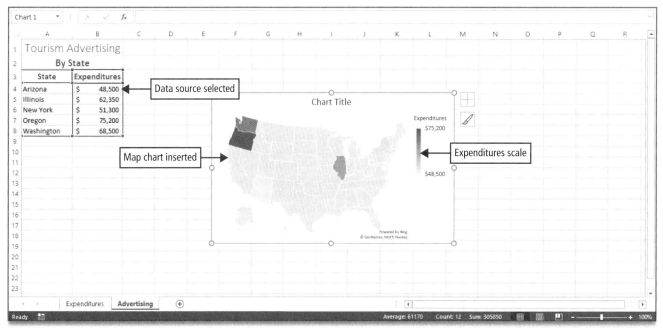

Figure 3.44

6 Click the **Chart Title**, and then select the title text. Type **Tourism Advertising by State** and then click outside of the title so that it is not selected.

7 Point to the map chart to display the [pointer icon] pointer, and then drag the chart so that its upper left corner aligns with the upper left corner of cell **D1**. On the **Format tab**, in the **Height** box [icon], type **2** and then click in the **Width** box [icon]. Type **4** and then press Enter to resize the chart. **Save** [icon], and then compare your screen with Figure 3.45.

Figure 3.45

Activity 3.22 | Creating and Sizing a Funnel Chart

MOS
Expert 4.1.2

As a promotional event, the Pacifica Bay Tourism Office recently invited travel agents, event planners, and wedding planners from the five states in which the city advertises to come to tour the city and see its attractions and venues. The guests were provided with lodging for two days. Invitations were sent to 125 individuals. To track the success of this promotional event, you will create a funnel chart to illustrate the number of invited guests, the number of guests that indicated they would attend, and the number of guests that actually attended.

1 In cell **A12**, type **Travel Agent Event** and then click cell **A1**. On the **Home tab**, in the **Clipboard group**, click **Format Painter** 🖌, and then click cell **A12** to copy the format from cell **A1** to **A12**. Click cell **A13**. Type **Invitation Analysis** and then use **Format Painter** to copy the format from cell **A2** to **A13**.

2 In the range **A15:B17**, type the following data:

Invited	125
Responded Yes	78
Attended	65

3 Select the range **A15:B17**, and then on the **Insert tab**, in the **Charts group**, click **Insert Waterfall, Funnel, Stock, Surface, or Radar Chart** 📊. Click **Funnel** to insert a funnel chart. Compare your screen with Figure 3.46.

The funnel chart displays to the right of the data and slightly overlaps the map chart. Each rectangle in the funnel chart indicates a corresponding value from the data series. The invited guests represent the largest number and the attending guests represent the smallest number.

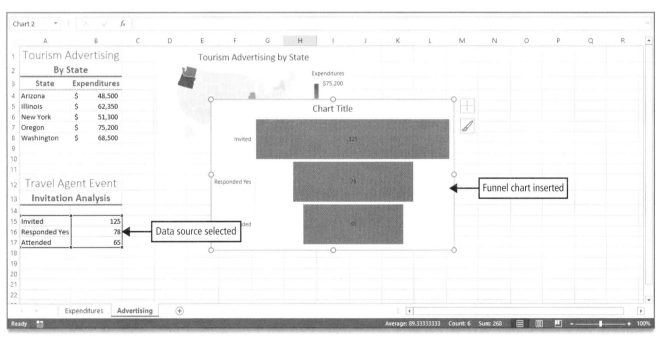

Figure 3.46

4 On the **Format tab**, select the number in the **Height box** 📏. Type **2.5** and then select the number in the **Width box** 📏. Type **4** and then press Enter.

5 Click the **Chart Title**, and then select the title text. Type **Promotional Event** and then click outside of the title so that it is not selected.

6 Point to the funnel chart to display the 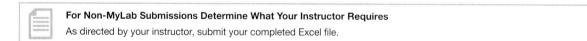 pointer, and then drag the chart so that its upper left corner aligns with the upper left corner of cell **D12**. Compare your screen with Figure 3.47.

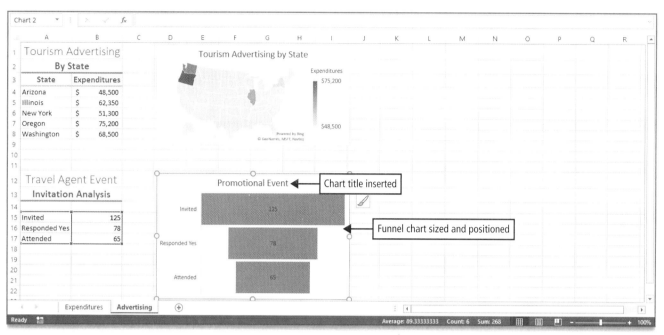

Figure 3.47

7 Group the two worksheets. Click the **Page Layout tab**, and then in the **Scale to Fit group**, click the **Width arrow**. Click **1 page**. In the **Page Setup group**, click **Margins**, and then click **Custom Margins**. In the **Page Setup** dialog box, on the **Margins tab**, under **Center on page**, select the **Horizontally** check box.

8 Click the **Header/Footer tab**, and then in the center of the dialog box, click **Custom Footer**. In the **Footer** dialog box, with your insertion point blinking in the **Left section**, on the row of buttons, click **Insert File Name** 🖹.

9 Click **OK** two times. Display the workbook **Properties**. As the **Tags**, type **tourism spending** and as the **Subject**, type your course name and section number. Be sure your name displays as the **Author**.

10 **Save** the workbook and then **Close** Excel.

For Non-MyLab Submissions Determine What Your Instructor Requires
As directed by your instructor, submit your completed Excel file.

---

11 In **MyLab IT**, in your **Course Materials**, locate and click the Grader Project **Excel 3B Tourism**. In **step 3**, under **Upload Completed Assignment**, click **Choose File**. In the **Open** dialog box, navigate to your **Excel Chapter 3 folder**, and then click your **Student_Excel_3B_Tourism** file one time to select it. In the lower right corner of the **Open** dialog box, click **Open**.

The name of your selected file displays above the Upload button.

12 To submit your file to **MyLab IT** for grading, click **Upload**, wait a moment for a green **Success!** message, and then in **step 4**, click the blue **Submit for Grading** button. Click **Close Assignment** to return to your list of **Course Materials**.

You have completed Project 3B END

Objective   Analyze Trends with a Line Chart

ALERT   Working with Web-Based Applications and Services

Computer programs and services on the web receive continuous updates and improvements, so the steps to complete this web-based Activity may differ from the ones shown. You can often look at the screens and the information presented to determine how to complete the Activity.

 If you do not already have a Google account, you will need to create one before you begin this Activity. Go to **http://google.com** and, in the upper right corner, click Sign In. On the Sign In screen, click Create Account. On the Create your Google Account page, complete the form, read and agree to the Terms of Service and Privacy Policy, and then click Next step. On the Welcome screen, click Get Started.

Activity │ Create a Line Chart

1 1 From the desktop, open your browser, navigate to http://google.com, and then click **Google apps** ▦ . Click **Drive** ☁ , and then if necessary, sign in to your Google account.

2 Open your **GO! Web Projects** folder—or click New to create and then open this folder if necessary. Click **New**, and then click **File upload**. Navigate to your student data files, click **e03_3B_Web**, and then click **Open**.

3 Right-click the file you uploaded, point to **Open with**, and then click **Google Sheets**.

4 Drag to select the years and values in the range **A4:F5**, and then on the menu bar, click the **Insert tab**. Click **Chart** and notice that based on the selected data, a line chart is inserted.

5 Point to the chart, and then drag down and to the left to position the chart so that its upper left corner is aligned with the upper left corner of cell **A21**.

6 Select the existing chart title text. Type **Tourism Spending 2016 to 2020** and then press Enter.

7 In the **Chart editor**, with the **CUSTOMIZE** tab selected, click **Legend**. Click **Auto** and then click **None** to remove the legend. In the **Chart Editor**, click **Vertical Axis**. Click in the **Min** box, type **2500000** and then press Enter so that the lowest value on the Vertical Axis is $2,500,000.

8 In the **Chart Editor**, click **Series**. Click the **Line thickness**, and then click **4px**. Click **Point size**, and then click **10px**. **Close** the **Chart editor**, and then compare your screen with Figure A.

9 Submit your file as directed by your instructor. Sign out of your Google account and close your browser.

Figure A

»»» **GO!** To Work

Microsoft Office Specialist (MOS) Skills in this Chapter	
Project 3A	**Project 3B**
5.1.1 Create charts 5.1.2 Create chart sheets 5.2.3 Add and modify chart elements	2.1.1 Paste data by using special paste options 2.1.3 Insert and delete multiple columns or rows 2.2.3 Format cells by using Format Painter 5.2.1 Add data series to charts Expert 3.4.2 Perform what-if analysis by using Goal Seek and Scenario Manager Expert 4.1.2 Create and modify charts including Box & Whisker, Combo, Funnel, Histogram, Map, Sunburst, and Waterfall charts

Build Your E-Portfolio

An E-Portfolio is a collection of evidence, stored electronically, that showcases what you have accomplished while completing your education. Collecting and then sharing your work products with potential employers reflects your academic and career goals. Your completed documents from the following projects are good examples to show what you have learned: 3G, 3K, and 3L.

GO! for Job Success

Video: Workplace Etiquette

Your instructor may assign this video to your class, and then ask you to think about, or discuss with your classmates, these questions:

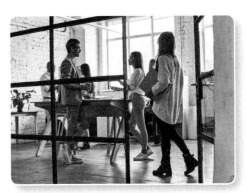

g-stockstudio/Shutterstock

> Name three specific ways that Rachel demonstrated a lack of professionalism in this video. Be as specific as possible.

> As a manager, what would you do to address Rachel's unprofessional behavior?

> In what ways does Rachel exhibit a lack of respect for the lines of authority in her office?

End of Chapter

Summary

Use pie charts when you want to show the relationship of each part to a whole. Consider using a pie chart when you have only one data series to plot and you do not have more than seven categories.

To create a pie chart, you must select two ranges. One range contains the labels for each pie slice; the other contains the values that add up to a total. Both ranges must have the same number of cells.

In formulas, Excel follows rules called the order of operations; expressions within parentheses are processed first, and multiplication and division are performed before addition and subtraction.

Use a line chart when you want to show trends over time. Time displays along the bottom axis and the data point values connect with a line. The curve and direction of the line make trends obvious.

GO! Learn It Online

Review the concepts, key terms, and MOS skills in this chapter by completing these online challenges, which you can find at **MyLab IT**.

> **Chapter Quiz:** Answer matching and multiple choice questions to test what you learned in this chapter.

> **Lessons on the GO!:** Learn how to use all the new apps and features as they are introduced by Microsoft

> **MOS Prep Quiz:** Answer questions to review the MOS skills that you practiced in this chapter.

GO! Collaborative Team Project (Available in Instructor Resource Center)

If your instructor assigns this project to your class, you can expect to work with one or more of your classmates—either in person or by using internet tools—to create work products similar to those that you created in this chapter. A team is a group of workers who work together to solve a problem, make a decision, or create a work product. Collaboration is when you work together with others as a team in an intellectual endeavor to complete a shared task or achieve a shared goal.

Monkey Business Images/Fotolia

Your instructor will assign Projects from this list to ensure your learning and assess your knowledge.

	Project Guide for Excel Chapter 3		
Project	**Apply Skills from These Chapter Objectives**	**Project Type**	**Project Location**
3A MyLab IT	Objectives 1–4 from Project 3A	**3A Instructional Project (Grader Project)** **Instruction** Guided instruction to learn the skills in Project 3A.	In **MyLab IT** and in text
3B MyLab IT	Objectives 5–8 from Project 3B	**3B Instructional Project (Grader Project)** **Instruction** Guided instruction to learn the skills in Project 3B.	In **MyLab IT** and in text
3C	Objectives 1–4 from Project 3A	**3C Skills Review (Scorecard Grading)** **Review** A guided review of the skills from Project 3A.	In text
3D	Objectives 5–8 from Project 3B	**3D Skills Review (Scorecard Grading)** **Review** A guided review of the skills from Project 3B.	In text
3E MyLab IT	Objectives 1–4 from Project 3A	**3E Mastery (Grader Project)** **Mastery and Transfer of Learning** A demonstration of your mastery of the skills in Project 3A with extensive decision making.	In **MyLab IT** and in text
3F MyLab IT	Objectives 5–8 from Project 3B	**3F Mastery (Grader Project)** **Mastery and Transfer of Learning** A demonstration of your mastery of the skills in Project 3B with extensive decision making.	In **MyLab IT** and in text
3G MyLab IT	Objectives 1–8 from Project 3A and 3B	**3G Mastery (Grader Project)** **Mastery and Transfer of Learning** A demonstration of your mastery of the skills in Projects 3A and 3B with extensive decision making.	In **MyLab IT** and in text
3H	Combination of Objectives from Projects 3A and 3B	**3H GO! Fix It (Scorecard Grading)** **Critical Thinking** A demonstration of your mastery of the skills in Projects 3A and 3B by creating a correct result from a document that contains errors you must find.	IRC
3I	Combination of Objectives from Projects 3A and 3B	**3I GO! Make It (Scorecard Grading)** **Critical Thinking** A demonstration of your mastery of the skills in Projects 3A and 3B by creating a result from a supplied picture.	IRC
3J	Combination of Objectives from Projects 3A and 3B	**3J GO! Solve It (Rubric Grading)** **Critical Thinking** A demonstration of your mastery of the skills in Projects 3A and 3B, your decision-making skills, and your critical thinking skills. A task-specific rubric helps you self-assess your result.	IRC
3K	Combination of Objectives from Projects 3A and 3B	**3K GO! Solve It (Rubric Grading)** **Critical Thinking** A demonstration of your mastery of the skills in Projects 3A and 3B, your decision-making skills, and your critical thinking skills. A task-specific rubric helps you self-assess your result.	In text
3L	Combination of Objectives from Projects 3A and 3B	**3L GO! Think (Rubric Grading)** **Critical Thinking** A demonstration of your understanding of the chapter concepts applied in a manner that you would outside of college. An analytic rubric helps you and your instructor grade the quality of your work by comparing it to the work an expert in the discipline would create.	In text
3M	Combination of Objectives from Projects 3A and 3B	**3M GO! Think (Rubric Grading)** **Critical Thinking** A demonstration of your understanding of the chapter concepts applied in a manner that you would outside of college. An analytic rubric helps you and your instructor grade the quality of your work by comparing it to the work an expert in the discipline would create.	IRC
3N	Combination of Objectives from Projects 3A and 3B	**3N You and GO! (Rubric Grading)** **Critical Thinking** A demonstration of your understanding of the chapter concepts applied in a manner that you would in a personal situation. An analytic rubric helps you and your instructor grade the quality of your work.	IRC
3O	Combination of Objectives from Projects 3A and 3B	**3O Collaborative Team Project for EXCEL Chapter 2** **Critical Thinking** A demonstration of your understanding of concepts and your ability to work collaboratively in a group role-playing assessment, requiring both collaboration and self-management.	IRC
Capstone Project for EXCEL Chapters 1-3	Combination of Objectives from Chapters 1-3	A demonstration of your mastery of the skills in Chapters 1-3 with extensive decision making. **(Grader Project)**	In **MyLab IT** and IRC

Glossary

Glossary of Chapter Key Terms

3-D The shortened term for *three-dimensional*, which refers to an image that appears to have all three spatial dimensions—length, width, and depth.

Absolute cell reference A cell reference that refers to cells by their fixed position in a worksheet; an absolute cell reference remains the same when the formula is copied.

Axis A line that serves as a frame of reference for measurement and which borders the chart plot area.

Base The starting point when you divide the amount of increase by it to calculate the rate of increase.

Bevel A shape effect that uses shading and shadows to make the edges of a shape appear to be curved or angled.

Category axis The area along the bottom of a chart that identifies the categories of data; also referred to as the x-axis.

Chart area The entire chart and all of its elements.

Chart sheet A workbook sheet that contains only a chart.

Data marker A column, bar, area, dot, pie slice, or other symbol in a chart that represents a single data point; related data points form a data series.

Data point A value that originates in a worksheet cell and that is represented in a chart by a data marker.

Data series Related data points represented by data markers; each data series has a unique color or pattern represented in the chart legend.

Enterprise fund A municipal government fund that reports income and

expenditures related to municipal services for which a fee is charged in exchange for goods or services.

Explode The action of pulling out one or more pie slices from a pie chart for emphasis.

Formula AutoComplete An Excel feature which, after typing an = (equal sign) and the beginning letter or letters of a function name, displays a list of function names that match the typed letter(s).

Fund A sum of money set aside for a specific purpose.

Funnel chart A type of chart that shows values across the stages in a process.

General fund The term used to describe money set aside for the normal operating activities of a government entity such as a city.

Goal Seek A what-if analysis tool that finds the input needed in one cell to arrive at the desired result in another cell.

Legend A chart element that identifies the patterns or colors that are assigned to the categories in the chart.

Line chart A chart type that displays trends over time; time displays along the bottom axis and the data point values are connected with a line.

Major unit The value in a chart's value axis that determines the spacing between tick marks and between the gridlines in the plot area.

Map chart A type of chart that compares values and shows categories across geographical regions; for example, across countries, states, counties, and regions.

Order of operations The mathematical rules for performing multiple calculations within a formula.

Percent for new value = base percent + percent of increase The formula for calculating a percentage by which a value increases by adding the base percentage—usually 100%—to the percent increase.

Percentage rate of increase The percent by which one number increases over another number.

Pie chart A chart that shows the relationship of each part to a whole.

Plot area The area bounded by the axes of a chart, including all the data series.

Rate = amount of increase/base The mathematical formula to calculate a rate of increase.

Relative cell reference In a formula, the address of a cell based on the relative positions of the cell that contains the formula and the cell referred to in the formula.

Value after increase = base x percent for new value The formula for calculating the value after an increase by multiplying the original value—the base—by the percent for new value (see the *Percent for new value* formula).

Value axis A numerical scale on the left side of a chart that shows the range of numbers for the data points; also referred to as the y-axis.

What-if analysis The process of changing the values in cells to see how those changes affect the outcome of formulas in a worksheet.

x-axis Another name for the category axis.

y-axis Another name for the value axis.

Chapter Review

Apply 3A skills from these Objectives:

1. Chart Data with a Pie Chart
2. Format a Pie Chart
3. Edit a Workbook and Update a Chart
4. Use Goal Seek to Perform What-If Analysis

In the following Skills Review, you will edit a worksheet for Jerry Silva, City Parks Manager, which details the revenue generated from city parks and structures. Your completed worksheets will look similar to Figure 3.48.

Project Files

For Project 3C, you will need the following file:

e03C_Parks

You will save your workbook as:

Lastname_Firstname_3C_Parks

Project Results

Figure 3.48

(continues on next page)

Chapter Review

1 Start Excel. From your student data files, open the file **e03C_Parks**. Save the file in your **Excel Chapter 3** folder as **Lastname_Firstname_3C_Parks**

a. Click cell **D5**, and then type = to begin a formula. Click cell **C5**, type / and then click cell **C11**. Press [F4] to make the reference to the value in cell **C11** absolute. On the **Formula Bar**, click **Enter**, and then fill the formula down through cell **D10**. (Mac users, press [command ⌘] + [T] to make the cell reference absolute.)

b. With the range **D5:D10** selected, on the **Home tab**, click **Percent Style** and **Center**.

2 Select the nonadjacent ranges **A5:A10** and **C5:C10** to select the park names and the projected revenue. Click the **Insert tab**, and then in the **Charts group**, click **Insert Pie or Doughnut Chart**. Under **3-D Pie**, click the chart type **3-D Pie**.

a. On the **Design tab**, in the **Location group**, click **Move Chart**. In the **Move Chart** dialog box, click the **New sheet** option button. In the **New sheet** box, replace the highlighted text *Chart1* by typing **Projected Park Revenue Chart** and then click **OK**.

b. Click the text *Chart Title*. Type **Projected Park Revenue** and then press [Enter] to create the new chart title. (Mac users, drag to select the title text, type the new text and then click outside of the title.)

c. If necessary, select the title. On the **Format tab**, in the **WordArt Styles group**, click **More** to display the gallery. In the second row, select the fifth style, and then change the **Font Size** to **32**.

d. Click in a white area of the chart to deselect the chart title. Click **Chart Elements**, and then click the **Legend** check box to remove the legend. (Mac users, on the Chart Design tab, click Add Chart Element, point to Legend, and then click None.)

e. In the list of **Chart Elements**, point to **Data Labels**, click the **arrow** that displays, and then click **More Options**. In the **Format Data Labels** pane on the right, under **Label Options**, select the **Category Name** and **Percentage** check boxes, and *clear* all other checkboxes. Under **Label Position**, click **Center**. (Mac users, to display the Format Data Labels Pane, on the Chart Design tab, click Add Chart Element, point to Data Labels, and then click More Options.)

f. With the data labels selected, on the **Home tab**, change the **Font Size** to **11** and then apply **Bold** and **Italic**.

3 In any pie slice, point anywhere outside the selected label, and then double-click to display the **Format Data Series** pane. Under **Series Options**, click **Effects**, and then click **3-D Format**.

a. Click the **Top bevel arrow**, and then under **Bevel**, click the first button. Apply the same bevel to the **Bottom bevel**.

b. Set the **Width** and **Height** of both the **Top bevel** and the **Bottom bevel** to **512 pt**

c. Scroll down, click the **Material arrow**, and then under **Standard**, click the third material—**Plastic**.

d. Scroll to the top of the **Format Data Series** pane, click **Shadow**, and then click the **Presets arrow**. Scroll down, and then under **Perspective**, in the first row, click the third effect—**Perspective: Below**.

e. In the **Format Data Series** pane, under **Series Options**, click the third button—**Series Options**. Set the **Angle of first slice** to **50**

f. On the pie chart, click the **Diamond League Fields** slice to select only that slice, and then in the **Format Data Point** pane, set the **Point Explosion** to **10%**

g. With the **Diamond League Fields** slice still selected, in the **Format Data Point** pane, under **Series Options**, click **Fill & Line**, and then click **Fill** to expand the options.

h. Click the **Gradient fill** option button, click the **Preset gradients arrow**, and then in the fourth row, click the third gradient.

4 Point to the white area just inside the border of the chart to display the ScreenTip *Chart Area*, and then click one time to display the **Format Chart Area** pane.

a. Under **Chart Options**, click **Fill & Line**, and be sure the **Fill** options are still displayed.

b. Click the **Gradient fill** option button, click the **Preset gradients arrow**, and then in the first row, click the fifth gradient.

c. In the **Format Chart Area** pane, click **Fill** to collapse the options, and then click **Border** to expand the options.

d. Click the **Solid line** option button, click the **Color arrow**, and then in the fifth column, click the last color. Set the **Width** of the border to **5 pt** Close the pane, and then **Save** your workbook.

(continues on next page)

Chapter Review

5 In the sheet tab area at the bottom of the workbook, click the **Sheet1 tab**.

a. Click cell **C11**. On the **Data tab**, in the **Forecast group**, click **What-If Analysis**, and then click **Goal Seek**. In the **Goal Seek** dialog box, verify that the Set cell box displays **C11**. press Tab to move to the **To value** box, and then type **17,800,000**

b. Press Tab to move the insertion point to the **By changing cell** box, and then click cell **C10**. Click **OK**. In the displayed **Goal Seek Status** dialog box, click **OK** to set the total projected revenue to $17,800,000 by changing the projected revenue for the Community Center.

6 With your worksheet displayed, in the sheet tab area, double-click *Sheet1* to select the text, and then type **Projected Park Revenue Data** and press Enter.

a. Click the **Page Layout tab**. In the **Page Setup Group**, click **Margins**, click **Custom Margins**, and then in the **Page Setup** dialog box, on the **Margins tab**, under **Center on page**, select the **Horizontally** check box.

b. Click the **Header/Footer tab**, click **Custom Footer**, and then with your insertion point in the **Left section**, on the row of buttons, click **Insert File Name**. Click **OK** two times.

c. Display the **Projected Park Revenue Chart**, and then display the **Page Setup** dialog box.

d. Click the **Header/Footer tab**, click **Custom Footer**, and then in the **Left section**, click the **Insert File Name** button. Click **OK** two times.

e. Click the **File tab**, and then display the workbook **Properties**. As the **Tags**, type **park revenue** As the **Subject**, type your course name and section number. Be sure your name displays as the **Author**.

f. **Save** and **Close** your workbook. Print or submit your workbook electronically as directed by your instructor.

You have completed Project 3C   END

Chapter Review

Skills Review | Project 3D Housing Permits

Apply 3B skills from these Objectives:

5. Design a Worksheet for What-If Analysis
6. Answer What-If Questions by Changing Values in a Worksheet
7. Chart Data with a Line Chart
8. Create a Map Chart and a Funnel Chart

In the following Skills Review, you will edit a worksheet that forecasts the revenue from new housing permits that the City of Pacifica Bay expects to collect in the five-year period 2020-2024. Your completed worksheet will look similar to Figure 3.49.

Project Files

For Project 3D, you will need the following file:

e03D_Housing_Permits

e03D_Housing

You will save your workbook as:

Lastname_Firstname_3D_Housing_Permits

Project Results

Figure 3.49

(continues on next page)

Chapter Review

1 Start Excel. From your student data files, open **e03D_Housing_Permits**. Using your own name, save the file in your **Excel Chapter 3** folder as **Lastname_Firstname_3D_Housing_Permits**

a. In cell **B4**, type **2016** and then press [Tab]. In cell **C4**, type **2017** and then press [Enter].

b. Use the fill handle to fill the remaining years through **column F** so that the last year that displays is **2020**.

2 Click cell **C6**. Being sure to include the parentheses, type **=(c5-b5)/b5** and then press [Enter]. Select cell **C6**, and then apply **Percent Style**.

a. With cell **C6** selected, drag the fill handle to the right through cell **F6**.

b. In cell **A8**, type **Projected Future Housing Permit Revenue** and then press [Enter]. Click cell **A2**. On the **Home tab**, in the **Clipboard group**, click **Format Painter**, and then click cell **A8**. In cell **A10**, type **Forecasted Increase** and then click **A12**. Type **Year**

c. In cell **A13**, type **Projected Permit Revenue** and then in cell **B12**, type **2020** and press [Tab]. In cell **C12**, type **2021** and then press [Tab]. Select the range **B12:C12**, and then drag the fill handle through cell **F12** to extend the pattern of years to *2024*. Apply **Bold** to the selection.

d. Right-click cell **F5**, and then click **Copy**. Right-click over cell **B13**, and then click **Paste**. (Mac users, press [control] and then click to display the shortcut menu.)

e. In cell **B10**, type **7%** which is the percent of increase from 2019 to 2020. Select the range **A10:B10**, and then apply **Bold** and **Italic**.

3 Click cell **C13**. Type **=b13*(100%+b10)** and then on the **Formula Bar**, click **Enter** to keep the cell active. With cell **C13** as the active cell, drag the fill handle to copy the formula to the range **D13:F13**.

a. Click cell **B13**. On the **Home tab**, click **Format Painter**, and then select the range **C13:F13**.

b. Click cell **A15**. Type **Forecasted Revenue Estimates 2020 to 2024** and then press [Enter]. Use **Format Painter** to copy the format from cell **A8** to cell **A15**.

c. In the range **A17:A19**, type the following row titles:

Year
7% Increase
8% Increase

4 Select the range **B12:F12**, and then on the **Home tab**, in the **Clipboard group**, click **Copy**. **Paste** the selection to the range **B17:F17**.

a. Select the range **B13:F13**, right-click over the selection, and then on the shortcut menu, click **Copy**. Point to cell **B18**, right-click, and then from the shortcut menu, point to **Paste Special**. Under **Paste Values**, click the second button—**Values & Number Formatting**. Press [Esc] to cancel the moving border. (Mac users, on the Home tab, click the Paste *arrow*, and then click Values & Number Formatting.)

b. Click cell **B10**. Type **8** and then press [Enter]. Copy the new values in the range **B13:F13**. Point to cell **B19**, right-click, and then point to **Paste Special**. Under **Paste Values**, click **Values & Number Formatting**. **Save** your workbook.

5 In the **row header area**, point to **row 8** to display the pointer, and then drag down to select **rows 8:24**. Right-click over the selection to display the shortcut menu, and then click **Insert** to insert the same number of blank rows as you selected. Under the selection area near cell **A25**, click **Insert Options**, and then click the **Clear Formatting** option button to clear any formatting from these rows. (Mac users, on the Home tab, click Clear, and then click Clear Formats.)

a. On the **Page Layout tab**, in the **Themes group**, click the **Colors arrow**, and then click **Yellow**. Select the range **A5:F5**. On the **Insert tab**, in the **Charts group**, click **Insert Line or Area Chart**. In the displayed gallery of line charts, click the **Line with Markers** chart type to create the chart.

b. Point to the border of the chart to display the [pointer icon] pointer, and then drag the chart so that its upper left corner is positioned in cell **A9**, aligned approximately under the *c* in the word *Projected* above.

c. Point to the **Chart Title** *Permit Revenue* and right-click. On the shortcut menu, click **Edit Text**. With the insertion point positioned at the beginning of the title, type **Pacifica Bay Housing** and then press [Spacebar]. Click at the end of the title after the word *Revenue*, and then press [Enter] to create a second line. Type **2016 to 2020**

d. Click the dashed border around the chart title to change it to a solid border, right-click over the title, and then on the shortcut menu, click **Font**. In the **Font** dialog box, change the **Font style** to **Bold**, and change the **Size** to **16**. Click **OK**.

(continues on next page)

Chapter Review

6 ▶ At the bottom of the chart, point to any of the numbers *1* through *5*, and then right-click. On the shortcut menu, click **Select Data**. On the right side of the **Select Data Source** dialog box, click **Edit**. In the worksheet, select the years in the range **B4:F4**, and then click **OK** two times to enter the years as the category labels. (Mac users, in the Select Data Source dialog box, click in the Horizontal (Category) axis labels box, and then select the range B4:F4.)

a. With the **Horizontal (Category) Axis** still selected, click **Chart Elements**, point to **Axes**, click the **arrow**, and then click **More Options**. In the **Format Axis** pane, under **Axis Options**, click **Fill & Line**. If necessary, click Line to expand the options. Click the **No line** option button, and then **close** the **Format Axis** pane. (Mac users, on the Chart Design tab, click Add Chart Element, point to Axes, and then click More Axis Options.)

b. On the left side of the chart, point to any of the dollar values, right-click, and then click **Format Axis**. In the **Format Axis** pane, under **Bounds**, select the text in the **Minimum** box, and then type **1900000**

c. Under **Units**, in the **Major** box, select the existing text. Type **50000** and then press Enter.

d. Near the top of the **Format Axis** pane, click the **Axis Options arrow**, and then click **Chart Area** to display the **Format Chart Area** pane. Click **Fill & Line**. (Mac users, point to the upper right corner of the chart to display the Chart Area ScreenTip, and then click to display the Format Chart Area pane.)

e. In the **Format Chart Area** pane, click **Fill** to expand the options, and then click the **Picture or texture fill** option button. Under **Insert picture from**, click **File**. In the **Insert Picture** dialog box, navigate to the student data files, and then click **e03D_Housing**. Click **Insert**.

f. In the **Format Chart Area** pane, click **Fill** to collapse the options, and then if necessary, click Border to expand the Border section. Click the **Solid line** option button. Set the **Width** to **4 pt** Scroll to the bottom of the pane, and then select the **Rounded corners** check box.

g. Select the chart title text, and then on the **Home tab**, click the **Font Color arrow**. In the first column, click the first color.

7 ▶ To the right of the chart, click **Chart Elements**, point to **Gridlines**, click the **arrow**, and then click **More Options** to display the **Format Major Gridlines** pane. (Mac users, on the Chart Design tab, click Add Chart Element, point to Gridlines, and then click More Gridline Options.)

a. Under **Line**, click the **Solid line** option button. Set the **Width** to **1 pt**

b. In the chart, point to any of the dollar values on the **Vertical (Value) Axis**, right-click, and then click **Font**. In the **Font** dialog box, change the **Font style** to **Bold**, and the **Font Color** to the first color in the first row.

c. By using the same technique, apply **Bold** to the **Horizontal (Category) Axis** and change the font color to the first color in the first row. **Close** the **Format Axis** pane, and then click cell **A1** to deselect the chart.

d. Click the **Page Layout tab**. In the **Page Setup group**, click **Margins**, and then click **Custom Margins**. On the **Margins tab**, select the **Horizontally** check box. Click the **Header/Footer tab**, click **Custom Footer**, and then in the **Left section**, insert the file name. Click **OK** two times.

8 ▶ Click the **Permit Analysis** sheet tab. To create a map chart that shows the revenue from permits issued to out of state developers, select the range **A3:B7**. On the **Insert tab**, in the **Charts group**, click **Maps**, and then click **Filled Map**.

a. Select the chart title and type **Housing Permits Issued by State**

b. Click the **Chart Tools Format tab**, and then in the **Size group**, click in the **Height box**. Type **2** and then click in the **Width box**. Type **4** and then press Enter.

c. Drag the chart so that its upper left corner aligns with the upper left corner of cell **D1**.

9 ▶ Select the range **A15:B17**. On the **Insert tab**, in the **Charts group**, click **Insert Waterfall, Funnel, Stock, Surface, or Radar Chart**, and then click **Funnel**. Select the chart title and type **Housing Permit Applications**

a. Click the **Chart Tools Format tab**, and then in the **Size group**, click in the **Height box**. Type **2.5** and then click in the **Width box**. Type **4** and then press Enter.

(continues on next page)

Chapter Review

b. Drag the chart so that its upper left corner aligns with the upper left corner of cell **D12**. Click cell **A1**.

c. On the **Page Layout tab**, in the **Page Setup group**, click **Orientation**, and then click **Landscape**.

d. In the **Page Setup group**, click **Margins**, and then click **Custom Margins**. On the **Margins tab**, select the **Horizontally** check box. Click the **Header/Footer tab**, click **Custom Footer**, and then in the **Left section**, insert the file name. Click **OK** two times.

e. Display the **Properties**. As the **Tags**, type **housing permit revenue** In the **Subject** box, type your course name and section number. Be sure your name displays as the **Author**.

f. **Save** and **Close** your workbook. Print or submit your workbook electronically as directed by your instructor.

You have completed Project 3D   END

Content-Based Assessments (Mastery and Transfer of Learning)

Apply 3A skills from these Objectives:

1. Chart Data with a Pie Chart
2. Format a Pie Chart
3. Edit a Workbook and Update a Chart
4. Use Goal Seek to Perform What-If Analysis

In the following project, you will edit a worksheet that summarizes the revenue budget for the City of Pacifica Bay. Your completed worksheets will look similar to Figure 3.50.

Project Files for **MyLab IT** Grader

1. In your **MyLab IT** course, locate and click **Excel 3E Revenue,** Download Materials, and then Download All Files.
2. Extract the zipped folder to your Excel Chapter 3 folder. Close the Grader download screens.
3. Take a moment to open the downloaded **Excel_3E_Revenue_Instructions**; note any recent updates to the book.

Project Results

Figure 3.50

For Non-MyLab Submissions

For Project 3E, you will need:

e03E_Revenue

In your Excel Chapter 3 folder, save your workbook as:

Lastname_Firstname_3E_Revenue

If your instructor requires a workbook with formulas, save as:

Lastname_Firstname_3E_Revenue_formulas

After you have named and saved your workbook on the next page, begin with Step 2.
After Step 13, save and submit your file as directed by your instructor.

(continues on next page)

Content-Based Assessments (Mastery and Transfer of Learning)

1 Navigate to your **Excel Chapter 3 folder**, and then double-click the Excel file you downloaded from **MyLab IT** that displays your name—**Student_Excel_3E_Revenue**.

2 In cell **D5**, construct a formula to calculate the **% of Total Projected Revenue** from **Taxes** by dividing the **Projected Revenue for Next Fiscal Year** for **Taxes** by the **Total Projected Revenue for Next Fiscal Year**. Use absolute cell references as necessary, format the result in **Percent Style**, and **Center** the percentage. Fill the formula down through cell **D9**.

3 Select the nonadjacent ranges **A5:A9** and **C5:C9** as the data for a pie chart, and then insert a **3-D Pie** chart. Move the chart to a **New sheet** named **Projected Revenue Chart**

4 As the text for the **Chart Title** element, type **Projected Revenue** Format the **Chart Title** with a **WordArt Style**—in the first row, click the second style. Change the **Font Size** to **32**.

5 Remove the **Legend** chart element, and then add the **Data Labels** chart element formatted so that only the **Category Name** and **Percentage** display positioned in the **Center**. Format the data labels with a **Font style** of **Bold** and a **Font Size** of **14**.

6 Format the **Data Series** using a **3-D Format** effect. Change the **Top bevel** and **Bottom bevel** to the first bevel in the first row. Set the **Top bevel Width** and **Height** to **350 pt** and then set the **Bottom bevel Width** and **Height** to **0 pt** Change the **Material** to the second **Special Effect**—**Soft Edge**.

7 Display the **Series Options**, and then set the **Angle of first slice** to **115** so that the **Taxes** slice is in the front of the pie.

8 Select the **Services** slice, and then explode the slice **10%**. Change the **Fill Color** of the **Services** slice to a **Solid fill**—in the eighth column, click the first color.

9 Format the **Chart Area** by applying a **Gradient fill** using the **Preset gradients**—in the first column, click the first gradient style. Format the **Border** of the **Chart Area** by applying a **Solid line** border—in the fifth column, click the first color. Change the **Width** to **5 pt**. Close any panes that are open on the right.

10 Display the **Page Setup** dialog box, and then for this chart sheet, insert a **Custom Footer** in the **left section** with the file name.

11 Display the **Revenue Sources** sheet. Click cell **C10**, and then use **Goal Seek** to determine the projected amount of *Other* revenue in cell **C9** if the value in **C10** is **150,125,000**

12 Display the **Page Setup** dialog box, center the worksheet **Horizontally**, and then insert a custom footer in the **left section** with the file name.

13 Display the workbook **Properties**, and then as the **Tags**, type **revenue sources** As the **Subject**, type your course name and section number. Be sure your name displays as the **Author**. **Save** your workbook and **Close** Excel.

14 In **MyLab IT**, locate and click the Grader Project **Excel 3E Revenue**. In **step 3**, under **Upload Completed Assignment**, click **Choose File**. In the **Open** dialog box, navigate to your **Excel Chapter 3 folder**, and then click your **Student_Excel_3E_Revenue** file one time to select it. In the lower right corner of the **Open** dialog box, click **Open**.

The name of your selected file displays above the Upload button.

15 To submit your file to **MyLab IT** for grading, click **Upload**, wait a moment for a green **Success!** message, and then in **step 4**, click the blue **Submit for Grading** button. Click **Close Assignment** to return to your list of **Course Materials**.

You have completed Project 3E END

Content-Based Assessments (Mastery and Transfer of Learning)

Apply 3B skills from these Objectives:

5. Design a Worksheet for What-If Analysis
6. Answer What-If Questions by Changing Values in a Worksheet
7. Chart Data with a Line Chart
8. Create a Map Chart and a Funnel Chart

In the following project, you will edit a worksheet that the City of Pacifica Bay Facilities Director will use to prepare a five-year forecast of the costs associated with street maintenance. Your completed worksheet will look similar to Figure 3.51.

Project Files for **MyLab IT** Grader

1. In your **MyLab IT** course, locate and click **Excel 3F Streets,** Download Materials, and then Download All Files.
2. Extract the zipped folder to your Excel Chapter 3 folder. Close the Grader download screens.
3. Take a moment to open the downloaded **Excel_3F_Streets_Instructions**; note any recent updates to the book.

Project Results

Figure 3.51

📄 **For Non-MyLab Submissions**

For Project 3F, you will need:
e03F_Streets

In your Excel Chapter 3 folder, save your workbook as:
Lastname_Firstname_3F_Streets
If your instructor requires a workbook with formulas, save as:
Lastname_Firstname_3F_Streets_formulas

After you have named and saved your workbook on the next page, begin with Step 2.
After Step 15, save and submit your file as directed by your instructor.

(continues on next page)

Content-Based Assessments (Mastery and Transfer of Learning)

1 Navigate to your **Excel Chapter 3 folder**, and then double-click the Excel file you downloaded from **MyLab IT** that displays your name—**Student_Excel_3F_Streets**.

2 Change the **Theme Colors** to **Blue Green**. On the **Housing Revenue** sheet, in the range **B4:F4**, fill the year range with the values **2016** through **2020**.

3 In cell **C6**, construct a formula to calculate the percent of increase in annual street maintenance costs from 2016 to 2017. Format the result with the **Percent Style** and then fill the formula through cell **F6** to calculate the percent of increase in each year.

4 In the range **B12:F12**, use the fill handle to enter the years **2020** through **2024**. Use **Format Painter** to apply the format from cell **B4** to the range **B12:F12**.

5 **Copy** the value in cell **F5** to cell **B13**. In cell **B10**, type **6%** which is the projected increase estimated by the City financial analysts. To the range **A10:B10**, apply **Bold** and **Italic**.

6 In cell **C13**, construct a formula to calculate the annual projected street maintenance costs for the year 2021 after the projected increase of 6% is applied. Use absolute cell references as necessary. Fill the formula through cell **F13**, and then use **Format Painter** to copy the formatting from cell **B13** to the range **C13:F13**.

7 Use **Format Painter** to copy the format from cell **A8** to cell **A15**. **Copy** the range **B12:F12**, and then **Paste** the selection to **B17:F17**.

8 Copy the range **B13:F13** and then paste the **Values & Number Formatting** to the range **B18:F18**. Complete the Projected Estimates section of the worksheet by changing the *Projected Increase* in **B10** to **4%** and then copying and pasting the **Values & Number Formatting** to the appropriate range in the worksheet. **Save** your workbook.

9 Select **rows 8:24**, and then **Insert** the same number of blank rows as you selected. **Clear Formatting** from the inserted rows. By using the data in **A5:F5**, insert a **Line with Markers** chart in the worksheet. Move the chart so that its upper left corner is positioned in cell **A9** and visually centered under the data above.

10 Display the **Select Data Source** dialog box, and then edit the **Horizontal (Category) Axis Labels** using the range that contains the years in **B4:F4**. Format the **Bounds** of the **Vertical (Value) Axis** so that the **Minimum** is **2000000** and the **Major unit** is **200000**

11 Format the **Chart Area** with a **Border** by applying a **Solid line**. In the fifth column, click the last color. Change the **Width** of the border to **2 pt**.

12 Click cell **A1** to deselect the chart. Center the worksheet **Horizontally**, and then insert a **Custom Footer** in the **left section** with the file name.

13 Display the **Permit Analysis** worksheet. Select the range **A4:B7** and then insert a **Funnel** chart that depicts the number of bids in each stage of the bid process. Change the chart title to **2020 Contract Bids** and then drag the chart so that the upper left corner aligns with the upper left corner of cell **D1**. Change the chart **Height** to **2** and the **Width** to **4**

14 Deselect the chart, and then change the **Orientation** to **Landscape**. Center the worksheet **Horizontally**, and then insert a **Custom Footer** in the **left section** with the file name.

15 Display the workbook **Properties**, and then as the **Tags**, type **street maintenance costs** As the **Subject**, type your course name and section number. Be sure your name displays as the **Author**. **Save** your workbook and then **Close** Excel.

16 In **MyLab IT**, locate and click the Grader Project **Excel 3F Streets**. In **step 3**, under **Upload Completed Assignment**, click **Choose File**. In the **Open** dialog box, navigate to your **Excel Chapter 3 folder**, and then click your **Student_Excel_3F_Streets** file one time to select it. In the lower right corner of the **Open** dialog box, click **Open**.

The name of your selected file displays above the Upload button.

17 To submit your file to **MyLab IT** for grading, click **Upload**, wait a moment for a green **Success!** message, and then in **step 4**, click the blue **Submit for Grading** button. Click **Close Assignment** to return to your list of **Course Materials**.

You have completed Project 3F **END**

Content-Based Assessments (Mastery and Transfer of Learning)

| MyLab IT Grader | **Mastering Excel** | **Project 3G Expenses** |

Apply a combination of 3A and 3B skills:

1. Chart Data with a Pie Chart
2. Format a Pie Chart
3. Edit a Workbook and Update a Chart
4. Use Goal Seek to Perform What-If Analysis
5. Design a Worksheet for What-If Analysis
6. Answer What-If Questions by Changing Values in a Worksheet
7. Chart Data with a Line Chart
8. Create a Map Chart and a Funnel Chart

In the following project, you will you will edit a workbook for Jennifer Carson, City Finance Manager, that analyzes Recreation Department annual expenses, workshop enrollments, and County partnerships in the State of California. Your completed worksheets will look similar to Figure 3.52.

Project Files for **MyLab IT** Grader

1. In your **MyLab IT** course, locate and click **Excel 3G Expenses,** Download Materials, and then Download All Files.
2. Extract the zipped folder to your Excel Chapter 3 folder. Close the Grader download screens.
3. Take a moment to open the downloaded **Excel_3G_Expenses_Instructions**; note any recent updates to the book.

Project Results

Figure 3.52

For Non-MyLab Submissions

For Project 3G, you will need:
e03G_Expenses

In your Excel Chapter 3 folder, save your workbook as:
Lastname_Firstname_3G_Expenses

If your instructor requires a workbook with formulas, save as:
Lastname_Firstname_3G_Expenses_formulas

After you have named and saved your workbook on the next page, begin with Step 2.

After Step 17, save and submit your file as directed by your instructor.

(continues on next page)

Mastering Excel: Project 3G Expenses (continued)

1 Navigate to your **Excel Chapter 3 folder**, and then double-click the Excel file you downloaded from **MyLab IT** that displays your name—**Student_Excel_3G_Expenses**.

2 In the **Expenses** worksheet, calculate row totals for each Expense item in the range **F5:F9**. Calculate column totals for each quarter and for the Annual Total in the range **B10:F10**. Be sure that **F6:F9** are formatted with **Comma Style** and zero decimal places.

3 In cell **G5**, construct a formula to calculate the **Percent of Total** by dividing the **Annual Total** for **Salaries and Benefits** by the **Annual Total** for all quarters. Use absolute cell references as necessary, format the result in **Percent Style**, and then **Center**. Fill the formula down through cell **G9**.

4 Use a **3-D Pie** chart to chart the **Annual Total** for each item. Move the chart to a **New sheet**; name the sheet **Annual Expenses Chart**

5 As the text for the **Chart Title** element, type **Summary of Annual Expenses** and then change the **Font Size** to **28**.

6 Remove the **Legend** from the chart, and then add **Data Labels** formatted so that only the **Category Name** and **Percentage** display positioned in the **Center**. Format the data labels by applying a **Font style** of **Bold** and **Italic** and a **Font Size** of **12**.

7 Format the **Data Series** using a **3-D Format** effect. Change the **Top bevel** and **Bottom bevel**—under **Bevel**, in the first row, apply the first bevel effect. Set the **Top bevel Width** and **Height** to **50 pt** and then set the **Bottom bevel Width** and **Height** to **256 pt**.

8 Display the **Series Options**, and then set the **Angle of first slice** to **125** so that the **Salaries and Benefits** slice is in the front of the pie. Select the **Salaries and Benefits** slice, and then explode the slice **10%**.

9 Format the **Chart Area** by applying a **Gradient fill** using the **Preset gradients**—in the first column, apply the second gradient. Format the **Border** of the **Chart Area** by adding a **Solid line** border—in the fourth column, apply the first color. Change the **Width** to **3 pt**.

10 Display the **Page Setup** dialog box, and then for this chart sheet, insert a **Custom Footer** in the **left section** with the file name. **Save** your workbook.

11 Display the **Expenses** worksheet, and then by using the Quarter names and the Totals by Quarter, insert a **Line with Markers** chart in the worksheet. Do *not* include the Annual Total. Move the chart so that its upper left corner is positioned slightly inside the upper left corner of cell **A12**. Change the **Width** of the chart to **7.5** and then as the **Chart Title**, type **Recreation Department Expense Summary**

12 Format the **Bounds** of the **Vertical (Value) Axis** so that the **Minimum** is **2100000** and the **Major unit** is **50000** Apply **Bold** to the values on the **Vertical (Value) Axis** and to the labels on the **Horizontal (Category) Axis**. Close any open panes, click cell **A1** to deselect the chart, and then **Save** your workbook.

13 **Copy** the **Annual Total** in cell **F10** and then use **Paste Special** to paste **Values & Number Formatting** in cell **B35**. In cell **C35**, construct a formula to calculate the **Projected Expenses** after the forecasted increase of **3.5%** in cell **B31** is applied. Fill the formula through cell **F35**, and then use **Format Painter** to copy the formatting from cell **B35** to the range **C35:F35**.

14 Change the **Orientation** of this worksheet to **Landscape**, and then use the **Scale to Fit** options to fit the **Height** to **1 page**. In the **Page Setup** dialog box, center this worksheet **Horizontally**, and insert a **Custom Footer** in the **left section** with the file name. **Save** your workbook.

15 Display the **Enrollment** worksheet. Insert a **Funnel chart** that shows resident workshop participation for the year using the range **A4:B6**. Change the **Height** of the chart to **2.5** and the **Width** to **3** and then drag the chart so that the upper left corner aligns with the upper left corner of **A9**. Change the chart title to **Enrollment Analysis** and then click cell **A1**. Center the worksheet **Horizontally** and insert a **Custom Footer** in the left section with the file name.

16 Display the **County Partnership** worksheet. The City of Pacifica Bay is partnering with the County to offer workshops to residents. The Recreation Department staff will visit several cities with similar partnership agreements. Using the range **A3:B9**, insert a **Filled Map** chart. Change the chart title to **Partnership Analysis** and then drag the chart so that the upper left corner aligns with the upper left corner of **D1**. Change the chart **Width** to **4** and then deselect the chart. Change the **Orientation** of this worksheet to **Landscape**.

(continues on next page)

Mastering Excel: Project 3G Expenses (continued)

17 Center this worksheet **Horizontally** and insert a **Custom Footer** in the left section with the file name. Display the workbook **Properties**. As the **Tags**, type **recreation workshops, expenses** and as the **Subject**, type your course name and section number. Be sure your name displays as the **Author**. **Save** your workbook and then **Close** Excel.

18 In **MyLab IT**, locate and click the Grader Project **Excel 3G Expenses**. In **step 3**, under **Upload Completed Assignment**, click **Choose File**. In the **Open** dialog box, navigate to your **Excel Chapter 3 folder**, and then click

your **Student_Excel_3G_Expenses** file one time to select it. In the lower right corner of the **Open** dialog box, click **Open**.

The name of your selected file displays above the Upload button.

19 To submit your file to **MyLab IT** for grading, click **Upload**, wait a moment for a green **Success!** message, and then in **step 4**, click the blue **Submit for Grading** button. Click **Close Assignment** to return to your list of **Course Materials**.

You have completed Project 3G `END`

Content-Based Assessments (Critical Thinking)

Apply a combination of the 3A and 3B skills.

GO! Fix It	**Project 3H Schools**	IRC
GO! Make It	**Project 3I Tax**	IRC
GO! Solve It	**Project 3J Staffing**	IRC
GO! Solve It	**Project 3K Water Usage**	

Project Files

For Project 3K, you will need the following file:

New blank Excel workbook

You will save your workbook as:

Lastname_Firstname_3K_Water_Usage

Pacifica Bay is a growing community and the City Council has requested an analysis of future resource needs. In this project, you will create a worksheet for the Department of Water and Power that illustrates residential water usage over a five-year period. Create a worksheet with the following data:

	2016	2017	2018	2019	2020
Water Use in Acre Feet	62518	65922	71864	76055	82542

Calculate the percent increase for the years 2017 to 2020. Below the Percent Increase, insert a line chart that illustrates the city's water usage from 2016 to 2020. Format the chart and worksheet attractively with a title and subtitle and apply appropriate formatting. Include the file name in the footer and enter appropriate document properties. Save the workbook as **Lastname_Firstname_3K_Water_Usage** and submit as directed.

		Performance Level		
		Exemplary: You consistently applied the relevant skills	**Proficient: You sometimes, but not always, applied the relevant skills**	**Developing: You rarely or never applied the relevant skills**
Performance Criteria	**Create formulas**	All formulas are correct and are efficiently constructed.	Formulas are correct but not always constructed in the most efficient manner.	One or more formulas are missing or incorrect; or only numbers were entered.
	Insert and format line chart	Line chart created correctly and is attractively formatted.	Line chart was created but the data was incorrect or the chart was not appropriately formatted	No line chart was created.
	Format attractively and appropriately	Formatting is attractive and appropriate.	Adequately formatted but difficult to read or unattractive.	Inadequate or no formatting.

You have completed Project 3K | END

Outcomes-Based Assessments (Critical Thinking)

Rubric

The following outcomes-based assessments are open-ended assessments. That is, there is no specific correct result; your result will depend on your approach to the information provided. Make Professional Quality your goal. Use the following scoring rubric to guide you in how to approach the problem and then to evaluate how well your approach solves the problem.

The *criteria*—Software Mastery, Content, Format and Layout, and Process—represent the knowledge and skills you have gained that you can apply to solving the problem. The *levels of performance*—Professional Quality, Approaching Professional Quality, or Needs Quality Improvements—help you and your instructor evaluate your result.

	Your completed project is of Professional Quality if you:	Your completed project is Approaching Professional Quality if you:	Your completed project Needs Quality Improvements if you:
1-Software Mastery	Choose and apply the most appropriate skills, tools, and features and identify efficient methods to solve the problem.	Choose and apply some appropriate skills, tools, and features, but not in the most efficient manner.	Choose inappropriate skills, tools, or features, or are inefficient in solving the problem.
2-Content	Construct a solution that is clear and well organized, contains content that is accurate, appropriate to the audience and purpose, and is complete. Provide a solution that contains no errors of spelling, grammar, or style.	Construct a solution in which some components are unclear, poorly organized, inconsistent, or incomplete. Misjudge the needs of the audience. Have some errors in spelling, grammar, or style, but the errors do not detract from comprehension.	Construct a solution that is unclear, incomplete, or poorly organized, contains some inaccurate or inappropriate content, and contains many errors of spelling, grammar, or style. Do not solve the problem.
3-Format and Layout	Format and arrange all elements to communicate information and ideas, clarify function, illustrate relationships, and indicate relative importance.	Apply appropriate format and layout features to some elements, but not others. Overuse features, causing minor distraction.	Apply format and layout that does not communicate information or ideas clearly. Do not use format and layout features to clarify function, illustrate relationships, or indicate relative importance. Use available features excessively, causing distraction.
4-Process	Use an organized approach that integrates planning, development, self-assessment, revision, and reflection.	Demonstrate an organized approach in some areas, but not others; or, use an insufficient process of organization throughout.	Do not use an organized approach to solve the problem.

Rubric | **Excel** 515

Apply a combination of the 3A and 3B skills.

GO! Think	Project 3L Employment

Project Files

For Project 3L, you will need the following file:

New blank Excel workbook

You will save your workbook as:

Lastname_Firstname_3L_Employment

Sandy Ingram, the Director of the Employment Development Department for the city of Pacifica Bay, has requested an analysis of employment sectors in the city. Employment data for the previous two years is listed below:

Job Sector	2020 Employment	2021 Employment
Government	1,795	1,524
Healthcare	2,832	2,952
Retail	2,524	2,480
Food Service	3,961	3,753
Industrial	1,477	1,595
Professional	2,515	2,802

Create a workbook to provide Sandy with the employment information for each sector and the total employment for each year. Insert a column to calculate the percent change from 2020 to 2021. Note that some of the results will be negative numbers. Format the percentages with two decimal places. Insert a pie chart in its own sheet that illustrates the 2021 employment figures, and format the chart attractively. Format the worksheet so that it is professional and easy to read and understand. Insert a footer with the file name and add appropriate document properties. Save the file as **Lastname_Firstname_3L_Employment** and print or submit as directed by your instructor.

You have completed Project 3L	END

GO! Think!	Project 3M Population	IRC
You and GO!	Project 3N Expense Analysis	IRC
GO! Cumulative Team Project	Project 3O Bell Orchid Hotels	IRC

Introduction to Microsoft Access 2019

ACCESS 2019

Mego studio/Shutterstock

Access 2019: Introduction Introduction to Access

Microsoft Access 2019 provides a convenient way to organize data that makes it easy for you to utilize and present information. Access uses tables to store the data; like Excel spreadsheets, data is stored in rows and columns in a table. So why use a database rather than an Excel spreadsheet? By using a database, you can manipulate and work with data in a more robust manner. For example, if you have thousands of records about patients in a hospital, you can easily find all of the records that pertain to the patients who received a specific type of medicine on a particular day. Information from one table can be used to retrieve information from another table.

For example, by knowing a patient's ID number, you can view immunization records or view insurance information or view hospitalization records. Having information stored in an Access database enables you to make bulk changes to data at one time even when it is stored in different tables.

It's easy to get started with Access by using one of the many prebuilt database templates. For example, a nonprofit organization can track events, donors, members, and donations for a nonprofit organization. A small business can use a prebuilt database to track inventory, create invoices, monitor projects, manage pricing, track competitors, and manage quotes.

Getting Started with Microsoft Access 2019

1

ACCESS 2019

PROJECT **1A**

Outcomes
Create a new database.

Objectives

1. Identify Good Database Design
2. Create a Table and Define Fields in a Blank Desktop Database
3. Change the Structure of Tables and Add a Second Table
4. Create a Query, Form, and Report
5. Close a Database and Close Access

PROJECT **1B**

Outcomes
Create a database from a template.

Objectives

6. Use a Template to Create a Database
7. Organize Objects in the Navigation Pane
8. Create a New Table in a Database Created with a Template
9. View a Report

Rawpixel.com/Shutterstock

In This Chapter

GO! To Work
with Access

In this chapter, you will use Microsoft Access 2019 to organize a collection of related information. You will create new databases, create tables, and enter data into the tables. You will create a query, a form, and a report—all of which are Access objects that make a database useful for locating and analyzing information. You will also create a complete database from a template that is provided, or that you can modify to meet your needs. In this chapter, you will also learn how to apply good database design principles to your Access database and to define the structure of a database.

The projects in this chapter relate to **Texas Lakes Community College**, which is located in the Austin, Texas area. Its four campuses serve over 30,000 students and offer more than 140 certificate programs and degrees. The college has a highly acclaimed Distance Education program and an extensive Workforce Development program. The college makes positive contributions to the community through cultural and athletic programs and has significant partnerships with businesses and nonprofit organizations. Popular fields of study include nursing and health care, solar technology, computer technology, and graphic design.

PROJECT 1A

Student Advising Database with Two Tables

Project Activities

In Activities 1.01 through 1.17, you will assist Dr. Daniel Martinez, Vice President of Student Services at Texas Lakes Community College, in creating a new database for tracking students and their faculty advisors. Your completed Navigation Pane will look similar to Figure 1.1.

Project Files for MyLab IT Grader

1. In your storage location, create a folder named **Access Chapter 1**.
2. In your **MyLab IT** course, locate and click **Access 1A Advising**, Download Materials, and then Download All Files.
3. Extract the zipped folder to your Access Chapter 1 folder. Close the Grader download screens.
4. Take a moment to open the downloaded **Access_1A_Advising_Instructions**; note any recent updates to the book.

Project Results

GO! Project 1A
Where We're Going

Figure 1.1 Project 1A Advising

For Non-MyLab Submissions

For Project 1A, you will need the following files:

Blank database
a01A_Students (Excel workbook)
a01A_Faculty_Advisors (Excel workbook)

Start with a new blank Access database

In your storage location, create a folder named **Access Chapter 1**
In your Access Chapter 1 folder, save your database as:

Lastname_Firstname_1A_Advising

After you have named and saved your workbook, on the next page begin by comparing your screen with Figure 1.4 in Step 3.

NOTE	If You Are Using a Touch Screen

Tap an item to click it.

Press and hold for a few seconds to right-click; release when the information or commands display.

Touch the screen with two or more fingers and then pinch together to zoom out or stretch your fingers apart to zoom in.

Slide your finger on the screen to scroll—slide left to scroll right and slide right to scroll left.

Slide to rearrange—similar to dragging with a mouse.

Swipe to select—slide an item a short distance with a quick movement—to select an item and bring up commands, if any.

Objective 1 Identify Good Database Design

ALERT   Because Office 365 is a cloud-based subscription service that receives continuous updates, you may encounter some variations in what appears on your screen and what is shown in this instruction. Microsoft Office 365 is fully installed on your PC or Mac; no internet access is necessary to create or edit documents. When you *are* connected to the internet, you will receive monthly upgrades and new features, so you always have the latest versions of Office apps as soon as they are available. Your subscription gives you continuous free access to the latest innovations and refinements.

GO! Learn How

Video A1-1

A *database* is an organized collection of *data*—facts about people, events, things, or ideas—related to a specific topic or purpose. *Information* is data that is accurate, timely, and organized in a useful manner. Your contact list is a type of database, because it is a collection of data about one topic—the people with whom you communicate. A simple database of this type is called a *flat database* because it is not related or linked to any other collection of data. Another example of a simple database is your music collection. You do not keep information about your music collection in your contact list because the data is not related to the people in your contact list.

A more sophisticated type of database is a *relational database*, because multiple collections of data in the database are related to one another—for example, data about the students, the courses, and the faculty members at a college. Microsoft Access 2019 is a relational *database management system*—also referred to as a *DBMS*—which is software that controls how related collections of data are stored, organized, retrieved, and secured.

Activity 1.01 | Using Good Design Techniques to Plan a Database

Before creating a new database, the first step is to determine the information you want to keep track of by asking yourself, *What questions should this database be able to answer?* The purpose of a database is to store the data in a manner that makes it easy to find the information you need by asking questions. For example, in a student database for Texas Lakes Community College, the questions to be answered might include:

- How many students are enrolled at the college?
- How many students have not yet been assigned a faculty advisor?
- Which students live in Austin, Texas?
- Which students owe money for tuition?
- Which students are majoring in Information Systems Technology?

Tables are the foundation of an Access database because all of the data is stored in one or more tables. A table is similar in structure to an Excel worksheet because data is organized into rows and columns. Each table row is a *record*—all of the categories of data pertaining to one person, place, event, thing, or idea. Each table column is a *field*—a single piece of information for every record. For example, in a table storing student contact information, each row forms a record for only one student. Each column forms a field for every record—for example, the student ID number or the student last name.

When organizing the fields of information in your table, break each piece of information into its smallest, most useful part. For example, create three fields for the name of a student—one field for the last name, one field for the first name, and one field for the middle name or initial.

The *first principle of good database design* is to organize data in the tables so that *redundant*—duplicate—data does not occur. For example, record the student contact information in only *one* table, so that if a student's address changes, you can change the information in just one place. This conserves space, reduces the likelihood of errors when inputting new data, and does not require remembering all of the places where a student's address is stored.

The *second principle of good database design* is to use techniques that ensure the accuracy and consistency of data as it is entered into the table. Proofreading data is critical to maintaining accuracy in a database. Typically, many different people enter data into a database—think of all the people who enter data about students at your college. When entering a state in a student contacts table, one person might enter the state as *Texas*, while another might enter the state as *TX*. Use design techniques to help those who enter data into a database to enter the data more accurately and consistently.

Normalization is the process of applying design rules and principles to ensure that your database performs as expected. Taking the time to plan and create a database that is well designed will ensure that you can retrieve meaningful information from the database.

The tables of information in a relational database are linked or joined to one another by a *common field*—a field in two or more tables that stores the same data. For example, a Students table includes the Student ID, name, and full address of every student. The Student Activities table includes the club name and the Student ID of members, but not the name or address, of each student in the club. Because the two tables share a common field—Student ID—you can use the data together to create a list of names and addresses of all of the students in a particular club. The names and addresses are stored in the Students table, and the Student IDs of the club members are stored in the Student Activities table.

Objective 2 Create a Table and Define Fields in a Blank Desktop Database

GO! Learn How
Video A1-2

Three methods are used to create a new Access database. One method is to create a new database using a *database template*—a preformatted database designed for a specific purpose. A second method is to create a new database from a *blank desktop database*. A blank desktop database is stored on your computer or other storage device. Initially, it has no data and has no database tools; you create the data and the tools as you need them. A third method is to create a *custom web app* database from scratch or by using a template that you can publish and share with others over the Internet.

Regardless of the method you use, you must name and save the database before you can create any *objects* in it. Objects are the basic parts of a database; you create objects to store your data, to work with your data, and to display your data. The most common database objects are tables, queries, forms, and reports. Think of an Access database as a container for the objects that you create.

1 Start Microsoft Access 2019. Take a moment to compare your screen with Figure 1.2 and study the parts of the Microsoft Access opening screen described in the table in Figure 1.3.

From this Access opening screen, you can open an existing database, create a blank database, or create a new database from a template.

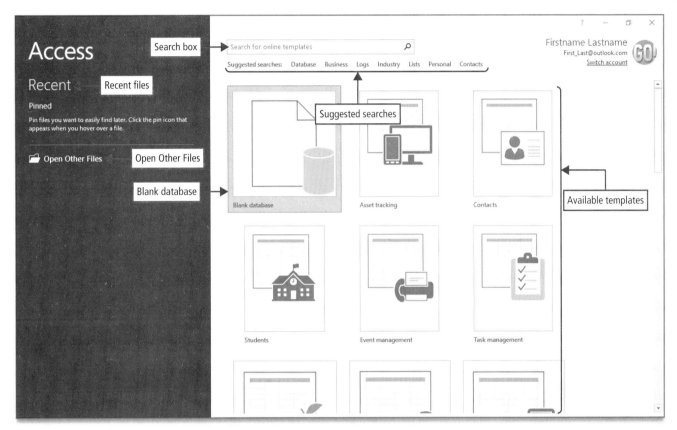

Figure 1.2

Screen Element	Description
Available templates	Starts a database for a specific purpose that includes built-in objects and tools ready for use.
Blank database	Starts a blank database that is stored on your computer or on a portable storage device.
Open Other Files	Enables you to open a database file from your computer, a shared location, or other location that you have designated.
Recent files	Displays a list of database files that have been recently opened.
Search box	Enables you to search the Microsoft Office website for templates.
Suggested searches	Enables you to click on a category to start an online search for a template.

Figure 1.3

2 Navigate to your **Access Chapter 1 folder**, and then double-click the Access file that you downloaded from **MyLab IT** that displays your name—**Student_Access_1A_Advising**. In your blank database, if necessary, click **Enable Content** at the top.

3 Click the **Create tab**. In the **Tables group**, click **Table**. Compare your screen with Figure 1.4, and then take a moment to study the screen elements described in the table in Figure 1.5.

Recall that a table is an Access object that stores data in columns and rows, similar to the format of an Excel worksheet. Table objects are the foundation of a database because tables store data that is used by other database objects.

Figure 1.4

Access Window Element	Description
Navigation Pane	Displays the database objects that can be opened in the object window.
Object tab	Identifies the open object.
Object window	Displays the active or open object(s), including tables, queries, or other objects.
Close button for object	Closes the active object.
Ribbon	Displays commands grouped by related tasks and stored on different tabs.
Status bar	Indicates the active view and the status of action occurring within the database on the left; provides buttons on the right to switch between Datasheet view and Design view.
Table Tools	Provides tools on two tabs for working with the active table object, these are contextual tabs—only available when a table object is active.
Close button for application (Access)	Closes the active database and Access.

Figure 1.5   Microsoft Access Database Window Elements

Activity 1.03 | Assigning the Data Type and Name to Fields

MOS
2.4.1, 2.4.5

After you have named and saved your database, the next step is to consult your database design plan and then create the tables for your data. Limit the data in each table to *one* subject. For example, in this project, your database will have two tables—one for student information and one for faculty advisor information.

Recall that each column in a table is a field; field names display at the top of each column of the table. Recall also that each row in a table is a record—all of the data pertaining to one person, place, thing, event, or idea. Each record is broken up into its smallest usable parts—the fields. Use meaningful names for fields; for example, *Last Name*.

1 Notice the new blank table that displays in Datasheet view, and then take a moment to study the elements of the table's object window. Compare your screen with Figure 1.6.

The table displays in ***Datasheet view***, which displays the data in columns and rows similar to the format of an Excel worksheet. Another way to view a table is in ***Design view***, which displays the underlying design—the ***structure***—of the table's fields. The ***object window*** displays the open object—in this instance, the table object.

In a new blank database, there is only one object—a new blank table. Because you have not yet named this table, the ***object tab*** displays a default name of *Table1*. Access creates the first field and names it *ID*. In the ID field, Access assigns a unique sequential number—each number incremented by one—to each record as it is entered into the table.

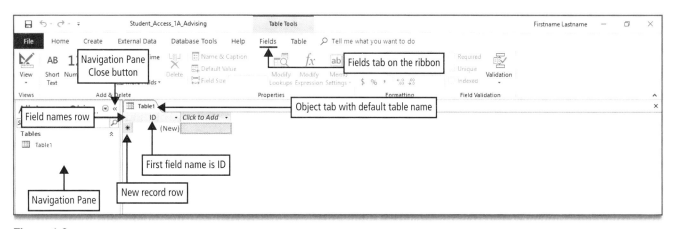

Figure 1.6

2 In the **Navigation Pane**, click **Shutter Bar Open/Close** [«] to collapse the **Navigation Pane** to a narrow bar on the left.

The ***Navigation Pane*** displays and organizes the names of the objects in a database. From the Navigation Pane, you can open objects. Collapse or close the Navigation Pane to display more of the object—in this case, the table.

ANOTHER WAY Press [F11] to close or open the Navigation Pane.

3 In the field names row, click anywhere in the text *Click to Add* to display a list of data types. Compare your screen with Figure 1.7.

A ***data type*** classifies the kind of data that you can store in a field, such as numbers, text, or dates. A field in a table can have only one data type. The data type of each field should be included in your database design. After selecting the data type, you can name the field.

ANOTHER WAY   To the right of *Click to Add*, click the arrow.

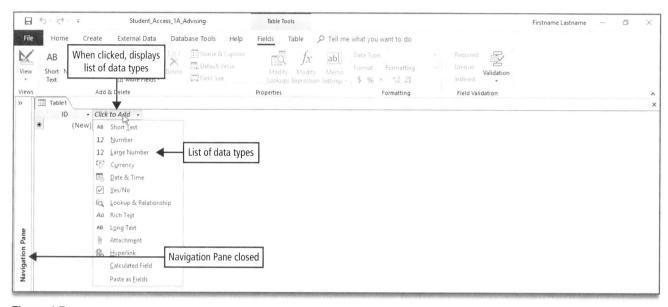

Figure 1.7

4 In the list of data types, click **Short Text**, and notice that in the second column, *Click to Add* changes to *Field1*, which is selected. Type **Last Name** and then press Enter.

The second column displays *Last Name* as the field name, and, in the third column, the data types list displays. The ***Short Text data type*** describes text, a combination of text and numbers, or numbers that do not represent a quantity or are not used in calculations, such as the Postal Code. This data type enables you to enter up to 255 characters in the field.

ANOTHER WAY   With the list of data types displayed, type the character that is underscored to select the data type. For example, type *t* to select Short Text or type *u* to select Currency.

5 In the third field name box, type **t** to select *Short Text*, type **First Name** and then press Enter.

6 In the fourth field name box, click **Short Text**, type **Middle Initial** and then press Enter.

7 Create the remaining fields from the table below by first selecting the data type, typing the field name, and then pressing Enter. The field names in the table will display on one line–do not be concerned if the field names do not completely display in the column; you will adjust the column widths later.

Data Type		Short Text	Short Text	Short Text	Short Text	Short Text	Short Text	Short Text	Short Text	Short Text	Short Text	Currency
Field Name	ID	Last Name	First Name	Middle Initial	**Address**	**City**	**State**	**Postal Code**	**Phone**	**Email**	**Faculty Advisor ID**	**Amount Owed**

The Postal Code and Phone fields are assigned a data type of Short Text because the numbers are never used in calculations. The Amount Owed field is assigned the *Currency data type*, which describes monetary values and numeric data that can be used in calculations and that have one to four decimal places. A U.S. dollar sign ($) and two decimal places are automatically included for all of the numbers in a field with the Currency data type.

8 If necessary, scroll to bring the first column—ID—into view, and then compare your screen with Figure 1.8.

Access automatically created the ID field, and you created 11 additional fields in the table.

Figure 1.8

MORE KNOWLEDGE | **Create Fields by Entering Data**

You can create a new field in Datasheet view by typing the data in a new column. Access automatically assigns a data type based on the data you enter. For example, if you enter a date, Access assigns the Date & Time data type. If you enter a monetary amount, Access assigns the Currency data type. If Access cannot determine the data type based on the data entered, the Short Text data type is assigned. You can always change the data type if an incorrect data type is assigned. If you use this method to create fields, you must check the assigned data types to be sure they are correct. You must also rename the fields because Access assigns the names as *Field1*, *Field2*, and so on.

Activity 1.04 | Renaming Fields, Changing Data Types, and Setting Field Size in a Table

2.4.3, 2.4.4, 2.4.5

Once a table has been created, the field structure can be edited in Datasheet view. As you change data types and field sizes, you need to be sure that any existing data meets the new restrictions. In this Activity, you will modify the default ID field that displayed when you created the new table.

1 In the first column, click anywhere in the text *ID*. On the ribbon, under **Table Tools**, on the **Fields tab**, in the **Properties group**, click **Name & Caption**. In the **Enter Field Properties** dialog box, in the **Name** box, change *ID* to **Student ID**

The field name *Student ID* is a more precise description of the data contained in this field. In the Enter Field Properties dialog box, you have the option to use the *Caption* property to display a name for a field different from the one that displays in the Name box. Many database designers do not use spaces in field names; instead, they might name a field *LastName* or *LName* and then create a caption for the field so it displays as *Last Name* in tables, forms, or reports. In the Enter Field Properties dialog box, you can also provide a description for the field.

🔄 **ANOTHER WAY** Right-click the field name to display the shortcut menu, and then click Rename Field; or, double-click the field name to select the existing text, and then type the new field name.

2 Click **OK** to close the **Enter Field Properties** dialog box. On the ribbon, in the **Formatting group**, notice that the **Data Type** for the **Student ID** field is *AutoNumber*. Click the **Data Type arrow**, and then click **Short Text**.

> In the new record row, the Student ID field is selected. By default, Access creates an ID field for all new tables and sets the data type for the field to AutoNumber. The **AutoNumber data type** describes a unique sequential or random number assigned by Access as each record is entered. Changing the data type of this field to Short Text enables you to enter a custom student ID number.
>
> When records in a database have *no* unique value, such as a book ISBN or a license plate number, the AutoNumber data type is a useful way to automatically create a unique number. In this manner, you are sure that every record is different from the others.

3 On the ribbon, in the **Properties group**, click in the **Field Size** box to select the text *255*, and then type **7** Press [Enter], and then compare your screen with Figure 1.9.

> This action limits the size of the Student ID field to no more than seven characters. The default field size for a Short Text field is 255. Limiting the Field Size property to seven ensures that no more than 7 characters can be entered for each Student ID. However, this does not prevent someone from entering seven characters that are incorrect or entering fewer than seven characters. Setting the proper data type for the field and limiting the field size are two ways to help reduce errors during data entry.

Figure 1.9

Activity 1.05 | Adding a Record to a Table

1.1.2

A new contact list is not useful until you fill it with names and phone numbers. Likewise, a new database is not useful until you **populate** it by filling one or more tables with data. You can populate a table with records by typing data directly into the table.

1 In the new record row, click in the **Student ID** field to display the insertion point, type **1023045** and then press [Enter]. Compare your screen with Figure 1.10.

> The pencil icon [✎] in the **record selector box** indicates that a record is being entered or edited. The record selector box is the small box at the left of a record in Datasheet view. When clicked, the entire record is selected.

↻ **ANOTHER WAY**   Press [Tab] to move the insertion point to the next field.

Figure 1.10

2 With the insertion point positioned in the **Last Name** field, type **Fresch** and then press Tab.

Pressing Enter or Tab will move the insertion point from field to field in the record.

NOTE **Correcting Typing Errors**

Correct any typing errors you make by using the techniques you have practiced in other Office applications. For example, use Backspace to remove characters to the left of the insertion point. Use Del to remove characters to the right of the insertion point. Or select the text you want to replace and type the correct information. Press Esc to exit out of a record that has not been completely entered.

---

3 In the **First Name** field, type **Jenna** and then press Enter.

4 In the **Middle Initial** field, type **A** and then press Enter.

5 In the **Address** field, type **7550 Douglas Ln** and then press Enter.

Do not be concerned if the data does not completely display in the column. As you progress in your study of Access, you will adjust column widths so that you can view all of the data.

6 Continue entering data in the fields as indicated in the table below, pressing Enter to move to the next field.

City	State	Postal Code	Phone	Email	Faculty Advisor ID
Austin	**TX**	**78749**	**(512) 555-7550**	**jfresch@tlcc.edu**	**FAC-2289**

NOTE **Format for Typing Telephone Numbers in Access**

Access does not require a specific format for typing telephone numbers in a record. The examples in this textbook use the format of Microsoft Outlook. Using such a format facilitates easy transfer of Outlook information to and from Access.

---

7 In the **Amount Owed** field, type **250** and then press Enter. Compare your screen with Figure 1.11.

Pressing Enter or Tab in the last field moves the insertion point to the next row to begin a new record. Access automatically saves the record as soon as you move to the next row; you do not have to take any specific action to save a record.

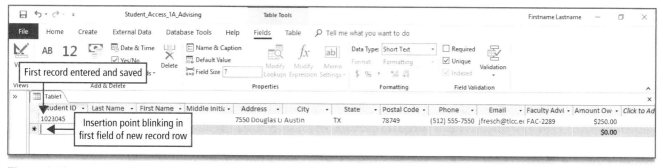

Figure 1.11

> **8** To give your table a meaningful name, click the **File tab**, and, on the left, click **Save As**. Under *Save As*, double-click **Save Object** As In the **Save As** dialog box, in the **Table Name** box, replace the selected text by typing **1A Students**
>
> > Save each database object with a name that identifies the data that it contains. When you save objects within a database, it is not necessary to use underscores in place of the spaces between words. Notice that the object tab—located directly above the *Student ID* field name—displays the table name.

MORE KNOWLEDGE **Renaming or Deleting a Table**

To change the name of a table, close the table, display the Navigation Pane, right-click the table name, and then click Rename. Type the new name or edit as you would any selected text. To delete a table, close the table, display the Navigation Pane, right-click the table name, and then click Delete.

Activity 1.06 | Adding Additional Records to a Table

> **1** In the new record row, click in the **Student ID** field, and then enter the data for two additional students as shown in the table below. Press Enter or Tab to move from field to field. The data in each field will display on one line in the table.

Student ID	Last Name	First Name	Middle Initial	Address	City	State	Postal Code	Phone	Email	Faculty Advisor ID	Amount Owed
2345677	Ingram	Joseph	S	621 Hilltop Dr	Leander	TX	78646	(512) 555-0717	jingram@ tlcc.edu	FAC-2377	378.5
3456689	Snyder	Amanda	J	4786 Bluff St	Buda	TX	78610	(512) 555-9120	asnyder@ tlcc.edu	FAC-9005	0

> **2** Press Enter, and compare your screen with Figure 1.12.

Figure 1.12

Activity 1.07 | Importing Data from an Excel Workbook into an Existing Access Table

2.1.1

You can type records directly into a table. You can also **import** data from a variety of sources. Importing is the process of copying data from one source or application to another application. For example, you can import data from a Word table or an Excel spreadsheet into an Access database because the data is arranged in columns and rows, similar to a table in Datasheet view.

In this Activity, you will *append*—add on—data from an Excel spreadsheet to your *1A Students* table. To append data, the table must already be created, and it should be closed.

1 In the upper right corner of the table, below the ribbon, click **Object Close** ⊠ to close your **1A Students** table. Notice that no objects are open.

2 On the ribbon, click the **External Data tab**. In the **Import & Link group**, click the **New Data Source** arrow, point to **From File**, and then click **Excel**. In the **Get External Data – Excel Spreadsheet** dialog box, click **Browse**.

3 In the **File Open** dialog box, navigate to your student files, double-click the Excel file **a01A_Students**, and then compare your screen with Figure 1.13.

The path to the *source file*—the file being imported—displays in the File name box. There are three options for importing data from an Excel spreadsheet: import the data into a *new* table in the current database, append a copy of the records to an existing table, or link the data from the spreadsheet to a linked table in the database. A *link* is a connection to data in another file. When linking, Access creates a table that maintains a link to the source data, so that changes to the data in one file are automatically made in the other—linked—file.

ANOTHER WAY   Click the file name, and then in the File Open dialog box, click Open.

Figure 1.13

4 Click the **Append a copy of the records to the table** option button, and then, in the box to the right, click the **arrow**.

Currently, your database has only one table, so no other tables display on the list. However, when a database has multiple tables, click the arrow to select the table to which you want to append records. The table into which you import or append data is referred to as the *destination table*.

5 Press [Esc] to cancel the list, and in the dialog box, click **OK**. Compare your screen with Figure 1.14.

The first screen of the Import Spreadsheet Wizard displays. A *wizard* is a feature in a Microsoft Office program that walks you step by step through a process. The presence of scroll bars in the window indicates that records and fields are out of view. To append records from an Excel workbook to an existing database table, the column headings in the Excel worksheet or spreadsheet must be identical to the field names in the table. The wizard identified the first row of the spreadsheet as column headings, which are equivalent to field names.

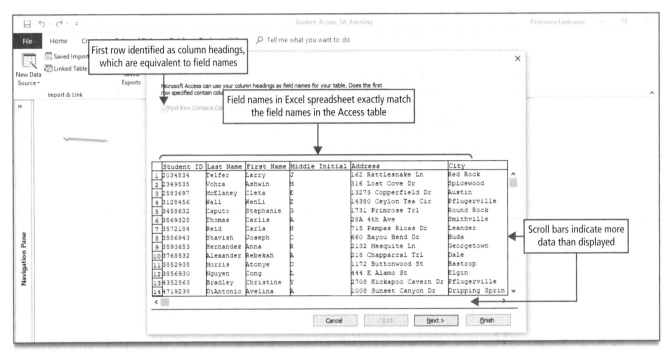

Figure 1.14

6 In the lower right corner of the wizard, click **Next**. Notice that the name of your table displays under **Import to Table**. In the lower right corner of the wizard, click **Finish**.

7 In the **Get External Data – Excel Spreadsheet** dialog box, click **Close**. Open [»] the **Navigation Pane**, and then compare your screen with Figure 1.15.

Figure 1.15

8 In the **Navigation Pane**, double-click your **1A Students** table to open the table in Datasheet view, and then **Close** [«] the **Navigation Pane**.

🔄 **ANOTHER WAY** To open an object from the Navigation Pane, right-click the object name, and then click Open.

9 In the lower left corner of your screen, locate the navigation area, and notice that there are a total of **25** records in the table—you entered three records and imported 22 additional records. Compare your screen with Figure 1.16.

The records that you entered and the records you imported from the Excel spreadsheet display in your table; the first record in the table is selected. The *navigation area* indicates the number of records in the table and has controls in the form of arrows that you click to move through the records.

Figure 1.16

Objective 3 **Change the Structure of Tables and Add a Second Table**

GO! Learn How

Video A1-3

Recall that the structure of a table is the underlying design of the table and includes field names and data types. You can create or modify a table in Datasheet view. To define and modify fields, many database experts prefer to work in Design view, where you have more options for defining fields in a table.

Activity 1.08 | Deleting a Table Field in Design View

MOS

2.4.1

In a recent meeting, the Student Services department has decided that the Students table does not need to include a field for the middle initial. In this Activity, you will delete the *Middle Initial* field from the table.

1 Click the **Home tab**, and then in the **Views group**, click the **View arrow** to display a list of views.

There are two views for tables: Datasheet view and Design view. Other objects have different views. On the list, Design view is represented by a picture of a pencil, a ruler, and an angle. Datasheet view is represented by a picture of a table arranged in columns and rows. In the Views group, if the top of the View button displays the pencil, ruler, and angle, clicking View will switch your view to Design view. Likewise, clicking the top of the View button that displays as a datasheet will switch your view to Datasheet view.

2 On the list, click **Design View**, and then compare your screen with Figure 1.17.

Design view displays the underlying design—the structure—of the table and its fields. In Design view, the records in the table do not display. You can only view the information about each field's attributes. Each field name is listed, along with its data type. You can add explanatory information about a field in the Description column, but it is not required.

You can decide how each field should look and behave in the Field Properties area. For example, you can set a specific field size in the Field Properties area. In the lower right corner, information displays about the active selection—in this case, the Field Name.

Figure 1.17

3 In the **Field Name** column, to the left of **Middle Initial**, point to the row selector box to display the ➡ pointer, and then click one time to select the entire row.

4 On the **Design tab**, in the **Tools group**, click **Delete Rows**. Read the warning in the message box, and then click **Yes**.

Deleting a field deletes both the field and its data. After you save the changes, you cannot undo this action, so Access prompts you to be sure you want to proceed. If you change your mind after deleting a field and saving the changes, you must add the field back into the table and then reenter the data for that field for every record.

 ANOTHER WAY   In Design view, right-click the selected row, and then click Delete Rows; or, in Datasheet view, select the field—column—and on the Home tab, in the Records group, click Delete.

Activity 1.09 | Adding Field Descriptions and Changing Field Size

2.2.3, 2.4.4

Typically, many different individuals have the ability to enter data into a table. For example, at your college, many Registration Assistants enter and modify student and course information daily. Two ways to help reduce errors are to restrict what can be typed in a field and to add descriptive information to help the individuals when entering the data.

1 With your table still displayed in **Design** view, in the **Field Name** column, click anywhere in the **Student ID** field name.

2 In the **Student ID** row, click in the **Description** box, type **Seven-digit Student ID number** and then press Enter. Compare your screen with Figure 1.18.

Descriptions for fields in a table are optional. Include a description if the field name does not provide an obvious explanation of the type of data to be entered. If a description is provided for a field, when data is being entered in that field in Datasheet view, the text in the Description displays on the left side of the status bar to provide additional information for the individuals who are entering the data.

When you enter a description for a field, a Property Update Options button displays below the text you typed, which enables you to copy the description for the field to all other database objects that use this table as an underlying source.

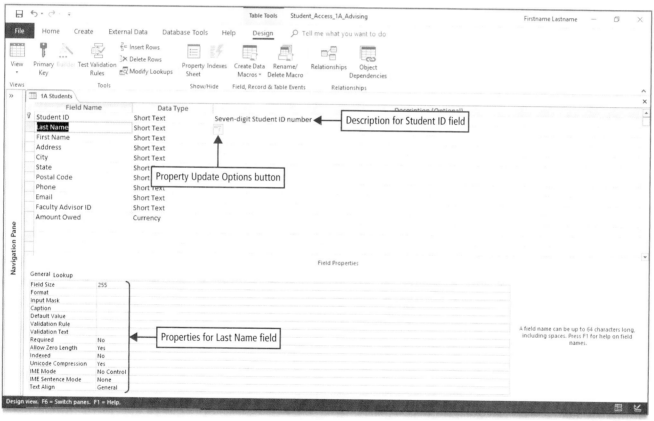

Figure 1.18

3 Click in the **State** field name box. In the lower area of the screen, under **Field Properties**, click in the **Field Size** box to select the text **255**, and type **2** Click in the **Description** box for this field, type **Two-character state abbreviation** and then press (Enter).

> Recall changing the size of a field limits the number of characters that the field will accept. *Field properties* control how the field displays and how data can be entered into the field. You can define properties for each field in the Field Properties area by first clicking on the field name to display the properties for that specific data type.

4 Click in the **Faculty Advisor ID** field name box. In the **Field Properties** area, change the **Field Size** to **8** and in the **Description** box for this field, type **Eight-character ID of the instructor assigned as advisor** and then press (Enter).

MORE KNOWLEDGE **Add a Table Description**

You can create a description to provide more information to users regarding the entire table. With the table displayed in Design view, click the Design tab. In the Show/Hide group, click Property Sheet. Click in the Description box, type the table description, and then press Enter. Close the Property Sheet.

---

5 On the Quick Access Toolbar, click **Save** 🖫 to save the design changes to your table, and then notice the message.

> The message indicates that the field size property of one or more fields has changed to a shorter size. If more characters are currently present in the State, or Faculty Advisor ID fields than you have allowed, the data will be *truncated*—cut off or shortened—because the fields were not previously restricted to these specific number of characters.

6 In the message box, click **Yes**.

Activity 1.10 | Viewing the Primary Key in Design View

Primary key refers to the required field in the table that uniquely identifies a record. For example, in a college registration database, your Student ID number identifies you as a unique individual—every student has a student number and no other student at the college has your exact student number. In the 1A Students table, the Student ID uniquely identifies each student.

When you create a table using the blank database template, Access designates the first field as the primary key field and names the field ID. It is good database design practice to establish a primary key for every table, because doing so ensures that you do not enter the same record more than once. You can imagine the confusion if another student at your college had the same Student ID number as you do.

1 With your table still displayed in **Design** view, in the **Field Name** column, click in the **Student ID** box. To the left of the box, notice the small icon of a key, as shown in Figure 1.19.

Access automatically designates the first field as the primary key field, but you can set any field as the primary key by clicking the field name, and then in the Tools group, clicking Primary Key.

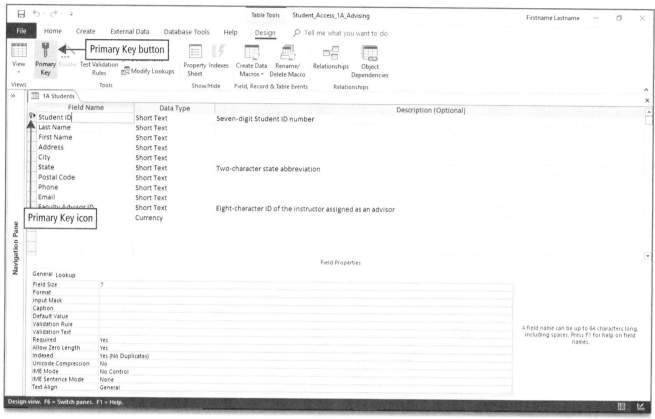

Figure 1.19

2 On the **Design tab**, in the **Views group**, notice that the View button displays a picture of a datasheet, indicating that clicking View will switch the view to Datasheet view. Click the top of the **View** button.

If you make design changes to a table and switch views without first saving the table, Access will prompt you to save the table before changing views.

Activity 1.11 | Adding a Second Table to a Database by Importing an Excel Spreadsheet

1.1.1

Many Microsoft Office users track data in an Excel spreadsheet. The sorting and filtering capabilities of Excel are useful for a simple database where all of the information resides in one large Excel spreadsheet. However, Excel is limited as a database management tool because it cannot *relate* the information in multiple spreadsheets in a way that you can ask a question and get a meaningful result. Because data in an Excel spreadsheet is arranged in columns and rows, the spreadsheet can easily convert to an Access table by importing the spreadsheet.

1 On the ribbon, click the **External Data tab**. In the **Import & Link group**, click the **New Data Source** arrow, point to **From File**, and then click **Excel**. In the **Get External Data – Excel Spreadsheet** dialog box, to the right of the **File name** box, click **Browse**.

2 In the **File Open** dialog box, navigate to the location where your student data files are stored, and then double-click **a01A_Faculty_Advisors**. Compare your screen with Figure 1.20.

Figure 1.20

3 Be sure that the **Import the source data into a new table in the current database** option button is selected, and then click **OK**.

The Import Spreadsheet Wizard displays the spreadsheet data.

4 In the upper left corner of the wizard, select the **First Row Contains Column Headings** check box.

The Excel data is framed, indicating that the first row of Excel column titles will become the Access table field names, and the remaining rows will become the individual records in the new Access table.

Click **Next**. Notice that the first column—*Faculty ID*—is selected, and in the upper area of the wizard, the **Field Name** and the **Data Type** display. Compare your screen with Figure 1.21.

In this step, under Field Options, you can review and change the name or the data type of each selected field. You can also identify fields in the spreadsheet that you do not want to import into the Access table by selecting the Do not import field (Skip) check box.

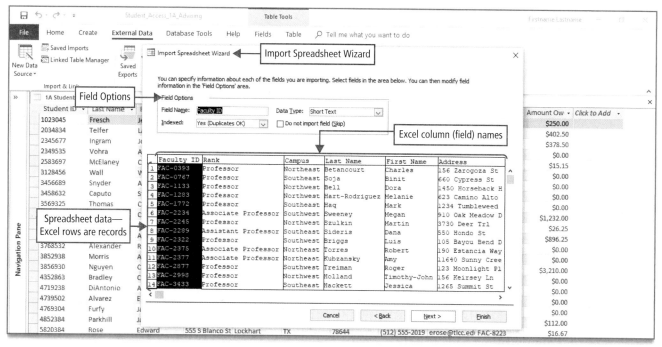

Figure 1.21

6 Click **Next**. In the upper area of the wizard, click the **Choose my own primary key** option button, and then verify that **Faculty ID** displays.

In the new table, Faculty ID will be the primary key. Every faculty member has a Faculty ID and no two faculty members have the same Faculty ID. By default, Access selects the first field as the primary key, but you can click the arrow and select a different field.

7 Click **Next**. In the **Import to Table** box, type **1A Faculty Advisors** and then click **Finish**.

8 In the **Get External Data – Excel Spreadsheet** dialog box, click **Close. Open** ⊠ the **Navigation Pane**.

9 In the **Navigation Pane**, double-click your **1A Faculty Advisors** table to open it in Datasheet view, and then **Close** ⊠ the **Navigation Pane**.

Two tables that are identified by their object tabs are open in the object window. Your 1A Faculty Advisors table is the active table and displays the 29 records that you imported from the Excel spreadsheet.

10 In your **1A Faculty Advisors** table, click in the **Postal Code** field in the first record. On the ribbon, under **Table Tools**, click the **Fields tab**. In the **Formatting group**, click the **Data Type arrow**, and then click **Short Text**. Compare your screen with Figure 1.22.

When you import data from an Excel spreadsheet, check the data types of all fields to ensure they are correct. Recall that if a field, such as the Postal Code, contains numbers that do not represent a quantity or are not used in calculations, the data type should be set to Short Text. To change the data type of a field, click in the field in any record.

Figure 1.22

Activity 1.12 | Adjusting Column Widths and Viewing a Table in Print Preview

You can adjust the column widths in a table displayed in Datasheet view by using techniques similar to those you use for Excel spreadsheets.

1 In the object window, click the **object tab** for your **1A Students** table to make it the active object and to display it in the object window.

Clicking an object tab along the top of the object window enables you to display the open object and make it active so that you can work with it. All of the columns in the datasheet are the same width, regardless of the length of the data in the field, the length of the field name, or the field size that was set. If you print the table as currently displayed, some of the data or field names will not print completely, so you will want to adjust the column widths.

2 In the field names row, point to the right edge of the **Address** field to display the ⊞ pointer, and then compare your screen with Figure 1.23.

Figure 1.23

3 With the ⊞ pointer positioned as shown in Figure 1.23, double-click the right edge of the **Address** field.

> The column width of the Address field widens to display the longest entry in the field fully. In this manner, the width of a column can be increased or decreased to fit its contents in the same manner as a column in an Excel spreadsheet. In Access, adjusting the column width to fit the contents is referred to as *Best Fit*.

4 Point to the **City** field name to display the ↓ pointer, right-click to select the entire column and display the shortcut menu. Click **Field Width**, and then in the **Column Width** dialog box, click **Best Fit**.

> This is a second way to adjust column widths.

5 If necessary, scroll to the right to view the last three fields. Point to the **Email** field name to display the ↓ pointer, hold down the left mouse button, and then drag to the right to select this column, the **Faculty Advisor ID** column, and the **Amount Owed** column. Point to the right edge of any of the selected columns to display the ⊞ pointer, and then double-click to apply **Best Fit** to all three columns.

> You can select multiple columns and adjust the widths of all of them at one time by using this technique or by right-clicking any of the selected columns, clicking Field Width, and clicking Best Fit in the Column Width dialog box.

6 If necessary, scroll to the left to view the **Student ID** field. To the left of the **Student ID** field name, click **Select All** ▢. Notice that all of the fields are selected.

7 On the ribbon, click the **Home tab**. In the **Records group**, click **More**, and then click **Field Width**. In the **Column Width** dialog box, click **Best Fit**. Click anywhere in the **Student ID** field, and then compare your screen with Figure 1.24.

> Using the More command is a third way to adjust column widths. By using Select All, you can adjust the widths of all of the columns at one time. Adjusting the width of columns does not change the data in the table's records; it only changes the *display* of the data.

Figure 1.24

NOTE   Adjusting Column Widths

After adjusting column widths, scroll horizontally and vertically to be sure that all of the data displays in all of the fields. Access adjusts column widths to fit the screen size based on the displayed data. If data is not displayed on the screen when you adjust column widths—even if you use Select All—the column width may not be adjusted adequately to display all of the data in the field. After adjusting column widths, click in any field to remove the selection of the column or columns, and then save the table before performing other tasks.

> **8** On the Quick Access Toolbar, click **Save** to save the table design changes—changing the column widths.
>
> > If you do not save the table after making design changes, Access prompts you to save it when you close the table.

Activity 1.13 | Viewing a Table in Print Preview

MOS
1.3.1

> There are times when you will want to print a table, even though a report may look more professional. For example, you may need a quick reference, or you may want to proofread the data that has been entered. In Access, it is best to preview a table before printing to make any necessary layout changes.

> **1** On the ribbon, click the **File tab**, click **Print**, and then click **Print Preview**. Compare your screen with Figure 1.25.
>
> > The table displays in Print Preview with the default zoom setting of One Page, a view that enables you to see how your table will print on the page. It is a good idea to view any object in Print Preview before printing so that you can make changes to the object if needed before actually printing it. In the navigation area, the Next Page button is darker (available), an indication that more than one page will print.

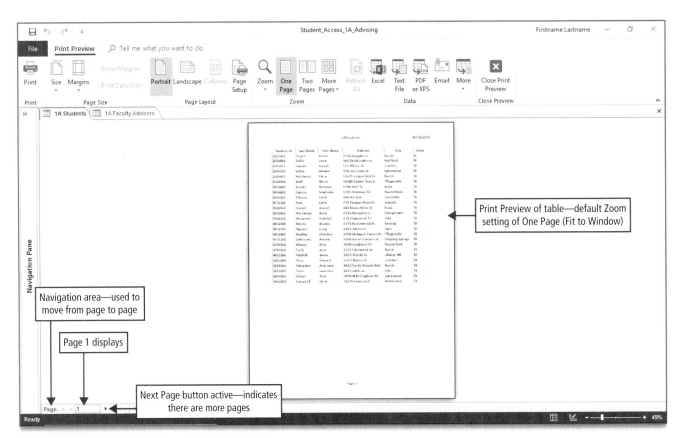

Figure 1.25

> **NOTE**   **Headers and Footers in Access Objects**
>
> The headers and footers in Access tables and queries are controlled by default settings; you cannot enter additional information or edit the information. The object name displays in the center of the header area, and the current date displays on the right. Adding your name to the object name is helpful in identifying your paper printouts or electronic results. The page number displays in the center of the footer area. The headers and footers in Access forms and reports are more flexible; you can add to and edit the information.

2 In the navigation area, click **Next Page** ▶ to display Page 2. Point to the top of the page to display the 🔍 pointer, click one time to zoom in, and then compare your screen with Figure 1.26.

The Print Preview display enlarges, and the Zoom Out pointer displays. The second page of the table displays the last five fields. The Next Page button is dimmed, indicating that the button is unavailable because there are no more pages after Page 2. The Previous Page button is available, indicating that a page exists before this page.

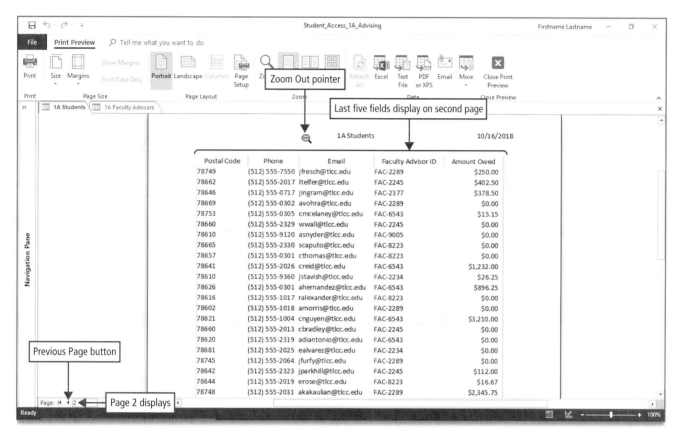

Figure 1.26

3 On the ribbon, on the **Print Preview tab**, in the **Zoom group**, click **Zoom** to change the zoom setting back to the default setting of One Page.

ANOTHER WAY With the 🔍 pointer displayed on the page, click to zoom back to the One Page setting.

4 In the **Page Layout group**, click **Landscape**, and notice that there are only three fields on Page 2. In the navigation area, click **Previous Page** to display Page 1, and then compare your screen with Figure 1.27.

The orientation of the page to be printed changes. The header on the page includes the table name and current date, and the footer displays the page number. The change in orientation from portrait to landscape is not saved with the table. Each time you print, you must check the page orientation, the margins, and any other print parameters so that the object prints as you intend.

Figure 1.27

NOTE   Creating a PDF Electronic Image of Your Database Object That Looks Like a Printed Document

Display the object (table, query, form, report, and so on) in Print Preview and adjust margins and orientation as needed. On the Print Preview tab, in the Data group, click PDF or XPS. In the Publish as PDF or XPS dialog box, navigate to your chapter folder. Use the default file name, or follow your instructor's directions to name the object. If you wish to view the PDF file, in the dialog box, select the Open file after publishing check box. In the Publish as PDF or XPS dialog box, click Publish. If necessary, close any windows that try to display your PDF—Adobe Reader, Adobe Acrobat, or the Microsoft Edge browser, and then close the Export – PDF dialog box. On the ribbon, click Close Print Preview; your electronic image is saved. Close the Save Export Steps dialog box.

---

5 On the ribbon, in the **Close Preview group**, click **Close Print Preview**. In the upper right corner of the object window, click **Close Object** to close your **1A Students** table. Notice that the **1A Faculty Advisors** table is the active object in the object window.

ANOTHER WAY   In the object window, right-click the 1A Students object tab, and then click Close.

6 In your **1A Faculty Advisors** table, to the left of the **Faculty ID** field name, click **Select All** to select all of the columns. On the **Home tab**, in the **Records group**, click **More**, and then click **Field Width**. In the **Column Width** dialog box, click **Best Fit** to adjust the widths of all of the columns so that all of the data displays. Click in any field in the table to cancel the selection. Scroll horizontally and vertically to be sure that all of the data displays in each field; if necessary, use the techniques you practiced to apply Best Fit to individual columns. **Save** the changes you made to the table's column widths, and then click in any record to cancel the selection, if necessary.

7 On the ribbon, click the **File tab**, click **Print**, and then click **Print Preview**. On the **Print Preview tab**, in the **Page Layout group**, click **Landscape**. Notice that the table will print on more than one page. In the **Page Size group**, click **Margins**, click **Normal**, and then notice that one more column moved to the first page—your results may differ depending upon your printer's capabilities.

> In addition to changing the page orientation to Landscape, you can change the margins to Normal to see if all of the fields will print on one page. In this instance, there are still too many fields to print on one page, although the Postal Code field moved from Page 2 to Page 1.

8 On the ribbon, in the **Close Preview group**, click **Close Print Preview**. In the object window, **Close** your **1A Faculty Advisors** table, saving changes if necessary.

> All of your database objects—your *1A Students* table and your *1A Faculty Advisors* table—are closed; the object window is empty.

Objective 4 | Create a Query, Form, and Report

GO! Learn How
Video A1-4

Recall that tables are the foundation of an Access database because all of the data is stored in one or more tables. You can use the data stored in tables in other database objects such as queries, forms, and reports.

Activity 1.14 | Creating a Query by Using the Simple Query Wizard

3.1.7

A *query* is a database object that retrieves specific data from one or more database objects—either tables or other queries—and then, in a single datasheet, displays only the data that you specify when you design the query. Because the word *query* means *to ask a question*, think of a query as a question formed in a manner that Access can answer.

A *select query* is one type of Access query. A select query, also called a *simple select query*, retrieves (selects) data from one or more tables or queries and then displays the selected data in a datasheet. A select query creates a subset of the data to answer specific questions; for example, *Which students live in Austin, TX?*

The objects from which a query selects the data are referred to as the query's *data source*. In this Activity, you will create a simple query using a wizard that walks you step by step through the process. The process involves selecting the data source and indicating the fields that you want to include in the query results. The query—the question you want to ask—is *What is the name, email address, phone number, and Student ID of every student?*

1 On the ribbon, click the **Create tab**, and then in then in the **Queries group**, click **Query Wizard**. In the **New Query** dialog box, be sure **Simple Query Wizard** is selected, and then click **OK**. Compare your screen with Figure 1.28.

In the wizard, the displayed table or query name is the object that was last selected on the Navigation Pane. The last object you worked with was your 1A Faculty Advisors table, so that object name displayed in the wizard.

Figure 1.28

2 In the wizard, click the **Tables/Queries arrow**, and then click your **Table: 1A Students**.

To create a query, first select the data source—the object from which the query is to select the data. The information you need to answer the question is stored in your 1A Students table, so this table is your data source.

3 Under **Available Fields**, click **Last Name**, and then click **Add Field** `>` to move the field to the **Selected Fields** list on the right. Double-click the **First Name** field to add the field to the **Selected Fields** list.

Use either method to add fields to the Selected Fields list—you can add fields in any order.

4 By using **Add Field** `>` or by double-clicking the field name, add the following fields to the **Selected Fields** list in the order specified: **Email**, **Phone**, and **Student ID**. Compare your screen with Figure 1.29.

Selecting these five fields will answer the question, *What is the name, email address, phone number, and Student ID of every student?*

Figure 1.29

5 In the wizard, click **Next**. Click in the **What title do you want for your query?** box. Edit as necessary so that the query name is **1A All Students Query** and then compare your screen with Figure 1.30.

Figure 1.30

6 In the wizard, click **Finish**. Select all of the columns, apply **Best Fit**, and then **Save** 🖫 the query. In the first record, click in the **Last Name** field to cancel the selection. Compare your screen with Figure 1.31.

Access **runs** the query—performs the actions indicated in your query design—by searching the records in the specified data source, and then finds the records that match specified criteria. The records that match the criteria display in a datasheet. A select query *selects*—pulls out and displays—only the information from the data source that you request, including the specified fields. In the object window, Access displays every student from your 1A Students table—the data source— but displays *only* the five fields that you moved to the Selected Fields list in the Simple Query Wizard.

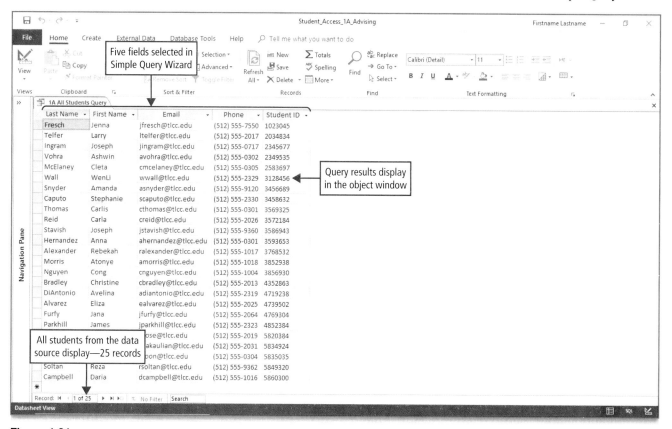

Figure 1.31

7 In the object window, **Close** ⨯ the query.

Activity 1.15 | Creating a Form

1.3.1, 4.1.1

A *form* is an Access object with which you can enter data, edit data, or display data from a table or query. In a form, the fields are laid out in an attractive format on the screen, which makes working with the database easier for those who must enter and look up data.

One type of form displays only one record at a time. Such a form is useful not only to the individual who performs the data entry—typing in the records—but also to anyone who has the job of viewing information in the database. For example, when you visit the Records office at your college to obtain a transcript, someone displays your record on the screen. For the viewer, it is much easier to look at one record at a time using a form than to look at all of the student records in the database table.

1 Open ⟩ the **Navigation Pane**. Notice that a table name displays with a datasheet icon, and a query name displays an icon of two overlapping datasheets. Right-click your **1A Students** table, and then compare your screen with Figure 1.32.

Figure 1.32

2 On the shortcut menu, click **Open** to display the table in the object window, and then **Close** ⟨ the **Navigation Pane** to maximize your object window space.

 ANOTHER WAY   In the Navigation Pane, double-click the object name to open it.

3 Notice that there are 11 fields in the table. On the **Create tab**, in the **Forms group**, click **Form**. Compare your screen with Figure 1.33.

The Form tool creates a form based on the currently selected object—your 1A Students table. The form displays all of the fields from the underlying data source—one record at a time—in a simple top-to-bottom format with all 11 fields in a single column. You can use this form as it displays, or you can modify it. Records that you create or edit in a form are automatically added to or updated in the underlying table or data source.

The new form displays in *Layout view*—the Access view in which you can make changes to elements of an object while it is open and displaying the data from the data source. Each field in the form displayed in Figure 1.33 displays the data for the first student record—*Jenna Fresch*—in your 1A Students table.

Figure 1.33

NOTE   The Property Sheet Displays

If the Property sheet was displayed the last time you were viewing a form in Access, it will display by default with the new form.

---

4 At the right side of the status bar, notice the three buttons. Point to each button to display its ScreenTip, and notice that **Layout View** ▦ is active, indicating that the form is displayed in Layout view.

5 In the status bar, click **Form View** ▦.

In *Form view*, you can view the records, create a new record, edit a record, and delete a record. You cannot change the layout or design of the form. Form view is useful for individuals who *access records* in your database. Layout view is useful for individuals who *design* the form.

⟳ **ANOTHER WAY**   On the Design tab, or on the Home tab, in the Views group, click View when the button displays an icon of a form.

---

6 In the navigation area, click **Next record** ▶ two times to display the third record—the record for *Joseph Ingram*.

> Use the navigation buttons to scroll among the records and to display any single record.

7 Save 🖫 the form as **1A Student Form**

8 On the ribbon, click the **File tab**, click **Print**, and then on the right, click **Print**—do *not* click Print Preview because you are going to print a *single* record—not all of the records.

9 In the **Print** dialog box, under **Print Range**, click the **Selected Record(s)** option button, and then click **Setup**.

10 In the **Page Setup** dialog box, click the **Columns tab**. Under **Column Size**, double-click in the **Width** box, type **7.5** and then click **OK**.

> Forms are usually not printed, so the default width for a form created with the Form command is larger than most printers can handle to print on one page. If you do not change the width, the form will print on two pages because the column flows over the margins allowed by the printer. If, after changing the Width to 7.5, your form still prints on two pages, try entering a different value for Width; for example, 7 or 6.5.

11 Unless instructed to print your objects, click Cancel.

> After printing, along the left edge of the record, the narrow bar—the *record selector bar*—displays in black, indicating that the record is selected.

NOTE   Printing a Single Form in PDF

On the File tab, click Print, and then on the right, click Print. In the Print dialog box, click Setup. In the Page Setup dialog box, click the Columns tab. Under Column Size, double-click in the Width box, type **7.5** and then click OK. In the Print dialog box, click Cancel. On the left edge of the form, click the record selector bar so that it is black—selected.

On the ribbon, click the External Data tab. In the Export group, click PDF or XPS. In the Publish as PDF or XPS dialog box, navigate to your chapter folder, and at the lower right corner of the dialog box, click Options. In the Options dialog box, under Range, click the Selected records option button, and then click OK. In the Publish as PDF or XPS dialog box, click Publish. If necessary, close Adobe Reader, Adobe Acrobat, or the Microsoft Edge browser.

---

12 Close ✕ the form object; leave your **1A Students** table open.

Activity 1.16 │ Creating and Modifying a Report

5.1.1, 5.1.2, 5.2.3

A *report* is a database object that displays the fields and records from a table or query in an easy-to-read format suitable for printing. Create professional-looking reports to summarize database information.

1 Open ⏵⏵ the **Navigation Pane**, and then open your **1A Faculty Advisors** table by double-clicking the table name or by right-clicking the table name and clicking Open. **Close** ⏴⏴ the **Navigation Pane**.

2 On the **Create tab**, in the **Reports group**, click **Report**.

> The Report tool creates a report in Layout view and includes all of the fields and all of the records in the data source—your 1A Faculty Advisors table. Dotted lines indicate how the report would break across pages if you print it now. In Layout view, you can make quick changes to the report layout while viewing the data from the table.

3 Click the **Faculty ID** field name, and then on the ribbon, under **Report Layout Tools**, click the **Arrange tab**. In the **Rows & Columns group**, click **Select Column**, and then press Del. Using the same technique, delete the **Rank** field.

> The Faculty ID and Rank fields, along with the data, are deleted from the report. The fields readjust by moving to the left. Deleting the fields from the report does *not* delete the fields and data from the data source—your 1A Faculty Advisors table.

ANOTHER WAY   Right-click the field name, click Select Entire Column, and then press Del.

4 Click the **Address** field name, and then by using the scroll bar at the bottom of the screen, scroll to the right to display the **Cell Phone** field; be careful not to click in the report.

5 Hold down Shift, and then click the **Cell Phone** field name to select all of the fields from *Address* through *Cell Phone*. With the field names selected—surrounded by a colored border—in the **Rows & Columns group**, click **Select Column**, and then press Del.

> Use this method to select and delete multiple columns in Layout view.

6 Scroll to the left and notice that the four remaining fields display within the dotted lines— they are within the margins of the report. Click the **Campus** field name. Hold down Shift, and then click the **First Name** field name to select the first three fields. In the **Rows & Columns group**, click **Select Column** to select all three fields.

7 On the ribbon, click the **Design tab**, and then in the **Tools group**, click **Property Sheet**.

> The *Property Sheet* for the selected columns displays on the right side of the screen. Every object and every item in an object has an associated Property Sheet where you can make precise changes to the properties—characteristics—of selected items.

8 In the **Property Sheet**, if necessary, click the **Format tab**. Click **Width**, type **1.5** and then press Enter. Compare your screen with Figure 1.34.

> The width of the three selected fields changes to 1.5", and the fields readjust by moving to the left. You can change the Width property if you need to move columns within the margins of a report. In this report, the fields already displayed within the margins, but some reports may need this minor adjustment to print on one page.

ANOTHER WAY   Select the column, and then drag the right edge of the column to the left to decrease the width of the field, or, drag to the right to increase the width of the field.

Figure 1.34

9 > Close ☒ the **Property Sheet**. Click the **Last Name** field name. On the ribbon, click the **Home tab**, and then in the **Sort & Filter group**, click **Ascending**.

> Access sorts the report in ascending alphabetical order by the Last Name field. By default, tables are sorted in ascending order by the primary key field—in this instance, the Faculty ID field. Changing the sort order in the report does *not* change the sort order in the underlying table.

10 > At the top of the report, to the right of the green report icon, click anywhere in the title of the report to select the title. On the **Home tab**, in the **Text Formatting group**, click the **Font Size arrow**, and then click **14**. Save 🖫 the report. In the **Save As** dialog box, in the **Report Name** box, add **Report** to the end of *1A Faculty Advisors*, and then click **OK**.

11 > On the **File tab**, click **Print**, and then click **Print Preview**. On the **Print Preview tab**, in the **Zoom group**, click **Two Pages**, and then compare your screen with Figure 1.35

> As currently formatted, the report will print on two pages, because the page number at the bottom of the report is positioned beyond the right margin of the report.

Figure 1.35

12 > In the **Close Preview group**, click **Close Print Preview**. Scroll down to display the bottom of the report, and then, if necessary, scroll right to display the page number. Click the page number—**Page 1 of 1**—and then press ⌫Del.

> Because all of the data will print on one page, the page number is not necessary for this report. If you want the page number to display, you can drag it within the margins of the report.

13 > Display the report in **Print Preview**, and notice that the report will now print on one page. In the **Zoom group**, click **One Page**. Click Save 🖫 to save the changes to the design of the report. Click **Close Print Preview**.

> When you create a report by using the Report tool, the default margins are 0.25 inch. Some printers require a greater margin, so your printed report may result in two pages. As you progress

in your study of Access, you will practice making these adjustments. Also, if a printer is not installed on your system, the electronic PDF printout might result in a two-page report.

14 In the object window, right-click any **object tab**, and then click **Close All** to close all of the open objects. Notice that the object window is empty.

Objective 5 Close a Database and Close Access

GO! Learn How
Video A1-5

When you close a table, any changes made to the records are saved automatically. If you made changes to the structure or adjusted column widths, you will be prompted to save the table when you close the table or when you switch views. Likewise, you will be prompted to save queries, forms, and reports if you make changes to the layout or design. If the Navigation Pane is open when you close Access, it will display when you reopen the database. When you are finished using your database, close the database, and then close Access.

Activity 1.17 | Closing a Database and Closing Access

1 Open ⟩⟩ the **Navigation Pane**. Notice that your report object displays with a green report icon. Compare your screen with Figure 1.36.

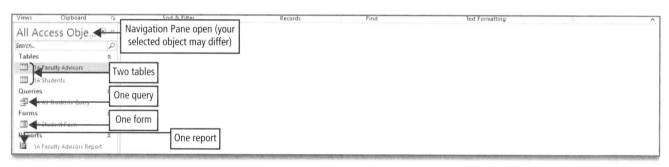

Figure 1.36

2 On the **File tab**, click **Close** to close the database but leave Access open. This action enables you to continue working in Access with another database if you want to do so. In the Access opening screen, in the upper right corner, click **Close** ▇ to close Access.

For Non-MyLab Submissions: Determine What Your Instructor Requires for Submission
As directed by your instructor, submit your completed database file.

---

3 In **MyLab IT**, locate and click the Grader Project **Access 1A Advising**. In **step 3**, under **Upload Completed Assignment**, click **Choose File**. In the **Open** dialog box, navigate to your **Access Chapter 1 folder**, and then click your **Student_Access_1A_Advising** file one time to select it. In the lower right corner of the **Open** dialog box, click **Open**.

The name of your selected file displays above the Upload button.

4 To submit your file to **MyLab IT** for grading, click **Upload**, wait a moment for a green **Success!** message, and then in **step 4**, click the blue **Submit for Grading** button. Click **Close Assignment** to return to your list of **Course Materials**.

You have completed Project 1A ▇ END

»» GO! With Google

Objective	**Export an Access Table to an Excel Spreadsheet, Open as a Google Sheet, Edit a Record, and Save to Your Computer**

Access web apps are designed to work with Microsoft's **SharePoint**, a service for setting up websites to share and manage documents. Your college may not have SharePoint installed, so you will use other tools to share objects from your database so that you can work collaboratively with others. Recall that Google Drive is Google's free, web-based word processor, spreadsheet, slide show, form, and data storage and sharing service. For Access, you can **export** a database object to an Excel worksheet, a PDF file, or a text file, and then save the file to Google Drive.

ALERT   Working with Web-Based Applications and Services

Computer programs and services on the web receive continuous updates and improvements. Therefore, the steps to complete this web-based Activity may differ from the ones shown. You can often look at the screens and the information presented to determine how to complete the Activity.

If you do not already have a Google account, you will need to create one before you begin this Activity. Go to **http://google.com** and in the upper right corner, click **Sign In**. On the Sign In screen, click **Create Account**. On the Create your Google Account page, complete the form, read and agree to the Terms of Service and Privacy Policy, and then click **Next step**. On the Welcome screen, click **Get Started**.

Activity | Exporting an Access Table to an Excel Spreadsheet, Saving the Spreadsheet to Google Drive, Editing a Record in Google Drive, and Saving to Your Computer

In this Activity, you will export your 1A Faculty Advisors table to an Excel spreadsheet, upload your Excel file to Google Drive as a Google Sheet, edit a record in the Google Sheet, and then download a copy of the edited spreadsheet to your computer.

1 Start Access, navigate to your **Access Chapter 1** folder, and then **Open** your **1A_Advising** database file. If necessary, on the Message Bar, click Enable Content. In the **Navigation Pane**, click your **1A Faculty Advisors** table to select it—do not open it.

2 On the ribbon, click the **External Data tab**, and then in the **Export group**, click **Excel**. In the **Export – Excel Spreadsheet** dialog box, click **Browse**, and then navigate to your **Access Chapter 1** folder. In the **File Save** dialog box, click in the **File name** box, type **Lastname_Firstname_a1A_Web** and then click **Save**.

3 In the **Export – Excel Spreadsheet** dialog box, under **Specify export options**, select the first two check boxes—**Export data with formatting and layout** and **Open the destination file after the export operation is complete**—and then click **OK**. Take a moment to examine the data in the file, and then **Close** Excel. In the **Export – Excel Spreadsheet** dialog box, click **Close**, and then **Close** Access.

4 Open your browser, navigate to **http://drive.google.com**, and sign in to your Google account; if necessary,

create a new Google account and then sign in. On the right side of the screen, click **Settings** ⚙, and then click **Settings**. In the **Settings** dialog box, to the right of *Convert uploads*, if necessary, select the **Convert uploaded files to Google Docs editor format** check box. In the upper right, click **Done**

It is necessary to select this setting; otherwise, your document will upload as a pdf file and cannot be edited without further action.

5 Open your **GO! Web Projects** folder—or create and then open this folder by clicking **New** and then **Folder**. On the left, click **New**, and then click **File upload**. In the **Open** dialog box, navigate to your **Access Chapter 1** folder, and then double-click your **a1A_Web** Excel file to upload it to Google Drive. When the message *1 upload complete* displays, **Close** the message box.

6 Double-click your **Lastname_Firstname_a1A_Web** file to display the file, and then compare your screen with Figure A. The worksheet displays column letters, row numbers, and data.

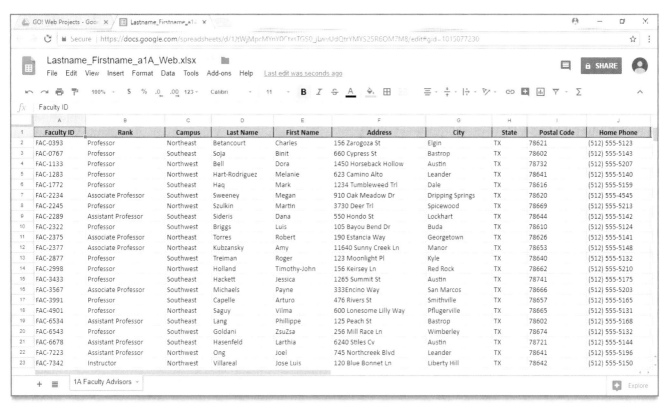

Figure A

7 Click in cell **C2** and replace the current Campus with **Southwest** Click in cell **D2** and replace Betancourt with your last name. Press [Tab] and then replace Charles with your first name.

8 Above row **1** and to the left of column **A**, click **Select All** [____]. On the menu bar, click **Format**, and then click **Clear formatting** so that the default font is applied to all data; the cell borders are removed, and the formatting of the field names are removed.

9 In the column headings row, click **I** to select the entire column. On the menu bar, click **Format**, point to **Number**, and then click **Plain text** to format every number in the columns as text. Click in cell **A1** to deselect the column.

Recall that in Access, numbers that are not used in calculations should be formatted as Short Text. Because the formatting is cleared, you can enter new records into the spreadsheet in the same format as the existing records.

10 Click **File** to display the menu, point to **Download as**, and then click **Microsoft Excel (.xlsx)**. Click **Enable Content**. Click **File**, and then click **Save As**. In the **Save As** dialog box, navigate to your **Access Chapter 1** folder, click in the **File name** box, and type **Lastname_ Firstname_a1A_Web_Download** and then click **Save**. **Close** the message box.

NOTE Saving the Downloaded File to the Access Chapter 1 Folder

Depending on the browser you are using, you may need to open the file in Excel and then save the a1A_Web_Download worksheet to your Access Chapter 1 folder.

11 In Google Drive, at the top right corner of your screen, click your user name, and then click **Sign out**. **Close** your browser window.

12 Start Excel. In the Excel opening screen, click **Open Other Workbooks**, and then click **Browse**. Navigate to your **Access Chapter 1** folder, and then double-click your **a1A_Web** Excel file. Notice that this file is the original file—the record is not edited. If you

are required to print your documents, use one of the methods in the following Note. **Close** your Excel file; and, if prompted, save the changes to your worksheet. Then **Open** and print your **a1A_Web_Download** Excel file using one of the methods in the following Note. **Close** Excel; and, if prompted, save the changes to your worksheet. As directed by your instructor, submit your two workbooks and the two paper printouts or PDF electronic images that are the results of this project.

NOTE **Adding the File Name to the Footer and Printing or Creating an PDF Electronic Image of an Excel Spreadsheet on One Page**

Click the File tab, click Print, and then click Page Setup. In the Page Setup dialog box, on the Page tab, under Orientation, click Landscape. Under Scaling, click the Fit to option button. In the Page Setup dialog box, click the Header/Footer tab, and then click Custom Footer. With the insertion point blinking in the Left section box, click the Insert File Name button, and then click OK. In the Page Setup dialog box, click OK.

To print on paper, click Print. To create an electronic file of your printout, on the left side of your screen, click Export. Under Export, be sure Create PDF/XPS Document is selected, and then click Create PDF/XPS. Navigate to your Access Chapter 1 folder, and then click Publish to save the file with the default name and an extension of pdf.

Student Workshops Database

Project Activities

In Activities 1.18 through 1.24, you will assist Dr. Miriam Yong, Director of Student Activities, in creating a database to store information about student workshops held at Texas Lakes Community College campuses. You will use a database template that tracks event information, add workshop information to the database, and then print the results. Your completed Navigation Pane will look similar to Figure 1.37.

Project Files for MyLab IT Grader

1. In your **MyLab IT** course, locate and click **Access 1B Student Workshops**, Download Materials, and then Download All Files. Close the Grader download screens.
2. Extract the zipped folder to your Access Chapter 1 folder.
3. Take a moment to open the downloaded **Access_1B_Student_Workshops_Instructions**; note any recent updates to the book.

Project Results

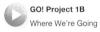

GO! Project 1B
Where We're Going

Figure 1.37
Project 1B Student Workshops

For Non-MyLab Submissions
For Project 1B, you will need the following files:
a01B_Event_Template
a01B_Workshops (Excel workbook)

Start with an Access Data File
In your Access Chapter 1 folder, save your workbook as:
Lastname_Firstname_1B_Student_Workshops

After you have saved your database, open it to launch Access. On the next page, begin with Activity 1.19.

GO! Learn How
Video A1-6

A database template contains prebuilt tables, queries, forms, and reports that perform a specific task, such as tracking events. For example, your college may hold events such as athletic contests, plays, lectures, concerts, and club meetings. Using a predefined template, your college's Activities Director can quickly create a database to manage these events. The advantage of using a template to start a new database is that you do not have to create the objects—all you need to do is enter the data and modify the prebuilt objects to suit your needs.

The purpose of the database in this project is to track the student workshops that are held by Texas Lakes Community College. The questions to be answered might include:

- What workshops will be offered and when will they be offered?
- In what rooms and on what campuses will the workshops be held?
- Which workshop locations have a computer projector for PowerPoint presentations?

Activity 1.18 | Using a Template to Create a Database

ALERT   Because Office 365 is a cloud-based subscription service that receives continuous updates, you may encounter some variations in what appears on your screen and what is shown in this instruction. Microsoft Office 365 is fully installed on your PC or Mac; no internet access is necessary to create or edit documents. When you *are* connected to the internet, you will receive monthly upgrades and new features, so you always have the latest versions of Office apps as soon as they are available. Your subscription gives you continuous free access to the latest innovations and refinements.

These templates can be used to create databases that will be stored on your desktop. Because the templates available change so often, in this activity, you will use a previously saved template to create your database.

1 Start Access. In the Access opening screen, scroll down to display an **Inventory** template and a **Nutrition tracking** template. Compare your screen with Figure 1.38.

These templates are included with the Access program. To create a database to manage inventory on your desktop, select the *Inventory* template; to manage what you eat, select the *Nutrition tracking* template.

You can search the Microsoft Office website for more templates. You can also click on a category under the search box, where templates will be suggested.

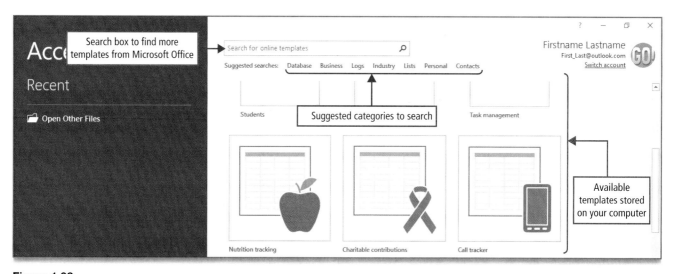

Figure 1.38

> **2** On the left, click **Open Other Files**, and then click **Browse**. Navigate to your **Access Chapter 1 folder**, and then double-click the Access file that you downloaded from **MyLab IT** that displays your name—**Student_Access_1B_Student_Workshops**. If necessary, at the top click **Enable Content**.

Activity 1.19 | Building a Table by Entering Records in a Multiple-Items Form and a Single-Record Form

2.3.1

One purpose of a form is to simplify the entry of data into a table—either for you or for others who enter data. In Project 1A, you created a simple form that enabled you to display or enter records in a table one record at a time. The Desktop Event management template creates a *multiple-items form* that enables you to display or enter *multiple* records in a table, but with an easier and simplified layout rather than typing directly into the table itself. The form opens when the database opens.

> **1** In the new record row, click in the **Title** field. Type **Your Online Reputation** and then press Tab. In the **Start Time** field, type **3/9/23 7p** and then press Tab.

> Access formats the date and time. As you enter dates and times, a small calendar displays to the right of the field. You can use the calendar to select a date instead of typing it.

> **2** In the **End Time** field, type **3/9/23 9p** and then press Tab. In the **Description** field, type **Internet Safety** and then press Tab. In the **Location** field, type **Northeast Campus** and then press Tab three times to move to the **Title** field in the new record row. Compare your screen with Figure 1.39.

> Because the workshops have no unique value, Access uses the AutoNumber data type in the ID field to assign a unique, sequential number to each record.

Figure 1.39

3 In the form, directly above the field names row, click **New Event**.

> A *single-record form* with the name *Event Details* displays, similar to the simple form you created in Project 1A. A single-record form enables you to display or enter one record at a time into a table.

4 Using Tab to move from field to field, enter the following record in the **Event Details** form—press Tab two times to move from the **Title** field to the **Description** field, and then click the **Location** field. Then compare your screen with Figure 1.40.

Title	Description	Location	Start Time	End Time
Writing a Research Paper	Computer Skills	Southwest Campus	3/10/23 4p	3/10/23 6p

Figure 1.40

5 In the **Event Details** single-record form, in the Menu bar, click **Close**, and notice that the new record displays in the multiple-items form—*Event List*.

6 Enter the following records by using either the **Event List** form—the multiple-items form—or the **Event Details** form—the single-record form that is accessed by clicking the *New Event* command on the Event List form. Be sure the multiple-items form displays, and then compare your screen with Figure 1.41.

ID	Title	Start Time	End Time	Description	Location
3	**Resume Writing**	**3/18/23 2p**	**3/18/23 4p**	**Job Skills**	**Northwest Campus**
4	**Careers in the Legal Profession**	**3/19/23 2p**	**3/19/23 4p**	**Careers**	**Southeast Campus**

Figure 1.41

7 In the object window, click **Close** [×] to close the **Event List** form.

Activity 1.20 | Appending Records by Importing from an Excel Spreadsheet

MOS
2.1.1

In this Activity, you will append records to the table storing the data that displays in the Events List form. You will import the records from an Excel spreadsheet.

1 On the ribbon, click the **External Data tab**. In the **Import & Link group**, click **New Data Source**, point to **From File**, and then click **Excel**.

2 In the **Get External Data – Excel Spreadsheet** dialog box, click **Browse**. Navigate to the location where your student data files are stored, and then double-click **a01B_Workshops**.

3 Click the second option button—**Append a copy of the records to the table:**—and then click **OK**.

The table that stores the data is named *Events*. Recall that other objects, such as forms, queries, and reports, display data from tables; so the Event Details form displays data that is stored in the Events table.

4 In the **Import Spreadsheet Wizard**, click **Next**, and then click **Finish**. In the **Get External Data – Excel Spreadsheet** dialog box, click **Close**.

5 ▶ Double-click **Event List** to open the form that displays data from the Events table, and then **Close** [«] the **Navigation Pane**. Compare your screen with Figure 1.42.

A total of 12 records display; you entered four records, and you appended eight records from the a01B_Workshops Excel workbook. The data displays truncated in several fields because the columns are not wide enough to display all of the data.

Figure 1.42

6 ▶ To the left of the **ID** field name, click **Select All** [ ] to select all of the columns and rows.

7 ▶ In the field names row, point to the right edge of any of the selected columns to display the [+] pointer, and then double-click to apply Best Fit to all of the columns. Click in any field to cancel the selection, and then **Save** [ ] the form.

Objective 7   Organize Objects in the Navigation Pane

GO! Learn How
Video A1-7

Use the Navigation Pane to open objects, organize database objects, and perform common tasks, such as renaming an object or deleting an object.

Activity 1.21 | Grouping Database Objects in the Navigation Pane

1.1.3

The Navigation Pane groups and displays your database objects and can do so in predefined arrangements. In this Activity, you will group your database objects using the *Tables and Related Views* category, which groups objects by the table to which the objects are related. This grouping is useful because you can determine easily the table that is the data source of queries, forms, and reports.

1 ▶ **Open** 〉〉 the **Navigation Pane**. At the top of the **Navigation Pane**, click **More** ⊙. On the list, under **Navigate To Category**, click **Tables and Related Views**. Compare your screen with Figure 1.43.

In the Navigation Pane, you can see the number of objects that are included in the Desktop Events Management template, including the table named *Events*. Other objects in the database that display data from the Events table include one query, two forms, and five reports. In the Navigation Pane, the Event List form is selected because it is open in the object window and is the active object.

Other objects might display on the Navigation Pane; for example, Filters and Unrelated Objects. These filters are objects created for use by the Desktop Event management template.

Figure 1.43

2 ▶ In the **Navigation Pane**, point to **Events: Table**, right-click, and then click **Open** to display the records in the underlying table.

The Events table is the active object in the object window. Use the Navigation Pane to open objects for use. The 12 records that display in the Event List multiple-items form are stored in this table. Recall that tables are the foundation of your database because your data must be stored in a table. You can enter records directly into a table or you can use a form to enter records.

🔄 **ANOTHER WAY**   Double-click the table name to open it in the object window.

3 ▶ In the object window, click the **Event List tab** to display the form as the active object in the object window.

Recall that a form presents a more user-friendly screen for entering records into a table.

4 In the **Navigation Pane**, double-click the **Current Events** *report* (green icon) to open the report. Compare your screen with Figure 1.44.

> An advantage of using a template to create a database is that many objects, such as reports, are already designed for you.

Figure 1.44

5 In the object window, **Close** ☒ the **Current Events** report.

6 By double-clicking or right-clicking, from the **Navigation Pane**, open the **Events by Week** report.

> In this predesigned report, the events are displayed by week. After entering records in the form or table, the preformatted reports are updated with the records from the table.

7 In the object window, right-click any one of the **object tabs**, and then click **Close All** to close all of the objects. **Close** ☒ the **Navigation Pane**.

Objective 8 Create a New Table in a Database Created with a Template

GO! Learn How
Video A1-8

The Desktop Event management template included only one table—the *Events* table. It is easy to start a database with a template, and then you can add additional objects as needed.

Activity 1.22 | Using the Table Tool to Create a New Table

2.4.1, 2.4.5

Dr. Yong has information about the various locations where workshops are held. For example, on the Northeast Campus, she has information about the room, seating arrangements, number of seats, and multimedia equipment. In the Events table, workshops are scheduled in rooms at each of the four campuses. It would not make sense to store information about the campus rooms multiple times in the same table. It is *not* considered good database design to have duplicate information in a table.

When data becomes redundant, it is usually an indication that you need a new table to contain that information. In this Activity, you will create a table to track the workshop locations, the equipment, and the seating arrangements in each location.

1 On the ribbon, click the **Create tab**, and then in the **Tables group**, click **Table**.

2 In the field names row, click **Click to Add**, click **Short Text**, type **Campus/Location** and then press Enter.

3 In the third column, click **Short Text**, type **Room** and then press Enter. In the fourth column, click **Number**, type **Seats** and then press Enter.

> The *Number data type* describes numbers that represent a quantity and may be used in calculations. For the Seats field, you may need to determine how many seats remain after reservations are booked for a room. In the new record row, a *0* displays in the field.

4 In the fifth column, type **t** to select *Short Text*, type **Room Arrangement** and then press Enter. In the sixth column, type **t** and then type **Equipment** On your keyboard, press ↓.

> With the data type list displayed, you can select the data type by either clicking it or typing the letter that is underscored for the data type.

> This table has six fields. Access automatically creates the first field in the table—the ID field—to ensure that every record has a unique value. Before naming each field, you must define the data type for the field.

5 Right-click the **ID** field name, and then click **Rename Field**. Type **Room ID** and then press Enter. On the **Fields tab**, in the **Formatting group**, click the **Data Type arrow**, and then click **Short Text**. On the ribbon, in the **Field Validation group**, notice that **Unique** is selected.

> Recall that, by default, Access creates the ID field with the AutoNumber data type so that the field can be used as the primary key. Here, this field will store a unique room ID that is a combination of letters, symbols, and numbers; therefore, it is appropriate to change the data type to Short Text. In Datasheet view, the primary key field is identified by the selection of the Unique check box.

MORE KNOWLEDGE **Create a Table from a Template with Application Parts**

To create a table using the Application parts gallery, click the Create tab, and in the Templates group, click Application Parts. Under Quick Start, click Comments. In the Create Relationships dialog box, specify a relationship between the Comments table and an associated table, click Next to choose the lookup column, and then click Create to create the table. If you choose No relationship, click Create to create the table. The Comments table displays in the Navigation Pane.

Activity 1.23 │ Entering Records Into a New Table

1 In the new record row, click in the **Room ID** field. Enter the following record, pressing Enter or Tab to move from one field to the next. Do not be concerned that all of your text does not display; you will adjust the column widths later. After entering the record, compare your screen with Figure 1.45.

> Recall that Access saves a record when you move to another row within the table. You can press either Enter or Tab to move between fields in a table.

Room ID	Campus/ Location	Room	Seats	Room Arrangement	Equipment
NE-01	**Northeast Campus**	**H265**	**150**	**Theater**	**Computer Projector, Surround Sound, Microphone**

Figure 1.45

2 In the **Views group**, click the top of the **View** button to switch to **Design** view. In the **Save As** dialog box, in the **Table Name** box, using your own name, type **1B Workshop Locations** and then click **OK**.

> Recall that when you switch views or when you close a table, Access prompts you to save the table if you have not previously saved it.

ANOTHER WAY On the right side of the status bar, click Design View ⬚ to switch to Design view.

> **3** In the **Field Name** column, to the left of **Room ID**, notice the key icon.
>
> In Design view, the key icon indicates that the field—Room ID—is the primary key field.
>
> **4** In the **Views group**, click the top of the **View** button to switch back to **Datasheet** view.

ANOTHER WAY On the right side of the status bar, click Datasheet View ⬚ to switch to Datasheet view.

> **5** In the new record row, click in the **Room ID** field. Enter the following records, pressing Enter or Tab to move from one field to the next.

Room ID	Campus/Location	Room	Seats	Room Arrangement	Equipment
SW-01	Southwest Campus	A15	35	Lecture Classroom	Computer Projector
NW-01	Northwest Campus	C202	50	Lecture Classroom	Smart Board
SE-01	Southeast Campus	D148	20	U-shaped	White Board
NE-02	Northeast Campus	B105	25	U-shaped	25 Computers, Projector

> **6** To the left of the **Room ID** field name, click **Select All** ⬚ to select all of the columns and rows in the table. On the **Home tab**, in the **Records group,** click **More**, and then click **Field Width**. In the **Column Width** dialog box, click **Best Fit** to display all of the data in each column. Click in any field to cancel the selection, and then **Save** 🖫 the changes to the table. In the object window, **Close** × your **1B Workshop Locations** table.
>
> **7** Open » the **Navigation Pane** and notice that your new table displays in its own group. Point to the right edge of the **Navigation Pane** to display the ⬚ pointer. Drag to the right to increase the width of the **Navigation Pane** so that your entire table name displays. Compare your screen with Figure 1.46.
>
> Recall that organizing the Navigation Pane by Tables and Related Views groups the objects by each table and displays the related objects under each table name.

Figure 1.46

Objective 9 View a Report

GO! Learn How
Video A1-9

Recall that one advantage to starting a new database with a template, instead of from a blank database, is that many report objects are already created for you.

Activity 1.24 | Viewing a Report

MOS
5.1.3

1 ▶ In the **Navigation Pane**, double-click the report (not the form) name **Event Details** to open it in the object window.

This prebuilt Event Details report displays in an attractively arranged format.

2 ▶ **Close** ⌧ the **Event Details** report. Open the **All Events** report, and then **Close** ⌧ the **Navigation Pane**. On the **Home** tab, in the **Views group**, click the top of the **View** button to switch to **Layout** view.

Recall that Layout view enables you to make changes to an object while viewing the data in the fields. Each prebuilt report displays the records in the table in different useful formats.

ANOTHER WAY On the right side of the status bar, click Layout View ▤ to switch to Layout view.

3 ▶ At the top of the report, click the title—*All Events*—to display a colored border around the title. Click to the left of the letter *A* to place the insertion point there. Type **1B** and then press Spacebar. Press Enter, and then **Save** ⌧ the report.

4 ▶ **Close** ⌧ your **1B All Events** report. For the convenience of the next individual opening the database, **Open** ⌧ the **Navigation Pane**.

Notice the report name *All Events* did not change in the Navigation Pane. You changed the title of the report as it would print.

5 ▶ On the right side of the title bar, click **Close** ⌧ to close the database and to close Access.

For Non-MyLab Submissions : Determine What Your Instructor Requires for Submission
As directed by your instructor, submit your completed database file.

---

6 ▶ In **MyLab IT**, locate and click the Grader Project **Access 1B Student Workshops**. In **step 3**, under **Upload Completed Assignment**, click **Choose File**. In the **Open** dialog box, navigate to your **Access Chapter 1 folder**, and then click your **Student_Access_1B_Student_Workshops** file one time to select it. In the lower right corner of the **Open** dialog box, click **Open**.

The name of your selected file displays above the Upload button.

7 ▶ To submit your file to **MyLab IT** for grading, click **Upload**, wait a moment for a green **Success!** message, and then in **step 4**, click the blue **Submit for Grading** button. Click **Close Assignment** to return to your list of **Course Materials**.

You have completed Project 1B ▪ **END**

»» GO! With Google

Access web apps are designed to work with Microsoft's SharePoint, a service for setting up websites to share and manage documents. Your college may not have SharePoint installed, so you will use other tools to share objects from your database so that you can work collaboratively with others. Recall that Google Drive is Google's free, web-based word processor, spreadsheet, slide show, form, and data storage and sharing service. For Access, you can export a database object to an Excel worksheet, a PDF file, or a text file, and then save the file to Google Drive.

ALERT **Working with Web-Based Applications and Services**

Computer programs and services on the web receive continuous updates and improvements. Therefore, the steps to complete this web-based Activity may differ from the ones shown. You can often look at the screens and the information presented to determine how to complete the Activity.

Activity | Exporting an Access Table to a Word Document, Saving the Document to Google Drive, Adding a Record in Google Drive, and Saving to Your Computer

In this activity, you will export your 1B Workshop Locations table to a Word document, upload your Word file to Google Drive as a Google Doc, add a record in Google Drive, and then download a copy of the edited document to your computer.

1 Start Access, navigate to your **Access Chapter 1** folder, and then **Open** your **1B_Student_Workshops** database file. If necessary, on the Message Bar, click Enable Content, and then **Close** the **Event List** form. In the **Navigation Pane**, click your **1B Workshop Locations** table to select it—do not open it.

2 On the ribbon, click the **External Data tab**. In the **Export group**, click **More**, and then click **Word**. In the **Export – RTF File** dialog box, click **Browse**, and then navigate to your **Access Chapter 1** folder. In the **File Save** dialog box, click in the **File name** box, using your own name, type **Lastname_Firstname_a1B_Web** and then click **Save**.

3 In the **Export – RTF File** dialog box, under **Specify export options**, select the second check box—**Open the destination file after the export operation is complete**—and then click **OK**. Take a moment to examine the data in the file.

Notice that the table is too wide to display fully with Portrait orientation.

4 **Close** Word. In the **Export – RTF File** dialog box, click **Close**, and then **Close** Access.

5 Open your browser, navigate to **http://drive.google .com**, and sign in to your Google account; if necessary, create a new Google account and then sign in. On the right side of the screen, click **Settings** ⚙, and then click **Settings**. In the **Settings** dialog box, to the right of *Convert uploads*, if necessary, select the **Convert uploaded files to Google Docs editor format** check box. In the upper right, click **Done**

It is necessary to select this setting; otherwise, your document will upload as a pdf file and cannot be edited without further action.

6 Open your **GO! Web Projects** folder—or create and then open this folder by clicking **New** and then clicking **New folder**. On the left, click **New**, and then click **File upload**. In the **Choose File to Upload** dialog box, navigate to your **Access Chapter 1** folder, and then double-click your **a1B_Web** Word file to upload it to Google Drive. When the title bar of the message box indicates *1 upload complete*, **Close** the message box.

7 Double-click your **a1B_Web** file to open the file in Google Docs. Notice that the table is not fully displayed on the page, and compare your screen with Figure A.

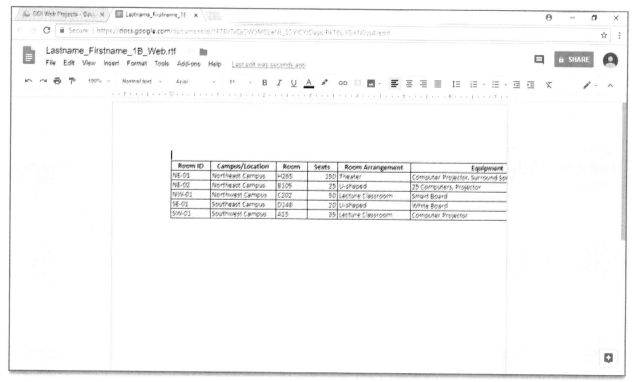

Figure A

8 Click **File** to display a menu, and then click **Page setup**. In the **Page setup** dialog box, under **Orientation**, click **Landscape**. Click **OK**.

The table displays fully with Landscape orientation.

Field	Room ID	Campus/Location	Room	Seats	Room Arrangement	Equipment
	SE-02	**Southeast Campus**	**D120**	**20**	**Testing Lab**	**20 Computers**

9 Click in the last cell in the table, and press Tab. Add the following record.

10 On the menu, click **File**, point to **Download as**, and then click **Microsoft Word (.docx)**. In the message box—usually displays at the bottom of your screen—click the **Save arrow**, and then click **Save as**. In the **Save As** dialog box, navigate to your **Access Chapter 1** folder, click in the **File name** box, and type Lastname_Firstname_a1B_Web_Download and then click **Save**. If necessary, click OK to upgrade to the newest file format.

11 In Google Drive, at the top right corner of your screen, click your user name, and then click **Sign out**. **Close** your browser window.

12 Start Word. In the Word opening screen, click **Open**. Under **Open**, click **Browse**. Navigate to your **Access Chapter 1** folder, and then double-click your **a1B_Web** Word file. Notice that this file is the original file—the new record is not entered. If you are required to print your documents, use one of the methods in following Note. **Close** your Word file; and, if prompted, save the changes to your document. Then **Open** and print your **a1B_Web_Download** Word file using one of the methods in the following Note. **Close** Word; and, if prompted, save the changes to your document. As directed by your instructor, submit your two documents and the two paper printouts or PDF electronic images that are the results of this project.

NOTE   Adding the File Name to the Footer and Printing or Creating a PDF Electronic Image

Click the Insert tab. In the Header & Footer group, click Footer, and then click Blank. With Type here selected, in the Insert group, click Document Info, and then click File Name. Close the Footer window. Click the Layout tab. In the Page Setup group, click Orientation, and then click Landscape.

To print on paper, click File, and then click Print. To create a pdf electronic image of your printout, click File, and then click Export. Under Export, be sure Create PDF/XPS Document is selected, and then click Create PDF/XPS. Navigate to your Access Chapter 1 folder, and then click Publish to save the file with the default name and an extension of pdf.

››› GO! To Work

wavebreakmedia/Shutterstock, Monkey Business Images/Fotolia, Ivanko80/Shutterstock, Monkey Business Images/Shutterstock

Microsoft Office Specialist (MOS) Skills in This Chapter

Project 1A	Project 1B
1.1.1 Import objects or data from other sources	**1.1.3** Hide and display objects in the Navigation Par
1.1.2 Delete database objects	**2.1.1** Import data into tables
1.3.1 Configure print options for records, forms, and reports	**5.1.3** Add and modify labels on reports
2.1.1 Import data into tables	
2.2.3 Add table descriptions	
2.4.1 Add or remove fields	
2.4.3 Change field captions	
2.4.4 Change field sizes	
2.4.5 Change field data types	
2.4.6 Configure fields to auto-increment	
3.1.7 Run queries	
4.1.1 Add, move and remove form controls	
5.1.2 Add report controls	
5.1.3 Add and modify labels on reports	
5.2.3 Format report elements	

Build Your E-Portfolio

An E-Portfolio is a collection of evidence, stored electronically, that showcases what you have accomplished while completing your education. Collecting and then sharing your work products with potential employers reflects your academic and career goals. Your completed documents from the following projects are good examples to show what you have learned: 1G, 1K, and 1L.

GO! For Job Success

Video: Customer Service

Your instructor may assign this video to your class, and then ask you to think about, or discuss with your classmates, these questions:

g-stockstudio/Shutterstock

How did Lee's responses demonstrate both good and bad customer service skills?

How well did Christine, the supervisor, handle Karen's situation? Provide specific examples.

Based on this call, what can SunTel Systems do to provide a better customer service experience? Provide two examples.

End of Chapter

Summary

Principles of good database design, also known as normalization, help ensure that the data in your database is accurate and organized in a way that you can retrieve information that is useful.

You can create databases from scratch by using the blank desktop database template or a custom web app or by using a template that contains prebuilt tables, queries, forms, reports, and other objects.

Tables are the foundation of a database, but before entering records in a table, you must define the data type and name the field. Common data types are Short Text, Number, Currency, and Date/Time.

Use forms to enter data into a table or view the data in a table. Use queries to retrieve information from tables. Reports display information from tables in a professional-looking format.

GO! Learn It Online

Review the concepts, key terms, and MOS skills in this chapter by completing these online challenges, which you can find at **MyLab IT**.

Chapter Quiz: Answer matching and multiple-choice questions to test what you learned in this chapter.

Lessons on the GO!: Learn how to use all the new apps and features as they are introduced by Microsoft.

MOS Prep Quiz: Answer questions to review the MOS skills that you practiced in this chapter.

GO! Collaborative Team Project (Available in Instructor Resource Center)

If your instructor assigns this project to your class, you can expect to work with one or more of your classmates—either in person or by using Internet tools—to create work products similar to those that you created in this chapter. A team is a group of workers who work together to solve a problem, make a decision, or create a work product. Collaboration is when you work together with others as a team in an intellectual endeavor to complete a shared task or achieve a shared goal.

Monkey Business Images/ Fotolia

Project Guide for Access Chapter 1

Your instructor will assign Projects from this list to ensure your learning and assess your knowledge.

Project	Apply Skills from These Chapter Objectives	Project Type		Project Location
1A MyLab IT	Objectives 1–5 from Project 1A	**1A Instructional Project (Grader Project)** A guided review of the skills from Project 1A.	Instruction	In **MyLab IT** and in text
1B MyLab IT	Objectives 6–9 from Project 1B	**1B Instructional Project (Grader Project)** A guided review of the skills from Project 1B.	Instruction	In **MyLab IT** and in text
1C	Objectives 1–5 from Project 1A	**1C Chapter Review (Scorecard Grading)** A guided review of the skills from Project 1A.	Review	In text
1D	Objectives 6–9 from Project 1B	**1D Chapter Review (Scorecard Grading** A guided review of the skills from Project 1B.	Review	In text
1E MyLab IT	Objectives 1–5 from Project 1A	**1E Mastery (Grader Project)** A demonstration of your mastery of the skills in Project 1A with extensive decision-making.	Mastery and Transfer of Learning	In **MyLab IT** and in text
1F MyLab IT	Objectives 6–9 from Project 1B	**1F Mastery (Grader Project)** A demonstration of your mastery of the skills in Project 1B with extensive decision-making.	Mastery and Transfer of Learning	In **MyLab IT** and in text
1G MyLab IT	Combination of Objectives from Projects 1A and 1B	**1G Mastery (Grader Project)** A demonstration of your mastery of the skills in Projects 1A and 1B with extensive decision-making.	Mastery and Transfer of Learning	In **MyLab IT** and in text
1H	Combination of Objectives from Projects 1A and 1B	**1H GO! Fix It (Scorecard Grading)** A demonstration of your mastery of the skills in Projects 1A and 1B by creating a correct result from a document that contains errors you must find.	Critical Thinking	IRC
1I	Combination of Objectives from Projects 1A and 1B	**1I GO! Make It (Scorecard Grading)** A demonstration of your mastery of the skills in Projects 1A and 1B by creating a result from a supplied picture.	Critical Thinking	IRC
1J	Combination of Objectives from Projects 1A and 1B	**1J GO! Solve It (Rubric Grading)** A demonstration of your mastery of the skills in Projects 1A and 1B, your decision-making skills, and your critical thinking skills. A task-specific rubric helps you self-assess your result.	Critical Thinking	IRC
1K	Combination of Objectives from Projects 1A and 1B	**1K GO! Solve It (Rubric Grading)** A demonstration of your mastery of the skills in Projects 1A and 1B, your decision-making skills, and your critical thinking skills. A task-specific rubric helps you self-assess your result.	Critical Thinking	In text
1L	Combination of Objectives from Projects 1A and 1B	**1L GO! Think (Rubric Grading)** A demonstration of your understanding of the Chapter concepts applied in a manner that you would outside of college. An analytic rubric helps you and your instructor grade the quality of your work by comparing it to the work an expert in the discipline would create.	Critical Thinking	In text
1M	Combination of Objectives from Projects 1A and 1B	**1M GO! Think (Rubric Grading)** A demonstration of your understanding of the Chapter concepts applied in a manner that you would outside of college. An analytic rubric helps you and your instructor grade the quality of your work by comparing it to the work an expert in the discipline would create.	Critical Thinking	IRC
1N	Combination of Objectives from Projects 1A and 1B	**1N You and GO! (Rubric Grading)** A demonstration of your understanding of the Chapter concepts applied in a manner that you would in a personal situation. An analytic rubric helps you and your instructor grade the quality of your work.	Critical Thinking	IRC
1O	Combination of Objectives from Projects 1A and 1B	**1O Cumulative Team Project for Access Chapter 1** A demonstration of your understanding of concepts and your ability to work collaboratively in a group role-playing assessment, requiring both collaboration and self-management.		IRC

Glossary

Glossary of Chapter Key Terms

Append To add on to the end of an object; for example, to add records to the end of an existing table.

AutoNumber data type A data type that describes a unique sequential or random number assigned by Access as each record is entered and that is useful for data that has no distinct field that can be considered unique.

Best Fit An Access command that adjusts the width of a column to accommodate the column's longest entry.

Blank desktop database A database that has no data and has no database tools—you must create the data and tools as you need them; the database is stored on your computer or other storage device.

Caption A property setting that displays a name for a field in a table, query, form, or report different from the one listed as the field name.

Common field A field included in two or more tables that stores the same data.

Currency data type An Access data type that describes monetary values and numeric data that can be used in mathematical calculations involving values with one to four decimal places.

Custom web app A database that you can publish and share with others over the Internet.

Data Facts about people, events, things, or ideas.

Data source The table or tables from which a query, form, or reports gathers its data.

Data type Classification identifying the kind of data that can be stored in a field, such as numbers, text, or dates.

Database An organized collection of facts about people, events, things, or ideas related to a specific topic or purpose.

Database management system (DBMS) Database software that controls how related collections of data are stored, organized, retrieved, and secured; also known as a DBMS.

Database template A preformatted database that contains prebuilt tables, queries, forms, and reports that perform a specific task, such as tracking events.

Datasheet view The Access view that displays data organized in columns and rows similar to an Excel worksheet.

DBMS An acronym for database management system.

Design view An Access view that displays the detailed structure of a table, query, form, or report. For forms and reports, may be the view in which some tasks must be performed, and only the controls, and not the data, display in this view.

Destination table The table to which you import or append data.

Export The process of copying data from one file into another file, such as an Access table into an Excel spreadsheet.

Field A single piece of information that is stored in every record; represented by a column in a database table.

Field properties Characteristics of a field that control how the field displays and how data can be entered in the field; vary for different data types.

First principle of good database design A principle of good database design stating that data is organized in tables so that there is no redundant data.

Flat database A simple database file that is not related or linked to any other collection of data.

Form An Access object you can use to enter new records into a table, edit or delete existing records in a table, or display existing records.

Form view The Access view in which you can view records, but you cannot change the layout or design of the form.

Import The process of copying data from another file, such as a Word table or an Excel workbook, into a separate file, such as an Access database.

Information Data that is accurate, timely, and organized in a useful manner.

Layout view The Access view in which you can make changes to a form or report while the data from the underlying data source displays.

Link A connection to data in another file.

Multiple-items form A form that enables you to display or enter multiple records in a table.

Navigation area An area at the bottom of the Access window that indicates the number of records in the table and contains controls in the form of arrows that you click to move among the records.

Navigation Pane An area of the Access window that displays and organizes the names of the objects in a database; from here, you open objects for use.

Normalization The process of applying design rules and principles to ensure that your database performs as expected.

Number data type An Access data type that represents a quantity, how much or how many, and may be used in calculations.

Object tab In the object window, a tab that identifies the object and which enables you to make an open object active.

Object window An area of the Access window that displays open objects, such as tables, queries, forms, or reports; by default, each object displays on its own tab.

Objects The basic parts of a database that you create to store your data and to work with your data; for example, tables, queries, forms, and reports.

Populate The action of filling a database table with records.

Primary key A required field that uniquely identifies a record in a table; for example, a Student ID number at a college.

Property Sheet A list of characteristics—properties—for fields or controls on a form or report in which you can make precise changes to each property associated with the field or control.

Query A database object that retrieves specific data from one or more database objects—either tables or other queries—and then, in a single datasheet, displays only the data you specify.

Record All of the categories of data pertaining to one person, place, event, thing, or idea; represented by a row in a database table.

Record selector bar The bar at the left edge of a record when it is displayed in a form, and which is used to select an entire record.

Record selector box The small box at the left of a record in Datasheet view that, when clicked, selects the entire record.

Redundant In a database, information that is duplicated in a manner that indicates poor database design.

Relational database A sophisticated type of database that has multiple collections of data within the file that are related to one another.

Report A database object that summarizes the fields and records from a table or query in an easy-to-read format suitable for printing.

Glossary

Run The process in which Access searches the records in the table(s) included in the query design, finds the records that match the specified criteria, and then displays the records in a datasheet; only the fields that have been included in the query design display.

Second principle of good database design A principle stating that appropriate database techniques are used to ensure the accuracy and consistency of data as it is entered into the table.

Select query A type of Access query that retrieves (selects) data from one or more tables or queries, displaying the selected data in a datasheet; also known as a simple select query.

SharePoint A Microsoft application used for setting up web sites to share and manage documents.

Short Text data type An Access data type that describes text, a combination of text and numbers, or numbers that are not used in calculations, such as the Postal Code.

Simple select query Another name for a select query.

Single-record form A form that enables you to display or enter one record at a time from a table.

Source file When importing a file, refers to the file being imported.

Structure In Access, the underlying design of a table, including field names, data types, descriptions, and field properties.

Table A format for information that organizes and presents text and data in columns and rows; the foundation of a database.

Tables and Related Views An arrangement in the Navigation Pane that groups objects by the table to which they are related.

Truncated Data that is cut off or shortened because the field or column is not wide enough to display all of the data or the field size is too small to contain all of the data.

Wizard A feature in Microsoft Office that walks you step by step through a process.

Chapter Review

Skills Review | Project 1C College Administrators

Apply 1A skills from these Objectives:

Apply 1A skills from these Objectives:

1. Identify Good Database Design
2. Create a Table and Define Fields in a Blank Desktop Database
3. Change the Structure of Tables and Add a Second Table
4. Create a Query, Form, and Report
5. Close a Database and Close Access

In the following Skills Review, you will create a database to store information about the administrators of Texas Lakes Community College and their departments. Your completed Navigation Pane will look similar to Figure 1.47.

Project Files

For Project 1C, you will need the following files:

Blank database
a01C_Administrators (Excel workbook)
a01C_Departments (Excel workbook)

You will save your database as:

Lastname_Firstname_1C_College_Administrators

Project Results

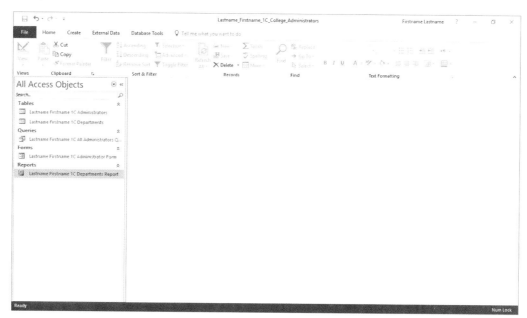

Figure 1.47

(continues on next page)

Chapter Review

1 ▶ Start Access. In the Access opening screen, click **Blank database**. In the **Blank database** dialog box, to the right of the **File Name** box, click **Browse**. In the **File New Database** dialog box, navigate to your **Access Chapter 1** folder. In the **File New Database** dialog box, click in the **File name** box, type **Lastname_Firstname_1C_College_Administrators** and then press Enter. In the **Blank database** dialog box, click **Create**.

a. **Close** the **Navigation Pane**. In the field names row, click in the text *Click to Add*, and then click **Short Text**. Type **Title** and then press Enter.

b. In the third field name box, click **Short Text**, type **Last Name** and then press Enter. In the fourth field name box, click **Short Text**, type **First Name** and then press Enter. Create the remaining fields shown in Table 1, pressing Enter after the last field name. All of the data is typed on one line.

Table 1

Data Type		Short Text	Short Text	Short Text	Short Text	Short Text	Short Text	Short Text	Short Text	Short Text	Short Text	Currency
Field Name	ID	Title	Last Name	First Name	**Middle Initial**	Address	City	State	Postal Code	Phone Number	Department ID	Salary

c. If necessary, scroll to bring the first column into view, and then click the **ID** field name. On the **Fields tab**, in the **Properties group**, click **Name & Caption**. In the **Name** box, change *ID* to **Employee ID** and then click **OK**. On the ribbon, in the **Formatting group**, click the **Data Type arrow**, and then click **Short Text**.

d. In the new record row, click in the **Employee ID** field, type, **ADM-9200** and press Enter. In the **Title** field, type **Vice President** and press Enter. Continue entering data in the fields shown in Table 2, pressing Enter or Tab to move to the next field and to the next row.

Table 2

Last Name	First Name	Middle Initial	Address	City	State	Postal Code	Phone Number	Department ID	Salary
Shaffer	**Lonnie**	**J**	**489 Ben Ave**	**Austin**	**TX**	**78734**	**(512) 555-6185**	**AS**	**123500**

e. On the Quick Access Toolbar, click **Save**. In the **Save As** dialog box, in the **Table Name** box, using your own name, replace the selected text by typing **Lastname Firstname 1C Administrators** and then click **OK**.

f. In the new record row, enter the data for two college administrators shown in Table 3, pressing Enter or Tab to move from field to field and to the next row.

Table 3

Employee ID	Title	Last Name	First Name	Middle Initial	Address	City	State	Postal Code	Phone Number	Department ID	Salary
ADM-9201	**Associate Vice President**	**Holtz**	**Diann**	**S**	**8416 Spencer Ln**	**George town**	**TX**	**78627**	**(512) 555-1069**	**AS**	**101524**
ADM-9202	**Director, Enrollment Services**	**Fitchette**	**Sean**	**H**	**3245 Deer Trl**	**Spice wood**	**TX**	**78669**	**(512) 555-9012**	**SS**	**45070**

g. **Close** your **1C Administrators** table. On the **External Data tab**, in the **Import & Link group**, click **New Data Source**, point to **From File**, and then click **Excel**. In the **Get External Data – Excel Spreadsheet** dialog box, click **Browse**. In the **File Open** dialog box, navigate to your student data files, and then double-click the **a01C_Administrators** Excel file.

h. Click the **Append a copy of the records to the table** option button, and then click **OK**. In the **Import Spreadsheet Wizard**, click **Next**, and then click **Finish**. In the **Get External Data – Excel Spreadsheet** dialog box, click **Close**.

(continues on next page)

Chapter Review

i. **Open** the **Navigation Pane**. Resize the Navigation Pane so that the entire table name displays. In the **Navigation Pane**, double-click your **1C Administrators** table to open it, and then **Close** the **Navigation Pane**—there are 30 records in this table.

2 ▶ Click the **Home tab**, and then in the **Views group**, click the top of the **View** button to switch to **Design** view. In the **Field Name** column, to the left of **Middle Initial**, click the row selector box to select the entire row. On the **Design tab**, in the **Tools group**, click **Delete Rows**. In the message box, click **Yes**.

a. Click in the **Employee ID** field name box. Under **Field Properties**, click **Field Size** to select the existing text. Type **8** and then in the **Employee ID** field row, click in the **Description** box. Type **Eight-character Employee ID** and then press Enter.

b. Click in the **State** field name box. In the **Field Properties** area, click **Field Size**, and then type **2** In the **State Description** box, type **Two-character state abbreviation** and then press Enter.

c. **Save** the design changes to your table, and in the message box, click **Yes**. On the **Design tab**, in the **Views group**, click the top of the **View** button to switch to **Datasheet** view.

d. On the ribbon, click the **External Data tab**, and then in the **Import & Link group**, click **New Data Source**, point to **From File**, and then click **Excel**. In the **Get External Data – Excel Spreadsheet** dialog box, to the right of the **File name** box, click **Browse**. In the **File Open** dialog box, navigate to your student data files, and then double-click **a01C_Departments**. Be sure that the **Import the source data into a new table in the current database** option button is selected, and then click **OK**.

e. In the upper left corner of the wizard, select the **First Row Contains Column Headings** check box, and then click **Next**. Click **Next** again. Click the **Choose my own primary key** option button, be sure that **Department ID** displays, and then click **Next**. In the **Import to Table** box, type **1C Departments** and then click **Finish**. In the **Get External Data – Excel Spreadsheet** dialog box, click **Close**.

f. **Open** the **Navigation Pane**, double-click your **1C Departments** table, and then **Close** the **Navigation Pane**. There are 12 records in your **1C Departments** table.

g. To the left of the **Department** field name, click **Select All**. On the ribbon, click the **Home tab**, and in the **Records group**, click **More**, and then click **Field Width**. In the **Column Width** dialog box, click **Best Fit**. Click in any field to cancel the selection, and then **Save** your table. In the object window, click the **object tab** for your **1C Administrators** table. Using the techniques you just practiced, apply **Best Fit** to the columns, cancel the selection, and then **Save** the table.

h. With your **1C Administrators** table displayed, on the ribbon, click the **File tab**, click **Print**, and then click **Print Preview**. On the **Print Preview tab**, in the **Page Layout group**, click **Landscape**. Click **Close Print Preview**, and then **Close** your **1C Administrators** table.

i. With your **1C Departments** table displayed, view the table in **Print Preview**. Change the orientation to **Landscape**, and then create a paper printout or PDF electronic image as directed by your instructor—one page results. Click **Close Print Preview**, and then **Close** your **1C Departments** table.

3 ▶ On the ribbon, click the **Create tab**, and then in the **Queries group**, click **Query Wizard**. In the **New Query** dialog box, be sure **Simple Query Wizard** is selected, and then click **OK**. In the wizard, click the **Tables/Queries arrow**, and then click your **Table: 1C Administrators**.

a. Under **Available Fields**, click **Last Name**, and then click **Add Field** to move the field to the **Selected Fields** list on the right. Double-click the **First Name** field to move it to the **Selected Fields** list. By using **Add Field** or by double-clicking the field name, add the following fields to the **Selected Fields** list in the order specified: **Title**, **Department ID**, and **Phone Number**. This query will answer the question, *What is the last name, first name, title, Department ID, and phone number of every administrator?*

b. In the wizard, click **Next**. Click in the **What title do you want for your query?** box. Using your own name, edit as necessary so that the query name is **1C All Administrators Query** and then click **Finish**. If necessary, apply Best Fit to the columns, and then Save the query. Display the query in **Print**. Click **Close Print Preview**, and then **Close** the query.

(continues on next page)

Chapter Review

c. **Open** the **Navigation Pane**, right-click your **1C Administrators** table, and then click **Open** to display the table in the object window. **Close** the **Navigation Pane**. Notice that the table has 11 fields. On the ribbon, click the **Create tab**, and in the **Forms group**, click **Form**. On the Quick Access Toolbar, click **Save**. In the **Save As** dialog box, click in the **Form Name** box, edit to name the form **Lastname Firstname 1C Administrator Form** and then click **OK**.

d. In the navigation area, click **Last record**, and then click **Previous record** two times to display the record for *Diann Holtz*. By using the instructions in Activity 1.15, print or create an PDF electronic image of only this record on one page. **Close** the form object, saving it if prompted. Your **1C Administrators** table object remains open.

e. **Open** the **Navigation Pane**, open your **1C Departments** table by double-clicking the table name or by right-clicking the table name and clicking Open. **Close** the **Navigation Pane**. On the **Create tab**, in the **Reports group**, click **Report**.

f. Click the **Department ID** field name, and then on the ribbon, under **Report Layout Tools**, click the **Arrange tab**. In the **Rows & Columns group**, click **Select Column**, and then press Del. Using the same technique, delete the **Department Email** field.

g. Click the **Department Phone** field name. Hold down Shift, and then click the **Suite Number** field name to select the last three field names. In the **Rows & Columns group**, click **Select Column**. On the ribbon, click the **Design tab**, and then in the **Tools group**, click **Property Sheet**. In the **Property Sheet**, on the **Format tab**, click **Width**, type **1.5** and then press Enter. **Close** the **Property Sheet**.

h. Click the **Department Name** field name. On the ribbon, click the **Home tab.** In the **Sort & Filter group**, click **Ascending** to sort the report in alphabetic order by *Department Name*. At the bottom of the report, on the right side, click **Page 1 of 1**, and then press Del.

i. **Save** the report as **Lastname Firstname 1C Departments Report** and then click **OK**. Display the report in **Print**. Click **Close Print Preview**. In the object window, right-click any **object tab**, and then click **Close All** to close all open objects, leaving the object window empty.

4 **Open** the **Navigation Pane**. If necessary, increase the width of the Navigation Pane so that all object names display fully. On the right side of the title bar, click **Close** to close the database and to close Access. As directed by your instructor, submit your database for grading.

You have completed Project 1C **END**

Chapter Review

In the following Skills Review, you will create a database to store information about certification test preparation events at Texas Lakes Community College. Your completed Navigation Pane will look similar to Figure 1.48.

Apply 1B skills from these Objectives:

6. Use a Template to Create a Database
7. Organize Objects in the Navigation Pane
8. Create a New Table in a Database Created with a Template
9. View a Report

Project Files

For Project 1D, you will need the following files:

a01D_Certification_Template
a01D_Certification_Events (Excel workbook)

You will save your database as:

Lastname_Firstname_1D_Certification_Events

Project Results

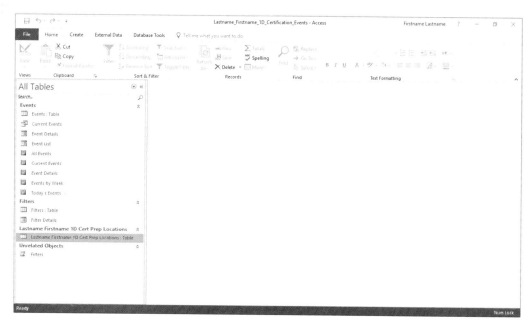

Figure 1.48

(continues on next page)

Chapter Review

1 Start Access. On the left, click **Open Other Files**, and then click **Browse**. Navigate to your student data for this chapter, and open the database named **a01D_Certification_Template**. On the ribbon, click the **File tab**, on the left, click **Save As**, and then, under *Save Database As*, click **Save As**. In the **Save As dialog** box, navigate to your **Access Chapter 1** folder, and then using your own name, type **Lastname_Firstname_1D_Certification_Events** and then click **Save**. Under the ribbon, on the **Message Bar**, click **Enable Content**.

a. In the first row, click in the **Title** field, type **Word 2019** and then press [Tab]. In the **Start Time** field, type **7/9/23 10a** and then press [Tab]. In the **End Time** field, type **7/9/23 4p** and then press [Tab]. In the **Description** field, type **Office 2019** and then press [Tab]. In the **Location** field, type **Southwest Campus** and then press [Tab] three times to move to the **Title** field in the new record row.

b. In the form, directly above the field names row, click **New Event** to open the **Event Details** single-record form. Using [Tab] to move from field to field, enter the record shown in **Table 1**. Press [Tab] three times to move from the **End Time** field to the **Description** field.

Table 1

Title	Location	Start Time	End Time	Description
Excel 2019	Northeast Campus	7/16/23 10a	7/16/23 4p	Office 2019

c. In the **Events Detail** form, click **Close**. Using either the **Event List** multiple-items form or the **Event Details** single-record form, enter the records shown in **Table 2**. If you use the Event Details form, be sure to close it after entering records to display the records in the Event List form.

Table 2

ID	Title	Start Time	End Time	Description	Location
3	Access 2019	7/23/23 12p	7/23/23 6p	Office 2019	Southeast Campus
4	PowerPoint 2019	7/30/23 9a	7/30/23 3p	Office 2019	Northwest Campus

d. **Close** the Event List form. On the ribbon, click the **External Data tab**, in the **Import & Link group**, click **New Data Source**, point to **From File**, and then click **Excel**. In the **Get External Data – Excel Spreadsheet** dialog box, click **Browse**. Navigate to your student data files, and then double-click **a01D_Certification_Events**. Click the second option button—**Append a copy of the records to the table: Events**—and then click **OK**.

e. In the **Import Spreadsheet Wizard**, click **Next**, and then click **Finish**. In the **Get External Data – Excel Spreadsheet** dialog box, click **Close**. **Open** the **Navigation Pane**, and then double-click **Event List** to open the form that displays data stored in the Events table—12 total records display. **Close** the **Navigation Pane**.

f. To the left of the **ID** field name, click **Select All**. In the field names row, point to the right edge of any of the selected columns to display the ✛ pointer, and then double-click to apply **Best Fit** to all of the columns. Click in any field to cancel the selection, and then **Save** the form.

2 **Open** the **Navigation Pane**. At the top of the Navigation Pane, click **More**. On the list, under **Navigate To Category**, click **Tables and Related Views**.

a. In the **Navigation Pane**, point to **Events: Table**, right-click, and then click **Open** to display the records in the underlying table. In the **Navigation Pane**, double-click the **Current Events** *report* (green icon) to view this predesigned report. From the **Navigation Pane**, open the **Events by Week** report to view this predesigned report.

b. In the object window, right-click any of the **object tabs**, and then click **Close All**. **Close** the **Navigation Pane**.

3 On the ribbon, click the **Create tab**, and in the **Tables group**, click **Table**.

a. In the field names row, click **Click to Add**, click **Short Text**, type **Campus Location** and then press [Enter]. In the third column, click **Short Text**, type **Lab** and then press [Enter]. In the fourth column, click **Number**, type **# Computers** and then press [Enter]. In the fifth column, click **Short Text**, type **Additional Equipment** and then press [↓].

(continues on next page)

Chapter Review

b. Right-click the **ID** field name, and then click **Rename Field**. Type **Lab ID** and then press Enter. On the **Fields tab**, in the **Formatting group**, click the **Data Type arrow**, and then click **Short Text**.

c. In the new record row, click in the **Lab ID** field, and then enter the records shown in **Table 3**, pressing Enter or Tab to move from one field to the next.

Table 3

Lab ID	Campus Location	Lab	# Computers	Additional Equipment
NW-L01	Northwest Campus	H202	35	3 printers, DVD player
SE-L01	Southeast Campus	E145	25	Projector, document camera, smart board
NE-L01	Northeast Campus	F32	40	4 printers, smart board, instructor touch screen
SW-L01	Southwest Campus	G332	30	Projector, 4 digital displays
SE-L02	Southeast Campus	A225	25	Projector, white board, instructor touch screen

d. In the **Views group**, click the upper portion of the **View** button to switch to **Design** view. In the **Save As** dialog box, in the **Table Name** box, using your own name, type **Lastname Firstname1D Cert Prep Locations** and then click **OK**. Notice that the **Lab ID** field is the **Primary Key**. On the **Design tab**, in the **Views group**, click the upper portion of the **View** button to switch to **Datasheet** view.

e. To the left of the **Lab ID** field name, click **Select All** to select all of the columns and rows in the table. On the **Home tab**, in the **Records group**, click **More**, and then click **Field Width**. In the **Column Width** dialog box, click **Best Fit**. Click in any field to cancel the selection, and then **Save** the changes to the table. **Close** the table, and then **Open** the Navigation Pane. Increase the width of the **Navigation Pane** so that your entire table name displays.

4 In the Navigation Pane, double-click the **All Events** report to open it in the object window. **Close** the **Navigation Pane**. On the **Home tab**, in the **Views** group, click the top of the **View** button to switch to **Layout** view. At the top of the report, click the title—*All Events*—to display a colored border around the title. Click to the left of the letter *A* to place the insertion point there. Using your name, type **Lastname Firstname 1D** and then press Spacebar. Press Enter, and then **Save** the report.

a. On the right side of the status bar, click **Print Preview**, and notice that the report will print on one page. Click **Close Print Preview**, and then **Close** the report.

b. **Open** the Navigation Pane, double-click your **1D Cert Prep Locations** table, and then **Close** the Navigation Pane. On the ribbon, click the **File tab**, click **Print**, and then click **Print Preview**. On the **Print Preview tab**, in the **Page Layout group**, click **Landscape**. **Close Print Preview**. Close your **1D Cert Prep Locations** table.

c. **Open** the Navigation Pane. On the right side of the title bar, click **Close** to close the database and to close Access. As directed by your instructor, submit your database for grading.

You have completed Project 1D **END**

Mastering Access Project 1E Kiosk Inventory

Apply 1A skills from these Objectives:

1. Identify Good Database Design
2. Create a Table and Define Fields in a Blank Desktop Database
3. Change the Structure of Tables and Add a Second Table
4. Create a Query, Form, and Report
5. Close a Database and Close Access

In the following Mastering Access project, you will create a database to track information about the inventory of items for sale in the kiosk located in the Snack Bar at the Southeast Campus of Texas Lakes Community College. Your completed Navigation Pane will look similar to Figure 1.49.

Project Files for MyLab IT Grader

1. In your **MyLab IT** course, locate and click **Access 1E Kiosk Inventory**, Download Materials, and then Download All Files. Close the Grader download screens.
2. Extract the zipped folder to your Access Chapter 1 folder.
3. Take a moment to open the downloaded **Access_1E_Kiosk_Inventory_Instructions**; note any recent updates to the book.

Project Results

Figure 1.49

 For Non-MyLab Submissions

For Project 1E, you will need these starting file:

Blank database
a01E_Inventory (Excel workbook)
a01E_Inventory_Storage (Excel workbook)

Start with a New Blank Access Database

In your Access Chapter 1 folder, save your database as:

Lastname_Firstname_1E_Kiosk_Inventory

After you have saved your database, open it to launch Access. On the next page, begin with Step 2.

After Step 11, submit your database as directed by your instructor.

(continues on next page)

Content-Based Assessments (Mastery and Transfer of Learning)

Mastering Access: Project 1E Kiosk Inventory (continued)

1 Start Access. Navigate to your **Access Chapter 1 folder**, and then double-click the downloaded file that displays your name—**Student_1E_Kiosk_Inventory**. If necessary, at the top, click Enable Content.

2 **Close** the **Navigation Pane**. Create a new table in Datasheet view, and create the fields shown in **Table 1**.

Table 1

Data Type		Short Text	Short Text	Short Text	Short Text	Currency	Number
Field Name	ID	**Item**	**Category**	**Campus**	**Storage Location**	**Price**	**Quantity in Stock**

3 For the **ID** field, change the **Data Type** to **Short Text**, rename the field to **Item ID** and then enter the records shown in **Table 2.**

Table 2

Item ID	Item	Category	Campus	Storage Location	Price	Quantity in Stock
C-1	**Chocolate Bar**	**Candy**	**Southeast**	**SE100A**	.89	250
C-2	**Lollipop**	**Candy**	**Southeast**	**SE100A**	.5	500
T-1	**T-shirt**	**Clothing**	**Southeast**	**SE100B**	17.5	100

4 **Save** the table as **1E Inventory** and **Close** the table. From your student data files, import and then **Append** the data in the Excel file **a01E_Inventory** to your **1E Inventory** table. After importing, open your **1E Inventory** table—17 records display.

5 In **Design** view, delete the **Campus** field, which is redundant data. For the **Category** field, change the **Field Size** to **25** and enter a **Description** of **Enter the category of the item** For the **Item ID** field, change the **Field Size** to **10** and then **Save** the changes to your table. Switch to **Datasheet** view, apply **Best Fit** to all of the fields in the table, and then **Save** your changes. Display the table in **Print Preview**, change the orientation to **Landscape**. **Close Print Preview**, and then **Close** the table.

6 From your student data files, import the **Excel** file **a01E_Inventory_Storage** into the database as a new table; designate the first row as column headings and the **Category** field as the primary key. In the wizard, name the table **1E Inventory Storage** and then open your **1E Inventory Storage** table—five records display. In **Design** view, for the **Location Detail** field, change the **Field Size** to **35** and enter a **Description** of **Room and bin number or alternate location of inventory item** Save the design changes, switch to **Datasheet** view, apply **Best Fit** to all of the fields, and then **Save** your changes. **Close** the table.

7 Create a **Simple Query**, by using the **Query Wizard**, based on your **1E Inventory** table. Include only the three fields that will answer the question, *For all items, what is the storage location and quantity in stock?* In the wizard, accept the default name for the query. Display the query in **Print Preview**, create a paper printout or PDF electronic image as directed, **Close Print Preview**, and then **Close** the query.

8 Open your **1E Inventory** table, and then **Create** a **Form** for this table. **Save** the form as **1E Inventory Form** and then view the records. **Close** the form object, saving changes if prompted.

9 With your **1E Inventory** table open, **Create** a **Report**. Delete the **Category** and **Price** fields, and then sort the **Item ID** field in **Ascending** order. Using the **Property Sheet**, for the **Item ID** field, change the **Width** to **0.75** and then for the **Storage Location** field, change the **Width** to **1.5** Scroll to display the bottom of the report, if necessary, and then delete the page number— **Page 1 of 1**. **Save** the report as **1E Inventory Report** **Close** the report.

10 **Close All** open objects. **Open** the **Navigation Pane** and be sure that all object names display fully.

11 **Close** the database, and then **Close** Access.

(continues on next page)

Content-Based Assessments (Mastery and Transfer of Learning)

12 In **MyLab IT**, locate and click the Grader Project **Access 1E Kiosk Inventory**. In **step 3**, under **Upload Completed Assignment**, click **Choose File**. In the **Open** dialog box, navigate to your **Access Chapter 1 folder**, and then click your **Student_Access_1E_Kiosk_Inventory** file one time to select it. In the lower right corner of the **Open** dialog box, click **Open.**

13 To submit your file to **MyLab IT** for grading, click Upload, wait a moment for a green **Success!** message, and then in **step 4**, click the blue **Submit for Grading** button. Click **Close Assignment** to return to your list of **Course Materials**.

You have completed Project 1E   **END**

Content-Based Assessments (Mastery and Transfer of Learning)

Mastering Access Project 1F Recruitment Events

Apply 1B skills from these Objectives:

6. Use a Template to Create a Database
7. Organize Objects in the Navigation Pane
8. Create a New Table in a Database Created with a Template
9. View a Report

In the following Mastering Access project, you will create a database to store information about the recruiting events that are scheduled to attract new students to Texas Lakes Community College. Your completed Navigation Pane will look similar to Figure 1.50.

Project Files for MyLab IT Grader

1. In your **MyLab IT** course, locate and click **Access 1F Recruitment Events**, Download Materials, and then Download All Files. Close the Grader download screens.
2. Extract the zipped folder to your Access Chapter 1 folder.
3. Take a moment to open the downloaded **Access_1F_Recruitment_Events_Instructions**; note any recent updates to the book.

Project Results

Figure 1.50

For Non-MyLab Submissions

For Project 1F, you will need these starting files:

a01F_Recruitment_Template

a01F_Recruiting_Events (Excel workbook)

Start with an Access Data File

In your Access Chapter 1 folder, save your database as:

Lastname_Firstname_1F_Recruitment_Events

After you have saved your database, open it to launch Access. On the next page, begin with Step 2.
After Step 9, submit your database as directed by your instructor.

(continues on next page)

Content-Based Assessments (Mastery and Transfer of Learning)

1 Start Access. Navigate to your **Access Chapter 1 folder**, and then double-click the downloaded file that displays your name—**Student_1F_Recruitment_ Events**. If necessary, at the top, click Enable Content.

2 In the **Event List** multiple-items form or the **Event Details** single-record form—open by clicking **New Event** on the Event List form—enter the records shown in **Table 1**.

Table 1

ID	Title	Start Time	End Time	Description	Location
1	Health Professions	6/1/23 8a	6/1/23 12p	Science Students	Hill Country High School
2	New Students	6/1/23 10a	6/1/23 3p	College Fair	Brazos Convention Center
3	Information Technology	6/2/23 9a	6/2/23 12p	Technical Students	Round Rock Technical Center
4	International Students	6/2/23 2p	6/2/23 5p	Open House	Southeast Campus

3 **Close** the **Event List** form. From your student data files, import and **Append** the data from the **Excel** file **a01F_Recruiting_Events** to the **Events** table. **Open** the **Navigation Pane**, organize the objects by **Tables and Related Views**, and then open the **Events** table to display 13 records. **Close** the table, and then **Close** the **Navigation Pane**.

4 **Create** a new **Table** defining the new fields shown in **Table 2**.

Table 2

Data Type		Short Text	Short Text	Short Text	Short Text	Short Text
Field Name	ID	Location	Last Name	First Name	Email Address	Business Phone

5 For the **ID** field, change the **Data Type** to **Short Text**, rename the field to **Recruiter ID** and then enter the records shown in **Table 3**.

Table 3

Recruiter ID	Location	Last Name	First Name	Email Address	Business Phone
R-01	Hill Country High School	Rostamo	Robyn	rrostamo@hillcohs.sch	(512) 555-3410
R-02	Brazos Convention Center	Hart	Roberto	rlhart@brazosconv.ctr	(512) 555-1938
R-03	Round Rock Technical Center	Sedlacek	Belinda	bsedlacek@rrocktech.sch	(512) 555-0471
R-04	Southeast Campus	Nguyen	Thao	tnguyen@tlcc.edu	(512) 555-2387

6 Apply **Best Fit** to all of the columns. **Save** the table as **1F Recruiters** and then **Close** the table.

7 From the **Navigation Pane**, open the **Event Details** *report* (green icon). Switch to **Layout** view. In the report, click in the title—*Event Details*—and then click to position the insertion point to the left of the word *Event*. **1F** and then press Spacebar and Enter. **Save** and **Close** the report.

8 From the **Navigation Pane**, open the **Events** table, select all of the columns, and then apply **Best Fit** to all of the columns by double-clicking the right edge of any of the selected columns. Cancel the selection, and then **Save** the table. Display the table in **Print Preview**, change the orientation to **Landscape**, change the **Margins** to **Normal**. **Save** and **Close** the table.

(continues on next page)

Content-Based Assessments (Mastery and Transfer of Learning)

9 In the **Navigation Pane**, be sure that all object names display fully. **Close** the database and **Close** Access.

10 In In **MyLab IT**, locate and click the Grader Project **Access 1F Recruitment Events**. In **step 3**, under **Upload Completed Assignment**, click **Choose File**. In the **Open** dialog box, navigate to your **Access Chapter 1 folder**, and then click your **Student_Access_1F_Recruitment_Events** file one time to select it. In the lower right corner of the **Open** dialog box, click **Open**.

11 To submit your file to **MyLab IT** for grading, click **Upload**, wait a moment for a green **Success!** message, and then in **step 4**, click the blue **Submit for Grading** button. Click **Close Assignment** to return to your list of **Course Materials**.

You have completed Project 1F   **END**

Mastering Access   **Project 1G College Construction**

In the following Mastering Access project, you will create one database to store information about construction projects for Texas Lakes Community College and a second database to store information about the public events related to the construction projects. Your completed Navigation Pane will look similar to Figure 1.51.

Project Files for MyLab IT Grader

1. In your **MyLab IT** course, locate and click **Access 1G College Construction** Download Materials, and then Download All Files. Close the Grader download screens.
2. Extract the zipped folder to your Access Chapter 1 folder.
3. Take a moment to open the downloaded **Access_1G_College_Construction_Instructions**; note any recent updates to the book.

Project Results

Figure 1.51

For Non-MyLab Submissions
For Project 1G, you will need these starting files:
a01G_College_Construction
a01G_Projects (Excel workbook)
a01G_Contractors (Excel workbook)

Start with an Access Data File
In your Access Chapter 1 folder, save your database as:
Lastname_Firstname_1G_College_Construction

After you have saved your database, open it to launch Access. On the next page, begin with Step 2.
After Step 13, submit your database as directed by your instructor.

(continues on next page)

Content-Based Assessments (Mastery and Transfer of Learning)

1 Navigate to your **Access Chapter 1 folder**, and then double-click the downloaded file that displays your name—**Student_Access_1G_College_Construction**. If necessary, at the top, click Enable Content.

2 **Close** the **Navigation Pane**. Create a new table with the fields shown in **Table 1**.

Table 1

Data Type		Short Text	Short Text	Short Text	Currency
Field Name	ID	Building Project	Site	Contractor	Budget Amount

3 For the **ID** field, change the **Data Type** to **Short Text**, rename the field to **Project ID** and change the **Field Size** to **5** Enter the three records shown in **Table 2**.

Table 2

Project ID	Building Project	Site	Contractor	Budget Amount
P-356	Student Center, 3-story	Northeast Campus	RR Construction	61450000
P-823	Student Center, 2-story	Southeast Campus	RR Construction	41960000
P-157	Health Professions Center	Northwest Campus	Marshall Ellis Construction	42630000

4 **Save** the table as **1G Projects** and **Close** the table. From your student data files, import and then **Append** the data in the **Excel** file **a01G_Projects** to your **1G Projects** table. After importing, open your **1G Projects** table—eight records display.

5 In **Design** view, for the **Project ID** field, enter a **Description** of **Enter the Project ID using the format P-###** For the **Site** field, change the field size to **25** and enter a **Description** of **Campus location Save** the changes to your table. Switch to **Datasheet** view, apply **Best Fit** to all of the fields in the table, and then **Save** your changes. Display the table in **Print Preview**, change the orientation to **Landscape. Close Print Preview,** and then **Close** the table.

6 From your student data files, import the **Excel** file **a01G_Contractors** into the database as a new table; designate the first row as column headings and the **CO ID** field as the primary key. In the wizard, name the table **1G Contractors** and then open your **1G Contractors** table—four records display. Apply **Best Fit** to all of the fields, and then **Save** your changes. Display the table in **Print Preview**, change the orientation to **Landscape. Close Print Preview**, and then **Close** the table.

7 **Create**, by using the **Query Wizard**, a **Simple Query** based on your **1G Projects** table. Include only the three fields that will answer the question, *For every site, what is the building project and the budget amount?* In the wizard, accept the default name for the query. **Close** the query.

8 Open your **1G Projects** table, and then **Create** a **Form** for this table. **Save** the form as **1G Project Form** and **Close** the form object.

9 With your **1G Projects** table open, **Create** a **Report**. Delete the **Budget Amount** field, and then sort the **Building Project** field in **Ascending** order. For the **Building Project**, **Site**, and **Contractor** fields, using the **Property Sheet**, change the **Width** of all three fields to **2** At the bottom of the report, delete the page number—**Page 1 of 1**. Change the **Report title** to **1G Project Report Save** the report as **1G Project Report**

10 Open the Navigation Pane, open the **Event List** form, and then close the Navigation Pane. In the Event List multiple-items form, enter the following two records (the Start Time and End Time data will reformat automatically):

Table 3

ID	Title	Start Time	End Time	Location	Description
1	Groundbreaking	6/13/22 10a	6/13/22 11a	Northeast Campus	Student Center groundbreaking
2	Dedication	8/26/22 12:30p	8/26/22 2p	Southwest Campus	Gymnasium building dedication

(continues on next page)

Mastering Access: Project 1G College Construction (continued)

11 In the **Event List** form, click **New Event**, and in the **Event Details** single-record form, enter the following record (the Start Time and End Time data will reformat automatically):

Table 4

ID	Title	Start Time	End Time	Location	Description
3	**Community Arts Expo**	**10/5/21 6p**	**10/5/22 9p**	**Southeast Campus**	**Book and Art Expo at Library Location**

12 **Close All** open objects. **Open** the **Navigation Pane**, arrange the objects by **Tables and Related Views**, and be sure that all object names display fully.

13 In the **Navigation Pane**, be sure that all object names display fully. **Close** the database and **Close** Access.

14 In In **MyLab IT**, locate and click the Grader Project **Access 1G College Construction**. In **step 3**, unde **Upload Completed Assignment**, click **Choose File**. In the **Open** dialog box, navigate to your **Access Chapter 1 folder**, and then click your **Student_Access_1G_College_ Construction** file one time to select it. In the lower right corner of the **Open** dialog box, click **Open**.

15 To submit your file to **MyLab IT** for grading, click **Upload**, wait a moment for a green **Success!** message, and then in **step 4**, click the blue **Submit for Grading** button. Click **Close Assignment** to return to your list of **Course Materials**.

You have completed Project 1G `END`

Content-Based Assessments (Critical Thinking)

Apply a combination of the 1A and 1B skills.

GO! Fix It	**Project 1H Scholarships**	IRC
GO! Make It	**Project 1I Theater Events**	IRC
GO! Solve It	**Project 1J Athletic Scholarships**	IRC
GO! Solve It	**Project 1K Student Activities**	

Project Files

For Project 1K, you will need the following files:

Event management template

a01K_Student_Activities (Word document)

You will save your database as:

Lastname_Firstname_1K_Student_Activities

Use the Event management template to create a database, and then save it in your Access Chapter 1 folder as **Lastname_Firstname_1K_Student_Activities** From your student data files, use the information in the Word document a01K_Student_Activities to enter data into the Event List multiple-items form. Each event begins at 7 p.m. and ends at 10 p.m.

After entering the records, close the form, and arrange the Navigation Pane by Tables and Related Views. Open the Event Details *report*, and then add your **Firstname Lastname 1K** to the beginning of the report title. Decrease the font size of the title so that it displays on one line. Create a paper printout or PDF electronic image as directed—two pages result. As directed, submit your database for grading.

Performance Criteria		Performance Level		
		Exemplary	**Proficient**	**Developing**
	Create database using Event management template and enter data	Database created using the correct template, named correctly, and all data entered correctly.	Database created using the correct template, named correctly, but not all data entered correctly.	Database created using the correct template, but numerous errors in database name and data.
	Modify report	Event Details report title includes name and project on one line.	Event Details report title includes name and project, but not on one line.	Event Details report title does not include name and project and does not display on one line.
	Create report printout	Event Details report printout is correct.	Event Details printout is incorrect.	Event Details report printout not created.

You have completed Project 1K END

Outcomes-Based Assessments (Critical Thinking)

Rubric

The following outcomes-based assessments are *open-ended assessments*. That is, there is no specific correct result; your result will depend on your approach to the information provided. Make *Professional Quality* your goal. Use the following scoring rubric to guide you in how to approach the problem and then to evaluate how well your approach solves the problem.

The *criteria*—Software Mastery, Content, Format & Layout, and Process—represent the knowledge and skills you have gained that you can apply to solving the problem. The *levels of performance*—Professional Quality, Approaching Professional Quality, or Needs Quality Improvements—help you and your instructor evaluate your result.

	Your completed project is of Professional Quality if you:	Your completed project is Approaching Professional Quality if you:	Your completed project Needs Quality Improvements if you:
1-Software Mastery	Choose and apply the most appropriate skills, tools, and features and identify efficient methods to solve the problem.	Choose and apply some appropriate skills, tools, and features, but not in the most efficient manner.	Choose inappropriate skills, tools, or features, or are inefficient in solving the problem.
2-Content	Construct a solution that is clear and well organized, contains content that is accurate, appropriate to the audience and purpose, and is complete. Provide a solution that contains no errors of spelling, grammar, or style.	Construct a solution in which some components are unclear, poorly organized, inconsistent, or incomplete. Misjudge the needs of the audience. Have some errors in spelling, grammar, or style, but the errors do not detract from comprehension.	Construct a solution that is unclear, incomplete, or poorly organized, contains some inaccurate or inappropriate content, and contains many errors of spelling, grammar, or style. Do not solve the problem.
3-Format and Layout	Format and arrange all elements to communicate information and ideas, clarify function, illustrate relationships, and indicate relative importance.	Apply appropriate format and layout features to some elements, but not others. Overuse features, causing minor distraction.	Apply format and layout that does not communicate information or ideas clearly. Do not use format and layout features to clarify function, illustrate relationships, or indicate relative importance. Use available features excessively, causing distraction.
4-Process	Use an organized approach that integrates planning, development, self-assessment, revision, and reflection.	Demonstrate an organized approach in some areas, but not others; or, use an insufficient process of organization throughout.	Do not use an organized approach to solve the problem.

Outcomes-Based Assessments (Critical Thinking)

Apply a combination of the 1A and 1B skills.

GO! Think   **Project 1L Student Clubs**

Project Files

For Project 1L, you will need the following files:

Blank database
a01L_Clubs (Word document)
a01L_Student_Clubs (Excel workbook)
a01L_Club_Presidents (Excel workbook)
You will save your database as
Lastname_Firstname_1L_Student_Clubs

Dr. Daniel Martinez, Vice President of Student Services, needs a database that tracks information about student clubs. The database should contain two tables—one for club information and one for contact information for the club presidents.

Create a desktop database, and then save the database in your Access Chapter 1 folder as **Lastname_Firstname_1L_Student_Clubs** From your student data files, use the information in the Word document a01L_Clubs to create the first table and to enter two records. Name the table appropriately to include your name and 1L, and then append the 23 records from the Excel workbook a01L_Student_Clubs to your table. For the Club ID and President ID fields, add a description and change the field size.

Create a second table in the database by importing 25 records from the Excel workbook a01L_Club_Presidents, and then name the table appropriately to include your name and 1L. For the State and Postal Code fields, add a description and change the field size. Be sure that the field data types are correct—recall that numbers that are not used in calculations should have a data type of Short Text. Be sure all of the data and field names display in each table.

Create a simple query based on the Clubs table that answers the question, *What is the club name, meeting day, meeting time, campus, and Room ID for all of the clubs?* Create a form based on the Clubs table, saving it with an appropriate name that includes your name and 1L. Create a report based on the Presidents table, saving it with an appropriate name that includes your name and 1L, that displays the president's last name (in ascending order), the president's first name, and the phone number of every president. Change the width of the three fields so that there is less space between them, but being sure that each record prints on a single line.

Create paper printout or PDF electronic images of the two tables, the query, only Record 21 of the form, and the report as directed being sure that each object prints on one page. Organize the objects on the Navigation Pane by Tables and Related Views, and be sure that all object names display fully. As directed, submit your database for grading.

You have completed Project 1L   **END**

GO! Think   **Project 1M Faculty Training Online**   IRC

You and GO!   **Project 1N Personal Contacts Online**   IRC

GO! Cumulative Group Project   **Project 1O Bell Orchid Hotels Online**   IRC

Sort and Query a Database

PROJECT 2A

Outcomes
Sort and query a database

Objectives
1. Open and Save an Existing Database
2. Create Table Relationships
3. Sort Records in a Table
4. Create a Query in Design View
5. Create a New Query From an Existing Query
6. Sort Query Results
7. Specify Criteria in a Query

PROJECT 2B

Outcomes
Create complex queries

Objectives
8. Specify Numeric Criteria in a Query
9. Use Compound Criteria in a Query
10. Create a Query Based on More Than One Table
11. Use Wildcards in a Query
12. Create Calculated Fields in a Query
13. Calculate Statistics and Group Data in a Query
14. Create a Crosstab Query
15. Create a Parameter Query

Spiroview Inc./Shutterstock

In This Chapter

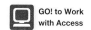

GO! to Work with Access

In this chapter, you will sort Access database tables and create and modify queries. To convert data into meaningful information, you must manipulate your data in a way that you can answer questions. One question might be: *Which students have a grade point average of 3.0 or higher?* With this information, you could send information about scholarships or internships to students who meet the grade point average criteria.

The projects in this chapter relate to **Texas Lakes Community College**, which is located in the Austin,

Texas, area. Its four campuses serve over 30,000 students and offer more than 140 certificate programs and degrees. The college has a highly acclaimed Distance Education program and an extensive Workforce Development program. The college makes positive contributions to the community through cultural and athletic programs and has maintained partnerships with businesses and non-profit organizations.

Instructors and Courses

Project Activities

In Activities 2.01 through 2.16, you will assist Dr. Carolyn Judkins, Dean of the Business Division at the Northeast Campus of Texas Lakes Community College, in locating information about instructors and summer courses offered in the Division. Your completed Navigation Pane will look similar to Figure 2.1.

 ## Project Files for MyLab IT Grader

1. In your storage location, create a folder named **Access Chapter 2**.
2. In your **MyLab IT** course, locate and click **Access 2A Instructors and Courses**, Download Materials, and then Download All Files.
3. Extract the zipped folder to your Access Chapter 2 folder. Close the Grader download screens.
4. Take a moment to open the downloaded **Access_2A_Instructors_Courses_Instructions**; note any recent updates to the book.

Project Results

GO! Project 2A
Where We're Going

Figure 2.1 Project 2A Instructors and Courses

For Non-MyLab Submissions

For Project 2A, you will need this starting file:
a02A_Instructors_Courses

Start with an Access Data File

In your storage location, create a folder named **Access Chapter 2**
In your Access Chapter 2 folder, save your database as:
Lastname_Firstname_2A_Instructors_Courses

After you have saved your database, launch Access and open the database. On the next page, begin with Step 2.

ALERT   Because Office 365 is a cloud-based subscription service that receives continuous updates, you may encounter some variations in what appears on your screen and what is shown in this instruction. Microsoft Office 365 is fully installed on your PC or Mac; no internet access is necessary to create or edit documents. When you *are* connected to the internet, you will receive monthly upgrades and new features, so you always have the latest versions of Office apps as soon as they are available. Your subscription gives you continuous free access to the latest innovations and refinements.

GO! Learn How

Video A2-1

There will be instances where you need to work with a database and still keep the original, unaltered version of the database. Like the other Microsoft Office 2019 applications, you can open a database file and save it with another name.

Activity 2.01 | Opening an Existing Database and Resolving Security Alerts

1 Start Access. In the Access opening screen, click **Open Other Files**. Navigate to your **Access Chapter 2 folder**, and then double-click the Access file that you downloaded from **MyLab IT** that displays your name—**Student_Access_2A_Instructors_Courses**.

2 In the **Navigation Pane**, notice that this database contains two table objects.

The 2A Instructors table contains information about the instructors at Texas Lakes Community College. The 2A Schedule table outlines the course schedule information.

3 On the **Message Bar**, notice the **SECURITY WARNING**. Compare your screen with Figure 2.2.

The *Message Bar* is the area directly below the ribbon that displays information such as security alerts when there is potentially unsafe, active content in an Office document that you open. Settings that determine the alerts that display on your Message Bar are set in the Access *Trust Center*, an area in Access where you can view the security and privacy settings for your Access installation.

Figure 2.2

4 On the **Message Bar**, click **Enable Content**.

> When working with the student data files that accompany this textbook, repeat this action each time you see the security warning. Databases for this textbook are safe to use on your computer.

Objective 2 Create Table Relationships

GO! Learn How
Video A2-2

Access databases are relational databases because the tables in the database can relate—actually connect—to other tables through common fields. Recall that common fields are fields in one or more tables that store the same data; for example, a Student ID number may be stored in two tables in the same database.

After you have a table for each subject in your database, you must provide a way to connect the data in the tables when you need to obtain meaningful information from the stored data. To do this, create common fields in the related tables, and then define table ***relationships***. A relationship is an association that you establish between two tables based on common fields. After the relationship is established, you can create a query, form, or report that displays information from more than one related table.

Activity 2.02 | Selecting the Tables and Common Field to Establish the Table Relationship

1.2.1, 1.2.5

In this Activity, you will select the two tables in the database that will be used to establish the table relationship and identify the common field that is used to connect the tables.

1 In the **Navigation Pane**, double-click your **2A Instructors** table to open it in the object window. Examine the fields in the table. Double-click your **2A Schedule** table to open it and examine the fields in the table.

> In the 2A Instructors table, *Instructor ID* is the primary key field, which ensures that each instructor has only one record in the table. No two instructors have the same Instructor ID, and the table is sorted by Instructor ID.

> In the 2A Schedule table, *Schedule ID* is the primary key field. Every scheduled course section during an academic term has a unique Schedule ID. The courses are sorted by Schedule ID.

2 In the **2A Schedule** table, scroll to display the **Instructor ID** field, and then compare your screen with Figure 2.3.

> Both the 2A Instructors table and the 2A Schedule table include the *Instructor ID* field, which is the common field of the two tables. Because *one* instructor can teach *many* different courses, *one* Instructor ID can be present *many* times in the 2A Schedule table. When the relationship is established, it will be a ***one-to-many relationship***, which is the most common type of relationship in Access.

Figure 2.3

3 In the object window, right-click either **object tab**, and then click **Close All** to close both tables. Click the **Database Tools tab**, and then in the **Relationships group**, click **Relationships**. Compare your screen with Figure 2.4.

The Show Table dialog box displays in the Relationships window. In the Show Table dialog box, the Tables tab displays the two tables that are in this database.

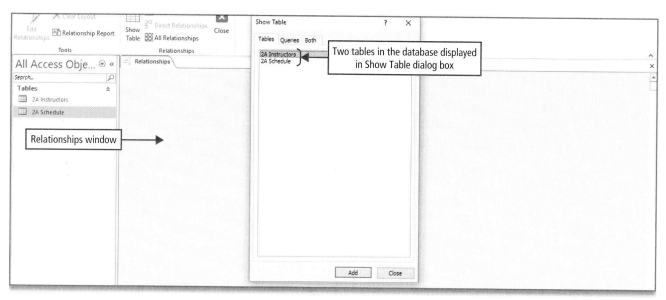

Figure 2.4

4 Point to the title bar of the **Show Table** dialog box, and then, holding down the left mouse button, drag downward and slightly to the right to move the dialog box away from the top of the **Relationships** window. Release the mouse button.

Moving the Show Table dialog box enables you to see the tables as they are added to the Relationships window.

5 In the **Show Table** dialog box, if necessary, click your **2A Instructors** table, and then click **Add**. In the **Show Table** dialog box, double-click your **2A Schedule** table to add it to the **Relationships** window. In the **Show Table** dialog box, click **Close**, and then compare your screen with Figure 2.5.

You can use either technique to add a table to the Relationships window; tables are displayed in the order in which they are added. A *field list*—a list of the field names in a table—for each of the two table objects displays, and each table's primary key is identified by a key icon. Although this database has only two tables, it is not uncommon for larger databases to have many tables. Scroll bars in a field list indicate that there are fields in the table that are not currently in view.

Figure 2.5

6 In the **2A Schedule** field list—the field list on the right—point to the title bar to display the ⬦ pointer. Drag the field list to the right until there is about one inch of space between the field lists.

7 In the **2A Instructors** field list—the field list on the left—point to the lower right corner of the field list to display the ⬦ pointer, and then, holding down the left mouse button, drag downward and to the right to increase the height and width of the field list until the entire name of the table in the title bar displays and all of the field names display. Release the mouse button and all of the field names display as shown in Figure 2.6.

This action enables you to see all of the available fields and removes the vertical scroll bar. Recall that *one* instructor can teach *many* scheduled courses. The arrangement of field lists in the Relationships window displays the *one table* on the left side and the *many table* on the right side. Recall also that the primary key in each table is the required field that contains the data that uniquely identifies each record in the table. In the 2A Instructors table, each instructor is uniquely identified by the Instructor ID. In the 2A Schedule table, each scheduled course section is uniquely identified by the Schedule ID.

Figure 2.6

8 In the **2A Instructors** field list, point to **Instructor ID**, and then, holding down the left mouse button, drag the field name downward and to the right into the **2A Schedule** field list until the ⬦ pointer's arrow is on top of **Instructor ID**. Release the mouse button to display the **Edit Relationships** dialog box.

As you drag, a small graphic displays to indicate that you are dragging a field name from one field list to another. A table relationship works by matching data in two fields—the common field. In these two tables, the common field has the same name—*Instructor ID*. Common fields are not required to have the same name; however, they must have the same data type and field size.

🔄 **ANOTHER WAY**   On the Design tab, in the Tools group, click Edit Relationships. In the Edit Relationships dialog box, click Create New. In the Create New dialog box, designate the tables and fields that will create the relationship.

9 Point to the title bar of the **Edit Relationships** dialog box, and then, holding down the left mouse button, drag the dialog box to the right below the two field lists as shown in Figure 2.7. Release the mouse button.

> By dragging the common field, you create the *one-to-many* relationship. In the 2A Instructors table, Instructor ID is the primary key. In the 2A Schedule table, Instructor ID is the *foreign key* field. The foreign key is the field in the related table used to connect to the primary key in another table. The field on the *one* side of the relationship is typically the primary key.

Figure 2.7

Activity 2.03 | Setting Relationship Options

MOS
1.2.4

In this Activity, you will set relationship options that will enable you to work with records in the related tables.

1 In the **Edit Relationships** dialog box, click to select the **Enforce Referential Integrity** check box. Notice that the two options under **Enforce Referential Integrity** are now available.

> *Referential integrity* is a set of rules that Access uses to ensure that the data between related tables is valid. Enforcing referential integrity ensures that an Instructor ID cannot be added to a course in the 2A Schedule table if the Instructor ID is *not* included in the 2A Instructors table first. Similarly, enforcing referential integrity ensures that you cannot delete an instructor from the 2A Instructors table if there is a course that has been assigned to that instructor in the 2A Schedule table. After selecting Enforce Referential Integrity, *cascade options*—relationship options that enable you to update records in related tables when referential integrity is enforced—become available for use.

2 In the **Edit Relationships** dialog box, click to select the **Cascade Update Related Fields** check box.

> The *Cascade Update Related Fields* option enables you to change the data in the primary key field for the table on the *one* side of the relationship, and updates automatically change any fields in the related table that store the same data. For example, in the 2A Instructors table, if you change the data in the Instructor ID field for one instructor, Access automatically finds every scheduled course assigned to that instructor in the 2A Schedule table and changes the data in the common field, in this case, the Instructor ID field. Without this option, if you try to change the ID number for an instructor, an error message displays if there is a related record in the related table on the *many* side of the relationship.

3 In the **Edit Relationships** dialog box, click to select the **Cascade Delete Related Records** check box, and then compare your screen with Figure 2.8.

The *Cascade Delete Related Records* option enables you to delete a record in the table on the *one* side of the relationship and also delete all of the related records in related tables. For example, if an instructor retires or leaves the college and the courses that the instructor teaches must be canceled because no other instructor can be found, you can delete the instructor's record from the 2A Instructors table, and then all of the courses that are assigned to that instructor in the 2A Schedule table are also deleted. Without this option, an error message displays if you try to delete the instructor's record from the 2A Instructors table. Use caution when applying this option; in many instances another instructor would be found so you would not want the course to be deleted. In this instance, you would need to change the Instructor ID in the related records before deleting the original instructor from the 2A Instructors table.

Figure 2.8

4 In the **Edit Relationships** dialog box, click **Create**, and then compare your screen with Figure 2.9.

A *join line*—the line connecting or joining the two tables—displays between the two tables. The join line connects the primary key field—Instructor ID—in the 2A Instructors field list to the common field—Instructor ID—in the 2A Schedule field list. On the join line, *1* indicates the *one* side of the relationship, and the infinity symbol (∞) indicates the *many* side of the relationship. These symbols display when referential integrity is enforced.

Figure 2.9

MORE KNOWLEDGE **Edit or Delete a Relationship**

To modify or delete an existing relationship, right-click the join line. On the shortcut menu, click Delete to remove the join line and the relationship. If you want to edit the relationship options, click Edit Relationship to display the Edit Relationships dialog box.

Activity 2.04 | Saving a Relationship Report

1.0.1, 1.2.2

The Relationships window provides a map of how your database tables are related, and you can print and save this information as a report.

1 On the **Design tab**, in the **Tools group**, click **Relationship Report**.

The report is created and displays in the object window in Print Preview.

2 On the **Print Preview tab**, in the **Page Size group**, click **Margins**, and then click **Normal** to increase the margins slightly—some printers cannot print with narrow margins. Compare your screen with Figure 2.10.

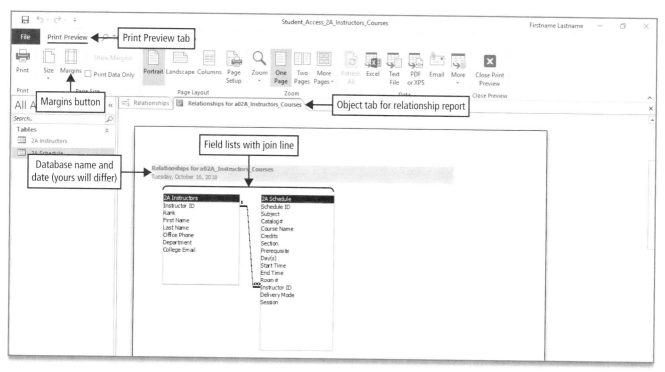

Figure 2.10

3 On the **Quick Access Toolbar**, click **Save** 🔲. In the **Save As** dialog box, click **OK** to accept the default report name. On the **Print Preview** tab, click **Close Print Preview**.

The report name displays in the Navigation Pane under *Unrelated Objects*. Because the report is just a map of the relationship between the tables, and not a report containing records from a table, it is not associated or related with any tables.

4 In the object window, click **Close** ⊠ to close the report, and then **Close** ⊠ the **Relationships** window.

NOTE　**Close Print Preview and the Relationship Report**

If you click Close Print Preview when the report is displayed in Print Preview, the Relationship report will display in Design view in the object window. If this happens, you can Close the object while it is displayed in this view.

Activity 2.05 | Displaying Subdatasheet Records

When you open the table on the *one* side of the relationship, the related records from the table on the *many* side are available for you to view and to modify.

1 In the **Navigation Pane**, double-click your **2A Instructors** table to open it in the object window, and then **Close** ⟪ the **Navigation Pane**.

2 On the left side of the first record—*Instructor ID* of *1224567*—click **+**, and then compare your screen with Figure 2.11.

A plus sign (+) to the left of a record in a table indicates that *related* records may exist in another table. Click the plus sign to display the related records in a ***subdatasheet***. In the first record for *Craig Fresch*, you can see that related records exist in the 2A Schedule table—he is scheduled to teach five LGL (Legal) courses. The plus signs display because you created a relationship between the two tables using the Instructor ID field—the common field.

When you click + to display the subdatasheet, the symbol changes to a minus sign (-), an indication that the subdatasheet is expanded. Click - to collapse the subdatasheet.

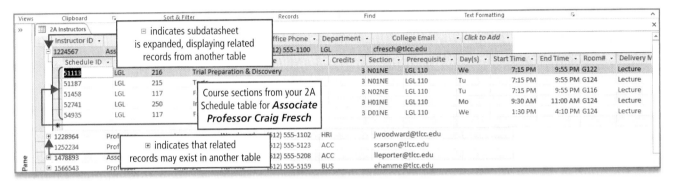

Figure 2.11

MORE KNOWLEDGE **Other Types of Relationships: One-to-One and Many-to-Many**

The type of relationship is determined by the placement of the primary key field. A one-to-one relationship exists between two tables when a record in one table is related to only one record in a second table. In this case, both tables use the same field as the primary key. This is most often used when data is placed in a separate table because access to that information is restricted; for example, using an Employee ID field as the primary key field, there is one table for contact information, and a second table with payroll information.

A many-to-many relationship between tables exists where many records in one table can be related to many records in another table. For example, many students can enroll in many courses. To create a many-to-many relationship, you must create a third table that contains the primary key fields from both tables. In the Relationships window, you create a join line from this table to the other two tables. In effect, you create multiple one-to-many relationships.

Activity 2.06 | **Testing Cascade Options**

Recall that cascade options enable you to make changes to records on the *one* side table of the relationship and update or delete records in the table on the *many* side of the relationship. In this Activity, you will change the data in the Instructor ID field—the primary key field—for one instructor, and then delete all of the records associated with another instructor from both tables.

1 In the subdatasheet for the first record—*Instructor ID* of *1224567*—notice that the first course that the instructor is scheduled to teach has a *Schedule ID* of *51113—LGL 216*. In the **2A Instructors** table, to the left of the first record, click **–** (minus sign) to collapse the subdatasheet.

2 If necessary, in the first record, in the **Instructor ID** field, select the data—**1224567**. Type **8224567** and then press ↓ to save the record.

If you had not enabled Cascade Update Related Fields in the Edit Relationships dialog box, an error message would have displayed.

3 Open » the **Navigation Pane**. In the **Navigation Pane**, double-click your **2A Schedule** table to open it, and then **Close** « the **Navigation Pane**.

🔄 **ANOTHER WAY**   Press [F11] to open or close the Navigation Pane.

4 Scroll to locate the record with a **Schedule ID** of **51113**—*LGL 216*. If necessary, scroll to the right to display the **Instructor ID** field, and notice that for this record, the **Instructor ID** is **8224567**. Compare your screen with Figure 2.12.

The Cascade Update Related Fields option enables you to change the data in the primary key field in your 2A Instructors table, and the five related records for *Craig Fresch* in the 2A Schedule table were updated to store his Instructor ID of *8224567*.

Figure 2.12

5 **Close** × your **2A Schedule** table. In your **2A Instructors** table, scroll to display the last few records. On the left side of the record for **Instructor ID** of **6145288**—*Professor Ivey Clarke*— click ⊞ to display the subdatasheet. Notice that this instructor is scheduled to teach two courses—*Schedule ID* of *42837* and *42930*.

6 Click ⊟ to collapse the subdatasheet. For the same record—**Instructor ID** of **6145288**— point to the record selector box to display the ➡ pointer, and then click to select the record. On the **Home tab**, in the **Records group**, click **Delete**.

A message displays warning you that this record and related records in related tables will be deleted. The record you selected does not display in the table, and the next record is selected. If you had not enabled Cascade Delete Related Records, an error message would have displayed, and you would not be able to delete the record for Professor Ivey Clarke without assigning her courses to another instructor first.

🔄 **ANOTHER WAY**   With the record selected, press [Del] or with the record selected, right-click, and then click Delete Record.

7 In the message box, click **Yes**.

The record for *Instructor ID* of *6145288* is deleted. On the Quick Access Toolbar, the Undo button is unavailable—if you mistakenly delete the wrong record and the related records, you must enter them again in both tables. Access cannot use Undo to undo a Delete.

8 Open » the **Navigation Pane**, open your **2A Schedule** table, and then **Close** « the **Navigation Pane**. Scroll through the records and notice that the records for a **Schedule ID** of **42837** and **42930** have been deleted from the table.

The Cascade Delete Related Records option in the Edit Relationships dialog box enables you to delete a record in the table on the *one* side of the relationship—2A Instructors—and simultaneously delete the records in the table on the *many* side of the relationship—2A Schedule—that are related to the deleted record.

9 In the object window, right-click either **object tab**, and then click **Close All** to close both tables.

> **NOTE**   Cascade Options—Record Must Be Edited or Deleted in Correct Table
>
> Changes in the data in the common field must be made in the primary key field in the table on the *one* side of the relationship—
> you cannot change the data in the common field in the table on the *many* side of the relationship. To delete a record and all
> of its associated records in another table, you must delete the record in the table on the *one* side of the relationship. You can,
> however, delete a related record from the table on the *many* side of the relationship—the related record in the table on the *one*
> side of the relationship is not deleted.

Objective 3   Sort Records in a Table

GO! Learn How

Video A2-3

Sorting is the process of arranging data in a specific order based on the value in a field. For example, you can sort the names in your contact list alphabetically by each person's last name, or you can sort your music collection by the artist. As records are entered into an Access table, they display in the order in which they are added to the table. After you close the table and reopen it, the records display in order by the primary key field.

Activity 2.07 | Sorting Records in a Table in Ascending or Descending Order

2.3.2

In this Activity, you will determine the departments of the faculty in the Business Division by sorting the data. Data can be sorted in either *ascending order* or *descending order*. Ascending order sorts text alphabetically (A to Z) and sorts numbers from the lowest number to the highest number. Descending order sorts text in reverse alphabetical order (Z to A) and sorts numbers from the highest number to the lowest number.

1 Open ⟩⟩ the **Navigation Pane**, open your **2A Instructors** table, and then **Close** ⟨⟨ the **Navigation Pane**. Notice that the records in the table are sorted in ascending order by the **Instructor ID** field, which is the primary key field.

2 In the field names row, click the **Department arrow**, click **Sort A to Z**, and then compare your screen with Figure 2.13.

> To sort records in a table, click the arrow to the right of the field name in the column on which you want to sort, and then click the sort order. After a field is sorted, a small arrow in the field name box indicates the sort order. For the Department field, the small arrow points up, indicating an ascending sort, and on the ribbon, Ascending is selected.

> The records display in alphabetical order by the Department field. Because the department names are now grouped together, you can quickly scroll through the table to see the instructors for each department. The first record in the table has no data in the Department field because the *Instructor ID* of 9999999 is reserved for *Staff*, a designation that is used until a scheduled course has been assigned to a specific instructor.

 ANOTHER WAY   Click in the field in any record, and then on the Home tab, in the Sort & Filter group, click Ascending; or right-click in the field in any record, and then click Sort A to Z.

Figure 2.13

> **3** ▸ On the **Home tab**, in the **Sort & Filter group**, click **Remove Sort** to clear the sort and return the records to the default sort order, which is by the primary key field—*Instructor ID*.

> **4** ▸ Click the **Last Name arrow**, and then click **Sort Z to A**.

> The records in the table are sorted by the Last Name field in reverse alphabetical order. The small arrow in the field name box points down, indicating a descending sort. On the ribbon, Descending is selected.

> **5** ▸ In the **Sort & Filter group**, click **Remove Sort** to clear the sort.

Activity 2.08 | Sorting Records in a Table on Multiple Fields

2.3.2

To sort a table on two or more fields, first identify the fields that will act as the *outermost sort field* and the *innermost sort field*. The outermost sort field is the first level of sorting, and the innermost sort field is the second or final level of sorting. To alphabetize a table by Last Name and then First Name (also called First Name within Last Name), the Last Name field is identified as the outermost sort field. If there are duplicate last names, the records should be further sorted by the First Name field—the innermost sort field. For tables, you sort the innermost field first and then sort the outermost field.

In this Activity, you will sort the records by Last Name (innermost sort field) within the Department (outermost sort field).

> **1** ▸ In the **Last Name** field, click in any record. On the **Home tab**, in the **Sort & Filter group**, click **Ascending**.

> The records are sorted in ascending order by Last Name—the innermost sort field.

2 Point anywhere in the **Department** field, right-click, and then click **Sort Z to A**. Compare your screen with Figure 2.14.

The records are sorted in descending order first by Department—the outermost sort field. Within each Department grouping, the records are sorted in ascending order by Last Name—the innermost sort field. Records can be sorted on multiple fields using both ascending and descending order.

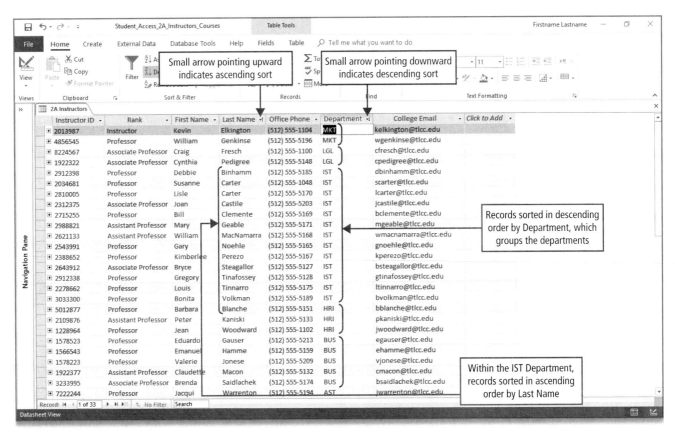

Figure 2.14

3 On the ribbon, click the **File tab**, click **Print**, and then click **Print Preview**. In the **Page Layout** group, click **Landscape**. In the **Zoom group**, click **Two Pages**, and notice that the table will print on two pages.

4 In the **Close Preview group**, click **Close Print Preview**. In the object window, **Close** × the table. In the message box, click **Yes** to save the changes to the sort order.

Tables are not always stored with the data sorted. In some cases, queries are created that sort the data, and then reports are created to display the sorted data.

Objective 4   Create a Query in Design View

GO! Learn How
Video A2-4

Recall that a select query is a database object that retrieves (selects) specific data from one or more tables and then displays the specified data in a table in Datasheet view. A query answers a question such as *Which instructors teach courses in the IST department?* Unless a query has already been designed to ask this question, you must create a new query.

Database users rarely need to see all of the records in all of the tables. That is why a query is so useful; it creates a *subset* of records—a portion of the total records—according to your specifications, and then displays only those records.

Activity 2.09 | Creating a New Select Query in Design View

Previously, you created a query using the Query Wizard. To create queries with more control over the results that are displayed, use Query Design view. The table or tables from which a query selects its data is referred to as the *data source*.

1 On the ribbon, click the **Create tab**, and then in the **Queries group**, click **Query Design**. Compare your screen with Figure 2.15.

A new query opens in Design view, and the Show Table dialog box displays, which lists both tables in the database.

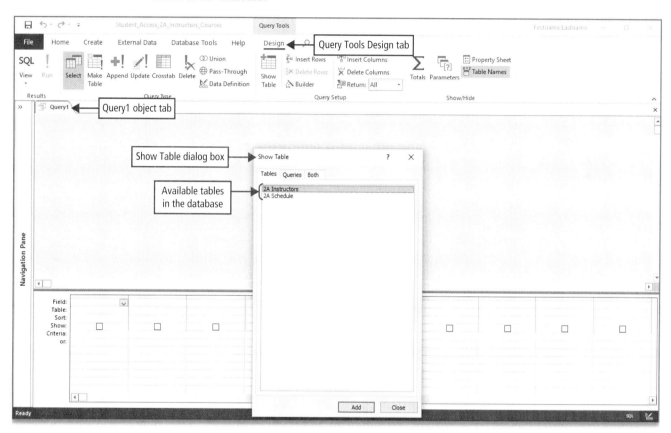

Figure 2.15

2 In the **Show Table** dialog box, double-click **2A Instructors**, and then, in the dialog box, click **Close**.

A field list for your 2A Instructors table displays in the upper area of the Query window. Instructor ID is the primary key field in this table. The Query window has two parts: the *table area* (upper area), which displays the field lists for tables that are used in the query, and the *design grid* (lower area), which displays the design of the query.

ALERT   Is there more than one field list in the table area?

If you double-click a table more than one time, a duplicate field list displays in the table area of the Query window. To remove a field list from the Query window, right-click the title bar of the field list, and then click Remove Table.

3 Point to the lower right corner of the field list to display the pointer, and then, holding down the left mouse button, drag downward and to the right to resize the field list, displaying all of the field names and the entire table name. Release the mouse button. In the **2A Instructors** field list, double-click **Rank**, and then look at the design grid.

The Rank field name displays in the design grid in the Field row. You limit the fields that display in the query results by placing only the desired field names in the design grid.

4 In the **2A Instructors** field list, point to **First Name**, holding down the left mouse button, drag the field name down into the design grid until the ⬚ pointer displays in the **Field** row in the second column, and then release the mouse button. Compare your screen with Figure 2.16.

This is a second way to add field names to the design grid. When you release the mouse button, the field name displays in the Field row.

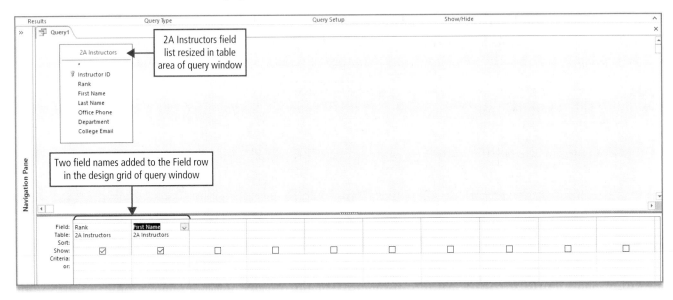

Figure 2.16

5 In the design grid, in the **Field** row, click in the third column, and then click the **arrow** that displays. From the list, click **Last Name** to add the field to the design grid.

This is a third way to add field names to the design grid.

6 Using one of the three techniques you just practiced, add the **Office Phone** field to the fourth column and the **Department** field to the fifth column in the design grid.

ALERT   Is there a duplicate field name or an incorrect field name in the design grid?

If you double-click a field name more than one time, a duplicate field name displays in the design grid. To remove a duplicate field name, in the design grid, in the Field row, right-click the duplicate field name, and then click Cut. Use this same method to delete a field name that you placed in the design grid by mistake. As you progress in your study of query design, you will learn alternate ways to delete field names from the design grid.

Activity 2.10 | Running, Saving, and Closing a Query

3.1.1, 3.1.6, 3.1.7

Once a query is designed, you **run** it to display the results. When you run a query, Access looks at the records in the table (or tables) you have included in the query, finds the records that match the specified conditions (if any), and displays only those records in a datasheet. Only the fields that you have added to the design grid display in the query results. The query always runs using the current table or tables, presenting the most up-to-date information.

1 ▶ On the **Design tab**, in the **Results group**, click **Run**, and then compare your screen with Figure 2.17.

> This query answers the question, *What is the rank, first name, last name, office phone number, and department of all of the instructors in the 2A Instructors table?* A query is a subgroup of the records in the table, arranged in Datasheet view, using the fields and conditions that you specify in the design grid. The five fields you specified in the design grid display in columns, and the records from the 2A Instructors table display in rows.

⟳ **ANOTHER WAY** On the Design tab, in the Results group, click the upper portion of the View button, which runs the query by switching to Datasheet view.

Figure 2.17

2 ▶ On the **Quick Access Toolbar**, click **Save** 🖫. In the **Save As** dialog box, type **2A Instructors Query** and then click **OK**.

> The query name displays on the object tab in the object window. Save your queries if you are likely to ask the same question again; doing so will save you the effort of creating the query again to answer the same question—just run the query again.

3 ▶ Click the **File tab**, click **Print**, and then click **Print Preview**.

> Queries answer questions and gather information from the data in tables. Typically, queries are created as a basis for a report, but query results can be printed like any table of data.

4 ▶ **Close** Print Preview. **Close** ✕ the query. **Open** » the **Navigation** Pane. At the top of the Navigation Pane, click **More** ⊙. On the list, under **Navigate To Category**, click **Tables and Related Views**. Notice that your **2A Instructors Query** object displays under your **2A Instructors** table object.

> The new query name displays in the Navigation Pane under the table with which it is related—the 2A Instructors table, which is the data source. Only the design of the query is saved; the records reside in the table object. Each time you open a query, Access runs it and displays the results based on the data stored in the data source. Thus, the results of the query always reflect the most up-to-date information.

Objective 5 | **Create a New Query From an Existing Query**

GO! Learn How
Video A2-5

You can create a new query from scratch or you can open an existing query, save it with a new name, and modify the design to answer another question. Using an existing query saves you time if your new query uses all or some of the same fields and conditions in an existing query.

Activity 2.11 | Copying an Existing Query

MOS
3.1.6

1 In the **Navigation Pane**, right-click your **2A Instructors Query**, and then click **Copy**.

2 In the **Navigation Pane**, point to a blank area, right-click, and then click Paste.

The Paste As dialog box displays, which enables you to name the copied query.

> **ANOTHER WAY** To create a copy of the query, in the Navigation Pane, click the query name to select it. On the Home tab, in the Clipboard group, click Copy. On the Home tab, in the Clipboard group, click the upper portion of the Paste button.

3 In the **Paste As** dialog box, type **2A Instructor IDs Query** and then click **OK**.

A new query, based on a copy of your 2A Instructors Query, is created and displays in the object window and in the Navigation Pane under its data source—your 2A Instructors table.

> **MORE KNOWLEDGE** **Rename a Query**
>
> If the query name is not correct, you can rename it as long as the query is closed. In the Navigation Pane, right-click the query name, and then click Rename. Edit the current name or type a new name, and then press Enter to accept the change.

4 In the **Navigation Pane**, double-click your **2A Instructor IDs Query** to run the query and display the query results in **Datasheet** view. **Close** « the **Navigation Pane**.

> **ANOTHER WAY** To create a copy of a query using a new name, click the File tab, and then click Save As. Under Save As, double-click Save Object As. In the Save As dialog box, click in the Name box and type the name of the new query.

Activity 2.12 | Modifying the Design of a Query

MOS
3.2.1, 3.1.6, 3.1.7

1 On the **Home tab**, in the **Views group**, click **View** to switch to **Design** view.

> **ANOTHER WAY** On the Home tab, in the Views group, click the View arrow, and then click Design View; or on the right side of the status bar, click the Design View button.

2 In the design grid, point to the thin gray selection bar above the **Office Phone** field name to display the ↓ pointer, and then compare your screen with Figure 2.18.

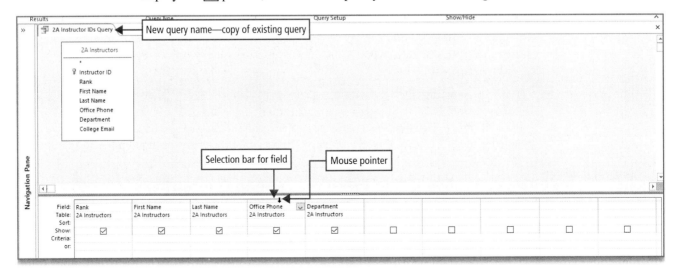

Figure 2.18

3 With the ⬇ pointer displayed in the selection bar above the **Office Phone** field name, click to select the column, and then press Del.

> This action deletes the field from the query design only—it has no effect on the field in the data source—2A Instructors table. The Department field moves to the left. Similarly, by using the selection bar, you can drag to select multiple fields and delete them at one time.

ANOTHER WAY In the design grid, click in the field name. On the Design tab, in the Query Setup group, click Delete Columns; or right-click the field name, and then click Cut; or click in the field name, and on the Home tab, in the Records group, click Delete.

4 Point to the selection bar above the **First Name** column, and then click to select the column. In the selected column, point to the selection bar to display the �by pointer, and then drag to the right until a dark vertical line displays on the right side of the **Last Name** column. Release the mouse button to position the **First Name** field in the third column.

> To rearrange fields in a query, first select the field to move, and then drag it to a new position in the design grid.

5 Using the technique you just practiced, move the **Department** field to the left of the **Rank** field.

6 From the field list, drag the **Instructor ID** field down to the first column in the design grid until the 🔖 pointer displays, and then release the mouse button. Compare your screen with Figure 2.19.

> The Instructor ID field displays in the first column, and the remaining four fields move to the right. Use this method to insert a field to the left of a field already displayed in the design grid.

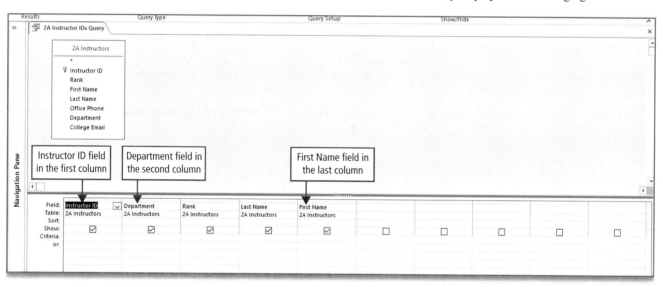

Figure 2.19

7 On the **Design tab**, in the **Results group**, click **Run**.

> This query answers the question, *What is the instructor ID, department, rank, last name, and first name of every instructor in the 2A Instructors table?* The results of the query are a subgroup of the records stored in the 2A Instructors table. The records are sorted by the table's primary key field—Instructor ID.

8 **Close** ✕ the query. In the message box, click **Yes** to save the changes to the query design—deleting a field, moving two fields, and adding a field. **Open** » the **Navigation Pane**.

> The query is saved and closed, and the query name displays in the Navigation Pane under the related table. Recall that only the *design* of the query is saved; the records reside in the related table or tables.

Objective 6 | Sort Query Results

You can sort the results of a query in ascending or descending order in either Datasheet view or Design view. Use Design view if your query results should always display in a specified sort order, or if you intend to use the sorted results in a report.

Activity 2.13 | Sorting Query Results

MOS

3.2.2, 3.1.7, 3.1.6

In this Activity, you will save an existing query with a new name, and then sort the query results by using the Sort row in Design view.

1 In the **Navigation Pane**, right-click your **2A Instructor IDs Query**, and then click **Copy**. In the **Navigation Pane**, point to a blank area, right-click, and then click **Paste**.

2 In the **Paste As** dialog box, type **2A Department Sort Query** and then click **OK**.

A new query is created based on a copy of your 2A Instructor IDs Query; that is, the new query includes the same fields in the same order as the query on which it is based. The query does not need to be open to save it with another name; you can select the object name in the Navigation Pane.

3 In the **Navigation Pane**, right-click your **2A Department Sort Query**, and then click **Design View**. **Close** ⟪ the **Navigation Pane**.

Use this technique to display the query in Design view if you are redesigning the query. Recall that if you double-click a query name in the Navigation Pane, Access runs the query and displays the query results in Datasheet view.

4 In the design grid, in the **Sort** row, under **Last Name**, click to display the insertion point and an arrow. Click the **arrow**, click **Ascending**, and then compare your screen with Figure 2.20.

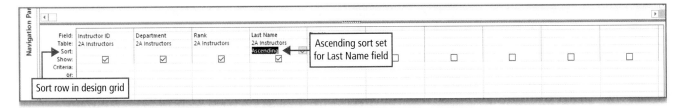

Figure 2.20

5 On the **Design tab**, in the **Results group**, click **Run**.

In the query results, the records are sorted in ascending order by the Last Name field, and two instructors have the same last name of *Carter—Susanne* and *Lisle*.

6 On the **Home tab**, in the **Views group**, click the upper portion of the **View** button to switch to **Design** view.

7 In the design grid, click in the **Sort** row under **First Name**, click the **arrow**, and then click **Ascending**. **Run** the query.

In the query results, the records are sorted first by the Last Name field. If two instructors have the same last name, then those records are sorted by the First Name field. The two instructors with the same last name of *Carter* are sorted by their first names, and the two records with the same last name of *Fresch* are sorted by their first names.

8 Switch to **Design** view. In the design grid, click in the **Sort** row under **Department**, click the **arrow**, and then click **Descending**. **Run** the query, and then compare your screen with Figure 2.21.

In Design view, fields with a Sort setting are sorted from left to right. That is, the sorted field on the left becomes the outermost sort field, and the sorted field on the right becomes the innermost sort field. Thus, the records in this query are sorted first in descending order by the Department field—the leftmost sort field. Then, within each department, the records are sorted in ascending order by the Last Name field. And, finally, within each duplicate last name, the records are sorted in ascending order by the First Name field.

If you run a query and the sorted results are not what you intended, be sure the fields are displayed from left to right according to the groupings that you desire.

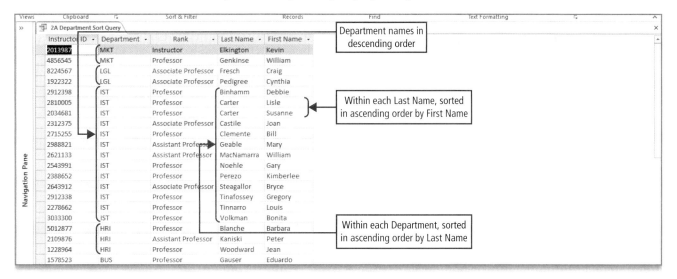

Figure 2.21

9 **Close** ⊠ the query. In the message box, click **Yes** to save the changes to the query design.

MORE KNOWLEDGE **Sorting in Design View or Datasheet View**

If you add a sort order to the *design* of a query, it remains as a permanent part of the query design. If you use the sort buttons in Datasheet view, the sort order will override the sort order of the query design and can be saved as part of the query.
A sort order designated in Datasheet view does not display in the Sort row of the query design grid. As with sorting tables, in Datasheet view, a small arrow displays to the right of the field name to indicate the sort order of the field.

Objective 7 **Specify Criteria in a Query**

GO! Learn How
Video A2-7

Queries locate information in a table based on ***criteria*** that you specify as part of the query design. Criteria are conditions that identify the specific records for which you are looking. Criteria enable you to ask a more specific question; therefore, you will get a more specific result. For example, to find out how many instructors are in the IST department, limit the results to display only that specific department by entering criteria in the design grid.

Activity 2.14 | **Specifying Text Criteria in a Query**

3.1.1, 3.2.1, 3.2.3,
3.1.6, 3.1.7

In this Activity, you will assist Dean Judkins by creating a query to answer the question, *Which instructors are in the IST Department?*

1 On the ribbon, click the **Create tab**, and then in the **Queries group**, click **Query Design**.

2 In the **Show Table** dialog box, double-click your **2A Instructors** table to add it to the table area, and then **Close** the **Show Table** dialog box.

3 By dragging the lower right corner, resize the field list to display all of the field names and the table name. Add the following fields to the design grid in the order given: **Department**, **Instructor ID**, **Rank**, **First Name**, and **Last Name**.

4 In the design grid, click in the **Criteria** row under **Department**, type **IST** and then press Enter. Compare your screen with Figure 2.22.

Access places quotation marks around the criteria to indicate that this is a *text string*—a sequence of characters. Use the Criteria row to specify the criteria that will limit the results of the query to your exact specifications. The criteria is not case sensitive; you can type *ist* instead of *IST*.

Figure 2.22

5 **Run** the query, and then compare your screen with Figure 2.23.

Thirteen records display. There are 13 instructors in the IST Department; or, more specifically, there are 13 records that have *IST* in the Department field.

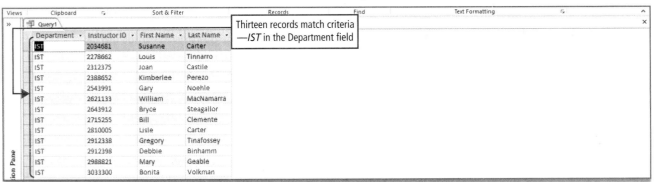

Figure 2.23

6 **Save** 🔲 the query as **2A IST Query**

7 **Close** ✕ the query, **Open** » the **Navigation Pane**, and then notice your **2A IST Query** object.

Recall that in the Navigation Pane, queries display an icon of two overlapping datasheets.

Activity 2.15 | Specifying Criteria and Hiding the Field in the Query Results

3.1.1, 3.2.1,
3.2.2, 3.2.3,
3.1.6, 3.1.7

So far, all of the fields that you included in the query design have also been included in the query results. There are times when you need to use the field in the query design, but you do not need to display that field in the results—usually, when the data in the field is the same for all of the records. In this Activity, you will create a query to answer the question, *Which instructors have a rank of Professor?*

1 **Close** ⟨«⟩ the **Navigation Pane.** On the **Create tab**, in the **Queries group**, click **Query Design**.

2 In the **Show Table** dialog box, double-click your **2A Instructors** table to add it to the table area, and then **Close** the **Show Table** dialog box.

3 Resize the field list, and then add the following fields to the design grid in the order given: **Instructor ID**, **First Name**, **Last Name**, and **Rank**.

4 Click in the **Sort** row under **Last Name**, click the **arrow**, and then click **Ascending**.

5 Click in the **Criteria** row under **Rank**, type **professor** and then press ⏎. Compare your screen with Figure 2.24.

> Recall that criteria is not case sensitive. As you start typing *professor*, a list of functions displays, from which you can select if a function is included in your criteria. After pressing ⏎, the insertion point moves to the next criteria box, and quotation marks are added around the text string that you entered.

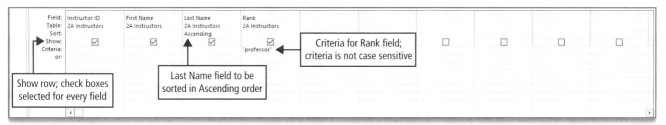

Figure 2.24

6 In the design grid, in the **Show** row, notice that a check box is selected for every field. **Run** the query.

> Eighteen records meet the criteria—*professor* in the *Rank* field. In the Rank column, every record displays *Professor*, and the records are sorted in ascending order by the Last Name field.

7 Switch to **Design** view. In the design grid, in the **Show** row under **Rank**, click to clear the check box.

> Because it is repetitive and not particularly useful to display *Professor* for every record in the query results, clear the Show check box so that the field is hidden or does not display. You should, however, always run the query first before clearing the Show check box to be sure that the correct records display.

8 **Run** the query, and then notice that the *Rank* field does not display even though it was used to specify criteria in the query.

> The same 18 records display, but the *Rank* field is hidden from the query results. Although the Rank field is included in the query design so that you could specify the criteria of *professor*, it is not necessary to display the field in the results. When appropriate, clear the Show check box to avoid cluttering the query results with data that is not useful.

9 **Save** 💾 the query as 2A Professors Query **Close** ⟨×⟩ the query.

Activity 2.16 | Using *Is Null* Criteria to Find Empty Fields

MOS
3.1.1, 3.2.1,
3.2.2, 3.2.3,
3.1.6, 3.1.7, 3.2.3

Sometimes you must locate records where data is missing. You can locate such records by using *Is Null* as the criteria in a field. *Is Null* is used to find empty fields. Additionally, you can display only the records where data has been entered in the field by using the criteria of *Is Not Null*, which excludes records where the specified field is empty. In this Activity, you will design a query to answer the question, *Which scheduled courses have no credits listed?*

> **1** On the **Create tab**, in the **Queries group**, click **Query Design**. In the **Show Table** dialog box, double-click your **2A Schedule** table to add it to the table area, and then **Close** the **Show Table** dialog box.

> **2** Resize the field list, and then add the following fields to the design grid in the order given: **Subject**, **Catalog#**, **Section**, **Course Name**, and **Credits**.

> **3** Click in the **Criteria** row under **Credits**, type **is null** and then press Enter.

> Access capitalizes *is null*. The criteria *Is Null* examines the Credits field and locates records that do *not* have any data entered in the field.

> **4** Click in the **Sort** row under **Subject**, click the **arrow**, and then click **Ascending**. **Sort** the **Catalog#** field in **Ascending** order, and then **Sort** the **Section** field in **Ascending** order. Compare your screen with Figure 2.25.

Figure 2.25

> **5** **Run** the query, and then compare your screen with Figure 2.26.

> Four scheduled courses do not have credits listed—the Credits field is empty. The records are sorted in ascending order first by the Subject field, then by the Catalog# field, and then by the Section field. Using the information displayed in the query results, a course scheduler can more easily locate the records in the table and enter the credits for these courses.

Figure 2.26

> **6** **Save** the query as **2A No Credits Query**

> **7** **Close** the query. **Open** the **Navigation Pane**, and then notice that your **2A No Credits Query** object displays under your **2A Schedule** table object, its data source. At the top of the **Navigation Pane**, click **More**. On the list, under **Navigate To Category**, click **Object Type**. Notice that the queries are now grouped together.

> **8** **Close** the database and **Close** Access.

For Non-MyLab Submissions : Determine What Your Instructor Requires for Submission

As directed by your instructor, submit your completed database file.

9 In **MyLab IT**, locate and click the Grader Project **Access 2A Instructors and Courses**. In **step 3**, under **Upload Completed Assignment**, click **Choose File**. In the **Open** dialog box, navigate to your **Access Chapter 2 folder**, and then click your **Student_Access_2A_Instructors_ Courses** file one time to select it. In the lower right corner of the **Open** dialog box, click **Open**.

The name of your selected file displays above the Upload button.

10 To submit your file to **MyLab IT** for grading, click **Upload**, wait a moment for a green **Success!** message, and then in **step 4**, click the blue **Submit for Grading** button. Click **Close Assignment** to return to your list of **Course Materials**.

You have completed Project 2A   END

Objective	**Export a Relationship Report to a PDF File, Save the PDF File to Google Drive, and then Share the File**

Access web apps are designed to work with Microsoft's SharePoint, a service for setting up websites to share and manage documents. Your college may not have SharePoint installed, so you will use other tools to share objects from your database so that you can work collaboratively with others. Recall that Google Drive is Google's free, web-based word processor, spreadsheet, slide show, form, and data storage and sharing service. For Access, you can export a database object to an Excel worksheet, a PDF file, or a text file, and then save the file to Google Drive.

ALERT **Working with Web-Based Applications and Services**

Computer programs and services on the web receive continuous updates and improvements, so the steps to complete this web-based Activity may differ from the ones shown. You can often look at the screens and the information presented to determine how to complete the Activity.

If you do not already have a Google account, you will need to create one before you begin this Activity. Go to **http://google.com** and in the upper right corner, click **Sign In**. On the Sign In screen, click **Create Account**. On the Create your Google Account page, complete the form, read and agree to the Terms of Service and Privacy Policy, and then click **Next step**. On the Welcome screen, click **Get Started**.

Activity | Exporting a Relationship Report to a PDF File, Saving the PDF file to Google Drive, and Sharing the File

In this Activity, you will export your Relationships Report object to a PDF file, upload your PDF file to Google Drive, and then share the file.

1 Start Access, navigate to your **Access Chapter 2** folder, and then open your **2A_Instructors_Courses** database file. On the **Message Bar**, click **Enable Content**. In the **Navigation Pane**, click your **Relationships for 2A_Instructors_Courses** object to select it.

2 On the ribbon, click the **External Data tab**, and then in the **Export group**, click **PDF or XPS**. In the **Publish as PDF or XPS** dialog box, navigate to your **Access Chapter 2** folder. In the **Publish as PDF or XPS** dialog box, click in the **File name** box, and then using your own name, type **Lastname_Firstname_AC_2A_Web** and be sure that the **Open file after publishing** check box is selected and the **Minimum size (publishing online)** option button is selected. Click **Publish**.

The PDF file is created and opens in your browser, Adobe Reader, or Adobe Acrobat, depending on the software that is installed on your computer.

3 If necessary, close the view of the PDF file. In the **Export – PDF** dialog box, click **Close**, and then **Close** ⌧ Access.

4 From the desktop, open your browser, navigate to **http://google.com**, and then sign in to your Google account. Click the **Google Apps** menu ⊞, and then click **Drive** △. Open your **GO! Web Projects** folder— or click New to create and then open this folder if necessary.

5 On the left, click **New**, click **File upload**. In the **Open** dialog box, navigate to your **Access Chapter 2** folder, and then double-click your **Lastname_Firstname_AC_2A_Web** file to upload it to Google Drive. When the title bar of the message box indicates *1 upload complete*, **Close** the message box. A second message box may display t emporarily.

6 In the file list, click your **Lastname_Firstname_AC_2A_Web** PDF file one time to select it.

7 Right-click the file name. On the shortcut menu, click **Share**.

8 In the Share with others dialog box, with your insertion point blinking in the **Enter names or email addresses** box, type the email address that you use at your college. To the right of the email address, click **Edit files directly** 🖉▾, and click **Can comment**. Click in the **Add a note** box, and then type **This relationship report identifies tables that can be used together to create other objects in the database.** Compare your screen with Figure A.

If you upload a table that you exported as an Excel spreadsheet or Word document and that you want to enable others to add records, be sure that you set the Sharing permission to *Can edit*.

9 Start the **Snipping Tool**. In the **Snipping Tool** dialog box, click the **New arrow**, and then click **Full-screen Snip**.

10 On the **Snipping Tool** toolbar, click the **Save Snip** button 🖫. In the **Save As** dialog box, navigate to your **Access Chapter 2** folder. Click in the **File name** box, type **Lastname_Firstname_AC_2A_Web_Snip** be sure that the **Save as type** box displays **JPEG file**, and then click **Save**. **Close** ⊠ the **Snipping Tool** window.

11 In the **Share with others** dialog box, click **Send**.

If your college is not using Google accounts, you may have to confirm sending the message with a link.

12 In Google Drive, click your Google Drive name, and then click **Sign out**. **Close** your browser window.

13 If directed to submit a paper printout of your PDF and snip file, follow the directions given in the Note below. As directed by your instructor, submit your pdf file and your snip file that are the results of this project. Your instructor may also request that you submit a copy of the email that was sent to you notifying you of the shared file.

Figure A

NOTE   **Printing your PDF and Snip .JPG File**

Using File Explorer, navigate to your Access Chapter 2 folder. Locate and double-click your AC_2A_Web file. On the toolbar, click the Print file button. Then Close your default PDF reader. In your Access Chapter 2 folder, locate and double-click your AC_2A_Web_Snip file. If this is the first time you have tried to open a .jpg file, you will be asked to identify a program. If you are not sure which program to use, select Paint or Windows Photo Viewer. From the ribbon, menu bar, or toolbar, click the Print command, and then Close the program window.

Athletic Scholarships Database

Project Activities

In Activities 2.17 through 2.32, you will assist Roberto Garza, Athletic Director for Texas Lakes Community College, in creating queries to locate information about athletic scholarships that have awarded to students. Your completed Navigation Pane will look similar to Figure 2.27.

Project Files for MyLab IT Grader

1. In your **MyLab IT** course, locate and click **Access 2B Athletes and Scholarships**, Download Materials, and then Download All Files.
2. Extract the zipped folder to your Access Chapter 2 folder. Close the Grader download screens.
3. Take a moment to open the downloaded **Access 2B_Athletes_Scholarships_Instructions**; note any recent updates to the book.

Project Results

GO! Project 2B
Where We're Going

Figure 2.27 Project 2B Athletic Scholarships

For Non-MyLab Submissions

For Project 2B, you will need:
a02B_Athletes_Scholarships
a02B_Athletes (Excel workbook)

Start with an Access Data File

In your Access Chapter 2 folder, save your database as:
Lastname_Firstname_2B_Athletes_Scholarships

After you have saved your database, launch Access and open the database. On the next page, begin with Step 2.

| Objective 8 | **Specify Numeric Criteria in a Query** |

ALERT   Because Office 365 is a cloud-based subscription service that receives continuous updates, you may encounter some variations in what appears on your screen and what is shown in this instruction. Microsoft Office 365 is fully installed on your PC or Mac; no internet access is necessary to create or edit documents. When you *are* connected to the internet, you will receive monthly upgrades and new features, so you always have the latest versions of Office apps as soon as they are available. Your subscription gives you continuous free access to the latest innovations and refinements.

GO! Learn How

Video A2-8

Criteria can be set for fields containing numeric data. When you design your table, set the appropriate data type for fields that will contain numbers, currency, or dates so that mathematical calculations can be performed.

Activity 2.17 | Opening an Existing Database and Importing a Spreadsheet as a New Table

MOS

1.1.1, 1.2.3, 2.4.5

In this Activity, you will import an Excel spreadsheet as a new table in the database.

1 Start Access. In the Access opening screen, click **Open Other Files**. Navigate to your **Access Chapter 2 folder**, and then double-click the Access file that you downloaded from **MyLab IT** that displays your name—**Student_Access_2B_Athletes_Scholarships**.

2 On the **Message Bar**, click **Enable Content**. Double-click the **2B Scholarships Awarded** table to open it in **Datasheet** view. **Close** ❮ the **Navigation Pane**, and then examine the data in the table. Compare your screen with Figure 2.28.

In this table, Mr. Garza tracks the names and amounts of scholarships awarded to student athletes. Students are identified only by their Student ID numbers, and the primary key is the Scholarship ID field.

Figure 2.28

3 **Close** ✕ the table. On the ribbon, click the **External Data tab**. In the **Import & Link group**, click the **New Data Source** arrow, point to **From File**, and then click **Excel**. In the **Get External Data – Excel Spreadsheet** dialog box, to the right of the **File name** box, click **Browse**.

4 In the **File Open** dialog box, navigate to your student data files, and then double-click **a02B_Athletes**. Be sure that the **Import the source data into a new table in the current database** option button is selected, and then click **OK**.

The Import Spreadsheet Wizard opens and displays the spreadsheet data.

5 In the upper left area of the wizard, select the **First Row Contains Column Headings** check box. In the wizard, click **Next**, and then click **Next** again.

6 In the wizard, click the **Choose my own primary key** option button, and then verify that **Student ID** displays in the box.

> In the new table, Student ID will be designated as the primary key. No two students have the same Student ID.

7 Click **Next**. With the text selected in the **Import to Table** box, type **2B Athletes** and then click **Finish**. In the **Get External Data – Excel Spreadsheet** dialog box, click **Close**.

8 Open ⟩⟩ the **Navigation Pane**. In the **Navigation Pane**, right-click your **2B Athletes** table, and then click **Design View**. **Close** ⟨⟨ the **Navigation Pane**.

9 To the right of **Student ID**, click in the **Data Type** box, click the **arrow**, and then click **Short Text**. For the **Postal Code** field, change the **Data Type** to **Short Text**, and in the **Field Properties** area, click **Field Size**, type **5** and then press Enter. In the **Field Name** column, click **State**, set the **Field Size** to **2** and then press Enter. Compare your screen with Figure 2.29.

> Recall that numeric data that does not represent a quantity and is not used in a calculation, such as the Student ID and Postal Code, should be assigned a data type of Short Text.

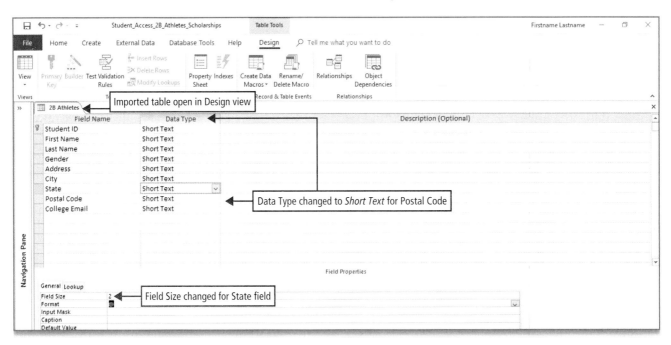

Figure 2.29

10 On the **Design tab**, in the **Views group**, click the top half of the **View button** to switch to **Datasheet** view. In the message box, click **Yes** to save the table. In the second message box, click **Yes**—no data will be lost. Take a moment to examine the data in the imported table.

11 In the datasheet, to the left of the **Student ID** field name, click the **Select All** button. On the **Home tab**, in the **Records group**, click **More**, and then click **Field Width**. In the **Column Width** dialog box, click **Best Fit**. Click in any record to cancel the selection, **Save** the layout changes to the table, and then **Close** × the table.

Activity 2.18 | Creating a One-to-Many Table Relationship

In this Activity, you will create a one-to-many relationship between your 2B Athletes table and your 2B Scholarships Awarded table by using the common field—*Student ID*.

1 Click the **Database Tools tab**, and then in the **Relationships group**, click **Relationships**.

2 In the **Show Table** dialog box, double-click your **2B Athletes** table, and then double-click your **2B Scholarships Awarded** table to add both tables to the **Relationships** window. **Close** the **Show Table** dialog box.

3 Point to the title bar of the field list on the right, and then drag the field list to the right until there is approximately one inch of space between the field lists. By dragging the lower right corner of the field list, resize each field list to display all of the field names and the entire table name.

Repositioning and resizing the field lists are not required but doing so makes it easier for you to view the field names and the join line when creating relationships.

4 In the **2B Athletes** field list, point to **Student ID**, and then, holding down the left mouse button, drag the field name into the **2B Scholarships Awarded** field list on top of **Student ID**. Release the mouse button to display the **Edit Relationships** dialog box.

5 Point to the title bar of the **Edit Relationships** dialog box, and then drag it to the right of the two field lists. In the **Edit Relationships** dialog box, verify that **Student ID** displays as the common field for both tables.

Repositioning the Edit Relationships dialog box is not required but doing so enables you to see the field lists. The Relationship Type is *One-To-Many—one* athlete can have *many* scholarships. The common field in both tables is the *Student ID* field. In the 2B Athletes table, Student ID is the primary key. In the 2B Scholarships Awarded table, Student ID is the foreign key.

6 In the **Edit Relationships** dialog box, click to select the **Enforce Referential Integrity** check box, the **Cascade Update Related Fields** check box, and the **Cascade Delete Related Records** check box. Click **Create**, and then compare your screen with Figure 2.30.

The one-to-many relationship is established. The *1* and ∞ symbols indicate that referential integrity is enforced, which ensures that a scholarship cannot be awarded to a student whose Student ID is not included in the 2B Athletes table. Recall that the Cascade options enable you to update and delete records automatically on the *many* side of the relationship when changes are made in the table on the *one* side of the relationship.

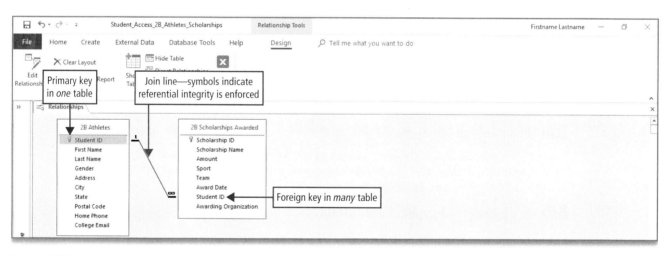

Figure 2.30

7 On the **Design tab**, in the **Tools group**, click **Relationship Report**. On the **Print Preview tab**, in the **Page Size group**, click **Margins**, and then click **Normal**. **Save** 🖫 the report as **2B Relationships**

8 In the object window, right-click either **object tab**, and then click **Close All** to close the Relationships Report and the Relationships window.

9 **Open** 》 the **Navigation Pane**, double-click your **2B Athletes** table to open it, and then **Close** 《 the **Navigation Pane**. On the left side of the first record, click **+** (plus sign) to display the subdatasheet for the record.

In the first record, for *Joel Barthmaier*, one related record exists in the 2B Scholarships Awarded table. Joel has been awarded the *Austin Jump Ball Award* in the amount of *$300*. The subdatasheet displays because you created a relationship between the two tables using Student ID as the common field.

10 ▸ **Close** ⊠ the **2B Athletes** table.

When you close the table, the subdatasheet will collapse—you do not need to click – (minus sign) before closing a table.

Activity 2.19 | Specifying Numeric Criteria in a Query

3.1.1, 3.2.1, 3.2.2, 3.2.3, 3.1.7

In this Activity, you will create a query to answer the question regarding scholarships awarded, *Which scholarships are in the amount of $300, and for which sports?*

1 ▸ Click the **Create tab**. In the **Queries group**, click **Query Design**.

2 ▸ In the **Show Table** dialog box, double-click your **2B Scholarships Awarded** table to add it to the table area, and then **Close** the **Show Table** dialog box. Resize the field list to display all of the fields and the entire table name.

3 ▸ Add the following fields to the design grid in the order given: **Scholarship Name**, **Sport**, and **Amount**.

4 ▸ Click in the **Sort** row under **Sport**, click the **arrow**, and then click **Ascending**.

5 ▸ Click in the **Criteria** row under **Amount**, type **300** and then press Enter. Compare your screen with Figure 2.31.

When you enter currency values as criteria, do not type the dollar sign. Include a decimal point only if you are looking for a specific amount that includes cents; for example, 300.49. Access does not insert quotation marks around the criteria because the data type of the field is Currency, which is a numeric format.

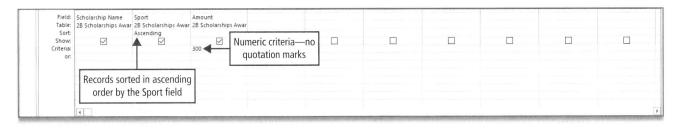

Figure 2.31

6 ▸ On the **Design tab**, in the **Results group**, click **Run** to display the query results.

Five scholarships in the exact amount of $300 were awarded to student athletes. In the navigation area, *1 of 5* displays—1 represents the first record that is selected, and 5 represents the total number of records that meet the criteria.

7 ▸ On the **Home tab**, in the **Views group**, click **View** to switch to **Design** view.

Activity 2.20 | Using Comparison Operators in Criteria

3.1.6, 3.2.3

Comparison operators are symbols that are used to evaluate data in the field to determine whether it is the same (=), greater than (>), less than (<), or in between a range of values as specified by the criteria. If no comparison operator is specified, equal (=) is assumed. For example, in the previous Activity, you created a query to display only those records where the *Amount* is *300*. The comparison operator of = was assumed, and the query results displayed only those records that had values in the Amount field equal to 300.

1 ▸ In the design grid, in the **Criteria** row under **Amount**, select the existing criteria—*300*— and then type **>300** and press Enter. **Run** the query.

Fourteen records display, and each has a value *greater than* $300 in the Amount field; there are no records for which the Amount is *equal to* $300.

2 Switch to **Design** view. In the **Criteria** row under **Amount**, select the existing criteria—*>300*. Type **<300** and then press [Enter]. **Run** the query.

> Eleven records display, and each has a value *less than* $300 in the Amount field; there are no records for which the Amount is *equal to* $300.

3 Switch to **Design** view. In the **Criteria** row under **Amount**, select the existing criteria–*<300*. Type **>=300** and then press [Enter]. **Run** the query, and then compare your screen with Figure 2.32.

> Nineteen records display, including the records for scholarships in the exact amount of $300. The records include scholarships *greater than* or *equal to* $300. In this manner, comparison operators can be combined. This query answers the question, *Which scholarships have been awarded in the amount of $300 or more, and for which sports, arranged alphabetically by sport?*

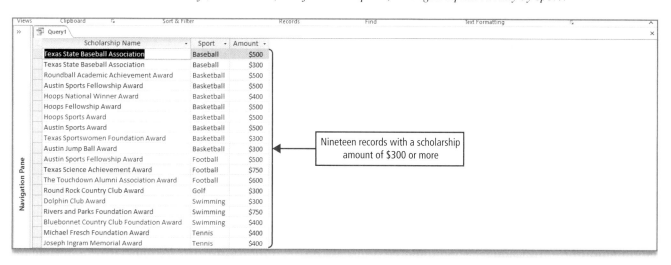

Figure 2.32

4 **Save** 🖫 the query as **2B $300 or More Query** and then display the query results in **Print Preview**.

5 Click **Close Print Preview**. **Close** ⨯ the query. **Open** ❯❯ the **Navigation Pane**, and notice that this new query displays under *2B Scholarships Awarded*, its data source.

Activity 2.21 | Using the Between . . . And Comparison Operator

3.1.6, 3.1.7, 3.2.3

The ***Between . . . And operator*** is a comparison operator that looks for values within a range. It is useful when you need to locate records that are within a range of dates; for example, scholarships awarded between May 1 and June 30.

In this Activity, you will create a new query from an existing query, and then add criteria to look for values within a range of dates. The query will answer the question, *Which scholarships were awarded between May 1 and June 30?*

1 In the **Navigation Pane**, click your **2B $300 or More Query** object to select it. On the **Home tab**, in the **Clipboard** group, click **Copy**. In the **Navigation Pane**, point to a blank area, right-click, and then click **Paste**.

2 In the **Paste As** dialog box, type **2B Awards May-June Query** and then click **OK**.

> A new query, based on a copy of your 2B $300 or More Query, is created and displays in the Navigation Pane under its data source—your 2B Scholarships Awarded table.

3 In the **Navigation Pane**, right-click your **2B Awards May-June Query**, click **Design View**, and then **Close** ⟪ the **Navigation Pane**.

4 In the **2B Scholarships Awarded** field list, double-click **Award Date** to add it to the fourth column in the design grid.

5 In the **Criteria** row under **Amount**, select the existing criteria—*>=300*—and then press Del so that the query is not restricted by a monetary value.

6 Click in the **Criteria** row under **Award Date**, type **between 5/1/22 and 6/30/22** and then press Enter.

7 In the selection bar of the design grid, point to the right edge of the **Award Date** column to display the ⊞ pointer, and then double-click to apply Best Fit to this column. Compare your screen with Figure 2.33.

> The width of the Award Date column is increased to fit the longest entry in the column, which enables you to see all of the criteria. Access places pound signs (#) around the dates and capitalizes *between* and *and*. This criteria instructs Access to look for values in the Award Date field that begin with 5/1/22 and end with 6/30/22. Both the beginning and ending dates will be included in the query results.

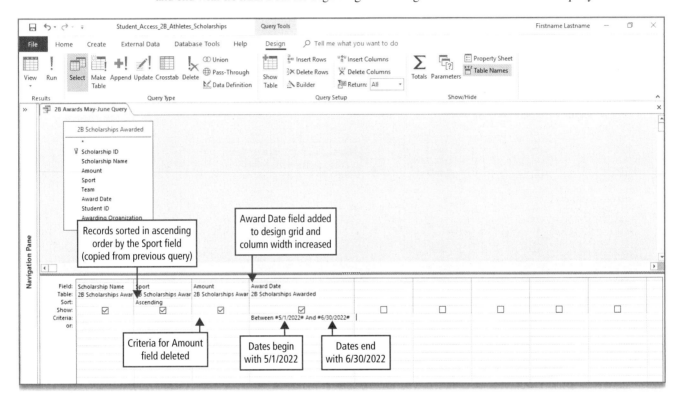

Figure 2.33

8 **Run** the query, and notice that eight scholarships were awarded between 5/1/2022 and 6/30/2022.

9 **Close** × the query, and in the message box, click **Yes** to save the changes to the query design.

Objective 9 | **Use Compound Criteria in a Query**

GO! Learn How
Video A2-9

You can specify more than one condition—criteria—in a query; this is called ***compound criteria***. Compound criteria use AND and OR ***logical operators***. Logical operators enable you to enter multiple criteria for the same field or for different fields.

Activity 2.22 | Using AND Criteria in a Query

3.1.1, 3.2.1,
3.2.3, 3.1.6, 3.1.7

The ***AND condition*** is an example of a compound criteria used to display records that match all parts of the specified criteria. In this Activity, you will help Mr. Garza answer the question, *Which scholarships over $500 were awarded for football?*

1 Click the **Create tab**, and in the **Queries group**, click **Query Design**. In the **Show Table** dialog box, double-click your **2B Scholarships Awarded** table to add it to the table area, and then **Close** the **Show Table** dialog box. Resize the field list to display all of the fields and the table name.

2 Add the following fields to the design grid in the order given: **Scholarship Name**, **Sport**, and **Amount**.

3 Click in the **Criteria** row under **Sport**, type **football** and then press Enter.

4 In the **Criteria** row under **Amount**, type **>500** and then press Enter. Compare your screen with Figure 2.34.

> You create the AND condition by placing the criteria for both fields on the same line in the Criteria row. The criteria indicates that records should be located that contain *Football* in the Sport field AND a value greater than *500* in the Amount field. Both conditions must exist or be true for the records to display in the query results.

Figure 2.34

5 **Run** the query, and notice that two records display that match both conditions—*Football* in the Sport field AND a value greater than *$500* in the Amount field.

6 **Save** 🖫 the query as **2B Football AND Over $500 Query** and then **Close** ✕ the query.

7 **Open** » the **Navigation Pane**, and then click to select the **2B Football AND Over $500 Query** object. Click the **File tab**, click **Print**, and then click **Print Preview**.

> You can view an object in Print Preview or print any selected object in the Navigation Pane—the object does not need to be open in the object window to print it.

8 Click **Close Print Preview**. **Close** the query. **Close** « the **Navigation Pane**.

Activity 2.23 | Using OR Criteria in a Query

3.1.1, 3.2.1,
3.2.3, 3.1.6, 3.1.7

The *OR condition* is an example of a compound criteria used to display records that meet one or more parts of the specified criteria. The OR condition can specify criteria in a single field or in different fields. In this Activity, you will help Mr. Garza answer the question, *Which scholarships over $200 were awarded for volleyball or golf, and what is the award date of each?*

1 On the **Create tab**, in the **Queries group**, click **Query Design**.

2 In the **Show Table** dialog box, double-click your **2B Scholarships Awarded** table to add it to the table area, and then **Close** the **Show Table** dialog box. Resize the field list, and then add the following fields to the design grid in the order given: **Scholarship Name**, **Sport**, **Amount**, and **Award Date**.

3 In the design grid, click in the **Criteria** row under **Sport**, type **volleyball** and then press ↓.

> The insertion point is blinking in the *or* row under Sport.

4 In the **or** row under **Sport**, type **golf** and then press Enter. **Run** the query.

> Six records were located in the 2B Scholarships Awarded table that have either *volleyball* OR *golf* stored in the Sport field. This is an example of using the OR condition to locate records that meet one or more parts of the specified criteria in a single field—*Sport*.

5 Switch to **Design** view. In the **or** row under **Sport**, select *"golf"* and then press Del. In the **Criteria** row under **Sport**, select and delete *"volleyball"*. Type **volleyball or golf** and then press Enter.

6 In the **Criteria** row under **Amount**, type **>200** and then press [Enter]. Compare your screen with Figure 2.35.

This is an alternative way to enter the OR condition in the Sport field and is a good method to use when you add an AND condition to the criteria. Access will locate records where the Sport field contains *volleyball* OR *golf* AND where the Amount field contains a value greater than *200*.

If you enter *volleyball* in the Criteria row, and *golf* in the or row for the Sport field, then you must enter *>200* in both the Criteria row and the or row for the Amount field so that the correct records are located when the query is run.

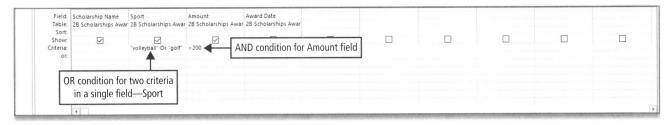

Figure 2.35

7 **Run** the query.

Two records were located in the 2B Scholarships Awarded table that have either *Volleyball* OR *Golf* stored in the Sport field AND a value greater than $200 in the Amount field. This is an example of using the OR condition in combination with an AND condition.

8 **Save** 🖫 the query as **2B Volleyball OR Golf AND Over $200 Query Close** ☒ the query.

Objective 10 Create a Query Based on More Than One Table

GO! Learn How
Video A2-10

In a relational database, you can retrieve information from more than one table. Recall that a table in a relational database contains all of the records about a single topic. Tables are joined to one another by relating the primary key in one table to the foreign key in another table. This common field is used to create the relationship and is used to find records from multiple tables when the query is created and run.

For example, the Athletes table stores all of the data about the student athletes—name, address, and so on. The Scholarships Awarded table stores data about the scholarship name, the amount, and so on. When an athlete receives a scholarship, only the Student ID of the athlete is used to identify the athlete in the Scholarships Awarded table. It is not necessary to include any other data about the athlete in the Scholarships Awarded table; doing so would result in redundant data.

Activity 2.24 | Creating a Query Based on More Than One Table

3.1.1, 3.2.1,
3.2.3, 3.2.2,
3.1.5, 3.1.6, 3.1.7

In this Activity, you will create a query that selects records from two tables. This is possible because you created a relationship between the two tables in the database. The query will answer the questions, *What is the name, email address, and phone number of athletes who have received a scholarship for tennis or swimming, and what is the name and amount of the scholarship?*

1 On the **Create tab**, in the **Queries group**, click **Query Design**. In the **Show Table** dialog box, double-click your **2B Athletes** table, and then double-click your **2B Scholarships Awarded** table to add both tables to the table area. In the **Show Table** dialog box, click **Close**. Resize each field list to display all of the field names and the entire table name.

The join line displays because you created a one-to-many relationship between the two tables using the common field of Student ID; *one* athlete can have *many* scholarships.

2 From the **2B Athletes** field list, add the following fields to the design grid in the order given: **First Name**, **Last Name**, **College Email**, and **Home Phone**.

3 From the **2B Scholarships Awarded** field list, add the following fields to the design grid in the order given: **Scholarship Name**, **Sport**, and **Amount**.

4 Click in the **Sort** row under **Last Name**, click the **arrow**, and then click **Ascending** to sort the records in alphabetical order by the last names of the athletes.

5 Click in the **Criteria** row under **Sport**, type **tennis or swimming** and then press Enter.

6 In the selection bar of the design grid, point to the right edge of the **Scholarship Name** column to display the ✛ pointer, and then double-click to increase the width of the column and to display the entire table name on the **Table** row. Using the same technique, increase the width of the **Sport** column. Compare your screen with Figure 2.36.

> When locating data from multiple tables, the information in the Table row is helpful, especially when different tables include the same field name, such as Address. Although the field name is the same, the data may be different—for example, an athlete's address or a coach's address from two different related tables.

Figure 2.36

7 **Run** the query, and then compare your screen with Figure 2.37.

> Eight records display for athletes who received either a Swimming *or* Tennis scholarship, and the records are sorted in ascending order by the Last Name field. Because the common field of Student ID is included in both tables, Access can locate the specified fields in both tables by using one query. Two students—*Carla Reid* and *Florence Zimmerman*—received two scholarships, one for swimming and one for tennis. Recall that *one* student athlete can receive *many* scholarships.

Figure 2.37

8 **Save** 🖫 the query as **2B Tennis OR Swimming Query** and then display the query results in **Print Preview**. Change the orientation to **Landscape**, and the **Margins** to **Normal**. **Close** Print Preview.

9 ▶ **Close** ⊠ the query, **Open** ⊠ the **Navigation Pane**. If necessary, resize the Navigation Pane so all object names are visible, and then compare your screen with Figure 2.38.

Your *2B Tennis OR Swimming Query* object name displays under both tables from which it selected records.

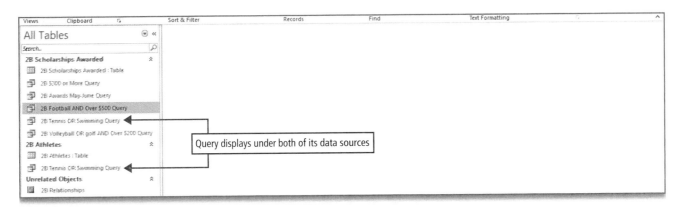

Figure 2.38

10 ▶ **Close** ⊠ the **Navigation Pane**.

Objective 11 | Use Wildcards in a Query

GO! Learn How
Video A2-11

A **wildcard character** is used to represent one or more unknown characters in a string. When you are unsure of the specific character or set of character to include in the criteria for a query, use a wildcard character in place of the character.

Activity 2.25 | Using a Wildcard in a Query

MOS
3.1.1, 3.1.5,
3.2.1, 3.2.3,
3.1.6, 3.1.7

Use the asterisk (*) wildcard character to represent one or more unknown characters. For example, entering Fo* as the criteria in a last name field will result in displaying records containing last names of Foster, Forrester, Fossil, or any other last name that begins with *Fo*. In this Activity, you will use the asterisk (*) wildcard character in criteria to answer the question related to organizations that award scholarships, *Which athletes received scholarships from local rotary clubs, country clubs, or foundations?*

1 ▶ On the **Create tab**, in the **Queries group**, click **Query Design**. In the **Show Table** dialog box, double-click your **2B Athletes** table, and then double-click your **2B Scholarships Awarded** table to add both tables to the table area. In the **Show Table** dialog box, click **Close**. Resize each field list to display all of the field names and the entire table name.

2 ▶ From the **2B Athletes** field list, add the following fields to the design grid in the order given: **First Name** and **Last Name**. From the **2B Scholarships Awarded** field list, add the **Awarding Organization** field to the design grid.

3 ▶ Click in the **Sort** row under **Last Name**, click the **arrow**, and then click **Ascending** to sort the records in alphabetical order by the last names of the athletes.

4 ▶ Click in the **Criteria** row under **Awarding Organization**, type **rotary*** and then press [Enter].

The * wildcard character is a placeholder used to match one or more unknown characters. After pressing [Enter], Access adds *Like* to the beginning of the criteria.

5 ▸ **Run** the query, and then compare your screen with Figure 2.39.

Three athletes received scholarships from a rotary club from different cities. The results are sorted alphabetically by the Last Name field.

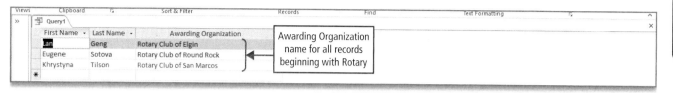

Figure 2.39

6 ▸ Switch to **Design** view. Click in the **or** row under **Awarding Organization**, type ***country club** and then press `Enter`.

The * wildcard character can be used at the beginning, middle, or end of the criteria. The position of the * determines the location of the unknown characters. By entering *country club*, you will locate records where the Awarding Organization name ends in *Country Club*.

7 ▸ **Run** the query.

Six records display for students receiving scholarships; three from organizations with a name that begins with *Rotary*, and three from organizations with a name that ends with *Country Club*.

8 ▸ Switch to **Design** view. In the design grid under **Awarding Organization** and under **Like "*country club"**, type ***foundation*** and then press `Enter`. Compare your screen with Figure 2.40.

This query will also display records where the Awarding Organization has *Foundation* anywhere in the organization name—at the beginning, middle, or end. Three *OR* criteria have been entered for the Awarding Organization field. When run, this query will locate records where the Awarding Organization has a name that begins with *Rotary*, OR ends with *Country Club*, OR that has *Foundation* anywhere in its name.

Figure 2.40

9 ▸ **Run** the query.

Twenty-eight scholarships were awarded from organizations where the name of the organization begins with Rotary, ends with Country Club, or has Foundation anywhere in its name. The records are sorted alphabetically by the Last Name field.

10 ▸ **Save** 🖫 the query as **2B Wildcard Query** and then display the query results in **Print Preview**. Click **Close Print Preview**.

11 ▸ **Close** ☒ the query, and then **Open** ≫ the **Navigation Pane**. Notice that your **2B Wildcard Query** displays under both tables because the query selected data from both tables—the data sources.

MORE KNOWLEDGE | **Using the ? Wildcard Character to Search for a Single Unknown Character**

The question mark (?) wildcard character is used to search for a single unknown character. For each question mark included in the criteria, any character can be located. For example, entering *b?d* as the criteria will result in the display of words such as *bed*, *bid*, or *bud*, or any three-character word that begins with *b* and ends with *d*. Entering *b??d* as the criteria will results in the display of words such as *bard*, *bend*, or *bind*, or any four-character word that begins with *b* and ends with *d*.

Objective 12 Create Calculated Fields in a Query

GO! Learn How
Video A2-12

Queries can create calculated values that are stored in a ***calculated field***. A calculated field stores the value of a mathematical operation. For example, you can multiply the value stored in a field named Total Hours Worked by the value stored in a field named Hourly Pay to display the Gross Pay value for each work study student.

There are two steps to create a calculated field in a query. First, name the field that will store the results of the calculation. Second, enter the ***expression***—the formula—that will perform the calculation. When entering the information for the calculated field in the query, the new field name must be followed by a colon (:), and each field name from the table used in the expression must be enclosed within its own pair of brackets.

Activity 2.26 │ Creating a Calculated Field in a Query

MOS

3.1.1, 3.2.1,
3.2.2, 3.1.6, 3.1.7

For each scholarship received by student athletes, the Texas Lakes Community College Alumni Association will donate an amount equal to 50 percent of each scholarship. In this Activity, you will create a calculated field to determine the amount that the alumni association will donate for each scholarship. The query will answer the question, *How much money will the alumni association donate for each student athlete who is awarded a scholarship?*

1 ▶ **Close** « the **Navigation Pane**. On the **Create tab**, in the **Queries group**, click **Query Design**. In the **Show Table** dialog box, double-click your **2B Scholarships Awarded** table to add the table to the table area, **Close** the **Show Table** dialog box, and then resize the field list.

2 ▶ Add the following fields to the design grid in the order given: **Student ID**, **Scholarship Name**, and **Amount**. Click in the **Sort** row under **Student ID**, click the **arrow**, and then click **Ascending**.

3 ▶ In the **Field** row, right-click in the first empty column to display a shortcut menu, and then click **Zoom**.

Although the calculation can be typed directly in the empty Field box, the Zoom dialog box gives you more working space and enables you to see the entire calculation as you enter it.

4 ▶ In the **Zoom** dialog box, type **Alumni Donation:[Amount]*0.5** and then compare your screen with Figure 2.41.

The first element, *Alumni Donation*, is the new field name that will identify the result of the calculation when the query is run; the field is not added back to the table. The new field name is followed by a colon (:), which separates the new field name from the expression. *Amount* is enclosed in brackets because it is an existing field name in your 2B Scholarships Awarded table; it contains the numeric data on which the calculation is performed. Following the right square bracket is the asterisk (*), the mathematical operator for multiplication. Finally, the percentage expressed as a decimal—*0.5*—displays.

Figure 2.41

> **5** In the **Zoom** dialog box, click **OK**, **Run** the query, and then compare your screen with Figure 2.42.

> The query results display three fields from your 2B Scholarships Awarded table and a fourth field—*Alumni Donation*—that displays a calculated value. Each calculated value equals the value in the Amount field multiplied by 0.5 or 50%.

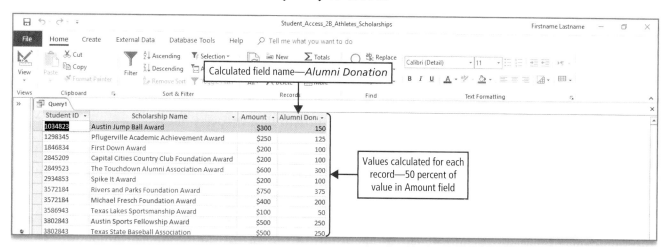

Figure 2.42

ALERT   Do your query results differ from Figure 2.42?

If your new field name does not display or if the results of the calculation do not display as shown in Figure 2.42, switch to Design view and carefully examine the expression you entered. Spelling or syntax errors prevent calculated fields from working properly.

> **6** Notice the formatting of the values in the **Alumni Donation** field—there are no dollar signs to match the formatting in the **Amount** field; you will adjust the formatting of this field later.

> When using a number, such as 0.5, in an expression, the values that display in the calculated field may not be formatted the same as the existing field that was part of the calculation.

Activity 2.27 | Creating a Second Calculated Field in a Query

3.2.1, 3.1.7

> In this Activity, you will create a calculated field to determine the total value of each scholarship after the alumni association donates an additional 50% based on the amount awarded by various organizations. The query will answer the question, *What is the total value of each scholarship after the alumni association donates an additional 50%?*

> **1** Switch to **Design** view. In the **Field** row, right-click in the first empty column to display a shortcut menu, and then click **Zoom**.

> **2** In the **Zoom** dialog box, type **Total Scholarship:[Amount]+[Alumni Donation]** and then compare your screen with Figure 2.43.

> Each existing field name—*Amount* and *Alumni Donation*—must be enclosed in separate pairs of brackets.

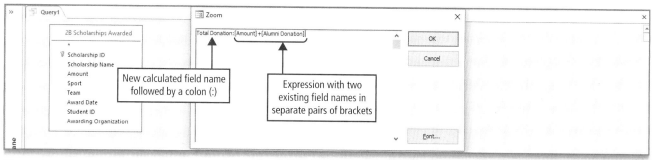

Figure 2.43

3 In the **Zoom** dialog box, click **OK**, and then **Run** the query.

> The value in the *Total Scholarship* field is calculated by adding together the values in the Amount field and the Matching Donation field. The values in the Total Scholarship field are formatted with dollar signs, commas, and decimal points, which is carried over from the Currency format in the Amount field.

Activity 2.28 | Formatting Calculated Fields

3.1.6, 3.1.7, 3.2.4

In this Activity, you will format the calculated fields so that the values display in a consistent manner as currency.

1 Switch to **Design** view. In the **Field** row, click in the **Alumni Donation** field name box.

2 On the **Design tab**, in the **Show/Hide group**, click **Property Sheet**.

> The Property Sheet displays on the right side of your screen. Recall that a Property Sheet enables you to make precise changes to the properties—characteristics—of selected items, in this case, a field.

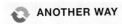 **ANOTHER WAY** In the design grid, on the Field row, right-click in the Alumni Donation field name box, and then click Properties.

3 In the **Property Sheet**, with the **General tab** active, click **Format**. In the property setting box, click the **arrow**, and then compare your screen with Figure 2.44.

> A list of available formats for the Alumni Donation field displays.

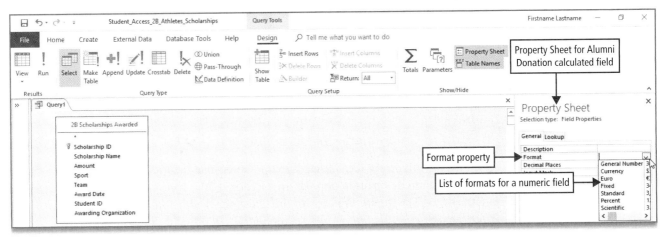

Figure 2.44

4 In the list, click **Currency**. In the **Property Sheet**, click **Decimal Places**. In the property setting box, click the **arrow**, and then click **0**.

5 In the design grid, in the **Field** row, click in the **Total Scholarship** field name. In the **Property Sheet**, set the **Format** property setting to **Currency** and the **Decimal Places** property setting to **0**.

6 Close ⊠ the **Property Sheet**, and then **Run** the query.

> The Alumni Donation and Total Scholarship fields are formatted as Currency with 0 decimal places.

7 To the left of the **Student ID** field name, click the **Select All** ☐ button. On the **Home tab**, in the **Records group**, click **More**, and then click **Field Width**. In the **Column Width** dialog box, click **Best Fit**. Click in any field, and then **Save** ☐ the query as **2B Alumni Donations Query**

> The field widths are adjusted to display fully the calculated field names.

8 Close ⊠ the query.

Objective 13 Calculate Statistics and Group Data in a Query

GO! Learn How
Video A2-13

Queries can be used to perform statistical calculations known as *aggregate functions* on a group of records. For example, you can find the total or average amount for a group of records, or you can find the lowest or highest number in a group of records.

Activity 2.29 | Using the Min, Max, Avg, and Sum Functions in a Query

MOS
3.1.1, 3.1.7, 3.2.4

In this Activity, you will use aggregate functions to find the lowest and highest scholarships amounts and the average and total scholarship amounts. The last query in this Activity will answer the question, *What is the total dollar amount of all scholarships awarded?*

1 ▶ On the **Create tab**, in the **Queries group**, click **Query Design**. In the **Show Table** dialog box, double-click your **2B Scholarships Awarded** table to add the table to the table area, **Close** the **Show Table** dialog box, and then resize the field list.

2 ▶ Add the **Amount** field to the design grid.

Include only the field to summarize in the design grid, so that the aggregate function is applied only to that field.

3 ▶ On the **Design tab**, in the **Show/Hide group**, click **Totals** to add a **Total** row as the third row in the design grid. Notice that in the design grid, on the **Total** row under **Amount**, *Group By* displays.

Use the Total row to select an aggregate function for the selected field.

4 ▶ In the **Total** row under **Amount**, click in the box that displays *Group By*, and then click the **arrow** to display a list of aggregate functions. Compare your screen with Figure 2.45, and then take a moment to review the available aggregate functions and the purpose of each function as shown in the table in Figure 2.46.

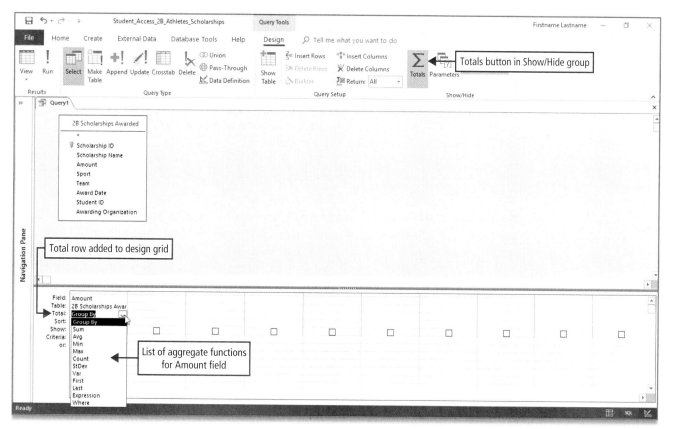

Figure 2.45

Function Name	Purpose
Group By	Combines data based on matching data in the selected field.
Sum	Totals the values in a field.
Avg	Averages the values in a field.
Min	Locates the smallest value in a field.
Max	Locates the largest value in a field.
Count	Displays the number of records based on a field.
StDev	Calculates the standard deviation for the values in a field.
Var	Calculates the variance for the values in a field.
First	Displays the first value in a field for the first record.
Last	Displays the last value in a field for the last record.
Expression	Creates a calculated field that includes an aggregate function.
Where	Limits the records to those that match a condition specified in the Criteria row of a field.

Figure 2.46

5 In the list of functions, click **Min**, and then **Run** the query. Point to the right edge of the first column to display the ⊞ pointer, and then double-click to apply Best Fit to the field.

> Access locates the minimum (smallest) value--*$100*—in the Amount field for all of the records in the 2B Scholarships Awarded table. The field name *MinOfAmount* is automatically created. This query answers the question, *What is the minimum (smallest) scholarship amount awarded to athletes?*

6 Switch to **Design** view. In the **Total** row under **Amount**, click the **arrow**, and then click **Max**. **Run** the query.

> The maximum (largest) value for a scholarship award amount is *$750.00*.

7 Switch to **Design** view. In the **Total** row, select the **Avg** function, and then **Run** the query.

> The average scholarship award amount is *$358.33*.

8 Switch to **Design** view. In the **Total** row, select the **Sum** function, and then **Run** the query.

> The values in the Amount field for all records is summed and displays a result of *$10,750.00*. The field name *SumOfAmount* is automatically created. The query answers the question, *What is the total dollar amount of all scholarships awarded?*

Activity 2.30 | Grouping Records in a Query

3.2.4, 3.2.2, 3.1.6, 3.1.7

You can use aggregate functions and group the records by the data in a field. For example, to group (summarize) the amount of scholarships awarded to each student, you include the Student ID field in addition to the Amount field. Using the Sum aggregate function, the records will be grouped by the Student ID so you can see the total amount of scholarships awarded to each student. Similarly, you can group the records by the Sport field so you can see the total amount of scholarships awarded for each sport.

1 Switch to **Design** view. From the field list, drag the **Student ID** field to the first column of the design grid—the **Amount** field moves to the second column. In the **Total** row under **Student ID**, notice that *Group By* displays.

> This query will group—organize—the records by Student ID and will calculate a total amount for each student.

2 **Run** the query, and then compare your screen with Figure 2.47.

The query calculates the total amount of all scholarships for each student.

Figure 2.47

3 Switch to **Design** view. In the design grid, above **Student ID**, point to the selection bar to display the ⬇ pointer. Click to select the column, and then press Del to remove the **Student ID** field from the design grid.

4 From the field list, drag the **Sport** field to the first column in the design grid—the **Amount** field moves to the second column. Click in the **Sort** row under **Amount**, click the **arrow**, and then click **Descending**.

5 On the **Design tab**, in the **Show/Hide group**, click **Property Sheet**. In the **Property Sheet**, set the **Format** property to **Currency**, and then set the **Decimal Places** property to **0**. **Close** ☒ the **Property Sheet**.

6 **Run** the query, and then compare your screen with Figure 2.48.

Access groups—summarizes—the records by each sport and displays the groupings in descending order by the total amount of scholarships awarded for each sport. Basketball scholarships were awarded the largest total amount--*$3,500*—and Volleyball scholarships were awarded the smallest total amount--*$650*.

Figure 2.48

7 **Save** 🖫 the query as **2B Total by Sport Query** and then **Close** ☒ the query.

Objective 14 | Create a Crosstab Query

GO! Learn How
Video A2-14

A *crosstab query* uses an aggregate function for data that can be grouped by two types of information, and displays the data in a compact, spreadsheet-like format with column headings and row headings. A crosstab query always has at least one row heading, one column heading, and one summary field. Use a crosstab query to summarize a large amount of data in a compact space that is easy to read.

Activity 2.31 | Creating a Crosstab Query Using the Query Wizard

3.1.2, 3.2.4

In this Activity, you will create a crosstab query that displays the total amount of scholarships awarded for each sport and for each type of team—men's or women's.

1 On the **Create tab**, in the **Queries group**, click **Query Wizard**.

2 In the **New Query** dialog box, click **Crosstab Query Wizard**, and then click **OK**.

3 In the **Crosstab Query Wizard**, click your **Table: 2B Scholarships Awarded**, and then click **Next**.

4 In the wizard under **Available Fields**, double-click **Sport** to group the scholarship amounts by the sports—the sports will display as row headings. Click **Next**, and then compare your screen with Figure 2.49.

The sport names will be grouped and displayed as row headings, and you are prompted to select column headings.

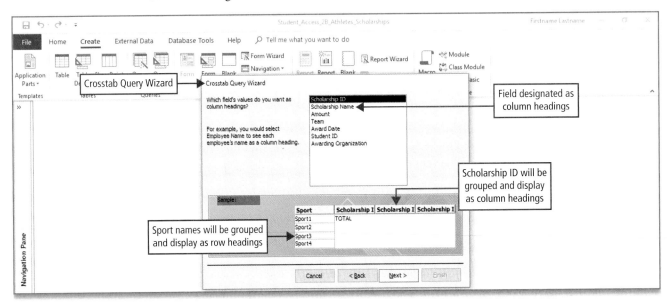

Figure 2.49

5 In the wizard, in the field list, click **Team** to select the column headings. Click **Next**, and then compare your screen with Figure 2.50.

The Team types—*Men's* and *Women's*—will display as column headings, and you are prompted to select a field to summarize.

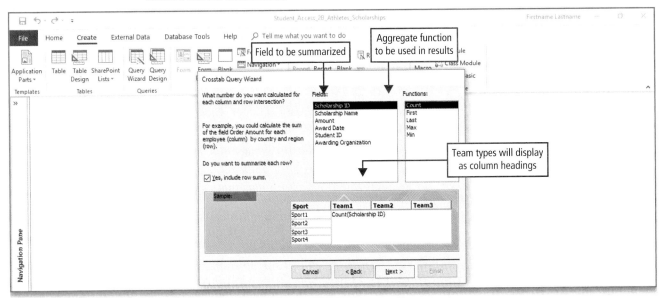

Figure 2.50

6 In the wizard under **Fields**, click **Amount**. Under **Functions**, click **Sum**.

The crosstab query will calculate the total scholarship amount for each sport and for each type of team.

7 Click **Next**. In the **What do you want to name your query?** box, select the existing text, type **2B Sport and Team Crosstab Query** and then click **Finish**. Apply **Best Fit** to the datasheet, click in any field to cancel the selection, **Save** the query, and then compare your screen with Figure 2.51.

The field widths are adjusted to display fully the calculated field names.

Figure 2.51

8 Close × the query.

MORE KNOWLEDGE **Creating a Crosstab Query Using Data From Two Related Tables**

To create a crosstab query using fields from more than one table, you must first create a select query with the fields from both tables, and then use the query as the data source for the crosstab query.

Objective 15 **Create a Parameter Query**

GO! Learn How
Video A2-15

A *parameter query* prompts you for criteria before running the query. For example, you need to display the records for students who live in different cities serviced by Texas Lakes Community College. You can create a select query and enter the criteria for a city such as Austin, but when you open the query, only the records for those students who live in Austin will display. To find the students who live in Round Rock, you must open the query in Design view, change the criteria, and then run the query again.

A parameter query eliminates the need to change the design of a select query. You create a single query that prompts you to enter the city; the results are based upon the criteria you enter when prompted.

Activity 2.32 | Creating a Parameter Query With One Criteria

3.1.3, 3.2.2,
3.1.6, 3.1.7

In this Activity, you will create a parameter query that displays student athletes from a specific city in the areas serviced by Texas Lakes Community College each time it is run.

1 On the **Create tab**, in the **Queries group**, click **Query Design**.

2 In the **Show Table** dialog box, double-click your **2B Athletes** table to add it to the table area, **Close** the **Show Table** dialog box, and then resize the field list.

3 Add the following fields to the design grid in the order given: **First Name**, **Last Name**, **Address**, **City**, **State**, and **Postal Code**.

4 In the **Sort** row under **Last Name**, click the **arrow**, and then click **Ascending**.

5 In the **Criteria** row under **City**, type **[Enter a City]** and then press Enter. Compare your screen with Figure 2.52.

The bracketed text indicates a *parameter*—a value that can be changed—rather than specific criteria.

Figure 2.52

6 **Run** the query. In the **Enter Parameter Value** dialog box, type **austin** and then compare your screen with Figure 2.53.

The Enter Parameter Value dialog box prompts you to *Enter a City*, which is the text enclosed in brackets that you entered in the criteria row under City. The city you enter will be set as the criteria for the query. Because you are prompted for the criteria, you can reuse this query without having to edit the criteria row in Design view. The value you enter is not case sensitive—you can enter *austin*, *Austin*, or *AUSTIN*.

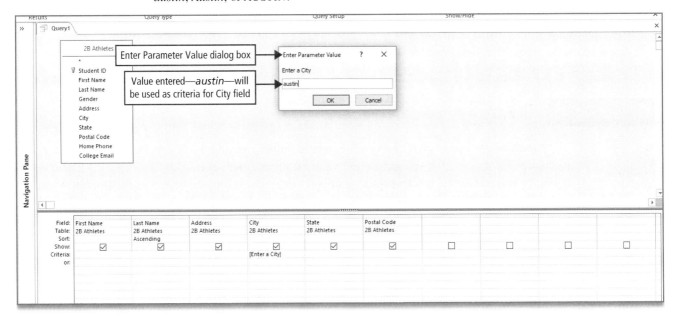

Figure 2.53

ALERT **Did the Enter Parameter Value dialog box not display?**

If the Enter Parameter Value dialog box does not display, you may have typed the parameter incorrectly in the design grid. Common errors include using parentheses or curly braces instead of brackets around the parameter text, which Access interprets as specific criteria, resulting in no records matching the criteria. If you typed curly braces instead of brackets, the query will not run. To correct, display the query in Design view and change the parameter entered in the Criteria row.

7 In the **Enter Parameter Value** dialog box, click **OK**.

Twenty-three students live in the city of Austin, and the records are sorted in alphabetical order by the Last Name field.

8 **Save** 🖫 the query as **2B City Parameter Query**, and then **Close** ⨯ the query.

9 Open the **Navigation Pane**. In the **Navigation Pane**, under your **2B Athletes** table, double-click your **2B City Parameter Query**. In the **Enter Parameter Value** dialog box, type **round rock** and then click **OK**. **Close** the **Navigation Pane**. Compare your screen with Figure 2.54.

Nine students live in the city of Round Rock. Every time you open a parameter query, you are prompted to enter criteria. You may have to apply Best Fit to the columns if all of the data in the fields does not display and you wish to print the query results—the length of the data in the fields changes as new records display depending upon the criteria entered. Recall that only the query design is saved; each time you open a query, it is run using the most up-to-date information in the data source.

Figure 2.54

10 **Close** ⊠ the query.

MORE KNOWLEDGE **Parameter Query Prompts**

Be sure that the parameter you enter in the Criteria row as a prompt is not the same as the field name. For example, do not use *[City]* as the parameter. Access interprets this as the field name of *City*. Recall that you entered a field name in brackets when creating a calculated field in a query. If you use a field name as the parameter, the Enter Parameter Value dialog box will not display, and all of the records will display.

The parameter should inform the individual running the query of the data required to display the correct results. If you want to use the field name by itself as the prompt, type a question mark at the end of the text; for example, *[City?]*. You cannot use a period, exclamation mark (!), curly braces ({ }), another set of brackets ([ ]), or the ampersand (&) as part of the parameter.

---

11 Open the **Navigation Pane**, and, if necessary increase the width of the pane so that all object names display fully. **Close** ⊠ the database and **Close** Access.

For Non-MyLab Submissions : Determine What Your Instructor Requires for Submission
As directed by your instructor, submit your completed database file.

---

12 In **MyLab IT**, locate and click the Grader Project **Access 2B Athletes and Scholarships**. In **step 3**, under **Upload Completed Assignment**, click **Choose File**. In the **Open** dialog box, navigate to your **Access Chapter 2 folder**, and then click your **Student_Access_2B_Athletes_Scholarships** file one time to select it. In the lower right corner of the **Open** dialog box, click **Open**.

The name of your selected file displays above the Upload button.

13 To submit your file to **MyLab IT** for grading, click **Upload**, wait a moment for a green **Success!** message, and then in **step 4**, click the blue **Submit for Grading** button. Click **Close Assignment** to return to your list of **Course Materials**.

You have completed Project 2B   **END**

Objective	**Export an Access Query to an Excel Spreadsheet, Save it in Google Drive, and Create a Chart**

Access web apps are designed to work with Microsoft's SharePoint, a service for setting up websites to share and manage documents. Your college may not have SharePoint installed, so you will use other tools to share objects from your database so that you can work collaboratively with others. Recall that Google Drive is Google's free, web-based word processor, spreadsheet, slide show, form, and data storage and sharing service. For Access, you can export a database object to an Excel worksheet, a PDF file, or a text file, and then save the file to Google Drive.

> **ALERT**   **Working with Web-Based Applications and Services**
>
> Computer programs and services on the web receive continuous updates and improvements, so the steps to complete this web-based Activity may differ from the ones shown. You can often look at the screens and the information presented to determine how to complete the Activity.
>
> If you do not already have a Google account, you will need to create one before you begin this Activity. Go to **http://google.com** and in the upper right corner, click **Sign In**. On the Sign In screen, click **Create Account**. On the Create your Google Account page, complete the form, read and agree to the Terms of Service and Privacy Policy, and then click **Next step**. On the Welcome screen, click **Get Started**.

Activity | Exporting an Access Query to an Excel Spreadsheet, Saving the Spreadsheet to Google Drive, Editing a Record in Google Drive, and Saving to Your Computer

In this Activity, you will export your 2B Sport and Team Crosstab Query table to an Excel spreadsheet, upload the Excel file to your Google Drive as a Google Sheet, edit a record in Google Drive, and then download a copy of the edited spreadsheet to your computer.

1 Start Access, navigate to your **Access Chapter 2** folder, and then open your **2B_Athletes_Scholarships** database file. If necessary, on the Message Bar, click **Enable Content**. In the **Navigation Pane**, click your **2B Sport and Team Crosstab Query** one time to select it—do not open it.

2 Click the **External Data tab**, and then in the **Export group**, click **Excel**. In the **Export – Excel Spreadsheet** dialog box, click **Browse**, and then navigate to your **Access Chapter 2** folder. In the **File Save** dialog box, click in the **File name** box, type **Lastname_Firstname_AC_2B_Web** and then click **Save**.

3 In the **Export – Excel Spreadsheet** dialog box, under **Specify export options**, select the first two check boxes—**Export data with formatting and layout** and **Open the destination file after the export operation is complete**—and then click **OK**. Take a moment to examine the data in the file, and then **Close** Excel. In the **Export – Excel Spreadsheet** dialog box, click **Close**, and then **Close Access**.

4 From the desktop, open your browser, navigate to **http://google.com**, and then sign in to your Google account. Click the **Google Apps** menu ▦, and then click **Drive** △. Open your **GO! Web Projects** folder—or click New to create and then open this folder if necessary.

5 In the upper right corner, click **Settings** ⚙, and then on the menu click **Settings**. In the **Settings** dialog box, next to *Convert uploads*, be sure that **Convert uploaded files to Google Docs editor format** is selected. In the upper right, click **Done**.

> If this setting is not selected, your document will upload as a pdf file and cannot be edited without further action.

6 On the left, click **New**, and then click **File upload**. In the **Open** dialog box, navigate to your **Access Chapter 2** folder, and then double-click your **AC_2B_Web** Excel file to upload it to Google Drive. In the lower right corner, when the title bar of the message box indicates *Uploads completed*, **Close** the message box. A second message box may display temporarily.

7 In the file list, double-click your **Lastname_Firstname_AC_2B_Web** file to open it in Google Sheets. Compare your screen with Figure A.

The worksheet displays column letters, row numbers, and data.

8 Select the range **A1:B8**. On the menu bar, click **Insert**, and then click **Chart**.

The chart is placed in the spreadsheet, covering some of the data.

Figure A

9 Click the **Chart title**, type **Total Scholarships by Sport**. In the **Chart editor**, click **Legend**. Click the arrow next to *Right*, and then click **None**.

10 Click to select the chart, if necessary. Point to the top of the chart window until the pointer displays. Hold down the left mouse button, and then drag the chart below the data in the spreadsheet.

11 On the menu, click **File**, point to **Download as**, and then click **Microsoft Excel (.xlsx)**. Use your browser commands to save the file in your **Access Chapter 2** folder as **Lastname_Firstname_AC_2B_Web_Download**

> **NOTE** **Saving The Downloaded File to the Access Chapter 2 Folder**
>
> Depending on the browser you are using, you may need to open the file in Excel and then save the AC_2B_Web_Download worksheet to your Access Chapter 2 folder.

12 On the Taskbar, click the icon for your browser. In Google Drive, in the upper right corner, click your name, and then click **Sign out**. **Close** your browser window.

13 If necessary, start Excel. In the Excel opening screen, in the lower left corner, click **Open Other Workbooks**. Navigate to your **Lastname_Firstname_AC_2B_Web_Download** file and then open the file.

14 If directed to submit a paper printout of your Lastname_Firstname_AC_2B_Web_Download file, follow the directions given in the Note below. As directed by your instructor, submit your Excel file created of this project.

> **NOTE** **Printing or Creating an PDF electronic image of an Excel Spreadsheet**
>
> To print on paper, click Print. To create a PDF electronic image of your printout, on the left side of your screen, click Export. Under Export, be sure Create PDF/XPS Document is selected, and then click Create PDF/XPS. Navigate to your Access Chapter 2 folder, and then click Publish to save the file with the default name and an extension of pdf.

»» GO! To Work

Microsoft Office Specialist (MOS) Skills in this Chapter	
Project 2A	**Project 2B**
1.2.1 Understand relationships	**1.1.1** Import objects or data from other sources
1.2.2 Display relationships	**1.2.1** Understand relationships
1.2.4 Enforce referential integrity	**1.2.2** Display relationships
1.2.5 Set foreign keys	**1.2.3** Set Primary Keys
1.3.1 Configure print options for records, forms, and reports	**1.2.4** Enforce referential integrity
2.3.2 Sort records	**1.2.5** Set foreign keys
3.1.1 Create simple queries	**3.1.1** Create simple queries
3.1.6 Save queries	**3.1.2** Create basic crosstab queries
3.1.7 Run queries	**3.1.3** Create basic parameter queries
3.2.1 Add, hide, and remove fields in queries	**3.1.5** Create basic multi-table queries
3.2.2 Sort data within queries	**3.1.6** Save queries
3.2.3 Filter data within queries	**3.1.7** Run queries
	3.2.1 Add, hide, and remove fields in queries
	3.2.2 Sort data within queries
	3.2.3 Filter data within queries
	3.2.4 Format fields within queries

Build Your E-Portfolio

An E-Portfolio is a collection of evidence, stored electronically, that showcases what you have accomplished while completing your education. Collecting and then sharing your work products with potential employers reflects your academic and career goals. Your completed documents from the following projects are good examples to show what you have learned: 2G, 2K, and 2L.

▶ GO! For Job Success

Video: Preparing for Meetings

Your instructor may assign this video to your class, and then ask you to think about, or discuss with your classmates, these questions:

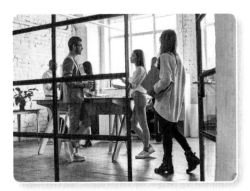

g-stockstudio/Shutterstock

> Out of the four employees, which one demonstrated appropriate meeting behavior? Provide specific examples.

> How did technology assist the meeting and how did technology hinder the meeting?

> What perception of the company may the client have from the conference call? Provide two examples.

End of Chapter

Summary

Table relationships are created by joining the common fields in tables providing a means for you to modify data simultaneously and use data from multiple tables to create queries, forms, and reports.

Queries are created to answer questions and to extract information from your database tables; saving a query with your database saves you time when you need to answer the question many times.

Queries range from simple queries where you ask a single question to complex queries where you use compound criteria, wildcard characters, logical operators, and create calculated fields.

A crosstab query displays information grouped by two fields, an easy way to display complex data, and a parameter query prompts you to enter the criteria each time you open or run the query.

GO! Learn It Online

Review the concepts and key terms in this chapter by completing these online challenges, which you can find at **MyLab IT**.

> **Chapter Quiz:** Answer matching and multiple choice questions to test what you learned in this chapter.

> **Lessons on the GO!:** Learn how to use all the new apps and features as they are introduced by Microsoft.

> **MOS Prep Quiz:** Answer questions to review the MOS skills that you practiced in this chapter.

GO! Collaborative Team Project (available in Instructor Resource Center)

If your instructor assigns the project to your class, you can expect to work with one or more of your classmates—either in class or by using Internet tools—to create work products similar to those you created in this chapter. A team is a group of workers who work together to solve a problem, make a decision, or create a work product. Collaboration is when you work together with others as a team in an intellectual endeavor to complete a shared task or achieve a shared goal.

Monkey Business Images/Fotolia

Project Guide for Access Chapter 2

Your instructor will assign Projects from this list to ensure your learning and assess your knowledge.

	Project Guide for Access Chapter 2		
Project	**Apply Skills from These Chapter Objectives**	**Project Type**	**Project Location**
2A **MyLab IT**	Objectives 1–7 from Project 2A	**2A Instructional Project (Grader Project)** **Instruction** A guided review of the skills from Project.	**MyLab IT** and in text
2B **MyLab IT**	Objectives 8–15 from Project 2B	**2B Instructional Project (Grader Project)** **Instruction** A guided review of the skills from Project.	**MyLab IT** and in text
2C	Objectives 1–7 from Project 2A	**2C Chapter Review (Scorecard Grading)** **Review** A guided review of the skills from Project 2A.	In text
2D	Objectives 8–15 from Project 2B	**2D Chapter Review (Scorecard Grading)** **Review** A guided review of the skills from Project 2B.	In text
2E **MyLab IT**	Objectives 1–7 from Project 2A	**2E Mastery (Grader Project)** **Mastery and Transfer of Learning** A demonstration of your mastery of the skills in Project 2A with extensive decision-making.	**MyLab IT** and in text
2F **MyLab IT**	Objectives 8–15 from Project 2B	**2F Mastery (Grader Project)** **Mastery and Transfer of Learning** A demonstration of your mastery of the skills in Project 2B with extensive decision-making.	**MyLab IT** and in text
2G **MyLab IT**	Combination of Objectives from Projects 2A and 2B	**2G Mastery (Grader Project)** **Mastery and Transfer of Learning** A demonstration of your mastery of the skills in Projects 2A and 2B with extensive decision-making.	**MyLab IT** and in text
2H	Combination of Objectives from Projects 2A and 2B	**2H GO! Fix It (Scorecard Grading)** **Critical Thinking** A demonstration of your mastery of the skills in Projects 2A and 2B by creating a correct result from a document that contains errors you must find.	IRC
2I	Combination of Objectives from Projects 2A and 2B	**2I GO! Make It (Scorecard Grading)** **Critical Thinking** A demonstration of your mastery of the skills in Projects 2A and 2B by creating a result from a supplied picture.	IRC
2J	Combination of Objectives from Projects 2A and 2B	**2J GO! Solve It (Rubric Grading)** **Critical Thinking** A demonstration of your mastery of the skills in Projects 2A and 2B, your decision-making skills, and your critical thinking skills. A task-specific rubric helps you self-assess your result.	IRC
2K	Combination of Objectives from Projects 2A and 2B	**2K GO! Solve It (Rubric Grading)** **Critical Thinking** A demonstration of your mastery of the skills in Projects 2A and 2B, your decision-making skills, and your critical thinking skills. A task-specific rubric helps you self-assess your result.	In text
2L	Combination of Objectives from Projects 2A and 2B	**2L GO! Think (Rubric Grading)** **Critical Thinking** A demonstration of your understanding of the Chapter concepts applied in a manner that you would outside of college. An analytic rubric helps you and your instructor grade the quality of your work by comparing it to the work an expert in the discipline would create.	In text
2M	Combination of Objectives from Projects 2A and 2B	**2M GO! Think (Rubric Grading)** **Critical Thinking** A demonstration of your understanding of the Chapter concepts applied in a manner that you would outside of college. An analytic rubric helps you and your instructor grade the quality of your work by comparing it to the work an expert in the discipline would create.	IRC
2N	Combination of Objectives from Projects 2A and 2B	**2N You and GO! (Rubric Grading)** **Critical Thinking** A demonstration of your understanding of the Chapter concepts applied in a manner that you would in a personal situation. An analytic rubric helps you and your instructor grade the quality of your work.	IRC
2O	Combination of Objectives from Projects 2A and 2B	**2O Cumulative Group Project for Access Chapter 2** A demonstration of your understanding of concepts and your ability to work collaboratively in a group role-playing assessment, requiring both collaboration and self-management.	IRC

Glossary

Glossary of Chapter Key Terms

Aggregate functions Calculations such as Min, Max, Avg, and Sum that are performed on a group of records.

AND condition A compound criteria used to display records that match all parts of the specified criteria.

Ascending order A sorting order that arranges text alphabetically (A to Z) and numbers from the lowest number to the highest number.

Between . . . And operator A comparison operator that looks for values within a range.

Calculated field A field that stores the value of a mathematical operation.

Cascade Delete Related Records A cascade option that enables you to delete a record in a table and also delete all of the related records in related tables.

Cascade options Relationship options that enable you to update records in related tables when referential integrity is enforced.

Cascade Update Related Fields A cascade option that enables you to change the data in the primary key field in the table on the *one* side of the relationship and update that change to any fields storing that same data in related tables.

Comparison operators Symbols that are used to evaluate data in the field to determine if it is the same (=), greater than (>), less than (<), or in between a range of values as specified by the criteria.

Compound criteria Multiple conditions in a query or filter.

Criteria Conditions in a query that identify the specific records you are looking for.

Crosstab query A query that uses an aggregate function for data that can be grouped by two types of information and displays the data in a compact, spreadsheet-like format with column headings and row headings.

Data source The table or tables from which a form, query, or report retrieves its data.

Descending order A sorting order that arranges text in reverse alphabetical order (Z to A) and numbers from the highest number to the lowest number.

Design grid The lower area of the query window that displays the design of the query.

Expression A formula that will perform the calculation.

Field list A list of field names in a table.

Foreign key The field that is included in the related table so the field can be joined with the primary key in another table for the purpose of creating a relationship.

Innermost sort field When sorting on multiple fields in Datasheet view, the field that will be used for the second level of sorting.

Is Not Null A criteria that searches for fields that are not empty.

Is Null A criteria that searches for fields that are empty.

Join line In the Relationships window, the line joining two tables that visually indicates the common fields and the type of relationship.

Logical operators Operators that combine criteria using AND and OR. With two criteria, AND requires that both conditions be met and OR requires that either condition be met for the record to display in the query results.

Message Bar The area directly below the ribbon that displays information such as security alerts when there is potentially unsafe, active content in an Office document that you open.

One-to-many relationship A relationship between two tables where one record in the first table corresponds to many records in the second table—the most common type of relationship in Access.

OR condition A compound criteria used to display records that match at least one of the specified criteria.

Outermost sort field When sorting on multiple fields in Datasheet view, the field that will be used for the first level of sorting.

Parameter A value that can be changed.

Parameter query A query that prompts you for criteria before running the query.

Referential integrity A set of rules that Access uses to ensure that the data between related tables is valid.

Relationship An association that you establish between two tables based on common fields.

Run The process in which Access looks at the records in the table(s) included in the query design, finds the records that match the specified criteria, and then displays the records in a datasheet; only the fields included in the query design display.

Sorting The process of arranging data in a specific order based on the value in a field.

Subdatasheet A format for displaying related records when you click the plus sign (+) next to a record in a table on the *one* side of the relationship.

Subset A portion of the total records available.

Table area The upper area of the query window that displays field lists for the tables that are used in a query.

Text string A sequence of characters.

Trust Center An area of Access where you can view the security and privacy settings for your Access installation.

Wildcard character In a query, a character that represents one or more unknown characters in criteria; an asterisk (*) represents one or more unknown characters, and a question mark (?) represents a single unknown character.

Chapter Review

Skills Review | Project 2C Freshman Orientation

Apply 2A skills from these Objectives:

1. Open and Save an Existing Database
2. Create Table Relationships
3. Sort Records in a Table
4. Create a Query in Design View
5. Create a New Query From an Existing Query
6. Sort Query Results
7. Specify Criteria in a Query

In the following Skills Review, you will assist Dr. Wendy Bowie, the Director of Counseling at the Southwest Campus, in using her database to answer several questions about the freshman orientation sessions that will be held prior to class registration. Your completed Navigation Pane will look similar to Figure 2.55.

Project Files

For Project 2C, you will need the following file:

a02C_Freshman_Orientation

You will save your database as:

Lastname_Firstname_2C_Freshman_Orientation

Project Results

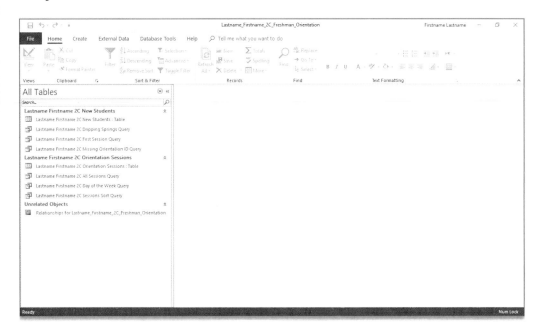

Figure 2.55

(continues on next page)

Chapter Review

1 Start Access. In the Access opening screen, click **Open Other Files**. Under **Open**, click Browse, and then navigate to the location where your student data files are stored. Double-click **a02C_Freshman_Orientation** to open the database.

a. Click the **File tab**, and then click **Save As**. Under **File Types**, be sure **Save Database As** is selected. On the right, under **Database File Types**, be sure **Access Database** is selected, and then click **Save As**.

b. In the **Save As** dialog box, navigate to your **Access Chapter 2** folder. Click in the **File name** box, type **Lastname_Firstname_2C_Freshman_Orientation** and then press [Enter]. On the **Message Bar**, click **Enable Content**.

c. In the **Navigation Pane**, right-click **2C New Students**, and then click **Rename**. With the table name selected and using your own name, type **2C New Students** and then press [Enter]. **Rename** the **2C Orientation Sessions** table to **Lastname Firstname 2C Orientation Sessions** and resize the **Navigation Pane** to display both tables names fully.

2 In the **Navigation Pane**, double-click your **Lastname Firstname 2C New Students** table to open it in the object window, and examine the fields in the table. Double-click your **Lastname Firstname 2C Orientation Sessions** table and examine the fields in the table. In the object window, right-click either **object tab**, and then click **Close All** to close both tables. **Close** the **Navigation Pane**.

a. Click the **Database Tools tab**, and then in the **Relationships group**, click **Relationships**.

b. In the **Show Table** dialog box, click your **Lastname Firstname 2C Orientation Sessions** table, and then click **Add**. In the **Show Table** dialog box, double-click your **Lastname Firstname 2C New Students** table to add it to the **Relationships** window. In the **Show Table** dialog box, click **Close**.

c. In the **Lastname Firstname 2C New Students** field list, point to the lower right corner of the field list to display the [icon] pointer, and then drag downward and to the right to resize the field list and display all of the field names and the entire table name. Use the same technique to resize the **Lastname Firstname 2C Orientation Sessions** field list—the field list on the left—so that the table name displays fully. In the

Lastname Firstname 2C New Students field list— the field list on the right—point to the title bar, and holding down the left mouse button, drag the field list to the right until there are approximately one inch of space between the field lists.

d. In the **Lastname Firstname 2C Orientation Sessions** field list, point to **Orientation ID**, and, holding down the left mouse button, drag the field name downward and to the right into the **Lastname Firstname 2C New Students** field list until the [icon] pointer's arrow is on top of **Orientation ID**. Release the mouse button to display the **Edit Relationships** dialog box. Drag the **Edit Relationships** dialog box downward and to the right below the two field lists.

e. In the **Edit Relationships** dialog box, click to select the **Enforce Referential Integrity** check box, the **Cascade Update Related Fields** check box, and the **Cascade Delete Related Records** check box. In the **Edit Relationships** dialog box, click **Create** to create a one-to-many relationship—*one* orientation session can be scheduled for *many* new students.

f. On the **Design tab**, in the **Tools group**, click **Relationship Report**. On the **Print Preview tab**, in the **Page Size group**, click **Margins**, and then click **Normal**. On the **Quick Access Toolbar**, click the **Save** button. In the **Save As** dialog box, click **OK** to accept the default report name. In the object window, **Close** the report, and then **Close** the **Relationships** window.

g. **Open** the **Navigation Pane**, double-click your **Lastname Firstname 2C Orientation Sessions** table to open it in the object window, and then **Close** the **Navigation Pane**. On the left side of the last record—*Orientation ID* of *OS-01*—click **+** to display the subdatasheet and notice that 13 new students are scheduled to attend this orientation session. Click **-** to collapse the subdatasheet.

h. In the last record, in the **Orientation ID** field, select the existing data—*OS-01*—and then type **OS-001** to make the data consistent with the Orientation IDs of the other sessions; the 13 related records are updated with the new Orientation ID because you selected Cascade Update Related Fields in the Edit Relationships dialog box.

(continues on next page)

Chapter Review

i. Display the subdatasheet for the record with an **Orientation ID** of **OS-010** and notice that one student—*Student ID* of *8273485*—is scheduled for this orientation session. Collapse the subdatasheet. To the left of the record, point to the record selector box to display the ➡ pointer, and then click to select the record. On the **Home tab**, in the **Records group**, click **Delete**. In the message box, click **Yes** to delete this record and the related student record in the **Lastname Firstname 2C New Students** table.

3 In the **Date** field, click in any record. On the **Home tab**, in the **Sort & Filter group**, click **Ascending** to sort the records by the date. In the field names row, click the **Room arrow**, and then click **Sort Z to A** to sort the rooms from Room 203 to Room 201. The records are sorted first by the Room and then by the Date. On the **File tab**, click **Print**, and then click **Print Preview**. Create a paper or PDF electronic image as directed, and then click **Close Print Preview**. On the **Home tab**, in the **Sort & Filter group**, click **Remove Sort**. **Close** the table, and in the message box, click **No**; you do not need to save any design changes to the table.

4 Click the **Create tab**, and then in the **Queries group**, click **Query Design**. In the **Show Table** dialog box, double-click your **Lastname Firstname 2C Orientation Sessions** table, and then **Close** the **Show Table** dialog box. Resize the field list, displaying all of the field names and the entire table name.

a. In the field list, double-click **Date** to add the field to the first column in the design grid. In the design grid, in the **Field** row, click in the second column, click the **arrow**, and then click **Day of Week** to add the field to the design grid. In the field list, point to **Room**, drag the field name down into the design grid until the 🔲 pointer displays in the **Field** row in the first column, and then release the mouse button. Using one of the three techniques you just practiced, add the **Time** field to the fourth column

b. On the **Design tab**, in the **Results group**, click **Run**. This query answers the question, *What is the room, date, day of week, and time for all of the orientation sessions in the Lastname Firstname 2C Orientation Sessions table?*

c. On the **Quick Access Toolbar**, click **Save**. In the **Save As** dialog box, type **Lastname Firstname 2C All Sessions Query** and then click **OK**. **Close** the query.

5 **Open** the **Navigation Pane**. Right-click the **Lastname Firstname 2C All Sessions Query** and click **Copy**. Right-click in a blank area of the **Navigation Pane**, and then click **Paste**. In the **Paste As** dialog box, type **Lastname Firstname 2C Day of Week Query** and then click **OK** to create a new query based on an existing query. **Close** the **Navigation Pane**.

a. In the **Navigation Pane**, right-click the **Lastname Firstname 2C Day of the Week Query** and click **Design View**. In the design grid, point to the thin gray selection bar above the **Room** field name to display the ⬇ pointer, click to select the column, and then press Delete.

b. Point to the selection bar above the **Day of Week** field name to display the 🔲 pointer, and then drag to the left until a dark vertical line displays on the left side of the **Date** column. Release the mouse button to position the **Day of Week** field in the first column.

c. **Run** the query. The query results display three fields. This query answers the question, *What is the day of week, date, and time for every orientation session in the Lastname Firstname 2C Orientation Sessions table?*

d. **Close** the query, and in the message box, click **Yes** to save the changes to the design—you deleted one field and moved another field. **Open** the **Navigation Pane**.

6 Right-click the **Lastname Firstname 2C Day of the Week Query** and click **Copy**. Right-click in a blank area of the **Navigation Pane**, and then click **Paste**. In the **Paste As** dialog box, type **Lastname Firstname 2C Sessions Sort Query** and then click **OK** to create a new query based on an existing query. Increase the width of the **Navigation Pane** so that the names of all of the objects display fully.

a. In the **Navigation Pane**, right-click your **Lastname Firstname 2C Sessions Sort Query**, click **Design View**, and then **Close** the **Navigation Pane**. In the field list, drag the **Room** field to the left of the **Day of Week** field to position it in the first column. In the design grid, in the **Sort** row under **Room**, click the **arrow**, and then click **Descending**. In the **Sort** row under **Date**, click the **arrow**, and then click **Ascending**.

b. **Run** the query. This query answers the question, *For every session, within each room (with the Room field sorted in descending order), what is the day of week, date (with the Date field sorted in ascending order), and time?*

c. **Close** the query, and in the message box, click **Yes** to save the changes to the query design.

(continues on next page)

Chapter Review

7 Click the **Create tab**, and then in the **Queries group**, click **Query Design**. In the **Show Table** dialog box, double-click your **Lastname Firstname 2C New Students** table to add it to the table area, and then **Close** the **Show Table** dialog box. Resize the field list to display all of the field names and the table name. Add the following fields to the design grid in the order given: **Student ID**, **Last Name**, **First Name**, and **Orientation ID**.

a. In the design grid, click in the **Criteria** row under **Orientation ID**, type **OS-001**—the first character is the letters *O* and *S* followed by a hyphen, two zeros, and the number *1*—and then press Enter.

b. **Run** the query to display 13 records that meet the specified criteria—records that have *OS-001* in the *Orientation ID* field. **Save** the query as **Lastname Firstname 2C First Session Query** and then **Close** the query.

c. On the **Create tab**, in the **Queries group**, click **Query Design**. In the **Show Table** dialog box, double-click your **Lastname Firstname 2C New Students** table to add it to the table area, and then **Close** the **Show Table** dialog box. Resize the field list, and then add the following fields to the design grid in the order given: **Student ID**, **First Name**, **Last Name**, **Phone Number**, **Email Address**, and **City**. Click in the **Criteria** row under **City**, type **dripping springs** and then press Enter.

d. **Run** the query to display the five new students who live in *Dripping Springs*. Switch to **Design** view. In the design grid, in the **Show** row under **City**, click to clear the check box. Recall that if all of the results use the same criteria, such as *dripping springs*, it is not necessary to display that field in the query results. **Run** the query again. **Save** the query as **Lastname Firstname 2C Dripping Springs Query** and then **Close** the query.

e. On the **Create tab**, in the **Queries group**, click **Query Design**. In the **Show Table** dialog box, double-click your **Lastname Firstname 2C New Students** table to add it to the table area, and then **Close** the **Show Table** dialog box. Resize the field list, and then add the following fields to the design grid in the order given: **Student ID**, **First Name**, **Last Name**, **Email Address**, **Phone Number**, and **Orientation ID**. Click in the **Sort** row under **Last Name**, click the **arrow**, and then click **Ascending**. Click in the **Criteria** row under **Orientation ID**, type **is null** and then press Enter.

f. **Run** the query to display the three new students who have not signed up for an orientation session. **Save** the query as **Lastname Firstname 2C Missing Orientation ID Query** and then **Close** the query.

g. **Open** the **Navigation Pane**. If necessary, increase the width of the pane so that all object names display fully. On the right side of the title bar, click **Close** to close the database and to close Access. As directed by your instructor, submit your database for grading.

You have completed Project 2C   **END**

Chapter Review

Apply 2B skills from these Objectives:

8. Specify Numeric Criteria in a Query
9. Use Compound Criteria in a Query
10. Create a Query Based on More Than One Table
11. Use Wildcards in a Query
12. Create Calculated Fields in a Query
13. Calculate Statistics and Group Data in a Query
14. Create a Crosstab Query
15. Create a Parameter Query

In the following Skills Review, you will assist Dr. Michael Bransford, the Student Activities Director for Texas Lakes Community College, in answering his questions about fundraisers, clubs, donations, dates of fundraiser events, and fundraiser locations. Your completed Navigation Pane will look similar to Figure 2.56.

Project Files

For Project 2D, you will need the following files:

a02D_Club_Fundraisers

a02D_Club (Excel workbook)

You will save your database as:

Lastname_Firstname_2D_Club_Fundraisers

Project Results

Figure 2.56

(continues on next page)

Chapter Review

1 Start Access. In the Access opening screen, click **Open Other Files**. Under **Open**, click **Browse** and then navigate to the location where your student data files are stored. Double-click **a02D_Club_Fundraisers** to open the database.

a. Click the **File tab**, and then click **Save As**. Under **File Types**, be sure **Save Database As** is selected. On the right, under **Database File Types**, be sure **Access Database** is selected, and then at the bottom of the screen, click **Save As**. In the **Save As** dialog box, navigate to your **Access Chapter 2** folder. Click in the **File name** box, type **Lastname_ Firstname_2D_Club_Fundraisers** and then press Enter. On the **Message Bar**, click **Enable Content**.

b. In the **Navigation Pane**, right-click **2D Fundraisers**, click **Rename**, type **Lastname Firstname 2D Fundraisers** and then press Enter. Increase the width of the **Navigation Pane** to display the entire table name. Double-click the table name to open it, examine the fields in the table, and then **Close** the table.

c. Click the **External Data tab**, and then in the **Import & Link group**, click **Excel**. In the **Get External Data – Excel Spreadsheet** dialog box, to the right of the **File name** box, click **Browse**. In the **File Open** dialog box, navigate to your student data files, and then double-click **a02D_Clubs**. Be sure that the **Import the source data into a new table in the current database** option button is selected, and then click **OK**.

d. In the upper left area of the wizard, select the **First Row Contains Column Headings** check box. In the wizard, click **Next**, and then click **Next** again. In the wizard, click the **Choose my own primary key** option button, be sure that **Club ID** displays, and then click **Next**. With the text selected in the **Import to Table** box, type **Lastname Firstname 2D Clubs**, and then click **Finish**. In the **Import Spreadsheet Wizard**, click **Next**, and then click **Finish**. In the **Get External Data – Excel Spreadsheet** dialog box, click **Close**.

e. In the **Navigation Pane**, right-click your **Lastname Firstname 2D Clubs** table, and then click **Design View**. **Close** the **Navigation Pane**. In the **Field Name** column, click **Club ID**. In the **Field Properties** area, click **Field Size**, type **8** and then press Enter. On the **Design tab**, in the **Views group**,

click **View** to switch to **Datasheet** view. In the message box, click **Yes** to save the design changes. In the second message box, click **Yes**—no data will be lost. Examine the fields and data in the table. To the left of the **Club ID** field name, click the **Select All** button. On the **Home tab**, in the **Records group**, click **More**, and then click **Field Width**. In the **Column Width** dialog box, click **Best Fit**. Click in any record to cancel the selection, **Save** the table, and then **Close** the table.

f. Click the **Database Tools tab**, and then in the **Relationships group**, click **Relationships**. In the **Show Table** dialog box, double-click your **Lastname Firstname 2D Clubs** table, and then double-click your **Lastname Firstname 2D Fundraisers** table to add both tables to the **Relationships** window. **Close** the **Show Table** dialog box. By dragging the lower right corner of the field list, resize each field list to display all of the field names and the entire table name. Point to the title bar of the field list on the right, and drag the field list to the right until there are approximately one inch of space between the field lists.

g. In the **Lastname Firstname 2D Clubs** field list, point to **Club ID**, drag the field name into the **Lastname Firstname 2D Fundraisers** table on top of **Club ID**, and then release the mouse button. Point to the title bar of the **Edit Relationships** dialog box, and then drag it downward below the two field lists. In the **Edit Relationships** dialog box, select the **Enforce Referential Integrity** check box, the **Cascade Update Related Fields** check box, the **Cascade Delete Related Records** check box, and then click **Create**. A *one-to-many* relationship is established; *one* student club can raise money for *many* fundraising events.

h. On the **Design tab**, in the **Tools group**, click **Relationship Report**. On the **Print Preview tab**, in the **Page Size group**, click **Margins**, and then click **Normal**. **Save** the report as **Lastname Firstname 2D Relationships** and then click **Close All**.

2 Click the **Create tab**. In the **Queries group**, click **Query Design**. In the **Show Table** dialog box, double-click your **Lastname Firstname 2D Fundraisers** table to add it to the table area, and then **Close** the **Show Table** dialog box. Resize the field list. Add the following fields to the design grid in the order given: **Fundraiser Name**, **Donation**, and **Fundraiser Location**.

(continues on next page)

Chapter Review

a. Click in the **Sort** row under **Fundraiser Name**, click the **arrow**, and then click **Ascending**. Click in the **Criteria** row under **Donations**, type **>=1000** and then press Enter. **Run** the query and notice that seven records match the criteria. This query answers the question, *Where was each fundraiser held (in alphabetical order by the Fundraiser Name field) for fundraisers with donations greater than or equal to $1,000?*

b. **Save** the query as **Lastname Firstname 2D $1000 or More Donations Query**. **Close** the query.

c. In the **Navigation Pane**, right-click your **Lastname Firstname 2D $1000 or More Donations Query**, and click **Copy**. In a blank area in the Navigation Pane, right-click and click **Paste**. In the **Paste As** dialog box, type **Lastname Firstname 2D Fundraisers June-July Query** and then click **OK**. In the **Navigation Pane**, right-click your **Lastname Firstname 2D Fundraisers June-July Query** query, and then click **Design View**.

d. In the **Lastname Firstname 2D Fundraisers** field list, double-click **Date** to add it to the fourth column in the design grid. Click in the **Sort** row under **Fundraiser Name**, click the **arrow**, and then click **(not sorted)**. Click in the **Sort** row under **Date**, click the **arrow**, and then click **Ascending**.

e. In the **Criteria** row under **Donation**, select the existing criteria, *>=1000*, and then press Del so that the query results are not restricted by a monetary value. Click in the **Criteria** row under **Date**, type **between 6/1/22 and 7/31/22** and then press Enter. **Run** the query, and notice that four records match the criteria. This query answers the question, *What is the fundraiser name, donation, fundraiser location, and date (in chronological order) for events held between June 1, 2022 and July 31, 2022?*

f. **Close** the query, and in the message box, click **Yes** to save the changes to the query design.

3 Click the **Create tab**, and in the **Queries group**, click **Query Design**. In the **Show Table** dialog box, double-click your **Lastname Firstname 2D Fundraisers** table to add it to the table area, and then **Close** the **Show Table** dialog box. Resize the field list. Add the following fields to the design grid in the order given: **Fundraiser Name**, **Fundraiser Location**, **Donation**, and **Club ID**.

a. Click in the **Sort** row under **Fundraiser Name**, click the **arrow**, and then click **Ascending**. Click in the **Criteria** row under **Club ID**, type **club-109**

and then press Enter. Click in the **Criteria** row under **Donation**, type **<=1000** and then press Enter. **Run** the query, and notice that two records match the criteria. Switch back to **Design** view, and in the **Show** row under **Club ID**, clear the check box. **Run** the query again. This query answers the question, *Which fundraiser events with their locations listed had donations of $1,000 or less raised by CLUB-109?*

b. **Save** the query as **Lastname Firstname 2D CLUB-109 Donations <=1000 Query** and **Close** the query.

c. On the **Create tab**, in the **Queries group**, click **Query Design**. In the **Show Table** dialog box, double-click your **Lastname Firstname 2D Fundraisers** table to add it to the table area, and then **Close** the **Show Table** dialog box. Resize the field list. Add the following fields to the design grid in the order given: **Club ID**, **Fundraiser Name**, **Date**, and **Donation**.

d. Click in the **Sort** row under **Date**, click the **arrow**, and then click **Ascending**. Click in the **Criteria** row under **Club ID**, type **club-107 or club-115** and then press Enter. Click in the **Criteria** row under **Donation**, type **>1000** and then press Enter. **Run** the query, and notice that two records match the criteria. This query answers the question, *Which fundraiser events received donations over $1,000 from either CLUB-107 or CLUB-115, and on what dates (in chronological order) were the fundraiser events held?*

e. **Save** the query as **Lastname Firstname 2D CLUB 107 or 115 Over $1000 Query** and **Close** the query.

4 On the **Create tab**, in the **Queries group**, click **Query Design**. In the **Show Table** dialog box, double-click your **Lastname Firstname 2D Clubs** table, and then double-click your **Lastname Firstname 2D Fundraisers** table to add both tables to the table area. **Close** the **Show Table** dialog box. Drag the field list on the right side to the right until there are approximately one inch of space between the field lists, and then resize each field list.

a. From the **Lastname Firstname 2D Clubs** field list, add the following fields to the design grid in the order given: **Club Name**, **Campus**, and **Club Email**. From the **Lastname Firstname 2D Fundraisers** field list, add the following fields to the design grid in the order given: **Fundraiser Name**, **Date**, and **Donation**. In the design grid, drag the **Donation** field to position it as the first column.

(continues on next page)

Chapter Review

b. Click in the **Sort** row under **Donation**, click the **arrow**, and then click **Descending**. Click in the **Criteria** row under **Campus**, type **southeast** and then press Enter. Click in the **or** row under **Campus**, type **northeast** and then press Enter. **Run** the query, and notice that 10 records match the criteria. This query answers the question, *For the Southeast and Northeast campuses, what is the donation (in descending order), club name, campus name, club email address, fundraiser name, and date of all fundraising events?*

c. **Save** the query as **Lastname Firstname 2D SE or NE Donations Query** and then display the query results in **Print Preview**. In the **Page Layout group**, click **Landscape**. In the **Page Size group**, click **Margins**, and then click **Normal**. **Close** the query.

5 On the **Create tab**, in the **Queries group**, click **Query Design**. In the **Show Table** dialog box, double-click your **Lastname Firstname 2D Clubs** table, and then double-click your **Lastname Firstname 2D Fundraisers** table to add both tables to the table area. **Close** the **Show Table** dialog box. Drag the field list on the right side to the right until there are approximately two inches of space between the field lists, and then resize each field list. From the **Lastname Firstname 2D Clubs** field list, add the **Club Name** field to the design grid. From the **Lastname Firstname 2D Fundraisers** field list, add the **Fundraiser Name** field to the design grid.

a. Click in the **Sort** row under **Club Name**, click the **arrow**, and then click **Ascending**. Click in the **Criteria** row under **Club Name**, type **phi*** and then press Enter. In the **Criteria** row under **Fundraiser Name**, type ***walk*** and then press Enter. **Run** the query, and notice that two records match the criteria—Club Name begins with *Phi* and Fundraiser Name has *Walk* anywhere in its name. This query answers the question, *Which clubs (in alphabetical order) that have names starting with Phi have raised money for fundraisers that involve walking?*

b. **Save** the query as **Lastname Firstname 2D Phi Walk Query** and then **Close** the query.

6 On the **Create tab**, in the **Queries group**, click **Query Design**. In the **Show Table** dialog box, double-click your **Lastname Firstname 2D Clubs** table, and then double-click your **Lastname Firstname 2D Fundraisers** table to add both tables to the table area. **Close** the **Show Table** dialog box. Drag the field list on the right side to the right until there are approximately two inches of space between the field lists, and then resize each field list. From the field lists, add the following fields to the design grid in the order given: **Fundraiser ID**, **Club Name**, and **Donation**.

a. Click in the **Sort** row under **Fundraiser ID**, click the **arrow**, and then click **Ascending**. Alumni will donate an additional 25 percent based on the value in the Donation field. In the **Field** row, right-click in the fourth column, and then click **Zoom**. In the **Zoom** dialog box, type **Alumni Donation:[Donation]*0.25** and then click **OK**. **Run** the query to be sure the new field—*Alumni Donation*—displays. In the first record, the *Alumni Donation* displays as *156.25*.

b. Switch to **Design** view. In the **Field** row, right-click in the first empty column, and then click **Zoom**. In the **Zoom** dialog box, type **Total Donation:[Donation]+[Alumni Donation]** and then click **OK**. **Run** the query to be sure that the new field—*Total Donation*—displays. In the first record, the *Total Donation* displays as *$781.25*.

c. Switch to **Design** view. In the **Field** row, click in the **Alumni Donation** field name box. On the **Design tab**, in the **Show/Hide group**, click **Property Sheet**. In the **Property Sheet**, click **Format**. In the property setting box, click the **arrow**, and then click **Currency**. **Close** the **Property Sheet**, and then **Run** the query. This query answers the question, *In ascending order by Fundraiser ID, what is the club name, donation, alumni donation, and total donation for each fundraising event if the alumni donate an additional 25 percent based on the value in the Donation field?*

d. To the left of the **Fundraiser ID** field name, click the **Select All** button. On the **Home tab**, in the **Records group**, click **More**, and then click **Field Width**. In the **Column Width** dialog box, click **Best Fit**. Click in any field to cancel the selection, **Save** the query as **Lastname Firstname 2D Alumni Donation Query** and **Close** the query.

7 On the **Create tab**, in the **Queries group**, click **Query Design**. In the **Show Table** dialog box, double-click your **Lastname Firstname 2D Fundraisers** table to add the table to the table area. **Close** the **Show Table** dialog box. Resize the field list, and then add the **Donation** field to the design grid.

(continues on next page)

Chapter Review

a. On the **Design tab**, in the **Show/Hide group**, click **Totals** to add a **Total** row as the third row in the design grid. In the **Total** row under **Donation**, click in the box that displays *Group By*, click the **arrow**, and then click **Sum**. In the **Show/Hide group**, click **Property Sheet**. In the **Property Sheet**, set **Decimal Places** to **0**, and then **Close** the **Property Sheet**. **Run** the query. Apply Best Fit to the field. The sum of the Donations field is *$20,259*.

b. Switch to **Design** view. From the field list, drag the **Club ID** field to the first column in the design grid— the **Donation** field moves to the second column. **Run** the query. This query answers the question, *For each club ID, what are the total donations?*

c. **Save** the query as **Lastname Firstname 2D Total Donations by Club Query** and then **Close** the query.

8 On the **Create tab**, in the **Queries group**, click **Query Wizard**. In the **New Query** dialog box, click **Crosstab Query Wizard**, and then click **OK**. In the **Crosstab Query Wizard**, click your **Table: Lastname Firstname 2D Fundraisers**, and then click **Next**. In the wizard under **Available Fields**, double-click **Fundraiser ID** to group the records by this field and display the Fundraiser IDs as row headings. Click **Next**.

a. In the wizard, in the field list, click **Club ID** to select the column headings, and then click **Next**. Under **Fields**, click **Donation**. Under **Functions**, click **Sum**, and then click **Next**. In the **What do you want to name your query?** box, select the existing text, type **Lastname Firstname 2D Fundraisers and Clubs Crosstab Query** and then click **Finish**.

b. Click the **Home** tab, and then switch to **Design** view. In the design grid, click in the **Donation** column. On the **Design tab**, in the **Show/Hide group**, click **Property Sheet**. In the **Property Sheet**, set **Decimal Places** to **0**, and then **Close** the **Property Sheet**. **Run** the query. Select all of the columns, apply **Best Fit**, and then **Save** the query. This query answers the question, *Grouped by Fundraiser ID and Club ID, what are the total donations?*

c. **Close** the query.

9 On the **Create tab**, in the **Queries group**, click **Query Design**. In the **Show Table** dialog box, double-click your **Lastname Firstname 2D Fundraisers** table to add the table to the table area. **Close** the **Show Table** dialog box, and then resize the field list. Add the following fields to the design grid in the order given: **Club ID**, **Fundraiser Location**, and **Date**.

a. In the **Sort** row under **Date**, click the **arrow**, and then click **Ascending**. In the **Criteria** row under **Club ID**, right-click, and then click **Zoom**. In the **Zoom** dialog box, type **[Enter a Club ID in the format club-###]** and then click **OK**. **Save** the query as **Lastname Firstname 2D Club ID Parameter Query**

b. **Run** the query. In the **Enter Parameter Value** dialog box, type **club-109** and then click **OK**. Three records match the criteria. **Close** the query.

c. **Open** the **Navigation Pane**, and increase the width of the pane so that all object names display fully. On the right side of the title bar, click **Close** to close the database and **Close** Access. As directed by your instructor, submit your database for grading.

You have completed Project 2D **END**

Content-Based Assessments (Mastery and Transfer of Learning)

MyLab IT Grader

Mastering Access **Project 2E Biology Supplies**

Apply 2A skills from these Objectives:

1. Open and Save an Existing Database
2. Create Table Relationships
3. Sort Records in a Table
4. Create a Query in Design View
5. Create a New Query From an Existing Query
6. Sort Query Results
7. Specify Criteria in a Query

In the following Mastering Access project, you will assist Greg Franklin, Chair of the Biology Department at the Southwest Campus, in using his database to answer questions about biology laboratory supplies. Your completed Navigation Pane will look similar to Figure 2.57.

Project Files for MyLab IT Grader

1. In your **MyLab IT** course, locate and click **Access 2E Biology Supplies**, Download Materials, and then Download All Files.
2. Extract the zipped folder to your Access Chapter 2 folder. Close the Grader download screens.
3. Take a moment to open the downloaded **Access_2E_Biology_Supplies_Instructions**; note any recent updates to the book.

Project Results

Figure 2.57

For Non-MyLab Submissions

For Project 2E, you will need:
a02E_Biology_Supplies

Start with an Access Data File

In your Access Chapter 2 folder, save your database as:
Lastname_Firstname_2E_Biology_Supplies

After you have saved your database, open it to launch Access. On the next page, begin with Step 2.
After Step 10, submit your file as directed by your instructor.

(continues on next page)

Content-Based Assessments (Mastery and Transfer of Learning)

1 Navigate to your **Access Chapter 2 folder**, and then double-click the downloaded file that displays your name—**Student_2E_Biology Supplies** and then enable the content.

2 Open both tables to examine the fields and data, and then **Close** both tables. Create a *one-to-many* relationship between your **2E Vendors** table and your **2E Biology Lab Supplies** table using the common field **Vendor ID**. **Enforce Referential Integrity**, and enable both cascade options. *One* vendor can supply *many* supplies. Create a **Relationship Report** with **Normal Margins**. Save it as **2E Relationships**

3 **Close All** open objects. Open your **2E Vendors** table. In the last record, in the **Vendor ID** field, select **V-100**, type **V-001** and then press ⬇ to save the record. **Close** the table.

4 Open your **2E Biology Lab Supplies** table. Sort the records first in **Descending** order by **Price Per Item** and then in **Ascending** order by **Category**. **Close** the table, saving changes to the table.

5 **Create** a query in **Query Design** view using your **2E Biology Lab Supplies** table to answer the question, *What is the item ID, item name, room, location, and quantity in stock for all of the items, sorted in ascending order by the Room field and the Location field?* Display the fields in the order listed in the question. **Save** the query as **2E Items by Room Query Close** the query.

6 In the **Navigation Pane**, use your **2E Items by Room Query** to create a new query object named **2E Item Categories Query** and then redesign the query to answer the question, *What is the item ID, item name, category, vendor ID, and quantity in stock for all items, sorted in ascending order by the Category field and the Vendor ID field?* Display only the fields necessary to answer the question and in the order listed in the question. **Close** the query, saving the design changes.

7 In the **Navigation Pane**, use your **2E Items by Room Query** to create a new query object named **2E Supplies Sort Query** and then open the new query in **Design** view. Redesign the query to answer the question,

What is the item name, category, price per item, and quantity in stock for all supplies, sorted in ascending order by the Category field and then in descending order by the Price Per Item field? Display only the fields necessary to answer the question and in the order listed in the question. **Close** the query, saving the design changes.

8 Using your **2E Supplies Sort Query**, create a new query object named **2E Kits Query** and then redesign the query to answer the question, *What is item name, category, price per item, quantity in stock, and vendor ID for all items that have a category of kits, sorted in ascending order by the Item Name field?* Do not display the **Category** field in the query results. Display the rest of the fields in the order listed in the question. Six records match the criteria. **Close** the query, saving the design changes.

9 **Create** a query in **Query Design** view using your **2E Vendors** table to answer the question, *What is the vendor ID, vendor name, and phone number where the phone number is blank, sorted in ascending order by the Vendor Name field?* Display the fields in the order listed in the question. Two records match the criteria. **Save** the query as **2E Missing Phone Query Close** the query.

10 Be sure all objects are closed. **Open** the **Navigation Pane**, be sure that all object names display fully, and then **Close** Access.

11 In **MyLab IT**, locate and click the Grader Project **Access 2E Biology Supplies**. In **step 3**, under **Upload Completed Assignment**, click **Choose File**. In the **Open** dialog box, navigate to your **Access Chapter 2 folder**, and then click your **Student_Access_2E_Biology_Supplies** file one time to select it. In the lower right corner of the **Open** dialog box, click **Open**. The name of your selected file displays above the Upload button.

12 To submit your file to **MyLab IT** for grading, click **Upload**, wait a moment for a green **Success!** message, and then in **step 4**, click the blue **Submit for Grading** button. Click **Close Assignment** to return to your list of **Course Materials**.

You have completed Project 2E **END**

Content-Based Assessments (Mastery and Transfer of Learning)

Mastering Access | **Project 2F Student Publications**

In the following Mastering Access project, you will assist Siabhon Reiss, the English Writing Lab Coordinator, in using her database to answer questions about student publications. Your completed Navigation Pane will look similar to Figure 2.58.

Apply 2B skills from these Objectives:

8. Specify Numeric Criteria in a Query
9. Use Compound Criteria in a Query
10. Create a Query Based on More Than One Table
11. Use Wildcards in a Query
12. Create Calculated Fields in a Query
13. Calculate Statistics and Group Data in a Query
14. Create a Crosstab Query
15. Create a Parameter Query

Project Files for MyLab IT Grader

1. In your **MyLab IT** course, locate and click **Access 2F Student Publications**, Download Materials, and then Download All Files.
2. Extract the zipped folder to your Access Chapter 2 folder. Close the Grader download screens.
3. Take a moment to open the downloaded **Access_2F_Student_Publications_Instructions**; note any recent updates to the book.

Project Results

Figure 2.58

For Non-MyLab Submissions

For Project 2F, you will need:
a02F_Student_Publications
a02F_Student_Papers (Excel workbook)

Start with an Access Data File

In your Access Chapter 2 folder, save your database as:
Lastname_Firstname_2F_Student_Publications

After you have saved your database, open it to launch Access. On the next page, begin with Step 2.
After Step 10, submit your file as directed by your instructor.

(continues on next page)

Content-Based Assessments (Mastery and Transfer of Learning)

1 Navigate to your **Access Chapter 2 folder**, and then double-click the downloaded file that displays your name—**Student_2F_Student_Publications** and then enable the content.

2 From your student data files, import **a02F_ Student_Papers** as a new table in the database. Designate the first row of the spreadsheet as column headings, and designate **Paper ID** as the primary key. Name the new table **2F Student Papers**

Open your **2F Student Papers** table in **Design** view. For the **Student ID** field, change the **Data Type** to **Short Text**. Switch to **Datasheet** view, apply **Best Fit** to all of the columns, and then **Save** the table. Examine the fields and data in this table. Open your **2F Publishers** table, examine the fields and data, and then **Close All** open objects.

Create a *one-to-many* relationship between your **2F Publishers** table and your **2F Student Papers** table using the common field **Publisher ID**. **Enforce Referential Integrity** and enable both cascade options. *One publisher can publish many student papers.* Create a **Relationship Report** with **Normal Margins**, saving it as **2F Relationship Report Close All** open objects.

3 Create a query in **Query Design** view using your **2F Student Papers** table to answer the question, *What is the student ID, home campus, award paid, and publisher ID for awards greater than or equal to $50, sorted in ascending order by the Student ID field?* Display the fields in the order listed in the question. Five records match the criteria. **Save** the query as **2F Awards $50 or More Query**

4 Using your **2F Awards $50 or More Query**, create a new query object named **2F 2nd Qtr NW Students Query** and then redesign the query to answer the questions, *Which students (Student ID) from the Northwest campus had papers published between 4/1/22 and 6/30/22, and what was the paper name, the award paid, and the category, sorted in ascending order by the Publication Date field?* Do not display the **Home Campus** field in the query results. Display the rest of the fields in the order listed in the question. Three records match the criteria. **Close** the query, saving the design changes.

5 Create a query in **Query Design** view using your **2F Student Papers** table to answer the question, *Which paper IDs, paper names, and category for students from the Southeast and Northeast campuses were published that had an award paid greater than $25, sorted in descending order by the Award Paid field?* Display the fields in the order listed in the question. Six records match the criteria. **Save** the query as **2F SE or NE Over $25 Query Close** the query.

6 Create a query in **Query Design** view using both tables to answer the questions, *Which paper names were published with a publisher name that has Texas as part of its name, what is the contact name and contact phone number, and what was the award paid, sorted in descending order by the Award Paid field?* (Hint: Use a wildcard character in the criteria row.) Display the fields in the order listed in the question. Eight records match the criteria. **Save** the query as **2F Texas Publishers Query Close** the query.

7 The college's Federation of English Faculty will donate money to the English Writing Lab based on 50 percent of the awards paid to the students. **Create** a query in **Query Design** view using your **2F Student Papers** table to answer the question, *In ascending order by the Paper ID field, what will be the total of each donation to the Writing Lab if the Federation donates an additional 50 percent of each award paid to students?* (Hint: First calculate the amount of the donation, naming the new field **Federation Donation**, and then run the query to be sure the correct results display. Then calculate the total donation, naming the new field **Total Donation**.) Change the property settings of the **Federation Donation** field to display with a **Format** of **Currency** and with **Decimal Places** set to **2**. For the **Publisher ID** of **P-20**, the *Federation Donation* is *$22.50*, and the *Total Donation* is *$67.50*. Apply **Best Fit** to all of the columns, **Save** the query as **2F Federation Donation Query Close** the query.

8 Create a query in **Query Design** view using your **2F Student Papers** table and the **Sum** aggregate function to answer the question, *What are the total awards paid for each category, sorted in descending order by the Award Paid field?* Display the fields in the order listed in the question. Change the property settings of the **Award Paid** field to display with a **Format** of **Currency** and with **Decimal Places** set to **0**. For the **Category** of **Student Life**, total awards paid are *$265*. Apply **Best Fit** to the **SumOfAward Paid** column. **Save** the query as **2F Awards by Category Query Close** the query.

(continues on next page)

Content-Based Assessments (Mastery and Transfer of Learning)

9 By using the **Query Wizard**, create a crosstab query based on your **2F Student Papers** table. Select **Home Campus** as the row headings and **Category** as the column headings. **Sum** the **Award Paid** field. Name the query **2F Campus and Category Crosstab Query** In **Design** view, change the property settings of the last two fields to display with a **Format** of **Currency** and with **Decimal Places** set to **0**. This query answers the question, *What are the total awards paid for student publications by each home campus and by each category?* Apply **Best Fit** to all of the columns, and then **Save** the query. **Close** the query.

10 **Create** a query in **Query Design** view using your **2F Student Papers** table that prompts you to **Enter the Home Campus**, and then answers the question, *What is the home campus, student ID, paper name, category, and publication date for student publications, sorted in ascending order by the Publication Date field?* Display the fields in the order listed in the question. **Run** the query, entering **southwest** when prompted for criteria. Seven records match the criteria. **Save** the query as **2F Campus Parameter Query Close** the query.

11 Open the **Navigation Pane** and be sure that all object names display fully. **Close** Access.

12 In **MyLab IT**, locate and click the Grader Project **Access 2F Student Publications**. In **step 3**, under **Upload Completed Assignment**, click **Choose File**. In the **Open** dialog box, navigate to your **Access Chapter 2 folder**, and then click your **Student_Access_2F_Student_Publications** file one time to select it. In the lower right corner of the **Open** dialog box, click **Open**. The name of your selected file displays above the Upload button.

13 To submit your file to **MyLab IT** for grading, click **Upload**, wait a moment for a green **Success!** message, and then in **step 4**, click the blue **Submit for Grading** button. Click **Close Assignment** to return to your list of **Course Materials**.

You have completed Project 2F **END**

Content-Based Assessments (Mastery and Transfer of Learning)

Mastering Access   **Project 2G Student Scholarships**

Apply 2A and 2B skills from these Objectives:

1. Open and Save an Existing Database
2. Create Table Relationships
3. Sort Records in a Table
4. Create a Query in Design View
5. Create a New Query From an Existing Query
6. Sort Query Results
7. Specify Criteria in a Query
8. Specify Numeric Criteria in a Query
9. Use Compound Criteria in a Query
10. Create a Query Based on More Than One Table
11. Use Wildcards in a Query
12. Create Calculated Fields in a Query
13. Calculate Statistics and Group Data in a Query
14. Create a Crosstab Query
15. Create a Parameter Query

In the following Mastering Access project, you will assist Kim Ngo, Director of Academic Scholarships, in using her database to answer questions about scholarships awarded to students. Your completed Navigation Pane will look similar to Figure 2.59.

Project Files for MyLab IT Grader

1. In your **MyLab IT** course, locate and click **Access 2G Student Scholarships**, Download Materials, and then Download All Files.
2. Extract the zipped folder to your Access Chapter 2 folder. Close the Grader download screens.
3. Take a moment to open the downloaded **Access_2G_Student_Scholarships_Instructions**; note any recent updates to the book.

Project Results

Figure 2.59

For Non-MyLab Submissions	**Start with an Access Data File**
For Project 2G you will need:	In your Access Chapter 2 folder, save your Access as:
a02G_Student_Scholarships	**Lastname_Firstname_2G_Student_Scholarships**

After you have saved your database, open it to launch Access. On the next page, begin with Step 2.
After Step 12, submit your file as directed by your instructor.

(continues on next page)

Content-Based Assessments (Mastery and Transfer of Learning)

Mastering Access: Project 2G Student Scholarships

1 Navigate to your **Access Chapter 2 folder**, and then double-click the downloaded file that displays your name—**Student_2G_Student_Scholarships** and then enable the content.

2 Open both tables to examine the fields and data, and then **Close** both tables. Create a *one-to-many* relationship between your **2G Students** table and your **2G Scholarships Awarded** table using the common field **Student ID**. **Enforce Referential Integrity** and enable both cascade options. *One* student can have *many* scholarships. Create a **Relationship Report** with **Normal Margins**, saving it as **2G Relationships**. Create a paper or PDF electronic image as directed, and then **Close All** open objects. Open your **2G Students** table. In the last record, in the **Student ID** field, select **9999999**, type **2839403** and then press ↓ to save the record. **Close** the table.

3 Create a query in **Query Design** view using your **2G Scholarships Awarded** table to answer the question, *What is the scholarship name, amount, and major for scholarships greater than or equal to $500, sorted in ascending order by the Scholarship Name field?* Display the fields in the order listed in the question. Eight records match the criteria. **Save** the query as **2G Amount $500 or More Query Close** the query.

4 Use your **2G Amount $500 or More Query** to create a new query object named **2G Awards 4th Qtr Query** and then redesign the query to answer the question, *Which scholarships (Scholarship Name) were awarded between 10/1/22 and 12/31/22, for what amount, and for which student (Student ID), sorted in ascending order by the Award Date field?* Display only the fields necessary to answer the question and in the order listed in the question. Do not restrict the results by amount, and sort only by the field designated in the question. Five records match the criteria. **Close** the query, saving the design changes.

5 Create a query in **Query Design** view using your **2G Scholarships Awarded** table to answer the question, *Which scholarships (Scholarship Name) were awarded for either Math or Business majors for amounts of more than $200, sorted in descending order by the Amount field?* Display the fields in the order listed in the question. Four records match the criteria. (Hint: If six records display, switch to Design view and combine the majors on one criteria line using OR.) **Save** the query as **2G Math or Business More Than $200 Query Close** the query.

6 Create a query in **Query Design** view using your **2G Students** table to answer the question, *What is the city, student ID, first name, and last name of students from cities that begin with the letter L, sorted in ascending order by the City field and by the Last Name field?* Display the fields in the order listed in the question. Five records match the criteria. **Save** the query as **2G L Cities Query Close** the query.

7 Create a query in **Query Design** view using your **2G Students** table and all of the fields to answer the question, *For which students is the Postal Code missing?* Three records match the criteria. **Save** the query as **2G Missing Postal Code Query** and **Close** the query.

8 The Board of Trustees for the college will donate an amount equal to 50 percent of each scholarship amount. **Create** a query in **Query Design** view using both tables to answer the question, *In ascending order by the Scholarship Name field, and including the first name and last name of the scholarship recipient, what will be the total value of each scholarship if the Board of Trustees donates an additional 50 percent of each award paid to students?* (Hint: First calculate the amount of the donation, naming the new field **Board Donation**, and then run the query to be sure the correct results display. Then calculate the total donation, naming the new field **Total Donation**.) Change the property settings of the appropriate fields to display with a **Format** of **Currency** and with **Decimal Places** set to **0**. For the **Scholarship Name** of **Amanda Snyder Foundation Scholarship**, the *Board Donation* is *$125*, and the *Total Donation* is *$375*. Apply **Best Fit** to all of the columns, **Save** the query as **2G Board Donation Query** and **Close** the query.

9 Create a query in **Query Design** view using your **2G Scholarships Awarded** table and the **Sum** aggregate function to answer the question, *For each major, what is the total scholarship amount, sorted in descending order by the Amount field?* Display the fields in the order listed in the question. Change the property settings of the **Amount** field to display with a **Format** of **Currency** and with **Decimal Places** set to **0**. For the **Major** of **History**, the total scholarship amount is *$1,850*. Apply **Best Fit** to all of the columns. **Save** the query as **2G Amount by Major Query** and **Close** the query.

(continues on next page)

Content-Based Assessments (Mastery and Transfer of Learning)

10 By using the **Query Wizard**, create a crosstab query based on your **2G Scholarships Awarded** table. Select **Student ID** as the row headings and **Major** as the column headings. **Sum** the **Amount** field. Name the query **2G Student ID and Major Crosstab Query** In **Design** view, change the property settings of the last two fields to display with a **Format** of **Currency** and with **Decimal Places** set to **0**. This query answers the question, *What are the total scholarship amounts paid by each student ID and by each major?* Apply **Best Fit** to all of the columns, and then **Save** the query. **Close** the query.

11 **Create** a query in **Query Design** view using your **2G Scholarships Awarded** table that prompts you to enter the **Major** of the student, and then answers the question, *What is the scholarship name and amount for a major, sorted in ascending order by the Scholarship Name field?* Display the fields in the order listed in the question. **Run** the query, entering **history** when prompted for criteria. Four records match the criteria. Hide the **Major** field from the results, and then **Run** the query again, entering **history** when prompted for criteria. **Save** the query as **2G Major Parameter Query** and **Close** the query.

12 Open the **Navigation Pane** and be sure that all object names display fully. **Close** Access.

13 In **MyLab IT**, locate and click the Grader Project **Access 2G Student Scholarships**. In **step 3**, under **Upload Completed Assignment**, click **Choose File**. In the **Open** dialog box, navigate to your **Access Chapter 2 folder**, and then click your **Student_Access_2G_ Student_Scholarships** file one time to select it. In the lower right corner of the **Open** dialog box, click **Open**. The name of your selected file displays above the Upload button.

14 To submit your file to **MyLab IT** for grading, click **Upload**, wait a moment for a green **Success!** message, and then in **step 4**, click the blue **Submit for Grading** button. Click **Close Assignment** to return to your list of **Course Materials**.

You have completed Project 2G   **END**

Content-Based Assessments (Critical Thinking)

Apply a combination of the 2A and 2B skills.

GO! Fix It	**Project 2H Social Sciences**	IRC
GO! Make It	**Project 2I Faculty Awards**	IRC
GO! Solve It	**Project 2J Student Refunds**	IRC
GO! Solve It	**Project 2K Leave**	

Project Files

For Project 2K, you will need the following file:

a02K_Leave

You will save your database as:

Lastname_Firstname_2K_Leave

Start Access, navigate to your student data files, open a02K_Leave, and then save the database in your Access Chapter 2 folder as **Lastname_Firstname_2K_Leave** Add your Lastname Firstname to the beginning of both table names, create a one-to-many relationship with cascade options between the two tables—*one* employee can receive *many* leave transactions—and then create a relationship report saving it as **Lastname Firstname 2K Relationships**

Create and save four queries to answer the following questions; be sure that all data displays fully:

- What is the last name and first name of employees who have used personal leave, sorted in ascending order by the Last Name field? Do not display the Leave field in the query results.

- What is the last name, first name, and email address of employees who have no phone number listed, sorted in ascending order by the Last Name and First Name fields?

- Grouped by the Leave Classification field, what is the total of each type of leave used? (Hint: Use the aggregate function Count.)

- What is the total number of leave transactions grouped in rows by the Employee# field and grouped in columns by the Leave Classification field?

Verify that the object names display fully in the Navigation Pane. As directed, submit your database for grading.

(continues on next page)

Content-Based Assessments (Critical Thinking)

GO! Solve It. Project 2K Leave (continued)

		Performance Level		
		Exemplary	**Proficient**	**Developing**
Performance Criteria	**Create relationship and relationship report**	Relationship and relationship report created correctly.	Relationship and relationship report created with one error.	Relationship and relationship report created with two or more errors, or missing entirely.
	Create Personal Leave query	Query created with correct name, fields, sorting, and criteria.	Query created with one element incorrect.	Query created with two or more elements incorrect, or missing entirely.
	Create Missing Phone query	Query created with correct name, fields, sorting, and criteria.	Query created with one element incorrect.	Query created with two or more elements incorrect, or missing entirely.
	Create Type of Leave query	Query created with correct name, fields, and aggregate function.	Query created with one element incorrect.	Query created with two or more elements incorrect, or missing entirely.
	Create Crosstab query	Query created with correct name, row headings, column headings, and aggregate function.	Query created with one element incorrect.	Query created with two or more two elements incorrect, or missing entirely.

You have completed Project 2K | END |

Outcomes-Based Assessments (Critical Thinking)

Rubric

The following outcomes-based assessments are open-ended assessments. That is, there is no specific correct result; your result will depend on your approach to the information provided. Make Professional Quality your goal. Use the following scoring rubric to guide you in how to approach the problem and then to evaluate how well your approach solves the problem.

The *criteria*—Software Mastery, Content, Format and Layout, and Process—represent the knowledge and skills you have gained that you can apply to solving the problem. The *levels of performance*—Professional Quality, Approaching Professional Quality, or Needs Quality Improvements—help you and your instructor evaluate your result.

	Your completed project is of Professional Quality if you:	Your completed project is Approaching Professional Quality if you:	Your completed project Needs Quality Improvements if you:
1-Software Mastery	Choose and apply the most appropriate skills, tools, and features and identify efficient methods to solve the problem.	Choose and apply some appropriate skills, tools, and features, but not in the most efficient manner.	Choose inappropriate skills, tools, or features, or are inefficient in solving the problem.
2-Content	Construct a solution that is clear and well organized, contains content that is accurate, appropriate to the audience and purpose, and is complete. Provide a solution that contains no errors of spelling, grammar, or style.	Construct a solution in which some components are unclear, poorly organized, inconsistent, or incomplete. Misjudge the needs of the audience. Have some errors in spelling, grammar, or style, but the errors do not detract from comprehension.	Construct a solution that is unclear, incomplete, or poorly organized, contains some inaccurate or inappropriate content, and contains many errors of spelling, grammar, or style. Do not solve the problem.
3-Format and Layout	Format and arrange all elements to communicate information and ideas, clarify function, illustrate relationships, and indicate relative importance.	Apply appropriate format and layout features to some elements, but not others. Overuse features, causing minor distraction.	Apply format and layout that does not communicate information or ideas clearly. Do not use format and layout features to clarify function, illustrate relationships, or indicate relative importance. Use available features excessively, causing distraction.
4-Process	Use an organized approach that integrates planning, development, self-assessment, revision, and reflection.	Demonstrate an organized approach in some areas, but not others; or, use an insufficient process of organization throughout.	Do not use an organized approach to solve the problem.

Outcomes-Based Assessments (Critical Thinking)

Apply a combination of the 2A and 2B skills.

| GO! Think | Project 2L Coaches |

Project Files

For Project 2L, you will need the following file:

a02L_Coaches

You will save your database as

Lastname_Firstname_2L_Coaches

Start Access, navigate to your student data files, open a02L_Coaches, and then save the database in your Access Chapter 2 folder as **Lastname_Firstname_2L_Coaches** Add to the beginning of both table names, create a one-to-many relationship with cascade options between the two tables—*one* coach can participate in *many* activities—and then create a relationship report saving it as **Lastname Firstname 2L Relationships**

Create queries to assist Randy Garza, the Athletic Director, answer the following questions about the coaches at Texas Lakes Community College:

- What is the last name and first name of every coach involved in *Dive* activities, sorted in ascending order by the Last Name field? Do not display the activity name.
- What is the last name and first name of every coach involved in basketball or football activities, sorted in ascending first by the Activity Name field and then by the Last Name field?
- Grouped by division, what is the total number of activity names, sorted in descending order by the total number? (Hint: Use the Count aggregate function.)
- What is the skill specialty, first name, last name, and phone number for coaches in a specified position that is entered when prompted for the Position, sorted in ascending order first by the Skill Specialty field and then by the Last Name field? (When prompted, enter the position of *director*)

Verify that the object names display fully in the Navigation Pane. As directed, submit your database for grading.

You have completed Project 2L | **END**

| GO! Think | Project 2M Club Donations | IRC |

| You and GO! | Project 2N Personal Inventory | IRC |

| GO! Cumulative Group Project | Project 2O Bell Orchid Hotels | IRC |

Forms, Filters, and Reports

ACCESS 2019

PROJECT 3A

Outcomes
Create forms to enter and delete records and to display data in a database.

Objectives

1. Create and Use a Form to Add and Delete Records
2. Filter Records
3. Create a Form by Using the Form Wizard
4. Modify a Form in Layout View and in Design View

PROJECT 3B

Outcomes
Create reports to display database information.

Objectives

5. Create a Report by Using the Report Tool and Modify the Report in Layout View
6. Create a Report by Using the Report Wizard
7. Modify the Design of a Report
8. Keep Grouped Data Together in a Printed Report

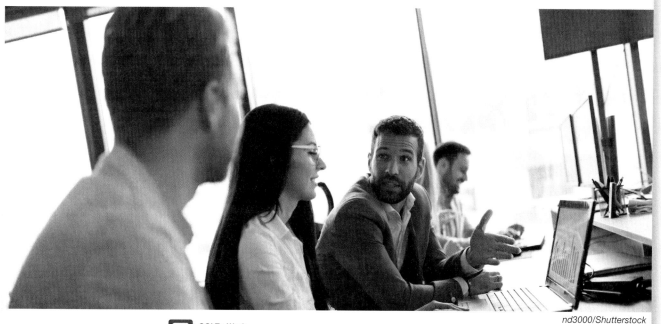

nd3000/Shutterstock

In This Chapter

GO! To Work with Access

In this chapter, you will create forms to enter and delete data and to view data in database tables. Forms can display one record at a time with fields placed in the same order to match a paper source document. Records in a form or table can be filtered to display a subset of the records based on matching specific values. You will modify forms by adding fields, changing field widths, and adding labels to the forms. You will create professional-looking reports that summarize the data from query or table. You will modify the reports by changing the fields in the report, by changing the layout of the report, by grouping data, and by making sure that groupings of data stay together on the printed page.

The projects in this chapter relate to **Texas Lakes Community College**, which is located in the Austin, Texas area. Its four campuses serve over 30,000 students and offer more than 140 certificate programs and degrees. The college has a highly acclaimed Distance Education program and an extensive Workforce Development program. The college makes positive contributions to the community through cultural and athletic programs, and has significant partnerships with businesses and nonprofit organizations. Popular fields of study include nursing and health care, solar technology, computer technology, and graphic design.

MyLab IT
Project 3A Grader for Instruction
Project 3A Simulation for Training and Review

Project Activities

In Activities 3.01 through 3.15, you will assist Sean Fitchette, Director of Enrollment Services at Texas Lakes Community College, in using his Access database to track new students and their major fields of study. Your completed Navigation Pane will look similar to Figure 3.1.

Project Files for MyLab IT Grader

1. In your storage location, create a folder named **Access Chapter 3**.
2. In your **MyLab IT** course, locate and click **Access 3A Students and Majors**, Download Materials, and then Download All Files.
3. Extract the zipped folder to your Access Chapter 3 folder. Close the Grader download screens.
4. Take a moment to open the downloaded **Access_3A_Students_Majors_Instructions**; note any recent updates to the book.

Project Results

GO! Project 3A
Where We're Going

Figure 3.1 Project 3A Students and Majors

	For Non-MyLab Submissions	**Start with an Access Data File**
	For Project 3A, you will need this starting file:	In your storage location, create a folder named **Access Chapter 3**
	a03A_Students_Majors	In your Access Chapter 3 folder, save your database as:
		Lastname_Firstname_3A_Students_Majors

After you have saved your database, launch Access and open the database. On the next page, begin with Step 2.

Objective 1 | Create and Use a Form to Add and Delete Records

ALERT   Because Office 365 is a cloud-based subscription service that receives continuous updates, you may encounter some variations in what appears on your screen and what is shown in this instruction. Microsoft Office 365 is fully installed on your PC or Mac; no internet access is necessary to create or edit documents. When you *are* connected to the internet, you will receive monthly upgrades and new features, so you always have the latest versions of Office apps as soon as they are available. Your subscription gives you continuous free access to the latest innovations and refinements.

GO! Learn How
Video A3-1

A *form* is a database object that you can use to display existing records in a table, or to edit, delete, or enter new records into a table. A form is useful to control access to the data. For example, you can design a form for college registration assistants so that they can see and enter the courses scheduled and fees paid by an individual student. However, they cannot see or enter grades for a student.

Some forms display only one record at a time; other forms display multiple records at the same time. A form that displays only one record at a time is useful not only to the individual who performs the *data entry*—entering the actual records—but also to anyone who has the job of viewing information in a database. For example, when you request a transcript from your college, someone displays your record on the screen. For the individual viewing your transcript, it is much easier to look at one record at a time, using a form, than to look at all of the student transcripts in the database.

Activity 3.01 | Opening and Saving an Existing Database and Viewing a Table Relationship

MOS
1.2.2

1▶ Start Access. In the Access opening screen, click **Open Other Files**. Navigate to your **Access Chapter 3 folder**, and then double-click the Access file that you downloaded from **MyLab IT** that displays your name—**Student_Access_3A_Students_Majors**. On the **Message Bar**, click **Enable Content**.

2▶ On the ribbon, click the **Database Tools tab**. In the **Relationships group**, click **Relationships**. If the relationships do not display, under Relationship Tools, on the Design tab, in the Relationships group, click All Relationships.

If you rename the tables, the field lists do not automatically display in the Relationships window.

3 In the **Relationships** window, click the **join line** between the two field lists. In the **Tools group**, click **Edit Relationships**. Point to the title bar of the **Edit Relationships** dialog box and drag the dialog box to the right of the two field lists. Compare your screen with Figure 3.2.

One major is associated with *many* students. A one-to-many relationship is established between your 3A Majors table and your 3A New Students table using the Major ID field as the common field. Recall that Cascade Update Related Fields enables you to change the primary key in the 3A Majors table, and then the data in the foreign key field in the 3A New Students field is automatically updated. Recall that Cascade Delete Related Records enables you to delete a record in the 3A Majors table, and then all related records in the 3A New Students table are automatically deleted.

ANOTHER WAY In the Relationships window, double-click the join line to display the Edit Relationships dialog box.

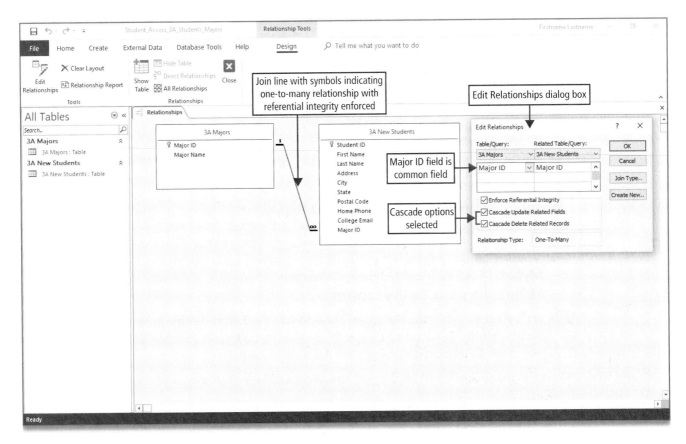

Figure 3.2

ALERT   Is your Edit Relationships dialog box empty?

The Edit Relationships dialog box does not display any information if you do not first click the join line. If this happens, close the Edit Relationships dialog box, and then be sure that you click the join line—when selected, the join line is darker.

4 **Close** ☒ the **Edit Relationships** dialog box, and then **Close** ☒ the **Relationships** window. If necessary, in the message box, click Yes to save changes to the layout of the relationships.

Activity 3.02 | Creating a Form and Viewing Records

4.2.2

There are several ways to create a form in Access, but the fastest and easiest way is to use the *Form tool*. With a single mouse click, all fields from the data source are placed on the form. You can modify the form in Layout view or in Design view, or you can switch to Form view and use the new form immediately.

The Form tool uses all of the field names and all of the records from an existing table or query. Records that you create or edit using a form are automatically updated in the underlying table or tables. In this Activity, you will create a form and then view records from the underlying New Students table—the data source—so the staff can access information easily.

1 In the **Navigation Pane**, double-click your **3A New Students** table to open it. Scroll as needed to view all 10 fields—*Student ID, First Name, Last Name, Address, City, State, Postal Code, Home Phone, College Email,* and *Major ID.* **Close** ⊠ the table.

2 In the **Navigation Pane**, be sure your **3A New Students** table is selected. On the ribbon, click the **Create tab**, and then in the **Forms group**, click **Form**. **Close** « the **Navigation Pane**, and then compare your screen with Figure 3.3.

The form is created based on the currently selected object—your 3A New Students table—and displays in *Layout view*. In Layout view, you can modify the form with the data displayed in the fields. For example, you can adjust the size of the text boxes to fit the data.

The form is created in a simple top-to-bottom layout, with all 10 fields from your 3A New Students table lined up in a single column. The data for the first record in the data source displays.

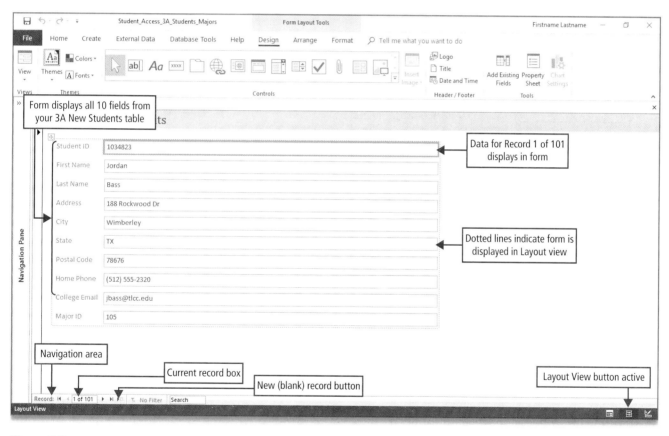

Figure 3.3

3 In the navigation area, click **Next record** ▶ four times to display the fifth record—*Student ID 1298345.* In the navigation area, select the text in the Current record box, type **62** and then press Enter to display the record for *Student ID 5720358.* In the navigation area, click **Last record** ▶ to display the record for *Student ID 9583924,* and then click **First record** ◀ to display the record for *Student ID 1034823.*

Use the navigation buttons to scroll among the records or the Current record box to display any single record.

4 Save 🖫 the form as **3A New Student Form** and then **Close** ⊠ the form object.

5 Open ⟫ the **Navigation Pane**. Notice that your new form displays under the table with which it is related—your **3A New Students** table.

Activity 3.03 | Creating a Second Form

4.2.2

In this Activity, you will use the Form tool to create a form for your 3A Majors table so the enrollment services staff can review student information relative to his or her major.

1 In the **Navigation Pane**, click your **3A Majors** table to select it. On the ribbon, click the **Create tab**, and then in the **Forms group**, click **Form**. **Close** ⟪ the **Navigation Pane**, and then compare your screen with Figure 3.4.

Because a one-to-many relationship is established, the form displays related records in the 3A New Students table for each record in the 3A Majors table. Five new students have selected a major of *Diagnostic Medical Sonography—Major ID 105.*

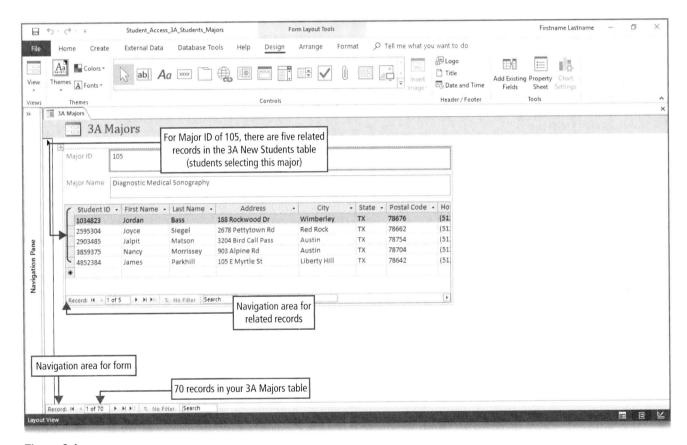

Figure 3.4

2 **Close** ⊠ your **3A Majors** form. In the message box, click **Yes**. In the **Save As** dialog box, in the **Form Name** box, type **3A Major Form** and then click **OK**.

Recall that if you do not save an object, you are prompted to do so when you close the object.

3 Open ⟫ the **Navigation Pane**. Notice that your new form displays under the table with which it is related—your **3A Majors** table.

Activity 3.04 | Adding Records to a Table by Using a Form

By using a single-record form to add, modify, and delete records, you can reduce the number of data entry errors, because the individual performing the data entry is looking at only one record at a time. Recall that your database is useful only if the information is accurate—just like your contact list is useful only if it contains accurate phone numbers and email addresses.

Forms are based on—also referred to as **bound** to—the table where the records are stored. When a record is entered in a form, the new record is added to the underlying table. The reverse is also true—when a record is added to the table, the new record can be viewed in the related form.

In this Activity, you will add a new record to both tables by using the forms that you just created.

1 In the **Navigation Pane**, double-click your **3A New Student Form** object to open it, and then **Close** « the **Navigation Pane**. In the navigation area, click **New (blank) record** ▶ to display a new blank form.

When you double-click to open a form, the first record in the underlying table displays in *Form view*, which is used to view, add, modify, and delete records stored in the table.

2 In the **Student ID** field, type **9712345** and then press Tab.

Use the Tab key to move from field to field in a form. *Tab order* is the order in which the insertion point moves from one field to the next when you press the Tab key. As you start typing, the pencil icon displays in the *record selector bar* at the left—the bar used to select an entire record. The pencil icon displays when a record is being created or edited.

ANOTHER WAY Press the Enter key, provided there are no special links on the form, such as a link to create a new form or a link to print the form.

3 Using your own first name and last name and using the first initial of your first name and your last name for the *College Email* field, continue entering the data shown in the following table, and then compare your screen with Figure 3.5.

Student ID	First Name	Last Name	Address	City	State	Postal Code	Home Phone	College Email	Major ID
9712345	**First Name**	**Last Name**	5820 Sweet Basil Ct	**Austin**	**TX**	78726	(512) 555-5712	**flastname@tlcc.edu**	339

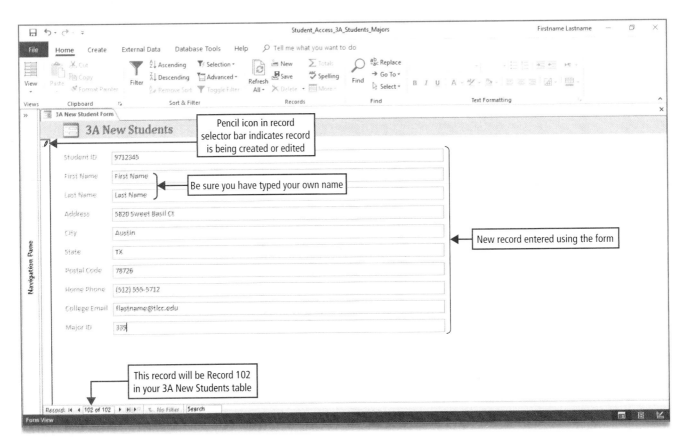

Figure 3.5

4 With the insertion point positioned in the last field, press Enter to save the record and display a new blank record. **Close** × your **3A New Student Form** object.

5 **Open** » the **Navigation Pane**, and then double-click your **3A New Students** table to open it. In the navigation area, click **Last record** ▶| to verify that the record you entered in the form is stored in the underlying table. **Close** × your **3A New Students** table.

6 In the **Navigation Pane**, double-click your **3A Major Form** object to open it. At the bottom of the screen, in the navigation area for the form—*not* the navigation area for the subdatasheet—click **New (blank) record** ▶✱. In the blank form, enter the data shown in the following table:

Major ID	Major Name
339.555.22	**Network Security**

7 **Close** × your **3A Major Form** object. In the **Navigation Pane**, double-click your **3A Majors** table, and then scroll to verify that the record for *Major ID 339.555.22 Network Security* displays in the table—records are sorted by the *Major ID* field. **Close** × the table.

Activity 3.05 | Deleting Records from a Table by Using a Form

You can delete records from a database table by using a form. In this Activity, you will delete the record for *Major ID 800.03* because the program has been discontinued.

1 In the **Navigation Pane**, double-click your **3A Major Form** object to open it, and then **Close** « the **Navigation Pane**. On the **Home tab**, in the **Find group**, click **Find** to open the **Find and Replace** dialog box.

🔄 **ANOTHER WAY** Press Ctrl + F to open the Find and Replace dialog box.

2 In the **Look In** box, notice that *Current field* displays. In the **Find What** box, type **800.03** and then click **Find Next**. Compare your screen with Figure 3.6, and then verify that the record for *Major ID 800.03* displays.

Because the insertion point was positioned in the *Major ID* field before opening the dialog box, Access will search for data in this field—the *Current field*.

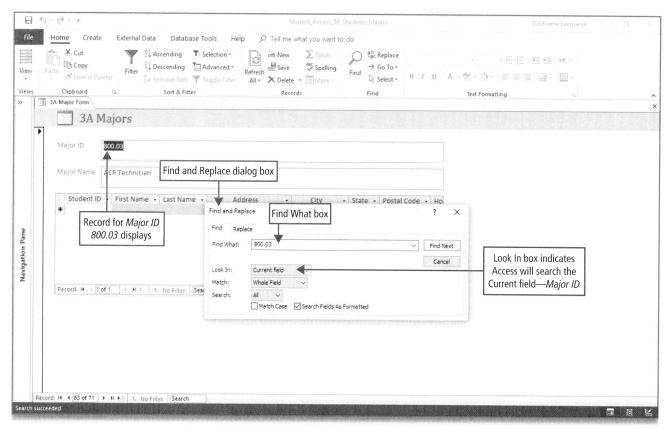

Figure 3.6

3 **Close** × the **Find and Replace** dialog box. On the **Home tab**, in the **Records group**, click the **Delete arrow**, and then click **Delete Record**.

The record is removed from the screen, and a message displays alerting you that you are about to delete *1 record(s)*. Once you click *Yes*, you cannot click Undo to reverse this action. If you delete a record by mistake, you must re-create the record by reentering the data. Because no students are associated with this major and the program is being discontinued, you can delete it from the table.

4 In the message box, click **Yes** to delete the record. In the navigation area for the form, notice that the total number of records in the table is *70*. **Close** × your **3A Major Form** object.

5 Open the **Navigation Pane**, and then double-click your **3A Majors** table to open it. Examine the table to verify that the *Major ID 800.03* record has been deleted from the table, and then **Close** ⊠ the table.

> Adding and deleting records in a form updates the records stored in the underlying table.

Objective 2 Filter Records

GO! Learn How

Video A3-2

Filtering records in a form displays only a portion of the total records—a *subset*—based on matching specific values. Filters are commonly used to provide a quick answer to a question, and the result is not generally saved for future use. For example, by filtering records in a form, you can quickly display a subset of records for students majoring in Information Systems Technology, which is identified by the Major ID of 339.

A form provides an interface for the database. For example, because of security reasons, the registration assistants at your college may not have access to the entire student database. Rather, by using a form, they can access and edit only some information—the information necessary for them to do their jobs. Filtering records within a form provides individuals who do not have access to the entire database a way to ask questions of the database without constructing a query. You can save the filter with the form if you are going to use the filter frequently.

Activity 3.06 | Filtering Data by Selection of One Field

MOS

2.3.3

In this Activity, you will assist a counselor at the college who wants to see records for students majoring in Information Systems Technology. In a form, you can use the *Filter By Selection* command to display only the records that contain the value in the selected field and to hide the records that do *not* contain the value in the selected field.

1 Open the **Navigation Pane**, double-click your **3A New Student Form** object to open it in **Form** view, and then **Close** ⊠ the **Navigation Pane**.

2 In the first record, click the **Major ID** field name—or you can click in the text box. Press Ctrl + F to display the **Find and Replace** dialog box. In the **Find What** box, type **339** If necessary, in the Match box, click the arrow, and then click Whole Field. Click **Find Next**, and then compare your screen with Figure 3.7.

> This action finds and displays a record with a *Major ID* of *339*—the major of *Information Systems Technology*. You will use this action to filter the records using the value of *339*.

Figure 3.7

3 ▶ **Close** ☒ the **Find and Replace** dialog box. On the **Home tab**, in the **Sort & Filter group**, click **Selection**, and then click **Equals "339"**. Compare your screen with Figure 3.8.

Seven records match the contents of the selected Major ID field—*339*—the Major ID for the Information Systems Technology major. In the navigation area, *Filtered* with a funnel icon displays next to the number of records. *Filtered* also displays on the right side of the status bar to indicate that a filter is applied. On the Home tab, in the Sort & Filter group, Toggle Filter is active.

ANOTHER WAY   With the data selected in the field, right-click the selection, and then click Equals "339".

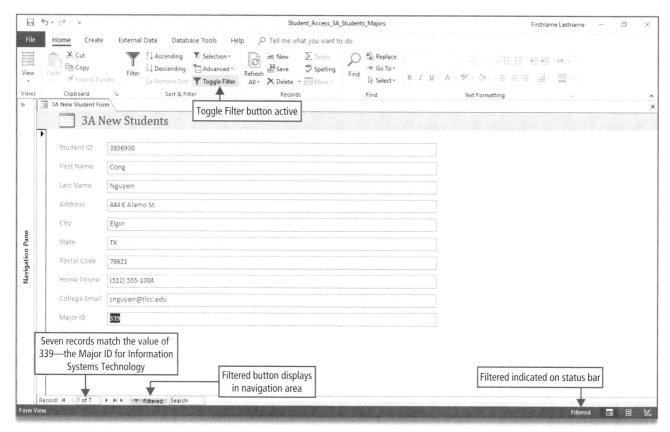

Figure 3.8

4 ▶ On the **Home tab**, in the **Sort & Filter group**, click **Toggle Filter** to remove the filter and display all 102 records. Notice *Unfiltered* in the navigation area, which indicates a filter is created but is not active.

ANOTHER WAY   Click Filtered in the navigation area to remove the filter.

NOTE   The Toggle Filter Button

On the Home tab, in the Sort & Filter group, the Toggle Filter button is used to apply or remove a filter. If no filter is created, the button is not available. After a filter is created, the button becomes available. Because it is a toggle button used to apply or remove a filter, the ScreenTip that displays for this button alternates between Apply Filter—when a filter is created but is not currently applied—and Remove Filter—when a filter is applied.

5 Be sure that the first record—for *Jordan Bass*—displays. On the **Home tab**, in the **Sort & Filter group**, click **Toggle Filter** to reapply the filter. In the navigation area, click **Last record** to display the last of the seven records that match a Major ID of *339*.

> The record for *Student ID 9712345* displays—the record with your name. Use Toggle Filter to apply or remove filters as needed.

6 In the navigation area, click **Filtered** to remove the filter and display all of the records.

> In the navigation area, *Filtered* changes to *Unfiltered*.

7 In the first record for *Jordan Bass*, in the **Last Name** field, select the first letter—**B**—in *Bass*. In the **Sort & Filter group**, click **Selection**, and then click **Begins with "B"**.

> A new filter is applied that displays eight records in which the *Last Name* begins with the letter *B*.

 ANOTHER WAY With the letter *B* selected, right-click the selection, and then click Begins with "B".

8 Use either **Toggle Filter** in the **Sort & Filter group** or **Filtered** in the navigation area to remove the filter and display all of the records.

9 In the **Sort & Filter group**, click **Advanced**, and then click **Clear All Filters**. Notice, that in the navigation area, *Unfiltered* changed to *No Filter*.

> The filter is removed from the form and must be recreated to apply it. If you toggle the filter off and save the form, the filter is saved with the form even though the filter is not currently applied.

Activity 3.07 | Using Filter By Form

MOS
2.3.3

Use the *Filter By Form* command to filter the records based on one or more fields, or based on more than one value in the same field. The Filter By Form command offers greater flexibility than the Filter By Selection command and can be used to answer a question that requires matching multiple values. In this Activity, you will filter records to help Mr. Fitchette determine how many students live in Dripping Springs or Austin.

1 ▶ On the **Home tab**, in the **Sort & Filter group**, click **Advanced**, and then click **Filter By Form**. Compare your screen with Figure 3.9.

The Filter by Form window displays all of the field names, but without any data. In the empty text box for each field, you can type a value or select a value from a list. The *Look for* and *Or* tabs display at the bottom.

Figure 3.9

2 ▶ In the form, click the **City** field name to position the insertion point in the **City** field box. At the right edge of the **City** field box, click the **arrow**, and then click **Dripping Springs**. In the **Sort & Filter group**, click **Toggle Filter**.

As displayed in the navigation area, four student records have *Dripping Springs* stored in the City field.

3 In the **Sort & Filter group**, click **Advanced**, and then click **Filter By Form**. In the lower left corner of the form, click the **Or tab**. Click the **City** field box **arrow**, and then click **Austin**. In the **Sort & Filter group**, click **Toggle Filter**, and then compare your screen with Figure 3.10.

> As displayed in the navigation area, 28 student records have either *Dripping Springs* OR *Austin* stored in the City field. You have created an *OR condition*; that is, records display where, in this instance, either of two values—Dripping Springs *or* Austin—is present in the selected field.

🔄 **ANOTHER WAY**   Click in the field box, and type the criteria separated by the word *or*. For example, in the City field box, type *Dripping Springs or Austin*.

Figure 3.10

4 In the **Sort & Filter group**, click **Advanced**, and then click **Clear All Filters** to display all 102 records.

Activity 3.08 | Using Advanced Filter/Sort

2.3.3

In this Activity, you will assist the enrollment services assistant by using the Advanced Filter/ Sort command to filter records to locate students who live in Austin with a Major ID of *339*— Information Systems Technology.

1 In the **Sort & Filter group**, click **Advanced**, and then click **Advanced Filter/Sort**. In the table area, resize the field list so that the entire table name and all of the field names display.

> The Advanced Filter design grid displays, which is similar to the query design grid, although not all rows display in the bottom half of the window. A field list for the underlying table of the form displays.

2 In the **3A New Students** field list, double-click **City**, and then double-click **Major ID** to add both fields to the design grid. In the **Criteria** row, under **City**, type **Austin** and then press Enter. In the **Criteria** row, under **Major ID**, type **339** and then press Enter. Compare your screen with Figure 3.11.

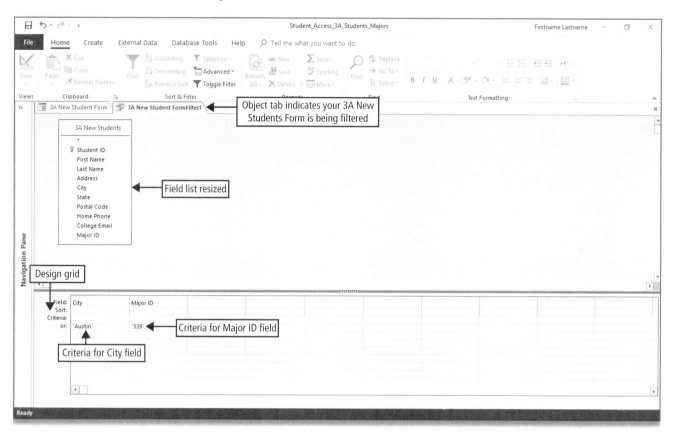

Figure 3.11

3 In the **Sort & Filter group**, click **Toggle Filter** to display the filtered records.

Three records match the criteria. You have created an **_AND condition_**; that is, only records where both values—Austin _and_ 339—are present in the selected fields display. There are three students who live in Austin who have declared a major of Information Systems Technology.

4 In the **Sort & Filter group**, click **Toggle Filter** to remove the filter and to display all of the records.

In the navigation area, _Unfiltered_ displays, which indicates that a filter has been created for this form. Unless you click Clear All Filters, the filter is saved with the form when the form is closed. When you reopen the form, you can click Toggle Filtered or Unfiltered to reapply the filter.

5 **Close** ☒ your **3A New Student Form** object and notice that the Advanced Filter grid also closes.

MORE KNOWLEDGE **Using the Filter Button**

You can filter a table in a manner similar to the way you filter records in a form. With a table open in Datasheet view, click in the field you wish to use for the filter. On the Home tab, in the Sort & Filter group, click Filter to display a shortcut menu. Select the (Select All) check box to clear the option, and then select the data by which you want to filter your records by clicking the check boxes preceding the data. To remove the filter, redisplay the menu, and then select the (Select All) check box.

GO! Learn How
Video A3-3

The **Form Wizard** walks you step by step through the creation of a form and gives you more flexibility in the design, layout, and number of fields in a form than the Form tool. Design a form for the individuals who use the form—either for entering new records or viewing records. For example, when your college counselor displays student information, it may be easier for the counselor to view the information if the fields are arranged in a layout that more closely matches a paper form.

Activity 3.09 | Creating a Form by Using the Form Wizard

In this Activity, you will create a form to match the layout of a paper form that a student at Texas Lakes Community College completes when that student changes his or her major. This will make it easier for the individual who changes the data in the database.

1 On the ribbon, click the **Create tab**, and then in the **Forms group**, click **Form Wizard**.

The Form Wizard walks you step by step through the process of creating a form by asking questions. In the first wizard screen, you select the fields to include on the form. The fields can come from more than one table or query.

2 In the **Tables/Queries** box, click the **arrow** to display a list of available tables and queries from which you can create the form.

There are two tables in the database from which you can create a new form. The selected table is the one that you last worked with.

3 Click **Table: 3A New Students**, and then compare your screen with Figure 3.12.

In the Available Fields list, the field names from your 3A New Students table display.

Figure 3.12

4 In the **Available Fields** list, double-click the following field names in the order given to move them to the **Selected Fields** list: **First Name**, **Last Name**, and **Major ID**. Compare your screen with Figure 3.13.

Three field names from your 3A New Students table display in the Selected Fields list.

🔄 **ANOTHER WAY**   Click the field name, and then click Add Field ⟩ to move a field from the Available Fields list to the Selected Fields list.

Figure 3.13

5 Click **Next**. In the wizard, be sure **Columnar** is selected as the layout, and then click **Next**. In the **What title do you want for your form?** box, select the existing text, type **3A Student Major Change Form** and then click **Finish** to close the wizard and create the form.

The three fields and the data from the first record in your 3A New Students table display in Form view.

6 Open ⟩⟩ the **Navigation Pane**. Compare your screen with Figure 3.14.

In the Navigation Pane, the form displays under its data source—your 3A New Students table.

Figure 3.14

Objective 4   **Modify a Form in Layout View and in Design View**

GO! Learn How
Video A3-4

After you create a form, you can make changes to it. For example, you can group the fields, resize the fields, add more fields to the form, and change the style of the form. Layout view enables you to see the data in the form as you modify the form. Most changes to a form can be made in Layout view.

Activity 3.10 | Grouping Controls in Layout View

4.1.2

In this Activity, you will group *controls* in the form so that you can work with them as one unit. Controls are objects on a form that display data or text, perform actions, and let you view and work with information.

1 ▶ **Close** « the **Navigation Pane** and be sure that your **3A Student Major Change Form** object displays in the object window. On the **Home tab**, in the **Views group**, click the top portion of the **View** button to switch to **Layout** view. If the Field List pane displays on the right side of your screen, click Close ✕ to close the pane. Compare your screen with Figure 3.15.

The field names and data for the first record in your 3A New Students record display in controls. The data for the first record displays in *text box controls*. The most commonly used control is the text box control, which typically displays data from a field in the underlying table. A text box control is a *bound control*—its data comes from a field in a table or query.

The field names—*First Name*, *Last Name*, and *Major ID*—display in *label controls*. A label control displays to the left of a text box control and contains descriptive information that displays on the form, usually the field name. A control that does not have a data source is an *unbound control*. Another example of an unbound control is a label control that displays the title of a form.

🔄 **ANOTHER WAY**   On the right side of the status bar, click Layout View ▤ to switch from Form view to Layout view.

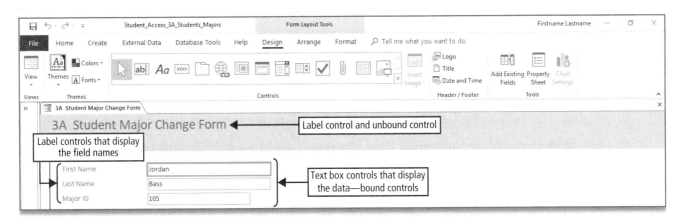

Figure 3.15

2 ▶ Click the **First Name label control**. Hold down Shift, and then click the **Last Name label control**, the **Major ID label control**, and the three **text box controls** to select all of the label and text box controls on the form.

ALERT   **Do your controls change order when selecting?**

If, when selecting multiple controls, the controls change order, click Undo, and then select the controls again. Be careful not to drag the mouse when you are selecting multiple controls.

3 With all six controls selected—surrounded by a colored border—on the ribbon, under **Form Layout Tools**, click the **Arrange tab**. In the **Table group**, click **Stacked**. Click the **First Name label control** to cancel the selection of all of the controls and to surround the **First Name label control** with a colored border. Compare your screen with Figure 3.16.

This action groups the controls together in the *Stacked layout* format—a layout similar to a paper form, with labels to the left of each field. Because the controls are grouped, you can move and edit the controls more easily as you redesign your form.

A dotted line forms a border around the controls, which indicates that the controls are grouped together. Above and to the left of the first label control that displays *First Name*, the *layout selector* displays. The layout selector is used to select and move or format the entire group of controls.

Figure 3.16

Activity 3.11 | Applying a Theme and Formatting a Form in Layout View

4.1.3

In this Activity, you will apply a *theme* to the form in Layout view. A theme is a predesigned set of colors, fonts, lines, and fill effects that look good together and that can be applied to all of the objects in the database or to individual objects in the database.

1 Under **Form Layout Tools**, click the **Design tab**. In the **Themes group**, click **Themes**. In the **Themes** gallery, using the ScreenTips, point to the **Retrospect** theme, right-click, and then click **Apply Theme to This Object Only**.

Right-click a theme so that you can apply the theme to an individual object within the database. Apply a theme before formatting any other controls in your form.

NOTE Applying a Theme to an Object and Determining the Applied Theme

If you click a theme rather than right-clicking it and selecting an option, the theme is applied to all objects in the database. You cannot click Undo to cancel the application of the theme to all objects. To determine the applied theme, in the Themes group, point to Themes. The ScreenTip displays the name of the current theme.

2 Click anywhere in the title of the form—*3A Student Major Change Form*—to select the title. Under **Form Layout Tools**, click the **Format tab**. In the **Font group**, click the **Font Size arrow**, and then click **14**. In the **Font group**, click **Bold** **B**. Click the **Font Color arrow**, and then under **Theme Colors**, in the fourth column, click the last color.

Activity 3.12 | Adding, Resizing, and Moving Controls in Layout View

4.1.1, 4.1.2, 4.1.3

In Layout view, you can change the form's *control layout*—the grouped arrangement of controls. After reviewing this form, Sean has requested a few changes. In this Activity, you will add the Student ID field and reorganize the form.

1 Be sure that your **3A Student Major Change Form** object displays in **Layout** view. On the **Design tab**, and in the **Tools group**, click **Add Existing Fields**. Compare your screen with Figure 3.17.

The Field List pane displays, which lists the fields in the underlying table—your 3A New Students table.

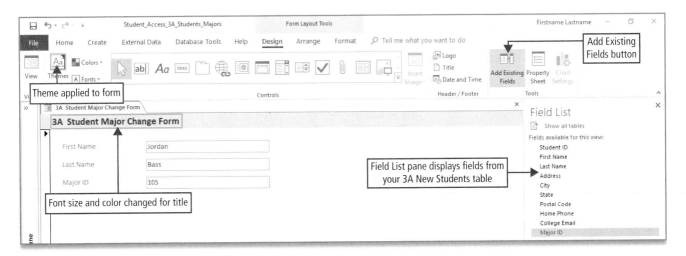

Figure 3.17

2 In the **Field List** pane, click **Student ID**, and then drag the field name to the left until the pointer displays above the **First Name label control** and a colored line displays above the control. Release the mouse button, and then compare your screen with Figure 3.18. If you are not satisfied with the result, click Undo, and begin again.

This action adds the Student ID label control and text box control to the form above the First Name controls.

Figure 3.18

3 Close ⊠ the **Field List** pane. Click the **Student ID text box control**, which displays *1034823*, to surround it with a border and to remove the border from the label control.

4 On the **Design tab**, in the **Tools group**, click **Property Sheet**.

The Property Sheet for the Student ID text box control displays. Recall that each control has an associated Property Sheet where precise changes to the properties—characteristics—of selected controls can be made. At the top of the Property Sheet, to the right of *Selection type: Text Box* displays because you selected the Student ID text box control.

5 In the **Property Sheet**, if necessary, click the **Format tab**. Click **Width** to select the property setting, type **1.5** and then press Enter to decrease the width of the text box controls. Compare your screen with Figure 3.19.

All four text box controls are resized simultaneously. Because the controls are grouped together in a stacked layout, you can adjust the width of all of the text box controls at one time without having to select all of the controls. By decreasing the width of the text box controls, you have more space in which to rearrange the form controls. Because you can see the data in Layout view, you can determine visually that the space you have allotted is adequate to display all of the data in every field for every record.

ANOTHER WAY   With the text box control selected, point to the right edge of the text box control until the ⟺ pointer displays, and then drag left to the desired location.

Figure 3.19

6 Close ⊠ the **Property Sheet**. Click the **Last Name text box control**, which displays *Bass*. Under **Form Layout Tools**, click the **Arrange tab**, and in the **Rows & Columns group**, click **Select Row** to select the text box control and its associated label control.

7 In the **Move group**, click **Move Up** to move both controls above the **First Name** controls, and then compare your screen with Figure 3.20.

 ANOTHER WAY Drag the selected controls to the desired location and then release the mouse button.

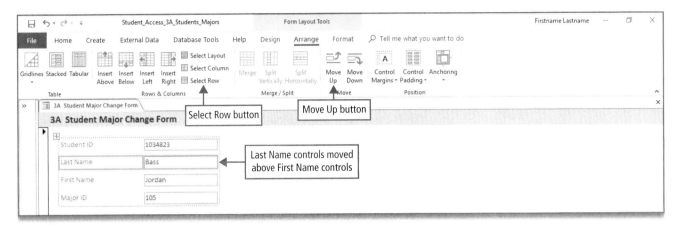

Figure 3.20

ALERT   Did the Last Name Label Control not move with the Last Name Text Box Control?

Be sure to select both the text box control and the label control before moving the controls; otherwise, only one of the controls will move. If this happens, click Undo, select both controls, and try again. Controls are stacked from top to bottom, not right to left.

8 Save 🔲 the changes you have made to the design of your form.

Activity 3.13 │ Formatting Controls in Layout View

4.1.2, 4.1.3

In this Activity, you will format and change the property settings for multiple controls.

1 With the form displayed in **Layout** view, click the **Student ID text box control**, which displays *1034823*. On the **Arrange tab**, in the **Rows & Columns group**, click **Select Column** to select all four text box controls.

 ANOTHER WAY Click the first text box control, hold down Shift, and then click the last text box control to select all four text box controls.

2 With all four text box controls selected, on the **Format tab**, in the **Font group**, click the **Background Color arrow** ⬜▾. Under **Theme Colors**, in the last column, click the second color.

All of the text box controls display a background color. This formatting is not applied to the label controls on the left.

3 Click the **Student ID label control**. On the ribbon, click the **Arrange tab**, and then in the **Rows & Columns group**, click **Select Column**. On the **Format tab**, click the **Font Color arrow**—*not* the Background Color arrow. Under **Theme Colors**, in the fourth column, click the first color. Click **Bold** ⓑ. Click in a blank area of the form to cancel the selection, and then compare your screen with Figure 3.21.

Figure 3.21

4 Click any **label control** to display the **layout selector** ⊞, and then click the **layout selector** ⊞ to select all of the grouped controls.

Recall that the layout selector, which displays to the left and above the Student ID label control, enables you to select and move the entire group of controls in Layout view.

ANOTHER WAY Click any control, and then on the Arrange tab, in the Rows & Columns group, click Select Layout.

5 On the **Format tab**, in the **Font group**, click the **Font Size arrow**, and then click **12** to change the font size of all of the text in all of the controls.

6 With all of the controls still selected, click the **Design tab**. In the **Tools group**, click **Property Sheet**, and then compare your screen with Figure 3.22.

The Property Sheet for the selected controls displays. At the top of the Property Sheet, to the right of *Selection type: Multiple selection* displays because you have more than one control selected.

Figure 3.22

7 In the **Property Sheet**, click **Height**, type **0.25** and then press Enter to change the height of each selected control.

8 Click the **Student ID label control** to cancel the selection of all of the controls and to select only this label control. In the **Property Sheet**, click **Width**, type **1.25** and then press Enter.

The width of every label control changed to 1.25 inches. Recall that because the label controls are arranged in a stacked layout, you can change the width of all controls by selecting only one control. This is one of the few properties that can be changed without first selecting the column.

9 **Close** ✕ the **Property Sheet**, and then **Save** 🖫 the design changes to your form.

Activity 3.14 | Modifying a Form in Design View

4.1.2, 4.2.4,
4.1.1, 4.1.3

Design view presents a detailed view of the structure of your form. Because the form is not actually running when displayed in Design view, the data does not display in the text box controls. However, some tasks, such as resizing sections, must be completed in Design view.

1 On the status bar, click **Design View** ![icon], and then compare your screen with Figure 3.23.

The form in Design view displays three sections, each designated by a ***section bar*** at the top of each section. The ***Form Header*** contains information, such as the form title, that displays at the top of the screen in Form view or Layout view and is printed at the top of the first page when records are printed as forms. The ***Detail section*** displays the records from the underlying table, and the ***Form Footer*** displays at the bottom of the screen in Form view or Layout view and is printed after the last detail section on the last page of a printout.

> **ANOTHER WAY** On the Home tab, in the Views group, click the View arrow, and then click Design view; or right-click the object tab, and then click Design View.

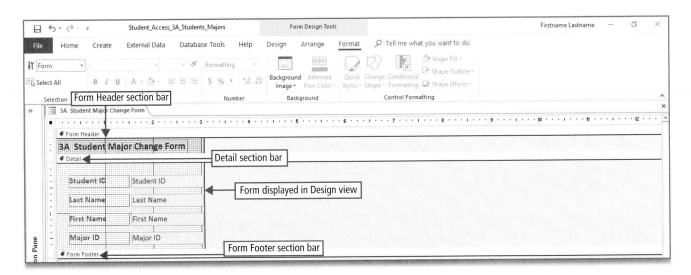

Figure 3.23

2 ▶ At the bottom of the form, click the **Form Footer section bar** to select it. On the ribbon, click the **Design tab**, and in the **Tools group**, click **Property Sheet** In the **Property Sheet**, on the **Format tab**, click **Height**, type **0.5** and then press [Enter]. Compare your screen with Figure 3.24.

> In addition to properties for controls, you can make precise changes to sections of the form. Because you selected the Form Footer section bar, the Property Sheet displays a *Selection type* of *Section*, and the section is identified as *Form Footer*.

ANOTHER WAY   At the bottom of the form, point to the lower edge of the Form Footer section bar to display the ⊞ pointer, and then drag downward approximately 0.5 inch to increase the height of the section.

Figure 3.24

3 ▶ On the **Design tab**, in the **Controls group**, click **Label** [Aa]. Move the ⁺A pointer into the **Form Footer** section and then position the plus sign of the ⁺A pointer at approximately **0.25 inch on the horizontal ruler** and even with the lower edge of the **Form Footer section bar**—the position does not need to be precise. Compare your screen with Figure 3.25.

Figure 3.25

4 Click one time. Type **Texas Lakes Community College** and then press Enter. With the **label control** selected, click the **Format tab**. In the **Font group**, click **Bold** B. Click the **Font Color arrow**, and then under **Theme Colors**, in the fourth column, click the first color.

5 With the **label control** still selected, in the **Property Sheet**, click **Top**, type **0.1** and then press Enter. In the **Property Sheet**, in the **Left** property setting, type **0.6** and then press Enter. **Close** × the **Property Sheet**, and then **Save** 🖫 the design changes to your form.

The top edge of the label control in the Form Footer section displays 0.1 inch from the lower edge of the Form Footer section bar. The left edge of the label control aligns at 0.6 inch from the left margin of the form. In this manner, you can place a control in a specific location on the form.

6 On the right side of the status bar, click **Form View** 🖽, and then compare your screen with Figure 3.26.

Form Footer text displays on the screen at the bottom of the form and prints only on the last page if all of the forms are printed. Recall, that in Form view, you can add, modify, or delete records stored in the underlying table.

 ANOTHER WAY   On the Home tab, in the Views group, click the View arrow, and then click Form View; or right-click the object tab, and then click Form View.

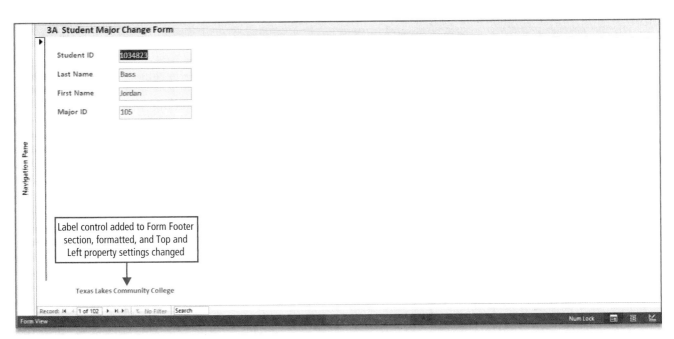

Figure 3.26

7 In the navigation area, click **Last record** ▶❘ to view the record containing your name.

8 **Close** × all open objects. **Resize** the **Navigation Pane** so all object names display fully. **Close** the database, and then **Close** Access.

For Non-MyLab Submissions : Determine What Your Instructor Requires for Submission

As directed by your instructor, submit your completed database file. If you are completing the optional activity, do so before submitting your database to your instructor.

---

9 In **MyLab IT**, locate and click the Grader Project **Access 3A Students and Majors**. In **step 3**, under **Upload Completed Assignment**, click **Choose File**. In the **Open** dialog box, navigate to your **Access Chapter 3 folder**, and then click your **Student_Access_3A_Students_Majors** file one time to select it. In the lower right corner of the **Open** dialog box, click **Open**.

> The name of your selected file displays above the Upload button.

10 To submit your file to **MyLab IT** for grading, click **Upload**, wait a moment for a green **Success!** message, and then in **step 4**, click the blue **Submit for Grading** button. Click **Close Assignment** to return to your list of **Course Materials**.

You have completed Project 3A   **END**

Activity 3.15 | Printing a Single Form

ALERT   **This Activity is optional**

This Activity is optional. Check with your instructor to see if you should complete this Activity. This Activity is not included in the MyLab IT Grader system for this project; however, you may want to practice this on your own to learn how to print a form for a single record within your database.

MOS

4.2.3

When a form is displayed, clicking Print causes *all* of the records to print in the form layout. In this Activity, you will print only *one* record.

1 Start Access. Under *Recent*, click your **3A_Students_Majors** database to open it.

2 **Open** |»| the **Navigation Pane**. In the **Navigation Pane**, double-click your **3A New Student Form** object to open it. Press Ctrl + F to open the **Find and Replace** dialog box. In the **Find What** box, type **9712345** and then click **Find Next** to display the record with your name. **Close** |×| the **Find and Replace** dialog box.

3 On the **File tab**, click **Print**, and then on the right, click **Print**. In the **Print** dialog box, under **Print Range**, click the **Selected Record(s)** option button. In the lower left corner of the dialog box, click **Setup**.

4 In the **Page Setup** dialog box, click the **Columns tab**. Under **Column Size**, double-click in the **Width** box to select the existing value, type **7.5** and then compare your screen with Figure 3.27.

> Change the width of the column in this manner so that the form prints on one page. Forms are not typically printed, so the width of the column in a form might be greater than the width of the paper on which you are printing. The maximum column width that you can enter is dependent upon the printer that is installed on your system. This setting is saved when you save or close the form.

Figure 3.27

5 In the **Page Setup** dialog box, click **OK**. To create a paper printout, in the **Print** dialog box click **OK**. To create a PDF electronic image of this single form, click **Cancel** and then follow the instructions in the Note below.

NOTE   Printing a Single Form as a PDF Electronic Image

To create a PDF electronic image of a single form as a PDF electronic image, change the column width to 7.5 as described in Step 3 above, and then in the Print dialog box, click Cancel. On the left side of the form, click the Record Selector bar so that it is black—selected. Click the External Data tab. In the Export group, click PDF or XPS.

In the Publish as PDF or XPS dialog box, navigate to your chapter folder. In the File name box, the file has the same name as the form. Be sure that the Open file after publishing check box is selected, and that the Minimum size (publishing online) option button is selected. In the Publish as PDF or XPS dialog box, click Options. In the Options dialog box, under Range, click the Selected records option button, click OK, and then click Publish. Close the Windows Edge Reader, Adobe Reader or Adobe Acrobat window, and then submit the file as directed by your instructor.

6 Open ⏩ the **Navigation Pane**, and then double-click your **3A Major Form** object to open it.

7 Use the techniques you just practiced to **Find** the record for the **Major ID** of **339.555.22**, and then create a paper or electronic printout as directed by your instructor of that record only on one page.

If there are no related records in the subdatasheet, the empty subdatasheet does not display in the printed form.

8 In the **Navigation Pane**, double-click your **3A Student Major Change Form** object to open it. With the first record displayed, create a paper or electronic printout as directed by your instructor of that record only on one page.

9 **Close** ✕ all open objects, and then **Open** ⏩ the **Navigation Pane**. If necessary, resize the **Navigation Pane** so all object names display fully. On the right side of the title bar, click Close ✕ to close the database and to close Access. As directed by your instructor, submit your database for grading.

You have completed the optional portion of Project 3A   END

Objective	**Export an Access Form to an Excel Spreadsheet, Save to Google Drive as a Google Sheet, Edit a Record, and Save to Your Computer**

Access web apps are designed to work with Microsoft's SharePoint, a service for setting up websites to share and manage documents. Your college may not have SharePoint installed, so you will use other tools to share objects from your database so that you can work collaboratively with others. Recall that Google Drive is Google's free, web-based word processor, spreadsheet, slide show, form, and data storage and sharing service. For Access, you can export a database object to an Excel worksheet, a PDF file, or a text file, and then save the file to Google Drive.

ALERT   Working with Web-Based Applications and Services

Computer programs and services on the web receive continuous updates and improvements, so the steps to complete this web-based activity may differ from the ones shown. You can often look at the screens and the information presented to determine how to complete the activity.

If you do not already have a Google account, you will need to create one before you begin this activity. Go to http://google.com and in the upper-right corner, click Sign In. On the Sign In screen, click Create account. On the Create your Google Account page, complete the form, read and agree to the Terms of Service and Privacy Policy, and then click Next step. On the Welcome screen, click Get Started.

Activity | **Exporting an Access Form to an Excel Spreadsheet, Saving the Spreadsheet to Google Drive, Editing a Record in Google Sheets, and Saving to Your Computer**

In this Activity, you will export your 3A Student Major Change Form object to an Excel spreadsheet, upload your Excel file to Google Drive, edit a record in Google Sheets, and then download a copy of the edited spreadsheet to your computer.

1 Start Access, on the left click **Open Other Files**, navigate to your **Access Chapter 3** folder, and then **Open** your **3A_Students_Majors** database file. If necessary, on the **Message Bar**, click **Enable Content**. In the **Navigation Pane**, click your **3A Student Major Change Form** object to select it.

2 On the **External Data tab**, in the **Export group**, click **Excel**. In the **Export – Excel Spreadsheet** dialog box, click **Browse**, and then navigate to your **Access Chapter 3** folder. In the **File Save** dialog box, click in the **File name** box, type **Lastname_Firstname_AC_3A_Web** and then click **Save**.

3 In the **Export – Excel Spreadsheet** dialog box, under **Specify export options**, select the second check box—**Open the destination file after the export operation is complete**—and then click **OK**.

The records from the underlying table of the form display in Excel. When you export a form to Excel, the formatting and layout are automatically saved. For example, notice the olive green background color of the cells, which was the color that was applied to the text box controls in the form.

4 In the **Microsoft Excel** window, in the column headings row, to the left of column **A**, click **Select All**. On the **Home tab**, in the **Cells group**, click **Format**, and then click **AutoFit Column Width**. Click in cell **A1** to cancel the selection, and then compare your screen with Figure A.

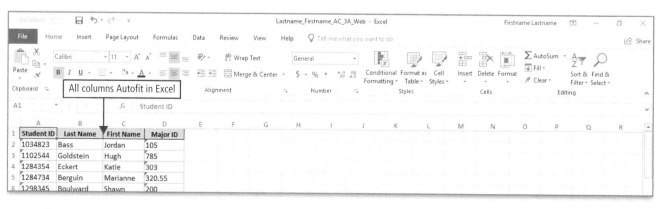

Figure A

»»» **GO!** With Google continues on next page

5 **Save** the workbook, and then **Close** Excel. In the **Export – Excel Spreadsheet** dialog box, click **Close**, and then **Close** Access.

6 From the desktop, open your browser, navigate to http://google.com, and then sign in to your Google account. Click the Google Apps menu [▦], and then click Drive [☁]. Open your **GO! Web Projects** folder—or click New to create and then open this folder if necessary.

7 In the upper right corner, click **Settings** [⚙], and then on the menu click **Settings**. In the **Settings** dialog box, next to **Convert uploads**, be sure that **Convert uploaded files to Google Docs editor format** is selected. In the upper right, click **Done**.

If this setting is not selected, your document will upload as a pdf file and cannot be edited without further action.

8 On the left, click **New**, and then click **File upload**. In the **Open** dialog box, navigate to your **Access Chapter 3** folder, and then double-click your **Lastname_ Firstname_AC_3A_Web** file to upload it to Google Drive. When the title bar of the message box indicates *1 upload complete*, **Close** the message box.

9 In your **GO! Web Projects** folder, double-click your **Lastname_Firstname_AC_3A_Web** file to open it in Google Sheets.

10 In the second record (row 3), click in the **Last Name** field, using your own last name, type **Lastname** and then press Enter. In the **First Name** field, using your own first name, type Firstname and then press Enter to save the record. Compare your screen with Figure B.

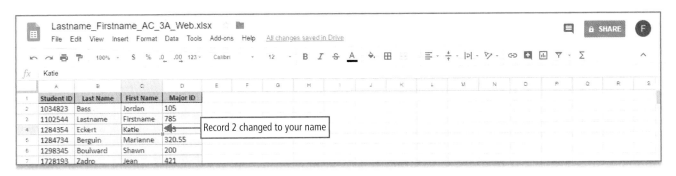

Figure B

11 On the menu bar, click **File**, point to **Download as**, and then click **Microsoft Excel (.xlsx)**. As necessary, open the downloaded file in Excel, enable editing, and then **Save** the file in your **Access Chapter 3** folder as **Lastname_Firstname_AC_3A_Web_Download**

12 Close Excel. In Google Drive, in the upper right corner, click your user name, and then click **Sign out**. **Close** your browser window.

13 As directed by your instructor, submit your two workbooks.

NOTE   **Printing or Creating an PDF electronic image of an Excel Spreadsheet**

To print on paper, click Print. To create a PDF electronic image of your printout, on the left side of your screen, click Export. Under Export, be sure Create PDF/XPS Document is selected, and then click Create PDF/XPS. Navigate to your Access Chapter 3 folder, and then click Publish to save the file with the default name and an extension of pdf.

Job Openings Database

Project Activities

In Activities 3.16 through 3.23, you will assist Jack Woods, director of the Career Center for Texas Lakes Community College, in using his Access database to track the employees and job openings advertised for the annual job fair. Your completed Navigation Pane will look similar to Figure 3.28.

Project Files for MyLab IT Grader

1. In your **MyLab IT** course, locate and click **Access 3B Job Openings**, Download Materials, and then Download All Files.
2. Extract the zipped folder to your Access Chapter 3 folder. Close the Grader download screens.
3. Take a moment to open the downloaded **Access_3B_Job_Openings_Instructions**; note any recent updates to the book.

Project Results

GO! Project 3B
Where We're Going

Figure 3.28 Project 3B Job Openings

For Non-MyLab Submissions	**Start with an Access Data File**
For Project 3B, you will need this starting file:	In your Access Chapter 3 folder, save your database as:
a03B_Job_Openings	**Lastname_Firstname_3B_Job_Openings**

After you have saved your database, launch Access and open the database. On the next page, begin with Step 2.

ALERT Because Office 365 is a cloud-based subscription service that receives continuous updates, you may encounter some variations in what appears on your screen and what is shown in this instruction. Microsoft Office 365 is fully installed on your PC or Mac; no internet access is necessary to create or edit documents. When you *are* connected to the internet, you will receive monthly upgrades and new features, so you always have the latest versions of Office apps as soon as they are available. Your subscription gives you continuous free access to the latest innovations and refinements.

GO! Learn How
Video A3-5

A *report* is a database object that summarizes the fields and records from a query or from a table in an easy-to-read format suitable for printing. A report consists of information extracted from queries or tables and report design controls, such as labels, headings, and graphics. The queries or tables that provide the underlying data for a report are referred to as the report's *record source*.

Activity 3.16 | Opening and Saving an Existing Database, Renaming Objects, and Viewing a Table Relationship

1.2.2

1 Start Access. In the Access opening screen, click **Open Other Files**. Under **Open**, click **Browse**, navigate to your **Access Chapter 3 folder**, and then double-click the Access file that you downloaded from **MyLab IT** that displays your name—**Student_Access_3B_Job_Openings**. On the **Message Bar**, click **Enable Content**.

2 On the **Database Tools tab**, in the **Relationships group**, click **Relationships**. If the relationships do not display, under Relationship Tools, on the Design tab, in the Relationships group, click All Relationships. If necessary, resize and move the field lists so that the entire table name and fields display for each field list.

3 In the **Relationships** window, click the **join line** between the two field lists. In the **Tools group**, click **Edit Relationships**. Point to the title bar of the **Edit Relationships** dialog box, and then drag the dialog box to the right of the **3B Job Openings** field list. Compare your screen with Figure 3.29.

One employer is associated with *many* job openings. Thus, a one-to-many relationship is established between the 3B Employers table and the 3B Job Openings table by using Employer ID as the common field. Referential integrity is enforced, and cascade options are selected.

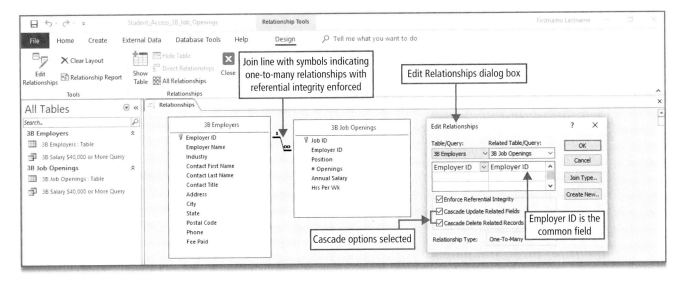

Figure 3.29

4 Close ⊠ the **Edit Relationships** dialog box, and then **Close** ⊠ the **Relationships** window. If necessary, in the message box, click Yes to save changes to the layout of the relationships.

5 In the **Navigation Pane**, double-click each table, and then examine the fields and data in each table. Double-click the query object to run the query and examine the query results, apply **Best Fit** to the query results, and then **Save** the query. Switch to **Design** view to examine the design grid.

> The query answers the question, *What is the Job ID, position, employer name, number of job openings, and annual salary for job openings that have an annual salary of $40,000 or more, in ascending order by the Employer Name field within the Position field?*

6 In the object window, right-click any **object tab**, and then click **Close All**.

Activity 3.17 | Creating a Report by Using the Report Tool and Applying a Theme to the Report

5.1.2, 5.2.3

The ***Report tool*** is the fastest way to create a report, because it displays all of the fields and records from the record source that you select. You can use the Report tool to look at the underlying data quickly in an easy-to-read format, after which you can save the report and modify it in Layout view or in Design view.

In this Activity, you will use the Report tool to create a report from a query that lists all of the job openings with an annual salary of at least $40,000 and apply a theme to the report.

1 In the **Navigation Pane**, if necessary, click to select your **3B Salary $40,000 or More Query** object. On the **Create tab**, in the **Reports group**, click **Report**. **Close** « the **Navigation Pane**, and then compare your screen with Figure 3.30.

> The report is created using the query as the record source and displays in Layout view. The report includes all of the fields and all of the records from the query and the title of the query. In Layout view, the broken lines indicate the page margins in the report.

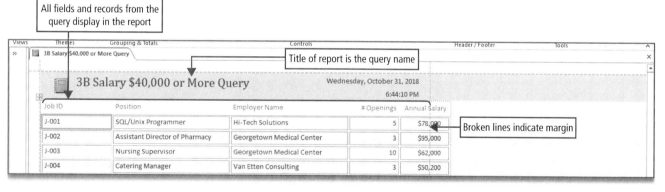

Figure 3.30

2 Under **Report Layout Tools**, on the **Design tab**, in the **Themes group**, click **Themes**. In the **Themes** gallery, use the ScreenTips to locate the **Integral** theme, right-click the **Integral** theme, and then click **Apply Theme to This Object Only**.

> Recall that right-clicking a theme enables you to apply a predefined format to the active object only, which is a quick way to apply a professional look to a report. Apply a theme before formatting any other controls on the report.

ALERT **You applied the theme to the entire database instead of a single object.**

If you applied the theme to the entire database, you cannot undo that selection. To correct the theme, under Report Layout Tools, on the Design tab, in the Themes group, click Themes. In the Themes gallery, click the Office theme to apply it to the entire database. Return to Step 2 above to apply the Integral theme to a single object.

Activity 3.18 | Modifying a Report in Layout View

5.2.1, 5.1.2,
5.2.5, 5.1.1, 5.2.3

After you create a report, you can make changes to it. For example, you can add or delete fields, resize the fields, and change the style of the report. Layout view enables you to see the data in the report as you modify the report. Most changes to a report can be made in Layout view.

1 ► Click the **Job ID** field name. On the **Report Layout Tools**, click the **Arrange tab**, in the **Rows & Columns group**, click **Select Column** to select the field name and all of the data for each record in the field. Press Del to remove the field from the report.

The Job ID field is deleted, and the remaining fields move to the left. No fields extend beyond the right margin of the report.

 ANOTHER WAY With the column selected, on the Home tab, in the Records group, click Delete; or right-click the selected column, and then click Delete or Delete Column.

2 ► In the **Employer Name** field, click in the **text box control** that displays *Monroe Heating & Air Conditioning* to select all of the text box controls in this field.

3 ► On the **Report Layout Tools**, click the **Design tab**, and in the **Tools group**, click **Property Sheet**. In the **Property Sheet**, on the **Format tab**, click **Width**, type **2.5** and then press Enter. Compare your screen with Figure 3.31.

Recall that you can use the Property Sheet to make precise changes to control properties.

ANOTHER WAY Point to the right edge of the text box control to display the ⟷ pointer. Drag to the right slightly until the data in the text box control displays on correctly.

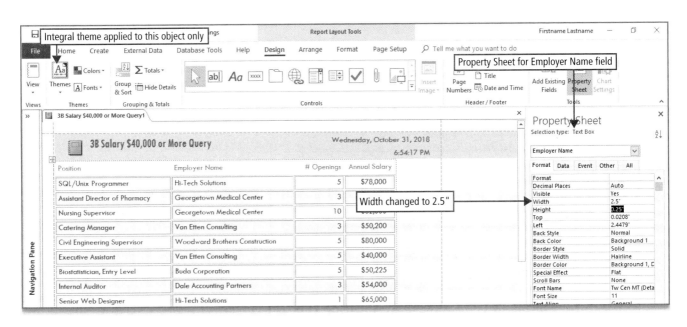

Figure 3.31

4 ► **Close** ⊠ the **Property Sheet**. Click the **Position** field name, and then on the **Home tab**, in the **Sort & Filter group**, click **Ascending** to sort the records in ascending order by the Position field.

ANOTHER WAY Right-click the selected field name and then click Sort A to Z.

5 Scroll to the bottom of the report, and then click the **calculated control** that displays *$2,157,625*, which is shortened at the bottom cutting off part of the data. Press Del to remove this control.

> In a report created by using the Report tool, a *calculated control* is automatically created to sum any field that is formatted as currency. A calculated control contains an expression, often a formula or a function. Here, the total is not a useful number and thus can be deleted.

6 Scroll to the bottom of the report again, and then under the last column, click the horizontal line that is the border between the last record and the calculated control that you deleted. Press Del to remove this line, and then scroll to the bottom of the report to verify that the line has been deleted.

7 Scroll to the top of the report, and then click the **# Openings** field name. On the **Design tab**, in the **Grouping & Totals group**, click **Totals**, and then click **Sum**.

8 Scroll to the bottom of the report, and then click the **calculated control** that displays *100*. On the **Design tab**, in the **Tools group**, click **Property Sheet**. In the **Property Sheet**, on the **Format tab**, click **Height**, type **0.25** and then press Enter. Compare your screen with Figure 3.32.

> The total number of job openings for positions with a salary of $40,000 or more is 100.

ANOTHER WAY Point to the lower edge of the text box control to display the ⇕ pointer, and then double-click to resize the control, or drag downward to increase the height of the control.

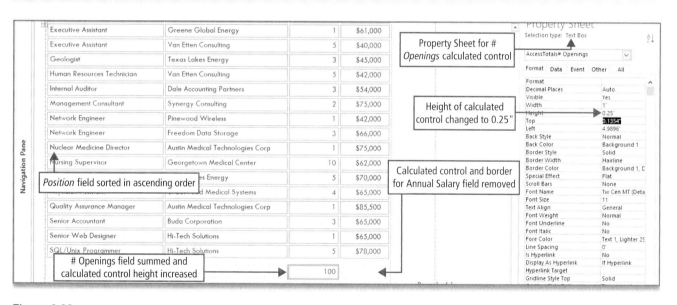

Figure 3.32

9 At the bottom of the report to the right of the calculated control, notice that the control that displays the page number does not fit entirely within the margins of the report. Click the **control** that displays *Page 1 of 1*. In the **Property Sheet**, click **Left**, type **2.5** and then press Enter.

> The control moves within the margins of the report with the left edge of the control 2.5 inches in from the left margin of the report. When you click on different controls in a report or form, the Property Sheet changes to match the selected control. Before printing, always scroll through the report to be sure that all of the controls display on one page and not outside of the margins.

ANOTHER WAY Click the control, point to the selected control to display the ▧ pointer, and then drag the control to the left within the margins of the report.

10 Scroll to the top of the report, and then click the **label control** that displays the title of the report—*3B Salary $40,000 or More Query*. On the **Report Layout Tools**, click the **Format tab**. In the **Font group**, click the **Font Size arrow**, and then click **14**.

11 With the **label control** for the title still selected, double-click **Query** to select the word, type **Report** and then press Enter to change the name of the report to *3B Salary $40,000 or More Report*.

12 Click the **Position** field name. In the **Property Sheet**, click **Left**, type **0.5** and then press Enter to move this field 0.5 inch in from the left margin of the report. Compare your screen with Figure 3.33.

> The other fields adjust by moving to the right. The fields are centered approximately within the margins of the report.

ANOTHER WAY   Click the layout selector ⊞ to select all of the controls, and then drag it slightly downward and to the right until the columns are visually centered between the margins of the report. If your columns rearrange, click Undo and begin again.

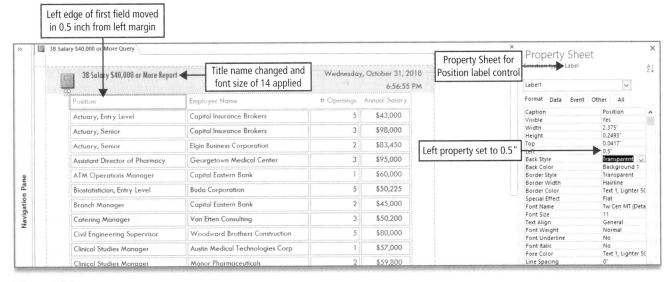

Figure 3.33

13 Close × the **Property Sheet**, and then Save 🖫 the report as **3B Salary $40,000 or More Report** Close × the report, and then Open » the **Navigation Pane**.

> The report displays under both tables from which the query was created. The report object name displays with a small green notebook icon.

14 Close « the **Navigation Pane**.

| Objective 6 | Create a Report by Using the Report Wizard |

GO! Learn How
Video A3-6

Use the ***Report Wizard*** when you need more flexibility in the design of your report. You can group and sort data by using the wizard and use fields from more than one table or query if you have created the relationships between tables. The Report Wizard is similar to the Form Wizard; the wizard walks you step by step through the process of creating the report by asking you questions and then designs the report based on your answers.

Activity 3.19 | Creating a Report by Using the Report Wizard

In this Activity, you will prepare a report for Mr Woods that displays the employers, grouped by industry, and the total fees paid by employers for renting a booth at the Job Fair.

1 On the **Create tab**, in the **Reports group**, click **Report Wizard**.

In the first wizard screen, you select the fields to include on the report. The fields can come from more than one table or query.

2 In the **Tables/Queries** box, click the **arrow**, and then click **Table: 3B Employers**. In the **Available Fields** list, double-click the following field names in the order given to move them to the **Selected Fields** list: **Industry**, **Employer Name**, and **Fee Paid** (scroll as necessary to locate the *Fee Paid* field). Compare your screen with Figure 3.34.

Three field names from your 3B Employers table display in the Selected Fields list.

🔄 **ANOTHER WAY**   Click the field name, and then click One Field [>] to move a field from the Available Fields list to the Selected Fields list.

Figure 3.34

3 Click **Next**. In the wizard, notice that you can add grouping levels and that a preview of the grouping level displays on the right.

Grouping data helps to organize and summarize the data in your report.

4 On the left, double-click **Industry**, and then compare your screen with Figure 3.35.

The preview displays how the data will be grouped in the report. Grouping data in a report places all of the records that have the same data in a field together as a group—in this instance, the records will be grouped by *Industry*. Within each Industry name, the Employer Name and Fee Paid will display.

Figure 3.35

5 ▶ Click **Next**. Click the **1** box **arrow**, click **Employer Name**, and then compare your screen with Figure 3.36.

In this step of the wizard, you indicate how you want to sort the records and summarize the information. You can sort up to four fields. The Summary Options button displays because the data is grouped, and at least one of the fields—*Fee Paid*—contains numerical or currency data. Within each Industry grouping, the records will be sorted alphabetically by the Employer Name. Sorting records in a report presents a more organized view of the records.

Figure 3.36

6 ▶ In the wizard, click **Summary Options**, and then compare your screen with Figure 3.37.

The Summary Options dialog box displays. The *Fee Paid* field can be summarized by selecting one of the four check boxes for Sum, Avg, Min, or Max. You can also display only summary information or display both the details—each record—and the summary information. The default setting is to display *Detail and Summary*.

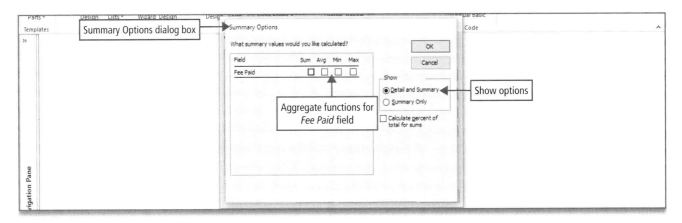

Figure 3.37

7 ▶ In the **Summary Options** dialog box, click to select the **Sum** check box. Under **Show**, verify that **Detail and Summary** is selected, and then click **OK**. In the wizard, click **Next**.

In this step of the wizard, you select the layout and page orientation. A preview of the layout displays on the left.

8 ▶ Click each **Layout** option button, noticing the changes in the preview, and then click **Stepped** to select it as the layout for your report. Under **Orientation**, be sure that **Portrait** is selected. At the bottom of the wizard, be sure that the **Adjust the field width so all fields fit on a page** check box is selected, and then click **Next**.

9 In the **What title do you want for your report?** box, select the existing text, type **3B Booth Fees by Industry Report** and then click **Finish**. Compare your screen with Figure 3.38.

The report is saved and displays in Print Preview using the specifications you defined in the Report Wizard. The records are grouped by Industry. Within each Industry, the records display in ascending order by the Employer Name. Within each Industry grouping, the Fee paid is summed or totaled—the word *Sum* displays at the end of each grouping.

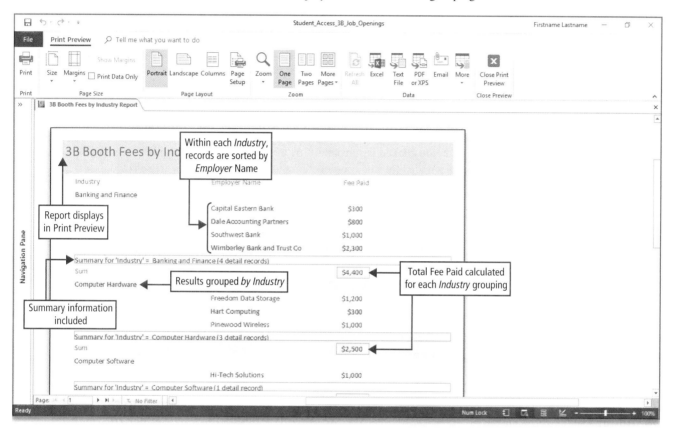

Figure 3.38

10 In the object window, right-click the **object tab** for the report, and then click **Layout View**.

 ANOTHER WAY On the status bar, click Layout View 🔲; or click Close Print Preview, and then on the Home tab or the Design tab, click the View arrow, and then click Layout View.

Objective 7 Modify the Design of a Report

GO! Learn How
Video A3-7

You can modify the design of a report that is created using the Report Wizard by using the same techniques and tools that you use to modify a report created with the Report tool. Recall that most report modifications can be made in Layout view.

Activity 3.20 | Formatting and Deleting Controls in Layout View

MOS
5.2.3

In this Activity, you will apply a theme to the report, format the title of the report, and delete the summary information controls.

1 Be sure that your **3B Booth Fees by Industry Report** object is displayed in **Layout** view. Under **Report Layout Tools**, on the **Design tab**, in the **Themes group**, click **Themes**. In the **Themes** gallery, use the ScreenTips to locate the **Ion Boardroom** theme, right-click the **Ion Boardroom** theme, and then click **Apply Theme to This Object Only**.

Recall that you should apply a theme before applying any other formatting changes. Also, recall that if you click a theme—instead of right-clicking—the theme is applied to all of the objects in the database.

2 At the top of the report, click the title—*3B Booth Fees by Industry Report*—to display a border around the label control. On the **Report Layout Tools**, click the **Format tab**. In the **Font group**, click the **Font Size arrow**, and then click **14**. In the **Font group**, click **Bold** ⓑ.

By changing the font size, the report name is no longer truncated and includes the word *Report*.

3 Within each *Industry* grouping, notice the **Summary for 'Industry'** information.

Because you selected Summary Options, a summary line is included at the end of each grouping that details what is being summarized—in this case, summed—and the number of records that are included in the summary total. Now that Mr. Woods has viewed the report, he has decided that this information is not necessary and can be removed.

4 Click any one of the controls that begins with **Summary for 'Industry'**.

The control that you clicked is surrounded by a border, and all of the other summary information controls are surrounded by paler borders to indicate that all controls are selected.

5 Press Del to remove the controls from the report, and then compare your screen with Figure 3.39.

🔄 **ANOTHER WAY** Right-click any of the selected controls, and then click Delete to remove the controls from the report.

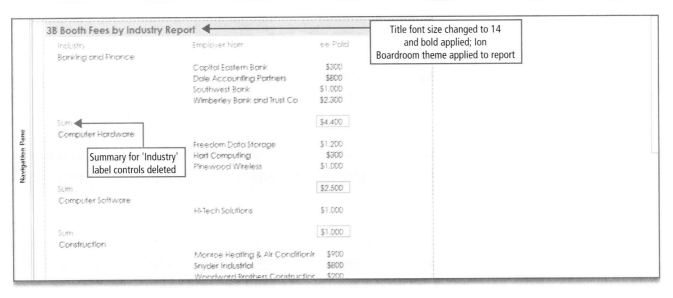

Figure 3.39

6 Save 💾 the changes you have made to the design of the report.

Activity 3.21 | Modifying Controls in Layout View

MOS
5.2.2, 5.2.3, 5.1.3

In this Activity, you will modify the text in controls, move controls, resize controls, and add a control to the report in Layout view.

1 On the left side of the report, click a **Sum label control**, which selects all of the related controls. Double-click the control to select the text—*Sum*. Type **Total Booth Fees by Industry** and then press [Enter]. Compare your screen with Figure 3.40.

This text states more clearly what is being summed.

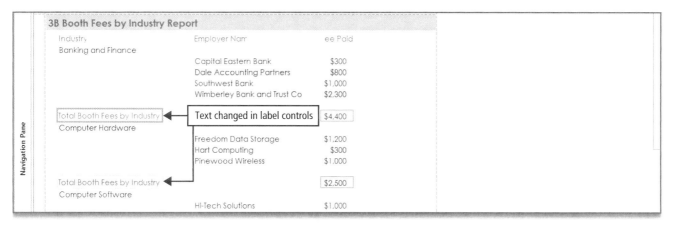

Figure 3.40

2 At the top of the report, click the **Industry label control** to select it. Hold down [Shift], click the **Employer Name label control**, and then click the **Fee Paid label control** to select all three field names. On the **Format tab**, in the **Font group**, click **Bold** [B].

Applying bold also increases the size of the controls so that the text is no longer truncated.

3 At the top of the report, under the **Fee Paid label control**, click the **text box control** that displays *$300* to select the text box controls for all of the records for this field. On the **Design tab**, in the **Tools group**, click **Property Sheet**. In the **Property Sheet**, on the **Format tab**, click **Left**, type **7** and then press [Enter]. Compare your screen with Figure 3.41.

All of the Fee Paid text box controls move to the right—7" in from the left margin. Do not be concerned that the summary total and the field name are not aligned with the data; you will correct this in the next Activity. The field is moved to the right so that you can increase the width of the Employer Name text box controls so that all of the data for every record displays.

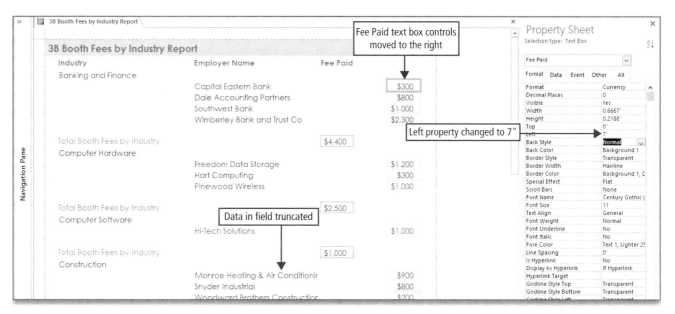

Figure 3.41

4 Scroll to view the bottom of the report. Click to select the **calculated control** for the **Grand Total**, which displays *20,400* and part of the dollar symbol. In the **Property Sheet**, click **Width**, type **0.8** and then press Enter.

> The width of the calculated control increases to display the dollar symbol. Do not be concerned that the right edge of the control no longer aligns with the control above it; you will correct this in the next Activity. Recall that a calculated control contains an expression—a formula or function—that displays the result of the expression when the report is displayed in Report view, Print Preview, or Layout view.

ANOTHER WAY Point to the left edge of the control to display the ⟷ pointer. Drag to the left slightly to increase the width of the calculated control.

5 At the bottom of the report, on the left side, click the **Grand Total label control**. In the **Property Sheet**, click **Width**, type **1** and then press Enter. Compare your screen with Figure 3.42.

> The width of the label control is increased so that all of the text displays.

ANOTHER WAY Point to the right edge of the control to display the ⟷ pointer, and then double-click to resize the control.

Figure 3.42

6 Scroll to the top to display the Industry grouping of **Construction**, and then notice that the first and third records have truncated data in the **Employer Name** field. In the **Construction** grouping, click the **Employer Name text box control** that starts with *Monroe Heating* to select all of the text box controls for this field.

7 In the **Property Sheet**, click **Width**, type **3** and then press Enter. **Save** 🖫 the design changes to your report, and then compare your screen with Figure 3.43.

> The width of the Employer Name text box controls is increased so that all of the data in this field for every record displays. Recall that you moved the Fee Paid text box controls to the right to make room for the increased width of these controls.

Figure 3.43

Activity 3.22 | Aligning Controls in Design View

5.2.2, 5.2.3, 5.1.3

Design view gives you a more detailed view of the structure of your report. You can see the header and footer sections for the report, for the page, and for groups. In Design view, your report is not running, so you cannot see the data from the table in the controls. In the same manner as forms, you can add labels to the Page Footer section or increase the height of sections. Some tasks, such as aligning controls, must be completed in Design view.

1 **Close** ☒ the **Property Sheet**. On the status bar, click **Design View** ◢, and then compare your screen with Figure 3.44.

Design view for a report is similar to Design view for a form. You can modify the layout of the report in this view, and then use the dotted grid pattern to align controls. This report has several sections. The ***Report Header*** displays information at the top of the *first page* of a report. The ***Page Header*** displays information at the top of *every page* of a report. The ***Group Header*** displays the name of data in the field by which the records are grouped; in this case, the *Industry* name. The Detail section displays the data for each record. The ***Group Footer*** displays the summary information for each grouping; in this case, the Industry name. The ***Page Footer*** displays information at the bottom of *every page* of the report. The ***Report Footer*** displays information at the bottom of the *last page* of the report.

If you do not group data in a report, the Group Header section and Group Footer section will not display. If you do not summarize the data, the Group Footer section will not display.

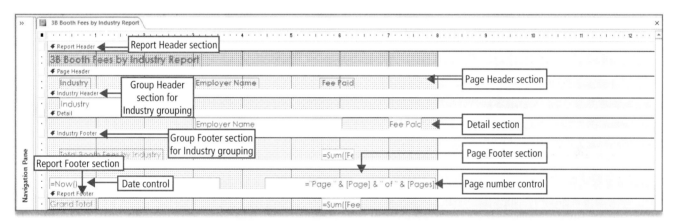

Figure 3.44

2 In the **Page Footer** section of the report, examine the two controls in this section. Recall that information in the Page Footer section displays at the bottom of every page in the report.

On the left side, the ***date control*** displays *=Now( )*, which inserts the current date each time the report is opened. On the right side, the ***page number control*** displays *="Page " & [Page] & " of " & [Pages]*, which inserts the page number, for example *Page 1 of 2*, when the report is displayed in Print Preview or when printed. Both of these controls contain examples of functions that are used by Access to create controls in a report.

3 In the **Industry Footer** section, click the **Total Booth Fees by Industry label control**. Hold down Shift, and in the **Report Footer** section, click the **Grand Total label control** to select both label controls.

4 Under **Report Design Tools**, click the **Arrange tab**. In the **Sizing & Ordering group**, click **Align**, and then click **Left**.

The left edge of the *Grand Total label control* is aligned with the left edge of the *Total Booth Fees by Industry label control*. When using the Align Left command, the left edges of the selected controls are aligned with the control that is the farthest to the left in the report.

5 In the **Page Header** section, click the **Fee Paid label control**. Hold down Shift while you click the following: in the **Detail** section, click the **Fee Paid text box control**; in the **Industry Footer** section, click the **calculated control** that begins with =*Sum*; and in the **Report Footer** section, click the **calculated control** that begins with =*Sum*.

Four controls are selected.

6 On the **Arrange tab**, in the **Sizing & Ordering group**, click **Align**, and then click **Right**. **Save** 🖫 the design changes to your report, and then compare your screen with Figure 3.45.

The right edges of the four selected controls are aligned with the right edge of the *Fee Paid text box control*. When using the Align Right command, the right edges of the selected controls are aligned with the control that is the farthest to the right in the report.

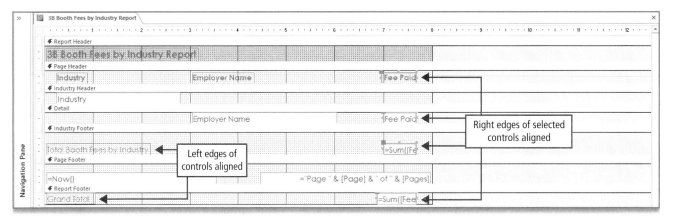

Figure 3.45

7 On the status bar, click **Layout View** 🗏 to display the underlying data in the controls. Scroll to view the bottom of the report. On the left side, notice that the **Total Booth Fees by Industry label control** and the **Grand Total label control** are left aligned. Also, notice the right alignment of the controls in the **Fee Paid** column.

Objective 8 | **Keep Grouped Data Together in a Printed Report**

GO! Learn How
Video A3-8

Before you print a report, examine the report in Print Preview to be sure that all of the labels and data display fully and to be sure that all of the data is properly grouped. Sometimes a page break occurs in the middle of a group of data, leaving the labels on one page and the data or summary information on another page.

Activity 3.23 | Keeping Grouped Data Together in a Printed Report

In this Activity, you will preview the document and then will keep the data in each group together so a grouping is not split between two pages of the report. This is possible if the data in a grouping does not exceed the length of a page.

1 On the status bar, click **Print Preview** 🔍. On the **Print Preview tab**, in the **Zoom group**, click **Two Pages**, and then compare your screen with Figure 3.46.

The report will print on two pages. For the Industry grouping of *Hotel and Food Service*, one record and the summary data display at the top of Page 2 and is separated from the rest of the grouping that displays at the bottom of Page 1. Your display may differ depending upon your printer configuration.

In Print Preview, the One Page or Two Pages Zoom view causes the records to be compressed slightly and might display with the bottoms of records truncated. The records, however, will print correctly.

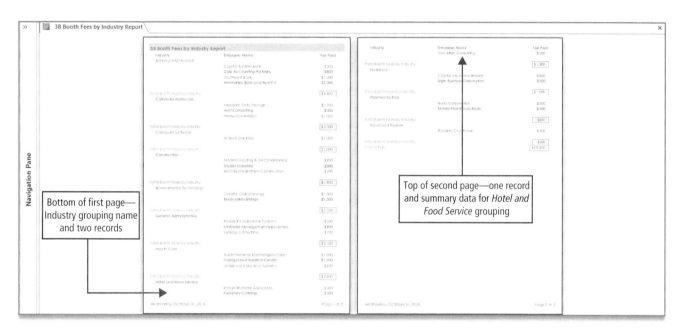

Figure 3.46

2 Click **Close Print Preview** to return to **Layout** view. On the **Design tab**, in the **Grouping & Totals group**, click **Group & Sort**.

At the bottom of the screen, the *Group, Sort, and Total pane* displays. This pane is used to control how information is grouped, sorted, or totaled. Layout view is the preferred view in which to accomplish these tasks because you can see how the changes affect the display of the data in the report.

3 In the **Group, Sort, and Total** pane, on the **Group on Industry** bar, click **More**. To the right of **do not keep group together on one page**, click the **arrow**, and then compare your screen with Figure 3.47.

The *keep whole group together on one page* command keeps each industry group together, from the name in the Group Header section through the summary information in the Group Footer section. The default setting is *do not keep group together on one page*. Next to *Group on Industry*, *with A on top* indicates that the industry names are sorted in ascending order.

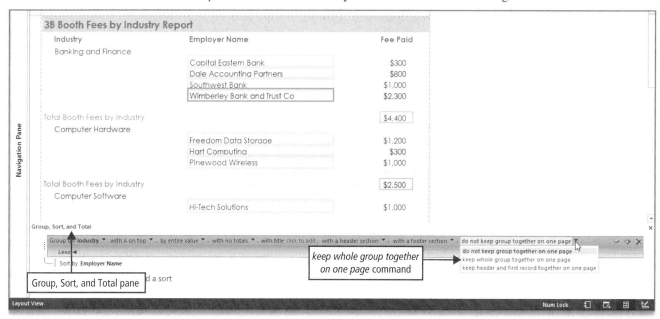

Figure 3.47

4 Click **keep whole group together on one page**. On the **Design tab**, in the **Grouping & Totals group**, click **Group & Sort** to close the **Group, Sort, and Total** pane.

5 On the status bar, click **Print Preview** 🔲. If necessary, in the **Zoom group**, click **Two Pages**. Compare your screen with Figure 3.48.

The entire grouping for the Industry of *Hotel and Food Service* displays at the top of page 2. The grouping no longer breaks between page 1 and page 2. Recall that even though the bottoms of records display truncated because of the compressed Print Preview setting of Two Pages, the records will print correctly.

Figure 3.48

6 Save ⊟ the design changes to your report.

7 Close ⊠ the report, and then Open ⟫ the **Navigation Pane**. If necessary, increase the width of the Navigation Pane so that all object names display fully.

8 On the right side of the title bar, click **Close** ⊠ to close the database and to close Access.

For Non-MyLab Submissions : Determine What Your Instructor Requires for Submission
As directed by your instructor, submit your completed database file.

9 In **MyLab IT**, locate and click the Grader Project **Access 3B Job Openings**. In **step 3**, under **Upload Completed Assignment**, click **Choose File**. In the **Open** dialog box, navigate to your **Access Chapter 3 folder**, and then click your **Student_Access_3B_Job_Openings** file one time to select it. In the lower right corner of the **Open** dialog box, click **Open**.

The name of your selected file displays above the Upload button.

10 To submit your file to **MyLab IT** for grading, click **Upload**, wait a moment for a green **Success!** message, and then in **step 4**, click the blue **Submit for Grading** button. Click **Close Assignment** to return to your list of **Course Materials**.

You have completed Project 3B   **END**

»» GO! With Google

Access web apps are designed to work with Microsoft's SharePoint, a service for setting up websites to share and manage documents. Your college may not have SharePoint installed, so you will use other tools to share objects from your database so that you can work collaboratively with others. Recall that Google Drive is Google's free, web-based word processor, spreadsheet, slide show, form, and data storage and sharing service. For Access, you can export a database object to an Excel worksheet, a PDF file, or a text file, and then save the file to Google Drive.

ALERT   Working with Web-Based Applications and Services

Computer programs and services on the web receive continuous updates and improvements, so the steps to complete this web-based activity may differ from the ones shown. You can often look at the screens and the information presented to determine how to complete the activity.

If you do not already have a Google account, you will need to create one before you begin this activity. Go to http://google.com and in the upper-right corner, click Sign In. On the Sign In screen, click Create account. On the Create your Google Account page, complete the form, read and agree to the Terms of Service and Privacy Policy, and then click Next step. On the Welcome screen, click Get Started.

Activity | Exporting an Access Report to a Word File, Uploading the Word File to OneDrive, and Editing the Report in Google Docs

In this Activity, you will export your 3B Salary $40,000 or More Report object to a Word file, upload your Word file to OneDrive, and then edit the report in Google Docs.

1 Start Access, on the left click **Open Other Databases**, navigate to your **Access Chapter 3** folder, and then open your **3B_Job_Openings** database file. If necessary, on the Message Bar, click Enable Content. In the **Navigation Pane**, click one time to select the report **3B Salary $40,000 or More Report** object to select it.

2 On the **External Data tab**, in the **Export group**, click **More**, and then click **Word**.

The report will be exported as a *Rich Text Format (RTF)*—a standard file format that contains text and some formatting such as underline, bold, italic, font sizes, and colors. RTF documents can be opened in many word processing programs and text editors.

3 In the **Export – RTF File** dialog box, click **Browse**, and then navigate to your **Access Chapter**

3 folder. In the **File Save** dialog box, click in the **File name** box to select the existing text. Type **Lastname_Firstname_AC_3B_Web** and then click **Save**. In the **Export – RTF File** dialog box, select the **Open the destination file after the export operation is complete** check box, and then click **OK**.

4 In Word, click the **File tab**, click **Save As**, and then click **Browse**. In the **Save As** dialog box, navigate to your **Access Chapter 3** folder. In the **File name** box, type **Lastname_Firstname_AC_3B_Web_Word** and then in the **Save as** type box, click the arrow and select **Word Document**. In the **Save As** dialog box, click **Save**. In the message box, click **OK**, and then compare your screen with Figure A.

The file is saved as a Word document in the .docx format to preserve the formatting of the document originally created in Access.

Figure A

5 **Close** Word. In the **Export – RTF File** dialog box, click **Close**, and then **Close** Access.

6 From the desktop, open your browser, navigate to http://google.com, and then sign in to your Google account. Click the **Google Apps** menu ⊞, and then click **Drive** . Open your **GO! Web Projects** folder—or click New to create and then open this folder if necessary.

7 In the upper right, click **Settings** , and then on the menu click **Settings**. In the **Settings** dialog box, next to *Convert uploads*, be sure that **Convert uploaded files to Google Docs editor format** is selected. In the upper right, click **Done**.

If this setting is not selected, your document will upload as a pdf file and cannot be edited without further action.

8 On the left, click **New**, and then click **File upload**. In the **Open** dialog box, navigate to your **Access Chapter 3** folder, and then double-click your **Lastname_Firstname_AC_3B_Web_Word** file to upload it to Google Drive. In the lower right corner, when the title bar of the message box indicates *1 upload complete*, **Close** the message box.

9 In the file list, double-click your **AC_3B_Web_Word** file to open it in Google Docs.

10 Drag across the four column headings—**Position**, **Employer Name**, **# Openings**, and **Annual Salary**—to select them, and then on the toolbar, click **Bold** and **Underline** . Click in the report title to deselect the row, and compare your screen with Figure B.

Figure B

11 Start the **Snipping Tool**. In the Snipping Tool dialog box, click the **New arrow**, and then click **Full-screen Snip**.

12 On the Snipping Tool toolbar, click **Save Snip** . In the **Save As** dialog box, navigate to your **Access Chapter 3** folder. Click in the **File name** box, type **Lastname_Firstname_AC_3B_Web_Snip** and then be sure

that the **Save as type** box displays **JPEG file**. Click **Save**. **Close** ✕ the Snipping Tool window.

13 In **Google Drive**, at the upper right, click your user name, and then click **Sign out**. **Close** your browser window.

14 Submit your file as directed by your instructor.

»»» GO! To Work

wavebreakmedia/Shutterstock, Monkey Business Images/Fotolia, Ivanko80/Shutterstock, Monkey Business Images/Shutterstock

Microsoft Office Specialist (MOS) Skills in This Chapter	
Project 3A	**Project 3B**
1.2.2 Display relationships	**1.2.2** Display relationships
2.3.1 Find and replace data	**5.1.1** Group and sort fields on reports
2.3.3 Filter records	**5.1.2** Add report controls
4.1.1 Add, move, and remove form controls	**5.1.3** Add and modify labels on reports
4.1.2 Set form control properties	**5.2.2** Modify report positioning
4.1.3 Add and modify form labels	**5.2.3** Format report elements
4.2.2 Set records by form field	**5.2.5** Insert information in report headers and footers
4.2.3 Modify form positioning	
4.2.4 Insert images in form headers and footers	

Build Your E-Portfolio

An E-Portfolio is a collection of evidence, stored electronically, that showcases what you have accomplished while completing your education. Collecting and then sharing your work products with potential employers reflects your academic and career goals. Your completed documents from the following projects are good examples to show what you have learned: 3G, 3K, and 3L.

▶ GO! For Job Success

Video: Tough Interview Questions

Your instructor may assign this video to your class, and then ask you to think about, or discuss with your classmates, these questions:

g-stockstudio/Shutterstock

How would you answer an illegal interview question like *Are you married or single*?

How would you handle an interview question about a missing reference?

Why is it important to always be open, honest, and to the point in an interview?

End of Chapter

Summary

A form is a database object that you can use to enter new records into a table, or to edit, delete, or display existing records in a table and can be used to control access to the data in a database.

Filter records in a form to display only a subset of the total records based on matching specific values to provide a quick answer to a question. Filters are generally not saved with a form.

A report is a database object that summarizes the fields and records from a query or from a table, in an easy-to-read format suitable for printing. You can group records and summarize the data in a report.

Most changes to forms and reports can be done in Layout view where the underlying data displays in the controls; however, some modifications, such as aligning controls, must be done in Design view.

GO! Learn It Online

Review the concepts and key terms in this chapter by completing these online challenges, which you can find at **MyLab IT**.

Chapter Quiz: Answer matching and multiple choice questions to test what you learned in this chapter.

Learn it on the GO!: Learn how to use all the new apps and features as they are introduced by Microsoft.

MOS Prep Quiz: Answer questions to review the MOS skills that you practiced in this chapter.

GO! Collaborative Team Project (Available in Instructor Resource Center)

If your instructor assigns this project to your class, you can expect to work with one or more of your classmates—either in person or by using internet tools—to create work products similar to those that you created in this chapter. A team is a group of workers who work together to solve a problem, make a decision, or create a work product. Collaboration is when you work together with others as a team in an intellectual endeavor to complete a shared task or achieve a shared goal.

Monkey Business Images/ Fotolia

Project Guide for Access Chapter 3

Your instructor will assign Projects from this list to ensure your learning and assess your knowledge.

		Projetct Guide for Access Chapter 3	
Project	**Apply Skills from These Chapter Objectives**	**Project Type**	**Project Location**
3A MyLab IT	Objectives 1–4 from Project 3A	**3A Instructional Project (Grader Project)** **Instruction** A guided review of the skills from Project 3A.	In **MyLab IT** and in text
3B MyLab IT	Objectives 5–8 from Project 3B	**3B Instructional Project (Grader Project)** **Instruction** A guided review of the skills from Project 3B.	In **MyLab IT** and in text
3C	Objectives 1–4 from Project 3A	**3C Chapter Review (Scorecard Grading)** **Review** A guided review of the skills from Project 3A.	In text
3D	Objectives 5–8 from Project 3B	**3D Chapter Review (Scorecard Grading)** **Review** A guided review of the skills from Project 3B.	In text
3E MyLab IT	Objectives 1–4 from Project 3A	**3E Mastery (Grader Project)** **Mastery and Transfer of Learning** A demonstration of your mastery of the skills in Project 3A with extensive decision-making.	In **MyLab IT** and in text
3F MyLab IT	Objectives 5–8 from Project 3B	**3F Mastery (Grader Project)** **Mastery and Transfer of Learning** A demonstration of your mastery of the skills in Project 3B with extensive decision-making.	In **MyLab IT** and in text
3G MyLab IT	Combination of Objectives from Projects 3A and 3B	**3G Mastery (Grader Project)** **Mastery and Transfer of Learning** A demonstration of your mastery of the skills in Projects 3A and 3B with extensive decision-making.	In **MyLab IT** and in text
3H	Combination of Objectives from Projects 3A and 3B	**3H GO! Fix It (Scorecard Grading)** **Critical Thinking** A demonstration of your mastery of the skills in Projects 3A and 3B by creating a correct result from a document that contains errors you must find.	IRC
3I	Combination of Objectives from Projects 3A and 3B	**3I GO! Make It (Scorecard Grading)** **Critical Thinking** A demonstration of your mastery of the skills in Projects 3A and 3B by creating a result from a supplied picture.	IRC
3J	Combination of Objectives from Projects 3A and 3B	**3J GO! Solve It (Rubric Grading)** **Critical Thinking** A demonstration of your mastery of the skills in Projects 3A and 3B, your decision-making skills, and your critical thinking skills. A task-specific rubric helps you self-assess your result.	IRC
3K	Combination of Objectives from Projects 3A and 3B	**3K GO! Solve It (Rubric Grading)** **Critical Thinking** A demonstration of your mastery of the skills in Projects 3A and 3B, your decision-making skills, and your critical thinking skills. A task-specific rubric helps you self-assess your result.	In text
3L	Combination of Objectives from Projects 3A and 3B	**3L GO! Think (Rubric Grading)** **Critical Thinking** A demonstration of your understanding of the Chapter concepts applied in a manner that you would outside of college. An analytic rubric helps you and your instructor grade the quality of your work by comparing it to the work an expert in the discipline would create.	In text
3M	Combination of Objectives from Projects 3A and 3B	**3M GO! Think (Rubric Grading)** **Critical Thinking** A demonstration of your understanding of the Chapter concepts applied in a manner that you would outside of college. An analytic rubric helps you and your instructor grade the quality of your work by comparing it to the work an expert in the discipline would create.	IRC
3N	Combination of Objectives from Projects 3A and 3B	**3N You and GO! (Rubric Grading)** **Critical Thinking** A demonstration of your understanding of the Chapter concepts applied in a manner that you would in a personal situation. An analytic rubric helps you and your instructor grade the quality of your work.	IRC
3O	Combination of Objectives from Projects 3A and 3B	**3O Cumulative Team Project for Access Chapter 1** A demonstration of your understanding of concepts and your ability to work collaboratively in a group role-playing assessment, requiring both collaboration and self-management.	IRC
Capstone Project for Access Chapters 1-3	Combination of Objectives from Projects 1A, 1B, 2A, 2B, 3A, and 3B	A demonstration of your mastery of the skills in Chapters 1-3 with extensive decision making. **(Grader Project)**	In **MyLab IT** and IRC

Glossary

Glossary of Chapter Key Terms

AND condition A condition in which records display only when all of the specified values are present in the selected fields.

Bound A term used to describe objects and controls that are based on data that is stored in tables.

Bound control A control that retrieves its data from an underlying table or query; a text box control is an example of a bound control.

Calculated control A control that contains an expression, often a formula or function, that most often summarizes a field that contains numerical data.

Control An object on a form or report that displays data or text, performs actions, and lets you view and work with information.

Control layout The grouped arrangement of controls on a form or report; for example, the Stacked layout.

Data entry The action of entering the data into a record in a database table or form.

Date control A control on a form or report that inserts the current date each time the form or report is opened.

Design view The Access view that displays the detailed structure of a query, form, or report; for forms and reports, may be the view in which some tasks must be performed, and displays only the controls, not the data.

Detail section The section of a form or report that displays the records from the underlying table or query.

Filter by Form An Access command that filters the records in a form based on one or more fields, or based on more than one value in the field.

Filter by Selection An Access command that displays only the records that contain the value in the selected field and hides the records that do not contain the value.

Filtering The process of displaying only a portion of the total records (a subset) based on matching specific values to provide a quick answer to a question.

Form A database object that you can use to enter new records into a table, or to edit, delete, and display existing records in a table.

Form Footer Information displayed at the bottom of the screen in Form view or Layout view that is printed after the last detail section on the last page of a printout.

Form Header Information such as a form's title that displays at the top of the screen in Form view or Layout view and is printed at the top of the first page when records are printed as forms.

Form tool An Access tool that creates a form with a single mouse click, which includes all of the fields from the underlying data source (table or query).

Form view The Access view in which you can view, modify, delete, or add records in a table but you cannot change the layout or design of the form.

Form Wizard An Access tool that walks you step by step through the creation of a form and that gives you more flexibility in the design, layout, and number of fields in a form.

Group Footer Information printed at the end of each group of records to display summary information for the group.

Group Header Information printed at the beginning of each new group of records; for example, the group name.

Group, Sort, and Total pane A pane that displays at the bottom of the window in Design view in which you can control how information is sorted and grouped in a report; provides the most flexibility for adding or modifying groups, sort orders, or totals options on a report.

Label control A control on a form or report that contains descriptive information, usually a field name or title.

Layout selector A small symbol that displays in the upper left corner of a selected control layout in a form or report that is displayed in Layout view or Design view and is used to move or format an entire group of controls.

Layout view The Access view in which you can make changes to a form or report while the data from the underlying data source displays.

OR condition A condition in which records display that match at least one of the specified values.

Page Footer Information printed at the bottom of every page in a report and most often includes the page number.

Page Header Information printed at the top of every page in a report.

Page number control A control on a form or report that inserts the page number when displayed in Print Preview or when printed.

Record selector bar The vertical bar at the left edge of a record used to select an entire record in Form view.

Record source The tables or queries that provide the underlying data for a form or report.

Report A database object that summarizes the fields and records from a query or table in an easy-to-read format suitable for printing.

Report Footer Information printed at the bottom of the last page of a report.

Report Header Information printed on the first page of a report that is used for logos, titles, and dates.

Report tool An Access tool that creates a report with one mouse click and displays all of the fields and records from the record source that you select.

Report Wizard An Access tool that walks you step by step through the creation of a report and that gives you more flexibility in the design, layout, and number of fields in a report.

Rich Text Format (**RTF**) A standard file format that contains some formatting such as underline, bold, font sizes, and colors. RTF documents can be opened in many applications.

Section bar In Design view, a bar in a form or report that identifies and separates one section from another; used to select the section and to change the size of the section.

Stacked layout A control layout format that is similar to a paper form, with label controls placed to the left of each text box control; the controls are grouped together for easy editing.

Subset A portion of the total records available.

Tab order The order in which the insertion point moves from one field to another in a form when you press the Tab key.

Text box control A bound control on a form or report that displays the data from the underlying table or query.

Theme A predesigned set of colors, fonts, lines, and fill effects that look good together and that can be applied to all of the objects in the database or to individual objects in the database.

Unbound control A control that does not have a source of data, such as the title in a form or report.

Chapter Review

Apply 3A skills from these Objectives:

1. Create and Use a Form to Add and Delete Records
2. Filter Records
3. Create a Form by Using the Form Wizard
4. Modify a Form in Layout View and in Design View

In the following Skills Review, you will assist Erinique Jerlin, the Dean of Business at the Northwest Campus, in using her database to track business students and their internship placements for the current semester. Your completed Navigation Pane will look similar to Figure 3.49.

Project Files

For Project 3C, you will need the following file:

a03C_Student_Internships

You will save your database as:

Lastname_Firstname_3C_Student_Internships

Project Results

Figure 3.49

(continues on next page)

Chapter Review

Skills Review: Project 3C Student Internships (continued)

1 ▶ Start Access. In the Access opening screen, click **Open Other Files**. Under **Open**, click **Browse** and then navigate to the location where your student data files are stored. Double-click **a03C_Student_Internships** to open the database.

a. On the **File tab**, click **Save As**. Under **File Types**, be sure **Save Database As** is selected. On the right, under **Database File Types**, be sure **Access Database** is selected, and then click **Save As**.

b. In the **Save As** dialog box, navigate to your **Access Chapter 3** folder. In the **File name** box, replace the existing text with **Lastname_Firstname_3C_Student_Internships** and then press Enter. On the **Message Bar**, click **Enable Content**.

c. In the **Navigation Pane**, right-click **3C Students**, and then click **Rename**. With the table name selected and using your own name, type **Lastname Firstname 3C Students** and then press Enter. **Rename** the **3C Internships** table to **Lastname Firstname 3C Internships** and then point to the right edge of the **Navigation Pane** to display the ⟺ pointer. Drag to the right to increase the width of the pane until both tables names display fully.

d. On the **Database Tools tab**, in the **Relationships group**, click **Relationships**. Under **Relationship Tools**, on the **Design tab**, in the **Relationships group**, click **All Relationships**. Resize and move the field lists so that the entire table name and fields display for each field list. In the **Relationships** window, click the **join line** between the two field lists. In the **Tools group**, click **Edit Relationships**. Point to the title bar of the **Edit Relationships**

dialog box, and then drag the dialog box downward below the two field lists. Notice that a *one-to-many* relationship is established between the two tables by using *Internship ID* as the common field. **Close** the **Edit Relationships** dialog box, and then **Close** the **Relationships** window. In the message box, click **Yes** to save changes to the layout of the relationships.

e. In the **Navigation Pane**, click your **3C Students** table to select it. On the **Create tab**, and then in the **Forms group**, click **Form**. **Save** the form as **Lastname Firstname 3C Student Form** and then **Close** the form object.

f. In the **Navigation Pane**, click your **3C Internships** table to select it. On the **Create tab**, and then in the **Forms group**, click **Form**. Notice that for the first record—*Internship ID INTERN-1000* for *Lakes Realty Inc*—there are two student records in the subdatasheet—two students have been assigned internships for this employer. **Close** the form, and in the message box, click **Yes** to save the form. In the **Save As** dialog box, type **Lastname Firstname 3C Internship Company Form** and then press Enter. If necessary, increase the width of the Navigation Pane so that all object names display fully.

g. In the **Navigation Pane**, double-click your **3C Student Form** object to open it, and then **Close** the **Navigation Pane**. In the navigation area, click **New (blank) record** to display a new blank form. In the **Student ID** field, type **3120045** and then press Enter. Using your own last name and first name, continue entering the data as shown in **Table 1**.

Table 1

Student ID	Last Name	First Name	Phone Number	Email	Internship ID
3120045	**Lastname**	**Firstname**	**(512) 555-3263**	**ns3120@tlcc.edu**	**INTERN-1000**

h. With the insertion point positioned in the last field, press Enter to save the record and display a new blank record. **Close** your **3C Student Form** object, and then **Open** the **Navigation Pane**. Double-click your **3C Internship Company Form** object to open it, and then **Close** the **Navigation Pane**. Notice that for the

first record, in the subdatasheet, the record you just entered displays. Scroll to view the bottom of the form. In the navigation area for the form—*not* the navigation area for the subdatasheet—click **New (blank) record**. In the blank form, using your own first name and last name, enter the data as shown in **Table 2**.

Table 2

Internship ID	Employer Name	Contact First Name	Contact Last Name	Address	City	State	Postal Code	Phone	Hrs Per Week
INTERN-1027	**College Suppliers**	**Firstname**	**Lastname**	**1700 College Cres**	**Austin**	**TX**	**78755**	**(512) 555-3133**	**10**

(continues on next page)

Chapter Review

i. In the navigation area for the form, click **First record**. Click in the **Employer Name** field, and then on the **Home tab**, in the **Find group**, click **Find**. In the **Find and Replace** dialog box, in the **Find What** box, type **Jones Consulting** and then click **Find Next**. **Close** the **Find and Replace** dialog box. On the **Home tab**, in the **Records group**, click the **Delete arrow**, and then click **Delete Record**. In the message box, click **Yes** to delete the record. In the navigation area for the form, notice that the total number of records is *27*.

j. Use the technique you just practiced to **Find** the form for the **Internship ID** of **INTERN-1027**, and then **Close** the **Find and Replace** dialog box. On the **File tab**, click **Print**, and then on the right, click **Print**. In the **Print** dialog box, under **Print Range**, click the **Selected Record(s)** option button. In the lower left corner of the dialog box, click **Setup**. In the **Page Setup** dialog box, click the **Columns tab**. Under **Column Size**, double-click in the **Width** box to select the existing value, type **7.5** and then click **OK**.

k. **Close** your **3C Internship Company Form** object, and then **Open** the **Navigation Pane**. In the **Navigation Pane**, double-click your **3C Student Form** object to open it, and then **Close** the **Navigation Pane**. Use the **Find** command to display the record where the **Last Name** field contains your last name, and then create a paper or electronic printout of only that record, being sure to change the **Column Size Width** to **7.5**

2 With your **3C Student Form** object displayed in **Form** view, in the navigation area, click **First record**, and then click the **Internship ID** field name to select the text in the field box. Press [Ctrl] + [F] to display the **Find and Replace** dialog box. In the **Find What** box, type **INTERN-1009** and then click **Find Next** to find and display the record for *Michael Fresch*. **Close** the **Find and Replace** dialog box. On the **Home tab**, in the **Sort & Filter group**, click **Selection**, and then click **Equals "INTERN-1009"**. In the navigation area, notice that two students are assigned internships with the company identified as INTERN-1009.

a. In the **Sort & Filter group**, click **Toggle Filter** to remove the filter and display all 52 records. **Close** the form. If prompted, click **Yes** to save the form.

b. **Open** the **Navigation Pane**, double-click your **3C Internship Company Form** object to open it, and then **Close** the **Navigation Pane**. On the **Home tab**, in the **Sort & Filter group**, click **Advanced**,

and then click **Filter By Form**. In the form, click the **City** field name to position the insertion point in the **City** field box, click the **arrow**, and then click **Georgetown**. In the **Sort & Filter group**, click **Toggle Filter** to display the filtered records. In the navigation area for the form, notice that three internships are located in the *City* of *Georgetown*.

c. In the **Sort & Filter group**, click **Advanced**, and then click **Filter By Form**. In the lower left corner of the form, click the **Or tab**. Click the **City** field box **arrow**, and then click **Elgin**. In the **Sort & Filter group**, click **Toggle Filter**. In the navigation area for the form, notice that five internships are located in either *Georgetown* or *Elgin*. In the **Sort & Filter group**, click **Advanced**, and then click **Clear All Filters** to display all 27 records.

d. In the **Sort & Filter group**, click **Advanced**, and then click **Advanced Filter/Sort**. Resize the field list. In the **3C Internships** field list, double-click **City**, and then double-click **Hrs Per Week** to add both fields to the design grid. Click in the **Criteria** row under **City**, type **Austin** In the **Criteria** row under **Hrs Per Week**, type **>10** In the **Sort & Filter group**, click **Toggle Filter** to display the filtered records, and notice that that there are five internships in the *City* of *Austin* offering *more than 10* hours per week of work. In the **Sort & Filter group**, click **Toggle Filter** to remove the filter and display all 27 records. **Save** and then **Close** your **3C Internship Company Form** object, which also closes the Advanced Filter grid.

3 On the **Create tab**, and in the **Forms group**, click **Form Wizard**. In the **Tables/Queries** box, click the **arrow**, and then click **Table: Lastname Firstname 3C Students**. In the **Available Fields** list, double-click the following field names in the order given to move them to the **Selected Fields** list: **First Name**, **Last Name**, and **Internship ID**. Click **Next**. In the wizard, be sure **Columnar** is selected as the layout, and then click **Next**. In the **What title do you want for your form?** box, select the existing text, type **Lastname Firstname 3C Student Internship Form** and then click **Finish** to close the wizard and create the form.

4 On the **Home tab**, in the **Views group**, click the top portion of the **View** button to switch to **Layout** view. If the **Field List** pane displays on the right side of your screen, close the pane. If the Property Sheet displays, Close it. Click the **First Name label control**. Hold down [Shift], and then click the **Last Name label control**, the **Internship ID label**

(continues on next page)

Chapter Review

control, and the three **text box controls** to select all of the controls. On the **Form Layout Tools**, click the **Arrange tab**. In the **Table group**, click **Stacked** to group all of the controls. Click the **First Name label control** to cancel the selection of all of the controls.

a. On the **Form Layout Tools**, click the **Design tab**. In the **Themes group** click **Themes**. In the **Themes** gallery, using the ScreenTips, point to the **Wisp** theme, right-click, and then click **Apply Theme to This Object Only**. Click anywhere in the title—*Lastname Firstname 3C Student Internship Form*—to select the title. On the **Form Layout Tools**, click the **Format tab**, and in the **Font group**, click the **Font Size arrow**, and then click **14**. In the **Font group**, click **Bold**. Click the **Font Color arrow**, and then under **Theme Colors**, in the sixth column, click the last color.

b. On the **Design tab**, in the **Tools group**, click **Add Existing Fields**. In the **Field List** pane, click **Student ID**, and then drag the field name to the left until the 🔾 pointer displays above the **First Name label control** and a colored line displays above the control. Release the mouse button to add the *Student ID* controls to the form, and then **Close** the **Field List** pane.

c. Click the **First Name text box control**, which displays *Jordan*, to select it. On the **Design tab**, in the **Tools group**, click **Property Sheet**. In the **Property Sheet**, on the **Format tab**, click **Width**, type **1.75** and then press [Enter] to decrease the width of the text box controls. **Close** the **Property Sheet**. Be sure that the **First Name text box control** is still selected. On the **Arrange tab**, in the **Rows & Columns group**, click **Select Row**. In the **Move group**, click **Move Down** to move both controls below the **Last Name** controls. **Save** the changes you have made to the design of your form.

d. Click the **Student ID text box control**, which displays *1010101*. On the **Arrange tab**, in the **Rows & Columns group**, click **Select Column** to select all four text box controls. On the **Format tab**, in the **Font group**, click the **Background Color arrow**. Under **Theme Colors**, in the fourth column, click the second color.

e. Click the **Student ID label control**, and then click the **Arrange tab**. In the **Rows & Columns group**, click **Select Column** to select all four label controls. Click the **Format tab**, and then click the **Font Color arrow**—*not* the **Background Color arrow**. Under **Theme Colors**, in the fourth column, click the first color. In the **Font group**, click **Bold**.

f. Click the **layout selector** ⊞ to select all of the controls. In the **Font group**, click the **Font Size arrow**, and then click **12**. With all of the controls still selected, on the ribbon, click the **Design tab**, and in the **Tools group**, click **Property Sheet**. In the **Property Sheet**, on the **Format tab**, click **Height**, type **0.25** and then press [Enter] to change the height of each selected control.

g. Click the **Student ID label control** to select only that control. In the **Property Sheet**, click **Width**, type **1.75** and then press [Enter] to change the width of all of the label controls. **Save** the design changes to your form.

h. On the status bar, click **Design View**. At the bottom of the form, click the **Form Footer section bar** to select it. In the **Property Sheet**, click **Height**, type **0.5** and then press [Enter] to increase the height of the **Form Footer** section.

i. Under **Form Layout Tools**, click the **Design tab**. In the **Controls group**, click **Label**. Move the pointer into the **Form Footer** section and then position the plus sign of the pointer at approximately **0.25 inch on the horizontal ruler** and even with the lower edge of the **Form Footer section bar**—the placement does not need to be precise. Click one time, type **Texas Lakes Community College** and then press [Enter].

j. With the **label control** selected, click the **Format tab**. In the **Font group**, click **Bold**. Click the **Font Color arrow**, and then under **Theme Colors**, in the fourth column, click the first color. If necessary, double-click the right edge of the label control to resize the control so that all of the data displays.

k. With the **label control** still selected, in the **Property Sheet**, click **Top**, type **0.1** and then press [Enter]. In the **Property Sheet**, in the **Left** property setting box, type **0.9** and then press [Enter]. **Close** the **Property Sheet**, and then **Save** the design changes to your form.

l. On the right side of the status bar, click **Form View**. In the navigation area, click **Last record** to display the record containing your name. On the **File tab**, click **Print**. In the **Print** dialog box, under **Print Range**, click the **Selected Records(s)** option button. Because you changed the field widths, you do not need to change the Column Size Width in the **Print** dialog box.

5 **Close** all open objects, and then **Open** the **Navigation Pane**. If necessary, increase the width of the pane so that all object names display fully. On the right side of the title bar, click **Close** to close the database and to close Access.

6 As directed by your instructor, submit your database for grading.

You have completed Project 3C   **END**

Chapter Review

Skills Review	Project 3D Student Parking

In the following Skills Review, you will assist Carlos Medina, Chief of Security, in using his Access database to track the details about students who have paid for parking in designated lots at the Southeast Campus of Texas Lakes Community College. Your completed Navigation Pane will look similar to Figure 3.50.

Apply 3B skills from these Objectives:

5. Create a Report by Using the Report Tool and Modify the Report in Layout View
6. Create a Report by Using the Report Wizard
7. Modify the Design of a Report
8. Keep Grouped Data Together in a Printed Report

Project Files

For Project 3D, you will need the following file:

a03D_Student_Parking

You will save your database as:

Lastname_Firstname_3D_Student_Parking

Project Results

Figure 3.50

(continues on next page)

Chapter Review

1 ▶ Start Access. In the Access opening screen, click **Open Other Files**. Under **Open**, click **Browse** and then navigate to the location where your student data files are stored. Double-click **a03D_Student_Parking** to open the database.

a. On the **File tab**, click **Save As**. Under **File Types**, be sure **Save Database As** is selected. On the right, under **Database File Types**, be sure **Access Database** is selected, and then at the bottom of the screen, click **Save As**. In the **Save As** dialog box, navigate to your **Access Chapter 3** folder. In the **File name** box, replace the existing text with **Lastname_Firstname_3D_Student_Parking** and then press Enter. On the **Message Bar**, click **Enable Content**.

b. In the **Navigation Pane**, right-click the **3D Parking Lots** table, and then click **Rename**. Using your own name, type **Lastname Firstname 3D Parking Lots** and then press Enter. Use this same technique to add your last name and first name to the beginning of the names of the two queries and the **3D Students** table. Increase the width of the **Navigation Pane** so that all object names display fully.

c. On the **Database Tools tab**, in the **Relationships group**, click **Relationships**. On the **Design tab**, in the **Relationships group**, click **All Relationships**. Resize and move the field lists so that the entire table name and fields display for each field list. In the **Relationships** window, click the **join line** between the two field lists. In the **Tools group**, click **Edit Relationships**. Point to the title bar of the **Edit Relationships** dialog box, and then drag the dialog box downward below the two field lists. Notice that a *one-to-many* relationship is established between the two tables by using *Lot ID* as the common field. **Close** the **Edit Relationships** dialog box, and then **Close** the **Relationships** window. In the message box, click **Yes** to save changes to the layout of the relationships.

d. In the **Navigation Pane**, double-click each table to open them, and then examine the fields and data in each table. In the **Navigation Pane**, double-click your **3D Building G Student Parking Query** object to run the query and view the results. Apply **Best Fit** to the query results, and then **Save** the query. Switch to **Design** view to examine the design grid. This query answers the question, *What is the lot ID, lot location, student ID, student last name, student first name, license plate, and semester fee for students who have paid for parking in front of Building G, in ascending order by the Last Name field?*

In the **Navigation Pane**, double-click your **3D Student Parking by Lots Query** object, apply **Best Fit** to the query results, **Save** the query, and then switch to **Design** view to examine the design grid. This query answers the question, *What is the lot ID, student ID, student last name, student first name, license plate, state, and semester fee for all students?* In the object window, right-click any **object tab**, and then click **Close All**.

e. In the **Navigation Pane**, click to select your **3D Building G Student Parking Query** object. On the **Create tab**, in the **Reports group**, click **Report**. **Close** the Navigation Pane. Under **Report Layout Tools**, on the **Design tab**, in the **Themes group**, click **Themes**. In the **Themes** gallery, use the ScreenTips to locate the **Retrospect** theme, right-click the **Retrospect** theme, and then click **Apply Theme to This Object Only**.

f. Click the **Lot Location** field name. On the **Report Layout Tools**, click the **Arrange tab**. In the **Rows & Columns group**, click **Select Column** to select the field name and all of the data for each record in the field. Press Del to remove the field from the report.

g. Click the **Last Name** field name, hold down Shift, and then click the **First Name** field name. On the **Design tab**, in the **Tools group**, click **Property Sheet**. In the **Property Sheet**, on the **Format tab**, click **Width**, type **1.25** and then press Enter to decrease the width of the two fields. **Close** the **Property Sheet**.

h. Click the **Last Name** field name to cancel the selection of both fields and to select only this field. On the **Home tab**, in the **Sort & Filter group**, click **Ascending** to sort the records in ascending order by the Last Name field.

i. If necessary, scroll to the bottom of the report, and notice that the *Semester Fee* column is automatically totaled. At the top of the report, click the **Student ID** field name. On the **Design tab**, in the **Grouping & Totals group**, click **Totals**, and then click **Count Records**. If necessary, scroll to the bottom of the report, and notice that *14* students have paid for parking in front of Building G.

(continues on next page)

Chapter Review

j. At the bottom of the report, under **Student ID**, click the **calculated control** that displays *14*. Hold down Ctrl, and then under **Semester Fee**, click the **calculated control** that displays *$1,075*—the two calculated controls are selected. On the **Design tab**, in the **Tools group**, click **Property Sheet**. In the **Property Sheet**, click **Height**, type **0.25** and then press Enter to increase the height of both controls. At the bottom of the report, to the right of the **calculated control** that displays *$1,075*, click the **control** that displays *Page 1 of 1*. In the **Property Sheet**, click **Left**, type **2.5** and then press Enter to move the page number within the margins of the report.

k. At the top of the report, click the **label control** that displays the title of the report—*Lastname Firstname 3D Building G Student Parking Query*. On the **Report Layout Tools**, click the **Format tab**. In the **Font group**, click the **Font Size arrow**, and then click **14**. With the **label control** still selected, double-click **Query** to select the word, type **Report** and then press Enter to change the title of the report to *Lastname Firstname 3D Building G Student Parking Report*.

l. Click the **Lot ID** field name. In the **Property Sheet**, click **Left**, type **0.25** and then press Enter to move all of the fields slightly to the right from the left margin. **Close** the **Property Sheet**, and then **Save** the report as **Lastname Firstname 3D Building G Student Parking Report**.

m. On the right side of the status bar, click **Print Preview**. On the **Print Preview tab**, in the **Zoom group**, click **Two Pages**, and notice that the report will print on one page. **Close Print Preview**, and then **Close** the report.

2 On the **Create tab**, in the **Reports group**, click **Report Wizard**. In the **Tables/Queries** box, click the **arrow**, and then click **Query: Lastname Firstname 3D Student Parking by Lots Query**. In the **Available Fields** list, double-click the following field names in the order given to move them to the **Selected Fields** list: **Lot ID**, **Last Name**, **First Name**, **Student ID**, and **Semester Fee**.

a. Click **Next**. In the **How do you want to view your data?** box, click **by Lastname Firstname 3D Students**, and then click **Next**. In the list on the left, double-click **Lot ID** to group the records by this field, and then click **Next**. Click the **1** box **arrow**, and then click **Last Name** to sort the records by the student's last name within each Lot ID.

b. In the wizard, click **Summary Options**. In the **Summary Options** dialog box, to the right of **Semester Fee**, click to select the **Sum** check box. Under **Show**, be sure that **Detail and Summary** is selected, and then click **OK**. In the wizard, click **Next**.

c. In the wizard, under **Layout**, be sure that **Stepped** is selected. Under **Orientation**, click **Landscape**. At the bottom of the wizard, be sure that the **Adjust the field width so all fields fit on a page** check box is selected, and then click **Next**. In the **What title do you want for your report?** box, select the existing text, type **Lastname Firstname 3D Fees by Parking Lot Report** and then click **Finish**. In the object window, right-click the **object tab** for the report, and then click **Layout View**.

3 Under **Report Layout Tools**, on the **Design tab**, in the **Themes group**, click **Themes**. In the **Themes** gallery, use the ScreenTips to locate the **Ion Boardroom** theme, right-click the **Ion Boardroom** theme, and then click **Apply Theme to This Object Only**. In the report, click the title—*Lastname Firstname 3D Fees by Parking Lot*—to display a border around the label control. On the **Report Layout Tools**, click the **Format tab**. In the **Font group**, click the **Font Size arrow**, and then click **14**. In the **Font group**, click **Bold**. In the body of the report, click any one of the controls that begins with **Summary for 'Lot ID'**, and then press Del. **Save** the design changes to your report.

a. On the left side of the report, click a **Sum label control**, which will select all of the related controls. Double-click the control to select the text—*Sum*. Type **Total Fees by Parking Lot** and then press Enter.

b. At the top of the report, click the **Lot ID label control** to select it. Hold down Shift, and then click each one of the four other label controls that display the field names to select all five label controls. On the **Format tab**, in the **Font group**, click **Bold**.

c. In the report, under **Last Name**, click the **text box control** that displays *Dolensky*. Hold down Shift, and then under **First Name**, click the **text box control** that displays *Adam*. On the **Design tab**, in the **Tools group**, click **Property Sheet**. In the **Property Sheet**, click **Width**, type **1.5** and then press Enter.

(continues on next page)

Chapter Review

d. In the report, click the **Student ID label control**. In the **Property Sheet**, click **Left**, type **7.25** and then press Enter. Do not be concerned that the data in the field is not aligned with the field name; you will adjust this later in this project. Scroll to the bottom of the report, and then click the **Grand Total label control**. In the **Property Sheet**, click **Width**, type **1** and then press Enter. **Close** the **Property Sheet**, and then **Save** the design changes to your report.

e. On the status bar, click **Design View**. In the **Lot ID Footer** section, click the **Total Fees by Parking Lot label control**. Hold down Shift, and in the **Report Footer** section, click the **Grand Total label control** to select both controls. Under **Report Design Tools**, click the **Arrange tab**. In the **Sizing & Ordering group**, click **Align**, and then click **Left**.

f. In the report, in the **Page Header** section, click the **Student ID label control**. Hold down Shift, and in the **Detail** section, click the **Student ID text box control**. On the **Arrange tab**, in the **Sizing & Ordering group**, click **Align**, and then click **Left**. On the status bar, click **Layout View** and notice the left alignment of the two sets of controls.

4 On the status bar, click **Print Preview**. On the **Print Preview tab**, in the **Zoom group**, click **More Pages**, and then click **Four Pages** to view how your report is currently laid out. In the **Zoom group**, click the **Zoom arrow**, and then click **50%**. Notice at the bottom of Page 1 and the top of Page 2, that the grouping for **LOT-2B** breaks across these two pages. Notice at the bottom of Page 2 and the top of Page 3, that the grouping for **LOT-6A** breaks across these two pages. Your pages may display differently depending upon the printer that is installed on your system.

a. **Close Print Preview** to return to **Layout** view. On the **Design tab**, in the **Grouping & Totals group**, click **Group & Sort**. In the **Group, Sort, and Total** pane, on the **Group on Lot ID** bar, click **More**. Click the **do not keep group together on one page arrow**, and then click **keep whole group together on one page**. On the **Design tab**, in the **Grouping & Totals group**, click **Group & Sort** to close the **Group, Sort, and Total** pane. **Save** the design changes to your report.

b. On the status bar, click **Print Preview**. Notice that the entire grouping for **LOT-2B** displays at the top of Page 2. Keeping this group together forced the groupings for **LOT-5C** and **LOT-6A** to move to the top of Page 3—your groupings may display differently depending upon the printer that is installed on your system.

c. **Close** the report, and then **Open** the **Navigation Pane**. If necessary, increase the width of the pane so that all object names display fully. On the right side of the title bar, click **Close** to close the database and to close Access.

5 As directed by your instructor, submit your database for grading.

You have completed Project 3D **END**

Mastering Access   Project 3E Textbook Publishers

Apply 3A skills from these Objectives:

1. Create and Use a Form to Add and Delete Records
2. Filter Records
3. Create a Form by Using the Form Wizard
4. Modify a Form in Layout View and Design view

In the following Mastering Access project, you will assist Donna Rider, Bookstore Manager, in using her database to track textbooks and publishers for courses being offered by the Science Department at the Northeast Campus of Texas Lakes Community College. Your completed Navigation Pane will look similar to Figure 3.51.

Project Files for MyLab IT Grader

1. In your **MyLab IT** course, locate and click **Access 3E Textbook Publishers**, Download Materials, and then Download All Files.
2. Extract the zipped folder to your Access Chapter 3 folder. Close the Grader download screens.
3. Take a moment to open the downloaded **Access_3E_Textbook_Publishers_Instructions**; note any recent updates to the book.

Project Results

Figure 3.51

For Non-MyLab Submissions	**Start with an Access Data File**
For Project 3E, you will need this starting file:	In your Access Chapter 3 folder, save your database as:
a03E_Textbook_Publishers	**Lastname_Firstname_3E_Textbook_Publishers**

After you have saved your database, open it to launch Access. On the next page, begin with Step 2.

After Step 12, save and submit your file as directed by your instructor.

(continues on next page)

Content-Based Assessments (Mastery and Transfer of Learning)

1 Start Access. From your student data files, open **Student_Access_3E_Textbook_Publishers** and **Enable Content**.

2 View the relationship between the *3E Publishers* table and the *3E Science Textbooks* table; *one* publisher can provide *many* textbooks for the science courses. If necessary, resize the field lists so all table and field names are fully visible. Save the changes to the layout of the relationships.

3 Based on your **3E Publishers** table, use the **Form** tool to create a form. **Save** the form as **3E Publisher Form** and then switch to **Form** view. Using the form, add a new record to the underlying table as shown in **Table 1**.

Table 1

Publisher ID	Publisher Name	Address	City	State	Postal Code	Phone Number	Publisher Web Site
PUB-1008	Hidden Hills Publishing Co	5100 Live Oak St	Dallas	TX	75201	(214) 555-0857	http://www.hhpubco.pub

4 Display the first record, and then click in the **Publisher ID** field. **Find** the record for the **Publisher ID** of **PUB-1006**, and then **Delete** the record. **Find** the record for the **Publisher ID** of **PUB-1008**, and change the **Column Size Width** in the **Print** dialog box to **7.5**. **Save** the design changes to your form.

5 Use the **Filter By Form** tool in your **3E Publisher Form** object to create a filter that displays records with a **State** of **CA** or **TX**. After verifying that three records match this criteria, click **Toggle Filter** to display all seven records. **Save** your form, and then **Close** your form.

6 Use the **Form Wizard** to create a form based on your **3E Science Textbooks** table that includes the following fields in the order given: **Course(s)**, **Textbook Name**, **Publisher ID**, **Price Per Book**, and **# Books**. Apply a **Columnar** layout, and then name the form **3E Science Textbook Form**.

7 In **Layout** view, apply the **Stacked** layout to all of the controls, and then apply the **Ion Boardroom** theme to this object (Form) only. For the title of the form, change the **Font Size** to **16**, apply **Bold**, and then change the **Font Color** to **Dark Purple, Text 2**—under **Theme Colors**, in the fourth column, the first color. **Save** the design changes to the form.

8 From the **Field List** pane, add the **Textbook ID** field to the form directly above the **Textbook Name** field. Move the **# Books** controls directly above the **Price Per Book** controls. **Close** the **Field List** pane. Display Record 9—this record's textbook name is the longest entry of all records. Click the **Textbook Name text box control**, set the **Width** property to **4** and then **Save** the design changes to your form.

9 Select all six **text box controls**, and, change the **Background Color**. Under **Theme colors**, in the eighth column, select the second color. Select all six **label controls**, and change the **Font Color**. Under **Theme Colors**, in the eighth column, select the last color. With the **label controls** still selected, set the **Width** property to **1.75** and then select all of the **label controls** and all of the **text box controls**. Change the **Font Size** to **12**, set the **Height** property to **0.25** and then **Save** the design changes to your form.

10 In **Design** view, set the **Form Footer** section **Height** property to **0.5** Add a **Label control** to the **Form Footer** section that displays **Texas Lakes Science Books** For this **label control**, change the **Font Color**; under **Theme Colors**, in the eighth column, select the last color—and then apply **Bold**. For this **label control**, set the **Width** property to **2.25** set the **Top** property to **0.1** and then set the **Left** property to **1.95**

11 Close the **Property Sheet**. **Save** your form.

12 Close all open objects, and then **Open** the **Navigation Pane**. If necessary, increase the width of the pane so that all object names display fully. **Close** Access.

13 In **MyLab IT**, locate and click the Grader Project **Access 3E Textbook Publishers**. In **step 3**, under **Upload Completed Assignment**, click **Choose File**. In the **Open** dialog box, navigate to your **Access Chapter 3 folder**, and then click your **Student_Access_3E_Textbook_Publishers** file one time to select it. In the lower right corner of the **Open** dialog box, click **Open**.

14 To submit your file to **MyLab IT** for grading, click **Upload**, wait a moment for a green **Success!** message, and then in **step 4**, click the blue **Submit for Grading** button. Click **Close Assignment** to return to your list of **Course Materials**.

You have completed Project 3E | END

Content-Based Assessments (Mastery and Transfer of Learning)

Mastering Access   **Project 3F Degrees and Students**

Apply 3B skills from these Objectives:

5. Create a Report by Using the Report Tool and Modify the Report in Layout View
6. Create a Report by Using the Report Wizard
7. Modify the Design of a Report
8. Keep Grouped Data Together in a Printed Report

In the following Mastering Access project, you will assist Tom Catogrides, the Registrar, in using his database to track degrees and grade point averages for honor students in the health professions program in preparation for graduation. Your completed Navigation Pane will look similar to Figure 3.52.

Project Files for MyLab IT Grader

1. In your **MyLab IT** course, locate and click **Access 3F Degrees and Students**, Download Materials, and then Download All Files.
2. Extract the zipped folder to your Access Chapter 3 folder. Close the Grader download screens.
3. Take a moment to open the downloaded **Access_3F_Degrees_Students_Instructions**; note any recent updates to the book.

Project Results

Figure 3.52

For Non-MyLab Submissions

For Project 3F, you will need this starting file:
a03F_Degrees_Students

Start with an Access Data File

In your Access Chapter 3 folder, save your database as:
Lastname_Firstname_3F_Degrees_Students

After you have saved your database, open it to launch Access. On the next page, begin with Step 2.
After Step 7, save and submit your file as directed by your instructor.

(continues on next page)

Content-Based Assessments (Mastery and Transfer of Learning)

1 Start Access. From your student data files, open **Student_Access_3F_Degrees_Students** and then **Enable Content**.

2 View the relationship that is established between the *3F Degrees* tables and the *3F Students* table—*one* type of degree can be awarded to *many* students. If necessary, resize the field lists so all table and field names are fully visible. Save the changes to the layout of the relationships. **Run** each query to display the query results, apply **Best Fit**, and then **Save** each query.

Open each query in **Design** view to examine the design grid. The *3F Summa Cum Laude Graduates Query* answers the question, *What is the GPA, student ID, last name, first name, degree, and program for students graduating with a grade point average of 3.8 or higher, in descending order by GPA and ascending order by Last Name?* The *3F GPAs by Degree Program Query* answers the question, *What is the program, last name, first name, and GPA for all students, in ascending order by the Last Name field within the Program field?* **Close All** objects.

3 Based on your **3F Summa Cum Laude Graduates Query** object, use the **Report** tool to create a report. Apply the **Facet** theme to only this object (report). Delete the **Student ID** field from the report. For the **Last Name**, **First Name**, and **Degree text box controls**, set the **Width** property to **1.25** and then **Sort** the **Last Name** field in **Ascending** order. For the **Program text box controls**, set the **Width** property to **2.5**

At the bottom of the report, for the **calculated control**, which displays *8*, set the **Height** to **0.25** and then for the **page number control**, set the **Left** property to **5** For the title of the report, set the **Font Size** to **14** and change the word *Query* to **Report** For the **GPA** field, set the **Left** property to **0.25** to approximately center the fields within the margins of the report. **Save** the report as **3F Summa Cum Laude Graduates Report Close Print Preview**, **Close** the **Property Sheet**, and then **Close** the report.

4 Use the **Report Wizard** to create a report based on your **3F GPAs by Degree Program Query** object that includes the following fields in the order given: **Program**, **GPA**, **Last Name**, and **First Name**. View your data by **3F Degrees** and do not apply any additional grouping. Sort first in **Descending** order by **GPA**, and second in **Ascending** order by **Last Name**. Summarize the report by averaging the **GPA** field for each degree. Be sure the layout is **Stepped** and the orientation is **Portrait**. For the report title, type **3F GPAs by Program Report** and then switch to **Layout** view.

5 Apply the **Wisp** theme to only this object (report). For the report title, change the **Font Size** to **16**, and then apply **Bold**. Delete the controls that begin with *Summary for 'Program'*. Under **Program**, for the **text box controls**, set the **Width** property to **2.75** At the top of the report, select the four **label controls** that display the field names, and then apply **Bold**. Select the **GPA label control**, the **GPA text box controls**, and the **calculated controls** for the average GPA, and then set the **Width** property to **1** and the **Left** property to **3 Close** the **Property Sheet**. Display the report in **Design** view. Under **Program Header**, click the **Program text box control**, hold down Shift, and under **Program Footer**, click the **Average GPA by Program label control**. **Align** the controls on the **Right**, and then **Save** the design changes to your report.

6 Switch to **Print Preview**, **Zoom** to display **Two Pages** of the report, and examine how the groupings break across the pages. Switch to **Layout** view, display the **Group, Sort, and Total** pane, select **keep whole group together on one page**, and then close the **Group, Sort, and Total** pane. Switch to **Print Preview**, and then notice that the groupings are not split between pages. **Save** the report.

7 **Close Print Preview**, and then **Close** the report. **Open** the **Navigation Pane**, and, if necessary, increase the width of the pane so that all object names display fully.

8 In **MyLab IT**, locate and click the Grader Project **Access 3F Degrees and Students**. In **step 3**, under **Upload Completed Assignment**, click **Choose File**. In the **Open** dialog box, navigate to your **Access Chapter 3 folder**, and then click your **Student_Access_3F_Degrees_Students** file one time to select it. In the lower right corner of the **Open** dialog box, click **Open**.

9 To submit your file to **MyLab IT** for grading, click **Upload**, wait a moment for a green **Success!** message, and then in **step 4**, click the blue **Submit for Grading** button. Click **Close Assignment** to return to your list of **Course Materials**.

You have completed Project 3F   **END**

Mastering Access Project 3G Career Books

Apply 3A and 3B skills from these Objectives:

1. Create and Use a Form to Add and Delete Records
2. Filter Records
3. Create a Form by Using the Form Wizard
4. Modify a Form in Layout View and in Design View
5. Create a Report by Using the Report Tool and Modify the Report in Layout View
6. Create a Report by Using the Report Wizard
7. Modify the Design of a Report
8. Keep Grouped Data Together in a Printed Report

In the following Mastering Access project, you will assist Rebecca Hennelly, Head Librarian at the Southwest Campus of Texas Lakes Community College, in using her database to track publishers and book titles that assist students in finding employment. Your completed Navigation Pane will look similar to Figure 3.53.

Project Files for MyLab IT Grader

1. In your **MyLab IT** course, locate and click **Access 3G Career Books**, Download Materials, and then Download All Files.
2. Extract the zipped folder to your Access Chapter 3 folder. Close the Grader download screens.
3. Take a moment to open the downloaded **Access_3G_Career_Books_Instructions**; note any recent updates to the book.

Project Results

Figure 3.53

For Non-MyLab Submissions

For Project 3G, you will need this starting file:
a03G_Career_Books

Start with an Access Data File

In your Access Chapter 3 folder, save your database as:
Lastname_Firstname_3G_Career_Books

After you have saved your database, open it to launch Access. On the next page, begin with Step 2.

After Step 20, save and submit your file as directed by your instructor.

(continues on next page)

Content-Based Assessments (Mastery and Transfer of Learning)

1 Start Access. From your student data files, open **Student_Access_3G_Career_Books**. and then **Enable Content**.

2 View the relationship that is established between the *3G Publishers* table and the *3G Career Books* table—*one* publisher can publish *many* career books. If necessary, resize the field lists so all table and field names are fully visible. Save the changes to the layout of the relationships.

3 Open the **3G Resume or Interview Books Query**, apply **Best Fit**, and then **Save** the query. Switch the query to **Design** view, examine the design of the query, and then **Close** the query object.

4 Based on your **3G Career Books** table, use the **Form** tool to create a form. **Save** the form as **3G Career Book Form** and then switch to **Form** view. Using the form, add a new record to the underlying table as shown in **Table 1**.

Table 1

Title ID	Title	Author Last Name	Author First Name	Publisher ID	Category	Copies On Hand	Value of Books
T-25	Effective Networking	Nunez	Charlene	PUB-109	Job Search	6	180

5 Display the first record and click in the **Title ID** field. **Find** the record for the **Title ID** of **T-19**, and then **Delete** the record. Display the record you entered for **T-25** and change the **Column Size Width** in the **Print** dialog box to **7.5 Save** the design changes to your form.

6 Use the **Filter By Form** tool in your **3G Career Book Form** object to create a filter that displays records with a **Category** of **Interviewing Strategies** or **Resumes**. After verifying that 10 records match this criteria, click **Toggle Filter** to display all 24 records. **Save** the form, and then **Close** the form.

7 Use the **Form Wizard** to create a form based on your **3G Publishers** table that includes the following fields in the order given: **Company Name**, **Rep Last Name**, **Rep First Name**, **Job Title**, and **Phone Number**. Apply a **Columnar** layout, and name the form **3G Publisher Form**

8 In **Layout** view, apply the **Stacked** layout to all of the controls, and then apply the **Integral** theme to this form only. For the title of the form, change the **Font Size** to **16**, apply **Bold**, and then change the **Font Color**— under **Theme Colors**, in the fourth column, select the last color. **Save** the design changes to the form.

9 From the **Field List** pane, add the **Publisher ID** field to the form directly above the **Company Name** field. **Close** the **Field List** pane. Move the **Rep First Name** controls directly above the **Rep Last Name** controls. Click the **Job Title text box control**, set the **Width** property to **2.5** and then **Save** the design changes to your form.

10 Select all six **text box controls**, and change the **Background Color**; under **Theme Colors**, in the fifth column, select the second color. Select all six **label controls**, and change the **Font Color**— under **Theme Colors**, in the fourth column, select the last color. Apply **Bold** to the **label controls**. With the **label controls** still selected, set the **Width** property to **1.75** and then select all of the **label controls** and all of the **text box controls**. Change the **Font Size** to **12**, set the **Height** property to **0.25** and then **Save** the design changes to your form.

11 In **Design** view, set the **Form Footer** section **Height** property to **0.5** Add a **Label** control to the **Form Footer** section that displays **Texas Lakes Southwest Campus**. For this **label control**, change the **Font Color**; under **Theme Colors**, in the fourth column, select the last color —and then apply **Bold**. For this **label control**, set the **Width** property to **2.2** set the **Top** property to **0.1** and then set the **Left** property to **1.25 Close** the **Property Sheet**, **Save** your form, and then switch to **Form** view. Using the form, add a new record to the underlying table as shown in **Table 2**.

Table 2

Publisher ID	Company Name	Rep First Name	Rep Last Name	Job Title	Phone Number
PUB-111	Associated Publishers	Marquis	Sullivan	Sales Associate	(512) 555-7373

(continues on next page)

12 View the record that you just created. **Close** the form.

13 Based on your **3G Resume or Interview Books Query** object, use the **Report** tool to create a report. Apply the **Retrospect** theme to only this report. Delete the following fields from the report: **Publisher ID**, **Category**, and **Company Name**. For the **Title text box controls**, set the **Width** property to **3** and then **Sort** the **Title** field in **Ascending** order. For the **Author Last Name text box controls** and the **Author First Name text box controls**, set the **Width** property to **1.5**

14 Click the **Title** field name, and then add a calculated control that counts the number of records. At the bottom of the report, for the **calculated control**, which displays *10*, set the **Height** to **0.25** and then for the **page number control**, set the **Left** property to **5** For the title of the report, set the **Font Size** to **14** and change the word *Query* to **Report**. Click the **Title** field name, and then set the **Left** property to **0.75** to move all of the controls to the right. **Save** the report as **3G Resume or Interview Books Report Close** the **Property Sheet**, and then **Close** the report.

15 Use the **Report Wizard** to create a report based on your **3G Career Books** table that includes the following fields in the order given: **Category**, **Title**, and **Value of Books**. Group your data by **Category**, sort in **Ascending** order by **Title**, and then summarize the report by summing the **Value of Books** field. Be sure the layout is **Stepped** and the orientation is **Portrait**. For the report title, type **3G Book Values by Category Report** and then switch to **Layout** view.

16 Apply the **Ion Boardroom** theme to only this report. For the report title, change the **Font Size** to **14**, and then apply **Bold**. Delete the controls that begin with **Summary for 'Category'**. Select the **Category**, **Title**, and **Value of Books label controls**, and then apply **Bold**. Under **Title**, for the **text box controls**, set the **Width** property to **3.5** For the **Value of Books label control**, set the **Left** property to **6** and then **Save** the design changes to your report.

17 At the bottom of the report in the last column, select the following three controls: **text box control** that displays *$420*, **calculated control** that displays *$945*, and the **calculated control** that displays *7,730 (Grand Total control, may be too small to view number)*. Set the **Width** property to **1.25** and the **Left** property to **6** For the **Grand Total label control**, set the **Width** property to **1** and then change the text in the **Sum label control** to **Total Value of Books by Category** Click any **Title text box control**, set the **Height** property to **0.35** and then **Save** your report.

18 **Close** the **Property Sheet**, and then display your report in **Design** view. Under **Category Footer**, click the **label control** that displays *Total Value of Books by Category*, hold down ⇧Shift, and then under **Report Footer**, click the **Grand Total label control**. **Align** the controls on the **Left**, and then **Save** the design changes to your report.

19 Switch to **Print Preview**, **Zoom** to display **Two Pages** of the report, and examine how the groupings break across the pages. Switch to **Layout** view, display the **Group, Sort, and Total** pane, select **keep whole group together on one page**, and then close the **Group, Sort, and Total** pane. Switch to **Print Preview** and notice that the groupings are no longer split between pages. **Save** the report.

20 **Close Print Preview**, and then **Close** the report. **Open** the **Navigation Pane**, and, if necessary, increase the width of the pane so that all object names display fully. On the right side of the title bar, click **Close** to close the database and to close Access.

21 In **MyLab IT**, locate and click the Grader Project **Access 3G Career Book**. In **step 3**, under **Upload Completed Assignment**, click **Choose File**. In the **Open** dialog box, navigate to your **Access Chapter 3 folder**, and then click your **Student_Access_3G_Career_Books** file one time to select it. In the lower right corner of the **Open** dialog box, click **Open**.

22 To submit your file to **MyLab IT** for grading, click **Upload**, wait a moment for a green **Success!** message, and then in **step 4**, click the blue **Submit for Grading** button. Click **Close Assignment** to return to your list of **Course Materials**.

You have completed Project 3G   **END**

Content-Based Assessments (Critical Thinking)

Apply a combination of the 3A and 3B skills.

GO! Fix It	**Project 3H Resume Workshops**	IRC
GO! Make It	**Project 3I Study Abroad**	IRC
GO! Solve It	**Project 3J Job Offers**	IRC
GO! Solve It	**Project 3K Financial Aid**	

Project Files

For Project 3K, you will need the following file:

a03K_Financial_Aid

You will save your database as:

Lastname_Firstname_3K_Financial_Aid

Start Access, navigate to your student data files, open **a03K_Financial_Aid**, and then save the database in your **Access Chapter 3** folder as **Lastname_Firstname_3K_Financial_Aid**. Using your own name, add **Lastname Firstname** to the beginning of both table names and the query name. Sivia Long, the Financial Aid Director, would like you to create an attractive form and a report for this database, using the following guidelines:

- The form will be used to update student records in the 3K FA Students table. Be sure that the Last Name field displays above the First Name field. After the form is created, enter a new record using your own information with a Student ID of **9091246** and Financial Aid ID of **FA-07** and a Home Phone of **(512) 555-9876** and a College Email of **ns246@tlcc.edu** Create a filter that when toggled on displays the records for those students whose last names begin with the letter *S*. Add a footer to the form that displays **Texas Lakes Community College Financial Aid** Save the form as **Lastname Firstname 3K FA Student Update Form**.

- The report should use the query and list the Award Name, the Student ID, and the Award Amount for financial aid offered to students, viewed by students, grouped by the Award Name field, and sorted in ascending order by Student ID. Include a total for the Award Amount field, save the report as **Lastname Firstname 3K FA Amount by Award Report** and be sure the groupings do not break across pages when the report is printed.

Open the Navigation Pane, be sure that all object names display fully, and then close Access. As directed, submit your database for grading.

		Performance Level		
		Exemplary: You consistently applied the relevant skills	**Proficient:** You sometimes, but not always, applied the relevant skills	**Developing:** You rarely or never applied the relevant skills
Performance Criteria	**Create 3K FA Student Update Form**	Form created with correct fields, new record, footer, and filter in an attractive format.	Form created with no more than two missing elements.	Form created with more than two missing elements.
	Create 3K FA Amount by Award Report	Report created with correct fields, grouped, sorted, and summarized correctly, with groupings kept together in an attractive format.	Report created with no more than two missing elements.	Report created with more than two missing elements.

You have completed Project 3K | END

Outcomes-Based Assessments (Critical Thinking)

Rubric

The following outcomes-based assessments are *open-ended assessments*. That is, there is no specific correct result; your result will depend on your approach to the information provided. Make *Professional Quality* your goal. Use the following scoring rubric to guide you in *how* to approach the problem and then to evaluate *how well* your approach solves the problem.

The *criteria*—Software Mastery, Content, Format and Layout, and Process—represent the knowledge and skills you have gained that you can apply to solving the problem. The *levels of performance*—Professional Quality, Approaching Professional Quality, or Needs Quality Improvements—help you and your instructor evaluate your result.

	Your completed project is of Professional Quality if you:	Your completed project is Approaching Professional Quality if you:	Your completed project Needs Quality Improvements if you:
1-Software Mastery	Choose and apply the most appropriate skills, tools, and features and identify efficient methods to solve the problem.	Choose and apply some appropriate skills, tools, and features, but not in the most efficient manner.	Choose inappropriate skills, tools, or features, or are inefficient in solving the problem.
2-Content	Construct a solution that is clear and well organized, contains content that is accurate, appropriate to the audience and purpose, and is complete. Provide a solution that contains no errors of spelling, grammar, or style.	Construct a solution in which some components are unclear, poorly organized, inconsistent, or incomplete. Misjudge the needs of the audience. Have some errors in spelling, grammar, or style, but the errors do not detract from comprehension.	Construct a solution that is unclear, incomplete, or poorly organized, contains some inaccurate or inappropriate content, and contains many errors of spelling, grammar, or style. Do not solve the problem.
3-Format and Layout	Format and arrange all elements to communicate information and ideas, clarify function, illustrate relationships, and indicate relative importance.	Apply appropriate format and layout features to some elements, but not others. Overuse features, causing minor distraction.	Apply format and layout that does not communicate information or ideas clearly. Do not use format and layout features to clarify function, illustrate relationships, or indicate relative importance. Use available features excessively, causing distraction.
4-Process	Use an organized approach that integrates planning, development, self-assessment, revision, and reflection.	Demonstrate an organized approach in some areas, but not others; or, use an insufficient process of organization throughout.	Do not use an organized approach to solve the problem.

Outcomes-Based Assessments (Critical Thinking)

Apply a combination of the 3A and 3D skills.

GO! Think	Project 3L Food Services

Project Files

For Project 3L, you will need the following file:

a03L_Food_Services

You will save your database as:

Lastname_Firstname_3L_Food_Services

Start Access, navigate to your student data files, open **a03L_Food_Services**, save the database in your **Access Chapter 3** folder as **Lastname_Firstname_3L_Food_Services** and then enable the content. Using your own name, add **Lastname Firstname** to the beginning of both table names. Luciano Gonzalez, the Hospitality Director, would like you to create to create an attractive form and a report to assist him with the staff scheduling of food services for a two-day student orientation workshop using the following guidelines:

- The form will be used to update records in the 3L Staff table. Be sure that the Last Name field displays above the First Name field. After the form is created, enter a new record using your own last name and first name with a Staff ID of **STAFF-1119** and a Phone Number of **(512) 555-0845** and a Title of **Server** Create a filter that when toggled on displays the records for staff with a Title of *Server*. Add a footer to the form that displays **Texas Lakes Community College Hospitality Services** Save the form as **Lastname Firstname 3L Staff Update Form** and then create a paper or PDF electronic image of your record only.

- The report will be used by Mr. Gonzalez to call staff members when the schedule changes, so it should be grouped by title. Add a report footer that displays **Texas Lakes Community College Hospitality Services** and then save the report as **Lastname Firstname 3L Staff Phone List** Create a paper or PDF electronic image as directed.

Open the Navigation Pane, be sure that all object names display fully, and then close Access. As directed, submit your database for grading.

	You have completed Project 3L	END

GO! Think	Project 3M Donor Gifts	IRC
You and GO!	Project 3N Personal Inventory	IRC
GO! Cumulative Group Project	Project 3O Bell Orchid Hotels	IRC

Introducing Microsoft PowerPoint 2019

Sunshine Studio/Shutterstock

PowerPoint 2019: Introduction

 Introduction to PowerPoint

Communication skills are critical to your success in many careers, and when it comes to communicating *your* ideas, presentation is everything! Whether you are planning to deliver your presentation in person or online—to a large audience or to a small group—Microsoft PowerPoint 2019 is a versatile business tool that will help you create presentations that make a lasting impression. Additionally, collaborating with others to develop a presentation is easy because you can share the slides you create by using your free Microsoft OneDrive cloud storage.

Microsoft PowerPoint 2019 includes a variety of themes that you can apply to a new presentation. Each theme includes several theme variants that coordinate colors, fonts, and effects. The benefit of this approach is that the variations evoke different moods and responses, yet the basic design remains the same. As a result, you can use a similar design within your company to brand your presentations, while still changing the colors to make the presentation appropriate to the audience and topic. You do not have to determine which colors work well together in the theme you choose, because professional designers have already done that for you. So you can concentrate on how best to communicate your message. Focus on creating dynamic, interesting presentations that keep your audience engaged!

Getting Started with Microsoft PowerPoint

1

POWERPOINT
2019

PROJECT 1A

Outcomes
Create a company overview presentation.

Objectives
1. Create a New Presentation
2. Edit a Presentation in Normal View
3. Add Pictures to a Presentation
4. Print and View a Presentation

PROJECT 1B

Outcomes
Create a new product announcement presentation.

Objectives
5. Edit an Existing Presentation
6. Format a Presentation
7. Use Slide Sorter View
8. Apply Slide Transitions

Bety X/Shuttestock

In This Chapter

GO! To Work
with PowerPoint

In this chapter, you will use Microsoft PowerPoint to study presentation skills, which are among the most important skills you will learn. Good presentation skills enhance your communications—written, electronic, and interpersonal. In this technology-enhanced world, communicating ideas clearly and concisely is a critical personal skill. Microsoft PowerPoint 2019 is presentation software with which you create electronic slide presentations. Use PowerPoint to present information to your audience effectively. You can start with a new, blank presentation and add content, pictures, and themes, or you can collaborate with colleagues by inserting slides that have been saved in other presentations.

The projects in this chapter relate to **Kodiak West Travel**, which is a travel agency with offices in Juneau, Anchorage, and Victoria. Kodiak West Travel works closely with local vendors to provide clients with specialized adventure travel itineraries. The company was established in 2001 in Juneau and built a loyal client base that led to the expansion into Anchorage and Victoria. As a full-service travel agency, Kodiak West Travel agents strive to provide their clients with travel opportunities that exceed their expectations. The company works with all major airlines, cruise lines, hotel chains, and vehicle rental companies as well as with small, specialized, boutique hotels.

Company Overview Presentation

Project Activities

In Activities 1.01 through 1.16, you will create the first five slides of a new presentation that Kodiak West Travel tour manager Ken Dakano is developing to introduce the tour services that the company offers. Your completed presentation will look similar to Figure 1.1.

Project Files for **MyLab IT** Grader

1. In your storage location, create a folder named **PowerPoint Chapter 1**.
2. In your **MyLab IT** course, locate and click **PowerPoint 1A KWT Overview**, Download Materials, and then Download All Files.
3. Extract the zipped folder to your PowerPoint Chapter 1 folder. Close the Grader download screens.
4. Take a moment to open the downloaded **PowerPoint_1A_KWT_Overview_Instructions**; note any recent updates to the book.

Project Results

GO! Project 1A
Where We're Going

Figure 1.1 Project 1A KWT Overview

For Non-MyLab Submissions

For Project 1A, you will need:
p01A_KWT_Overview
p01A_Bay
p01A_Glacier

In your storage location, create a folder named **PowerPoint Chapter 1**
In your PowerPoint Chapter 1 folder, save your presentation as:
Lastname_Firstname_1A_KWT_Overview

After you have named and saved your presentation, close the file and then, on the next page, begin with Step 1.

NOTE   If You Are Using a Touch Screen

Tap an item to click it.

Press and hold for a few seconds to right-click; release when the information or commands display.

Touch the screen with two or more fingers and then pinch together or stretch your fingers apart to zoom in and out.

Slide your finger on the screen to scroll—slide left to scroll right and slide right to scroll left.

Slide to rearrange—similar to dragging with a mouse.

Swipe to select—slide an item a short distance with a quick movement—to select an item and bring up commands, if any.

Objective 1   Create a New Presentation

ALERT   Because Office 365 is a cloud-based subscription service that receives continuous updates, you may encounter some variations in what appears on your screen and what is shown in this instruction. Microsoft Office 365 is fully installed on your PC or Mac; no internet access is necessary to create or edit documents. When you *are* connected to the internet, you will receive monthly upgrades and new features, so you always have the latest versions of Office apps as soon as they are available. Your subscription gives you continuous free access to the latest innovations and refinements.

GO! Learn How
Video P1-1

Microsoft PowerPoint 2019 is software you can use to present information to your audience effectively. You can edit and format a blank presentation by adding text, a presentation theme, and pictures. When you start PowerPoint, presentations you have recently opened, if any, display on the left. On the right you can select either a blank presentation or a *theme*—a set of unified design elements that provides a look for your presentation by applying colors, fonts, and effects. A presentation consists of one or more slides. Similar to a page in a document—a presentation *slide* can contain text, pictures, tables, charts, and other multimedia or graphic objects.

Activity 1.01 | **Identifying Parts of the PowerPoint Window**

In this Activity, you will start PowerPoint and identify the parts of the PowerPoint window.

1 Start PowerPoint. In the list of templates, click **Facet** to view a preview of the Facet theme and the color variations associated with this theme. If Facet is not visible, use the Search templates box to search for it. Below the theme preview, click either the left- or right-pointing **More Images** ◀ and ▶ arrows to view how various types of slides in this theme display. To the right of the preview, click each of the color variations. After you have viewed each color, click the original green color.

MAC TIP   There is no color preview available in the Mac version of PowerPoint.

2 On either the left or right side of the preview window, notice the arrow, and then compare your screen with Figure 1.2. Click the right- or left-pointing arrow several times to view other available themes, and then return to the **Facet** theme.

You can use the arrows to the left and right of the preview window to scroll through the available themes.

MAC TIP   Scroll down on the opening screen to view other themes.

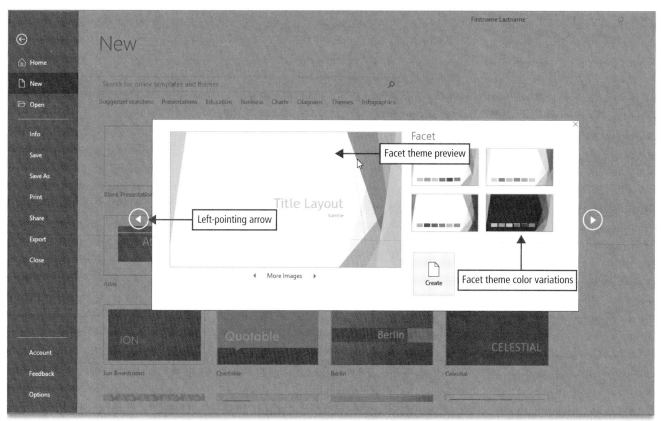

Figure 1.2

3 In the lower right area of the preview window, click **Create** to begin a new presentation using the **Facet** theme.

4 Compare your screen with Figure 1.3, and then take a moment to study the parts of the PowerPoint window described in the table in Figure 1.4.

The presentation displays in *normal view*, which is the primary editing view in PowerPoint where you write and design your presentations. On the left, a pane displays miniature images—*thumbnails*—of the slides in your presentation. On the right, the *Slide pane* displays a larger image of the active slide.

MAC TIP   To display group names on the ribbon, display the menu, click PowerPoint, click Preferences, click View, select the Show group titles check box.

Figure 1.3

Microsoft PowerPoint Screen Elements	
Screen Element	**Description**
Slide pane	Displays a large image of the active slide.
Slide thumbnails	Miniature images of each slide in the presentation. Clicking a slide thumbnail displays the slide in the Slide pane.
Status bar	Displays, in a horizontal bar at the bottom of the presentation window, the current slide number, number of slides in a presentation, Notes button, View buttons, Zoom slider, and Fit slide to current window button; you can customize this area to include additional information.
View buttons	Control the look of the presentation window with a set of commands.
Zoom slider	Zooms the slide displayed in the Slide pane, in and out.
Fit slide to current window button	Fits the active slide to the maximum view in the Slide pane.

Figure 1.4

5 In the upper right corner of your screen, click **Close** ⊠ to close PowerPoint. Do not save your file. Navigate to your **PowerPoint Chapter 1 folder**, and then double-click the PowerPoint file you downloaded from MyLab IT that displays your name—**Student_PowerPoint_1A_KWT_ Overview**. In your presentation, if necessary, at the top, click **Enable Editing**.

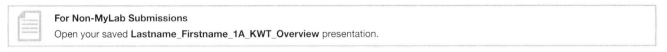

For Non-MyLab Submissions
Open your saved **Lastname_Firstname_1A_KWT_Overview** presentation.

Activity 1.02 | Entering Presentation Text

When you create a new presentation, PowerPoint displays a new blank presentation with a single slide—a title slide in Normal view. The *title slide* is usually the first slide in a presentation; it introduces the presentation topic.

1 In the **Slide pane**, click in the text *Click to add title*, which is the title placeholder.

A *placeholder* is a box on a slide with dotted or dashed borders that holds title and body text or other content such as charts, tables, and pictures. This slide contains two placeholders, one for the title and one for the subtitle.

2 Type **Kodiak West** and then click in the subtitle placeholder. Type **Your Travel** and then press Enter to create a new line in the subtitle placeholder. Type **Your Way** and then compare your screen with Figure 1.5.

Figure 1.5

3 On the **Quick Access Toolbar**, click **Save** 🖫.

Activity 1.03 | Applying a Presentation Theme

A theme is a set of unified design elements that provides a look for your presentation by applying colors, fonts, and effects. After you create a presentation, you can change the look of your presentation by applying a different theme. Kodiak West Travel wants a theme that evokes a feeling of nature.

1 On the ribbon, click the **Design tab**. In the **Themes group**, click **More** 🔽 to display the **Themes** gallery. Compare your screen with Figure 1.6.

The themes displayed on your system may differ from Figure 1.6.

Figure 1.6

2 ▶ In the gallery, point to several of the themes and notice that a ScreenTip displays the name of each theme, and the Live Preview feature displays how each theme would look if applied to your presentation.

The first theme that displays is the Office Theme.

 MAC TIP   Live previews do not display in the Mac version of PowerPoint.

3 ▶ Use the ScreenTips to locate the **Organic** theme shown in Figure 1.7.

Figure 1.7

4 ▶ Click **Organic** to change the presentation theme and then **Save** 🖫 your presentation.

ALERT   If your system does not have the Organic theme, use the theme file downloaded with your data files from **MyLab IT**. In the themes gallery, click Browse for Themes, navigate to your PowerPoint Chapter 1 folder, locate the Organic.thmx file and click Apply.

Objective 2   Edit a Presentation in Normal View

GO! Learn How
Video P1-2

Editing is the process of modifying a presentation by adding and deleting slides or by changing the contents of individual slides.

Activity 1.04 | **Inserting a New Slide**

MOS
2.1.3

Your presentation consists of a single slide. Most presentations consist of multiple slides. This presentation will highlight the company and consist of five slides when finished.

1 ▶ On the **Home tab**, in the **Slides group**, point to the **New Slide arrow**—the lower part of the New Slide button. Compare your screen with Figure 1.8.

The New Slide button is a *split button*—a type of button in which clicking the main part of the button performs a command and clicking the arrow opens a menu, list, or gallery. The upper, main part of the New Slide button, when clicked, inserts a slide without displaying any options. The lower part—the New Slide arrow—when clicked, displays a gallery of slide *layouts*— the arrangement of elements, such as title and subtitle text, lists, pictures, tables, charts, shapes, and movies, on a slide.

Figure 1.8

> **2** In the **Slides group**, click the lower portion of the **New Slide** button—the **New Slide arrow**—to display the gallery, and then compare your screen with Figure 1.9.

Figure 1.9

> **3** In the gallery, click the **Panoramic Picture with Caption** layout to insert a new slide. Notice that the new blank slide displays in the **Slide pane**, and a slide thumbnail displays at the left. Compare your screen with Figure 1.10.

BY TOUCH In the gallery, tap the desired layout to insert a new slide.

Figure 1.10

4 On the new slide, below the picture placeholder, click the text *Click to add title*, and then type **Your Dreams**

5 Below the title placeholder, click in the text placeholder. Type **Whether you want to trek on a glacier or spend your time in quiet solitude, Kodiak West Travel can make your dream a reality.** Compare your screen with Figure 1.11.

Figure 1.11

6 On the **Home tab**, in the **Slides group**, click the **New Slide arrow** to display the gallery, and then click **Title and Content**. In the title placeholder, type **Our Expertise** and then below the title placeholder, click in the content placeholder. Type **Over 20 years of experience in the travel industry**

7 Save 🖫 your presentation.

Activity 1.05 | Increasing and Decreasing List Levels

3.1.3

You can organize text in a PowerPoint presentation according to *list levels*. List levels, each represented by a bullet symbol, are similar to outline levels. On a slide, list levels are identified by the bullet style, indentation, and the size of the text. The first level on an individual slide is the title.

Increasing the list level of a bullet point increases its indent and results in a smaller text size. Decreasing the list level of a bullet point decreases its indent and results in a larger text size. Use list levels to organize information.

1 ▶ On **Slide 3**, if necessary, click at the end of the first bullet point after the word *industry*, and then press Enter to insert a new bullet point.

2 ▶ Press Tab, and then notice that the bullet is indented. Type **Certified Travel Associates**

By pressing Tab at the beginning of a bullet point, you can increase the list level and indent the bullet point.

3 ▶ Press Enter and notice that a new bullet point displays at the same level as the previous bullet point.

4 ▶ On the **Home tab**, in the **Paragraph group**, click **Decrease List Level** [icon]. Type **Specializing in land and sea travel** and then compare your screen with Figure 1.12.

The indent is removed and the size of the text increases.

Figure 1.12

5 ▶ Press Enter, and then on the **Home tab**, click **Increase List Level** [icon]. Type **Pacific Northwest including U.S. and Canada**

You can use the Increase List Level button to indent the bullet point.

6 ▶ Compare your screen with Figure 1.13, and then **Save** [icon] your presentation.

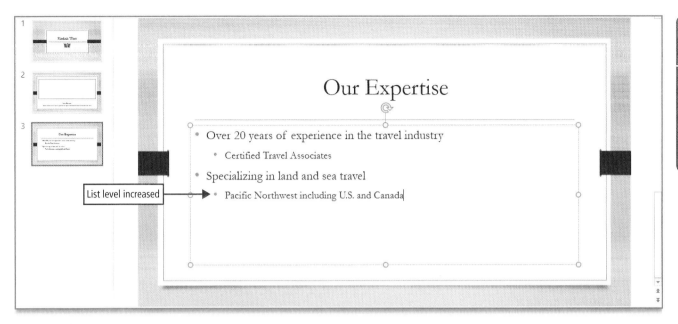

Figure 1.13

Activity 1.06 | Adding Speaker Notes to a Presentation

The ***Notes pane*** is an area of the Normal view window that displays below the Slide pane with space to type notes about the active slide. You can refer to these notes while making a presentation, reminding you of the important points that you want to discuss. This will be helpful when employees of Kodiak West give the presentation before new customers.

1 With **Slide 3** displayed, in the **Status bar**, click **Notes** ⬛, and then notice that below the Slide pane, the Notes pane displays. Click in the **Notes** pane, and then type **Kodiak West Travel has locations in Juneau, Anchorage, and Victoria.**

The Notes button is a toggle button. Clicking once will display the Notes pane, clicking again will hide it.

2 **Save** 💾 your presentation, and then compare your screen with Figure 1.14.

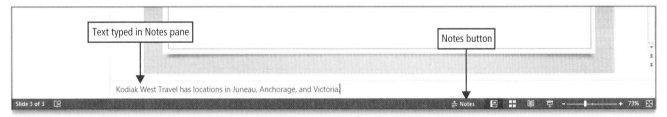

Figure 1.14

Activity 1.07 | Displaying and Editing Slides in the Slide Pane

1 On the left side of the PowerPoint window, look at the slide thumbnails, and then notice that the presentation contains three slides. On the right side of the PowerPoint window, in the vertical scroll bar, point to the scroll box, and then hold down the left mouse button to display a ScreenTip indicating the slide number and title.

2 Drag the scroll box up until the ScreenTip displays *Slide: 2 of 3 Your Dreams*. Compare your slide with Figure 1.15, and then release the mouse button to display **Slide 2**.

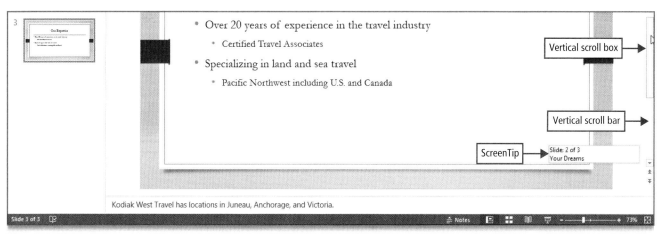

Figure 1.15

3 At the bottom of the slide, in the content placeholder, click at the end of the sentence, after the period. Press Spacebar, and then type **If you can dream it, we can help you get there.**

4 On the left side of the PowerPoint window, in the slide thumbnails, point to **Slide 3**, and then notice that a ScreenTip displays the slide title. Compare your screen with Figure 1.16.

Figure 1.16

5 Click **Slide 3** to display it in the Slide pane. On the **Home tab**, in the **Slides group**, click the **New Slide arrow** to display the **Slide Layout** gallery, and then click **Section Header**.

A *section header* is a type of slide layout that changes the look and flow of a presentation by providing text placeholders that do not contain bullet points.

6 Click in the title placeholder, and then type **About Our Company**

7 Click in the content placeholder below the title, and then type **Kodiak West Travel was established in May of 2001 by Ken Dakona and Mariam Dorner, two Alaska residents whose sense of adventure and commitment to ecotourism is an inherent aspect of their travel itineraries.** Compare your screen with Figure 1.17.

The placeholder text is resized to fit within the placeholder. The AutoFit Options button displays.

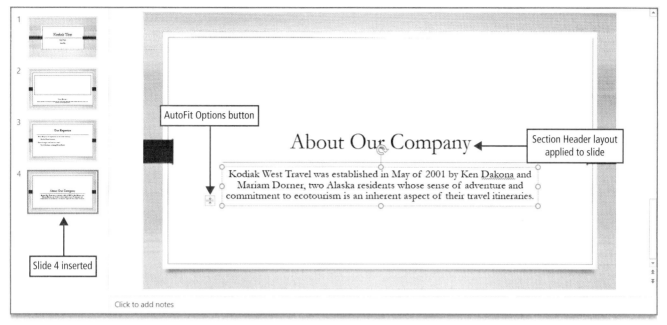

Figure 1.17

8 Click **AutoFit Options** 🔄, review the AutoFit options and then click outside the menu to close it.

The *AutoFit Text to Placeholder* option keeps the text contained within the placeholder by reducing the size of the text. The *Stop Fitting Text to This Placeholder* option turns off the AutoFit option so that the text can flow beyond the placeholder border; the text size remains unchanged. You can also choose to split the text between two slides, continue on a new slide, or divide the text into two columns.

MAC TIP To adjust AutoFit, on the Shape Format tab, click More Formats to open the Format pane. On the Format pane, click Text Options, and click the Text Box tab.

9 In the slide thumbnails, click **Slide 1** to display it in the Slide pane, and then in the slide title, click at the end of the word *West*. Press Spacebar, and then type **Travel**

Clicking a slide thumbnail is the most common method used to display a slide in the Slide pane.

10 **Save** 💾 your presentation.

Objective 3 Add Pictures to a Presentation

GO! Learn How
Video P1-3

Photographic images add impact to a presentation and help the audience visualize your message. Photos can be inserted from files or from online sources, and format and enhance the images using tools built into PowerPoint.

Activity 1.08 | Inserting a Picture from a File

Many slide layouts in PowerPoint accommodate digital picture files so that you can easily add pictures you have stored. The travel agency has a collection of photographs to be inserted in the presentation that highlights the beauty of the region.

1 Display **Slide 2**, and then compare your screen with Figure 1.18.

In the center of the picture placeholder, the *Pictures* button displays.

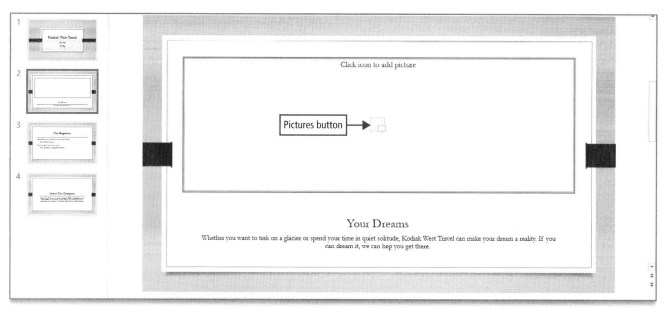

Figure 1.18

> **2** In the picture placeholder, click **Pictures** 🖼 to open the **Insert Picture** dialog box. Navigate to the data files downloaded with this project, click **p01A_Glacier**, and then click **Insert** to insert the picture in the placeholder. If necessary, close the Design Ideas pane. Compare your screen with Figure 1.19.
>
> > Small circles—*sizing handles*—surround the inserted picture and indicate that the picture is selected and can be modified or formatted. The *rotation handle*—a circular arrow above the picture—provides a way to rotate a selected image. The Picture Tools are added to the ribbon, providing picture formatting commands.

NOTE   Design Ideas Pane

The Design Ideas pane may open each time you insert a picture. The pane includes ideas for ways to format and lay out a slide. In this project you will not use these suggestions, so you can close the pane each time it opens.

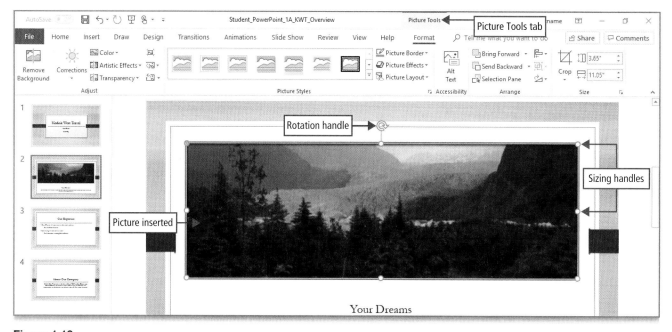

Figure 1.19

3 ▸ Display **Slide 3**. On the **Home tab**, in the **Slides group**, click the **New Slide arrow**, and then click **Title and Content**. In the title placeholder, type **Your Vacation**

4 ▸ In the content placeholder, click **Pictures** . Navigate to the data files for this project, and then click **p01A_Bay**. Click **Insert**, **Save** 🖫 the presentation, and then compare your screen with Figure 1.20.

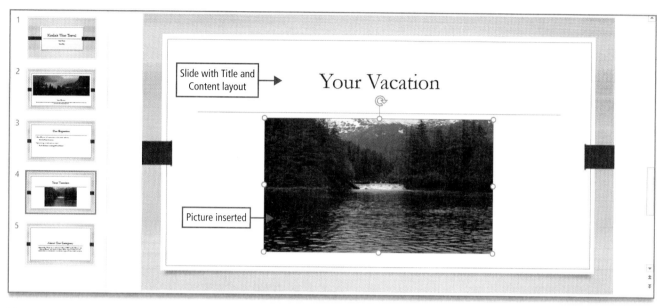

Figure 1.20

Activity 1.09 │ Applying a Style to a Picture

MOS
3.3.2

When you select a picture, the Picture Tools display, adding the Format tab to the ribbon. The Format tab provides numerous styles that you can apply to your pictures. A *style* is a collection of formatting options that you can apply to a picture, text, or an object.

1 ▸ With **Slide 4** displayed, if necessary, click the picture to select it. On the ribbon, notice that the *Picture Tools* are active and the *Format* tab displays.

2 ▸ On the **Picture Tools Format tab**, in the **Picture Styles group**, click **More** ▾ to display the **Picture Styles** gallery, and then compare your screen with Figure 1.21.

Figure 1.21

3 In the gallery, point to several of the picture styles to display the ScreenTips and to view the effect on your picture. Point to each style to display a ScreenTip, and then locate and click **Simple Frame, Black**. Click in a blank area of the slide, compare your screen with Figure 1.22, and then **Save** 🖫 the presentation.

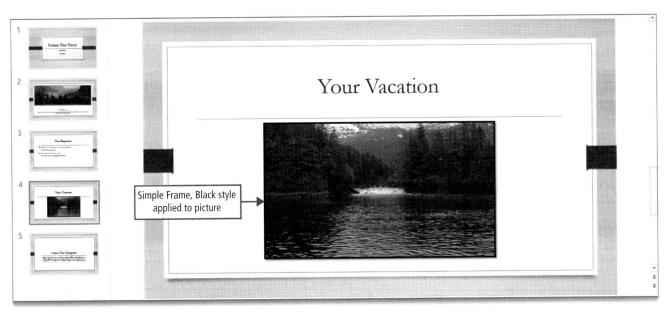

Figure 1.22

Activity 1.10 | Applying and Removing Picture Artistic Effects

3.3.2

Artistic effects are formats applied to images that make pictures resemble sketches or paintings.

1 On **Slide 4**, click the picture to select it. On the **Picture Tools Format tab**, in the **Adjust group**, click **Artistic Effects** to display the **Artistic Effects** gallery. Compare your screen with Figure 1.23.

Figure 1.23

2 In the gallery, point to several of the artistic effects to display the ScreenTips and to have Live Preview display the effect on your picture. Then, locate and click the **Glow Diffused** effect.

3 With the picture still selected, on the **Format tab**, in the **Adjust group**, click **Artistic Effects** again to display the gallery. In the first row, click the first effect—**None**—to remove the effect from the picture and restore the previous formatting. **Save** 🖫 the presentation.

Objective 4   Print and View a Presentation

GO! Learn How
Video P1-4

There are several print options in PowerPoint. For example, you can print full page images of your slides, presentation handouts to provide your audience with copies of your slides, or Notes pages displaying speaker notes below an image of the slide.

Activity 1.11 | Viewing a Slide Show

MOS
1.2.2

When you view a presentation as an electronic slide show, the entire slide fills the computer screen, and an audience can view your presentation if your computer is connected to a projection system.

1 On the ribbon, click the **Slide Show tab**. In the **Start Slide Show group**, click **From Beginning**. Compare your slide with Figure 1.24.

> The first slide fills the screen, displaying the presentation as the audience would see it if your computer was connected to a projection system.

ANOTHER WAY   Press [F5] to start the slide show from the beginning. Or, display the first slide you want to show and click the Slide Show button on the lower right side of the status bar.

MAC TIP   On the Slide Show tab click Play from Start.

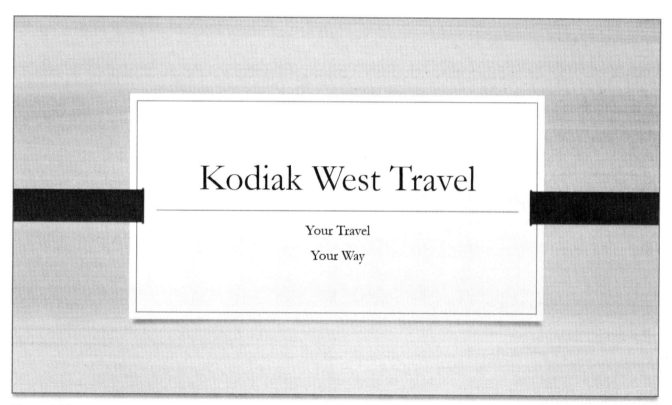

Figure 1.24

2 Click the left mouse button or press [Spacebar] to advance to the second slide.

3 Continue to click or press [Spacebar] until the last slide displays, and then click or press [Spacebar] one more time to display a ***black slide***—a slide that displays after the last slide in a presentation indicating that the presentation is over.

4 With the black slide displayed, click the left mouse button to exit the slide show and return to the presentation.

ANOTHER WAY   Press (Esc) to exit the slide show.

Activity 1.12 | Using Presenter View

1.4.5

Presenter View shows the full-screen slide show on one monitor or projection screen for the audience to see, while enabling the presenter to view a preview of the next slide, notes, and a timer on another monitor.

1 On the **Slide Show tab**, in the **Monitors** group, if necessary, select the Use Presenter View check box. Hold down (Alt) and press (F5). Take a moment to study the parts of the PowerPoint Presenter View window described in the table in Figure 1.25.

If you do not have two monitors, you can practice using Presenter View by pressing (Alt) + (F5). You will see only the presenter's view—not the audience's view—in this mode.

ALERT   Alt + F5 does not open Presenter View

On a notebook computer, you may need to press the Fn or Function Lock key to override the preassigned function of the F5 key.

MAC TIP   On the Slide Show tab, click Presenter View. Point to the current slide to display Presenter View tools.

Microsoft PowerPoint Presenter View Elements	
Screen Element	**Description**
0:00:00 ‖ ↻	**Timer:** running time, pause timer, and reset timer options
✎	**Pen and laser pointer tools:** point to or annotate slides during a presentation
⊞	**See all slides:** displays all slides on the screen to easily navigate between them
🔍	**Zoom into the slide:** focus on a part of a slide while presenting
🖥	**Black or unblack slide show:** hide or unhide the presentation
⊙	**More slide show options:** including hide presenter view, help, pause, and end show
◉ and ▶	**Navigation buttons:** move back and forth through the presentation
⟲ SHOW TASKBAR ⟱ DISPLAY SETTINGS ▼ ⟱ END SLIDE SHOW	**Presenter View ribbon:** controls slide presentation display options
A˄	**Notes pane text size adjustment:** make notes text larger or smaller

Figure 1.25

2 Below the current slide, click the **Advance to the next animation or slide arrow** ▶ to display **Slide 2**.

👆 **BY TOUCH**   Advance to the next slide by swiping the current slide to the left.

3 In the upper right corner of the **Presenter View** window, point to the next slide—*Our Expertise*—and then click. Notice that the notes that you typed on **Slide 3** display. Compare your screen with Figure 1.26.

Clicking the image of the next slide advances the presentation.

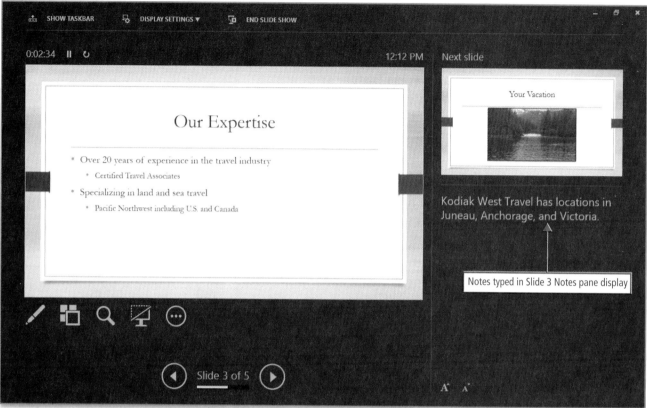

Figure 1.26

4 Below the notes, click **Make the text larger** to increase the font size of the notes in Presenter view to make the notes easier to read.

5 Below the current slide, click the second button—**See all slides** . Compare your screen with Figure 1.27.

A thumbnail view of all of the slides in your presentation displays. Here you can quickly move to another slide, if for example, you want to review a concept or answer a question related to a slide other than the current slide.

MAC TIP All slides are visible below the current slide in Presenter View.

Figure 1.27

6 ▸ Click **Slide 4** to make Slide 4 the current slide in Presenter View. Below the current slide, click the third button—**Zoom into the slide** 🔍. Move the 🔍 pointer to the middle of the picture on the current slide, and then click to zoom in on the picture. Notice that the 🖑 pointer displays. Compare your slide with Figure 1.28.

> With the 🖑 pointer displayed, you can move the zoomed image to draw close-up attention to a specific part of your slide.

BY TOUCH   Touch the current slide with two fingers and then pinch together to zoom in or stretch your fingers apart to zoom out.

MAC TIP   The Zoom into the slide feature is not available in the Mac version of PowerPoint.

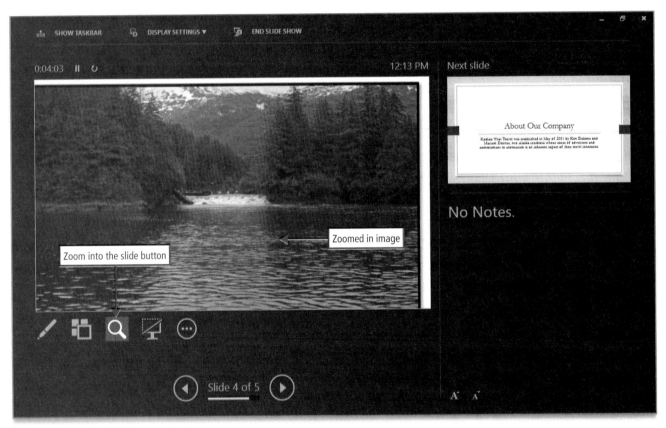

Figure 1.28

7 ▸ Below the current slide, click the **Advance to the next animation or slide arrow** 🔘 to display **Slide 5.** At the top of the **Presenter View** window, click **END SLIDE SHOW** to return to your presentation.

Activity 1.13 | Inserting Headers and Footers on Slide Handouts

A *header* is text that prints at the top of each sheet of *slide handouts* or *notes pages*. Slide handouts are printed images of slides on a sheet of paper. These can be given to customers to follow along and take notes during the presentation. Notes pages are printouts that contain the slide image on the top half of the page and notes that you have created in the Notes pane in the lower half of the page.

In addition to headers, you can insert *footers*—text that displays at the bottom of every slide or that prints at the bottom of a sheet of slide handouts or notes pages.

1 Click the **Insert tab**, in the **Text group**, click **Header & Footer** to display the **Header and Footer** dialog box.

2 In the **Header and Footer** dialog box, click the **Notes and Handouts tab**. Under **Include on page**, select the **Date and time** check box, and as you do so, watch the Preview box in the upper right corner of the Header and Footer dialog box.

> The two narrow rectangular boxes at the top of the Preview box are placeholders for the header text and date. When you select the Date and time check box, the placeholder in the upper right corner is outlined, indicating the location in which the date will display.

3 Be sure that the **Update automatically** option button is selected so that the current date prints on the notes and handouts each time the presentation is printed. If it is not selected, click the Update automatically option button.

4 Verify that the **Page number** check box is selected and select it if it is not. If necessary, clear the Header check box to omit this element. Notice that in the **Preview** box, the corresponding placeholder is not selected.

5 Select the **Footer** check box, and then click in the **Footer** box. Type **1A_KWT_Overview** so that the file name displays as a footer, and then compare your dialog box with Figure 1.29.

Figure 1.29

6 In the lower right corner of the dialog box, click **Apply to All**. Save your presentation.

Activity 1.14 | Inserting Slide Numbers on Slides

MOS
1.2.3,
2.2.3

In this Activity, you will insert the slide numbers on the presentation slides.

1 Display **Slide 1**. On the **Insert tab**, in the **Text group**, click **Header & Footer** to display the **Header and Footer** dialog box.

2 In the **Header and Footer** dialog box, if necessary, click the Slide tab. Under **Include on slide**, select the **Slide number** check box, and then select the **Don't show on title slide** check box. Verify that all other check boxes are cleared, and then compare your screen with Figure 1.30.

> Selecting the *Don't show on title slide* check box omits the slide number from the first slide in a presentation.

Figure 1.30

3. Click **Apply to All**, and then notice that on the first slide, the slide number does not display.

4. Display **Slide 2**, and then notice that the slide number displays in the lower right area of the slide. Display each slide in the presentation and notice the placement of the slide number.

   The position of the slide number and other header and footer information is determined by the theme applied to the presentation.

5. Click **File** to redisplay **Backstage** view. On the Info tab, click **Show All Properties**. In the list of **Properties**, click to the right of **Tags**, and then type company overview

6. Click to the right of **Subject**, and then type your course name and section number. Under **Related People**, be sure that your name displays as the author, and edit if necessary.

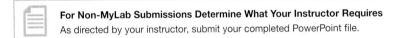 **MAC TIP**   Click the File menu, click Properties, click the Summary tab, and instead of Tags, use the Keywords box.

7. Click **Save** 🖫. If you will not be completing the following optional Activity, on the right end of the title bar, click **Close** ✕ to close the presentation and close PowerPoint.

For Non-MyLab Submissions Determine What Your Instructor Requires
As directed by your instructor, submit your completed PowerPoint file.

---

8. In **MyLab IT**, in your **Course Materials**, locate and click the Grader Project **PowerPoint 1A KWT Overview**. In **step 3**, under **Upload Completed Assignment**, click **Choose File**. In the **Open** dialog box, navigate to your **PowerPoint Chapter 1 folder**, and then click your **Student_PowerPoint_1A_KWT_Overview** file one time to select it. In the lower right corner of the **Open** dialog box, click **Open**.

   The name of your selected file displays above the Upload button.

9. To submit your file to **MyLab IT** for grading, click **Upload**, wait a moment for a green **Success!** message, and then in **step 4**, click the blue **Submit for Grading** button. Click **Close Assignment** to return to your list of **Course Materials**.

ALERT Optional Activities for Non-MyLab IT Submissions

Activities 1.15 and 1.16, in which you print handouts and notes, are optional. Check with your instructor to see if you should complete these Activities. These Activities are not available as MyLab IT Grader projects.

Activity 1.15 │ Printing Presentation Handouts

MOS
1.3.3

Use Backstage view to preview the arrangement of slides and to print your presentation.

1 If necessary, open your **Student_PowerPoint_1A_KWT_Overview** presentation. Display **Slide 1**. Click **File** to display **Backstage** view, and then click **Print**.

The Print tab displays the tools you need to select your settings and view a preview of your presentation. On the right, Print Preview displays your presentation exactly as it will print. If your system is not connected to a color printer, your slide may display in black and white.

2 Under **Settings**, click **Full Page Slides**, and then compare your screen with Figure 1.31.

The gallery displays either the default print setting—Full Page Slides—or the most recently selected print setting.

MAC TIP In the Print window, click Show Details. Under Layout, click Slides.

Figure 1.31

3 In the gallery, under **Handouts**, click **6 Slides Horizontal**. Notice that the **Print Preview** on the right displays the slide handout, and that the current date, file name, and page number display in the header and footer. Compare your screen with Figure 1.32.

In the Settings group, the Portrait Orientation option displays; here you can change the print orientation from Portrait to Landscape.

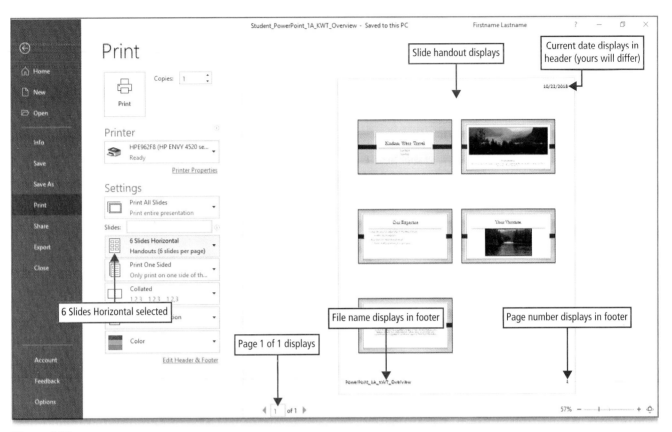

Figure 1.32

4 To create an electronic image of your handouts that looks like printed handouts, skip this step and continue to Step 5. To print your handout document on paper using the default printer on your system, in the upper left portion of the screen, click **Print**.

> The handout will print on your default printer—on a black and white printer, the colors will print in shades of gray. To save the cost of color ink, you can print in grayscale by clicking the Color button. Backstage view closes and your file redisplays in the PowerPoint window.

5 To create an electronic image of your presentation that looks like a printed document, on the left click **Export**. On the right, click the **Create PDF/XPS** button to display the **Publish as PDF or XPS** dialog box.

6 In the **Publish as PDF or XPS** dialog box, click **Options.** Under **Publish what**, click the **Slides arrow**, and then click **Handouts.** Be sure **Slides per page** is set to **6** and **Order** is set to **Horizontal.** Click **OK.**

MAC TIP   In the Print window, click the PDF arrow, and then click Save as PDF.

7 Navigate to your **PowerPoint Chapter 1** folder, and then click **Publish**. If your Adobe Acrobat or Reader program displays your PDF, close the PDF file. If your PDF displays in Microsoft Edge, in the upper right corner click Close ⊠. Notice that your presentation redisplays in PowerPoint.

Activity 1.16 | Printing Speaker Notes

1 On the **Print tab**, under **Settings**, click **6 Slides Horizontal**, and then under **Print Layout**, click **Notes Pages** to view the presentation notes for **Slide 1**; recall that you created notes for **Slide 3**.

Indicated below the Notes page are the current slide number and the number of pages that will print when Notes Pages is selected. You can use the Next Page and Previous Page arrows to display each Notes page in the presentation.

2 At the bottom of the **Print Preview**, click **Next Page** ▶ two times so that **Page 3** displays. Notice that the notes that you typed for Slide 3 display below the image of the slide. Compare your screen with Figure 1.33.

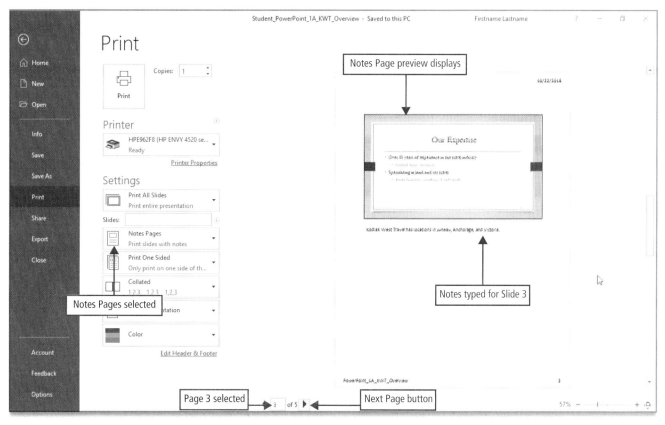

Figure 1.33

3 Under **Settings**, click in the **Slides box**. Type **3** and then click **Notes Pages**. In the lower section, click **Frame Slides**. Under **Printer**, click the printer arrow, click **Microsoft Print to PDF**, and then click **Print** to print your presentation to a PDF file.

Microsoft Print to PDF is an automatically installed printer option in Windows 10, which enables you to create an image that looks like a printed document.

ALERT   No Microsoft Print to PDF Printer Option Available

If you are using Windows 7 or 8, select the Microsoft XPS Document Writer printer instead to print your presentation to the XPS format, a Microsoft file format that also creates an image of your document and that opens in the XPS viewer.

4 Navigate to the location where you store your files for this chapter, name the file **Lastname_Firstname_1A_KWT_Overview_Notes** and then click **Save** 🖫. **Close** PowerPoint.

You have completed Project 1A   **END**

»» GO! With Google Slides

Objective   Create a Company Overview Presentation in Google Slides

ALERT   Working with Web-Based Applications and Services

Computer programs and services on the web receive continuous updates and improvements, so the steps to complete this web-based activity may differ from the ones shown. You can often look at the screens and the information presented to determine how to complete the activity.

 If you do not already have a Google account, you will need to create one before you begin this activity. Go to http://google.com and in the upper right corner, click Sign in. On the Sign In screen, click Use another account, click Create Account. On the Create your Google Account page, complete the form, read and agree to the Terms of Service and Privacy Policy, and then click Next step. On the Welcome screen, click Get Started.

Activity │ Creating a Company Overview Presentation in Google Slides

 In this Activity, you will use Google Slides to create a presentation similar to the one you created in Project 1A.

1 From the desktop, open your browser, navigate to **http://google.com**, and sign in to your Google account. Click **Google apps** ⬚ and click Drive ⬤. Open your **GO! Web Projects** folder—or click New to create and then open this folder if necessary.

2 In the left pane, click **New**, and then click **Google Slides**. In the **Themes** pane, click **Tropic**. If this theme is not available, select another theme. **Close** the **Themes** pane.

3 At the top of the window, click **Untitled presentation** and then, using your own name, type **Lastname_Firstname_1A_Google_Slides** as the file name and then press Enter.

4 In the title placeholder, type **Kodiak West Travel** and then in the subtitle placeholder type **Your Travel - Your Way**

5 On the **toolbar**, click the **New slide with layout arrow** ⊞ , and then click **Caption**.

6 On the **toolbar**, click **Image** 🖼. Click **Upload from computer**. Navigate to your student data files, and then click **p01A_Glacier**. Click **Open**.

7 In the text placeholder, type **Your Dreams**

8 On the **toolbar**, click the **New slide with layout arrow** ⊞ , and then click **Title and body**. In the title placeholder, type **Our Expertise**

9 Click in the content placeholder. On the toolbar, if necessary, click More, and click **Bulleted list** ▤ . In the placeholder, type **Over 20 years of experience in the travel industry** and then press Enter. Press Tab. Type **Certified Travel Associates** and then press Enter. On toolbar, if necessary, click More, and then click **Decrease indent** ⬚ . Type **Specializing in land and sea travel** and then press Enter. Press Tab and then type **Pacific Northwest including U.S. and Canada**

10 Below the slide, click in the **Notes** pane. Type **Kodiak West Travel has locations in Juneau, Anchorage, and Victoria.** Compare your screen to Figure A.

11 In the upper right, click the **Present button arrow**, click **Present from beginning**. Click the left mouse button to progress through the presentation. When the last slide displays, press Esc or click **Exit**.

12 Your presentation will be saved automatically. If you are instructed to submit your file, click the File menu, point to Download as, and then click Microsoft PowerPoint, PDF Document, or another format as directed by your instructor. The file will download to your default download folder as determined by your browser settings. Sign out of your Google account and close your browser.

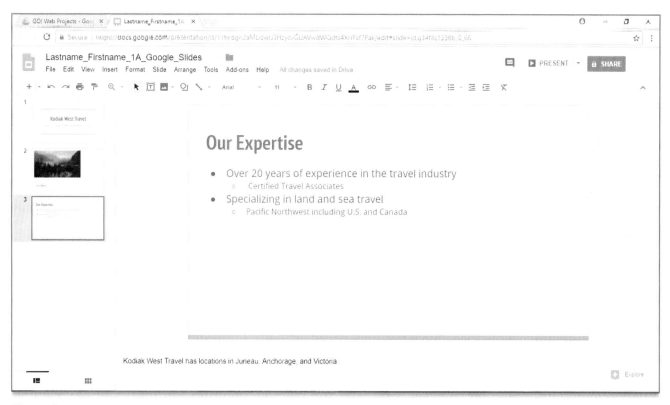

Figure A

PROJECT
1B

Itinerary
Presentation

MyLab IT
Project 1B Grader for Instruction
Project 1B Simulation for Training and Review

Project Activities

In Activities 1.17 through 1.33, you will combine two presentations that the marketing team at Kodiak West Travel developed describing itinerary ideas when visiting Seattle before or after a cruise. You will insert slides from one presentation into another, and then you will rearrange and delete slides. You will also apply font formatting and slide transitions to the presentation. Your completed presentation will look similar to Figure 1.34.

 ## Project Files for MyLab IT Grader

1. In your **MyLab IT** course, locate and click **PowerPoint 1B Seattle**, Download Materials, and then Download All Files.
2. Extract the zipped folder to your PowerPoint Chapter 1 folder. Close the Grader download screens.
3. Take a moment to open the downloaded **PowerPoint_1B_Seattle_Instructions**; note any recent updates to the book.

Project Results

Figure 1.34 Project 1B Seattle

For Non-MyLab Submissions

For Project 1B, you will need:
p01B_Seattle
p01B_Slides

In your PowerPoint Chapter 1 folder, save your presentation as:
Lastname_Firstname_1B_Seattle

After you have named and saved your presentation, on the next page, begin with Step 2.

Objective 5 | Edit an Existing Presentation

ALERT Because Office 365 is a cloud-based subscription service that receives continuous updates, you may encounter some variations in what appears on your screen and what is shown in this instruction. Microsoft Office 365 is fully installed on your PC or Mac; no internet access is necessary to create or edit documents. When you *are* connected to the internet, you will receive monthly upgrades and new features, so you always have the latest versions of Office apps as soon as they are available. Your subscription gives you continuous free access to the latest innovations and refinements.

GO! Learn How
Video P1-5

Recall that editing refers to the process of adding, deleting, and modifying presentation content. You can edit presentation content in either the Slide pane or in the presentation outline.

Activity 1.17 | Changing Slide Size

1.2.1

Presentations created with one of the new themes in PowerPoint default to a widescreen format using a 16:9 *aspect ratio*—the ratio of the width of a display to the height of the display. This slide size is similar to most television and computer monitor screens. Previous versions of PowerPoint used a squarer format with a 4:3 aspect ratio.

1 Navigate to your **PowerPoint Chapter 1 folder**, and then double-click the downloaded PowerPoint file that displays your name—**Student_PowerPoint_1B_Seattle**. In your presentation, if necessary, at the top click **Enable Editing**.

2 Notice that **Slide 1** displays in a squarish format.

3 On the **Design tab**, in the **Customize group**, click **Slide Size**, and then click **Widescreen (16:9)**. Compare your screen with Figure 1.35 and notice that the slide fills the slide pane. **Save** the presentation.

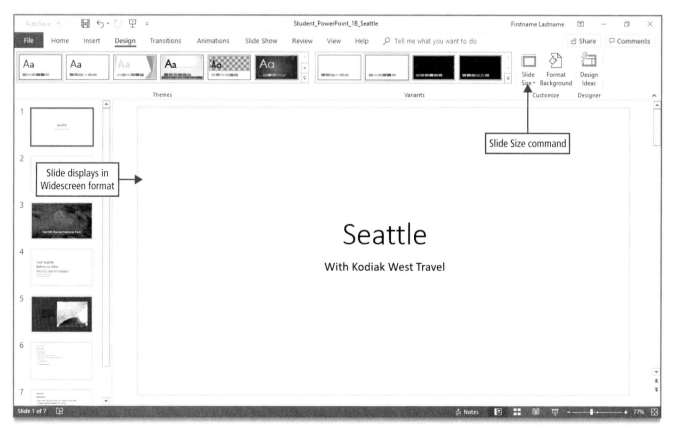

Figure 1.35

Activity 1.18 | Inserting Slides from an Existing Presentation

2.1.2

Presentation content is commonly shared among group members in an organization. Rather than re-creating slides, you can insert slides from an existing presentation into the current presentation. In this Activity, you will insert slides from an existing presentation into your 1B_Seattle presentation.

1 With **Slide 1** displayed, on the **Home tab**, in the **Slides group**, click the **New Slide arrow** to display the **Slide Layout** gallery and additional commands for inserting slides. Compare your screen with Figure 1.36.

Figure 1.36

2 Below the gallery, click **Reuse Slides** to open the Reuse Slides pane on the right side of the PowerPoint window.

3 In the **Reuse Slides** pane, click **Browse**. In the **Browse** dialog box, navigate to the data files downloaded with this project, and then double-click **p01B_Slides** to display the slides from this presentation in the Reuse Slides pane.

4 At the bottom of the **Reuse Slides** pane, be sure that the **Keep source formatting** check box is *cleared*, and then compare your screen with Figure 1.37.

When the *Keep source formatting* check box is cleared, the theme formatting of the presentation into which the slides are inserted is applied. When the *Keep source formatting* check box is selected, you retain the formatting of the slides when inserted into the presentation.

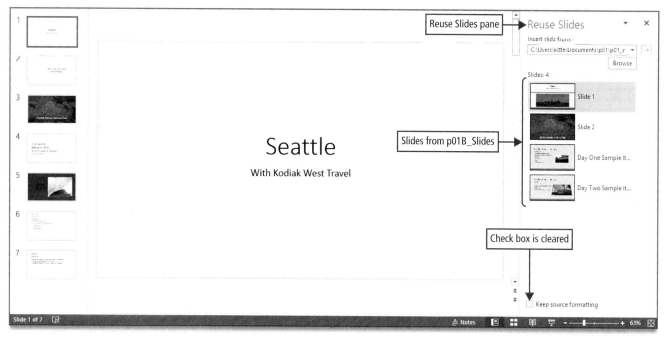

Figure 1.37

5 In the **Reuse Slides** pane, point to each slide to view a ScreenTip displaying the file name and the slide title.

6 In the **Reuse Slides** pane, click the first slide to insert the slide after **Slide 1** in your Seattle presentation. Notice that the inserted slide adopts the color of your Seattle presentation theme.

NOTE   Inserting Slides

You can insert slides into your presentation in any order; remember to display the slide that will come before the slide that you want to insert.

MAC TIP   Mac users can only insert all slides from an existing presentation. With Slide 1 selected, on the Home tab, click the New Slide arrow, click Reuse Slides, and navigate to the data files for this project. Double-click p01B_Slides to insert all four slides into your presentation after Slide 1. Select and press (delete) to delete Slide 3—*Visit Mt. Rainier National Park!* and Slide 4—*Day One Sample Itinerary*. Drag the new Slide 3—*Day Two Sample Itinerary* after the existing Slide 7. Skip to Step 9.

7 In your **1B_Seattle** presentation, in the slide thumbnails, click **Slide 7** to display it in the **Slide pane**.

8 In the **Reuse Slides** pane, click the fourth slide, *Day Two Sample Itinerary*, to insert it after **Slide 7**.

Your presentation contains nine slides. When a presentation contains a large number of slides, a scroll box displays to the right of the slide thumbnails so that you can scroll and then select the thumbnails.

9 **Close** ⊠ the **Reuse Slides** pane, and then **Save** 🖫 the presentation.

MORE KNOWLEDGE   Inserting All Slides

You can insert all of the slides from an existing presentation into the current presentation at one time. In the Reuse Slides pane, right-click one of the slides that you want to insert, and then click Insert All Slides.

Activity 1.19 | Displaying and Editing the Presentation Outline

MOS
1.2.2

Outline View displays the presentation outline to the left of the Slide pane. You can use the outline to edit the presentation text. Changes that you make in the outline are immediately displayed in the Slide pane.

1 To the right of the slide thumbnails, if necessary, drag the scroll box up, and then click **Slide 1** to display it in the Slide pane. On the **View tab**, in the **Presentation Views group**, click **Outline View**. Compare your screen with Figure 1.38.

The outline displays at the left of the PowerPoint window in place of the slide thumbnails. Each slide in the outline displays the slide number, slide icon, and the slide title in bold. Slides that do not display a slide title in the outline use a slide layout that does not include a title, for example, the Blank layout.

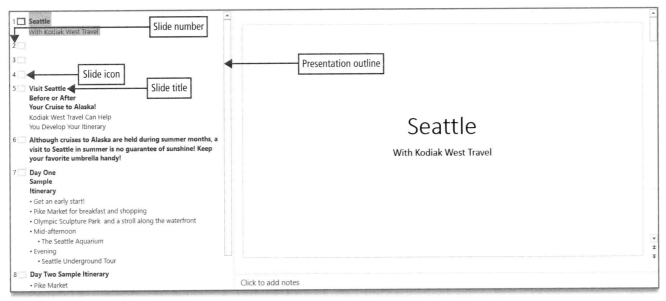

Figure 1.38

2 In the **Outline**, in **Slide 7**, drag to select the text of the second and third bullet points—*Pike Market for breakfast and shopping*, and *Olympic Sculpture Park and a stroll along the waterfront*. Compare your screen with Figure 1.39.

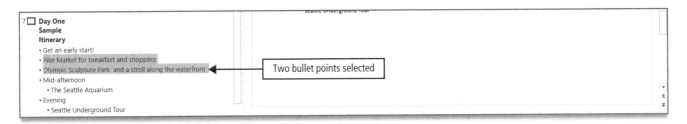

Figure 1.39

3 On the **Home tab**, in the **Paragraph group**, click **Increase List Level** one time to increase the list level of the selected bullet points.

When you type in the outline or change the list level, the changes also display in the Slide pane.

4 In the **Outline**, in **Slide 7**, click at the end of the last bullet point after the word *Tour*. Press Enter to create a new bullet point at the same list level as the previous bullet point. Type **Pike Place Market for dinner** and then compare your screen with Figure 1.40.

Figure 1.40

5 In the **Status bar**, click **Normal** 🔲 to close Outline View and redisplay the slide thumbnails. **Save** 🔲 the presentation.

> You can type text in the Slide pane or in the Outline. Displaying the Outline enables you to view the entire flow of the presentation text.

Activity 1.20 | Deleting and Moving a Slide

MOS
2.3.2

1 To the right of the slide thumbnails, locate the vertical scroll bar and scroll box. If necessary, drag the scroll box down so that **Slide 9** displays in the slide thumbnails. Click **Slide 9** to display it in the Slide pane. Press Delete to delete the slide from the presentation.

> Your presentation contains eight slides.

2 If necessary, scroll the slide thumbnails so that **Slide 4** displays. Point to **Slide 4**, hold down the left mouse button, and then drag down to position the **Slide 4** thumbnail below the **Slide 8** thumbnail. Release the mouse button, and then compare your screen with Figure 1.41. **Save** 🔲 the presentation.

> You can easily rearrange your slides by dragging a slide thumbnail to a new location in the presentation.

BY TOUCH   Use your finger to drag the slide you want to move to a new location in the presentation.

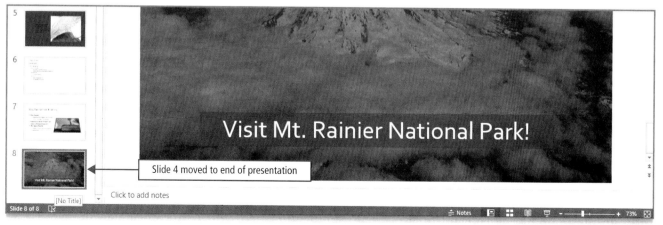

Figure 1.41

Activity 1.21 | Finding and Replacing Text

The Replace command enables you to locate all occurrences of specified text and replace it with alternative text.

1 Display **Slide 1**. On the **Home tab**, in the **Editing group**, click **Replace**. In the **Replace** dialog box, in the **Find what** box, type **Pike Market** and then in the **Replace with** box, type **Pike Place Market** Compare your screen with Figure 1.42.

MAC TIP Find and Replace are in the Edit menu.

Figure 1.42

2 In the **Replace** dialog box, click **Replace All** to display a message box indicating that two replacements were made.

3 In the message box, click **OK**. **Close** ☒ the **Replace** dialog box, and then click **Save** 🖫.

Objective 6 **Format a Presentation**

GO! Learn How
Video P1-6

Formatting refers to changing the appearance of the text, layout, and design of a slide. Recall that a theme is a set of unified design elements that provides a look for your presentation by applying colors, fonts, and effects.

Activity 1.22 | Applying a Theme Variant

Each PowerPoint theme includes several *variants*—variations on the theme style and color. The themes and variants that are available on your system may vary.

1 On the **Design tab**, in the **Variants group**, notice that four variants of the current theme display and the second variant is applied.

2 Point to each of the variants to view the change to **Slide 1**.

If you do not see the same variants, refer to the figures for this activity.

3 With **Slide 1** displayed, in the **Variants group**, point to the **third variant**, and then right-click. Compare your screen with Figure 1.43.

The shortcut menu displays options for applying the variant.

Figure 1.43

> **4** Click **Apply to Selected Slides** to apply the variant to **Slide 1** only. Compare your screen with Figure 1.44.

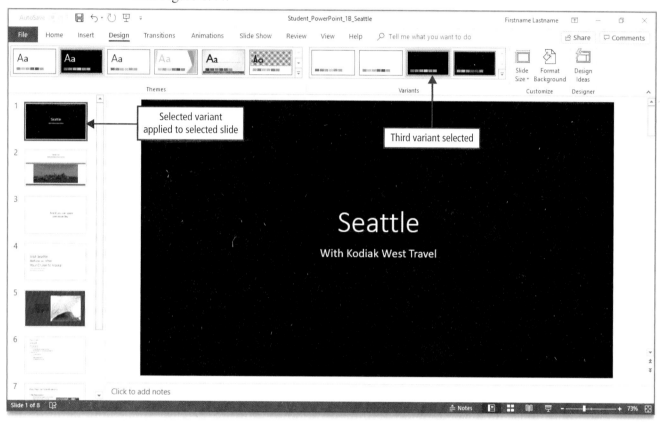

Figure 1.44

> **5** In the **Variants group**, right-click the **second variant**. On the shortcut menu, click **Apply to All Slides** so that the original variant color is applied to all of the slides in the presentation. **Save** your presentation.

🔄 **ANOTHER WAY**   Click Undo to remove the variant you applied in step 4.

Activity 1.23 | Changing Fonts and Font Sizes

A font is a set of characters with the same design and shape and fonts are measured in points. Font styles include bold, italic, and underline, and you can apply any combination of these styles to presentation text. Font styles and font color are useful to provide emphasis and are a visual cue to draw the reader's eye to important text.

> **1** Display **Slide 2**. Select all of the text in the title placeholder, point to the mini toolbar, and then click the **Font arrow** to display the available fonts. Scroll the font list, and then click **Georgia**.

🖥 **MAC TIP**   Use the formatting options on the Home tab.

2 Select the first line of the title—*Seattle*. On the mini toolbar, click the **Font Size arrow** and then click **80**.

3 Select the second line of the title—*Making the Most of Your First Port*. On the **Home tab**, in the **Font group**, click the **Font Size arrow**, and then click **36**. Click in a blank area of the slide to cancel your selection, and then compare your screen with Figure 1.45. **Save** 🖫 your presentation.

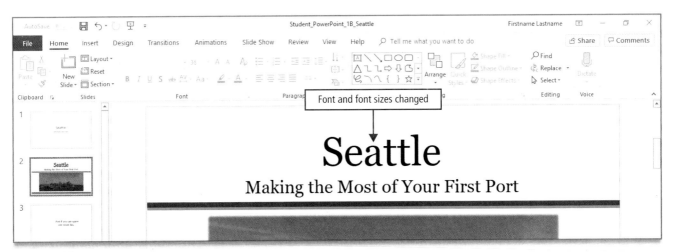

Figure 1.45

Activity 1.24 | Changing Font Styles and Font Colors

Font styles include bold, italic, and underline, and you can apply any combination of these styles to presentation text. Font styles and font color are useful to provide emphasis and are a visual cue to draw the reader's eye to important text.

1 Display **Slide 3**, and then select both lines of text. On the **Home tab**, in the **Font group**, click the **Font Color arrow** 🔺 and then compare your screen with Figure 1.46.

The colors in the top row of the color gallery are the colors associated with the presentation theme—*Frame*. The colors in the rows below the first row are light and dark variations of the theme colors.

Figure 1.46

2 ▶ Point to several of the colors and notice that a ScreenTip displays the color name and Live Preview displays the selected text in the color to which you are pointing.

3 ▶ Under Theme Colors, in the fifth column of colors, click the last color to change the font color. Notice that on the **Home tab**, the lower part of the **Font Color** button displays the most recently applied font color.

> When you click the Font Color button instead of the Font Color button arrow, the color displayed in the lower part of the Font Color button is applied to selected text without displaying the color gallery.

4 ▶ With the two lines of text still selected, right-click within the selected text to redisplay the mini toolbar, and then from the mini toolbar, apply **Bold** and **Italic**.

5 ▶ Display **Slide 4**, and then select the title—*Visit Seattle Before or After Your Cruise to Alaska!* On the mini toolbar, click **Font Color** [A ▾] to apply the most recently applied font color to the selection. Select the subtitle—*Kodiak West Travel Can Help You Develop Your Itinerary*—and then change the **Font Color** to most recently applied color. Compare your screen with Figure 1.47. **Save** [💾] your presentation.

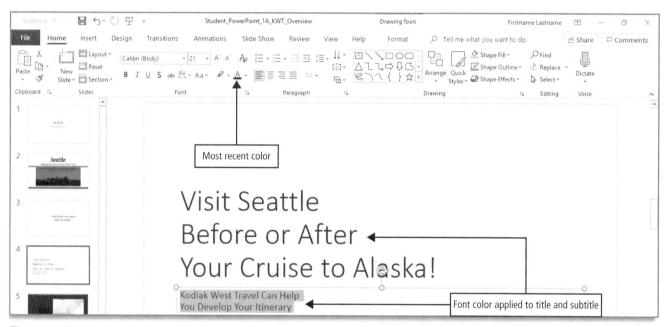

Figure 1.47

Activity 1.25 | Aligning Text

In PowerPoint, ***text alignment*** refers to the horizontal placement of text within a placeholder. You can align text left, centered, right, or justified.

1 ▶ Display **Slide 5**, and then select all of the text in the paragraph. Click the **Font Color arrow** [A ▾] and change the font color to the first color in the first column.

2 ▶ On the **Home tab**, in the **Paragraph group**, click **Center** [≡] to center the text within the placeholder.

3 ▶ Display **Slide 4**, and then click anywhere in the slide title. Press [Ctrl] + [E] to use the keyboard shortcut to center the text.

4 On **Slide 4**, using one of the methods that you practiced, **Center** the subtitle. Click in a blank area of the slide. Compare your screen with Figure 1.48 and then **Save** 🖫 the presentation.

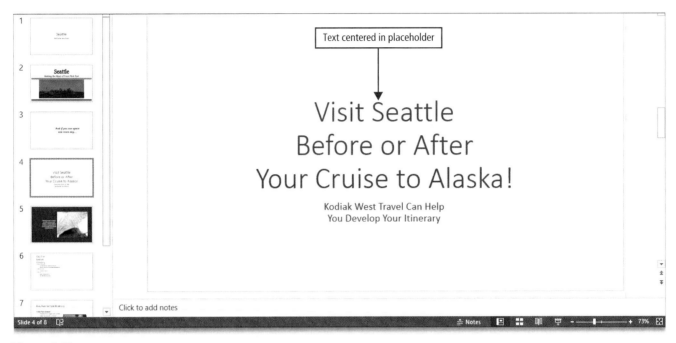

Figure 1.48

Activity 1.26 │ Changing Line Spacing

1 Display **Slide 5**, and then click anywhere in the paragraph. On the **Home tab**, in the **Paragraph group**, click **Line Spacing** 🔳▾. In the list, click **2.0** to change from single spacing to double spacing between lines of text. Compare your screen with Figure 1.49.

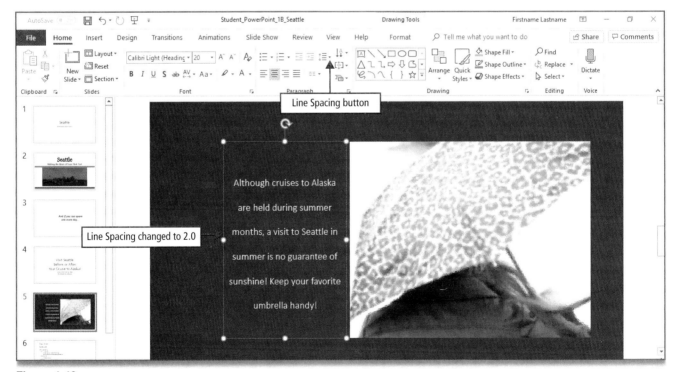

Figure 1.49

2 **Save** 🖫 your presentation.

Activity 1.27 | Changing the Slide Layout

The slide layout defines the placement of the content placeholders on a slide. PowerPoint includes predefined layouts that you can apply to your slide for arranging slide elements. For example, a Title Slide contains two placeholder elements—the title and the subtitle. When you design your slides, consider the content that you want to include, and then choose a layout with the elements that will display the message you want to convey in the best way.

1 ▶ Display **Slide 1**. On the **Home tab**, in the **Slides group**, click **Layout** to display the **Slide Layout** gallery. Notice that *Title Slide* is selected, indicating the layout of the current slide.

2 ▶ Click **Section Header** to change the slide layout. Compare your screen with Figure 1.50, and then **Save** 🖫 your presentation.

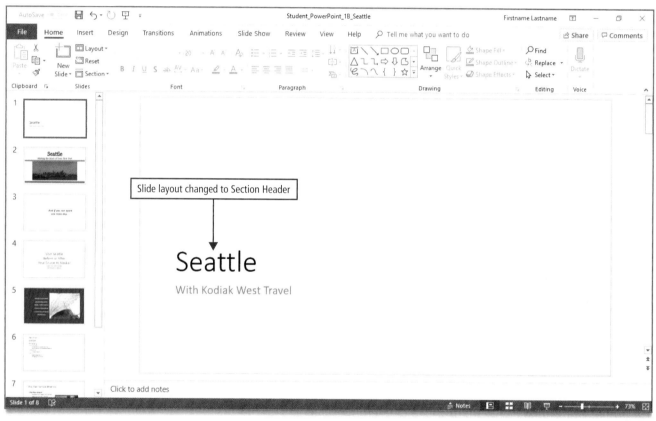

Figure 1.50

Objective 7 | Use Slide Sorter View

GO! Learn How
Video P1-7

Slide Sorter view displays thumbnails of all of the slides in a presentation. Use Slide Sorter view to rearrange and delete slides and to apply formatting to multiple slides.

Activity 1.28 | Deleting Slides in Slide Sorter View

1 In the lower right corner of the PowerPoint window, click **Slide Sorter** ⊞ to display all of the slide thumbnails. Compare your screen with Figure 1.51.

Your slides may display larger or smaller than those shown in Figure 1.51.

> 🔄 **ANOTHER WAY** On the View tab, in the Presentation Views group, click Slide Sorter.

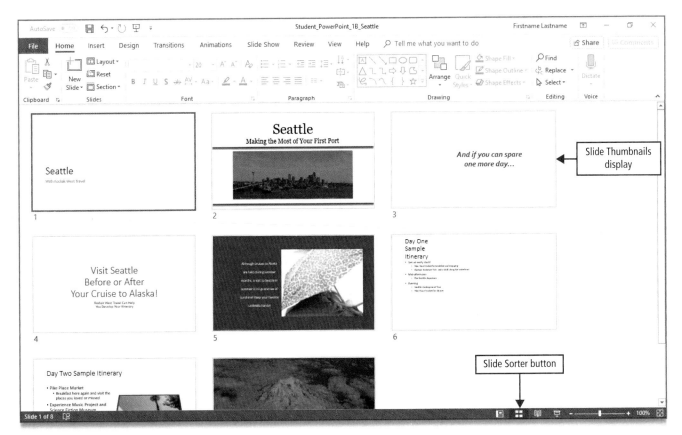

Figure 1.51

2 If necessary, click Slide 1, and notice that a thick outline surrounds the slide, indicating that it is selected. On your keyboard, press ⌞Delete⌝ to delete the slide. Click **Save** 💾.

Activity 1.29 | Moving a Single Slide in Slide Sorter View

1 With the presentation displayed in Slide Sorter view, point to **Slide 2**. Hold down the left mouse button, and then drag to position the slide to the right of **Slide 6**, as shown in Figure 1.52.

Figure 1.52

> **2** Release the mouse button to move the slide to the **Slide 6** position in the presentation. **Save** 🖫 your presentation.

Activity 1.30 | Selecting Contiguous and Noncontiguous Slides and Moving Multiple Slides

MOS
2.3.2

Contiguous slides are slides that are adjacent to each other in a presentation. *Noncontiguous slides* are slides that are not adjacent to each other in a presentation.

> **1** Click **Slide 2**, hold down Ctrl, click **Slide 4**, release Ctrl. Notice that both slides are selected.

The noncontiguous slides—Slides 2 and 4—are outlined, indicating that both are selected. By holding down Ctrl, you can select noncontiguous slides.

⌐⌐ **MAC TIP** Hold down command ⌘ + click.

> **2** Click **Slide 3**, so that only Slide 3 is selected. Hold down Shift, click **Slide 5**, and then release Shift. Compare your screen with Figure 1.53.

The contiguous slides—Slides 3, 4, and 5—are outlined, indicating that all three slides are selected. By holding down Shift, you can create a group of contiguous selected slides.

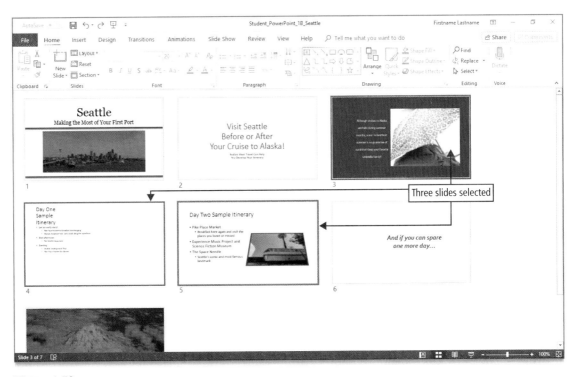

Figure 1.53

3 With **Slides 3, 4,** and **5** selected, hold down Ctrl, and then click **Slide 3**. Notice that only **Slides 4** and **5** are selected.

With a group of selected slides, you can press Ctrl and then click a selected slide to *deselect* it.

4 Point to either of the selected slides, hold down the left mouse button, and then drag to position the two slides to the right of **Slide 2**. Compare your screen with Figure 1.54.

The selected slides are dragged as a group, and the number 2 in the upper left area of the selected slides indicates the number of slides that you are moving.

Figure 1.54

5 Release the mouse button to reposition the slides. On the View tab, click **Normal** 🔲 to return to Normal view. **Save** 🔲 your presentation.

<table>
<tr><td>**Objective 8**</td><td>**Apply Slide Transitions**</td></tr>
</table>

GO! Learn How
Video P1-8

Slide transitions are the motion effects that occur in Slide Show view when you move from one slide to the next during a presentation. You can choose from a variety of transitions, and you can control the speed and method with which the slides advance.

Activity 1.31 | Applying Slide Transitions to a Presentation

MOS
5.1.1, 5.1.2

In this Activity, you will apply a slide transition to all the slides in the presentation.

1 Display **Slide 1**. On the **Transitions tab**, in the **Transition to This Slide group**, click **More** to display the **Transitions** gallery. Compare your screen with Figure 1.55.

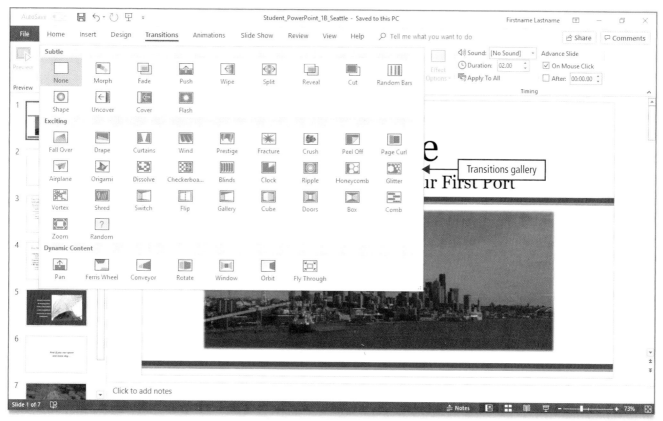

Figure 1.55

2 Under **Subtle**, click **Fade** to apply and view the transition. In the **Transition to This Slide group**, click **Effect Options** to display the way the slide enters the screen. Click **Smoothly**. In the **Timing group**, click **Apply To All** to apply the *Fade, Smoothly* transition to all of the slides in the presentation. **Save** 🔲 your presentation.

The Effect Options vary depending on the selected transition. In the slide thumbnails, a star displays below the slide number providing a visual cue that a transition has been applied to the slide.

Activity 1.32 | Setting Slide Transition Timing Options

MOS
5.3.2

In this Activity, you will modify the duration of the transition—the amount of time it takes for the transition to complete.

1 In the **Timing group**, notice that the **Duration** box displays *00.70*, indicating that the transition lasts 0.70 seconds. Click the **Duration up spin arrow** several times until *01.75* displays. Under **Advance Slide**, verify that the **On Mouse Click** check box is selected. Compare your screen with Figure 1.56.

With On Mouse Click selected, the presenter controls when the current slide advances to the next slide by clicking the mouse button or by pressing Spacebar.

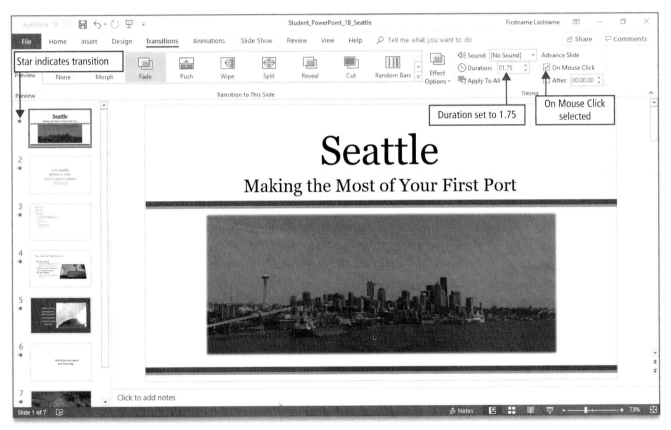

Figure 1.56

2 In the **Timing group**, click **Apply To All** so that the Duration of *1.75* seconds transition is applied to all of the slides in the presentation.

3 Click the **Slide Show tab**. In the **Start Slide Show group**, click **From Beginning**, and then view your presentation, clicking the mouse button to advance through the slides. When the black slide displays, click the mouse button one more time to display the presentation in Normal view. **Save** your presentation.

MORE KNOWLEDGE **Applying Multiple Slide Transitions**

You can apply more than one type of transition in your presentation by displaying the slides one at a time, and then clicking the transition that you want to apply instead of clicking Apply To All.

Activity 1.33 | Displaying a Presentation in Reading View

MOS
1.2.2, 1.2.3

Organizations frequently conduct online meetings when participants are unable to meet in one location. The *Reading view* in PowerPoint displays a presentation in a manner similar to a slide show but the taskbar, title bar, and status bar remain available in the presentation window. Thus, a presenter can easily facilitate an online conference by switching to another window without closing the slide show. This is useful for Kodiak West Travel because employees are frequently on the road and attend online meetings.

1 In the lower right corner of the PowerPoint window, click **Reading View** 📖. Compare your screen with Figure 1.57.

In Reading view, the status bar contains the Next and Previous buttons, which are used to navigate in the presentation, and the Menu button which is used to print, copy, and edit slides.

ANOTHER WAY On the View tab, in the Presentation Views group, click Reading View.

MAC TIP Reading view is not available in the Mac version of PowerPoint. Skip to Step 4.

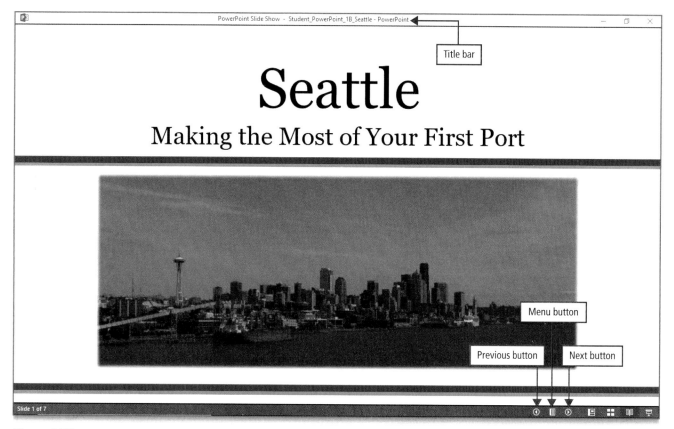

Figure 1.57

2 Press Spacebar to display **Slide 2**. Click the left mouse button to display **Slide 3**. In the status bar, click **Previous** ◯ to display **Slide 2**.

3 In the status bar, click **Menu** 🔳 to display the Reading view menu, and then click **End Show** to return to Normal view.

4 On the **Insert tab**, in the **Text group**, click **Header & Footer**, and then click the **Notes and Handouts tab**. Under **Include on page**, select the **Date and time** check box, and if necessary, select Update automatically. If necessary, select the **Page number** check box and clear the **Header** check box. Select the **Footer** check box, in the **Footer** box, type **1B_Seattle** and then click **Apply to All**.

5 Display **Backstage** view. On the Info tab, on the right, at the bottom of the **Properties** list, click **Show All Properties**. On the list of properties, click to the right of **Tags**, and then type **Seattle** To the right of **Subject**, type your course name and section number. Under **Related People**, be sure that your name displays as the author; edit if necessary.

6 On the left, scroll up as necessary, and then click **Save** 🖫.

For Non-MyLab Submissions Determine What Your Instructor Requires
As directed by your instructor, submit your completed PowerPoint presentation.

---

7 **Close** ⊠ PowerPoint.

8 In **MyLab IT**, in your **Course Materials**, locate and click the Grader Project **PowerPoint 1B Seattle**. In **step 3**, under **Upload Completed Assignment**, click **Choose File**. In the **Open** dialog box, navigate to your **PowerPoint Chapter 1 folder**, and then click your **Student_PowerPoint_1B_Seattle** file one time to select it. In the lower right corner of the **Open** dialog box, click **Open**.

The name of your selected file displays above the Upload button.

9 To submit your file to **MyLab IT** for grading, click **Upload**, wait a moment for a green **Success!** message, and then in **step 4**, click the blue **Submit for Grading** button. Click **Close Assignment** to return to your list of **Course Materials**.

You have completed Project 1B **END**

Objective | **Create an Itinerary Presentation in Google Slides**

ALERT **Working with Web-Based Applications and Services**

Computer programs and services on the web receive continuous updates and improvements, so the steps to complete this web-based activity may differ from the ones shown. You can often look at the screens and the information presented to determine how to complete the activity.

If you do not already have a Google account, you will need to create one before you begin this activity.

Activity | Creating an Itinerary Presentation in Google Slides

In this Activity, you will use Google Slides to create a presentation similar to the one you created in Project 1B.

1 From the desktop, open your browser, navigate to **http://google.com**, and then sign in to your Google account. Click the **Google apps** icon [⠿] and then click **Drive** [△].

Open your **GO! Web Projects** folder—or create and then open this folder, if necessary.

2 In the left pane, click **New**, and then click **File upload** [🗋]. Navigate to your student data files, click **p01_1B_Web**, and then click **Open**.

3 Wait a moment for the upload to complete, point to the uploaded file **p01_1B_Google_Slides.pptx**, and then right-click. On the shortcut menu, click **Rename**. Delete the existing text, and then using your own last name and first name, type **Lastname_Firstname_1B_Google_Slides** Click **OK** to rename the file.

4 Right-click the file that you just renamed, point to **Open with**, and then click **Google Slides**.

5 On **Slide 1**, in the Title placeholder, drag to select the two lines of text. On the **toolbar**, click the **Font arrow** [▾], and then click **Georgia**.

6 Select the text *Making the Most of Your First Port*. On the **toolbar**, click the **Font Size arrow** [10], and then click **24**.

7 Click **Slide 2**. Click the **Edit menu**, and then click **Delete** to remove the slide from the presentation.

8 With **Slide 2**—*Seattle Weather*—displayed, press [Delete] to remove the slide from your presentation. Notice that the presentation contains seven slides.

9 Display **Slide 3**, and then click in the paragraph on the left side of the slide. Drag to select the text, and then on the **toolbar**, click **Text color** [A]. Under **Theme**,

click the second color—**Theme Color white**. With the paragraph still selected, on the toolbar, click **Bold** [B] and **Italic** [I]. Click **Align** [≡ ▾] and click **Center** [≡]. Click anywhere in a blank area of the slide to cancel the selection and view your changes.

10 In the slide thumbnails, point to **Slide 4**, hold down the left mouse button, and then drag up slightly. Notice that a black bar displays above **Slide 4**. Continue to drag up until the black bar displays above **Slide 3**. Release the mouse button to move the slide.

11 Using the technique that you just practiced, move **Slide 5** to position it above **Slide 4**.

12 Display **Slide 6**. Select all three lines of text. Click **Align** [≡ ▾], and then click **Center** [≡]. Click anywhere on the slide to cancel the selection. Click **Slide 1** and compare your screen with Figure A.

13 Display **Slide 1**. At the right end of the toolbar, click **Transition** to open the **Animations** pane. On the right, in the Animations pane, click **No transition button**, click **Slide from right**, and then click **Apply to all slides**.

14 To the right of the **menu bar**, click the **Present button arrow**, and then click **Present from beginning**. If necessary, click Allow. Click the left mouse button to progress through the presentation. When the last slide displays, press [Esc] or in the lower left corner, click **Exit**.

15 Your presentation will be saved automatically. Download as Microsoft PowerPoint, PDF Document, or another format, and submit as directed by your instructor. Sign out of your Google account and close your browser.

»» GO! With Google Slides continues on next page

»»» GO! With Google Slides

Figure A

wavebreakmedia/Shutterstock, Monkey Business Images/Fotolia, Ivanko80/Shutterstock, Monkey Business Images/Shutterstock

Microsoft Office Specialist (MOS) Skills in This Chapter	
Project 1A	**Project 1B**
1.2.2 Display presentations in different views	**1.2.1** Change slide size
1.2.3 Set basic file properties	**1.2.2** Display presentations in different views
1.3.2 Print notes pages	**1.2.3** Set basic file properties
1.3.3 Print handouts	**2.1.2** Insert slides from another presentation
1.4.5 Present slide shows by using Presenter View	**2.3.2** Modify slide order
2.1.3 Insert slides and select slide layouts	**5.1.1** Apply basic and 3D slide transitions
2.2.3 Insert slide headers, footers, and page numbers	**5.1.2** Configure transition effects
3.1.3 Create bulleted and numbered lists	**5.3.2** Configure transition start and finish options
3.3.2 Apply built-in styles and effects to images	

Build Your E-Portfolio

An E-Portfolio is a collection of evidence, stored electronically, that showcases what you have accomplished while completing your education. Collecting and then sharing your work products with potential employers reflects your academic and career goals. Your completed documents from the following projects are good examples to show what you have learned: 1G, 1K, and 1L.

GO! for Job Success

Video: Personal Branding

Your instructor may assign this video to your class, and then ask you to think about, or discuss with your classmates, these questions:

g-stockstudio/Shutterstock

How do you suggest job seekers communicate their unique value—their personal brand—to potential employers online?

What are the best ways to network online and offline?

What are some of the biggest pitfalls in using social media to communicate a personal brand?

End of Chapter

Summary

In this chapter, you started a new presentation in PowerPoint. You inserted slides with various layouts, and you entered, edited, and formatted text. You also inserted text from another PowerPoint file.

Use a presentation theme to establish a unified presentation design. You can change the color of the presentation theme by applying one of the predefined variants that are supplied with each theme.

Presentations are often organized in a manner similar to outlines. List levels represent outline levels and are identified by the bullet style, indentation, and text size.

Slide layout defines the placement of content placeholders on a slide. Each presentation theme includes predefined layouts that you can apply to slides for the purpose of arranging slide elements.

GO! Learn It Online

Review the concepts, key terms, and MOS skills in this chapter by completing these online challenges, which you can find at **MyLab IT**.

Chapter Quiz: Answer matching and multiple choice questions to test what you learned in this chapter.

Lessons on the GO!: Learn how to use all the new apps and features as they are introduced by Microsoft.

MOS Prep Quiz: Answer questions to review the MOS skills that you practiced in this chapter.

GO! Collaborative Team Project (Available in Instructor Resource Center)

If your instructor assigns this project to your class, you can expect to work with one or more of your classmates—either in person or by using internet tools—to create work products similar to those that you created in this chapter. A team is a group of workers who work together to solve a problem, make a decision, or create a work product. Collaboration is when you work together with others as a team in an intellectual endeavor to complete a shared task or achieve a shared goal.

Monkey Business Images/Fotolia

Project Guide for PowerPoint Chapter 1

Your instructor will assign Projects from this list to ensure your learning and assess your knowledge.

	Apply Skills from These Chapter Objectives	Project Type		Project Location
Project Guide for PowerPoint Chapter 1				
1A **MyLab IT**	Objectives 1–4 from Project 1A	**1A Instructional Project (Grader Project)** **Instruction** Guided instruction to learn the skills in Project A.		In **MyLab IT** and in text
1B **MyLab IT**	Objectives 5–8 from Project 1B	**1B Instructional Project (Grader Project)** **Instruction** Guided instruction to learn the skills in Project B.		In **MyLab IT** and in text
1C	Objectives 1–4 from Project 1A	**1C Skills Review (Scorecard Grading)** **Review** A guided review of the skills from Project 1A.		In text
1D	Objectives 5–8 from Project 1B	**1D Skills Review (Scorecard Grading)** **Review** A guided review of the skills from Project 1B.		In text
1E **MyLab IT**	Objectives 1–4 from Project 1A	**1E Mastery (Grader Project)** **Mastery and Transfer of Learning** A demonstration of your mastery of the skills in Project 1A with extensive decision making.		In **MyLab IT** and in text
1F **MyLab IT**	Objectives 5–8 from Project 1B	**1F Mastery (Grader Project)** **Mastery and Transfer of Learning** A demonstration of your mastery of the skills in Project 1B with extensive decision making.		In **MyLab IT** and in text
1G **MyLab IT**	Objectives 1–8 from Projects 1A and 1B	**1G Mastery (Grader Project)** **Mastery and Transfer of Learning** A demonstration of your mastery of the skills in Projects 1A and 1B with extensive decision making.		In **MyLab IT** and in text
1H	Combination of Objectives from Projects 1A and 1B	**1H GO! Fix It (Scorecard Grading)** **Critical Thinking** A demonstration of your mastery of the skills in Projects 1A and 1B by creating a correct result from a document that contains errors you must find.		IRC
1I	Combination of Objectives from Projects 1A and 1B	**1I GO! Make It (Scorecard Grading)** **Critical Thinking** A demonstration of your mastery of the skills in Projects 1A and 1B by creating a result from a supplied picture.		IRC
1J	Combination of Objectives from Projects 1A and 1B	**1J GO! Solve It (Rubric Grading)** **Critical Thinking** A demonstration of your mastery of the skills in Projects 1A and 1B, your decision-making skills, and your critical thinking skills. A task-specific rubric helps you self-assess your result.		IRC
1K	Combination of Objectives from Projects 1A and 1B	**1K GO! Solve It (Rubric Grading)** **Critical Thinking** A demonstration of your mastery of the skills in Projects 1A and 1B, your decision-making skills, and your critical thinking skills. A task-specific rubric helps you self-assess your result.		In text
1L	Combination of Objectives from Projects 1A and 1B	**1L GO! Think (Rubric Grading)** **Critical Thinking** A demonstration of your understanding of the chapter concepts applied in a manner that you would outside of college. An analytic rubric helps you and your instructor grade the quality of your work by comparing it to the work an expert in the discipline would create.		In text
1M	Combination of Objectives from Projects 1A and 1B	**1M GO! Think (Rubric Grading)** **Critical Thinking** A demonstration of your understanding of the chapter concepts applied in a manner that you would outside of college. An analytic rubric helps you and your instructor grade the quality of your work by comparing it to the work an expert in the discipline would create.		IRC
1N	Combination of Objectives from Projects 1A and 1B	**1N You and GO! (Rubric Grading)** **Critical Thinking** A demonstration of your understanding of the chapter concepts applied in a manner that you would in a personal situation. An analytic rubric helps you and your instructor grade the quality of your work.		IRC
1O	Combination of Objectives from Projects 1A and 1B	**1O Collaborative Team Project for PowerPoint Chapter 1** **Critical Thinking** A demonstration of your understanding of concepts and your ability to work collaboratively in a group role-playing assessment, requiring both collaboration and self-management.		IRC

Glossary

Glossary of Chapter Key Terms

Artistic effects Formats applied to images that make pictures resemble sketches or paintings.

Aspect ratio The ratio of the width of a display to the height of the display.

Black slide A slide that displays after the last slide in a presentation indicating that the presentation is over.

Contiguous slides Slides that are adjacent to each other in a presentation.

Editing The process of modifying a presentation by adding and deleting slides or by changing the contents of individual slides.

Footer Text that displays at the bottom of every slide or that prints at the bottom of a sheet of slide handouts or notes pages.

Formatting The process of changing the appearance of the text, layout, and design of a slide.

Header Text that prints at the top of each sheet of slide handouts or notes pages.

Layout The arrangement of elements, such as title and subtitle text, lists, pictures, tables, charts, shapes, and movies, on a slide.

List level An outline level in a presentation represented by a bullet symbol and identified in a slide by the indentation and the size of the text.

Noncontiguous slides Slides that are not adjacent to each other in a presentation.

Normal view The primary editing view in PowerPoint where you write and design your presentations.

Notes page A printout that contains the slide image on the top half of the page and notes that you have created on the Notes pane in the lower half of the page.

Notes pane An area of the Normal view window that displays below the Slide pane with space to type notes regarding the active slide.

Outline view A PowerPoint view that displays the presentation outline to the left of the Slide pane.

Placeholder A box on a slide with dotted or dashed borders that holds title and body text or other content such as charts, tables, and pictures.

Presenter view A view that shows the full-screen slide show on one monitor or projection screen while enabling the presenter to view a preview of the next slide, notes, and a timer on another monitor.

Reading view A view in PowerPoint that displays a presentation in a manner similar to a slide show but in which the taskbar, title bar, and status bar remain available in the presentation window.

Rotation handle A circular arrow that provides a way to rotate a selected image.

Section header A type of slide layout that changes the look and flow of a presentation by providing text placeholders that do not contain bullet points.

Sizing handles Small circles surrounding a picture that indicate that the picture is selected.

Slide A presentation page that can contain text, pictures, tables, charts, and other multimedia or graphic objects.

Slide handout Printed images of slides on a sheet of paper.

Slide pane A PowerPoint screen element that displays a large image of the active slide.

Slide Sorter view A presentation view that displays thumbnails of all of the slides in a presentation.

Slide transitions Motion effects that occur in Slide Show view when you move from one slide to the next during a presentation.

Split button A type of button in which clicking the main part of the button performs a command and clicking the arrow opens a menu, list, or gallery.

Style A collection of formatting options that you can apply to a picture, text, or an object.

Text alignment The horizontal placement of text within a placeholder.

Theme A set of unified design elements that provides a look for your presentation by applying colors, fonts, and effects.

Thumbnails Miniature images of presentation slides.

Title slide A slide layout—most commonly the first slide in a presentation—that provides an introduction to the presentation topic.

Variant A variation on the presentation theme style and color.

Chapter Review

Skills Review Project 1C Glaciers

Apply 1A skills from these Objectives:

1. Create a New Presentation
2. Edit a Presentation in Normal View
3. Add Pictures to a Presentation
4. Print and View a Presentation

In the following Skills Review, you will create a new presentation by inserting content and pictures, adding notes and footers, and applying a presentation theme. Your completed presentation will look similar to Figure 1.58.

Project Files

For Project 1C, you will need:

New blank PowerPoint presentation
p01C_Glacier_Bay
p01C_Ice
p01C_Ship

You will save your presentation as:

Lastname_Firstname_1C_Glaciers

Project Results

Figure 1.58 Project 1C Glaciers

(continues on next page)

Chapter Review

1 Start PowerPoint. On the right, if necessary, click Find More, click **Slice**, and then click **Create.** On the **Quick Access Toolbar**, click **Save** 🖫. Under **Save As**, click **Browse**. Navigate to your **PowerPoint Chapter 1** folder. In the **File name** box, using your own name, replace the existing text with **Lastname_Firstname_1C_Glaciers** and then click **Save**. In the **Slide pane**, click in the text *Click to add title*. Type **Glacier Bay** and then click in the subtitle placeholder. Type **Part One in a Series of Alaskan Passage Adventures**

a. On the **Home tab**, in the **Slides group**, click the **New Slide arrow**, and then in the gallery, click **Two Content**. Click the text *Click to add title*, and then type **About the Park**

2 On the left side of the slide, click in the content placeholder. Type **Located in the Southeast Alaskan Wilderness** and then press ⌅. Press ⭾. Type **3.3 million acres** and then press ⌅. Type **A national park and preserve** and then press ⌅.

a. On the **Home tab**, in the **Paragraph group**, click **Decrease List Level**. Type **Visitor season** and then press ⌅. On the **Home tab**, in the **Paragraph group**, click **Increase List Level**. Type **May to September**

b. On the **Home tab**, in the **Slides group**, click the **New Slide arrow**, and then in the gallery, click **Panoramic Picture with Caption**. In the lower portion of the slide, click the text *Click to add title*, and then type **Prepare to be Amazed!**

c. Click in the text placeholder. Type **Before you reach Glacier Bay, walk around your cruise ship to find the best viewing locations. Make sure your camera battery is charged!**

d. On the **Home tab**, in the **Slides group**, click the **New Slide arrow**, and then in the gallery, click **Content with Caption**. In the title placeholder, type **Learn More!**

e. Click in the text placeholder on the right, and then type **A national park ranger will board your ship during your visit to Glacier Bay. Check your ship's itinerary for presentation information and locations.**

3 With **Slide 4** displayed, in the **Status bar**, click **Notes**. Click in the **Notes pane**, and then type **Your cruise ship will spend between 6 and 8 hours in Glacier Bay.**

a. On the left side of the PowerPoint window, in the slide thumbnails, click **Slide 1**. Click in the subtitle placeholder after the *n* in *Alaskan*. Press ⌴, and then type **Inside**

b. In the slide thumbnails, click **Slide 2**, and then click at the end of the last bullet point after the word *September*. Press ⌅, and then type **Be prepared for rain**

4 With **Slide 2** displayed, in the placeholder on the right side of the slide, click **Pictures**. Navigate to your data files for this project, and then click **p01C_Glacier_Bay**. Click **Insert**. If necessary, close the Design Ideas pane.

a. With the picture selected, on the **Format tab**, in the **Picture Styles group**, click **More** ⛛ to display the **Picture Styles** gallery. Point to several styles to display a ScreenTip, and then locate and click **Beveled Oval, Black**.

b. Display **Slide 3**. In the Picture placeholder, click **Pictures**. Navigate to your student data files, and then click **p01C_Ice**. Click **Insert**.

c. Display **Slide 4**. In the content placeholder on the left side of the slide, click **Pictures**. Navigate to the data files for this project, and then insert **p01C_Ship**. On the **Format tab**, in the **Picture Styles group**, click **More** ⛛ to display the **Picture Styles** gallery. Point to each style to display a ScreenTip, and then locate and click **Soft Edge Rectangle**.

d. With the picture still selected, on the **Format tab**, in the **Adjust group**, click **Artistic Effects** to display the gallery. Point to each effect to display a ScreenTip, and then locate and click **Crisscross Etching**.

5 On the **Slide Show tab**, in the **Start Slide Show group**, click **From Beginning**. (Mac users click Play from Start.)

a. Click the left mouse button or press ⌴ to advance to the second slide. Continue to click or press ⌴ until the last slide displays, and then click or press ⌴ one more time to display a black slide.

b. With the black slide displayed, click the left mouse button or press ⌴ to exit the slide show and return to the presentation.

(continues on next page)

Chapter Review

6 ▶ Click the **Insert tab**, and then in the **Text group**, click **Header & Footer** to display the **Header and Footer** dialog box.

a. In the **Header and Footer** dialog box, click the **Notes and Handouts tab**. Under **Include on page**, select the **Date and time** check box. If necessary, click the Update automatically option button so that the current date prints on the notes and handouts.

b. Select the **Page number** check box. If necessary, clear the Header check box to omit this element. Select the **Footer** check box. In the **Footer** box, type **1C_Glaciers** and then click **Apply to All**.

c. In the upper left corner of your screen, click the **File** tab to display **Backstage** view.On the right, at the bottom of the **Properties list**, click **Show All**

Properties. (Mac users, click the File menu, click Properties, click the Summary tab, and instead of Tags, use the Keywords box.)

d. On the list of Properties, click to the right of **Tags** to display an empty box, and then type **Glacier Bay** Click to the right of **Subject** to display an empty box, and then type your course name and section number. Under **Related People**, be sure that your name displays as the author; edit if necessary.

e. **Save** your presentation. As directed by your instructor, create and submit a paper printout or an electronic image of your presentation that looks like a printed document; or, submit your completed PowerPoint file. **Close** PowerPoint.

You have completed Project 1C   END

Chapter Review

Skills Review **Project 1D Photography**

Apply 1B skills from these Objectives:

5. Edit an Existing Presentation
6. Format a Presentation
7. Use Slide Sorter View
8. Apply Slide Transitions

In the following Skills Review, you will edit an existing presentation by inserting slides from another presentation, applying font and slide formatting, and applying slide transitions. Your completed presentation will look similar to Figure 1.59.

Project Files

For Project 1D, you will need:

p01D_Photography
p01D_Photography_Slides

You will save your presentation as:

Lastname_Firstname_1D_Photography

Project Results

Figure 1.59 Project 1D Photography

(continues on next page)

Chapter Review

1 From your student data files, double-click **p01D_Photography** to open it. On the **File tab**, click **Save As**, navigate to your **PowerPoint Chapter 1** folder, and then using your own name, save the file as **Lastname_Firstname_1D_Photography**

a. On the **Design tab**, in the **Customize group**, click **Slide Size**, and then click **Widescreen (16:9)**.

b. With **Slide 1** displayed, on the **Home tab**, in the **Slides group**, click the **New Slide arrow**, and then click **Reuse Slides**. In the **Reuse Slides** pane, click **Browse**. In the **Browse** dialog box, navigate to the data files for this project, and then double-click **p01D_Photography_Slides** to display the slides from this presentation in the **Reuse Slides** pane.

c. At the bottom of the **Reuse Slides** pane, be sure that the **Keep source formatting** check box is *cleared*. In the **Reuse Slides** pane, click the first slide—*Alaskan Wildlife*—to insert the slide after Slide 1.

d. At the left of your screen, in the slide thumbnails, click **Slide 6** to display it in the **Slide pane**. In the **Reuse Slides** pane, click the second slide—*Be Careful*—to insert it after **Slide 6**. **Close** the **Reuse Slides** pane. (Mac users click the New Slide arrow, click Reuse Slides, and navigate to the data files for this project. Double-click p01D_Photography_ Slides to insert all four slides into your presentation after Slide 1. Delete Slide 4—*Lights, Camera, Action*—and Slide 5— *Be aware of the scenery*. Drag the new Slide 3—*Be Careful*—after Slide 6.)

2 Display **Slide 1**. On the **View tab**, in the **Presentation Views group**, click **Outline View**.

a. In the **Outline**, in **Slide 7**, drag to select the second and third bullet points—beginning with *Never approach* and ending with *animal's home*.

b. On the **Home tab**, in the **Paragraph group**, click **Decrease List Level** one time.

c. In the **Outline**, in the same slide, click at the end of the first bullet point after the word *sense*. Press Spacebar, and then type **when photographing wildlife**

d. In the **Status bar**, click **Normal** to display the slide thumbnails.

3 Display **Slide 8**, and then press Delete to delete the slide from the presentation.

a. Display **Slide 1**. On the **Home tab**, in the **Editing group**, click **Replace**. In the **Replace** dialog box, in the **Find what** box, type **home** and then in the **Replace with** box, type **habitat**

b. In the **Replace** dialog box, click **Replace All** to display a message box indicating that one replacement was made. In the message box, click **OK**. **Close** the **Replace** dialog box. (Mac users, click the Edit menu, point to Find, and then click Replace.)

c. On the **Design tab**, in the **Variants group**, right-click the first variant. On the shortcut menu, click **Apply to All Slides** so that the variant color is applied to all of the slides in the presentation.

4 Display **Slide 5**. Select all of the text in the placeholder. On the **Home tab**, in the **Font group**, click the **Font arrow**, scroll the font list, and then click **Arial**. Click the **Font Size arrow**, and then click **32**. In the **Paragraph group**, click **Line Spacing**, and then click **1.5**.

a. Display **Slide 2**. On the **Home tab**, in the **Slides group**, click **Layout** to display the **Slide Layout** gallery. Click **Title Slide** to change the slide layout.

b. On **Slide 2**, select the title—*Alaskan Wildlife*. On the **Home tab**, in the **Font group**, click the **Font Color arrow**. In the fifth column, click the first color— **Dark Red, Accent 1**.

c. Display **Slide 3**, and then select the title—*Lights, Camera, Action*. On the mini toolbar, click **Font Color** to apply the font color **Dark Red, Accent 1**.

d. Display **Slide 4**, and then, click anywhere in the text. On the **Home tab**, in the **Paragraph group**, click **Center** to center the text within the placeholder.

e. Display **Slide 6**, and then select the subtitle. From the mini toolbar, apply **Bold** and **Italic**.

f. In the slide thumbnails, point to **Slide 7**, hold down the left mouse button, and then drag up to position the slide between **Slides 3** and **4**.

5 In the lower right corner of the PowerPoint window, click **Slide Sorter** to display all of the slide thumbnails. Click **Slide 1**, so that it is selected. On your keyboard, press Delete to delete the slide.

a. Click **Slide 4**, and then hold down Ctrl and click **Slide 5**. With both slides selected, point to either of the selected slides, hold down the left mouse button, and then drag to position the two slides to the right of **Slide 6**. Release the mouse button to move the two slides. In the status bar, click **Normal** to return to Normal view.

b. Display **Slide 1**. On the **Transitions tab**, in the **Transition to This Slide group**, click **More** to display the **Transitions** gallery.

(continues on next page)

Chapter Review

c. Under **Exciting**, click **Gallery** to apply and view the transition. In the **Transition to This Slide group**, click **Effect Options**, and then click **From Left**. In the **Timing group**, click **Apply To All** to apply the *Gallery, From Left* transition to all of the slides in the presentation.

d. In the **Timing group**, click the **Duration up spin arrow** so that *01.75* displays. Under **Advance Slide**, verify that the **On Mouse Click** check box is selected; select it if necessary. In the **Timing group**, click **Apply To All**.

e. Click the **Slide Show tab**. In the **Start Slide Show group**, click **From Beginning**, and then view your presentation, clicking the mouse button to advance through the slides. When the black slide displays, click the mouse button one more time to display the presentation in Normal view. (Mac users click Play from Start.)

6 On the **Insert tab**, in the **Text group**, click **Header & Footer** to display the **Header and Footer** dialog box.

a. In the **Header and Footer** dialog box, click the **Notes and Handouts tab**. Under **Include on page**, select the **Date and time** check box. If necessary,

click the Update automatically option button so that the current date prints on the notes and handouts.

b. Select the **Page number** check box. If necessary, clear the Header check box to omit this element. Select the **Footer** check box. In the **Footer** box, type **1D_Photography** and then click **Apply to All**.

c. In the upper left corner of your screen, click the **File** tab to display **Backstage** view.On the right, at the bottom of the **Properties list**, click **Show All Properties**.

d. On the list of Properties, click to the right of **Tags**, and then type **photography** Click to the right of **Subject**, and then type your course name and section number. Under **Related People**, be sure that your name displays as the author. If necessary, right-click the author name, click Edit Property, type your name, and click OK. (Mac users, click the File menu, click Properties, click the Summary tab, and instead of tags, use the Keywords box.)

e. **Save** your presentation. As directed by your instructor, create and submit a paper printout or an electronic image of your presentation that looks like a printed document; or, submit your completed PowerPoint file. **Close** the presentation.

You have completed Project 1D **END**

Content-Based Assessments (Mastery and Transfer of Learning)

Mastering PowerPoint | **Project 1E Juneau**

In the following Mastering PowerPoint project, you will create a new presentation that Kodiak West Travel will use in their promotional materials to describe activities in the city of Juneau. Your completed presentation will look similar to Figure 1.60.

Apply 1A skills from these Objectives:

1. Create a New Presentation
2. Edit a Presentation in Normal View
3. Add Pictures to a Presentation
4. Print and View a Presentation

Project Files for MyLab IT Grader

1. In your **MyLab IT** course, locate and click **PowerPoint 1E Juneau**, Download Materials, and then Download All Files.
2. Extract the zipped folder to your PowerPoint Chapter 1 folder. Close the Grader download screens.
3. Take a moment to open the downloaded **PowerPoint_1E_Juneau_Instructions**; note any recent updates to the book.

Project Results

Figure 1.60 Project 1E Juneau

For Non-MyLab Submissions

For Project 1E, you will need:

p01E_Juneau
p01E_Glacier
p01E_Whale
p01E_Falls

In your PowerPoint Chapter 1 folder, save your presentation as:

Lastname_Firstname_1E_Juneau

After you have named and saved your presentation on the next page, begin with Step 2.

After Step 14, save and submit your file as directed by your instructor.

(continues on next page)

Mastering PowerPoint: Project 1E Juneau (continued)

1 Navigate to your **PowerPoint Chapter 1 folder** and then double-click the PowerPoint file you downloaded from **MyLab IT** that displays your name—**Student_PowerPoint_1E_Juneau**. If necessary, at the top, click **Enable Editing**.

2 As the title of this presentation, type **Juneau Alaska** and as the subtitle, type **Kodiak West Travel**

3 Insert a **New Slide** using the **Content with Caption** layout. In the title placeholder, type **The View from Above**

4 In the content placeholder on the right side of the slide, from the files downloaded with this project, insert the picture **p01E_Aerial_View**. Format the picture with the **Rotated, White** picture style.

5 In the text placeholder on the left, type **View a glacial ice field from above by plane or helicopter. If you are more adventurous, try glacier trekking in Juneau where you can land on a glacier and climb an ice wall.**

6 Insert a **New Slide** using the **Two Content** layout. In the title placeholder, type **On Land and Sea**

7 In the content placeholder on the right, type the following text, increasing and decreasing the list level as shown below. In this presentation theme, the first level bullet points do not include a bullet symbol.

> **On the water**
>> **Whale watching**
>> **Kayaking**
> **Mount Roberts tramway**
>> **Spectacular views of Juneau**
>> **Recreational hiking trails**

8 In the content placeholder on the right, from the files downloaded with this project, insert the picture **p01E_Whale**. Apply the **Reflected Rounded Rectangle** picture style.

9 Insert a new slide with the **Picture with Caption** layout. In the title placeholder, type **Mendenhall Glacier** and then in the picture placeholder, from the files downloaded with this project, insert the picture **p01E_Falls**.

10 In the text placeholder, type **Walk to Mendenhall Glacier from the Visitor Center to get a close-up view of Nugget Falls.**

11 In the **Notes pane**, type **Mendenhall Glacier is the most famous glacier in Juneau and in some years is visited by over 400,000 people.**

12 Insert a **Header & Footer** on the **Notes and Handouts**. Include the **Date and time** updated automatically, the **Page number**, and a **Footer** with the text **1E_Juneau** and apply to all the slides.

13 Display the **Document Properties**. As the **Tags** type **Juneau** As the **Subject** type your course and section number. Be sure your name is indicated as the Author. (Mac users use the Keywords box.)

14 **Save** your presentation, and then view the slide show from the beginning. **Close** the presentation and close PowerPoint.

15 In **MyLab IT**, in your **Course Materials**, locate and click the Grader Project **PowerPoint 1E Juneau**. In **step 3**, under **Upload Completed Assignment**, click **Choose File**. In the **Open** dialog box, navigate to your **PowerPoint Chapter 1 folder**, and then click your **Student_PowerPoint_1E_Juneau** file one time to select it. In the lower right corner of the **Open** dialog box, click **Open**.

The name of your selected file displays above the Upload button.

16 To submit your file to **MyLab IT** for grading, click **Upload**, wait a moment for a green **Success!** message, and then in **step 4**, click the blue **Submit for Grading** button. Click **Close Assignment** to return to your list of **Course Materials**.

You have completed Project 1E **END**

Content-Based Assessments (Mastery and Transfer of Learning)

Mastering PowerPoint   Project 1F Refuge

Apply 1B skills from these Objectives:

5. Edit an Existing Presentation
6. Format a Presentation
7. Use Slide Sorter View
8. Apply Slide Transitions

In the following Mastering PowerPoint project, you will edit a presentation regarding a wildlife refuge where Kodiak West Travel conducts tours. Your completed presentation will look similar to Figure 1.61.

Project Files for **MyLab IT** Grader

1. In your **MyLab IT** course, locate and click **PowerPoint 1F Refuge**, Download Materials, and then Download All Files.
2. Extract the zipped folder to your PowerPoint Chapter 1 folder. Close the Grader download screens.
3. Take a moment to open the downloaded **PowerPoint_1F_Refuge_Instructions**; note any recent updates to the book.

Project Results

Figure 1.61 Project 1F Refuge

For Non-MyLab Submissions

For Project 1F, you will need:
p01F_Refuge
p01F_Excursions

In your PowerPoint Chapter 1 folder, save your workbook as:
Lastname_Firstname_1F_Refuge

After you have named and saved your presentation on the next page, begin with Step 2.
After Step 14, save and submit your file as directed by your instructor.

(continues on next page)

Content-Based Assessments (Mastery and Transfer of Learning)

1 Navigate to your **PowerPoint Chapter 1 folder** and then double-click the PowerPoint file you downloaded from **MyLab IT** that displays your name—**Student_PowerPoint_1F_Refuge**. If necessary, at the top, click **Enable Editing**.

2 Change the **Slide Size** to **Widescreen (16:9)**.

3 Display the presentation **Outline**. In the **Outline**, on **Slide 2**, increase the list level of the third and the fifth bullet points. Click at the end of the last bullet point after the word *roads*, and then type **or facilities**

4 Return the presentation to **Normal view**, and then display **Slide 4**. Display the **Reuse Slides** pane. Browse to open from the files downloaded with this project, **p01F_Excursions**. Make sure the **Keep source formatting** check box is *cleared*. With **Slide 4** in your presentation displayed, insert the last two slides from the **Reuse Slides** pane. (Mac users insert all slides and delete Slide 5—*Wildlife and Excursions*.)

5 Display **Slide 1**, and then change the layout to **Title Slide**.

6 Select the subtitle—*Experience Alaska with Kodiak West Travel*. Change the **Font** to **Arial**, and the **Font Size** to **28**. Change the **Font Color** to **Black, Text 1**. **Center** the title and the subtitle.

7 Display **Slide 5**, and then select the paragraph in the content placeholder. Apply **Bold** and **Italic**, and then change the **Font Size** to **16**.

8 **Center** the paragraph text, and then change the **Line Spacing** to **1.5**. **Center** the slide title.

9 In **Slide Sorter** view, delete **Slide 3**. Move **Slide 5** to position it after **Slide 2**.

10 Move **Slide 4** to the end of the presentation.

11 In **Normal** view, display **Slide 1**. Apply the **Split** transition and change the **Effect Options** to **Horizontal Out**. Change the **Duration** to **1.75** and apply the transition to all of the slides in the presentation. View the slide show from the beginning.

12 Insert a **Header & Footer** on the **Notes and Handouts**. Include the **Date and time** updated automatically, the **Page number**, and a **Footer** with the text **1F_Refuge**

13 Display the **Document Properties**. As the **Tags** type **refuge, tours** As the **Subject** type your course and section number. Be sure your name is indicated as the **Author**. (Mac users use the Keywords box.) **Save** your presentation.

14 In the upper right corner of your screen, click **Close** ☒ to close PowerPoint.

15 In **MyLab IT**, in your **Course Materials**, locate and click the Grader Project **PowerPoint 1F Refuge**. In **step 3**, under **Upload Completed Assignment**, click **Choose File**. In the **Open** dialog box, navigate to your **PowerPoint Chapter 1 folder**, and then click your **Student_PowerPoint_1F_Refuge** file one time to select it. In the lower right corner of the **Open** dialog box, click **Open**.

The name of your selected file displays above the Upload button.

16 To submit your file to **MyLab IT** for grading, click **Upload**, wait a moment for a green **Success!** message, and then in **step 4**, click the blue **Submit for Grading** button. Click **Close Assignment** to return to your list of **Course Materials**.

You have completed Project 1F   **END**

| MyLab IT Grader | **Mastering PowerPoint** Project 1G Northern Lights |

Apply 1A and 1B skills from these Objectives:

1. Create a New Presentation
2. Edit a Presentation in Normal View
3. Add Pictures to a Presentation
4. Print and View a Presentation
5. Edit an Existing Presentation
6. Format a Presentation
7. Use Slide Sorter View
8. Apply Slide Transitions

In the following Mastering PowerPoint project, you will edit an existing presentation that describes the Northern Lights and ideal viewing areas. Your completed presentation will look similar to Figure 1.62.

Project Files for MyLab IT Grader

1. In your **MyLab IT** course, locate and click **PowerPoint 1G Northern Lights**, Download Materials, and then Download All Files.
2. Extract the zipped folder to your PowerPoint Chapter 1 folder. Close the Grader download screens.
3. Take a moment to open the downloaded **PowerPoint_1G_Northern_Lights_Instructions**; note any recent updates to the book.

Project Results

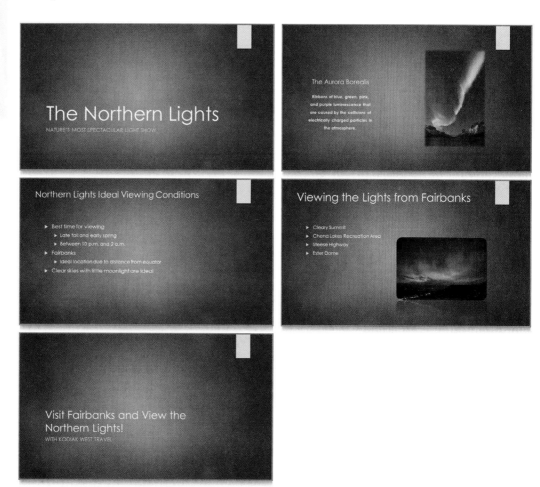

Figure 1.62 Project 1G Northern Lights

For Non-MyLab Submissions

For Project 1G, you will need:
p01G_Northern_Lights
p01G_Lights
p01G_Slides

In your PowerPoint Chapter 1 folder, save your presentation as:
Lastname_Firstname_1G_Northern_Lights

After you have named and saved your presentation on the next page, begin with Step 2.
After Step 17, save and submit your file as directed by your instructor.

Mastering PowerPoint: Project 1G Northern Lights (continued)

1 Navigate to your **PowerPoint Chapter 1 folder,** and then double-click the PowerPoint file you downloaded from **MyLab IT** that displays your name—**Student_PowerPoint_1G_Northern_Lights**. If necessary, at the top, click **Enable Editing**.

2 Replace all occurrences of the text **North** with **Northern** and then change the layout of **Slide 1** to **Title Slide**.

3 Apply the **Ion** theme, with the second, blue variant option.

4 Change the **Slide Size** to **Widescreen (16:9)**.

5 Display **Slide 2**, open the **Reuse Slides** pane, and then from the files downloaded with this project, browse for and open the presentation **p01G_Slides**. If necessary, clear the Keep source formatting check box, and then insert the last two slides from the **p01G_Slides** file. (Mac users insert all slides and delete Slide 3—*Alaska Slides.)*

6 Display **Slide 2**. In either the slide pane or in the slide outline, click at the end of the first bullet point after the word *time*. Add the words **for viewing** and then in the same slide, increase the list level of the second and third bullet points.

7 With **Slide 2** still displayed, select the title and change the **Font Size** to **32**. In the **Notes pane**, type the following notes: **The lights reach their peak in September and March.**

8 Display **Slide 3**. Select the paragraph of text, and then change the **Font Color** to **Green, Accent 6, Lighter 60%**—in the last column, the third color. Change the **Font Size** to **16**, and then apply **Bold**.

9 Change the paragraph **Line Spacing** to **1.5**, and then **Center** the paragraph and the slide title.

10 With **Slide 3** still displayed, format the picture with the **Soft Edge Rectangle** picture style and the **Marker** artistic effect.

11 Display **Slide 4**. In the content placeholder on the right, from your student data files, insert the picture **p01G_Lights**. Apply the **Reflected Rounded Rectangle** picture style.

12 Move **Slide 3** between **Slides 1** and **2**.

13 Display **Slide 4**. Insert a **New Slide** with the **Section Header** layout. In the title placeholder type **Visit Fairbanks and View the Northern Lights!** In the text placeholder, type **With Kodiak West Travel**

14 Apply the **Uncover** transition and change the **Effect Options** to **From Top**. Change the **Timing** by increasing the **Duration** to **01.25**. Apply the transition effect to all of the slides. View the slide show from the beginning.

15 Insert a **Header & Footer** on the **Notes and Handouts**. Include the **Date and time** updated automatically, the **Page number**, and a **Footer**, using your own name, with the text **1G_Northern_Lights**

16 Display the **Document Properties**. As the **Tags,** type **northern lights, Fairbanks** As the **Subject,** type your course and section number. Be sure your name is indicated as the Author. (Mac users use the Keywords box.) **Save** your presentation.

17 In the upper right corner of your screen, click **Close** to close PowerPoint.

18 In **MyLab IT**, in your **Course Materials**, locate and click the Grader Project **PowerPoint 1G Refuge**. In **step 3**, under **Upload Completed Assignment**, click **Choose File**. In the **Open** dialog box, navigate to your **PowerPoint Chapter 1 folder**, and then click your **Student_PowerPoint_1G_Refuge** file one time to select it. In the lower right corner of the **Open** dialog box, click **Open**.

The name of your selected file displays above the Upload button.

19 To submit your file to **MyLab IT** for grading, click **Upload**, wait a moment for a green **Success!** message, and then in **step 4**, click the blue **Submit for Grading** button. Click **Close Assignment** to return to your list of **Course Materials**.

You have completed Project 1G | END

Content-Based Assessments (Critical Thinking)

Apply a combination of the 1A and 1B skills.

GO! Fix It	**Project 1H Rain Forest**	IRC
GO! Make It	**Project 1I Eagles**	IRC
GO! Solve It	**Project 1J Packrafting**	IRC
GO! Solve It	**Project 1K Packing**	

Project Files

For Project 1K, you will need:

p01K_Packing

You will save your presentation as:

Lastname_Firstname_1K_Packing

Open the file p01K_Packing and save it as **Lastname_Firstname_1K_Packing** Complete the presentation by applying a theme and changing the variant. Format the presentation attractively by applying appropriate font formatting and by changing text alignment and line spacing. Change the layout of the last slide to an appropriate layout. On Slide 2, insert a picture that you have taken yourself, or use one of the pictures in your student data files that you inserted in other projects in this chapter. Apply a style to the picture. Apply slide transitions to all of the slides in the presentation, and then insert a header and footer that includes the date and time updated automatically, **1K_Packing** in the footer, and the page number. Add your name, your course name and section number, and the tags **packing, weather** to the properties. Save and print or submit as directed by your instructor.

		Performance Level	
	Exemplary	**Proficient**	**Developing**
Apply a theme and a variant	An appropriate theme and variant were applied to the presentation.	A theme was applied but the variant was not changed.	Neither a theme nor the variant theme were applied.
Apply font and slide formatting	Font and slide formatting is attractive and appropriate.	Adequately formatted but difficult to read or unattractive.	Inadequate or no formatting.
Use appropriate pictures and apply styles attractively	An appropriate picture was inserted and a style is applied attractively.	A picture was inserted but a style was not applied.	Picture was not inserted.
Apply appropriate slide layout to Slide 4	An appropriate layout was applied to the last slide.	The slide layout was changed but is not appropriate for the type of slide.	The slide layout was not changed.

Performance Criteria (vertical label)

You have completed Project 1K | END

Rubric

The following outcomes-based assessments are open-ended assessments. That is, there is no specific correct result; your result will depend on your approach to the information provided. Make Professional Quality your goal. Use the following scoring rubric to guide you in how to approach the problem, and then to evaluate how well your approach solves the problem.

The *criteria*—Software Mastery, Content, Format and Layout, and Process—represent the knowledge and skills you have gained that you can apply to solving the problem. The *levels of performance*—Professional Quality, Approaching Professional Quality, or Needs Quality Improvements—help you and your instructor evaluate your result.

	Your completed project is of Professional Quality if you:	Your completed project is Approaching Professional Quality if you:	Your completed project Needs Quality Improvements if you:
1-Software Mastery	Choose and apply the most appropriate skills, tools, and features and identify efficient methods to solve the problem.	Choose and apply some appropriate skills, tools, and features, but not in the most efficient manner.	Choose inappropriate skills, tools, or features, or are inefficient in solving the problem.
2-Content	Construct a solution that is clear and well organized, contains content that is accurate, appropriate to the audience and purpose, and is complete. Provide a solution that contains no errors of spelling, grammar, or style.	Construct a solution in which some components are unclear, poorly organized, inconsistent, or incomplete. Misjudge the needs of the audience. Have some errors in spelling, grammar, or style, but the errors do not detract from comprehension.	Construct a solution that is unclear, incomplete, or poorly organized, contains some inaccurate or inappropriate content, and contains many errors of spelling, grammar, or style. Do not solve the problem.
3-Format and Layout	Format and arrange all elements to communicate information and ideas, clarify function, illustrate relationships, and indicate relative importance.	Apply appropriate format and layout features to some elements, but not others. Overuse features, causing minor distraction.	Apply format and layout that does not communicate information or ideas clearly. Do not use format and layout features to clarify function, illustrate relationships, or indicate relative importance. Use available features excessively, causing distraction.
4-Process	Use an organized approach that integrates planning, development, self-assessment, revision, and reflection.	Demonstrate an organized approach in some areas, but not others; or, use an insufficient process of organization throughout.	Do not use an organized approach to solve the problem.

Content-Based Assessments (Critical Thinking)

Apply a combination of the 1A and 1B skills.

GO! Think   Project 1L Bears

Project Files

For Project 1L, you will need:

New blank PowerPoint presentation

p01L_Bear

You will save your presentation as:

Lastname_Firstname_1L_Bears

Cindy Barrow, Tour Operations Manager for Kodiak West Travel, is developing a presentation describing brown bear viewing travel experiences that the company is developing. In the presentation, Cindy will be describing the brown bear habitat and viewing opportunities.

Kodiak bears are the largest known size of brown bears on record; they can weigh as much as 2,000 pounds and can get as large as polar bears. Kodiak bears are active during the day and are generally solitary creatures. The Kodiak Bear Travel Experience is a small, personalized travel adventure available to only eight participants at a time. It is an opportunity to peer into the life of these majestic mammals.

The adventure takes place on Kodiak Island near a lake with a high concentration of salmon, making it the perfect natural feeding ground for the Kodiak bears. Travelers can view the bears from boats, kayaks, and recently constructed viewing platforms, and guides are available.

This is a true wildlife experience as the area is home to deer, fox, and river otter. Accommodations are available at the Kodiak West Breakfast Inn from mid-June to the end of August. Peak season is early August, and reservations can be made up to one year in advance. The cost is $1,800 per person for one week, and includes all meals, use of watercraft, and guided tours.

Using the preceding information, create a presentation that Cindy can show at a travel fair. The presentation should include four to six slides describing the travel experience. Apply an appropriate theme and use slide layouts that will effectively present the content. Insert at least one picture and apply appropriate picture formatting. You may use your own image file, search for one online, or from your student data files, use the file p01L_Bear. Apply font formatting and slide transitions and modify text alignment and line spacing as necessary.

Save the file as **Lastname_Firstname_1L_Bears** and then insert a header and footer that include the date and time updated automatically, **1L_Bears** in the footer, and the page number. Add your name, your course name and section number, and the tags **bears, tours** to the properties. Save and print or submit as directed by your instructor.

You have completed Project 1L   END

Content-Based Assessments (Critical Thinking)

GO! Think	**Project 1M Sitka**	IRC
You and GO!	**Project 1N Travel**	IRC
GO! Cumulative Team Project	**Project 1O Bell Orchid Hotels**	IRC

Formatting PowerPoint Presentations

POWERPOINT
2019

Outcomes
Format a presentation to add visual interest and clarity.

Objectives

1. Format Numbered and Bulleted Lists
2. Insert Online Pictures
3. Insert Text Boxes and Shapes
4. Format Objects

Outcomes
Enhance a presentation with WordArt and SmartArt.

Objectives

5. Remove Picture Backgrounds and Insert WordArt
6. Create and Format a SmartArt Graphic
7. Insert a 3D Object

Antonio V. Oquias/Shutterstock

In This Chapter

GO! To Work
with PowerPoint

A well-designed PowerPoint presentation helps the audience understand complex information while keeping them focused on your message. Color is an important element that enhances your slides and draws the audience's interest by creating focus. When designing the background and element colors for your presentation, be sure that the colors you use provide contrast so that the text is visible on the background. Use elements such as images, shapes, and other graphics to enhance your presentation and illustrate your message.

The projects in this chapter relate to **Sensation Park Entertainment Group**, an entertainment company that operates 15 regional theme parks across the United States, Mexico, and Canada. Park types include traditional theme parks, water parks, and animal parks. This year the company will launch three of its new "Sensation Parks" where attractions combine fun and the discovery of math and science information, and where teens and adults enjoy the free Friday night concerts. The company focuses on safe and imaginative attractions that appeal to guests with a variety of entertainment interests, including adventure, science, and the arts.

Employee Training Presentation

Project Activities

In Activities 2.01 through 2.21, you will format a presentation for Marc Johnson, Director of Operations for Sensation Park Entertainment Group, which describes important safety guidelines for employees. Your completed presentation will look similar to Figure 2.1.

Project Files for **MyLab IT** Grader

1. In your storage location, create a folder named **PowerPoint Chapter 2**.
2. In your **MyLab IT** course, locate and click **PowerPoint 2A Safety**, Download Materials, and then Download All Files.
3. Extract the zipped folder to your PowerPoint Chapter 2 folder. Close the Grader download screens.
4. Take a moment to open the downloaded **PowerPoint_2A_Safety_Instructions**; note any recent updates to the book.

Project Results

GO! Project 2A
Where We're Going

Figure 2.1 Project 2A Safety

For Non-MyLab Submissions

For Project 2A, you will need:

p02A_Safety

In your storage location, create a folder named **PowerPoint Chapter 2**

In your PowerPoint Chapter 2 folder, save your presentation as:

Lastname_Firstname_2A_Safety

After you have named and saved your presentation, on the next page, begin with Step 2.

NOTE   If You Are Using a Touch Screen

Tap an item to click it.

Press and hold for a few seconds to right-click; release when the information or commands display.

Touch the screen with two or more fingers and then pinch together or stretch your fingers apart to zoom in and out.

Slide your finger on the screen to scroll—slide left to scroll right and slide right to scroll left.

Slide to rearrange—similar to dragging with a mouse.

Swipe to select—slide an item a short distance with a quick movement—to select an item and bring up commands, if any.

Objective 1   Format Numbered and Bulleted Lists

ALERT   Because Office 365 is a cloud-based subscription service that receives continuous updates, you may encounter some variations in what appears on your screen and what is shown in this instruction. Microsoft Office 365 is fully installed on your PC or Mac; no internet access is necessary to create or edit documents. When you *are* connected to the internet, you will receive monthly upgrades and new features, so you always have the latest versions of Office apps as soon as they are available. Your subscription gives you continuous free access to the latest innovations and refinements.

GO! Learn How
Video P2-1

The font, color, and style of a numbered or bulleted list are determined by the presentation theme; however, you can format these elements by changing the bulleted and numbered list styles and colors. A ***bulleted list***, sometimes called an unordered list, is a list of items preceded by small dots or other shapes, which do not indicate order or rank. In a ***numbered list***, or ordered list, items are preceded by numbers, which indicate sequence or rank of the items.

Activity 2.01 | Selecting Placeholder Text

A placeholder is a box on a slide with dotted or dashed borders that holds title and body text or other content such as charts, tables, and pictures. You can format placeholder contents by selecting text or by selecting the entire placeholder.

> **1** Navigate to your **PowerPoint Chapter 2 folder**, and then double-click the PowerPoint file you downloaded from **MyLab IT** that displays your name—**Student_PowerPoint_2A_Safety**. In your presentation, if necessary, at the top click **Enable Editing**.

> **2** Display **Slide 2**, and then click anywhere in the content placeholder with the single bullet point.

> **3** Point to the dashed border surrounding the placeholder to display the 🔛 pointer, and then click one time to display the border as a solid line. Compare your screen with Figure 2.2.

> When a placeholder's border displays as a solid line, all of the text in the placeholder is selected, and any formatting changes that you make will be applied to *all* of the text in the placeholder.

⬜ **MAC TIP**   The border may not display as a dashed line; however, clicking the border will select all text in the placeholder.

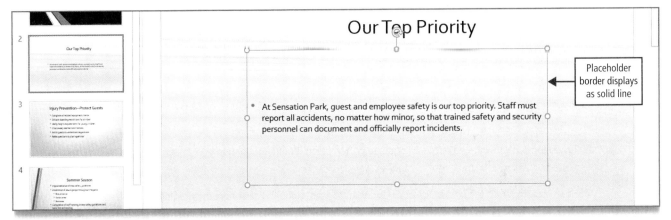

Figure 2.2

> **4** With the border of the placeholder displaying as a solid line, change the **Font Size** [60 ▾] to **24**. Notice that the font size of *all* of the placeholder text increases.

> **5** **Save** your presentation.

Activity 2.02 | Changing a Bulleted List to a Numbered List

3.1.3

You can easily change a bulleted list to a numbered list. In this safety presentation, the list of steps to follow should be a numbered list, such as the rules employees should follow for injury prevention.

> **1** Display **Slide 3**, and then click anywhere in the bulleted list. Point to the placeholder dashed border to display the ⟨pointer⟩ pointer, and then click one time to display the border as a solid line indicating that all of the text is selected.

> **2** On the **Home tab**, in the **Paragraph group**, click **Numbering** and then compare your slide with Figure 2.3. **Save** your presentation.

> All of the bullet symbols are converted to numbers. The color of the numbers is determined by the presentation theme.

⌨ **MAC TIP** If group names do not display on your ribbon, open PowerPoint. On the menu, click PowerPoint, and then click Preferences. Click View, and then in the View dialog box, select the Show group titles check box. Close the dialog box to display group names on the ribbon.

Figure 2.3

Activity 2.03 | Changing the Shape and Color of a Bulleted List Symbol

MOS
3.1.3

The presentation theme includes default styles for the bullet points in content placeholders. You can customize a bullet by changing its style, color, and size. It is good practice to create presentations that use styles, colors, and other formatting that represent the brand of the company.

1 Display **Slide 4**, and then select the three second-level bullet points—*Ride entrances*, *Visitor center*, and *Rest areas*.

2 On the **Home tab**, in the **Paragraph group**, click the **Bullets button arrow** to display the **Bullets** gallery, and then compare your screen with Figure 2.4.

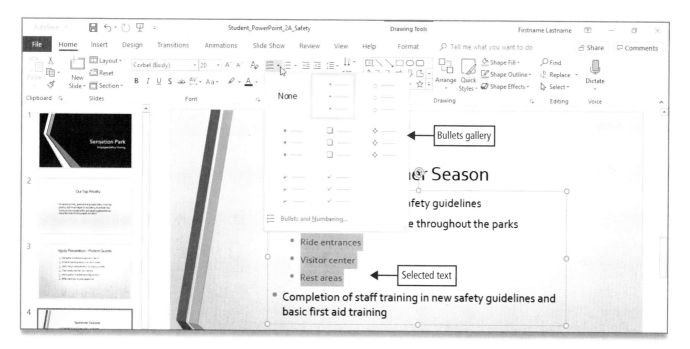

Figure 2.4

3 Below the **Bullets** gallery, click **Bullets and Numbering**. In the **Bullets and Numbering** dialog box, point to several bullet styles to display each ScreenTip. Then, in the second row, click **Star Bullets**. If the Star Bullets are not available, in the second row of bullets, click the second bullet style, and then click the Reset button.

4 Below the gallery, click **Color**. Under **Theme Colors**, in the eighth column, click the last color. In the **Size** box, select the existing number, type **100** and then compare your dialog box with Figure 2.5.

Figure 2.5

> **5** Click **OK** to apply the bullet style, and then **Save** 🔲 your presentation.

MORE KNOWLEDGE **Using Other Symbols as Bullet Characters**

Many bullets styles are available to insert in your presentation. In the Bullets and Numbering dialog box, click Customize to view additional bullet styles.

Activity 2.04 | **Removing a Bullet Symbol from a Bullet Point**

The Bullets button is a toggle, enabling you to turn the bullet symbol on and off. A slide that contains a single bullet point can be formatted as a single paragraph *without* a bullet symbol.

> **1** Display **Slide 2**, and then click in the paragraph. On the **Home tab**, in the **Paragraph group**, click **Bullets** ☷ ▾. Compare your screen with Figure 2.6.

The bullet symbol no longer displays, and the Bullets button is no longer selected. Additionally, the indentation associated with the list level is removed.

Figure 2.6

2 ▶ Click the dashed border to display the solid border and to select all of the text in the paragraph, and then apply **Bold** B and **Italic** I. In the **Paragraph group**, click **Line Spacing** ⌁▾, and then click **2.0**. **Center** ≡ the paragraph, and then **Save** 💾 your presentation.

Objective 2 | **Insert Online Pictures**

▶ **GO! Learn How**
Video P2-2

There are many sources from which you can insert images and other media into a presentation. One type of image that you can insert is a *clip*—a single media file such as art, sound, animation, or a movie.

Activity 2.05 | Inserting Online Pictures in a Content Placeholder

PowerPoint searches Bing when you insert an online picture. You can use various keywords to find online images that are appropriate for your documents.

1 ▶ Display **Slide 5**. In the placeholder on the right side of the slide, click **Online Pictures** 🖼 to display the **Online Pictures** dialog box. With the insertion point in the **Search** box, type **pouring water** Press Enter to search for images that contain the keywords *pouring water* and then compare your screen with Figure 2.7.

💻 **MAC TIP** The Mac version of PowerPoint does not include this feature. Open your browser, navigate to Bing.com, click Images, and search for images that contain the keywords pouring water. Select a vertical image of water being poured, similar to Figure 2.8. Save the file to your computer and use the Insert Picture icon in the content placeholder to insert your downloaded image. For this Activity you can insert the picture p02A_Pouring_Water that is included with the data files for this project.

Figure 2.7

2 ▶ Select a vertical image of water being poured, similar to Figure 2.8.

The results shown indicate the images are licensed under Creative Commons, which, according to www.creativecommons.org is "a nonprofit organization that enables the sharing and use of creativity and knowledge through free legal tools." Creative Commons helps people share and use their photographs, but not allow companies to sell them. For your college assignments, you can use these images so long as you are not profiting by selling the images.
To find out more about Creative Commons, go to *https://creativecommons.org* and watch their video.

NOTE Unable to Locate Similar Image

If you are unable to locate a suitable image or would prefer to have your project match this text exactly, you can insert the picture p02A_Pouring_Water that is included with the data files for this project.

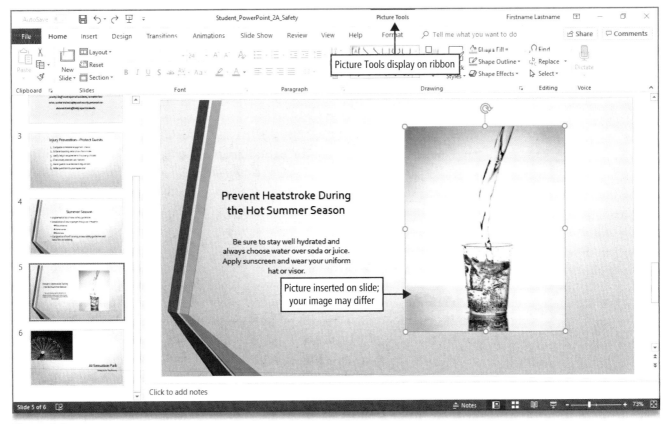

Figure 2.8

> **3** With the water picture selected, click **Insert**. If necessary, close the Design Ideas pane.
>
> On the ribbon, the Picture Tools display, and the pouring water image is surrounded by sizing handles, indicating that it is selected. Your ribbon may also display the Drawing Tools tab.

BY TOUCH Tap the picture that you want to insert, and then tap Insert.

NOTE **Design Ideas Pane**

The Design Ideas pane may open each time you insert a picture. The pane includes ideas for ways to format and layout a slide. In this project you will not use these suggestions, so you can close the pane each time it opens.

NOTE **Credit Line Below Inserted Image**

When you insert an online image, PowerPoint may include a credit line below the image. This includes copyright information such as author name and CC (Creative Commons) licenses. When using the work of others, you should appropriately cite your sources. For this exercise, you can delete this information so that your screen will match the figures in this text more closely.

> **4** If necessary, select only the textbox below the inserted image, and then press Delete. **Save** 🖫 your presentation.

Activity 2.06 | Inserting Pictures in Any Location on a Slide

1 Display **Slide 1**. On the **Insert tab**, in the **Images group**, click **Pictures**.

 MAC TIP Click Pictures and then click Picture from File.

2 In the **Insert Picture** dialog box, navigate to the data files for this project, click **p02A_Red_Light**, and then click **Insert**. Compare your screen with Figure 2.9. **Save** 💾 your presentation.

When you insert an image from the ribbon instead of from the button in a content placeholder, PowerPoint inserts the image in the center of the slide.

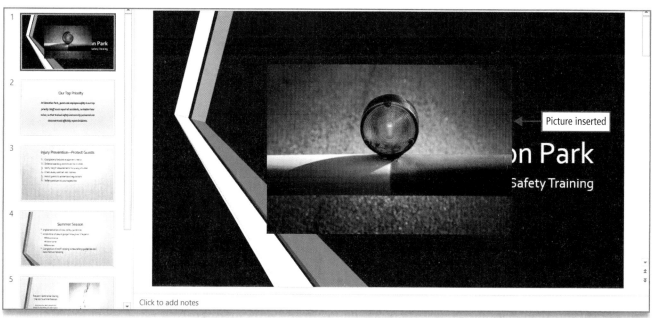

Figure 2.9

Activity 2.07 | Sizing a Picture

MOS
3.3.1

A selected image displays sizing handles that you can drag to resize the image. You can also resize an image using the Shape Height and Shape Width boxes on the Format tab.

1 If necessary, select the picture of the red light. On the **Picture Tools Format tab**, in the **Size group**, click in the **Shape Height** box, and then replace the selected number with **3.5**

2 Press Enter to resize the image. Notice that the picture is resized proportionately, and the **Width** box of this image displays *5.26*. Compare your screen with Figure 2.10. **Save** 💾 your presentation.

When a picture is resized in this manner, the width adjusts in proportion to the picture height.

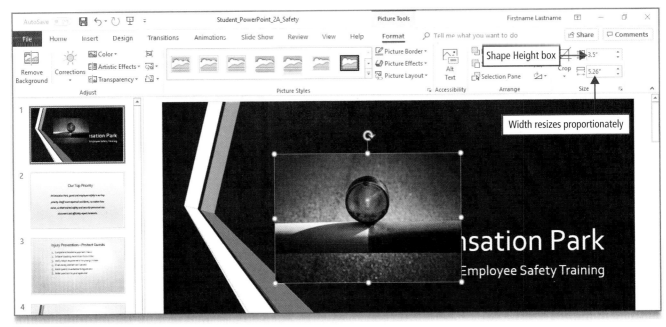

Figure 2.10

🖐 **BY TOUCH**   Drag the corner sizing handle with your finger or mouse to resize the picture proportionately.

Activity 2.08 | Using Smart Guides and the Ruler to Position a Picture

[MOS]
3.5.4

Smart guides are dashed lines that display on your slide when you are moving an object to assist you with alignment.

1 On **Slide 1**, on the **View tab**, in the **Show group**, verify that the **Ruler** check box is selected and if necessary, select the check box. On the horizontal and vertical rulers, notice that *0* displays in the center. Point to the picture, and then drag up so that the top edge of the picture aligns with the top edge of the slide. Compare your screen with Figure 2.11.

Horizontally, the PowerPoint ruler indicates measurements from the center of the slide *out* to the left and to the right. Vertically, the PowerPoint ruler indicates measurements from the center up and down.

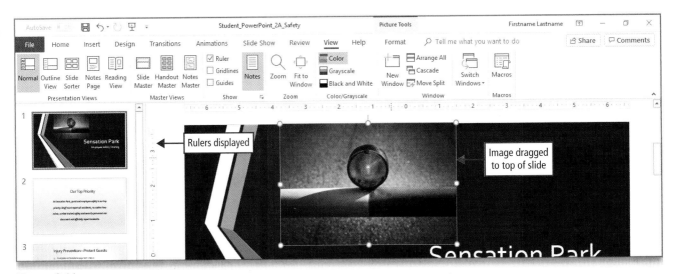

Figure 2.11

2 ▶ Point to the picture to display the ⊕ pointer. Hold down Shift, and then slowly drag the picture to the right and notice that dashed red Smart Guides periodically display along the edges of the picture. When the dashed red Smart Guide displays on the right edge of the picture at approximately **6 inches to the right of zero on the horizontal ruler**, compare your screen with Figure 2.12, and then release the mouse button. **Save** 🖫 the presentation.

Smart Guides display when you move an object and it is aligned with another object on the slide. Here, the Smart Guide displays because the right edge of the picture is aligned with the right edge of the title placeholder. Pressing Shift while dragging an object constrains object movement in a straight line either vertically or horizontally. Here, pressing Shift maintains the vertical placement of the picture at the top edge of the slide.

Figure 2.12

🔄 **ANOTHER WAY**   On the Picture Tools Format tab, in the Size group, click More to open the Format Picture pane. On the Size and Properties tab, and set the position by entering values in the Horizontal position and Vertical position boxes measured from the top left corner or the center of the slide. For this Activity, enter 7.5 in the Horizontal position box and 0 in the Vertical position box.

MORE KNOWLEDGE   **Moving an Object by Using the Arrow Keys**

You can use the directional arrow keys on your keyboard to move a picture, shape, or other object in small increments. Select the object so that its outside border displays as a solid line. Then, on your keyboard, press the directional arrow keys to move the selected object in small, precise increments.

Activity 2.09 | Cropping a Picture

3.3.1

When you *crop* a picture, you remove unwanted or unnecessary areas of the picture.

1 ▶ Display **Slide 6**, and then select the Ferris wheel picture. On the **Picture Tools Format tab**, in the **Size group**, click the upper portion of the **Crop** button to display the crop handles on the edges of the picture. Compare your screen with Figure 2.13.

Use the *crop handles* like sizing handles to remove unwanted areas of the picture.

Figure 2.13

> **2** Point to the center right crop handle to display the crop pointer ⊩. Compare your screen
> with Figure 2.14.
>
> The ***crop pointer*** is the mouse pointer that displays when cropping areas of a picture.

Figure 2.14

> **3** With the crop pointer displayed, hold down the left mouse button and drag to the left to
> approximately **1.5 inches to the left of zero on the horizontal ruler**, and then release the
> mouse button. Compare your screen with Figure 2.15.
>
> The portion of the picture to be removed by the crop displays in gray.

Figure 2.15

4 On the **Picture Tools Format tab**, in the **Size group**, click the upper portion of the **Crop** button to apply the crop, and then **Save** 🖫 your presentation.

🔄 **ANOTHER WAY** Press [Enter] or click outside the picture to apply the crop.

Activity 2.10 | Using the Crop to Shape Command to Change the Shape of a Picture

An inserted picture is typically rectangular in shape; however, you can modify a picture by changing its shape.

1 Display **Slide 1**, and then select the picture. On the **Picture Tools Format tab**, in the **Size group**, click the lower portion of the Crop button—the **Crop arrow**—and then compare your screen with Figure 2.16.

Figure 2.16

2 Point to **Crop to Shape** to display a gallery of shapes. Under **Basic Shapes**, in the first row, click the first shape—**Oval**—to change the picture's shape to an oval. Compare your screen with Figure 2.17.

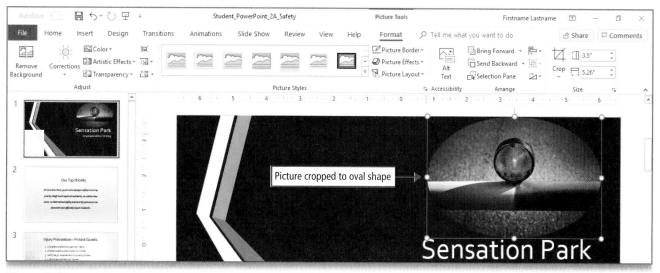

Picture cropped to oval shape

Figure 2.17

3 **Save** 🖫 your presentation.

Insert Text Boxes and Shapes

GO! Learn How
Video P2-3

You can use objects, including text boxes and shapes, to draw attention to important information or to serve as containers for slide text. Many shapes, including lines, arrows, ovals, and rectangles, are available to insert and position anywhere on your slides.

Activity 2.11 │ Inserting a Text Box

3.4.3

A *text box* is an object with which you can position text anywhere on a slide.

1 Display **Slide 3** and verify that the rulers display. On the **Insert tab**, in the **Text group**, click **Text Box**.

2 Move the ⏐↓⏐ pointer to several different places on the slide, and as you do so, in the horizontal and vertical rulers, notice that *ruler guides*—dotted red vertical and horizontal lines that display in the rulers indicating the pointer's position—move also.

Use the ruler guides to help you position objects on a slide.

3 Position the pointer so that the ruler guides are positioned on the **left half of the horizontal ruler at 4.5 inches** and on the **lower half of the vertical ruler at 2 inches**, and then compare your screen with Figure 2.18.

Figure 2.18

4 Click one time to create a narrow rectangular text box surrounded by sizing handles. With the insertion point blinking inside the text box, type **If Safety is Questionable** Notice that as you type, the width of the text box expands to accommodate the text. Compare your screen with Figure 2.19.

Do not be concerned if your textbox is not positioned exactly as shown in the figure.

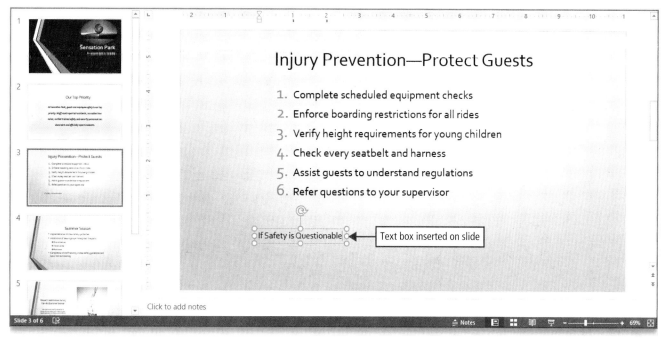

Figure 2.19

5 Select the text that you typed, change the **Font Size** to **24** and then **Save** your presentation.

> You can format the text in a text box by using the same techniques that you use to format text in any other placeholder. For example, you can change the font, font style, font size, and font color.

Activity 2.12 │ Inserting and Sizing a Shape

3.4.1, 3.4.4

Shapes are slide objects such as lines, arrows, boxes, callouts, and banners. You can size and move a shape using the same techniques that you use to size and move pictures.

1 With **Slide 3** displayed, on the **Insert tab**, in the **Illustrations group**, click **Shapes** to display the **Shapes** gallery. Under **Block Arrows**, click the first shape—**Arrow: Right**. Move the pointer into the slide until the ⊞ pointer—called the *crosshair pointer*—displays, indicating that you can draw a shape.

2 Move the ⊞ pointer to position the ruler guides at approximately **0 on the horizontal ruler** and on the **lower half of the vertical ruler at 2 inches**. Compare your screen with Figure 2.20.

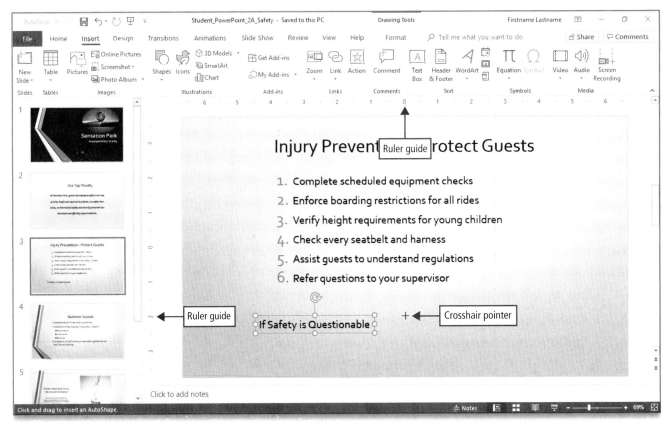

Figure 2.20

> **3** ▸ Click to insert the arrow. On the **Drawing Tools Format tab**, in the **Size group**, click in the **Shape Height** box 🔳 to select the number. Type **0.5** click in the **Shape Width** box 🔳. Type **2** and then press [Enter] to resize the arrow. Compare your screen with Figure 2.21.

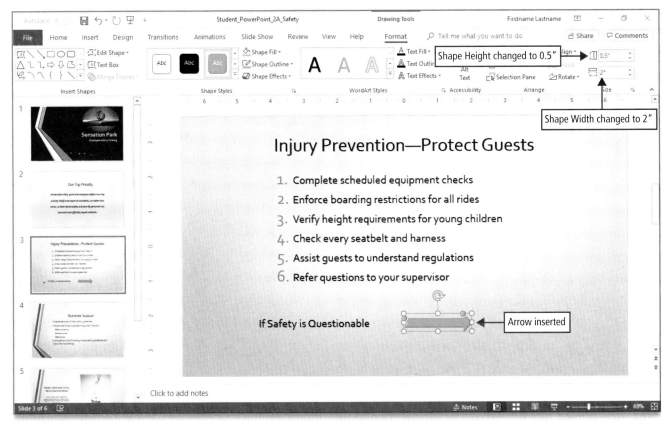

Figure 2.21

4 On the **Drawing Tools Format tab**, in the **Insert Shapes group**, click **More** ⬚. In the gallery, under **Basic Shapes**, in the first row, click the second to last shape—**Octagon**.

5 Move the ✛ pointer to position the ruler guides on the **right half of the horizontal ruler at 3.5 inches** and on the **lower half of the vertical ruler at 1 inch**, and then click one time to insert an octagon.

6 On the **Drawing Tools Format tab**, in the **Size group**, click in the **Shape Height** box ⬚ to select the number. Type **2** and then click in the **Shape Width** box ⬚. Type **2** and then press Enter to resize the octagon. Compare your slide with Figure 2.22.

Do not be concerned if your shapes are not positioned exactly as shown in the figure. The exact size and location are not important as you will adjust both in a later step.

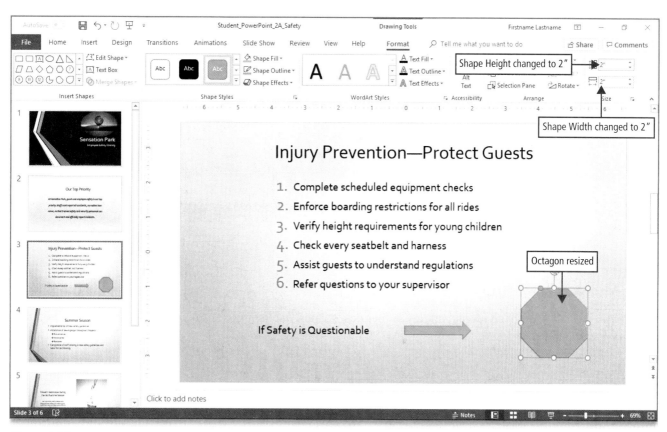

Figure 2.22

7 **Save** ⬚ your presentation.

Activity 2.13 | Adding Text to Shapes

Shapes can serve as a container for text. After you add text to a shape, you can change the font and font size, apply font styles, and change text alignment.

1 On **Slide 3**, if necessary, click the octagon so that it is selected. Type **STOP** and notice that the text is centered within the octagon.

2 Select the text *STOP*, and then change the **Font Size** to **32**.

3 Click in a blank area of the slide to cancel the selection, and then compare your screen with Figure 2.23. **Save** 💾 your presentation.

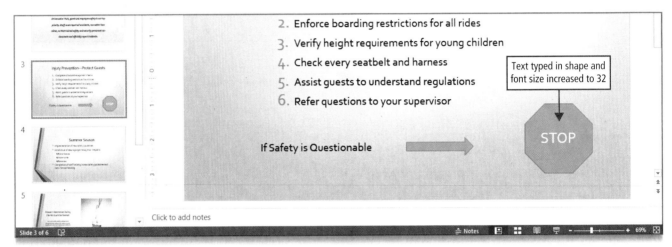

Figure 2.23

Objective 4 **Format Objects**

GO! Learn How
Video P 2-4

Apply styles and effects to pictures, shapes, and text boxes to complement slide backgrounds and colors.

Activity 2.14 | Applying Shape Fills and Outlines

MOS
3.4.5, 3.4.6

A distinctive way to format a shape is by changing the *fill color*—the inside color of text or of an object—and the outside line color. You can use *shape styles* to apply predefined combinations of these fill and line colors and to apply other effects.

1 Display **Slide 2**, and then click anywhere in the paragraph of text to select the content placeholder.

2 On the **Drawing Tools Format tab**, in the **Shape Styles group**, click the **Shape Fill arrow**. Point to several of the theme colors and watch as Live Preview changes the inside color of the text box. In the fifth column, click the second color.

🖥 **MAC TIP**   Use the commands on the Shape Format tab.

3 In the **Shape Styles group**, click the **Shape Outline arrow**. Point to **Weight**, click **3 pt**, and notice that a thick outline surrounds the text placeholder. Click in a blank area of the slide so that nothing is selected, and then compare your slide with Figure 2.24. **Save** 💾 your presentation.

You can use combinations of shape fill, outline color, and weight to format an object.

Shape fill applied to content placeholder

Shape outline applied

Figure 2.24

Activity 2.15 │ Using the Eyedropper to Change Color

The *eyedropper* is a tool that captures the exact color from an object on your screen and then applies it to any shape, picture, or text. You can use the eyedropper to give your presentation a cohesive look by matching a font color, fill color, border color, or other slide element to any color on any slide.

1 Display **Slide 6**, and then select the title text—*At Sensation Park*.

2 On the **Home tab**, in the **Font group**, click the **Font Color arrow** 🅰▾. Below the gallery, click **Eyedropper**, and then move the 🖊 pointer into the upper right corner of the Ferris wheel picture. Compare your screen with Figure 2.25.

A small square displays next to the pointer indicating the exact color to which you are pointing. When you hover over a color, it's **RGB** color coordinates display in a ScreenTip, replacing the block of color. RGB is a color model in which the colors red, green, and blue are added together to form another color.

Figure 2.25

3 With the ✐ pointer in the upper right corner of the picture, click one time. Notice that the color is applied to the selected text. Click a blank area of the slide to deselect the text and compare your screen with Figure 2.26.

Figure 2.26

4 Display **Slide 5**, and then select the title. On the **Home tab**, click the **Font Color arrow** 🄰▾. Under **Recent Colors**, notice that the color you selected with the eyedropper displays. Point to the color to display the ScreenTip—*Dark Blue*. Click **Dark Blue** to apply the color to the selection.

> After a color has been selected with the eyedropper, it remains available in the presentation each time the color gallery is displayed. When you use the eyedropper in this manner, you can consistently apply the same color throughout your presentation.

5 Save 💾 your presentation.

Activity 2.16 | Applying Shape Styles

MOS
3.4.6

The default style of the inserted shapes can easily be changed. For example, in this presentation, the octagon shape is blue, but changing it to red will make it stand out and look like a Stop sign.

1 Display **Slide 3**, and then select the **arrow shape**. On the **Drawing Tools Format tab**, in the **Shape Styles group**, click **More** ⊡ to display the **Shape Styles** gallery. Under **Theme Styles**, in the last row, click the second style.

2 Click anywhere in the text *If Safety is Questionable* to select the text box. On the **Drawing Tools Format tab**, in the **Shape Styles group**, click **More** ⊡.

3 Under **Theme Styles**, in the last row, click the fifth style.

4 Select the **octagon shape**, and then apply the same style you applied to the text box.

5 **Save** 🖫 your presentation and then compare your screen with Figure 2.27.

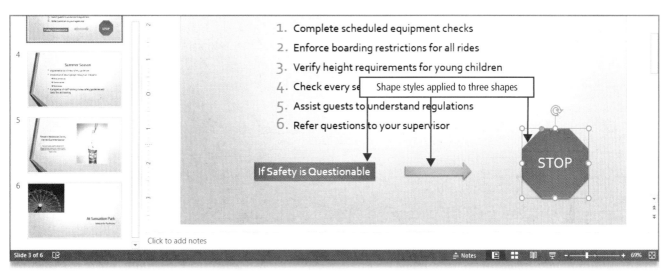

Figure 2.27

Activity 2.17 | Applying Shape and Picture Effects

MOS
3.3.2, 3.4.5

1 Display **Slide 1**, and then select the picture. On the **Picture Tools Format tab**, in the **Picture Styles group**, click **Picture Effects**.

A list of effects that you can apply to pictures displays. These effects can also be applied to shapes and text boxes.

2 Point to **Soft Edges**, and then in the **Soft Edges** gallery, point to each style to view its effect on the picture. Click the last **Soft Edges** effect—**50 Point**, and then compare your screen with Figure 2.28.

The soft edges effect softens and blurs the outer edge of the picture so that it blends into the slide background.

Figure 2.28

> 3 ▶ Display **Slide 2**, and then select the light blue content placeholder. On the **Drawing Tools Format tab**, in the **Shape Styles group**, click **Shape Effects**. Point to **Bevel** to display the **Bevel** gallery. Point to each bevel to view its ScreenTip and to use Live Preview to examine the effect of each bevel on the content placeholder. Then, in the last row, click the last bevel—**Round Convex**. On some systems, this effect may be called Art Deco.

> 4 ▶ Click in a blank area of the slide and then compare your screen with Figure 2.29.

Figure 2.29

> 5 ▶ Display **Slide 5**, and then select the picture. On the **Picture Tools Format tab**, in the **Picture Styles group**, click **Picture Effects**, and then point to **Glow**.

> 6 ▶ Point to several of the effects to view the effect on the picture, and then under **Glow Variations**, in the second row, click the first glow effect—**Glow: 8 point; Blue, Accent color 1**.

> The glow effect applies a colored, softly blurred outline to the selected object.

> 7 ▶ **Save** 🖫 your presentation.

Activity 2.18 | Duplicating Objects

> 1 ▶ Display **Slide 6**, and then select the picture.

> 2 ▶ Press and hold down Ctrl, and then press D one time. Release Ctrl.

> Ctrl + D is the keyboard shortcut to duplicate an object. A duplicate of the picture overlaps the original picture and the duplicated image is selected.

MAC TIP   Press command ⌘ and D

> **3** Compare your screen with Figure 2.30. **Save** 🖫 your presentation.

Figure 2.30

Activity 2.19 | Aligning and Distributing Objects Relative to the Slide

MOS
3.5.2

You can select multiple slide objects, and then use ribbon commands to align and distribute the objects precisely.

> **1** With **Slide 6** displayed, if necessary click the image in the upper left corner of the slide to select it. Hold down Shift and then click the second image so that both images are selected. Release the Shift key, and then compare your slide with Figure 2.31.

ANOTHER WAY   Position the pointer in the gray area of the Slide pane just outside the upper left corner of the slide to display the ⌖ pointer. Drag down and to the right to draw a transparent, gray, selection rectangle that encloses both pictures.

Figure 2.31

2 ▶ On the **Picture Tools Format tab**, in the **Arrange group**, click **Align** ⊟. At the bottom of the menu, click **Align to Slide** to activate this setting. Click **Align** ⊟ again, click **Align Left**, and then compare your screen with Figure 2.32.

The *Align to Slide* setting tells PowerPoint to align each selected object with the slide, rather than with each other. In combination with the Align Left option, this aligns the left edge of each picture with the left edge of the slide.

Figure 2.32

3 ▶ With both pictures still selected, on the **Picture Tools Format tab**, in the **Arrange group**, click **Align** ⊟, and then click **Distribute Vertically**.

The pictures are distributed evenly down the left edge of the slide between the top and bottom edges of the slide.

4 ▶ With both pictures selected, on the **Picture Tools Format tab**, in the **Picture Styles group**, click **Picture Effects**. Point to **Soft Edges**, use the ScreenTips to locate and then click **50 Point** to apply the picture effect to both images. Click in a blank area of the slide and compare your screen with Figure 2.33.

Figure 2.33

5 **Save** the presentation.

Activity 2.20 | Aligning and Distributing Objects Relative to Each Other

MOS
3.5.2

Using the commands in the Arrange group is a more precise way of aligning objects than positioning the objects manually.

1 Display **Slide 3**, hold down Shift, and then at the bottom of the slide, click the **text box**, the **arrow**, and the **octagon** to select all three objects. Release Shift.

BY TOUCH Tap the text box, hold down Shift, and then tap the arrow and the octagon.

2 With the three objects selected, on the **Drawing Tools Format tab**, in the **Arrange group**, click **Align** . Click **Align Selected Objects**.

The *Align Selected Objects* option will cause the objects that you select to align relative to each other, rather than relative to the edges of the slide.

3 On the **Drawing Tools Format tab**, in the **Arrange group**, click **Align** , and then click **Align Middle**. Click **Align** again, and then click **Distribute Horizontally**.

The midpoint of each object aligns and the three objects are distributed evenly between the left edge of the leftmost object—the text box—and the right edge of the rightmost object—the octagon.

4 Click anywhere on the slide so that none of the objects are selected. Compare your screen with Figure 2.34, and then **Save** the presentation.

Figure 2.34

Activity 2.21 | Grouping Objects

MOS
3.5.3

You can select multiple objects and group them so that they can be formatted and edited as one object.

1 With **Slide 3** displayed, click the **text box**, hold down Shift, and then click the **arrow** and the **octagon** so that all three objects are selected.

Sizing handles surround each individual object.

2 On the **Drawing Tools Format tab**, in the **Arrange group**, click **Group**, and then click **Group**. Compare your screen with Figure 2.35.

The sizing handles surround all three shapes as one, indicating that the three shapes are grouped into one object. The individual objects are not selected. The grouped object can be formatted, aligned, and moved as one object.

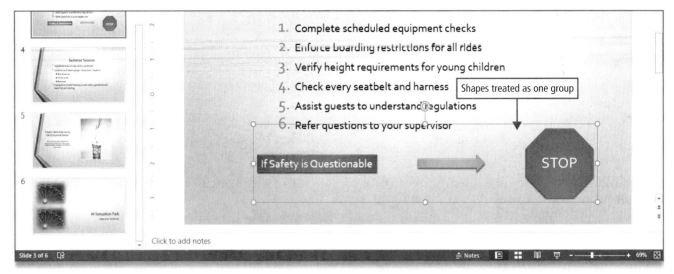

Figure 2.35

3 On the **Drawing Tools Format tab**, in the **Arrange group**, click **Align**, and then click **Align Center**.

The group is centered horizontally on the slide.

4 On the **Slide Show tab**, in the **Start Slide Show group**, click **From Beginning**, and then view the slide show. When the black slide displays, press Esc.

5 On the **Insert tab**, in the **Text group**, click **Header & Footer** to display the **Header and Footer** dialog box. Click the **Notes and Handouts tab**. Under **Include on page**, select the **Date and time** check box, and then select **Update automatically**. Verify the **Header** check box is not selected, and the **Page number** check box is selected. Select the **Footer** check box. In the **Footer** box, type **2A_Safety** and then click **Apply to All**.

6 Display the document properties. As the **Tags** type **safety presentation** and as the **Subject**, type your course and section number. Click to the right of **Subject**, and then type your course name and section number. Under **Related People**, be sure that your name displays as the author, and edit if necessary.

For Non-MyLab Submissions Determine What Your Instructor Requires
As directed by your instructor, submit your completed PowerPoint file.

---

7 Click **Save**. On the right end of the title bar, click **Close** ⊠ to close the presentation and close PowerPoint.

8 In **MyLab IT**, in your **Course Materials**, locate and click the Grader Project **PowerPoint 2A Safety**. In **step 3**, under **Upload Completed Assignment**, click **Choose File**. In the **Open** dialog box, navigate to your **PowerPoint Chapter 2 folder**, and then click your **Student_PowerPoint_2A_Safety** file one time to select it. In the lower right corner of the **Open** dialog box, click **Open**.

The name of your selected file displays above the Upload button.

9 To submit your file to **MyLab IT** for grading, click **Upload**, wait a moment for a green **Success!** message, and then in **step 4**, click the blue **Submit for Grading** button. Click **Close Assignment** to return to your list of **Course Materials**.

You have completed Project 2A | END

| Objective | Create an Informational Presentation in Google Slides |

ALERT   **Working with Web-Based Applications and Services**

Computer programs and services on the web receive continuous updates and improvements, so the steps to complete this web-based activity may differ from the ones shown. You can often look at the screens and the information presented to determine how to complete the activity.

If you do not already have a Google account, you will need to create one before you begin this activity. Go to http://google.com and in the upper-right corner, click **Sign In**. On the Sign In screen, click **Create Account**. On the Create your Google Account page, complete the form, read and agree to the Terms of Service and Privacy Policy, and then click **Next step**. On the Welcome screen, click **Get Started**.

Activity | Creating an Informational Presentation in Google Slides

In this Activity, you will use Google Slides to create a presentation similar to the one you created in Project 2A.

1 From the desktop, open your browser, navigate to **http://google.com**, and then sign in to your Google account. Click **Google apps** ⊞, and then click **Drive** ⬠. Open your **GO! Web Projects** folder—or if necessary, click New to create and then open this folder.

2 In the left pane, click **New**, click **File upload** 🗋, and then in the **Open** dialog box, navigate to your student data files. Select **p02_2A_Google_Slides**. Click **Open**. When the upload is complete and the file name displays in the file list, right-click **p02_2A_ Google_Slides**, and then click **Rename**. In the **Rename** dialog box, select and delete the text. Using your own name, as the file name, type **Lastname_ Firstname_2A_Google_Slides** and then press Enter. Right-click your file, point to **Open with**, and then click **Google Slides**.

3 Display **Slide 5**. On the **toolbar**, click **Image** 🖼. Click **Search the web**. In the **Search for Google Images** box, type **pouring water** and then press Enter. Select a picture similar to the one that you inserted in Project 2A, and then in the lower left, click **INSERT**. Drag the image to the right and use the sizing handles to position and resize the image so that there is an even amount of space above, below, and to the right of the image. Alternatively, you can insert the picture p02A_Pouring_Water from your student data files.

4 Display **Slide 2**, and then click anywhere in the paragraph. At the right end of the toolbar, if necessary, click More ⋯ , and then click **Bulleted list** ≔ to remove the bullet symbol from the paragraph.

5 If necessary, click More. Click **Align** ▤, click **Center** ▤, and then select the entire paragraph. Change the **Font size** to **24** and apply **Bold**.

6 With **Slide 2** displayed and the paragraph selected, on the **toolbar**, click **Fill color** 🖌, and then in the eighth column, select the fifth color—**light blue 1**.

7 Click **Border color** ✏, and then, in the eighth column, select the second color—**blue**. Click **Border weight** ▤, and then click **4px**. Click a blank area of the slide to deselect the text box, and then compare your screen with Figure A.

8 Display **Slide 3**, and then click in the bulleted list. If necessary, click More ⋯ , and then click **Numbered list** ≔ to apply numbers to all of the bullet points. It is not necessary to select the text; bullets and numbering are applied to all of the bullet points in a content placeholder.

9 With **Slide 3** displayed, on the **toolbar**, click **Text box** 🔡 to insert a text box in your slide. Click below the content placeholder and drag to create the textbox near the bottom of the slide—the exact size and placement need not be precise.

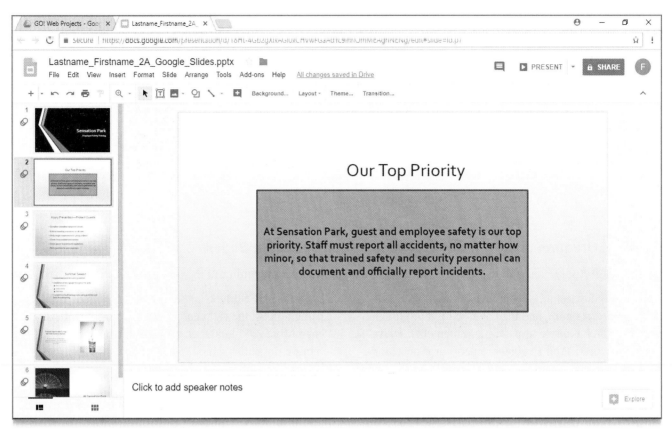

Figure A

10 With the insertion point blinking in the text box, type **If Safety is Questionable** and then on the **toolbar**, click **Fill color** [icon]. In the first column, click the fourth color—**light red berry 2**. If necessary, drag the sizing handles of the textbox to shorten the text box to fit the text. Click outside the text box to deselect it.

11 On the **toolbar**, click **Shape** [icon], point to **Arrows**, and then click **Right Arrow**. Position the mouse pointer to the right of the text box and click to insert an arrow in the middle of your slide. Drag the arrow so that it is aligned horizontally with the text box—a red guide will display to assist you—and its left edge aligns with the *y* in *your*. and then on the **toolbar**, click **Fill color** [icon]. In the eighth column, click the second color—**blue**.

12 On the **toolbar**, click **Shape** [icon], point to **Shapes**, and then click **Octagon**. Position the mouse pointer to the right of the arrow, and then click to insert an octagon on your slide. Drag the octagon so that its center sizing handle aligns with the arrow point and its left edge aligns with the *s* in *regulations*, and then on the **toolbar**, click **Fill color** [icon]. In the first column, click the fourth color— **light red berry 2**.

13 Click in the octagon. Type **STOP**, select the text, change the **Font size** to 18, **Align Center**, and then click in a blank area of the slide. Compare your screen with Figure B and make adjustments to the position of the shapes as necessary.

14 Your presentation will be saved automatically. If you are instructed to submit your file, click the File menu, point to Download, and then click PDF or PowerPoint as directed by your instructor. The file will download to your default download folder as determined by your browser settings. Sign out of your Google account.

Figure B

Event Announcement

Project Activities

In Activities 2.22 through 2.35, you will format slides in a presentation for the Sensation Park Entertainment Group Marketing Director that informs employees about upcoming events at the company's amusement parks. You will enhance the presentation using SmartArt and WordArt graphics. Your completed presentation will look similar to Figure 2.36.

Project Files for MyLab IT Grader

1. In your **MyLab IT** course, locate and click **PowerPoint 2B Celebrations**, Download Materials, and then Download All Files.
2. Extract the zipped folder to your PowerPoint Chapter 2 folder. Close the Grader download screens.
3. Take a moment to open the downloaded **PowerPoint_2B_Celebrations_Instructions**; note any recent updates to the book.

Project Results

GO! Project 2B

Where We're Going

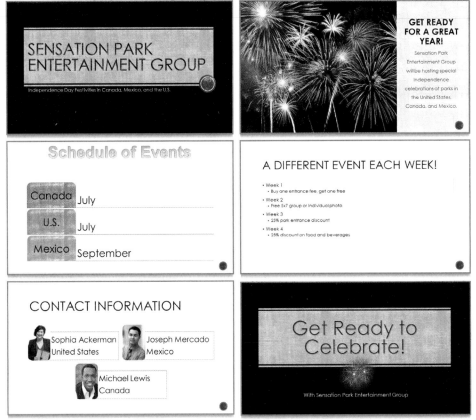

Figure 2.36 Project 2B Celebrations

For Non-MyLab Submissions

For Project 2B, you will need:
p02B_Canada_Contact
p02B_Celebrations
p02B_Mexico_Contact
p02B_US_Contact

In your PowerPoint Chapter 2 folder, save your presentation as:
Lastname_Firstname_2B_Celebrations

After you have named and saved your presentation, on the next page, begin with Step 2.

Objective 5 | Remove Picture Backgrounds and Insert WordArt

ALERT Because Office 365 is a cloud-based subscription service that receives continuous updates, you may encounter some variations in what appears on your screen and what is shown in this instruction. Microsoft Office 365 is fully installed on your PC or Mac; no internet access is necessary to create or edit documents. When you *are* connected to the internet, you will receive monthly upgrades and new features, so you always have the latest versions of Office apps as soon as they are available. Your subscription gives you continuous free access to the latest innovations and refinements.

GO! Learn How
Video P2-5

To avoid the boxy look that results when you insert an image into a presentation, use the ***Background Removal*** command, which removes unwanted portions of a picture so that the picture does not appear as a self-contained rectangle. This enables you to flow a picture into the content of the presentation.

WordArt is a gallery of text styles with which you can create decorative effects, such as shadowed or mirrored text. You can choose from the gallery of WordArt styles to insert a new WordArt object or you can customize existing text by applying WordArt formatting.

Activity 2.22 | Removing the Background from a Picture and Applying Soft Edge Options

MOS
3.3.2

1 Navigate to your **PowerPoint Chapter 2 folder**, and then double-click the downloaded PowerPoint file that displays your name—**Student_PowerPoint_2B_Celebrations**. In your presentation, if necessary, at the top click **Enable Editing**.

2 Display **Slide 6**. Click the fireworks picture to select it, and then on the **Picture Tools Format tab**, in the **Adjust group**, click **Remove Background**. Compare your screen with Figure 2.37.

PowerPoint determines what portion of the picture is the foreground—the portion to keep—and which portion is the background—the portion to remove. The background is overlaid in magenta, leaving the remaining portion of the picture as it will look when the background removal is complete. A rectangular selection area displays that can be moved and sized to select additional areas of the picture. The Background Removal options display in the Refine group on the ribbon.

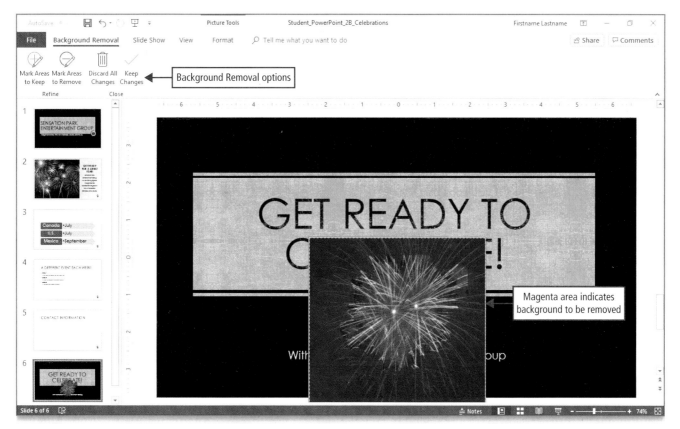

Figure 2.37

3 On the **Background Removal tab**, in the **Close group**, click **Keep Changes** to remove the background.

4 With the picture selected, on the **Picture Tools Format tab**, in the **Picture Styles group**, click **Picture Effects**, point to **Soft Edges**, and then click **50 Point**. **Save** 🖫 your presentation, and then compare your slide with Figure 2.38.

Figure 2.38

Activity 2.23 | Applying WordArt Styles to Existing Text

3.1.1

1 On **Slide 6**, click anywhere in the word *Get* to activate the title placeholder, and then select the title—*Get Ready to Celebrate!* Click the **Drawing Tools Format tab**, and then in the **WordArt Styles group**, click **More** ⊡ to display the WordArt gallery.

2 Point to several WordArt styles to view the change to the slide title. In the first row, click the first style. Click anywhere on the slide outside the title placeholder.

3 **Save** 🖫 your presentation, and then compare your screen with Figure 2.39.

Figure 2.39

Activity 2.24 | Changing the Text Fill and Text Outline Colors of a WordArt Object

You can modify a WordArt object by changing the colors of the text fill and text outline.

1 On **Slide 6**, select the title. On the **Drawing Tools Format tab**, in the **WordArt Styles group**, click **Text Fill**. Under **Theme Colors**, in the sixth column, click the fifth color.

2 With the text still selected, in the **WordArt Styles group**, click **Text Outline**. In the second column, click the first color. Click anywhere on the slide to deselect the title.

3 **Save** 🖫 your presentation, and then compare your screen with Figure 2.40.

Figure 2.40

Activity 2.25 | Inserting and Aligning a WordArt Object

In addition to formatting existing text using WordArt, you can insert a new WordArt object anywhere on a slide.

1 Display **Slide 3**. On the **Insert tab**, in the **Text group**, click **WordArt**. In the gallery, in the second row, click the third WordArt style.

In the center of your slide, a WordArt placeholder displays *Your text here*. Text that you type will replace this text and the placeholder will expand to accommodate the text. The WordArt is surrounded by sizing handles with which you can adjust its size.

2 Type **Schedule of Events** to replace the WordArt placeholder text. Compare your screen with Figure 2.41.

Figure 2.41

3 With the WordArt selected, on the **Drawing Tools Format tab**, in the **Arrange group**, click **Align** , and then click **Align Top** to move the WordArt to the top of the slide.

4 Click in a blank area of the slide, and then compare your screen with Figure 2.42.

Figure 2.42

> **5** Save 🖫 your presentation.

Activity 2.26 | Adding Text Effects to a WordArt

Text effects are formats applied to text that include shadows, reflections, glows, bevels, and 3-D rotations.

> **1** With **Slide 3** displayed, select the **WordArt** text. Change the **Font** to **Arial** and the **Font Size** to **66**.

> **2** On the **Drawing Tools Format tab**, in the **WordArt Styles group**, click **Text Effects**. Point to **Shadow**, and then compare your screen with Figure 2.43.

Figure 2.43

3 Under **Outer**, click the last style—**Offset: Top Left**. Click in a blank area of the slide, and then compare your screen with Figure 2.44.

Figure 2.44

4 **Save** 🔲 your presentation.

Objective 6 Create and Format a SmartArt Graphic

GO! Learn How
Video P2-6

A **SmartArt graphic** is a visual representation of information that you create by choosing from among various layouts to communicate your message or ideas effectively. SmartArt graphics can illustrate processes, hierarchies, cycles, lists, and relationships. You can include text and pictures in a SmartArt graphic, and you can apply colors, effects, and styles that coordinate with the presentation theme.

Activity 2.27 | Creating a SmartArt Graphic from Bulleted Points

MOS
4.3.2

You can convert an existing bulleted list into a SmartArt graphic. When you create a SmartArt graphic, consider the message that you are trying to convey, and then choose an appropriate layout. The table in Figure 2.45 describes types of SmartArt layouts and suggested purposes.

Microsoft PowerPoint SmartArt Graphic Types		
Graphic Type	**Example Layout**	**Purpose of Graphic**
List		Shows non-sequential information
Process		Shows steps in a process or timeline
Cycle		Shows a continual process

Microsoft PowerPoint SmartArt Graphic Types		
Graphic Type	**Example Layout**	**Purpose of Graphic**
Hierarchy		Shows a decision tree or displays an organization chart
Relationship		Illustrates connections
Matrix		Shows how parts relate to a whole
Pyramid		Shows proportional relationships with the largest component on the top or bottom
Picture		Includes pictures in the layout to communicate messages and ideas
Office.com		Additional layouts available from Office.com

Figure 2.45

1 Display **Slide 4**, and then click anywhere in the bulleted list in the content placeholder. On the **Home tab**, in the **Paragraph group**, click **Convert to SmartArt Graphic** ⊞. Below the gallery, click **More SmartArt Graphics**.

Three sections comprise the Choose a SmartArt Graphic dialog box. The left section lists the SmartArt graphic types. The center section displays the SmartArt layouts according to type. The third section displays the selected SmartArt graphic, its name, and a description of its purpose.

ANOTHER WAY Right-click on a bulleted list to display the shortcut menu, point to Convert to SmartArt, and then click More SmartArt Graphics.

2 On the left side of the **Choose a SmartArt Graphic** dialog box, click **List**. Use the ScreenTips to locate and then click **Tab List**. Compare your screen with Figure 2.46.

MAC TIP Choose Vertical Box List.

ALERT Tab List Layout Missing?

If the Tab List option is not available, choose Vertical Box List or a similar list style.

Figure 2.46

3 In the **Choose a SmartArt Graphic** dialog box, click **OK**. If necessary, close the Text pane on the left. **Save** 💾 your presentation, and then compare your screen with Figure 2.47.

It is not necessary to select all of the text in the list. By clicking in the list, PowerPoint converts all of the bullet points to the selected SmartArt graphic. On the ribbon, the SmartArt contextual tools display two tabs—Design and Format. The thick border surrounding the SmartArt graphic indicates that it is selected and displays the area that the object will cover on the slide.

Figure 2.47

Activity 2.28 | Adding Shapes in a SmartArt Graphic

4.3.3

If a SmartArt graphic does not have enough shapes to illustrate a concept or display the relationships, you can add more shapes.

1 Click in the shape that contains the text *Week 3*. On the **SmartArt Tools Design tab**, in the **Create Graphic group**, click the **Add Shape arrow**, and then click **Add Shape After** to insert a shape at the same level. Type **Week 4**

The text in each of the SmartArt shapes resizes to accommodate the added shape.

🔄 **ANOTHER WAY**   Right-click the shape, point to Add Shape, and then click Add Shape After.

2 On the **SmartArt Tools Design tab**, in the **Create Graphic group**, click **Add Bullet** to add a bullet to the right of the *Week 4* shape.

3 Type **25% discount on food and beverages** Click a blank area of the slide and compare your slide with Figure 2.48.

Figure 2.48

4 **Save** 💾 your presentation.

Activity 2.29 | Inserting a SmartArt Graphic Using a Content Layout

4.3.1

1 Display **Slide 5**. In the center of the content placeholder, click **Insert a SmartArt Graphic** 🖼 to open the **Choose a SmartArt Graphic** dialog box.

2 On the left, click **Picture**, and then scroll as necessary and use the ScreenTips to locate, and then click **Picture Strips**. Compare your screen with Figure 2.49.

Figure 2.49

3 Click **OK** to insert the SmartArt graphic.

You can type text directly into the shapes or you can type text in the Text Pane, which may display to the left of your SmartArt graphic. You can toggle the Text Pane display by clicking the Text Pane tab—the small left arrow on the left side of the SmartArt graphic border—or by clicking the Text Pane button in the Create Graphic group.

Activity 2.30 | Inserting Pictures and Text in a SmartArt Graphic

1 In the SmartArt graphic, in the upper left text rectangle shape, type **Sophia Ackerman** and then press Enter. Type **United States** and then click in the text rectangle on the right. Type **Joseph Mercado** and then press Enter. Type **Mexico** and then click in the lower text rectangle. Type **Michael Lewis** and then press Enter. Type **Canada**

2 In the top left picture placeholder, click **Insert Picture** . In the **Insert Pictures** dialog box, click **From a file**. Navigate to your student data files, click **p02B_US_Contact**, and then click **Insert** to insert the picture.

3 Using the technique you just practiced, in the right picture placeholder, insert **p02B_Mexico_Contact**. In the lower picture placeholder, insert **p02B_Canada_Contact**.

4 **Save** your presentation, and then compare your screen with Figure 2.50.

Figure 2.50

Activity 2.31 | Changing the Size and Shape of SmartArt Elements

You can select individual or groups of shapes in a SmartArt graphic and make them larger or smaller, and you can change selected shapes to another type of shape.

1 With **Slide 5** displayed, click the picture of *Sophia Ackerman*. Hold down Shift, and then click the pictures of *Joseph Mercado* and *Michael Lewis* so that all three pictures are selected. Release Shift.

2 On the **SmartArt Tools Format tab**, in the **Shapes group**, click **Larger** two times to increase the size of the three pictures.

3 With the three pictures selected, on the **SmartArt Tools Format tab**, in the **Shapes group**, click **Change Shape**. Under **Rectangles**, click the second shape—**Rectangle: Rounded Corners**.

4 Click a blank area of the slide, and then compare your screen with Figure 2.51.

Figure 2.51

> 5 **Save** 🖫 your presentation.

Activity 2.32 | Changing the SmartArt Layout

> 1 Display **Slide 3**, and then click anywhere in the SmartArt graphic. On the **SmartArt Tools Design tab**, in the **Layouts group**, click **More** ⏷, and then click **More Layouts**. In the **Choose a SmartArt Graphic** dialog box, click **List**. Scroll up or down as necessary to locate and then click **Vertical Block List**. Compare your screen with Figure 2.52.

Figure 2.52

> 2 Click **OK**, and then **Save** 🖫 the presentation.

Activity 2.33 | Changing the Color and Style of a SmartArt Graphic

SmartArt Styles are combinations of formatting effects that you can apply to SmartArt graphics.

> 1 With **Slide 3** displayed, if necessary, select the SmartArt. On the **SmartArt Tools Design tab**, in the **SmartArt Styles group**, click **Change Colors**. In the color gallery, under **Colorful**, click the second style—**Colorful Range - Accent Colors 2 to 3**—to change the colors.

> 2 On the **SmartArt Tools Design tab**, in the **SmartArt Styles group**, click **More** ⏷ to display the **SmartArt Styles gallery**. Under **Best Matches for Document**, click the third style, **Subtle Effect**. Compare your slide with Figure 2.53.

Figure 2.53

> **3** Save 💾 your presentation.

Activity 2.34 | Converting a SmartArt to Text

> **1** Display **Slide 4**, and then click anywhere in the SmartArt graphic. On the **SmartArt Tools Design tab**, in the **Reset group**, click **Convert**, and then click **Convert to Text** to convert the SmartArt graphic back to a bulleted list. Compare your screen with Figure 2.54.

Figure 2.54

> **2** Insert a **Header & Footer** on the **Notes and Handouts**. Include the **Date and time updated automatically**, the **Page number**, and a **Footer** with the text 2B_Celebrations

> **3** Display the document properties. As the **Tags** type Independence Day, celebrations and as the **Subject** type your course and section number. Be sure your name displays as the author, and then **Save** your file. Mac users use the Keywords box for tags.

> **4** View the slide show from the beginning, and then make any necessary adjustments. **Save** 💾 your presentation.

5 If you will be completing the next optional Activity, leave the presentation open. Otherwise, **Close** ☒ PowerPoint.

6 In **MyLab IT**, in your **Course Materials**, locate and click the Grader Project **PowerPoint 2B Celebrations**. In **step 3**, under **Upload Completed Assignment**, click **Choose File**. In the **Open** dialog box, navigate to your **PowerPoint Chapter 2 folder**, and then click your **Student_PowerPoint_2B_ Celebrations** file one time to select it. In the lower right corner of the **Open** dialog box, click **Open**.

The name of your selected file displays above the Upload button.

7 To submit your file to **MyLab IT** for grading, click **Upload**, wait a moment for a green **Success!** message, and then in **step 4**, click the blue **Submit for Grading** button. Click **Close Assignment** to return to your list of **Course Materials**.

Objective 7 Insert a 3D Object

ALERT Optional Activity for Non-MyLab IT submissions.

The remaining Activity in this chapter is optional. Check with your instructor to see if you should complete this Activity. This Activity is not available as a MyLab IT Grader project or Simulation.

 MAC TIP The Mac version of PowerPoint does not support 3D models. Skip this Activity.

GO! Learn How

Video P2-7

One type of image that you can insert is a 3D object. You can insert a 3D object from a file or download from an online gallery. Microsoft Windows 10 includes Paint 3D, with which you can create your own 3D objects.

Activity 2.35 | Inserting 3D Objects

4.4.1, 4.4.2

In this Activity, you will insert and position a 3D object from a file.

1 Display **Slide 4**. On the **Insert tab**, in the **Illustrations group**, click the **3D Models arrow**, and then click **From a File**. From your files for this project, insert the 3D model **p02B_Balloon**.

2 If necessary, click the **3D Model Tools Format tab** and compare your screen with Figure 2.55.

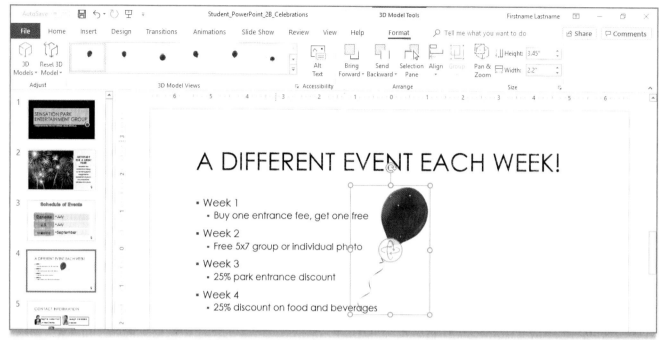

Figure 2.55

3 Point to the 3D handle in the middle of the balloon object to display the rotation pointer. Click and drag to change the view of the object.

> You can rotate a 3D object to view the object from perspective.

4 Drag the balloon to position it in the white space on the right side of the slide. On the **3D Model Tools Format tab**, in the **3D Model Views group**, click **More**. In the gallery, point to each view to display the ScreenTip. Locate and click **Above Front** to position the balloon.

5 Save 🖫 your presentation and submit as directed by your instructor.

You have completed Project 2B   **END**

»» GO! With Google Slides

| Objective | Create an Advertisement Presentation in Google Slides |

ALERT   **Working with Web-Based Applications and Services**

Computer programs and services on the web receive continuous updates and improvements, so the steps to complete this web-based activity may differ from the ones shown. You can often look at the screens and the information presented to determine how to complete the activity.

   If you do not already have a Google account, you will need to create one before you begin this activity. Go to http://google.com and in the upper right corner, click **Sign In**. On the Sign In screen, click **Create Account**. On the Create your Google Account page, complete the form, read and agree to the Terms of Service and Privacy Policy, and then click **Next step**. On the Welcome screen, click **Get Started**.

Activity | Creating an Advertisement Presentation in Google Slides

   In this Activity, you will use Google Slides to format a presentation similar to the one you created in Project 2B.

1 From the desktop, open your browser, navigate to **http://google.com**, and then sign in to your Google account. Click **Google apps** ⊞, and then click **Drive** ☁. Open your **GO! Web Projects** folder—or create and then open this folder if necessary.

2 On the left, click **New**, and then click **File upload**. Navigate to your student data files, click **p02_2B_Google_Slides**, and then click **Open**. When the upload is complete and file name displays in the file list, right click **p02_2B_Google_Slides**, and then click **Rename**. In the **Rename** dialog box, select and delete the existing text. Using your own name, as the file name, type **Lastname_Firstname_2B_Google_Slides** and then press **Enter**. Right-click the file that you just renamed, point to **Open with**, and then click **Google Slides**.

3 Display **Slide 5**. Click the picture to select it, and then on the **toolbar**, click the **Mask image arrow** ▾, point to **Callouts**, and then click **Explosion 1**.

4 With the picture selected, on the **toolbar**, click **Format options**, and then, under **Adjustments**, drag the **Transparency** slider to **20%**. **Close** the **Format options** pane.

5 Display **Slide 3**. On the **Insert** menu, click **Word art**. In the center of your slide, with your insertion point blinking in the placeholder, type **Schedule of Events** and press **Enter**. The Word art is surrounded by sizing handles with which you can adjust its size.

6 With the **Word art** selected, on the **toolbar**, click **Fill color** 🖌, and then in the first column, click the eighth color – **dark red berry 3**. On the **toolbar**, click **Border color** ✏, and then in the first column, click the third color—**light red berry 3**.

7 Drag the **Word art** upward until there is an even amount of white space above and below it. On the menu bar, click **Arrange**, point to **Center on page**, and then click **Horizontally**.

8 With **Slide 3** displayed, select the Word art. On the **toolbar**, change the **Font** to **Georgia**. Compare your screen to Figure A.

9 Your presentation will be saved automatically. Download as a PDF or PowerPoint file and submit as instructed by your instructor. Sign out of your Google account.

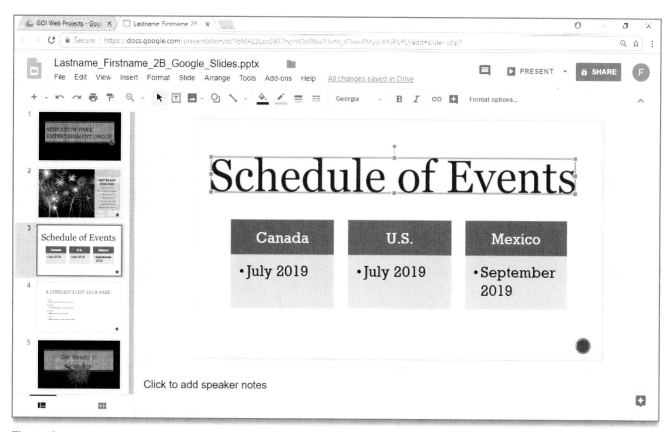

Figure A

POWERPOINT

»»» GO! To Work

wavebreakmedia/Shutterstock, Monkey Business Images/Fotolia, Ivanko80/Shutterstock, Monkey Business Images/Shutterstock

Microsoft Office Specialist (MOS) Skills in This Chapter	
Project 2A	**Project 2B**
3.1.3 Create bulleted and numbered lists	**3.1.1** Apply built-in styles to text
3.3.1 Resize and crop images	**3.3.2** Apply built-in styles and effects to images
3.3.2 Apply built-in styles and effects to images	**4.3.1** Insert SmartArt graphics
3.4.1 Insert and change shapes	**4.3.2** Convert lists to SmartArt graphics
3.4.3 Add text to shapes and text boxes	**4.3.3** Add and modify SmartArt graphic content
3.4.4 Resize shapes and text boxes	**4.4.1** Insert 3D models
3.4.5 Format shapes and text boxes	**4.4.2** Modify 3D models
3.4.6 Apply built-in styles to shapes and text boxes	
3.5.2 Align shapes, images, and text boxes	
3.5.3 Group shapes and images	
3.5.4 Display alignment tools	

Build Your E-Portfolio

An E-Portfolio is a collection of evidence, stored electronically, that showcases what you have accomplished while completing your education. Collecting and then sharing your work products with potential employers reflects your academic and career goals. Your completed documents from the following projects are good examples to show what you have learned: 2G, 2K, and 2L.

Go! For Job Success

Video: Business Lunch Etiquette

Your instructor may assign this video to your class, and then ask you to think about, or discuss with your classmates, these questions:

g-stockstudio/Shutterstock

In what specific ways did Sara and Jordan demonstrate improper interpersonal communication during their lunch with Karen?

As a manager, did Chris follow the rules of interpersonal communication with his client? Explain your answer.

In what ways did Sara, Jordan, and Theo demonstrate proper or improper *nonverbal* communication skills?

End of Chapter

Summary

Use numbered and bulleted lists in a presentation to focus attention on specific items. The theme that you select includes default styles for bullets, but you can change the shape and color of the symbols.

Use pictures to illustrate an idea. The Online Pictures feature enables you to search the web for images that emphasize important points. Using good keywords is critical to a successful search to find a great picture!

Objects are easily modified in PowerPoint. Removing the picture background and cropping eliminate unnecessary picture parts. Smart guides and alignment options are used to position pictures and shapes.

Use SmartArt graphics to present information to illustrate processes, hierarchies, cycles, lists, and relationships. SmartArt graphics may include text and pictures, and can be formatted with styles and color combinations for maximum impact.

GO! Learn It Online

Review the concepts and key terms, and MOS skills in this chapter by completing these online challenges, which you can find in **MyLab IT**.

Chapter Quiz: Answer matching and multiple choice questions to test what you learned in this chapter.

Lessons on the GO!: Learn how to use all the new apps and features as they are introduced by Microsoft.

MOS Prep Quiz: Answer questions to review the MOS skills that you practiced in this chapter.

GO! Collaborative Team Project (Available in Instructor Resource Center)

If your instructor assigns this project to your class, you can expect to work with one or more of your classmates--either in person or by using Internet tools--to create work products similar to those that you created in this chapter. A team is a group of workers who work together to solve a problem, make a decision, or create a work product. Collaboration is when you work together with others as a team in an intellectual endeavor to complete a shared task or achieve a shared goal.

Monkey Business Images/Fotolia

Project Guide for PowerPoint Chapter 2

Your instructor may assign one or more of these projects to help you review the chapter and assess your mastery and understanding of the chapter.

Project	Apply Skills from These Chapter Objectives	Project Type		Project Location
2A MyLab IT	Objectives 1–4 from Project 2A	**2A Instructional Project (Grader Project)** Guided instruction to learn the skills in Project A.	Instruction	In **MyLab IT** and in text
2B MyLab IT	Objectives 5–7 from Project 2B	**2B Instructional Project (Grader Project)** Guided instruction to learn the skills in Project B.	Instruction	In **MyLab IT** and in text
2C	Objectives 1–4 from Project 1A	**2C Skills Review (Scorecard Grading)** A guided review of the skills from Project 1A.	Review	In text
2D	Objectives 5–7 from Project 1B	**2D Skills Review (Scorecard Grading)** A guided review of the skills from Project 1B.	Review	In text
2E MyLab IT	Objectives 1–4 from Project 2A	**2E Mastery (Grader Project)** A demonstration of your mastery of the skills in Project 2A with extensive decision making.	Mastery and Transfer of Learning	In **MyLab IT** and in text
2F MyLab IT	Objectives 5–7 from Project 2B	**2F Mastery (Grader Project)** A demonstration of your mastery of the skills in Project 2B with extensive decision making.	Mastery and Transfer of Learning	In **MyLab IT** and in text
2G MyLab IT	Objectives 1–7 from Projects 2A and 2B	**2G Mastery (Grader Project)** A demonstration of your mastery of the skills in Projects 2A and 2B with extensive decision making.	Mastery and Transfer of Learning	In **MyLab IT** and in text
2H	Combination of Objectives from Projects 2A and 2B	**2H GO! Fix It (Scorecard Grading)** A demonstration of your mastery of the skills in Projects 2A and 2B by creating a correct result from a document that contains errors you must find.	Critical Thinking	IRC
2I	Combination of Objectives from Projects 2A and 2B	**2I GO! Make It (Scorecard Grading)** A demonstration of your mastery of the skills in Projects 2A and 2B by creating a result from a supplied picture.	Critical Thinking	IRC
2J	Combination of Objectives from Projects 2A and 2B	**2J GO! Solve It (Rubric Grading)** A demonstration of your mastery of the skills in Projects 2A and 2B, your decision-making skills, and your critical thinking skills. A task-specific rubric helps you self-assess your result.	Critical Thinking	IRC
2K	Combination of Objectives from Projects 2A and 2B	**2K GO! Solve It (Rubric Grading)** A demonstration of your mastery of the skills in Projects 2A and 2B, your decision-making skills, and your critical thinking skills. A task-specific rubric helps you self-assess your result.	Critical Thinking	In text
2L	Combination of Objectives from Projects 2A and 2B	**2L GO! Think (Rubric Grading)** A demonstration of your understanding of the chapter concepts applied in a manner that you would outside of college. An analytic rubric helps you and your instructor grade the quality of your work by comparing it to the work an expert in the discipline would create.	Critical Thinking	In text
2M	Combination of Objectives from Projects 2A and 2B	**2M GO! Think (Rubric Grading)** A demonstration of your understanding of the chapter concepts applied in a manner that you would outside of college. An analytic rubric helps you and your instructor grade the quality of your work by comparing it to the work an expert in the discipline would create.	Critical Thinking	IRC
2N	Combination of Objectives from Projects 2A and 2B	**2N You and GO! (Rubric Grading)** A demonstration of your understanding of the chapter concepts applied in a manner that you would in a personal situation. An analytic rubric helps you and your instructor grade the quality of your work.	Critical Thinking	IRC
2O	Combination of Objectives from Projects 2A and 2B	**2O Collaborative Team Project for PowerPoint Chapter 2** A demonstration of your understanding of concepts and your ability to work collaboratively in a group role-playing assessment, requiring both collaboration and self-management.	Critical Thinking	IRC

Glossary

Glossary of Chapter Key Terms

Align to Slide A setting tells PowerPoint to align each selected object with the slide, rather than with each other.

Background Removal A feature that removes unwanted portions of a picture so that the picture does not appear as a self-contained rectangle.

Bulleted list A list of items preceded by small dots or other shapes, which do not indicate order or rank. Sometimes called unordered lists.

Clip A single media file such as art, sound, animation, or a movie.

Crop A command that removes unwanted or unnecessary areas of a picture.

Crop handles Handles used to remove unwanted areas of a picture.

Crop pointer The pointer used to crop areas of a picture.

Crosshair pointer The pointer used to draw a shape.

Eyedropper A tool that captures the exact color from an object on your screen and then applies it to any shape, picture, or text.

Fill color The inside color of text or of an object.

Numbered list A list of items preceded by numbers, which indicate sequence or rank of the items. Sometimes called ordered lists.

RGB A color model in which the colors red, green, and blue are added together to form another color.

Ruler guides Dotted red vertical and horizontal lines that display in the rulers indicating the pointer's position.

Shape A slide object such as a line, arrow, box, callout, or banner.

Shape style Predefined combination of shape fill, line colors, and other effects.

Smart guides Dashed lines that display on your slide when you are moving an object to assist you with alignment.

SmartArt graphic A visual representation of information that you create by choosing from among various layouts to communicate your message or ideas effectively.

SmartArt Styles Combinations of formatting effects that you can apply to SmartArt graphics.

Text box An object with which you can position text anywhere on a slide.

Text effects Formats applied to text that include shadows, reflections, glows, bevels, and 3-D rotations.

WordArt A gallery of text styles with which you can create decorative effects, such as shadowed or mirrored text.

Chapter Review

Apply 2A skills from these Objectives:

1. Format Numbered and Bulleted Lists
2. Insert Online Pictures
3. Insert Text Boxes and Shapes
4. Format Objects

In the following Skills Review, you will format a presentation that describes annual Concert in the Park events at several Sensation Park Entertainment Group amusement parks. Your completed presentation will look similar to Figure 2.55.

Project Files

For Project 2C, you will need:

p02C_Concerts

p02C_Drums

p02C_Guitar

p02C_Music (optional)

You will save your presentation as:

Lastname_Firstname_2C_Concerts

Project Results

Figure 2.55 Project 2C Concerts

(continues on next page)

Chapter Review

1 Start PowerPoint. From the student data files, locate and open **p02C_Concerts**. On the **File tab**, click **Save As**, navigate to your **PowerPoint Chapter 2** folder, and then using your own name, save the file as **Lastname_Firstname_2C_Concerts**

a. If necessary, display the rulers. With **Slide 1** displayed, on the **Insert tab**, in the **Illustrations group**, click **Shapes**, and then under **Basic Shapes**, in the second row, click the fifth shape—**Frame**.

b. Move the pointer to align the ruler guides with the **left half of the horizontal ruler at 3 inches** and with the **upper half of the vertical ruler at 2.5 inches**, and then click to insert the Frame.

c. On the **Format tab**, in the **Size group**, click in the **Shape Height** box to select the number, and then type **1.7** Click in the **Shape Width** box. Replace the selected number with **5.5** and then press [Enter] to resize the shape.

d. With the frame selected, type **Sensation Park Entertainment Group** and then change the **Font Size** to **28**. Change the **Font Color** to **Light Gray, Background 2**—under Theme Colors, in the third column, the first color. On the **Format tab** in the **Shape Styles group**, click **Shape Fill**, and then under **Theme Colors**, in the third column, click the first color— **Light Gray, Background 2**

2 On the **Insert tab**, in the **Images group**, click **Online Pictures**. In the **Bing Image Search** box, type **sheet music** and then press [Enter].

(Mac users, open your browser, navigate to Bing.com, click Images, search for **sheet music** and download an appropriate image. Save the file to your computer and use the Insert Picture icon in the content placeholder to insert your downloaded image. For this Activity you can insert the picture *p02C_Music* that is included with the data files for this project.)

a. Click a horizontal picture of lines of music on a music sheet of your choosing, and then click **Insert**. If necessary, click to select the credit line below the image and press [Delete]. If you are unable to find a suitable online image or prefer your screen to match the figure for this project, you can insert the picture *p02C_Music* that is included with the data files for this project.

b. On the **Format tab**, in the **Size group**, click in the **Shape Height** box. Replace the selected number with **2.5** and then press [Enter] to resize the image.

c. Drag the picture down and to the right until intersecting red dashed Smart Guides display, indicating that the picture is center aligned with the title and its top edge aligns with the bottom edge of the title placeholder.

d. With the picture selected, on the **Format tab**, in the **Size group**, click the **Crop arrow**, and then point to **Crop to Shape**. Under **Basic Shapes**, click the first shape— **Oval**. In the **Picture Styles group**, click **Picture Effects**, point to **Soft Edges**, and then click **25 Point**.

e. With the picture selected, hold down [Shift], and the click the **frame shape** and the **title placeholder** so that all three objects are selected. On the **Format tab**, in the **Arrange group**, click **Align**, and then click **Align to Slide**. Click **Align** again, and then click **Align Center**. **Save** the presentation.

3 Display **Slide 2**. On the **Insert tab**, in the **Images group**, click **Pictures**. In the **Insert Picture** dialog box, navigate to the data files for this project, click **p02C_Drums**, and then click **Insert**. (Mac users click Pictures and then click Picture from File.)

a. With the picture selected, on the **Format tab**, in the **Size group**, click the **Crop arrow**, and then point to **Crop to Shape**. Under **Basic Shapes**, click the first shape— **Oval**. In the **Picture Styles group**, click **Picture Effects**, point to **Soft Edges**, and then click **50 Point**.

b. Click in the placeholder containing the text *Every Friday in June and July*. On the **Home tab**, in the **Paragraph group**, click **Bullets** to remove the bullet symbol from the title.

c. Select the text *Every Friday in June and July*. On the **Home tab**, in the **Font group**, click the **Font Color button arrow**. Below the gallery, click **Eyedropper**, and then move the eyedropper pointer so that it is pointing to any bright colored area of the drum on the right side of the picture. Click one time to apply the color to the selected text. Apply **Bold** and **Italic** and change the **Font Size** to **32**.

4 Display **Slide 3**, and then select the third and fourth bullet points—*Seating is limited* and *Reserved seating is available*.

a. On the **Home tab**, in the **Paragraph group**, click the **Bullets button arrow**, and then click **Bullets and Numbering**. In the second row, click the first style—**Hollow Square Bullets**. Replace the number in the **Size** box with **90** and then click the **Color arrow**. Under **Recent Colors**, apply the color chosen using the eyedropper on Slide 2. Click **OK**.

(continues on next page)

Chapter Review

Skills Review | **Project 2D Corporate Events**

Apply 2B skills from these Objectives:

5. Remove Picture Backgrounds and Insert WordArt
6. Create and Format a SmartArt Graphic
7. Insert a 3D Object

In the following Skills Review, you will format a presentation by inserting and formatting WordArt and SmartArt graphics. Your completed presentation will look similar to Figure 2.56.

Project Files

For Project 2D, you will need:

p02D_Corporate_Events

You will save your presentation as:

Lastname_Firstname_2D_Corporate_Events

Project Results

Figure 2.56 Project 2D Corporate Events

(continues on next page)

Chapter Review

1 Start PowerPoint. From your student data files, locate and open **p02D_Corporate_Events**. **Save** the presentation in your **PowerPoint Chapter 2** folder as **Lastname_Firstname_2D_Corporate_Events**

a. With **Slide 1** displayed, select the text *Corporate Event Planning*. On the **Format tab**, in the **WordArt Styles group**, click **More**. In the third row, click the last style—**Fill: Brown, Background color 2; Inner Shadow**. Click outside the placeholder.

b. On the **Insert tab**, in the **Text group**, click **WordArt**. In the **WordArt gallery**, in the first row, click the fourth style—**Fill: White; Outline: Tan, Accent color 5; Shadow**. With the text *Your text here* selected, type **Sensation Park**

c. With the WordArt selected, hold down Shift, and then click the subtitle. On the **Format tab**, in the **Arrange group**, click **Align**, and then click **Align Selected Objects**. Click **Align** again, and then click **Align Left**.

2 Display **Slide 3**. In the center of the content placeholder, click **Insert a SmartArt Graphic** to open the **Choose a SmartArt Graphic** dialog box. On the left, click **List**, and then scroll as necessary and locate and click **Horizontal Bullet List**. Click **OK**.

a. In the SmartArt graphic, in the first gold rectangle, click **Text**. Type **Days and Times** and then click in the rectangle below the text you typed. Type **Weeknights** and then click in the second bullet point. Type **7 to 11 p.m.**

b. In the second gold rectangle, type **Packages** and then click in the rectangle below the text you typed. Type **Admission, parking, and dinner** and then delete the second text bullet point in the rectangle.

c. In the third gold rectangle, type **Capacity** and then click in the rectangle below the text you typed. Type **Maximum 750 guests** and then delete the second text bullet point in the rectangle.

d. On the **SmartArt Tools Design tab**, in the **SmartArt Styles group**, click **Change Colors**, and then under **Colorful**, click the last style **Colorful Range - Accent Colors 5 to 6**. In the **SmartArt Styles group**, click **More**, and then under **3-D**, in the first row, click the fourth style—**Powder**.

e. Click in the **Days and Times** rectangle, hold down Shift, and then click the **Packages** and **Capacity** rectangles. On the **SmartArt Tools Format tab**, in the **Shapes group**, click **Change Shape**. Under **Rectangles**, click the fourth shape—**Rectangle: Top Corners Snipped.**

3 Display **Slide 4**, and then click anywhere in the bulleted list. On the **Home tab**, in the **Paragraph group**, click **Convert to SmartArt**. At the bottom of the gallery, click **More SmartArt Graphics**. On the left side of the **Choose a SmartArt Graphic** dialog box, click **List**. Locate and click **Grouped List**, and then click **OK** to convert the list to a SmartArt graphic.

(Mac users, choose the first SmartArt style. On the SmartArt Design tab, below the style gallery, click More. Scroll to List and click Grouped List.)

a. Under **Family Evening**, click in the **Dinner and Dessert** shape, and then on the **SmartArt Tools Design tab**, in the **Create Graphic group**, click **Add Shape**. In the inserted shape, type **Special children's events**

b. With the *Special children's events* shape selected, add another shape, and then type **All ages**

c. On the **SmartArt Tools Design tab**, in the **SmartArt Styles group**, click **Change Colors**. In the **Color** gallery, under **Colorful**, click the last style—**Colorful Range - Accent Colors 5 to 6**.

d. On the **Design tab**, in the **SmartArt Styles group**, click **More** to display the **SmartArt Styles gallery**. Under **3-D**, in the first row, click the third style—**Cartoon**.

4 Display **Slide 5**. Select the picture of the admission tickets, and then on the **Format tab**, in the **Adjust group**, click **Remove Background**. In the **Close group**, click **Keep Changes**.

a. With the picture selected, on the **Format tab**, in the **Picture Styles group**, click **Picture Effects**. Point to **Soft Edges**, and then click **25 Point**.

b. Insert a **Header & Footer** on the **Notes and Handouts**. Include the **Date and time updated automatically**, a **Page number**, and a **Footer** with the text **2D_Corporate_Events**

c. Display the document properties. As the **Tags** type **corporate events** and as the **Subject** type your course and section number. Be sure your name displays as author, and then **Save** your file.

(Mac users, instead of tags, use the Keywords box.)

d. View the slide show from the beginning. As directed by your instructor, create and submit a paper printout or an electronic image of your presentation that looks like a printed document; or, submit your completed PowerPoint file. **Close** PowerPoint.

You have completed Project 2D | END

Content-Based Assessments (Mastery and Transfer of Learning)

| MyLab IT Grader | **Mastering PowerPoint** | **Project 2E Coasters** |

In the following Mastering PowerPoint project, you will format a presentation describing new roller coasters being constructed at several Sensation Park Entertainment Group amusement parks. Your completed presentation will look similar to Figure 2.57.

Apply 2A skills from these Objectives:

1. Format Numbered and Bulleted Lists
2. Insert Online Pictures
3. Insert Text Boxes and Shapes
4. Format Objects

Project Files for MyLab IT Grader

1. In your **MyLab IT** course, locate and click **PowerPoint 2E Coasters**, Download Materials, and then Download All Files.
2. Extract the zipped folder to your PowerPoint Chapter 2 folder. Close the Grader download screens.
3. Take a moment to open the downloaded **PowerPoint_2E_Coasters_Instructions**; note any recent updates to the book.

Project Results

Figure 2.57 Project 2E Coasters. (Christian Müller/Fotolia)

For Non-MyLab Submissions

For Project 2E, you will need:
p02E_Coasters

In your PowerPoint Chapter 2 folder, save your presentation as:
Lastname_Firstname_2E_Coasters

After you have named and saved your presentation, on the next page, begin with Step 2.
After Step 13, save and submit your presentation as directed by your instructor.

(continues on next page)

1 Navigate to your **PowerPoint Chapter 2 folder** and then double-click the PowerPoint file you downloaded from **MyLab IT** that displays your name—**Student_PowerPoint_2E_Coasters**

2 On **Slide 2**, remove the bullet symbol from the paragraph, and then **Center** the paragraph.

3 With the content placeholder selected, display the **Shape Styles** gallery, and then apply the **Subtle Effect – Blue-Gray, Accent 5** style. Apply the **Round Convex** beveled shape effect to the placeholder.

Note—this may be named Art Deco on your system.

4 On **Slide 3**, apply **Numbering** to the first-level bullet points—*Intensity, Hang Time,* and *Last Chance*. Change all of the second-level bullets to **Star Bullets**, and then change the bullet color to the fourth color in the fifth column under Theme Colors.

5 On **Slide 3**, select the title. Using the **Eyedropper**, select the light yellow color of the stripe on the roller coaster car at the right side of the picture and change the font color of the title. On **Slides 1** and **2**, apply the same light yellow color to the slide title on each slide.

6 On **Slide 3**, apply the **Glow: 5 point; Aqua, Accent color 2** picture effect to the picture.

7 Display **Slide 4**. Insert an **Online Picture** by searching for **roller coaster** and then insert a picture of people riding a roller coaster. **Crop** the picture by dragging the crop handles so that it's roughly square in shape.

Note—alternatively, search for an image in a web browser, and then download and insert a relevant image from the results or insert the image *p02E_Roller_Coaster* downloaded with the data files for this project.

8 Align the upper left corner of the picture with the top left corner of the slide, and then change the **Height** to **4.5** Modify the **Picture Effect** by applying a **50 Point Soft Edges** effect.

9 Duplicate the picture, and then use the **Align to Slide** option to align the pictures with the left edge of the slide and to distribute the pictures vertically.

10 Insert a **Text Box** aligned with the **horizontal ruler at 0 inches** and with the **lower half of the vertical ruler at 2.5 inch**. In the text box, type **Starting Summer 2022!** Change the **Font Size** to **28**. Change the **Shape Fill** to the sixth color in the last column under Theme Colors.

11 Select the title and the text box, and then, using the **Align Selected Objects** option, apply **Align Right** alignment.

12 **Insert** a **Header & Footer** on the **Notes and Handouts**. Include the **Date and time updated automatically**, the **Page number**, and a **Footer** with the text **2E_Coasters**

13 Display the document properties. As the **Tags** type **coasters** and as the **Subject** type your course and section. (Mac users enter keywords instead of tags.) Be sure your name displays as author, and then **Save** your file. **Close** PowerPoint.

14 In **MyLab IT**, in your **Course Materials**, locate and click the Grader Project **PowerPoint 2E Coasters**. In **step 3**, under **Upload Completed Assignment**, click **Choose File**. In the **Open** dialog box, navigate to your **PowerPoint Chapter 2 folder**, and then click your **Student_PowerPoint_2E_ Coasters** file one time to select it. In the lower right corner of the **Open** dialog box, click **Open**.

The name of your selected file displays above the Upload button.

15 To submit your file to **MyLab IT** for grading, click **Upload**, wait a moment for a green **Success!** message, and then in **step 4**, click the blue **Submit for Grading** button. Click **Close Assignment** to return to your list of **Course Materials**.

You have completed Project 2E **END**

Content-Based Assessments (Mastery and Transfer of Learning)

| MyLab IT Grader | Mastering PowerPoint | Project 2F Attractions |

In the following Mastering PowerPoint project, you will format a presentation describing new attractions at several of the Sensation Park Entertainment Group amusement parks. Your completed presentation will look similar to Figure 2.58.

Apply 2B skills from these Objectives:

5. Remove Picture Backgrounds and Insert WordArt
6. Create and Format a SmartArt Graphic
7. Insert a 3D Object

Project Files for MyLab IT Grader

1. In your **MyLab IT** course, locate and click **PowerPoint 2F Attractions**, Download Materials, and then Download All Files.
2. Extract the zipped folder to your PowerPoint Chapter 2 folder. Close the Grader download screens.
3. Take a moment to open the downloaded **PowerPoint_2F_Attractions_Instructions**; note any recent updates to the book.

Project Results

Figure 2.58 Project 2F Attractions

For Non-MyLab Submissions

For Project 2F, you will need: In your PowerPoint Chapter 2 folder, save your presentation as:
p02F_Attractions   **Lastname_Firstname_2F_Attractions**

After you have named and saved your presentation, on the next page, begin with Step 2.
After Step 13, save and submit your presentation as directed by your instructor.

(continues on next page)

Mastering PowerPoint: Project 2F Attractions (continued)

1 Navigate to your **PowerPoint Chapter 2 folder** and then double-click the PowerPoint file you downloaded from **MyLab IT** that displays your name—**Student_PowerPoint_2F_Attractions**. If necessary, at the top, click **Enable Editing**.

2 On **Slide 1**, select the title and display the **WordArt** gallery. In the third row, apply the first WordArt style. Change the **Text Outline** by applying under Theme Colors, in the fourth column, the fourth color.

3 On **Slide 2**, in the content placeholder, insert a **List** type **SmartArt** graphic—**Vertical Bullet List**. In the first Text placeholder, type **Location** and then in the bullet point, type **Brookside** In the second placeholder, type **Availability** and then in the bullet point, type **June 2022**

4 Click the *Availability* placeholder, and then add a shape after the placeholder. In the new placeholder, type **Specifications** and then add a bullet. Type **Course located around park perimeter**

5 Change the SmartArt color to **Colorful Range - Accent Colors 4 to 5**, and then apply the **3-D Polished** style.

6 Select the three shapes, and then change the shapes to the **Right Arrow** shape. On the **Format tab**, in the **Shapes group**, click the **Smaller** button one time to decrease the size of the arrows.

7 On **Slide 3**, convert the bulleted list to a **SmartArt** graphic by applying the **Vertical Box List** graphic. (Mac users, convert to Vertical Bullet List and then change to Vertical Box List)

8 Change the SmartArt color to **Colorful Range - Accent Colors 4 to 5**, and then apply the **Polished 3-D** SmartArt style.

9 On **Slide 5**, insert a **WordArt** using the last style in the first row. Replace the WordArt text with **To Accept the Challenge?** Change the **Font Size** to **48**.

10 Drag the WordArt down so that its top edge is positioned on the **lower half of the vertical ruler at 1**. Align center.

11 Insert a **Header & Footer** on the **Notes and Handouts**. Include the **Date and time updated automatically**, the **Page number**, and a **Footer** with the text **2F_Attractions**

12 Display the document properties. As the **Tags** type **zip line, rock wall** and as the **Subject,** type your course and section. Be sure your name displays as author, and then **Save** your file. (Mac users enter keywords instead of tags.)

13 In the upper right corner of your screen, click **Close** ⊠ to close PowerPoint.

14 In **MyLab IT**, in your **Course Materials**, locate and click the Grader Project **PowerPoint_2F_Attractions**. In **step 3**, under **Upload Completed Assignment**, click **Choose File**. In the **Open** dialog box, navigate to your **PowerPoint Chapter 2 folder**, and then click your **Student_PowerPoint_2F_ Attractions** file one time to select it. In the lower right corner of the **Open** dialog box, click **Open**.

The name of your selected file displays above the Upload button.

15 To submit your file to **MyLab IT** for grading, click **Upload**, wait a moment for a green **Success!** message, and then in **step 4**, click the blue **Submit for Grading** button. Click **Close Assignment** to return to your list of **Course Materials**.

You have completed Project 2F **END**

Content-Based Assessments (Mastery and Transfer of Learning)

Mastering PowerPoint   **Project 2G Orientation**

Apply 2A and 2B skills from these Objectives:

1. Format Numbered and Bulleted Lists
2. Insert Online Pictures
3. Insert Text Boxes and Shapes
4. Format Objects
5. Remove Picture Backgrounds and Insert WordArt
6. Create and Format a SmartArt Graphic
7. Insert a 3D Object

In the following Mastering PowerPoint project, you will edit an existing presentation that is shown to Sensation Park Entertainment Group employees on their first day of a three-day orientation. Your completed presentation will look similar to Figure 2.59.

Project Files for MyLab IT Grader

1. In your **MyLab IT** course, locate and click **PowerPoint 2G Orientation**, Download Materials, and then Download All Files.
2. Extract the zipped folder to your PowerPoint Chapter 2 folder. Close the Grader download screens.
3. Take a moment to open the downloaded **PowerPoint_2G_Orientation_Instructions**; note any recent updates to the book.

Project Results

Figure 2.59 Project 2G Orientation

For Non-MyLab Submissions

For Project 2G, you will need:
p02G_Orientation

In your PowerPoint Chapter 2 folder, save your presentation as:
Lastname_Firstname_2G_Orientation

After you have named and saved your presentation, on the next page, begin with Step 2.
After Step 17, save and submit your presentation as directed by your instructor.

(continues on next page)

1 Navigate to your **PowerPoint Chapter 2 folder** and then double-click the PowerPoint file you downloaded from **MyLab IT** that displays your name—**Student_PowerPoint_2G_Orientation**. If necessary, at the top, click **Enable Editing**.

2 On **Slide 1**, format the subtitle—*New Employee Orientation*—as **WordArt** using the last style in the first row.

3 Select the picture and then **Crop** the image from the left side so that the center-left crop handle aligns with the **left half of the horizontal ruler at 5 inches**.

4 Change the picture **Height** to **3.5** and then apply a **Glow: 8 point; Turquoise, Accent color 1** picture effect to the image. Use the **Align Selected Objects** command to apply **Align Middle** to the title and the picture.

5 On **Slide 2**, remove the bullet symbol from the paragraph, and then change the **Shape Fill** to the second color in the third column under Theme Colors, and the **Shape Outline** to the first color in the second column under Theme Colors.

6 On **Slide 3**, convert the bulleted list to the **Hierarchy** type **SmartArt** graphic—**Hierarchy List**. Change the color to **Colorful Range - Accent Colors 3 to 4**, and then apply the **3-D Inset** style.

7 On **Slide 4**, change the two bulleted lists to **Numbering**.

8 On **Slide 5**, change the bullet symbols to **Filled Square Bullets**, change the **Color** to the fourth color in the third column under Theme Colors, and then change the **Size** to **100**

9 On **Slide 5**, in the placeholder on the right, insert an **Online Picture** by searching for **fire alarm** and then insert a picture of a fire alarm with a background.

Note—alternatively, insert the image *p02G_Alarm* downloaded with the data files for this project.

10 If the option is available, remove the background from the picture, and then apply the **Glow: 18 point, Bright Green, Accent color 3** picture effect.

11 On **Slide 5**, insert a **Text Box** below the content placeholder on the left side of the slide. In the text box, type **All employees will be tested on park safety procedures!** Using the **Align to Slide** option **Align Center** the text box and apply **Align Bottom**.

12 On **Slide 6**, from the **Shapes** gallery, under **Basic Shapes**, insert a **Diamond** of any size anywhere on the slide. Resize the diamond so that its **Shape Height** is **6** and its **Shape Width** is **8**

13 Using the **Align to Slide** option, apply **Align Center**, and **Align Middle** to the diamond shape. Apply the **Moderate Effect – Bright Green, Accent 3** shape style.

14 In the diamond, type **Sensation Park Entertainment Group Welcomes You!** Change the **Font Size** to **28**, and then apply the **Round Convex Bevel** effect to the diamond shape. **Note**—this effect may be called Art Deco on some systems.

15 Insert a **Header & Footer** on the **Notes and Handouts**. Include the **Date and time updated automatically**, the **Page number**, and a **Footer** with the text **2G_Orientation**

16 Display the document properties. As the **Tags** type **orientation** and as the **Subject** type your course and section number. (Mac users use the Keywords box.) Be sure your name displays as author, and then **Save** your file.

17 In the upper right corner of your screen, click **Close** ☒ to close PowerPoint.

18 In **MyLab IT**, in your **Course Materials**, locate and click the Grader Project **PowerPoint 2G Orientation**. In **step 3**, under **Upload Completed Assignment**, click **Choose File**. In the **Open** dialog box, navigate to your **Excel Chapter 2 folder**, and then click your **Student_PowerPoint_2G_Orientation** file one time to select it. In the lower right corner of the **Open** dialog box, click **Open**.

The name of your selected file displays above the Upload button.

19 To submit your file to **MyLab IT** for grading, click **Upload**, wait a moment for a green **Success!** message, and then in **step 4**, click the blue **Submit for Grading** button. Click **Close Assignment** to return to your list of **Course Materials**.

You have completed Project 2G **END**

Content-Based Assessments (Critical Thinking)

Apply a combination of the 2A and 2B skills.

GO! Fix It	**Project 2H Summer Jobs**	IRC
GO! Make It	**Project 2I Renovation Plans**	IRC
GO! Solve It	**Project 2J Business Summary**	IRC
GO! Solve It	**Project 2K Hotel**	

Project Files

For Project 2K, you will need:

p02K_Hotel

You will save your presentation as:

Lastname_Firstname_1K_Packing

Open the file p02K_Hotel and save it in your **PowerPoint Chapter 2** folder as **Lastname_Firstname_2K_Hotel** Complete the presentation by inserting an online picture on the first slide and applying appropriate picture effects. On Slide 2, format the bullet point as a single paragraph and apply a shape style, and then on Slide 3, convert the bulleted list to an appropriate SmartArt graphic. Change the SmartArt color and apply a style. On Slide 4, insert and attractively position a WordArt with the text Save the Date! On the Notes and Handouts, insert a header and footer that includes the date and time updated automatically, the file name in the footer, and the page number. Add your name, your course name and section number, and the tags **hotel, accommodations** to the Properties area. Save your presentation. As directed by your instructor, create and submit a paper printout or an electronic image of your presentation that looks like a printed document; or, submit your completed PowerPoint file.

		Performance Level		
		Exemplary	**Proficient**	**Developing**
Performance Criteria	**Insert and format an appropriate online picture**	An appropriate online picture was inserted and formatted in the presentation.	An online picture was inserted but was not appropriate for the presentation or was not formatted.	An online picture was not inserted.
	Insert and format appropriate SmartArt graphic	Appropriate SmartArt graphic was inserted and formatted in the presentation.	SmartArt graphic was inserted but was not appropriate for the presentation or was not formatted.	SmartArt graphic was not inserted.
	Insert and format appropriate WordArt	Appropriate WordArt was inserted and formatted in the presentation.	WordArt was inserted but was not appropriate for the presentation or was not formatted.	WordArt was not inserted.
	Remove bullet point and apply appropriate shape style	Bullet point was removed and an appropriate shape style was applied.	Either the bullet point was not removed or the shape style was not applied.	Bullet point was not removed and a shape style was not applied.

You have completed Project 2K | END

Outcomes-Based Assessments (Critical Thinking)

Rubric

The following outcomes-based assessments are *open-ended assessments*. That is, there is no specific correct result; your result will depend on your approach to the information provided. Make *Professional Quality* your goal. Use the following scoring rubric to guide you in *how* to approach the problem and then to evaluate *how well* your approach solves the problem.

The *criteria*—Software Mastery, Content, Format and Layout, and Process—represent the knowledge and skills you have gained that you can apply to solving the problem. The *levels of performance*—Professional Quality, Approaching Professional Quality, or Needs Quality Improvements—help you and your instructor evaluate your result.

	Your completed project is of Professional Quality if you:	Your completed project is Approaching Professional Quality if you:	Your completed project Needs Quality Improvements if you:
1-Software Mastery	Choose and apply the most appropriate skills, tools, and features and identify efficient methods to solve the problem.	Choose and apply some appropriate skills, tools, and features, but not in the most efficient manner.	Choose inappropriate skills, tools, or features, or are inefficient in solving the problem.
2-Content	Construct a solution that is clear and well organized, contains content that is accurate, appropriate to the audience and purpose, and is complete. Provide a solution that contains no errors of spelling, grammar, or style.	Construct a solution in which some components are unclear, poorly organized, inconsistent, or incomplete. Misjudge the needs of the audience. Have some errors in spelling, grammar, or style, but the errors do not detract from comprehension.	Construct a solution that is unclear, incomplete, or poorly organized, contains some inaccurate or inappropriate content, and contains many errors of spelling, grammar, or style. Do not solve the problem.
3-Format and Layout	Format and arrange all elements to communicate information and ideas, clarify function, illustrate relationships, and indicate relative importance.	Apply appropriate format and layout features to some elements, but not others. Overuse features, causing minor distraction.	Apply format and layout that does not communicate information or ideas clearly. Do not use format and layout features to clarify function, illustrate relationships, or indicate relative importance. Use available features excessively, causing distraction.
4-Process	Use an organized approach that integrates planning, development, self-assessment, revision, and reflection.	Demonstrate an organized approach in some areas, but not others; or, use an insufficient process of organization throughout.	Do not use an organized approach to solve the problem.

Outcomes-Based Assessments (Critical Thinking)

Apply a combination of the 2A and 2B skills.

GO! Think   **Project 2L Interactive Ride**

Project Files

For Project 2L, you will need:
New blank PowerPoint presentation
You will save your presentation as:
Lastname_Firstname_2L_Interactive_Ride

As part of its mission to combine fun with the discovery of math and science, Sensation Park Entertainment Group is opening a new, interactive roller coaster at its South Lake Tahoe location. Sensation Park's newest coaster is designed for maximum thrill and minimum risk. In a special interactive exhibit located next to the coaster, riders can learn about the physics behind this powerful coaster and even try their hand at building a coaster.

Guests will begin by selecting the height of the first hill, which determines the coaster's maximum potential energy to complete its journey. Next they will plan the exit path, and build additional hills, loops, and corkscrews. When completed, riders can submit their coaster for a safety inspection to find out whether the ride passes or fails.

Whether the ride passes or fails, riders can take a virtual tour of the ride they created to see the maximum speed achieved, the amount of negative G-forces applied, the length of the track, and the overall thrill factor. They can also see how their coaster compares with other Sensation Park coasters, and they can email the coaster simulation to their friends.

Using the preceding information, create a presentation that Marketing Director, Annette Chosek, will present at a travel fair describing the new attraction. The presentation should include four to six slides with at least one SmartArt graphic and one online picture. Apply an appropriate theme and use slide layouts that will effectively present the content, and use text boxes, shapes, and WordArt if appropriate. Apply font formatting and slide transitions, and modify text alignment and line spacing as necessary. Save the file as **Lastname_Firstname_2L_Interactive_Ride** and then insert a header and footer that includes the date and time updated automatically, the file name in the footer, and the page number. Add your name, your course name and section number, and the tags **roller coaster, new rides** to the Properties area. As directed by your instructor, create and submit a paper printout or an electronic image of your presentation that looks like a printed document; or, submit your completed PowerPoint file.

You have completed Project 2L   END

Outcomes-Based Assessments (Critical Thinking)

GO! Think	**Project 2M Research**	IRC
You and GO!	**Project 2N Theme Park**	IRC
GO! Cumulative Team Project	**Project 2O Bell Orchid Hotels**	IRC

Enhancing a Presentation with Animation, Video, Tables, and Charts

POWERPOINT 2019

PROJECT 3A

Outcomes
Customize a presentation with animation and video

Objectives
1. Customize Slide Backgrounds and Themes
2. Animate a Slide Show
3. Insert a Video

PROJECT 3B

Outcomes
Create a presentation that includes data in tables and charts

Objectives
4. Create and Modify Tables
5. Create and Modify Charts

fotoGN/Shutterstock

In This Chapter

 GO! To Work with PowerPoint

In this chapter, you will learn how to customize a presentation by modifying the theme, formatting the slide background, and applying animation to slide elements. Additionally, you will learn how to enhance your presentations by inserting tables and charts that help your audience understand numeric data and trends just as pictures and diagrams help illustrate a concept. The data that you present should determine whether a table or a chart would most appropriately display your information. Styles applied to your tables and charts unify these slide elements by complementing your presentation theme.

The projects in this chapter relate to the city of **Pacifica Bay**, a coastal city south of San Francisco. The city's access to major transportation provides both residents and businesses an opportunity to compete in the global marketplace. The city's mission is to create a more beautiful and more economically viable community for its residents. Each year the city welcomes a large number of tourists who enjoy exploring the rocky coastline and seeing the famous landmarks in San Francisco. The city encourages best environmental practices and partners with cities in other countries to promote sound government at the local level.

<table>
<tr><td>PROJECT
3A</td><td># Parks and Trails
Presentation</td><td>**MyLab IT**
Project 3A Grader for Instruction
Project 3A Simulation for Training and Review</td></tr>
</table>

Project Activities

In Activities 3.01 through 3.17, you will edit and format a presentation that Carol Lehman, Director of Pacifica Bay Parks and Recreation, has created to inform residents about the benefits of using the city's parks and trails. Your completed presentation will look similar to Figure 3.1.

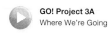 ## Project Files for **MyLab IT Grader**

1. In your storage location, create a folder named **PowerPoint Chapter 3**.
2. In to your **MyLab IT** course, locate and click **PowerPoint 3A Trails**, Download Materials, and then Download All Files.
3. Extract the zipped folder to your PowerPoint Chapter 3 folder. Close the Grader download screens.
4. Take a moment to open the downloaded **PowerPoint_3A_Trails_Instructions**; note any recent updates to the book.

Project Results

GO! Project 3A
Where We're Going

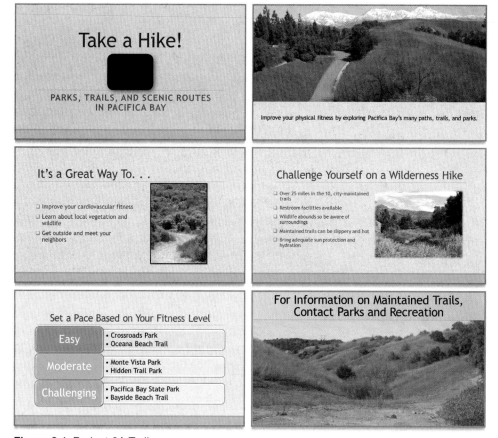

Figure 3.1 Project 3A Trails

 For Non-MyLab Submissions

For Project 3A, you will need:
p03A_Trails
p03A_Hills
p03A_Video

In your storage location, create a folder named **PowerPoint Chapter 3**
In your PowerPoint Chapter 3 folder, save your presentation as:
Lastname_Firstname_3A_Trails

After you have named and saved your presentation, on the next page, begin with Step 2.

Objective 1   Customize Slide Backgrounds and Themes

ALERT   Because Office 365 is a cloud-based subscription service that receives continuous updates, you may encounter some variations in what appears on your screen and what is shown in this instruction. Microsoft Office 365 is fully installed on your PC or Mac; no internet access is necessary to create or edit documents. When you *are* connected to the internet, you will receive monthly upgrades and new features, so you always have the latest versions of Office apps as soon as they are available. Your subscription gives you continuous free access to the latest innovations and refinements.

GO! Learn How
Video P3-1

You have practiced customizing presentations by applying themes with unified design elements, backgrounds, and colors that provide a consistent look in your presentation. Additional ways to customize a slide include changing theme fonts and colors, applying a background style, modifying the background color, or inserting a picture on the slide background.

Activity 3.01 | Changing Theme Colors

The presentation theme is a coordinated, predefined set of colors, fonts, lines, and fill effects. In this activity, you will open a presentation in which the Retrospect theme is applied, and then you will change the *theme colors*—a set of coordinating colors that are applied to the backgrounds, objects, and text in a presentation. For this presentation about parks and trails, a green theme is more appropriate than the orange theme.

1 Navigate to your **PowerPoint Chapter 3 folder**, and then double-click the PowerPoint file you downloaded from **MyLab IT** that displays your name—**Student_PowerPoint_3A_ Trails**. In your presentation, if necessary, at the top click **Enable Editing**.

2 Click the **Design tab**, and then in the **Variants group**, click **More** ⏷. Point to **Colors** to display the sets of theme colors. Point to several sets and notice the color changes on **Slide 1**.

MAC TIP   To display group names on the ribbon, display the menu, click PowerPoint, click Preferences, click View, and select the Show group titles check box.

MAC TIP   Live Preview is not available in the Mac version of PowerPoint.

3 Click **Green** to change the presentation colors, and then compare your screen with Figure 3.2. **Save** 🖫 your presentation.

Changing the colors does not change the overall design of the presentation. In this presentation, the *Retrospect* presentation theme is still applied to the presentation. By modifying the theme colors, you retain the design of the *Retrospect* theme but apply colors that coordinate with the pictures in the presentation, and that are available as text, accent, and background colors.

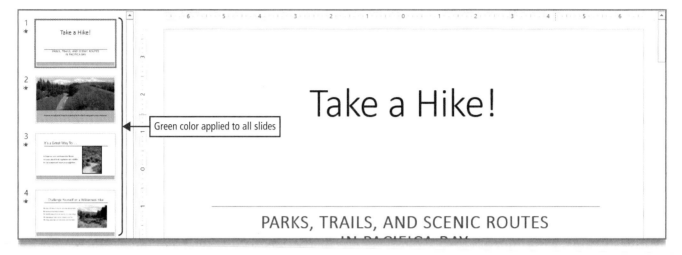

Figure 3.2

Activity 3.02 | **Changing Theme Fonts**

In addition to theme colors, every presentation theme includes ***theme fonts*** that determine the font to apply to two types of slide text—headings and body. The ***Headings font*** is applied to slide titles and the ***Body font*** is applied to all other text. When you apply a new theme font to the presentation, the text on every slide is updated with the new heading and body fonts.

1 With **Slide 1** displayed, click anywhere in the title placeholder. On the **Home tab**, in the **Font group**, click the **Font arrow**. Notice that at the top of the **Font** list, under **Theme Fonts**, Calibri Light (Headings) and Calibri (Body) display. Compare your screen with Figure 3.3.

Figure 3.3

2 Click anywhere on the slide to close the Font list. On the **Design tab**, in the **Variants group**, click **More** ⊡ Point to **Fonts**.

> This list displays the name of each theme and the pair of fonts in the theme. The first and larger font in each pair is the Headings font and the second and smaller font in each pair is the Body font.

3 Point to several of the themes and watch as Live Preview changes the title and subtitle text. Scroll to the bottom of the **Fonts** list, and then click **TrebuchetMS**. **Save** 🔲 your presentation and then compare your screen with Figure 3.4.

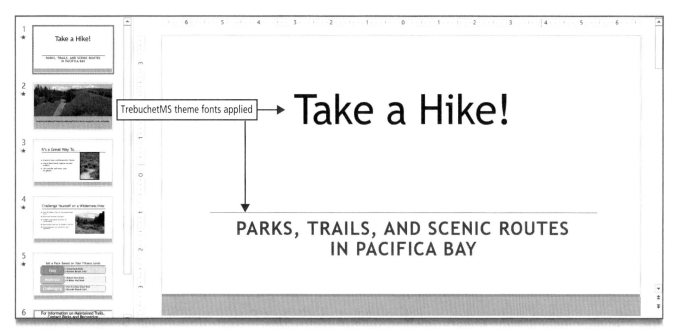

Figure 3.4

Activity 3.03 | Applying a Background Style

A ***background style*** is a predefined slide background fill variation that combines theme colors in different intensities or patterns.

1 With **Slide 1** displayed, on the **Design tab**, in the **Variants group**, click **More** ⊡. Point to **Background Styles**, and then compare your screen with Figure 3.5.

Figure 3.5

2 Point to each of the background styles to view the style on **Slide 1**. Then, in the first row, click **Style 2** Compare your screen with Figure 3.6.

The background style is applied to all the slides in the presentation.

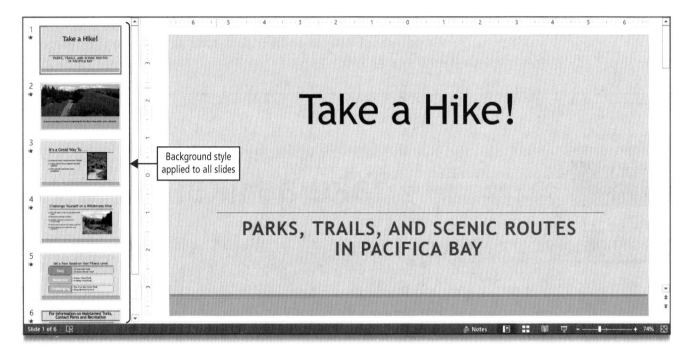

Background style applied to all slides

Figure 3.6

3 Display **Slide 5**. On the **Design tab**, in the **Variants group**, click **More** ⌄. Point to **Background Styles**, and then in the third row, right-click the third style—**Style 11**—to display the shortcut menu. On the shortcut menu, click **Apply to Selected Slides** to apply the style to Slide 5.

You can select individual slides to which you apply a background style.

MAC TIP The Mac version of PowerPoint does not enable you to apply a Background Style to selected slides, but only to the entire presentation. To customize one slide, click Format Background to open the Format Background pane. Apply the solid fill color—Dark Green, Text 2.

4 **Save** 🖫 your presentation.

Activity 3.04 | Hiding Background Graphics

2.2.2

Many PowerPoint themes contain graphic elements that display on the slide background. In the Retrospect theme applied to this presentation, the background includes a rectangle shape and line. Sometimes the background graphics interfere with or clash with the slide content. When this happens, you can hide the background graphics.

1 Display **Slide 2**, and notice the bright green rectangle and line at the bottom of the slide.

2 On the **Design tab**, in the **Customize group**, click **Format Background** to display the Format Background pane.

You can customize a slide background by changing the formatting options in the Format Background pane.

3 ▸ In the **Format Background** pane, be sure that under **Fill**, the fill options display, and if necessary, click Fill to display the options. Under **Fill**, select the **Hide Background Graphics** check box. Compare your slide with Figure 3.7.

The background objects—the rectangle and line below the picture—no longer display.

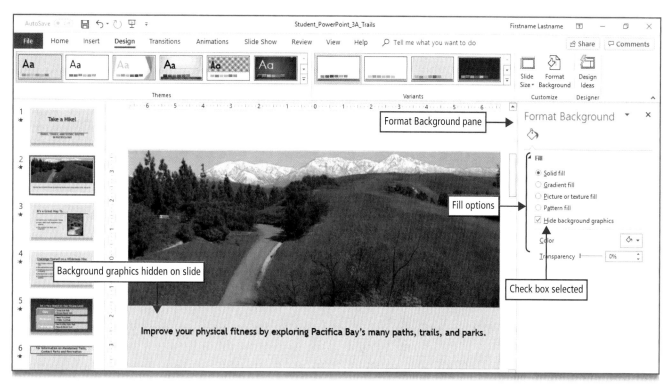

Figure 3.7

4 ▸ Leave the Format Background pane open for the next Activity, and then **Save** 🔚 your presentation.

MORE KNOWLEDGE **Hiding Background Objects from All Slides in a Presentation**

To hide the background objects from all of the slides in a presentation, in the Format Background pane, select the Hide background graphics check box, and then at the bottom of the Format Background pane, click Apply to All.

Activity 3.05 │ Applying a Background Fill Color to a Slide

2.2.2

In addition to applying predefined background styles, you can apply a fill color to one or all of the slides in your presentation.

1 ▸ Display **Slide 1**.

2 In the **Format Background** pane, under **Fill**, verify that **Solid fill** is selected, and selcct it if it is not. To the right of **Color**, click **Fill Color** 🎨. Under **Theme Colors**, in the third column, click the second color. Compare your screen with Figure 3.8.

The slightly darker solid fill color is applied to the slide background.

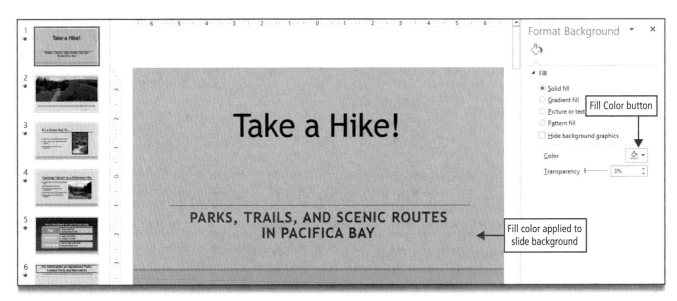

Figure 3.8

3 Leave the **Format Background** pane open for the next Activity. **Save** 💾 your presentation.

MORE KNOWLEDGE | **Applying a Fill Color to All the Slides in a Presentation**

To apply a fill color to all of the slides in a presentation, in the Format Background pane, select the fill color that you want to apply, and then at the bottom of the Format Background pane, click Apply to All.

2.2.2

Activity 3.06 | Applying a Background Texture

PowerPoint includes a selection of textures you can use to fill the slide background for visual interest.

1 Display **Slide 2**, hold down ⇧Shift and then in the slide thumbnails, click **Slide 4** to select **Slides 2**, **3**, and **4**.

Recall that you can select contiguous slides in this manner.

2 In the **Format Background** pane, under **Fill**, click **Picture or texture fill**.

A background picture that is part of the Retrospect theme may display on the slide background of the three selected slides.

3 Under **Insert picture from**, to the right of **Texture**, click **Texture** 🖼. In the **Texture gallery**, in the third row, point to the fourth texture—**Recycled paper**. Compare your screen with Figure 3.9.

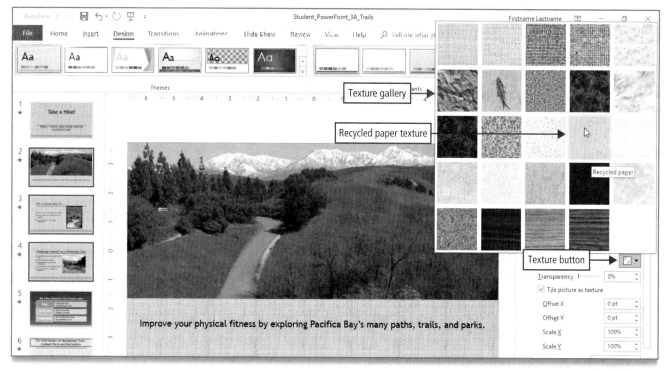

Figure 3.9

4 Click **Recycled paper** to apply the textured background to the three selected slides.

5 Leave the **Format Background** pane open for the next Activity, and then **Save** 🖫 your presentation.

Activity 3.07 | Applying a Picture to the Slide Background and Adjusting Transparency

MOS
2.2.2

You can insert a picture on a slide background so that the image fills the entire slide.

1 Display **Slide 6**. In the **Format Background** pane, select the **Hide background graphics** check box.

2 Under **Fill**, click **Picture or texture fill**. Under **Insert picture from**, click **File**. Navigate to your data files downloaded with this project, click **p03A_Hills**, and then click **Insert**. Compare your slide with Figure 3.10 and notice that the picture displays as the background of Slide 6.

When a picture is applied to a slide background using the Format Background option, the picture is not treated as an object. The picture fills the entire background and you cannot move it or size it.

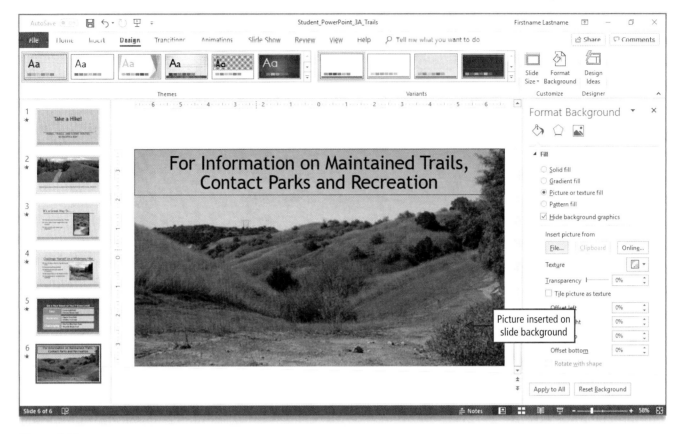

Figure 3.10

3 In the **Format Background** pane, to the right of **Transparency**, notice that *0%* displays, indicating that the picture is inserted in full color. Click in the **Transparency box**, and then replace the number with **50**

> The transparency setting lightens the picture on the slide background. You can use the transparency option when there are other objects on the slide that do not display well against the slide background.

ANOTHER WAY Drag the Transparency slider to the left or right to adjust the transparency figure.

4 Replace the number in the **Transparency box** with **10**

> The 10% transparency setting provides good contrast for the title while still displaying the picture in a vibrant color.

5 Click in the title placeholder. On the **Drawing Tools Format tab**, in the **Shape Styles group**, click **More**. In the fourth row, click the second style. Click anywhere on the slide outside of the title placeholder. Compare your screen with Figure 3.11.

> Adequate contrast between the slide background and slide text is important as it improves slide readability. Use combinations of transparency and text placeholder styles and fills to improve contrast.

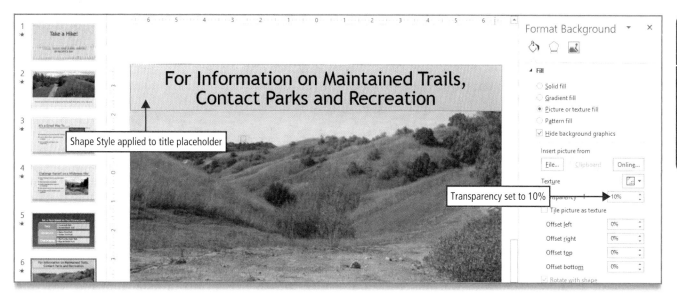

Figure 3.11

6 Leave the **Format Background** pane open for the next Activity. **Save** 🖫 your presentation.

Activity 3.08 | Resetting a Slide Background

1 Display **Slide 5**. At the bottom of the **Format Background** pane, click **Reset Background**, and then compare your slide with Figure 3.12.

> After making changes to a slide background, you may decide that the original formatting is the best choice for displaying the text and graphics on a slide. The Reset Background feature restores the theme and color theme formatting to a slide.

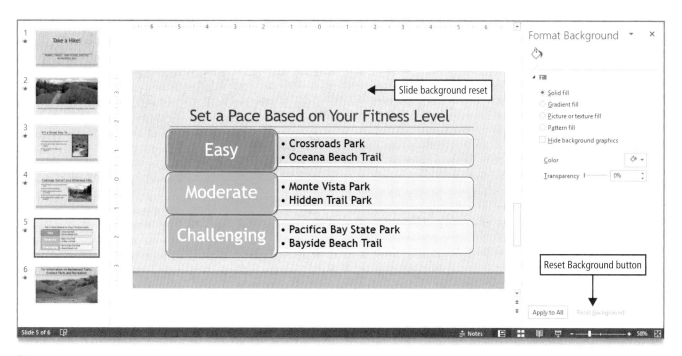

Figure 3.12

2 **Close** ☒ the **Format Background** pane, and then **Save** 🖫 your presentation.

Animation is a visual or sound effect added to an object or text on a slide. Use animation to focus the audience's attention, providing the speaker with an opportunity to emphasize important points using the slide element as an effective visual aid.

GO! Learn How
Video P3-2

Activity 3.09 | Applying Animation Entrance Effects and Effect Options

5.2.1, 5.2.3,
5.2.4

Entrance effects are animations that bring a slide element onto the screen. Use the animation Effect Options command to modify an entrance effect.

1 Display **Slide 3**, and then click anywhere in the bulleted list placeholder. On the **Animations tab**, in the **Animation group**, click **More** , and then compare your screen with Figure 3.13.

An entrance effect is animation that brings an object or text onto the screen. An *emphasis effect* is animation that emphasizes an object or text that is already displayed. An *exit effect* is animation that moves an object or text off the screen.

Figure 3.13

2 ▶ Under **Entrance**, click **Fly In**, and then notice the animation applied to the list. Compare your screen with Figure 3.14.

The numbers *1, 2,* and *3* display to the left of the bulleted list placeholder, indicating the order in which the bullet points will be animated during the slide show.

MAC TIP The Fly In animation is in the Basic group.

ALERT   **Are animation numbers missing?**

Make sure to select the Animation tab. If the animation numbers still do not appear on your slide, Save the file to a local drive on your computer, close the file, and reopen it. If the numbers still do not display, continue with the Activity, following along with the figures.

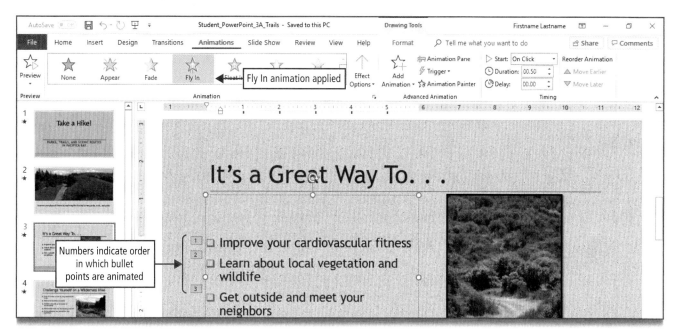

Figure 3.14

3 ▶ In the **Animation group**, click **Effect Options**, and then compare your screen with Figure 3.15.

The Effect Options control the direction and sequence in which the animation displays. Additional options may be available with other entrance effects.

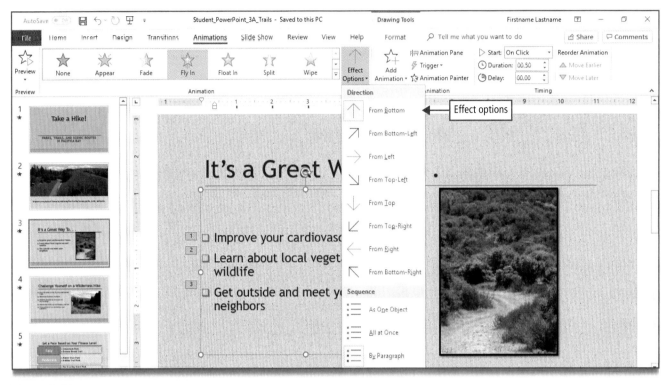

Figure 3.15

> **4** Click **From Top** and notice the bullets enter from the top of the slide.

> **5** Select the picture. In the **Animation group**, click **More** ⟨⟩, and then below the gallery, click **More Entrance Effects**. In the lower left corner of the **Change Entrance Effect** dialog box, verify that the **Preview Effect** check box is selected. Compare your screen with Figure 3.16.

> The Change Entrance Effect dialog box displays additional entrance effects grouped in four categories: Basic, Subtle, Moderate, and Exciting.

Figure 3.16

6 Under **Subtle**, click **Fade**, and then watch as Live Preview displays the picture with the selected entrance effect. Click **OK**

The number *4* displays next to the picture, indicating that it is fourth in the slide animation sequence.

7 Click in the title placeholder. On the **Animations tab**, in the **Animation group**, click **More** ⬇, and then under **Entrance**, click **Fade** to apply the animation to the title.

The number 5 displays next to the title, indicating that it is fifth in the slide animation sequence.

8 **Save** 🖫 the presentation.

Activity 3.10 | Reordering Animation

1 With **Slide 3** displayed, on the **Animations tab**, in the **Preview group**, click **Preview**.

The list displays first, followed by the picture, and then the title. The order in which animation is applied is the order in which objects display during the slide show.

2 Click in the title placeholder. On the **Animations tab**, in the **Timing group**, under **Reorder Animation**, click **Move Earlier** two times, until the sequence number displays 1, and then compare your screen with Figure 3.17.

🖥 **MAC TIP** In the Animations pane, click *5 It's a Great Way to..* and then click the up arrow two times.

To the left of the title placeholder, the number *1* displays. You can use the Reorder Animation buttons to change the order in which text and objects are animated during the slide show.

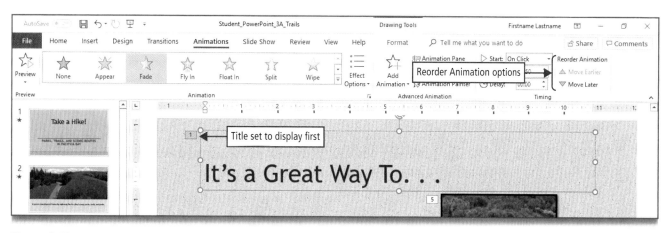

Figure 3.17

Activity 3.11 | Setting Animation Start Options

Timing options control when animated items display in the animation sequence.

1 If necessary, click in the title placeholder. On the **Animations tab**, in the **Timing group**, click the **Start arrow** to display three options—*On Click*, *With Previous*, and *After Previous*. Compare your screen with Figure 3.18.

The *On Click* option begins the animation sequence for the selected slide element when the mouse button is clicked or the [Spacebar] is pressed. The *With Previous* option begins the animation sequence at the same time as the previous animation or slide transition. The *After Previous* option begins the animation sequence for the selected slide element immediately after the completion of the previous animation or slide transition.

Figure 3.18

2 Click **After Previous**, and then notice that next to the title, the number *1* is changed to *0*, indicating that the animation will begin immediately after the slide transition; the presenter does not need to click the mouse button or press Spacebar to display the title.

3 Select the picture, and then in the **Timing group**, click the **Start arrow**. Click **With Previous** and notice that the number is changed to *3*, indicating that the animation will begin at the same time as the last bullet in the bulleted list.

4 On the **Animations tab**, in the **Preview group**, click **Preview** and notice that the title displays first, and that the picture displays at the same time as the last bullet in the bulleted list.

5 Display **Slide 1**, and then click in the title placeholder. On the **Animations tab**, in the **Animation group**, click the **Entrance** effect **Fly In**, and then click **Effect Options**. Click **From Top**. In the **Timing group**, click the **Start arrow**, and then click **After Previous**.

The number *0* displays to the left of the title indicating that the animation will begin immediately after the slide transition.

6 **Save** your presentation.

Activity 3.12 | Setting Animation Duration and Delay Timing Options

MOS
5.3.1

1 On **Slide 1**, if necessary, click in the title placeholder. On the **Animation tab**, in the **Timing group**, click the **Duration up arrow** so that *00.75* displays in the **Duration** box. Compare your screen with Figure 3.19.

Duration controls the speed of the animation. You can set the duration of an animation by typing a value in the Duration box, or you can use the spin box arrows to increase and decrease the duration in 0.25-second increments. When you decrease the duration, the animation speed increases. When you increase the duration, the animation is slowed.

Figure 3.19

2 Click anywhere in the subtitle, and then in the **Animation group**, apply the **Fade** entrance effect. In the **Timing group**, click the **Start arrow**, and then click **After Previous**. In the **Timing group**, select the value in the **Delay** box, type.**50** and then press Enter. Compare your screen with Figure 3.20.

MAC TIP The Delay option is in the Timing section of the Animations pane.

You can use Delay to begin a selected animation after a specified amount of time has elapsed. Here, the animation is delayed by one-half of a second after the completion of the previous animation—the title animation. You can type a value in the Delay or Duration boxes, or you can use the up and down arrows to change the timing.

Figure 3.20

3 View the slide show from the beginning and notice the animation on Slides 1 and 3. When the black slide displays, press Esc to return to Normal view, and then **Save** your presentation.

Activity 3.13 | Using Animation Painter and Removing Animation

Animation Painter is a feature that copies animation settings from one object to another.

1 Display **Slide 3**, and then click anywhere in the bulleted list. On the **Animations tab**, in the **Advanced Animation group**, click **Animation Painter**. Display **Slide 4**, and then point anywhere in the bulleted list placeholder to display the Animation Painter pointer. Compare your screen with Figure 3.21.

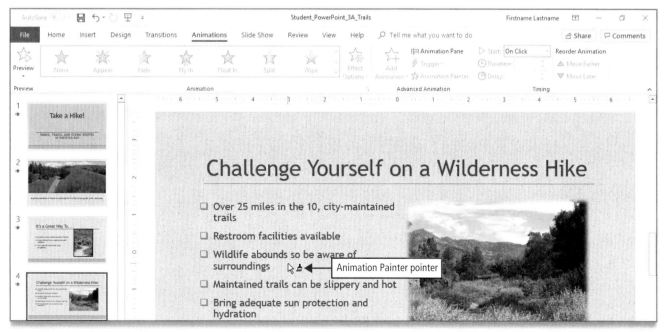

Figure 3.21

2 Click the bulleted list to copy the animation settings from the list on **Slide 3** to the list on **Slide 4.**

3 Display **Slide 3**, and then select the picture. Using the technique that you just practiced, use **Animation Painter** to copy the animation from the picture on **Slide 3** to the picture on **Slide 4**. With **Slide 4** displayed, compare your screen with Figure 3.22.

> The numbers displayed to the left of the bulleted list and the picture indicate that animation is applied to the objects.

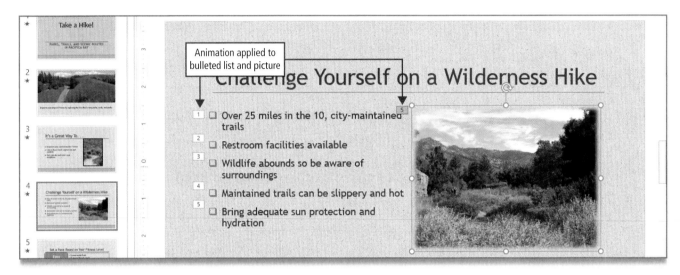

Figure 3.22

4 Display **Slide 3**, and then click in the title placeholder. On the **Animations tab**, in the **Animation group**, click **None** to remove the animation from the title placeholder. Compare your screen with Figure 3.23, and then **Save** 🖫 your presentation.

MAC TIP In the Animations pane, under ANIMATIONS, select the title and then click the red X to remove the animation.

Figure 3.23

Objective 3 Insert a Video

GO! Learn How

Video P3-3

You can insert, size, and move videos in a PowerPoint presentation, and you can format videos by applying styles and effects. Video editing features in PowerPoint enable you to trim parts of a video and to compress the video to make the presentation easier to share.

Activity 3.14 | Inserting a Video and Using Media Controls

MOS

4.5.1

1 Display **Slide 1**. On the **Insert tab**, in the **Media group**, click **Video**, and then click **Video on My PC**. In the **Insert Video** dialog box, navigate to the files downloaded with this project, and then click **p03A_Video**. Click **Insert**, and then compare your screen with Figure 3.24.

The video displays in the center of the slide, and media controls display in the control panel below the video.

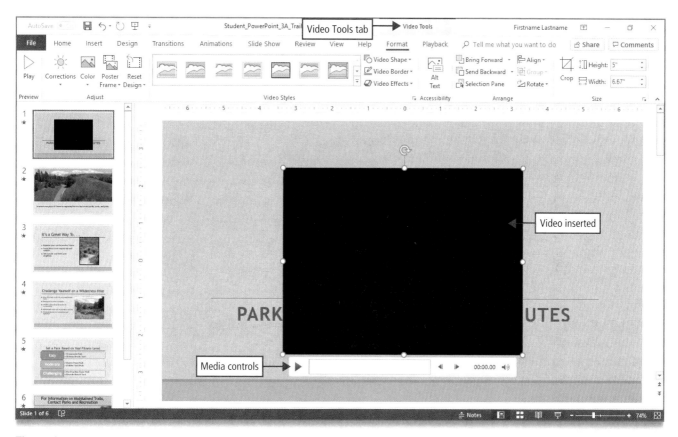

Figure 3.24

2 Below the video, in the media controls, click **Play/Pause** ▶ to view the video and notice that as the video plays, the media controls display the time that has elapsed since the start of the video.

3 View the slide show from the beginning. On **Slide 1**, after the subtitle displays, point to the video to display the 🖑 pointer, and then compare your screen with Figure 3.25.

When you point to the video during the slide show, the media controls display.

Figure 3.25

> **4** With the 🖑 pointer displayed, click the mouse button to view the video. Move the pointer away from the video and notice that the media controls no longer display. When the video is finished, press Esc to exit the slide show.

> **5** **Save** 💾 your presentation.

Activity 3.15 | Sizing and Aligning a Video

> **1** With the video selected, on the **Video Tools Format tab**, in the **Size group**, click in the **Height** box 🔲. Type **2** and then press Enter. Notice that the video width adjusts proportionately.

> **2** On the **Video Tools Format tab**, in the **Arrange group**, click **Align** 🖼, and then click **Align Center**. Click **Align** 🖼 again, and then click **Align Middle**. Compare your screen with Figure 3.26. **Save** 💾 your presentation.

> The video is centered horizontally and vertically on the slide.

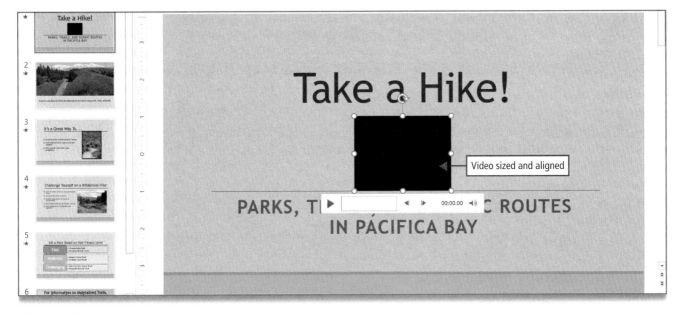

Figure 3.26

You can apply styles and effects to a video and change the video shape and border. You can also recolor a video so that it coordinates with the presentation theme.

1 On **Slide 1**, if necessary, select the video. On the **Video Tools Format tab**, in the **Video Styles group**, click **More** ⊡ to display the **Video Styles** gallery.

2 Using the ScreenTips to view the style name, under **Subtle**, click the last style—**Drop Shadow Rectangle**. Compare your screen with Figure 3.27.

Figure 3.27

3 In the **Video Styles group**, click **Video Shape**, and then under **Rectangles**, click the second shape—**Rectangle: Rounded Corners**. Compare your screen with Figure 3.28.

You can format a video with any combination of styles, shapes, and effects.

▭ **MAC TIP** Click the Crop arrow, point to Change Shape, and then click Rounded Rectangle.

Figure 3.28

Activity 3.17 | Trimming and Compressing a Video and Setting Playback Options

MOS

1.5.5, 4.5.2, 4.5.3

You can *trim*—delete parts of a video to make it shorter—and you can compress a video file to reduce the file size of your PowerPoint presentation. You can trim the video from the beginning and the end.

1 If necessary, select the video. On the **Video Tools Playback tab**, in the **Editing group**, click **Trim Video**, and then compare your screen with Figure 3.29.

At the top of the displayed Trim Video dialog box, the file name and the video duration display. Below the video, a timeline displays with start and end markers indicating the video start and end time. Start Time and End Time boxes display the current start and end of the video. The Previous Frame and Next Frame buttons move the video forward and backward one frame at a time.

Figure 3.29

2 In the **End Time** box, replace the number with **00:09.425** and then compare your screen with Figure 3.30.

The blue section of the timeline indicates the portion of the video that will play during the slide show. The gray section indicates the portion of the video that is trimmed. The image in the Trim Video dialog box displays the last frame in the video based on the trim setting.

MAC TIP Drag the End Trim slider to adjust the duration. The duration counter is above the video preview in the trim window.

Figure 3.30

> **3** Click **OK** to apply the trim settings.

> **4** Click **File**, and then click **Compress Media**. Read the description of each video quality option, and then click **Standard Quality**. Depending on your system, this may be named Low Quality. Compare your screen with Figure 3.31.

> The Compress Media dialog box displays the slide number on which the selected video is inserted, the video file name, the original size of the video file, and when compression is complete, the amount that the file size was reduced. Because this video is an MP4 video format, which is a compressed format, your dialog box Status may indicate Already Compressed.

MAC TIP The Compress Media feature is not available in the Mac version of PowerPoint.

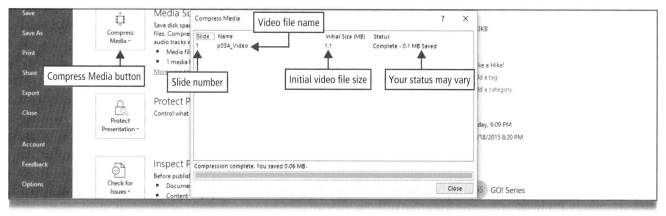

Figure 3.31

5 In the **Compress Media** dialog box, click **Close**, and then on the left, click **Save**.

6 If necessary, select the video. On the **Video Tools Playback tab**, in the **Video Options group**, click the **Start arrow**, and then click **Automatically** so that during the slide show, the video will begin automatically. Compare your screen with Figure 3.32.

Figure 3.32

7 Click the **Slide Show tab**, in the **Start Slide Show group**, click **From Beginning**, and then view the slide show. Notice that on Slide 1, the video begins playing immediately after the subtitle displays. After you view the video, click the mouse button to advance to the next slide and then continue to view the presentation. Press Esc when the black slide displays.

8 Insert a **Header & Footer** on the **Notes and Handouts**. Include the **Date and time** updated automatically, the **Page Number**, and a **Footer**. In the **Footer** box, type **3A_Trails** and then click **Apply to All**.

9 Display the document properties. As the **Tags**, type **walking trails** and as the **Subject**, type your course and section number. Be sure your name displays as author, and then **Save** your file. **Close** PowerPoint.

For Non-MyLab Submissions Determine What Your Instructor Requires
As directed by your instructor, submit your completed PowerPoint presentation.

---

10 In **MyLab IT**, in your **Course Materials**, locate and click the Grader Project **PowerPoint 3A Trails**. In **step 3**, under **Upload Completed Assignment**, click **Choose File**. In the **Open** dialog box, navigate to your **PowerPoint Chapter 3 folder**, and then click your **Student_PowerPoint_3A_Trails** file one time to select it. In the lower right corner of the **Open** dialog box, click **Open**.

The name of your selected file displays above the Upload button.

11 To submit your file to **MyLab IT** for grading, click **Upload**, wait a moment for a green **Success!** message, and then in **step 4**, click the blue **Submit for Grading** button. Click **Close Assignment** to return to your list of **Course Materials**.

You have completed Project 3A `END`

Objective | Create an Informational Presentation Using Google Slides

ALERT Working with Web-Based Applications and Services

Computer programs and services on the web receive continuous updates and improvements, so the steps to complete this web-based activity may differ from the ones shown. You can often look at the screens and the information presented to determine how to complete the activity.

If you do not already have a Google account, you will need to create one before beginning this activity.

Activity | Creating an Informational Presentation in Google Slides

In this Activity, you will use Google Slides to create a presentation similar to the one you created in Project 3A.

1 From the desktop, open your browser, navigate to **http://google.com**, and then sign in to your Google account. Click **Google apps**, and then click **Drive**. Open your **GO! Web Projects** folder—or click New to create and then open this folder, if necessary.

2 In the left pane, click **New**, click **File upload**, and then in the **Open** dialog box, navigate to your student data files. Select **p03_3A_Google_Slides**. Click **Open**. When the upload is complete, if necessary, close the Uploads completed message box. Right-click **p03_3A_ Google_Slides**, and then click **Rename**. Using your own name, as the file name, type **Lastname_Firstname_3A_ Google_Slides** and then press Enter. Right-click your file, point to **Open with**, and then click **Google Slides**.

3 On the toolbar, click **Background**, click the **Color arrow**, in the fifth column, click the fourth color—**light green 2**. Click **Done** to apply the light green background to Slide 1.

4 On **Slide 1**, in the title placeholder, select the title text—*Take a Hike!* Click the **Font arrow**, and then click **Georgia**.

5 Display **Slide 2**, and then at the bottom of the slide, click in the text placeholder. On the toolbar, click **Fill color**, and then in the fifth column, click the fourth color—**light green 2**. Select the text, and then change the **Font Size** to **36**.

6 With the placeholder selected, point to the center-left sizing handle, and then drag as far to the left as possible without exceeding the left edge of the slide. Repeat this process on the right side of the slide, and then click outside of the placeholder.

7 Display **Slide 3**, and then click anywhere in the bulleted list. On the menu bar click **View**, and then click **Animations** to display the **Animations pane**. On the **Animations pane**, if necessary, click Select an object to animate, click **Add animation**, click the **Fade in arrow**, and then click **Fly in from right**.

8 Click the picture, if necessary, click Select an object to animate, click **Add animation**, click the **Fade in arrow**, and then click **Appear**.

9 Click anywhere in the title text, if necessary, click Select an object to animate, click **Add animation**, click the **Fade in arrow**, and then click **Fly in from top**. Notice the animation sequencing in the Animations pane, which indicates that the title animation Fly in from top will display last. At the bottom of the **Animations pane**, click the **Play** button, and then point to the slide and click the slide four times to preview the animations in sequence.

10 With **Slide 3** displayed, with the title selected, in the **Animations pane**, click the title animation *Fly in from top* and drag it to the top of the list so that it will appear first. At the bottom of the **Animations pane**, click the **Play** button, and then point to the slide and click the slide four times to preview the animations in sequence.

11 Display **Slide 4**, and then click the title. On the **Animations pane**, click **Add animation**, click the **Fade in arrow**, and then click **Fly in from top**.

12 Click the bulleted list. On the **Animations pane**, click **Add animation**, click the **Fade in arrow**, and then click **Fly in from right**.

13 Click the picture, click **Add animation**, click the **Fade in arrow**, and then click **Appear**.

14 Display **Slide 6**, and then click in the title. On the **Animations pane**, click **Add animation**, click the **Fade in arrow**, and then click **Fly in from top**.

15 On the **Animations pane**, if necessary, click ▶ to expand **Slide: No transition**. Click the **No transition arrow**, click **Slide from left**, and then click **Apply to all slides**. **Close** × the **Animations pane**.

16 Display **Slide 1** In the upper right, click the **Present arrow**, click **Present from beginning**. If necessary, click **Allow**. Click the left mouse button to progress through the presentation. When the last slide displays, press [Esc] or click **Exit**.

17 Your presentation will be saved automatically. If you are instructed to submit your file, click the File menu, point to Download as, and then click PDF or PowerPoint as directed by your instructor. The file will download to your default download folder as determined by your browser settings. Sign out of your Google account and close your browser.

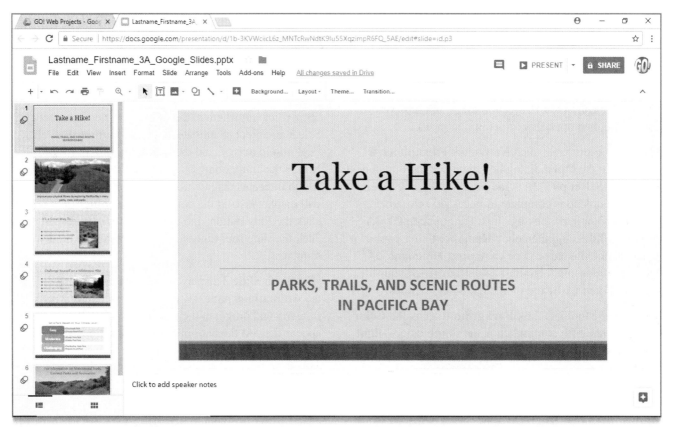

Figure A

Summary and Analysis Presentation

Project Activities

In Activities 3.18 through 3.30, you will add a table and two charts to a presentation that Mindy Walker, Director of Parks and Recreation, is creating to inform the City Council about enrollment trends in Pacifica Bay recreation programs. Your completed presentation will look similar to Figure 3.33.

Project Files for MyLab IT Grader

1. In your **MyLab IT** course, locate and click **PowerPoint 3B Enrollment**, Download Materials, and then Download All Files.
2. Extract the zipped folder to your PowerPoint Chapter 3 folder. Close the Grader download screens.
3. Take a moment to open the downloaded **PowerPoint_3B_Enrollment_Instructions**; note any recent updates to the book.

Project Results

GO! Project 3B
Where We're Going

Figure 3.33 Project 3B Enrollment

For Non-MyLab Submissions

For Project 3B, you will need this starting file: In your PowerPoint Chapter 3 folder, save your presentation as:
p03B_Enrollment   **Lastname_Firstname_3B_Enrollment**

After you have named and saved your presentation, on the next page, begin with Step 2.

Objective 4 | Create and Modify Tables

ALERT Because Office 365 is a cloud-based subscription service that receives continuous updates, you may encounter some variations in what appears on your screen and what is shown in this instruction. Microsoft Office 365 is fully installed on your PC or Mac; no internet access is necessary to create or edit documents. When you *are* connected to the internet, you will receive monthly upgrades and new features, so you always have the latest versions of Office apps as soon as they are available. Your subscription gives you continuous free access to the latest innovations and refinements.

GO! Learn How
Video P3-4

A *table* is a format for information that organizes and presents text and data in columns and rows. The intersection of a column and row is referred to as a *cell* and is the location in which you type text in a table. Tables are a useful way to organize information.

Activity 3.18 | Creating a Table

4.1.1

There are several ways to insert a table in a PowerPoint slide. For example, you can insert a slide with a Content Layout and then click the Insert Table button. Or, click the Insert tab and then click Table. In this presentation, a table will be used to summarize the recreation program.

1 Navigate to your **PowerPoint Chapter 3 folder**, and then double-click the downloaded PowerPoint file that displays your name—**Student_PowerPoint_3B_Enrollment**. In your presentation, if necessary, at the top, click **Enable Editing**.

2 Display **Slide 2**. In the content placeholder, click **Insert Table** 🖽 to display the **Insert Table** dialog box. In the **Number of columns** box, type **3** and then press Tab. In the **Number of rows** box, if necessary, type **2** and then compare your screen with Figure 3.34.

> Enter the number of columns and rows that you want the table to contain.

Figure 3.34

3 Click **OK** to create a table with three columns and two rows. Notice that the insertion point is blinking in the upper left cell of the table.

> The table extends from the left side of the content placeholder to the right side, and the three columns are equal in width. By default, a style is applied to the table.

ALERT Did You Press Enter instead of Tab?
In a table, pressing Enter creates another line in the same cell. If you press Enter by mistake, you can remove the extra line by pressing Backspace.

4 With the insertion point positioned in the first cell of the table, type **Athletics** and then press Tab.

Pressing Tab moves the insertion point to the next cell in the same row.

5 With the insertion point positioned in the second cell of the first row, type **Leisure** and then press Tab. Type **Arts** and then press Tab to move the insertion point to the first cell in the second row. Compare your table with Figure 3.35.

Figure 3.35

6 With the insertion point positioned in the first cell of the second row, type **Team sports** and then press Tab. Type **Personal development classes** and then press Tab. Type **Music and dance classes**

7 Save your presentation.

Activity 3.19 │ Inserting Rows and Columns in a Table

MOS
4.1.2

You can modify the layout of a table by inserting or deleting rows and columns.

1 With the insertion point positioned in the last cell of the table, press Tab and notice that a new blank row is inserted.

When the insertion point is positioned in the last cell of a table, pressing Tab inserts a new blank row at the bottom of the table.

2 In the first cell of the third row, type **Youth** and then press Tab. Type **Older adults** and then press Tab. Type **Young adults** and then compare your table with Figure 3.36.

Figure 3.36

ALERT **Did You Add an Extra Row to the Table?**

When the insertion point is positioned in the last cell of the table, pressing Tab inserts a new blank row. If you inadvertently inserted a blank row in the table, on the Quick Access Toolbar, click Undo.

3 Click in any cell in the first column, and then click the **Table Tools Layout tab**. In the **Rows & Columns group**, click **Insert Left**.

A new first column is inserted and the width of the columns is adjusted so that all four columns are the same width.

4 In the second row, click in the first cell, and then type **Largest Enrollments**

5 In the third row, click in the first cell, type **Primary Market** and then compare your table with Figure 3.37.

Figure 3.37

6 With the insertion point positioned in the third row, on the **Table Tools Layout tab**, in the **Rows & Columns group**, click **Insert Above** to insert a new third row. In the first cell, type **Average Enrollment** and then press Tab. Type the remaining three entries, pressing Tab to move from cell to cell: **85% of capacity** and **62% of capacity** and **78% of capacity**

7 Save your presentation.

MORE KNOWLEDGE | **Deleting Rows and Columns**

To delete a row or column from a table, click in the row or column that you want to delete. Click the Layout tab, and then in the Rows & Columns group, click Delete. In the displayed list, click Delete Columns or Delete Rows.

Activity 3.20 | Sizing a Table

A selected table is surrounded by sizing handles and can be resized in the same manner in which a shape or picture is resized.

1 Point to the bottom, center sizing handle to display the pointer. Compare your screen with Figure 3.38.

Figure 3.38

2 Hold down the left mouse button, and then drag down until the ruler guide is positioned on the **lower half of the vertical ruler at 2 inches**. Compare your screen with Figure 3.39.

A dim border and the red dotted ruler guides display, indicating the size of the table.

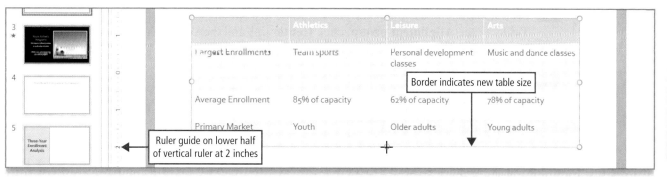

Figure 3.39

3 Release the mouse button to size the table, and then **Save** 🖫 your presentation.

🔄 **ANOTHER WAY** On the Layout tab, in the Table Size group, type 3.5 in the Height box.

Activity 3.21 │ Distributing Rows and Aligning Table Text

By default, table text is aligned left and the rows adjust as you enter text. This can result in a table with rows of unequal height, which may be visually unappealing or difficult to read. You can adjust the text alignment within the table cells—both horizontally and vertically. You can use the Distribute Rows command so the rows are of equal height.

1 Click in the first cell of the table. On the **Table Tools Layout tab**, in the **Cell Size group**, click **Distribute Rows**. Compare your table with Figure 3.40.

The Distribute Rows command adjusts the height of the rows in the table so that they are equal.

Figure 3.40

2 On the **Table Tools Layout tab**, in the **Table group**, click **Select**, and then click **Select Table**. In the **Alignment group**, click **Center** ▤, and then click **Center Vertically** ▤.

All of the table text is centered horizontally and vertically within the cells.

3 **Save** 🖫 your presentation.

> **MORE KNOWLEDGE** **Distributing Columns**
>
> To distribute columns, click anywhere in the table, and then on the Table Tools Layout tab, in the Cell Size group, click Distribute Columns.

Activity 3.22 | Applying and Modifying a Table Style

4.1.3

You can modify the design of a table by applying a *table style*. A table style formats the entire table so that it is consistent with the presentation theme. There are color categories within the table styles—Best Match for Document, Light, Medium, and Dark.

1 Click in any cell in the table. On the **Table Tools Design tab**, in the **Table Styles group**, click **More** ⌄. In the **Table Style**s gallery, point to several of the styles to view the Live Preview of the style.

2 Under **Light**, in the third row, click the fourth style—**Light Style 3 – Accent 3**—to apply the style to the table.

3 On the **Table Tools Design tab**, in the **Table Style Options group**, clear the **Banded Rows** check box, and then select the **Banded Columns** check box. Compare your screen with Figure 3.41. **Save** 🖫 the presentation.

The check boxes in the Table Style Options group control where Table Style formatting is applied.

Figure 3.41

Activity 3.23 | Applying Table Effects and Font Formatting

1 Move the pointer outside of the table so that it is positioned to the left of the first row in the table to display the ➡ pointer, as shown in Figure 3.42.

Figure 3.42

2 With the ➡ pointer pointing to the first row in the table, click the mouse button to select the entire row so that you can apply formatting to the selection.

3 With the first row still selected, on the **Table Tools Design tab**, in the **Table Styles group**, click **Effects**. Point to **Cell Bevel**, and then under **Bevel**, click the first bevel—**Round**. Depending on your version of PowerPoint, this may be named *Circle*. With the first table row selected, point to the selection and right-click. On the mini toolbar, change the **Font Size** to **28**.

MAC TIP   Click the Home tab to change the font.

4 Select the first column, and then right-click to display the mini toolbar and shortcut menu. Apply **Bold**.

5 Click in a blank area of the slide, and then compare your slide with Figure 3.43. **Save** 🖫 the presentation.

Figure 3.43

GO! Learn How
Video P3-5

A ***chart*** is a graphic representation of numeric data. Commonly used chart types include bar and column charts, pie charts, and line charts. A chart that you create in PowerPoint is stored in an Excel worksheet that is incorporated into the PowerPoint file.

Activity 3.24 | Inserting a Column Chart

MOS
4.2.1

A ***column chart*** is useful for illustrating comparisons among related numbers. In this Activity, you will create a column chart that compares enrollment in each category of recreation activities by season.

1 Display **Slide 4**. In the content placeholder, click **Insert Chart** ▮ to display the **Insert Chart** dialog box. Compare your screen with Figure 3.44.

> Along the left side of the dialog box, the types of charts that you can insert in your presentation display. Along the top of the dialog box, subtypes of the selected chart type display. By default, Column is selected and a Clustered Column chart displays in the preview area on the right side of the dialog box.

Figure 3.44

2 Along the top of the dialog box, point to each column chart to view the ScreenTip. Then, with the **Clustered Column** chart selected, click **OK**. Compare your screen with Figure 3.45.

> The PowerPoint window displays a column chart in the content placeholder. A *Chart in Microsoft PowerPoint* worksheet window displays with cells, columns, and rows. A cell is identified by the intersecting column letter and row number, forming the ***cell reference***.
> The worksheet contains sample data from which the chart on the PowerPoint slide is generated. The column headings—*Series 1*, *Series 2*, and *Series 3* display in the chart ***legend*** and the row headings—*Category 1*, *Category 2*, *Category 3*, and *Category 4*—display as ***category labels***. The legend identifies the patterns or colors that are assigned to the data series in the chart. The category labels display along the bottom of the chart to identify the categories of data.

Figure 3.45

Activity 3.25 | Entering Chart Data

1 In the **Chart in Microsoft PowerPoint** worksheet window, in cell **B1**, which contains the text *Series 1,* type **Athletics** and then press [Tab] to move to cell **C1**.

Below the chart, the chart legend is updated to reflect the change in the Excel worksheet.

2 In cell **C1**, which contains the text *Series 2,* type **Leisure** and then press [Tab] to move to cell **D1**. Type **Arts** and then press [Tab]. Notice that cell **A2**, which contains the text *Category 1*, is selected. Compare your screen with Figure 3.46.

The outlined cells define the area in which you are entering data. When you press [Tab] in the rightmost cell, the first cell in the next row becomes active.

Figure 3.46

3 Beginning in cell **A2**, type the following data (starting with *Spring*), pressing Tab to move from cell to cell. Notice that as you enter the data, the chart columns resize to display the entered amounts.

	Athletics	Leisure	Arts
Spring	895	630	720
Summer	1250	350	820
Fall	1490	585	690
Winter	1130	750	

4 In cell **D5**, which contains the value 5, type **710** and then press Enter.

Pressing Enter in the last cell of the outlined area maintains the existing data range.

ALERT   Did You Press Tab After the Last Entry?

If you pressed Tab after entering the data in cell D5, you expanded the chart range. In the Chart in Microsoft PowerPoint window, click Undo ↻.

5 Compare your worksheet and your chart with Figure 3.47. Correct any typing errors by clicking in the cell that you want to change, and then retype the data.

Each of the 12 cells containing the numeric data that you entered is a ***data point***—a value that originates in a worksheet cell. Each data point is represented in the chart by a ***data marker***—a column, bar, area, dot, pie slice, or other symbol in a chart that represents a single data point. Related data points form a ***data series***; for example, there is a data series for *Athletics*, *Leisure*, and *Arts*. Each data series has a unique color or pattern represented in the chart legend. A placeholder for the chart title displays above the chart.

To the right of the chart, three buttons display. The ***Chart Elements button*** ⊞ enables you to add, remove, or change chart elements such as the title, legend, gridlines, and data labels. The ***Chart Styles button*** 🖌 enables you to set a style and color scheme for your chart. The ***Chart Filters button*** ▽ enables you to change which data displays in the chart.

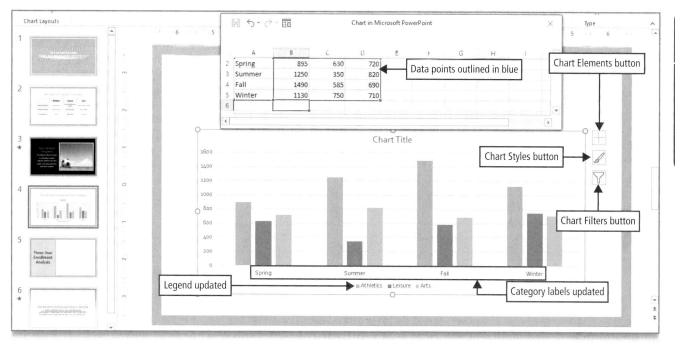

Figure 3.47

6 In the upper right corner of the **Chart in Microsoft PowerPoint** worksheet window, click **Close** ⊠. **Save** 🖫 the presentation.

When you save the presentation, the worksheet data is saved with it.

MORE KNOWLEDGE | **Editing the Chart Data After Closing the Worksheet**

You can redisplay the worksheet and make changes to the data after you have closed it. To do so, click the chart to select it, and then on the Chart Tools Design tab in the Data group, click Edit Data.

Activity 3.26 | Applying a Chart Style and Modifying Chart Elements

4.2.2

A *chart style* is set of predefined formats applied to a chart, including colors, backgrounds, and effects. *Chart elements* are the various components of a chart, including the chart title, axis titles, data series, legend, chart area, and plot area.

1 Click the outer edge of the chart, if necessary, to select it. On the **Chart Tools Design tab**, in the **Chart Styles group**, click **More** ⊽ to display the **Chart Styles** gallery.

2 In the **Chart Styles** gallery, point to each style to Live Preview the style. Notice that as you point to a chart style, a ScreenTip indicates the chart style number. Click **Style 5**. Compare your screen with Figure 3.48.

This style includes lightly shaded column data markers. Horizontal gridlines display behind the columns.

Figure 3.48

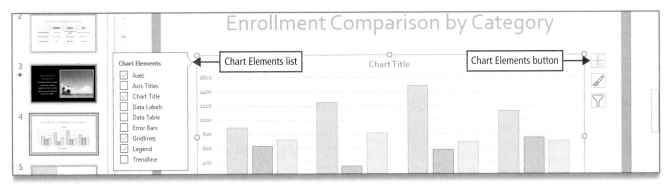 To the right of the chart, click **Chart Elements** ⊞, and then compare your screen with Figure 3.49.

A list of chart elements displays to the left of the chart. You can select the chart elements that you wish to display in your chart. In this slide, the slide title describes the chart so a chart title is not necessary.

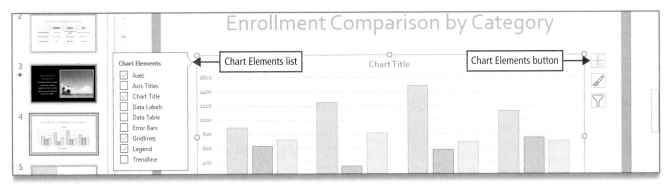

Figure 3.49

Under **Chart Elements**, click **Chart Title** to clear the check box and remove the chart title placeholder from the chart. Click **Chart Elements** ⊞ to close the Chart Elements list.

⌐ **MAC TIP** On the Chart Design tab, click Add Chart Element.

Click in a blank area of the slide, and then compare your screen with Figure 3.50. **Save** 🖫 your presentation.

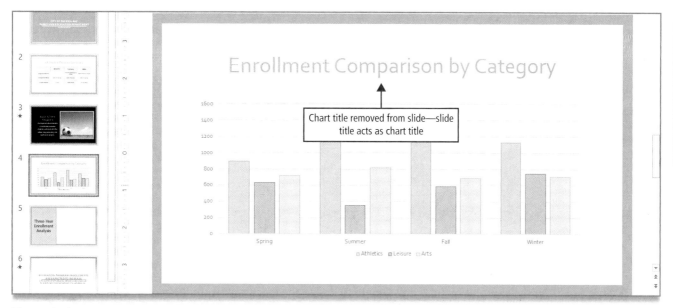

Enrollment Comparison by Category

Chart title removed from slide—slide title acts as chart title

Figure 3.50

Activity 3.27 | Creating a Line Chart and Deleting Chart Data

4.2.1

To analyze and compare annual data over a three-year period, the presentation requires an additional chart. Recall that there are a number of different types of charts that you can insert in a PowerPoint presentation. In this activity, you will create a *line chart*, which is commonly used to illustrate trends over time.

1 Display **Slide 5**. In the content placeholder, click **Insert Chart**. On the left side of the **Insert Chart** dialog box, click **Line**, and then on the right, click the fourth chart—**Line with Markers**. Click **OK**.

2 In the worksheet, in cell **B1**, which contains the text *Series 1*, type **Youth** and then press Tab. In cell **C1**, type **Adult** and then press Tab. In cell **D1**, type **Senior** and then press Tab.

3 Beginning in cell **A2**, type the following data, pressing Tab to move from cell to cell. If you make any typing errors, click in the cell that you want to change, and then retype the data.

	Youth	Adult	Senior
2022	3822	1588	2240
2023	4675	1833	2534
2024	4535	1925	2897

4 In the worksheet, position the pointer over **row heading 5** so that the ➡ pointer displays. Compare your screen with Figure 3.51.

Figure 3.51

> **5** With the ➡ pointer displayed, right-click to select the row and display the shortcut menu. On the shortcut menu, click **Delete** to delete the extra row from the worksheet, and then compare your screen with Figure 3.52.

> The data in the worksheet contains four columns and four rows, and the outline area defining the chart data range is resized. You must delete columns and rows from the sample worksheet data that you do not want to include in the chart. You can add additional rows and columns by typing column and row headings and then entering additional data. When data is typed in cells adjacent to the chart range, the range is resized to include the new data.

Figure 3.52

Activity 3.28 | Formatting a Line Chart

1 Close ☒ the worksheet window. To the right of the chart, click **Chart Styles** 🖌. Compare your screen with Figure 3.53.

> The Chart Style gallery displays on the left side of the chart and the Style tab is active. The chart styles display in a vertical gallery.

Figure 3.53

2 In the **Chart Style** gallery, be sure that **Style** is selected. Scroll the list, and point to various styles to view the ScreenTips and the effect of the style on the chart. Click **Style 6** and then click anywhere outside of the chart to close the Chart Style gallery.

> The styles that display when you click the Chart Styles button are the same as those that display in the Chart Styles gallery on the ribbon. Apply chart styles using the technique that you prefer.

🖥 **MAC TIP** On the Chart Design tab, click More.

3 In the chart, click the text **Chart Title**, and then type **By Age Category**

4 Click in a blank area of the slide, and then compare your screen with Figure 3.54. **Save** 🖫 your presentation.

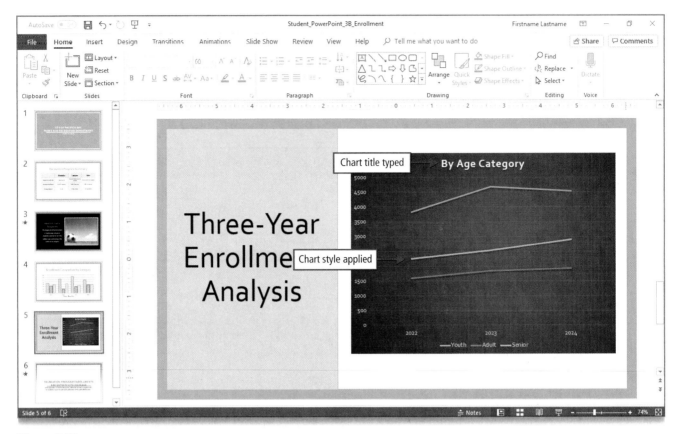

Figure 3.54

Activity 3.29 | Animating a Chart

5.2.1, 5.2.3

1 Display **Slide 4**, and then click the column chart placeholder to select it. On the **Animations tab**, in the **Animation group**, click **More** �死, and then under **Entrance**, click **Fade**.

2 In the **Animation group**, click **Effect Options**, and then under **Sequence**, click **By Series**. In the **Preview group**, click **Preview** to preview the By Series effect. On **Slide 4**, notice the chart animation sequence. Compare your screen with Figure 3.55.

The By Series option displays the chart one data series at a time, and the numbers 1, 2, 3, and 4 to the left of the chart indicate the four parts of the chart animation sequence. The chart animation sequence includes the background, followed by the Athletics data series for each season, and then the Leisure series, and then the Arts series.

Figure 3.55

3 In the **Animation group**, click **Effect Options**, and then under **Sequence**, click **As One Object**. View the slide show from the beginning. On **Slide 4**, notice the chart animation sequence returns to a *1*. Save your presentation.

Activity 3.30 | Animating a Chart with the Morph Transition

MOS
5.2.1

You have applied animation effects to charts, to make them move in a specified manner as they enter the slide. Another way to animate objects is by making duplicate slides and applying the Morph transition.

1 Display **Slide 5**, press Ctrl + D to duplicate the slide.

2 On **Slide 5**, click to select the chart. On the **Chart Tools Design tab**, click **Edit Data** to open the **Chart in Microsoft PowerPoint** window. Edit the data in the range **A2:D4** using the following:

2019	3715	1457	1549
2020	4247	1291	1785
2021	4412	1369	2452

3 Close the **Chart in Microsoft PowerPoint** window.

4 Display **Slide 6**. on the **Transitions tab**, in the **Transition to This Slide group**, point to **Morph**, to display the ScreenTip. Compare your screen with. Figure 3.56

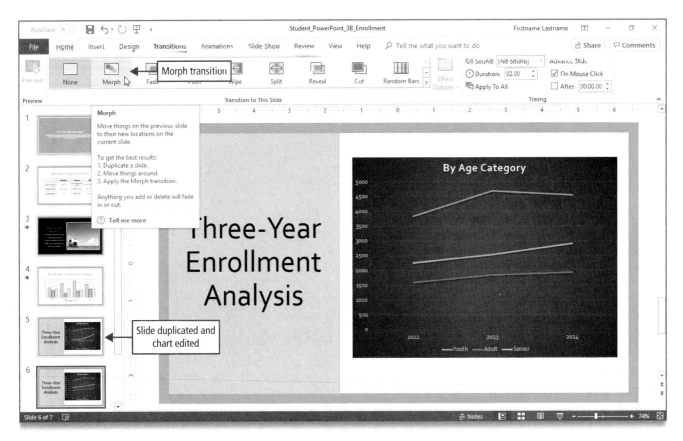

Figure 3.56

> **5** Click **Morph**. Change the Duration to 1.00.

> **6** Display **Slide 5**. On the **Slide Show tab**, in the **Start Slide Show group**, click **From Current Slide**. Click to advance to **Slide 6** and notice the morph transition of the graph.

> The lines appear to move as you advance the slides.

> **7** Press (Esc) to return to your presentation.

> **8** Insert a **Header & Footer** on the **Notes and Handouts**. Include the **Date and time** updated automatically, the **Page Number**, and a **Footer**. In the Footer box, type **3B_Enrollment** and then click **Apply to All**.

> **9** Display the document properties. As the **Tags**, type **recreation enrollment** and as the **Subject**, type your course and section number. Be sure your name displays in as author, and then **Save** your file.

For Non-MyLab Submissions Determine What Your Instructor Requires

As directed by your instructor, submit your completed PowerPoint presentation.

---

10 Close ⊠ PowerPoint.

11 In **MyLab IT**, in your **Course Materials**, locate and click the Grader Project **PowerPoint 3B Enrollment**. In **step 3**, under **Upload Completed Assignment**, click **Choose File**. In the **Open** dialog box, navigate to your **PowerPoint Chapter 3 folder**, and then click your **Student_PowerPoint_3B_ Enrollment** file one time to select it. In the lower right corner of the **Open** dialog box, click **Open**.

The name of your selected file displays above the Upload button.

12 To submit your file to **MyLab IT** for grading, click **Upload**, wait a moment for a green **Success!** message, and then in **step 4**, click the blue **Submit for Grading** button. Click **Close Assignment** to return to your list of **Course Materials**.

You have completed Project 3B **END**

Objective | Create a Summary and Analysis Presentation in Google Slides

ALERT **Working with Web-Based Applications and Services**

Computer programs and services on the web receive continuous updates and improvements, so the steps to complete this web-based activity may differ from the ones shown. You can often look at the screens and the information presented to determine how to complete the activity.

If you do not already have a Google account, you will need to create one before beginning this activity.

Activity | Creating a Summary and Analysis Presentation in Google Slides

In this Activity, you will use Google Slides to create a presentation similar to the one you created in Project 3B.

1 From the desktop, open your browser, navigate to **http://google.com**, and then sign in to your Google account. Click **Google apps** ⊞, and then click **Drive** 🔺. Open your **GO! Web Projects** folder—or click New to create and then open this folder if necessary.

2 In the left pane, click **New**, click **File upload**, and then in the **Open** dialog box, navigate to your student data files. Select **p03_3B_Google_Slides**. Click **Open**. When the upload is complete, if necessary, close the Uploads complete message box. Right-click **p03_3B_Google_Slides**, and then click **Rename**. Using your own name, as the file name type **Lastname_Firstname_3B_Googles_Slides** and then press [Enter]. Right-click your file, point to **Open with**, and then click **Google Slides**.

3 Display **Slide 2**. On the menu bar, click **Insert**, point to **Table**, and drag the mouse to the right to highlight four columns and drag down to highlight four rows. Click to insert a 4 X 4 column table. Type the text in Table 1 at the bottom of the page.

4 Display **Slide 4**. On the menu bar, click **Insert**, point to **Chart**, and then click **Column**. In the upper right of the chart, click the link arrow and then click **Open source.** In the Google Sheet, beginning in cell **B1**, type:

	Athletics	Leisure	Arts
Spring	895	630	720
Summer	1250	350	820
Fall	1490	585	690
Winter	1130	750	710

5 In the sheet, double-click the chart to open the **Chart editor** pane. On the **DATA** tab, click **Add Series**. With the **What data?** box displayed, drag to select the range **D1:D5**, the Arts column. Click **OK**. Click the **CUSTOMIZE** tab. Click to open **Chart & axis titles**, and delete the text **Points Scored**.

6 **Close** ⊠ the Google Sheet and return to the Google Slide presentation. In the chart, click **UPDATE**. On the menu bar, click **Arrange**, point to **Center on page**, and then click **Horizontally**.

Table 1

	Athletics	Leisure	Arts
Largest Enrollments	Team sports	Personal development classes	Music and dance classes
Average Enrollment	85% of capacity	62% of capacity	78% of capacity
Primary Market	Youth	Older adults	Young adults

7 Display **Slide 5**. On the menu bar, click **Insert**, point to **Chart**, and then click **Line**. Click the link arrow and then click **Open source**. In the Google Sheet, beginning in cell **B1**, type the following text:

	Youth	Adult	Senior
2022	3822	1588	2240
2023	4675	1833	2534
2024	4535	1925	2897

8 Double-click the chart to open the **Chart editor**. On the **DATA** tab, change the **Data range** to **A1:D4**. Click the **CUSTOMIZE** tab, click **Chart & axis titles**, and then delete the title text. **Close** ⨯ the Google Sheet and return to the Google Slide presentation. In the chart, click **UPDATE**. Drag the chart to position it in the white area of the slide.

9 Your presentation will be saved automatically. If you are instructed to submit your file, click the File menu, point to Download as, and then click PDF or PowerPoint as directed by your instructor. The file will download to your default download folder as determined by your browser settings. Sign out of your Google account.

Figure A

»» GO! To Work

wavebreakmedia/Shutterstock, Monkey Business Images/Fotolia, Ivanko80/Shutterstock, Monkey Business Images/Shutterstock

Microsoft Office Specialist (MOS) Skills in this Chapter	
Project 3A	**Project 3B**
1.5.5 Preserve presentation content	**4.1.1** Create and insert tables
2.2.2 Modify individual slide backgrounds	**4.1.2** Insert and delete table rows and columns
4.5.1 Insert audio and visual clips	**4.1.3** Apply built-in table styles
4.5.2 Create and insert screen recordings	**4.2.1** Create and insert charts
4.5.3 Configure media playback options	**4.2.2** Modify charts
5.2.1 Animate text and graphic elements	**5.2.1** Animate text and graphic elements
5.2.3 Configure animation effects	**5.2.3** Configure animation effects
5.2.4 Configure animation paths	
5.2.5 Reorder animations on a slide	
5.3.1 Set transition effect duration	
5.3.2 Configure transition start and finish options	

Build Your E-Portfolio

An E-Portfolio is a collection of evidence, stored electronically, that showcases what you have accomplished while completing your education. Collecting and then sharing your work products with potential employers reflects your academic and career goals. Your completed documents from the following projects are good examples to show what you have learned: 3G, 3K, and 3L.

GO! For Job Success

Video: Preparing for a Video Conference Interview

Your instructor may assign this video to your class, and then ask you to think about, or discuss with your classmates, these questions:

g-stockstudio/Shutterstock

What are the possible benefits and potential drawbacks of a video-conference interview?

What mistakes did Talia make in preparing for this type of interview? What mistakes did she make during the interview itself?

How would you prepare for a video-conference interview to avoid making those mistakes?

End of Chapter

Summary

There are many ways to modify a presentation theme and customize a presentation. You can apply background styles, insert pictures and textures on slide backgrounds, and change theme fonts and colors.

One way to enhance a presentation and engage an audience is by inserting interesting and informative video. Styles, shapes, and effects can be applied to videos. A video can be trimmed and compressed to make the file size smaller.

Use animation to focus audience attention on a particular slide element in order to draw attention to important points. Apply animation to slide elements in the order in which you want them to display.

Use tables to present information in an organized and attractive manner. Use charts to visually represent data. Apply styles to charts and tables to give your presentations a consistent and informative look.

POWERPOINT 3

GO! Learn It Online

Review the concepts and key terms, and MOS skills in this chapter by completing these online challenges, which you can find in **MyLab IT**.

> **Chapter Quiz:** Answer matching and multiple-choice questions to test what you learned in this chapter.

> **Lessons on the GO!:** Learn how to use all the new apps and features as they are introduced by Microsoft.

> **MOS Prep Quiz:** Answer questions to review the MOS skills that you practiced in this chapter.

GO! Collaborative Team Project (Available in Instructor Resource Center)

If your instructor assigns this project to your class, you can expect to work with one or more of your classmates—either in person or by using Internet tools—to create work products similar to those that you created in this chapter. A team is a group of workers who work together to solve a problem, make a decision, or create a work product. Collaboration is when you work together with others as a team in an intellectual endeavor to complete a shared task or achieve a shared goal.

Monkey Business Images/ Fotolia

Project Guide for PowerPoint Chapter 3

Your instructor may assign one or more of these projects to help you review the chapter and assess your mastery and understanding of the chapter.

Project Guide for PowerPoint Chapter 3			

Project	Apply Skills from These Chapter Objectives	Project Type	Project Location
3A MyLab IT	Objectives 1–3 from Project 3A	**3A Instructional Project (Grader Project)** **Instruction** Guided instruction to learn the skills in Project A.	In **MyLab IT** and in text
3B MyLab IT	Objectives 4–5 from Project 3B	**3B Instructional Project (Grader Project)** **Instruction** Guided instruction to learn the skills in Project B.	In **MyLab IT** and in text
3C	Objectives 1–3 from Project 3A	**3C Skills Review (Scorecard Grading)** **Review** A guided review of the skills from Project 3A.	In text
3D	Objectives 4-5 from Project 3A	**3D Skills Review (Scorecard Grading)** **Review** A guided review of the skills from Project 3B.	In text
3E MyLab IT	Objectives 1–3 from Project 3A	**3E Mastery (Grader Project)** **Mastery and Transfer of Learning** A demonstration of your mastery of the skills in Project 3A with extensive decision making.	In **MyLab IT** and in text
3F MyLab IT	Objectives 4–5 from Project 3A	**3F Mastery (Grader Project)** **Mastery and Transfer of Learning** A demonstration of your mastery of the skills in Project 3B with extensive decision making.	In **MyLab IT** and in text
3G MyLab IT	Combination of Objectives from Projects 3A and 3B	**3G Mastery (Grader Project)** **Mastery and Transfer of Learning** A demonstration of your mastery of the skills in Projects 3A and 3B with extensive decision making.	In **MyLab IT** and in text
3H	Combination of Objectives from Projects 3A and 3B	**3H GO! Fix It (Scorecard Grading)** **Critical Thinking** A demonstration of your mastery of the skills in Projects 3A and 3B by creating a correct result from a document that contains errors you must find.	IRC
3I	Combination of Objectives from Projects 3A and 3B	**3I GO! Make It (Scorecard Grading)** **Critical Thinking** A demonstration of your mastery of the skills in Projects 3A and 3B by creating a result from a supplied picture.	IRC
3J	Combination of Objectives from Projects 3A and 3B	**3J GO! Solve It (Rubric Grading)** **Critical Thinking** A demonstration of your mastery of the skills in Projects 3A and 3B, your decision-making skills, and your critical thinking skills. A task-specific rubric helps you self-assess your result.	IRC
3K	Combination of Objectives from Projects 3A and 3B	**3K GO! Solve It (Rubric Grading)** **Critical Thinking** A demonstration of your mastery of the skills in Projects 3A and 3B, your decision-making skills, and your critical thinking skills. A task-specific rubric helps you self-assess your result.	In text
3L	Combination of Objectives from Projects 3A and 3B	**3L GO! Think (Rubric Grading)** **Critical Thinking** A demonstration of your understanding of the chapter concepts applied in a manner that you would outside of college. An analytic rubric helps you and your instructor grade the quality of your work by comparing it to the work an expert in the discipline would create.	In text
3M	Combination of Objectives from Projects 3A and 3B	**3M GO! Think (Rubric Grading)** **Critical Thinking** A demonstration of your understanding of the chapter concepts applied in a manner that you would outside of college. An analytic rubric helps you and your instructor grade the quality of your work by comparing it to the work an expert in the discipline would create.	IRC
3N	Combination of Objectives from Projects 3A and 3B	**3N You and GO! (Rubric Grading)** **Critical Thinking** A demonstration of your understanding of the chapter concepts applied in a manner that you would in a personal situation. An analytic rubric helps you and your instructor grade the quality of your work.	IRC
3O	Combination of Objectives from Projects 3A and 3B	**3O Collaborative Team Project for PowerPoint Chapter 3** **Critical Thinking** A demonstration of your understanding of concepts and your ability to work collaboratively in a group role-playing assessment, requiring both collaboration and self-management.	IRC
Capstone Project for PowerPoint Chapters 1–3	Combination of Objectives from Projects Chapters 1–3	A demonstration of your mastery of the skills in Chapters 1–3 with extensive decision making. **(Grader Project)**	In **MyLab IT** and IRC

Glossary

Glossary of Chapter Key Terms

After Previous An animation option that begins the animation sequence for the selected slide element immediately after the completion of the previous animation or slide transition.

Animation A visual or sound effect added to an object or text on a slide.

Animation Painter A feature that copies animation settings from one object to another.

Background style A predefined slide background fill variation that combines theme colors in different intensities or patterns.

Body font A font that is applied to all slide text except slide titles.

Category labels Text that displays along the bottom of a chart to identify the categories of data.

Cell The intersection of a column and row in a table.

Cell reference The intersecting column letter and row number that identify a cell.

Chart A graphic representation of numeric data.

Chart elements The various components of a chart, including the chart title, axis titles, data series, legend, chart area, and plot area.

Chart Elements button A button that displays options for adding, removing, or changing chart elements.

Chart Filters button A button that displays options for changing the data displayed in a chart.

Chart style A set of predefined formats applied to a chart, including colors, backgrounds, and effects.

Chart Styles button A button that displays options for setting the style and color scheme for a chart.

Column chart A type of chart used for illustrating comparisons among related numbers.

Data marker A column, bar, area, dot, pie slice, or other symbol in a chart that represents a single data point.

Data point A chart value that originates in a worksheet cell.

Data series A group of related data points.

Emphasis effect Animation that emphasizes an object or text that is already displayed.

Entrance effect Animation that brings a slide element onto the screen.

Exit effect Animation that moves an object or text off the screen.

Headings font A font that is applied to all slide title text.

Legend A chart element that identifies the patterns or colors that are assigned to the data series in the chart.

Line chart A type of chart commonly used to illustrate trends over time.

On Click An animation option that begins the animation sequence for the selected slide element when the mouse button is clicked or the Spacebar is pressed.

Table A format for information that organizes and presents text and data in columns and rows.

Table style A format applied to a table that is consistent with the presentation theme.

Theme colors A set of coordinating colors that are applied to the backgrounds, objects, and text in a presentation.

Theme fonts The fonts that apply to two types of slide text—headings and body.

Timing options Animation options that control when animated items display in the animation sequence.

Trim A command that deletes parts of a video to make it shorter.

With Previous An animation option that begins the animation sequence at the same time as the previous animation or slide transition.

Chapter Review

Apply 3A skills from these Objectives:

1. Customize Slide Backgrounds and Themes
2. Animate a Slide Show
3. Insert a Video

In the following Skills Review, you will format a presentation by applying slide background styles, colors, pictures, and animation. Your completed presentation will look similar to Figure 3.57.

Project Files

For Project 3C, you will need:

p03C_Park

p03C_Park_Scenery

p03C_Park_Video

You will save your presentation as:

Lastname_Firstname_3C_Park

Project Results

Figure 3.57 Project 3C Park

(continues on next page)

Chapter Review

1 ▶ Navigate to your student data files, double-click **p03C_Park**, and then **Save** the presentation in your **PowerPoint Chapter 3** folder as **Lastname_Firstname_3C_Park**

a. On the **Design tab**, in the **Variants group**, click **More**, point to **Colors**, and then click **Orange Red** to change the theme colors.

b. On the **Design tab**, in the **Variants group**, click **More**, point to **Fonts**, and then click **Candara** to change the theme fonts.

c. On the **Design tab**, in the **Customize group**, click **Format Background**. In the **Format Background** pane, under **Fill**, click **Picture or texture fill**. Under **Insert picture from**, to the right of **Texture**, click **Texture**, and then in the third row, click the fourth texture—**Recycled Paper**.

d. **Close** the **Format Background** pane.

2 ▶ Display **Slide 2**. Hold down Ctrl and click **Slide 4** so that both **Slides 2** and **4** are selected. On the **Design tab**, in the **Variants group**, click **More**, and then point to **Background Styles**. In the second row, right-click the third style—**Style 7**, and then on the shortcut menu, click **Apply to Selected Slides**. (Mac users, click Slide 2. On the Design tab, in the Customize group, click Format Background. Under Fill, click Solid fill. To the right of Color, click Fill Color, and under theme colors, in the third column click the fifth color—Gray, Background 2, Darker 25%.)

a. Display **Slide 3**. On the **Design tab**, in the **Customize group**, click **Format Background**. Under **Fill**, select the **Hide Background Graphics** check box.

b. In the **Format Background** pane, under **Fill**, click **Picture or texture fill**. Under **Insert picture from**, click **File**, and then navigate to your student data files. Click **p03C_Park_Scenery**, and then click **Insert**.

c. In the **Transparency** box, type **10%**

3 ▶ Display **Slide 5**. If necessary, display the Format Background pane.

a. In the **Format Background** pane, under **Fill**, verify that **Solid Fill** is selected.

b. To the right of **Color**, click **Fill Color**. In the third column, click the first color.

c. **Close** the **Format Background** pane.

4 ▶ With **Slide 5** displayed, on the **Insert tab**, in the **Media group**, click **Video**, and then click **Video on My PC**. Navigate to your student data files, and then click **p03C_Park_Video**. Click **Insert** to insert the video.

a. With the video selected, on the **Format tab**, in the **Size group**, replace the value in the **Height** box with **2.5** and then press Enter.

b. On the **Format tab**, in the **Arrange group**, click **Align**, and then click **Align Center**. Click **Align** again, and then click **Align Bottom** so that the video is centered and aligned with the lower edge of the slide.

c. With the video selected, on the **Format tab**, in the **Video Styles** group, click **More**, and then under **Subtle**, click the third style—**Soft Edge Rectangle**.

d. In the **Video Styles group**, click **Video Shape**, and then under **Rectangles**, click the second shape—**Rectangle: Rounded Corners**. (Mac users click the Crop arrow, point to Change Shape, and then click Rounded Rectangle.)

e. With the video selected, on the **Playback tab**, in the **Video Options group**, click the **Start arrow**, and then click **Automatically**.

f. On the **Playback tab**, in the **Editing group**, click **Trim Video**. Select the number in the **End Time** box, and then type **00:14** and notice that the video ends with a picture of the park. Click **OK** to apply the trim settings. (Mac users drag the End Trim slider to the left until the Duration counter is roughly 0:14:000, and then click Trim.)

5 ▶ Display **Slide 2**, and then select the text in the bulleted list placeholder. On the **Home tab**, in the **Font group**, click **Font Color**, and then in the second column, click the first color so that the text displays with more contrast against the slide background.

a. With the bulleted list selected, on the **Animations tab**, in the **Animation group**, click **More**, and then under **Entrance**, click **Split**.

b. In the **Animation group**, click **Effect Options**, and then click **Vertical Out**.

c. In the **Timing group**, click the **Start arrow**, and then click **After Previous** so that the list displays after the slide transition.

(continues on next page)

Chapter Review

d. In the **Timing group**, click the **Duration up arrow** two times so that *01.00* displays in the **Duration** box. Click the **Delay up arrow** one time so that *00.25* displays in the **Delay** box. (Mac users, in the Animations pane, click to expand Timing to adjust the **Delay** value.)

6 ▶ Display **Slide 3**, and then click in the title placeholder. On the **Animations tab**, in the **Animation group**, click **More**, and then under **Entrance**, click **Wipe**. In the **Timing group**, click the **Start arrow**, and then click **After Previous** so that the title displays immediately after the slide transition.

a. With the title selected, in the **Advanced Animation group**, click **Animation Painter**. Click **Slide 1**, and then click the subtitle—*Remodel Update*—to apply the animation effect to the subtitle.

b. On **Slide 1**, select the title. On the **Animations tab**, in the **Animation group**, click **More**, and then click **None** to remove the animation from the title. (Mac users, in the Animations pane, under ANIMATIONS, select the title and then click the red X to remove the animation.)

c. Insert a **Header & Footer** for the **Notes and Handouts**. Include the **Date and time updated automatically**, the **Page number**, and a **Footer** with the text **3C_Park**

d. On the **Slide Show tab**, in the **Start Slide Show group**, click **From Beginning**, and then view your presentation, clicking the mouse button to advance through the slides. When the video on Slide 5 finishes, press (Esc) to return to the presentation.

7 ▶ Click the **File tab**, and then click **Compress Media**. Click **Standard Quality** to make the presentation size smaller and easier to submit. Depending on your system, this may be named Low Quality. When the compression is complete, in the **Compress Media** dialog box, click **Close**. (Mac users, the Compress Media feature is not available in the Mac version of PowerPoint.)

a. Display the document properties. As the **Tags,** type **park remodel** and as the **Subject,** type your course and section number. Be sure your name displays as author, and then **Save** your file.

b. As directed by your instructor, submit your completed PowerPoint presentation. **Close** PowerPoint.

You have completed Project 3C **END**

Chapter Review

Skills Review | **Project 3D Budget**

Apply 3B skills from these Objectives:

4. Create and Modify Tables
5. Create and Modify Charts

In the following Skills Review, you will format a presentation by inserting and formatting a table, a column chart, and a line chart. Your completed presentation will look similar to Figure 3.58.

Project Files

For Project 3D, you will need:

p03D_Budget

You will save your presentation as:

Lastname_Firstname_3D_Budget

Project Results

Figure 3.58 Project 3D Budget

(continues on next page)

Chapter Review

1 Navigate to your student data files, double-click **p03D_Budget**, and then **Save** the presentation in your **PowerPoint Chapter 3** folder as **Lastname_Firstname_3D_Budget**

a. Display **Slide 2**. In the content placeholder, click **Insert Table** to display the **Insert Table** dialog box. In the **Number of columns box**, type **3** and then press Tab. In the **Number of rows** box, if necessary, type **2** and then click **OK** to create the table.

b. In the first row of the table, click in the second cell. Type **City Hall** and then press Tab. Type **School District** and then press Tab to move the insertion point to the first cell in the second row.

c. With the insertion point positioned in the first cell of the second row, type **Network Upgrade** and then press Tab. Type **75% complete** and then press Tab. Type **50% complete** and then press Tab to insert a new blank row. In the first cell of the third row, type **Software Training** and then press Tab. Type **50% complete** and then press Tab. Type **20% complete**

d. With the insertion point positioned in the last column, on the **Layout tab**, in the **Rows & Columns group**, click **Insert Left** to insert a new column. Click in the top cell of the inserted column, and then type **Library** In the second and third rows of the inserted column, type **85% complete** and **65% complete**

e. With the insertion point positioned in the third row, on the **Layout tab**, in the **Rows & Columns group**, click **Insert Above**. Click in the first cell of the row you inserted, type **Software Testing** and then press Tab. Type the remaining three entries in the row as follows: **Complete** and **Complete** and **40% complete**

2 At the center of the lower border surrounding the table, point to the sizing handle, and make the table larger by dragging down until the lower edge of the table aligns **on the lower half of the vertical ruler at 2 inches**.

a. Click in the first cell of the table. On the **Layout tab**, in the **Cell Size group**, click **Distribute Rows**.

b. On the **Layout tab**, in the **Table group**, click **Select**, and then click **Select Table**. In the **Alignment group**, click **Center**, and then click **Center Vertically**.

c. On the **Table Tools Design tab**, in the **Table Styles group**, click **More**. Under **Medium**, in the third row, click the second style—**Medium Style 3 – Accent 1**—to apply the style to the table.

d. Move the pointer outside of the table so that it is positioned to the left of the first row in the table to display the ➡ pointer, and then click one time to select the entire row. On the **Design tab**, in the **Table Styles group**, click **Effects**. Point to **Cell Bevel**, and then under **Bevel**, click the first bevel—**Round**. Depending on your version of PowerPoint, this may be named **Circle**. Change the **Font Size** of the text in the first row to **24**.

3 Display **Slide 3**. In the content placeholder, click **Insert Chart** to display the **Insert Chart** dialog box. With the **Clustered Column** chart selected, click **OK**.

a. In the worksheet window, click in cell **B1**, which contains the text *Series 1*. Type **City Hall** and then press Tab to move to cell **C1**.

b. In cell **C1**, which contains the text *Series 2*, type **Library** and then press Tab to move to cell **D1**, which contains the text *Series 3*. Type **School District** and then press Tab.

c. Beginning in cell **A2**, type the following data, pressing Tab to move from cell to cell.

	City Hall	Library	School District
Budget	235650	110500	185635
Actual	275895	95760	192570

d. In the worksheet window, position the pointer over **row heading 4** so that the ➡ pointer displays. Then, drag down to select both **rows 4** and **5**. Right-click in one of the selected the rows to display the shortcut menu. On the shortcut menu, click **Delete**. **Close** the worksheet window. (Mac users press command ⌘ and click.)

e. With the chart selected, on the **Chart Tools Design tab**, in the **Chart Styles group**, click **More**. In the **Chart Styles** gallery, in the second row, click **Style 13** to apply the style to the chart.

f. To the right of the chart, click **Chart Elements**, and then *clear* the **Chart Title** box to remove it from the chart. Select the **Data Labels** box to add the data labels to the chart. (Mac users, on the Chart Design tab, click Add Chart Element, point to Chart Title, and then click None. Click Add Chart Element, point to Data Labels, and then click Outside End.)

(continues on next page)

Chapter Review

g. With the chart selected, click the **Animations tab**, and then in the **Animation group**, click **More**. Under **Entrance**, click **Split**. In the **Animation group**, click **Effect Options**, and then under **Sequence**, click **By Series**.

4 Display **Slide 4**. In the content placeholder, click **Insert Chart**. On the left side of the displayed **Insert Chart** dialog box, click **Line**, and then under **Line**, click the fourth chart—**Line with Markers**. Click **OK**.

a. In the worksheet, click in cell **B1**, which contains the text *Series 1*. Type **City Hall** and then press Tab. Type **Library** and then press Tab. Type **School District**

b. Beginning in cell **A2**, type the following data. After you finish entering the data, close the worksheet window.

	City Hall	Library	School District
Quarter 1	76575	8265	50665
Quarter 2	89670	18675	52830
Quarter 3	53620	41730	31560
Quarter 4	56030	27090	57515

c. Click in the **Chart Title**, and then type **Information Technology**

d. Insert a **Header & Footer** for the **Notes and Handouts**. Include the **Date and time updated automatically**, the **Page number**, and a **Footer** with the file name **3D_Budget**

e. Display the document properties. As the **Tags,** type **technology budget** and as the **Subject,** type your course and section number. Be sure your name displays as author, and then **Save** your file.

f. As directed by your instructor, submit your completed PowerPoint presentation. **Close** PowerPoint.

You have completed Project 3D **END**

Mastering PowerPoint Project 3E Gardens

In the following Mastering PowerPoint project, you will format a presentation created by the Pacifica Bay Public Relations department that describes the City of Pacifica Bay Botanical Gardens. Your completed presentation will look similar to Figure 3.59.

Apply 3A skills from these Objectives:

1. Customize Slide Backgrounds and Themes
2. Animate a Slide Show
3. Insert a Video

Project Files for MyLab IT Grader

1. In your **MyLab IT** course, locate and click **PowerPoint 3E Garden**, Download Materials, and then Download All Files.
2. Extract the zipped folder to your PowerPoint Chapter 3 folder. Close the Grader download screens.
3. Take a moment to open the downloaded **PowerPoint_3E Garden_Instructions**; note any recent updates to the book.

Project Results

Figure 3.59 Project 3E Garden

For Non-MyLab Submissions

For Project 3E, you will need:
New blank PowerPoint presentation
p03E_Garden
p03E_Flower
p03E_Video

In your PowerPoint Chapter 3 folder, save your presentation as:
Lastname_Firstname_3E_Garden

After you have named and saved your presentation, on the next page, begin with Step 2.
After Step 15, save and submit your presentation as directed by your instructor.

(continues on next page)

Content-Based Assessments (Mastery and Transfer of Learning)

1 Navigate to your **PowerPoint Chapter 3 folder** and then double-click the PowerPoint file you downloaded from **MyLab IT** that displays your name—**Student_PowerPoint_3E_Garden**

2 Change the **Colors** for the presentation to **Green**, and the **Fonts** to **Cambria**.

3 On **Slide 1**, format the background by changing the **Fill Color** to **Tan, Text 2, Darker 90%**—in the fourth column, the last color.

4 Select **Slides 2** and **3**, and then format the background of the two selected slides with the **Canvas Texture**.

5 On **Slide 2**, select the paragraph on the right side of the slide, and then apply the **Split** entrance effect. Change the **Effect Options** to **Horizontal Out**. Change the **Start** setting to **After Previous**, and then change the **Duration** to **01.00**.

6 Use the **Animation Painter** to apply the same animation from the paragraph on **Slide 2** to the bulleted list on **Slide 3**. Then, on Slide 3, remove the animation from the title.

7 On **Slide 4,** hide the background graphics, and then format the background with a picture from your student data files—**p03E_Flower**. Change the **Transparency** to **50%**.

8 Format the title placeholder with a **Shape Fill** color—in the fifth column, the last color.

9 From your student data files, insert the video **p03E_Video**. Change the **Video Height** to **5**

10 Using the **Align to Slide** option, apply the **Align Center** and **Align Middle** options.

11 Format the video by applying, from the **Video Styles** gallery, a **Moderate** style—**Beveled Oval, Black**.

12 Change the video **Start** setting to **Automatically**, and then trim the video to **00:12** Compress the video using the **Standard Quality** setting or Low Quality depending on your version of PowerPoint. Note— The Compress Media feature is not available in the Mac version of PowerPoint.

13 Insert a **Header & Footer** on the **Notes and Handouts**. Include the **Date and time updated automatically**, the **Page number**, and a **Footer** with the text **3E_Garden**

14 Display the document properties. As the **Tags,** type **botanical gardens** and as the **Subject,** type your course and section number. Be sure your name displays in the **Author box**, and then **Save** your file.

15 View the slide show from the beginning. **Close** PowerPoint.

16 In **MyLab IT**, in your **Course Materials**, locate and click the Grader Project **PowerPoint 3E Garden**. In **step 3**, under **Upload Completed Assignment**, click **Choose File**. In the **Open** dialog box, navigate to your **PowerPoint Chapter 3 folder**, and then click your **Student_PowerPoint_3E_Garden** file one time to select it. In the lower right corner of the **Open** dialog box, click **Open**.

The name of your selected file displays above the Upload button.

17 To submit your file to **MyLab IT** for grading, click **Upload**, wait a moment for a green **Success!** message, and then in **step 4**, click the blue **Submit for Grading** button. Click **Close Assignment** to return to your list of **Course Materials**.

You have completed Project 3E   **END**

Mastering PowerPoint **Project 3F Report**

In the following Mastering PowerPoint project, you will format several of the slides in a presentation that the City Manager is developing for an upcoming City Council meeting. Your completed presentation will look similar to Figure 3.60.

Project Files for **MyLab IT** Grader

1. In your **MyLab IT** course, locate and click **PowerPoint 3F Report**, Download Materials, and then Download All Files.
2. Extract the zipped folder to your PowerPoint Chapter 3 folder. Close the Grader download screens.
3. Take a moment to open the downloaded **PowerPoint_3F_Report_Instructions**; note any recent updates to the book.

Project Results

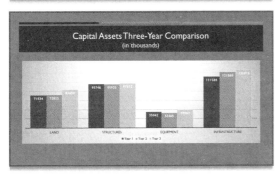

Figure 3.60 Project 3F Report

For Non-MyLab Submissions

For Project 3F, you will need: In your PowerPoint Chapter 3 folder, save your presentation as:
p03F_Report   **Lastname_Firstname_3F_Report**

After you have named and saved your presentation, on the next page, begin with Step 2.

After Step 14, save and submit your presentation as directed by your instructor.

(continues on next page)

Content-Based Assessments (Mastery and Transfer of Learning)

1 Navigate to your **PowerPoint Chapter 3 folder** and then double-click the PowerPoint file you downloaded from **MyLab IT** that displays your name—**Student_PowerPoint_3F_Report**. If necessary, at the top, click **Enable Editing**.

2 On **Slide 3**, in the content placeholder, insert a **Line with Markers** chart. In the worksheet, in cell **B1**, type **Taxes** and then enter the following data:

	Taxes	City Fees	Capital Grants
Quarter 1	8074	4154	3525
Quarter 2	6380	3092	3785
Quarter 3	6695	3260	4150
Quarter 4	7382	6958	2795

3 **Close** the worksheet window. Apply **Chart Style 7**, and then apply the **Wipe** entrance effect to the chart.

4 Including the parentheses, change the **Chart Title** to **(IN THOUSANDS)**

5 On **Slide 4**, in the content placeholder, insert a **Table** with **2 columns** and **5 rows**, and then type the text in **Table 1** at the bottom of the page.

6 Change the height of the table to **4.36"** Align the table text so that it is centered horizontally and vertically within the cells.

7 Apply table style **Medium Style 3 - Accent 2**, and then apply a **Round Bevel** to the first row. Note—Depending on your version of PowerPoint, this may be named Circle Bevel. Change the **Font Size** of the text in the first row to **24**.

8 On **Slide 5**, in the content placeholder, insert a **Clustered Column** chart. In the worksheet, in cell **B1**, type **Year 1** and then enter the following data:

	Year 1	Year 2	Year 3
Land	71534	72823	83653
Structures	95746	95920	97812
Equipment	35042	33465	39767
Infrastructure	111586	121860	125873

9 Apply **Chart Style 4** to the chart, and then remove the **Chart Title** element.

10 Apply the **Wipe** entrance effect to the chart. Change the **Effect Options** so that the animation is applied **By Series**.

11 Change chart animation **Timing** so that the animation starts **After Previous**.

12 **Insert** a **Header & Footer** on the **Notes and Handouts**. Include the **Date and time updated automatically**, the **Page number**, and a **Footer** with the text **3F_Report**

13 Display the document properties. As the **Tags**, type **city council report** and as the **Subject**, type your course and section number. Be sure your name displays as author, and then **Save** your file.

14 View the slide show from the beginning. **Close** PowerPoint.

15 In **MyLab IT**, in your **Course Materials**, locate and click the Grader Project **PowerPoint 3F Report**. In **step 3**, under **Upload Completed Assignment**, click **Choose File**. In the **Open** dialog box, navigate to your **PowerPoint Chapter 3 folder**, and then click your **Student_PowerPoint_3F_Report** file one time to select it. In the lower right corner of the **Open** dialog box, click **Open**.

The name of your selected file displays above the Upload button.

16 To submit your file to **MyLab IT** for grading, click **Upload**, wait a moment for a green **Success!** message, and then in **step 4**, click the blue **Submit for Grading** button. Click **Close Assignment** to return to your list of **Course Materials**.

Table 1

Item	Description
Street Improvements	Monroe Avenue asphalt, signage, and street lighting
City Buildings	Infrastructure upgrades
Flood Control	Main Street storm drain replacement
City Parks	Monterey Park installation of two baseball diamonds

You have completed Project 3F | **END**

Content-Based Assessments (Mastery and Transfer of Learning)

Mastering PowerPoint   Project 3G Travel

In the following Mastering PowerPoint project, you will format a presentation that the Pacifica Bay Travel and Tourism Director will show at a conference for California Travel Agents. Your completed presentation will look similar to Figure 3.61.

Project Files for MyLab IT Grader

1. In your **MyLab IT** course, locate and click **PowerPoint 3G Travel**, Download Materials, and then Download All Files.
2. Extract the zipped folder to your Excel Chapter 3 folder. Close the Grader download screens.
3. Take a moment to open the downloaded **PowerPoint_3G_Travel_Instructions**; note any recent updates to the book.

Project Results

Figure 3.61 Project 3G Travel

For Non-MyLab Submissions

For Project 2G, you will need:
p03G_Travel
p03G_Video
p03G_Background

In your PowerPoint Chapter 3 folder, save your presentation as:
Lastname_Firstname_3G_Travel

After you have named and saved your workbook, open it to launch Excel, and then on the next page, begin with Step 2.

After Step 18, save and submit your presentation as directed by your instructor.

(continues on next page)

Content-Based Assessments (Mastery and Transfer of Learning)

Mastering PowerPoint: Project 3G Travel (continued)

1 Navigate to your **PowerPoint Chapter 3 folder** and then double-click the PowerPoint file you downloaded from **MyLab IT** that displays your name—**Student_PowerPoint_3G_Travel**. If necessary, at the top, click **Enable Editing**.

2 Change the **Colors** for the presentation to **Blue Green**.

3 On **Slide 1**, format the background with the **Water droplets Texture**, and then change the **Transparency** to **50%**.

4 Select **Slides 2 through 4**, and then apply a **Solid fill** to the background of the selected slides—in the second to last column, the third color.

5 On **Slide 2**, hide the background graphics.

6 Insert a **Table** with **3 columns** and **4 rows**. Apply table style **Medium Style 3 - Accent 3**, and then type the information in **Table 1** at the bottom of this page, into the inserted table.

7 Resize the table so that its lower edge extends to **3 inches on the lower half of the vertical ruler (height 4.72")**, and then distribute the table rows. Align the table text so that it is centered horizontally and vertically within the cells.

8 Change the **Font Size** of the first row of the table text to **24**. Apply a **Divot Cell Bevel** to the first row.

9 On **Slide 3**, animate the picture using the **Wipe** entrance effect starting **After Previous**. Change the **Duration** to **01:00**. Apply the **Split** entrance effect to the bulleted list placeholder, and then change the **Effect Options** to **Vertical Out**.

10 On **Slide 4**, insert a **Clustered Column** chart. In the worksheet, in cell **B1**, type **Year 1** and then enter the following data:

	Year 1	Year 2	Year 3
Spring	75600	72300	81460
Summer	105300	128730	143600
Fall	35900	58300	58320
Winter	41600	58430	67300

11 Apply **Chart Style 8** to the chart, and then remove the **Chart Title** element. Apply the **Wipe** entrance effect to the chart and change the **Effect Options** to **By Series**.

12 On **Slide 5**, apply the **Style 1** background style to this slide only. (Mac users, format the background using Solid Fill color White, Background 1.)

13 From your student data files, insert the video **p03G_Video**. Change the **Video Height** to **6** and use the **Align Center** and **Align Top** options to position the video. Apply the **Simple Beveled Rectangle** video style.

14 On the **Playback tab**, change the **Video Options** to **Start** the video **Automatically**. **Trim** the video so that the **End Time** is **00:09** and then compress the media in **Standard Quality** or Low Quality depending on your version of PowerPoint. (Mac users, the Compress Media feature is not available in the Mac version of PowerPoint.)

15 On **Slide 6**, hide the background graphics, and then format the slide background by inserting a picture from your downloaded project files—**p03G_Background**. Set the **Transparency** to **0%**

16 Insert a **Header & Footer** on the **Notes and Handouts**. Include the **Date and time updated automatically**, the **Page number**, and a **Footer** with the text **3G_Travel**

17 Display the document properties. As the **Tags,** type **travel, tourism** and as the **Subject,** type your course and section number. Be sure your name displays as author, and then **Save** your file.

18 View the slide show from the beginning. **Close** PowerPoint.

19 In **MyLab IT**, in your **Course Materials**, locate and click the Grader Project **PowerPoint 3G Travel**. In **step 3**, under **Upload Completed Assignment**, click **Choose File**. In the **Open** dialog box, navigate to your **PowerPoint Chapter 3 folder**, and then click your **Student_PowerPoint_3G_Travel** file one time to select it. In the lower right corner of the **Open** dialog box, click **Open**.

The name of your selected file displays above the Upload button.

20 To submit your file to **MyLab IT** for grading, click **Upload**, wait a moment for a green **Success!** message, and then in **step 4**, click the blue **Submit for Grading** button. Click **Close Assignment** to return to your list of **Course Materials**.

Table 1

Trip Type	Day One	Day Two
Adventure Seeker	Kayak and Snorkel	Nature Preserve Hike
Family-Friendly	Pacifica Bay Zoo	Beach Day and Horseback Riding
Arts & Culture	Pacifica Bay Art Museum	Artisan Walk

You have completed Project 3G **END**

Content-Based Assessments (Critical Thinking)

Apply a combination of the 3A and 3B skills.

GO! Fix It	**Project 3H Housing Developments**	IRC
GO! Make It	**Project 3I Water Usage**	IRC
GO! Solve It	**Project 3J Aquatic Center**	IRC
GO! Solve It	**Project 3K Power**	

Project Files

For Project 3K, you will need:

p03K_Power

p03K_Tower

You will save your presentation as:

Lastname_Firstname_3K_Power

Open the file p03K_Power and save it as **Lastname_Firstname_3K_Power** Complete the presentation by applying a theme and then formatting the slide background for the title slide with the picture found in your student data files—p03K_Tower. Adjust the size, position, fill color, and font color on the title slide as necessary so that the title text displays attractively against the background picture. Format the background of at least one other slide using a background style, solid fill color, or texture. On Slide 3, insert a table with the following information:

Power Sources	Percent Used by City
Natural gas	32%
Hydroelectric	17%
Renewables	18%
Coal	23%
Nuclear	10%

On Slide 4, insert and format an appropriate chart to demonstrate the revenue collected from residential power sales over the past three years. Revenue in 2018 was 35.5 million dollars, in 2019 revenue was 42.6 million dollars, and in 2020 revenue was 48.2 million dollars. Apply appropriate animation and slide transitions to the slides. Insert a header and footer that includes the date and time updated automatically, **3K_Power** in the footer, and the page number. Add your name, your course name and section number, and the keywords **power sources, revenue** to the Properties area. Save and then as directed by your instructor, create and submit a paper printout or an electronic image of your presentation that looks like a printed document—either as the Notes and Handouts or as the presentation slides—or, submit your completed PowerPoint file. Close PowerPoint.

Content-Based Assessments (Critical Thinking)

		Performance Level		
		Exemplary	**Proficient**	**Developing**
		You consistently applied the relevant skills	You sometimes, but not always, applied the relevant skills	You rarely or never applied the relevant skills
Performance Elements	**Format two slide backgrounds with pictures and styles**	Two slide backgrounds were formatted attractively and text displayed with good contrast against backgrounds.	Slide backgrounds were formatted but text did not display well against the chosen background, or only one slide background was formatted.	Slide backgrounds were not formatted with pictures or styles.
	Insert and format appropriate table and chart	Appropriate table and chart were inserted and formatted and the entered data was accurate.	A table and a chart were inserted but were not appropriate for the presentation or either a table or a chart was omitted.	Table and chart were not inserted.
	Apply appropriate animation	Appropriate animation was applied to the presentation.	Animation was applied but was not appropriate for the presentation.	Animation was not applied.

You have completed Project 3K **END**

Rubric

The following outcomes-based assessments are open-ended assessments. That is, there is no specific correct result; your result will depend on your approach to the information provided. Make Professional Quality your goal. Use the following scoring rubric to guide you in how to approach the problem and then to evaluate how well your approach solves the problem.

The *criteria*—Software Mastery, Content, Format and Layout, and Process—represent the knowledge and skills you have gained that you can apply to solving the problem. The *levels of performance*—Professional Quality, Approaching Professional Quality, or Needs Quality Improvements—help you and your instructor evaluate your result.

	Your completed project is of Professional Quality if you:	Your completed project is Approaching Professional Quality if you:	Your completed project Needs Quality Improvements if you:
1-Software Mastery	Choose and apply the most appropriate skills, tools, and features and identify efficient methods to solve the problem.	Choose and apply some appropriate skills, tools, and features, but not in the most efficient manner.	Choose inappropriate skills, tools, or features, or are inefficient in solving the problem.
2-Content	Construct a solution that is clear and well organized, contains content that is accurate, appropriate to the audience and purpose, and is complete. Provide a solution that contains no errors of spelling, grammar, or style.	Construct a solution in which some components are unclear, poorly organized, inconsistent, or incomplete. Misjudge the needs of the audience. Have some errors in spelling, grammar, or style, but the errors do not detract from comprehension.	Construct a solution that is unclear, incomplete, or poorly organized, contains some inaccurate or inappropriate content, and contains many errors of spelling, grammar, or style. Do not solve the problem.
3-Format and Layout	Format and arrange all elements to communicate information and ideas, clarify function, illustrate relationships, and indicate relative importance.	Apply appropriate format and layout features to some elements, but not others. Overuse features, causing minor distraction.	Apply format and layout that does not communicate information or ideas clearly. Do not use format and layout features to clarify function, illustrate relationships, or indicate relative importance. Use available features excessively, causing distraction.
4-Process	Use an organized approach that integrates planning, development, self-assessment, revision, and reflection.	Demonstrate an organized approach in some areas, but not others; or, use an insufficient process of organization throughout.	Do not use an organized approach to solve the problem.

Outcomes-Based Assessments (Critical Thinking)

Apply a combination of the 3A and 3B skills.

GO! Think   **Project 3L Animal Sanctuary**

Project Files

For Project 3L, you will need:

New blank PowerPoint presentation

You will save your presentation as:

Lastname_Firstname_3L_Animal_Sanctuary

The Pacifica Bay Animal Sanctuary, a nonprofit organization, provides shelter and care for animals in need, including dogs, cats, hamsters, and guinea pigs. The Sanctuary, which celebrates its tenth anniversary in July, has cared for more than 12,000 animals since it opened and is a state-of-the-art facility. Funding for the Sanctuary comes in the form of business sponsorships, individual donations, and pet adoption fees. The following table indicates revenue generated by the Sanctuary during the past three years.

	Fees	Donations	Sponsorships
2018	125,085	215,380	175,684
2019	110,680	256,785	156,842
2020	132,455	314,682	212,648

In addition to shelter services, the Sanctuary offers community service and training programs, veterinarian services, and vaccine clinics. Examples of these services include Canine Obedience classes, microchipping ($25 fee), and the Healthy Pet Hotline (free). Canine Obedience classes are for puppies and adult dogs to improve obedience, socialization, and behavior. Classes last two, three, or four months and cost $150 to $250.

Using the preceding information, create the first five slides of a presentation that the director of the Pacifica Bay Animal Sanctuary will show at an upcoming pet fair. Apply an appropriate theme and use slide layouts that will effectively present the content. Include a line chart with the revenue data, a table with the community service programs information, and at least one slide formatted with a dog or cat on the slide background. Apply styles to the table and chart, apply animation and slide transitions to the slides. Use the techniques that you practiced in this chapter so that your presentation is professional and attractive. Save the file as **Lastname_Firstname_3L_Animal_Sanctuary** and then insert a header and footer that includes the date and time updated automatically, the **3L_Animal_Sanctuary** in the footer, and the page number. Add your name, your course name and section number, and the keywords **animals, pets** to the properties. As directed by your instructor, submit your completed PowerPoint presentation. Close PowerPoint.

You have completed Project 3L   **END**

Outcomes-Based Assessments (Critical Thinking)

GO! Think	**Project 3M Water Sources**	IRC
You and GO!	**Project 3N Recreation Programs**	IRC
GO! Cumulative Team Project	**Project 3O Bell Orchid Hotels**	IRC

Integrating Word, Excel, Access, and PowerPoint

OFFICE
INTEGRATED
PROJECTS

PROJECT 1A

Outcomes
Create an Excel workbook that includes data exported from Access and data copied from Word and PowerPoint.

Objectives
1. Export Access Data to Excel
2. Create an Excel Worksheet from a Word Table
3. Copy and Paste an Excel Chart into Other Programs
4. Copy and Paste an Object from PowerPoint into Excel

PROJECT 1B

Outcomes
Link Excel data to a Word document and complete a mail merge in Word using Access data.

Objectives
5. Link Excel Data to a Word Document
6. Modify Linked Data and Update Links
7. Create a Table in Word from Access Data
8. Use Access Data to Complete a Mail Merge in Word

EpicStockMedia/Fotolia

In This Chapter

GO! To Work with Integrated Projects

By design, all applications in a software suite, for example, Microsoft Office, work well with one another. You can input data or create objects, such as a chart or table, in one application and then export the data to another application without retyping the data or re-creating the object. It is important to identify the appropriate software within the suite to produce solutions that best utilize the functions of the various applications. In this chapter, you will copy and paste data and objects between applications. You will link, modify, and update data and use mail merge to create individualized documents.

The projects in this chapter relate to **Ultimate Action Sports Gear**, one of the country's leading retailers of sports equipment and outdoor recreational merchandise. The company has a growing online business in addition to large retail stores in Colorado, New Mexico, Oregon, and Washington. Major merchandise categories include fishing, camping, golf, rock climbing, winter sports, action sports, aquatic sports, team sports, racquet sports, fitness and athletic apparel, and footwear. Inventory is constantly updated to provide customers with the newest products in the action sports industry.

State Sales

MyLab IT
Project 1A Grader for Instruction

Integrated Projects are now available as Grader Projects in MyLab IT. To complete this Project as a Grader, download the instructions and files from MyLab IT and follow the steps for completion and submission.

Project Activities

In Activities 1.01 through 1.12, you will export Access data into an Excel workbook, and then you will copy and paste Word data into the Excel workbook. In Excel, you will create a chart based on the data, and then copy the chart into a PowerPoint presentation. Your completed documents will look similar to Figure 1.1.

Project Files

For Non-MyLab Submissions

For Project 1A, you will need the following files:

i01A_Store_Locations (Access database)
i01A_State_Sales (Word document)
i01A_Sales_Presentation (PowerPoint presentation)
i01A_Store_Locations_by_Manager_FOR_MAC_USERS

In your storage location, create a folder named **Integrated Projects**

You will save your files as:

Lastname_Firstname_1A_Sales_Chart (Excel workbook)
Lastname_Firstname_1A_Store_Locations (Access database, not necessary to submit)
Lastname_Firstname_1A_State_Sales (Word document)
Lastname_Firstname_1A_Sales_Presentation (PowerPoint presentation)

Project Results

Figure 1.1 Project 1A State Sales

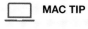

NOTE   If You Are Using a Touch Screen

Tap an item to click it.

Press and hold for a few seconds to right-click; release when the information or commands display.

Touch the screen with two or more fingers and then pinch together to zoom out or stretch your fingers apart to zoom in.

Slide your finger on the screen to scroll—slide left to scroll right and slide right to scroll left.

Slide to rearrange—similar to dragging with a mouse.

Swipe to select—slide an item a short distance with a quick movement—to select an item and bring up commands, if any.

Objective 1   **Export Access Data to Excel**

Access includes a tool to export data from an Access database into an Excel workbook. When you export Access data, you create a copy of the data in Excel.

Activity 1.01 | **Exporting Access Data to Excel**

In the following Activity, you will export Access data into an Excel workbook.

MAC TIP   Because you do not have Access on a Mac, locate and open the Excel file i01A_Store_Locations_by_Manager_FOR_MAC_USERS and in rows 18-21 replace Firstname and Lastname with your own name. Save the workbook in your folder, using your own name, as Lastname_Firstname_1A_Sales_Chart and in the sheet tab area, rename the worksheet Store Locations by Manager. Then move to Activity 1.02.

1 Start Access. On the left of the opening screen, click the command to open other Access files, and then click **Browse**. In the **Open** dialog box, navigate to the files you downloaded for this project, and then open the Access database **i01A_Store_Locations**. If necessary, click Enable Content. Click the **File tab**, and then click **Save As**. On the **Save As** screen, with **Save Database As** selected, on the right, click **Save As**.

2 In the **Save As** dialog box, navigate to the location where you are saving your files. In the **File name** box, using your own name, type **Lastname_Firstname_1A_Store_Locations** and then press Enter. If necessary, on the **Message Bar** that displays a Security Warning, click **Enable Content**.

3 In the **Navigation Pane**, double-click the **Managers** table. At the bottom of the table, select **Firstname**, and then type your own first name. Press Tab to select **Lastname**, type your own last name, and then press Enter.

4 ▶ In the **Navigation Pane**, double-click the query **Store Locations by Manager**, and then be sure that your name displays. Compare your screen with Figure 1.2.

Figure 1.2

5 ▶ On the **External Data tab**, in the **Export group**, click **Excel**. In the **Export - Excel Spreadsheet** dialog box, click **Browse**. Navigate to your **Integrated Projects** folder, using your own name, type the file name **Lastname_Firstname_1A_Sales_Chart** and then click **Save**.

6 ▶ In the **Export - Excel Spreadsheet** dialog box, be sure that the **File format** is **Excel Workbook (*.xlsx)**. Select the **Export data with formatting and layout** check box, and then compare your screen with Figure 1.3.

Figure 1.3

7 ▶ In the **Export – Excel Spreadsheet** dialog box, click **OK**. In the dialog box, be sure that the **Save export steps** check box is *not* selected, and then click **Close**.

8 ▶ **Close** ⊠ Access.

9 Start Excel. On Excel's opening screen, click the command to open other files, and then click **Browse**. In the **Open** dialog box, navigate to your **Integrated Projects** folder, and then open the Excel workbook **Lastname_Firstname_1A_Sales_Chart**.

> The sheet tab at the bottom of the worksheet indicates that the worksheet name is changed to the exported Access query name—*Store Locations by Manager*.

Activity 1.02 | Creating and Sorting an Excel Table

To easily manage and analyze a group of related data, you can convert a range of cells to an Excel table. An Excel table typically contains data in a series of rows and columns; the Excel table can be managed independently from the data in other rows and columns in the worksheet. In the following Activity, you will change a range of data into an Excel table, and then sort the data.

1 Click cell **A1**. On the **Insert tab**, in the **Tables group**, click **Table**. In the **Create Table** dialog box, under **Where is the data for your table?**, be sure that the range is =$A$1:$E$21 and that the **My table has headers** check box is selected. Compare your screen with Figure 1.4.

Figure 1.4

2 In the **Create Table** dialog box, click **OK**.

3 Click cell **E1**, click ▼, and then click **Sort A to Z** to sort the entire table alphabetically by City name. Compare your screen with Figure 1.5.

> After a column is sorted in ascending or descending order, a small arrow displays on the Filter button to indicate the sort order.

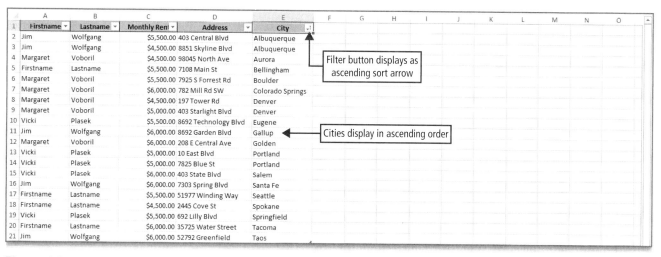

Figure 1.5

4 **Save** 🖫 your Excel workbook.

Activity 1.03 | Inserting a Total Row in an Excel Table

To quickly total the data in the columns of an Excel table, display a total row at the end of the table, and then use the functions that are provided for each cell in the total row.

1 If necessary, click cell **E1**, and then on the **Design tab**, in the **Table Style Options group**, select the **Total Row** check box. Click cell **E22**, and then compare your screen with Figure 1.6.

Cell E22 displays the number *20*. Because the values in Column E are not numbers, instead of totaling, Excel counts the number of cells containing text in column E. The header row is not included in the Total Row calculations.

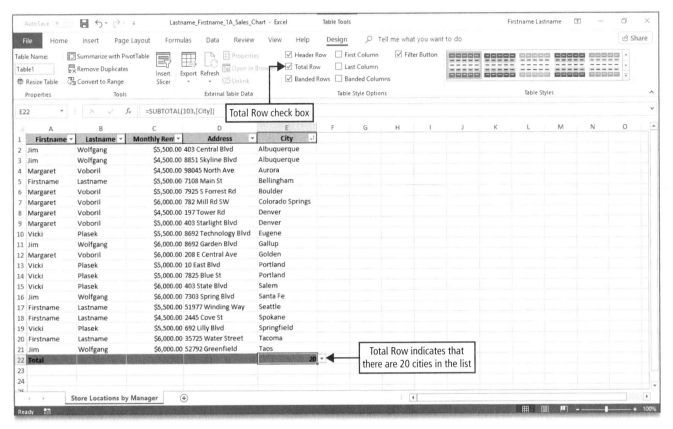

Figure 1.6

2 To the right of cell **E22**, click the arrow ▼, and then click **None**.

Because the cells in column E contain text, a calculation is not required.

3 Click cell **C22**. To the right of cell **C22**, click the arrow ▼, and then click **Sum**. Compare your screen with Figure 1.7.

The total Monthly Rent revenue for all locations displays in cell C22.

Figure 1.7

4 **Save** 🖫 your Excel workbook.

Objective 2   Create an Excel Worksheet from a Word Table

You can use data stored in one file in a different file so that you do not have to reenter the data.

Activity 1.04 | Formatting a Word Table

1 With your Excel workbook still open, start Word. On Word's opening screen, click the command to open other files, click **Browse**, navigate to the files you downloaded with this project, and then open the document **i01A_State_Sales**. Click the **File tab**, click **Save As**, navigate to your **Integrated Projects** folder, and then using your own name, **Save** the document as **Lastname_Firstname_1A_State_Sales**

2 With the Word document displayed, on the **Insert tab**, in the **Header & Footer group**, click **Footer**. At the bottom of the **Footer** gallery, click **Edit Footer**. On the ribbon, under **Header & Footer Tools**, on the **Design tab**, in the **Insert group**, click **Document Info**, and then click **File Name**. In the **Close group**, click **Close Header and Footer**. Display the ruler and formatting marks, if necessary.

3 Scroll down to view the table. Click anywhere in the first cell in the table, and then compare your screen with Figure 1.8.

When the entire table or a table element is selected, the Table Tools tabs—Design and Layout—display.

Figure 1.8

4 On the ribbon, under **Table Tools**, on the **Design tab**, in the **Table Styles group**, click **More**. In the **Table Styles** gallery, scroll down, and then under **List Tables**, in the third row, click the last style—**List Table 3 - Accent 6**.

5 On the **Table Tools Layout tab**, in the **Cell Size group**, click **AutoFit**, and then click **AutoFit Contents**. In the **Table group**, click **Properties**. In the **Table Properties** dialog box, under **Alignment**, click **Center**. Compare your screen with Figure 1.9.

Figure 1.9

6 In the **Table Properties** dialog box, click **OK** to center the table horizontally on the page.

7 Save 🖫 your Word document.

Activity 1.05 | Copying and Pasting a Word Table into an Excel Workbook

After entering data in a Word document, you might decide that you can manipulate the data better in another program, such as Excel. Instead of starting over and retyping the data, you can copy the data from the Word document, and then paste the data into an Excel workbook.

> **NOTE   Working with Multiple Open Windows**
>
> In this chapter, you will work with a number of different files and will have a number of different windows open. When you have completed the work in one file, save the file, and then minimize the window. When you need to use the file again, click the appropriate program icon on the taskbar to maximize that window.

1 Be sure that Word is the active window. On the **Table Tools Layout tab**, in the **Table group**, click **Select**, and then click **Select Table**. On the **Home tab** in the **Clipboard group**, click **Copy** 🗐.

The entire table is selected and copied.

2 On the taskbar, click the **Excel** icon 🗷 to make the Excel window active.

3 At the bottom of the worksheet, click **New sheet** ⊕ to insert a new blank worksheet. Right-click the **Sheet1** worksheet tab, and then click **Rename**. Type **Sales** and then press Enter. Compare your screen with Figure 1.10.

Figure 1.10

4 On the **Page Layout tab**, in the **Themes group**, click **Themes**, and then under **Office**, click **Office**.

5 Click cell **A4** to make it the active cell. On the **Home tab**, in the **Clipboard group**, click the upper portion of the **Paste** button. Compare your screen with Figure 1.11.

The Word data is pasted into the Excel worksheet, starting in cell A4—the active cell.

The pound sign (#) will display if a column is not wide enough to display an entire number.

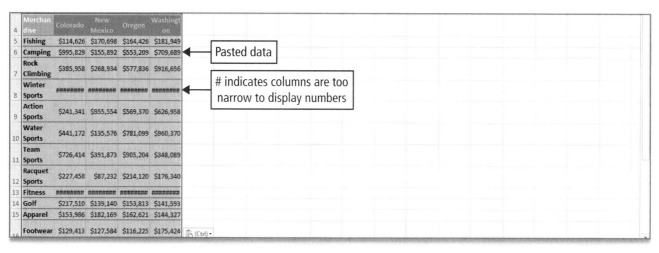

Figure 1.11

6 Click cell **A4**. On the **Home tab**, in the **Cells group**, click **Format**, and then click **Column Width**. In the **Column Width** dialog box, type **16** and then click **OK**.

7 Select the range **B4:E4**. In the **Cells group**, click **Format**, and then click **Column Width**. In the **Column Width** dialog box, type **12** and then click **OK**.

By widening the columns, all data displays in the worksheet.

8 Select the range **A4:A16**. In the **Cells group**, click **Format**, and then click **Row Height**. In the **Row Height** dialog box, type **17** and then click **OK**. Click in an empty cell, and then compare your screen with Figure 1.12.

Merchandise	Colorado	New Mexico	Oregon	Washington
Fishing	$114,626	$170,698	$164,426	$181,949
Camping	$995,829	$155,892	$553,209	$709,689
Rock Climbing	$385,958	$268,934	$577,836	$916,656
Winter Sports	$1,311,794	$1,235,790	$1,529,598	$1,482,004
Action Sports	$241,341	$955,554	$569,370	$626,958
Water Sports	$441,172	$135,576	$781,099	$960,370
Team Sports	$726,414	$391,873	$905,204	$348,089
Racquet Sports	$227,458	$87,232	$214,120	$176,340
Fitness	$1,705,677	$1,057,227	$1,991,815	$1,675,831
Golf	$217,510	$139,140	$153,813	$141,593
Apparel	$153,986	$182,169	$162,621	$144,327
Footwear	$129,413	$127,584	$116,225	$175,424

Column widths adjusted

Row heights adjusted

Figure 1.12

9 In cell **A1**, type **Ultimate Action Sports Gear** and then press Enter. In cell **A2**, type **Sales by State** and then press Enter. Select the range **A1:F1**, and then on the **Home tab**, in the **Alignment group**, click **Merge & Center**. In the **Styles group**, click **Cell Styles**, and then click **Accent 6**. In the **Font group**, click the **Font Size button arrow** 11, and then click **16**.

10 Select the range **A2:F2**. Click **Merge & Center**, apply the cell style **60% - Accent 6**, and then change the **Font Size** to **14** and change the **Font Color** to **White, Background 1**. Compare your screen with Figure 1.13.

Formatted cells in rows 1 and 2

	A	B	C	D	E	F
1	Ultimate Action Sports Gear					
2	Sales by State					
3						
4	Merchandise	Colorado	New Mexico	Oregon	Washington	
5	Fishing	$114,626	$170,698	$164,426	$181,949	

Figure 1.13

11 **Save** 💾 your Excel workbook.

Activity 1.06 | Using the SUM Function and Fill Handle in Excel

In the following Activity, you will use the SUM function to add numbers.

1 Click cell **F4**, type **Total Sales** and then press Enter.

2 Be sure that **F5** is the active cell. On the **Home tab**, in the **Editing group**, click **Sum**, and then on the **Formula Bar**, click **Enter** ✓ to confirm the entry and keep cell **F5** as the active cell. Using the technique you previously practiced, change the width of **column F** to **13**

> **ALERT** **The Formula Bar May Not Display**
>
> If the Formula Bar does not display, on the View tab, in the Show group, select the Formula Bar check box.

3 In cell **F5**, point to the fill handle until the ➕ pointer displays, hold down the left mouse button, and then drag down to cell **F16**. Release the mouse button. In the **Font group**, click **Increase Font Size** 🄰 one time, and then compare your screen with Figure 1.14.

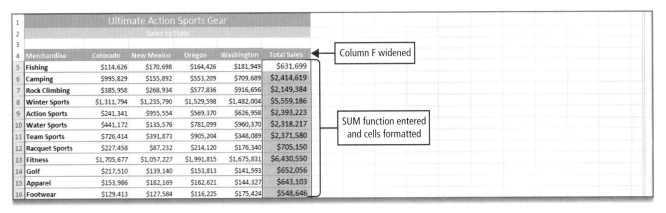

Column F widened

SUM function entered and cells formatted

	Merchandise	Colorado	New Mexico	Oregon	Washington	Total Sales
1	Ultimate Action Sports Gear					
2	Sales by State					
3						
4	Merchandise	Colorado	New Mexico	Oregon	Washington	Total Sales
5	Fishing	$114,626	$170,698	$164,426	$181,949	$631,699
6	Camping	$995,829	$155,892	$553,209	$709,689	$2,414,619
7	Rock Climbing	$385,958	$268,934	$577,836	$916,656	$2,149,384
8	Winter Sports	$1,311,794	$1,235,790	$1,529,598	$1,482,004	$5,559,186
9	Action Sports	$241,341	$955,554	$569,370	$626,958	$2,393,223
10	Water Sports	$441,172	$135,576	$781,099	$960,370	$2,318,217
11	Team Sports	$726,414	$391,873	$905,204	$348,089	$2,371,580
12	Racquet Sports	$227,458	$87,232	$214,120	$176,340	$705,150
13	Fitness	$1,705,677	$1,057,227	$1,991,815	$1,675,831	$6,430,550
14	Golf	$217,510	$139,140	$153,813	$141,593	$652,056
15	Apparel	$153,986	$182,169	$162,621	$144,327	$643,103
16	Footwear	$129,413	$127,584	$116,225	$175,424	$548,646

Figure 1.14

4 ▸ Click cell **A17**, type **Total** and then press ⌐Tab⌐.

5 ▸ With cell **B17** selected, in the **Editing group**, click **Sum**, and then on the **Formula Bar**, click **Enter** ✓. Using the technique you just practiced, use the fill handle to copy the formula to cells **C17:F17**.

6 ▸ Select the range **A5:E16**. In the **Font group**, click the **Border button arrow** [▦ ▾], and then click **No Border**. Select the range **A17:F17**. In the **Styles group**, click **Cell Styles**, and then under **Titles and Headings**, click **Total**. In the **Font group**, click **Increase Font Size** [A⁺] one time. Click in an empty cell, and then compare your screen with Figure 1.15.

4	Merchandise	Colorado	New Mexico	Oregon	Washington	Total Sales		
5	Fishing	$114,626	$170,698	$164,426	$181,949	$631,699		
6	Camping	$995,829	$155,892	$553,209	$709,689	$2,414,619		
7	Rock Climbing	$385,958	$268,934	$577,836	$916,656	$2,149,384	◂	No border applied
8	Winter Sports	$1,311,794	$1,235,790	$1,529,598	$1,482,004	$5,559,186		
9	Action Sports	$241,341	$955,554	$569,370	$626,958	$2,393,223		
10	Water Sports	$441,172	$135,576	$781,099	$960,370	$2,318,217		
11	Team Sports	$726,414	$391,873	$905,204	$348,089	$2,371,580		
12	Racquet Sports	$227,458	$87,232	$214,120	$176,340	$705,150		
13	Fitness	$1,705,677	$1,057,227	$1,991,815	$1,675,831	$6,430,550		
14	Golf	$217,510	$139,140	$153,813	$141,593	$652,056	◂	SUM function entered
15	Apparel	$153,986	$182,169	$162,621	$144,327	$643,103		and cells formatted
16	Footwear	$129,413	$127,584	$116,225	$175,424	$548,646		
17	Total	$6,651,178	$4,907,669	$7,719,336	$7,539,230	$26,817,413	◂	

Figure 1.15

7 ▸ Save [💾] your Excel workbook.

Objective 3 | **Copy and Paste an Excel Chart into Other Programs**

A chart displays numerical data in a visual format. You can copy an Excel chart, and then paste it in files created with other applications.

Activity 1.07 | **Creating and Formatting a Bar Chart in Excel**

In the following Activity, you will create and format a bar chart showing a comparison of merchandise sales by state.

1 Select the range **A4:E16**. On the **Insert tab**, in the **Charts group**, click the **Insert Column or Bar Chart arrow** ⬛, and then under **3-D Bar**, click the first chart—**3-D Clustered Bar**. On the **Design tab**, in the **Location group**, click **Move Chart**. In the **Move Chart** dialog box, click the **New sheet** option button, type **Merchandise Chart** and then click **OK**. Compare your screen with Figure 1.16.

A 3-D bar chart is created and moved to a new chart sheet named Merchandise Chart.

Figure 1.16

2 In the chart, click the text *Chart Title*, click in the **Formula Bar**, type **Retail Sales by State** and then press Enter. Click in a blank area of the chart to deselect the chart title.

3 To the right of the chart, click **Chart Styles** ✎. In the **Style** gallery, scroll down, and then by using the ScreenTips, locate and click **Style 10**.

4 To the right of the chart, click **Chart Elements** ⊞. Under **Chart Elements**, point to **Legend**, click the **Legend arrow**, and then click **Top**.

5 ▶ Under **Chart Elements**, point to **Axes**, click the **Axes arrow**, and then click **More Options**. In the **Format Axis** pane, under **Axis Options**, click **Size & Properties** 📊. Under **Alignment**, in the **Custom angle** box, type **30** and then press ⏎. Compare your screen with Figure 1.17.

The numbers on the horizontal axis display at an angle of 30 degrees.

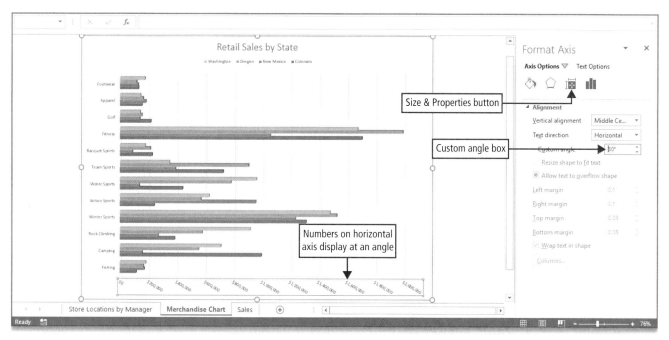

Figure 1.17

6 ▶ **Close** ✕ the **Format Axis** pane.

7 ▶ **Save** 💾 your Excel workbook.

Activity 1.08 | Creating and Formatting a Pie Chart in Excel

In the following Activity, you will create a pie chart to show each state's percentage of total sales.

1 ▶ Click the **Sales** worksheet tab. Select the range **B4:E4**, press and hold ⌃, and then select the range **B17:E17**.

The range B4:E4 and the range B17:E17 are selected. Recall that holding down ⌃ enables you to select nonadjacent cells.

2 ▶ On the **Insert tab**, in the **Charts group**, click **Insert Pie or Doughnut Chart** 🥧 ▾, and then under **3-D Pie**, click **3-D Pie**. On the ribbon, under **Chart Tools**, on the **Design tab**, in the **Location group**, click **Move Chart**. In the **Move Chart** dialog box, click the **New sheet** option button, type **State Sales Chart** and then click **OK**.

3 To the right of the chart, click **Chart Styles** 🖊. In the **Style** gallery, scroll down, and then click **Style 5**. Press Esc to close the gallery. Compare your screen with Figure 1.18.

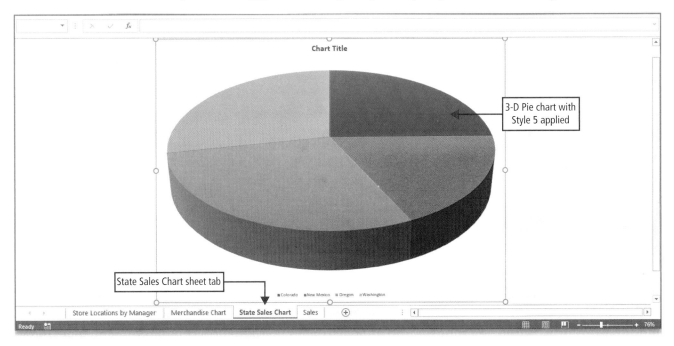

Chart Title

3-D Pie chart with Style 5 applied

State Sales Chart sheet tab

Colorado New Mexico Oregon Washington

Store Locations by Manager | Merchandise Chart | **State Sales Chart** | Sales ⊕

Ready

76%

Figure 1.18

4 In the chart, click the text *Chart Title*, click in the **Formula Bar**, type **State Sales** and press Enter. Click in a blank area of the chart.

5 Click **Chart Elements** ⊞, and then under **Chart Elements**, click **Legend** to remove the legend from the chart.

6 Under **Chart Elements**, select the **Data Labels** check box. Click the **Data Labels arrow**, and then click **More Options**. In the **Format Data Labels** pane, if necessary, expand **Label Options**. Under **Label Contains** select the **Category Name** check box, deselect the **Value** check box, and then click the **Percentage** check box. Under **Label Position**, click the **Center** option button. With the data labels selected, on the **Home tab**, change the **Font Size** 11 ▾ to **16**. Click in a blank area just inside chart to deselect the data labels.

The Format Chart Area pane displays on the right.

7 In the **Format Chart Area** pane, under **Chart Options**, click **Fill & Line** 🖌. Click **Fill**, and then click the **Gradient fill** option button. Click the **Preset gradients arrow**, and then in the first row, click the third gradient—**Light Gradient – Accent 3**. **Close** ✕ the **Format Chart Area** pane, and then compare your screen with Figure 1.19.

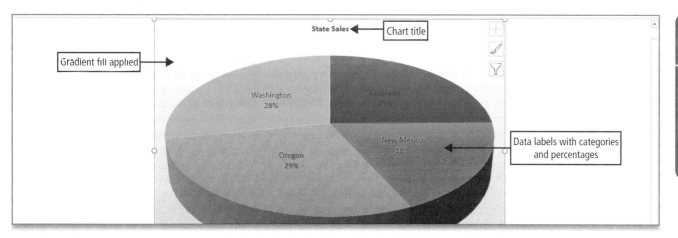

Figure 1.19

8 Press and hold Ctrl, and then click the **Merchandise Chart** sheet tab.

Both chart sheets are selected.

9 On the **Page Layout tab**, in the **Page Setup** group, click the **Dialog Box Launcher** ⬚. In the **Page Setup** dialog box, click the **Header/Footer tab**, and then click **Custom Footer**. In the **Footer** dialog box, be sure that the insertion point is in the *Left section*, and then click **Insert File Name** ⬚. Compare your screen with Figure 1.20.

In the Left section box, the file name is inserted—*&[File]* displays.

Figure 1.20

10 In the **Footer** dialog box, click **OK**, and then in the **Page Setup** dialog box, click **OK**.

The file name is inserted in the footer of both chart sheets.

11 Click the **Sales** worksheet tab to make it the active worksheet and to deselect the chart sheets. Press and hold Ctrl, and then click the **Store Locations by Manager** worksheet tab.

12 On the **Page Layout tab**, in the **Page Setup** group, click the **Dialog Box Launcher** ⬚. In the **Page Setup** dialog box, click the **Header/Footer tab**, and then click **Custom Footer**. In the **Footer** dialog box, with the insertion point in the *Left section*, click **Insert File Name** ⬚. Click **OK** two times to close the dialog boxes.

You must insert footers in worksheets separately from inserting them in chart sheets. In this instance, the file name is inserted in the footer of both worksheets.

13 Press Ctrl + Home to display the top of the worksheet. Right-click the **Sales** sheet tab, and then click **Ungroup Sheets**.

14 Save ⬚ your Excel workbook.

1 On the **Home tab**, in the **Clipboard group**, click the **Dialog Box Launcher** ⌐ to display the Clipboard pane. In the **Clipboard** pane, click **Clear All**. Click the **State Sales Chart** sheet tab, and then click the border of the pie chart to select the chart. On the **Home tab** in the **Clipboard group**, click **Copy** ⌐. Compare your screen with Figure 1.21.

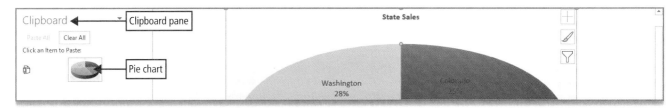

Figure 1.21

2 Click the **Merchandise Chart** sheet tab, and then click the border of the bar chart to select the chart. In the **Clipboard group**, click **Copy** ⌐.

3 At the bottom of the screen, on the taskbar, click the **Word** icon ⌐. Press Ctrl + End to move the insertion point to the end of the document.

4 Press Ctrl + Enter.

A new blank Page 2 is inserted.

5 With the insertion point at the top of **Page 2**, type **In the chart below, our state sales managers can view their sales results**. Press Enter.

6 On the **Home tab**, in the **Clipboard group**, click the **Dialog Box Launcher** ⌐ to display the Clipboard pane, as shown in Figure 1.22.

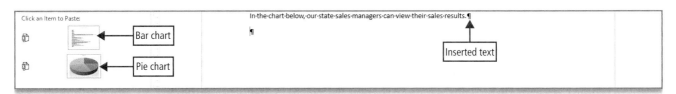

Figure 1.22

7 In the **Clipboard** pane, click the **bar chart**.

The bar chart is pasted into the Word document.

8 **Close** ☒ the **Clipboard** pane, and then press Ctrl + Home.

9 Click the **File tab**, and then in the lower right portion of the screen, at the bottom of the **Properties** list, click **Show All Properties**. In the **Tags** box, type **memo, state sales chart** and in the **Subject** box, type your course name and section number. Be sure your name displays as the author; edit if necessary.

10 On the left, click **Save**, and then **Close** ☒ Word.

Activity 1.10 | Pasting an Excel Chart in PowerPoint

1 With your Excel workbook still open, start PowerPoint. On PowerPoint's opening screen, on the left, click the command to open other presentations, click **Browse**, navigate to the files you downloaded with this project, and then open the presentation **i01A_Sales_Presentation**. Click the **File tab**, on the left, click **Save As**, and then click **Browse** to display the **Save As** dialog box. Navigate to your **Integrated Projects** folder, and then using your own name, **Save** the presentation as **Lastname_Firstname_1A_Sales_Presentation**

2 On the **Insert tab**, in the **Text group**, click **Header & Footer**. In the **Header and Footer** dialog box, click the **Notes and Handouts** tab. Select the **Footer** check box, click in the **Footer** box, using your own name, type **Lastname_Firstname_1A_Sales_Presentation** and then compare your screen with Figure 1.23.

Figure 1.23

3 Click **Apply to All**.

4 Display **Slide 2**. On the **Home tab**, in the **Slides group**, click the **New Slide button arrow**, and then from the **Slides** gallery, click **Blank**. On the **Design tab**, in the **Customize group**, click **Format Background**. In the **Format Background** pane, under **Fill**, select the **Hide background graphics** check box. Compare your screen with Figure 1.24.

A new blank Slide 3 is inserted into the presentation, and the background graphics do not display.

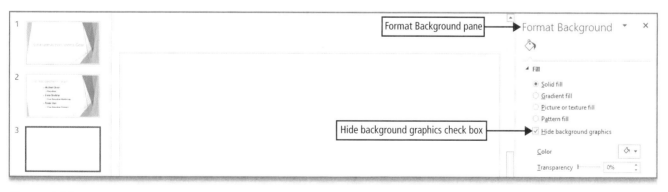

Figure 1.24

5 **Close** ☒ the **Format Background** pane. On the **Home tab**, in the **Clipboard group**, click the **Dialog Box Launcher** ⬚. In the **Clipboard** pane, click the bar chart.

The bar chart is pasted into Slide 3 of the presentation.

6 On the **Home tab**, in the **Slides group**, click the **New Slide button arrow**, and then from the **Slides** gallery, click **Blank**. Using the technique you practiced, select the **Hide background graphics** check box. In the **Clipboard** pane, click the pie chart. Compare your screen with Figure 1.25.

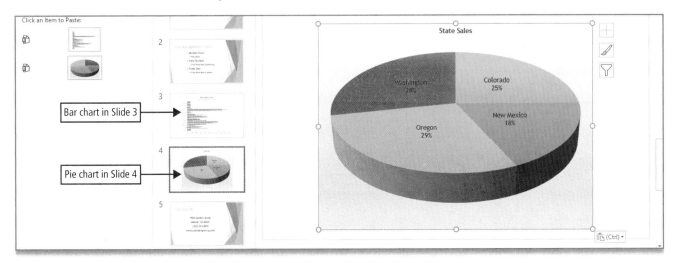

Figure 1.25

7 **Close** ⊠ the **Clipboard** pane, and then **Save** 🖫 the presentation.

Objective 4 **Copy and Paste an Object from PowerPoint into Excel**

In PowerPoint, you can convert bullet points into a SmartArt graphic to illustrate your message visually. After you create a SmartArt graphic in PowerPoint, you can copy the graphic and paste it into a file created with another program. This can save you time because there is no need to re-create the graphic.

Activity 1.11 | **Inserting a SmartArt Graphic**

1 Click **Slide 2** to make it the active slide. Click in the placeholder containing the names of the managers. On the **Home tab**, in the **Paragraph group**, click **Convert to SmartArt Graphic**. In the **SmartArt** gallery, locate and click **Target List**. If the Text Pane displays to the left of the SmartArt placeholder, click Close ⊠.

2 On the ribbon, under **SmartArt Tools**, on the **Design tab**, in the **SmartArt Styles group**, click **More** ▾. In the **SmartArt Styles** gallery, under **3-D**, locate and click **Cartoon**.

3 With the **SmartArt** graphic selected, on the **Animations tab**, in the **Animation group**, click **More** [⌄]. In the **Animation** gallery, under **Entrance**, click **Wheel**. Click in a blank area of the slide to deselect the SmartArt graphic, and then compare your screen with Figure 1.26.

> The number 1 displays to the left of the SmartArt graphic, which indicates that an animation effect is applied to the object.

Figure 1.26

4 On the **Slide Show tab**, in the **Start Slide Show group**, click **From Beginning** to view the presentation. Press Enter to view the second slide.

5 Continue to press Enter to view the remaining slides, and then press Enter to return to **Normal** view.

6 **Save** [💾] the presentation.

Activity 1.12 | Copying and Pasting a SmartArt Graphic

After you create an object in one file, you can copy the object and paste it in a file created with a different program. In this Activity, you will copy the SmartArt graphic in the PowerPoint presentation, and then paste it in an Excel workbook.

1 Click the border of the SmartArt graphic.

> By clicking the border of an object, you select the entire object, not just a part of the object.

2 On the **Home tab**, in the **Clipboard group**, click **Copy** [📋▾].

3 On the taskbar, click the **Excel** icon [📊].

4 In **Excel**, click the **Sales** worksheet tab, and then click cell **A20**. On the **Home tab**, in the **Clipboard group**, click the upper portion of the **Paste** button.

The SmartArt graphic is pasted into the Sales worksheet. The top left corner of the graphic is in cell A20.

5 Scroll down to view the entire graphic. On the ribbon, under **SmartArt Tools**, on the **Format tab**, click **Size**, if necessary. Click in the **Height** box, and then type **3.5** Click in the **Width** box, type **5.5** and then press Enter.

6 Right-click the border of the SmartArt graphic, and then above the shortcut menu, click **Color**. In the **Color** gallery, under **Colorful**, click the fourth color—**Colorful Range – Accent Colors 4 to 5**. Compare your screen with Figure 1.27.

Figure 1.27

7 In the **Clipboard** pane, click **Clear All**, and then **Close** ⊠ the **Clipboard** pane.

8 Click the **File tab**, and then at the right, at the bottom of the **Properties** list, click **Show All Properties**. In the **Tags** box, type **charts, SmartArt** In the **Subject** box, type your course name and section number. Be sure your name displays as the author; edit if necessary.

9 On the left, click **Save**, and then **Close** ⊠ Excel.

10 If necessary, in PowerPoint, **Close** ⊠ the **Clipboard** pane.

11 Click the **File tab**, and then at the right, at the bottom of the **Properties** list, click **Show All Properties**. In the **Tags** box, type **company info, charts, SmartArt** In the **Subject** box, type your course name and section number. Be sure your name displays as the author; edit if necessary.

12 On the left, click **Save**, and then **Close** ⊠ PowerPoint.

13 Submit your printed or electronic files as directed by your instructor. You will have an Excel workbook with four worksheets, a two-page Word document, and a five-slide PowerPoint presentation. You need not submit the Access database.

You have completed Project 1A **END**

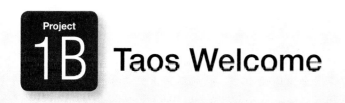

MyLab IT

Project 1B Grader for Instruction

Integrated Projects are now available as Grader Projects in MyLab IT. To complete this Project as a Grader, download the instructions from MyLab IT and follow the steps for completion and submission.

Project Activities

In Activities 1.13 through 1.19, you will link and update Excel data in a Word document. Because Microsoft Office programs work together, you can quickly create individualized documents in Word using data stored in a different application. You will use Word's mail merge feature and data stored in an Access database to create individualized memos. Your completed files will look similar to Figure 1.28.

Project Files

For Non-MyLab Submissions

For Project 1B, you will need the following files:

i01B_Welcome_Memo (Word document)
i01B_Taos_Inventory (Excel workbook)
i01B_All_Associates (Access database)
i01B_Sales_Associates_List_FOR_MAC_USERS
i01B_Store_Location_RTF_FOR_MAC_USERS

In your storage location, create a folder named **Integrated Projects**
You will save your files as:

Lastname_Firstname_1B_Welcome_Memo (Word document)
Lastname_Firstname_1B_Taos_Memo (Word document)
Lastname_Firstname_1B_Taos_Inventory (Excel workbook)
Lastname_Firstname_1B_All_Associates (Access database, do not submit)
Lastname_Firstname_1B_Store_Location (Word document)

Project Results

Figure 1.28 Project 1B Taos Welcome

Use the linking tools in Office to connect the data in an Excel worksheet to a Word document. When you link an Excel workbook to a Word document, changes you make to data in the Excel workbook will be updated in the linked Word document. Information about the link is saved with the Word document. By default, when you open the Word document, Word checks all linked files and prompts you to apply any changes.

Activity 1.13 | Using Paste Special to Link Files

In this Activity, you will insert Excel data into a Word document. By selecting options in the Paste Special dialog box, you can link your Word document to the data in the Excel workbook.

1 Navigate to the files you downloaded with this project, and then open the document **i01B_Welcome_Memo**. Display the **Save As** dialog box, and then using your own name, **Save** the document in your **Integrated Projects** folder as **Lastname_Firstname_1B_Welcome_Memo** If necessary, display the ruler and formatting marks.

2 With your Word document displayed, open File Explorer, navigate to the files you downloaded with this project, and then open the Excel workbook **i01B_Taos_Inventory**. Display the **Save As** dialog box, and then using your own name, **Save** the workbook in your **Integrated Projects** folder as **Lastname_Firstname_1B_Taos_Inventory**

3 On the **Page Layout tab**, in the **Page Setup group**, click the **Dialog Box Launcher** ⬚. In the **Page Setup** dialog box, click the **Header/Footer tab**, and then click **Custom Footer**. In the **Footer** dialog box, with the insertion point in the **Left section**, click **Insert File Name** ⬚—&[File] displays. Click **OK** two times to close the dialog boxes.

4 Click cell **A1**, and then **Save** ⬚ the Excel workbook.

5 Select the range **A3:B22**. On the **Home tab** in the **Clipboard group**, click **Copy** ⬚. Compare your screen with Figure 1.29.

	Item	Cost
3		
4	Basic Goggles	$99.49
5	Basic Scarf	$29.49
6	Basic Sunglasses	$79.49
7	Brim/Baseball Hat	$26.99
8	Men's Basic Gloves	$49.99
9	Men's Basic Jacket	$479.49
10	Men's Basic Pant	$469.99
11	Men's Liner Gloves	$24.99
12	Men's Pipe Gloves	$39.99	← Range A3:B22 selected and copied
13	Women's Basic Gloves	$49.99
14	Women's Basic Jacket	$479.49
15	Women's Basic Pant	$469.99
16	Women's Liner Gloves	$19.99
17	Women's Pipe Gloves	$39.99
18	Youth Basic Boys Jacket	$169.49
19	Youth Basic Girls Jacket	$169.49
20	Youth Basic Girls Pant	$99.49
21	Youth Basic Gloves	$19.99
22	Youth Liner Gloves	$14.49

Figure 1.29

6 On the taskbar, click the **Word** icon ⬚. In the Word document, below the paragraph that begins *I am pleased to welcome you*, click in the blank paragraph.

7 On the **Home tab**, in the **Clipboard group**, click the **Paste button arrow**, and then click **Paste Special**. In the **Paste Special** dialog box, click the **Paste link** option button, and then under **As**, click **Microsoft Excel Worksheet Object**. Compare your screen to Figure 1.30.

Figure 1.30

8 In the **Paste Special** dialog box, click **OK**.

The linked data from Excel is pasted into the Word document.

9 Click the edge of the inserted table to select the object (sizing handles display), and then on the **Home tab**, in the **Paragraph group**, click **Center**.

10 Save your Word document.

11 Click the **File tab**, and then click **Close** to close the document but leave Word open.

NOTE   Updating Links

From this point forward, when you reopen a Word document that has a link to an external file, a Security Notice will automatically display. The notice will inform you that the file contains links and you have the option of updating the links or not updating them. If you trust the source of the file, you can update links. If you do not know where a file originated, you should cancel the update and investigate where the file came from before continuing.

12 In Word, click the **File tab**, click **Open**, click **Browse**, navigate to your **Integrated Projects** folder, and then open the your file **Lastname_Firstname_1B_Welcome_Memo**. A message box displays, as shown in Figure 1.31.

The message box informs you that the Word document is linked to another file, and it asks whether you want to update the data in the document.

Figure 1.31

13 In the message box, click **Yes**.

The linked information is updated.

It is common to make changes to your data in saved files. You can modify the data in the source file and all linked data to that source file is updated to reflect the changes.

Activity 1.14 | Updating the Linked Data

In the following Activity, you will edit data in the linked Excel workbook, and then verify that the updated data displays in the Word document.

1 Double-click the pasted data table in the Word document to display the source file—the linked Excel workbook.

Excel becomes the active window.

2 If necessary, maximize the Excel worksheet, and then press Esc to cancel the moving border. Click cell **B9**, type **389.99** and then press Enter. Click cell **B14**, type **379.99** and then press Enter. Compare your screen with Figure 1.32.

Figure 1.32

3 Save the Excel workbook.

4 On the taskbar, click the **Word** icon. Compare your screen to Figure 1.33.

The changes made in the Excel workbook are reflected in the linked Word document.

ALERT   **What If the Data Is Not Updated?**

If you do not see the new numbers in the Word document, click one time in the data to select it, and then press F9 to update the Excel data.

Figure 1.33

5 Save the Word document.

6 On the taskbar, click the **Excel** icon to display the workbook.

7 Click the **File tab**, and then at the right, at the bottom of the **Properties** list, click **Show All Properties**. In the **Tags** box, type **edited data, linked** In the **Subject** box, type your course name and section number. Under Related People, if your name does not display as the author, right-click the author name, click Edit Property, type your name, and then click OK.

8 On the left, click **Save**, and then **Close** Excel. Your Word document remains open.

Objective 7 | Create a Table in Word from Access Data

You can export data from an Access file to another file—for example, an Excel worksheet, a Word document, or another database. Exporting is similar to copying and pasting. In Access, you can export large amounts of data by selecting the name of the object that contains the data you want to export. Exporting data eliminates the need to retype information; and, as a result, the possibility of data entry errors is reduced.

Activity 1.15 | Exporting an Access Table to an RTF File

MAC TIP Skip to Activity 1.16. In Step 2, from the files you downloaded with this project, use the file i01B_Store_Location_RTF_FOR_MAC_USERS.

1 From the files you downloaded with this project, open the Access database **i01B_All_Associates**. Click the **File tab**, click **Save As**, and then with **Save Database** selected, click **Save As**.

2 In the **Save As** dialog box, navigate to your **Integrated Projects** folder, and then using your own name, **Save** the database as **Lastname_Firstname_1B_All_Associates** On the **Message Bar** that displays a Security Warning, click **Enable Content**.

3 In the **Navigation Pane**, click the **Store Location** table one time to select it. On the **External Data tab**, in the **Export group**, click **More**, and then click **Word**.

The Export - RTF File dialog box displays.

4 In the **Export – RTF File** dialog box, click **Browse**, and then navigate to your **Integrated Projects** folder. In the **File name** box, using your own name, type **Lastname_Firstname_1B_Store_Location** and then click **Save**. Compare your screen with Figure 1.34.

The Access table is saved as a rich text format file. Rich text format is a universal file format, using the .rtf file extension, which can be read by many word processing programs.

Figure 1.34

5 In the **Export – RTF File** dialog box, click **OK**. In the dialog box asking if you want to save these export steps, be sure the **Save export steps** check box is not selected. Click **Close**. Leave your Access database open.

Activity 1.16 | Inserting Access Data into a Word Document

1 On the taskbar, click the **Word** icon [W]. Press Ctrl + End to move to the blank paragraph at end of the document.

2 On the **Insert tab**, in the **Text group**, click the **Object button arrow**, and then click **Text from File**. In the **Insert File** dialog box, navigate to your **Integrated Projects** folder, click the file name **Lastname_Firstname_1B_Store_Location**, and then click **Insert**. Compare your screen with Figure 1.35.

Store ID¤	Address¤	City¤	State¤	¤
CO19¤	197·Tower·Rd¤	Denver¤	CO¤	¤
CO20¤	208·E·Central·Ave¤	Golden¤	CO¤	¤
CO40¤	403·Starlight·Blvd¤	Denver¤	CO¤	¤
CO78¤	782·Mill·Rd·SW¤	Colorado·Springs¤	CO¤	¤
CO79¤	7925·S·Forrest·Rd¤	Boulder¤	CO¤	¤
CO98¤	98045·North·Ave¤	Aurora¤	CO¤	¤
NM40¤	403·Central·Blvd¤	Albuquerque¤	NM¤	¤
NM52¤	52792·Greenfield¤	Taos¤	NM¤	¤
NM73¤	7303·Spring·Blvd¤	Santa·Fe¤	NM¤	¤
NM86¤	8692·Garden·Blvd¤	Gallup¤	NM¤	¤
NM88¤	8851·Skyline·Blvd¤	Albuquerque¤	NM¤	¤
OR10¤	10·East·Blvd¤	Portland¤	OR¤	¤
OR40¤	403·State·Blvd¤	Salem¤	OR¤	¤
OR69¤	692·Lilly·Blvd¤	Springfield¤	OR¤	¤
OR78¤	7825·Blue·St¤	Portland¤	OR¤	¤
OR86¤	8692·Tech·Blvd¤	Eugene¤	OR¤	¤
WA24¤	2445·Cove·St¤	Spokane¤	WA¤	¤
WA35¤	35725·Water·Street¤	Tacoma¤	WA¤	¤
WA51¤	51977·Winding·Way¤	Seattle¤	WA¤	¤
WA71¤	7108·Main·St¤	Bellingham¤	WA¤	¤

Table inserted in Word document

Figure 1.35

3 In the inserted table, click in the first cell, **Store ID**, to make the cell the active cell. On the ribbon, under **Table Tools**, on the **Design tab**, in the **Table Styles group**, click **More** [▾]. In the **Table Styles** gallery, scroll down, and then under **List Tables**, in the third row, click the third style—click **List Table 3 - Accent 2**.

4 Click in the cell **Store ID**, and then on the **Table Tools Layout tab**, in the **Rows & Columns group**, click **Delete**. On the displayed list, click **Delete Columns** to delete the Store ID column.

5 On the **Table Tools Layout tab**, in the **Cell Size group**, click **AutoFit**, and then click **AutoFit Contents**.

The columns are automatically resized to fit the contents of the cells.

6 In the **Table group**, click **Properties**, and then on the **Table tab**, under **Alignment**, click **Center**. Click **OK**, and then compare your screen with Figure 1.36.

The table is centered horizontally on the page.

Address¤	City¤	State¤	¤
197·Tower·Rd¤	Denver¤	CO¤	¤
208·E·Central·Ave¤	Golden¤	CO¤	¤
403·Starlight·Blvd¤	Denver¤	CO¤	¤
782·Mill·Rd·SW¤	Colorado·Springs¤	CO¤	¤
7925·S·Forrest·Rd¤	Boulder¤	CO¤	¤
98045·North·Ave¤	Aurora¤	CO¤	¤
403·Central·Blvd¤	Albuquerque¤	NM¤	¤
52792·Greenfield¤	Taos¤	NM¤	¤
7303·Spring·Blvd¤	Santa·Fe¤	NM¤	¤
8692·Garden·Blvd¤	Gallup¤	NM¤	¤
8851·Skyline·Blvd¤	Albuquerque¤	NM¤	¤
10·East·Blvd¤	Portland¤	OR¤	¤
403·State·Blvd¤	Salem¤	OR¤	¤
692·Lilly·Blvd¤	Springfield¤	OR¤	¤
7825·Blue·St¤	Portland¤	OR¤	¤
8692·Tech·Blvd¤	Eugene¤	OR¤	¤
2445·Cove·St¤	Spokane¤	WA¤	¤
35725·Water·Street¤	Tacoma¤	WA¤	¤
51977·Winding·Way¤	Seattle¤	WA¤	¤
7108·Main·St¤	Bellingham¤	WA¤	¤

AutoFit and style applied to table

Table horizontally centered on page

Figure 1.36

7 **Save** 🖫 your Word document.

Objective 8 Use Access Data to Complete a Mail Merge in Word

If you already have information in an existing data source—for example, an Access database—you do not need to enter the data again during the mail merge process. You can filter data to quickly find a portion of the total records available. Filtered data displays only the records that meet the conditions you specify and hides the records that do not meet the conditions.

Activity 1.17 | Adding Records to an Access Table

One of the most powerful features of Access is the ability to add, edit, or delete existing records without changing the structure of the existing objects—tables, queries, forms, and reports—in the database. In the following activity, you will use a form to add a record to a database.

MAC TIP Skip to Activity 1.18, and then in Steps 3 and 4, from the files downloaded with this project, use the file i01B_Sales_Associates_List.

1 On the taskbar, click the **Access** icon 🔢. In the **Navigation Pane**, double-click the **Sales Associates Form**.

2 In the navigation area at the bottom of the form, click the **New (blank) record** button ▸. In the **ID** field, type **10-60531** and then press Tab. Type your own first name, press Tab, type your own last name, and then press Tab. Type **Sales Associate** press Tab, type **NM52** and then compare your screen with Figure 1.37.

Figure 1.37

> **3** Press Tab to accept your record.

> **4** In the **Navigation Pane**, double-click the report **Store Associates by Location**. Scroll through the report and be sure that your name displays under **NM** for the **Taos** location.

> **5** **Close** ⊠ Access.

> Access automatically saves records that have been added to a database; there is no need to save the file before closing Access.

Activity 1.18 │ Starting Mail Merge in Word

Mail Merge can be used to add placeholders for inserting a data field into a document to make each document unique. In the following Activity, you will start the mail merge process in Word and filter the Access records.

> **1** If necessary, on the taskbar, click the Word icon ⊞ to display the Word document.

> **2** Press Ctrl + Home. On the **Mailings tab**, in the **Start Mail Merge group**, click **Select Recipients**, and then click **Use an Existing List**.

> **3** In the **Select Data Source** dialog box, navigate to your **Integrated Projects** folder, select your **Lastname_Firstname_1B_All_Associates** database, and then click **Open** to display the **Select Table** dialog box. Compare your screen with Figure 1.38.

> The Access database contains more than one table. You need to select which table will be used for the mail merge.

Figure 1.38

> **4** In the **Select Table** dialog box, be sure that **Sales Associates** is selected, and then click **OK**.

> **5** In the **Start Mail Merge group**, click **Edit Recipient List**.

> You can add or edit fields in the Mail Merge Recipients dialog box.

> **6** In the **Mail Merge Recipients** dialog box, under **Refine recipient list**, click **Filter**.

7 In the **Filter and Sort** dialog box, with the **Filter Records tab** selected, click the **Field arrow**, and then click **Store ID**. Under **Comparison**, be sure that *Equal to* is selected. In the **Compare to** box, type **NM52** and then compare your screen with Figure 1.39.

You can filter on any of the fields.

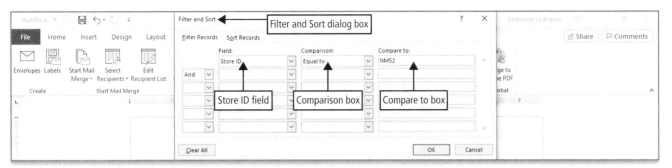

Figure 1.39

8 At the bottom of the **Filter and Sort** dialog box, click **OK**.

The three Taos records—including your record—display.

9 In the **Mail Merge Recipients** dialog box, click **OK**.

Activity 1.19 | Inserting Merge Fields

You can add merge fields as placeholders in the Word document for the information that will be inserted from the Access database. In the mail merge process, you combine a data source and a main document to create a new Word document—for example, a document that contains individualized memos, letters, or mailing labels.

1 Near the top of the document, in the heading *TO*, click to position the insertion point to the left of the paragraph mark.

2 On the **Mailings tab**, in the **Write & Insert Fields group**, click the **Insert Merge Field button arrow**, and then click **Firstname**. Compare your screen with Figure 1.40.

The Firstname field is inserted in the memo.

A merge field is surrounded by double angle brackets (« »). These formatting marks help distinguish the merge fields in the main document and do not display in the final document—after the merge process is completed.

Figure 1.40

3 Press [Spacebar]. Click the **Insert Merge Field button arrow**, and then click **Lastname**.

This is the location in the memo where the sales associate names will be inserted.

4 In the **Preview Results group**, click **Preview Results**. In the **Preview Results group**, click **Next Record** ▷ two times to preview the three memos.

The memo—the main document—displays with changes based on each record in the filtered data source—in this case, the sales associate's name.

5 In the **Preview Results** group, click **Preview Results** to turn off the feature. Notice the merge fields display in the document.

6 In the **Finish group**, click **Finish & Merge**, and then click **Edit Individual Documents**. In the **Merge to New Document** dialog box, be sure that the **All** option button is selected, and then click **OK**. Compare your screen with Figure 1.41.

A new Word document—Letters1—displays. The six-page document contains three individualized memos and is no longer connected to the Access database. The associate's first name and last name in the first record display on Page 1.

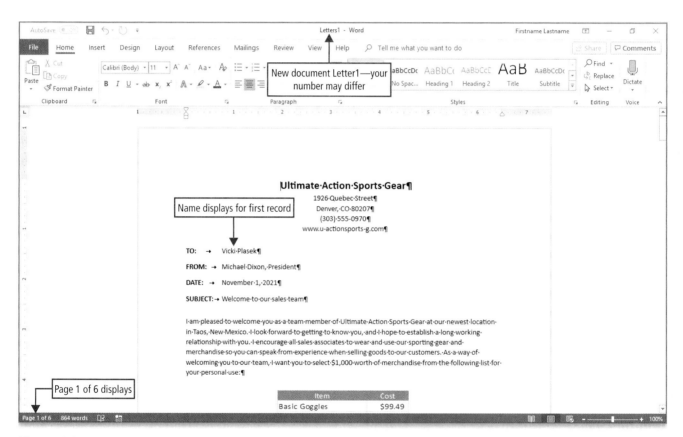

Figure 1.41

7 Display the **Save As** dialog box, and then save the new merged document in your **Integrated Projects** folder with the file name **Lastname_Firstname_1B_Taos_Memo**

8 Right-click in the footer area, and then click **Edit Footer**. On the ribbon, under **Header & Footer Tools**, on the **Design tab**, in the **Insert group**, click **Document Info**, and then click **File Name**. In the **Close group**, click **Close Header and Footer**.

9 Click the **File tab**, and then at the right, at the bottom of the **Properties** list, click **Show All Properties**. In the **Tags** box, type linked table, merged In the **Subject** box, type your course name and section number. Be sure your name displays as the author; edit if necessary.

10 On the left, click **Save**. With the Word document redisplayed, click the **File tab**, and then on the left, click **Close** to close the file and display your **1B_Welcome_Memo** document.

11 In your **Lastname_Firstname_1B_Welcome_Memo**, right-click in the footer area, and then click **Edit Footer**. On the ribbon, under **Header & Footer Tools**, on the **Design tab**, in the **Insert group**, click **Document Info**, and then click **File Name**. In the **Close group**, click **Close Header and Footer**.

12 Click the **File tab**, and then at the right, at the bottom of the **Properties** list, click **Show All Properties**. In the **Tags** box, type linked table, merge fields In the **Subject** box, type your course name and section number. Be sure your name displays as the author; edit if necessary.

13 On the left, click **Save**, and then **Close** ⊠ Word.

14 Submit your printed or electronic files as directed by your instructor. You will have three Word documents and one Excel workbook. You need not submit your Access database.

You have completed Project 1B   **END**

Appendix

MICROSOFT OFFICE SPECIALIST WORD			
Obj Number	**Objective text**	**GO! Activity**	**Page Number**
1.0 Manage Documents			
1.1	**Navigate within documents**		
1.1.1	Search for text	2.16, 3.11	197, 250
1.1.2	Link to locations within documents	OFW 1.17	39
1.1.3	Move to specific locations and objects in documents	3.11	250
1.1.4	Show and hide formatting symbols and hidden text	1.01, 2.01	105, 171
1.2	**Format documents**		
1.2.1	Set up document pages	OFW 1.10, Ch1 1.17	25, 127
1.2.2	Apply style sets	2.22	207
1.2.3	Insert and modify headers and footers	1.15, 2.01	120, 171
1.2.4	Configure page background elements	1.05	110
1.3	**Save and share documents**		
1.3.1	Save documents in alternative file formats	3.14	255
1.3.2	Modify basic document properties	1.16, 2.10, 2.20, 3.12	122, 183, 205, 251
1.3.3	Modify print settings	Word Supplemental Project 1	
1.3.4	Share documents electronically	Word Supplemental Project 4	
1.4	**Inspect documents for issues**		
1.4.1	Locate and remove hidden properties and personal information	OFW 1.16	38
1.4.2	Locate and correct accessibility issues	OFW 1.16	38
1.4.3	Locate and correct compatibility issues	OFW 1.16	38
2.0 Insert and Format Text, Paragraphs, and Sections			
2.1	**Insert text and paragraphs**		197
2.1.1	Find and replace text	2.16	276
2.1.2	Insert symbols and special characters	3.25	
2.2	**Format text and paragraphs**		
2.2.1	Apply text effects	3.24	275
2.2.2	Apply formatting by using Format Painter	2.04	176
2.2.3	Set line and paragraph spacing and indentation	1.19, 1.20, 1.21, 3.01, 3.02	130, 131, 132, 237, 238
2.2.4	Apply built-in styles to text	2.22	207
2.2.5	Clear formatting	1.11	116

MICROSOFT OFFICE SPECIALIST WORD			
Obj Number	**Objective text**	**GO! Activity**	**Page Number**
2.3	**Create and configure document settings**		
2.3.1	Format text in multiple columns	3.15, 3.16	262, 263
2.3.2	Insert page, section, and column breaks	3.08, 3.15, 3.17	248, 262, 265
2.3.3	Change page setup options for a section	Word Supplemental Project 3	
3.0 Manage Tables and Lists			
3.1	**Create tables**		
3.1.1	Convert text to tables	Word Supplemental Project 1	
3.1.2	Convert tables to text	Word Supplemental Project 3	
3.1.3	Create tables by specifying rows and columns	2.01	171
3.2	**Modify tables**		
3.2.1	Sort table data	Word Supplemental Project 3	
3.2.2	Configure cell margins and spacing	2.07	179
3.2.3	Merge and split cells	2.07	179
3.2.4	Resize tables, rows, and columns	2.05	177
3.2.5	Split tables	Word Supplemental Project 3	
3.2.6	Configure a repeating row header	Word Supplemental Project 3	
3.3	**Create and modify lists**		
3.3.1	Format paragraphs as numbered and bulleted lists	1.22, 1.23. 2.04	134, 135, 176
3.3.2	Change bullet characters and number formats	1.24	137
3.3.3	Define custom bullet characters and number formats	Word Supplemental Project 2	
3.3.4	Increase and decrease list levels	2.04	176
3.3.5	Restart and continue list numbering	Word Supplemental Project 4	
3.3.6	Set starting number values	Word Supplemental Project 2	
4.0 Create and Manage References			
4.1	**Create and manage reference elements**		
4.1.1.	Insert footnotes and endnotes	3.03	240
4.1.2	Modify footnote and endnote properties	3.04	241
4.1.3	Create and modify bibliography citation sources	3.05, 3.06	244, 245
4.1.4	Insert citations for bibliographies	3.05, 3.07, 3.09	244, 247, 249

MICROSOFT OFFICE SPECIALIST WORD			
Obj Number	**Objective text**	**GOI Activity**	**Page Number**
4.2	**Create and manage reference tabs**		
4.2.1	Insert tables of contents	Word Supplemental Project 1	
4.2.2	Customize tables of contents	Word Supplemental Project 1	
4.2.3	Insert bibliographies	3.09	249
5.0 Insert and Format Graphic Elements			
5.1	**Insert illustrations and text boxes**		
5.1.1	Insert shapes	1.11	116
5.1.2	Insert pictures	1.04, 3.19	109, 268
5.1.3	Insert 3D models	OFW 1.17	127
5.1.4	Insert SmartArt graphics	1.27	143
5.1.5	Insert screenshots and screen clippings	3.23	274
5.1.6	Insert text boxes	1.13	118
5.2	**Format illustrations and text boxes**		
5.2.1	Apply artistic effects	1.09	114
5.2.2	Apply picture effects and picture styles	1.08	114
5.2.3	Remove picture backgrounds	3.20	271
5.2.4	Format graphic elements	1.12, 1.14, 3.21, 3.22	117, 119, 272, 273
5.2.5	Format SmartArt graphics	1.28	144
5.2.6	Format 3D models	OFW 1.17	39
5.3	**Add text to graphic elements**		
5.3.1	Add and modify text in text boxes	1.13	118
5.3.2	Add and modify text in shapes	1.12	117
5.3.3	Add and modify SmartArt graphic content	1.27	143
5.4	**Modify graphic elements**		
5.4.1	Position objects	1.07, 3.18, 3.19	112, 266, 268
5.4.2	Wrap text around objects	1.05, 3.18	110, 266
5.4.3	Add alternative text to objects for accessibility	OFW 1.14	
6.0 Manage Document Collaboration			
6.1	**Add and manage comments**		
6.1.1	Add comments	Word Supplemental Project 4	
6.1.2	Review and reply to comments	Word Supplemental Project 4	
6.1.3	Resolve comments	Word Supplemental Project 4	
6.1.4	Delete comments	Word Supplemental Project 4	

MICROSOFT OFFICE SPECIALIST WORD			
Obj Number	Objective text	GO! Activity	Page Number
6.2	**Manage change tracking**		
6.2.1	Track changes	Word Supplemental Project 4	
6.2.2	Review tracked changes	Word Supplemental Project 4	
6.2.3	Accept and reject tracked changes	Word Supplemental Project 4	
6.2.4	Lock and unlock change tracking	Word Supplemental Project 4	

MICROSOFT OFFICE SPECIALIST EXCEL			
Obj Number	**Objective text**	**Activity**	**Page Number**
1.0 Manage Worksheets and Workbooks			
1.1	**Import data into workbooks**		
1.1.1	Import data from .txt files	Excel Supplemental Project 1	
1.1.2	Import data from .csv files	Excel Supplemental Project 4	
1.2	**Navigate within workbooks**		
1.2.1	Search for data within a workbook	2.11	399
1.2.2	Navigate to named cells, ranges, or workbook elements	1.02 Excel Supplemental Project 1	320
1.2.3	Insert and remove hyperlinks	Excel Supplemental Project 2	
1.3	**Format worksheets and workbooks**		
1.3.1	Modify page setup	1.14, 1.17	339, 342
1.3.2	Adjust row height and column width	1.04, 1.17, 1.26	323, 342, 359
1.3.3	Customize headers and footers	1.14	339
1.4	**Customize options and views**		
1.4.1	Customize the Quick Access toolbar	Excel Supplemental Project 4	
1.4.2	Display and modify workbook content in different views	Excel Supplemental Project 3	
1.4.3	Freeze worksheet rows and columns	2.13	400
1.4.4	Change window views	2.19	406
1.4.5	Modify basic workbook properties	1.15	341
1.4.6	Display formulas	1.17	342
1.5	**Configure content for collaboration**		
1.5.1	Set a print area	1.16	342
1.5.2	Save workbooks in alternative file formats	Excel Supplemental Project 2	
1.5.3	Configure print settings	1.16, 1.17, 2.20	
1.5.4	Inspect workbooks for issues	Excel Supplemental Projects 1 & 4	
2.0 Manage Data Cells and Ranges			
2.1	**Manipulate data in worksheets**		
2.1.1	Paste data by using special paste options	3.16	480
2.1.2	Fill cells by using Auto Fill	1.03	321
2.1.3	Insert and delete multiple columns or rows	1.25, 2.01, 3.17	358, 387, 482
2.1.4	Insert and delete cells	Excel Supplemental Project 1	
2.2	**Format cells and ranges**		
2.2.1	Merge and unmerge cells	1.08, 2.07	329, 394

MICROSOFT OFFICE SPECIALIST EXCEL			
Obj Number	Objective text	Activity	Page Number
2.2.2	Modify cell alignment, orientation, and indentation	1.24, 2.07	357, 394
2.2.3	Format cells by using Format Painter	3.14	478
2.2.4	Wrap text within cells	1.26, 2.25	359, 418
2.2.5	Apply number format	1.05, 1.09, 1.21	325, 330, 352
2.2.6	Apply cell formats from the Format Cells dialog box	2.07	394
2.2.7	Apply cell styles	1.08, 1.09, 1.18, 1.21	329, 330, 348, 352
2.2.8	Clear cell formatting	2.23	416
2.3	**Define and reference named ranges**		
2.3.1	Define a named range	Excel Supplemental Project 2	
2.3.2	Name a table	Excel Supplemental Project 2	
2.4	**Summarize data visually**		
2.4.1	Insert sparklines	1.13, 2.33	338, 427
2.4.2	Apply built-in conditional formatting	2.10	397
2.4.3	Remove conditional formatting	Excel Supplemental Project 2	
3.0 Manage Tables and Table Data			
3.1	**Create and format tables**		
3.1.1	Create Excel tables from cell ranges	2.14	402
3.1.2	Apply table styles	2.14	402
3.1.3	Convert tables to cell ranges	Excel Supplemental Project 1	
3.2	**Modify tables**		
3.2.1	Add or remove table rows and columns	Excel Supplemental Project 3	
3.2.2	Configure table style options	Excel Supplemental Project 3	
3.2.3	Insert and configure total rows	2.16	404
3.3	**Filter and sort table data**		
3.3.1	Filter records	2.16	404
3.3.2	Sort data by multiple columns	2.15	403
4.0 Perform Operations by using Formulas and Functions			
4.1	**Insert references**		
4.1.1	Insert relative, absolute, and mixed references	1.07, 1.22, 2.31	328, 354, 425
4.1.2	Reference named ranges and named tables in formulas	Excel Supplemental Project 2	

MICROSOFT OFFICE SPECIALIST EXCEL			
Obj Number	Objective text	Activity	Page Number
4.2	**Calculate and transform data**		
4.2.1	Perform calculations by using the AVERAGE(), MAX(), MIN(), and SUM() functions	1.06, 2.03, 2.05	326, 389, 392
4.2.2	Count cells by using the COUNT(), COUNTA(), and COUNTBLANK() functions	Excel Supplemental Projects 2 & 3	
4.2.3	Perform conditional operations by using the IF() function	2.09	396
4.3	**Format and modify text**		
4.3.1	Format text by using RIGHT(), LEFT(), and MID() functions	Excel Supplemental Project 3	
4.3.2	Format text by using UPPER(), LOWER(), and LEN() functions	Excel Supplemental Project 3	
4.3.3	Format text by using the CONCAT() and TEXTJOIN() functions	Excel Supplemental Projects 2 & 3	
5.0 Manage Charts			
5.1	**Create charts**		
5.1.1	Create charts	1.11, 3.02	332, 462
5.1.2	Create chart sheets	3.02	462
5.2	**Modify charts**		
5.2.1	Add data series to charts	3.18	484
5.2.2	Switch between rows and columns in source data	1.11	332
5.2.3	Add and modify chart elements	1.12	335
5.3	**Format charts**		
5.3.1	Apply chart layouts	1.12, 3.04	335, 464
5.3.2	Apply chart styles	Excel Supplemental Project 4	Supplemental
5.3.3	Add alternative text to charts for accessibility	1.19	350

MICROSOFT OFFICE EXPERT ACCESS

Obj Number	Objective text	GO! Activity	Page Number
1.0 Manage Databases			
1.1	**Modify database structure**		
1.1.1	Import objects or data from other sources	GO! Access Comprehensive 1.11, 2.17, 9.04, 9.06	537, 622
1.1.2	Delete database objects	1.05	528
1.1.3	Hide and display objects in the Navigation Pane	GO! Access Comprehensive 1.21, 10.08	563
1.2	**Manage table relationship and keys**		
1.2.1	Understand relationships	GO! Access Comprehensive 2.02, 2.18, 5.18, 5.19	598, 623
1.2.2	Display relationships	GO! Access Comprehensive 2.04, 2.18, 3.01, 3.16, 5.11, 5.15	603, 623, 673, 702
1.2.3	Set primary keys	GO! Access Comprehensive 2.17, 4.03, 4.13, 6.01, 9.02, 9.03, 10.02	622
1.2.4	Enforce referential integrity	2.03, 2.18	601, 623
1.2.5	Set foreign keys	2.03, 2.18	601, 623
1.3	**Print and export data**		
1.3.1	Configure print options for records, forms, and reports	1.13, 1.15, 2.04, 3.15	542, 548, 603, 697
1.3.2	Export objects to alternative formats	GO! Access Comprehensive 9.09, 9.10, 9.11, 9.12, 9.14, 9.15	GO! Access Comprehensive
2.0 Create and Modify Tables			
2.1	**Create tables**		
2.1.1	Import data into tables	GO! Access Comprehensive 1.07, 1.20, 4.04, 9.02, 9.03	530, 562
2.1.2	Create linked tables from external sources	GO! Access Comprehensive 9.08	GO! Access Comprehensive
2.1.3	Import tables from other databases	GO! Access Comprehensive 4.06, 9.07	GO! Access Comprehensive
2.2	**Manage tables**		
2.2.1	Hide fields in tables	GO! Access Comprehensive 6.11	GO! Access Comprehensive
2.2.2	Add total rows	GO! Access Comprehensive 8.12	GO! Access Comprehensive
2.2.3	Add table descriptions	GO! Access Comprehensive 1.09, 4.04	535
2.3	**Manage table records**		
2.3.1	Find and replace data	GO! Access Comprehensive 3.05, 4.07, 4.08	677

MICROSOFT OFFICE EXPERT ACCESS			
Obj Number	**Objective text**	**GO! Activity**	**Page Number**
2.3.2	Sort records	GO! Access Comprehensive 2.07, 2.08, 4.03, 5.15, 5.16, 5.17, 10.02	606, 607
2.3.3	Filter records	3.06, 3.07, 3.08	680, 683, 684
2.4	**Create and modify fields**		
2.4.1	Add or remove fields	GO! Access Comprehensive 1.03, 1.08, 1.22, 4.03, 4.05, 4.09, 4.14	525, 533, 564
2.4.2	Add validation rules to fields	GO! Access Comprehensive 4.22	GO! Access Comprehensive
2.4.3	Change field captions	GO! Access Comprehensive 1.04, 4.13	527
2.4.4	Change field sizes	GO! Access Comprehensive 1.09, 4.13, 4.14	535
2.4.5	Change field data types	GO! Access Comprehensive 1.03, 1.04, 1.22, 2.17, 4.03, 4.05, 4.09, 4.11, 4.12, 4.13, 4.14, 4.15, 4.16, 4.18, 9.02	525, 527, 564, 622
2.4.6	Configure fields to auto-increment	1.04	527
2.4.7	Set default values	GO! Access Comprehensive 4.22	GO! Access Comprehensive
2.4.8	Apply built-in input masks	GO! Access Comprehensive 4.17, 4.18	GO! Access Comprehensive
3.0 Create and Modify Queries			
3.1	**Create and run queries**		
3.1.1	Create simple queries	GO! Access Comprehensive 2.09, 2.14, 2.15, 2.16, 2.19, 2.23, 2.24, 2.25, 2.26, 2.29, 5.03, 5.04, 5.05	609, 615, 616, 617, 625, 628, 629, 631, 633, 636
3.1.2	Create basic crosstab queries	GO! Access Comprehensive 2.31, 5.06	638
3.1.3	Create basic parameter queries	GO! Access Comprehensive 2.32, 5.09, 5.10	640
3.1.4	Create basic action queries	GO! Access Comprehensive 5.12, 5.13, 5.14, 5.15, 5.16, 5.17	GO! Access Comprehensive
3.1.5	Create basic multi-table queries	GO! Access Comprehensive 2.24, 2.25, 5.04, 5.05, 5.09, 5.10, 5.11, 5.13, 5.17, 5.18 10.13, 10.14, 10.15, 10.16, 10.17	629, 631
3.1.6	Save queries	GO! Access Comprehensive 1.14, 2.10, 2.12, 2.13, 2.14, 2.15, 2.16, 2.20, 2.21, 2.22, 2.23, 2.24, 2.26, 2.28, 2.30, 2.32, 5.01, 5.03, 5.04, 5.05, 5.10, 5.12, 5.13, 5.16, 5.18, 9.05, 10.03, 10.13, 10.14, 10.18	545, 610, 612, 614, 615, 616, 617, 625, 626, 627, 628, 629, 633, 635, 637, 640

MICROSOFT OFFICE EXPERT ACCESS			
Obj Number	Objective text	GO! Activity	Page Number
3.1.7	Run queries	GO! Access Comprehensive 1.14, 2.10, 2.12, 2.13, 2.14, 2.15, 2.16, 2.19, 2.21, 2.22, 2.23, 2.24, 2.25, 2.26, 2.27, 2.29, 2.30, 2.32, 5.01, 5.03, 5.04, 5.05, 5.09, 5.10, 5.12, 5.13, 5.16, 5.17, 5.18, 5.19, 9.05, 9.12, 10.03, 10.13, 10.14, 10.17, 10.18	545, 610, 612, 614, 615, 616, 617, 625, 626, 627, 628, 629, 631, 633, 634, 636, 637, 640
3.2	**Modify queries**		
3.2.1	Add, hide, and remove fields in queries	GO! Access Comprehensive 2.09, 2.12, 2.14, 2.15, 2.16, 2.19, 2.22, 2.23, 2.24, 2.25, 2.26, 2.27, 5.01, 5.03, 5.04, 5.05, 5.07, 5.08, 5.11, 5.13, 5.15, 5.16, 5.17, 5.18, 5.19	609, 612, 615, 616, 617, 625, 627, 628, 629, 631, 633, 636
3.2.2	Sort data within queries	GO! Access Comprehensive 2.13, 2.15, 2.16, 2.19, 2.24, 2.26, 2.30, 5.05, 5.15, 5.18, 10.13, 10.15	614, 616, 617, 625, 629, 633, 637
3.2.3	Filter data within queries	GO! Access Comprehensive 2.14, 2.15, 2.16, 2.19, 2.20, 2.21, 2.22, 2.23, 2.25, 2.32, 5.02, 5.07, 5.08, 5.09, 5.10, 5.11, 5.13, 5.15, 5.16, 5.17, 10.13, 10.14, 10.17	615, 616, 617, 625, 625, 626, 627, 628, 631, 640,
3.2.4	Format fields within queries	GO! Access Comprehensive 2.28, 2.29, 2.30, 5.02	635, 636, 637
4.0 Modify Forms in Layout View			
4.1	**Configure from controls**		
4.1.1	Add, move, and remove form controls	GO! Access Comprehensive 1.15, 3.09, 3.12, 3.14, 6.01, 6.03, 6.04, 7.02, 7.03, 7.04, 7.05, 7.06, 7.07, 8.05, 8.06	548, 686, 690, 694
4.1.2	Set form control properties	GO! Access Comprehensive 3.10, 3.12, 3.13, 3.14, 6.01, 6.03, 6.04, 6.05, 6.07, 6.08, 6.09, 6.10, 7.02, 7.05, 7.06, 8.02, 8.05, 8.06, 8.11	688, 690, 692, 694
4.1.3	Add and modify form labels	GO! Access Comprehensive 3.11, 3.12, 3.13, 3.14, 6.04, 6.07, 7.07, 10.01	689, 690, 692, 694
4.2	**Format forms**		
4.2.1	Modify tab order on forms	GO! Access Comprehensive 6.1	GO! Access Comprehensive
4.2.2	Set records by form field	GO! Access Comprehensive 3.02, 3.03, 6.01, 6.03, 6.10, 7.02, 7.03	674, 676
4.2.3	Modify form positioning	GO! Access Comprehensive 3.15, 6.10, 7.03	697

MICROSOFT OFFICE EXPERT ACCESS			
Obj Number	Objective text	GO! Activity	Page Number
4.2.4	Insert information in form headers and footers	GO! Access Comprehensive 3.14, 6.02	694
4.2.5	Insert images on forms	GO! Access Comprehensive 6.02, 6.04, 7.05	GO! Access Comprehensive
5.0 Modify Reports in Layout View			
5.1	**Configure report controls**		
5.1.1	Group and sort fields on reports	GO! Access Comprehensive 3.18, 3.19, 3.23, 6.17, 7.14	704, 706, 715
5.1.2	Add report controls	GO! Access Comprehensive 1.16, 3.17, 3.18, 3.19, 6.11, 6.13, 6.15, 6.18, 7.08, 7.09, 7.10, 7.11, 7.12	550, 703, 704, 706
5.1.3	Add and modify labels on reports	GO! Access Comprehensive 1.16, 3.21, 3.22, 6.12, 6.14, 6.15, 6.18, 7.08, 7.09, 7.11, 7.12, 7.13, 7.14	550, 710, 713
5.2	**Format reports**		
5.2.1	Format a report into multiple columns	GO! Access Comprehensive 3.18, 6.11, 9.05, 10.18	704
5.2.2	Modify report positioning	GO! Access Comprehensive 3.21, 3.22, 6.13, 6.16, 6.17, 6.18, 7.11	710, 713
5.2.3	Format report elements	GO! Access Comprehensive 1.16, 3.17, 3.20, 3.21, 3.22, 6.12, 6.13, 6.16, 7.10, 7.11, 7.12, 9.07	550, 703, 709, 710, 713
5.2.4	Change report orientation	GO! Access Comprehensive 6.14, 6.16	GO! Access Comprehensive
5.2.5	Insert information in report headers and footers	GO! Access Comprehensive 3.18, 7.11, 7.13	704
5.2.6	Insert images on reports	GO! Access Comprehensive 6.14, 6.16, 7.13	GO! Access Comprehensive

MICROSOFT OFFICE SPECIALIST POWERPOINT			
Obj Number	Objective text	GO! Activity Introductory	Page Number
1.0 Manage Presentations			
1.1	**Modify slide masters, handout masters, and notes masters**		
1.1.1	Change the slide master theme or background	GO! PowerPoint Comprehensive 4.01, 4.02, 4.04	GO! PowerPoint Comprehensive
1.1.2	Modify the slide master content	GO! PowerPoint Comprehensive 4.03, 4.11	GO! PowerPoint Comprehensive
1.1.3	Create slide layouts	GO! PowerPoint Comprehensive 4.05	GO! PowerPoint Comprehensive
1.1.4	Modify slide layouts	GO! PowerPoint Comprehensive 4.06	GO! PowerPoint Comprehensive
1.1.5	Modify the handout master	GO! PowerPoint Comprehensive 4.07	GO! PowerPoint Comprehensive
1.1.6	Modify the notes master	GO! PowerPoint Comprehensive 4.08	GO! PowerPoint Comprehensive
1.2	**Change presentation options and views**		
1.2.1	Change slide size	1.17	773
1.2.2	Display presentations in different views	1.11, 1.19, 1.28, 1.33	761, 776, 783, 787
1.2.3	Set basic file properties	1.14, 1.33	765, 787
1.3	**Configure print settings for presentations**		
1.3.1	Print all or part of a presentation	GO! PowerPoint Comprehensive 6.16	GO! PowerPoint Comprehensive
1.3.2	Print notes pages	1.16	769
1.3.3	Print handouts	1.15	767
1.3.4	Print in color, grayscale, or black and white	1.15	767
1.4	**Configure and present slide shows**		
1.4.1	Create custom slide shows	GO! PowerPoint Comprehensive 6.1	GO! PowerPoint Comprehensive
1.4.2	Configure slide show options	GO! PowerPoint Comprehensive 6.15	GO! PowerPoint Comprehensive
1.4.3	Rehearse slide show timing	GO! PowerPoint Comprehensive 6.15	GO! PowerPoint Comprehensive
1.4.4	Set up slide show recording options	GO! PowerPoint Comprehensive 6.15	GO! PowerPoint Comprehensive
1.4.5	Present slide shows by using Presenter View	1.12	762
1.5	**Prepare presentations for collaboration**		
1.5.1	Restrict editing	GO! PowerPoint Comprehensive 4.21	GO! PowerPoint Comprehensive
1.5.2	Protect presentations by using passwords	GO! PowerPoint Comprehensive 4.20,	GO! PowerPoint Comprehensive
1.5.3	Inspect presentations for issues	GO! PowerPoint Comprehensive 4.17, 4.18, 4.19	GO! PowerPoint Comprehensive

MICROSOFT OFFICE SPECIALIST POWERPOINT			
Obj Number	Objective text	GO! Activity Introductory	Page Number
1.5.4	Add and manage comments	GO! PowerPoint Comprehensive 4.12, 4.13, 4.14	GO! PowerPoint Comprehensive
1.5.5	Preserve presentation content	3.17	898
1.5.6	Export presentations to other formats	GO! PowerPoint Comprehensive 8.05, 8.06, 8.07, 8.08, 8.09	GO! PowerPoint Comprehensive
2.0 Manage Slides			
2.1	**Insert slides**		
2.1.1	Import Word document outlines	GO! PowerPoint Comprehensive 8.01	GO! PowerPoint Comprehensive
2.1.2	Insert slides from another presentation	1.18	774
2.1.3	Insert slides and select slide layouts	1.04	751
2.1.4	Insert Summary Zoom slides	PowerPoint Supplemental Project 1	
2.1.5	Duplicate slides	GO! PowerPoint Comprehensive 6.12	GO! PowerPoint Comprehensive
2.2	**Modify slides**		
2.2.1	Hide and unhide slides	GO! PowerPoint Comprehensive 6.12	GO! PowerPoint Comprehensive
2.2.2	Modify individual slide backgrounds	3.03, 3.04, 3.05, 3.06, 3.07	881, 882, 883, 884, 885
2.2.3	Insert slide headers, footers, and page numbers	1.14	765
2.3	**Order and group slides**		
2.3.1	Create sections	GO! PowerPoint Comprehensive 7.1	GO! PowerPoint Comprehensive
2.3.2	Modify slide order	1.20, 1.29, 1.30	777, 784, 784
2.3.3	Rename sections	GO! PowerPoint Comprehensive 7.1	GO! PowerPoint Comprehensive
3.0 Insert and Format Text, Shapes, and Images			
3.1	**Format text**		
3.1.1	Apply built-in styles to text	2.23	844
3.1.2	Format text in multiple columns	GO! PowerPoint Comprehensive 8.04	GO! PowerPoint Comprehensive
3.1.3	Create bulleted and numbered lists	1.05, 2.03	754, 817
3.2	**Insert links**		
3.2.1	Insert hyperlinks	GO! PowerPoint Comprehensive 6.06, 6.07, 6.08, 6.11	GO! PowerPoint Comprehensive
3.2.2	Insert Section Zoom links and Slide Zoom links	PowerPoint Supplemental Project 1	

MICROSOFT OFFICE SPECIALIST POWERPOINT			
Obj Number	**Objective text**	**GO! Activity Introductory**	**Page Number**
3.3	**Insert and format images**		
3.3.1	Resize and crop images	2.07, 2.09, 2.10	821, 823, 825
3.3.2	Apply built-in styles and effects to images	1.09, 1.10, 2.17, 2.22	759, 760, 833, 843
3.3.3	Insert screenshots and screen clippings	PowerPoint Supplemental Project 1	
3.4	**Insert and format graphic elements**		
3.4.1	Insert and change shapes	2.12	827
3.4.2	Draw by using digital ink	GO! PowerPoint Comprehensive 6.14	GO! PowerPoint Comprehensive
3.4.3	Add text to shapes and text boxes	2.11	826
3.4.4	Resize shapes and text boxes	2.12	827
3.4.5	Format shapes and text boxes	2.14, 2.17	830, 833
3.4.6	Apply built-in styles to shapes and text boxes	2.14, 2.16	830, 833
3.4.7	Add alt text to graphic elements for accessibility	GO! PowerPoint Comprehensive 4.17, 5.15	GO! PowerPoint Comprehensive
3.5	**Order and group objects on slides**		
3.5.1	Order shapes, images, and text boxes	GO! PowerPoint Comprehensive 5.01	GO! PowerPoint Comprehensive
3.5.2	Align shapes, images, and text boxes	2.19, 2.20	835, 837
3.5.3	Group shapes and images	2.21	837
3.5.4	Display alignment tools	2.08	822
4.0 Insert Tables, Charts, SmartArt, 3D Models, and Media			
4.1	**Insert and format tables**		
4.1.1	Create and insert tables	3.18	904
4.1.2	Insert and delete table rows and columns	3.19	905
4.1.3	Apply built-in table styles	3.22	908
4.2	**Insert and modify charts**		
4.2.1	Create and insert charts	3.24, 3.27	910, 915
4.2.2	Modify charts	3.26, 3.28	913, 917
4.3	**Insert and format SmartArt graphics**		
4.3.1	Insert SmartArt graphics	2.29	850
4.3.2	Convert lists to SmartArt graphics	2.27	847
4.3.3	Add and modify SmartArt graphic content	2.28, 2.30	850, 851
4.4	**Insert and modify 3D models**		
4.4.1	Insert 3D models	2.35	854
4.4.2	Modify 3D models	2.35	854

MICROSOFT OFFICE SPECIALIST POWERPOINT			
Obj Number	**Objective text**	**GO! Activity Introductory**	**Page Number**
4.5	**Insert and manage media**		
4.5.1	Insert audio and visual clips	3.14	895
4.5.2	Create and insert screen recordings	3.17	898
4.5.3	Configure media playback options	3.17	898
5.0 Apply Transitions and Animations			
5.1	**Apply and configure slide transitions**		
5.1.1	Apply basic and 3D slide transitions	1.31	786
5.1.2	Configure transition effects	1.31	786
5.2	**Animate slide content**		
5.2.1	Animate text and graphic elements	3.09, 3.29, 3.30	888, 918, 919
5.2.2	Animate 3D models	PowerPoint Supplemental Project 1	
5.2.3	Configure animation effects	3.09, 3.29	888, 918
5.2.4	Configure animation paths	3.09	888
5.2.5	Reorder animations on a slide	3.10	891
5.3	**Set timing for transitions and animations**		
5.3.1	Set transition effect duration	3.12	892
5.3.2	Configure transition start and finish options	1.32, 3.11	786, 891

Glossary

3-D The shortened term for *three-dimensional*, which refers to an image that appears to have all three spatial dimensions—length, width, and depth.

3D models A new kind of shape that you can insert from an online library of ready-to-use, three-dimensional graphics.

Absolute cell reference A cell reference that refers to cells by their fixed position in a worksheet; an absolute cell reference remains the same when the formula is copied.

Accounting Number Format The Excel number format that applies a thousand comma separator where appropriate, inserts a fixed U.S. dollar sign aligned at the left edge of the cell, applies two decimal places, and leaves a small amount of space at the right edge of the cell to accommodate a parenthesis for negative numbers.

Active cell The cell, surrounded by a black border, ready to receive data or be affected by the next Excel command.

Address bar In a File Explorer window, the area that displays your current location in the folder structure as a series of links separated by arrows.

After Previous An animation option that begins the animation sequence for the selected slide element immediately after the completion of the previous animation or slide transition.

Aggregate functions Calculations such as Min, Max, Avg, and Sum that are performed on a group of records.

Align to Slide A setting tells PowerPoint to align each selected object with the slide, rather than with each other.

Alignment The placement of paragraph text relative to the left and right margins.

Alignment guides Green lines that display when you move an object to assist in alignment.

Alt text Text added to a picture or object that helps people using a screen reader understand what the object is; also called *alternative text*.

Alternative text Text added to a picture or object that helps people using a screen reader understand what the object is; also called *alt text*.

American Psychological Association (APA) One of two commonly used style guides for formatting research papers.

AND condition A compound criteria used to display records that match all parts of the specified criteria.

Animation A visual or sound effect added to an object or text on a slide.

Animation Painter A feature that copies animation settings from one object to another.

Append To add on to the end of an object; for example, to add records to the end of an existing table.

Application A computer program that helps you perform a task for a specific purpose.

Arguments The values that an Excel function uses to perform calculations or operations.

Arithmetic operators The symbols +, −, *, /, %, and ^ used to denote addition, subtraction (or negation), multiplication, division, percentage, and exponentiation in an Excel formula.

Artistic effects Formats applied to images that make pictures resemble sketches or paintings.

Ascending order A sorting order that arranges text alphabetically (A to Z) and numbers from the lowest number to the highest number.

Aspect ratio The ratio of the width of a display to the height of the display.

Auto Fill An Excel feature that generates and extends values into adjacent cells based on the values of selected cells.

AutoCalculate A feature that displays three calculations in the status bar by default—Average, Count, and Sum—when you select a range of numerical data.

AutoComplete A feature that speeds your typing and lessens the likelihood of errors; if the first few characters you type in a cell match an existing entry in the column, Excel fills in the remaining characters for you.

AutoCorrect A feature that corrects common typing and spelling errors as you type, for example changing *teh* to *the*.

AutoFit An Excel feature that adjusts the width of a column to fit the cell content of the widest cell in the column.

AutoNumber data type A data type that describes a unique sequential or random number assigned by Access as each record is entered and that is useful for data that has no distinct field that can be considered unique.

AutoSave An Office 365 feature that saves your document every few seconds—if saved on OneDrive, OneDrive for Business, or SharePoint Online—and enables you to share the document with others for real-time co-authoring.

AutoSum A button that provides quick access to the SUM function.

AVERAGE function An Excel function that adds a group of values, and then divides the result by the number of values in the group.

Axis A line that serves as a frame of reference for measurement and that borders the chart plot area.

Background Removal A feature that removes unwanted portions of a picture so that the picture does not appear as a self-contained rectangle.

Background style A predefined slide background fill variation that combines theme colors in different intensities or patterns.

Backstage tabs The area along the left side of Backstage view with tabs to display screens with related groups of commands.

Backstage view A centralized space for file management tasks; for example, opening, saving, printing, publishing, or sharing a file.

Base The starting point when you divide the amount of increase by it to calculate the rate of increase.

Best Fit An Access command that adjusts the width of a column to accommodate the column's longest entry.

Between . . . And operator A comparison operator that looks for values within a range.

Bevel A shape effect that uses shading and shadows to make the edges of a shape appear to be curved or angled.

Bibliography A list of cited works in a report or research paper; also referred to as Works Cited, Sources, or References, depending upon the report style.

Bing Microsoft's search engine.

Black slide A slide that displays after the last slide in a presentation indicating that the presentation is over.

Blank desktop database A database that has no data and has no database tools—you must create the data and tools as you need them; the database is stored on your computer or another storage device.

Body The text of a letter.

Body font A font that is applied to all slide text except slide titles.

Bookmark A command that marks a word, section, or place in a document so that you can jump to it quickly without scrolling.

Booting the computer The process of turning on the computer.

Bound A term used to describe objects and controls that are based on data that is stored in tables.

Bound control A control that retrieves its data from an underlying table or query; a text box control is an example of a bound control.

Brightness The relative lightness of a picture.

Bulleted list A list of items with each item introduced by a symbol such as a small circle or check mark, and which is useful when the items in the list can be displayed in any order; also referred to as unordered lists.

Bullets Text symbols such as small circles or check marks that precede each item in a bulleted list.

Calculated control A control that contains an expression, often a formula or function, that most often summarizes a field that contains numerical data.

Calculated field A field that stores the value of a mathematical operation.

Caption A property setting that displays a name for a field in a table, query, form, or report different from the one listed as the field name.

Cascade Delete Related Records A cascade option that enables you to delete a record in a table and also delete all of the related records in related tables.

Cascade options Relationship options that enable you to update records in related tables when referential integrity is enforced.

Cascade Update Related Fields A cascade option that enables you to change the data in the primary key field in the table on the *one* side of the relationship and update that change to any fields storing that same data in related tables.

Category axis The area along the bottom of a chart that identifies the categories of data; also referred to as the x-axis.

Category labels The labels that display along the bottom of a chart to identify the categories of data; Excel uses the row titles as the category names.

Cell The intersection of a column and a row.

Cell (Word) The intersection of a column and row in a table.

Cell address Another name for a cell reference.

Cell content Anything typed into a cell.

Cell margins The space inside a table cell between the text and the cell borders—top, bottom, left, and right.

Cell reference The identification of a specific cell by its intersecting column letter and row number.

Cell style A defined set of formatting characteristics, such as font, font size, font color, cell borders, and cell shading.

Center alignment The alignment of text or objects centered horizontally between the left and right margin.

Chart The graphic representation of data in a worksheet; data presented as a chart is usually easier to understand than a table of numbers.

Chart area The entire chart and all of its elements.

Chart elements The various components of a chart, including the chart title, axis titles, data series, legend, chart area, and plot area.

Chart Elements button A button that enables you to add, remove, or change chart elements such as the title, legend, gridlines, and data labels.

Chart Filters button A button that displays options for changing the data displayed in a chart.

Chart layout The combination of chart elements that can be displayed in a chart such as a title, legend, labels for the columns, and the table of charted cells.

Chart sheet A workbook sheet that contains only a chart.

Chart style The overall visual look of a chart in terms of its graphic effects, colors, and backgrounds; for example, you can have flat or beveled columns, colors that are solid or transparent, and backgrounds that are dark or light.

Chart Styles button A button that displays options for setting the style and color scheme for a chart.

Chart Styles gallery A group of predesigned chart styles that you can apply to an Excel chart.

Chart types Various chart formats used in a way that is meaningful to the reader; common examples are column charts, pie charts, and line charts.

Check Accessibility A command that checks a document for content that people with disabilities might find difficult to read.

Check Compatibility A command that searches your document for features that may not be supported by older versions of Office.

Citation A note inserted into the text of a research paper that refers the reader to a source in the bibliography.

Click The action of pressing the left button of the mouse pointing device.

Clip A single media file such as art, sound, animation, or a movie.

Clipboard A temporary storage area that holds text or graphics that you select and then cut or copy.

Cloud computing Applications and services that are accessed over the internet.

Cloud storage Online storage of data so that you can access your data from different places and devices.

Collaboration The action of working together with others as a team in an intellectual endeavor to complete a shared task or achieve a shared goal.

Column A vertical group of cells in a worksheet.

Column break indicator A dotted line containing the words *Column Break* that displays at the bottom of the column.

Column chart A chart in which the data is arranged in columns and that is useful for showing data changes over a period of time or for illustrating comparisons among items.

Column heading The letter that displays at the top of a vertical group of cells in a worksheet; beginning with the first letter of the alphabet, a unique letter or combination of letters identifies each column.

Column Width A Learning Tools command that changes the width of the line length to fit more or less text on each line; options include Very Narrow, Narrow, Moderate, or Wide.

Comma Style The Excel number format that inserts thousand comma separators where appropriate and applies two decimal places; Comma Style also leaves space at the right to accommodate a parenthesis when negative numbers are present.

Commands An instruction to a computer program that causes an action to be carried out.

Common field A field included in two or more tables that stores the same data.

Comparison operators Symbols that are used to evaluate data in the field to determine if it is the same (=), greater than (>), less than (<), or in between a range of values as specified by the criteria.

Complimentary closing A parting farewell in a business letter.

Compound criteria Multiple conditions in a query or filter.

Compressed files Files that have been reduced in size, take up less storage space, and can be transferred to other computers faster than uncompressed files.

Compressed Folder Tools Command available in File Explorer with which you can extract compressed files.

Conditional format A format that changes the appearance of a cell—for example, by adding cell shading or font color—based on a condition; if the condition is true, the cell is formatted based on that condition, and if the condition is false, the cell is *not* formatted.

Constant value Numbers, text, dates, or times of day that you type into a cell.

Content pane In a File Explorer window, another name for the file list.

Context menus Menus that display commands and options relevant to the selected text or object; also called *shortcut menus*.

Context sensitive A command associated with the currently selected or active object; often activated by right-clicking a screen item.

Context-sensitive commands Commands that display on a shortcut menu that relate to the object or text that is selected.

Contextual tab A tab added to the ribbon automatically when a specific object is selected and that contains commands relevant to the selected object.

Contiguous slides Slides that are adjacent to each other in a presentation.

Contrast The difference between the darkest and lightest area of a picture.

Control An object on a form or report that displays data or text, performs actions, and lets you view and work with information.

Control layout The grouped arrangement of controls on a form or report; for example, the Stacked layout.

Copy A command that duplicates a selection and places it on the Clipboard.

Cortana Microsoft's intelligent personal assistant in Windows 10 and also available on other devices; named for the intelligent female character in the video game Halo.

COUNT function A statistical function that counts the number of cells in a range that contains numbers.

COUNTIF function A statistical function that counts the number of cells within a range that meet the given condition and that has two arguments—the range of cells to check and the criteria.

Cover letter A document that you send with your resume to provide additional information about your skills and experience.

Criteria Conditions in a query that identify the specific records you are looking for; or, conditions that you specifiy in a logical function.

Crop A command that removes unwanted or unnecessary areas of a picture.

Crop handles Handles used to remove unwanted areas of a picture.

Crop pointer The pointer used to crop areas of a picture.

Crosshair pointer The pointer used to draw a shape.

Crosstab query A query that uses an aggregate function for data that can be grouped by two types of information and displays the data in a compact, spreadsheet-like format with column headings and row headings.

Currency data type An Access data type that describes monetary values and numeric data that can be used in mathematical calculations involving values with one to four decimal places.

Custom web app A database that you can publish and share with others over the Internet.

Cut A command that removes a selection and places it on the Clipboard.

Dashboard The right side of the Start menu that is a one-screen view of links to information and programs that matter to you.

Data (Windows) The documents, worksheets, pictures, songs, and so on that you create and store during the day-to-day use of your computer.

Data (Access) Facts about people, events, things, or ideas.

Data (Excel) Text or numbers in a cell.

Data bar A cell format consisting of a shaded bar that provides a visual cue to the reader about the value of a cell relative to other cells; the length of the bar represents the value in the cell—a longer bar represents a higher value and a shorter bar represents a lower value.

Data entry The action of entering the data into a record in a database table or form.

Data management The process of managing files and folders.

Data marker A column, bar, area, dot, pie slice, or other symbol in a chart that represents a single data point.

Data point A value that originates in a worksheet cell and that is represented in a chart by a data marker.

Data series Related data points represented by data markers; each data series has a unique color or pattern represented in the chart legend.

Data source (Word) A document that contains a list of variable information, such as names and addresses, that is merged with a main document to create customized form letters or labels.

Data source (Access) The table or tables from which a form, query, or report retrieves its data.

Data type Classification identifying the kind of data that can be stored in a field, such as numbers, text, or dates.

Database management system (DBMS) Database software that controls how related collections of data are stored, organized, retrieved, and secured; also known as a DBMS.

Database An organized collection of facts about people, events, things, or ideas related to a specific topic or purpose.

Database template A preformatted database that contains prebuilt tables, queries, forms, and reports that perform a specific task, such as tracking events.

Datasheet view The Access view that displays data organized in columns and rows similar to an Excel worksheet.

Date & Time A command with which you can automatically insert the current date and time into a document in variety of formats.

Date control A control on a form or report that inserts the current date each time the form or report is opened.

Dateline The first line in a business letter that contains the current date and which is positioned just below the letterhead if a letterhead is used.

DBMS An acronym for database management system.

Default The term that refers to the current selection or setting that is automatically used by a computer program unless you specify otherwise.

Descending order A sorting order that arranges text in reverse alphabetical order (Z to A) and numbers from the highest number to the lowest number.

Deselect The action of canceling the selection of an object or block of text by clicking outside of the selection.

Design grid The lower area of the query window that displays the design of the query.

Design view An Access view that displays the detailed structure of a table, query, form, or report. For forms and reports, may be the view in which some tasks must be performed, and only the controls, and not the data, display in this view.

Desktop A simulation of a real desk that represents your work area; here you can arrange icons such as shortcuts to files, folders, and various types of documents in the same manner you would arrange physical objects on top of a desk.

Desktop app A computer program that is installed on your PC and requires a computer operating system such as Microsoft Windows to run; also known as a *desktop application*.

Desktop application A computer program that is installed on your PC and requires a computer operating system such as Microsoft Windows to run; also known as a *desktop app*.

Desktop shortcuts Desktop icons that can link to items accessible on your computer such as a program, file, folder, disk drive, printer, or another computer.

Destination table The table to which you import or append data.

Detail section The section of a form or report that displays the records from the underlying table or query.

Detail sheets The worksheets that contain the details of the information summarized on a summary sheet.

Details pane When activated in a folder window, displays—on the right—the most common file properties associated with the selected file.

Details view A command that displays a list of files or folders and their most common properties.

Dialog box A small window that displays options for completing a task.

Dialog Box Launcher A small icon that displays to the right of some group names on the ribbon and that opens a related dialog box or pane providing additional options and commands related to that group.

Dictate A feature in Word, PowerPoint, Outlook, and OneNote for Windows 10; when you enable Dictate, you start talking and as you talk, text appears in your document or slide.

Displayed value The data that displays in a cell.

Document properties Details about a file that describe or identify it, including the title, author name, subject, and keywords that identify the document's topic or contents; also known as *metadata*.

Dot leader A series of dots preceding a tab that guides the eye across the line.

Double-click The action of pressing the left mouse button two times in rapid succession while holding the mouse still.

Download The action of transferring or copying a file from another location—such as a cloud storage location, your college's Learning Management System, or from an internet site—to your computer.

Drag The action of holding down the left mouse button while moving your mouse.

Drag-and-drop A technique by which you can move, by dragging, selected text from one location in a document to another.

Drawing objects Graphic objects, such as shapes, diagrams, lines, or circles.

Drive An area of storage that is formatted with a file system compatible with your operating system and is identified by a drive letter.

Edit The process of making changes to text or graphics in an Office file.

Editing The process of modifying a presentation by adding and deleting slides or by changing the contents of individual slides.

Editor A digital writing assistant in Word and Outlook that displays misspellings, grammatical mistakes, and writing style issues.

Ellipsis A set of three dots indicating incompleteness; an ellipsis following a command name indicates that a dialog box will display if you click the command.

Em dash A punctuation symbol used to indicate an explanation or emphasis.

Emphasis effect Animation that emphasizes an object or text that is already displayed.

Enclosures Additional documents included with a business letter.

Endnote In a research paper, a note placed at the end of a document or chapter.

Enhanced ScreenTip A ScreenTip that displays useful descriptive information about the command.

Enterprise fund A municipal government fund that reports income and expenditures related to municipal services for which a fee is charged in exchange for goods or services.

Entrance effect Animation that brings a slide element onto the screen.

Excel pointer An Excel window element with which you can display the location of the pointer.

Excel table A series of rows and columns that contains related data that is managed independently from the data in other rows and columns in the worksheet.

Exit effect Animation that moves an object or text off the screen.

Expand Formula Bar button An Excel window element with which you can increase the height of the Formula Bar to display lengthy cell content.

Expand horizontal scroll bar button An Excel window element with which you can increase the width of the horizontal scroll bar.

Explode The action of pulling out one or more pie slices from a pie chart for emphasis.

Export The process of copying data from one file into another file, such as an Access table into an Excel spreadsheet.

Expression A formula that will perform the calculation.

Extract To decompress, or pull out, files from a compressed form.

Eyedropper A tool that captures the exact color from an object on your screen and then applies it to any shape, picture, or text.

Field A single piece of information that is stored in every record; represented by a column in a database table.

Field list A list of field names in a table.

Field properties Characteristics of a field that control how the field displays and how data can be entered in the field; vary for different data types.

Fields In a mail merge, the column headings in the data source.

File Information stored on a computer under a single name.

File Explorer The Windows program that displays the contents of locations, folders, and files on your computer.

File Explorer window A window that displays the contents of the current location and contains helpful parts so that you can navigate—explore within the file organizing structure of Windows.

File list In a File Explorer window, the area that displays the contents of the current location.

File name extension A set of characters at the end of a file name that helps Windows understand what kind of information is in a file and what program should open it.

File properties Information about a file, such as the author, the date the file was last changed, and any descriptive tags.

Fill The inside color of an object.

Fill color The inside color of text or of an object.

Fill handle The small black square in the lower right corner of a selected cell.

Filter The process of displaying only a portion of the data based on matching a specific value to show only the data that meets the criteria that you specify.

Filter by Form An Access command that filters the records in a form based on one or more fields, or based on more than one value in the field.

Filter by Selection An Access command that displays only the records that contain the value in the selected field and hides the records that do not contain the value.

Filtered list A display of files that is limited based on specified criteria.

Filtering The process of displaying only a portion of the total records (a subset) based on matching specific values to provide a quick answer to a question.

Find and Replace A command that searches the cells in a worksheet—or in a selected range—for matches and then replaces each match with a replacement value of your choice.

First principle of good database design A principle of good database design stating that data is organized in tables so that there is no redundant data.

Flash Fill Recognizes a pattern in your data, and then automatically fills in values when you enter examples of the output that you want. Use it to split data from two or more cells or to combine data from two cells.

Flat database A simple database file that is not related or linked to any other collection of data.

Flip A command that creates a reverse image of a picture or object.

Floating object A graphic that can be moved independently of the surrounding text characters.

Folder A container in which you can store files.

Folder structure The hierarchy of folders.

Folder window A window that typically displays the File List for a folder.

Font A set of characters with the same design and shape.

Font styles Formatting emphasis such as bold, italic, and underline.

Footer (PowerPoint) Text that displays at the bottom of every slide or that prints at the bottom of a sheet of slide handouts or notes pages.

Footer (Word) A reserved area for text or graphics that displays at the bottom of each page in a document.

Footnote In a research paper, a note placed at the bottom of the page.

Foreign key The field that is included in the related table so the field can be joined with the primary key in another table for the purpose of creating a relationship.

Form An Access object you can use to enter new records into a table, edit or delete existing records in a table, or display existing records.

Form Footer Information displayed at the bottom of the screen in Form view or Layout view that is printed after the last detail section on the last page of a printout.

Form Header Information such as a form's title that displays at the top of the screen in Form view or Layout view and is printed at the top of the first page when records are printed as forms.

Form tool An Access tool that creates a form with a single mouse click, which includes all of the fields from the underlying data source (table or query).

Form view The Access view in which you can view, modify, delete, or add records in a table but you cannot change the layout or design of the form.

Form Wizard An Access tool that walks you step by step through the creation of a form and that gives you more flexibility in the design, layout, and number of fields in a form.

Format Changing the appearance of cells and worksheet elements to make a worksheet attractive and easy to read.

Format Painter The command to copy the formatting of specific text or to copy the formatting of a paragraph and then apply it in other locations in your document; when active, the pointer takes the shape of a paintbrush.

Formatting (PowerPoint) The process of changing the appearance of the text, layout, and design of a slide.

Formatting (Word) The process of applying Office commands to make your documents easy to read and to add visual touches and design elements to make your document inviting to the reader; establishes the overall appearance of text, graphics, and pages in an Office file—for example, in a Word document.

Formatting marks Characters that display on the screen, but do not print, indicating where the Enter key, the Spacebar, and the Tab key were pressed; also called *nonprinting characters*.

Formula An equation that performs mathematical calculations on values in a worksheet.

Formula AutoComplete An Excel feature which, after typing an = (equal sign) and the beginning letter or letters of a function name, displays a list of function names that match the typed letter(s).

Formula Bar An element in the Excel window that displays the value or formula contained in the active cell; here you can also enter or edit values or formulas.

Free-form snip From the Snipping Tool, a command that draws an irregular line such as a circle around an area of the screen.

Freeze Panes A command that enables you to select one or more rows or columns and freeze (lock) them into place; the locked rows and columns become separate panes.

Full-screen snip From the Snipping Tool, a command that captures the entire screen.

Function A predefined formula—a formula that Excel has already built for you—that performs calculations by using specific values in a particular order or structure.

Fund A sum of money set aside for a specific purpose.

Funnel chart A type of chart that shows values across the stages in a process.

Gallery An Office feature that displays a list of potential results.

General format The default format that Excel applies to numbers; this format has no specific characteristics—whatever you type in the cell will display, with the exception that trailing zeros to the right of a decimal point will not display.

General fund The term used to describe money set aside for the normal operating activities of a government entity such as a city.

Goal Seek A what-if analysis tool that finds the input needed in one cell to arrive at the desired result in another cell.

Gradient fill A fill effect in which one color fades into another.

Graphical user interface Graphics such as an image of a file folder or wastebasket that you click to activate the item represented.

Graphics Pictures, charts, or drawing objects.

Group Footer Information printed at the end of each group of records to display summary information for the group.

Group Header Information printed at the beginning of each new group of records; for example, the group name.

Group, Sort, and Total pane A pane that displays at the bottom of the window in Design view in which you can control how information is sorted and grouped in a report; provides the most flexibility for adding or modifying groups, sort orders, or totals options on a report.

Groups On the Office ribbon, the sets of related commands that you might need for a specific type of task.

GUI An abbreviation of the term graphical user interface.

Hamburger Another name for a hamburger menu.

Hamburger menu Another name for a menu icon, deriving from the three lines that bring to mind a hamburger on a bun.

Hanging indent An indent style in which the first line of a paragraph extends to the left of the remaining lines and that is commonly used for bibliographic entries.

Hard disk drive The primary storage device located inside your computer where some of your files and programs are typically stored, usually designated as drive C.

Header Text that prints at the top of each sheet of slide handouts or notes pages.

Headings font A font that is applied to all slide title text.

Hierarchy An arrangement where items are ranked and where each level is lower in rank than the item above it

Icons Small images that represent commands, files, applications, or other windows.

IF function A function that uses a logical test to check whether a condition is met, and then returns one value if true, and another value if false.

IFS function A function that checks whether one or more conditions— logical tests—are met, and then returns a value corresponding to the first TRUE condition.

Import The process of copying data from another file, such as a Word table or an Excel workbook, into a separate file, such as an Access database.

Indenting Moving the beginning of the first line of a paragraph to the right or left of the rest of the paragraph to provide visual cues to the reader to help divide the document text and make it easier to read.

Info tab The tab in Backstage view that displays information about the current file.

Information Data that is accurate, timely, and organized in a useful manner.

Inline object An object or graphic inserted in a document that acts like a character in a sentence.

Innermost sort field When sorting on multiple fields in Datasheet view, the field that will be used for the second level of sorting.

Insertion point A blinking vertical line that indicates where text or graphics will be inserted.

Inside address The name and address of the person receiving the letter and positioned below the date line.

Inspect Document A command that searches your document for hidden data of personal information that you might not want to share publicly.

Inverse A Page Color in Learning Tools that displays the text in white on a black background.

Is Not Null A criteria that searches for fields that are not empty.

Is Null A criteria that searches for fields that are empty.

Join line In the Relationships window, the line joining two tables that visually indicates the common fields and the type of relationship.

JPEG An acronym that stands for *Joint Photographic Experts Group* and that is a common file type used by digital cameras and computers to store digital pictures.

Jump List A display of destinations and tasks from a program's taskbar icon when you right-click the icon.

Justified alignment An arrangement of text in which the text aligns evenly on both the left and right margins.

Keyboard shortcut A combination of two or more keyboard keys, used to perform a task that would otherwise require a mouse.

KeyTip The letter that displays on a command in the ribbon and that indicates the key you can press to activate the command when keyboard control of the ribbon is activated.

Keywords Custom file properties in the form of words that you associate with a document to give an indication of the document's content.

Label Another name for a text value; it usually provides information about number values.

Label control A control on a form or report that contains descriptive information, usually a field name or title.

Landscape orientation A page orientation in which the paper is wider than it is tall.

Layout The arrangement of elements, such as title and subtitle text, lists, pictures, tables, charts, shapes, and movies, on a slide.

Layout Options A button that displays when an object is selected and that has commands to choose how the object interacts with surrounding text.

Layout selector A small symbol that displays in the upper left corner of a selected control layout in a form or report that is displayed in Layout view or Design view and is used to move or format an entire group of controls.

Layout view The Access view in which you can make changes to a form or report while the data from the underlying data source displays.

Leader character Characters that form a solid, dotted, or dashed line that fills the space preceding a tab stop.

Learning Tools Features in Word that add visual changes to assist with reading fluency and comprehension.

Left alignment (Excel) The cell format in which characters align at the left edge of the cell; this is the default for text entries and is an example of formatting information stored in a cell.

Left alignment (Word) An arrangement of text in which the text aligns at the left margin, leaving the right margin uneven.

Legend A chart element that identifies the patterns or colors that are assigned to the categories in the chart.

Lettered column headings The area along the top edge of a worksheet that identifies each column with a unique letter or combination of letters.

Letterhead The personal or company information that displays at the top of a letter, and that commonly includes a name, address, and contact information.

Line break indicator A formatting mark in the shape of a bent arrow that indicates a manual line break.

Line chart A chart type that displays trends over time; time displays along the bottom axis and the data point values are connected with a line.

Line spacing The distance between lines of text in a paragraph.

Link A connection to data in another file.

LinkedIn A professional networking website that focuses on business and employment-oriented services and on which you can build and share your professional identify and connect with others in your field of interest.

List level An outline level in a presentation represented by a bullet symbol and identified in a slide by the indentation and the size of the text.

Live Layout A feature that reflows text as you move or size an object so that you can view the placement of surrounding text.

Live Preview A technology that shows the result of applying an editing or formatting change as you point to possible results—*before* you actually apply it.

Live tiles Tiles that are constantly updated with fresh information.

Location Any disk drive, folder, or other place in which you can store files and folders.

Lock screen A background that fills the computer screen when the computer boots up or wakes up from sleep mode.

Logical functions A group of functions that test for specific conditions and that typically use conditional tests to determine whether specified conditions are true or false.

Logical operators Operators that combine criteria using AND and OR. With two criteria, AND requires that both conditions be met and OR requires that either condition be met for the record to display in the query results.

Logical test Any value or expression that can be evaluated as being true or false.

Mail merge A feature that joins a main document and a data source to create customized letters or labels.

Main document In a mail merge, the document that contains the text or formatting that remains constant.

Major unit The value in a chart's value axis that determines the spacing between tick marks and between the gridlines in the plot area.

Manual column break An artificial end to a column to balance columns or to provide space for the insertion of other objects.

Manual line break A line break that moves the text to the right of the insertion point to a new line while keeping the text in the same paragraph.

Manual page break The action of forcing a page to end and placing subsequent text at the top of the next page.

Map chart A type of chart that compares values and shows categories across geographical regions; for example, across countries, states, counties, and regions.

Margins The space between the text and the top, bottom, left, and right edges of the paper.

MAX function An Excel function that determines the largest value in a selected range of values.

Maximize A window control button that will enlarge the size of the window to fill the entire screen.

MEDIAN function An Excel function that finds the middle value that has as many values above it in the group as are below it; it differs from AVERAGE in that the result is not affected as much by a single value that is greatly different from the others.

Menu A list of commands within a category.

Menu bar A group of menus at the top of a program window.

Menu icon A button consisting of three lines that, when clicked, expands a menu; often used in mobile applications because it is compact to use on smaller screens—also referred to a *hamburger menu*.

Merge & Center A command that joins selected cells in an Excel worksheet into one larger cell and centers the contents in the merged cell.

Message Bar The area directly below the ribbon that displays information such as security alerts when there is potentially unsafe, active content in an Office document that you open.

Metadata Details about a file that describe or identify it, including the title, author name, subject, and keywords that identify the document's topic or contents; also known as *document properties*.

Microsoft account A user account with which you can sign in to any Windows 10 computer on which you have, or create, an account.

Microsoft Store app A smaller app that you download from the Microsoft Store.

MIN function An Excel function that determines the smallest value in a selected range of values.

Mini toolbar A small toolbar containing frequently used formatting commands that displays as a result of selecting text or objects.

Minimize A window control button that will keep a program open but will remove it from screen view.

Modern Language Association (MLA) One of two commonly used style guides for formatting research papers.

Mouse pointer Any symbol that displays on the screen in response to moving the mouse.

Move In File Explorer, the action of removing a file or folder from its original location and storing it in a new location.

MRU Acronym for *most recently used*, which refers to the state of some commands that retain the characteristic most recently applied; for example, the Font Color button retains the most recently used color until a new color is chosen.

Multiple-items form A form that enables you to display or enter multiple records in a table.

Name Box An element of the Excel window that displays the name of the selected cell, table, chart, or object.

Nameplate The banner on the front page of a newsletter that identifies the publication.

Navigate (Excel) The process of moving within a worksheet or workbook.

Navigate (Windows) A process for exploring within the file organizing structure of Windows.

Navigation area An area at the bottom of the Access window that indicates the number of records in the table and contains controls in the form of arrows that you click to move among the records.

Navigation pane The area on the left side of the File Explorer window to access your OneDrive, folders on your PC, devices and drives connected to your PC, and other PCs on your network.

Navigation Pane An area of the Access window that displays and organizes the names of the objects in a database; from here, you open objects for use.

Newsletter A periodical that communicates news and information to a specific group.

No Paragraph Space The built-in paragraph style—available from the Paragraph Spacing command—that inserts *no* extra space before or after a paragraph and uses line spacing of 1.

Noncontiguous slides Slides that are not adjacent to each other in a presentation.

Nonprinting characters Characters that display on the screen, but do not print, indicating where the Enter key, the Spacebar, and the Tab key were pressed; also called *formatting marks*.

Normal template The template that serves as a basis for all Word documents.

Normal view (Excel) A screen view that maximizes the number of cells visible on your screen and keeps the column letters and row numbers close to the columns and rows.

Normal view (PowerPoint) The primary editing view in PowerPoint where you write and design your presentations.

Normalization The process of applying design rules and principles to ensure that your database performs as expected.

Note In a research paper, information that expands on the topic, but that does not fit well in the document text.

Notepad A basic text-editing program included with Windows 10 that you can use to create simple documents.

Notes page A printout that contains the slide image on the top half of the page and notes that you have created on the Notes pane in the lower half of the page.

Notes pane An area of the Normal view window that displays below the Slide pane with space to type notes regarding the active slide.

NOW function An Excel function that retrieves the date and time from your computer's calendar and clock and inserts the information into the selected cell.

Number data type An Access data type that represents a quantity, how much or how many, and that may be used in calculations.

Number format A specific way in which Excel displays numbers in a cell.

Number values Constant values consisting of only numbers.

Numbered list A list of items preceded by numbers, which indicate sequence or rank of the items. Sometimes called ordered lists.

Numbered row headings The area along the left edge of a worksheet that identifies each row with a unique number.

Object A text box, picture, table, or shape that you can select and then move and resize.

Objects (Access) The basic parts of a database that you create to store your data and to work with your data; for example, tables, queries, forms, and reports.

Object anchor The symbol that indicates to which paragraph an object is attached.

Object tab In the object window, a tab that identifies the object and enables you to make an open object active.

Object window An area of the Access window that displays open objects, such as tables, queries, forms, or reports; by default, each object displays on its own tab.

Office 365 A version of Microsoft Office to which you subscribe for an annual fee.

Office Presentation Service A Word feature to present your Word document to others who can watch in a web browser.

On Click An animation option that begins the animation sequence for the selected slide element when the mouse button is clicked or the spacebar is pressed.

One-click Row/Column Insertion A Word table feature with which you can insert a new row or column by pointing to the desired location and then clicking.

One-to-many relationship A relationship between two tables where one record in the first table corresponds to many records in the second table—the most common type of relationship in Access.

OneDrive Microsoft's free cloud storage for anyone with a free Microsoft account.

Operating system A specific type of computer program that manages the other programs on a computing device such as a desktop computer, a laptop computer, a smartphone, a tablet computer, or a game console.

Operators The symbols with which you can specify the type of calculation you want to perform in an Excel formula.

Option button In a dialog box, a round button that enables you to make one choice among two or more options.

OR condition A compound criteria used to display records that match at least one of the specified criteria.

Order of operations The mathematical rules for performing multiple calculations within a formula.

Outermost sort field When sorting on multiple fields in Datasheet view, the field that will be used for the first level of sorting.

Outline view A PowerPoint view that displays the presentation outline to the left of the Slide pane.

Page break indicator A dotted line with the text *Page Break* that indicates where a manual page break was inserted.

Page Color A Learning Tools command that changes the color of the page to make the text easy to scan and consume.

Page Footer Information printed at the bottom of every page in a report and most often includes the page number.

Page Header Information printed at the top of every page in a report.

Page number control A control on a form or report that inserts the page number when displayed in Print Preview or when printed.

Page Width A command that zooms the document so that the width of the page matches the width of the window.

Pane A portion of a worksheet window bounded by and separated from other portions by vertical and horizontal bars.

Paragraph symbol The symbol ¶ that represents the end of a paragraph.

Parameter A value that can be changed.

Parameter query A query that prompts you for criteria before running the query.

Parent folder The location in which the folder you are viewing is saved.

Parenthetical references References that include the last name of the author or authors, and the page number in the referenced source.

Paste The action of placing cell contents that have been copied or moved to the Clipboard into another location.

Paste area The target destination for data that has been cut or copied using the Office Clipboard.

Paste Options gallery A gallery of buttons that provides a Live Preview of all the Paste options available in the current context.

Path A sequence of folders that leads to a specific file or folder.

PDF The acronym for Portable Document Format, which is a file format that creates an image that preserves the look of your file, but that cannot be easily changed; a popular format for sending documents electronically, because the document will display on most computers.

PDF Reflow The ability to import PDF files into Word so that you can transform a PDF back into a fully editable Word document.

Pen A pen-shaped stylus that you tap on a computer screen.

Percent for new value = base percent + percent of increase The formula for calculating a percentage by which a value increases by adding the base percentage—usually 100%—to the percent increase.

Percentage rate of increase The percent by which one number increases over another number.

Personal folder The folder created on the hard drive for each Windows 10 user account on a computer; for each user account—even if there is only one user on the computer—Windows 10 creates a personal folder labeled with the account holder's name.

Picture effects Effects that enhance a picture, such as a shadow, glow, reflection, or 3-D rotation.

Picture element A point of light measured in dots per square inch on a screen; 64 pixels equals 8.43 characters, which is the average number of characters that will fit in a cell in an Excel worksheet using the default font.

Picture styles Frames, shapes, shadows, borders, and other special effects that can be added to an image to create an overall visual style for the image.

Pie chart A chart that shows the relationship of each part to a whole.

Pixel The abbreviated name for a picture element.

Placeholder A box on a slide with dotted or dashed borders that holds title and body text or other content such as charts, tables, and pictures.

Placeholder text Non-printing text that holds a place in a document where you can type.

Plot area The area bounded by the axes of a chart, including all the data series.

.png file An image file type that can be transferred over the internet, an acronym for Portable Network Graphic.

Point-and-click The technique of constructing a formula by pointing to and then clicking cells; this method is convenient when the referenced cells are not adjacent to one another.

Point to The action of moving the mouse pointer over a specific area.

Pointer Any symbol that displays on your screen in response to moving your mouse.

Pointing device A mouse or touchpad used to control the pointer.

Points A measurement of the size of a font; there are 72 points in an inch.

Populate The action of filling a database table with records.

Portable Document Format A file format that creates an image that preserves the look of your file, but that cannot be easily changed; a popular format for sending documents electronically, because the document will display on most computers.

Portrait orientation A page orientation in which the paper is taller than it is wide.

Presenter view A view that shows the full-screen slide show on one monitor or projection screen while enabling the presenter to view a preview of the next slide, notes, and a timer on another monitor.

Primary key A required field that uniquely identifies a record in a table; for example, a Student ID number at a college.

Print Preview A view of a document as it will appear when you print it.

Print Titles An Excel command that enables you to specify rows and columns to repeat on each printed page.

Program A set of instructions that a computer uses to accomplish a task.

Progress bar A bar that displays in a dialog box—and also on the taskbar button—that indicates visually the progress of a task such as a copy process, a download, or a file transfer.

Property Sheet A list of characteristics—properties—for fields or controls on a form or report in which you can make precise changes to each property associated with the field or control.

pt The abbreviation for *point* when referring to a font size.

Query A database object that retrieves specific data from one or more database objects—either tables or other queries—and then, in a single datasheet, displays only the data you specify.

Quick access In the navigation pane in a File Explorer window, a list of files you have been working on and folders you use often.

Quick Analysis Tool A tool that displays in the lower right corner of a selected range, with which you can analyze your data by using Excel tools such as charts, color-coding, and formulas.

Range Two or more selected cells on a worksheet that are adjacent or nonadjacent; because the range is treated as a single unit, you can make the same changes or combination of changes to more than one cell at a time.

Range finder An Excel feature that outlines cells in color to indicate which cells are used in a formula; useful for verifying which cells are referenced in a formula.

Rate = amount of increase/base The mathematical formula to calculate a rate of increase.

Read Aloud A Learning Tools command that reads text out loud and highlights each word as it is read; this command is available in both Word and Outlook.

Read Mode A view in Word that optimizes the Word screen for the times when you are reading Word documents on the screen and not creating or editing them.

Reading view A view in PowerPoint that displays a presentation in a manner similar to a slide show but in which the taskbar, title bar, and status bar remain available in the presentation window.

Real-time co-authoring A process where two or more people work on the same file at the same time and see changes made by others in seconds.

Recolor A feature that enables you to change all colors in the picture to shades of a single color.

Recommended Charts An Excel feature that displays a customized set of charts that, according to Excel's calculations, will best fit your data based on the range of data that you select.

Record All of the categories of data pertaining to one person, place, event, thing, or idea; represented by a row in a database table.

Record selector bar The bar at the left edge of a record when it is displayed in a form and that is used to select an entire record.

Record selector box The small box at the left of a record in Datasheet view that, when clicked, selects the entire record.

Record source The tables or queries that provide the underlying data for a form or report.

Rectangular snip From the Snipping Tool, a command that draws a precise box by dragging the mouse pointer around an area of the screen to form a rectangle.

Recycle Bin The area where deleted items are stored until you empty the bin; enables you to recover deleted items until the bin is emptied.

Redundant In a database, information that is duplicated in a manner that indicates poor database design.

Referential integrity A set of rules that Access uses to ensure that the data between related tables is valid.

Relational database A sophisticated type of database that has multiple collections of data within the file that are related to one another.

Relationship An association that you establish between two tables based on common fields.

Relative cell reference In a formula, the address of a cell based on the relative positions of the cell that contains the formula and the cell referred to in the formula.

Removable storage device A device such as a USB flash drive used to transfer information from one computer to another.

Report A database object that summarizes the fields and records from a query or table in an easy-to-read format suitable for printing.

Report Footer Information printed at the bottom of the last page of a report.

Report Header Information printed on the first page of a report that is used for logos, titles, and dates.

Report tool An Access tool that creates a report with one mouse click and displays all of the fields and records from the record source that you select.

Report Wizard An Access tool that walks you step by step through the creation of a report and that gives you more flexibility in the design, layout, and number of fields in a report.

Researcher A Word feature that helps you find topics and reliable sources for a research paper; for sources that you select, citation information is available.

Resources The collection of the physical parts of your computer such as the central processing unit (CPU), memory, and any attached devices such as a printer.

Restore Down A command that resizes a window to its previous size.

Resume Assistant A feature in Word with which you can see suggestions from LinkedIn to help you update your resume.

RGB A color model in which the colors red, green, and blue are added together to form another color.

Ribbon In Office applications, displays a group of task-oriented tabs that contain the commands, styles, and resources you need to work in an Office desktop app. In a File Explorer window, the area at the top that groups common tasks on tabs. such as copying and moving, creating new folders, emailing and zipping items, and changing view on related tabs.

Rich Text Format (RTF) A standard file format that contains some formatting such as underline, bold, font sizes, and colors. RTF documents can be opened in many applications.

Right alignment An arrangement of text in which the text aligns at the right margin, leaving the left margin uneven.

Right-click The action of clicking the right mouse button one time.

Rotation handle A symbol with which you can rotate a graphic to any angle; displays above the top center sizing handle.

Rounding A procedure in which you determine which digit at the right of the number will be the last digit displayed and then increase it by one if the next digit to its right is 5, 6, 7, 8, or 9.

Row A horizontal group of cells in a worksheet.

Row heading The numbers along the left side of an Excel worksheet that designate the row numbers.

Ruler guides Dotted red vertical and horizontal lines that display in the rulers indicating the pointer's position.

Run The process in which Access looks at the records in the table(s) included in the query design, finds the records that match the specified criteria, and then displays the records in a datasheet; only the fields included in the query design display.

Salutation The greeting line of a business letter.

Sans serif font A font design with no lines or extensions on the ends of characters.

Scale A command that resizes a picture to a percentage of its size.

Scale to Fit Excel commands that enable you to stretch or shrink the width, height, or both, of printed output to fit a maximum number of pages.

Scaling The process of shrinking the width and/or height of printed output to fit a maximum number of pages.

Screen Clipping A tool with which you can take a quick snapshot of part of a screen, and then add it to your document.

Screen reader Software that enables visually impaired users to read text on a computer screen to understand the content of pictures.

Screenshot An image of an active window on your computer that you can paste into a document.

ScreenTip A small box that that displays useful information when you perform various mouse actions such as pointing to screen elements or dragging.

Scroll arrow An arrow found at either end of a scroll bar that can be clicked to move within the window in small increments.

Scroll bar A vertical bar that displays when the contents of a window or pane are not completely visible; a scroll bar can be vertical, displayed at the side of the window, or horizontal, displayed at the bottom of a window.

Scroll box Within a scroll bar, a box that you can move to bring the contents of the window into view.

Second principle of good database design A principle stating that appropriate database techniques are used to ensure the accuracy and consistency of data as it is entered into the table.

Section A portion of a document that can be formatted differently from the rest of the document.

Section bar In Design view, a gray bar in a form or report that identifies and separates one section from another; used to select the section and to change the size of the section.

Section break A double dotted line that indicates the end of one section and the beginning of another section.

Section header A type of slide layout that changes the look and flow of a presentation by providing text placeholders that do not contain bullet points.

Select To specify, by highlighting, a block of data or text on the screen with the intent of performing some action on the selection.

Select All box A box in the upper left corner of the worksheet grid that, when clicked, selects all the cells in a worksheet.

Select query A type of Access query that retrieves (selects) data from one or more tables or queries, displaying the selected data in a datasheet; also known as a simple select query.

Selecting Highlighting, by dragging with your mouse, areas of text or data or graphics, so that the selection can be edited, formatted, copied, or moved.

Sepia A Page Color command in Learning Tools that shades the screen in pale yellow with a print feel.

Series A group of things that come one after another in succession; for example, January, February, March, and so on.

Serif font A font design that includes small line extensions on the ends of the letters to guide the eye in reading from left to right.

Shape A line, arrow, star, banner, oval, rectangle, or other object with which you can illustrate an idea, a process, or a workflow.

Shape style Predefined combination of shape fill, line colors, and other effects.

SharePoint A Microsoft technology that enables employees in an organization to access information across organizational and geographic boundaries.

Sheet tab scrolling buttons Buttons to the left of the sheet tabs used to display Excel sheet tabs that are not in view; used when there are more sheet tabs than will display in the space provided.

Sheet tabs The labels along the lower border of the workbook window that identify each worksheet.

Short Text data type An Access data type that describes text, a combination of text and numbers, or numbers that are not used in calculations, such as the Postal Code.

Shortcut menu A menu that displays commands and options relevant to the selected text or object; also called a *context menu*.

Show Formulas A command that displays the formula in each cell instead of the resulting value.

Side to Side A Page Movement setting that enables you to see whole pages by sliding each page from right to left or left to right.

Simple select query Another name for a select query.

Single spacing The common name for line spacing in which there is *no* extra space before or after a paragraph; uses line spacing of 1.

Single-record form A form that enables you to display or enter one record at a time from a table.

Sizing handles Small circles surrounding a picture that indicate that the picture is selected.

Skype A Microsoft product with which you can make voice calls, make video calls, transfer files, or send messages—including instant messages and text messages—over the Internet.

Slide A presentation page that can contain text, pictures, tables, charts, and other multimedia or graphic objects.

Slide handout Printed images of slides on a sheet of paper.

Slide pane A PowerPoint screen element that displays a large image of the active slide.

Slide Sorter view A presentation view that displays thumbnails of all of the slides in a presentation.

Slide transitions Motion effects that occur in Slide Show view when you move from one slide to the next during a presentation.

Small caps A font effect that changes lowercase letters to uppercase letters, but with the height of lowercase letters.

Smart guides Dashed lines that display on your slide when you are moving an object to assist you with alignment.

Smart Lookup A Word feature with which you can get more information about text you select; shows definitions, images, and results from various online sources.

SmartArt A designer-quality visual representation of your information that you can create by choosing from among many different layouts to effectively communicate your message or ideas.

SmartArt graphic A visual representation of information that you create by choosing from among various layouts to communicate your message or ideas effectively.

SmartArt Styles Combinations of formatting effects that you can apply to SmartArt graphics.

Snap An action to arrange two or more open windows on your screen so that you can work with multiple screens at the same time.

Snap Assist A feature that displays all other open windows after one window is snapped.

Snip An image captured by the Snipping tool that can be annotated, saved, copied, or shared via email.

Snipping tool A Windows 10 program that captures an image of all or part of your computer's screen.

Sort The process of arranging data in a specific order based on the value in each field.

Source file When importing a file, refers to the file being imported.

Sparkline A tiny chart in the background of a cell that gives a visual trend summary alongside your data; makes a pattern more obvious.

Spin box A small box with an upward- and downward-pointing arrow that lets you move rapidly through a set of values by clicking.

Split Splits the window into multiple resizable panes that contain views of your worksheet. This is useful to view multiple distant parts of your worksheet at one time.

Split button A button divided into two parts and in which clicking the main part of the button performs a command and clicking the arrow opens a menu with choices.

Spreadsheet Another name for a worksheet.

Stacked layout A control layout format that is similar to a paper form, with label controls placed to the left of each text box control; the controls are grouped together for easy editing.

Start menu A Windows 10 menu that displays as a result of clicking the Start button and that displays a list of installed programs on the left and a customizable group of tiles on the right that can act as a user dashboard.

Statistical functions Excel functions, including the AVERAGE, MEDIAN, MIN, and MAX functions, that are useful to analyze a group of measurements.

Status bar The area along the lower edge of the Excel window that displays, on the left side, the current cell mode, page number, and worksheet information; on the right side, when numerical data is selected, common calculations such as Sum and Average display.

Structure In Access, the underlying design of a table, including field names, data types, descriptions, and field properties.

Style A group of formatting commands, such as font, font size, font color, paragraph alignment, and line spacing that can be applied to a paragraph with one command.

Style guide A manual that contains standards for the design and writing of documents.

Style set A collection of character and paragraph formatting that is stored and named.

Subdatasheet A format for displaying related records when you click the plus sign (+) next to a record in a table on the *one* side of the relationship.

Subfolder The term for a folder placed within another folder.

Subject line The optional line following the inside address in a business letter that states the purpose of the letter.

Subset A portion of the total records available.

SUM function A predefined formula that adds all the numbers in a selected range of cells.

Summary sheet A worksheet where totals from other worksheets are displayed and summarized.

Suppress A Word feature that hides header and footer information, including the page number, on the first page of a document.

Switch Row/Column A charting command to swap the data over the axis—data being charted on the vertical axis will move to the horizontal axis and vice versa

Syllables A Learning Tools command that shows breaks between syllables of words.

Synchronization The process of updating computer files that are in two or more locations according to specific rules—also called *syncing*.

Syncing The process of updating computer files that are in two or more locations according to specific rules—also called *synchronization*.

Synonyms Words with the same or similar meaning.

System tray Another term for the notification area on the taskbar that displays notification icons and the system clock and calendar.

Tab order The order in which the insertion point moves from one field to another in a form when you press the Tab key.

Tab stop A specific location on a line of text, marked on the Word ruler, to which you can move the insertion point by pressing the Tab key, and which is used to align and indent text.

Table (Access) A format for information that organizes and presents text and data in columns and rows; the foundation of a database.

Table (Excel) A format for information that organizes and presents text and data in columns and rows.

Table (Word) An arrangement of information organized into rows and columns.

Table area The upper area of the query window that displays field lists for the tables that are used in a query.

Table style A format applied to a table that is consistent with the presentation theme.

Tables and Related Views An arrangement in the Navigation Pane that groups objects by the table to which they are related.

Tabs (ribbon) On the Office ribbon, the name of each activity area.

Tags Custom file properties in the form of words that you associate with a document to give an indication of the document's content; used to help find and organize files. Also called keywords.

Task View A taskbar button that displays your desktop background with small images of all open programs and apps and from which you can see and switch between open apps, including desktop apps.

Taskbar The bar at the bottom of your Windows screen that contains buttons to launch programs and buttons for all open apps.

Team A group of workers tasked with working together to solve a problem, make a decision, or create a work product.

Tell Me A search feature for Microsoft Office commands that you activate by typing what you are looking for in the Tell Me box.

Tell me more A prompt within a ScreenTip that opens the Office online Help system with explanations about how to perform the command referenced in the ScreenTip.

Template An existing document that you use as a starting point for a new document; it opens a copy of itself, unnamed, and then you use the structure—and possibly some content, such as headings—as the starting point for a new document.

Text alignment The horizontal placement of text within a placeholder.

Text box A movable resizable container for text or that you can position anywhere in an Office file.

Text box control A bound control on a form or report that displays the data from the underlying table or query.

Text effects Decorative formats, such as shadowed or mirrored text, text glow, 3-D effects, and colors that make text stand out.

Text from File A command to insert text from another file into your document.

Text Highlight Color A Word command with which you can apply a highlight color to selected text.

Text pane A pane that displays to the left of a SmartArt graphic and is used to type text and edit text in a SmartArt graphic.

Text Spacing A Learning Tools command that increases the spacing between words, characters, and lines.

Text string A sequence of characters.

Text values Constant values consisting of only text, and which usually provide information about number values; also referred to as labels.

Text wrapping The manner in which text displays around an object.

Theme A predesigned combination of colors, fonts, and effects that look good together and that is applied to an entire document by a single selection.

Theme colors A set of coordinating colors that are applied to the backgrounds, objects, and text in a presentation.

Theme fonts The fonts that apply to two types of slide text—headings and body.

Thesaurus A research tool that provides a list of synonyms.

Thumbnail A reduced image of a graphic.

Tiles A group of square and rectangular boxes that display on the start menu.

Timeline A Windows 10 feature that when you click the Task view button, you can see activities you have worked on across your devices; for example, you can find a document, image, or video you worked on yesterday or a week ago.

Timing options Animation options that control when animated items display in the animation sequence.

Title bar The bar across the top of the window that displays the program, file, or app name.

Title slide A slide layout—most commonly the first slide in a presentation—that provides an introduction to the presentation topic.

Toggle button A button that can be turned on by clicking it once, and then turned off by clicking it again.

Toolbar A row, column, or block of buttons or icons that displays across the top of a window and that contains commands for tasks you perform with a single click.

Trim A command that deletes parts of a video to make it shorter.

Triple-click The action of clicking the left mouse button three times in rapid succession.

Truncated Data that is cut off or shortened because the field or column is not wide enough to display all of the data or the field size is too small to contain all of the data.

Trust Center An area of Access where you can view the security and privacy settings for your Access installation.

.txt file A simple file consisting of lines of text with no formatting that almost any computer can open and display.

Unbound control A control that does not have a source of data, such as the title in a form or report.

Underlying formula The formula entered in a cell and visible only on the Formula Bar.

Underlying value The data that displays in the Formula Bar.

Undo On the Quick Access Toolbar, the command that reverses your last action.

Unzip The process of extracting files that have been compressed.

User account A user on a single computer.

Value Another name for a constant value.

Value after increase = base × percent for new value The formula for calculating the value after an increase by multiplying the original value—the base—by the percent for new value (see the *Percent for new value* formula).

Value axis A numerical scale on the left side of a chart that shows the range of numbers for the data points; also referred to as the Y-axis.

Variant A variation on the presentation theme style and color.

Volatile A term used to describe an Excel function that is subject to change each time the workbook is reopened; for example, the NOW function updates itself to the current date and time each time the workbook is opened.

Wallpaper Another term for the Desktop background.

What-if analysis The process of changing the values in cells to see how those changes affect the outcome of formulas in a worksheet.

Wildcard character In a query, a character that represents one or more unknown characters in criteria; an asterisk (*) represents one or more unknown characters, and a question mark (?) represents a single unknown character.

Window snip From the Snipping Tool, a command that captures the entire displayed window.

Windows 10 An operating system developed by Microsoft Corporation that works with mobile computing devices and also with traditional desktop and laptop PCs.

With Previous An animation option that begins the animation sequence at the same time as the previous animation or slide transition.

Wizard A feature in Microsoft Office that walks you step by step through a process.

Word wrap The feature that moves text from the right edge of a paragraph to the beginning of the next line as necessary to fit within the margins.

WordArt A gallery of text styles with which you can create decorative effects, such as shadowed or mirrored text.

Workbook An Excel file that contains one or more worksheets.

Works Cited In the MLA style, a list of cited works placed at the end of a research paper or report.

Worksheet The primary document that you use in Excel to work with and store data, and which is formatted as a pattern of uniformly spaced horizontal and vertical lines.

Worksheet grid area A part of the Excel window that displays the columns and rows that intersect to form the worksheet's cells.

Writer's identification The name and title of the author of a letter placed near the bottom of the letter under the complimentary closing—also referred to as the *writer's signature block*.

Writer's signature block The name and title of the author of a letter placed near the bottom of the letter, under the complimentary closing—also referred to as the *writer's identification*.

X-axis Another name for the horizontal (category) axis.

XML Paper Specification A Microsoft file format that creates an image of your document and that opens in the XPS viewer.

XPS The acronym for *XML Paper Specification*—a Microsoft file format that creates an image of your document and that opens in the XPS viewer.

Y-axis Another name for the vertical (value) axis.

Zip The process of compressing files.

Zoom The action of increasing or decreasing the size of the viewing area on the screen.

Index

A

absolute cell references, 354–356, 461
Access, 517
  closing, 549–550
  creating Word tables from, 969–971
  database window elements, 524
  exporting data to Excel from, 947–949
  exporting queries to spreadsheets from, 644–645
  exporting tables to spreadsheets from, 551
  mail merges using data from, 971–975
  opening screen elements, 523
accessibility, 36–37
  checking, 38
Accounting Number Format, 42, 331, 423
Action Center, 52
active cells, 320
address bars, 56, 58, 73, 75, 209
addressing envelopes, 206–207
Advanced Filter/Sort command, 684–685
advertisement presentations, 856–857
After Previous timing option, 891–892
aggregate functions, 637
Align Selected Objects, 835–836
Align to Slide, 835
Align Top, 845
alignment
  in cells, 321
  center, 18, 128–129, 324
  in column text, 265
  defining, 18, 128
  formatting text with, 27–30
  justified, 128–129, 265
  objects, 835–837
  paragraphs, 128–130
  positioning pictures and, 113
  in presentations, 781–782
  tab, 139–140
  table text, 907–908
  text, 323–324, 781–782
  types of, 128, 129
  videos, 896
  WordArt objects, 845
alignment guides, 23, 111
All Files, 82
alt text, 36–37, 41–44
alternative text, 36–37
American Psychological Association (APA), 237, 245, 249
AND condition, 628–629, 685
animation
  charts, 918–920
  defining, 888
  duration and delay timing options, 892–893
  entrance effects and effect options, 888–891
  morph transitions, 919–920
  removing, 893–894

  reordering, 891
  start options, 891–892
Animation Painter, 893–894
APA. *See* American Psychological Association
append, 530
Application Parts, 561
applications, 46–47
apps
  Calculator, 67–68
  desktop, 3
    closing, 40–41
    Notepad, 82
    Snipping Tool, 54
    WordPad, 78
  Microsoft Store, 47
  Weather, 67–68
  web, 522
arguments, 390
  defining, 391
arithmetic operators, 351–352
Arrange group, 835, 837
Art Deco, 834
artistic effects, 114–115, 760
ascending order, 606–607
aspect ratio, 773
asterisk (*) wildcard character, 632–633
Auto Fill, 322
AutoCalculate, 352
AutoComplete, 321
AutoCorrect, 136–137
  adding entries, 194–195
AutoFit, 177–178, 343, 757, 970
AutoFormat, 136
automatic numbered lists, 136
automatic updates, 46
AutoNumber data type, 527
AutoSave, 6–7
AutoSum, 327–328, 353, 422–423, 426, 954–955
AVERAGE function, 389–391, 410
Avg function, 637–638
axis
  category, 335, 485
  defining, 485
  fonts, 490–491
  formatting, 485–488
  value, 335, 485

B

Back button, 76
background fill colors, applying to slides, 883–884
Background Removal command, 843–844
backgrounds
  desktop, 52
  hiding graphics, 882–883, 961

  hiding objects, 883
  pictures, 885–887
  resetting, 887
  styles, 881–882
  texture, 884–885
  transparency, 885–887
Backstage tabs, 8
Backstage view, 4, 8–9, 38, 407, 430–431
banding (rows/columns in Excel tables), 405
bar charts, 955–957
base (Excel formula value), 477–478
Best Fit column width, 538
Between . . . And comparison operator, 627–628
bevels, 467, 834
bibliographies, 244
Bing, 53
  online picture search with, 819–820
black slides, 761
blank desktop databases, 522
blank documents, 5
blank presentations, 747
body (of letters), 194
Body font, 880
bold, 29
bookmarks, inserting, 39
booting computers, 49
borders
  adding to paragraphs, 276–278
  applying to pictures, 272
  bottom, on paragraphs, 193
  page, 115–116
  table, 183–186
Borders and Shading dialog box, 115–116
bottom borders, applying to paragraphs, 193
bound (forms), 677
bound controls, 688
Bovee, Courtland, 195–197
brightness, 271–272
bullet characters, 817–818
  customizing, 137–139
Bullet Library, 138
bulleted lists, 134–135, 815
  changing to numbered lists, 816
  creating SmartArt graphics from, 847–848
  in Google Docs, 147–148
  symbol shapes and colors, 817
  in tables, 176–177
bullets, 134
  customizing, 137–139
  removing bullet symbols from, 818–819
  symbols, 817–818

Bullets gallery, 817
Business Communication Today (Bovee and Thill), 195
business letters, 192

C

calculated controls, 705, 711
calculated fields, 634–636
Calculator app, 67–68
Calibri Light font, 28
Cambria font, 27
Caption property, 527
Cascade Delete Related Records option, 602, 605, 625
cascade options, 602
  testing, 604–605
Cascade Update Related Fields option, 601, 605, 625
Cascade Update Related Records option, 601
category axis, 335, 485
category labels, 335, 911
cell addresses, 320
cell contents, 320
cell margins, 179–180
cell references, 320, 910
  absolute, 354–356, 461
  formula copying and, 354–356
  relative, 329, 461
Cell Styles, 330
  Percent, 357
Cell Styles gallery, 349
cells, 904
  alignment in, 321
  clearing
    contents, 416–417
    formatting, 416–417
  defining, 317
  formatting, 357
  merging, 179–180
center alignment, 18, 128–129, 324
centering text, 324
  worksheets, 339–340
chart elements, 913
Chart Elements button, 336, 464, 913
Chart Filters button, 336, 913
chart layouts, 336
chart sheets, 462–463
  printing workbooks with, 473
chart styles
  applying, 335–338, 913–914
  defining, 337, 913
  formatting line charts with, 917
Chart Styles button, 336, 913
Chart Styles gallery, 337
Chart Tools, applying chart styles with, 335–338
chart types, 333
charts
  from Access queries, 644–645
  alt text on, 41–44
  animating, 918–920

applying styles to, 335–338
bar, 955–957
category labels, 911
column, 333–335, 910
copying and pasting
  to other programs, 955–962
  into PowerPoint, 961–962
  into Word, 960
defining, 332
deleting data from, 915–916
editing data after closing worksheets, 913
formatting
  area of, 470
  elements of, 464–466
  titles, 464
funnel, 491, 493–494
inserting
  in presentations, 910–911
  with Recommended Charts, 332–335
legends, 910
line, 483–491, 495, 915–917
map, 491–492
morph transitions, 919–920
moving to chart sheets, 462–463
pie, 461–470, 957–959
shadow effects, 468
3-D effects, 466–467
updating, 470–471
Check Accessibility, 38
Check Compatibility, 38
Chrome browser, 11
citations
  for books, 244–245
  corporate authors, 245
  defining, 244
  editing, 245–247
  for websites, 247–248
Clear Formats, 416
click, defined, 51
clip, defined, 819
Clipboard, 32–36, 69
  files in, 86
cloud computing, 7
  saving files to cloud, 6
  storage, 7, 49, 54, 59
  subscription services, 3
collaboration, 150
Collapse the Ribbon, 25
Collections option, 61
Colorful theme, 3
colors
  changing with eyedropper, 831–832
  font, 780–781
  formatting text with, 27–30
  recent, 832
  text, 118, 844
  theme, 28, 360–362, 879–880
column break indicators, 265
column breaks, 265
column charts, 333–335, 345–346
  inserting in presentations, 910–911

column headings, 319, 343
  in File Explorer window, 73
  inserting columns and, 359
Column Layout feature (Read Mode), 255
Column Width command, 210
columns
  adjusting size of, 323–324
  adjusting widths, 177–178, 359–360, 537–539
  banding, 405
  defining, 319
  deleting, 358–359, 906
  distributing, 908
  formatting multiple, 264
  freezing, 401
  inserting, 358–359, 905–906
  justifying text in, 265
  manual breaks in, 262
  moving, 388–389
  selecting one, 182
  sparklines, 426–427
  of text, 262–264
  wrapping text in, 359–360
Comma Style, 331
commands
  context-sensitive, 14
  performing
    from dialog box, 15–17
    from Quick Access Toolbar, 19–20
    from Ribbon, 21–24
Comments, 6
common fields, 522, 600
Community group, 43
comparison operators, 396
  Between . . . And, 627–628
  criteria using, 626–627
complimentary closing, 194
compound criteria, 628–630
Compress Media, 899–900
compressed files, 10
Compressed Folder Tools, 10–11, 65, 74
compressing video, 898–900
computers
  booting, 49
  signing in, 49–52
conditional formatting, 397–398, 411
constant values, 320
content, defining, 101
content layout, inserting SmartArt graphics, 850
Content Layout, inserting tables into slides with, 904
content pane, 58
content placeholders, 756
context menus, 14, 57
context sensitive, defined, 322
context-sensitive commands, 14
contextual tabs, 24, 58
contiguous slides, 784–785
contrast, 272–273
controls
  adding, resizing, and moving in Layout View, 690–692

aligning in Design view, 712–714
bound, 688
calculated, 705, 711
date, 713
deleting in Layout view, 709–710
formatting in Layout view, 692–693, 709–710
grouping in Layout view, 688–689
label, 688, 689, 706, 710–711
layout, 690
media, 895–896
modifying in Layout view, 710–712
page number, 713
text box, 688, 691, 704, 705, 711
types of, 688
unbound, 688
copy, 32–36, 69
Excel charts, 955–962
files, 86, 89
SmartArt graphics, 963–964
copying files, 89–90
copyright information, 820
Cortana, 53
COUNT function, 395
COUNTIF function, 395, 410
cover letters, 192
creating, 194–201
cover pages, 252–255
creating electronic images, 41
creating folders, 87–88
Creative Commons, 819
credit lines, 820
criteria, 395
adding, 616
comparison operators in, 626–627
compound, 628–630
defining, 615
Is Null, 618–619
numeric, 626
in parameter queries, 641–643
specifying in queries, 615–619
text, 616
crop, 268, 823–825
crop handles, 268, 823
crop pointer, 268, 824
Crop to Shape command, 825
crosshair pointer, 827
crosstab queries, 639–641
Currency data type, 526
Custom Footer, 430
Custom Format, 398
custom web app, 522
Customize Quick Access Toolbar, 20
cut, 32–36

D

dashboards, 51
data, 521
creating Word tables from Access, 969–971
defining, 46, 320

deleting from charts, 915–916
displays of, 325
entering by range, 350–351
entering into worksheets, 320–326
field creation by entering, 526
grouping, in printed reports, 714–716
importing from Excel workbooks, 530–532
inserting into Word documents, 970–971
modifying linked, 968
moving, 393
using in mail merge, 971–975
data bar, 398
data entry, 673
Data Labels, 465
data management, 47
data markers, 336, 463, 912
data points, 336, 463, 913
data series, 336, 463, 912
formatting with shadow effects, 468
formatting with 3-D effects, 466–467
data source, 279, 542, 608, 973
data types
assigning to fields, 524–526
AutoNumber, 527
changing, 527
Currency, 526
defining, 525
Number, 560
Short Text, 526, 560
database management system (DBMS), 521
database templates, 522
databases, 517. *See also* **fields; records**
applying themes to, 703
blank desktop, 522
closing, 549–550
creating from templates, 555–556
design principles for, 522
flat, 521
forms as interface to, 679
opening and saving, 597, 673–674, 702–703
opening existing, 623
planning, 521–522
relational, 521, 630
starting with blank, 523–524
Datasheet view, 525
query results in, 612
sorting queries in, 615
date controls, 713
Date & Time command, 195
Date & Time functions, 400
dateline, 194
dates
entering and formatting, 414–416
Excel interpreting, 415
inserting, 195–197
DBMS. *See* **database management system**
default, 12
deleting files, 87, 94
descending order, 606–607

deselect, 18
design grid, 609
calculated field formatting in, 636
hiding fields in, 617–618
modifying queries in, 612–613
sorting queries in, 615
Design Ideas pane, 758, 820
Design view, 525
aligning controls in, 712–714
deleting table field in, 532–533
modifying forms in, 693–696
modifying queries in, 612–614
query creation in, 608–609
sorting queries in, 615
viewing primary key in, 535
desktop, 47, 52
desktop applications, 3
desktop apps, 3
closing, 40–41
Notepad, 82
Snipping Tool, 54
WordPad, 78
desktop backgrounds, 52, 53
desktop shortcuts, 82
destination tables, 530
Detail section, 694
detail sheets, 425
Details pane, 76, 77
Details view, 87
dialog box, 6
defining, 54, 80
elements of, 16–17, 81
performing commands from, 15–17
Dialog Box Launcher, 34
Dictate feature, 44
Display settings, 48
displayed values, 325
Distribute Horizontally, 837
Distribute Vertically, 836
Document Formatting group, 191
Document Info, 37–38
document properties, 8, 37–38, 251–252
adding, 122–123
for workbooks, 341
document settings, defaults, 106
documents
activating Show/Hide in, 12
blank, 5
creating electronic images of, 41
inspecting, 38
Documents folder, 82, 86, 87
dot leader, 142
double spacing, 130
double-click, 64
downloads
defining, 10
zipped files, 11–14, 65–66
drag, 13, 60
drag and drop, 393
moving text with, 199–200
drawing objects, 108
Drawing Tools Format tab, 828–829, 837

drives, 54
Drop Shadow Rectangle style, 24
duplicating objects, 834

E

edit, 10
Edit Alt Text, 36
Edit Relationships dialog box, 600,
   601–602, 625, 673–674
editing
   chart data after closing worksheet, 913
   citations, 245–247
   enable, 11, 105
   enabling, 11
   presentations, 751, 773–778
   relationships, 602
   slides, 755–757
   text, 11–14
   values
      with Formula Bar, 357
      in worksheet, 356–357
   workbooks, 470–471
Editor, 201–206
Editor pane, 14–15
Effect Options, 889–890
ellipsis, 16
em dashes, 275–276
emphasis effects, 888
empty fields, finding with *Is Null* criteria,
   618–619
Enable Editing, 11, 105
enclosures, 194
endnotes, 240
Enforce Referential Integrity option,
   601, 625
enhanced ScreenTip, 21
Enter Parameter Value dialog box, 642
entering dates, 414–416
entering numbers, 325
entering text, 11–14
enterprise funds, 461
entrance effects
   applying, 888–891
   defining, 888
envelopes, addressing and printing, 206–207
Error Checking, 354
error messages, resolving, 393
Excel, 313
   copying and pasting PowerPoint objects
      into, 962–964
   exporting Access data to, 947–949
   linking data to Word documents from,
      966–967
   pointer, 319
   resolving error messages, 393
   starting, 317–320
   window parts, 318
   workbook window elements, 319
Excel table
   converting to ranges, 405
   creating, 402, 949

filtering, 404–405
inserting total rows in, 950
sorting, 403, 949
exit effects, 888
Expand Formula Bar button, 319
Expand horizontal scroll bar
   button, 318
explode, 469
exporting
   Access data to Excel, 947–949
   Access queries to spreadsheets, 718–719
   Access tables to spreadsheets, 551
   to Excel spreadsheets, 948
   forms to spreadsheets, 698–699
   Relationship Report to PDF, 620–621
   reports to Word files, 718–719
   to RTF files, 969–970
   tables to spreadsheets, 551–552
expressions, 634
External Data tab, 948, 969
extract, 10
   with File Explorer, 73–74
   zipped files, 11–14, 65–66
Extract All, 11
Extract tab, 11
eyedropper, 831–832

F

Facet theme, 747
Few, Stephen, 313
field lists, 599, 600, 609
field properties, 534
fields
   changing data type, 527
   changing size of, 533–534
   common, 522, 600
   creating by entering data, 526
   in crosstab queries, 640
   data type and name assignment,
      524–526
   deleting, 532–533
   duplicate or incorrect names, 609
   filtering data by selection of one,
      679–680
   finding empty, 618–619
   hiding in query results, 617–618
   ID, 526
   inserting in footers, 120–121
   mail merge, 973–975
   renaming, 527
   selecting in Report Wizard, 707
   setting size of, 527
   structure of, 525
File Explorer, 11, 52, 55
   copying and moving files by snapping
      windows in, 92–93
   copying files in, 89–90
   displaying locations, folders, and files
      with, 74–78
   extracting zipped files with, 73–74
   navigating with, 71–73

OneDrive and, 54
parts of window, 56–57
searching, pinning, sorting, and filtering
   in, 84–85
window parts, 73
zipped folders in, 65
File Explorer window, 56
file lists, 56, 58, 64, 73, 76, 87–88
   All Files type in, 82
   quick access, 71
file name extensions, 82
file names, 64
   in footer, 37, 120–121
file properties, 76
File tab, 4, 6, 8
files, 6
   compressed, 10
   copying, 89–90
      from removable storage, 85–86
      by snapping windows, 92–93
   creating and saving, 59–65
   creating folder for storing, 54–59
   defining, 54
   deleting, 87, 94
   displaying with File Explorer, 74–78
   inserting text from, 173–176
   linking with Paste Special, 966–967
   moving, 85–86, 90–91
   opening, 80–83
   renaming, 87–88
   saving after naming, 9
   selecting, 91
   zipped, 11–14
fill colors, 830
   applying to slides, 883–884
Fill Effects dialog box, 16
fill handles, 954–955
   Auto Fill with, 322
   formula copying with, 328–329
Fill Series, 322
fills
   defining, 16
   gradient, 16
   slide backgrounds, 883–884
Filter By Form, 681–682
Filter By Selection command, 679
filtered lists, 85
filtering
   defining, 679
   Excel tables, 404–405
   in File Explorer, 84–85
   by one field, 679–680
   using Advanced Filter/Sort command,
      684–685
   using Filter By Form, 681–682
filters
   applying to Excel tables, 404–405
   clearing, 405
financial numbers, formatting, 330–332
Find and Replace dialog box, 198, 678
Find and Replace feature, 399
finding text, 197–199, 778

Firefox browser, 11
extracting files with, 65
Fit All Columns on One Page, 407–408
Flash Fill, 387–388
flat databases, 521
flip commands, 272
floating objects, 118
Fly In entrance effect, 889, 892
flyers, creating with Google Docs, 124–125
Focus mode, 255
folder structure, 70
folder windows, 72
folders, 6
creating, 87–88
for file storage, 7–10
new, 54–59
defining, 54
displaying with File Explorer, 74–78
Documents, 82, 86, 87
parent, 57
renaming, 87–88
font effects, small caps, 274–275
Font gallery, 28
fonts
axis, 490–491
body, 880
changing in presentations, 779–780
chart title formatting, 464
colors, 27–30, 780–781
default, 106
formatting text with, 27–30
headings, 880
sans serif, 28
serif, 28
sizes, 28, 106, 117, 779–780
styles, 27–30, 780–781
theme, 28, 880–881
footers
in Access objects, 539
adding file name to, 37, 120–121
custom, 430
defining, 37
form, 694, 695
group, 713
inserting, 37–38
fields in, 120–121
on slide handouts, 764–765
in objects, 539
page, 713
repeating, 429–431
report, 713
in worksheets, 339–340
footnotes
defining, 240
inserting, 240–241
modifying style, 241–244
symbols for, 241
foreign keys, 600, 630
Form Footer, 694, 695
Form Header, 694

Form Layout Tools
Arrange tab, 689, 691
Design tab, 690
Format tab, 690
Form tool, 674–675
Form view, 546, 676, 695
Form Wizard, 685–687
Format Background pane, 961
Fill, 884
Hide Background Graphics, 883
transparency, 886
Format Chart Area pane, 488–489
Format Data Labels pane, 465–466
Format Data Series pane, 466–467, 468–469
Format Painter, 478, 493
creating bulleted lists and, 176–177
customizing bullets, 138
formatting text with, 30–32
Format Picture pane, 823
formatting
axes, 485–488
bar charts, 955–957
calculated fields, 636
Cell Styles, 330
cells, 329–332
chart area, 470, 488–489
chart elements, 464–466
clearing existing, 109
clearing from cells, 416–417
conditional, 397–398, 411
controls, in Layout view, 692–693
dates, 414–416
defining, 15
exploding and coloring pie chart slices, 469
financial numbers, 330–332
footnotes, 241–244
with Format Painter, 30–32
forms, 690
grouped worksheets, 423
with individual commands, 332
line chart fonts, 490–491
line charts, 917
multiple columns, 264
multiple worksheets, 429–431
numbers, 325
objects, 830–838
Paste Special and, 481
picture styles, 759–760
pie charts, 464–470, 957–959
plot area gridlines, 490–491
presentations, 778–783
research paper, 237–240
Screen Clipping, 273
shadow effects, 468
shapes, 117–118
SmartArt graphics, 144–145
sparklines, 338–339
tables, 177–186, 951–952
text, 27–30
text boxes, 119–120

with text effects, 108
3-D effects, 466–467
worksheets, 358–362
formatting marks, 12, 106
showing, 105
forms
adding, resizing, and moving controls, 690–692
adding records using, 676–677
creating, 545–547, 674–675
creating with wizard, 685–687
as database interface, 679
defining, 673
deleting records using, 678
exporting to spreadsheets, 698–699
formatting in Layout view, 690
modifying
in Design view, 693–696
in Layout view, 687–692
multiple-items, 556–557
printing, 696–697
printing as PDFs, 547, 697
single-record, 556–557
Formula Auditing group, 342–343
Formula AutoComplete, 476
Formula Bar, 321–322, 327, 328, 348, 477
editing values with, 357
showing, 954
formulas, 320
absolute cell references and copying, 354–356
constructing, 326–328
copying, 328–329
displaying, 342–343
on grouped worksheets, 419–422
mathematical operations with, 351–356
parentheses in, 476–477
point and click method for constructing, 327
printing, 343–344
referring to cells in another worksheet, 425
underlying, 327
free-form snips, 62
Freeze Panes command, 401
freezing panes, 400–401
frequent folders area, 56
full-screen snips, 62
Function Arguments dialog box, 390
functions
AVERAGE, 389–391, 410
COUNT, 395
COUNTIF, 395, 410
Date & Time, 400
defining, 326
Google Sheets, 410
IF, 396–397, 410
IFS, 427–429
logical, 395
MAX, 392
MEDIAN, 391–392
MIN, 392

functions (*continued*)
  NOW, 400
  statistical, 387
  SUM, 326 328, 389–391, 410, 422, 423
  volatile, 400
funds, 461
funnel charts, 491, 493–494

G

galleries, 18
general formats, 325
general funds, 461
Glow, 834
Goal Seek, 471–472
Google Docs, 564, 644–645
  creating flyers with, 124–125
  creating information handouts with,
    147–148
  creating tables in, 212–213
  editing reports in, 718–719
  editing resumes in, 188–189
  formatting newsletters in, 284–285
  Research Bar, 259–260
Google Drive, 551, 564
Google Sheets, 345–346, 433–434,
  551–553, 699–700
  functions, 410
  inventory valuation reports using, 363–364
  line charts in, 495
  pie charts, 474
  summarizing inventory lists, 410–411
Google Slides, 770, 789
  advertisement presentations with,
    856–857
  informational presentations with,
    839–840, 901–902
  summary and analysis presentations with,
    922–923
gradient fills, 16, 845
grammar checking, 202–205
graphical user interface (GUI), 47
graphics, 108
  copying, 32
  cutting, 32
  hiding background, 882–883
gridlines, 183–186
Group, Sort, and Total pane, 715
Group Footer, 713
Group Header, 713
group names, 6
  displaying, 12
grouped worksheets
  formatting, 423
  formatting and constructing formulas on,
    419–422
  multiple totals on, 422–423
grouping
  data, in printed report, 714–716
  objects, 837–838
  records, in query, 638–639
groups, 19
GUI, 47

H

hamburger menus, 61
hamburgers, 61
  history of icon, 65
handouts
  inserting headers and footers on,
    764–765
  printing, 767–768
hard disk drives, 54
  copying files to, 85
Header and Footer dialog box, 765
Header & Footer tab, 340
headers
  in Access objects, 539
  form, 694
  group, 713
  inserting on slide handouts, 764–765
  page, 713
  report, 713
  section, 756
headings
  column, 73, 319, 343, 359
  in File Explorer window, 73
  fonts, 880
  row, 320, 358
Headings font, 880
Help buttons, 56
Help features, 41–44
Help panes, 42
Help & Support group, 43
hiding worksheets, 420
hierarchies, 70
Highlight Cells Rules, 398
Home tab, 4
horizontal rulers, 822–823, 826
  tab alignment and, 140
hyperlinks, 187, 273

I

icons, 47, 143
  inserting, 145–146
ID fields, 526
IF function, 396–397, 410
IFS function, 427–429
Illustrations group, 39
images, credit lines below, 820
Import Spreadsheet Wizard, 530,
  558, 623
importing
  adding tables to databases through,
    535–537, 623–624
  from Excel workbook to Access table,
    530–532
indenting
  defining, 239
  paragraphs, 131–133, 238–240
  in research paper formatting, 238–240
  text, 131–133
Info tab, 8, 38
information, 521
information handouts, 147–148

informational presentations, 839–840,
  901–902
inline objects, 109
innermost sort fields, 607
input devices, 47
Insert Chart dialog box, 333–335
Insert Hyperlink dialog box, 273
Insert tab, Illustrations group, 39
Insert Table dialog box, 904
Insert Video dialog box, 895
inserting 3D models, 39
inserting bookmarks, 39
inserting pictures from files, 757–759
insertion point, 11, 47
inside addresses, 194
Inspect Document, 38
Inverse page color, 210
Is Not Null **criteria, 618**
Is Null **criteria, 618–619**
italics, 29–30

J

join lines, 602, 702
JPEG files, 64
Jump List, 54
justified alignment, 128, 129
  in column text, 265

K

keep source formatting check box, 36,
  774
keyboards, 50
keyboard shortcuts, 13, 66, 323
  for movement, 33, 34
  using, 32–36
KeyTips, 25
keywords, 38

L

label controls, 688, 689, 706, 710–711
labels, 320
  formatting data, 465–466
landscape orientation, 25
Layout Options, 22
  text wrap settings in, 109
  wrapping text around picture using,
    110–111
layout selectors, 689
Layout view, 549, 674
  adding, resizing, and moving controls in,
    690–692
  applying themes to forms in, 690
  deleting controls in, 709–710
  formatting controls in, 692–693, 709–710
  formatting forms in, 690
  grouping controls in, 688–689
  modifying controls in, 710–711
  modifying forms in, 687–692
  modifying reports in, 704–706
layouts, 751

leader characters, 142
Learning Tools, 210–211
left alignment, 128, 129, 321
legends, 335, 463, 910
lettered column headings, 319
letterheads, 191
line break indicators, 192, 278
line charts
    analyzing trends with, 495
    creating, 482–485, 915–916
    defining, 482
    formatting, 917
        axes, 485–488
        chart area, 488–489
        plot area gridlines and fonts, 490–491
line spacing, 782
    default, 106
    options for, 130
    setting, 130–131
LinkedIn, 173–175
links, 530
    updating, 967, 968
list levels, 754
lists
    bulleted, 134–135, 147–148, 176–177,
        815, 816
    ending, 137
    filtered, 85
    numbered, 135–137, 147–148, 815, 816
Live Layout, 111–112
Live Preview, 18, 24, 82
live tiles, 51
locations, 6, 56
    displaying with File Explorer, 74–78
lock screen, 50
logical functions, 395
logical operators, 628
logical tests, 396, 428

M

mail merge, 279–283
    inserting fields for, 973–975
    starting, 972–973
    using Access data in, 971–975
Mail Merge Recipients dialog box,
    972–973
Mail Merge Wizard, 279–281
mailing labels, 279–283
main document, 279
Major unit, 487
manual column breaks, 262
manual line breaks, 191–193, 278
manual page breaks, 248
many-to-many relationships, 604
map charts, 491–492
margins
    cell, 179–180
    default, 106
    defining, 127
    setting, 127–128
MAX function, 392–393, 637–638

Maximize button, 56, 60
media controls, 895–896
MEDIAN function, 391–392
menu bars, 62
menu icons, 61
menus
    defining, 62
    hamburger, 61
Merge Cells, 180
Merge & Center, 329–330
merging table cells, 179–180
Message Bar, security warnings on,
    597–598
metadata, 8. See also document
    properties
Microsoft account, 48, 49
    creating, 7
    presenting Word documents online and,
        186
Microsoft Edge browser, 11, 52
    extracting files with, 65
Microsoft Mixed Reality, 61
Microsoft Office, 49
    checking file compatibility, 38
    color themes, 3
    exploring, 4–5
    help features, 41–44
    linking tools in, 966–967
Microsoft Print to PDF, 769
Microsoft Store, 52
Microsoft Store app, 47
Microsoft XPS Document Writer, 769
Min function, 637–638
MIN function, 392
mini toolbar, 13
    Styles on, 18
Minimize button, 56, 66
minimizing Ribbon, 25, 57, 72
MLA. See Modern Language Association
Modern Language Association (MLA),
    237, 245, 247–249
modifying linked data, 968
morph transitions, 919–920
most recently used, 29
mouse, 50
mouse pointer, 11, 51, 63
move, 90
movement keyboard shortcuts, 33, 34
moving files, 90–91
MRU, 29
multi-column newsletters, 262–273
multiple 1.08 spacing, 130
multiple-items forms, 556–557

N

name boxes, 321
nameplates, 263
navigate, 56, 413
    with File Explorer, 71–73
navigation area, 532

navigation pane, 9, 55, 57, 64, 71, 73, 84,
    87
    going to specific page with, 250–251
    quick access area of, 82
Navigation Pane, 525, 558
    copying queries, 612
    grouping objects in, 559–560
    viewing reports and, 563
network notification icons, 52
New Slide button, 751–753
newsletters
    formatting
        in Google Docs, 284–285
        multi-column, 262–273
    inserting pictures, 266–268
No Paragraph Space style, 192
noncontiguous slides, 785
nonprinting characters, 12, 106
Normal template, 208
normal view, 317, 748
normalization, 522
Notepad desktop app, 82
notes, 240
notes pages, 764
Notes pane, 755
notification areas, 52
NOW function, 400
Number data type, 560
number formats, 325
    Accounting, 42
number values, 320
numbered lists, 134, 135–137, 815
    automatic, 136
    changing bulleted list to, 816
    in Google Docs, 147–148
numbered row headings, 319
Numbering gallery, 817
numbers
    entering, 325
    formatting, 325
    formatting financial, 330–332
    slide, 765–766
numeric criteria, 626

O

object anchors, 110
Object dialog box, 107
object tabs, 525, 537
object windows, 525
Object Zoom, 255
objects, 22, 522
    aligning and distributing
        relative to each other, 837
        relative to slide, 835–837
    changing color with eyedropper, 831–832
    drawing, 108
    duplicating, 835
    floating, 118
    formatting, 830–838
    grouping, 838–839
        in Navigation Pane, 559–560

objects (*continued*)
headers and footers in, 539
hiding background, 883
inline, 109
moving with arrow keys, 823
PDF images of, 541
renaming, 702–703
WordArt, 844–845
Office 365, 3, 7, 46
Office 365 accounts, 59
Office Intelligent Services, 44, 253
Office Presentation Service, 186
On Click timing option, 891
One-click Row/Column Insertion, 178–179
OneDrive, 6–8, 49, 54, 57, 82, 87, 743
cloud storage with, 59
OneDrive for Business, 6
one-to-many relationships, 598, 600
creating, 624–626
one-to-one relationships, 604
Online 3D Models dialog box, 39
Online Pictures, inserting, 819–821
opening data files, 80–83
operating systems, 46
operators, 419
arithmetic, 351–352
comparison, 396
defining, 351
option buttons, 17
OR condition, 629–630, 681
order of operations, 476
outermost sort fields, 607
Outline View, 776–777

P

page borders, 115–116
page break indicators, 248
page breaks, 248
Page Color, 15–17, 210–211
Page Footer, 713
Page Header, 713
page number controls, 713
page numbering
in research paper formatting, 238–240
suppressing on first page of documents, 240
page orientation, changing, 25–26, 342–344
Page Setup, 127, 407
forms, 697
page orientation, 343
Page Width zoom, 25–26
panes
defining, 401
freezing and unfreezing, 400–401
splitting worksheet windows into, 406
Panoramic Picture with Caption layout, 752

paragraph symbol, 12
paragraphs
adding borders to, 276–278
adding shading to, 276–278
aligning, 128–130
bottom borders, 193
default spacing, 106
indenting, 131–133, 238–240
line spacing, 130–131
space before and after, 133–134
spacing, 133–134
parameters, defining, 642
parameter queries, 641–643
parent folders, 57
parentheses, in formulas, 476–477
parenthetical references, 245
Password box, 51
paste, 32–36
Excel charts, 955–962
files, 86, 89
SmartArt graphics, 963–964
paste area, 418
Paste dropdown menu, 34
Paste Options gallery, 34–36, 417–418
Paste Special, 480–482
linking files with, 966–967
paths, 59, 70
PDF files, 41, 769
creating from database objects, 541
exporting Relationship Report to, 620–621
printing single forms in, 547, 697
from spreadsheets, 553
PDF Reflow, 255–258
pens, 47
Pen button arrow, 63
percent for new value, 478–479
percent of increase, 479
Percent Style, 357
percentages, calculating, 356, 478–479
percentage rate of increase, 476
personal folders, 86
Picture Effects, 114, 833–835, 836
picture elements, 323
Picture Strips, 850
picture styles, 114
Picture Styles group, 24
Picture Tools, 22, 759
Format tab, 23, 24, 112, 823, 824, 835, 843–844
Size group, 823–825
pictures
adding to presentations, 757–760
aligning, 23, 113
applying borders to, 272
applying styles to, 759–760
applying to slide background, 885–887
artistic effects on, 114–115, 760
brightness and contrast of, 271–272
changing shape of, 825
cropping, 268–270, 823–825
flipping, 272

inserting
from file, 757–759
in newsletters, 266–268
in slides, 821
in SmartArt graphic, 850
in Word documents, 109
positioning, 112–113, 822–823
recoloring, 270–271
removing backgrounds from, 843–844
resizing, 111–112
scaling, 268–270
setting transparent colors, 270–271
sizing, 821–822
sizing and rotating, 758
wrapping text around, 110–111
pie charts, 957–959
calculating values for, 461–462
creating, 462–463
defining, 461
exploding and coloring slices, 469
formatting, 464–470
in Google Sheets, 474
rotating, 468
Pin to Quick access, 84
Pinned tab, 4
pinning, in File Explorer, 84–85
pixels, 323, 324
placeholder text, 143, 756
selecting, 815–816
placeholders, 749
content, 756
inserting Online Pictures in, 819–821
text alignment and, 781
playback options, for video in presentations, 898–900
plot areas, 485
formatting gridlines, 490–491
.png files, 68
point and click method, 327
point to, 51
pointers, 11, 47
pointing device, 47
points, 28
populate, 528
Portable Document Format, 41
Portable Network Graphic, 68
portrait orientation, 25
positioning
pictures, 112–113
text boxes, 119–120
PowerPoint, 743
copying and pasting Excel charts into, 961–962
copying and pasting objects into Excel from, 962–964
inserting saved files into, 66
Presenter View elements, 762
rulers, 822–823
window parts and screen elements, 747–749
Present Online, 187
Presentation Views group, 776

presentations, 743. *See also* **slides**
  adding pictures to, 757–760
  advertisement, 856–857
  applying slide transitions to, 786–788
  applying themes to, 750–751
  background styles, 881–882
  blank, 747
  changing fonts and font sizes, 779–780
  charts in, 910–911
  deleting and moving slides, 777
  displaying in Reading view, 787–788
  editing, 751, 773–778
  entering text, 749–750
  font styles and colors, 780–781
  formatting, 778–783
  in Google Slides, 770
  informational, 839–840, 901–902
  inserting new slides, 751–753
  inserting saved files into, 66
  inserting slides from existing, 774–775
  outlines, 776–777
  printing
    handouts, 767–768
    speaker notes, 769
  speaker notes in, 755
  summary and analysis, 922–923
  text alignment in, 781–782
  theme colors, 879–880
  theme fonts, 880–881
  themes, 747
  videos in, 895–900
  viewing, 761–766
Presenter View, 762–764
Preview pane, 77
primary keys, 630
  relationships and, 600
  viewing in Design view, 535
Print Layout view, 106
Print Preview, 40–41, 122–123, 430–431, 539–542, 602–603
  adding to Quick Access Toolbar, 20
  for presentation handouts, 767–768
  for speaker notes, 769
Print Titles, 406, 407–409
printing, 40–41
  adding commands to Quick Access Toolbar for, 20
  envelopes, 206–207
  forms, 696–697
  formulas, 343–344
  grouping data for, 714–716
  handouts, 767–768
  mail merge results, 282–283
  page color and, 17
  presentation handouts, 767–768
  speaker notes, 769
  Word documents, 122–123
  workbooks, 341, 431–432
    with chart sheets, 473
  worksheets, 431–432
    sections, 342
    titles, 407–409

programs, 46
  pinning to taskbar, 53–54
  starting, 78–79
progress bars, 86
proofing, activating, 201
Proofing group, 14, 203, 205, 350
Properties dialog box, 77
Property Sheet, 546, 548, 691
pt, 28
Publish as PDF or XPS, 768

Q

quantitative information, 313
queries
  aggregate functions in, 637–638
  calculated fields in, 634–636
  closing, 610–611
  copying, 612
  creating, 542–544
    in Design view, 608–609
    from existing, 611–613
  crosstab, 639–641
  defining, 542
  exporting to spreadsheets, 644–645
  grouping records in, 638–639
  hiding fields in results, 617–618
  modifying design of, 612–613
  multiple tables in, 630–632
  numeric criteria in, 626
  parameter, 641–643
  renaming, 612
  running, 544, 610–611
  saving, 610–611
  sorting results of, 614–615
  specifying criteria in, 615–619
  wildcard characters in, 632–633
Query Wizard, crosstab query creation with, 639–641
question mark (?) wildcard character, 633
quick access area, 57, 73, 82
Quick access location, 71
Quick Access Toolbar, 6, 9
  customizing, 19–20
  in File Explorer, 57
  performing commands from, 19–20
  removing items from, 38
  undo with, 19
Quick Analysis tool, 324, 352–353
Quick Layout button, 336–337

R

range finder, 354
ranges, 324
  converting tables to, 405
  data entry by, 350–351
  for pie charts, 463
rates, 477
rates of increase, 476–477
Read Aloud, 210–211

Read Mode, 255–258
Reading view, 787–788
real-time co-authoring, 7
Recent Colors, 832
Recent Locations button, 57
Recent tab, 4
recolor, 270
recoloring pictures, 270–271
Recommended Charts, 332–335, 491
record selector bar, 547, 676
record selector box, 528
record sources, 702
records, 522
  adding
    to tables, 528–529, 971–972
  adding using forms, 676–677
  appending by importing from spreadsheet, 558
  deleting using forms, 678
  entering into new table, 561–562
  filtering
    by one field, 679–680
    using Filter By Form, 681–682
  grouping in query, 638–639
  sorting, 606–608
  subdatasheet, 603
  viewing, 674–675
rectangular snip, 62
Recycle Bin, 52, 87, 94
redundant, 522
reference pages, creating, 249
referential integrity, 601
relational database, 521, 630
Relationship Report, 602–603
  exporting to PDF, 620–621
relationships
  creating, 598–600, 624–626
  defining, 598
  editing or deleting, 602
  many-to-many, 604
  one-to-many, 598, 600, 624–626
  one-to-one, 604
  setting options for, 601–602
  viewing, 673–674, 702–703
Relationships window, 599, 600
relative cell references, 329, 461
removable storage devices, 54
  copying files from, 85
renaming files, 87–88
renaming folders, 87–88
renaming objects, 702–703
renaming worksheets, 413–414, 952
Replace All, 399
Replace command, 778
replacing text, 197–199, 778
Report Design Tools, 713
Report Footer, 713
Report Header, 713
Report Layout Tools, 703, 704
Report Tool, 703
Report Wizard, 706–709

reports
applying themes to, 703
creating
and modifying, 547–549
with Report Tool, 703
with wizard, 706–709
defining, 702
exporting to Word files, 718–719
grouping data for printed, 714–716
modifying design of, 709–714
modifying in Layout view, 704–706
Relationship, 602–603
viewing, 563
Research Bar, 259–260
research papers
creating, 237–240
formatting
page numbering and paragraph
indents, 238–240
spacing and first-page information,
237–238
inserting footnotes, 240–241
managing and modifying sources,
249–250
modifying footnote style, 241–244
Researcher, 252–255
resetting slide backgrounds, 887
resolution, screen, 24, 48
resources, 47
Restore Down command, 92
Resume Assistant, 173–176
resumes
creating table for, 171–177
editing in Google Docs, 188–189
Retrospect theme, 879–880
Reuse Slides, 774–775
RGB, 831
Ribbon
Display Options, 6
displaying full, 5
in File Explorer window, 57, 73
group names in, 12
minimizing, 25, 57, 72
performing commands from, 21–24
size of groups on, 24
tabs, 6
ribbons
defining, 55
elements of, 19
in File Explorer, 57
Rich Text Format (RTF), 718
exporting Access table to, 969–970
right alignment, 128, 129
rotating pie charts, 468
rotating text, 394–395
rotation handles, 109, 758
Round Convex, 834
rounding, 328
row headings, 320
inserting rows and, 358
rows
banding, 405
defining, 320

deleting, 906
distributing, 907–908
freezing, 401
inserting, 905–906
inserting and deleting, 358–359,
483–485
Rows, inserting, 950
RTF. *See* **Rich Text Format**
ruler guides, 826
rulers, 822–823, 824, 826
showing, 105
tab alignment and, 140
Run, 610
running queries, 544

S

salutations, 194
sans serif fonts, 28
Save As command, 9
scale, 268
Scale to Fit, 406, 407–409
scaling, 343
for data slightly larger than printed pane,
409
pictures, 268–270
Screen Clipping, 93, 273
screen readers, 37
screen resolutions, 24, 48
screenshot, 53, 273
ScreenTip, 17, 71
color coordinates in, 831
enhanced, 21
for Layout Options, 22
for Picture Styles, 24
proofing errors, 202
Tell me more prompt, 42
scroll arrow, 60
scroll bar, 60
scroll box, 60
Search box, 53, 57, 73
searching
in File Explorer, 84–85
USB flash drives and, 87
searching commands, 6
section bars, 694, 695
section breaks, 264
section headers, 756
sections, 264
security alerts, resolving, 597–598
select, 13, 59, 91
Select All box, 319
Select All Sheets, 421
select queries, 542
creating in Design view, 608
selecting
one column, 182
placeholder text, 815–816
sentences, spacing between, 106
Sepia page color, 210
series, 322
data, 336, 463
serif fonts, 28

shading, 115–116
adding to paragraphs, 276–278
Shading styles, 17
shadow effects, 468
Shape Effects, 834–835
Shape Fill, 118, 830
Shape Height, 23, 827–828
Shape Outline, 118, 830–831
shape styles, 830–831
applying, 833
formatting text box with, 119–120
Shape Styles group, 118, 830, 833
Shape Width, 828
shapes
adding in SmartArt graphic, 850
adding text to, 830
fills and outlines, 830–831
formatting, 117–118
inserting, sizing, and positioning,
116–117
inserting and sizing, 827–829
typing text in, 117–118
Share dialog box, 6
Shared with Me tab, 4
SharePoint, 85, 551, 564, 644
SharePoint Online, 6
Sheet tab scrolling buttons, 318
sheet tabs, 318, 413
Short Text data type, 526, 560
shortcut menu, 14, 33, 57
Show All Properties, 430
Show Formulas command, 342, 343
show hidden icons, 53
Show Me the Numbers (Few), 313
Show/Hide, 12
Side to Side command, 254
side to side page movements,
252–255
signature blocks, 194
signed-in user, 6
Simple Query Wizard, 542–544
simple select queries, 542
single spacing, 130, 192
single-record forms, 556–557
sizing handles, 22, 109, 111, 758, 837
sizing pictures, 821–822
Skype, 49, 187
slide handouts, inserting headers and
footers on, 764–765
Slide Layout gallery, 783
slide layouts, section header, 756
slide numbers, 765–766
Slide pane, 748, 749
displaying and editing slides in,
755–757
slide shows
animating, 888–894
Presenter View, 762–764
viewing, 761–762
Slide Sorter view
deleting slides in, 783–784
moving slides in, 784
selecting slides in, 784–785

slide transitions
applying, 786
multiple, 787
timing options, 786–787
slides, 747
background
fill color, 883–884
style, 881–882
textures, 884–885
black, 761
changing fonts and font sizes, 779–780
changing layout of, 783
changing size of, 773
creating tables in, 904–905
deleting and moving, 777
deleting in Slide Sorter view, 783–784
displaying and editing, 755–757
distributing objects relative to, 835–837
font styles and colors, 780–781
inserting
column charts in, 910–911
from existing presentation, 774–775
new, 751–753
pictures in any location on, 821
slide numbers on, 765–766
layouts, 751
list levels in, 754
moving in Slide Sorter view, 784
resetting backgrounds, 887
selecting in Slide Sorter view, 784–785
text alignment in, 781–782
title, 749
small caps, 274–275
smart guides, 822–823
Smart Lookup, 252–255
SmartArt graphics, 847
adding shapes in, 850
changing color and style of, 852–853
changing layout, 852
changing size and shape of elements of, 851–852
converting to text, 853–854
copying and pasting, 963–964
creating from bulleted points, 847–848
inserting, 962–963
inserting in Word documents, 143–144
inserting text and pictures in, 850
inserting using content layouts, 850
sizing and formatting, 144–145
types of, 847
SmartArt Styles, 852
Snap, 66–70
Snap Assist, 68
snapping windows, 92–93
Snipping Tool, 53, 63–64
menu bar, 62
Snipping Tool Desktop app, 54
snips, 53, 62
Soft Edges, 114, 834, 836
options, 843–844
Sort & Filter group, 606–607, 679–680
Advanced Filter/Sort command, 684–685

sorting
in ascending or descending order, 606–607
Excel tables, 403, 949
in File Explorer, 84–85
on multiple fields, 607–608
query results, 614–615
of records in table, 606–608
source files, 530
Source Manager, 245–246, 249–250
spacing
line, 106, 782
before and after paragraphs, 133–134
for research paper formatting, 237–238
between sentences, 106
single, 130, 192
after tables, 181–183
before tables, 183–186
sparklines, 332
column, 426–427
creating and formatting, 338–339
speaker notes, 755
printing, 769
speakers icon, 53
special characters, 275–276
spellchecking, 14–15, 202–205
in worksheets, 348–350
spelling suggestions, 14
spin boxes, 111
split buttons, 34, 69, 751
Split command, 406
spreadsheets
adding tables to databases by importing, 535–537, 623–624
appending database records by importing from, 558
defining, 317
exporting Access queries to, 644–645
exporting Access table to, 551
exporting forms to, 698–699
PDF images of, 553
Stacked layout, 689
Star Bullets, 817
Start button, 53
Start menu
as dashboard, 82
displaying, 51
parts of, 52–53
starting programs, 78–79
statistical functions, 387
statistics, calculating in query, 637–638
status bars, 6, 73, 318
structures, 525
style guides, 237
style sets, 191
changing, 207–208
styles, 241
applying to pictures, 759–760
background, 881–882
cell, 330
chart, 335–338, 913–914, 917
defining, 18
fonts, 27–30, 780–781

picture, 114
shape, 119–120, 830, 833
table, 200–201, 908, 909
video, 897
subdatasheets, 603
subfolders, 70, 75
subject lines, 194
subsets, 608, 679
Suggestions, 204
Sum function, 637–638
SUM function, 326–328, 389–391, 410, 422, 954–955
populating cells with, 423
summary and analysis presentations, 922–923
Summary Options, 708
summary sheet, 424, 425–426, 429
suppress, 240
Switch Row/Column command, 334–335
Syllables, 210
symbols
bullet, 817–818
for footnotes, 241
inserting, 275–276
paragraph, 12
synching, 7
synchronization, 7
synonyms, 205
system date, 400
system tray, 52

T

Tab Alignment, 139–140
Tab List, 848
Tab order, 676
tab stops
modifying, 141–142
setting, 139–140
table areas, 609
table effects, 909
table move handles, 183
table styles, 908, 909
applying, 200–201
Table styles, 402
Table Tools, 172, 560–561
Design tab, 908, 909
tables (Access), 522
adding by importing spreadsheets, 535–537, 623–624
adding descriptions to, 534
adding field descriptions, 533–534
adding records to, 528–529, 971–972
adding records using forms, 676–677
adjusting column widths, 537–539
creating, 524, 560–561
creating relationships, 598–600
creating Word table from, 969–971
deleting, 529
deleting fields from, 532–533
deleting records using forms, 678
destination, 530
entering records into new, 561–562

tables (Access) (*continued*)
  exporting to RTF file, 969–970
  exporting to spreadsheets, *551*
  field size settings, 527, 533–534
  forms bound to, 676
  importing Excel workbooks into, 530–532
  queries based on multiple, 630–632
  renaming, 529, 673–674
  sorting records in, 606–608
  viewing in Print Preview, 539–542
tables (Excel)
  converting to range, 405
  creating, 402, 949
  filtering, 404–405
  inserting total row in, 950
  sorting, 403, 949
tables (PowerPoint)
  aligning text in, 907–908
  creating, 904–905
  distributing columns in, 908
  distributing rows in, 907–908
  inserting rows and columns in, 905–906
  sizing, 906–907
tables (Word)
  adjusting column widths, 177–178
  borders, 183–186
  bulleted lists in, 176–177
  converting to text, 186
  copying and pasting into workbook, 952–954
  creating
    from Access data, 969–971
    Excel worksheet from, 951–955
    in Google Docs, 212–213
    for resume, 171–177
  defining, 171
  formatting, 177–186, 951–952
  inserting
    by defining dimensions, 171–172
    into documents, 200–201
  merging cells, 179–180
  modifying dimensions with One-click Row/Column Insertion, 178–179
  setting tabs in, 181
  spacing
    after, 181–183
    before, 183–186
  typing text in, 172–173
  viewing gridlines in, 183–186
Tables and Related Views category, 559–560
tabs, 19
  contextual, 24, 58
  Ribbon, 6
  setting, in tables, 181
tags, 38, 76
Task View, 53, 66–70
taskbars
  defining, 53
  File Explorer button on, 71
  pinning program to, 53

teams, 150
telephone numbers, 528
Tell Me feature, 41–44
Tell me more, 41–44
Tell me what you want to do box, 41
templates, 4
  database, 522
  database creation from, 555–556
  Normal, 208
  Word, 208–210
text
  adding to shapes, 830
  aligning, 321, 323–324, 781–782
  aligning in tables, 907–908
  applying WordArt Styles to, 844
  centering, 324
  color, 118, 844
  columns of, 262–264
  converting SmartArt graphic to, 853–854
  converting tables to, 186
  copying, 32
  cutting, 32
  editing, 11–14
  entering, 11–14
  entering in worksheets, 320–321
  finding and replacing, 197–199, 778
  formatting, 27–30
    with Format Painter, 30–32
    with text effects, 108
  indenting, 131–133
  inserting
    from another document, 107
    from file, 173–176
    in SmartArt graphic, 850
  in list levels, 754
  moving, 199–200
  presentation, 749–750
  rotating, 394–395
  selecting, 199–200
  typing
    in shapes, 117–118
    in tables, 172–173
  wrapping
    in columns, 359–360
    around picture, 110–111
text alignment, 323–324, 781–782
text boxes, 116
  controls, 688, 691, 704–705, 711
  formatting, 119–120
  inserting, 118–119, 826–827
  sizing and positioning, 119–120
text criteria, 616
text effects
  applying, 18–19
  formatting text with, 108
  in WordArt, 847
Text Effects and Typography gallery, 19
Text Fill, 844
Text from File command, 173
Text Highlight Color, 252–255
Text Outline, 844
text strings, 616

Text That Contains, 398
text values, 320
text wrapping, 22
  in columns, 359–360
  around pictures, 110–111
  settings for, 109
textures, background, 884–885
theme colors, 28, 879–880
theme fonts, 28, 880–881
themes
  applying
    to databases, 703
    to forms, 690
    to presentations, 750–751
    to reports, 703
  changing colors, 360–362
  colors, 28, 879–880
  PowerPoint, 743
  presentations, 747
  variants, 778–779
  workbook, 332
thesaurus, 205–206
Thill, John, 195–197
This PC, 57, 71
3-D effects, 466–467
3-D Models, 39
thumbnails, 68, 748
tiles, 56
  live, 51
Timeline, 69
Timing group, 786–787
timing options
  duration and delay, 892–893
  setting, 891–892
title bars, 6, 66
title slides, 749
toggle buttons, 30, 137
Toggle Filter button, 681, 684
toolbars, 9
total rows, 950
touch screens
  accessing shortcut menus, 57
  accessing sign-in screen with, 50
  gestures for, 815
  Snipping Tool and, 53–54
training videos, 44
transitions, 786
transparency, slide backgrounds, 885–887
transparent color, 270–271
TrebuchetMS font, 881
trim, 898
trimming video, 898–900
triple-click, 29
truncated, 534
Trust Center, 597
.txt file, 82
typing errors, correcting, 528

U

unbound controls, 688
underlines, 29

underlying formulas, 327
underlying values, 325
undo, 18–19
unfreezing panes, 400–401
ungrouping worksheets, 423
unzip, 10
Up button, 57
updating links, 967, 968
URLs, 248
USB flash drives, 54, 55, 58, 84
   deleting files and, 87
   searching and, 87
Use Alignment guides, 23
user accounts
   Office 365, 59
   signed-in, 6, 8–9
   in Windows 10, 47–49

V

value after increase, 478
value axis, 335, 485
values, 320
   changing for what-if analysis,
      480–482
   displayed, 325
   editing
      with Formula Bar, 357
      in worksheet, 356–357
   percent for new, 478–479
   for pie chart, 461–462
   underlying, 325
Values & Number Formatting, 481
variants, 778–779
Vertical Box List, 848
vertical rulers, 822–823, 826
video
   changing styles and shapes of, 897
   inserting into presentations, 895–900
   playback options, 898–900
   sizing and aligning, 896
   trimming and compressing,
      898–900
View Gridlines, 183–184
viewing reports, 563
volatile functions, 400

W

wallpapers, 52
Weather app, 67, 68
web browsers, 11
what-if analysis, 471–472
   changing values in worksheet for,
      480–482
   worksheet design for, 476–479
wildcard characters, 632–633
window control buttons, 6
window snip, 62
windows
   snapping, 92–93
   working with multiple open, 952

Windows 10, 46
   Home version, 55
   lock screen, 50
   sign-in screen, 50–51
   user accounts in, 47–49
   variations in appearance, 49
   variations organization and
      functionality, 48
With Previous timing option, 891–892
wizards
   creating forms with, 686–687
   creating reports with, 706–709
   Form Wizard, 686–687
   Import Spreadsheet Wizard, 530,
      558, 623
   Mail Merge Wizard, 279–281
   Query Wizard, 639–641
   Report Wizard, 706–709
   Simple Query Wizard, 542–544
Word, 101
   copying and pasting Excel charts into, 960
   opening files with, 80–83
   using access data for mail merge in,
      971–975
Word documents
   aligning paragraphs, 128–130
   creating new, 105–106
   creating reference pages, 249
   default document settings, 106
   indenting text, 131–133
   inserting, sizing, and positioning shapes,
      116–117
   inserting Access data into, 970–971
   inserting icons, 145–146
   inserting mail merge fields, 973–975
   inserting pictures, 109
   inserting SmartArt graphics in, 143–144
   inserting tables into, 200–201
   inserting text from another, 107
   line spacing, 130–131
   linking Excel data to, 966–967
   lists, 134–139
   managing and modifying sources for,
      249–250
   page borders, 115–116
   paragraph spacing, 133–134
   presenting online, 186–187
   printing, 122–123
   setting margins, 127–128
Word Editor, 201–206
Word files
   exporting reports to, 718–719
   opening, 80–83
Word tables, creating Excel worksheet
   from, 951–955
Word templates, creating, 208–210
word wrap, 106
WordArt, 843
   changing text fill and text outline colors,
      844
   inserting and aligning, 845
   text effects in, 847

WordArt Styles, 464
   applying to existing text, 844
WordPad Desktop app, 78
workbooks
   changing theme colors, 360–362
   copying and pasting Word tables into,
      952–954
   defining, 317
   document properties for, 341
   editing, 470–471
   importing data into Access tables from,
      530–532
   linking to Word documents, 966–967
   naming and saving, 317–320
   navigating, 413–414
   printing, 341, 431–432, 473
   themes, 332
   window elements for, 319
Works Cited, 244, 245
worksheets
   centering, 339–340
   changing tab colors, 413–414
   chart, 462–463
   clearing entire, 417
   constructing formulas on grouped,
      419–422
   copying, 414
   creating from Word tables, 951–955
   defining, 317
   detail, 425–426
   editing chart data after closing, 913
   editing values in, 356–357
   entering data into, 320–326
   finding and replacing in, 399
   footers in, 339–340
   formatting, 358–362
      grouped, 419–422, 423
      multiple, 429–431
   formulas referring to cells in
      other, 425
   grid area, 318
   grouping, 418–419
   hiding, 420
   inserting, 424, 952
   modifying and shrinking view
      of, 406
   moving, 429–431
   multiple totals on grouped, 422–423
   navigating among, 413–414
   printing, 431–432
      sections of, 342
      titles, 407–409
   renaming, 413–414, 952
   scaling to fit, 407–409
   selecting all, 421
   spellchecking, 348–350
   splitting window into panes, 406
   summary, 425–426, 429
   ungrouping, 423
   for what-if analysis, 476–479
   what-if questions and values in,
      480–482

wrapping text, 22
    in columns, 359–360
    around pictures, 110–111
    settings for, 109
writer's identifications, 194
writer's signature blocks, 194

X

x-axis, 335, 485
XML Paper Specification, 41
XPS files, 41, 768

Y

y-axis, 335, 485

Z

zip, 10
zipped files
    downloading and extracting, 11–14,
        65–66
    extracting with File Explorer, 73–74
zipped folders, 65

zooms, 25
Zoom dialog box, 406
    calculated field creation in, 634, 635
zoom level
    changing, 25–26
    Object, 255
    Page Width, 25–26
Zoom slider, 25–26